WORLDCOMP'13
July 22-25, 2013
Las Vegas Nevada, USA
www.world-academy-of-science.org

PROCEEDINGS OF THE 2013 INTERNATIONAL CONFERENCE ON BIOINFORMATICS & COMPUTATIONAL BIOLOGY

BIOCOMP 2013

Editors

Hamid R. Arabnia
Quoc-Nam Tran

Associate Editors

George Jandieri
Ashu M. G. Solo, Fernando G. Tinetti

(An Imprint of Laxmi Publications Pvt. Ltd.)
An ISO 9001:2008 Company
BENGALURU • CHENNAI • COCHIN • GUWAHATI • HYDERABAD
JALANDHAR • KOLKATA • LUCKNOW • MUMBAI • RANCHI • NEW DELHI
BOSTON (USA) • ACCRA (GHANA) • NAIROBI (KENYA)

This volume contains papers presented at The 2013 International Conference on Bioinformatics & Computational Biology (BIOCOMP'13). Their inclusion in this publication does not necessarily constitute endorsements by editors or by the publisher.

Branches

✆	Bengaluru	080-26 75 69 30	
✆	Chennai	044-24 34 47 26,	24 35 95 07
✆	Cochin	0484-237 70 04,	405 13 03
✆	Guwahati	0361-254 36 69,	251 38 81
✆	Hyderabad	040-27 55 53 83,	27 55 53 93
✆	Jalandhar	0181-222 12 72	
✆	Kolkata	033-22 27 43 84	
✆	Lucknow	0522-220 99 16	
✆	Mumbai	022-24 91 54 15,	24 92 78 69
✆	Ranchi	0651-220 44 64	

Published in India by

An ISO 9001:2008 Company
113, GOLDEN HOUSE, DARYAGANJ,
NEW DELHI - 110002, INDIA
Telephone : 91-11-4353 2500, 4353 2501
Fax : 91-11-2325 2572, 4353 2528
www.laxmipublications.com info@laxmipublications.com

C—
Printed at:

Foreword

It gives us great pleasure to introduce this collection of papers to be presented at the 2013 International Conference on Bioinformatics and Computational Biology (BIOCOMP'13), July 22 through 25, 2013, at The New Tropicana Hotel, Las Vegas, USA.

An important mission of the World Congress in Computer Science, Computer Engineering, and Applied Computing (a federated congress to which this conference is affiliated with) includes *"Providing a unique platform for a diverse community of constituents composed of scholars, researchers, developers, educators, and practitioners. The Congress makes concerted effort to reach out to participants affiliated with diverse entities (such as: universities, institutions, corporations, government agencies, and research centers/labs) from all over the world. The congress also attempts to connect participants from institutions that have* ***teaching*** *as their main mission with those who are affiliated with institutions that have* ***research*** *as their main mission. The congress uses a quota system to achieve its institution and geography diversity objectives."* By any definition of diversity, this congress is among the most diverse scientific meeting in USA. We are proud to report that this federated congress has authors and participants from 82 different nations representing variety of personal and scientific experiences that arise from differences in culture and values. As can be seen (see below), the program committee of this conference as well as the program committee of all other tracks of the federated congress are as diverse as its authors and participants.

The program committee would like to thank all those who submitted papers for consideration. About 57% of the submissions were from outside the United States. Each submitted paper was peer-reviewed by two experts in the field for originality, significance, clarity, impact, and soundness. In cases of contradictory recommendations, a member of the conference program committee was charged to make the final decision; often, this involved seeking help from additional referees. In addition, papers whose authors included a member of the conference program committee were evaluated using the double-blinded review process. One exception to the above evaluation process was for papers that were submitted directly to chairs/organizers of pre-approved sessions/workshops; in these cases, the chairs/organizers were responsible for the evaluation of such submissions. The overall paper acceptance rate for regular papers was 27%; 14% of the remaining papers were accepted as poster papers (at the time of this writing, we had not yet received the acceptance rate for a few individual tracks.)

We are very grateful to the many colleagues who offered their services in organizing the conference. In particular, we would like to thank the members of the Program Committee of BIOCOMP'13, members of the congress Steering Committee, and members of the committees of federated congress tracks that have topics within the scope of BIOCOMP. Many individuals listed below, will be requested after the conference to provide their expertise and services for selecting papers for publication (extended versions) in journal special issues as well as for publication in a set of research books (to be prepared for publishers including: Springer, Elsevier, BMC, and others).

- *Dr. Selim Aissi (World Congress Steering Committee); formerly, Chief Strategist - Security, Intel Corp., USA; Senior Business Leader & Head of Global Enterprise Security Architecture, Visa Corporation, USA*
- *Prof. Babak Akhgar (World Congress Steering Committee); Fellow of the British Computer Society, CITP; Professor of Informatics; Co-Director of CENTRIC (Centre of Excellence in Terrorism, Resilience, Intelligence & organised Crime research), Sheffield Hallam University, Sheffield, UK*
- *Prof. Hussain Al-Asaad (PDPTA); Senior Member, IEEE; University of California at Davis, Davis, California, USA*
- *Prof. Nizar Al-Holou (World Congress Steering Committee); Professor and Chair, ECE Department; Vice Chair, IEEE/SEM-Computer Chapter; University of Detroit Mercy, Detroit, Michigan, USA*
- *Dr. Haider M. AlSabbagh (ICAI); University of Basra, Iraq*
- *Prof. Hamid R. Arabnia (World Congress Steering Committee); Professor, Computer Science; Editor-in-Chief, The Journal of Supercomputing (Springer); Elected Fellow, Int'l Society of Intelligent Biological Medicine (ISIBM); The University of Georgia, Department of Computer Science, USA*
- *Peyman Arebi; Assistant Professor, Department of Computer Engineering, Technical and Vocational University, Bushehr, Iran*

- *Prof. Ezendu Ariwa (Publicity Vice-Chair); Chair, IEEE Consumer Electronics Chapter, UK&RI; Visiting Professor, Gulf University, Bahrain and University of Lagos and Kano State Polytechnic, Nigeria*
- *Prof. Juan Jose Martinez Castillo; Director of The Acantelys Research Group and Coordinator of the Computer Engineering Department, Universidad Gran Mariscal de Ayacucho, Venezuela*
- *Dr. Hsi-Ya (Jerry) Chang (PDPTA); Division Chief, National Center for High-Performance Computing, Taiwan; Secretary General of ACCTA; Member, Council of the Taiwan Association of Cloud Computing (TACC); Taiwan, ROC*
- *Dr. Chun Chen; Interdisciplinary PhD Program in Genetics, Bioinformatics, and Computational Biology, Virginia Tech, Virginia, USA Associate Member, American Association for Cancer Research (AACR), USA*
- *Prof. Juan Cuadrado-Gallego; Universidad de Alcala, Edificio Politecnico, Madrid, Spain*
- *Prof. Kevin Daimi (World Congress Steering Committee); Director, Computer Science and Software Engineering Programs; Department of Mathematics, Computer Science and Software Engineering; University of Detroit Mercy, Detroit, Michigan, USA*
- *Somdip Dey (PDPTA); St. Xavier's College (Autonomous), India*
- *Prof. George A. Gravvanis; Democritus University of Thrace, Greece*
- *Dr. Bing He (PDPTA); Cisco System Inc., USA*
- *Dr. K. S. S. Iyer (PDPTA); Symbiosis Institute of Telecom Management, India*
- *Prof. George Jandieri (World Congress Steering Committee); Georgian Technical University, Tbilisi, Georgia; Chief Scientist, The Institute of Cybernetics, Georgian Academy of Science, Georgia; Editorial Board Member: International Journal of Microwaves and Optical Technology, Georgia*
- *Prof. Dong Hwa Kim; Department of Electronic and Control Engineering, Hanbat National University, Korea; Visiting Professor, Budapest University of Technology and Economic, Hungary; International Einstein awardee for Scientific achievement (2010)*
- *Prof. Dattatraya V. Kodavade (World Congress Steering Committee); Head of Computer Science and Engineering, D.K.T.E Society's Textile & Engineering Institute, Ichalkaranji, Maharashtra State, India*
- *Prof. Kun Chang Lee (World Congress Steering Committee); Professor of MIS and WCU Professor of Creativity Science, Business School and Department of Interaction Science, Sungkyunkwan University, Korea*
- *Dr. Ying Liu; St. John's University, Queens, New York, USA*
- *Dr. Bala Krishna Maddali; Univ. School of Information Technology, GGS Indraprastha University, India*
- *Muhammad Naufal Bin Mansor; University Malaysia Perlis, Perlis, Malaysia*
- *Arshad Mansoor (SWWS); Pakistan Aeronautical Complex, Pakistan*
- *Dr. Tao Mao (ICAI + GEM); Oracle America, Inc., USA*
- *Prof. Gevorg Margarov (PDPTA); State Engineering University of Armenia, Armenia*
- *Prof. George Markowsky (World Congress Steering Committee); Professor and Associate Director, School of Computing and Information Science; Chair International Advisory Board of IEEE IDAACS; Director 2013 Northeast Collegiate Cyber Defense Competition; Cooperating Professor Math and Statistics Department UMaine and School of Policy & International Affairs UMaine; University of Maine, Orono, Maine, USA*
- *Dr. Ehab Morsy (FCS); Suez Canal University, Egypt*
- *Dr. Ali Mostafaeipour; Yazd University, Iran*
- *Dr. Saurabh Mukherjee; Banasthali University, Banasthali, India*
- *Dr. Asoke Nath; Department of Computer Science, St. Xavier's College, India*
- *Prof. G. N. Pandey (World Congress Steering Committee); Vice-Chancellor, Arunachal University of Studies, Arunachal Pradesh, India; Adjunct Professor, Indian Institute of Information Technology, Allahabad, India*
- *Prof. James J. (Jong Hyuk) Park (World Congress Steering Committee); Professor of Computer Science and Engineering, Seoul National University of Science and Technology (SeoulTech), Korea; President, KITCS; President, FTRA; Editor-in-Chiefs: HCIS, JoC and IJITCC Journals*
- *Dr. Satish Penmatsa; University of Maryland - Eastern Shore, Maryland, USA*
- *Prof. R. Ponalagusamy; National Institute of Technology, India*
- *Prof. Junfeng Qu; Clayton State University, Georgia, USA*
- *Prof. B. V. A. N. S. S. Prabhakar Rao (ICAI + SERP); VIT University, India*
- *Dr. Ahmet Sacan; School of Biomedical Eng., Science and Health Systems; Drexel University, PA, USA*
- *Dr. Gerald Schaefer (Session Chair, IPCV); Loughborough University, UK*
- *Dr. Liang Shi; Senior Researcher, McAfee, USA*
- *Dr. Zhefu Shi (ICAI + PDPTA); Microsoft Corporation, Redmond, Washington, USA*
- *Dr. Marek Sikora (IKE); Silesian University of Technology, Poland*
- *Dr. Kok Swee Sim; Jalan Ayer Keroh Lama, Melaka, Malaysia*
- *Ashu M. G. Solo, (Publicity Chair); Fellow of British Computer Society, Principal/R&D Engineer, Maverick Technologies America Inc., USA*
- *Dr. Karthikeyan Swaminathan; R&D Bioinformatics - Agilent Technologies Inc., USA*

- *Dr. Jiao Tao (ICAI); Oracle USA*
- *Prof. Fernando G. Tinetti (World Congress Steering Committee); School of Computer Science, Universidad Nacional de La Plata, La Plata, Argentina; Co-editor, Journal of CS and Technology (JCS&T)*
- *Dr. Predrag Tosic (World Congress Steering Committee); Microsoft, Washington, USA*
- *Prof. Quoc-Nam Tran (Vice-Chair of BIOCOMP); Professor and Chair of Computer Science, The University of Texas at Tyler, Tyler, Texas, USA*
- *Prof. Vladimir Volkov (World Congress Steering Committee); The Bonch-Bruevich State University of Telecommunications, Saint-Petersburg, Russia*
- *Prof. Jongwook Woo; Director, High-Performance Information Computing Center (HiPiC), California State University, California, USA*
- *Prof. Jane You (Vice-Chair of IPCV); The Hong Kong Polytechnic University, Hong Kong*
- *Dr. Hao Zhao; Department of Bioinformatics and Computational Biology, MD Anderson Cancer Center, The University of Texas, Houston, Texas, USA*
- *Dr. Hao Zheng; Life Technologies, California, USA*

As Sponsors-at-large, partners, and/or organizers each of the followings (separated by semicolons) provided help for at least one track of the World Congress: Aldebaran Robotics Inc., USA (http://www.aldebaran-robotics.com); Altera Corporation, USA (http://www.altera.com/); Computer Science Research, Education, and Applications Press (CSREA); Impulse Accelerated Technologies, Inc., USA (http://www.impulseaccelerated.com/); NVIDIA Corporation, USA (http://www.nvidia.com/object/about-nvidia.html); Parallella Community, Supercomputing for Everyone, USA (http://forums.parallella.org/); Pico Computing, Inc., USA (http://picocomputing.com/); SemiWiki.com, The Semiconductor Wiki Project, USA (http://www.semiwiki.com/); Solarflare Communications, Inc., USA (http://www.solarflare.com/); Stream Computing, Performance Engineers, The Netherlands (http://streamcomputing.eu/); Taylor & Francis, UK (http://www.taylorandfrancis.com/); US Chapter of World Academy of Science (http://www.world-academy-of-science.org/) ; and WEBestSOL & Webest Solutions Ltd, UK (http://webestsol.com/). In addition, a number of university faculty members and their staff (names appear on the cover of the set of proceedings), several publishers of computer science and computer engineering books and journals, chapters and/or task forces of computer science associations/organizations from 5 countries, and developers of high-performance machines and systems provided significant help in organizing the conference as well as providing some resources. We are grateful to them all.

We express our gratitude to keynote, invited, and individual conference/tracks and tutorial speakers - the list of speakers appears on the conference web site. We would also like to thank the followings: UCMSS (Universal Conference Management Systems & Support, California, USA) for managing all aspects of the conference; Dr. Tim Field of APC for managing the printing of the proceedings; and the staff of the New Tropicana Hotel in Las Vegas for the professional service they provided. Last but not least, we would like to thank the Co-Editors and Associate Co-Editors of BIOCOMP'13: Prof. Hamid R. Arabnia, Prof. George Jandieri, Ashu M. G. Solo, Prof. Fernando G. Tinetti, and Prof. Quoc-Nam Tran.

We present the proceedings of BIOCOMP'13.

Steering Committee, 2013
http://www.world-academy-of-science.org/

Contents

SESSION: COMPUTATIONAL BIOLOGY AND MEDICAL APPLICATIONS, TOOLS AND SYSTEMS + HEALTH INFORMATICS AND RELATED ISSUES

SESSION: PROTEIN CLASSIFICATION AND STRUCTURE PREDICTION, FOLDING, AND COMPUTATIONAL STRUCTURAL BIOLOGY

SESSION: MODELING AND SIMULATION + NOVEL STUDIES

SESSION: DATA AND INFORMATION MINING + COMPUTATIONAL BIOLOGY + MEDICAL SCIENCE, MODELS, AND SYSTEMS + BIOMETRICS

SESSION: LATE BREAKING PAPERS - BIOINFORMATICS AND COMPUTATIONAL BIOLOGY - MICROARRAYS, DNA SEQUENCING, GENE REGULATORY NETWORKS, HEALTH AND MEDICAL INFORMATICS

SESSION: PROTEIN FOLDING, CANCER STUDIES, GENE REGULATORY NETWORKS, RECOGNITION SYSTEMS , DNA/RNA TRANSFORMATION, ACOUSTICS, AND ALGORITHMS

SESSION

COMPUTATIONAL BIOLOGY AND MEDICAL APPLICATIONS, TOOLS AND SYSTEMS + HEALTH INFORMATICS AND RELATED ISSUES

Chair(s)

TBA

Emulation on Motion Tracking of Endoscopic Capsule inside Small Intestine

Guanqun Bao, Liang Mi, and Kaveh Pahlavan, *Fellow, IEEE*
Center for Wireless Information Network Studies
Worcester Polytechnic Institute
Worcester, MA, 01609, USA
(gbao, lmi, kaveh)@wpi.edu

Abstract — Video capsule endoscopy (VCE) provides a noninvasive way to examine the intestinal lumen as the capsule moves along the gastrointestinal (GI) tract. However, this technology is unable to localize itself when an abnormality is found by the video source. Knowing how the capsule moves will greatly enhance the accuracy in localizing the capsule. In this paper, we develope a novel image processing technique to track the motion of the endoscopic capsule. The proposed method is based on analyzing the displacements of feature points between consecutive images captured by the camera while traveling through the GI tract. To validate the performance of our algorithm, we created a virtual cylindrical tube that looks exactly the same as a small intestine and placed a virtual camera inside the tube to emulate the transition of the video capsule. By processing the emulated images, our proposed method was proved to be able to accurately estimate the linear transition, tilt, and rotation of the video capsule.

***Index Terms* — Video capsule endoscopy (VCE), motion tracking, localization, feature matching.**

I. Introduction

Video capsule endoscopy (VCE) [1] has been in use for clinical procedure for more than 13 years. It provides a noninvasive imaging technology for examining the digestive system. During the capsule's several-hour journey, medical physicians can receive clear pictures at a frame rate of 2 frames / second and based on these pictures they can easily detect abnormalities such as bleeding or a tumor inside the GI tract. However, a big drawback of this technique is its inability of localizing the abnormality after it is found by the video source [2]. Physicians cannot tell the exact location of the capsule, which prevents them from administering immediate treatments or procedures. A commonly used approach for localizing the capsule is to attach many calibrated external antennas to the anterior abdominal wall to detect the UHF-band signal that is emitted by the wireless capsule [3] (as shown in Fig. 1). Metrics such as received signal strength (RSS) or time of arrival (TOA) of the direct path can be used to identify the distance between the transmitting end and receiving end. Given ranging estimates from three or more different antennas, the position of the capsule can be estimated by pattern matching algorithms such as the least square algorithm [4] and the maximum likelihood algorithm [5]. However, due to the non-homogeneity of the body medium, features of the received signal are poorly correlated with the distance. Thus, the existing ranging based RF localization techniques often end up providing discontinuous and scattered estimates with unacceptable amount of error [6]. In our previous work [7], we used a Kalman filter and a particle filter to integrate the RSS-based Wi-Fi localization and the movement models from inertial sensors for indoor geo-localization. The results were very promising since this method showed the potential to smooth the scattered RF localization results by adding the constraints of continuous motion tracking. However, inertial sensors that meet the accuracy requirement for the VCE applications are too large to be embedded inside a video capsule and even if they can be embedded when the assembly technology improves, the cost of the capsule will be increased dramatically. Therefore, we need to find an inexpensive and efficient way to track the motion of the capsule. In the localization literature, there has been a trend to extract motion parameters from consecutive image sequence to improve the performance of RF localization. This class of algorithms is known as video based simultaneous localization and mapping (SLAM) algorithms [8]. In the VCE application, since an endoscopic capsule continually takes pictures inside the GI tract with very short interval, it is possible to reconstruct the camera motion from image sequences to aid the existing RF localization infrastructure.

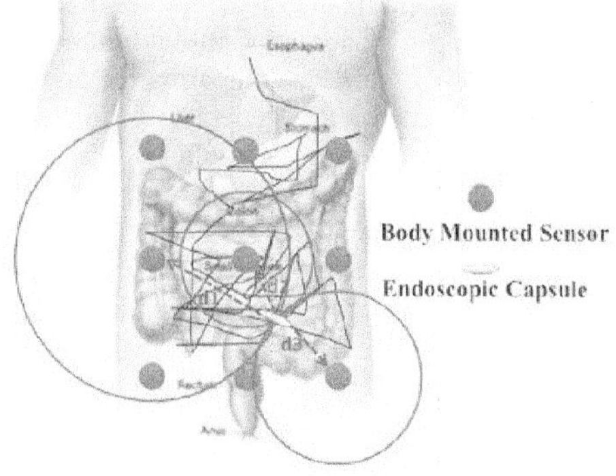

Fig. 1 An example of RF localization infrastructure. (Black polyline represents the estimated trajectory of the capsule based on the received RF signal. d1, d2, and d3 are the RSS ranging distances between the capsule and three body mounted sensors respectively.)

This research was funded by the National Institute of Standards and Technology (NIST), USA, under contract FON 2009-NIST-ARRA-MSE-Research-01, entitled "RF Propagation Measurement and Modeling for Body Area Networking".

During the past few years, there have been a few attempts to track the endoscopic camera motion. In [9], the authors developed a camera motion detection method to reduce diagnosis time by automatically detecting duplicated recordings caused by backward camera movement. In [10], an inverse projection method was proposed to give a better representation of the interior wall of the small intestine. Then, a motion estimation algorithm was applied to those projected images to eliminate the redundancy by finding overlapped portion between consecutive images. In [11], the authors proposed a method to estimate the relative movements of the VCE by applying the affine scale invariant feature transform (SIFT) feature detector and descriptor to a sequence of VCE images. However, the use of camera motion tacking algorithms in localization of the video capsule has been understudied in the literature and validation of the algorithm is very challenging since clinical experiments on the human body are extremely difficult and restricted [12].

In this paper, we propose a novel camera motion tracking algorithm to provide real time motion status of the VCE. In an image sequence captured with a small time interval, consecutive frames show transformations such as skew, scaling, and rotation etc. The nature and quantities of these transformations give an indication of the camera motion during that elapsed time. The proposed method detected and analyzed the displacements of unique portions of the scene, which are referred as "feature points" (FP) in the rest of this paper, between consecutive frames to reveal the camera motion during that elapsed time. To validate the performance of our algorithm, we created both physical and virtual test beds that looked exactly the same as a small intestine and placed an enteroscopy camera and a virtual camera inside the physical plastic tube and the virtual cylindrical tube respectively to emulate the transition of the video capsule. By processing the emulated images, the transition distance, tilt, and rotation of the video camera could be accurately estimated by the proposed method. The major contribution of this paper is that we explored the potential of extracting motion information from image sequence to aid the existing RF localization infrastructure. Another contribution of this paper is that we provide a practical emulation environment to validate the performance of our algorithm.

The rest of the paper is organized as follows: In section II, we talk about setup of the emulation environment to test our motion tracking algorithm. By comparing the physical test bed and corresponding graphically generated virtual test bed with the real endoscopic images, we are able to verify the feasibility and practicability of the proposed emulation platform. In section III, the methodology is described in detail to show how the motion information is estimated. An inverse projection scheme is used to project the original cylindrical image into an angle and radius plane to better represent the motion vectors. By recognizing the pattern of the motion vector distribution and quantitative calculation, the direction of motion, degree of tilting and rotation of the capsule can be accurately estimated. In section IV, both the experimental results and analytical discussion are presented to validate the performance of the proposed algorithm. Finally, conclusion and future work are addressed in section V.

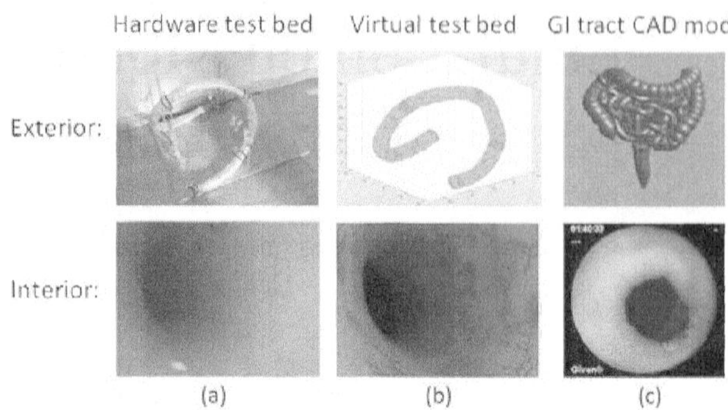

Fig.2 Emulation test beds. (Three upper pictures show the external appearance of hardware test bed, virtual test bed and the overall GI tract model respectively. Three lower pictures are the corresponding interior looks of the above three models.)

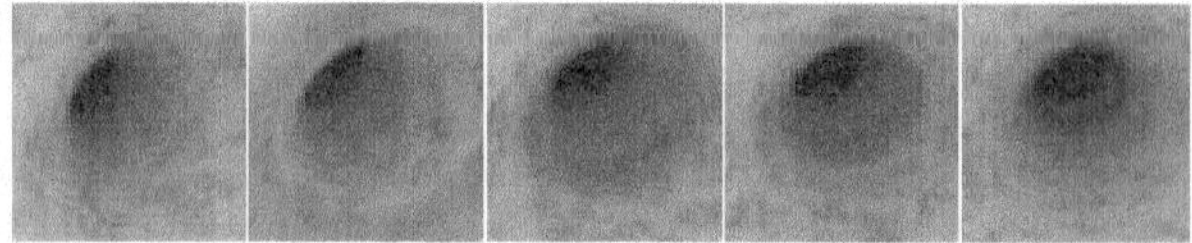

Fig. 3 A image sequence of 5 frames taken from the virtual test bed.

II. EMULATION TEST BED SET UP

Carrying out experiments on real human beings is extremely costly and restricted by law [2] [13]. Thus, the only way to test our algorithm is to build up emulation test beds. In our case, two test beds were established to emulate the motion of the capsule traveling inside a small intestine. One was the hardware test bed that is shown in Fig. 2 (a). This test bed was created by bending and twisting a 1.5 meter long 3 centimeter wide plastic tube into the shape of the small intestine, which looked like an intertwined snake (as shown on the top of Fig.2 (c)). The tube was painted flesh color to give it a more realistic interior look. Clinical data showed that the average length of a human small intestine was 7-9 meters long and the capsule stayed in the small intestine for around 3-4 hours. During the few hours the capsule was in the small intestine, it took pictures at 2 frames / second. If we assumed the capsule travels at a constant speed, then, the average step distance between two consecutive frames could be roughly calculated as 0.03 cm. To emulate the transition of the endoscopic capsule, we inserted a wired endoscopy camera equipped with four LED lights into the tube with the same constant speed of 0.06 cm / second and took 2 pictures per second. Since the abdominal cavity was an absolutely dark environment, we covered the tube with tinfoil paper to eliminate the influence of any light source from outside. In this way, the only light source was coming from the LED light that equipped on the video camera. Under this set up, tube surface that lied physically closer to the camera had a brighter intensity value and the brightness decreases as the distance increase. Eventually, in the far end of the tube a black hole would form representing the vanishing effect [14]. This was exactly what we observed from the real endoscopic images. A snap shot of the interior of the hardware test bed is shown at the bottom of Fig. 2 (a).

One problem with the hardware test bed was its inflexibility in camera control. Once the wired camera was inserted into the tube, we had limited control on how the camera moved rather than linear proceeding distance. To better implement rotation and tilting of the camera, an alternative way was to create a virtual test bed by generating the same cylindrical tube using Matlab graphic toolbox. As shown on the top of Fig.2 (b), the virtual test bed shared the same shape, size and color with the hardware test bed. In this virtual 3D space, we placed the camera view point inside the tube with its focal axis paralleled to the central line of the cylinder. Then, the movement of the camera could be adjusted by simply changing the parameters of the transition matrix as the camera moved along. Also, to create a similar illumination effect, we put a Phong light source behind the camera to emulate the LED light around the camera. What's more, we extracted the texture from the real endoscopic images and mapped it onto the interior surface of the tube to make it look even more realistic. The advantage of using a virtual test bed is that it has better camera control, more realistic interior texture, and quicker processing time and the topology of the tube can be changed as needed.

III. Methodology

3.1 *Feature Point Detection*

One important step in the motion tracking is feature point detection. The purpose of feature point detection is to track the transformations such as rotation, translation, and scaling between frames to reflect the motion of the camera. It is important that the feature points extracted from the reference frame can be accurately detected in the second frame even under geometric distortion and variations in illumination. There are many algorithms for feature points detection, such as edge detection [15], which detects the sharp changes in intensity values; corner detection [16], which detects the intersection of different edges within a local neighborhood; SIFT [17], which was first published by David Lowe, and is used to compare two images by rotation, translation and scale changes. Since the VCE images are suffered from illumination variations and geometric deformation problems. According to the literature [18], in a VCE application, more feature points can be detected by the affine SIFT algorithm than other algorithms, therefore, in this paper, we use affine SIFT to do feature point detection as well.

3.2 *Inverse Cylindrical Projection ("Image Unrolling")*

Since the camera is fully surrounded by the walls of the cylindrical tube, these walls are projected to the 2-D image plane as a bunch of circular rings [19] (as shown in Fig. 4 (b)). Under this image acquisition system, the points that are closer to the camera lie on circles with a larger radius compared to the points that are further down the cylinder. In Fig. 4 (a), C refers to the position of the camera, α refers to the half angle of view of the camera. Point M lies on the closest view that can be captured by the camera (when projected onto the cylindrical image, M has the largest radius value R as shown in Fig. 4 (b)).

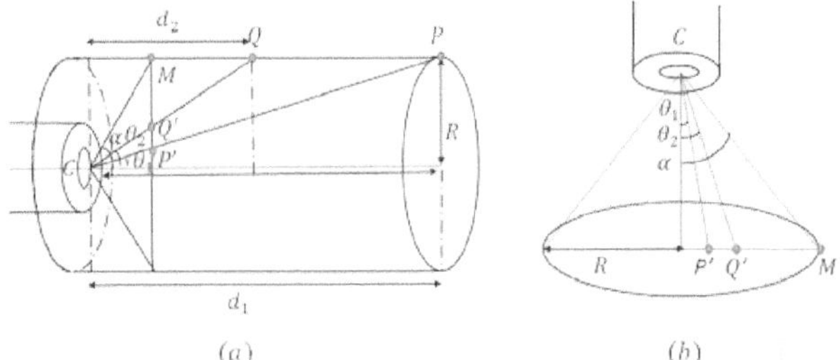

Fig. 4 Image acquisition system of VCE: (a) a horizontal view; (b) a vertical view

Point Q refers to a FP lying at a greater distance d_2 from the camera, line QC forms the "angular depth" of θ_2 with respect to the focal axis of the camera. Point P refers to a FP with even greater distance d_1, which forms a different angular depth of θ_1. It can be calculated that:

$$\theta_1 = tan^{-1}\left(\frac{R}{d_1}\right) \qquad \theta_2 = tan^{-1}\left(\frac{R}{d_2}\right) \tag{1}$$

It shows that a smaller angler depth indicates a larger distance.

After applying feature matching to consecutive frames, we can see that if the camera moves forward through the cylinder, the FPs move radially outward, indicating they are pointing toward rings with bigger radius. Similarly, when the camera moves backward, the positions of FPs are pointing toward the center of the rings. The magnitude of displacement of FPs is dependent on the relative distances of these points with respect to the camera. Points that lie physically closer to the camera show a greater apparent displacement when compared to the points further away during the same transition of the camera. These observations give us hints on analyzing the camera motion. To standardize the displacement of each FP pair, we need to perform an operation called "inverse cylindrical projection" [10] (also referred as "image unrolling" in [20]) to project the original image onto an angle and radius based coordinate system. Assuming that the cylinder is wrapped by a piece of paper, what the inverse cylindrical projection does is to "unroll" this piece of paper and present the content on this paper in a flatten view. The purpose of this process is to give a better visualization and to facilitate the calculation of angular depth.

Here is how to achieve this "unrolled" image mathematically. Consider a point P with cylindrical coordinates $(x,\ y)$ lying on a circle with radius r and origin $(x_0,\ y_0)$ as shown on the left of Fig. 5 (a). If P makes an angle $\emptyset$ with the horizontal axis, then:

$$r = \sqrt{(x - x_0)^2 + (y - y_0)^2} \tag{2}$$

$$\emptyset = tan^{-1}\left(\frac{y - y_0}{x - x_0}\right) \tag{3}$$

Let the size of the projected canvas to be $L \times H$. Point P would map to a point P' with coordinates (x', y') after the "unrolling" transformation by:

$$x' = \frac{L\emptyset}{2\pi} \qquad y' = H - r \tag{4}$$

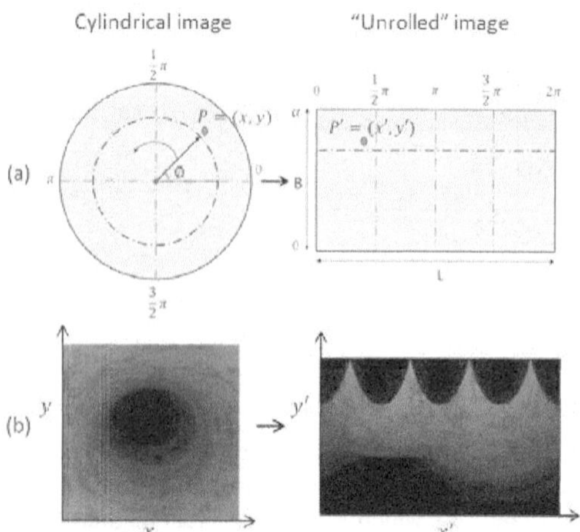

Fig. 5 The process of "unrolling" the cylindrical image.

In this transformed image plane, x' axis represents the radian in the cylindrical image whose value ranges from 0 (when $x' = 0$) to 2π (when $x' = L$); y' axis represents the count of the circle that is unrolled. In order to derive the angular depth of a selected FP, the y' coordinate of that FP in the unrolled domain is studied. After the projection, the circular rings in the cylindrical image are stacked up vertically in the unrolled domain. The largest circle in the image is captured at the maximum field of view of the camera α and has a radius of R. The depth of this circle in the unrolled domain is also given by R. A value of 0 in the y axis of the unrolled domain means an angular depth of 0°. The angular depths of the rest of the positions are calculated proportionally within this range of 0° and α. θ_1 and θ_2 are calculated using the y' coordinates of the FPs respectively, as shown below.

$$\theta = \left(\frac{y'}{H}\right)\alpha \tag{5}$$

3.3 Detect Linear Transition

As mentioned in previous sections, the motion of a video camera can be detected by measuring the displacement of the FPs and these displacements are better represented in the unrolled image domain. To explain better, we use Fig. 6 to illustrate the procedure of detecting linear transition of the camera.

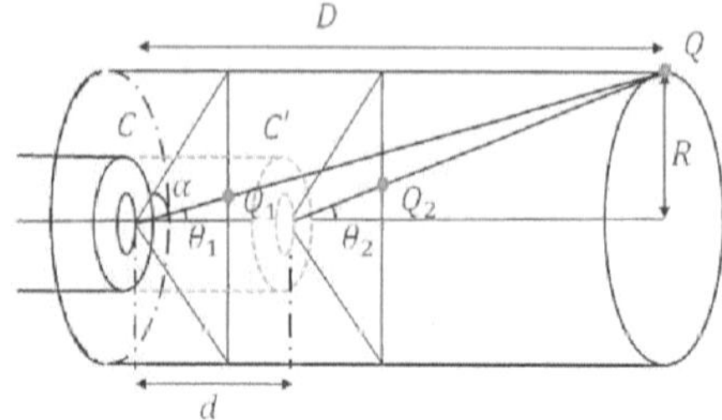

Fig. 6 Detection of linear transition of the video capsule

In Fig. 6, C refers to the initial position of the camera, α refers to the maximum field of view. Point Q refers to a FP lying at a distance D from the initial position of the camera. Q is projected to the image plane as Q_1 with angular depth of θ_1. After the camera moving forward by a distance d, point Q (which we will refer to as Q_2 to indicate the point Q viewed from the second camera position) now has a different angular depth of θ_2. ΔQ refers to the angular displacement of point Q when the camera is moved by d. This displacement ΔQ shows that a linear movement of the camera into the cylinder, which makes the FPs move radially outward. In the unrolled domain, this forward motion is reflected by vertical displacements of the FPs. For different depths of Q, the displacement ΔQ and the corresponding displacement in the unrolled domain are also of different magnitudes. So, we need to derive an expression for linear distance d traversed by the camera in terms of the initial depth of FP (θ_1) and final depth of FP (θ_2), so that the depth information D is factored out. Referring to Fig. 4 (a), we can deduce the following equations:

$$\theta_1 = tan^{-1}\left(\frac{R}{D}\right) \rightarrow D = \frac{R}{tan\theta_1} \tag{6}$$

$$\theta_2 = tan^{-1}\left(\frac{R}{D-d}\right) \tag{7}$$

Replacing D in Eq. 7 with Eq. 6, we get

$$d = \frac{R}{tan\theta_2}\left(1 - \frac{tan\theta_2}{tan\theta_1}\right) \tag{8}$$

From Eq. 6, it is seen that information on depth of FP is factored into the final expression of distance moved by camera. In this way, the actual displacement d of the camera is independent of the location of the FP chosen in the image. To reemphasize, the unrolling process facilitates the deriving of θ_1 and θ_2 in Eq. 8 and therefore facilitates the deduction of d. Similarly, the distance that the camera moves backward can be calculated in the same fashion.

3.4 Detect Rotation

Analysis of the images in the unrolled domain can be extended to study rotations of the camera. Any movement of the camera in the cylinder causes FPs to move in various directions. For the case of the camera's rotation about the focal axis, the displacements of all FPs would be horizontal in the unrolled domain (illustrated in Fig. 7 (c)). In our previous work [21], given the positions of the corresponding FPs in two cylindrical frames, we used Singular Value Decomposition (SVD) algorithm to reconstruct the rotation matrix in order to recover the rotation angle. Although this method is able to provide accurate estimate of the rotation, the algorithm is computationally costly and not easy to implement. On the contrast, when using inverse cylindrical projection, we can easily calculate the rotation angle by measuring the horizontal displacement of FPs in the unrolled plane. The greater is the horizontal component, the greater is the rotation and vice versa. For estimating rotations, there is no need for calculating angular depths. This is because irrespective of how deep the points are in the cylinder, the apparent rotations remain the same. Let us call the horizontal FP displacement as:

$$\Delta x' = x'_2 - x'_1 \qquad (9)$$

where x_1 and x_2 are x' coordinates of the same FP in the first frame and second frame respectively. The ratio of Δx to the length of the unrolled image directly translates into the rotation of the camera. The rotation angle $\emptyset$ can be calculated by:

$$\emptyset = \frac{\Delta x'}{L} 2\pi \qquad (10)$$

where L is the length of the unrolled image. The detectable rotation range is from 0 to 2π.

3.5 Detect Tilting

During the transition of the capsule, if the tube is not straight, the capsule will tilt toward the direction of the tube. In this case, the displacements of the FPs are still vertical stacked in the unrolled domain but with different magnitudes. As illustrated in Fig. 7, point P and point Q are at the same distance from the initial position of the camera C. After the camera moves to C' and tilted with angle φ , it can be seen that the angular depths of the two FPs are different in magnitude. Since the camera tilts downward the direction of Q, the angular displacement ΔP is obviously larger than the angular displacing ΔQ .

$$\Delta P = \theta_2 - \theta_1 \qquad \Delta Q = \beta_2 - \beta_1 \qquad (11)$$

where θ_1 and θ_2 are angular depths of P in the initial image plane and final image plane respectively. β_1 and β_2 are the angular depths of Q in the initial image plane and final image plane respectively. The magnitude of tilting can be roughly estimated by:

$$\varphi = abs\left(\frac{\Delta Q - \Delta P}{\max(\Delta Q,\ \Delta P)}\right)\alpha \qquad (12)$$

The range of tilt that can be detected is from 0 to α.

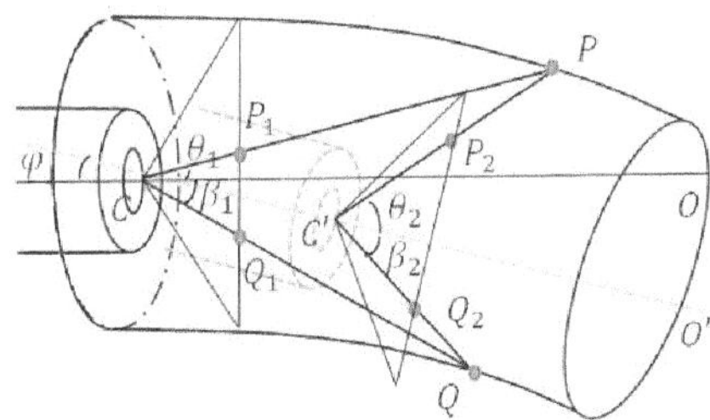

Fig. 7 Detection of tilts during the transition of the video capsule

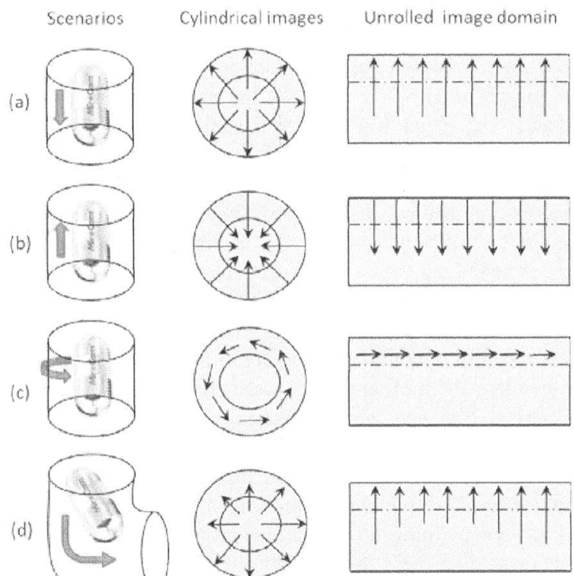

Fig. 8 Movement of FPs in different domains. (a) and (b) indicate the situations where the capsule moved forward and backward. (c) indicates the situation where the capsule rotated. (d) indicates the situation where the capsule tilted.

3.6 Summery

It has been shown that the displacements of FPs in the unrolled domain facilitate the motion tracking of the camera. If the camera moves forward, motion vectors in the original cylindrical image point to the outside. Correspondingly, in the unrolled domain, motion vectors are vertically stacked with their directions pointing upward (as shown in Fig, 8 (a)); the magnitudes of these motion vectors also reveal the distance the capsule travels during the two frames. Similarly, if the camera moves backward, motion vectors in the cylindrical image point to the center. In the unrolled domain, motion vectors are also vertically stacked but with their directions pointing downward (as shown in Fig, 8 (b)). If the camera rotates, motion vectors in the cylindrical image will form a circle around the focal axis. In this case, the corresponding motion vectors in the unrolled domain are pointed to either right or left which indicates a clockwise rotation or counterclockwise rotation respectively (as shown in Fig, 8 (c)). Lastly, if the capsule tilts or turns during the transition, the motion vector in the unrolled domain will still be vertically stacked, but the magnitude varies along the x' axis. The difference in magnitude indicates the degree that the capsule tilts. The x' coordinate with the smallest magnitude on average is the direction that the camera tilts to (as shown in Fig. 8 (d)).

IV. PERFORMANCE EVALUATION AND ANALYSIS

To verify the performance of our proposed method, we put the algorithm into test under the virtual test bed that was introduced in section II. The test bed was constructed in Matlab using graphic toolbox. The virtual camera was programmed to be traveling at a constant speed of 0.4 cm per step and the whole emulation took 160 steps. During the transition of the capsule, it took pictures at resolution of 420×560 pixels. For the purpose of inverse cylindrical projection, we only used the square portion (1:420, 71:490) of the original image. The radius of the cylindrical tube was set to be 1.5 cm, which was close to the actual radius of the small intestine. The view angle of the camera was 55°. The maximum field of view α in Fig. 4 (b) was 27.5^o. To extract features, an affine SIFT method was utilized to detect the same FPs in different images. On average, 76 feature points were detected per frame during the 160 steps. The size of the unrolled domain was set to be 500 (L) × 300 (H) pixels.

Fig. 9 shows some typical movements that were detected by the proposed motion tracking algorithm. In Fig. 9 (a), it can be seen that the motion vectors were pointed to the outside in cylindrical image while stacked vertically with their orientation pointing to the upward. Similarly, in Fig. 9 (b), motion vectors in the cylindrical image were pointed to the center and correspondingly, motion vectors in the unrolled domain are pointing downward, which indicated a backward movement. Fig. 9 (c) shows when the camera rotated, motion vectors in the cylindrical image formed a circle around the focal axis and the corresponding motion vectors in the unrolled domain were pointing to the right indicating a clockwise rotation. In Fig. 9 (d), the capsule tilted toward 120 degree, so the magnitudes of the motion vectors in this area were smaller than the others.

Experimental results show that the linear transitions and rotations can be inferred from the vertical component and horizontal component of the motion vectors in the unrolled domain respectively. Meanwhile, differences in the magnitude of motion vectors reflect tilting direction of the capsule. Based on the quantitative calculation presented throughout this paper, the tracking process was implemented as follows: given the initial position of the capsule, the subsequent positions of the capsule are estimated by multiply the current position with the transition matrix, which consists of distance, rotation, and tilt angle. The tracking results are illustrated in Fig. 10 compared with the ground truth path. Also, the MSE of estimated position of the capsule for each step is plotted in Fig.11. It can be seen from the plotting that the motion estimate for the first 50 steps were very accurate, whose average MSEs were below 1 cm. However, the error increased as the step went further. This was due to the accumulative characteristic of all motion tracking techniques. In every motion tracking technique, the next state is purely decided by the current state plus the current transition information, which is estimated from the displacements of FPs between consecutive image frames. If an error happens in the estimation of this transition information, even with very little magnitude, this error will accumulate and the overall error will keep increasing. This is what we call "drifting effect" in Robotics. Thus, we cannot judge the performance of a motion tracking algorithm based on the overall accuracy. Instead, we should evaluate the performance of an algorithm by measuring the accuracy of estimate within each step. Statistics in Table I show that our proposed algorithm worked accurately in calculating the proceeding distance and rotation angle for each step. The average distance error was 0.04 cm which was way below the unit step size, and the average rotation error was 1.8^o, which was also very small compared with average rotation angle of 7.8^o. The estimate of tilt was not as accurate because the differences in motion vectors were not always obvious and the range of smaller motion vectors may cover up to more than 45 degree of x'axis. Therefore, it was very hard to quantize the tilt angle which leaded to great calculation errors.

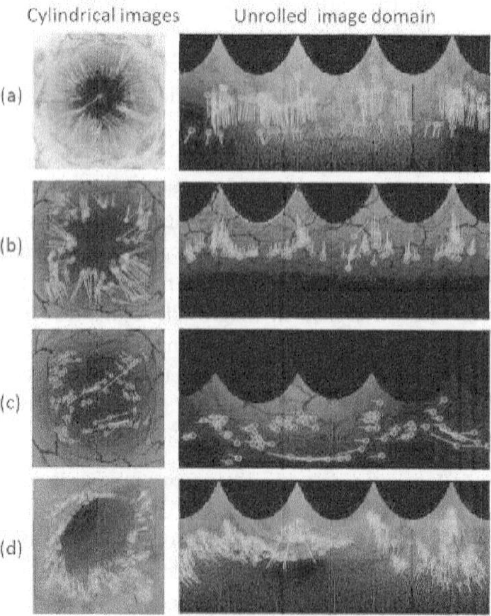

Fig. 9 Movement of FPs in different domains. (a) refers to moving forward; (b) refers to moving backward; (c) refers to rotation; (d) refers to tilt

TABLE I. MOTION TRACKING PERFORMANCE FOR EACH STEP

	Average estimates	**Average error**
Distance	0.41 cm	0.04cm
Rotation	7.8^o	1.8^o
Tilt	4.3^o	3.0^o

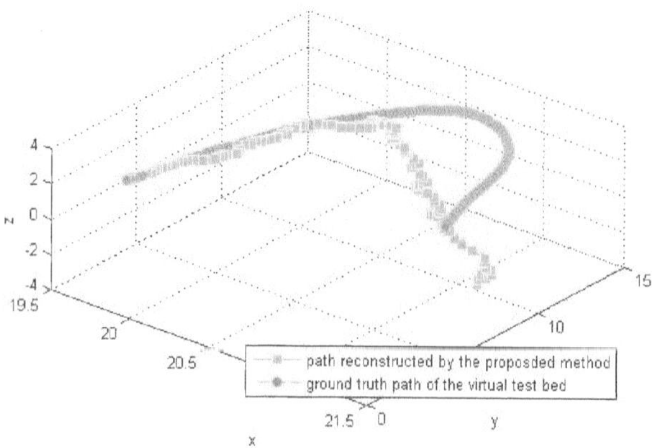

Fig. 10 Result of the motion tracking compared with ground truth.

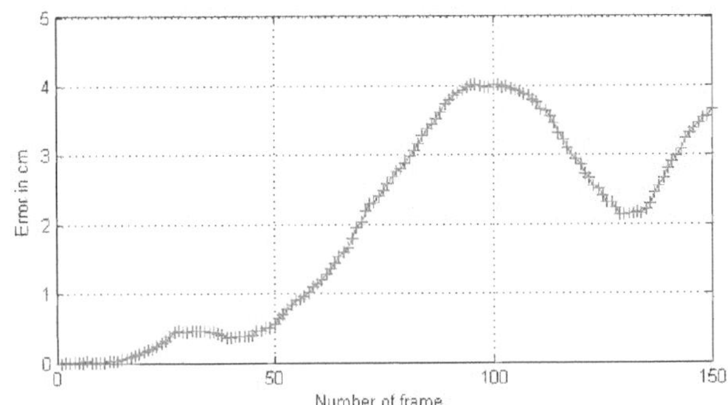

Fig. 11 Mean square error (MSE) in the motion racking process.

V. CONCLUSION AND FUTURE WORK

In this paper, we presented a novel image processing technique to track the motion of the VCE inside a virtual in-body environment. The major contribution of this work is that we presented the potential of using video source to aid the localization of the VCE. The proposed motion tracking technique is purely based on the image sequence that captured by the video camera which is already equipped on the capsule, thus, no extra components such as Inertial measurement units (IMUs) or magnetic coiled are needed. Experimental results show that by analyzing the transformations between consecutive video frames in the unrolled image plane, the direction, rotation and tilts of the camera can be accurately recovered. In the future, we will focus on refining this algorithm according to the clinical data and combining this technique with the existing RF localization approaches to provide a hybrid solution to the localization inside human body.

ACKNOWLEDGMENT

The authors would like to thank Dr. David Cave at UMass Memorial Medical Center for his precious suggestions, Jeffrey Elloian for his editing in English and the colleagues at the CWINS laboratory for their directly or indirectly help in preparation of the results presented in this paper.

REFERENCES

[1] D. O. Faigel and D. R. Cave, "*Capsule Endoscopy*", Saunders Elsevier Amsterdam, 2008.

[2] K. Pahlavan, G. Bao, Y. Ye, S. Makarov, U. Khan, P. Swar, D. Cave, A. Karellas, P. Krishnamurthy, and K. Sayrafian, "Rf Localization for Wireless Video Capsule Endoscopy," *International Journal of Wireless Information Networks*, vol. 19, no. 4, pp. 326–340, 2012.

[3] Y. Ye, P. Swar, K. Pahlavan, and K. Ghaboosi, "Accuracy of RSS-based RF Localization in Multi-capsule Endoscopy," *International Journal of Wireless Information Networks*, vol. 19, no. 3, pp. 229–238, 2012.

[4] Y. Huang, J. Benesty, G. W. Elko, and R. M. Mersereati, "Real-Time Passive Source Localization: A Practical Linear-correction Least-squares Approach," *IEEE Trans. Speech, Audio Process.*, vol. 9, pp. 943–956, Nov. 2001.

[5] S. Li, Y. Geng, J. He, K. Pahlavan, "Analysis of Three-Dimensional Maximum Likelihood Algorithm for Capsule Endoscopy Localization", *5th IEEE International Conference on Biomedical Engineering and Informatics (BMEI)*, Oct 2012.

[6] F. De Lorio, C. Malagelada, F. Azpiroz, M. Maluenda, C. Violanti, L. Igual, J. Vitrià4, J.-r. Malagelada. "Intestinal motor activity, Endoluminal Motion and Transit", *Neurogastroenterology & Motilit*, Vol. 21, Issue 12, pp. 1264-1271, Dec. 2009.

[7] K. Pahlavan, F. Akgul, Y. Ye, T. Morgan, F. Alizadeh-Shabdiz, M. Heidari, and C. Steger, "Taking Positioning Indoors Wi-Fi Localization and GNSS," *Inside GNSS*, vol. 5, no. 3, pp. 40–47, 2010.

[8] U. Frese, P. Larsson, and T. Duckett, "A Multilevel Relaxation Algorithm for Simultaneous Localization and Mapping," *IEEE Transactions on Robotics,* vol. 21, no. 2, pp. 196–207, April 2005.

[9] Y. Liu, T. Tillo, J Xiao, E. Lim, Z. Wang, "2D to Cylindrical Inverse Projection of the Wireless Capsule Endoscopy Images", 4th International Congress on Image and Signal Processing, Oct 2011.

[10] T. Tillo, E. Lim, Z. Wang, J. Hang, R. Qian, "Inverse Projection of the Wireless Capsule Endoscopy Images", International Conference on Biomedical Engineering and Computer Science (ICBECS), 2010.

[11] H. Lee, M. Choi, S. Lee, "Motion Analysis for Duplicate Frame Removal in Wireless Capsule Endoscope", Medical Imaging 2011: Image Processing, March 2011.

[12] G. Ciuti, M. Visentini-Scarzanella, A. Dore, A. Menciassi, P. Dario1 and G. Yang, "Intra-operative Monocular 3D Reconstruction for Image-Guided Navigation in Active Locomotion Capsule Endoscopy", The Fourth IEEE RAS/EMBS International Conference on Biomedical Robotics and Biomechatronics, Roma, Italy. June 2012

[13] L. France, J. Lenoir, A. Angelidis, P. Meseure, M.-P. Cani, F. Faure, C. Chaillou, "A Layered Model of a Virtual Human Intestine For Surgery Simulation", Medical Image Analysis, 9 (2005) 123–132.

[14] G. Bao and K. Pahlavan, "Motion Estimation of the Endoscopy Capsule using Region-based Kernel SVM Classifier", IEEE EIT conference, Rapid city, SD, 2013.

[15] J. Canny, "A computational approach to edge detection", IEEE PAMI, 8(6), 1986, 679-698.

[16] F. Mokhtarian and R. Suomela, "Robust image corner detection through curvature scale space," IEEE Trans. Pattern Anal. Mach. Intell., vol. 20, no. 12, pp. 1376–1381, Dec. 1998.

[17] D. Lowe, Object Recognition from Local Scale-Invariant Features, ICCV, pp. 1150-1157, 1999.

[18] Y. Fan, M. Meng, "3D reconstruction of the WCE images by affine SIFT method", 8th World Congress on Intelligent Control and Aut omation, June 2011.

[19] P. Szczypiński, R. Sriram, P. Sriram, D. Reddy, "A Model of Deformable Rings for Interpretation of Wireless Capsule Endoscopic Videos", Elsevier, Medical Image Analysis, 13 (2) (2009) 312-324.

[20] S. Sathyanarayana, S. Thambipillai, C. Clarke, "Real Time Tracking Of Camera Motion Through Cylindrical Passages", 15th IEEE International Conference on Digital Signal Processing, Jul 2007.

[21] G. Bao, Y. Ye, U. Khan, X. Zheng and K. Pahlavan, "Modeling of the Movement of the Endoscopy Capsule inside G.I. Tract based on the Captured Endoscopic Images", *International Conference on Modeling, Simulation and Visualization Methods*, Las Vegas, 2012.

My Smart Health: an integrated suite for Remote Self Monitoring of Diabetes

Maria Teresa Baldassarre[1], Giovanni Bruno[2], Danilo Caivano[1,2], Gennaro Del Campo[2], Massimiliano Morga[2], Giuseppe Visaggio[1,2]

Department of Informatics, University of Bari, Italy[1]
{baldassarre, caivano, visaggio}@di.uniba.it;

SER&Practices Spin Off, Bari, Italy[2]
{massimiliano.morga, giovanni.bruno, gennaro.delcampo}@serandpractices.com

***Abstract*—Diabetes mellitus is a constantly increasing disease. Evidences prove how self monitoring of blood glucose (SMBG) is associated to with better metabolic control in Type I diabetes patients. Nonetheless, there are several issues that limit the effectiveness and reliability of self monitoring such as: bulky devices for blood glucose checks, large amounts of data to report on log books and to interpret in real time, limited communication between diabetologist and patient, and scarce availability of data for medical and scientific use in evidence based medicine.**

"My Smart Health", proposed in this paper, is an integrated suite for remote SMBG. It aims to improve management of diabetes from several perspectives among which assure reliability of SMBG values collected, appropriateness of therapies identified, as well as timely communications with patients. The solution provides innovative software components and discrete hardware devices that enforce the traditional processes for blood glucose control and, at the same time, reduce the social impact of the disease, support the stakeholders involved (i.e. patients, diabetologists and GP) in defining and adopting the most appropriate therapy, readily analyze the data and assure real time feedback to patients after each blood glucose check.

***Index Terms*—Diabetes, SaaS, Evidence Based Medicine, blood glucose self monitoring**

I. INTRODUCTION

Diabetes mellitus is a chronic pathology largely diffused all over the world. According to the WHO, the last estimate of the number of diabetic subjects is about 270 million people [1, 2]. Nevertheless, this disease is increasing and the WHO forecasts that by 2015 the number of diabetics may even double. In Italy, approximately four million patients, with a recognized pathology, and about two million borderline ones, represent the diabetic population. Of this, 53.7% is male, and 59% is over 65 years of age, while about 33.7% is between 45 and 65 years, but over 7% is less than 35. The request for glycaemia strips, reimbursed by the National Health Service, has registered an increasing trend in the last years with a growth of 11% per year and a cost of 600 million euros. There is an increasing trend in the market of self-monitoring diabetes due to the impact of the pathology on the Italian population. In spite of the high cardiovascular risk of diabetic patients, it turns out that lipid profile monitoring (cholesterol and triglycerides) is carried out more systematically than blood glucose monitoring.

There are many evidences that prove how self monitoring of blood glucose is associated to a better metabolic control in patients with Type I diabetes, allowing for an adequate adjustment of the insulin doses, on behalf of healthcare providers, and most of all allowing the patient to self adjust the insulin dose according to the value collected. Indeed, such controls (as for glycaemia and arterial pressure) and their joint management with a GP may motivate the patent to constantly conform to a specific lifestyle (diet and exercise) and pharmacologic therapy.

In general, the aim of the Health Ministry in facing the diabetes emergency and the metabolism syndrome foresees structuring, for what is possible, local services that are able to reduce inconveniences for users, improve the quality of life of patients, allow for timely interventions of diagnosis and therapy and, in the perspective of reducing healthcare expenses, reduce the number of hospital accesses.

Domiciliary self monitoring of blood glucose has provided a very important contribution and is considered as a means for diabetes therapy, that helps and is integrated with other classic instruments such as diet, exercise, medicine and health care. Nevertheless, the other side of the medal consists in the way self monitoring is often carried out and its related issues which can be summarized as follows:

Methods and Techniques: there is no assurance and continuity in the control. Having to proceed autonomously on their own and without direct medical control, patients often forget to collect the vital parameters or they invert the values when reporting them on their blood glucose log book. In other cases, for example, when a patient is not at home and forgets something (glucose diary, value reader, pin-stick) he/she is not able to self monitor. Indeed this occurs for one third of the patients.

Instruments: collecting a blood sample for the test, by using a lancing device, monitoring system, test strips with control solution, is often lived as a trauma especially by children. Furthermore, each test requires specific ad hoc test strips that are not interchangeable from one device to another. As so, the current devices present many hygienic (sterile lancets and controlled disposal) and logistic limitations (diabetics must always have enough lancets with them), other than the ones related to traumatic and pain aspects.

Data Management and Knowledge Assets: doctors encounter objective difficulties in managing the large amount of the data. This is mostly due to the increasing number of diabetic patients and among them, the increasing number of domiciliary self monitoring patients. Each patient carries out from a minimum of one, up to to 5-6 checks per day (insulin dependents). Consequently, at each clinical control (usually every 2-3 months) the number of values that the doctor must analyze is considerable and this requires time for consultation. At the same time, given the characteristics of the blood glucose log books (paper, local files), the data contained cannot be shared by the scientific community and allow for large scale studies on the pathologies and the effectiveness of the treatments or therapies adopted.

In this sense, the "My Smart Health (MSH)" solution, illustrated in this paper consists in an integrated system for collecting diabetic patient parameters in mobility. This translates in practice to a better acknowledgement of the disease allowing patients to maintain a high quality of life, reducing at the same time healthcare costs for managing diabetes. MSH aims to improve self-monitoring of glycemic levels with easy to use devices. The benefits in terms of technological innovation are twofold. On one hand it improves patient's relation with the disease thanks to a discrete and reliable device that provides real time feedback on the measurements carried out; on the other, it allows diabetologists, to rapidly obtain information from the data collected and closely monitor their patients identifying critical situations and improvements on the course of the disease with attention to each single patient.

The rest of the paper is organized as follows: section II sets the state of art on currently available self monitoring systems, points out the benefits and advantages of the solution proposed with respect to the state of art on what literature and market offers; section III describes the MSH solution framework; section IV points out the innovations of the solution proposed and how it overcomes the issues raised in literature; section V illustrates how the concepts of evidence based medicine are implemented in MSH; finally, conclusions are drawn.

II. State of Art on Self-Monitoring systems

Traditional self monitoring devices have a set of problems that can be classified into three categories: size and low appeal; interpretation of the collected data delegated to the patient; difficulties in the analysis of historical data and its reliability. In the following we provide an analysis of the literature for what concerns these problems related to existing solutions.

A. Size and low appeal

Glucometers currently present on the market, although differing by manufacturer, reliability, speed of measurement and another, often have a non negligible dimension that does not allow for a discrete use of the device. As proof of how this aspect is a known problem, producers of diagnostic systems have attempted to solve it by proposing devices with reduced size. Bayer's CONTOUR® USB [3], is a pen drive that allows to save data via USB with an integrated meter and graphical display; OneTouch Verio® IQ [4] is also an alternative to traditional meters in terms of color, dimensions, and a layout similar to a MP3 player. Although these solutions are more discrete than traditional ones, the reduction of size is minimal and yet to be overcome. This issue should not be underestimated as it directly impacts on the social aspect of the disease. Often diabetic patients are embarrassed to carry out self monitoring when in public and not at home. This is especially true for young patients and may lead to a non measurement with enormous impact on disease management and prevention of hypo and hyperglycemia events. A recent product characterized by its small dimensions is the GMATE-IRIS meter [5] that transfers data through an audio jack to a last generation smartphone. The counterpart of this solution is that it is only compatible with two smartphones (IPhone 5 and Samsung Galaxy SIII), both quite pricy, making the solution is unfeasible for all users. Another limitation is the fact that the IRIS model recovers the energy it needs for its operations directly from the smartphone battery. It cannot be used connected to any other smartphone.

B. Interpretation of the collected data delegated to the patient

As stated previously, measurement of glucose values is a primary aspect for coping with diabetes. However, it must be supported by an effective interpretation of the collected data, as a mere detection of a value has no meaning and does not produce any effect on diabetes management if it is not contextualized and correctly interpreted. The meters currently on the market show the value to the patient who, if appropriately instructed by their healthcare professional, will be more or like able to adopt corrective actions with respect to the measured data. In each case, a correct interpretation cannot be context independent and requires consideration of other parameters such as type if meal, time from previous or next meal, exercise carried out, mood (stress surely influences glucose levels), other physical parameters such as sex, age, height, correlation with previous measures, trend of the last period, just to mention a few. Many of these parameters are not directly collectable by the patients who, consequently, will most likely not know the relation between measures collected and the appropriate action to undertake. On the other end, even though a diabetic specialist is aware of such correlations and of the patient's specific case, he is not able to readily analyze all of the measures collected and provide feedback in real time.

C. Difficulties in analyzing historical data and its reliability

The two issues discussed above not only impact on the single measures of self monitoring but also have consequences on the global management of the disease and of its course for a patient. A set of measures not carried out, not appropriately characterized with respect to the parameters mentioned, or falsified by the patient himself represent an information deficit for the diabetologist who, in turn, must analyze the patient's clinical situation, identify the most appropriate therapy and monitor the evolution of the disease. None of the meters commercially available are able to avoid the risk of falsification of the data. Indeed, a patient can manually report the (falsified) value on the blood glucose log book, or can change the content of the file produced after the measurement in case of electronic diary (falsifying the data).

Furthermore, even correct and timely collected measures are not able to express the entire information potential due to the restrictions of the meters: measures are reported manually in paper log books or extracted by specific software integrated with the glucometer and reported in an electronic diary. All of this data is analyzed by the diabetologist during the patient's medical visit. It is clear that the large amount of data, along with the short time available for the visit represent a limit for a complete and detailed analysis of the data collected over a long time span that goes at least from one visit to another.

Given these considerations, MSH aims to improve self monitoring measures of blood glucose levels, increase the ease of use of the devices involved and improve the general management of the data collected in time. In the next section a detailed description of the solution is provided.

III. My Smart Health Solution

MSH is a solution for self monitoring of blood glucose levels integrated with hardware and software tools for: synchronous collection and analysis, anti-falsification and proactive verification in mobility of physiological parameters of the metabolic syndrome aligned with various diagnostic therapeutic protocols.

Figure 1 illustrates the logical architecture and deploy of the MSH solution.

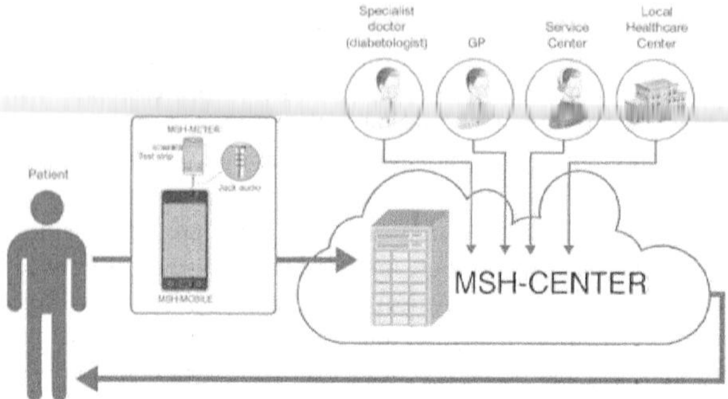

Fig. 1 Logical architecture of the MSH Solution

It is made up of the following components:

A. MSH-CENTER

This component is a software system provided as Software as a Service (SaaS) [6, 7] and accessible through a web portal by authorized users (diabetologist, patient, specialized operator, etc.) containing the following information: personal and physiological information of each patient; electronic log book of blood glucose measures; advanced report tools that allow to select and effectively present data included in the electronic log book; etc. Once logged into the system the diabetologist can select a patient from a list of patients and view information such as the blood glucose diary (Fig.2).

MSH-CENTER also includes a Feedback&Communication module used for detailed analysis of collected data, production of statistics and trends that support evidence based medicine [8, 9, 10]. This module will be further detailed in section IV.

B. MSH-MOBILE

This part of the system is made up of a software component installed on a certified and compatible smartphone, and a compatible audio jack able to visualize the physiological data collected by MSH-METER, save it locally in the electronic log book, elaborate and send it to the MSH-CENTER via GPRS/UMTS. MSH-MOBILE has a visual and vocal interface that guides the patient step by step in carrying out the self monitoring process (Fig.3). It also receives messages from the MSH-CENTER and therefore represents a means for communicating information to the patient (Fig.4).

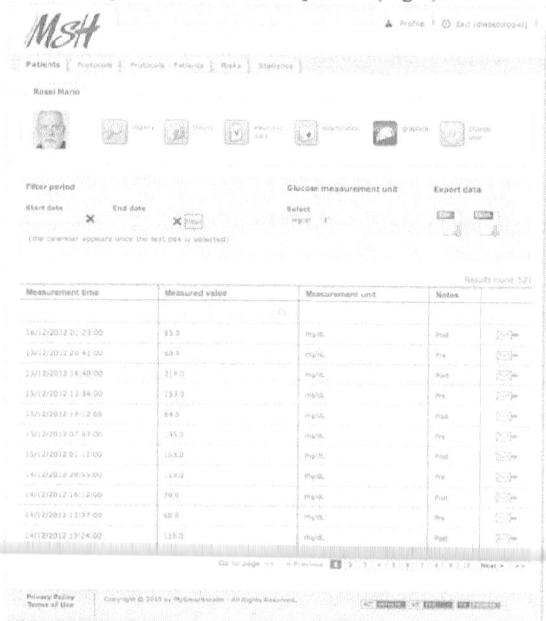

Fig.2. Blood Glucose diary of a selected patient

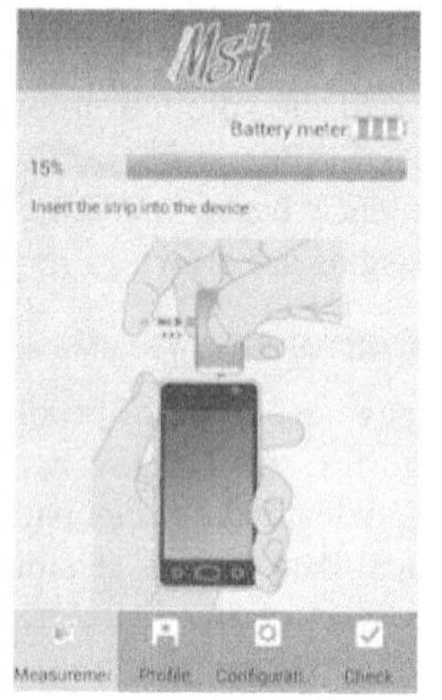

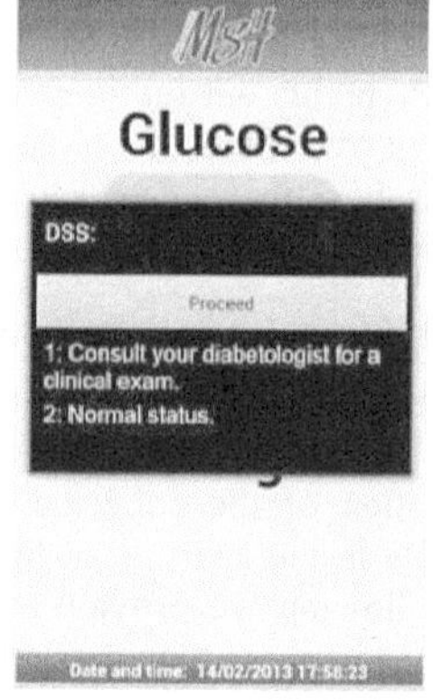

Fig.3 Guided interface

Fig.4 Message from MSH-CENTER

C. MSH-METER

This component is a self powered glucometer connected to the MSH-MOBILE through audio jack (Fig.5).

Fig.5 MSH METER

The component is able to collect the blood glucose values from a traditional test strip and communicate it to the MSH-MOBILE through the audio jack. A self control method assures interaction between MSH-METER and MSH-MOBILE which is installed on the smartphone.

The MSH architecture is based on two technological paradigms: Cloud Computing [11] and Future Internet [12] with particular attention to "internet of things". The first paradigm simplifies the administration and evolution of the system for doctors, patients and healthcare facility as it is managed by the MSH-CENTER. Furthermore, adoption of Future Internet maintains the communication between MSH-MOBILE, MSH-CENTER, diabetologists and service center in order to better control assistance to patients. This control is very reliable being based on an implementation of "internet of things" between MSH-METER and MSH-CENTER.

IV. Innovations of MSH

In this section we provide further insight as to how MSH overcomes the three categories of problems highlighted in section II.

A. Problem I: Size and low appeal

MSH-METER is a meter that combines ergonomic design with reduced dimensions, approximately half the size with respect to other commercially available devices, making it a suitable and discreet solution that preserves the social status of any diabetic patient. It assists self monitoring measurements and sends the data collected to the MSH-MOBILE component. Measurement is completed by simply connecting these two components through the audio jack of any smartphone. The connection allows for data transfer which consequently is: *reliable and secure*, in that it uses modulation frequency for transmission of signals, a stable and well known technology used for communication. Furthermore, the connection between MSH-METER and smartphone is mechanical, so it is not affected by poor reception or interferences as for wireless or infrared connections; *anonymous*, as transmission does not use radio frequencies or other types of signals (Bluetooth or WiFi) that may be intercepted and decoded. The data is collected from the MSH-METER and transferred AS-IS to the smartphone through audio signal.

Furthermore, unlike its competitor GMATE-IRIS, MSH-METER does not use the power of the smartphone to function, rather it is self powered by an internal lithium battery. Consequently it can be used on any smartphone with an audio jack that satisfies the OS requirements. The battery begins to supply power only after the self monitoring procedure has been activated through the MSH-MOBILE installed on the smartphone. Tests have shown that a battery lasts for about nine months of therapy of an average patient.

B. Problem II: Interpretation of the collected data delegated to the patient

MSH supports patients in interpreting the measurement values. After having completed the self measurement, MSH-MOBILE contextualizes the data and indicates if it is pre or post prandial as well as the elapsed time from the last meal (breakfast, lunch, dinner, snack). The data is locally saved in MSH-MOBILE and, at the same time, sent to MSH-CENTER and saved. Next, MSH-MOBILE will query MSH-CENTER with particular reference to the Feedback&Communication component, in order to receive feedback in real time on the measurement sent.

The Feedback&Communication component (Fig.6) is an analytical engine based on rules that allow to analyze the data received in real time and validate it with respect to one or more interpretation protocols defined by the diabetologist.

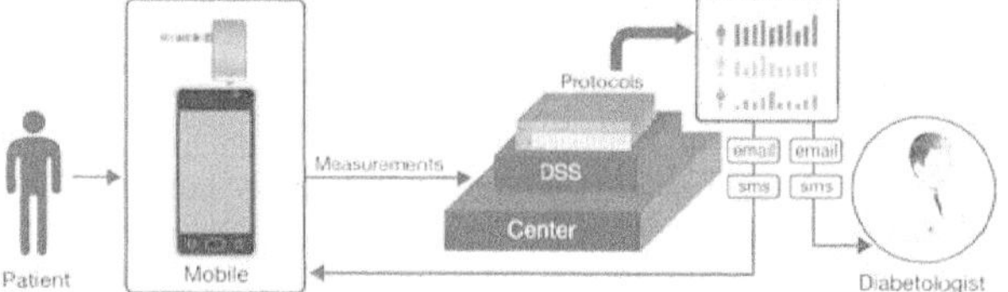

Fig.6 Feedback&Communication conceptual module

In practical terms, the MSH-CENTER is accessible through a webpage by authorized users, in this case the diabetologist. A protocol is a set of rules that the doctor creates with the assistance of a wizard that guides him in defining the decision rule(s) using a set of conditional operators (<, >, <=, >=) together with additional conditions that are taken into account for interpreting the data. The method and technology used to implement the decision support system is that of decision tables [13]. Here, the *conditions* are represented by indicators such as blood glucose measurements and eventually also other indicators such as sex, age, previous data values, pharmaceutical treatment undertaken etc.; the *conditional states* are the possible values for each condition; a *rule* or *action entry* is the combination of conditional states, i.e. the measurement values collected for each condition; the *actions* identified, represent the feedback information that is communicated to the patient and/or doctor after each measurement. The actions are classified according to a chromatic legend from most to less severe code: RED, ORANGE, YELLOW, GREEN. Figure 8 is the graphical interface that the diabetologist uses for defining a protocol in th MSH-CENTER. In this particular case the protocol expresses actions (rules) to undertake depending on the condition "blood glucose value" (<60=RED; between <60-100> = YELLOW; >200=RED; between <130-200>=YELLOW). Each time a protocol is defined, the diabetologist also specifies the recipient of the message among the possible user profiles (patient, doctor, service center, local healthcare unit, etc.) as well as where to send the message (sms, email, smartphone connected to the meter). As last step, the diabetologist assigns a protocol to each patient. To summarize, MSH-MOBILE collects the data from the meter, sends it to MSH-CENTER and queries the decision support system. Depending on the interpretation of the data, a message is sent to a specific recipient through a specific communication channel. So for e.g. if "Blood glucose value = 57", a RED CODE is activated and both diabetologist and patient are alerted with a message.

All of the communication messages sent out following to interpretations of the therapeutic protocols are saved in the Feedback&Communication module. Each time a measurement is carried out by a patient and transferred by the MSH-MOBILE, it activates a decision rule of the protocol, the system saves it in the archive of actions endorsed (made up of a temporal reference, the message sent and the communication channel used for sending it). All of the actions saved can be consulted in a specific section of MSH-CENTER which offers the following functionalities:

- Filter on actions. Actions per patient can be ordered and filtered according to date of issue, chromatic code of alert, etc;
- Detailed consultation of the action undertaken for each measurement collected;
- Mark notifications. The actions to carry out, that have been consulted by a patient can be marked as "already read".

The "Risks" section of the MSH-CENTER platform provides a summary of all the follow-up initiatives and feedback provided by the system based on the measurements received, according to the protocols defined by the diabetologists and applied to each patient. So, this section allows to monitor patients on a daily basis and readily take action in case of alert cases. Figure 8 summarizes the alert situations that have occurred for patient Mr. Mario Rossi specifying for each case, the date and alert code. It is also possible to have detailed information for each alert by clicking on it.

Fig. 7 Protocol Definition Interface

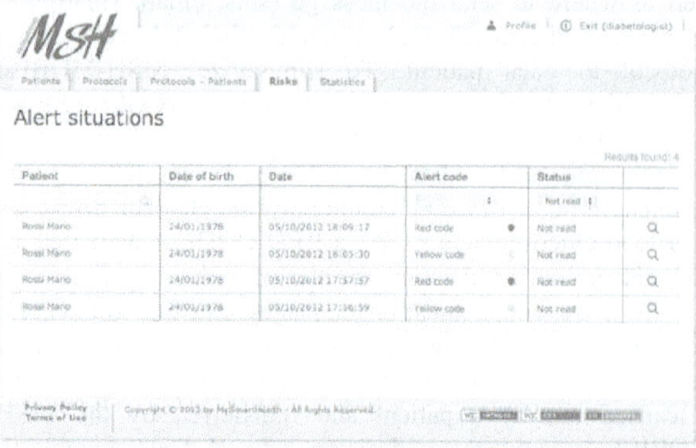

Fig. 8 Risks module for each patient

In this sense, this module not only provides a reference for the diabetologist who can control the general situation of any patient, but also and especially for a service center that is able to constantly monitor all registered patients in real time and promptly take action in case of emergency.

C. Problem III: Difficulties in analyzing historical data

The entire process of self monitoring, cataloging, collection, analysis, interpretation, and data management that characterizes the MSH-CENTER is a relevant contribution for the analysis of historical data and, consequently, plays an important role in validating the therapeutic treatment of each diabetic patient. Indeed, the MSH platform provides diabetologists a precise electronic log book of each patient without "falsifications" (every measurement reports the exact time it is taken at); furthermore, it also provides a consultation section dedicated to synthesis reports, graphical representations, trends of the data collected from the MSH-MOBILE unit, classified and stored in the MSH data bases of the MSH-CENTER component.

In particular, the module related to "Statistics" allows to define two types of graphs and is divided into two distinct logical areas: one dedicated to the representation of data related to single patients (Fig 9), and one for elaborating complex statistics on a wider range of patients (Fig.10) that belong to a specific cohort constantly monitored by the local healthcare center and by a diabetologist.

For what concerns the graphs on single patients, data points refer to a period of thirty days prior to the current one. It is also possible to create other graphs based on longer periods of observation such as monthly, three months, up to a six month period. For example, the graph in Fig. 9 provides textual information on the visualization date, reference period, number of days with at least one self monitoring data collected, number of self monitoring glucose level collected over the period, the risk baselines (60-200) in accordance to the OMS/NDDG criteria [14] and to the criteria for diagnosis of diabetes mellitus proposed by the ADA Expert Committee [15]. The graph shows the trend of the measures related to the patient (Mr. Mario Rossi) over at three month observation period. Other trends can be produced with respect to pre-post prandial values, mean, mean +/- standard deviation, or graphs that point out the distribution of the data points within reference intervals of glycemic values (for example: <60; <60-100>; <100-130>...).

It is evident that a graphical visualization of a patient's clinical situation is an added value for the diabetologist as he/she has a general picture of the trend of measurements in a unique interface that summarizes all the relevant information necessary for decision making, allowing to focus on a single data point if the case. Consequently, these functionalities reduce the effort of the diabetologist for analyzing the clinical data, and the effects of the therapy and eventually make any changes. Although such operations are also possible without the MSH suite, they obviously would request much more work, effort and data elaboration between various devices (paper/electronic log books, spreadsheets with data, statistical tool for elaborations etc.) with high risk of falsifications and errors.

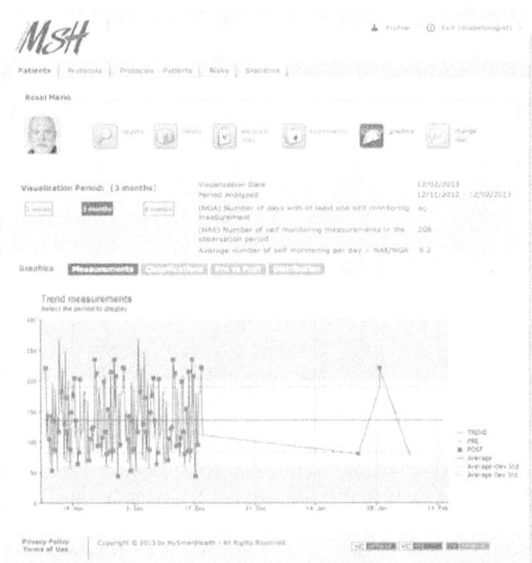

Fig. 9 Graph on trend of patient's self monitoring measurements

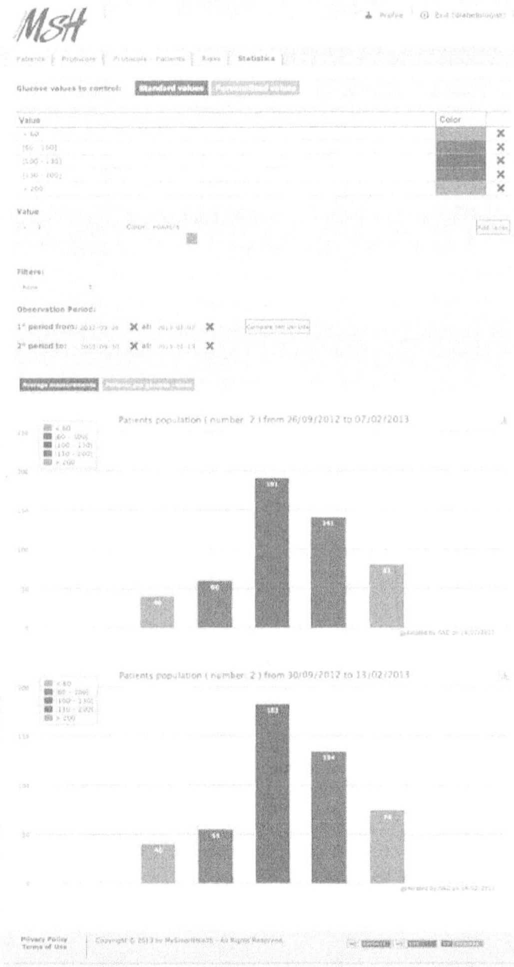

Fig. 10 Comparison of glucose values during two observation periods

MSH reduces such risks and allows for real time data elaboration and decision making based on the decision support system. Results are accessible via web and therefore consultable by various stakeholders (specialist, local healthcare center, patient, etc.) anywhere.

The graphs related to more complex elaborations on cohorts of patients can be seen as a Business Intelligence [16] subsystem, used by authorized personnel for epistemological analysis and wider investigations on entire populations of diabetic patients monitored by the healthcare center that uses MSH. This component provides various criteria for grouping and filtering data related to the population of patients. Possible filters are for example: age, sex, weight, type of diabetes, etc. So a type of graphical analysis that can be requested ad hoc may be to compare the averages of blood glucose levels of patients classified according to the intervals of the protocol during two different observation periods (Fig.10).

Availability of such information and data is important for the scientific community as it provides evidence on the effectiveness and validity of therapies defined and adopted. This concept is described in more detail in the next section.

V. Evidence Based Medicine in MSH

The MSH solution represents a valid support system for the diabetologist, as he/she can elaborate complex statistics on an entire cohort of patients and undertake common preventive initiatives and validate their effectiveness and evolution from both an epistemological and scientific perspective. All the information collected, the protocols defined and evolved in time, the decision support system created with decision models, the actions carried out, monitored and controlled in time make up the knowledge base of therapies and contribute to create the Evidence Based Medicine (EBM) [8, 9, 10] component. Moreover, EBM in this specific case constitutes an approach to the clinical practice, where the clinical decisions derive from the integration between the doctor's experience and the adoption of the best available evidence on therapies or protocols, mediated by the patient's experience.

This said, the EBM unit inside the proposed solution makes a cluster of statistical instruments available for doctors, diabetoligists, associations and authorized personnel, which are useful for analyzing the enormous quantity of clinical data collected by the system in order to determine, based on founded evidences, the best therapies to adopt. A general idea of the EBM concept is illustrated in Fig.11.

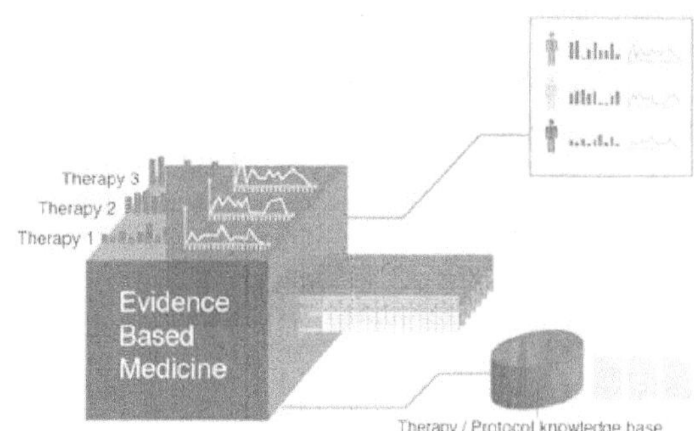

Fig. 11 Knowledge base of consultable therapies /protocols

As stated in the previous section the therapies/protocols associated to each patient are formalized through a decision table and are part of a decision support system. Consequently, by monitoring diabetic patients, it is possible to compare the effect of the different therapies and determine the best one; by studying a single patient, it is possible to check the effect that variations to a therapy/protocol (formally consisting in the change of a decision table) have on the patient's health condition. In this way, the doctor can immediately check the cause-effect relations between the therapy changes (for e.g. a different diet or a higher or lower injection of insulin) and the response of the patient. Furthermore, by studying the trend of the examined data, it is possible to go back to the therapy adopted and make the appropriate changes. For example, a trend showing a significant improvement of the glucose level pre and post-lunch, could encourage the doctor to revise the prescribed therapy and analyze its main features. The doctor could then decide to adopt it and experiment it on other patients as well. Finally, the EBM unit provides instruments for generating evidence and critical experience about the current therapies being adopted, and so, it can be seen as a valuable means for supporting continuous improvement of the clinical practice.

VI. Conclusions

"My Smart Health" is a solution made up of hardware devices and software components that allow data collection, synchronous and asynchronous analysis, proactive checking in mobility of physiological parameters involved in the monitoring process of glycemic values. It is a novel and innovative solution compared to competitor products currently available on the market. It reduces the social impact of diabetes and improves the support provided to patients during the definition and adoption of a diagnostic and therapeutic solution on behalf of all stakeholders such as diabetologists, general med doctors, pharmacists, and all the healthcare centers involved.

The advanced data analysis features along with the decision support system and therapies knowledge base provide considerable support towards scientific research for medical purposes on relevant amounts of data related to an entire cohort of patients. Moreover, the Feedback&Communication module allows to create and manage protocols, feedback and communications that can either be the same for all users or personalized per single patient, depending on the needs of the diabetologist and the clinical situation of the patient. Overall, the solution represents an effective means of communication towards patients allowing for a more effective action of therapeutic follow-up.

MSH has already been subjected to different cycles of verification and validation. First of all the software components have been tested through 3 types of tests: unit test, integration test, and system test. The unit test was conducted with a white box strategy while the remaining two in a black box mode. Then we carried out an on field investigation that involved a small group of 10 volunteers for a period of 6 months. They provided important feedbacks especially useful for improving the human-machine interface. We have recently started setting up a wider and more complex experiment involving 100 subjects. After this phase, we plan on starting a large-scale production and distribution of the product over national and international markets. Also the MSH-Meter was subject to multiple cycles of testing and prototyping that have allowed its validation and, above all, its evolution in order to be compatible with the largest number of smartphones on the market.

References

[1] T.Kuzuya, et al., "Report of the committee on the classification and diagnostic criteria of diabetes mellitus", Diabetes Research and Clinical Practice, 55(1), 2002, pp.65-85

[2] Report of a WHO Consultation, "Definition, diagnosis and classification of diabetes mellitus and its complications. Part 1", World Health Organization, Department of Noncommunicable Disease Surveillance, Geneva, 1999

[3] ContourUSB. www.byercontourusb.com

[4] OneTouch Verio. http://www.lifescan.it

[5] GMATE-IRIS, www.gmate.biz

[6] M.Turner, D.Budgen, P.Brereton, "Turning software into a service", IEEE Computer, 36 (10), 2003, pp.38-44.

[7] V.Choudhary, "Software as a service: implications for investment in software development", 40th Hawaii International Conference on System Sciences, 2007. HICSS 2007

[8] GH. Guyatt "Evidence-based medicine".ACP 1991; 114(2):A-16

[9] DL. Sackett, WMC Rosenberg, JAM Gray, et al. "Evidence-Based Medicine: What it is and what it isn't", BMJ 1996; 312:71-2 url: http://www.bmj.com/cgi/content/full/312/7023/71

[10] GH Guyatt, MO Meade, RZ Jaeschke, et al., "Practitioners of evidence based care". BMJ 2000; 320:954-955, url:http://www.bmj.com/cgi/content/full/320/7240/954

[11] T.Velte, A.Velte, R.Elsenpeter, *Cloud Computing, a practical approach*, McGraw Hill Inc., New York, 2010

[12] Future Internet. "Shaping Policies for a Digital World: The Seoul Declaration for the Future of the Internet Economy". OECD 2008, (http://www.oecd.org/FutureInternet/)

[13] J. Huysmans, K. Dejaeger, C.Mues, J.Vanthienen, B.Baesens, "An empirical evaluation of the comprehensibility of decision table, tree and rule based predictive models", Decision Support Systems, Volume 51, Issue 1, April 2011, Pages 141-154

[14] AA Motala, MA Omar, "Evaluation of WHO and NDDG criteria for impaired glucose tolerance", Diabetes Res Clin Practice, 1994; 23(2), pp.103-109.

[15] American Diabetes Association, "Diagnosis and classification of diabetes mellitus", Diabetes Care January 2010 vol. 33 no. Supplement 1 S62-S69, doi: 10.2337/dc10-S062

[16] L.T. Moss, S.Atre, *Business Intelligence Roadmap: the complete project lifecycle for decision support applications*, Addison Wesley, 2003, ISBN: 0201784203.

A novel method for finding sub-classification diagnosis biomarkers of ovarian cancer

Quoc-Nam Tran[†],
The University of Texas at Tyler, USA.

Abstract— *Ovarian cancer is the most lethal gynaecological malignancy, accounting for 5–6% of all cancer-related deaths. When ovarian cancer is diagnosed at early stages, the survival rate is very high - close to 90%. However, since ovarian cancer has few early or specific symptoms, the vast majority of patients are identified when they have late-stage disease. A typical molecular sub-classification method would have a low predictive accuracy of 68%-71%. Hence, discovering cost-effective biological markers that can be used to improve the diagnosis and prognosis of the disease is an important challenge.*

In this paper, we present a new statistical and data mining method, called the multi-pronged filter method, to find genetic markers and uses the markers to predict with up to 100% accuracy whether a patient has a sub-type of epithelial ovarian cancer. Our method overcomes many challenges arose from datasets of gene-expression profiles. The new method discovers novel genetic changes that occur in ovarian tumors using gene-expression profiles. We discovered that a small set of eleven gene-signatures (TFF3, FGFR4, TCOF1, EFNB2, GPRC5A, ANK1, ACTN1, PEG3, PBX1, ATP10B and MST4) from the dataset of 22,283 gene-expression profiles of ovarian tumors acts like an inference basis for ovarian cancer and hence can be used as genetic markers. Furthermore, our method discovers that a single gene - the MLF1 - can be used to differentiate the two sub-classes of Mucinous and Serous. These very small and previously unknown sets of biological markers gives an almost perfect predictive accuracy for the diagnosis of the disease.

Except for TFF3 and FGFR4, specific functions of proteins encoded by other gene-signatures for ovarian cancer have not yet been determined. Hence, this work opens new questions for structural and molecular biologists about the role of these gene-signatures for the disease.

Index Terms— **Biomarker, ovarian cancer, multi-pronged filter method, data mining, sub-classification diagnosis**

[†] Supported in part by NSF award CCF-0917257.

1. Introduction

Cancer has become a major public health problem in the United States as well as many other parts of the world [1, 2, 3]. Even though, ovarian cancer is not among the top five most common cancer-related deaths, it occurs in 1 of 2,500 post-menopausal women in the United States and is the most lethal gynaecological malignancy, accounting for 5–6% of all cancer-related deaths. When ovarian cancer is diagnosed at early stages, the survival rate is very high - close to 90%. However, since ovarian cancer has few early or specific symptoms, the vast majority of patients are identified when they have late-stage disease. It is estimated that there are 22,240 new cases and 14,030 deaths from ovarian cancer in the United States in 2013.

Researchers have not made many advances in extending overall survival durations over the past few decades [4]. Currently, the fundamental treatment of this cancer is surgery with the aim of reducing the tumor burden to microscopic disease. This is usually followed by adjuvant combination chemotherapy with platinum and taxane, which produces initial complete responses in 80% of patients [5]. However, abdominal and pelvic recurrence rates approach 80%, and response to further chemotherapy is limited. Attempts at using biologic agents to improve outcomes of this disease, including trap proteins, siRNA encapsulated in nanoparticles, and humanized antibodies, are ongoing [6, 7].

The most studied marker for ovarian cancer is CA125 and determination of its concentration in circulation is essential for monitoring response to treatment for ovarian cancer. Its expression is increased in many benign gynaecological diseases, such as endometriosis and outside of the female genital tract in tissues such as lung, breast and prostate. CA125 has been proposed as a possible screening test for ovarian cancer. However, this marker has low sensitivity, as its expression is increased in fewer than 50% of early-stage ovarian cancers and it is not expressed by tumor cells in 20% of women diagnosed. That said, discovering cost-effective biological markers that can be used to improve the diagnosis and prognosis of the disease is an important clinical challenge [8].

There are three main types of ovarian tumors: (a) Epithelial ovarian tumors are derived from the cells on the surface of the ovary. This is the most common form of ovarian cancer and occurs primarily in adults. (b) Germ cell ovarian tumors are derived from the egg producing cells within the body of the ovary. This occurs primarily in children and teens and is rare by comparison to epithelial ovarian tumors. (c) Sex cord stromal ovarian tumors are also rare in comparison to epithelial tumors and this class of tumors often produces steroid hormones.

Surface epithelial tumors account for 80-90% of malignant ovarian tumors. Surface epithelial neoplasms are classified into subtypes based on the type of epithelial differentiation that is present in the tumor. The subtypes include serous, mucinous, endometrioid, clear cell, and transitional cell.

Multiple techniques have evolved over the past few years allow rapid measurement of gene expression and simultaneous high-throughput measurement of thousands of genes from several hundred samples. Different parts of the gene-protein relationship can be measured such as messenger RNA levels, protein expression and cellular metabolic activity. Some of the available genomic technologies include gene expression arrays, serial analysis of gene expression, single-nucleotide polymorphism analysis, and high-throughput capillary sequencing [8].

Gene-expression array analysis methodologies developed over the last few years have demonstrated that expression data can be used in a variety of class discovery or class prediction biomedical problems including those relevant to tumor classification [9, 10, 11, 12]. Data mining and statistical techniques applied to gene expression data have been used to address the questions of distinguishing tumor morphology, predicting post treatment outcome, and finding molecular markers for disease [13, 14, 15, 16, 17, 18, 19].

However, gene expression profiles present many challenges for data mining both in finding differentially expressed genes, and in building predictive models because the datasets are highly multidimensional (22,283 dimensions in our study) and contain a small number of records (99 records in our study). Although microarray analysis tool can be used as an initial step to extract most relevant features, one has to avoid over-fitting the data and deal with the very large number of dimensions of the datasets. Other researchers also limited themselves in differentiate only two sub-types of ovarian cancer such as to compare gene expression profiles in ovarian cancers and normal ovaries.

This paper aims at a new statistical and data mining method, called the multi-pronged filter method, to find genetic markers and uses the markers to predict with up to 100% accuracy whether a patient has a sub-type of epithelial ovarian cancer. Our method overcomes many challenges arose from datasets of gene-expression profiles. This new method discovers novel genetic changes that occur in ovarian tumors using gene-expression profiles. We discovered that a small set of eleven gene-signatures (TFF3, FGFR4, TCOF1, EFNB2, GPRC5A, ANK1, ACTN1, PEG3, PBX1, ATP10B and MST4) from the dataset of 22,283 gene-expression profiles of ovarian tumors acts like an inference basis for ovarian cancer and hence can be used as genetic markers. Furthermore, our method discovers that a single gene - the MLF1 - can be used to differentiate the two sub-classes of Mucinous and Serous. These very small and previously unknown sets of biological markers gives an almost perfect predictive accuracy for the diagnosis of the disease.

While proteins encoded by some of these gene-signatures (e.g., TFF3 and FGFR4) have been showed to involve in the signal transduction of cells and proliferative control of normal cells, specific functions of proteins encoded by other gene-signatures have not yet been determined [20, 21, 22]. Hence, this work opens new questions for structural and molecular biologists about the role of these gene-signatures for the disease.

2. A Multi-pronged Filter Method for Significant Genes Selection & Sub-Classification

2.1 RNA Materials

We use the gene-expression profiles of ovarian tumors from the RNA expression profiles in GSE6008 [23] in that RNA expression of a total of 99 individual ovarian tumors (37 endometrioid, 41 serous, 13 mucinous, and 8 clear cell carcinomas) and 4 individual normal ovary samples were analyzed using one Affymetrix HG_U133A array per sample. Total RNA was extracted from the tissue lysate using an RNeasy kit (Qiagen). 3-5 µg of total RNA was processed to produce biotinylated cRNA targets using the standard Affymetrix procedures as hybridization protocol and scan protocol. Ann Arbor quantile-normalized trimmed-mean method was used for data processing. VALUE quantile-normalized trimmed-mean, log-transformed with log(max(x+50,0)+50) using base 10 logarithms.

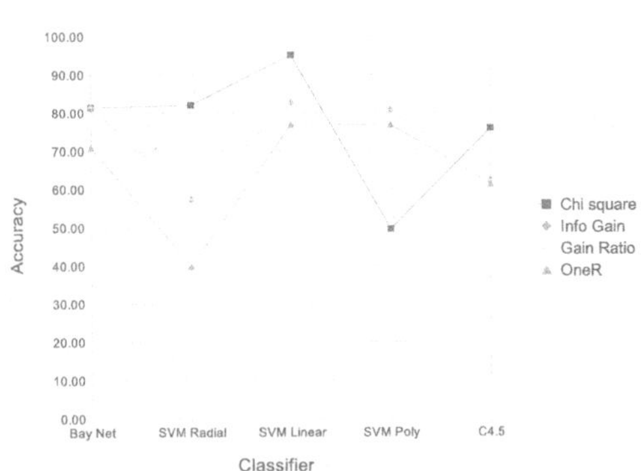

Fig. 1

ACCURACY OF KNOWN SUB-CLASSIFICATIONS FOR 5287 FILTERED GENES

2.2 Finding genetic markers

With 22,283 dimensions and only 99 records, these gene expression profiles for ovarian cancer presents many challenges for finding differentially expressed genes and for building predictive models. Although microarray analysis tool can be used as an initial step to extract most relevant features, one has to avoid over-fitting the data and deal with the very large number of dimensions of the datasets.

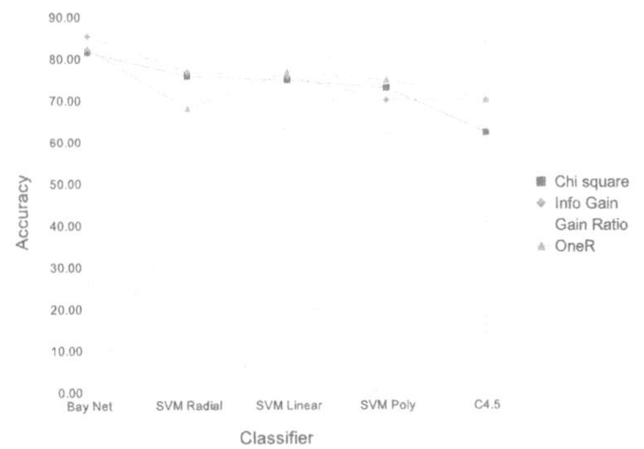

Fig. 2

ACCURACY OF KNOWN SUB-CLASSIFICATIONS FOR 100 FILTERED GENES

The most studied marker for ovarian cancer is CA125 and determination of its concentration in circulation is essential for monitoring response to treatment for ovarian cancer. Its expression is increased in many benign gynaecological diseases, such as endometriosis and outside of the female genital tract in tissues such as lung, breast and prostate. CA125 has been proposed as a possible screening test for ovarian cancer. However, this marker has low sensitivity, as its expression is increased in fewer than 50% of early-stage ovarian cancers and it is not expressed by tumor cells in 20% of women diagnosed.

Predictive classification of cancer tissue samples based upon gene expression data has advanced considerably in recent years. However, it faces great challenges to improve the accuracy. A typical molecular sub-classification method would have a low predictive accuracy of 68%-71%. Other researchers also limited themselves in differentiate only two sub-types of ovarian cancer such as to compare gene expression profiles in ovarian cancers and normal ovaries.

Hence, discovering cost-effective biological markers that can be used to improve the diagnosis and prognosis of the disease is an important clinical challenge [8]. Current research is looking at ways to combine tumor markers proteomics along with other indicators of disease such as radiology or symptoms to improve the accuracy.

It is well-known that not all of the 22,283 gene expression profiles are relevant for ovarian cancer. Therefore, reducing the dimensionality of the data will reduce the size of the hypothesis space and allows model building algorithms to operate faster and more effectively. Our goal is to find compact and cost-effective biological markers by removing irrelevant and redundant attributes in the dataset of gene expression profiles.

A simple approach for obtaining the smallest subset of gene expression profiles for predictive classifications is by analyzing all subsets of the gene expression profiles and select the one with highest accuracy. However, it is infeasible to do so because testing all combinatorial possibilities for 22,283 genes amounts to the building and testing of 10^{6707} predictive models - a task that would require many thousand years to finish even when all computers on the world are used together.

Many heuristic algorithms that perform feature selection as a pre-processing step prior to learning have been studied before. The wrapper approach employs statistical re-sampling techniques such as cross validation and uses a target predictive classification algorithm to estimate the accuracy of feature subsets [24, 25]. This approach has proved useful but is very slow to execute because the learning algorithm is called repeatedly. The filter approach operates independently of any learning algorithm in that undesirable features are filtered out of the dataset before induction commences [24, 26, 27, 28]. Filters typically make use of all the available training data when selecting a subset of features. Some filters look for consistency in the data such as a feature subset which is associated with a single class. Other filter methods attempt to rank features according to a relevancy score such as correlation, Chi square values, info gain values or gain ratios. Filters have proven to be much faster than wrappers and hence can be applied to large data sets containing many features. However, running correlation-based filters on our ovarian cancer dataset often produce large subsets with many hundreds gene attributes and require more than 100 CPU hours on a server with Intel Xeon W3520 CPU at 2.67 GHz running Linux Ubuntu 12.04 LTS. Furthermore, the filtered datasets provide low accuracy. Using the known filter methods, we filtered the ovarian cancer dataset by choosing the features with highest ranking using Chi square, info gain, gain ration and one rule methods. The results are not encouraging as we present the accuracy of five known different predictive classification algorithms on the filtered datasets in Figure 1, Figure 2 and Figure 3 where 5287, 100 and 10 highest ranking genes were selected, respectively. Discretization of gene expression values following [29] may help to improve the accuracy of the known sub-classification algorithms a bit. For example, the accuracy of the Bayesian Network classifier for the 10 genes with highest Chi square values will increase from 74.76% to 79.61% when the values are discretized.

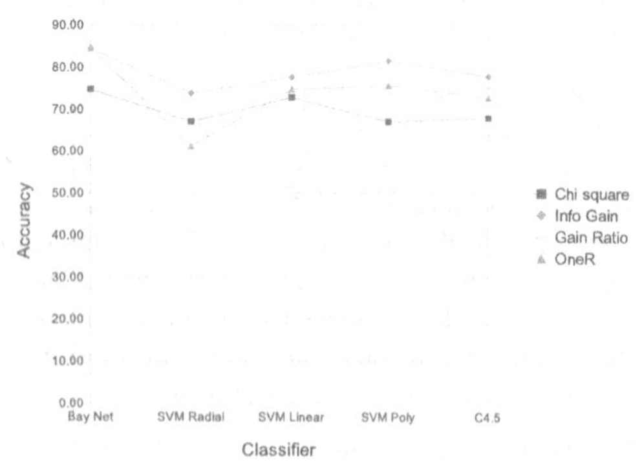

Fig. 3

ACCURACY OF KNOWN SUB-CLASSIFICATIONS FOR 10 FILTERED GENES

2.3 Results

To find compact and cost-effective biological markers with high accuracy, we use a multi-pronged filtering approach as depicted in Figure 4. We modified the ranking scheme for some filters (see Section-2.4 for details) to address challenges arose from datasets of gene-expression profiles and select several subsets of 250 genes with the highest scores using LorenzGini indexes, info gain, Chi square and one rule filters. To further reduce the size of the gene subsets and to improve the prediction accuracy, we evaluate different combinations of genes to identify an optimal subset in terms of accuracy for the Bayesian-based classification. The gene subsets to be evaluated are generated using different subset search techniques. We use Best First and Greedy search methods in the forward and backward directions. Greedy search considers changes local to the current subset through the addition or removal of genes. For a given parent set, a greedy search examines all possible child subsets through either the addition or removal of genes. The child subset that shows the highest goodness measure then replaces the parent subset, and the process is repeated. The process terminates when no more improvement can be made. Best First search is similar to greedy search in that it creates new subsets based on the addition or removal of genes to the current subset with the ability to backtrack along the subset selection path to explore different possibilities when the current path no longer shows improvement. To prevent the search from backtracking through all possibilities in the gene space, a limit is placed on the number of non-improving subsets that are considered. In our evaluation we chose a limit of five. This step reduces the candidate subset to between 20-30 genes.

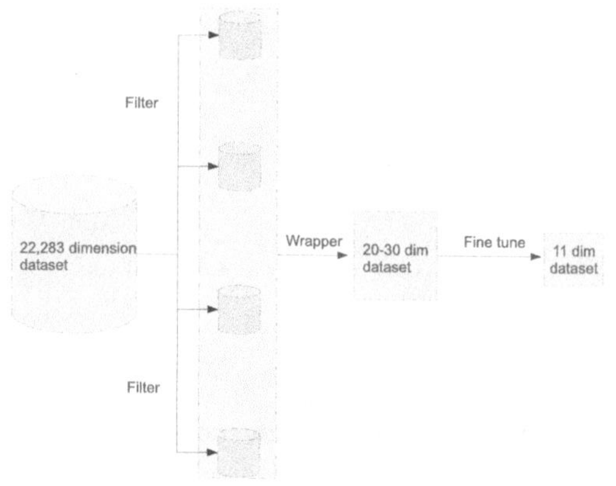

Fig. 4

MULTI-PRONGED FILTER APPROACH

Finally, the fine tune step of our multi-pronged filter method performs the exhaustive search to produce a subset of eleven gene-signatures (TFF3, FGFR4, TCOF1, EFNB2, GPRC5A, ANK1, ACTN1, PEG3, PBX1, ATP10B and MST4) from the dataset of 22,283 gene-expression profiles of ovarian tumors. This small subset of genes acts like an inference basis for ovarian cancer and hence can be used as genetic markers.

For a reliable evaluation of the accuracy, we use the well-known k-fold cross-validation approach. We test the classification algorithm for many values of k. More precisely, we test for $k = 7..10$. For each value of k, the data set D is randomly divided into k equal size subsets $D_1, D_2, \ldots, D_k$. We leave out one of the subsets D_i, $i = 1..k$ one at a time for being used as a separated test dataset for the validation. The remaining subsets $\cup_{j \neq i} D_j$ are used to build the model. This process is repeated k times, each time leaving one subset out for separated testing and the rest for training. The cross validation accuracy is given by the average of the accuracy of the k tested models. To ease the effects of the random partitions on the dataset, this whole process is repeated 10 times with different random seeds and the results are then averaged to give the estimated accuracy of the predictive sub-classification method.

During the validation process, all patients with clear cell type ovarian cancer were correctly predicted; all patients with endometrioid type ovarian cancer were correctly predicted; all patients with serous type ovarian cancer were correctly predicted; all patients with normal ovarian specimens were correctly predicted; and all but one patients with mucinous type ovarian cancer were correctly predicted. The only false prediction was a patient with mucinous type ovarian cancer but incorrectly predicted as serous type ovarian cancer.

To address this only false prediction, we apply the method again but for the reduced dataset with only two class labels of mucinous and serous. Our method returns a singleton set of one gene signature - the MLF1. This singleton set gives a perfect (100%) predictive accuracy for differentiating between mucinous and serous types ovarian cancer. The ROC curve with 1.0 area under the curve is presented in Figure 5.

As we can see, combining these very small sets of genes gives a perfect predictive accuracy for the sub-classification diagnosis of the disease. When the number of genes is further reduced or increased, the accuracy starts to declined. That said, this set of eleven genes acts like an inference basis for ovarian cancer and hence can be used as genetic markers. A summary of our approach is as follows:

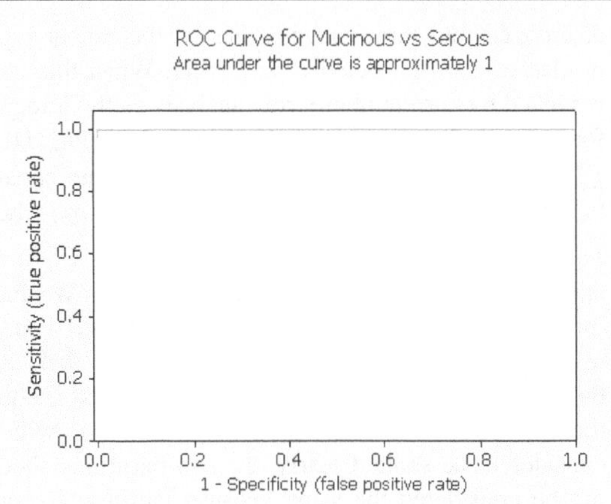

Fig. 5
RECEIVER OPERATOR CHARACTERISTIC (ROC) CURVE

Algorithm :

Input: A gene-expression profiles dataset D with 22823 gene-expression profiles.
OutputA small subset of genes as genetic markers and a prediction model for ovarian cancer
Step1: Select between 100-250 genes with highest ranking from multiple filters. Discretize the gene-expression profile values if needed.
Step2: Combine the filtered sets of genes. Apply wrappers and correlation-based feature selection methods to reduce the number of genes.
Step3: Fine tune the subset of genes using exhaustive search to produce the genetic markers.
Step3: Build the prediction model to classify patients using the genetic markers.

2.4 Methods

The first challenge that arose from the gene-expression datasets is the bias due to the order of cancer types or classes in data mining's terminology. Let's consider

Range/Class	C_1	C_2	C_3
R_1	4	6	30
R_2	6	30	4
R_3	0	4	16

Table 1
BIAS DUE TO THE ORDER OF CLASSES

a simple example of expression profiles for a gene in Table 1 where the gene dataset D has $d = 100$ elements and three classes. The gene expression values were discretized into three ranges. Clearly, the cancer types or classes can be labeled in any order. When this gene is ranked by current microarray analysis methodologies, for example by calculating the Gini index $gini_A(D) = \sum_{i=1}^{m} \frac{|R_i|}{d} \cdot gini(R_i)$, the first two rows contribute equally to the Gini index because $gini(R_i) = 1 - \sum_{j=1}^{n} p_{i,j}^2$ where $p_{i,j} = \frac{|C_{i,j}|}{|R_i|}$ is the relative frequency of class C_j in R_i, and $|\cdot|$ is the notation for cardinality [30]. We have the same problem when entropy is calculated instead of the Gini index. That said, when one just considers the probability distribution without taking into account the order of the classes, the first two partitions will be considered the same. Clearly, the two partitions should not be considered the same because Partition R_1 says that 75% of patients with gene expression values within this range are classified into Class C_3 while Partition R_2 says that 75% of patients with gene expression values within this range are classified into Class C_2. Hence, in order to have a robust gene selection method, one has to differentiate the partitions with different class orders because they have different amount of information.

To solve this problem, in [18] we generalized the well known Lorenz curves, a common measure in economics to gauge the inequalities in income and wealth. The Equality Polygon (Eq) is defined based on the percentages of elements in $|C_1|$, $|C_{1..2}| = |C_1| + |C_2|$, ..., $|C_{1..n}| = \sum_{j=1}^{n} |C_j|$ at x−coordinates 0, $1/n$, $2/n$, ..., 1, where n is the number of classes and $|C_1| \leq |C_2| \leq$, ..., $\leq |C_n|$. The Lorenz curve of a partition, say R_i, is defined based on the percentage of elements in $|C_{i,1}|$, $|C_{i,1}| + |C_{i,2}|$, ..., $\sum_{j=1}^{n} |C_{i,j}|$ at x−coordinates 0, $1/n$, $2/n$, ..., 1. The Gini coefficient of a partition, say R_i, is defined as $(\int_0^1 L(R_i) \cdot dx \text{-} \int_0^1 Eq \cdot dx) / \int_0^1 Eq \cdot dx$. One can easily see that the partitions with different class orders are now differentiated.

To evaluate the merit of a subset of features, we use

$$M_S = \frac{n \cdot \bar{r_{cf}}}{\sqrt{n + n \cdot (n-1) \cdot \bar{r_{ff}}}} \quad (1)$$

where M_S is the heuristic merit of a feature subset S containing n features, $\bar{r_{cf}}$ is the mean feature-class correlation for $f \in S$, and $\bar{r_{ff}}$ is the average feature-feature correlation. This merit value is actually the Pearson's correlation where all variables have been standardized [31, 28].

To build the classification model, we used Bayesian Network (BayesNet), which is structured as a combination of a directed acyclic graph of nodes and links, and a set of conditional probability tables. Nodes represent features or classes, while links between nodes represent the relationship between them. Conditional probability tables determine the strength of the links. There is one probability table for each node (feature) that defines the probability distribution for the node given its parent nodes. If a node has no parents the probability distribution is unconditional. If a node has one or more parents the probability distribution is a conditional distribution, where the probability of each feature value depends on the values of the parents.

3. Conclusion & Discussion

We presented a multi-pronged filter method that can find cost-effective biological markers as quantifiable measurements for a perfect predictive accuracy of five sub-types of epithelial ovarian cancers. As cancers are complicated, one can only predict the status using a combination of many genes. The genes we discovered as genetic markers for ovarian cancers (TFF3, FGFR4, TCOF1, EFNB2, GPRC5A, ANK1, ACTN1, PEG3, PBX1, ATP10B and MST4) are different with previously known results. Furthermore, proteins encoded by some of these gene-signatures (e.g., TFF3 and FGFR4) have been showed to involve in the signal transduction of cells and proliferative control of normal cells while specific functions of proteins encoded by other gene-signatures have not yet been determined. To differentiate the two sub-types of Mucinous and Serous, our method also discovers that a single gene - the MLF1 (myeloid leukemia factor 1) - can be used as a genetic marker. This genetic marker is not unique as another single gene - the WT1 (Wilms tumor 1) - can also be used as a genetic marker to differentiate the two sub-types of Mucinous and Serous. Finally, this work opens new questions for structural and molecular biologists about the role of these gene-signatures for the disease.

References

[1] A. Jemal, R. Siegel, E. Ward, T. Murray, J. Xu, and M. J. Thun, "Cancer statistics, 2007," *CA Cancer J Clin*, vol. 57, pp. 43–66, 2007.

[2] A. Jemal, R. Siegel, E. Ward, Y. Hao, J. Xu, and M. J. Thun, "Cancer statistics, 2009," *CA Cancer J Clin*, vol. 59, pp. 225–249, 2009.

[3] R. Siegel, A. Jemal, and D. Naishadham, "Cancer statistics, 2012," *CA Cancer J Clin*, vol. 62, pp. 10–29, 2012.

[4] T. M. Zaid, T.-L. Yeung, M. S. Thompson, C. S. Leung, T. Harding, N.-N. Co, R. S. Schmandt, S.-Y. Kwan, C. Rodriguez-Aguay, G. Lopez-Berestein, A. K. Sood, K.-K. Wong, M. J. Birrer, , and S. C. Mok, "Identification of fgfr4 as a potential therapeutic target for advanced-stage, high-grade serous ovarian cancer," *Clinical Cancer Research*, vol. 19, pp. 809–820, 2013.

[5] D. K. Armstrong, B. Bundy, L. Wenzel, H. Q. Huang, R. Baergen, S. Lele, L. J. Copeland, J. L. Walker, and R. A. Burger, "Intraperitoneal cisplatin and paclitaxel in ovarian cancer," *N Engl J Med*, vol. 354, pp. 34–43, 2006.

[6] T. Yap, C. Carden, and S. Kaye, "Beyond chemotherapy: targeted therapies in ovarian cancer," *Nat Rev Cancer*, vol. 9, no. 3, pp. 167–181, 2009.

[7] R. Burger, "Beyond chemotherapy: targeted therapies in ovarian cancer," *Gynecol Oncol*, vol. 121, no. 1, pp. 230–238, 2011.
[8] S. Singhal, D. Miller, S. Ramalingam, and S.-Y. Sun, "Gene expression profiling of non-small cell lung cancer," *Lung cancer*, vol. 60, no. 3, pp. 313–324, 2008.
[9] A. Butte, "The use and analysis of microarray data," *Nature Review Drug Discovery*, vol. 1, no. 12, pp. 951–960, 2002.
[10] G. Piatetsky-Shapiro and P. Tamayo, "Microarray data mining: Facing the challenges," *SIGKDD Explorations*, vol. 5, no. 2, 2003.
[11] S. Ramaswamy and T. R. Golub, "DNA microarrays in clinical oncology," *Journal of Clinical Oncology*, vol. 20, pp. 1932–1941, 2002.
[12] P. Tamayo and S. Ramaswamy, "Cancer genomics and molecular pattern recognition," in *Expression profiling of human tumors: diagnostic and research applications*, M. Ladanyi and W. Gerald, Eds. Humana Press, 2003.
[13] W. Dalton and S. Friend, "Cancer biomarkers–an invitation to the table," *Science*, vol. 312, no. 5777, pp. 1165–1168, 2006.
[14] T. J. Yeatman, "Predictive biomarkers: Identification and verification," *J Clin Oncol*, vol. 27, no. 17, pp. 2743–2744, 2009.
[15] K. Shedden, J. Taylor, S. Enkemann, M. Tsao, T. Yeatman, W. Gerald, S. Eschrich, I. Jurisica, T. Giordano, D. Misek, A. Chang, C. Zhu, S. D., S. Hanash, F. Shepherd, K. Ding, L. Seymour, K. Naoki, N. Pennell, B. Weir, R. Verhaak, C. Ladd-Acosta, T. Golub, M. Gruidl, A. Sharma, J. Szoke, M. Zakowski, V. Rusch, M. Kris, A. Viale, N. Motoi, W. Travis, B. Conley, V. Seshan, M. Meyerson, R. Kuick, K. Dobbin, T. Lively, J. Jacobson, and D. Beer, "Gene expression-based survival prediction in lung adenocarcinoma: A multi-site, blinded validation study," *Nat Med*, vol. 14, pp. 822–827, 2008.
[16] B. Kim, H. J. Lee, H. Y. Choi, Y. Shin, S. Nam, G. Seo, D.-S. Son, J. Jo, J. Kim, J. Lee, J. Kim, K. Kim, and S. Lee, "Clinical validity of the lung cancer biomarkers identified by bioinformatics analysis of public expression data," *Cancer Res*, vol. 67, pp. 7431–8, 2007.
[17] Q.-N. Tran, "Designing efficient many-core parallel algorithms for all-pairs shortest-paths using CUDA," in *Proceedings of IEEE-ITNG 2010 Conference*, Las Vegas, Nevada, 2010.
[18] ——, *Software Tools and Algorithms for Biological Systems.* Springer, 2011, ch. 9: Improving the Accuracy of Gene Expression Profile Classification, pp. 83–99.
[19] ——, "Microarray data mining: A new algorithm for gene selection using Gini ratios," in *Proceedings of IEEE-ITNG 2010 Conference*, Las Vegas, Nevada, 2010.
[20] M. Birrer, M. Johnson, K. Hao, K. Wong, D. Park, A. Bell, W. Welch, R. Berkowitz, and S. Mok, "Overview of anti-angiogenic agents in development for ovarian cancer," *J Clin Oncol*, vol. 25, no. 16, pp. 2281–7, 2007.
[21] S. Liao, J. Liu, P. Lin, T. Shi, R. Jain, and L. Xu, "Whole genome oligonucleotide-based array comparative genomic hybridization analysis identified fibroblast growth factor 1 as a prognostic marker for advanced-stage serous ovarian adenocarcinomas," *Clin Cancer Res*, vol. 17, no. 6, pp. 1415–24, 2011.
[22] "Integrated genomic analyses of ovarian carcinoma," *Nature*, vol. 474, pp. 609–15, 2011, by Cancer Genome Atlas Research Network.
[23] R. Kuick, "Human ovarian tumors and normal ovaries," Gene Expression Omnibus, 2007.
[24] H. John, R. Kohavi, and P. Pfleger, "Irrelevant features and the subset selection problem," in *Machine Learning: Proceedings of the Eleventh International Conference*, 1994.
[25] R. Kohavi and G. H. John, "Wrappers for feature subset selection," *Artificial Intelligence*, pp. 273–324, 1997. [Online]. Available: http://robotics.stanford.edu/users/ronnyk
[26] K. Kira and L. Rendell, "A practical approach to feature selection," in *Machine Learning: Proceedings of the Ninth International Conference*, 1992.
[27] D. Koller and M. Sahami, "Towards optimal feature selection," in *In Machine Learning: Proceedings of the Thirteenth International Conference*, 1996.
[28] M. A. Hall, *Correlation-based Feature Subset Selection.* NZ: Hamilton, 1998.
[29] M. Fayyad and B. Irani, "Multi-interval discretisation of continuous-valued attributes for classification learning," 1993.
[30] L. Breiman, J. H. Friedman, R. A. Olshen, and C. J. Stone, *Classification and regression trees.* Wadsworth & Brooks/Cole Advanced Books & Software, 1984, monterey, CA.
[31] E. Ghiselli, *Theory of Psychological Measurement.* McGraw-Hill, 1964.

Variable Color Environment System using Heart Rate Variability

Naoko Kanda, Daiki Sakuma, Masato Yoshimi, Tsutomu Yoshinaga, and Hidetsugu Irie
Network Computing, The University of Electro-Communications, Chofu, Tokyo, Japan

Abstract— *The color design of the working environment plays a supplementary role to a person's psychological or physiological condition in its effect on working performance. However, the color of the working environment is generally designed to match the preference of the majority of people, and does not take into account individual preferences. In addition, because the person's psychological and physiological state is constantly changing, the desired color environment also changes depending on the condition at that time. Therefore, for optimal working efficiency, it is necessary to construct an environment that changes color dynamically to suit personal preferences and physiological or psychological condition. Our system uses two conventionally researched relationships: (1) working efficiency estimation using HRV (heart rate variability) and (2) the effect of color on working efficiency. The results of the experiment showed that the system improved a user's working efficiency, increasing the possibility of performance acceleration by 13.9% compared with the conventional fixed-color environment. Using the proposed system, increases and prevention of deterioration in working efficiency were achieved.*

Keywords: HRV Analysis, Color Environment, Biofeedback System, State estimation

1. Introduction

Color is one of the most important factors that must be considered in the design of the working environment. Several studies have investigated how to obtain the appropriate color environment based on psychological and physiological effectiveness. It is well-known that the colors of offices and conference rooms are carefully designed to enhance user's working efficiency[1][2]. However, the color that best improves efficiency may well differ between individuals. Moreover, it can differ according to physiological or psychological state even for the same individual. Thus, a desirable outcome would be for the color of the environment to change based on the individual's state by exploiting bio-feedback variation such as HRV (heart rate variability) analysis.

Until relatively recently, measuring heartbeat has required large and expensive pieces of medical equipment such as an ECG (electrocardiograph). However, the popularity of smaller and more easily wearable devices that monitor heartbeat has increased in recent years. There are currently small and reasonably priced sensors available that can be mounted even while exercising, so obtaining HR (heart rate) information is not a burden on the user's daily life.

This paper proposes a system that changes the color of the working environment dynamically based on biological information direct from the user, exploiting HRV analysis to improve working efficiency. To construct the system, we conducted a preliminary experiment that examined the relationship between working efficiency and HRV so that an algorithm to determine whether the user is too relaxed or too stressed could be constructed. Based on this relationship, we outline our dynamic color changing environment system.

The paper is laid out as follows: Section 2 reviews relevant literature. Section 3 examines the relationship between color and working efficiency, and introduces the algorithm for estimating the user's mood based on HRV. Section 4 introduces our feedback system. Section 5 explains our evaluation method. Section 6 describes the evaluation experiment and shows the result. Section 7 summarizes the paper.

2. Related Work

2.1 Effect of the color of the working environment on humans

Vision accounts for 83% of the sensory information taken in by humans. The color information has a significant effect on human beings, and this has been studied in a variety of fields[2].

The color of the working environment is generally chosen to exploit psychological effects on feelings and physiological effects on the body. Omori et al. tried to clarify the effect that a color stimulus has on human psychology and physiology[3]. In this study, they used EEG (electroencephalography) and HRV as metrics for evaluating central nervous system and autonomic activity and also, for psychological evaluation, a factor analysis method called SD (semantic differential). They reported that HRV correlated with workload, and differences were observed in terms of the response to different colors.

Kato *et. al.* discussed the ways in which the color environment could reduce the stresses of VDT (Visual Display Terminal) work through analyzing the mind and body using HRV. They discovered that individual effectiveness is determined by three factors: (1) the color itself, (2) psychological characteristics, and (3) personal preference[4]. Fukazawa *et. al.* found that the color environment had a significant impact on bringing calm to the mind and body based on psychological indicators and aspects of the colors [5][6].

The effects of the color of the environment on working efficiency have been studied and discussed by Mizunoya et al. [7][6][8]. In their paper, the researchers conducted the Uchida-Kraepelin test of working efficiency in various color environments. They found that a difference in color environment produced a change in working efficiency.

2.2 Correlation between HRV and working efficiency

The beating of the heart is caused by the heart muscle contracting on a regular basis. This activity appears as an R-wave in the ECG, which shows that the "heart is beating". The time between beats is referred to as the "R-R Interval" (RRI).

The heartbeat of a healthy human is always fluctuating, and this fluctuation is defined as HRV. The result of frequency analysis of the RRI reflects the state of the autonomic nervous system. The HF (high frequency) component indicates the degree of activation of the sympathetic system, and LF/HF (LF is the low frequency component, LF/HF is the ratio of the HF to the LF) indicates the degree of activation of the parasympathetic system[9]. Therefore, HF and LF/HF are widely used as physiological indicators as follows[10][11]:

- HF: state of reduced fatigue or relaxation
- LF/HF: state of concentration or stress

There have been many attempts to clarify the correlation between mental load during work using the RRI.

Honda et al. evaluated the stress of working in the event of an emergency using physiological metrics. They discussed the correlation between subjective evaluation and physiological metrics, and between subjective evaluation and task results. In addition, Yajima et al. investigated the HF and LF/HF at the time of implementing a mental stress test, and their correlation with the results[12]. They showed that the LF/HF increased while working compared with prior to start working, and that there was a positive correlation between LF/HF and subjective motivation. The results demonstrate that if HF is reduced when a participant is challenged, the increase in both resting HF and LF/HF is reduced.

Ishibashi et al. investigated using HR as a metric of mental load[13] and showed that it tends to vary substantially in proportion to the difficulty of the intellectual task. As described above, there is a correlation between HRV and mental load, and both HF and LF/HF vary in response to the rise and fall of performance on the task. However, no studies have found a correlation between working efficiency and HF or LF/HF.

2.3 Biofeedback

The development of wearable devices and improvements in the calculation speed of computers have enabled real-time feedback. Based on these advances, attempts to provide feedback to the user based on physiological metrics are present in various fields, such as work support and entertainment. Such technology is crucial in constructing a virtual reality system that feeds back the physiological and psychological state of a human into a virtual space.

Sugita et al. proposed a system of altering audio or video information using physiological metrics [14], while Ushida et al. investigated the effect on the organism when the volume of the music played to a person is changed in real time based on the coefficient of variation of the RRI[15]. They found that changing the volume in proportion to the RRI variation coefficient had the effect of reducing the burden of operation on the subject, and increased their concentration.

Thus, there are many studies of biofeedback that show that it is possible to produce targeted effects depending on the person's current state.

3. Estimating Working Efficiency

3.1 Preliminary Experiment

To estimate working efficiency using RRI analysis, we first conducted a preliminary study following Uchida et al. The Uchida-Kraepelin test was performed 3 times on four subjects(who are laboratory students, male, twenties) in a sitting position in red, green and blue color environments.

First, subjects maintained a sitting posture with their eyes closed and stabilized their heartbeat for five minutes. Next, the Uchida-Kraepelin test was carried out for 15 minutes. After a 5-minute break with the eyes open, a second test was carried out for 15 minutes. Finally, subjects took a rest for 5 minutes. By measuring HF and LF/HF and comparing them to the number of answers per minute during the test, we obtained the time variation per minute of each question in the test. In addition, we calculated correlation coefficients between HF and LF/HF and the number of answers. As a means of quantifying the time-course of working efficiency, the Uchida-Kraepelin test was used. This test was performed every minute and involves the addition of successive pairs of digits in long rows of integers; it is widely used as a means of quantifying temporal changes in working efficiency.

The number of correct answers was used as a quantitative evaluation of working efficiency.

3.2 Results and Discussion

3.2.1 Correlation between HRV and working efficiency

We performed linear regressions on HF and LF/HF with the number of answers calculated by each subject for each color environment. Positive or negative slopes of the regression line indicated a rising or lowering HF and LF/HF, i.e., the working efficiency. Typically, LF/HF tended to increase with the number of answers over time on the Uchida-Kraepelin test, indicating increasing stress. This tendency accounted for 50% of the variance in the experimental results.

However, in the following cases the number of answers tended to decrease with time (Figure 1):

1) Too high LF/HF (the working efficiency increased as LF/HF decreased)
2) Increasing HF

The following five patterns were found (see Figure 1:

1) Increase in working efficiency as LF/HF increased
2) Decrease in working efficiency as LF/HF increased
3) Increase in working efficiency as LF/HF decreased
4) Decrease in working efficiency as HF increased
5) No increase or decrease in working efficiency

Patterns 2 and 3 indicate the result of a person's stress being excessive. For pattern 2, we hypothesize that the subject's working efficiency falls because of rising stress in an excessively high stress situation. For pattern 3, we hypothesize that the subject's working efficiency rises because of lowering stress in an excessively high stress situation. While concentrating on a task, LF/HF tends to rise[12]. In addition, in a state of high stress load in an emergency situation, LF/HF tends to show a high value when the motivation of the worker is high. However, LF/HF also reflects stress, and a person's working efficiency is reduced when they are under too much stress. Patterns 2 and 3 indicate states of too much stress. This result shows that increasing and decreasing working efficiency in excessively stressed states can be estimated from LF/HF. Pattern 4 shows that working efficiency is reduced depending on HF, and reflects the increase of relaxation without too much stress even though the subject is working[12]. Pattern 5 shows that working efficiency neither increased nor decreased ($Absolutevalueoftheslopeoftheregressionline < 0.01$). As we have seen, HRV can detect signs of performance degradation.

Correlation coefficients between the color of the environment and HF, the color of the environment and LF/HF, and the color of the environment and working efficiency were calculated. No significant differences between subjects were observed.

3.3 Algorithm for the estimation of working efficiency

Based on chapter 3.1, we determined our estimation algorithm as follows:

- LF/HF is greater than or equal to 1.5: When subjects are unduly stressed, working efficiency is reduced.
- LF/HF is less than 1.5 and HF is rising (slope of the regression line of HF is positive): When subjects are too relaxed, working efficiency is reduced.
- otherwise: Working efficiency is ideal.

Considering that the physiological and psychological effects of color are different depending on individual preference, in this system each user can choose colors that are calming, that motivate them, or that help them to concentrate from three colors (red, green, blue) in advance.

Based on the above, as shown in Figure 2, the system determines the color of the environment to be presented to the user at the correct time based on the feedback from the results of frequency analysis of HRV. A schematic is shown in Figure 7.

The color of the environment changes to "calming" when the user feels too much stress, and changes to "motivative" when the user feels too relaxed. Otherwise, the environment shows a neutral color that the user selected as "concentrative".

Decisions on when to display the colors are based on the estimated working efficiency. By estimating the increase or decrease of working efficiency, a suitable environment color is presented in line with the user's preferences. With this method, reductions in the user's working efficiency are prevented, and their overall efficiency is thus improved.

4. Proposal and implementation of dynamic color environment feedback system using HRV

4.1 System summary

To implement environment that dynamically changes color according to individual circumstances and personal preferences can be constructed, we propose a system for estimating the user's working efficiency from the real-time results of HRV analysis, and provide feedback as the appropriate color for the user's circumstances. The flowchart for this system is shown in Figure 3.

RRI data were obtained using the wearable device, and the latest series of RRI data that has sufficient length for a wavelet transform was analyzed. Working efficiency was estimated based on the HF and LF/HF obtained; this system results in the presentation of an environmental color according to the user's color preferences. By repeating this sequence of operations at constant intervals, real-time feedback is used to optimally change the color of the environment, assisting in work efficiency.

4.2 Real-time measurement of RRI

For the measurement of RRI, we used a GARMIN premium HR monitor (GARMIN, Inc.) . This device is intended to measure HR during exercise, and is used by winding it around the chest like a belt. RRI outputted from the device was received in real time by the computer using a USB ANT stick (GARMIN, Inc.).

4.3 HRV analysis

The outline of the algorithm is shown in Figure 5.

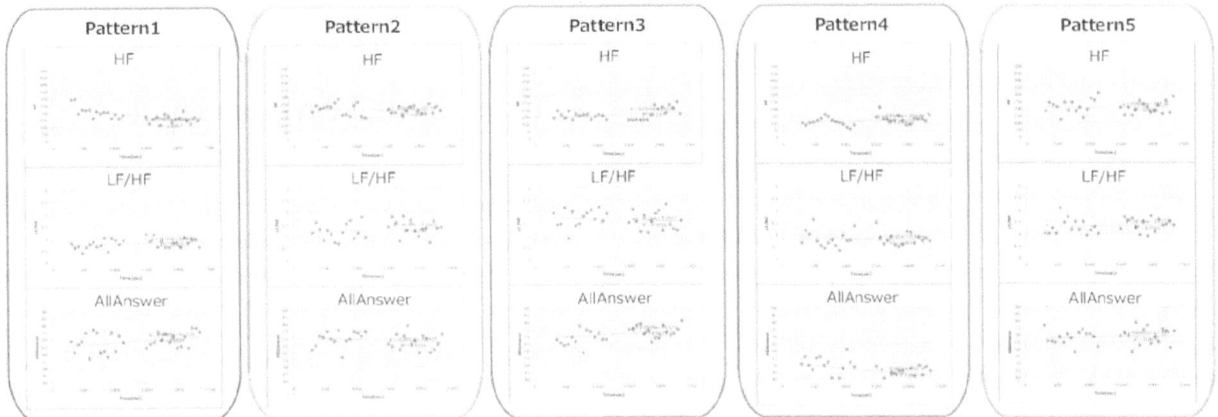

Fig. 1: Pattern of correlation between HRV and number of answers

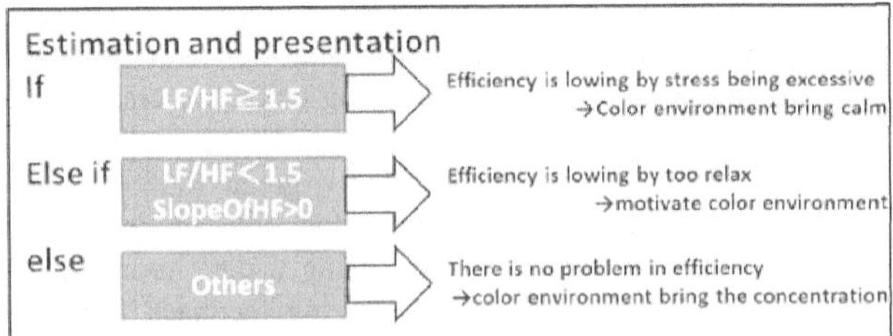

Fig. 2: Dynamic estimation of working efficiency and presentation color environment based on HRV

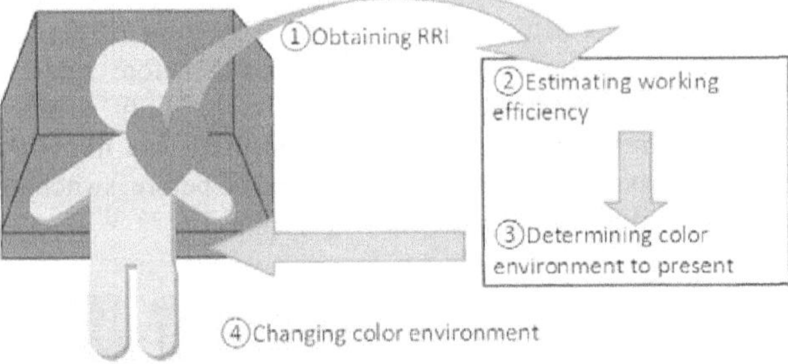

Fig. 3: System summary

4.3.1 Correction and interpolation of RRI

When frequency analysis using wavelet transform is performed on the RRI obtained by the premium HR monitor, significantly high values of HF and LF/HF may appear. Because such RRI values are not generally found as a result of the HRV analysis and tend to appear when the radio wave is of low quality, they can be considered as outliers and excluded.

To account for such values, a correction was performed on the data. First, RRI values lower than 450 and higher than 1250 were removed. Each value x_t was excluded as an outlier if it formed a steep mountain or valley shape. The threshold for outliers ws defined as 50 and 450 which are differences in x_{t+1} and x_{t+2}, respectively. Also, outliers could appear if data from the signal were lost from the HR monitor. In such a case, the HF and LF/HF values were removed.

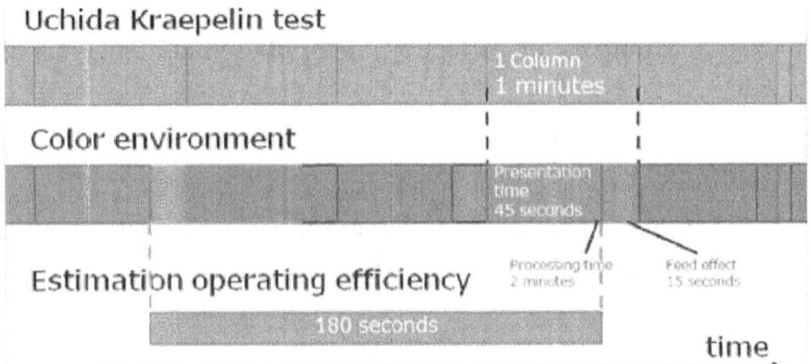

Fig. 4: Time interval of acquisition of HRV and presentation of feedback

When performing a frequency analysis using continuous wavelet transform, time series data analyzed must be equally spaced. The HR monitor transmits RRI at each heartbeat, and the RRI is received and recorded; therefore, it is necessary to correct the RRI data to be equally spaced. Since spline interpolation is often used in performing a frequency analysis when the data are not at evenly spaced time intervals, this interpolation strategy is used in our environment color construction system to account for irregular HRV feedback.

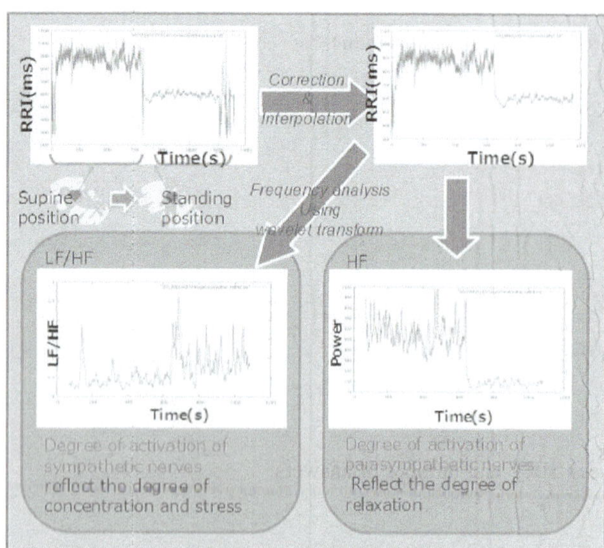

Fig. 5: Summary of correction, interpolation and analysis of RRI

4.3.2 Obtain the state of the autonomic nervous system using frequency analysis with the continuous wavelet transform

Continuous wavelet transform is used as a technique to analyze HRV. Conventionally, analysis of HRV has been done using autoregressive models and power spectrum analysis using FFT. However, It is difficult to capture non-stationary temporal changes in RRI with these methods. Nevertheless, by using a wavelet transform, we can capture the number of changes per second in autonomic nervous activity.

Referring to [16], we defined the total power in the power spectrum from 0.06 Hz to 0.15 Hz as LF, and from 0.15 Hz to 0.475 Hz as HF. Using the wavelet transform, we calculate HF and LF/HF per second and in this way, measuring change over time against the degree of activation, we can infer the activity of the parasympathetic nerves from HF and the activity of the sympathetic nerves from LF/HF.

Frequency analysis was performed on the last 180 seconds of the RRI time series (Figure 4). Feedback is triggered every minute but the first 180 seconds because of the analysis window. We used the program in [17] for continuous wavelet transform.

4.3.3 Dynamic presentation of color environment

The system presents an environment color that is determined based on the estimation of work efficiency, and changes color when the feedback timer is hit. The color change was performed using a fade effect that smoothly changes from one image to another by changing gradually across frames, using a program that can change the RGB color value in small steps. The aim of this effect is to make sure that a person is not distracted by the color change.

5. Experimental environment

To test our system we undertook a preliminary verification experiment, and to do so we constructed the following experimental environment. Figure 7 shows the appearance of the environment during the experiment.

We constructed a colored environment by creating a darkroom with a white interior, and placing the projector inside (Figure 6). External light was blocked by covering the outside with a blackout curtain. Inside the darkroom, we placed a white panel illuminated with a single color. Using this method, the field of view of the user was covered by a single color.

We used red, green, and blue colors in the experiment because they are the three primary colors. We built the colored environment by applying the color in the experiment to the color of the answer sheet and the color projected by the projector. For the illuminating color, we created and used image data consisting of only a single color based on Web Safe Colors: red (FF0000), green (008000), and blue (0000FF). Red, green and blue colored paper was used for the answer papers. By using a dark room in the verification experiments and outputting feedback from the proposed system to the projector, we were able to create an environment in which color changed dynamically based on feedback from the HRV.

The Uchida-Kraepelin test was applied to measure working efficiency. In the test, subjects switched the columns they had to calculate every minute. The color of the environment started to change 15 seconds before subjects switched between columns, so that it was fully changed by the time subjects actually switched. RRI data from 195 seconds before switching to 15 seconds before switching were used to estimate the state of a subject.

Fig. 6: Internal laboratory environment

Fig. 7: Appearance during the experiment (blue)

6. Experiment

6.1 Evaluation of the system

We use a wearable device that can transmit RRI to the computer in real time. We evaluated the system proposed in section 4.1. Experiments were carried out in the environment described in section 5.

Using the proposed system, an experiment similar to section 3.1 was conducted. The color of the environment presented by the proposed system was red, green or blue, the same as in the validation experiments and verification experiments. Subjects assigned red, green or blue to each color environment depending on whether it invoked feelings of calm, motivation or increased concentration. In this way, the color of the environment changed based on the preference of subjects.

6.1.1 Observed relationship

The overall result is shown in Figure 8. Results that show increasing working efficiency are shown in bold line, while results that show neither increasing nor decreasing working efficiency are shown in thin line ($Absolutevalueoftheslopeoftheregressionline < 0.01$). Working efficiency increased at a rate of 13.9% in the verification experiment, whereas in the evaluation experiment this value was 75 %. The subject's working efficiency was higher in the proposed color-changing environment system than in a single-color environment.

On the influence of feedback: it was observed frequently that working efficiency (number of answers) during one minute during the motivating environment color was higher than before the presentation of the motivating environment color by 71.4%(circled portion of Figure 8).

The frequency of the calming environment color being presented was low. No differences in working efficiency were observed in individuals or across the subjects as a whole before or during the presentation.

Furthermore, no differences were observed in subjects ' working efficiency in the concentrative environment color. The subjects reported the following after the experiment:

- Being distracted by the fade effect during the color changes.
- Having tired eyes compared with in the single environment color (verification experiment).
- When presented with the motivating color environment, being inspired.
- While the color of the environment is constant after the fade effect ends, feeling comfortable grappling with a task.
- Noticing low motivation.

6.2 discussion

In the verification experiment, the working efficiency increased by 61.1%. In the evaluation experiment, it increased by 75%. Compared with verification experiment, the working efficiency is higher than evaluation experiment.

When presented with the motivating environment color, working efficiency tended to be improved. Other environment colors had no effect on working efficiency. The effect of the calming environment color was smaller the more times it was presented, but by improving the threshold of determining how much stress is reflected by the LF/HF value depending on the individual ' s organism and the time, this color of environment may be more effective.

Operating efficiency as a whole in the proposed color-changing system increased more than in the single-color environment. Although the effects of color on biological metrics were not clearly detected in the fixed-color evaluation, our color-changing system produced good results. Thus, responding to the user ' s mood in real time improved the user ' s working efficiency.

7. conclusion

In this paper, we proposed a changing environment color system using feedback from HRV. Based on the estimation of working efficiency and personal preference, we tried to present the best color of environment in real time. The effect of environment color on working efficiency and the autonomic nervous system and the correlation between HRV and working efficiency were verified. As a result, though definite effects of the color of the environment were not clearly observed, we were able to estimate working efficiency based on HRV. In addition, the environmental color preferences for each subject were obtained.

The evaluation result revealed that introducing dynamic feedback improves working efficiency. Focusing on the timecourse of working efficiency, the proportion of time in which it increased was 75% of the total trial, which is greater than the 13.9% proportion in the static environment. Also, the proportion of time in which the working efficiency decreased was 0%, which was lower than the 19.4% in static environment.

Using the proposed system, increases and prevention of deterioration in working efficiency were achieved. Also, in terms of the influence of feedback, it was observed frequently in all subjects that working efficiency (number of answers) during one minute while in the motivating environment color was higher than that before this environment was prevented. This result shows that the notification of a stressed or relaxed condition by color is effective in spite of an ambiguous correlation between color and HRV. The effect of the calming environment color was smaller the more times it was presented, but by improving the threshold of determining how much stress is reflected by the LF/HF depending on the individual ' s organism and the time, this color of environment may be more effective. In this paper, we deal with work efficiency. Not only that, this research may be used to warn of high stress.

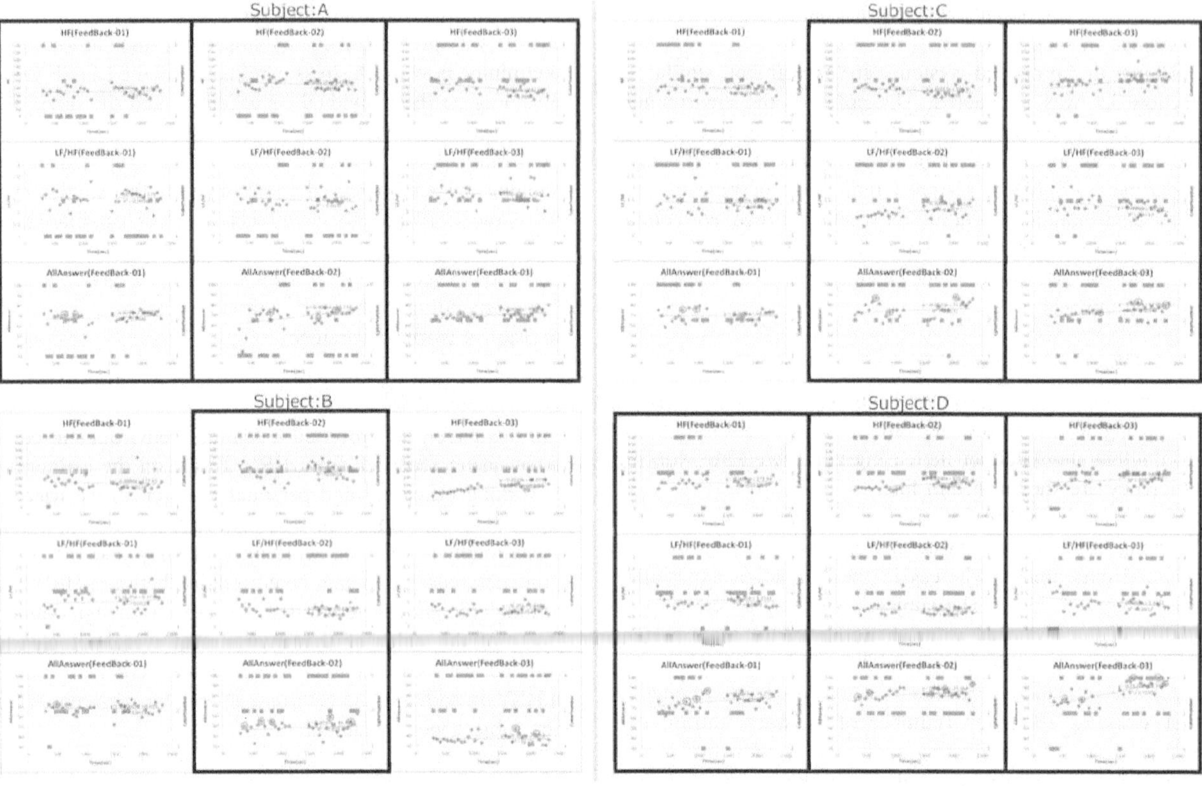

Fig. 8: Overall results

References

[1] A. T. Corporation, *A.F.T. Editorial committee of text to measure: A.F.T color test©sponsored by Ministry of Education Official text Grade 2*, 2010.

[2] A. TCorporation, *A.F.T. Editorial committee of text to measure: A.F.T color test©sponsored by Ministry of Education Official text Grade 3*, 2010.

[3] M. Omori, R. Hashimoto, and Y. Kato, "Relation between psychological and physiological responses on color stimulus," in *Color Science Association of Japan 26(2)*, 2002, pp. 50–63.

[4] C. Kato, N. Terada, T. Toyabe, and Y. Saito, "Analysis of influence of color environment on mind and body using heart rate variability -measurement of individual variation based on characteristic and preference-," in *The Visualization Society of Japan, 36*, 2008, pp. 143–146.

[5] K. Fukazawa, K. Takaya, and S. Tsuyako, "Physiological and emotional response of healthy adults to colors," *Yamanashi Nursing Journal*, vol. 8, no. 1, pp. 23–27, 2009.

[6] T. Mizunoya, S. Kubo, and A. Taguchi, "A study on the effect of color environment on psychology and operating efficiency," in *Ieice technical report Smart info-media system, 110(445)*, 2011, pp. 23–26.

[7] K. Syunpei, T. Mizunoya, and A. Taguchi, "A study on the effect of color environment on operating efficiency," in *The Institute of Electronics, Information and Communication Engineers, 219*, 2011, pp. 13–16.

[8] T. Mizunoya, S. Kubo, and A. Taguchi, "A study on the effect of color environment on psychology and operating effciency," in *The Color Science Association of Japan, 35(Supplement)*, 2011, pp. 34–35.

[9] H. M. Stauss, "Heart rate variability," *American Journal of Physiology-Regulatory, Integrative and Comparative Physiology*, vol. 285, no. 5, pp. R927–R931, 2003.

[10] M. Malik, J. T. Bigger, A. J. Camm, R. E. Kleiger, A. Malliani, A. J. Moss, and P. J. Schwartz, "Heart rate variability: Standards of measurement, physiological interpretation, and clinical use," *European Heart Journal*, vol. 17, no. 3, pp. 354–381, 1996. [Online]. Available: http://eurheartj.oxfordjournals.org/content/17/3/354.short

[11] M. Kumar, M. Weippert, R. Vilbrandt, S. Kreuzfeld, and R. Stoll, "Fuzzy evaluation of heart rate signals for mental stress assessment," *Fuzzy Systems, IEEE Transactions on*, vol. 15, no. 5, pp. 791–808, 2007.

[12] J. Yajima, N. Ogata, and A. Kawano, "Relationship between cardiac autonomic nervous activity interaction and subjective stress response under the mental stress testing," in *Bulletin of Beppu University Graduate School (12)*, 2010, pp. 31–39.

[13] T. Ishibashi, A. Ohtani, and M. Takeo, "Heart rate as an index of the mental load," in *Japan Society for Occupational Health, 10(7)*, 1968, pp. 377–379.

[14] N. Sugita, M. Yoshizawa, A. Tanaka, K. Abe, T. Yamabe, and S. Nitta, "Biofeedback of psychological and physiological index mediated by sound and image," in *SICE Tohoku Chapter 205st Workshop*, 2002, pp. 205–5.

[15] J. Ushida, K. Yokoyama, M. Mizuno, K. Shimada, and K. Takata, "Bio-feedback effects of background music controlled by heart rate variability during work," in *Institute of Electronics, Information and Communication Engineers 101(406)*, 2001, pp. 71–75.

[16] K. Honda and S. Wakai, "Study on heart rate variability analysis using wavelet transform : Power spectrum analysis of rapid change occasion between r-r interval," in *Bulletin of Graduate School of Social & Cultural Systems at Yamagata University*, vol. 3, 2006, pp. 35–43.

[17] H. Toda, Z. Zhang, and H. Kawabata, "Wavelet latest practical course:introduction and applications:from the basics to the latest theory of signal processing." SOFTBANK Creative Corp, "oct" 2005.

Advances in Performance Improvement of Time-Frequency Distributions for Doppler Ultrasound Blood Flow Instrumentation

F. García Nocetti, J. Solano González, E. Rubio Acosta
Universidad Nacional Autónoma de México, IIMAS, México D.F., 04510, México

Abstract: *Doppler ultrasound blood flow spectral estimation is a technique for non-invasive cardiovascular disease detection. Blood flow velocity and disturbance may be determined by measuring the spectral mean frequency and bandwidth respectively. Typical methods utilize Fourier Transform-based algorithms to estimate the spectral response of a signal. This practice suffers from poor frequency resolution when estimating non-stationary signals. The Cohen class of Time Frequency Distributions (TFD) has efficiently determined a very close estimation of the instantaneous frequency for quasi-stationary signals such as arterial blood flow. However, the computation complexity for each distribution is $O(N^3)$, where N is the sample length, this being not suitable for real-time applications. In this work a study is directed to evaluate the response of different distributions when truncating the TFD's generalized autocorrelation function. TFD such as Choi Williams, Bessel and Born Jordan are evaluated along with the Modified-B approach. The relationship with the precision obtained in the frequency estimation when considering particular distribution kernels is also studied. In order to define a truncation procedure, SNR and sample length are considered, this aims to minimize RMS error. Results are being applied to the development of a real-time spectrum analyzer for Doppler blood flow instrumentation.*

Keywords: Time-Frequency Distributions, spectral estimation, Doppler ultrasound blood flow.

1 Introduction

Conventional methods for real-time spectral analysis use Fourier Transform on consecutive or overlapping time segments, but this current practice suffers from poor frequency resolution as a result of the time segment duration and non-stationary. Other types of spectral estimators, called time-frequency distributions, have been developed [1]. Unlike conventional methods, these distributions are not limited to the use of stationary signals. Despite of this important advantage, the number of calculations involved in obtaining the spectral estimation increases substantially compared to the traditional methods. Therefore, it is desirable to simplify the formulation of the distributions in such a way that the computations can be reduced without any loss in the spectral resolution. Simplified expressions that calculate the time frequency distributions have been previously introduced [2][4][11]. Also, previous works have suggested that a controlled truncation of the time frequency distributions' autocorrelation function does not significantly affect the accuracy when estimating spectral parameters such as the pseudo instantaneous mean frequency and the RMS mean bandwidth [2][5]. On the contrary, it further diminishes the amount of calculations involved. This strategy may be usefully in order to achieve efficient real time algorithms suitable to be implemented in high performance architectures. This work accomplishes these studies and extends them with a performance evaluation using a real Doppler Ultrasound signal taken from the Carotid artery.

2 Time-Frequency Distributions

The time frequency distributions (TFD) of the Cohen class [1] considered in this work includes Bessel, Born Jordan, Choi Williams and Modified-B distributions. The discrete TFD of a complex signal $x(n)$ of length $2N$-1, whose elements are numbered from 1-N to N-1, when it is evaluated at discrete time $n=0$, and optimized [4] is:

$$DTFD(0,k,TI) = 4\,\mathrm{Re}\left[\sum_{\tau=0}^{N-1} W(\tau)W^{*}(-\tau) f_{GAF}(0,\tau,TI) e^{-j\frac{2\pi k\tau}{N}}\right] - 2W(0)W^{*}(0) f_{GAF}(0,0,TI) \quad (1)$$

where $f_{GAF}(n,\tau,TI)$ is the generalized autocorrelation function, TI is the truncation index of the $f_{GAF}(\bullet)$, $W(n)$ is a (Hanning) sampling window of length $2N$-1, and k is the discrete frequency taking integer values from 0 to N-1. Note that if $TI = N$-1, there is a non truncation effect; the exactly meaning of TI parameter is explained in section 3. The $f_{GAF}(\bullet)$ for the discrete Bessel TFD [6] is:

$$f_{GAF}(0,\tau,TI)=\sum_{\mu=\max\{-TI,-2\alpha|\tau|,-N+1+|\tau|\}}^{\min\{TI,2\alpha|\tau|,N-1-|\tau|\}}\left(\frac{1}{\pi\alpha|\tau|}\sqrt{1-\left(\frac{\mu}{2\alpha\tau}\right)^2}\right)x(\mu+\tau)x^*(\mu\ \ \tau) \quad (2)$$

where α is a scaling factor taking the half of any natural value. Note that $f_{GAF}(0,0,TI)=x(0)x^*(0)$.

The $f_{GAF}(\bullet)$ for the discrete Born Jordan TFD [1] is:

$$f_{GAF}(0,\tau,TI)=\sum_{\mu=\max\{-TI,-2\alpha|\tau|,-N+1+|\tau|\}}^{\min\{TI,2\alpha|\tau|,N-1-|\tau|\}}\left(\frac{1}{4\alpha|\tau|}\right)x(\mu+\tau)x^*(\mu-\tau) \quad (3)$$

where α is a scaling factor taking the half of any natural value. Note that $f_{GAF}(0,0,TI)=x(0)x^*(0)$.

The $f_{GAF}(\bullet)$ for the discrete Choi-Williams TFD [7] is:

$$f_{GAF}(0,\tau,TI)=\sum_{\mu=\max\{-TI,-N+1+|\tau|\}}^{\min\{TI,N-1-|\tau|\}}\left(\sqrt{\frac{1}{4\pi\tau^2/\sigma}}e^{-\frac{\mu^2}{4\tau^2/\sigma}}\right)x(\mu+\tau)x^*(\mu-\tau) \quad (4)$$

where σ is a scaling factor taking any positive real value. Note that $f_{GAF}(0,0,TI)=x(0)x^*(0)$.

The $f_{GAF}(\bullet)$ for the discrete Modified-B TFD [8] is:

$$f_{GAF}(0,\tau,TI)=\sum_{\mu=\max\{-TI,-N+1+|\tau|\}}^{\min\{TI,N-1-|\tau|\}}\frac{\Gamma(2\alpha)}{2^{2\alpha-1}\Gamma^2(\alpha)}\left(\frac{1}{\cosh^2(\mu)}\right)^{\alpha}x(\mu+\tau)x^*(\mu-\tau) \quad (5)$$

where α is a scaling factor with positive real value.

3 Truncation procedure

Observe that the generalized autocorrelation function in the equations (2) to (5) has a weighting factor that vanishes as index μ increases. Figures (1) to (4) show the weighting factors in the equations (2) to (5). As a consequence, a controlled truncation in the index μ results in a controlled decrement in the accuracy of TFD calculation. That controlled decrement in the accuracy of TFD calculation provokes a controlled increment in the spectral estimation errors but a decrement in the amount of calculations involved.

Such a truncation index *(TI)* has already been imposed in the summation respect to index μ in the equations (2) to (5). The admissible values of *TI* are from 0 to *N-1*. Note that *TI = 0* corresponds to the maximum truncation effect. Also, note that *TI ≥ N-1* has a non-truncation effect. Experimentally determined optimal scaling factors are considered in calculations; these are shown in Table 1 [3]:

Table 1. Optimal scaling factors of TFD.

Window Length	Modified B	Bessel
L = 63	$\alpha = 0.2$	$\alpha = 2$
L = 127	$\alpha = 0.05$	$\alpha = 2.5$
L = 255	$\alpha = 0.02$	$\alpha = 2.5$

Window Length	Born Jordan	Choi Williams
L = 63	$\alpha = 1$	$\sigma = 4$
L = 127	$\alpha = 1$	$\sigma = 5$

The number of addends in the following expression:

$$\sum_{\tau=0}^{N-1}\left(\sum_{\mu=\max\{-TI,-N+1+|\tau|\}}^{\min\{TI,N-1-|\tau|\}}(\bullet)\right) \quad (6)$$

which corresponds succinctly to the calculation of equation (1) for each *k*, according to the truncation index *(TI)* is:

$$\#addends=2(TI)N-(TI)^2+N\quad(TI) \quad (7)$$

If *TI=0*, the maximum truncation effect, then:

$$\#addends=N \quad (8)$$

If *TI=N-1*, a non-truncation effect, then:

$$\#addends=N^2 \quad (9)$$

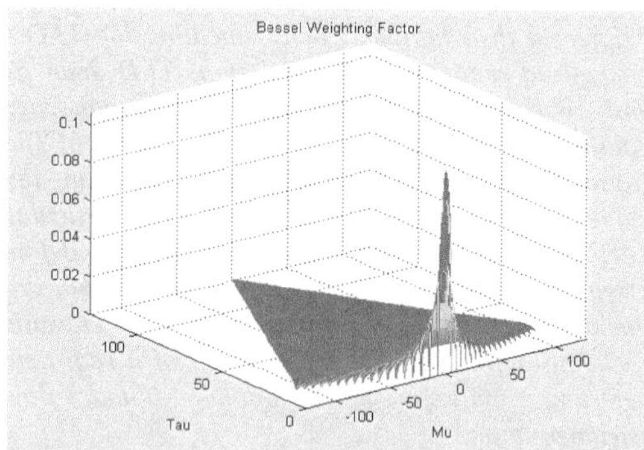

Figure 1. Bessel TFD weighting factor of the generalized autocorrelation function.

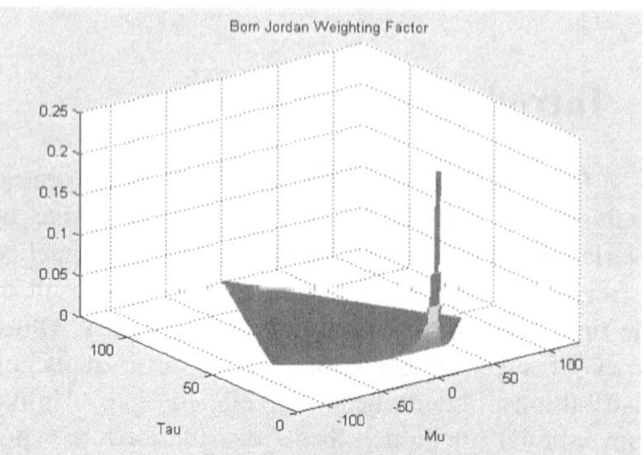

Figure 2. Born Jordan TFD weighting factor of the generalized autocorrelation function.

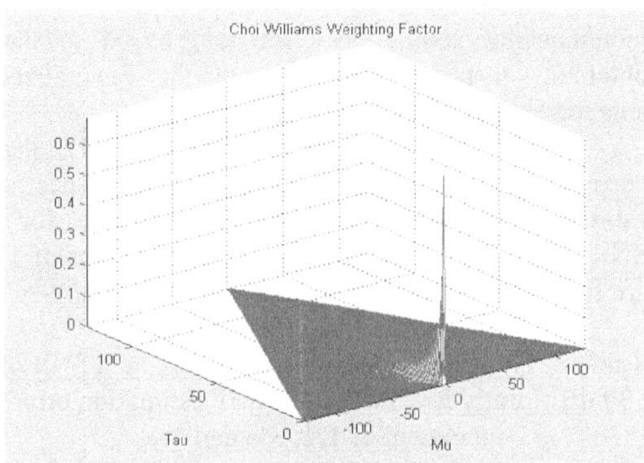

Figure 3. Choi Williams TFD weighting factor of the generalized autocorrelation function.

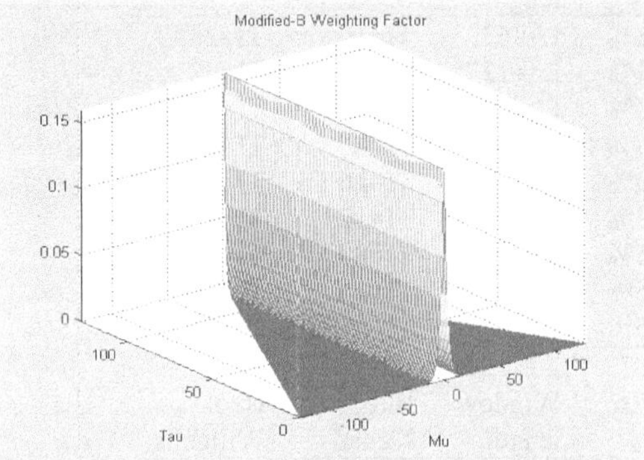

Figure 4. Modified-B TFD weighting factor of the generalized autocorrelation function.

4 Doppler US signal simulation

In order to depict the pseudo instantaneous mean frequency (PIMF) and the RMS mean bandwidth (RMSMB) error estimations when the TFD are used, it has been proposed the use of a simulated Doppler ultrasonic quasi-stationary signal that represents a typical blood flow in the Carotid artery.

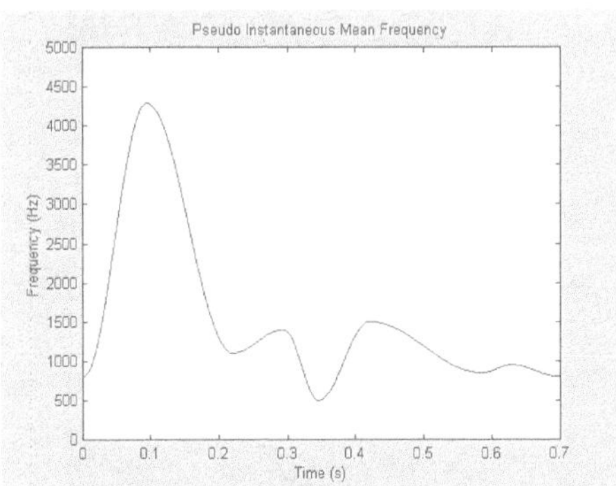

Figure 5. Signal's pseudo instantaneous mean frequency (PIMF) wave form of the simulated Doppler ultrasonic quasi-stationary signal that represents a typical blood flow in the Carotid artery.

Briefly, the signal's duration is *0.7s.*, indeed, it is the signal's mean period; it has a constant RMSMB of *100Hz* and its PIMF wave form is shown in figure 5. The simulation procedure is accurate described in [5]. In this work, a sampling rate $f_o=19200Hz$ is considered, i.e. $T=13440$ samples are taken. Note that the sampling rate must be four times the signal's maximum frequency when TFD are used.

A white noise is added to the whole signal before starting the signal analysis procedure, according to typically prescribed signal noise ratios (SNR). In this work, SNR of -10 dB, -20 dB, -30 dB and -40 dB are considered (the minus sign will be omitted); also, noiseless case is treated.

5 Spectral estimation

The spectral estimation of both the RMSMB and the PIMF is worked out as in [5][9]. Their procedures have a common part. First, a signal piece of length L is taken from the nth to the $(n+L-1)^{th}$ elements of the whole signal, it will be called the nth signal window. ÇIn this work, L can be *63*, *127* and *255*, and $L=2N-1$. The signal window's elements are numbered in the discrete time domain from $1-N$ to $N-1$. Second, the analytic signal of this signal window is calculated.

The analytic signal's elements are also numbered in the discrete time domain from $1-N$ to $N-1$. Third, the TFD of this analytic signal is calculated using equation (1) and (2), (3), (4) or (5) depending on the study case, considering prescribed truncation indexes TI and optimal scaling factors. The TFD's elements are numbered in the discrete frequency domain from 0 to $N-1$. Observe that the components corresponding to negative frequencies, which are numbered from $N/2$ to $N-1$, all are equal to zero.

Finally, the pseudo instantaneous power distribution (PIPD) of this TFD is calculated. Its elements are also numbered in the discrete frequency domain from 0 to $N-1$. The PIPD is defined as:

$$PIPD(0,k) = \begin{cases} TFD(0,k) & TFD(0,k) \geq 0 \\ 0 & TFD(0,k) < 0 \end{cases} \tag{10}$$

In case of the PIMF calculation, the pseudo instantaneous mean frequency associated to the nth window signal is stated by:

$$PIMF(n) = \frac{\sum_{k=0}^{N/2-1} f_k \bullet PIPD(0,k)}{\sum_{k=0}^{N/2-1} PIPD(0,k)} \tag{11}$$

where f_k is the real frequency associated to discrete frequency k. Observe that n can be considered as the whole signal's discrete time variable, running from 0 to $T-L$. Indeed, it represents the total amount of fully overlapped signal windows of length L in the whole signal (an overlapping of $L-1$ elements). That is, the PIMF(1) correspond to the 1st signal window; the PIMF(2), to the 2nd signal window; and so on. On the other hand, in case of the RMSMB calculation, the RMS mean bandwidth associated to the nth window signal is stated by:

$$RMSMB(n)=\sqrt{\frac{\sum_{k=0}^{N/2-1}(PIMF(n)-f_k)^2\bullet PIPD(0,k)}{\sum_{k=0}^{N/2-1}PIPD(0,k)}} \quad (12)$$

with the same considerations as in equation (11).

6 Error estimation

Typically, in any spectral estimation, the error has two independent components [5]. The first component represents the mean of the errors of the estimated values respect to the theoretic values. That error will be called the bias. The second component represents the standard deviation of those errors. Then, the root mean square (RMS) error is estimated according to:

$$error_{RMS}=\sqrt{bias^2+std^2} \quad (13)$$

In case of calculating the error estimation of the PIMF, it can be done with:

$$bias=\frac{1}{m}\sum_{n=0}^{m-1}\left(PIMF_{estimated}(n)-PIMF_{theoretic}(n)\right) \quad (14)$$

$$std^2=\frac{1}{m}\sum_{n=0}^{m-1}\left(PIMF_{estimated}(n)-PIMF_{theoretic}(n)\right)^2 \quad (15)$$

where m is the total amount of fully overlapped signal windows of length L in the whole signal of length T, in consequence, $m= T-L+1$. Whereas, in case of calculating the error estimation of the RMSMB, it can be done with:

$$bias=\frac{1}{m}\sum_{n=0}^{m-1}\left(RMSMB_{estimated}(n)-RMSMB_{theoretic}(n)\right) \quad (16)$$

$$std^2=\frac{1}{m}\sum_{n=0}^{m-1}\left(RMSMB_{estimated}(n)-RMSMB_{theoretic}(n)\right)^2 \quad (17)$$

with same considerations as in equations (14) , (15).

7 Results

Figures 6, 7, 8 and 9 show the detailed results obtained for the Bessel, Born Jordan, Choi Williams and Modified-B TFD, respectively. Each figure shows a set of graphs which relates the increment of jointly RMSMB and PIMF estimation error with the truncation index of the generalized autocorrelation function of the considered TFD. Note that the calculations are made involving the TFD's optimal scaling factors. Each graph takes in account several SNR (10 dB, 20 dB, 30 dB, 40 dB, noiseless), and several window lengths (63, 127, 255). The increment of estimation error is referred to that obtained when no truncation of the generalized autocorrelation function is involved.

Table 2 shows the truncation index *(TI)* that correspond to a jointly RMSMB and PIMF spectral estimation error increment of 5%, 3% and 1% for a SNR of 30 dB. Note that the admissible values of TI are from 0 to *N-1*, where window length is *L=2N-1*.

Table 2. Truncation index corresponding to a SNR of 30 dB. Jointly RMSMB and PIMF estimation error increment of 1%, 3% and 5%.

Error	Window length	Modified B	Bessel
1%	L = 63	TI=10	TI=26
1%	L = 127	TI=20	TI=52
1%	L = 255	TI=128	TI=80
3%	L = 63	TI=8	TI=24
3%	L = 127	TI=16	TI=44
3%	L = 255	TI=128	TI=72
5%	L = 63	TI=8	TI=22
5%	L = 127	TI=16	TI=36
5%	L = 255	TI=48	TI=72

Error	Window length	Born Jordan	Choi Williams
1%	L = 63	TI=20	TI=14
1%	L = 127	TI=44	TI=36
1%	L = 255	TI=88	TI=40
3%	L = 63	TI=16	TI=14
3%	L = 127	TI=44	TI=24
3%	L = 255	TI=56	TI=32
5%	L = 63	TI=16	TI=12
5%	L = 127	TI=44	TI=24
5%	L = 255	TI=48	TI=24

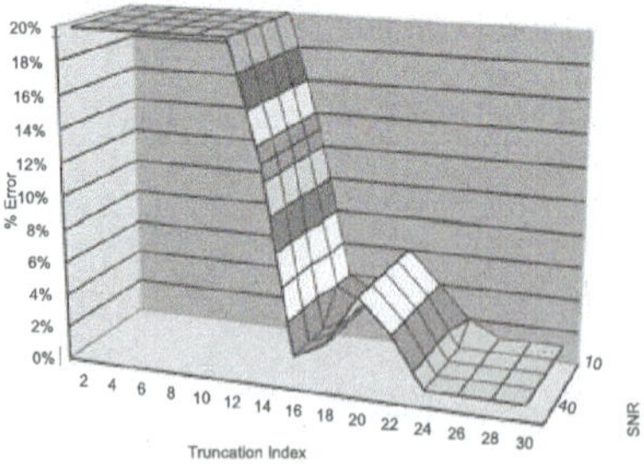

a

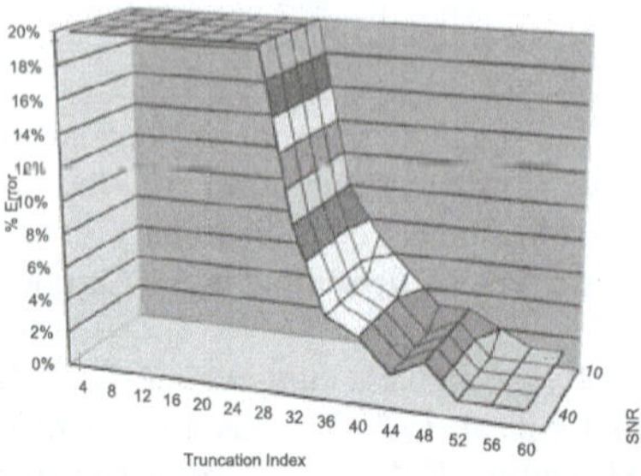

b

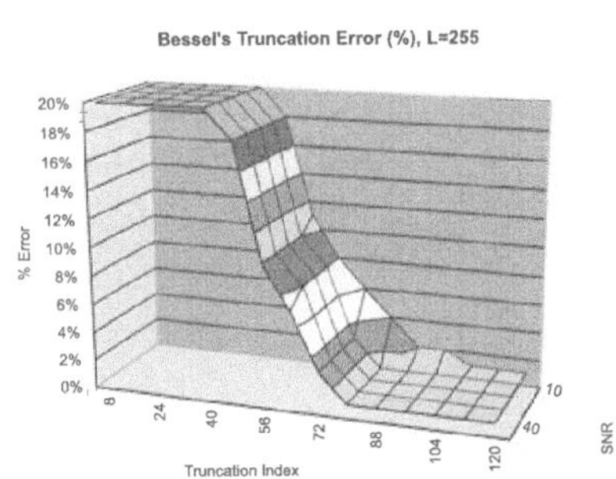

c

Figure 6. Bessel TFD increment of jointly RMSMB and PIMF estimation error vs. Truncation index for SNR (10dB, 20dB, 30dB, 40dB, noiseless), and window lengths of a) 63, b) 127, c) 255. Optimal scaling factors are considered.

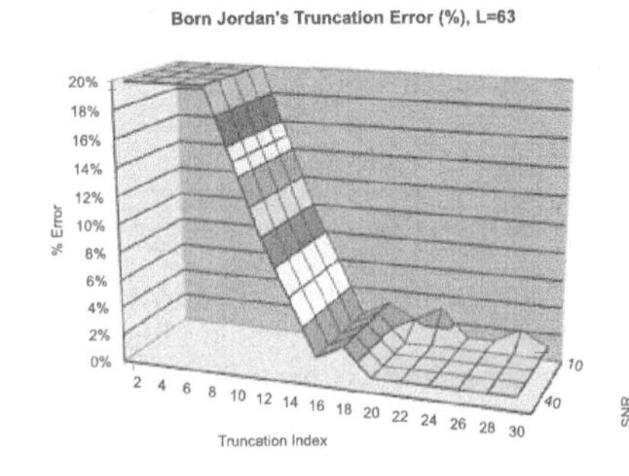

a

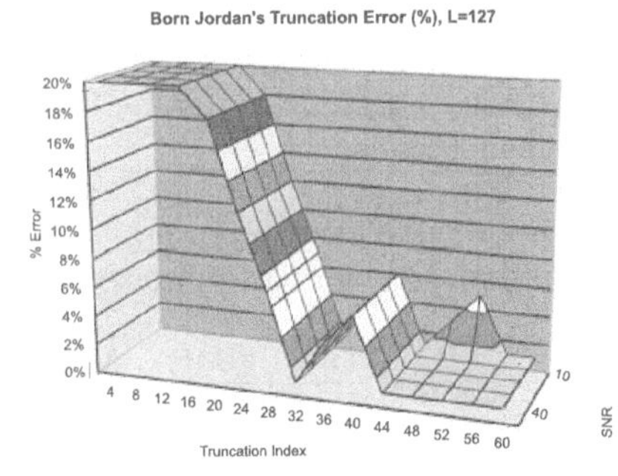

b

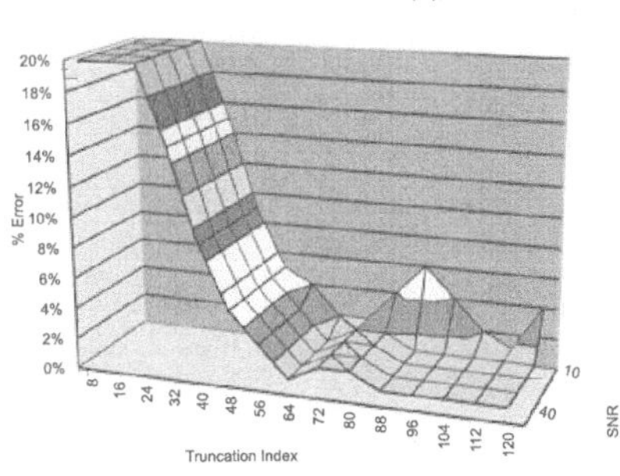

c

Figure 7. Born Jordan TFD increment of jointly RMSMB and PIMF estimation error vs. Truncation index for SNR (10dB, 20dB, 30dB, 40dB, noiseless), and window lengths of a) 63, b) 127, c) 255. Optimal scaling factors are considered.

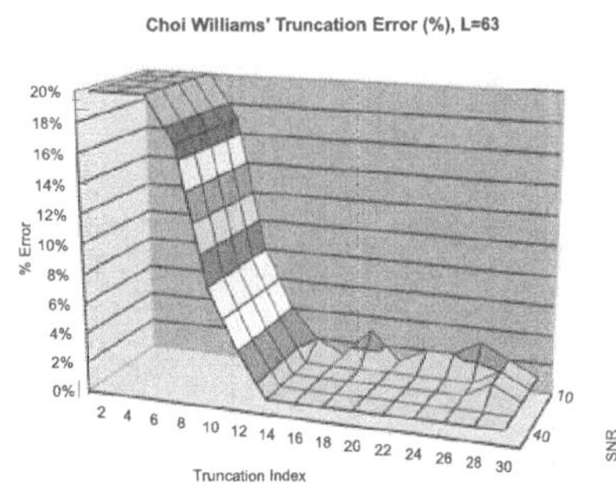

a

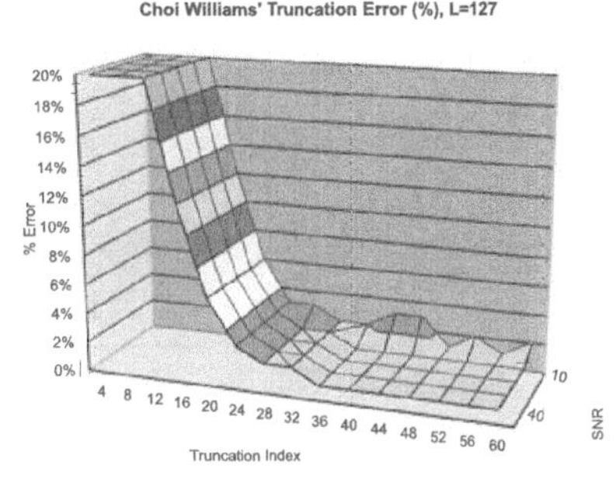

b

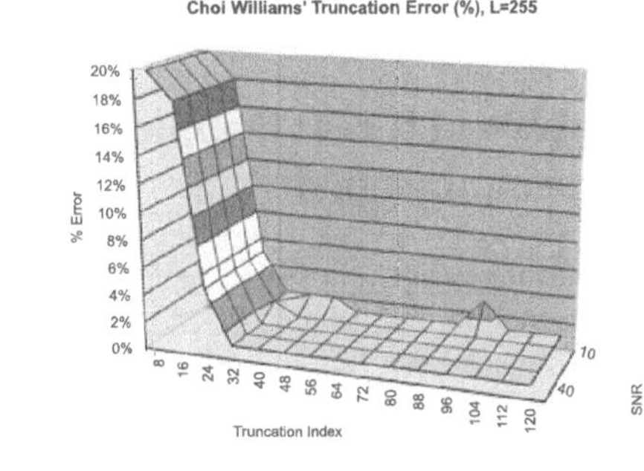

c

Figure 8. Choi Williams TFD increment of jointly RMSMB and PIMF estimation error vs. Truncation index for SNR (10dB, 20dB, 30dB, 40dB, noiseless), and window lengths of a) 63, b) 127, c) 255. Optimal scaling factors are considered.

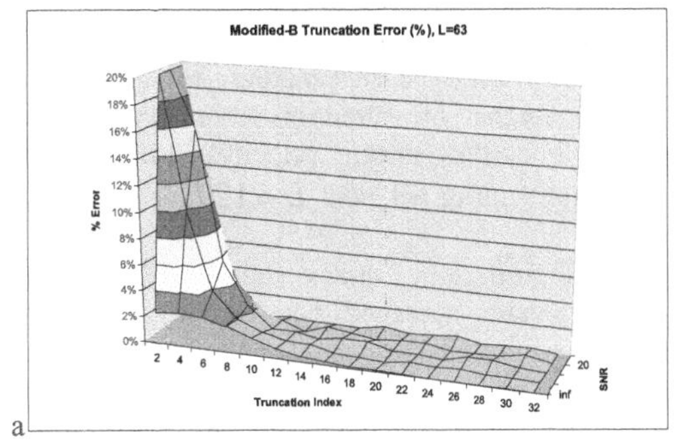

a

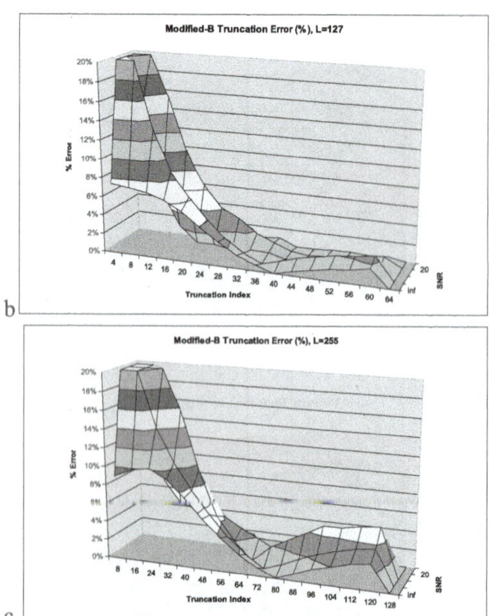

Figure 9. Modified-B TFD increment of jointly RMSMB and PIMF estimation error vs. Truncation index for SNR (10dB, 20dB, 30dB, 40dB, noiseless), and window lengths of a) 63, b) 127, c) 255. Optimal scaling factors are considered.

8 Analysis of a real Doppler ultrasound signal

This section analyses a real Doppler ultrasonic signal measured in the laboratory. Again, it is a signal that models the Carotid artery blood flow mean velocity. Figure 10 shows its PIPD using the Born Jordan distribution.

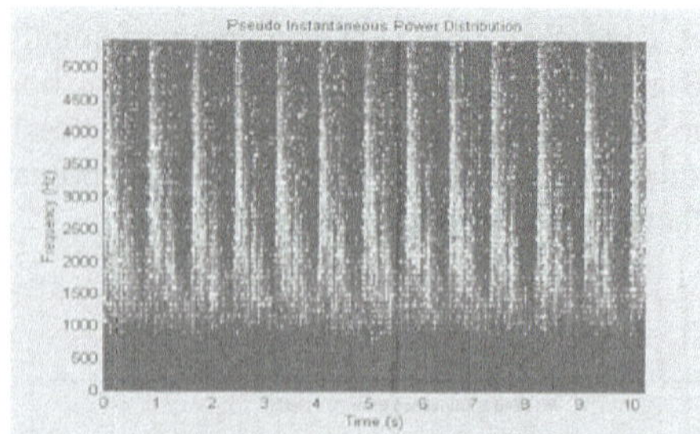

Figure 10. PIPD corresponding to a Doppler ultrasonic signal measured in laboratory (Carotid artery blood flow mean velocity). Born Jordan distribution with $\alpha = 1$, and $L = 127$ are used.

Figure 11.a shows the PIMF and the RMSMB, both averaged per cardiac cycle. An optimal scaling factor $\alpha = 1$, a window length $L = 127$ and no truncation ($TI = 63$) are used. Finally, figure 11.b shows the PIMF and the RMSMB but using a truncating index $TI = 44$. Similar waveforms are experimentally obtained using Bessel, Choi Williams and Modified-B distributions.

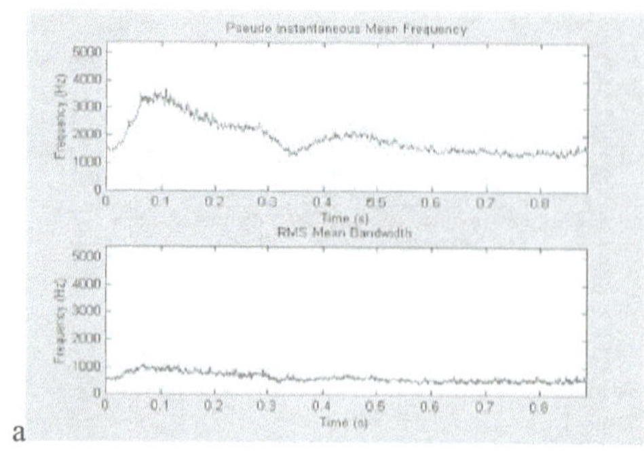

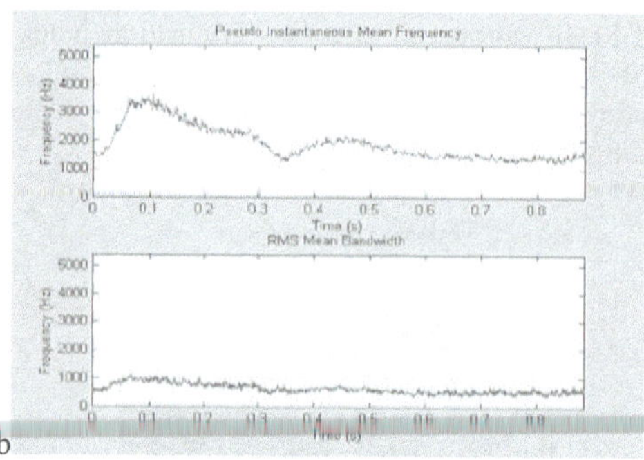

Figure 11. Averaged PIMF and RMSMB per cardiac cycle corresponding to a Doppler ultrasonic signal measured in laboratory (Carotid artery blood flow mean velocity). Born Jordan distribution with $\alpha = 1$, $L = 127$, a) no truncation and b) a truncating index $TI = 44$, are used.

Table 3 shows the RMS deviations obtained using truncation respect to the spectral estimations done without truncation.

Table 3. RMS deviations (Hz) using truncation respect to spectral estimations with not truncation.

	L	TI	PIMF	MBRMS
Bessel	63	26	0.00	0.00
		24	0.00	0.00
		22	2.43	3.85
	127	52	0.00	0.00
		44	3.06	3.21
		36	6.69	5.78
	255	80	3.08	2.77
		72	4.09	3.65
Born	63	20	0.00	0.00
Jordan		16	5.69	6.46
	127	44	0.00	0.00
	255	88	0.00	0.00
		56	3.32	2.76
		48	4.48	3.69
Choi	63	14	1.20	1.13
Williams		12	1.91	1.75
	127	36	0.09	0.09
		24	0.77	0.58
	255	40	0.60	0.46
		32	1.03	0.76
		24	1.77	1.32

Modified-B	63	10	0.38	1.01
		8	0.83	3.46
	127	20	3.80	6.24
		16	4.38	12.83
	255	128	0.00	0
		48	3.73	0.43

9 Conclusions

A controlled truncation in the index of the generalized autocorrelation function results in a controlled decrement in the accuracy of TFD calculation. Such a controlled reduction in the accuracy of TFD calculation produces a controlled increment in the spectral estimation errors but an important reduction in the amount of calculations involved. Four simplified expressions including an autocorrelation truncating index that calculate some TFD have been considered: the Bessel (2), the Born Jordan (3), the Choi Williams (4) and the Modified-B (5) distributions.

Optimal parameters of TFD, presented in Table 1 have been used. The case study considered is a simulated Doppler ultrasonic quasi-stationary signal that represents a typical blood flow in the Carotid artery. Figures 6, 7, 8 and 9 show the detailed results obtained. Those consist on the characterization of the increment of jointly PIMF and RMSBW estimation error as a function of the truncation index, the SNR and the sample window length.

Table 2 have showed the truncation index *(TI)* that correspond to a jointly RMSMB and PIMF spectral estimation error increment of 5%, 3% and 1% for a SNR of 30 dB, respectively. Note that the truncation of the autocorrelation function is more convenient for the Choi Williams distribution.

Finally, in section 8, a real Doppler ultrasound signal measured in laboratory is used for the TFD performance evaluation. The results corresponding to the Born Jordan distribution ($\alpha = 1$, $L = 127$) with and without truncation are shown in figure 11. Similar waveforms are experimentally obtained using Bessel, Choi Williams and Modified-B distributions. Table 3 has depicted the RMS deviations obtained using truncation respect to the spectral estimations done without truncation. Results are being applied to the development of a real-time spectrum analyzer for Doppler blood flow instrumentation [10].

10 Acknowledgments

The authors acknowledge projects DGAPA-UNAM PAPIIT (IN114710) and PAPIIT (IT101213) by the financial support. Also acknowledge to M. Fuentes, A. Contreras, S. Padilla, I. Sánchez and M. Vázquez for their technical support.

11 References

[1] Cohen, L. "Time-Frequency Distributions - A Review". *Proceedings of the IEEE*. **77**. 941-981, 1989.

[2] García-Nocetti F., Solano J., Rubio E., Moreno, E. "High Performance Computing of Time Frequency Distributions for Doppler Ulltrasound Signal Analysis". *Preprints of the 15th Triennial World Congress of the IFAC*, Barcelona Spain, July 2002

[3] García-Nocetti F., Solano J., Rubio E. "Precision enhancement of Doppler Ultrasound spectral estimation by finding TFD optimal parameters". *Forum Acusticum Sevilla. Special Issue of the Revista de Acústica*. **33**. Sevilla, Spain, September 2002.

[4] Boashash, B. and P. Black. "An Efficient Real-Time Implementation of the Wigner-Ville Distribution". *IEEE Transactions on Acoustics, Speech, and Signal Processing*. **ASSP-35**. 1611-1618, 1987.

[5] Cardoso, J. G. Ruano and P. Fish. "Nonstationary Broadening Reduction in Pulsed Doppler Spectrum Measurements Using Time-Frequency Estimators". *IEEE Transactions on Biomedical Engineering*. **43**. 1176-1186, 1996.

[6] Guo, Z., L. Durand and H. Lee. "The Time-Frequency Distributions of Nonstationary Signals Based on a Bessel Kernel". *IEEE Transactions on Signal Processing*. **42**. 1700-1707, 1994.

[7] Choi, H. and W. Williams. "Improved Time-Frequency Representation of Multicomponent Signals Using Exponential Kernels".*IEEE Transactions on Acoustics, Speech and Signal Processing*. **37**. 862-871, 1989.

[8] Hussain Z. And Boashash B. "Adaptive Instantaneous Frequency Estimation of Multicomponent FM Signals Using Quadratic Time-Frequenc Distributions".*IEEE Transactions on Signal Processing*. **50**. 1866-1876, 2002.

[9] Fan, L. and D. Evans. "Extracting Instantaneous Mean Frequency Information from Doppler Signals Using the Wigner Distribution Function". *Ultrasound in Med. & Biol.* **20**. 429-443, 1994.

[10] Solano J., Fuentes M., Villar A., Prohias J. and García-Nocetti F. "Doppler Ultrasound Blood Flow Measurement System for Assessing Coronary Revascularization". *Proceedings of the BIOCOMP'11, WORLDCOMP'11*, Las Vegas NV, USA. 429-433, July 2011.

[11] García-Nocetti F., Solano J., and Rubio E. "Improving Performance of a TFD-based Spectral Estimation Method in Doppler Ultrasound Blood Flow Measurement". *Proceedings of the BIOCOMP'12, WORLDCOMP'12*, Las Vegas NV, USA. 243-248, July 2012,

Characteristics of Brain Wave Changes by Affective Pictures

Ruoyu Du[1] **and Hyo Jong Lee**[1, 2]
[1]Division of Computer Science and Engineering, Chonbuk National University, Jeonju, Korea
[2]Center for Advanced Image & Information Technology, Chonbuk National University, Jeonju, Korea

Abstract - *Emotion status influences important areas in our daily lives. Many researchers reported successful emotion classifications. The aim of this study is to find out the neuro-physiological characteristics of the brain waves while affective pictures elucidate emotion. Four healthy college students volunteered the stimulus experiment with the standard IAPS affective pictures. All brain waves showed active pattern over the frontal and parietal lobes. The significances of emotion change were found frontal lobe and central gyri area for Alpha band. Beta band also showed significance for emotion change around parietal lobe. This study revealed only Alpha and Beta waves changed significantly at limited location due to changed emotional status.*

Keywords: Electroencephalogram (EEG); emotion; valence-arousal model; IAPS; ICA;

1 Introduction

Every human being expresses emotion daily lives. Emotions are an especially interesting phenomenon as a result of the huge impact they have on humans on a daily basis. Emotions play an important role in communication and affect our behaviors. Because of the importance of emotions, many researchers have investigated various psychological and physiological phenomena. An electroencephalogram (EEG) has been recognized as a useful tool because of its high time resolution and the direct information from a brain invasively. It also detects the abnormal brain waves or electrical activity of the brain. Many scientists reported various methods to retrieve emotion-related information from EEG signals with the advanced biomedical signal processing technology. This has resulted in the ability to detect a variety of psychological and physiological states.

EEG based emotion research is a challenging field within the area of biomedical signal processing. Recently several researches were performed to understand human emotion. Nie[1] et al. investigated the relationship between EEG signals and human emotions. They used EEG signals to classify either positive or negative emotions. A support vector machine (SVM) was applied to the extracted features from original EEG data. They reported 87% of accuracy between positive and negative emotion. Lin [2] et al. investigated EEG-based emotion elicited by auditory stimulus. Using the music-induced emotional responses, a comparative study was conducted to find out if hierarchical binary classifiers work better than nonhierarchical method. Kwon and Lee [3] used EEG signals which are stimulated while watching movie clips. Changes in alpha and gamma power have been interpreted to indicate differential valence pattern related to the frontal lobes. Liu [4] et al. proposed real-time algorithm of quantification of basic emotions using Arousal-Valence emotion model. An EEG-based web-enable music player was implemented, which can display the music according to the user's current emotion states.

Since an emotion elicitation procedure occurs in our mind by watching images or listening music, it is safe to assume the EEG signals reflect emotion-related brain activity. The signals provided by this procedure can then be processed to train and test the system of EEG based emotion recognition. However, these researches have not investigated neurophysiological phenomena arising inside a brain. To neuroscientists their feature data simply reflect unrecognizable numbers. A fuzzy approached training method or a SVM were trained with known emotion states and predict a subject's emotion condition based on trained numbers. The high classification rate means that randomly selected feature data were trained well. However, this does not mean that neurophysiological process, which occurred inside a brain, has been understood clearly.

The commonly practiced method for EEG of emotion research consists of three steps. First, EEG data are recorded and collected under predefined stimulus by using the biomedical related machine. Secord, preprocessing techniques are applied to signals to remove artifact noises, such as EOG, ECG and muscle movement signals. Third, each brain wave is extracted and analyzed in terms of power or patterns. The purpose of this paper is to find out neurophysiological characteristics of brain activity under emotional affection. For example, feature points can be extracted from alpha wave, beta wave or gamma wave in frontal lobes because all types of waves are activated under emotional condition. Through this study, the neurophysiological information will be able to distinguish which brain wave is prevalent and which wave will show significance during emotion changes.

2 Related Theory

2.1 Emotions

Two main approaches are commonly used to recognize emotions: the taxonomy approach and the dimensional approach. The taxonomy approach, in some cases is also known as the evolutionary approach [5].

The taxonomy approach derives from the non-cognitive theories, as well as from the somatic approaches. This approach considers emotions to be discrete and, therefore, characterization of each emotion is independent with regards of the others. Moreover, these discrete emotions would be useful responses to specific environmental situations, as a result of the evolution. Thus, this is also called the evolutionary approach.

The dimensional approach, derived from the cognitive theories, characterizes the state of mind of a person in terms of dimensions. Common dimensions are the valence of emotion (positive or negative) and the arousal level of emotion (active or passive). This 2D valence-arousal (V-A) emotion model is more expressible and general than the discrete emotion approaches.

In this paper, the V-A emotion model is used to classify emotion criterion. And the subjective assessment of emotion is represented from 0 to 9 as the level of evaluation, which is shown in Figure 1.

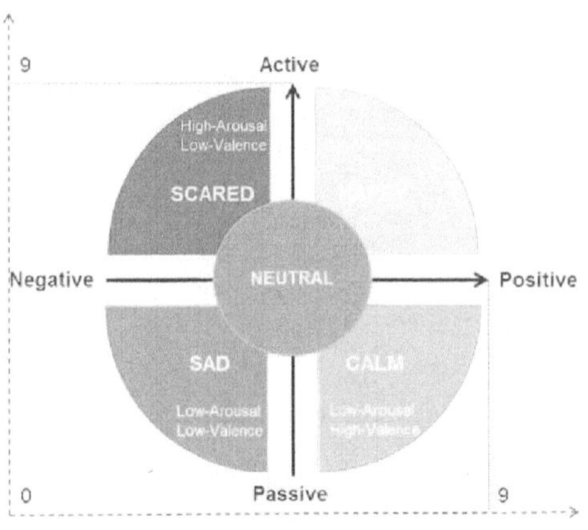

Fig. 1. Valence-Arousal Model

2.2 EEG and Brain waves

Electrical recordings from the surface of the brain, or even from the outer surface of the head, demonstrate that there are continuous electrical activities in the brain. Both the intensity and the patterns of this electrical activity depend on the level of excitation of different parts of the brain resulting from sleep, wakefulness, or brain diseases such as epilepsy or even psychoses. The undulations in the recorded electrical potentials are known as brain waves, and the entire record is called an EEG [6]. Intensity of EEG recording range from 0 to 200 microvolt on the surface of the scalp, and their frequency ranges from once every few seconds to 50 or more per second. The characteristics of the waves are dependent on the degree of activity in respective parts of the cerebral cortex. The waves change markedly between the states of emotions. Much of the time, the brain waves are irregular, and no specific pattern can be discerned in the EEG.

There are mainly five types of Brain waves: Delta waves (0.5-4 Hz) which are considered to be related to the deep sleep [7] in the adults or premature babies. It is usually found in the frontal region of brain in adults and posterior region in children. A common Theta wave (4-8 Hz) which occurs in children and adults when they are in emotional stress or they have deep midline disorders. It is found in parietal and occipital region. Another type of theta waves is named frontal midline theta. The theta waves exist during the various tasks which need the correlation of the increased mental effort and sustained concentration [8]. Alpha wave (8-13 Hz), which occurs in quiet resting state but not sleep, is found in the occipital region. Alpha waves can reflect the relaxation level a person is having. They are also believed to be responsible for the movement related brain activity. Another role of Alpha rhythms is to handle a perceptual processing, memory tasks, and emotions [7]. Beta wave (13-30 Hz) occurs in active and busy concentration or anxious thinking state. It is found in the frontal and parietal region and is related to the concentration level of people [5]. An increase in a beta power may reflect the increase of the arousal level of an emotional state [8]. Gamma wave (30-100 Hz) which occurs in certain cognitive or motor functions. It is often used for diagnosis of the certain brain illness [7].

2.3 Emotion in the Brain

Stimuli are transmitted into the brain at the brain stem. The limbic system around the brain stem is responsible for initial emotional interpretation of these signals from the autonomic nervous system. This part of the brain has also been found important for motivation and memory functions. Although motivation and memory also have their influence on the reaction to emotional stimuli, the rest of the text will focus on the limbic structures. They are also responsible for emotional reactions. The hypothalamus is responsible for processing the incoming signals and triggering the corresponding visceral physiological effects, like a raised heart rate or galvanic skin response [9]. From the hypothalamus the stimuli information is passed on to the amygdala, which is important for learning to stimulate emotional response (reward/fear) and evaluate the new stimulus by comparing their past experiences. The amygdala is thought to be important for processing emotion. However, since it is an underlying structure like the rest of the limbic system, it cannot be detected directly in recordings from the scalp. The amygdala is connected to the temporal and prefrontal cortices, which is considered to be the way visceral sensations are interpreted cognitively, resulting in a consciously experienced feeling of an emotion [9]. The temporal lobe is essential for hearing, language and emotion, and also plays an important role in memory. The prefrontal lobe (directly behind the forehead) is involved in the highest level of functioning. It is responsible for cognitive, emotional and motivational processes. The prefrontal lobe is part of the frontal cortex, which is allegedly known as the emotional control center and to even determine personality. It is involved in, among others, judgment and social behavior. These functions are very much effective based on the experience of emotions [10].

3 Materials and Methods

3.1 Subjects

In this experiment, four healthy males in the age group of 23-25 years old were recruited as subjects. They are all right-handed and have correct visions. All of the subjects were undergraduate students of the same institution and were informed about the purpose of this research. Once the consent forms were filled-up, the subjects were given a simple introduction about the research work and stages of experiment.

3.2 EEG Signal Acquisition

EEG signals were collected using the 10/20 internationally recognized placement system shown in Figure 2. This system is based on the relationship of various position of electrode placed on scalp and the underlying area of cerebral cortex [11].

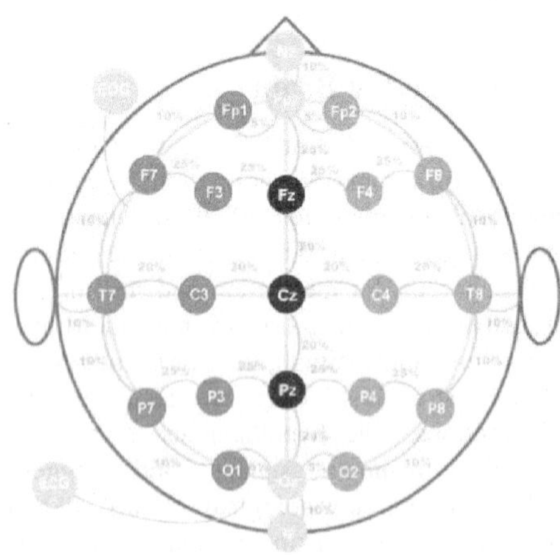

Fig. 2. The montage used in this research based on 10-20 system of electrode placement.

The EEG signals were recorded using a Brain Vision amplifier system (BrainProducts, Germany). Silver-silver-chloride-electrodes (Ag/AgCl) were used in association with the "Easy Cap System" (International 10-20 system shown in Figure 2, FMS Falk Minow Services, Herrsching-Breitbrunn, Germany). In this research, eighteen electrodes (Fp1, Fp2, F3, F4, Fz, F7, F8, C3, C4, Cz, T7, T8, P3, P4, P7, P8, O1, and O2) were inserted to record EEG signals using the Easy Cap which refer to Figure 2. The electrooculogram (EOG) was recorded from one additional electrodes placed below the outer canthi of left eye. Impedances were kept below 5 kΩ. Cardiac activity was recorded with an electrode from the left outer of neck, ECG drawn in Figure 2. An average reference was used. Brain Vision Recorder was used to record the data (0.5-70 Hz, 500 samples per second). Subjects were instructed to remain still and to blink or move their eyes and body as little as possible during the recording periods.

3.3 Experimental Procedure and Stimuli Construction

The whole experiment was designed to induct emotion within the valence (positive / approach versus negative / withdrawal) and arousal (calm versus excited) space. These two dimensions are a subset of the three-dimensional representation [12] [13] for collecting affective ratings for the IAPS. Figure 3 shows the relationships between arousal and valence of IAPS images. To make clear distinction among emotions, five affective states were selected: low arousal-low valence (LA_LV), low arousal-high valence (LA_HV), high arousal-high valence (HA_HV), high arousal-low valence (HA_LV) and middle arousal-middle valence (MA_MV). On the basis of these ratings, 35 pictures (7 pictures x 5 states) were selected from uniformly distributed clusters along the valence and arousal axes.

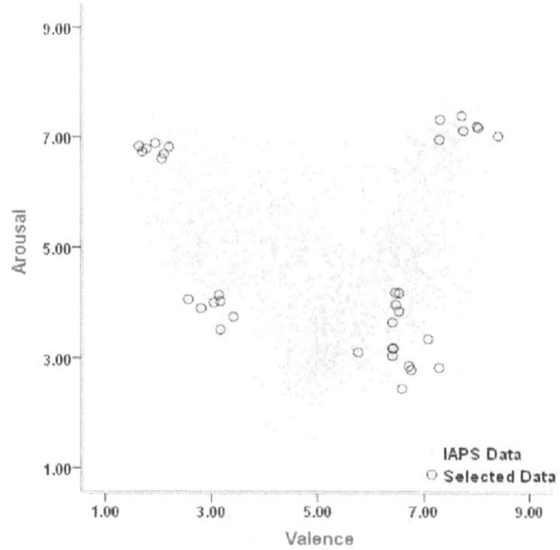

Fig. 3. Scatterplot of valence and arousal ratings (1–9 scales) for all available International Affective Picture System images. The circles denote the images selected in this study.

Figure 3 also shows the location of the pictures finally selected at the arousal-valence domain with the circles. During the experiment, the selected pictures were projected randomly for 4s following another 4s for resetting emotion with a blurred image. Due to its unknown emotional status before the projection of the first picture and after the projection of the last picture, a fixation mark (cross) was projected for eight seconds in the middle of the screen to attract the sight of the subject. Figure 4 shows the timing diagram of this experiment. The total time of collecting EEG recording in this experiment was 296 seconds. After all of the pictures were projected, a Self-Assessment Mannequin (SAM) [14] procedure took place. The EEG signals from each subject were recorded during the whole projection phase. It is important to distinguish between emotional stimulus and experienced emotion. IAPS stimuli are associated with "standard ratings", but the same picture may not induct the same level of arousal and valence. For this reason, the subjects were asked to rate their own emotional experience while being presented each stimulus. Each subject was told about the importance of these ratings, with particular emphasis on the importance to rate how the subject actually felt while viewing each picture.

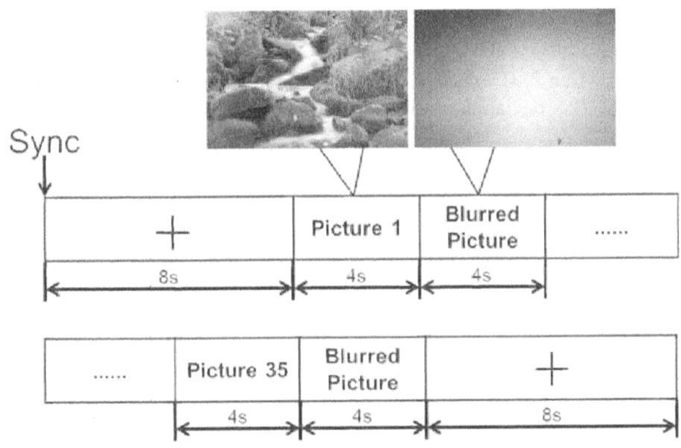

Fig. 4. Timing diagram for five different emotions. Each category has seven pictures totalling 35 pictures.

3.4 Preprocessing

An open source tool box named EEGLAB provided by SCCN lab [15], running under the cross platform of MATLAB environment (Mathworks, Inc.) is used for both preprocessing and analysis of the EEG data. It includes data collection functions, channel and event information management and data visualization tools, such as scrolling, scalp map and dipole model plotting and multi-trial ERP-image plots. Main preprocessing features are artifact rejection, filtering, epoch selection and averaging signals. It also provides high level analysis functions, such as PCA and ICA.

After the acquisition phase, the EEG data was at first referenced to Cz electrode while importing the EEG data files to the EEGLAB. Then the channel locations were imported for getting information about the recording electrodes which is necessary for plotting EEG scalp maps or to estimate source locations for data components. The data was then high-pass filtered with lower cut-off frequency of 4Hz and low-pass filtered with cutoff frequency of 50Hz. This band-pass filtering of continuous EEG data using linear FIR filter eliminated the power line noise, EMG and EOG artifacts.

3.5 Artifact Detection and Removal via ICA

ICA (Independent Component Analysis) algorithms have proven capable of separating artifacts and neural signals generated from EEG whose EEG contributions, across the training data, are maximally independent of one another. ICA is widely used in the EEG research community to detect and remove eye, muscle, and line noise artifacts and also to separate biologically plausible brain sources whose activity patterns are distinctly linked to behavioral phenomena. EEGLAB contains an automated version of the Infomax ICA algorithm with several enhancements. ICA finds a coordinate frame in which the data projections have minimal temporal overlap. The core mathematical concept of ICA is to minimize the mutual information among the data projections or maximize their joint entropy [15]. In this paper, ICA was applied to reduce the total number of features from 2000 (500Hz sampling rate, for 4 seconds), to first 20 components. For each of the number of independent components within this research, the classification procedure was applied, as the optimal number was unknown at this point.

ICA applied to a matrix of EEG scalp data finds an unmixing matrix of weights W which linearly decomposes the multichannel data into a sum of maximally temporally independent and spatially fixed components $u = Wx$. The rows of the output matrix u are courses of activation of the ICA components. These components account for artifacts, stimulus and response locked events and spontaneous EEG activity. The columns of the inverse matrix W^{-1} give the relative projection strengths of the respective components at each of the scalp sensors. This is the process of ICA decomposition of the data into maximally temporally independent processes, each with its distinct time series and scalp map. These scalp maps of projection strengths provide evidence for the components' physiological origin (e.g. ocular activity projects mainly to frontal sites). Selected components can be projected back onto the scalp using the relation $x_0 = W^{-1}u_0$, where u_0 is the matrix u with irrelevant components set to zero. Thereby brain signals accounted for by the selected components can be obtained in true polarity and amplitudes [16].

Eye movement artifacts result from the contamination of the EEG by the electrooculogram (EOG), a potential produced by movement of the eye or eyelid. Several methods have been proposed for removing ocular artifacts from the EEG, most of which make use of a separate EOG record. There are two main types of eye movement artifacts, those due to blinks and those due to saccadic movements [17-19]. Blink artifacts are due to contact of the eyelid with the cornea which alters ocular conductance. The influence of blink artifacts on recording electrodes decreases rapidly with distance from the eyes. Saccade artifacts arise from changes in orientation of the retina-corneal dipole. The cornea of the eye is positively charged relative to the retina. Rotation of the retina-corneal axis results in changes in electrical potential. The saccadic influence decreases much slower and shows a typical pattern of polarity difference between contra-lateral sites. ICA has already been used successfully for blind source separation of EEG data. Application of ICA to ERPs include artifact detection and removal [18] [20] [21] as well as analysis of event-related response averages [16] [22]. Application of ICA to single-trial ERPs is more recent [20] [23] [24]. In single-trial EEG analysis, the rows of the input matrix x are EEG and EOG signals recorded at different electrodes and the columns are measurements at different time points. There also have the other two types of artifact discussed here is due to cardiac and muscle activity. Compared to normal EEG activity, muscle artifact is characterized by high frequencies (over 15Hz) and often by high amplitude. Because of the cardiac signal have a regular wave. ICA can separate those artifacts easily and remove the interference [25]. Either conscious or unconscious muscle activity produces an electric potential called electromyogram (EMG). Muscle artifacts can be classified according to their spread in space (broad or localized) and time (transient or permanent) [26] which also can be removed by using ICA.

3.6 Data Analyses and Statistics

The power spectral density estimates were log-transformed (using the base 10 logarithm) in order to normalize their distribution. Spectral estimates were averaged within alpha (8-13 Hz), beta (13-30 Hz) and gamma (30-50 Hz) bands. For each epoch of each subject the spectral power data present the magnitude of signals at measurement points with colors. EEGLAB also shows the power spectrum of the brain model at the chosen frequency. Therefore, it is easy to know the activated parts on the brain during each event. In this paper, the power spectrum at the alpha frequency band, the beta frequency band and the gamma frequency band were plotted respectively to study the scalp distribution of power spectral density during stimuli. A probability of p<= 0.05 was accepted for being significant. All statistical analyses were performed by SPSS 19.0 (SPSS Inc. Chicago, Illinois, USA).

4 Results and Discussion

Figure 5 and 6 graphically presents the mean values of PSD (power spectrum density) in the frontal region and central gyri and parietal regions with standard deviation based on the different emotion states. Figure 7 and 8 displays also the mean of PSD in the frontal region for Beta and Gamma wave, respectively.

In order to determine significant correlation between the measured data and the visualization type, we employed paired 2-tailed T-tests. T-tests were used to determine the significance of spectral properties departing from the baseline measurements taken as well as spectral differences between visualization types. All statistical tests used the null hypothesis that there is no significant change in brain waves between the two emotions being analyzed. Table I and II displays T-test results with the mean and significance values for the alpha and beta waves between two emotions.

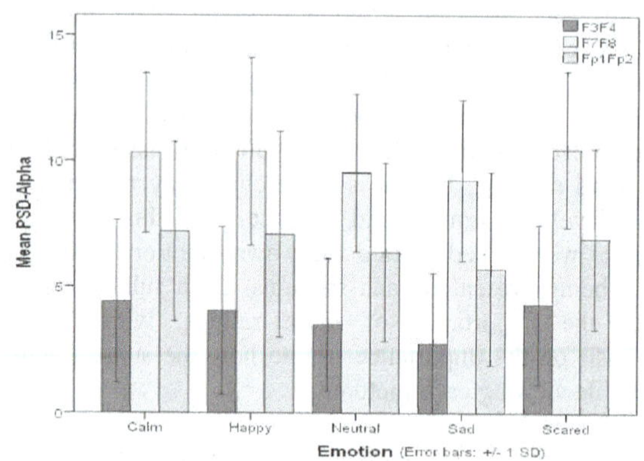

Fig. 5. Mean PSD values of Alpha wave in the frontal region with standard deviation based on the different emotion states.

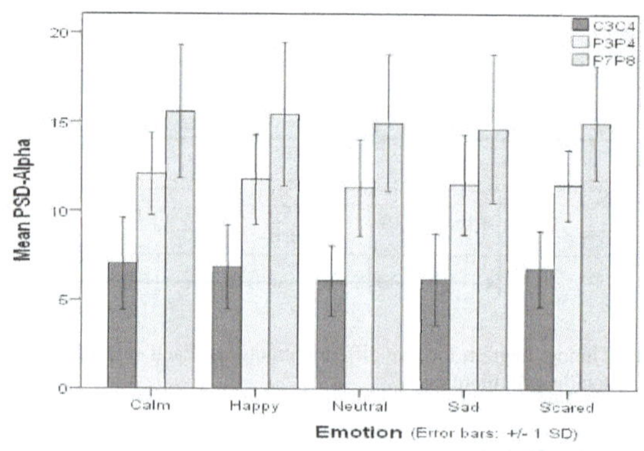

Fig. 6. Mean PSD values of Alpha wave in the central gyri and parietal regions with standard deviation based on the different emotion states.

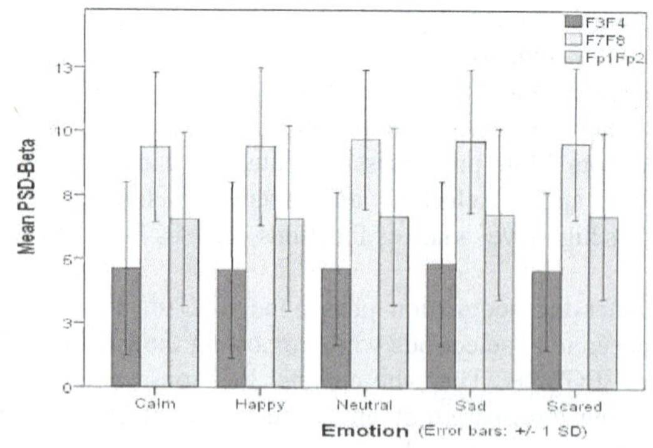

Fig. 7. Mean PSD values of Beta wave in the frontal region with standard deviation based on the different emotion states.

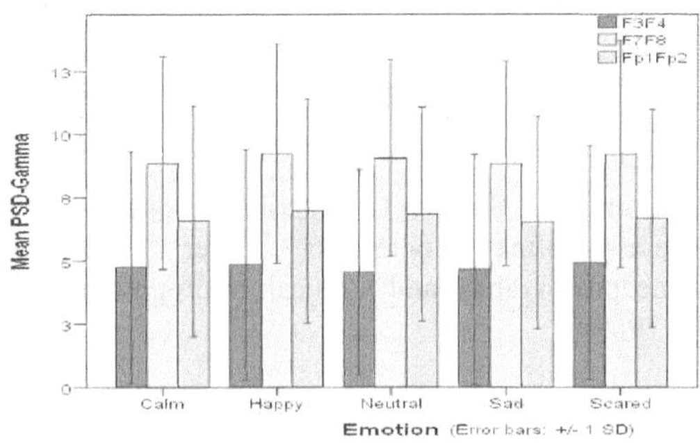

Fig. 8. Mean PSD values of Gamma wave in the frontal region with standard deviation based on the different emotion states.

TABLE I. EMOTION PAIRED SAMPLES STATISTIC RESULTS FOR ALPHA WAVE (SIGNIFICANT CHANGES ARE IN BOLD)

Location / Emotion	Fp1-Fp2		F3-F4		F7-F8	
	Mean	*Sig.(2-tailed)*	*Mean*	*Sig.(2-tailed)*	*Mean*	*Sig.(2-tailed)*
Neutral vs. Scared	6.648	.175	3.897	.062	10.002	**.035**
Sad vs. Scared	6.318	**.021**	3.524	**.002**	9.86	**.009**
Sad vs. Happy	6.403	**.014**	3.396	**.006**	9.81	**.032**
Sad vs. Calm	6.453	**.008**	3.579	**.002**	9.776	**.040**
Location / Emotion	**C3-C4**		**P3-P4**		**P7-P8**	
	Mean	*Sig.(2-tailed)*	*Mean*	*Sig.(2-tailed)*	*Mean*	*Sig.(2-tailed)*
Neutral vs. Scared	6.43	**.038**	11.389	.579	14.948	.931
Neutral vs. Calm	6.549	**.027**	11.687	**.042**	15.243	.231
Sad vs. Calm	6.592	**.035**	11.783	.155	15.091	.114

TABLE II. EMOTION PAIRED SAMPLES STATISTIC RESULTS FOR BETA WAVE (SIGNIFICANT CHANGES ARE IN BOLD)

Location / Emotion	P3-P4		P7-P8	
	Mean	*Sig.(2-tailed)*	*Mean*	*Sig.(2-tailed)*
Happy vs. Scared	11.611	**.037**	14.688	.225
Happy vs. Neutral	11.521	.115	15.168	**.045**

The mean PSDs of Alpha, Beta and Gamma waves show similar magnitude in the frontal lobes (Fig. 5, 7 and 8), while the PSD of Alpha wave shows larger in the parietal lobes (Fig. 6). Gamma wave showed strong PSD for every emotion in Figure 8. Consequently, changes of emotion status do not affect Gamma wave significantly.

Tables I and II summarized significances found according to each location for Alpha and Beta waves. Gamma wave did not show any significance anywhere due to steady pattern of brain waves. Table I shows that the emotion of sad causes significant changes most of in frontal lobes. Alpha waves in the parietal lobes are also significantly changed when there is a change from a neutral state to a scared or calm state. Table II shows that Beta wave change significantly in parietal lobes for emotion changes from happy to either scared or neutral state.

5 Conclusions

In this paper we investigate how brain waves change according to various emotional stimuli. Five affective states, low arousal-low valence, low arousal-high valence, high arousal-high valence, high arousal-low valence and middle arousal-middle valence were simulated with IAPS pictures. While those emotion statuses changed, Alpha, Beta, and Gamma brain waves are extracted and their power spectrum densities (PSD) were calculated over the whole brain region. Although every region showed active brain waves for changing emotional stimulus, significant changes were found in only a few regions, where emotional changes were dominant. The mean PSD of Alpha wave had significance when status change occurred as neutral-scared, sad-scared, sad-happy and sad-calm in frontal lobes. Another significance of Alpha wave was also found in parietal lobes as natural-scared, neutral-calm or sad-calm change occurred. The mean PSD of Beta wave showed significant changes only in the posterior parietal lobes for the emotion changes of happy-scared and happy-neutral. Gamma wave does not show significance for any changes of emotions.

Acknowledgment

This work was supported by the National Research Foundation of Korea (NRF) grant funded by the Korea government (MEST) (No. 2012R1A2A2A03).

References

[1] Dan Nie, Xia-Wei Wang, Li-Chen Shi, Bao-Liang Lu, "EEG-based emotion recognition during watching movies," Proceedings of the 5th international IEEE EMBS conference on Neural Engineering, pp. 667-670, 2011.

[2] Yuan-Pin Lin, Chi-Hong Wang, Tien-Lin Wu, Shyh-Kang Jeng, Jyh-Horng Cheng, "EEG-Based emotion recognition in music listening: A comparison of schemes for

multiclass support vector machine," Proceedings of IEEE International Conference on Acoustics, Speech, and signal Processing, pp. 489-492, 2009.

[3] Mingu Kwon and Minho Lee, "Emotion Understanding in movie clips based on EEG signal Analysis," Proceedings of ICONIP 2012, LNCS 7665, pp. 236-243, 2012.

[4] Yisi Liu, Olga Sourina, and Minh Khoa Nguyen, "Emotion Assessment: Arousal Evaluation Using EEG's and Peripheral Physiological Signals." Transactions on computational science XII, Springer-Verlag, Berlin Heidelberg, pp. 256-277, 2011.

[5] Larsen, R. J., & Buss, D. M.. Personality psychology. NewYork: McGraw-Hill, 2002.

[6] Guyton,A.C.,Hall J.E, Textbook Of Medical Physiology, Elsevier Inc., Philadelphia, 2005.

[7] S. Sanei and J. Chambers, EEG signal processing. Chichester, England, Hoboken, NJ: John Wiley & Sons, 2007.

[8] D. Sammler, M. Grigutsch, T. Fritz, and S. Koelsch, "Music and emotion: Electrophysiological correlates of the processing of pleasant and unpleasant music," Psychophysiology, vol. 44, pp. 293-304, 2007.

[9] E. R. Kandel, J. H. Schwartz, and T. M. Jessell.Principles of Neural Science. Mc Graw Hill, 2000.

[10] A. Bergsma and K. van Petersen. Het brein van A totZ. Hersenstichting Nederland / Het Spectrum B.V.,2003.

[11] Kennett R. Modern electroencephalography. J Neurol 2012;259:783-9.

[12] P. J. Lang, M. M. Bradley, and B. N. Cuthbert. International affective picture system (IAPS): stimuli, instruction manual and affective ratings. Technical Report A-4, The Center for Research in Psychophysiology, University of Florida, 1999.

[13] M. M. Bradley and P. J. Lang. International affective digitized sounds (IADS): stimuli,instruction manual and affective ratings. Technical Report B-2, The Center for Researchin Psychophysiology, University of Florida, 1999.

[14] J. D. Morris, "Observations: SAM the self-assessment mannequin-An efficient cross-cultural measurement of emotional response," Journal of Advertising Research, vol. 35, pp. 63-68, 1995.

[15] Delorme,A.,Makeig,S., EEGLAB: an open source toolbox for analysis of single-trial EEG dynamics including independent component analysis, Journal of Neuroscience Methods, vol 134 ,pp 9-21, 2004.

[16] Makeig S, Bell AJ, Jung T-P, and Sejnowski TJ, "Independent component analysis of electroencephalographic data." Advances in Neural Information Processing Systems, vol. 8, pp. 145-151, 1996.

[17] Overton D.A., Shagass C.: Distribution of eye movement and eye blink potentials over the scalp, Electroencephalography and Clinical Neurophysiology, vol. 27, 546, 1969.

[18] Jung T.-P., Makeig S., Humphries C., Lee T.-W., Mckeown M.J.,Iragui V., Sejnowski T.J.: Removing electroencephalographic artifacts by blindsource separation, Psychophysiology, vol. 37, pp. 163-178, 2000.

[19] Joyce C. A., Gorodnitsky I. F., Kutas M.: Automatic removal of eye movement and blink artifacts from EEG data using blind component separation, Psychophysiology, vol. 41, Issue 2, pp.313-325, 2004.

[20] Vigario R.N.: Extraction of ocular artefacts from EEG using independent component analysis, Electroencephalography and Clinical Neurophysiology, vol. 103, pp. 395-404, 1997.

[21] Jung T.-P., Humphries C., Lee T.-W., Makeig S., McKeown M.J., Iraguid V., Sejnowski T.J.: Extended ICA Removes Artifacts from Electroencephalographic Recordings, in Jordan M.I. et al., Advances in Neural Information Processing Systems 10 (NIPS'98), MIT Press/Bradford Books, Cambridge/London, pp.894, 1998.

[22] Makeig S., Jung T-P., Bell A.J., Ghahremani D., Sejnowski T.J.: Blind Separation of Auditory Event-related Brain Responses into Independent Components, Proc. of National Academy of Science USA, vol. 94, pp. 10979-10984, 1997.

[23] Jung T.-P., Makeig S., Westerfield M., Townsend J., Courchesne E., Sejnowski T.J.: Analyzing and Visualizing Single-Trial Event-Related Potentials, in Kearns M.S. et al. (eds.), Advances in Neural Information Processing Systems 11, MIT Press, 1999.

[24] Jung T.-P., Makeig S., Westerfield M., Townsend J., Courchesne E., Sejnowski T.J.: Analysis and Visualization of Single-Trial Event-RelatedPotentials, Human Brain Mapping, vol. 14, pp. 166-185, 2001.

[25] Chawla, M. P. S., H. K. Verma, and Vinod Kumar. "RETRACTED: A new statistical PCA–ICA algorithm for location of R-peaks in ECG." International journal of cardiology, vol. 129, no.1, pp. 146-148, 2008.

[26] Stern, John M., and Jerome Engel. Atlas of EEG patterns. Lippincott Williams & Wilkins, 2005.

Distributed Medical Images in Health Care Systems

Behrooz Seyed-Abbassi and Jesse Collins
School of Computing, University of North Florida, Jacksonville, Florida, USA

Abstract - *The capability to quickly share a patient's past records of medical examinations through an electronic medical record would allow medical facilities to offer a higher degree of service to their patients by enabling health care providers to view a patient's history and deliver more accurate health care. This research provides a method for image information to be transferred in a text format in a distributed environment among medical institutions for retrieval and analysis of the images. It creates a geographically distributed medical information system as a database with warehouse capability where the patient images are stored in a repository and then transferred for retrieval and selection of historical images by a healthcare provider or medical institutions. The method provides a fast mechanism for selection of the image before the image itself is transferred over the network.*

Keywords: Medical Image, Database Design, Data Warehouse, DICOM, Retrieval

1 Introduction

Until recently, computerized medical information systems have been used locally at the clinical level with electronic data minimally available as shared information among various health care professionals and institutions. As computerization rapidly expands into all areas of health care, effective techniques for utilizing and storing the varied types and often-substantial file size involved in health care data are essential for optimal patient care and research.

There is a growing expectation that all medical images could be readily managed in an efficient, organized structure and in digital form [1]. With the introduction of Computed Tomography (CT) [2] followed by other digital diagnostic imaging modalities (such as X-Ray, Computed Radiography (CR), Ultra Sound (US), Nuclear Medicine (NM), Magnetic Resonance Imaging (MRI), and Positron Emission Tomography (PET)) and the increased use of computers in clinical applications, the American College of Radiology (ACR) [3] and the National Electrical Manufacturers Association (NEMA) [4] both acknowledge the emerging need for a standard method to transfer images and associated information between devices that produce a variety of digital image formats and that are manufactured by different vendors.

At present, the storage structures used for imaging in most health care institutions are similar to the classical style of the folder systems using hierarchical organization. In larger health care groups, the radiology departments use a more sophisticated computerized system for medical imaging, called Picture Archiving and Communication Systems (PACS) [5], that was initiated in 1982 and later developed into a networked, computerized system dedicated to the storage, retrieval, distribution, and presentation of images.

In the 1990s, advancement was made towards achieving a filmless radiology by storing medical images in independent formats. The most common format for image storage is Digital Imaging and Communications in Medicine (DICOM) [6]. The initial DICOM standard as well as earlier versions of standards from ACR and NEMA contributed substantially to the progress made in reaching today's DICOM standards. Since the late 1990s, many file systems and database systems have been developed with DICOM support in medical imaging.

New initiatives in health care technology for a unified Electronic Health Record (EHR) and integration of medical information systems require a well-organized patient information system that includes radiological medical imaging. The proposed integrated imaging methodology in this research utilizes a DICOM file system to provide a better and more universal structure for health care specialists and database systems that use digital diagnostic imaging in various modalities. In Section 2, PACS technology and DICOM records including the types of information are discussed. Medical image research systems of different groups using DICOM records are introduced with their advantages and disadvantages in Section 3. A summary of data warehousing is given in Section 4, followed by Section 5 on medical data warehousing for medical imaging DICOM in a distributed network. The description of the design of a data warehouse for an efficient, electronic DICOM information system with the extraction and loading of DICOM records is presented in Section 5. Section 6 discusses information retrieval for analysis. Conclusions are presented in Section 7.

2 PACS technology and DICOM

The new generation of radiology devices provides more advanced utilization of the files and software system for various modalities including X-Ray, CT, CR, US, and PET. After capturing a patient's medical images and information, the devices enter the data into the standardized format of DICOM records. These records are sent to PACS to be stored in a file system for future retrieval and analysis. Both PACS and DICOM record technologies are well rooted within the medical community and are the prevailing technologies in their respective areas.

2.1 PACS technology

PACS is a computerized medical facility for the storage, retrieval, and distribution of medical images. PACS and the medical imaging devices work in conformance with the DICOM standard. The medical imaging devices directly feed the DICOM records into PACS for storage [7]. Data saved in PACS can be given unique patient identifiers, such as Medical Record Number (MRN) or Social Security Number, for accurate retrieval [8].

PACS is not involved with the distribution of medical records between referring medical facilities. This remains to be one of the largest hurdles facing the medical community [9]. Currently, the typical method of DICOM distribution is to send a physical copy from the source medical facility to the referring medical facility. Also, vast amounts of time and resources are used when DICOM files are retrieved from PACS for an individual patient due to the fact that every DICOM file for a patient is being retrieved rather than specific DICOM files.

2.2 DICOM record

Since the first version of the DICOM standard was published in 1985, there have been several revised versions with a significant revision and extension with the release of DICOM 3.0 Standard in 2000. In 1995, the name was changed from the ACR-NEMA Standard to the DICOM Standard. It remains an evolving standard that is maintained by the DICOM Standards Committee [4] [6].

As shown in Figure 1, the DICOM file structure begins with a 128-byte preamble, which is normally set to all zeros, and is followed by the letters "DICM," which determine if the file is a DICOM file. The DICOM file structure consists of two distinct sections. The header section stores information about the image, such as how and why the image was taken, annotations, patient name, type of scan, and image dimensions. The image section contains the actual image.

DICOM image data can be compressed (encapsulated) using lossy or lossless variants of the JPEG format, as well as a lossless Run-Length Encoding format to reduce the image size.

All the DICOM meta information is identified by tags. A tag is a unique identifier for an element of information composed of an ordered pair of numbers (a group number followed by an element number) that is used to identify attributes and corresponding data elements.

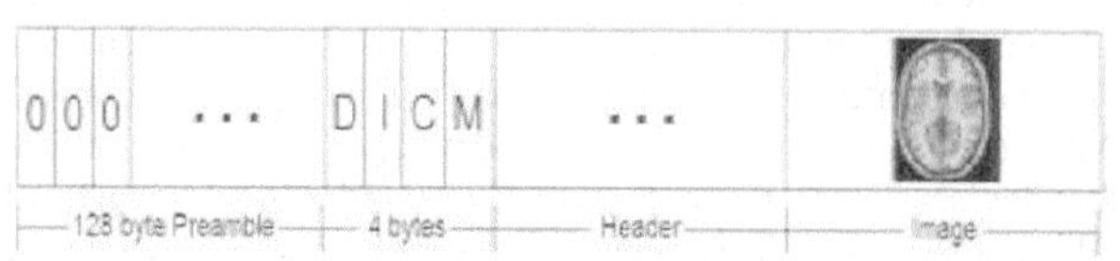

Figure 1. DICOM file structure

The DICOM header is organized into groups of data elements as shown in Figure 2. As a variable record, the DICOM header length varies and can contain any number of data elements. Each data element contains a data element tag, a value representation (VR), a value multiplicity (VM), and a value field. The DICOM data element tag is an ordered pair of hexadecimal numbers and is used to identify attributes and the corresponding data elements [4] [6]. The first hexadecimal number is called the group number and the second hexadecimal number is called the element number. Together, the group number and the element number make a unique combination, each with their own specific description. Currently, there are approximately over 2,000 standardized data element tags in the DICOM Data Dictionary [4] [6].

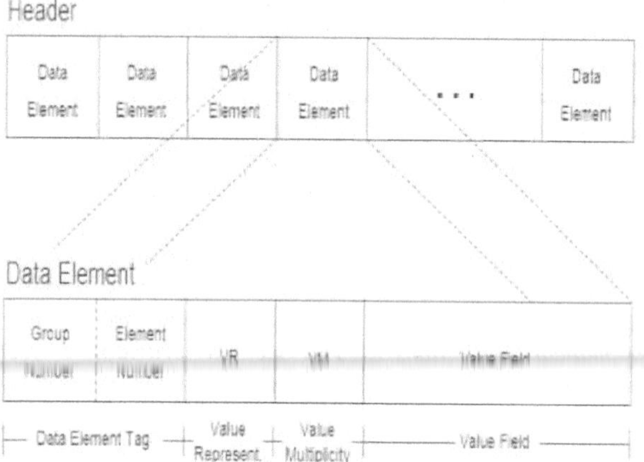

Figure 2. DICOM header and tag structure

The value representation (VR) specifies the data type/format of the value(s) contained in the value field. If used, the value multiplicity (VM) specifies the length of the value field that contains the actual data for that data element. The header can contain non-standardized data element tags that are not in the DICOM Data Dictionary. Normally, these unknown data element tags are private and only the creator (i.e. the clinic or hospital) knows what those tags represent.

Medical information using the PACS system allows the radiologist to view medical images (DICOM records) from devices or the files that have been recently loaded to the computer system for use. Due to the large size of the medical images, they cannot be stored as long-term files in the device or computer system and need to be moved to backup file systems for future uploads. When the patient is scheduled for an appointment, the medical images related to the patient's visit are uploaded to the device or computer system for the consultation or analysis needed to compare past and present images. Searching through the backup of medical images to locate the ones that are useful is often manual and tedious requiring human interaction. Different researchers and manufacturers have proposed various file systems and database systems as discussed in the next section.

3 Systems for medical images

With the adoption of PACS and DICOM technologies in medical information systems, numerous designs and implementations for utilization, storage, and retrieval have been proposed. There are two categories of distributed architectures utilized for remotely accessible medical information systems.

First, there are general distributed systems that are characterized as having a single system that acts as a centralized point of control. This system accepts remote connections and can consist of any number of servers, databases, and data file systems that maintain the medical records. Traditional distributed systems are widely utilized in all areas of computing for the storage and retrieval of data due to their proven technologies and simple architectures.

Second, there is an emerging distributed technology called the Grid. The Grid is characterized as having any number of independent and possibly heterogeneous systems that are capable of computing information and transferring resources transparently [10]. Distributed systems are much more complex yet offer far greater capabilities when compared to general distributed systems [11].

An early work was Open RIMS: Open Architecture Radiology Informatics Management System [12], which integrated Picture Archiving and Communication System/Radiology Information System (PACS/RIS) archive using open source tools and methods. Integration of PACS/RIS functionality decreased the risk of inconsistent data by reducing interfaces among databases that contained largely redundant information and with wide adoption hoped to promote standard data mining tools to reduce users need to learn multiple methods to perform the same task.

Research projects that are directly related in database or grid design for DICOM records of patient imaging information are the MammoGrid [13], eDiaMoND [14], and NDMA [15]. All the projects have the same goal of developing a geographically distributed database for digital medical records to aid in diagnosis and epidemiological studies. All the systems focus on the storage and retrieval of the non-proprietary DICOM format medical records.

These projects differ in the types of distributed architectures that they use. MammoGrid and eDiaMoND rely on the complicated distributed Grid architecture while NDMA utilizes the historically proven technology of a centralized server that accepts distributed connections. NDMA, MammoGrid, and eDiaMoND use relational databases for the storage of DICOM data. NDMA and eDiaMoND use IBM's relational database (DB2) whereas MammoGrid uses the open source relational database MySQL. However, traditional relational databases may lack the needed versatility that a comprehensive medical information system requires.

With eDiaMoND and MammoGrid's use of the Grid architecture, there would not be a centralized point of control and therefore the systems would not be plagued with bandwidth and storage issues. Yet, there would have to be a fairly sophisticated computer or collection of computers at each node. Therefore, each medical center or hospital would have to purchase an assortment of tools and technologies that may be obsolete within a few years given the Grid's early stages of development. Also, the multiple points of potential failure may require that each node has a specialized Grid technician that would maintain the system. NDMA's use of the general distributed system architecture includes the benefit of having a system that is simple when compared to the complex Grid architecture. Yet, NDMA's centralized point of control may have some serious bandwidth and storage issues when considering that every DICOM record is transmitted and stored at the centralized location. This is a problem that will likely get worse in the future.

MammoGrid and eDiaMoND are only capable of handling DICOM mammogram images. That was also true of NDMA until June 2005. The reason for systems not being capable of storing all types of DICOM modalities is most likely a direct effect of the DICOM header being highly heterogeneous and the projects use of a relational database to store the information. Therefore, a versatile technology for storing the DICOM header would alleviate the burdens of storing multiple types of DICOM modalities and allow a system to store more than just DICOM mammogram images.

Oracle [16] has recently expanded into the area of DICOM records and storage of the information in a database. Oracle 11g supports DICOM data type, but the database design and implementation are left to the designer or developer.

To provide a more efficient, integrated, and centralized database system, a database/data warehouse for DICOM header is proposed in this research and designed in relational database. The database contains a reference to the location of the original DICOM record. This reference includes the connection information for the medical facility that maintains the DICOM record and the information that is required to retrieve the file from PACS at the medical facility.

4 Database/data warehouse designs

The current systems discussed in Section 3 either use the general distributed system architecture that consists of a single system acting as a centralized point of control or the emerging Grid technology. Both types of technologies have their respective benefits and weaknesses. NDMA's use of the general distributed system architecture includes the benefit of having a simple system when compared to the complex Grid architecture. Yet, NDMA's centralized point of control has serious bandwidth and storage issues, since every DICOM record is transmitted and stored at the centralized location. Furthermore, this problem will get worse as more hospitals join the system and as DICOM records become larger.

The proposed medical information database system utilizes a combination of the general distributed system architecture and the Grid architecture as shown in Figure 3. The distributed architecture is displayed by the system containing a remotely accessible centralized server where all the medical facilities add and query information. Furthermore, a distributed Grid architecture is demonstrated by the medical facilities being geographically apart and being capable of exchanging information directly with each other as well as the centralized server.

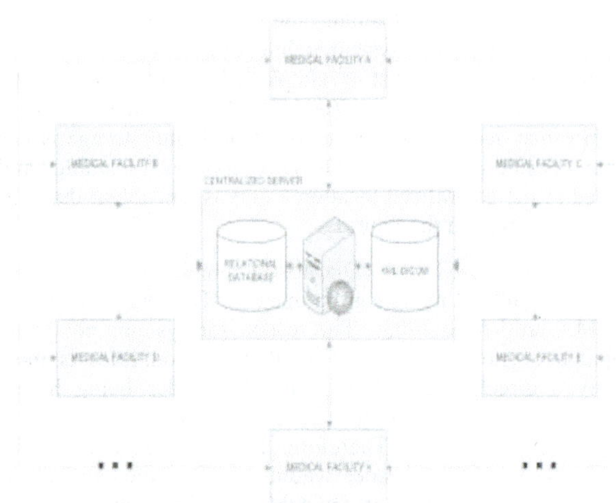

Figure 3. Design for integrated DICOM medical data

Each medical facility (such as A or 1) will have a medical information system client that communicates with the centralized server. The client will interact with the centralized server in two situations. First, the client will analyze each DICOM record after it is created by the imaging device(s) at the medical facility, and then transmit the DICOM header information to the centralized server for indexing and storage. Also, the client will interact with the centralized server when a medical technician is using the client to search and retrieve patient records. The medical information system client will interact with other medical facilities' clients when sending or receiving requested original DICOM records.

The design in Figure 3 also supports a data warehousing structure transparently as shown in Figure 4. The data warehouse can store DICOM header information as well as other clinical information, such as patient, image, medical facility, equipment, date, time and other related medical information, in a star schema [17] structure. The reason for selecting a star schema instead of a snowflake [18] is for the compact and optimized structure of the star schema to reduce the number of joins. The end result is an increase in the efficiency of the query response time for the Decision Support System (DSS).

5 DICOM medical data warehouse

The proposed database/data warehouse can perform a major role as a repository for radiological imaging of multiple medical organizations by keeping present and past patient images as a current and historical information system with the related radiological text comments, diagnoses, and recommendations. As a centralized system, the data warehouse the same as the centralized server shown in Figure 3 communicates with each medical facility through the process of extraction, transformation, and loading (ETL) and adds the header information to its main database repository as demonstrated in Figure 4 with data warehouse capabilities.

The centralized repository in Figure 3 and Figure 4 can contain each DICOM header information and a reference link to the medical facility (A, B, C, ... or 1, 2, 3, ...) PACS location with its related DICOM record's physical location. A medical facility could be in the same institution or multiple institutions as well as local or global locations networked together through a centralized database or data warehouse. Reference links can also be established to a medical facility DICOM record that does not have PACS software and has the DICOM information captured from its devices stored in a database or a file system as shown in the bottom left (Medical Facility 4) without PACS in Figure 4. In the designed system, a patient's radiology information would be available through a data warehouse for participating medical facilities on the network using a secure Internet connection by authorized medical personnel. A patient can receive care at any of the medical facilities with preservation of radiological history on body parts.

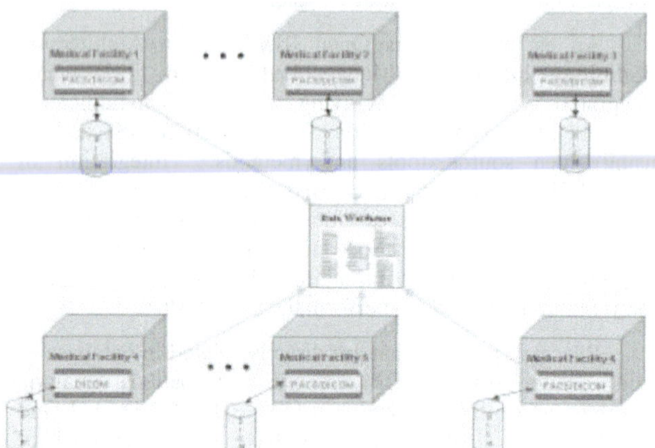

Figure 4. Integrated medical information for DICOM header distributed database/data warehouse

The DICOM data warehouse information as described in Section 4 can be categorized in a main repository using a star schema at the logical level shown in Figure 5. The star schema includes a DICOM fact table and dimensional entities/tables of DICOM header information, patient, medical facility, image, equipment, medical information, and date/time. Due to the large number of the attribute names in the DICOM header, only significant attribute names are shown in Figure 5 and all of the last attribute names in entities/tables are displayed with an extension of GroupID... to represent the continuation of attribute names.

The DICOM fact entity/table in Figure 5 displays the categorization of the most common structures for integration of the information available in the DICOM header record. Other fact entities/tables can be created based on particular subjects to associate different types of information from the data warehouse. Any of the medical facilities shown in Figure 4 could create their own additional fact entities/tables from data warehouse dimensional tables for a specific purpose. Since the data in dimensional tables are non-volatile, the information used in the fact table with historical values could have many positive results for patient wellness and medical research. For example, a subject could refer to a particular medical facility, body part, modality, age group, device radiation exposure, recommendation, or diagnostic test.

The use of the star schema provides more simplicity, ease of visualization, and better performance in comparison to snowflake schemas. Due to the centralized nature of the data warehouse structure, many studies in the radiology area can be formulated. The integrated repository allows creating various star schemas or snowflakes that could be further expand research areas. It should be mentioned that major considerations must be given to the security and protection of individual privacy as recommended by HIPAA privacy rules [19]. Due to the growing nature of a medical data warehouse and various possibilities for medical information in a decision support system, only the centalized server (Figure 3) implemention and comparisons are discussed in Sections 6 and 7 of this paper.

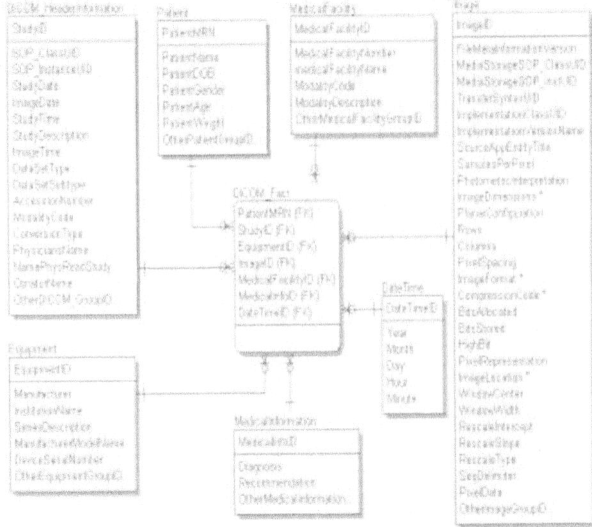

Figure 5. Logical level star schema for DICOM data warehouse

6 Implementation

The implementation of the medical information system prototype, named Distributed DICOM Database (disDicomDb) or Data Warehouse, was written entirely in Java and, therefore, can be run on any system hardware or operating system. The implementation consists of four interacting software applications, two of which are located at the centralized server while the other two are located at the clients. The software applications at the centralized server consist of a web service and a web application both running on a Java application server. The software applications at the client consist of a web service running on a Java application server and a command line utility that can be run at the Windows DOS prompt or Unix/Mac terminal. A DICOM file can be parsed and converted to XML file (XML-DICOM) and selected tags can be stored in the centralized server/ warehouse using ETL.

The web service located at the centralized server has the sole purpose of retrieving XML-DICOM records from medical facility clients. When the web service receives XML-DICOM records from medical facilities, it also extracts and adds the desired information to the database and saves the XML-DICOM record locally for future usage. The web application located at the centralized server is a graphical user interface (GUI) viewable by the users with their Internet browser.

6.1 Extraction, transformation, and loading

For extraction of DICOM header information, most radiological devices can generate text files or DCM files. If the device cannot create a text file, ezDICOM [20] or a similar tool is available to create the text file. After extraction, the DICOM text files are loaded to a named tables.

Figure 6 displays the steps the system takes when a new DICOM record is created at a medical facility.

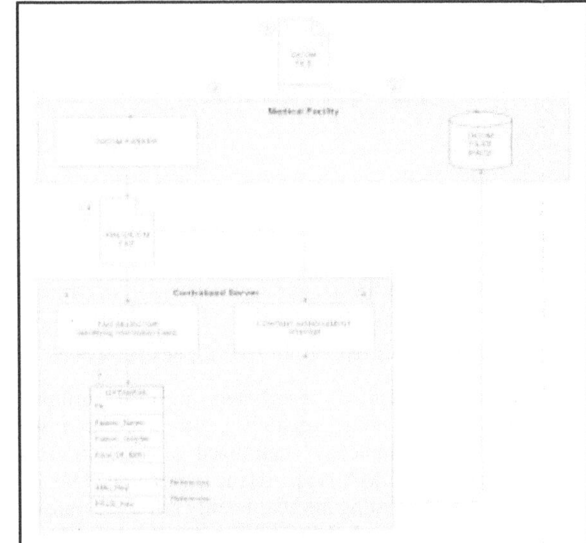

Figure 6. Detailed view of a new DICOM record being added to the medical information system

Below is a description of each of the steps.

1. A new DICOM record is created at a medical facility.
2. A process is executed in the medical information system client called the DICOM parser which analyzes the newly created DICOM record. The DICOM parser creates an XML-DICOM file that contains the header of the DICOM record.
3. The DICOM record is stored at the medical facility in the same fashion it would normally be handled, such as a PACS.
4. The XML-DICOM file is delivered via the Internet to the centralized server.
5. At the centralized server, a process called the tag selector selects tags from the XML-DICOM record in search of fields the system has deemed as "identifying information."
6. The XML-DICOM record is stored at the centralized server for later retrieval and usage.
7. The DICOM tags deemed as "identifying information," the location to retrieve the XML-DICOM record locally at the

centralized server, and the information on how to retrieve the original DICOM record from the medical facility are stored in the relational database as a single entry.

6.2 Information retrieval

Figure 7 is a screenshot of the results after the user selects to view the DICOM header. When the user selects to view the entire DICOM header, each header element consisting of the group number and element number is displayed, along with the description of that DICOM element and its value.

Figure 7. Display of software for header results

The implemented distributed medical information system, with warehouse capability, was compared with a mockup for a completely centralized medical information system, such as NDMA [15]. Hence, every DICOM record created at a participating medical facility has to be transmitted over the Internet and delivered to the centralized server. Furthermore, each record received by the centralized server must be stored indefinitely. Given the progressive size increase of medical images, this could become problematic for a large scale distributed medical information system.

Along with the implementation of database/data warehouse, a basic centralized medical information system was created to gain comparative statistics of medical record transmission times and storage requirements versus disDicomDb. In the comparison between disDicomDb and the emulated centralized medical information system, the Linux server for both systems ran on the same physical computer and the Command Line Utilities also ran on the same two physical computers. The server and both of the clients were running the Linux distribution Ubuntu [21] and one of the clients was running Ubuntu in a virtual machine using VMware's free VMware Player [22].

7 Comparison and result

The systems were compared based on the amount of data storage required to store a record added to the system. This comparison measured the amount of disk space required to store a record on a hard drive and did not include any archival devices or any type of compression techniques. Again, disDicomDb only stores the XML-DICOM file at the server whereas the emulated centralized system stores the original DICOM file at the server. In this comparison, 65 DICOM records were used for the initial testing.

Of the 65 records tested, the average DICOM record was approximately 5254 kB (5253662 bytes) whereas the average XML-DICOM record was 1.2 kB (11812 bytes). On average, the XML-DICOM record was .2% of the size of an original DICOM record. This reduction in size is due to the XML-DICOM record not containing the DICOM image. Figure 8 is a logarithmic scaled graph displaying the file size of the XML-DICOM files in comparison to the original DICOM files.

As displayed in Figure 8, the file sizes of the XML-DICOM files were approximately the same size regardless of how large the original DICOM files were.

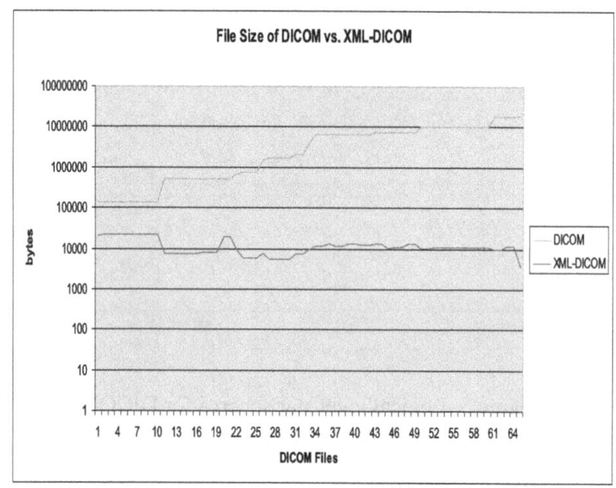

Figure 8. File size of DICOM vs. XML-DICOM

This is because the size of an XML-DICOM file is directly dependent upon how many data elements are within the DICOM header and the number of elements in a DICOM header is approximately the same with each DICOM record. Therefore, a system storing XML-DICOM records at the central server would not be concerned with the continuous rapid growth of DICOM record file size.

Further implementation of the database/data warehouse as a research initiative will allow medical doctors and professionals to retrieve available patient radiology information by body part or by particular date/time for comparisons and for medical recommendations.

8 Conclusion

Several of the most prevalent distributed medical information systems in development were analyzed to identify areas needing modification and improvement. All of the systems focused on the electronic medical imaging standard called DICOM and were capable of transmitting DICOM records between medical facilities to aid in patient diagnosis.

The proposed DICOM header database/data warehouse for handling distributed DICOM medical records provides enhancements for integration and an efficient method to centralize the radiology information in one place without migrating entire images. The method of only migrating DICOM header allows the health care professional to be selective based on header information and to decide which image needs to be seen or analyzed, and then retrieve that image. With the volume of medical imaging and future wave of enterprise medical information systems, the proposed database/data warehouse provides a better alternative to existing models for enhanced performance, comprehensive information, and integrated data in radiology.

9 Acknowledgment

Jesse Collins is currently a full time employee at Florida Blue (BCBSF).

10 References

[1] W. Burger and M. Burge. Digital Image Processing: An Algorithmic Introduction Using Java. Springer, 2008.

[2] Computed Tomography. Last accessed: May 2013. http://en.wikipedia.org/wiki/Computed_tomography.

[3] American College of Radiology. http://www.acr.org/. Last accessed: May 2013.

[4] National Electrical Manufacturers Association (NEMA). http://www.nema.org/about/. Last accessed: May 2013.

[5] Picture Archiving and Communication Systems (PACS). http://en.wikipedia.org/wiki/Picture_archiving_and_com munication_system. Last accessed: May 2013.

[6] NEMA- Digital Imaging and Communications in Medicine (DICOM) Part 18: Web Access to DICOM Persistent Objects (WADO). http://www.nema.org/ and index of ftp://medical.nema.org/medical/dicom/2009/ document 09_18pu.pdf. Last accessed: May 2013.

[7] S. Cohen, F. Gilboa, and U. Shani. "PACS and Electronic Health Records"; Medical Imaging 2002: PACS and Integrated Medical Information Systems: Design and Evaluation, Vol. 4685, pp. 288-298, May 2002.

[8] Medical Record Number. Last accessed: May 2013. http://www.ncvhs.hhs.gov/app7-8.htm.

[9] R. B. Elsberry. PACS Straight Talk. http://www.imagingeconomics.com/issues/articles/2001-03_05.asp. Last accessed: May 2013.

[10] M. Li and M. Baker. The Grid. John Wiley & Sons, West Sussex, 2005.

[11] I. Bilykh, Y. Bychkov, D. Dahlem, J. H. Jahnke, G. McCallum, C. Obry, A. Onabajo and C. Kuziemsky. "Can GRID Services Provide Answers to the Challenges of National Health Information Sharing?"; Proceedings of the 2003 Conference of the Centre for Advanced Studies on Collaborative Research, pp. 39-53, 2003.

[12] S. Langer. "OpenRIMS: An Open Architecture Radiology Informatics Management System"; Journal of Digital Imaging, Vol. 15, Issue 2, pp. 91-97, June 2002.

[13] F. Estrella, R. McClatchey and D. Rogulin. The MammoGrid Virtual Organization-Federating Distributed Mammograms, 2005.

[14] M. Brady, D. Gavaghan, A. Simpson, M. Parada and R. Highnam. "Chapter 41: e_DiaMoND: A Grid Enabled Federated Database of Annotated Mammograms"; Grid Computing: Making the Global Infrastructure a Reality. John Wiley and Sons, 2003.

[15] International Business Machines Corporation (IBM). http://www.ibm.com/innovation/guide/case_4_2b.shtm. Last accessed: May 2013.

[16] Oracle Database 11g DICOM Medical Image Support, http://www.oracle.com/technology/products/intermedia/pdf/11g_collate ral/dicom11g_twp.pdf. Last accessed: May 2013.

[17] W. H. Inmon. Building the Data Warehouse. John Wiley and Sons, 1996.

[18] S. Chaudhuri, and D. Umeshwar. "An Overview of Data Warehousing and OLAP Technology"; ACM SIGMOD Record, Vol. 26, Issue 1, pp. 6-74, June 1997.

[19] HIPAA Privacy Rule's protection. http://www.hhs.gov/ocr/privacy/hipaa/understanding/inde x.html. Last accessed: May 2013.

[20] ezDICOM. http://sourceforge.net/projects/ezdicom/. Last accessed: May 2013.

[21] Ubuntu. http://www.ubuntu.com/. Last accessed: May 2013.

[22] VMware. http://www.vmware.com/. Last accessed: May 2013.

A Path Analysis Method for Measuring the Resilience of Cancer Patients

Xiaodong Wang[1,3], and Jun Tian[2*]
[1]Faculty of Mathematics and Computer Science, Fuzhou University, Fuzhou, China
[2]School of Public Health, Fujian Medical University, Fuzhou, China
[3]Faculty of Mathematics and Computer Science, Quanzhou Normal University, Quanzhou, China
[*]Corresponding author E-mail: tianjunfjmu@126.com

Abstract - *This paper studies the relationship between resilience and quality of life (QOL) in digestive cancer patients. The patients' resilience, psychological distress, fatigue status, treatment side effects and QOL were measured during treatment. A relationship model of these variables was constructed using path analysis. The results showed that the relationship between resilience and QOL was statistically significant when psychological distress, fatigue, and side effects were absent from the model, whereas the regression coefficient of resilience was not statistically significant when these variables were added. These findings highlight the need to develop strategies that improve resilience in patients with digestive cancer.*

Keywords: Resilience; psychological distress; fatigue; quality of life; path analysis.

1 Introduction

Cancer is a disease that severely damages human physical and mental health. Its diagnosis significantly affects a patient's emotional and psychological status [1], with the patient's quality of life (QOL) often been affected considerably after surgery and chemotherapy/radiotherapy [2–4]. However, many studies have found that cancer patients with similar diseases and treatment status have significantly different QOLs [5, 6]. Psychologists believe that resilience is the main factor that causes patients with similar situations to have different perceptions of their QOL [7, 8].

Resilience is an individual's capacity to maintain his or her psychological and physical well-being in the face of adversity [8]. In recent years, the role of resilience in the process of cancer treatment has been given increasing attention [9–14]. Studies have found that resilience can powerfully predict patients' fatigue in the treatment [12], good resilience can help patients reduce treatment-induced damage to bodily functions and shorten the time of their recovery thereof [13], and patients with good resilience are able to treat their disease correctly and maintain relatively good mental and psychological states, thereby resulting in a better QOL [11, 12].

Although much research has shown that a relationship exists between QOL and resilience in cancer patients [11, 14–17], limited information is available on the nature of this relationship and the degree of the influence of resilience on QOL. Exploring whether resilience is an independent predictor of QOL and estimating the degree of its impact on QOL can make us understand the role of resilience in improving the QOL of cancer patients, as well as provide clinical staff with information on psychological intervention and psychological care programs for cancer patients.

In this study, we used path analysis to detect the relationships of resilience, psychological distress, fatigue, and treatment side effects with QOL. We drew a path map to show the paths of the influences of resilience, psychological distress, fatigue, and side effects on QOL and quantitatively estimated their direct and indirect effects on it. Our results may help explain whether strategies to improve resilience are important in promoting the QOL of cancer patients.

2 The Path Analysis

We selected patients with digestive tumors from Fujian Province for this study, because digestive cancer ranks as the leading cause of death in this area. They were recruited from five province-level hospitals in Fuzhou City during 2008–2011. The study sample was limited to patients whose tumors were located in the esophagus, stomach, or colorectum. The following eligibility criteria were used: (1) age between 18 and 70 years; (2) non-illiteracy; (3) absence of mental or psychological disease; and (4) with known diagnosis of cancer.

All participants provided their written informed consent. The study was approved by the relevant institutional review boards for human research from Fujian Medical University.

The RS-14, which was proposed by Wagnild [18], was used to measure the resilience of the participants. It is a 14-item questionnaire, and the score for each item ranges from 1 (not true) to 7 (true). Patients score the items based on their personal circumstances. The total score of the scale ranges from 14 to 98, with a high total score indicating good resilience. The RS-14 has been used for measuring an individual's degree of resilience in a wide variety of age groups [19], and its reliability and validity have been confirmed by many researchers [20]. In the present study, the Chinese version of this tool was found to have a reliability of 0.93.

The Hospital Anxiety and Depression Scale, which is a 14-item (7 for the anxiety subscale, 7 for the depression subscale) questionnaire, was used to evaluate the psychological distress of the participants [21]. The score for each item ranges from 0 to 3. Patients score the items based on their current situation. The total score of the scale ranges from 0 to 42, with a high total score indicating severe psychological distress. The Chinese version of this scale has been confirmed to be suitable for Chinese patients [22]. In the current study, this version had a reliability of 0.92.

The 20-item Multidimensional Fatigue Inventory Scale, developed by a Dutch research group [23], was used for measuring the fatigue of the participants. The score for each item ranges from 1 (true) to 5 (not true). Patients score the items based on their current situation. A high total score indicates severe fatigue. The Chinese version of this instrument has been confirmed to be suitable for Chinese patients [24].

Treatment side effects on the participants were examined from seven aspects: gastrointestinal system, respiratory system, liver and kidney, heart, hair, skin, and nervous system. The severity of side effects in each of these aspects had five ordinal scales: not at all, mild, moderate, a bit of severe, and severe, which were scored 1–5, respectively. The total score was the sum of the scores of the seven categories, with a high total score indicating severe side effects.

The European Organization for Research and Treatment of Cancer Core Questionnaire (Version 3.0) determines the QOL of cancer patients [25]. It is a 30-item questionnaire that includes 28 items scored from 1 to 4 and 2 items scored from 1 to 7. The Chinese version of this questionnaire has been confirmed to be suitable for Chinese cancer patients [25]. In the current study, the sum of the scores for Items 1–5 and Items 8–19 describes the physical aspect of QOL (QOL-Physical), the sum of the scores for Items 20–25 describes the mental aspect of QOL (QOL-Mental), and the sum of the scores for Items 6, 7, 26, and 27 describes the social aspect of QOL (QOL-Social). All these scores were transformed into values in the range of 0–100. A high total score indicates good QOL.

Data on each patient were collected in three periods: Before the first treatment cycle began (first period), the patient's resilience was measured by trained graduate students from Fujian Medical University; in the third week of treatment (second period), the patient's psychological distress, fatigue, and side effects were measured by trained nurses in the hospitals; and at the end of the first treatment cycle(third period), the patient's QOL was measured by trained graduate students from Fujian Medical University.

Low resilience affects mental health [26]. Poor mental health can increase side effects and fatigue [27] and, together with fatigue and side effects, influence the QOL of an individual [28, 29]. Therefore, we assumed that the models shown below describe the relationships between resilience (x), psychological distress (y1), fatigue (y2), side effects (y3), QOL-Social (z1), QOL-Mental (z2), and QOL-Physical (z3).

3 Results

In total, 970 participants, including 699 (72.06%) males and 271 (27.94%) females at an average age of 56.38 years (SD = 12.91), were included in this study. The percentages of participants with primary school, middle school, high school, and college education levels were 27.61%, 30.97%, 24.87%, and 16.54%, respectively. Among the 970 participants, 338 (34.84%) had esophageal cancer, 374 (38.56%) had gastric cancer, and 258 (26.60%) had colon cancer; in addition, 122 (12.56%), 343 (35.36%), 316 (32.58%), and 189 (19.48%) were in stages I–IV of their respective diseases. Moreover, 750 (77.32%) patients underwent surgery combined with chemotherapy, 85 (8.76%) underwent surgery combined with radiotherapy, and 135 (13.92%) underwent surgery combined with chemotherapy and radiotherapy. The average time of the first treatment cycle was 4 weeks.

One assumption was that psychological distress, fatigue, and treatment side effects were the main factors influencing QOL. To verify the correctness of this assumption, we analyzed the relationships between QOL as the dependent variable and psychological distress, fatigue, and side effects as the independent variables using multiple linear regression. The results revealed an adjusted R2 value of 0.524 for the model, indicating that psychological distress, fatigue, and side effects collectively could explain 52.4% of the variance in QOL and thus confirming that our assumption was appropriate. The other assumption in the model was that resilience had no direct effect on QOL. To verify the correctness of this assumption, we set resilience as the independent variable and QOL as the dependent variable in the regression model. The results showed that the regression coefficient of resilience, adjusted for age, sex, disease stage, psychological distress, fatigue, and side effects, was not statistically significant ($t = 1.562$, $P = 0.119$), indicating that resilience had no direct effect on QOL.

After adjusting for age, sex, and disease stage, the partial correlation coefficient between psychological distress and fatigue was $r12 = 0.440$ ($P < 0.001$), that between psychological distress and side effects was $r13 = 0.246$ ($P < 0.001$), and that between fatigue and side effects was $r23 = 0.178$ ($P < 0.001$).

The standardized coefficient for each path in the path map was estimated, and the standardized coefficients adjusted for age, sex, and disease stage are shown in Table 1. The square of the standardized coefficient of resilience revealed that it could explain 33.2% of the variance in psychological distress and 16.1% of that in fatigue. These results suggest that resilience is an important factor that affects both psychological distress and fatigue.

The standardized coefficients in Table 1 were written into the path map. The direct and indirect effects of resilience, psychological distress, fatigue, and side effects on QOL were calculated according to Equations (3) and (4) (Table 2). This table shows that psychological distress and fatigue had greater effects on the three dimensions of QOL. The direct effects of fatigue were the largest for QOL-Social and QOL-Physical, the direct effect of psychological distress was the largest for QOL-Mental, and side effects mainly influenced QOL-Physical.

By summing the direct effects on the three domains of QOL, we obtained the direct effects of psychological distress, fatigue, and side effects on QOL. By summing the indirect effects on the three domains of QOL, we obtained the indirect effects of psychological distress, fatigue, side effects, and resilience on QOL. Fatigue, psychological distress, and side effects accounted for 48.32%, 29.71%, and 21.97%, respectively, of the total direct effect on QOL. Of the total effect on QOL, fatigue accounted for 33.72%, psychological distress accounted for 28.94%, side effects accounted for 22.53%, and resilience accounted for 14.80%. These results suggest that psychological distress and fatigue produced in the course of treatment are important factors influencing the QOL of patients. Although resilience has a lower proportion of the total effect on QOL, it has significant effects on fatigue and psychological distress.

4 Conclusions

Resilience refers to an individual's capacity to maintain his or her psychological and physical well-being in the face of adversity. Resilience can be viewed as a defense mechanism that enables one to thrive amid the distress. Therefore, improving resilience may be an important target for disease treatment and prophylaxis [26]. Patients with cancer can show high levels of functioning in physical domains of QOL but not in others, suggesting that an individual's capacity to adjust and cope will influence his or her QOL. Individual differences in resilience cause patients to have different coping styles and adjustment capacities. [5] Therefore, it is necessary to introduce the concept of resilience into studies of the QOL of cancer patients.

QOL is an indicator of a patient's social, psychological, and physiological status and well-being [1]. In theory, resilience affects the psychological aspect of QOL [12, 16] and thus should have a direct effect on QOL. However, in this study, the regression coefficient of resilience (adjusted for age, sex, and disease stage) was statistically significant ($= 0.119$, $t = 4.499$, $P < 0.001$) when psychological distress, fatigue, and treatment side effects were absent from the regression model; the reverse was true ($t = 1.562$, $P > 0.05$) when these variables were added. These results suggest that the effect of resilience on QOL may be passed on by psychological distress, fatigue, and side effects and is therefore indirect. Further studies are necessary to confirm this conclusion.

In this study, we analyzed the patients in the following order: resilience psychological distress and fatigue and side effects QOL; that is, resilience was plotted on the left part of the path map, which means that if patients with low resilience can be identified early and are given good social support as well as psychological care, then their psychological distress will likely decrease. This would prompt them to actively respond to treatment-induced fatigue and side effects, thereby improving their QOL.

In summary, the data obtained by our epidemiological survey showed that although resilience is not an independent predictor of QOL in patients with digestive cancer and accounted for only 14.80% of the total effect on QOL, it is a main influencing factor of psychological distress and side effects. In addition, psychological distress and fatigue are important factors that affect QOL, indicating that the role of resilience in improving QOL cannot be ignored. In studying the QOL of patients with cancer, we should focus on strategies that improve their resilience.

5 References

[1] Bottomley A. The cancer patient and quality of life. Oncologist 2002; 7:120-5.

[2] Efficace F, Bottomley A, van Andel G. Health related quality of life in prostate carcinoma patients: a systematic review of randomized controlled trials. Cancer 2003; 97:377-88.

[3] Andersen BL. Quality of life for women with gynecologic cancer. Curr Opin Obstet Gynecol 1995; 7:69-76.

[4] Arora NK, Gustafson DH, Hawkins RP, McTavish F, Cella DF, Pingree S, Mendenhall JH, Mahvi DM. Impact of surgery and chemotherapy on the quality of life of younger women with breast carcinoma: a prospective study. Cancer 2001; 92:1288-1298.

[5] Joanne L, Christine E. Exploring links between the concepts of quality of life and resilience. Pediatric Rehabilitation 2001; 4(4):209-216.

[6] Epping-Jordan JE, Compas BE, Osowiecki DM, et al. Psychological adjustment in breast cancer processes of emotional distress. Health Psychology 1999; 18(4):315-326.

[7] Yi JP, Vitaliano PP, Smith RE, et al.The role of resilience on psychological adjustment and physical health in patients with diabetes. British Journal of Health Psychology 2008; 13:311-325.

[8] Richardson GE. The metatheory of resilience and resiliency. Journal of Clinic Psychology 2002; 58:307-321.

[9] Pearman T. Quality of life and psychosocial adjustment in gynecologic cancer survivors. Health and Quality of Life Outcomes 2003, 1:33 doi:10.1186/1477-7525-1-33.

[10] Bull AA, Meyerowitz BE, Hart S, et al. Quality of life in women with recurrent breast cancer. Breast Cancer Research Treat 1999; 54:47-57.

[11] Wenzel LB, Donnelly JP, Fowler JM, et al. Resilience, reflection, and residual stress in ovarian cancer survivorship: A gynecologic oncology group study. Psycho-Oncology 2002; 11:142-153.

[12] Strauss B, Brix C, Fischer S, et al. The influence of resilience on fatigue in cancer patients undergoing radiation therapy. Journal of cancer research and clinical oncology 2007; 133:511-518.

[13] Hou Wk, Law CC, Yin J, Fu YT. Resource loss, resource gain, and psychological resilience and dysfunction following cancer diagnosis: A growth mixture modeling approach. Healthy Psychology 2010; 29(5):484-495.

[14] 14. Costanzo ES, Ryff CD, Singer BH. Psychosocial adjustment among cancer survivors: Findings from a national survey of health and well-being. Health Psychology 2009; 28(2):147–156.

[15] Yang HC, Thornton LM, Shapiro CL, Andersen BL. Surviving Recurrence: Psychological and Quality-of-life Recovery. Cancer 2008; 112 (5): 1178-1187.

[16] Bull AA, Meyerowitz BE, Hart S, et al. Quality of life in women with recurrent breast cancer. Breast Cancer Res Treat 1999; 54:47-57.

[17] Antoni MH, Goodkin K. Host moderator variables in the promotion of cervical neoplasia-personality facets. J Psychosom Res 1988; 32:327-338.

[18] Wagnild GM. The Resilience Scale user's guide for the US English version of the Resilience Scale and the 14-Item Reselience Scale (RS-14). Montana: The Resilience Center, 2009.

[19] Ahern NR, Kiehl EM, Sole ML, Byers J. A review of instruments measuring resilience. Issues in Comprehensive Pediatric Nursing 2006; 29(2):103–125.

[20] Nishi1 D, Uehara R, Kondo M, Matsuoka Y. Reliability and validity of the Japanese version of the Resilience Scale and its short version. BMC Research Notes 2010; 3:310.

[21] Zigmond AS, Snaith PR. The hospital anxiety and depression scale. Acta Psychiatrica Scandinavica 1983; 67: 361-370.

[22] Leung CM, Ho S, Kan CS, Hung CH, Chen CN. Evaluation of the Chinese version of the Hospital Anxiety and Depression Scale. Across-cultural perspective. Int J psychsom 1993; 40: 29-34.

[23] Smets EM, Garssen B, Bonke B, De Haes JC. The Multidimensional Fatigue Inventory (MFI) psychometric qualities of an instrument to assess fatigue. J Psychosom Res 1995; 39: 315-325.

[24] Tian J, Hong JS. Validation of the Chinese version of Multidimensional Fatigue Inventory-20 in Chinese patients with cancer. Supportive Care in Cancer 2011, DOI 10.1007/s00520-011-1357-8.

[25] Zhen LC, Tian HR, Xie PZ. Medical Quality of survival Evaluation. Beijing: Junshi Yixue Kexue Press, 2000.

[26] Davydov DM, Stewart R, Ritchie K, Chaudieu I. Resilience and mental health. Clinical Psychology Review 2010; 30:479–495.

[27] Tian J, Chen ZC, Hang LF. Effects of nutritional and psychological status of gastrointestinal cancer patients on tolerance of the cancer treatments. World Journal of Gastroenterology 2007; 13(30): 4136-4140.

[28] Tian J, Chen ZC, Hang LF. The Effects of psychological status of the patients with digestive system cancers on prognosis of the disease. Cancer Nursing 2009; 32(3):230-235.

[29] Tian J, Chen ZC, Hang LF. Effects of nutritional and psychological status of the patients with Advanced Stomach cancer on Physical Performance Status. Supportive Care in Cancer 2009 ;17(10):1263-1268.

Local Phase Quantization Texture Descriptor for Protein Classification

Loris Nanni,[1] Michelangelo Paci,[2] Sheryl Brahnam,[3] Stefano Ghidoni,[1] and Emanuele Menegatti[1]

[1]DEI, University of Padua, viale Gradenigo 6, Padua, Italy. {loris.nanni, ghidoni,em}@unipd.it;
[2]DEI, Dipartimento di Ingegneria dell'Energia Elettrica e dell'InformazioneVia Venezia, 52 47521 - Cesena (FC) – Italy. michelangelo.paci@unibo.it;
[3]Computer Information Systems, Missouri State University, 901 S. National, Springfield, MO 65804, USA. sbrahnam@missouristate.edu

Abstract

In this work we proposed an ensemble of texture descriptors for virus image classification. Novel variants of texture descriptors, coupled with support vector machines as the classifier, are proposed. The novel variants of texture descriptors include: 1) a quinary coding of different local binary pattern variants; 2) two new approaches based on quinary coding (a selected multithreshold local quinary pattern and a selected multithreshold local quinary configuration pattern); 3) a new approach based on the co-occurrence matrix; and 4) an ensemble of local phase quantization variants with ternary encoding. Our system is compared with and shown to outperform several state of the art texture descriptors. These results are validated on a dataset of 1500 images with 15 classes. MATLAB code implementing our descriptors is publically available at http://www.dei.unipd.it/wdyn/?IDsezione=3314&IDgruppo_pass=124&preview=

Keywords: protein classification; texture descriptors; primary structure; local phase quantization; support vector machines.

1 Introduction

Negative stain transmission electron microscopy (TEM) is a microscopy technique that produces distinctive surface textures. TEM has proven to be very valuable in virus detection, discovery, and taxonomy [1, 2]. Until recently, classification of TEM images was exclusively performed at the microscope by human experts. Since expert inspection is expensive and results depend on the skills and experience of each inspector, automation of TEM image classification has become desirable.

TEM virus images are well suited to machine pattern analysis due to their properties of size, shape, and texture. For instance, virus shapes can range from icosahedral patterns to highly pleomorphic particles. Virus shape and size, alone, however, are not sufficient for confirming specific virus types. Texture provides indispensable information, as many viruses show distinct and recurring texture patterns.

In the last two decades, much work in computer vision has focused on image textures. Early texture classification methods explored the statistical analysis of images. Representative of these statistical approaches are methods based on the co-occurrence matrix [3] and filtering [4]. In [5], Ojala et al. proposed a Local Binary Pattern (LBP) histogram for rotation invariant texture classification. LBP, along with its variants, is a simple yet efficient operator for describing the local image pattern and has achieved impressive classification results on benchmark datasets (see, e.g., [6] for virus image classification and [7] for protein subcellular localization) and in real-world applications (see, e.g., [8, 9]). During the last decade, LBP has distinguished itself by its simplicity, effectiveness, and robustness in detection of textural and structural information.

Despite recent advances in image texture analysis and the crucial role texture plays in TEM virus classification, few papers have examined machine analysis of virus textures in TEM images. Ring filters in the Fourier power spectrum were used as features in [10] and higher order spectral features were used in [11] to differentiate four icosahedral viruses. In [12] a radical density profile (RDP) was used to distinguish intensity variations between three maturation stages of human cytomegalovirus capsids in TEM images of cell sections. Finally, in [6] an ensemble combining LBP and RDP is used to discriminate fifteen virus types.

In this paper we compare the performance of some recent local binary pattern (LBP) variants in classifying TEM virus images. For each method, we implement its quinary coding version [7], explained in detail in section 2.1. For two quinary based approaches (the multithreshold local quinary pattern and the multithreshold local quinary configuration pattern), sequential forward floating selection (SFFS) [13] is used to select a set of optimal parameters for building the ensemble. An ensemble is also built by combining the different local phase quantization descriptors (LPQ), i.e., by varying their parameters (not just their filter size), using a ternary coding scheme instead of a binary one [7]. This set of LPQ descriptors thus combined is likewise chosen by SFFS. Moreover, a variant of a very recent method [14, 15] where the features are extracted considering the co-occurrence matrix as a 3D shape (SHAPE) is proposed. The proposed system is tested on a publicly available dataset located http://www.cb.uu.se/~gustaf/ virustexture /index.html. It is composed of 1500 images with 15 different virus types.

2 Texture Descriptors

2.1 Multithreshold Local Quinary Pattern (MLQP)

MLQP operator is a development of the canonical Local Binary Pattern (LBP) operator [5] which assigns a binary label to each pixel of an image based on the local information extracted from a circular neighborhood of *P* pixels and radius *R* according to the following equation:

$$LBP(P,R) = \sum_{p=0}^{P-1} s(q_p - q_c) \cdot 2^p$$

where

$$s(x) = \begin{cases} 1, x \geq 0 \\ 0, x < 0 \end{cases}$$

First, we introduced into the binary coding *s(x)* two more thresholds (τ_1, τ_2), thus arriving at the following quinary coding:

$$s(x,\tau_1,\tau_2) = \begin{cases} 2, x \geq \tau_2 \\ 1, \tau_1 \leq x < \tau_2 \\ 0, -\tau_1 \leq x < \tau_1 \\ -1, -\tau_2 \leq x < -\tau_1 \\ -2, x < -\tau_2 \end{cases}$$

To reduce the verbosity of the quinary encoded labels assigned to each pixel of the image, the quinary labels are split into 4 sets of binary patterns, according to the binary function $b_c(x), c\in\{-2,-1,1,2\}$:

$$b_c(x) = \begin{cases} 1, x = c \\ 0, otherwise \end{cases}$$

By using the uniform rotation invariant (*riu2*) LBP mapping and considering the (P=8,R=1) and (P=16,R=2) neighborhoods, the final histogram is made of 112 bins.

The second step in defining MLQP is the threshold selection. As reported in [7], we chose a bunch of 25 threshold couples according to $\tau_1=\{1,3,5,7,9\}$ and $\tau_2=\{\tau_1+2, \ldots, 11\}$, with each of them producing a single 112 bin histogram, i.e., a 112 valued feature vector useful for classification tasks. In the case of a 2-class dataset, the 25 feature vectors obtained from the 25 threshold couples are then used for training 25 SVMs. The 25 different classification results are then fused together according to the sum rule. In case of a multiclass dataset (*m* classes), the "one vs all" classification method is used as follows:

- Train *m* SVMs for each of the 25 feature sets;
- Classify each feature set (out of 25) with its own group of *m* SVMs, getting *m* partial scores (each relative to one class).
- Fuse, according to the sum rule, the 25 partial scores relative to the *m*-th class, thus getting m different final scores;
- Assign the class out of the *m* classes according to the highest final score

2.2 Multithreshold Local Phase Quantization with Ternary Coding (MLPQ3)

A similar approach applied to the Local Phase Quantization (LPQ) operator produces the Multithreshold LPQ with Ternary Coding (MLPQ3). LPQ is based on the blur invariance of the Fourier Transform Phase [14], and it labels each pixel of an image with a binary label based on the real and imaginary parts of the 2D Fourier Transform computed at four specific 2D-frequencies ($\mathbf{F}_x = [\mathrm{Re}\{\mathbf{F}_x^c\}, \mathrm{Im}\{\mathbf{F}_x^c\}]^T$) for each neighborhood (size 3x3 or 5x5 pixels) centered in the pixel to be labeled. A detailed description of the operator is reported in [16].

We first replaced the original scalar quantizer:

$$q_j = \begin{cases} 1, g_j \geq 0 \\ 0, g_j < 0 \end{cases},$$

where g_j represents the j-th element out of the 8 components of $\mathbf{F}_x$, with its ternary version defined as:

$$q_j = \begin{cases} 1, g_j \geq \rho \cdot \tau \\ 0, -\rho \cdot \tau \leq g_j < \rho \cdot \tau \\ -1, g_j < -\rho \cdot \tau \end{cases},$$

where ρ is the standard deviation of the decorrelated F_x components, and τ is a threshold.

The quantized coefficients are then represented as integers in the interval 0-255 using the following binary codings:

$$b_+ = \sum_{j=1}^{8} (q == 1) \cdot 2^{j-1}$$

and

$$b_- = \sum_{j=1}^{8} (q == -1) \cdot 2^{j-1}$$

The b_+ and b_- values are then summarized in two distinct 256 bins histograms, which are concatenated to provide a 512 valued feature vector (i.e., for both the neighborhood of size 3 and 5; the final feature vector is 1024 bins).

We then apply the multithreshold approach by choosing five different thresholds $\tau\in\{0.2, 0.4, 0.6, 0.8, 1\}$ thereby obtaining five feature sets. As was done for MLQP, the "one vs all" classification method is used, considering the five feature sets (instead of the 25 feature sets used in MLQP).

We also build another ensemble, which we call MLQP-FE, by combining sets of LPQ descriptors using varying parameters for the filter size {3, 5}, the scalar frequency

{0.8, 1.2, 1.6, 2}, and the correlation coefficient between adjacent pixel values {0.75, 1.15, 1.55, 1.95}. A subset of all possible combinations is extracted using SFFS on the training data.

2.3 3D Shape

Texture is analyzed by means of the Gray Level Dependency Matrix (GLDM), which is a technique for measuring pixel transitions. Each element, or bin, of the matrix contains the number of occurrences of a specific transition between two grayscale levels, which are the bin coordinates in the matrix itself. Thus, GLDM is a 256 x 256 matrix irrespective of the dimension of the analyzed image. The pixel couples are chosen based on two parameters, the distance and the angle at which they are taken.

To simplify the texture analysis task, GLDM is analyzed by means of a number of features that represent a compact way of describing its shape. GLDM is a three-dimensional function that shows a strong and large peak along the principal diagonal, i.e., along the region representing pixel couples of very similar grey levels that are very likely to be found, as it can be seen in figure 1 (left). The shape of such a peak, also called the main (or principal) component, is analyzed by considering level curves of the GLDM at different heights. Since each curve can be made of more than one contour, the largest one is identified as the main component, which is approximated with an ellipse to simplify the analysis.

Once the main component has been evaluated at multiple heights, ranging from 1 to 20, features are calculated depending on the evolution of the shape of the ellipses over the different height values (obviously, the ellipses at lower heights will have larger areas). This is summarized in figure 1, in which a three-dimensional view of a GLDM is shown (left) together with the result of the main component detection at two different heights (center and right).

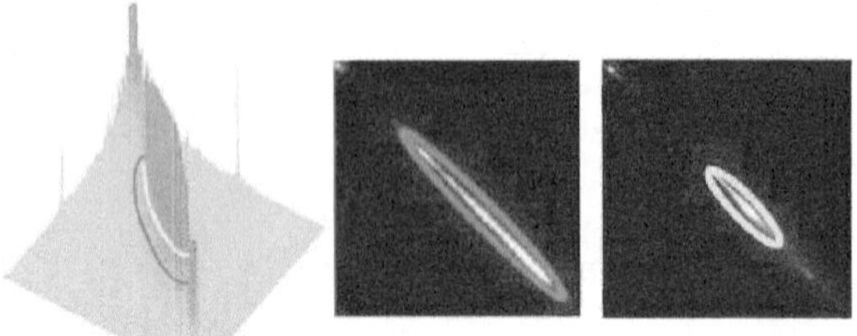

Figure 1: An example of GLDM (left) on which two level curves are considered. In the central and right images, the main component has been identified and approximated with an ellipse at the two heights.

The proposed features are used to measure the following characteristics (details in [7][8]):

1. Evenness: measures how evenly the minor axis of the ellipses decrease.
2. Minor axis spread: the difference between the minimum and maximum values for the ellipse minor axis.
3. Minimum value for the minor axis.
4. Average of the height/width ratio among all ellipses.
5. Total volume under the level curves.
6. Area of the smallest ellipse.
7. The ratio between the smallest and largest ellipses.
8. Volume of the peak, measured as the volume of the GLDM which is above the highest level curve.
9. Number of blank locations.

The above features measure the GLDM in several ways: some of them concentrate on its central part (features 1, 2, 4), while others aim at relating the upper and lower parts (7), and another group focuses on the upper part (3, 6, 8). Feature 5 considers the area under the highest level curve that is a general characteristic of the GLDM. Feature 9 is the only one that does not focus on the principal component but rather considers the surrounding area.

The process described above provides good performances when the GLDM has a large volume, i.e., when the sum of the bin heights is large, which leads to a well defined shape of the GLDM itself. Such a volume depends on the number of couples of the analyzed image pixels, which in turn depends on the size of the analyzed image and on the distance and orientation of the pixel couples. This last dependency is very weak; therefore, it is possible to approximate the GLDM volume with the number of pixels of the considered image. This means that the performance of the aforementioned process drops when it is applied to images with small dimensions. From practical experience, this problem appears when using input images composed of less than 10000 pixels, with each level curve composed of very few points, which makes it impossible to get a reasonable result for the elliptic fitting. This problem becomes more evident at higher levels, so it can happen that the analysis can be performed only on a reduced number of levels. In this situation it is still possible to perform the texture analysis by ignoring the levels for which the elliptic fitting cannot be obtained. This is accomplished by forcing the feature values to a conventional value of 0.

For the tested approaches, the GLDMs are obtained using d=1 and d=3 with an angle of {0°, 45°, 90°, 135°}. We test several methods based on the co-occurrence matrix:

- *5S*, where five shape based descriptors are combined (each used for training a different SVM, then the set of SVMs is combined by sum rule), the first extracted from the whole co-occurrence matrix; the others from subwindows of the GLDM (from the coordinates: (0, 0) to (127, 127); (128, 128) to (255, 255); (0, 0) to (191, 191); (64, 64) to (255, 255)).
- *13S*, where we combine thirteen shape based descriptors, the five of *5S*, and other eight extracted from sub-windows of the GLDM: (0, 0) to (63, 63); (31, 31) to (95, 95); (63, 63) to (127, 127); (95, 95) to (159, 159); (127, 127) to (191, 191); (159, 159) to (223, 223); (191, 191) to (255, 255); (63, 63) to (191, 191). Here the thirteen descriptors are combined by

weighted sum rule[1], the weights of the first five descriptors are 1, while the weight of the last eight descriptors is 0.5.

3 Experimental Results

In this work we used the "object scale" virus dataset tested in [6]. It is available at http://www.cb.uu.se/~gustaf/virustexture/index.html. The dataset is composed of 1500 images with fifteen different virus types, with the radius of each virus particle represented by 20 pixels (see [6] for more details).

The following approaches[2] are compared in Table 1a, using mean accuracy as the performance indicator:

- HAR, standard method based on thirteen features introduced by Haralick[3];
- 5S, the method defined in section 2.3;
- 13S, the method defined in section 2.3;
- NewH, the fusion by weighted sum rule between 13S and HAR[4], where the weight of HAR is 1 while the weight of 13S is 0.51;

The following approaches[5] are compared in Table 1b, using mean accuracy as the performance indicator:

- LBP, standard local binary patterns;
- LTP, standard local ternary patterns;
- ELB, the method proposed in [17];
- MLQP, standard multithreshold local quinary pattern [7];
- PLB, the method proposed in [18];
- PLQ, the variant of PLB where the quinary coding is used instead of the standard binary coding;
- NTB, the method proposed in [19];
- NTQ, the variant of NTB where the quinary coding is used instead of the standard binary coding;
- DLB, the method proposed in [20];
- DLQ, the variant of DLB where the quinary coding is used instead of the standard binary coding;
- LCP, the method proposed in [21];
- MLC, the variant of LCP where the quinary coding is used instead of the standard binary coding;
- FE1, a subset of the MLQP descriptors[6] is selected by SFFS for maximizing the performance using only the training data;
- FE2, as FE1 but is a subset of MLC to be selected.

The following approaches are compared in Table 1c:

- Morph, the method proposed in [22] (here we do not consider the features based on the Haralick's approach, since they are already reported in Table 1a);
- FRDP [6], it is the best method in the "object scale dataset" (i.e. the same used in this work) reported in [6]. We use the original code shared by the authors coupled with SVM. [7]
- LPQ, concatenation of the features extracted by local phase quantization with radius 3 and 5;
- MLPQ3, the multi-threshold approach proposed in [7] (exactly the same parameters).
- MLPQ3-FE, selection of a subset of the different descriptors LPQ descriptors varying different parameters (see section 2.2) by SFFS as in FE1.
- FUSION, fusion by sum rule (see footnote 4) among NewH, MLC, Morph and FRDP (the best four methods, each belong to a different type of descriptors).

From the results reported in the previous tables, we can draw the following conclusions:

- Multithreshold quinary approach outperforms the base approaches (i.e., MLQP outperforms LBP, PLQ outperforms PLB, NTLQ outperforms NTLB, DLQ outperforms DLB, and MLC outperforms LCP);
- Selection of the set of parameters boosts the performance of MLQP but does not improve MLC;
- In this classification problem, MLPQ3 works poorly since some feature sets composing the ensemble have low performances (the descriptors that belong to MLPQ3 obtains an accuracy of 62.9%, 58.9%, 52.7%, 49.6% and 48.2%) but MLPQ3-FE outperforms LPQ since the low performance descriptors are not selected by SFFS;
- The proposed NewH approach outperforms standard Haralik's features;

[1] Notice that the weights are not optimized in this dataset but we run experiments on ~10 different datasets using the same weighs, these experiments are not yet published.

[2] For all the tested approaches the uniform rotation invariant LBP mapping is used and considering the (P=8,R=1) and (P=16,R=2) neighborhoods

[3] Energy; Correlation; Inertia; Entropy; Inverse difference moment; Sum average; Sum variance; Sum entropy; Difference average; Difference variance; Difference entropy; Information measure of correlation 1; Information measure of correlation 2

[4] Before the fusion the scores of both the approaches are normalized to mean 0 and std 1

[5] For all the tested approaches the uniform rotation invariant LBP mapping is used and considering the (P=8,R=1) and (P=16,R=2) neighborhoods

[6] We have used more couple of thresholds with respect to standard MLQP:

```
for threshold=1:2:15
    for threshold2=threshold+2:19
.... Feature extraction with thresholds [threshold, threshold2]
    end
end
for threshold=1:2:15
    for threshold2=threshold+4:19
.... Feature extraction with thresholds [threshold, threshold2]
    end
end
```

[7] For this method we use a softmask (it is available in the code) shared by the authors of [6], instead of the mask (this is used for all the other methods excepts 5Sh and 13Sh) available at http://www.cb.uu.se/~gustaf/virustexture/index.html. Notice that for 5Sh and 13Sh we have NOT used masks.

- As widely reported in different classification problems, the fusion of different descriptors (i.e., the method named FUSION) obtains the best performance.

4 Conclusion

In this paper we compare different LBP variants, and for the first time we report the performance of their multithreshold quinary variants. The main novelty of the paper is the experimental assessment of the usefulness of the quinary coding coupled with different novel LBP-based descriptors. Another interesting result is that we show a method for improving the performance obtained with the information extracted from the co-occurrence matrix.

In the original paper [6], where the dataset used in this paper was proposed, the authors obtain a mean accuracy of 73.8% and a median accuracy of 79.0% (personal communication of the authors) using FRDP and performances lower than 60% with LBP and its variants (on the "object scale" dataset). In the "fixed scale" dataset (not available) the best result in [6] (median accuracy ~80%) is obtained by an LBP variant. Moreover, the authors report that it is useful to combine descriptors extracted from the "fixed scale" dataset with descriptors extracted from the "object scale" dataset.

Our tests on FRDP obtain lower performances, but our texture variants obtain good performance (mean accuracy) ~70% (notice that we have used the same 10-fold cross validation used by in [6]) and our fusion outperforms the result obtained in [6] using the "object scale" dataset (their best method obtains a mean accuracy of 73.8% while our fusion method obtains a mean accuracy of 80.7%).

a)

HAR	5Sh	13Sh	NewH
69.9	59. 3	60.5	71.7

b)

LBP	LTP	ELB	MLQP	PLB	PLQ	NTB	NTQ	DLB	DLQ	LCP	MLC	FE1	FE2
57.6	58.5	70.9	70.0	64.0	70.1	49.9	68.5	55.3	71.8	62.7	73.3	72.4	72.7

c)

Morph [1]	FRDP [3]	LPQ	MLPQ3	MLPQ3-FE	FUSION
71.7	70.0	63.3	57.9	64.5	80.7

Table 1. Comparison among the tested methods, (N.B. we report the mean accuracy among the classes and not the median as in [6]).

Acknowledgements

The authors would like to thank Dr. Gustaf Kylberg for sharing the virus dataset and his Matlab code as well as for the fruitful communication during the draft of this paper.

References

[1] C. S. Goldsmith and S. E. Miller, "Modern uses of electron microscopy for detection of viruses," *Clinical Microbiology Reviews,* vol. 22, pp. 552-563, 2009.

[2] S. S. Biel and D. Madeley, "Diagnostic virology-the need for electron microscopy: A discussion paper," *Journal of Clinical Virology* vol. 22, pp. 1-9, 2001.

[3] R. M. Haralick, K. Shanmugam, and I. Dinstein, "Texture features for image classification," *IEEE Transactions on Systems, Man, and Cybernetics,* vol. 3, pp. 610-621, 1973.

[4] T. Randen and J. H. Husy, "Filtering for texture classification: A comparative study," *IEEE Transactions on Pattern Analysis and Machine Intelligence,* vol. 21, pp. 291-310, 1999.

[5] T. Ojala, M. Pietikainen, and T. Maeenpaa, "Multiresolution gray-scale and rotation invariant texture classification with local binary patterns," *Ieee transactions on pattern analysis and machine intelligence,* vol. 24, pp. 971-987, 2002.

[6] G. Kylberg, M. Uppström, and I.-M. Sintorn, "Virus texture analysis using local binary patterns and radial density profiles," presented at the 18th Iberoamerican Congress on Pattern Recognition (CIARP), 2011.

[7] M. Paci, L. Nanni, A. Lathi, K. Aalto-Setälä, J. Hyttinen, and S. Severi, "Non-binary coding for texture descriptors in sub-cellular and stem cell image classification," *Current Bioinformatics,* 2013.

[8] N. Hervé, A. Servais, E. Thervet, J. C. Olivo-Marin, and V. Meas-Yedid, "Statistical color texture descriptors for histological images analysis.," presented at the Proc. of IEEE International Symposium on Biomedical Imaging (ISBI), 2011.

[9] B. Zhang, "Classification of subcellular phenotype images by decision templates for classifier ensemble," presented at the 2009 International Conference on Computational Models for Life Sciences (CMLS), 2010.

[10] B. J. Matuszewski and L. K. Shark, "Hierarchical iterative bayesian approach to automatic recognition of biological viruses in electron microscope images," presented at the 2001 International Conference on Image Processing (ICIP), 2001.

[11] H. C. L. Ong, "Virus recognition in electron microscope images using higher order spectral features," Ph.D. Thesis, Queensland University of Technology, 2006.

[12] I. M. Sintorn, M. Homman-Loudiyi, C. Söderberg-Nauclér, and G. Borgefors, "A refined circular template matching method for classification of human cytomegalovirus capsids in TEM images," *Computer Methods and Programs in Biomedicine,* vol. 76, 2004.

[13] P. Pudil, J. Novovicova, and J. Kittler, "Floating search methods in feature selection," *Pattern Recognition Letters,* vol. 5, pp. 1119-1125, 1994.

[14] S. Ghidoni, G. Cielniak, and E. Menegatti, "Texture-based crowd detection and localisation," presented at the International Conference on Intelligent Autonomous Systems (IAS-12), 2012.

[15] L. Nanni, S. Brahnam, S. Ghidoni, and E. Menegatti, "A comparison of methods for extracting information from the co-occurrence matrix for subcellular classification," submitted.

[16] V. Ojansivu and J. Heikkila, "Blur insensitive texture classification using local phase quantization," presented at the ICISP, 2008.

[17] L. Liu, L. Zhao, Y. Long, G. Kuang, and P. Fieguth, "Extended local binary patterns for texture classification," *Image and Vision Computing,* vol. 30, pp. 86-99, 2012.

[18] X. Qian, X.-S. Hua, P. Chen, and L. Ke, "PLBP: An effective local binary patterns texture descriptor with pyramid representation," *Pattern Recognition Letters,* vol. 44, pp. 2502-2515, 2011.

[19] A. Fathi and A. R. Naghsh-Nilchi, "Noise tolerant local binary pattern operator for efficient texture analysis," *Pattern Recognition Letters,* vol. 33, pp. 1093-1100, 2012.

[20] Y. Guo, G. Zhao, and M. Pietikainen, "Discriminative features for texture description," *Pattern Recognition Letters,* vol. 45, pp. 3834-3843, 2012.

[21] Y. Guo, G. Zhao, and M. Pietikainen, "Texture classification using a linear configuration model based descriptor," presented at the British Machine Vision Conference, 2011.

[22] P. Strandmark, J. Ulén, and F. Kahl, "HEp-2 Staining Pattern Classification," presented at the International Conference on Pattern Recognition (ICPR2012), 2012.

Improving Medical Diagnosis by Using Digital Data to Assess the Prior Probability of Disease

Robert A. Warner, MD

Tigard Research Institute,
12228 SW Chandler Drive,
Tigard, OR, 97224-2825
USA

Abstract

The study analyzed diagnostic data from 435 patients evaluated in the emergency department for shortness of breath. Electronically recorded heart sounds and brain natriuretic peptide (BNP) were analyzed to determine whether left ventricular systolic dysfunction (LVSD) with heart failure caused each patient's symptoms. Each patient's computerized electrocardiogram was used to determine the presence or absence of previous myocardial infarction. As expected, the data show that the electrocardiogram itself does not detect LVSD with heart failure. However, for both the recorded heart sounds and the BNP data, the diagnostic sensitivities at 98% specificity for LVSD with heart failure are significantly greater in the subgroup with previous myocardial infarction than they are in either the subgroup without previous myocardial infarction or in the entire group of subjects. Evaluating digital electrocardiographic evidence of previous myocardial infarction assesses the prior probability that LVSD with heart failure is the cause of a given patient's symptoms.

Keywords: diagnostic accuracy, digital data, prior probability

1 Introduction

In medicine, various diagnostic tests have been developed to detect specific diseases. In the present study, I tested the hypothesis that even though a particular diagnostic test does not itself detect a particular disease of interest, it can be used to assess the prior probability that the disease is present in the patients being tested. According to the principles of Bayesian statistics, the estimate of this prior probability can then be used to improve the diagnostic performances of the tests that are directly relevant to the disease of interest. For example, it is important to be able to detect left ventricular systolic dysfunction (LVSD), an abnormal condition in which the heart muscle often cannot contract strongly enough to meet the metabolic needs of the patient's body. In many cases, LVSD leads to heart failure that in turn eventuates in severe disability and premature death.

A number of diagnostic tests have been developed to detect LVSD and associated heart failure. One of these tests is the electronic recording of a patient's heart sounds. Specifically, these recordings can be used to detect an abnormal third heart sound by measuring the amount of acoustical energy that is present during a particular brief period of the cardiac cycle. The greater that acoustical energy, the greater is the likelihood that the patient has LVSD.

Another test for LVSD and associated heart failure is brain natriuretic peptide (BNP). BNP is measured in a small sample of the patient's blood and the higher the blood level of BNP that is measured, the greater is the likelihood that the patient has LVSD and heart failure.

The electrocardiogram (ECG) is an additional diagnostic test that is frequently used to evaluate patients with known or suspected heart disease. However, because of the nature of the data that the ECG acquires, the ECG itself cannot directly diagnose either LVSD or heart failure. In contrast, the ECG is an excellent tool for detecting the presence of previous myocardial infarction, i.e. a heart attack that has afflicted a patient at some time in the past. This is relevant in the present context because myocardial infarction often causes sufficient damage to the heart muscle that LVSD with heart failure ensues.[1-2] Therefore, LVSD is more common in patients with ECG evidence of previous myocardial infarction than it is in patients without such evidence.

An extremely common symptom associated with LVSD and heart failure is shortness of breath. However, shortness of breath often occurs in conditions other than LVSD and heart failure, e.g. chronic pulmonary disease, asthma, collapsed lung and acute anxiety reactions associated with hyperventilation. Since therapies that are appropriate for LVSD and heart failure are very different from those of each of the other causes of shortness of breath, it is crucial to diagnose LVSD and heart failure as accurately as possible.

Based on the above considerations, I tested the hypothesis that in a population of patients with shortness of breath, evidence of previous myocardial infarction provided by digital ECG data increases the prior probability that the combination of LVSD and heart failure is the cause of the shortness of breath. Accordingly, such an assessment of this prior probability would result in improved diagnostic accuracy of tests that have been developed to detect LVSD with heart failure, i.e. recorded third heart sound energy and BNP.

2 Materials and Methods

2.1 Selection of Patients

I studied a convenience sample of 435 patients (mean age = 59 years, 54% women) who presented to one of several different hospital emergency departments with the recent onset of shortness of breath. None of the patients had chest pain at the time of their evaluations.

2.2 Diagnostic Tests

All the subjects had an ECG obtained at the time of arrival in the emergency department and all had an echocardiogram within 24 hours of their arrival. The echocardiogram was used to determine whether LVSD was present or absent in each patient. The quantitative criterion for LVSD was a left ventricular ejection fraction <50% (the normal value being ≥65%). In addition, at the time of arrival in the emergency department, 432 (99%) of the patients had their heart sounds recorded electronically (Audicor™, Inovise Medical, Inc., Portland, OR, USA) and 374 (86%) of the patients had BNP measured. Digital ECG evidence of previous myocardial infarction was considered positive if the patient had a Selvester-Wagner Q Wave Score ≥1.[3]

2.3 Analysis of the Data

Receiver-operating characteristic curves were used to determine the diagnostic sensitivities at 98% specificity for LVSD for the heart sound data and for the BNP data, respectively. Chi square analysis was used to evaluate the statistical significance of any differences in diagnostic performance between the subgroup with digital ECG evidence of previous myocardial infarction vs. the entire group and vs. the subgroup with no digital ECG evidence of previous myocardial infarction. To avoid type 1 errors associated with multiple tests, an alpha <0.01 was a priori chosen to indicate statistical significance.

3 Results

Of all the patients, 215 (49%) had LVSD by echocardiogram and 220 (51%) did not. Of all the patients, 120 (28%) had previous myocardial infarction by digital ECG data and 315 (72%) did not. Of the 120 patients with previous myocardial infarction by ECG, 67 (56%) had LVSD and 53 (44%) did not (chi square = 2.7, p = NS. This supports the assertion that ECG evidence of previous myocardial infarction does not, in itself, detect LVSD. In contrast, the diagnostic performances exhibited by the tests that have been developed to detect LVSD, i.e. recorded heart sounds and BNP data, respectively, are shown in Tables 1 and 2. Tables 1 and 2 show that at 98% specificity, the diagnostic sensitivities of both the recorded heart sounds and BNP are statistically significantly greater in the subgroup with digital ECG evidence of previous myocardial infarction than they are in either the subgroup without previous myocardial infarction or in the entire group of patients. Concordantly, the tables also show that the threshold values of the recorded heart sounds and of BNP required to attain 98% diagnostic specificity are lower in the subgroup with digital ECG evidence of previous myocardial infarction than they are in either the subgroup without previous myocardial infarction or in the entire group of patients.

Table 1

Recorded 3rd Heart Sound Energy for Detecting LVSD

	All Patients (N = 432)	MI Absent (N = 313)	MI Present (N = 119)
Threshold*	5.66	6.00	5.19
Specificity	98%	98%	98%
Sensitivity	21%	16%	32%
Chi Square**	6.2	13.5	
P Value**	$1x10^{-2}$	$2x10^{-4}$	

*Proprietary sound energy display value, **Compared to MI Present

LVSD = left ventricular systolic dysfunction, MI = myocardial infarction

Table 2

Brain Natriuretic Peptide for Detecting LVSD

	All Patients (N = 374)	MI Absent (N = 274)	MI Present (N = 100)
Threshold*	1740	1740	779
Specificity	98%	98%	98%
Sensitivity	11%	11%	34%
Chi Square**	31.4	27.4	
P Value**	$2x10^{-8}$	$2x10^{-7}$	

*picograms/milliliter, **Compared to MI Present
LVSD = left ventricular systolic dysfunction, MI = myocardial infarction

4 Conclusions

The data of the present study show that using a test for one type of disease (previous myocardial infarction) can indirectly improve the diagnostic performances of tests intended to detect a different type of disease (LVSD with heart failure). The presence of previous myocardial infarction by computerized ECG increases the likelihood that a given patient's shortness of breath is caused by LVSD with heart failure, rather than by some other cause of shortness of breath. This is because ECG evidence of previous myocardial infarction in a patient is prima facie evidence that the patient has a type of heart disease that often results in LVSD with heart failure. For both the recorded heart sounds and the BNP tests for LVSD with heart failure, the diagnostic sensitivities at 98% specificity were statistically significantly greater not only in the previous myocardial infarction absent subgroup, but in the entire group of patients as well. In concert with this, the data in Tables 1 and 2 also show that the threshold values required to attain 98% specificity are lower in the previous myocardial infarction subgroup than they are in both the previous myocardial infarction absent subgroup and the entire group of patients.

Although a given body of evidence may be required to support a particular hypothesis, it does not follow that the same body of evidence necessarily supports only that hypothesis. In diagnostic testing, the hypothesis to be accepted or rejected is that the patient has a particular disease of interest. The evidence for or against that hypothesis is the body of data relevant to the parameter measured by an appropriate diagnostic test. In the present study, the hypothesis is that a given patient who presents to the emergency department with shortness of breath has LVSD with heart failure. The sets of data used to accept or reject this hypothesis are electronically recorded heart sound data and measured BNP values. Whereas it is highly likely that a given patient with LVSD and heart failure will have abnormal recorded heart sounds and elevated BNP values, the converse does not necessarily follow. This is because medical conditions other than LVSD with heart failure can also produce abnormal heart sounds and high BNP.[4-5]

Advocates of the Bayesian approach to statistics emphasize that the greater the prior probability that a hypothesis is correct, the greater is the likelihood that a body of relevant evidence supports that hypothesis. Therefore, I reasoned that the presence of one manifestation of heart disease (LVSD with heart failure) was more probable in patients in whom there was separate evidence for a different, but pathophysiologically relevant, manifestation of heart disease (previous myocardial infarction by ECG). The notion of considering the prior probability of disease when interpreting the results of diagnostic tests is important throughout the entire field of medicine. It helps one address such questions as, "Does a "positive" mammogram in a 30 year-old woman (in whose age group the prevalence of breast cancer is relatively low) have the same clinical significance as a "positive" mammogram in a 60 year-old woman (in whose age group the prevalence of breast cancer is relatively high)? Also, developers of diagnostic tests for all types of diseases often test their performances in disease-rich populations. This decreases the total number of subjects required to test for positive cases of the disease with a concomitant reduction in the cost of the testing. However, it is often uncertain to what extent these initially reported diagnostic results can be extrapolated to more typical populations, i.e. those that haven't been deliberately selected because of a high prevalence of the disease.

The use of digital ECG data to determine the prior probability of relevant heart disease is particularly advantageous. First, the ECG is non-invasive, widely available, inexpensive compared to many other diagnostic tests and does not require highly trained personnel to obtain. Furthermore, most ECGs are currently interpreted by computer algorithms whose accuracy has been well documented. Therefore, special expertise in electrocardiography is no longer required for the interpretation of most ECGs. Relevant to the present study, the diagnostic performances of modern ECG diagnostic algorithms for detecting previous myocardial infarction are particularly excellent.[6-8]

It should be noted that even before any ECG data were obtained, the patients in this study already had a high prior probability of LVSD with heart failure because they had chosen to visit an emergency department because of symptoms typical of that disorder. This is in contrast, for example, to a group of asymptomatic subjects who received screening tests for a disease of which they had no clinical manifestations. These observations emphasize the high incremental value of the digital ECG data for assessing the prior probability that LVSD with heart failure is the cause of a patient's symptoms.

5 Limitations of the Study

A limitation of the present study is that although the echocardiogram reliably detects LVSD, LVSD is not synonymous with heart failure. However, the presence of LVSD is necessary for the most important type of HF to occur. Also, using LVSD as a marker of highly probable heart failure in the appropriate context has the advantage that it is an objective diagnostic finding. This makes it superior to using the treating physicians' diagnoses of the presence or absence of HF as the diagnostic endpoint of the study. First, one or more of the treating physicians' diagnoses could easily be incorrect. Second, in making their diagnoses, the treating physicians may have used the S3 and/or BNP data. If so, any interpretation of the diagnostic efficacy of the S3 and BNP data would be circular. Finally, BNP is much more likely to be elevated in LVSD with heart failure than with LVSD alone.

Another possible objection is that recorded heart sound and BNP data were used to diagnose LVSD indirectly, rather than detecting LVSD directly with the echocardiogram. This is because the echocardiogram is expensive, requires highly trained personnel to obtain and is therefore often not readily available in the emergency department. This is substantiated by the fact that the electrocardiographic, heart sound and BNP data were obtained at the time of each patient's arrival in the emergency department, but the echocardiographic information required as long as 24 hours after arrival to obtain. This is especially important because LVSD with heart failure is often a life-threatening emergency that requires very prompt diagnosis and treatment.

6 References

1. Gheorghiade M, Bonow RO. Chronic heart failure in the United States: a manifestation of coronary artery disease. Circulation 97:282-289,1998.

2. He J; Ogden LG; Bazzano LA; Vupputuri S. Risk factors for congestive heart failure in US men and women: NHANES I epidemiologic follow-up study. Arch. Intern. Med. 161 (7): 996–1002, 2001.

3. Selvester RH, Wagner GS, Hindman NB. The Selvester qrs scoring system for estimating myocardial infarct size the development and application of the system. Arch Intern Med. 1985;145(10):1877-1881, 1985.

4. Waku S, Iida N, Ishihara T. Significance of brain natriuretic peptide measurement as a diagnostic indicator of cardiac function. Method Inform Med;39:249-53, 2000.

5. Marcus GM, Gerber L, McKeown BH. Association between phonocardiographic third and fourth heart sounds and objective measures of left ventricular function. JAMA 293:2238–44, 2005.

6. Warner RA, Hill NE. Optimized electrocardiographic criteria for prior inferior and an anterior myocardial infarction. J. Electrocardiol. 45:209-213, 2012.

7. Wagner GS, Maynard C, Andresen A, Anderson E, Myers R, Warner RA and Selvester RH. The evaluation of advanced electrocardiographic diagnostic software for detection of prior myocardial infarction. Amer. J. Cardiol. 89:75-79, Supplement 2002.

8. Elko P, Warner RA. Using directly-acquired digital EKG data to optimize the diagnostic criteria for anterior myocardial infarction. J. Electrocardiol. Supplemental Issue:S89-S92, 1994.

The Function of Phase Parameter in Sampling Data Analysis of BRATUNASS

A. Zhifu Tao[1], B. Yizhou Yao[2], C. Zhonglin Han[3], D. Meng Yao[3*], E. Huiyan Wang[4], F. Blair Fleet[5], G. Erik D. Goodman[5], H. Jinyao Yan[6], and I. John R. Deller[6]
[1] Dept of Elec Info Engineering, Suzhou Vocational University, Suzhou, China
[2]college of science, Shenyang University of technology, Shenyang, China
[3]School of Info Sci and Tech, East China Normal University, Shanghai, China
[4]School of Computer Sci and Info Egr, Zhejiang Gongshang University, Hangzhou, China
[5]BEACON Center, Michigan State University, East Lansing, MI, U.S.
[6]ECE Michigan State University, East Lansing, MI, U.S.
*Corresponding Author, e-mail: myao@ee.ecnu.edu.cn

Abstract - *This paper discusses the problem of the phase distribution of back scattering coefficient on microwave breast cancer detection method. In breast malignancy nidus area, the cell differentiation is low degree, the species of tissues is relative single and cell division is fast. That means the growth of cancerous tissues destroy the principle of tissues distribution composed by normal tissues. The malignancy degree is higher, the fractal dimension is greater and the tissues interface is more irregular. These characteristics indicate that the phase distributions have tremendous difference when microwave back scattering in normal tissues and malignancy tissues. Based on real case data acquired via BRATUMASS*[1], *finds the method of phase distribution of back scattering coefficient. Finally, we provided and analyzed typical detection results in three different state of Mammary gland disease condition (normal, fibromatosis and cancer) and verified the difference of those phase distribution.*

Keywords: Phase distribution, Complex dielectric constant, Back scattering coefficient, Circle mapping

1 Introduction

Cancer has become one of human terrible diseases. The existing research results show[2] the main difference between normal cells and cancerous cells. The former growth almost stops, and the latter division is abnormal fast, irregular, not harmonious, fuzzy and massed up. Interfaces of tissues are more fine structure, more irregular and rougher. Under the electromagnetic wave field it converts to the dielectric constant and conductivity of normal breast tissues and malignant tissues have great differences, especially in microwave frequency band. When the near-field microwave reach an area of cancerous tissue, the phase distribution of microwave back scattering in normal tissue interface and malignant tissue interface are larger differences, for the cancerous characteristics in tissue. So those can be used as physical basis for detection and imaging of breast cancer in microwave near field. BRATUMASS (Breast tumor microwave sensor system) was developed based on the above characteristics. This paper provides the difference of phase distribution between normal tissue and malignant tissue through analyzing the phase distribution of back-scattering signal in BRATUMASS. The difference can give reference to identify the tissues characteristics.

2 Back-scattering Signal Acquisition System in Microwave Near Field

BRATUMASS source signal uses the triangle (modulation period: 1 KHz) continuous frequency modulation method, carry frequency is 1.575GHz, bandwidth 100MHz. The generated FM signal divide into two. One signal passes through transmission antenna and becomes system transmission wave. The other signal after delay compensation arrives one input terminal of multiplying unit and becomes system direct wave. Transmission wave through transmission antenna enters into detection space and forms FM wave transmitted in breast. Then, this wave reaches receiver antenna after back-scattering on tissues target surface, and this back-scattering wave is named system received wave. The received wave through receiver antenna reaches the other input terminal of multiplying unit. The two signals, through multiplying unit and low-pass filter, become system signal and go to A/D sampler. We assume that $x(t)$ is an impulse signal of frequency modulation, whose center frequency, impulse width, bandwidth and amplitude are f_0, τ, B and A, respectively. Then $x(t)$ can be written as:

$$x(t) = Arect(t)\exp[j(2\pi f_0 t + \mu t^2 / 2)] \quad (1)$$

As shown in Figure 1, considering (1), the transmission signal at t moment is $x(t)$, so the scattering signal of l target should be $K_i x(t + \tau_i)$. Where, K_i is the scattering coefficient of i target. The output of multiplying unit at t moment is $\eta(\tau_i, t)$.

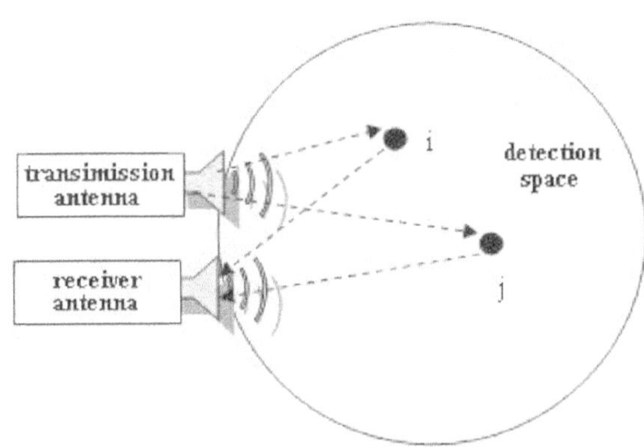

Fig.1 The detection principle of multi-targets of BRATUMASS

Reason, $\eta(\tau_i, t) = \boldsymbol{x^*(t) K_i x(t+\tau_i)}$, so there is:

$$\eta(\tau_i, t) = \begin{cases} \kappa_i A^2 \exp[j(2\pi f_0 \tau_i + \mu\tau_i t + \mu\tau_i^2/2)], \\ \quad \ldots\ldots \max(-\frac{\tau}{2}, -\frac{\tau}{2}+\tau_i) < t < \min(\frac{\tau}{2}, \frac{\tau}{2}+\tau_i) \\ 0, \quad\quad others \end{cases} \quad (2)$$

$$\eta(\tau_i, t) = \kappa_i A^2 \exp(j\mu\tau_i t + j\psi_i) \quad \max(-\frac{\tau}{2}, -\frac{\tau}{2}+\tau_i) < t < \min(\frac{\tau}{2}, \frac{\tau}{2}+\tau_i) \quad (3)$$

Where, $\psi_i = (2\pi f_0 \tau_i + \frac{\mu\tau_i^2}{2})$ calculates the Fourier transform of the parameter t in $\eta(\tau_i, t)$ of (3), there is:

$$\Pi(\tau_i, \omega) = \int_{-\infty}^{+\infty} \eta(\tau_i, t)\exp(-j\omega t)dt = \kappa_i A^2 \int_{-\infty}^{+\infty} \exp(j\mu\tau_i t + j\psi_i)\exp(-j\omega t)dt$$
$$= 2\pi\kappa_i A^2 \exp(j\psi_i)\delta(\omega - \mu\tau_i) \quad (4)$$

The amplitude spectrum of output of multiplying unit $|\Pi(\tau_i, \omega)|$ is:

$$|\Pi(\tau_i, \omega)| = 2\pi|\kappa_i| A^2 \delta(\omega - \mu\tau_i) \quad (5)$$

That is to say, if had target back wave, there will appear one impulse function in amplitude spectrum $|\Pi(\tau_i, \omega)|$, whose intensity is related to target characteristics. The frequencies of impulse function correspond to time delay. Because antenna detection tracks and detection targets have symmetrical characteristic, we just considers a kind of situation, which detection microwaves vertically arrive at the boundary of tissues. Fig.2 illustrates the relationship graph between reflection and transmission when incident microwave vertically arrives at interface of two different media. Where, P_i is the power of incidence wave, P_r is the power of reflect wave and P_t is the power of transmitted wave. The ratio is (the power of back-scattering signal and the power of incident signal) $P_r/P_t = |\Gamma|^2$. Consider Fig.2, the relationship as:

$$\Gamma = \frac{\eta_2 - \eta_1}{\eta_2 + \eta_2} \quad (6)$$

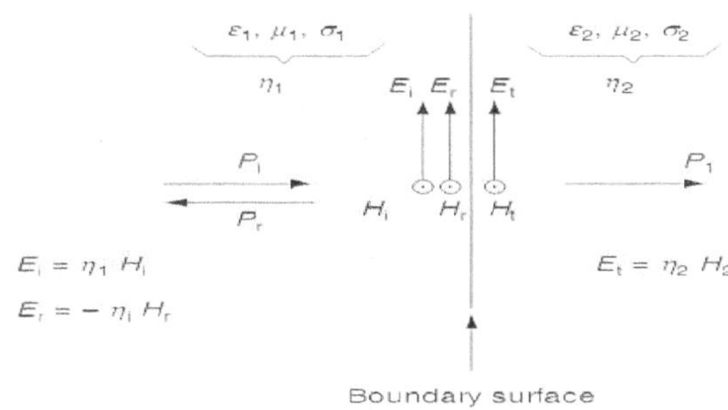

Fig. 2 The reflection and transmission of microwave in two media with different dielectric constant

Where, $\eta_1 = \sqrt{\mu_1/\varepsilon_1}, \eta_2 = \sqrt{\mu_2/\varepsilon_2}$. There is $\mu_1 = 1, \mu_2 = 1$ in non-magnetic medium.

$$|\Gamma| = \left|\frac{\sqrt{\varepsilon_2} - \sqrt{\varepsilon_1}}{\sqrt{\varepsilon_2} + \sqrt{\varepsilon_1}}\right| \quad (7)$$

As the back-scattering interface and the position of detection antenna are relatively fixed, the frequency of beat signal output by system multiplier (frequency mixing) is also relatively fixed. That means that an impulse, which is relative to interface characteristics, will appear in position of corresponding spectrum. If the interface is the boundary of scattering target i, there is:

$$P_i \propto A^2, \quad P_r \propto |\kappa_i|^2 A^2 \quad (8)$$

So, $$\frac{P_r}{P_i} = |\Gamma|^2 \propto |\kappa_i|^2 \quad (9)$$

$$|\kappa_i| \propto |\Gamma| = \left|\frac{\sqrt{\varepsilon_2} - \sqrt{\varepsilon_1}}{\sqrt{\varepsilon_2} + \sqrt{\varepsilon_1}}\right| \quad (10)$$

Where, K_i is the coefficient obtained from the ratio of amplitudes between actual back-scattering signals and transmitting signals, and Γ is the scattering coefficient in ideal condition. Aside the influent factors of transmission distance, it is:

$$|\kappa_i| = |\Gamma| = \left| \frac{\sqrt{\varepsilon_2} - \sqrt{\varepsilon_1}}{\sqrt{\varepsilon_2} + \sqrt{\varepsilon_1}} \right| \tag{11}$$

On the premise of not confusing, K_i and Γ are both called scattering coefficient (or back wave coefficient). If the value of ε_1 is known, the value of ε_2 can be calculated by (11). Calculation assumed as follow:

Other tissues (such as blood vessels, leaflets, breast ducts and malignant tissues) are all embedded in the normal breast tissue as background, and there are obvious interface between different media. The dielectric constant of normal breast tissue is ε_1. Considered the range of scattering target r, then the impact factor function of microwave transmission distance, H(r), (9) can be written as:

$$|\kappa_i| = |H(r) \times \Gamma| = |H(r)| \times \left| \frac{\sqrt{\varepsilon_2} - \sqrt{\varepsilon_1}}{\sqrt{\varepsilon_2} + \sqrt{\varepsilon_1}} \right| \tag{12}$$

It can be rewritten as:

$$\kappa(r) = H(r) \times \Gamma(r) \tag{13}$$

There have many scattering targets in practical detection space. Many targets, transmission loss and interference in microwave transmission will make the calculation become very complicated. The set of tissue units, which are corresponding to the same delay position in detection space, is called characteristic face (characteristic line in 2-dimension). In order to simplified problem, here only discusses a transceiver, as shown in Fig.3. The characteristic line l, whose distance from detection center is r, has two scattering targets i and j. There has:

$$\begin{aligned} \kappa_i(r) &= H(r) \times \Gamma_i(r) \\ \kappa_j(r) &= H(r) \times \Gamma_j(r) \end{aligned} \tag{14}$$

Where, $K_i(r)$ is the ith back-scattering coefficient measured by transceiver, $\Gamma_i(r)$ is ideal scattering coefficient of i target in tissues interface, $K_j(r)$ is the jth back-scattering coefficient measured by transceiver, $\Gamma_j(r)$ is ideal scattering coefficient of j target in tissues interface. The total back-scattering coefficient measured by transceiver is:

$$\kappa(r) = \kappa_i(r) + \kappa_j(r) = H(r)(\Gamma_i(r) + \Gamma_j(r)) \tag{15}$$

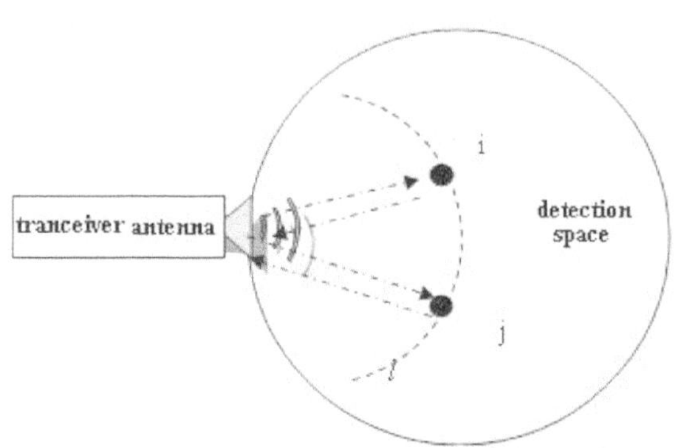

Fig. 3 The target characteristic of BRATUMASS in feature line

In the reality environment, scattering coefficient Γ in the tissues interface is often a complex number for the relationship of tissues conductivity [3]. So the scattering rate includes certain additional phase shift. The phase shift is related to the tissues conductivity. According to the above assumption, the tissue parameters of i are ε_i, σ_i the tissue parameters of j are ε_j, σ_j, the parameters of background are ε_i, σ_i. Then the complex dielectric constant of i target is:

$$\dot{\varepsilon}_i = \varepsilon_i + j\frac{\sigma_i}{\omega} \tag{16}$$

In the following text, a variable adding a dot represent a complex variable. Substitute it into (6),

$$\dot{\Gamma}_i = \frac{(\dot{\varepsilon}_1)^{0.5} - (\dot{\varepsilon}_i)^{0.5}}{(\dot{\varepsilon}_1)^{0.5} + (\dot{\varepsilon}_i)^{0.5}} = \frac{1 - |\dot{\varepsilon}_{i1}|^{0.5} \exp(j\arg(\dot{\varepsilon}_{i1}))}{1 + |\dot{\varepsilon}_{i1}|^{0.5} \exp(j\arg(\dot{\varepsilon}_{i1}))} = |\dot{\Gamma}_i| \exp(j\theta_i) \tag{17}$$

Where, $\dot{\varepsilon}_{i1} = \dot{\varepsilon}_i / \dot{\varepsilon}_1$, and θ_i is the principal value of compound angle. Consequently, (15) can be rewritten as:

$$\dot{\kappa}(r) = \dot{\kappa}_i(r) + \dot{\kappa}_j(r) = \dot{H}(r)[\dot{\Gamma}_i(r) + \dot{\Gamma}_j(r)] \tag{18}$$

$$\dot{\kappa}(r) = \dot{H}(r)\dot{\Gamma}(r) \tag{19}$$

Considering rewrite the Fourier transformation of system signal (4), there has:

$$\dot{\Pi}(\tau_i, \omega) = \dot{\Pi}(r, \omega) = 2\pi\dot{\kappa}(r)A^2 \exp(j\psi(r))\delta(\omega - \mu\frac{2r}{v}) \tag{20}$$

Where, the transmission range of τ_i is $2r$, v is the transmission velocity of electromagnetic wave in detection space. Substitute (9) into (20),

$$\dot{\Pi}(\tau_i,\omega) = \dot{\Pi}(r,\omega) = 2\pi \dot{H}(r)\dot{\Gamma}(r)A^2 \exp(j\psi(r))\delta(\omega - \mu\frac{2r}{v}) \quad (21)$$

If the distance influence function H(r) can be known, the synthesis of scattering coefficient $\dot{\Gamma}(r)$ in r position can be calculated with $\dot{\Pi}(r,\omega)$.

3 Components of the $\Pi(\tau_i, \omega)$ Phase

The phase Ψ_{Π_i} of $\Pi(\tau_i, \omega)$ can be divided into two parts: one is Ψ_i, produced by frequency modulation; the other is Ψ_{Ki}, produced by scattering coefficient K_i. Due to (3), Ψ_i can be rewritten as:

$$\psi_i = \omega_0\tau_i + \frac{(\mu\tau_i)^2}{2\mu} = \frac{\omega_0}{\mu}\omega + \frac{(\omega)^2}{2\mu} \quad (22)$$

Moreover, exp($j\Psi_i$) is a periodic function, which is circle mapping with T: $x \rightarrow f(x)$ (mod 2π). As shown in Fig. 4, the phase Ψ_i of $\Pi(\tau_i, \omega)$ will become complex in practical system. However, the Fourier transform of Ψ_i is relatively simple. Fig. 5 demonstrates that the Fourier transform of Ψ_i only appears one spectrum step near 200Hz (the center frequency of system is $\omega_0 = 2\pi \times 1.5GHz$). That is to say, the phase problem can be concise if discussed from the frequency spectrum.

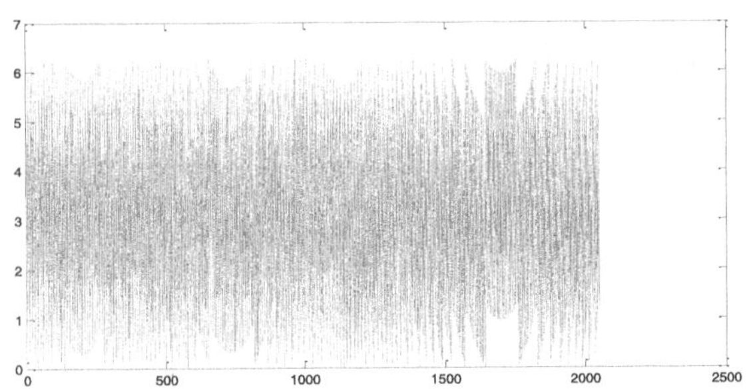

Figure. 4 The change of phase Ψ_i created by FM

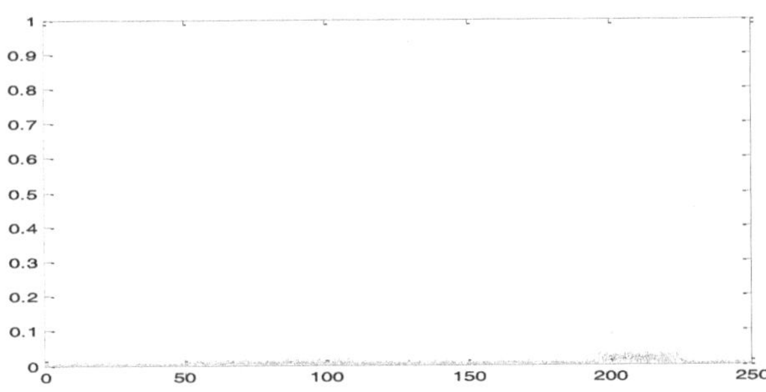

Figure. 5 The structure of Fourier transformation spectrum of phase Ψ_i

Ψ_{Ki} (r) is the phase produced by K_i, that is needed to extract by system. Considered the detection point i, the characteristic face, which the distance from sensor center is r, has N scattering units, which each scattering unit provides a corresponding scattering coefficient.

$$\Gamma_{im}(r) = |\Gamma_{im}(r)| \exp(j\theta_{im}(r)) \quad (23)$$

Where, $\theta_{im}(r)$ is the phase of scattering coefficient of the mth scattering unit. Then, N scattering unit is

$$\Gamma_{i\Sigma}(r) = |\Gamma_{i\Sigma}(r)| \exp(j\theta_{i\Sigma}(r)) = \sum_{m=1}^{N} |\Gamma_{im}(r)| \exp(j\theta_{im}(r)) \quad (24)$$

Sequence $\theta_{i1}(r), \theta_{i2}(r), \theta_{i3}(r), .. \theta_{iN}(r)$ has maximum and minimum value,

$$\theta_{i\min}(r) = \min(\theta_{i1}(r), \theta_{i2}(r), \theta_{i3}(r), .. \theta_{iN}(r)) \quad (25)$$

$$\theta_{i\max}(r) = \max(\theta_{i1}(r), \theta_{i2}(r), \theta_{i3}(r), .. \theta_{iN}(r)) \quad (26)$$

Phases, in $[\theta_{i\min}(r), \theta_{i\max}(r)]$, exist a statistical distribution $D_i(r, \theta)$. That reflects the tissues characteristics of scattering surface which distance from detection point i to detection center is r. From (19),

$$\dot{\kappa}_i(r) = \dot{H}_i(r)\dot{\Gamma}_i(r) \quad (27)$$

Both sides take logarithm,

$$\ln|\dot{\kappa}(r)| = \ln|\dot{H}(r)| + \ln|\dot{\Gamma}(r)| \quad (28)$$

$$\arg\dot{\kappa}(r) = \mathrm{mod}(\arg\dot{H}(r) + \arg\dot{\Gamma}(r), 2\pi) \quad (29)$$

As the logarithm function itself is multi valuedness, (29) actually has a principal value. If $H(r)$ is real function,

$$\arg\dot{\kappa}(r) = \arg\dot{\Gamma}(r) \quad (30)$$

There has:

$$\psi_{Ki}(r) = \theta_{i\Sigma}(r) \quad (31)$$

The variation law of phases, produced by K_i along the radial, represent the variation law of actual scattering phase angle along the radial. Both sides of (31) take Fourier transform for variable r,

$$\Psi_{Ki}(\lambda) = \Theta_{i\Sigma}(\lambda) \quad (32)$$

Where, $\Psi_{Ki}(\lambda)$ corresponds to Fourier transform of $\Psi_{Ki}(r)$, and $\Theta_{i\Sigma}(\lambda)$ corresponds to Fourier transform of $\theta_{i\Sigma}(r)$. Using this variation law along the radial, the phase distribution law can be obtained by joint inversion calculation of multipoint in detection space.

4 Data Processing of BRATUMASS in Practical

Based on analysis more than 50 cancerous breast cases and more than 10 normal breast cases, the Fourier transform $\Theta_{i\Sigma}(\lambda)$ of phase, whose are sampled from cancerous breast, have notable difference in signal characteristics compared with them of normal breast side. The typical results were discussed for clearly explaining these differences. Phase normalized distribution of sampling from three different state of Mammary gland disease condition's research cases (normal, fibromatosis and cancer).

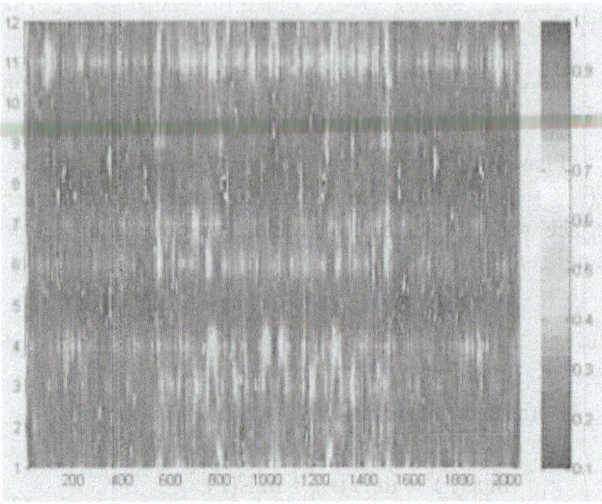

Figure. 6 The contour of phase normalized distribution of normal breast

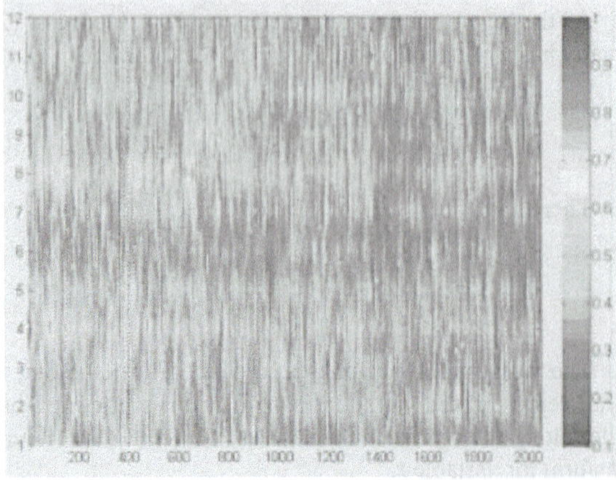

Figure. 7 The contour of phase normalized distribution of normal breast, removed influence of FM

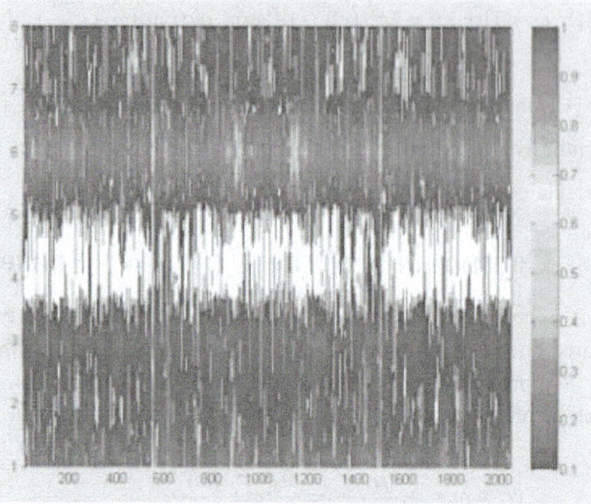

Figure. 8 The contour of phase normalized distribution of malignant breast

In figure 6 - 11, y-coordinate is the ordinal number i of sampling points, x-coordinate is the ordinal number of Fourier transform value, $\Theta_{i\Sigma}(\lambda)$, which can correspond to λ. Contrast phase contours of normal breast data (figure 6), cancerous breast data (figure 8) and fibroma breast data (figure 10), there have significant differences between them. In figure 6, the contour line of normal breast tissue distribute balance, all kinds of tissues distribute relative consistent and no special mighty tissues. Figure 7 shows that contour lines are uniformly distributed, removed the phase influence of frequency modulation. In figure 8, the 4th detection point, which directly faces cancerous tissue, lacks of contour line.

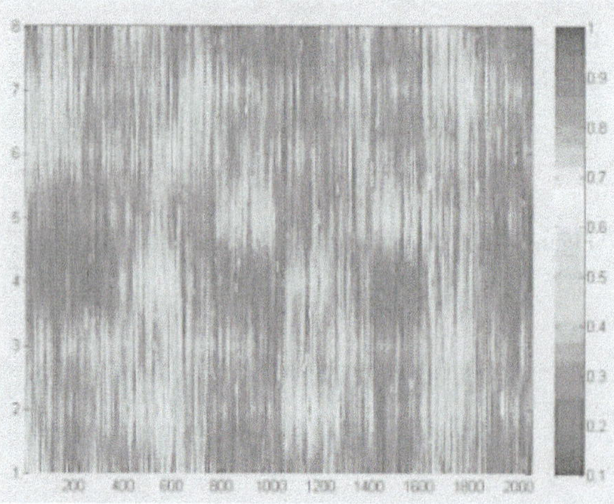

Figure. 9 The contour of phase normalized distribution of malignant breast, removed influence of FM

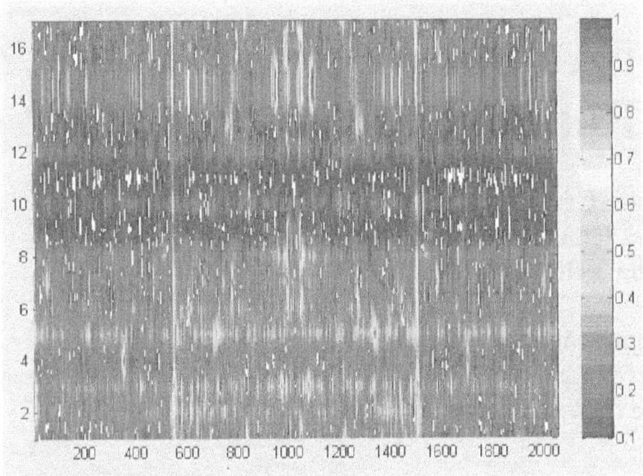

Figure. 10 The contour of phase normalized distribution of fibroma breast

That means, the model of target tissue distribution is prominent and suppresses models of other tissues distribution. Figure 9 indicates that contour lines are gathered round distribution, removed the phase influence of frequency modulation. In figure 10, the distribution of fibroma breast is not serious than cancerous breast, but it also lacks uniformity Figure 9 indicates that contour lines are gathered round distribution, removed the phase influence of frequency modulation. In figure 10, the distribution of fibroma breast is not serious than cancerous breast, but it also lacks uniformity compared to normal breast. Figure 11 demonstrates that the lack of uniformity is obvious, removed the phase influence of frequency modulation.

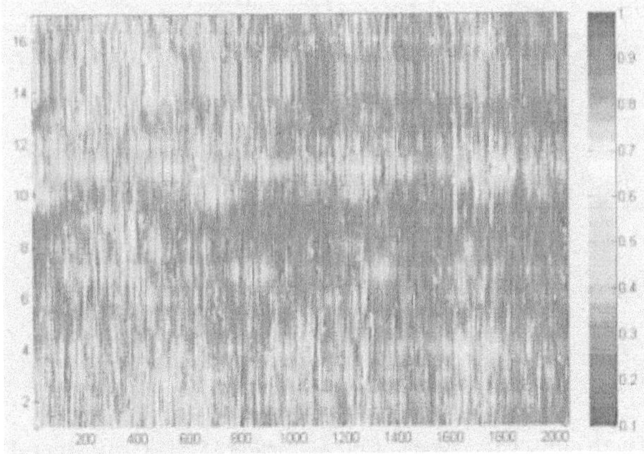

Figure. 11 The contour of phase normalized distribution of fibroma breast, removed influence of FM

5 Results and Discussion

This paper analyzes the relationship between the phase distribution of scattering coefficient of target tissue and system signals, based on the detection principle of BRATUMASS. Consequently, we obtain a result that the Fourier transform of phases of scattering coefficients corresponds to the Fourier transform of phases removed the influence of frequency modulation. Applied to existing practical sampling data (real case data), we find that the laws of phase distribution have great difference in three different state of Mammary gland disease condition ((normal, fibromatosis and cancer). And this difference is connected with variation of imaginary part of tissue complex dielectric constant. At the same time, tissues of cancer and fibroma destroy some kinds of uniformity of normal tissues; these just correspond to the law of phase distribution in BRATUMASS signal processing.

However, there have a few works to be studied in future. a) The form of microwave transmission function H(r) in breast tissues is not definition. In this paper, we assume that it is real function. However, it will be related to circle mapping [4] if it was complex function. This problem need to be further discussed and also need a large number of experimental data to support. b) How much suitable crowd can exactly suit these laws of phase distribution. This problem needs statistical analysis of abundance practical data. c) How to introduce these laws of phase distribution to reconstruction dielectric constant in the later work.

6 Acknowledge

This work has been performed while Prof. Meng Yao was a visiting Professor in Beacon Center, Michigan State University, thanks to a visiting research program from Prof. Erik D. Goodman. M. Yao would also like to acknowledge the support of Shanghai Science and Technology Development Foundation under the project grant numbers 03JC14026 and 08JC1409200, as well as the support of TI Co. Ltd through TI (China) Innovation Foundation. And this work is in part supported by National Science Foundation of China grant number 61002003.

7 References

[1] Zhongling Han et al. "Application of quarter Iteration of FRFT in BRATUMASS for Weak Signal Extraction". Proceedings of The 2011 International conference on Bioinformatics and Computational Biology 2011

[2] Surowiec A J, Stuchly S S, Barr J R and Swarup A. "1988 Dielectric properties of breast carcinoma and the surrounding tissues". IEEE Trans. Biomed. Eng. 35 257–63

[3] Mariya Lazebnik, Leah Mccartney , Dijana Popovic et al. "A large-scale study of the ultrawideband microwave dielectric properties of normal breast tissue obtained from reduction surgeries". Phys. Med. Biol. 52(2007) 2637-2656

R.S Mackay and C.Tresser. "Transition to topological chaos for circle maps". Physics 19D(1986)206-237

A Neuro-Fuzzy Approach for Automatic Detection of Breast Cancer Based on Raman Spectroscopy

Francisco Javier Luna Rosas[1], Julio Cesar Martínez Romo[1], Miguel Mora Gonzalez[2], Ricardo Mendoza Gonzalez[1], Valentín López Rivas[1] Gricelda Medina Veloz[3]

[1] Computer Science Department, Inst. Tec. Aguascalientes, Aguascalientes, México.
[2] Centro Universitario de los Lagos, Universidad de Guadalajara, México
[3]Universidad Tecnológica del Norte de Aguascalientes, México

Abstract – *The harmful presence of cancerous cells in the feminine breast brings as a result, breast cancer, illness that has spread widely lately, not only in Mexico, but in other parts of the planet. In this paper we present a method of automatic Breast cancer classification, in which a Raman signal is classified as coming from a biopsy of healthy tissue (class ω_1) or biopsy of diseased tissue (class ω_2); to do so, we created patterns from Raman spectra accurately measuring each Raman peak to provide naturally reduced data to a classifier; we used Adaptative Neuro-Fuzzy Inference System (ANFIS) classifier and high rates of correct classification were obtained. This provides the specialists with important clinical tools for a rapid and efficient automatic detection of breast cancer. We consider that our approach can be applicable to other kinds of cancer, e.g., lung, prostate, stomach.*

Keywords: ANFIS, Breast Cancer, Raman Spectroscopy, Automatic Detection.

1 Introduction

Cancer is the 10th most common cause of death in the world [2], it is estimated that cancer will kill 83.2 million people in the world before the year 2015. Cancer is associated with the presence of more than one hundred specific related conditions that appear in a cell, the basic unit of life. Cancer takes place when cells begin to grow without any order and without control. When cancer appears, the cells keep on growing and multiplying although new cells are not needed. Generally, the change of a normal cell into a cancerous cell begins with mutations in the DNA in the nucleus of the cell, known as genome. There are many factors that allow the appearance of different types of cancer in women; one of the latter is breast cancer, and it is the most common type of cancer after lung cancer, (10.4 %, considering both sexes) and the fifth cause of death [3]. In adult women, breast cancer is the most common type of death, approximately 16 % [3]. There is a malignant tumor that begins in the bust cells (see Fig 1). This illness appears generally in women, but it is not exclusive, it can also appear in men. The main components of the female breast are lobules connected to the nipple by ducts, fat cells, blood vessels and lymphatic vessels. The function of the lymphatic ganglions is to fight bacteria, cancerous cells and other harmful substances to the organism. When the normal cycle of the cells fails and the new cells keep on growing or the old cells do not die, these cells form a deformed mass called tumor. These abnormal tissues called tumors qualify as benign tumors (are neither cancerous nor spread through the organism) and malignant (are cancerous and put life in danger).

The majority of the types of breast cancer begin in the conduits, in the lobes and in the bordering tissues. The cancerous cells are spread into the lymphatic ganglions next to the breast and to almost any part of the body such as bones, liver, lungs and to the brain itself.

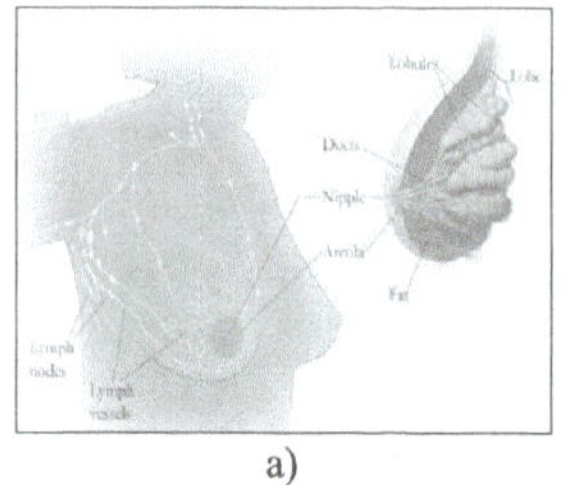

a)

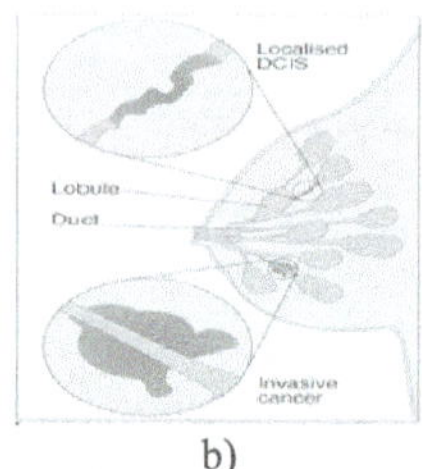

b)

Fig. 1. a) Feminine breast anatomy [1], b) Physical representation of Carcinoma ductal in situ (DCIS) [4]

1.1 Breast cancer types

There are several types of breast cancer [5], [3], [6]. **Ductal carcinoma in situ (DCIS)** is the most common type of non-invasive breast cancer where the cells of the ducts turn themselves into cancerous cells, (see fig. 1 b), and this is the first clinical diagnosis of breast cancer. **Lobular carcinoma in situ (LCIS):** [7], [8], begins in the milk-making glands but does not go through the wall of the lobules, (see Fig. 2a); although this is not a true cancer, having LCIS increases a woman's risk of developing cancer later. When the carcinogenic cells acquire the ability of penetrating membranes, the cancer is named **Invasive ductal carcinoma (IDC),** (see Fig. 2b), and it can have access to the blood and the nodules; it means a potential spread to different organs of the body, for this reason, it is the most common type of invasive breast cancer. Another kind is **Invasive lobular carcinoma (ILC),** the tumor grows in the lobes of the breast and it can spread to other parts of the body too, generally, it does not appear in the screening analysis and it is only detected in the physical explorations.

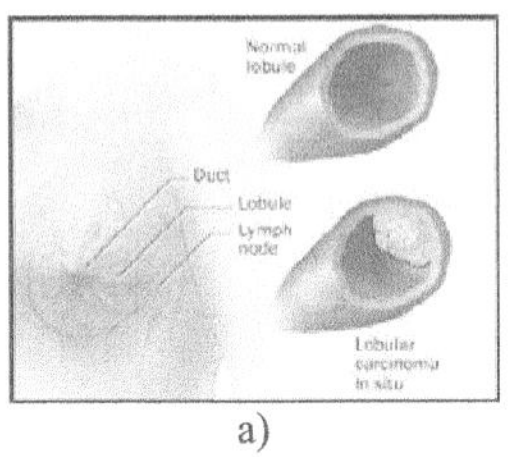

a)

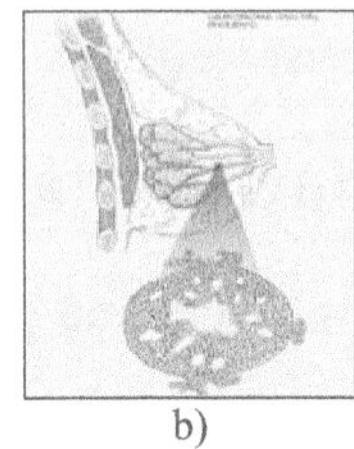
b)

Fig. 2. a) Physical representation of Lobular carcinoma in situ (LCIS) [9]. b) Physical representation of Invasive Ductual carcinoma zone (IDC) [10]

Other less common types of breast cancer that exist are: Inflammatory breast cancer (IBC), Fundamental Carcinoma, Illness of Paget of the nipple, Phyllodes Tumor and Tubular Carcinoma.

1.2 Physical examinations and screening

Early detection of breast cancer significantly reduces the risk of death. Tumors are found by physical examinations, by health professionals or by screening. Screening refers to checking for disease when there are no symptoms. Some screening tests and the current methods do not distinguish between a benign tumor and the malignant one, and for this reason they can be used to detect only suspicious injuries and not for diagnosis (to differentiate between a malignant or benign tumor at present specialized analyses through a biopsy are needed). Some tests are commonly used to screen for breast cancer, in this section some methods are mentoned. a) Breast self-exam (BSE) [12] and b) Clinical breast exam (CBE) [12] are exams made by the woman herself and by a health professional respectively, looking for lumps or anything else that seems unusual, c) Mammogram [11], [13] is an x-ray of the breast, it may find ductal carcinoma in situ (DCI), in symptomatic and asymptomatic women. d) Breast ultrasound [14] shows whether a lump is solid or fluid-filled. e) Magnetic Resonance Imaging (MRI) or (NMRI) [15], [16] a computer makes detailed pictures inside the breast area that show the difference between normal and diseased tissue.

1.3 Diagnosis

When the previous methods show abnormalities in the breast, some studies (tests) are made in tissues or blood samples to find whether the cells are cancerous. One of them is Breast biopsy or Tissue sampling (TS), [17], [18] where cells from breast tissue are examined under a microscope by a pathologist. With the purpose of limiting to the minimum the error of appreciation by the technician, alternative techniques of clinical diagnosis of breast cancer must be implemented. The use of optical diagnosis as the spectroscopy Raman [19] to provide additional information and to reinforce the diagnosis about the suspicious injury is an example. In recent years, several spectroscopic techniques such as Raman, Infrared and fluorescent have been used to examine tissues. Spectroscopy Raman (SR) uses beam laser that does not damage the cells of the tissue, but it provides information about its components [20], [21]; such is the case of cancerous tissues of breast [22], [23].

1.4 Raman Spectroscopy

The Raman Effect was described by Ch. V. Raman in 1982 [24]. The Raman spectroscopy analysis is a high-resolution technique that is based on the examination of the light dispersed by a material when affecting a monochrome beam of light; this provides chemical and structural information. Most of the dispersed light presents the same frequency that the incident light but a very small fraction displays a frequential change, result of the interaction of the light with the matter [24], [25]. The dispersed light that presents frequencies different from the incident radiation is that which provides information on the molecular composition of the sample (known as Raman dispersion).

1.5 Raman Spectroscopy and Breast Cancer

*Cancer Detection.*Various Raman spectroscopic studies on cancers have been reported, [26] and here we review one of the three most common cancers: breast cancer, the other two carcinomas (colorectal cancer and cervical cancer), are beyond the scope of this paper.

Breast Cancer. Breast cancer had the highest rate of occurrence in the United States among the female population in 2010 [26]. Numerous studies have investigated the application of Raman spectroscopy on the detection of normal, precancerous and cancerous breast tissues. For instance, Haka [27] and colleagues have demonstrated the ability of Raman spectroscopy to distinguish between normal, benign, and malignant lesions of breast ex vivo, with a sensitivity of 94% and a specificity of 96%. Tissues in four pathological conditions were examined and classified, including normal, fibrocystic change, fibroadenoma, and infiltrating carcinoma. Raman spectra of breast tissues were fitted to those of individual breast tissue components including fat, collagen, cell nucleus, epithelial cell cytoplasm, calcium oxalate, calcium hydroxyapatite, cholesterol-like lipid deposits, and β-carotene. Instead of examining breast tissues directly, Pichardo-Molina's group [28] studied serum samples from breast cancer patients and demonstrated the use of Raman spectroscopy for minimally invasive diagnostics. Seven Raman band ratios were used for classification, and spectral differences were observed between serum samples of breast cancer patients and normal healthy subjects. Using principal component analysis (PCA) and linear discriminant analysis (LDA), the sensitivity and specificity were reported to be 97% and 78%, respectively. However, the underlying molecular mechanism of these differences was not reported. Raman spectroscopic imaging technique has gained popularity recently in cancer research. Raman spectroscopic imaging is capable of visualizing the samples without extrinsic labeling, thus minimizing sample perturbation. In addition, the much-needed chemical and structural information about the sample are provided by Raman spectral analysis. Mariani and coworkers have applied Raman imaging to the detection of nuclear membrane lipid fluctuations in senescent epithelial breast cancer cells [28]. In this study, Raman images were composed based on the Raman peak intensity of CH-stretching. Another example is the proposed Abramczyk [30], in their study presents the most reliable statistical analysis based on Raman spectroscopy, data of normal breast tissue, benign and cancerous of 146 patients were found. In his article presents the first Raman optical biopsy images (RI) from normal and cancerous breast tissues from the same patient. The results presented demonstrate the ability of Raman spectroscopy to characterize exactly types of tissue (non-cancerous) or cancerous. The results provide evidence that the composition of lipids and carotenes differ significantly from non-cancerous and cancerous breast tissue that should be a key factor in the mechanisms that detect cancer.

Analysis methods. Raman spectra obtained from biological samples often contain significant amounts of fluorescence background. As Raman spectral differences between normal and diseased tissues are generally subtle, effective data-processing algorithms are often required for data analysis and interpretation.

Fluorescence background removal. As mentioned above, Raman spectra collected from tissues are composed mainly of Raman scattering and intrinsic tissue fluorescence. To eliminate the fluorescence background, a polynomial function that fits to the fluorescence profile is usually subtracted from the Raman spectra [31]. Although there is no consensus on the optimal order of the polynomial function, fourth- and fifth-order polynomials are most commonly employed [31].

Multivariate data analysis. Raman spectra contain various overlapping Raman bands. As a result, it is difficult to visually inspect and interpret the spectral data. Multivariate spectral analysis methods are often used to process the Raman spectra and facilitate data interpretation. Spectral analysis methods are generally categorized as either supervised or unsupervised. For unsupervised analyses, such as cluster analysis and PCA [28], no a priori knowledge of class characteristics is required but is to be determined from the analysis itself. In contrast, in a supervised analysis the number of classes and representative samples of each class are known a priori, as is the case in LDA [28], regression analysis, and artificial neural networks (ANNs).

2 Experimental methods

2.1 Subjects and protocol

Raw Raman spectra (Raman scattering plus background fluorescence) were provided to us by the Research Center in Optics (CIO, Centro de Investigaciones en Óptica, A.C.), and were taken from samples of cancerous and healthy breast tissue provided by the Cancer Institute of Jalisco, México; the samples were obtained by excisional biopsy of patients diagnosed with infiltrating ductal cancer and preserved in formalin; in order to obtain the Raman spectra, histological cuts were made on the samples. The Raman spectra were obtained using a Raman Renishaw system model 1000-B; this system uses a laser diode of λ = 830 nm and a grating of 600 lines mm-1. The laser was focused on the samples with a Leica microscope model DMLM (objective of 50x), at approximately 35mW of power. Each spectrum was collected in the region from 680 to 1780 cm-1, with an exposition time of 10s. Finally, the wavenumber resolution was of 2 cm-1 and the Raman system was calibrated with a silicon semiconductor at the Raman peak in 520 cm-1. With this experimental setup 100 Raman spectra were recorded from healthy and diseased tissue zones of the biopsies. For fluorescence removal, in this work, we adopted the Vancouver Raman Algorithm (VRA) [37], because it avoids the possible oscillations at the extreme points of the spectrum that other algorithms insert to the corrected Raman spectrum.

3 Results and Discussion

3.1 Highlighting Differences Raman Spectrum of Healthy Tissue Vs. Raman Spectrum of Damaged Tissue

In this section we present the results of Raman studies on normal breast tissue (noncancerous) and damaged (cancerous). Previous publications [30], [28], [33] have demonstrated that the Raman spectrum of normal breast tissue are dominated by lipids and carotenes. Healthy tissue spectrum show peaks in the bands 1004, 1080, 1158, 1259, 1266, 1304, 1444, 1518, 1660, 1750 and damaged tissue (cancerous tumors, invasive ductal carcinoma) gets less peak intensity. Fig. 3 compares a Raman spectrum of healthy and damaged breast tissue from the same patient. The most notorious differences can be observed in the regions of the bands 1158 and 1518 cm-1 assigned to carotenoids [30] and the regions of the bands 1444, 1660, 1750 cm-1that have been assigned to the lipids. A detailed inspection in Fig. 3 demonstrates that the Raman bands of the carotenoids are strong in healthy tissue while in damaged tissues they are not seen. Raman intensities of the peaks of lipids are significantly smaller in damaged tissue than in healthy tissue (bands 1444, 1750, 1259.1080) [30].

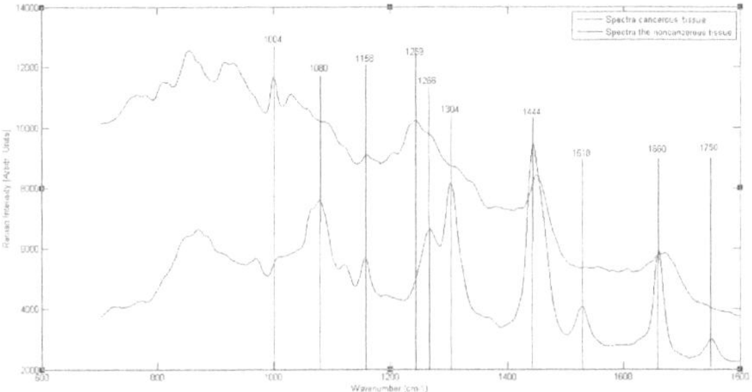

Fig. 3. Raman Spectrum of Normal and Damaged Breast Tissue (Invasive Ductal Carcinoma) of the Same Patient.

3.2 Analysis of Components Multivariate

Recently, multivariate methods have been applied to Raman spectroscopy to classify breast cancer tissue, noncancerous and cancerous. In Particular way the principal component analysis (PCA) has been used to differentiate healthy and damaged tissue [34].

Table 1. Feature Vectors for 86 Raman Spectrum Healthy and Damaged Breast Tissue.

Raman Scatter Region									
Region(Wavenumber in cm^{-1})									
1750	1660	1518	1444	1304	1266	1259	1158	1080	1004
0	1027.9	0	2011.2	0	0	469	0	0	403
0	782.1	0	1704	0	0	447	0	0	251
0	1597	0	3020	0	0	1154	0	0	1193
...	...	...	...	...	...	...	...	...	...
...	...	...	...	...	...	...	...	...	...
0	2408	0	4551	0	0	2171	0	0	1398
0	3070	0	5205	0	0	2004	0	0	1535

PCA is a multivariate technique that acts in an unsupervised manner, and is used to analyze the inherent structure of the data. PCA reduces the dimensionality of the data set to obtain an alternative set of coordenates: principal components (PCs). PCs are linear combinations of original variables which are orthogonal and are designed so that each one has the maximum variability in the data set [28].
As each of the spectrum contains a large amount of information we needed PCA help to extract important features or components. In PCA method each Raman spectrum is represented as a vector of intensity values of each wavelength. To make the multivariate component analysis (PCA), we obtained the Raman peak intensities of both healthy tissue and damaged tissue of the same patient´s biopsy. 86 vectors were formed with a features length (λ = 10), each feature is based on peaks intensity of the of their respective wave number (cm-1) as shown in Table 1. Once the feature vectors extracted from the 86 spectra based on Raman peak Intensities, we proceeded to a dimensions reduction, on which feature vectors that describe to Raman spectrum of healthy breast tissue as well as tissue damaged breast (Table 2).

Table 2. Principal Component Analysis in Three Dimensions.

Spectrum	pc1	pc2	pc3
1	523	-425	131
2	1223	-602	290
3	2137	-877	295
...	...	...	...
...	...	...	...
85	-1028	-503	3
86	-1053	-448	17

Fig 4 shows the new feature vectors distribution of Raman spectrum in the 86 tri-dimensional space in the first 3 principal components obtained from different parts of a breast cancer biopsy.

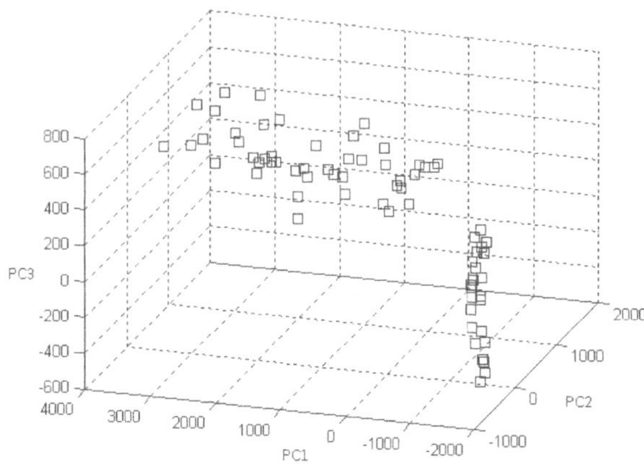

Fig. 4. PCA in Three Dimensions Retrieved from the Intensities of the Peaks Detected in Raman Spectrum 86.

3.3 Algorithm K-Means Clustering

Generally, PCA analysis by itself does not provide the meaning answer that each PCA component have, because the PCA does not group (Clustering) only reduces dimensions K-means is a clustering algorithm, which is an easy way to divide a given database in k groups (determined a priori).The main idea is to define k centroids (one for each group of the database and place them in the type of its nearest centroid. Next step is to recalculate the centroid of each group and redistribute all items according to the nearest centroid. The process is repeated until there are no changes in the groups from one step to the next. Detailed inspection of the algorithm can be observed in [35]. We apply the K-means algorithm to find the distribution of two kinds in our case these two kinds will be healthy breast tissue and damage breast tissue. For convenience each kind will be expressed as ω_1 and ω_2 respectively.

ω_1 = Healthy breast tissue.
ω_2 = Damaged breast tissue.

The K-means algorithm after 10 iterations grouped 44 feature vectors type ω_1 and 42 in ω_2 (Table 3). In the first column of Table 3 it´s shown the type to which belongs each feature vector of the Raman spectrum of healthy and damaged tissue.

Table 3. Structure for Feature Vectors

Class	Vector	Spectrum	pc1	pc2	pc3
ω_1	1	82	-1025	489	85
ω_1	2	83	-1074	815	30
ω_1	3	84	-1081	827	46
...	...	...	...	...	
...	...	...	...	...	...
ω_1	43	85	-1028	503	3
ω_1	44	86	-1053	448	17
ω_2	45	1	523	-425	131
ω_2	46	2	1223	-602	290
ω_2	47	3	2137	-877	295
...	...	...	...	...	...
...	...	...	...	...	...
ω_2	85	85	-1028	-503	3
ω_2	86	86	-1053	-448	17

The distribution of both types is shown in Fig. 5, as we can see in Fig. 5, the examples are from one of two distinctive groups, the left and right circles are separated according to healthy and damaged tissue. The left side circle exclusively represents normal breast tissue. The right circle represents damaged tissue.

Once the data is clustered the 86 Raman spectra are verified, Raman spectrum of normal breast tissue can be observed in Fig. 6 (a) and Raman spectrum of damage breast tissue can be seen in Fig. 6 (b).

Fig. 6 (a) and (b) clearly show many marked differences in the Raman spectrum of healthy and damaged tissue. The peaks of the Raman bands 1004, 1080, 1158, 1259, 1266, 1304, 1444, 1518, 1660, 1750 that have been assigned to lipids and carotenes are significantly different in healthy and damaged breast tissue.

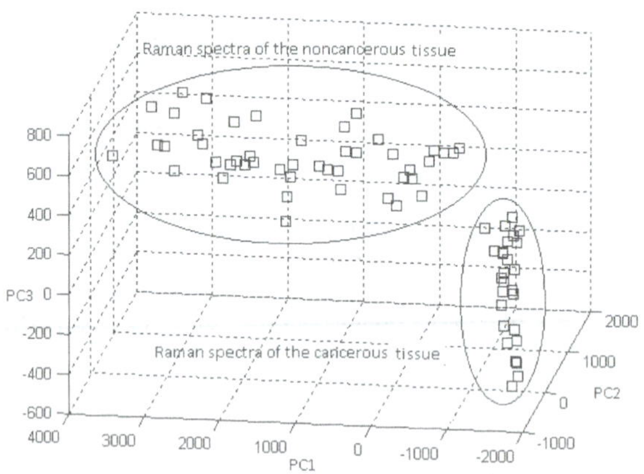

Fig. 5. Grouping of 86 Raman Spectrum with Healthy Breast Tissue (Left Side) and Breast Tissue with Invasive Ductal Carcinoma (Right Side).

As there are many marked differences in the Raman spectra of healthy and damaged breast tissue we considerate a Neuro-diffuse classifier (ANFIS).

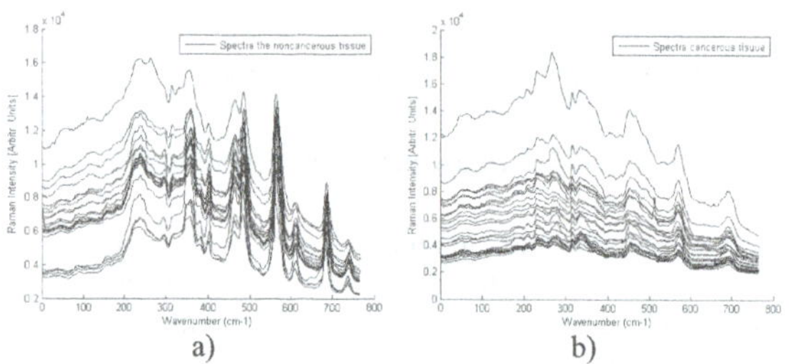

a) b)

Fig. 6. Raman Spectra of Healthy and Damage Breast Tissue Result of the Clustering Algorithm K-means Type.

As there are many marked differences in the Raman spectra of healthy and damaged breast tissue we considerate a Neuro-diffuse classifier (ANFIS).

3.4 ANFIS Architecture

Adaptative Neuro Fuzzy Inference System (ANFIS) is an architecture that is functionally equivalent to diffuse inferential systems (fuzzy), that is to say, is equivalent to the type of diffuse rules base of Takagi and Sugeno [36]. In the next section you will see results of ANFIS obtained from the evaluation of the 45 feature vectors of healthy tissue Raman spectra in Class ω_1 and 45 vectors of damaged tissue spectra associated with the class ω_2, using the technique of cross-validations. To evaluate the correct classification percentage it was performed the following confusion matrix:

Table 4. Confusion Matrix.

Class	ω_1	ω_2
ω_1	$VN_{(1,1)}$	$FP_{(1,2)}$
ω_2	$FN_{(2,1)}$	$VP_{(2,2)}$

Where:

TN (True Negative). The disease is not present and diagnosed as healthy.
FP (False Positive). The disease is not present and it´s diagnosed ill.
FN (False Negative). The disease is present but not detected.
TP (True Positive). The disease is present and detected.

Considering the confusion matrix previously described we can assess the *sensitivity* of our classifier to detect positive case of ill patients (percentage of patients correctly identified) and *specificity* that indicates the ability of our classifier to give as negative cases really healthy cases (percentage of correctly identified healthy patients).

$$Sensibilidad = \frac{VP}{VP + FN} * 100 \tag{1}$$

$$Especificidad = \frac{VN}{VN + FP} * 100 \tag{2}$$

The ANFIS classifier was evaluated with the membership functions Triangular, Trapezoidal, Gaussian and Bell. Having each one 10, 100 and 250 training epochs while fixing a threshold for classification. Table 5 shows the sensitivity and specificity of ANFIS classifier using the membership functions mentioned above.

Table 5. Sensitivity, Specificity and Predictive Accuracy Through ANFIS.

Membership Fuctions	Errors (case 18 bands + ANFIS)		Sensitivity	Specificity
	Healthy as cáncer(FP)	Cancer as healthy(FN)		
Triangular Membership	0/45	1/45	100%	97.77%
Trapezoid Membership	1/45	1/45	97.77%	97.77%
Gaussian Membership	1/45	2/45	97.77%	95.55%
Bell-shape Membership.	2/45	1/45	95.55%	97.77%

Fig. 7 shows the ANFIS classifier with a triangular membership function and 100 training epochs, in the figure we can observe that the classifier achieved a sensitivity of 100% and a specificity of 97.77%, with a classification error of 0% False Negatives (FN) and 2.23% for False Positives (FP).

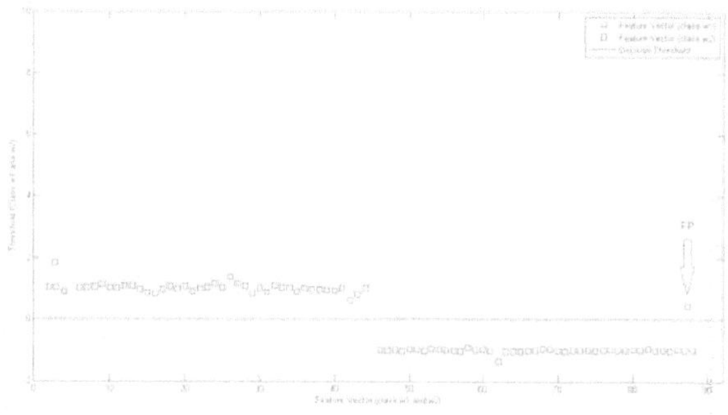

Fig. 7. Decision Threshold ANFIS with Triangular Membership Function 100 Epochs.

4. Conclusions

In this article we present a method for the automated detection of breast cancer in which a Raman signal is classified as healthy tissue biopsy (class ω_1) and damage tissue (type ω_2). An important aspect is the characteristic generating, using PCA, in the PCA method each Raman spectrum was represented as a vector of values of intensity for each wavelength, that represent Raman peaks both healthy tissue and damaged tissue. PCA analysis by itself does not provide the answer meaning that each component PCA have, as the PCA does not group (Clustering) only reduces the dimensions. We apply the K-means algorithm to find the distribution of two types, in our case these two types were damaged tissue and healthy tissue. For convenience each type was expressed as ω_1 and ω_2 respectively, after detecting types we tried a Neuro-diffuse classifier (ANFIS) and high correct classification rates were obtained.

5. References

[1] This National Cancer Institute (NCI) booklet (NIH Publication No. 05-1556). National Cancer Institute. (www.cancer.gov).
[2] An update of the global burden of disease in 2004. Geneva, World Health Organization (forthcoming).
[3] World Health Statistics, 2008. World Health Organization 2008. ISBN 978 92 4 156359 8.
[4] Ernster VL, Ballard-Barbash R, Barlow WE, et al (Oct 2002). "Detection of ductal carcinoma in situ in

women undergoing screening mammography". J Natl Cancer Inst 94 (20): 1546–54.

[5] Breast Cancer document. Technical Report. American Cancer Society. (www.cancer.org).

[6] Tumours of the breast and female genital organs, WHO. Classification of tumours, 2003.

[7] Foote FW, Stewart FW. Lobular carcinoma in situ: a rare form of mammary cancer. Am J Pathol1941; 17:491-496.

[8] Hutter RVP, Foote FW. Lobular carcinoma in situ. Long term follow-up. Cancer. 1969; 24, 1081.

[9] Causes of Lobular Carcinoma in situ. Mayo Foundation for Medical Education and Research (MFMER). Technical Report. (MayoClinic.com)

[10] Tests for Diagnosing IDC. www.breastcancer.org

[11] Breast cancer screening. Lyon, International Agency for Research on Cancer, 2002 (Handbooks on Cancer Prevention, Vol. 10)

[12] International Agency for Research on Cancer IARC. Technical Report. (screening.iarc.fr/)

[13] National Cancer Institute. Breast Cancer: Screening and Testing. Bethesda, MD: National Cancer Institute. Accessed: 25 September 2008. (www.cancer.gov)

[14] Wilson ARM. Ultrasound guidance boosts biopsy outcome. Diagnostic Imaging Europe: 40-45 & 50, December 1999.

[15] Lauterbur, P.C. (1973). "Image Formation by Induced Local Interactions: Examples of Employing Nuclear Magnetic Resonance". Nature 242: 190-191.

[16] Gould, RT-(R)(MR)(ARRT), Todd A. "How MRI Works." 01 April 2000. HowStuffWorks.com. (www.health.howstuffworks.com)

[17] Abeloff MD, Armitage JO, Niederhuber JE, Kastan MB, McKena WG. Clinical Oncology. 3rd ed. Orlando, Fl: Churchill Livingstone; 2004

[18] Whitman GJ. Ultrasound-guided breast biopsies. Ultrasound Clin. Dec 2006; 1(4); 603-615.

[19] K. E. Shafer-Peltier, A. S. Haka, M. Fitzmaurice, J. Crowe, J. Myles, R. R. Dasari, M. S. Feld, J. Raman Spectrosc. 33 (2002) 552.

[20] Parker FS (1983) Applications of infrared Raman, and resonance Raman spectroscopy in biochemistry. Plenum, New York.

[21] Das K, Stone N, Kendall C, Fowler C, Christie-Brown J. (2006) Raman spectroscopy of parathyroid tissue pathology. Lasers Med Sci 21(4):192–197

[22] Alfano RR, Liu CH et al (1991) Human breast tissue studied by IR Fourier transform Raman spectroscopy. Lasers in Life Sci 4:23–28

[23] Pichardo-Molina, et all. Raman spectroscopy and multivariate analysis of serum samples from breast cancer patients. (2006) Lasers Med Sci. DOI 10.1007/s10103-006-0432-8., Springer-Verlag.

[24] Raman, C. V., Nature, 108, 367, 1921

[25] C. V. Raman, K.S. Krishnan, A new type of Secondary Radiation, Nature, 121, 619, 1928.

[26] Qiang Tu, MS, Chang Chang. Diagnostic applications of Raman spectroscopy. Nanomedicine: Nanotechnology, Biology, and Medicine 8 (2012) 545–558.

[27] Haka AS, Shafer-Peltier KE, Fitzmaurice M, Crowe J, Dasari RR, Feld MS. Diagnosing breast cancer by using Raman spectroscopy. Proc Natl Acad Sci U S A 2005;102:12371-6.

[28] Pichardo-Molina JL, Frausto-Reyes C, Barbosa-Garcia O, Huerta-Franco R, Gonzalez-Trujillo JL, Ramirez-Alvarado CA, et al. Raman spectroscopy and multivariate analysis of serum samples from breast cancer patients. Lasers Med Sci 2007;22:229-36.

[29] Mariani MM, Maccoux LJ, Matthaus C, Diem M, Hengstler JG, Deckert V. Micro-Raman detection of nuclear membrane lipid fluctuations insenescent epithelial breast cancer cells. Anal Chem 2010;82:4259-63.

[30] Abramczyk Halina, Beata Brozek-Pluska, Jakub Surmacki, Joanna Jablonska-Gajewicz, Radzislaw Kordek. Raman 'optical biopsy' of human breast cancer. Progress in Biophysics and Molecular Biology. 108(2012) 74-81.

[31] Tu Q, Eisen J, Chang C. Surface-enhanced Raman spectroscopy study of indolic molecules adsorbed on gold colloids. J Biomed Opt 2010;020512:15.

[32] Robichaux-Viehoever A, Kanter E, Shappell H, Billheimer D, Jones III H, Mahadevan-Jansen A. Characterization of Raman spectra measured in vivo for the detection of cervical dysplasia. Appl Spectrosc 2007;61:986-93.

[33] B. Brożek-Płuska, I. Placek, K. Kurczewski, Z. Morawiec, M. Tazbir, H. Abramczyk. Breast cancer diagnostics by Raman spectroscopy, Journal of Molecular Liquids 141 (2008) 145–148

[34] H. Abramczyk, J. Surmacki, B. Bro_zek-Płuska Z. Morawiec M. Tazbir. The hallmarks of breast cancer by Raman spectroscopy, Journal of Molecular Structure 924–926 (2009) 175–182.

[35] K. Koutroumbas y S. Theodoridis, Pattern Recognition, 1st ed. California, E. U. A.: Academic Press, 1999.

[36] Roger, J.S., 1997. Neuro-fuzzy and Soft Computing. Prentice Hall. Nj, USA. ISBN 0-13-261066-3.

[37] J. Zhao, H. Lui, D. I. McLean, y H. Zeng, "Automated autofluorescence background subtraction algorithm for biomedical Raman spectroscopy", *Applied Spectroscopy*, vol. 61, no. 11, p. 1225–1232, 2007.

Constructing a Cloud-based ADHD Screening System: a Perspective of Norm Development

Kuo-Chung Chu*, **Lun-Ping Hung, and Chien-Fu Tseng**
Department of Information Management
National Taipei University of Nursing and Health Sciences
*e-mail: kcchu@ntunhs.edu.tw

Abstract - *Attention deficit hyperactivity disorder (ADHD) is a popular child psychiatry disorder; the main symptoms are inattention, unable to suppress their impulsive behavior and restlessness of the situation. Previous studies had revealed that the prevalence of ADHD in school-age is about 5-12%. Without early diagnosis and treatment, it may cause cognitive dysfunction, low academic achievement, frustration, loss of self-esteem and self-confidence, sleep disorder, deviant behavior, and so on. Theoretically, screening criteria should be different because of world areas vary. However, in Taiwan, the existing screening systems are imported and referred to European and American norm. As the reference to non-Asian norm, screening results are not fully consistent with the situation in Taiwan. Therefore, this paper proposes a cloud-based ADHD screening system, which not only can screen ADHD symptoms, but also builds a domestic ADHD norm. The proposed system will help to accurately assess symptoms. To validate the system, we jointly discuss sensitivity and specificity to maximize the system feasibility of clinical diagnosis.*

Keywords: ADHD; ADHD Norm; Cloud computing; Model development; System implementation; Screening system;

1 Introduction

If the children behave themselves improperly, they may be suffering from attention deficit hyperactivity disorder instead of deliberately naughty. Attention-deficit/hyperactivity disorder (ADHD) is a common childhood behavioral disorder; it causes inattention and will be easily fatigue. The ADHD children have significant difficulties with inattentive, hyperactive, or impulsive behaviors; they are often regarded as unruly child. Inattention and hyperactivity problems may persist over time, and there are potential risks for additional difficulties, including conduct disorders, peer relationship difficulties, educational problems and underachievement, employment problems, a lack of involvement in social activities, suicidal behaviors, and criminality [1, 2] [3]. Past studies have shown that the prevalence of ADHD, regardless of race, gender showed significant trend, ranging from 0.9% to 12% [4] [5]. Generally believed, this symptom is common in men, prevalence will vary because of the different races.

American Psychiatric Association (APA) reported that the prevalence of ADHD is 3~5% for pre-school children [6]. Naivety ADHD Taiwan association [7] estimated the prevalence is 5~7% in Taiwan, there are 2~4 ADHD students in a classroom. However, only less than 25% of children with ADHD have used specialist health services or been clinically diagnosed. Clinical diagnosis of ADHD is based on the Diagnostic and Statistical Manual of Mental Disorders (DSM-IV-TR). Attention deficit (hyperactivity disorder) symptoms can be categorized into three types: (1) compound: inattention, hyperactivity, impulsivity symptoms; (2) attention deficit (ADD): only single symptoms of inattention; (3) hyperactive/impulsive: symptoms of hyperactivity and impulsivity. ADHD diagnosis is quite complicated process several dimensions, including (1) DSM-IV-TR diagnostic criteria; (2) differential diagnosis; (3) rating scale (questionnaire); (4) objective assessment (computer system testing); (5) scenario discussion.

A joint expert team in which psychiatrist, professional clinical psychologist, special education, and pathology are involved conducts diagnosis and assessment. General diagnostics indicators, teachers scale and parents Scale, are provided by the APA DSM-IV to screen ADHD symptoms. The scales quickly help understanding of the children situation in the early stage. Associated scales are: Child Behavior Checklist (CBCL) and Teacher Report Form (TRF), Conner's Parent Rating Scale-Revised: Short Form (CPRS-R: S), Conner's Teacher Rating Scale-Revised: Short Form (CTRS-R: S), and SNAP-IV scale. By observing and determining performance of the patients in the school and the family is to assess whether they have the potential factors of ADHD. In the case of limited medical resources, after preliminary screening, the physician will further use of computer systems as a diagnostic tool.

CBCL is used in the evaluation of children with epilepsy and ADHD assessment, psychiatrists make use of the CBCL scale screening following symptoms, including social communication, physical factors, depression, childish, immature, schizophrenia, offensive, illegal, obesity, hyperactivity, adverse social, compulsion, cruelty, hostility, and anxiety.

Test of Variables of Attention (TOVA), an objective method for diagnosis of ADHD patients and therapeutic, is a diagnosis-supported computer system to assess attention efficacy of children and adults. TOVA Studies accurately identified 87% of the normal population, 84% of the non-hyperactive ADHD patients, and 90% of the hyperactive patients. The general clinical diagnosis is based on experience, interviews, behavioral score and symptom checklist, to comprehensive diagnosis and treatment of ADHD [8]. Continuous Performance Tests (CPT), another quick and effective screening tool for assessing inattention, is widely used in research and clinical assessment of ADHD subjects over the age of 6. The CPT indicators include inattention, impulsiveness, and vigilance difficult problems [9].

In existing diagnosis computer systems, most of them are exported from European and American (E-A), ADHD norm (reference database) could not fit for world-wide ADHD assessment because the clinical diagnostic criteria may be different in the different areas. Due to the limitation of non-Asian norm database, the diagnosis results are not fully consistent with the real situation. A possible case is that the criteria (ADHD norm) used in European-American area could be too low to differentiate the Asian patients; it leads to inaccurate assessment, Fig. 1. On the other hand, there are less data collected from domestic (Taiwan) patients, we need an ADHD norm to be a standard criteria for domestic diagnosis. This paper proposes a cloud-based diagnosis-supported ADHD (DS-ADHD) system which not only can screen ADHD symptoms, but also builds domestic ADHD norm.

The rest of this paper is organized as follows: section 2 gives methodology of constructing the cloud-based DS-ADHD system and section 3 shows the system validation approach. We conclude the paper in section 4 with remarks on future work.

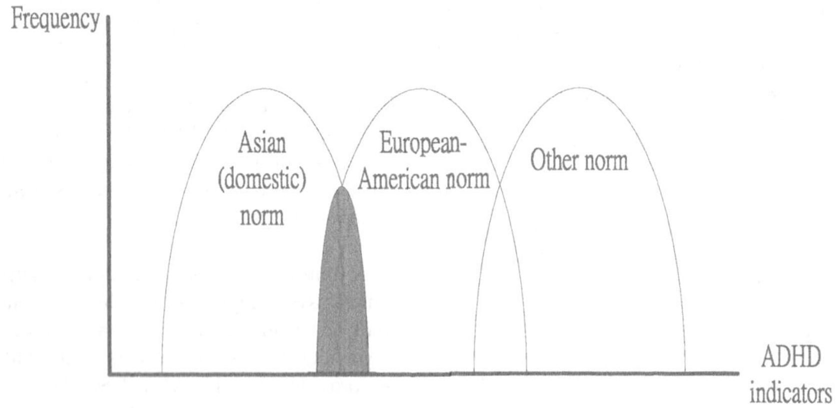

Fig. 1 The diagnosis difference of varied Norm

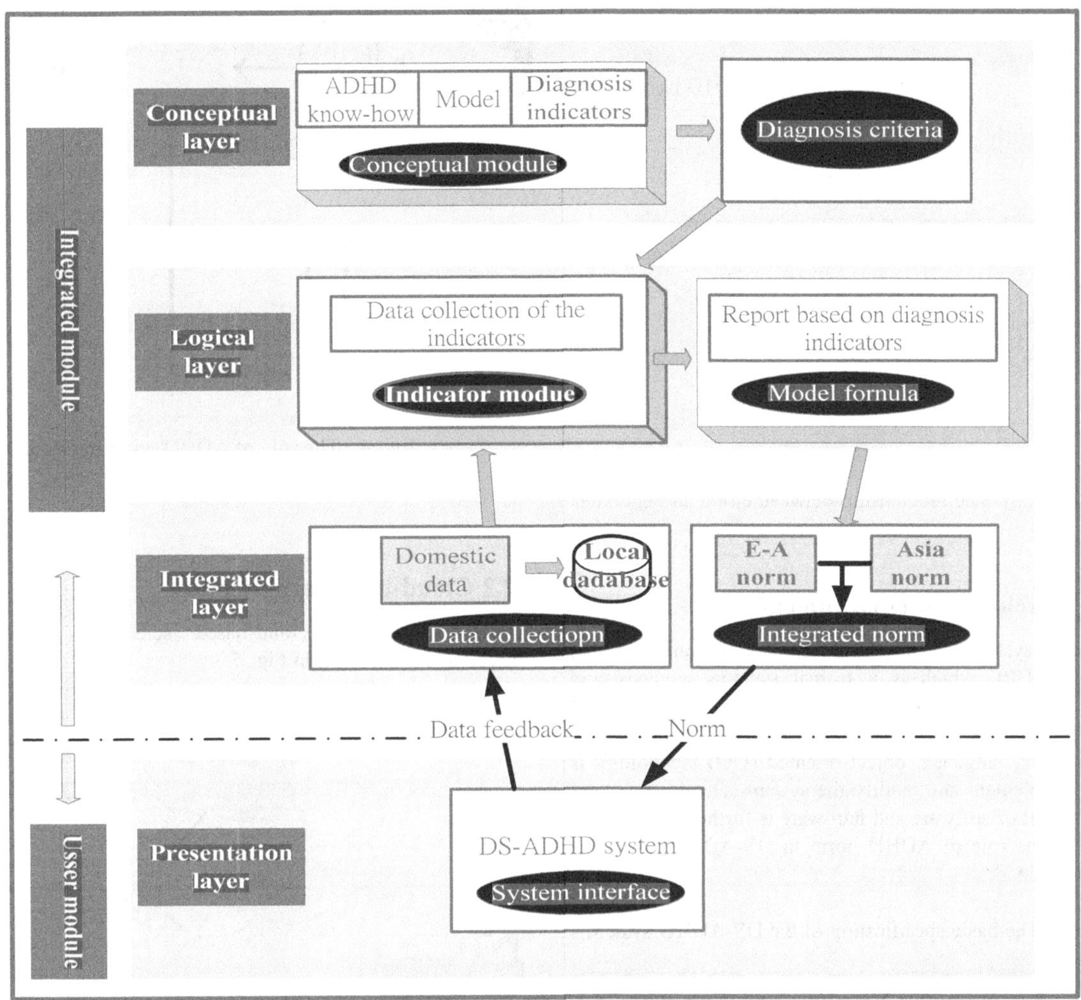

Fig. 2 Framework of DS-ADHD system

2 Methodology

2.1 ADHD system framework

The DS-ADHD system framework consists of four layers, Fig. 2:

- Conceptual layer: the conceptual mod el of the system. Based on literature survey and expert knowledge, we create screening standards (model indicators).
- Logical layer: using the indicators to build the system. Data collected from several end sites (hospitals) will be computed to generate indicators.
- Integrated layer: a local database is to collect diagnosis data, while integrated ADHD norm is a database to be compared with the diagnosis data. The integrated norm has two parts: 1) existing European-American norm; 2) domestic norm: a cloud-based norm (cloud site), which is periodically updated according to the local database. The relationship between cloud- and end- site is depicted in Fig. 3.
- Presentation layer: an operation interface of clinical diagnosis to collect data of ADHD patients.

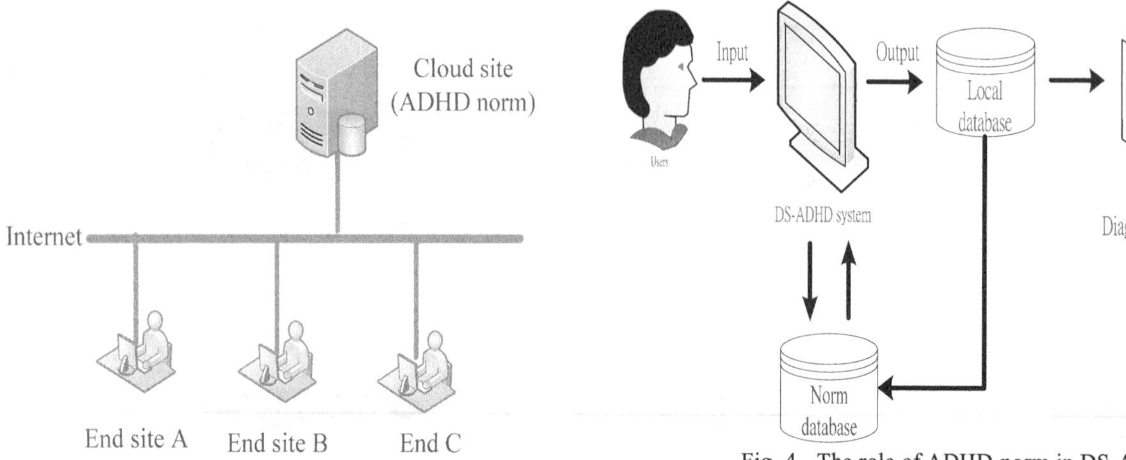

Fig. 3 The relationship between cloud and end site.

Fig. 4 The role of ADHD norm in DS-ADHD system

2.2 Development environment

The system development applies rational unified process (RUP), which is a formal systems analysis and design approach with the concept of the spiral model, and of the iterative and incremental development principle. In programming language, object-oriented (OO) technology is easy to implement and modify the system. The development environment of software and hardware is further described in Table 1. The role of ADHD norm in DS-ADHD system is shown in Fig. 4.

Table 1 The basic specification of the DS-ADHD system

Cloud site	Software	· Microsoft Windows Server 2005 (SP2) + · MS SQL 2008 · Visual Studio 2010 · Visual Basic 2008
	Hardware	· AMD Turion 64+ · 2GB 以上 DDR／RAM · 100 GB+ · CD-ROM
End site	Software	· Microsoft Windows XP (SP3) + · Microsoft Access 2007 +
	Hardware	· AMD Turion 64 + · 1GB+ DDR／RAM · HDD 100 GB+ · CD-ROM

2.2 Cloud-based architecture

To build a cloud-based screening system, the architecture is shown in Fig. 5.

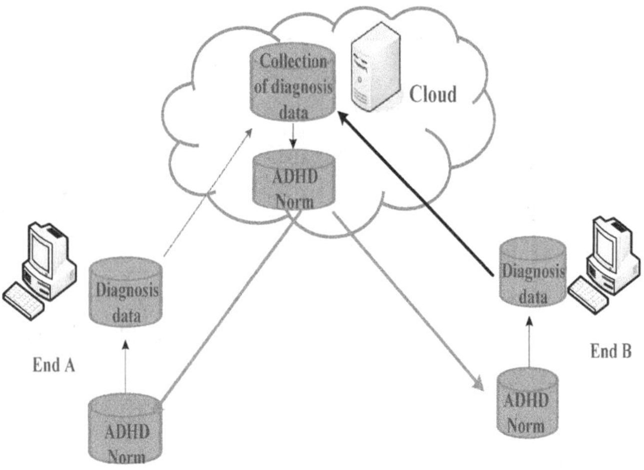

Fig. 5 Architecture of cloud-based ADHD norm development

3 System validation approach

Validity refers to the capability to measure the effectiveness of the system. The DS-ADHD validation is to discriminate the ADHD symptoms variables, including sensitivity and specificity. Sensitivity is the ability to correctly identify true ADHD cases; specificity is to the correctly identify normal (non-ADHD) cases. The higher the sensitivity, the higher the identification of ADHD symptoms; higher sensitivity is better to screen out those who may be suffering from ADHD cases. The higher the specificity, the lower the false positives (false alarm); higher specificity is more correctly discriminate from normal (non-ADHD) to abnormal (ADHD). There is a tradeoff (cutoff point) between sensitivity and specificity. When a value increases, the other value will be reduced. The tradeoff must be carefully determined. Fig. 6 is an example of tradeoff (cutoff point) between sensitivity and specificity, in which two samples (Sample1 and Sample2) are illustrated [10]. The objective of system validation is to choose a proper value of cutoff point to maximize the system feasibility of clinical diagnosis.

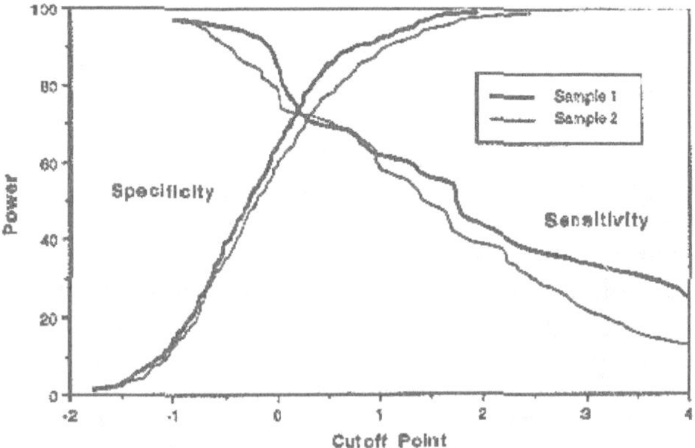

Fig. 6 Discrimination analysis of sensitivity and specificity

4 Conclusions

This paper propose a cloud-based ADHD screening system, it not only can screen ADHD symptoms, but also builds domestic ADHD norm. The system creates several ADHD indicators, including inattention, hyperactivity, impulsiveness, and vigilance. By collecting indicators data to build an ADHD norm, the system will help to accurately assess domestic patients. After screening out the patients, then joint expert team put limited resource to treat the patients on difficulties with inattentive, hyperactive, or impulsive behaviors. It will greatly avoid the waste of medical resources.

We integrate both the theoretical model and the practical application, and facilitate the domain cooperation for clinical medicine and informatics. This study provides a comprehensive mechanism to implement an ADHD screening system. To validate the proposed system, we discuss both sensitivity and specificity. Choosing a proper cutoff point between them will be a key successful factor, and e system feasibility of clinical diagnosis will be maximized. In the future, we intend to investigate other factors that will affect diagnosis results, including subject background (growth environment, lifestyle, drug habit) and user interface design (layout, targets size, displaying pattern and frequency).

5 References

[1] C. Merrell and P. B. Tymms, "Inattention, hyperactivity and impulsiveness: Their impact on academic achievement and progress," British Journal of Educational Psychology, vol. 71, pp. 43-56, Mar 2001.

[2] C. Galera, M. P. Bouvard, G. Encrenaz, A. Messiah, and E. Fombonne, "Hyperactivity-inattention symptoms in childhood and suicidal behaviors in adolescence: the Youth Gazel Cohort," Acta Psychiatrica Scandinavica, vol. 118, pp. 480-489, Dec 2008.

[3] W. J. Barbaresi, S. K. Katusic, R. C. Colligan, A. L. Weaver, and S. J. Jacobsen, "Long-term school outcomes for children with attention-deficit/hyperactivity disorder: A population-based perspective," Journal of Developmental and Behavioral Pediatrics, vol. 28, pp. 265-273, Aug 2007.

[4] J. C. Anderson, "DSM-III disorders in preadolescent children. Prevalence in a large sample from the general population," Arch Gen Psychiatry, vol. 44, pp. 69-76, 1987.

[5] E. J. Costello, "Psychopathology in pediatric primary care: the new hidden morbidity," Pediatrics, vol. 82, pp. 415-24, 1988.

[6] P. C. Buncher, "Attention-Deficit / Hyperactivity Disorder: A diagnosis for the '90s," Nurse Practitioner, vol. 21, pp. 43-64, 1996.

[7] Naivety-ADHD-Taiwan-association. (2010). Naivety ADHD Taiwan association. Available: http://www.adhd.org.tw

[8] J. B. Lawrence, R. A. Yomtovian, C. Dillman, S. R. Masarik, V. Chongkolwatana, R. J. Creger, et al., "Reliability of automated platelet counts: comparison with manual method and utility for prediction of clinical bleeding," Am J Hematol, vol. 48, pp. 244-50, Apr 1995.

[9] C. K. Conners, Ed., Conners' Continuous Performance Test (CPT II) Version 5 for Windows Technical Guide and Software Manual. 2004, p.^pp. Pages.

[10] L. M. Greenberg, C. L. Kindschi, T. R. Dupuy, and S. J. Hughes, T.O.V.A.® Clinical Manual Test Of Variables of Attention Continuous Performance Test, 2007.

Acknowledgements

This research was funded by the National Science Council of Taiwan (Grant No: NSC 101-2410-H-227 -008).

Computational Drug Screening in the Cloud Using HierVLS/PSVLS

Thomas Sitter[1], Darryl L. Willick[2,3], and Wely B. Floriano[4,5,*]
[1]Bioinformatics Program, Lakehead University, Thunder Bay, ON P7B 5E1, Canada
[2]SciReal LLC, Grand Marais, MN 55604, USA
[3]Technology Services Centre, Lakehead University, Thunder Bay, ON P7B 5E1, Canada
[4]Thunder Bay Regional Research Institute, Thunder Bay ON, P7A 7T1, Canada
[5]Department of Chemistry, Lakehead University, Thunder Bay, ON P7B 5E1, Canada
[*]corresponding author

Abstract - *Cloud computing is a rapidly growing platform for business and scientific software applications. It has key advantages over traditional high performance computers, particularly for smaller institutions without specialized staff and resources. This paper describes the transfer of scientific software used to calculate binding interactions of small molecules to proteins from a high performance computing environment to the OpenStack cloud computing environment.*

Keywords: cloud computing, virtual ligand screening, molecular docking, HPC, HierVLS, PSVLS.

1. Introduction

The number of genetic disorders with a known molecular basis is growing at an ever-quickening pace [1]. This growth in knowledge has allowed researchers to focus on personalized medicine and disease-specific molecular imaging agents (also known as molecular probes), both of which involve small molecules that bind selectively to proteins associated with a disease of interest. Currently, the discovery of new drugs and molecular probes is largely performed by experimentation using high-throughput screening, where millions of compounds are characterized in pharmacological tests looking for desired activity. This method is prohibitively expensive for many research institutions and requires advanced robotics and high-speed computers, and thus is normally only found in industry [2]. For small to medium sized institutions, it is therefore necessary to develop low cost methods for discovering drugs and molecular probes. A dramatic increase in the number of known protein structures over the last decade has enabled the development of entirely computational methods for high-throughput ligand screening. These methods are usually referred to as Virtual Ligand Screening (VLS) and involve molecular docking of libraries of chemical compounds into the three-dimensional (3D) structure of a protein target. The virtual libraries usually range from hundreds to hundreds of thousands of compounds. Although much cheaper than experimental high-throughput screening, VLS methods are computationally demanding and typically require high performance computing clusters (HPCCs) to run complex simulations. The costs associated with HPCC hardware purchase, maintenance and system administration is often out of reach for small institutions and research groups not focused on high performance computing. The recent boom in online services for on-demand computational infrastructure, called 'cloud computing', may present an affordable solution for many research groups to overcome the need for expensive high performance computers in virtual screening. In this paper, we report on the creation of a testbed cloud system using OpenStack and on the porting of a working implementation of a virtual screening suite of software HierVLS/PSVLS onto it.

2. The Virtual Ligand Screening Protocol HierVLS and its Multiple Binding Site Version PSVLS

HierVLS is a software suite that uses computational simulations to discover new molecular probes and medicinal drugs [3]. Originally designed to target a single binding site within the target protein, HierVLS was later expanded to screen the ligand library against all available binding pockets in the structure of the target protein, an approach referred to as Protein Scanning with Virtual Ligand Screening (PSVLS) [4-5]. PSVLS consists of three main software components used for finding potential ligand binding sites within the structure of a target protein, docking a ligand into a binding site, and calculating binding energy. Potential binding sites are found automatically using the experimentally determined model of a desired protein. Using progressively more complex calculations, 3D models of ligands are docked into the binding pockets in a variety of conformations and orientations. The binding energy and buried surface area are calculated and the least promising conformations and orientations are discarded prior to the next set of calculations. This minimizes the computational cost of virtual ligand screening while still ensuring the realistic binding scores are calculated for the most promising ligands. Because the simulations use a variety of individual software components, PSVLS must format and pass data files between programs to calculate binding potential of the library of small compounds. Since PSVLS can be complicated to configure and run, a graphical user interface (GUI) called Cassandra was developed to provide a user-friendly interface to set up and launch the calculations and to simplify the data handling and analysis [6]. PSVLS provides binding affinities and bound structures for each ligand in the virtual screening library in each one of the potential binding sites in the target protein.

3. High Performance Computing Clusters

A high performance computing cluster (HPCC) is a cluster of relatively inexpensive commodity computers, called “compute nodes”, connected together. The user interacts with a “head” node which controls the compute nodes. The more compute nodes an HPCC has, the more calculations it can perform at the same time. A head node includes resource management software which, among other things, monitors the status of compute nodes, dispatches (schedules) jobs, and retrieves and returns results to users. HierVLS/PSVLS were originally designed to work with the open source Torque/PBS resource manager (http://www.adaptivecomputing.com/products/open-source/torque/).

A discrete set of calculations submitted through the management software to the HPCC is often called a ‘job’. HierVLS/PSVLS is massively parallel, with the number of independent jobs equal to the number of identified binding sites in the 3D structure of the protein target multiplied by the number of ligands to be screened.

4. Cloud Computing

Cloud computing has been growing in popularity as an alternative to HPCCs. The usage demand for a HPCC can vary significantly over a period of time, especially for online businesses. This has created a market for dynamic and highly available computational resources. By renting computational resources on demand, companies use only as much computing resources as needed at any particular time. This contrasts with traditional HPCCs, where businesses have to buy a sufficiently sized system to handle peak usage, and then have the extra resources sitting unused during off hours. This need for highly available resources gave rise to "cloud computing": many commodity computers linked together with software so that they can be rented on an hourly basis as a service [7]. Virtualization software can be used to simulate multiple computers on one physical computer, transforming many commodity computers into effective computing resources. Computers with very different physical hardware can simulate identical virtual machines (VMs). VMs are assigned virtual memory and virtual CPUs from the physical computer. They can be provided with preinstalled software and settings. Complex software and configurations can be bundled in a virtual machine and then deployed many times over to emulate hundreds or thousands of physical computers. This architecture provides many unique advantages over high performance computers in terms of distribution and scalability.

Cloud services come in three major varieties: Software as a Service (SaaS), Platform as a Service (PaaS), and Infrastructure as a Service (IaaS). Software as a service is when the software and data are stored on cloud computers that can be accessed over the internet. The virtual machines running on the rented cloud computers have all the necessary software installed, so when demand increases more virtual systems are launched. This can save considerable effort and does not require specialized in-house staff to install and configure new systems. Some common examples of SaaS applications are Google Drive (drive.google.com), Apple iCloud (www.icloud.com), and DropBox (www.dropbox.com). IaaS allows customers to rent the physical computers so that they can provide their own virtual machines and provide Software as a Service. Platform as a Service provides an interface for customers to design and run software.

Some businesses construct their own cloud systems to meet their computational needs, a model called a "private cloud", in contrast to "public clouds" which are supplied by cloud providers. Others have constructed hybrid clouds, mixing private clouds for most of their needs with rented public clouds at peak demand. One reason for constructing a private cloud is data privacy. Since the security of the data stored in public clouds is not under the control of the business, the data may be vulnerable to untrusted access [8]. Another important aspect to consider is the dependency that may be created by developing software for a specific cloud vendor, which can make it difficult to transfer the software to a different cloud provider if the original one goes out of business or is no longer competitive [8]. To overcome this difficulty we chose a cloud provider, RackSpace, that uses open source cloud software that has open-standards used by other cloud providers such as HP Cloud Services (https://www.hpcloud.com) and Cloudscaling (www.cloudscaling.com).

Scientists around the world are now moving from the planning and testing phase to mature cloud systems [9-14]. For example, using IaaS, scientists at the Large Hadron Collider deploy approximately 500 virtual machines in parallel, with peaks up to 1,000 virtual machines to perform calculations [15]. This cloud system has been in operation for two years and completed over 500,000 jobs [15]. The virtualization technology allows them to create custom Linux images with older operating systems and software that are insulated from changing technology due to the virtualization software. Virtual machine images like this can also be used by other researchers who would like to perform those calculations using the software as a service cloud model. This is the model we have adopted for HierVLS/PSVLS.

5. Porting Software to Cloud Computers

As cloud computing becomes increasingly common, it is necessary to design scientific computational software that can use these resources instead of traditional HPCCs. In this context, methods for porting HPCC software over to cloud computers are becoming increasingly important. Because cloud computers use virtual machines, the first step in a port is the transfer of the software to a VM using virtualization software. VMs can be launched on local computers using virtualization software and show to produce consistent results within a small virtual HPCC environment before being launched on a cloud test environment. The final step is to launch a preconfigured VM onto an IaaS cloud. This allows the scientific software application to be offered as a SaaS for academic and industrial researchers. Currently, two major cloud providers specializing in IaaS are Amazon (http://aws.amazon.com/ec2/) and Rackspace (www.rackspace.com). Both providers have comparable prices, but Rackspace uses open source cloud software (OpenStack) and provides the Rackspace Private Cloud software for constructing local (or "private") clouds.This was another deciding factor to port HierVLS/PSVLS to OpenStack. The overall strategy adopted in this project is presented in *Figure 1*.

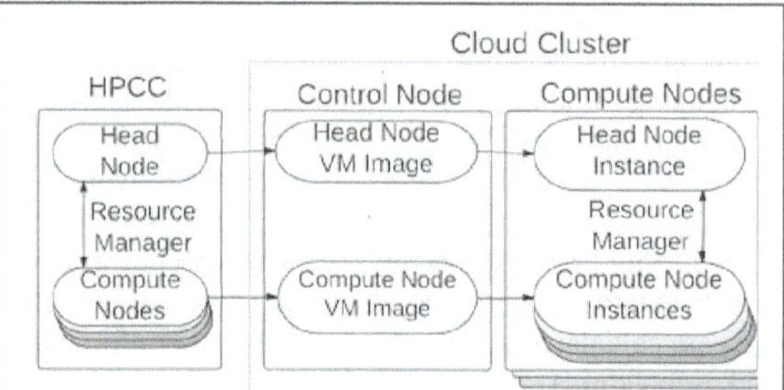

Figure 1. Schematic diagram of the various steps required to build a test cloud and deploy pre-configured instances into a virtual HPCC. VM images must be constructed of the Head and Compute nodes, and then they must be loaded in the Cloud image repository so that instances can be launched.

6. Strategy to Port HierVLS/PSVLS to a cloud environment

Prebuilt virtual machine images tested on OpenStack are freely available online from rackerjoe (https://github.com/rackerjoe/oz-image-build). The HPCC in our lab uses CentOS v5.3 (www.centos.org) to run HierVLS/PSVLS. CentOS is an open source Linux distribution based on Red Hat Enterprise Linux (www.redhat.com). Therefore, a Red Hat 5 update 6 image was chosen because it was the most closely related. To configure and test our virtual machines without having to rent cloud computers we constructed a private cloud using two nodes from a HPCC available in our lab. Our test cloud consisted of one control node (Intel Xeon E5520, 2.27 GHz, 12GB RAM) and one compute node (Intel Xeon X5550, 2.67 GHz, 24GB RAM). The cloud software used was Rackspace Private Cloud Alamo v2.0, an easy to install and configure cloud software distributed freely by Rackspace (http://www.rackspace.com). Included are services for managing virtual images, creating and launching virtual machine instances, and a graphical web interface for managing OpenStack cloud service called the Dashboard. The virtual machines must be configured to run the HierVLS/PSVLS calculations and emulate the behavior of a HPCC.

On our lab HPCC, the Operating System (OS) image is stored on the head node and pushed to the compute nodes when they are connected to it. Torque is the distributed resource management software used by HierVLS/PSVLS to manage the compute nodes. It is an open-source job scheduler based on the Portable Batch

System (PBS) originally developed by NASA. The head node has a Torque server daemon for submitting and managing jobs, as well as the Torque scheduler which implements a simple First In First Out (FIFO) protocol for jobs. Also available is a more advanced scheduler called Maui v3.2.5 (http://www.adaptivecomputing.com/products/open-source/maui/), which integrates with Torque v2.3.6 to queue jobs so that computing resources are used efficiently and fairly among multiple HPCC users.

7. Procedures

7.1. Determining Components and Dependencies

HierVLS uses a hierarchical approach to virtual ligand screening, i.e. there are multiple calculations with increasing complexity separated by filtering steps. HierVLS and Cassandra are not a bundled software package, but rather many software components linked together. A series of Perl and other scripts drive the necessary computations for virtual ligand screening. Perl is a common programming language with powerful tools for processing text, ideal for analyzing data generated from each program that comprises HierVLS and transferring it to the next component. Besides passing the data files between programs in the appropriate order, some other tasks may include converting file formats using an open source chemical data file converter called OpenBabel [16], scanning through ligand files to remove

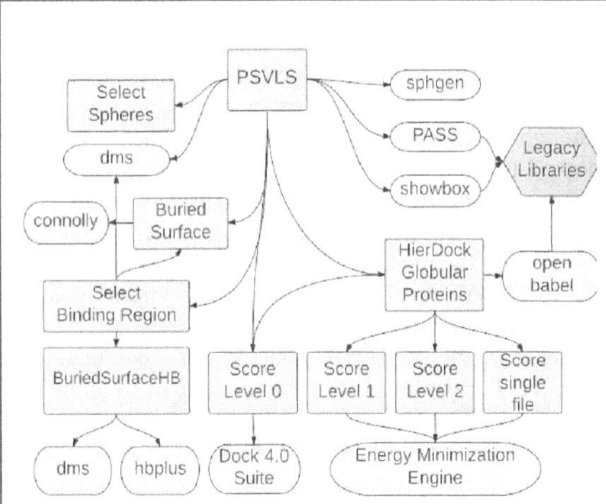

Figure 2. HierVLS/PSVLS components. Rectangles indicate Perl script components, ovals are compiled software components, and the hexagon represents specific libraries that must be included in the installation.

ones with poor binding scores, and consolidating the results at each step. The Cassandra GUI [6] allows users to input the chemical compounds and protein data files, which are then organized into a "Project" so that subsequent data analysis is simplified. Other components of HierVLS include compiled executable files, some of which rely on environmental variables, runtime libraries, and other files stored at specific locations (*Figure 2*). The function of each component can be seen in *Table 1*. The Perl script PSVLS launches the individual components and manages the application of HierVLS to each binding site available in the protein. Jobs are submitted to the HPCC via Torque/PBS.

Table 1. Main software components of HierVLS.

Component	Reference	Function
PASS	[17]	Identifies putative binding sites
Dock 4.0	[18]	Generates multiple ligand-protein docked configurations (> 10,000) without scoring or selection
Dms	[19]	Calculates molecular surface of a molecule
HBPlus	[20]	Calculates hydrogen bonds
Connolly	[21]	Calculates accessible surface area
OpenBabel	[16]	Converts chemical file formats

7.2. Creating an OpenStack Private Cloud

As a testbed, we used two nodes from our in-house HPCC cluster to construct an OpenStack cloud system. The Rackspace private cloud software Alamo v2.0 was used to install the OpenStack cloud software. Rackspace Alamo was installed with Ubuntu 12.04 as the host operating system, Chef for network configuration, and OpenStack Folsom release (http://www.openstack.org/software/folsom/). Using an Alamo install DVD allowed for a relatively easy installation process on bare hardware, creating a compute node with image object storage, block storage, and computing services, as well as the dashboard - a web interface for interacting with the control node to handle tasks such as launching and terminating virtual machine instances and creating virtual machine images.

Each node in an OpenStack cloud must have a connection to the internet during installation; one DVD is used to install both compute and control nodes so it is necessary to download the Ubuntu 12.04 image during installation. Due to our network setup, the easiest way to accomplish this was to connect each node to a network switch that then went through the head node of the existing HPCC, which acted as a router, and then out to the internet. More easily, nodes can be directly connected to a router. Intel VT-d hardware virtualization was enabled in the BIOS settings of the compute node to allow the OpenStack KVM hypervisor to run virtual machines (http://www.linux-kvm.org/page/Main_Page).

7.3. Creating and configuring the virtual nodes and connecting them into a virtual HPCC

A Red Hat 5 Update 6 image was downloaded from rackerjoe (https://github.com/rackerjoe/oz-image-build) and configured to act as either a head or compute node. The HierVLS software was installed on the image.

Essential library files and software components were installed/transferred to the virtual machine nodes. Environmental variables and symbolic links were set. Torque v4.1.3 was installed on the head and compute nodes. Users and passwords were created and configured for password-less SSH, which is required for Torque/PBS to transfer files between nodes. A user was created for running Cassandra on the compute nodes and the home directory from the head node was mounted on all compute nodes when they launch. A directory containing computational software was also mounted from the head node onto the compute nodes. This way, only the head node needs to have a complete copy of Cassandra, HierVLS, and its components. However, environmental variables and libraries were still configured independently on the compute node image.

Because HierVLS is controlled by the Cassandra GUI, X11 Forwarding had to be configured on the head node so that users can access the graphical interface.

7.4. Quality Control Data Set

A test data set was constructed using a relatively small protein - the N-terminal domain of the Human Papillomavirus 16 E6 oncoprotein (HPV16 E6), which has only two binding regions identified by PASS [17] in its experimentally determined structure (PDB code 2LJX) [22]. Four ligands were used in the test set: ethyl lactate, ethylene, ethyl acetate, and acetic acid. This data set was used to generate a quality control standard set of results used to validate HierVLS/PSVLS on each system.

Running the quality control data set gave results consistent with the physical HPCC indicating that HierVLS was installed correctly on the virtual test environment.

8. Discussion

HierVLS and Cassandra are not a bundled software package, but rather many software components linked together by scripts and controlled by a graphical user interface. Because of this, it can be difficult to ensure that all the required components are transferred to a new system. A successful installation must include all the necessary programs and libraries and settings in both head and compute nodes.

Originally the cloud environment chosen for this project was Amazon EC2 because it is the most popular cloud provider and it has extensive documentation. Amazon also offers compute instances with many powerful CPUs which would be ideal for high performance computing. Some papers, however, have noted that running multiple VMs with fewer CPUs can be just as effective as a single VM with many CPUs [23].

It was later decided that Rackspace would make a better cloud provider because they use open source cloud software, OpenStack, and also provide support and APIs for working with Amazon EC2 virtual machine images. Furthermore, Rackspace has a software bundle called the 'Rackspace private cloud' that allows users to quickly install a Rackspace OpenStack cloud running Ubuntu 12.04 on bare hardware, as long as they have an internet connection.

VirtualBox (www.virtualbox.org) machine images were constructed to test the transfer of the HierVLS system onto a virtual machine. Unfortunately, we could not launch the VirtualBox vdi images directly onto the OpenStack cloud, even though OpenStack has support for that format. The vdi images were then converted to qcow2 images using qemu. OpenStack was able to launch instances of the converted machine images, but connecting to the running instance was not successful, although there may be a way to do this. Instead we adopted the command-line only Red Hat 5.6 OpenStack images, which were launched and used without issue. This machine image was chosen because it was the most similar to the native CentOS 5.3 environment of HierVLS/PSVLS, and the VirtualBox virtual machine images used Centos 5.6.

Because the Red Hat images were command-line only, X11Forwarding had to be configured to allow user access to the Cassandra GUI through the users' computer, which is remotely connected to the cloud instance. We considered installing the Cassandra GUI directly on the host computer and modifying it to connect to the cloud instance. However, we decided to have Cassandra on the cloud and connect to it remotely, which allowed it to be used without any modifications. In the future, it would be convenient to create a web portal for users to interact with HierVLS and view results.

9. Conclusions

We have demonstrated that HierVLS/PSVLS has the ability to run in an OpenStack cloud environment. OpenStack networks virtual machine instances in an amenable manner for the HierVLS/PSVLS software. The Torque resource manager performed well in the cloud environment. No substantial modifications to the HierVLS/PSVLS source code were needed, and the ported software is still fully back-compatible with HPCCs.

Although there is still much to be done before HierVLS/PSVLs can be released as a SaaS product, we have demonstrated the feasibility of this endeavor. Next steps should be the development of a web interface for user interaction and displaying a more user-friendly analysis and presentation of binding results, as well as automatic creation and termination of compute nodes. Although no upper limit on the number of compute nodes was determined, we anticipate that the massively parallel nature of HierVLS/PSVLS is well complemented by the massive scale that can be leveraged by cloud computers.

10. Acknowledgements

This work was supported in part by a grant from the National Institutes of Health under a subcontract award (DC010105) to SciReal, LLC. Benchmarking calculations were performed using resources from SHARCNET under the auspices of Compute Canada. The authors would like to acknowledge Dr. Sabah Mohammed and Dr. Aicheng Chen for helpful discussions.

11. References

[1] A. Hamosh, *et al.*, "Online Mendelian Inheritance in Man (OMIM), a knowledgebase of human genes and genetic disorders," *Nucleic Acids Res,* vol. 33, pp. D514-7, Jan 1 2005.

[2] M. M. Hann and T. I. Oprea, "Pursuing the leadlikeness concept in pharmaceutical research," *Curr Opin Chem Biol,* vol. 8, pp. 255-63, Jun 2004.

[3] W. B. Floriano, *et al.*, "HierVLS hierarchical docking protocol for virtual ligand screening of large-molecule databases," *J Med Chem,* vol. 47, pp. 56-71, Jan 1 2004.

[4] S. Dadgar, *et al.*, "Paclitaxel Is an Inhibitor and Its Boron Dipyrromethene Derivative Is a Fluorescent Recognition Agent for Botulinum Neurotoxin Subtype A," *J Med Chem,* Mar 29 2013.

[5] X. Li, *et al.*, "Sweet taste receptor gene variation and aspartame taste in primates and other species," *Chem Senses,* vol. 36, pp. 453-75, Jun 2011.

[6] Z. H. Ramjan, *et al.*, "A cluster-aware graphical user interface for a virtual ligand screening tool," *Conf Proc IEEE Eng Med Biol Soc,* vol. 2008, pp. 4102-5, 2008.

[7] M. Armbrust, *et al.*, "Above the Clouds: A Berkeley View of Cloud Computing," EECS Department, University of California, Berkeley UCB/EECS-2009-28, February 10 2009.

[8] M. D. Dikaiakos, *et al.*, "Cloud Computing Distributed Internet Computing for IT and Scientific Research," *Ieee Internet Computing,* vol. 13, pp. 10-13, Sep-Oct 2009.

[9] S. Ostermann, *et al.*, "A Performance Analysis of EC2 Cloud Computing Services for Scientific Computing," *Cloud Computing,* vol. 34, pp. 115-131, 2010.

[10] H. Y. Chen, *et al.*, "An Investigation on Applications of Cloud Computing in Scientific Computing," *Information and Management Engineering, Pt V,* vol. 235, pp. 201-206, 2011.

[11] J. J. Rehr, *et al.*, "Scientific Computing in the Cloud," *Computing in Science & Engineering,* vol. 12, pp. 34-43, May-Jun 2010.

[12] J. Cohen, *et al.*, "RAPPORT: running scientific high-performance computing applications on the cloud," *Philosophical Transactions of the Royal Society a-Mathematical Physical and Engineering Sciences,* vol. 371, Jan 28 2013.

[13] K. Chine, "Scientific Computing Environments in the Age of Virtualization Toward a Universal Platform for the Cloud," *Proceedings 2009 Ieee International Workshop on Open-Source Software for Scientific Computation,* pp. 44-48, 2009.

[14] K. Jorissen, *et al.*, "A high performance scientific cloud computing environment for materials simulations," *Computer Physics Communications,* vol. 183, pp. 1911-1919, Sep 2012.

[15] A. A. R.J. Sobie, I. Gable, C. Leavett-Brown, M. Paterson, R. Taylor, A. Charbonneau, R. Impey, W. Podiama. (2013, Feb 2013). HTC Scientific Computing in a Distributed Cloud Environment. *arXiv:1302.1939 [cs.DC]*. Available: http://arxiv.org/abs/1302.1939

[16] N. M. O'Boyle, *et al.*, "Open Babel: An open chemical toolbox," *J Cheminform,* vol. 3, p. 33, 2011.

[17] G. P. Brady, Jr. and P. F. Stouten, "Fast prediction and visualization of protein binding pockets with PASS," *J Comput Aided Mol Des,* vol. 14, pp. 383-401, May 2000.

[18] T. J. Ewing, *et al.*, "DOCK 4.0: search strategies for automated molecular docking of flexible molecule databases," *J Comput Aided Mol Des,* vol. 15, pp. 411-28, May 2001.

[19] F. M. Richards, "Areas, volumes, packing and protein structure," *Annu Rev Biophys Bioeng,* vol. 6, pp. 151-76, 1977.

[20] I. K. McDonald and J. M. Thornton, "Satisfying hydrogen bonding potential in proteins," *Journal of Molecular Biology,* vol. 238, pp. 777-93, May 20 1994.

[21] M. L. Connolly, "Solvent-accessible surfaces of proteins and nucleic acids," *Science,* vol. 221, pp. 709-13, Aug 19 1983.

[22] K. Zanier, *et al.*, "Solution Structure Analysis of the HPV16 E6 Oncoprotein Reveals a Self-Association Mechanism Required for E6-Mediated Degradation of p53," *Structure,* vol. 20, pp. 604-617, Apr 4 2012.

[23] M. Alef and I. Gable, "HEP Specific Benchmarks of Virtual Machines on multi-core CPU Architectures," *17th International Conference on Computing in High Energy and Nuclear Physics (Chep09),* vol. 219, 2010.

A Novel Mathematical Model of Targeted Cancer Therapy along p53 Proteasomal Degradation Pathways

Prem Talwai
Department of Mathematics, American River College, Sacramento, CA, USA
Mira Loma High School, Sacramento, CA, USA

Abstract— *Overzealous MDM2-mediated ubiquitination of p53 characterizes and sustains over 50% of all human cancers. Targeted cancer therapy hinges on a thorough understanding of the ubiquitination process. Unfortunately, existing mathematical models inaccurately describe the ubiquitin-proteasome system, due to the underlying assumptions of steady-state and constant cellular concentrations of the ubiquitin-conjugating and ubiquitin ligase enzymes. This paper derives a novel non-steady-state mathematical model of sequential bi-substrate enzyme kinetics, which can be used to simulate the behavioral response of the ubiquitin-proteasome system to specific variations in the cellular concentrations of p53, MDM2, and ubiquitin-conjugated E2D3. From computer simulations of the derived model it was observed that the ubiquitin-ligase MDM2 accelerates the carcinogenic ubiquitination process, while ubiquitin-conjugated E2D3 inhibits it. The mathematical model was also shown to successfully reproduce the experimentally observed p53-MDM2 interaction. The derived model therefore suggests MDM2 as a prospective target for cancer therapy. In addition, the findings of this project propose recombinant E2D3-Ub as a new promising protein-based anticancer drug.*

Keywords: targeted cancer therapy, non-steady-state enzyme kinetic model, molecular inhibitor of p53 ubiquitination, protein-based anticancer drug, E2D3

1. Introduction

Overzealous MDM2-mediated ubiquitination of p53 characterizes and sustains over 50% of all human cancers [8]. Successful targeted cancer therapy hinges on a thorough understanding of the ubiquitination process.

The tumor suppressor protein p53, sometimes known as the "guardian of the genome", induces cell cycle arrest in response to cellular stress signals, such as DNA damage or hypoxia. p53 performs it vital function by inducing the transcription of certain genes whose proteins mediate the repair of the genome. Normally only a small amount of p53 actively participates in cellular processes, while the remainder is degraded by the E3 ubiquitin ligase MDM2 [2]. During emergency situations, however, MDM2 is phosphorylated and thus releases p53 to perform its function. A key characteristic of tumor cells is the overexpression of the oncogene MDM2, which results in excessive unregulated degradation of p53 even during abnormal cellular growth.

The crucial process of ubiquitination targets proteins for degradation by attaching chains of ubiquitin molecules to their lysine residues [11]. The process first begins with the activation of ubiquitin by the E1 activating enzyme, using energy in the form of ATP. The ubiquitin then leaves the E1 enzyme and forms a thioester linkage with the cysteine residue of an E2-conjugating enzyme. The latter enzyme transports the ubiquitin to an E3 ubiquitin ligase, which catalyzes the transfer of the ubiquitin (or pre-manufactured polyubiquitin chain) from the E2-conjugating enzyme to the target substrate protein. The ubiquitin binds to the target protein through an isopeptide bond with the substrate's lysine residue. E3 ubiquitin ligases possess either a HECT (Homologous to the E6-AP Carboxyl Terminus) or RING (Really Interesting New Gene) finger domain for binding with the E2 conjugase. This paper will focus specifically on the kinetics of RING finger ubiquitin ligases.

Unfortunately, existing mathematical models inaccurately describe the ubiquitin-proteasome system, due to the underlying assumptions of steady-state and constant cellular concentrations of the ubiquitin-conjugating and ubiquitin ligase enzymes [3]. The quasi-steady-state assumption underlying existing enzyme kinetic models requires that enzyme concentrations be infinitesimally small in comparison with the concentrations of the substrates [12]. However, in many overzealous ubiquitination processes (such as the degradation of p53), the oncogenic E3 ubiquitin ligase is expressed at much higher levels than the target substrate protein. This unique characteristic of many cancerous systems invalidates the quasi-steady-state assumption and therefore prohibits the use of current enzyme kinetic models.

In addition, current *in vitro* studies solely report the behavior of the ubiquitin-proteasome system at constant concentrations of the E3 ligase and ubiquitin-conjugated E2 [9]. However in actual cancer cells, the concentrations of these ubiquitination enzymes fluctuate considerably. Therefore, the results of such *in vitro* studies fail to accurately describe true protein ubiquitination. Furthermore, current multi-substrate enzyme kinetic models solely analyze the highly uncontrollable relationships between substrate activity and product formation rate during the course of enzyme catalysis. However, in most chemical reactors, the initial concentrations of the enzymes, substrates, and products are more easily varied in order to achieve optimal system performance.

This paper derives a novel *non-steady-state* mathematical model of sequential bi-substrate enzyme kinetics, which can be used to simulate the behavioral response of the ubiquitin-proteasome system (UPS) to specific variations in the cellular concentrations of targeted p53, MDM2, and ubiquitin-conjugated E2D3. The derived mathematical model may be used to analyze the effects of specific modifications in the initial conditions on the reaction progress curves for the enzyme, substrates, and products. Computational simulations of the derived mathematical model are provided in order to illustrate the effects of MDM2 and E2D3-Ub concentrations on the rates of multiple p53 ubiquitination processes (each generated by a different set of rate constants). The paper concludes with a detailed description of the implications of the aforementioned computational results on targeted cancer therapy and drug discovery.

2. Materials and Methods

MDM2-mediated ubiquitination of p53 follows a compulsory-order ternary complex mechanism [13]. The target protein p53 and the ubiquitin-conjugated E2D3 bind the E3 ligase MDM2, which transforms the latter substrates into their corresponding products (one of which is ubiquitinated p53). The general sequential bi-substrate enzyme mechanism can be summarized as follows :

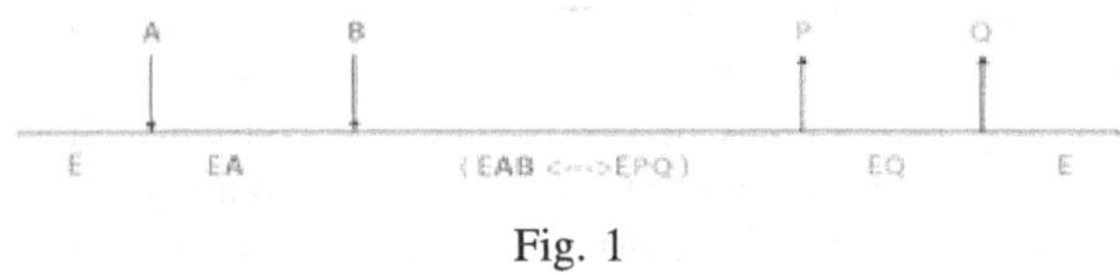

Fig. 1

where A and B are p53 and E2D3-Ub respectively and E is the RING finger enzyme MDM2. If we let C_1, C_2, C_3, and C_4 be the complexes EA, EAB, EPQ, and EQ, then the mechanism may be summarized by the following set of elementary reactions:

$$E + A + B \xrightarrow{k_1} C_1 + B$$
$$C_1 + B \xrightarrow{k_2} C_2$$
$$C_2 \underset{k_{-3}}{\overset{k_3}{\rightleftharpoons}} C_3$$
$$C_3 \xrightarrow{k_4} C_4 + P$$
$$C_4 + P \xrightarrow{k_5} E + P + Q$$

2.1 Construction of Model (System of Partial Differential Equations)

The Law of Mass Action was used to derive a nonlinear autonomous system of differential equations to model the reaction mechanism. Upon close investigation of this system of ODEs the following relationships were discovered:

$$\frac{dE}{dt} = \frac{dA}{dt} + \frac{dQ}{dt} \tag{1a}$$
$$\frac{dC_2}{dt} + \frac{dC_3}{dt} = -\left(\frac{dB}{dt} + \frac{dP}{dt}\right) \tag{1b}$$
$$\frac{dC_1}{dt} = \frac{dB}{dt} - \frac{dA}{dt} \tag{1c}$$
$$\frac{dC_4}{dt} = \frac{dP}{dt} - \frac{dQ}{dt} \tag{1d}$$

The concentrations of the various species throughout the reaction were allowed to depend not only on the time but also on the *initial concentrations* of the enzyme and substrates. This novel modification enables scientists to use the derived model for the investigation of precisely how the rates of certain enzyme-catalyzed reactions are affected by specific variations in the cellular concentrations of the enzymes and substrate proteins. By integrating both sides of the equations in (1), the concentrations of the enzyme and the intermediate complexes were expressed in terms of the concentrations of the substrates, products, and four unknown functions of the initial conditions. In the following derivations, let the variable s = the initial concentration of substrate A, the variable u = the initial concentration of substrate B, the variable v = the initial concentration of enzyme E, and the parameter P_0 = the initial concentration of the product P.

In order to determine the four unknown functions, the uncatalyzed reaction corresponding to the ordered bi-substrate enzyme mechanism was first analyzed. The substrate and product concentrations were then expressed in terms of the initial conditions and the extent of reaction. In addition, upon detailed comparison with the catalyzed reaction, the various states in which the substrates and products existed during the course of enzyme catalysis were discovered. It was noticed that the substrate A occurred in three states (a free state A and two bound states C_1 and C_2), the substrate B occurred in two states (a free state B and one bound state C_2), the product P occurred in two states (a free state P and one bound state C_3), and finally the product Q occurred in three states (a free state Q and two bound states C_3 and C_4). The total substrate and product concentrations were expressed as the sum of the concentrations of each of their respective free and bound states.

Using these derived relationships, the four unknown functions were determined and the concentrations of the product Q and intermediate complexes C_1, C_3, C_4 were precisely expressed in terms of the concentrations of the enzyme, substrates, complex C_2, product P, and the initial conditions. The equations were as follows:

$$Q = E - A - v + s \tag{2a}$$
$$C_1 = B - A + s - u \tag{2b}$$
$$C_3 = u + P_0 - (P + B + C_2) \tag{2c}$$
$$C_4 = P - E + A + v - s - P_0 \tag{2d}$$

The equations in (2) were then substituted into the original system of nine ODEs. This substitution enabled the elimination of four variables from the original system which rapidly simplified the computational simulation of the model and eliminated the need for inaccurate steady-state or constant-concentration assumptions. In addition, this substitution enabled the introduction of novel initial concentration variables into the mathematical model. The resulting nonlinear system of partial differential equations was as follows:

$$\frac{\partial E}{\partial t}(s,t,u,v) = k_5\left(P - E + A + v - s - P_0\right) - k_1 EA \quad (3a)$$

$$\frac{\partial A}{\partial t}(s,t,u,v) = -k_1 EA \quad (3b)$$

$$\frac{\partial B}{\partial t}(s,t,u,v) = -k_2 B\left(B - A + s - u\right) \quad (3c)$$

$$\frac{\partial C_2}{\partial t}(s,t,u,v) = k_2 B\left(B - A + s - u\right) + k_{-3}\left(u + P_0 - (P + B + C_2)\right) - k_3 C_2 \quad (3d)$$

$$\frac{\partial P}{\partial t}(s,t,u,v) = k_4\left(u + P_0 - (P + B + C_2)\right) \quad (3e)$$

Using the original system of ODEs and the relationships in (2), an equilibrium point for the nonlinear system in (3) was found to be $(v, 0, u - s, 0, s + P_0)$. The nonlinear system of PDEs was subsequently linearized about this equilibrium point and the following linear system was obtained:

$$\boxed{\vec{V}' = J\left(v, 0, u - s, 0, s + P_0\right)\vec{V}} \quad (4)$$

with $\vec{V}^T = \begin{bmatrix} E - v & A & B + s - u & C_2 & P - P_0 - s \end{bmatrix}$ and $\vec{V}^T(0) = \begin{bmatrix} 0 & s & s & 0 & -s \end{bmatrix}$. $J(v, 0, u - s, 0, s + P_0)$, the Jacobian of the nonlinear system at the equilibrium point, is given by:

$$\begin{bmatrix} -k_5 & -k_1 v + k_5 & 0 & 0 & k_5 \\ 0 & -k_1 v & 0 & 0 & 0 \\ 0 & k_2 u - k_2 s & k_2 s - k_2 u & 0 & 0 \\ 0 & k_2 s - k_2 u & k_2 u - k_2 s - k_{-3} & -k_{-3} - k_3 & -k_{-3} \\ 0 & 0 & -k_4 & -k_4 & -k_4 \end{bmatrix}$$

2.2 Solution to Model

The perturbed linear system was subsequently solved using conventional linear algebraic techniques. From the eigenvalues of the Jacobian $J(v, 0, u-s, 0, s+P_0)$, the equilibrium $(v, 0, u-s, 0, s+P_0)$ was found to be asymptotically stable for all biologically relevant conditions. The perturbations in each of the five variables were expressed as linear combinations of five exponential functions of time (whose growth "constants" depended on the initial conditions). The coefficients of these linear combinations (which were functions of the initial concentration variables) were determined through large-scale row reduction using the Mathematica program. In the interest of space, an abbreviated version of the final set of integrated rate laws will be provided in the results section. The complete model is incorporated into the computational simulations.

3. Results

The final mathematical model of the sequential bi-substrate enzyme mechanism was:

$$[MDM2] = n_1(s,u,v)e^{\lambda_1 t} + n_2(s,u,v)\frac{D_1 + D_2}{D_3 - D_4}e^{\lambda_2 t} + n_3(s,u,v)\frac{C_{13}}{C_{14}u - C_{14}s + C_{13}}e^{\lambda_3 t} + n_4(s,u,v)C_{15}e^{\lambda_4 t} + n_5(s,u,v)C_{16}e^{\lambda_5 t} + v \quad (5a)$$

$$[p53] = n_2(s,u,v)\frac{D_5 + D_6}{D_7}e^{\lambda_2 t} \quad (5b)$$

$$[E2D3 - Ub] = n_2(s,u,v)\frac{C_{27}v^3 + C_{28}v^2 + C_{29}v + C_{30}}{C_{31}v - C_{30}}e^{\lambda_2 t} + n_3(s,u,v)D_8 e^{\lambda_3 t} + u - s \quad (5c)$$

$$[C_2] = n_2(s,u,v)(C_{35}v^2 + C_{36}v)e^{\lambda_2 t} + n_3(s,u,v)D_9 e^{\lambda_3 t} + n_4(s,u,v)C_{39}e^{\lambda_4 t} + n_5(s,u,v)C_{40}e^{\lambda_5 t} \quad (5d)$$

$$[p53 - Ub] = n_2(s,u,v)e^{\lambda_2 t} + n_3(s,u,v)e^{\lambda_3 t} + n_4(s,u,v)e^{\lambda_4 t} + n_5(s,u,v)e^{\lambda_5 t} + P_0 + s \quad (5e)$$

where D_1, D_2, ..., D_9 are functions of s, u and v given by:

$$D_1 = C_1 v^5 + C_2' v^4 + C_3 v^3 + C_4 v^2 + C_5 v + C_6 uv^4 + C_7 uv^3 + C_8 uv^2 \quad (6a)$$

$$D_2 = C_9 uv - C_6 sv^4 - C_7 sv^3 - C_8 sv^2 - C_9 sv \quad (6b)$$

$$D_3 = C_{10} uv^2 + C_{11} u - C_{10} sv^2 \quad (6c)$$

$$D_4 = C_{12} sv + C_{11} s - C_{12} uv$$

$$D_5 = C_{17} v^4 + C_{18} v^3 + C_{19} v^2 + C_{20} v + C_{21} uv^3 + C_{22} uv^2 \quad (6d)$$

$$D_6 = C_{23} uv + C_{24} u - C_{21} sv^3 - C_{22} sv^2 - C_{23} sv - C_{24} s \quad (6e)$$

$$D_7 = C_{25} uv + C_{26} u - C_{25} sv - C_{26} s \quad (6f)$$

$$D_8 = C_{32} s^2 + C_{32} u^2 - 2C_{32} su + C_{33} s - C_{33} u + C_{34} \quad (6g)$$

$$D_9 = -C_{32} s^2 - C_{32} u^2 + 2C_{32} su - C_{37} s - C_{38} u \quad (6h)$$

λ_1, λ_2, ..., λ_5 are the eigenvalues of $J(v, 0, u - s, 0, s + P_0)$. The functions $n_1(s,u,v), n_2(s,u,v), \ldots, n_5(s,u,v)$ are omitted from this abbreviated model due to their length and complexity. Lengthy nonlinear expressions involving the rate constants are replaced by kinetic constants of the form C_i in order to aid parameter estimation (definitions of C_i and the aforementioned coefficient functions are incorporated into the computer simulations; definitions of C_i can also be found in Table 1). Note that in (5) the generic variables for the enzyme, substrates, and product have been replaced by the specific proteins that perform their functions in the process of p53 ubiquitination.

3.1 Computer Simulations of Mathematical Model

The mathematical model was simulated for several p53 ubiquitination processes by varying the values of the reaction rate constants (all given in min^{-1}). A detailed explanation and graphical representation of three such simulations is provided in Figure 2. From Figure 2, it is quite evident that the substrate E2D3-Ub inhibits overzealous p53 ubiquitination while the E3 ligase MDM2 accelerates this carcinogenic reaction. In addition it can be seen that E2D3-Ub is more effective inhibitor of p53 ubiquitination when present at higher concentrations (the curves are steepest in the right-most cluster of each substrate-velocity plot). However, the simulations also show that high concentrations of p53 can hinder the ability of E2D3-Ub to decelerate the reaction (an increase in the initial concentration of p53 makes the substrate-velocity curves more gradual).

3.2 Agreement with Experimental Results

The model accurately reproduces the experimentally observed p53-MDM2 interaction reported in various *in vitro* studies [7,5,1]. For example, in [10] it was observed that wild-type p53 ubiquitination increased rapidly when the MDM2 protein was overexpressed. The experimentally observed p53-MDM2 interaction was primarily reported qualitatively through Western Blot analysis. Since an ordered bi-bi mechanism produces both free and bound substrate and product states, distinction between the optical bands corresponding to these different states and subsequent densitometric quantification of the western blots becomes difficult [4]. Therefore empirical substrate-velocity curves for p53 ubiquitination were not obtainable for direct comparison against the derived model and an alternative method, known as sensitivity analysis [6], was used for model validation (please refer to Figure 3 for details).

4. Conclusion

Computer simulations of the derived model identify MDM2 as a potential target for cancer therapy and demonstrate that E2D3-Ub exhibits antitumor activity. Recombinant forms of E2D3-Ub may therefore function as a promising protein-based anticancer drug for targeting overzealous p53 ubiquitination. The derived model's successful duplication of the experimentally observed p53-MDM2 interaction confirms its validity in simulating less explored biochemical relationships, such as that between p53 and E2D3-Ub. Further *in vitro* experimentation is obviously necessary for additional verification of the therapeutic properties of ubiquitin-conjugated E2D3.

The non-steady-state mathematical model derived in this paper may be used for the kinetic analysis of various biochemical processes governed by ordered ternary-complex mechanisms, most notably the synthesis of DNA molecules by DNA polymerase, the detoxification of lipophilic xenobiotics by glutathione S-transferase, and the oxidation of NADH to NAD^+ by L-lactate dehydrogenase. Extrapolation of the model can be used to identify the most favorable initial conditions for generating optimal performance of many commercial chemical reactors. The findings of this paper may also be employed to determine treatment solutions for several other bacterial infections and inflammatory diseases (such as rheumatoid arthritis) characterized by an overzealous UPS. The model can be utilized for the discovery of new techniques to accelerate healthy biological processes and inhibit harmful protein activity. Finally, computational simulation of the derived model provides a safe, fast, and cost-effective preliminary alternative to expensive *in vitro* experimentation.

References

[1] D. Alarcon-Vargas, Z. Ronai, "p53–Mdm2—the Affair That Never Ends," *Carcinogenesis*, vol. 23, pp. 541-547, Apr. 2002.

[2] E. Barillot, L. Calzone, P. Hupe, J. Vert, and A. Zinovyev, *Computational Systems Biology of Cancer*, 1st ed., Boca Raton, USA: CRC Press, 2013.

[3] J. Brewer, "Investigations of the P53 Protein DNA Damage Network Using Mathematical Models," Ph.D. Comp. Biol. thesis, University College London, London, United Kingdom, Oct. 2002.

[4] M. Gassmann, B. Grenacher, B. Rodhe, and J. Vogel,"Quantifying Western Blots: Pitfalls of Densitometry," *Electrophoresis*, vol. 30, pp. 1845-1855, Jun. 2009.

[5] Y. Haupt, R. Maya, A. Kazaz, and M. Oren, "Mdm2 Promotes the Rapid Degradation of P53," *Nature*, vol. 387, pp. 266-269, May 1997.

[6] J. Kleijnen, "Verification and Validation of Simulation Models," *European Journal of Operational Research*, vol. 82, pp. 145-62, 1995

[7] M. Kubbutat, S. Jones, and K. Vousden, "Regulation of P53 Stability by Mdm2," *Nature*, vol. 387, pp. 299-303, May 1997.

[8] P. Kussie, S. Gorina, V. Marechal, B. Elenbaas, J. Moreau, A. Levine, and N. Pavletich, "Structure of the MDM2 Oncoprotein Bound to the P53 Tumor Suppressor Transactivation Domain," *Science*, vol. 274, pp. 948-53, Nov. 1996.

[9] Z. Lai, K. Ferry, M. Diamond, and K. Wee, "Human Mdm2 Mediates Multiple Mono-ubiquitination of P53 by a Mechanism Requiring Enzyme Isomerization,"*Journal of Biological Chemistry*, vol. 276, pp. 31357-31367, Jun. 2001.

[10] N. Lukashchuk and K. Vousden, "Ubiquitination and Degradation of Mutant P53," *Molecular and Cellular Biology*, vol. 27, pp. 8284-8295, Dec. 2007.

[11] C. Pickart, and M Eddins, "Ubiquitin: Structures, Functions, Mechanisms," *Biochimica Et Biophysica Acta (BBA) - Molecular Cell Research*,vol. 1695, pp. 55-72, Nov. 2004.

[12] L. Segel and M. Slemrod, "The Quasi-Steady-State Assumption: A Case Study in Perturbation," *SIAM Review*, vol. 31, pp. 446-477, Sep. 1989

[13] D. Swinney, M. Rose, A. Mak, I. Lee, L. Scarafia, and Y. Xu, "Bi-substrate Kinetic Analysis of an E3-Ligase–Dependent Ubiquitylation Reaction," *Methods in Enzymology*, vol. 399, pp. 323-333, 2005.

[14] X. Yu and D. Kem, "Proteasome Inhibition during Myocardial Infarction," *Cardiovascular Research*, vol. 35, pp. 310-320, Sep. 2009.

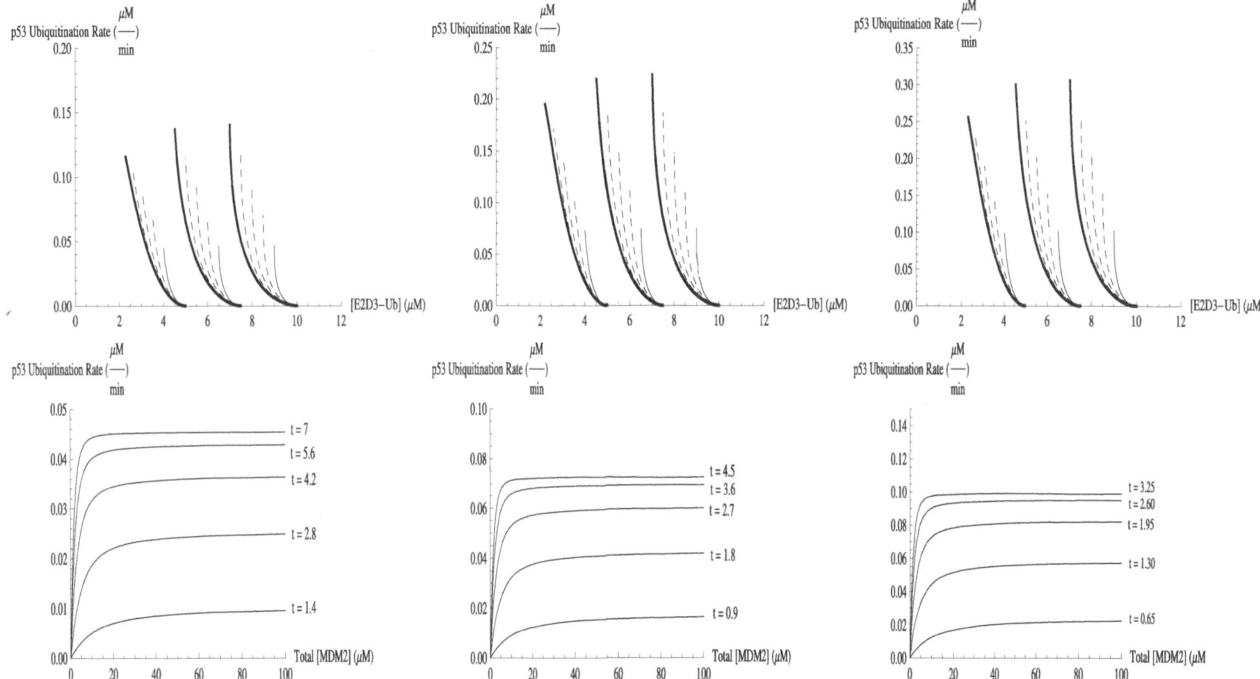

Fig. 2: Each column features a different simulation of the mathematical model. In each column, the top figure shows the influence of E2D3-Ub concentration on p53 ubiquitination rate for various initial concentrations of p53 and E2D3-Ub. The three distinct clusters of curves correspond to three different initial concentrations of E2D3-Ub: $5\,\mu M$, $7.5\,\mu M$, $10\,\mu M$. In each cluster, the dashed curves approach the thick curve as the initial concentration of p53 is increased from $1\,\mu M$ to $3\,\mu M$ (in increments of $0.5\,\mu M$) while the initial concentration of MDM2 is held fixed at $20\,\mu M$. The bottom figure shows the influence of total (initial) MDM2 concentration on p53 ubiquitination rate at different moments during the reaction. Note that in each simulation, the influence of E2D3-Ub concentration on ubiquitination rate was only investigated during the period of time before the substrate E2D3-Ub settled at a relatively steady concentration. The parameter values used to generate these simulations were: (Left) $k_1 = 0.15\,\mu M$, $k_2 = 0.175\,\mu M$, $k_3 = 0.125\,\mu M$, $k_{-3} = 0.1\,\mu M$, $k_4 = 0.2\,\mu M$, $k_5 = 0.25\,\mu M$ (Center) $k_1 = 0.25\,\mu M$, $k_2 = 0.275\,\mu M$, $k_3 = 0.225\,\mu M$, $k_{-3} = 0.2\,\mu M$, $k_4 = 0.3\,\mu M$, $k_5 = 0.35\,\mu M$ (Right) $k_1 = 0.35\,\mu M$, $k_2 = 0.375\,\mu M$, $k_3 = 0.325\,\mu M$, $k_{-3} = 0.3\,\mu M$, $k_4 = 0.4\,\mu M$, $k_5 = 0.45\,\mu M$

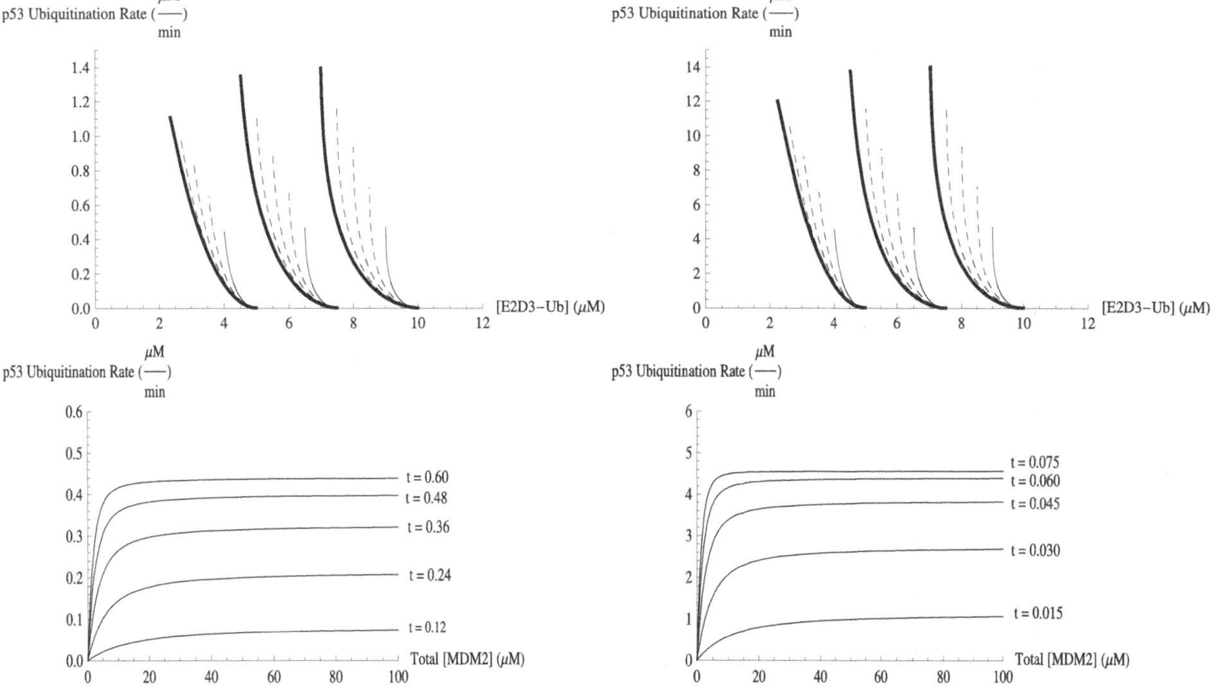

Fig. 3: Sensitivity analysis is used here to describe how the model responds to drastic changes in the input parameters. The rate constants use to generate the leftmost column of Figure 2 were modified by various powers of 10, and the effect on the simulated behavior of the p53 ubiquitination system was studied. It was observed that MDM2 continued to accelerate the ubiquitination process while E2D3-Ub persistently worked to inhibit it. Simulations for a modification by a factor of (Left) 10^1 and (Right) 10^2 are provided.

Table 1: Definitions of Model Parameters

Constants	Definitions
C_1	$-k_1^5$
C_2'	$2k_{-3}k_1^4 + k_1^4k_3 + k_1^4k_4 + k_1^4k_5$
C_3	$-k_{-3}^2k_1^3 - k_{-3}k_1^3k_3 - k_{-3}k_1^3k_4 - k_1^3k_3k_4 - 2k_{-3}k_1^3k_5 - k_1^3k_3k_5 - k_1^3k_4k_5$
C_4	$k_{-3}k_1^2k_3k_4 + k_{-3}^2k_1^2k_5 + k_{-3}k_1^2k_3k_5 + k_{-3}k_1^2k_4k_5 + k_1^2k_3k_4k_5$
C_5	$-k_{-3}k_1k_3k_4k_5$
C_6	$k_1^4k_2$
C_7	$-2k_{-3}k_1^3k_2 - k_1^3k_2k_3 - k_1^3k_2k_4 - k_1^3k_2k_5$
C_8	$k_{-3}^2k_1^2k_2 + k_{-3}k_1^2k_2k_3 + k_{-3}k_1^2k_2k_4 + k_1^2k_2k_3k_4 + 2k_{-3}k_1^2k_2k_5 + k_1^2k_2k_3k_5 + k_1^2k_2k_4k_5$
C_9	$-k_{-3}k_1k_2k_3k_4 - k_{-3}^2k_1k_2k_5 - k_{-3}k_1k_2k_3k_5 - k_{-3}k_1k_2k_4k_5$
C_{10}	$-k_1^2k_2k_3k_4$
C_{11}	$-k_{-3}k_2k_3k_4k_5$
C_{12}	$k_{-3}k_1k_2k_3k_4 + k_1k_2k_3k_4k_5$
C_{13}	k_5
C_{14}	$-k_2$
C_{15}	$\frac{2k_5}{-k_{-3}-k_3-k_4+\sqrt{-4k_3k_4+(k_{-3}+k_3+k_4)^2}+2k_5}$
C_{16}	$\frac{2k_5}{-k_{-3}-k_3-k_4-\sqrt{-4k_3k_4+(k_{-3}+k_3+k_4)^2}+2k_5}$
C_{17}	k_1^4
C_{18}	$-2k_{-3}k_1^3 - k_1^3k_3 - k_1^3k_4$
C_{19}	$k_{-3}^2k_1^2 + k_{-3}k_1^2k_3 + k_{-3}k_1^2k_4 + k_1^2k_3k_4$
C_{20}	$-k_{-3}k_1k_3k_4$
C_{21}	$-k_1^3k_2$
C_{22}	$2k_{-3}k_1^2k_2 + k_1^2k_2k_3 + k_1^2k_2k_4$
C_{23}	$-k_{-3}^2k_1k_2 - k_{-3}k_1k_2k_3 - k_{-3}k_1k_2k_4 - k_1k_2k_3k_4$
C_{24}	$k_{-3}k_2k_3k_4$
C_{25}	$k_1k_2k_3k_4$
C_{26}	$-k_{-3}k_2k_3k_4$
C_{27}	$-k_1^3$
C_{28}	$2k_{-3}k_1^2 + k_1^2k_3 + k_1^2k_4$
C_{29}	$-k_{-3}^2k_1 - k_{-3}k_1k_3 - k_{-3}k_1k_4 - k_1k_3k_4$
C_{30}	$k_{-3}k_3k_4$
C_{31}	$k_1k_3k_4$
C_{32}	$-\frac{k_2^2}{k_3k_4}$
C_{33}	$-\frac{k_{-3}k_2+k_2k_3+k_2k_4}{k_3k_4}$
C_{34}	-1
C_{35}	$\frac{k_1^2}{k_3k_4}$
C_{36}	$-\frac{k_{-3}k_1+k_1k_4}{k_3k_4}$
C_{37}	$-\frac{k_{-3}k_2+k_2k_4}{k_3k_4}$
C_{38}	$\frac{k_{-3}k_2+k_2k_4}{k_3k_4}$
C_{39}	$-\frac{2k_{-3}}{k_{-3}+k_3-k_4+\sqrt{-4k_3k_4+(k_{-3}+k_3+k_4)^2}}$
C_{40}	$-\frac{2k_{-3}}{k_{-3}+k_3-k_4-\sqrt{-4k_3k_4+(k_{-3}+k_3+k_4)^2}}$

Classification of Vocal Fold Diseases Using RASTA-PLP

Mansour Alsulaiman, Ghulam Muhammad and Zulfiqar Ali
Speech Processing Group, College of Computer and Information Sciences, King Saud University, Riyadh 11543, Saudi Arabia
Email: {msuliman, ghulam, zuali}@ksu.edu.sa

Abstract-*Various techniques of speech/speaker recognition has implemented in voice pathology assessment systems in the last decade. Classification of the vocal fold disorders is a difficult task as compares to disorder detection. In this paper, RASTA-PLP (Relative Spectral Transform Perceptual Linear Predictive) is deployed for the classification of four different types of vocal fold disorders. Sixty five dysphonic patients, containing male and female, of cyst, GERD, Polyp, and sulcus are taken into account. The diseases are classified by use of multi-class SVM. The results obtained are very encouraging. It is found that 100% classification rate can be achieved by choosing the suitable word for each disease.*

Keywords: Pathology classification, RASTA-PLP, multi-class SVM, Vector Quantization, Arabic digits.

1 Introduction

Assessment or diagnosis of voice disorders relies, besides other parameters, on the correct measurement of voice. There are two types of measurements, which are subjective and objective. Subjective measurement of voice quality is based on individual experience [1-3]. On the other hand, objective measurement that includes acoustical analysis is independent of human bias and can assess the voice quality more reliably by relating certain parameters to vocal fold behavior.

Current practices are therefore shifting towards developing new techniques of acoustic measures to improve the performance of an automatic voice disorder assessment system that should be capable of detecting the pathology, and classification the type of disorder. Many types of acoustic measures are reported in the literature to differentiate between disordered voice and normal voice. The acoustic measures can be divided mainly into three groups: temporal, frequency, and cepstral. Temporal features include amplitude perturbation (shimmer) and pitch perturbation (jitter) [4, 5]; frequency features include mean fundamental frequency, spectrum centroid, standard deviation of frequency, spectrum flatness, etc. [5]; and cepstral features include cepstral peak prominence (CPP) [6], CPP smoothed (CPPS) [7], etc. The use of RASTA-PLP for speech pathology was not reported in the literature. In [8], we performed digit recognition for dysphonic patients using RASAT-PLP and showed that it outperformed the other speech features, MFCC and LPCC. In this paper, the use of RASTA-PLP for disease classification is investigated.

Most of the work in speech pathology in the literature uses sustained vowel. Sustained vowel is useful for acoustic analysis in a controlled way; however, it is not an actual representation or way of talking in day to day life. Sustained vowel does not have prominent attributes such as voice onset and offset, voice breaks, pitch variation, etc. These attributes are equally important for the measurement of voice quality in everyday speech. In most of the available literature, acoustic measures are applied on sustained vowel, particularly /a/ vowel [9]. A few numbers of research works involving running speech compared to sustained vowel have been done so far in voice pathology detection [10], [11]. In this paper we use words as the speech to be analyzed.

Automatic speech/speaker recognition (ASR) framework has been used to detect voice pathology in most of the reported works [12-15] but only few researches tackled classification. An ASR system consists of two main components: feature extraction and classification. In [16], five pathologies, i.e., edema, nodules, polyps, cyst and paralysis are used for the classification. LPC and LPCC have provided correct appetence rates of 73% each, and the efficiencies were 85% and 80%, respectively, when the vocal folds edema was detected from other pathologies or normal voices. In [17], LPC and MFCC features are inputted to KNN and SVM for the classification of three classes. The sustained vowel /a/ was recorded to develop the database, and voice samples are labeled as healthy, nodular and diffuse. The best classification rate for LPC is 67.31%, and the rate for MFCC was 73.08%. An automatic voice disorder classification system by using vowels is proposed in [18]. Four features that include first two formants of two Arabic vowels are used in the system. The first vowel /a/ is called Al Fat'ha (َ) in Arabic language, second vowel /i/ is called Al Kasra (ِ). VQ and ANN are used as classification technique. ANN achieves higher classification rate, which is 67.86% for female speakers and 52.5% for male speakers.

The problem of classification the type of disorder needs more attention. In this paper, a difficult task is taken into account that voice disorder classification system is developed with the use of isolated words. In this system, RASTA-PLP coefficients are extracted from disordered voices and fed to multi-class SVM to determine the type of vocal fold disorder.

The rest of the paper is organized as follows: section 2 presents the proposed classification system. Section 3 describes experimental setup and discussion on the results. Finally, section 4 draws some conclusion.

2 Proposed Classification System

In the proposed classification system, RASTA_PLP is used to extract the features from digits. Before inputting the feature vector to multi-class SVM, the centroids of the highly representative vectors, are determined by using VQ. The database used to conduct the experiments contains the sample of four different types of voice disorder. Each patient has uttered nine Arabic digits.

2.1 Voice Disorder Database

The speech samples were recorded from patients with different voice disorders who attended the voice clinic at King Abdulaziz University Hospital between 2009 and 2010. A total of 65 speakers of four different types of voice disorders nine Arabic digits from one to nine. Table 1 lists the Arabic digits used in the experiments. The four types of voice disorders considered in this work were cysts, GERD, Polyp and sulcus vocalis. Table 2 gives the speakers' distribution according to their disease. The speakers' ages ranged from 18 to 50 years, and all of them were native Arabs. The speech samples were recorded in different sessions at Communication and Swallowing Disorders Unit, King Abdul Aziz University Hospital, King Saud University, Riyadh by experienced phoneticians in a sound proof room using a standardized recording protocol. All the patients' speech samples were recorded using the KayPentax computerized speech lab (CSL Model 4300). All the recorded voices were down sampled from 50 kHz to 16 kHz.

Table 1
List of Arabic numbers and their IPA

Numbers			
Symbol	Digit	Arabic writing	IPA
1	Wahed	واحد	wa:-ħid
2	Athnayn	أثنين	?iθ-ni:n
3	Thalathah	ثلاثة	θa-la:-θah
4	Arbaah	أربعة	?ar-ba-`ah
5	Khamsah	خمسة	xam-sah
6	Settah	ستة	Sit-tah
7	Sabaah	سبعة	sab-`ah
8	Thamanyah	ثمانية	θa-ma-ni-jah
9	Tesaah	تسعة	tis-`ah

Table 2
Number of Patients for each Disease

Disease	**Patients**	
	Male	*Female*
Cyst	6	6
GERD	19	3
Polyp	6	4
Sulcus	14	7
Total	45	20

2.2 Relative Spectral Transform Perceptual Linear Predictive Coefficients

The Perceptual Linear Predictive (PLP) [19] was proposed by Hermansky in 1990, and it demonstrates improvement over the LPCC. The PLP is based on the short term spectrum of speech. Linear prediction (LP) stresses on high frequencies while PLP emphasizes F1 and F2 and deemphasize high frequencies. PLP reduces disparity between voiced and unvoiced speech and they are also insensitive to the vocal tract length. [20].The The Relative Spectral Transformation (RASTA) is a way of warping spectra to minimize the differences between speakers while preserving the important speech information and makes PLP more robust to linear spectral distortion [21].

2.3 Vector Quantization

The RASTA-PLP features are compressed using VQ before inputting it to SVM. The features from all speakers of a specific disease for each digit are compressed using VQ. To achieve this, VQ [22] is implemented with the help of *kmeans* algorithm. Feature vectors, which are similar to each other makes a cluster and only one highly representative feature vector (the mean of these feature vectors) represents the whole cluster. This highly representative vector is called code vector and collection of these code vectors is called codebook. A codebook for each type of disease is constructed by using VQ. The generated codebooks are fed to multi-class SVM to generate the model for each voice disorder for training of the system.

2.4 Support Vector Machine

Support vector machine is proposed by Vapnik [23], and it can be used for pattern recognition just like multilayers perceptron and radial basis function networks [24]. SVM became popular due to its good performance and low computational cost as compared to GMM and HMM. The idea of SVM is to construct a decision surface (a hyper plane), where the dimension of a hyper plane depends on the dimension of the input vector, to maximize the distance between two classes, +1 and -1. To implement a multi-class SVM, the technique called 'One vs All' is used in this research.

3 Experimental Results and Discussion

Different experiments are performed to observe the performance of the developed classification system. The extracted RASTA-PLP coefficients are 12, 24 and 36, which are the features, the features with their first derivative, and the features with their first and second derivatives respectively. The size of VQ codebook is fixed at 250 after trying different sizes, i.e. 100, 150, 200, 250, and 300. The 'Linear' kernel is used to train the multi-class SVM. The accuracy of each digit with 12 RASTA-PLP is given in the Table 3.

Table 3
Voice Disorder Classification with 12 RASTA-PLP

Digits	Accuracy (%)				Avg. (%)
	Cyst	*GERD*	*Polyp*	*Sulcus*	
1	**75**	50	67	67	63
2	25	67	0	50	42
3	**75**	67	0	50	53
4	**75**	83	**100**	50	74
5	50	67	33	33	47
6	50	67	67	50	58
7	50	83	67	**83**	74
8	0	67	67	67	53
9	25	**100**	33	17	47

Bold values representing the maximum accuracy for a disorder

The accuracies of different disorders are varying for different digits. The maximum accuracy of cyst is 75% with digit 1, 3 and 4, for GERD it is 100% with digits 9, for polyp it is also 100% with digit 4, and for sulcus it is 83% with digit 7. A comparison between maximum accuracies for the digits is depicted in Fig.1.

An average accuracy of 72% and 78% is obtained for GERD and polyp, respectively, for digits 1, 4, and 7. The averaged classification rates for each disease for digits 1, 4, and 7 are provided in Table 4.

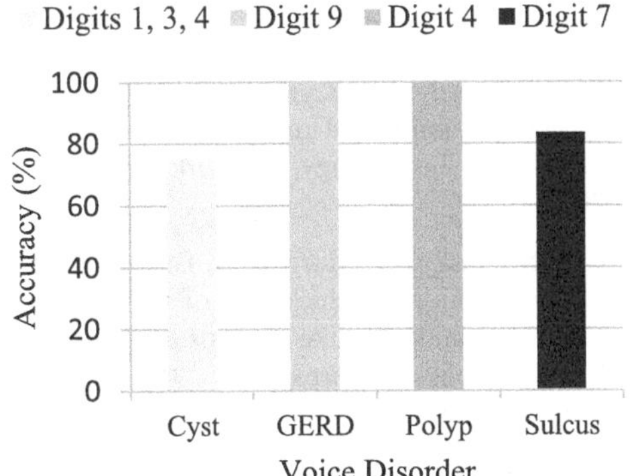

Fig. 1. Maximum Accuracies for Each Disease

Table 4
Voice Disorder Classification with 12 RASTA-PLP

Digits	Accuracy (%)				Avg. (%)
	Cyst	*GERD*	*Polyp*	*Sulcus*	
1	75	50	67	67	63
4	75	83	100	50	74
7	50	83	67	83	74
Avg.	67	72	78	67	70

Some experiments are performed with 24 and 36 RASTA-PLP coefficients, for each digit. The averages of the accuracies for all types of disorder are calculated for digits 1, 4, and 7. The trend of average accuracies of the three digits is depicted in Fig. 2. By observing Fig. 2, it can be concluded that the results with 12 coefficients are better than 24 and 36 coefficients.

4 Conclusion

Every Arabic digit has different set of vowels and consonant. This may be the reason that some digits performed well for certain disease. The average classification rates for the disorders, especially for GERD and polyp are encouraging with the group of digits 1, 4, and 7. By using RASTA-PLP the individual classification rates for GERD and polyp are 100% and achieved with digit 9 and digit 4, respectively. The maximum classification rate for cyst and sulcus is 75% and 83%, respectively.

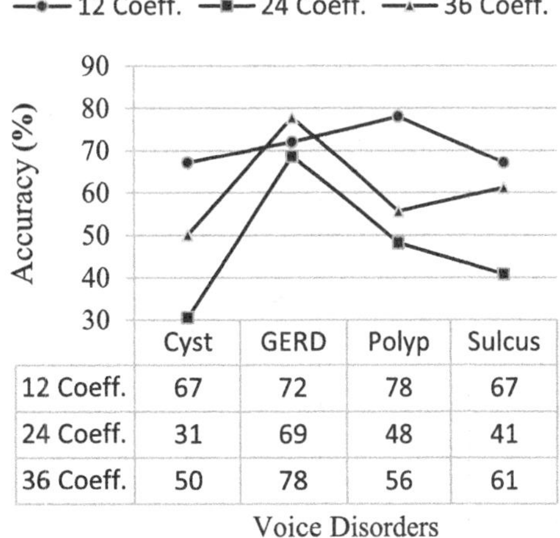

	Cyst	GERD	Polyp	Sulcus
12 Coeff.	67	72	78	67
24 Coeff.	31	69	48	41
36 Coeff.	50	78	56	61

Fig. 2. Trend of average accuracies for digits 1, 4, 7, and 9

Acknowledgment

This work is supported by the National Plan for Science and Technology in King Saud University under grant number 12-MED2474-02. The authors are grateful for this support.

References

[1] J. Kreiman, B. R. Gerratt, and K. Precoda, ''Listener experience and perception of voice quality," Journal Speech Hearing Research, vol. 33, pp. 103–115, 1990.

[2] R. C. Rabinov, J. Krieman, B. R. Gerratt, and S. Bielamowicz, "Comparing reliability of perceptual ratings of roughness and acoustic measures of jitter," Journal Speech Hearing Research, vol. 38, pp. 26–32, 1995.

[3] J. Kreiman, B. R. Gerratt, and K. Precoda, and G. S. Berke, "Individual differences in voice quality perception," Journal Speech Hearing Research, vol. 35, pp. 512–520, 1992.

[4] E. J. Wallen and J. H. L. Hansen, "A screening test for speech pathology assessment using objective quality measures," Proc. International Conference on Spoken Language Processing (ICSLP), vol. 2, pp. 776-779, October 1996.

[5] R. J. Moran, R. B. Reilly, P. Chazal, and P. D. Lacy, "Telephony-Based Voice Pathology Assessment Using Automated Speech Analysis," IEEE Trans. Biomedical Engineering, vol. 53, no. 3, pp. 468-477, 2006.

[6] Y. D. Heman-Ackah, R. J. Heuer, D. D. Michael, R. Ostrowski, M. Horman, M. Baroody, J. Hillenbrand, and R. T. Sataloff, "Cepstral peak prominence: a more reliable measure of dysphonia," Ann Otol Rhinol Laryngol., vol. 112, no. 4, pp. 324-333, 2003.

[7] R. Shrivastav and C. M. Sapienza, "Objective measures of breathy voice quality obtained using an auditory model," J. Acoustic Society America, vol. 114, no. 4, pp. 2217–2224, Oct. 2003.

[8] M. Alsulaiman, "Speech recognition for medically disordered voice", Proceedings of 24thInternational Conference on Computers and Their Applications in Industry and Engineering, CAINE, pp. 233-237, 2011.

[9] M. Vieira, F. Mclnnes, and M. Jack, "On the influence of laryngeal pathologies on acoustic and electroglottalgraphic jitter measures," Journal of Acoustic Society of America, vol. 111, no. 2, pp. 1045-1055, 2002.

[10] K. Umapathy, S. Krishnan, V. Parsa, and D. G. Jamieson, "Discrimination of pathological voices using a time-frequency approach," IEEE Trans. On Biomedical Engineering, vol. 52, no. 3, March 2005.

[11] S. Y. Lowell, R. H. Colton, R. T. Kelley, and Y. C. Hahn, "Spectral- and cepstral-based measures during continuous speech: capacity to distinguish dysphonia and consistency within a speaker," Journal of Voice, vol. 25, no. 5, pp. e223 - e232, 2011.

[12] S. C. Costa, B. G. Neto, J. M. Fechine, and S. Correia, "Parametric cepstral analysis for pathological voice assessment," Proc. Symposium on Applied Computing (SAC'08), pp. 1410-1414, 2008.

[13] J. I. Godino-Llorente, P. Gomes-Vilda, and M. Blanco-Velasco, "Dimensionality Reduction of a Pathological Voice Quality Assessment System Based on Gaussian Mixture Models and Short-Term Cepstral Parameters," IEEE Trans. on Biomedical Engineering, Vol. 53, No. 10, pp. 1943-1953, October 2006.

[14] A. Maier, T. Haderlein et al., "Automatic Speech Recognition Systems for the Evaluation of Voice and Speech Disorders in Head and Neck Cancer," EURASIP Journal on Audio, Speech, and Music Processing, Article ID 926951, 2010.

[15] J. I. G. Llorente and P. G. Vilda, "Automatic detection of voice impairments by means of short-term cepstral parameters and neural network based detectors," IEEE Tran. Biomedical Engineering, vol. 51, no. 2, pp. 380-384, Feb. 2004.

[16] B.G.A. Neto, S.C. Costa, J.M. Fechine and M. Muppah, "Feature estimation for vocal fold edema detection using short-term cepstral analysis", Proceedings of 7th International Conference on Bio-Informatics and Bio-Engineering, BIBE, pp. 1158-1162, 2007.

[17] A. Gelzinis, A. Verikas, and M. Bacauskiene ,"Automated speech analysis applied to laryngeal disease categorization", Journal of Computer Methods and Programs in Biomedicine, vol. 91, no. 1, pp. 36-47, July 2008.

[18] G. Muhammad, M. Alsulaiman, A. Mahmood and Z. Ali , "Automatic voice disorder classification using vowel formants", The 2011 IEEE International Conference on Multimedia and Expo (ICME 2011), Barcelona, July 11-15, 2011.

[19] H. Hermansky, "Perceptual linear predictive (PLP) analysis for speech", J. Acoust. Soc. Am., pp. 1738-1752, 1990.

[20] M. A. Anusuya, S. K. Katti, "Front end analysis of speech recognition: a review", International Journal of Speech Technology, vol. 14, pp. 99-145, Dec. 2010.

[21] H. Hermansky, N. Morgan, A. Bayya, and P. Kohn, "Compensation for the effect of the communication channel in auditory-like analysis of speech (RASTA-PLP)", Proc. of Eurospeech '91, pp. 1367-1371, Genova, Italy, 1991.

[22] Zulfiqar Ali, M. Aslam, A. M. M. Enriquez., "A Speaker Identification System using MFCC Features with VQ Technique", IITA 09, Nanchang, China, 2009.

[23] S. Haykin, McMaster University, Hamilton, Ontario, Canada, Neural Networks a Comprehensive Foundation, 2nd edition, pp.256-347.

[24] S. M. Kamruzzaman, A. N. M. RezaulKarim, Md. Saiful Islam And Md. EmadadulHaque, "Speaker Identification using MFCC-Domain support vector machine", International Journal of Electrical and Power Engineering, vol. 1, no. 3, pp. 274-278, 2007.

M.M.R SYSTEM

"Mass-Micro-Reconstruction"

Dr. Boucherit Taieb,
BOUCHERIT Laboratory, Oran, Algeria
53, road salhi houari "hipodromme" saint heugene, **Oran, Algeria**
Sponsored by **Dr. Boudiaf Abdelmalek** Prefect of Oran town , Algeria

Abstract – *The MMR system, or mass-micro reconstruction is an important discovery that allows us the reconstruction of an organ from the capture of its energy released by a physicochemical phenomenon, finally we will obtain a copy by composite material of the studied organ with all contained information's in this organ at the instant T when it was taken. The second step is the study and processing and reading of the taken photos from different angles of this composite by computer.*

1 Introduction

It is a discovery which allows us the reconstruction of any organ that we want to study, by a physicochemical process, starting from the emission of its energy without use any electronic or computer equipments at the first stage, it is only starting from the reconstitution of the organ and after taking photos of such organ obtained in composite that the computer intervenes for processing and analysis. The contribution of the contest of computers is crucial for the detailed imagery of this system

The reconstruction of the organ by a composite material is done from interior towards the external of the organ, in the direction of the cell to the organ itself

I put your at kind attention the images obtained by MMR system as well as the advance of all the procedure and you can even judge the quality of these images that are single in the world.

2 Material & Methods

2.1 Materials

The material is very simple; it consists of composite material as well as all the material of a physics laboratory, chemistry & computers.

2.2 Methods

- sensors.
- Materials chemical.
- Materials physics.
- Materials composites.
- The "organo-histo-*rebuilding*" makes it possible to manufactures the body in composite material starting from its emitted energy.
- The first stage of manufacture of the finished body, we proceed to the catch of photographs under various angles of the composite and the image processing is done by data-processing method.

2.3 Theory & explanation

We heard a lot of the memory of water,
It goes without saying that the opponents of this theory did not well understood the scope of such theory and the scientists who worked on the subject did not bring the formal and indisputable evidences to substantiate their discovery .

The problem was not well stated from the beginning since because to tackle the subject of the memory of water and to prove this theory, must basically take into account two distinct phenomena and prove their existence scientifically

- The existence of an energy contained and emitted in each cell, organ, and body
- Water memorizes and maintains this energy in its form since its composition intra cellular with the organ itself.

The energy of an organ emitted is collected and maintained in water during a given period of time before being dissolved, therefore if we manage to visualize the energy of this organ in water, we have to prove this theory, but the visualization of this energetic body is difficult the current instruments and means .
I state the problem in a different way, and I managed to find the experimental solution to prove this theory
Any organ emit an energy from the ultra cellular to the organ itself ; we can collect this energy by sensors, and carry out its "moulding" by a physicochemical process, we obtain at the end of the phase of "moulding" and this composite materials gives us the real certified copy of the organ.

2.4 **Process & technic:**

Each organ , from it's tiny or small unit to the mass itself, bathes in an energy , and any organ is made of material body and energetic body which is identical to the material body in it's minute details.

* The material body is visible and concrete

* The energetic body is invisible to the human eye as well as to the actual apparatuses of detection or visualization.
The energetic body present particular characteristics to know :
- It is formed of an unknown energy
- This energy fills the organism from the very small unit to the organism itself.
- It's volume is more important than the mass it occupies
- The mass bathes in this energy.
-This energy takes the form of the mass.
-The pressure is négative and it is characterized by a reversed.
-This energy is anchored in the mass it occupied
- The mass and energy duo is inseparable from each other making its coexistence vital.

- This unknown energy is invisible and to the naked eye and to the different existing equipement.

-This energy is formed of unknown particles .

Theses characteristics have been observed through experiences performed ,the big dificulty is that we can neither visualise nor mesure this energy nor with the equipements that technology may provide at the moment where which is a way to find the mean to make it visible even if it is impossible to do so ,the idea is to make such energy concrete .

After a long experiences ,we could understand different matters and particularly to know :

It may be captivated
- Water is the only environment that can preserve it in memory in it's whole state as it existed.
- It's memorizing in water stay a certain period of time before being disolved and disapper.

Taking a human head and visualize the head energy we obtain:

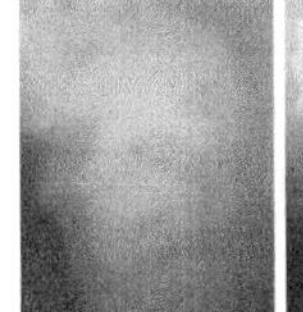
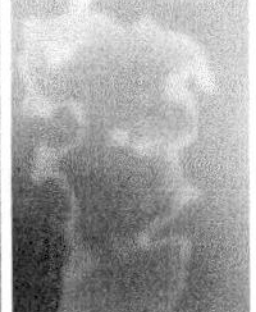
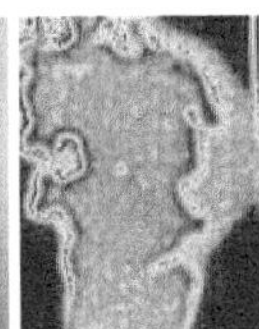
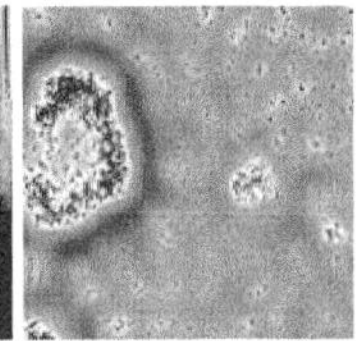

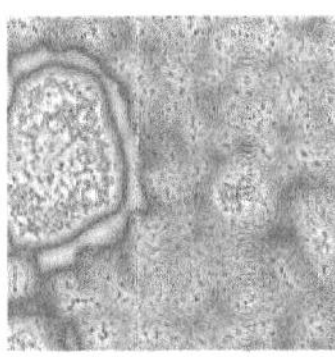
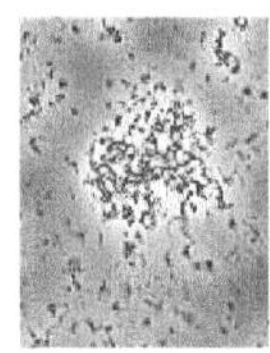
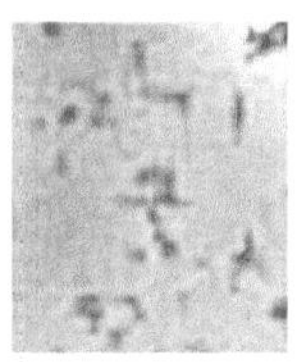

We observe that the composition of a such energy is made of unknown particles ,in practice,theses particles are always in movement ,giving the continual boiling aspect to this energy which is observable by the MMR system ,another thing was observed that this energy is found in it's structure and mobility in any organic body, vegetal, mineral.

example of the brain:

The red brain is the material brain as it really exists, while blue is the brain energetic. the red brain material bathed in the blue brain energetic. one is inseparable from the other, they are anchored and indivisible. the energetic brain is reversed in its configuration compared to material brain, The idea of capturing the energy emitted by the brain to be the image of the brain energy, that is to say inverted brain material. Our experience is captured the energy of a body for viewing, after extensive research it has been proven that the only environement capable of preserving this energy is water.
To illustrated this, we performed the uptake of energy of several organs readily recognizable that we put in water.
The next phase was the modeling of this energy to be able to compare the organ with the mold obtained

The organs of experiment are as follows:

- **The brain**
- **The kidney**
- **The liver**
- **The heart**
- **The ear**

We take these organs simply because they are easily recognizable.
After testing is obtained composite material:

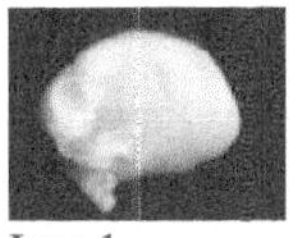
Img 1
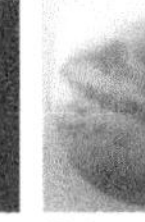
Img 2

Img 3

Img 4

Img 5

Img 1: brain
Img 2: Kidney
Img 3: liver
Img 4: Heart
Img 5: ear

The first stage is a physico-chemical, it allows us to obtain the composite organs from their énergie. the captur process is complex but easy to made, the energy released each organ can be captured and isolated in a specific environement which is the water,
the conservation of energy captured must be made by following a strict protocol that is to say that we should not other energies we will join in this case several composites of different energies, this is why the process must be mastered perfectly,
once the energy of the isolated organ in that particular setting, we proceeded to step visualization of the organ by a cast of this energy in a composite material, one obtains the body itself into a mold from his energy I want to digress by saying that this method of reproduction of the organ is revolutionary because it fact itself, and reproduces the organ in these exactness microscopic details.
(I do not describe the details here because this is a patent)
the proofs are the organs in composite materials of various organs. You can take any organ form the body or all humain body if desired.
More extraordinary still, we can replicate composite plants, and minerals.
We have taken as examples of experiments of human body organs easily recognizable.
After experimentation, we obtain:

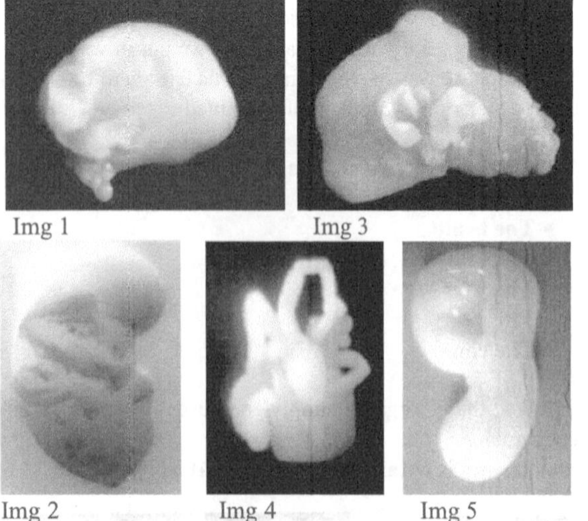

Img 1 Img 3
Img 2 Img 4 Img 5

Each energy emitted from a organ gives this organ of composite material with details of the infinitely small, with one fundamental difference, the resulting composite organ reproduces the real organ in reverse, in the example image is that of a gan that one back the other way, what is inside comes out and vice versa, to better understand it will take to every organ and its inverse which happens to be the real image of organ.

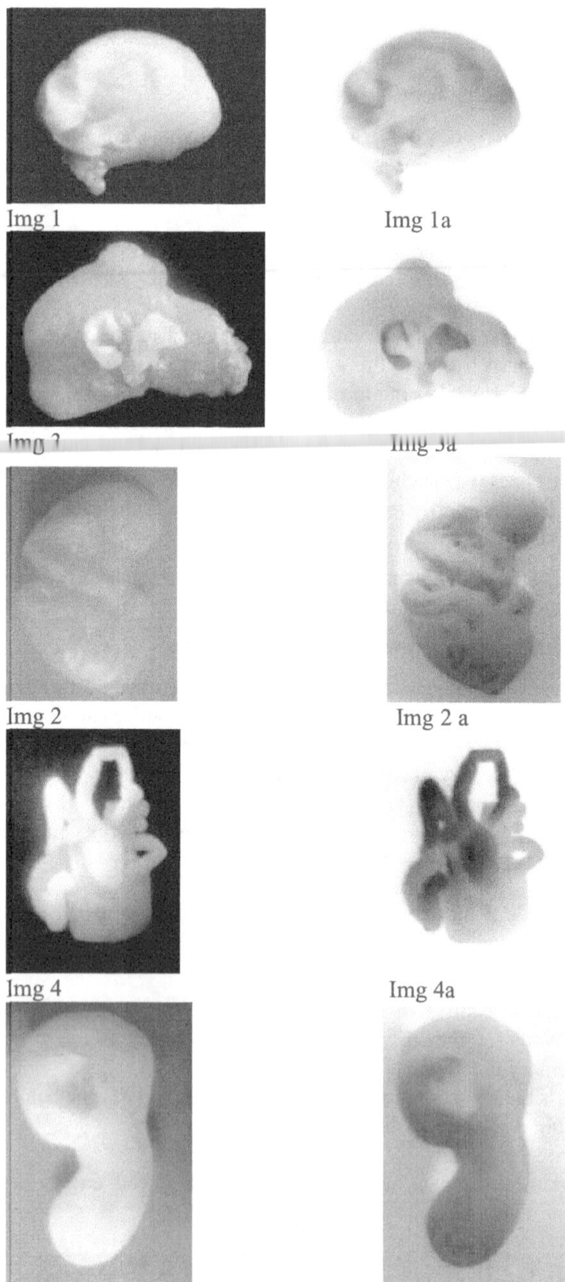

Img 1 Img 1a
Img 3 Img 3a
Img 2 Img 2 a
Img 4 Img 4a
Img 5 Img 5a

Img 1 : Brain image   Img 1a : Brain negative image
Img 2 : Kidney image   Img 2a : Kidney negative
Img 3 : Liver image   Img 3a : Liver negative image
Img 4 : Heart image   Img4 a : Heart negative image
Img 5 : Ear image   Img 5a : Ear negative image

2.5 Processing images

The images processing is achieved by computer processing, each obtained image is a "data bank" image, that's to say; it encloses an infinity number of images each one processing a précised information if we take a primary image; we can extract a secondary one, a tertiary and so on.

Image 1 ⟶ image 1.1
Image1.1 ⟶ image 1.2
Image1.2 ⟶ image 1.3
Image 1. (n-1) ⟶ image 1. (n)

2.5.1 The Brain

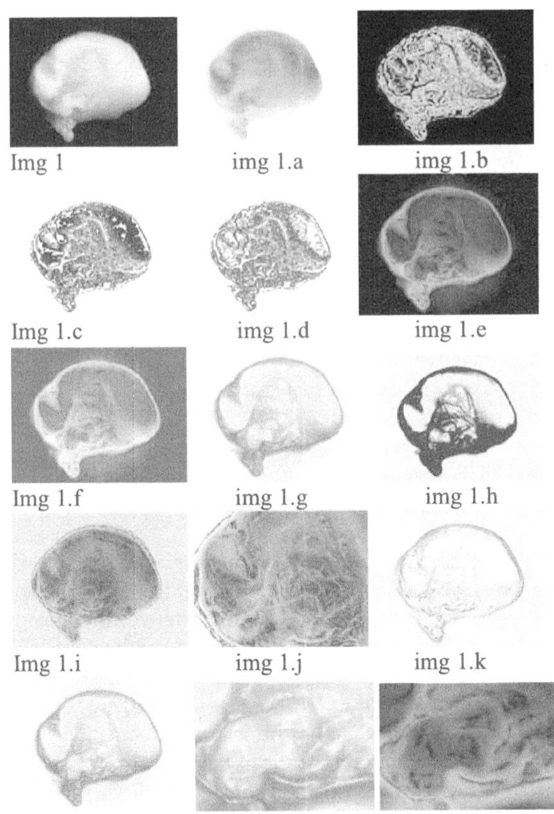

Img 1 | img 1.a | img 1.b
Img 1.c | img 1.d | img 1.e
Img 1.f | img 1.g | img 1.h
Img 1.i | img 1.j | img 1.k
Img 1.g | img 1.g Enlargement | img 1.g negative

Img 1 : Brain image   Img 1.a: Brain negative
Img 1.b: internal structure   Img 1.c: internal structure
Img 1.d: cranial arteries   Img 1.e : cranial arteries
Img 1.f : internal part   Img 1.g : internal structure
Img 1.h: ventricle   Img 1.i: cranial arteries
Img 1.j : enlargement   Img 1.k : negative image

In the brain case, from the first image which is a real one "data bank image", we can have an important number of images, each one treating a specified information, on contrary of the scan image that treat only a unique information, as this scanographic image is not real, it is the result of observed and approximative image in the data base of the scanner computer.

2.5.2 The Liver

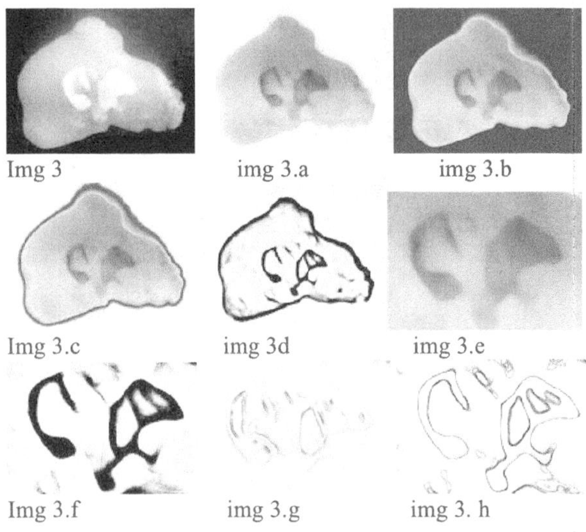

Img 3 | img 3.a | img 3.b
Img 3.c | img 3d | img 3.e
Img 3.f | img 3.g | img 3. h

img 3 : liver in composite material
img 3.a: negative
img 3.b: real image of the liver
img 3.c: image of the liver arteries
img 3.d: image sketches
img 3.e: image showing the hepatic artery below and above
img 3.f: hepatic artery below and above
img 3.g: hepatic arteries
img 3.h: sketches hepatic arteries

Same case for the brain image; the primary image of the liver after a computer processing give us "Data Bank images" that it lock up in order to explain them clearly. Each image is such a book, the first image is the page number 1, we turn the first page, the second page lock up the same image with a difference and so on.

The novelty in this system is a as soon we get a image of an organ with composit material, this image is energetic and no numeric, an energetic image is a real image that enclose an infinite number of images, that's why it is a "Data Bank image" on contrary of the numeric images that is unique and approximative and no real.

2.5.3 The Heart

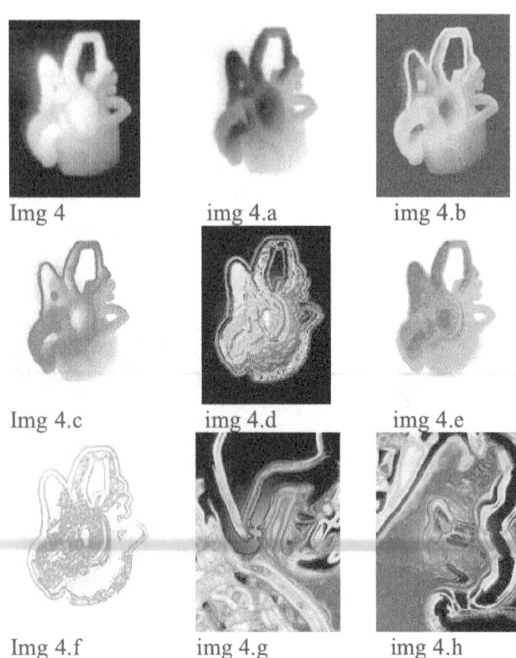

Img 4 img 4.a img 4.b
Img 4.c img 4.d img 4.e
Img 4.f img 4.g img 4.h

Img 4: Heart with vessels
img 4.a: negative image of the heart
img 4.b: appearance of internal structures of the heart
Img 4.c: negative image of the Heart
img 4.d: appearance of the internal structure of the heart
img 4.e: internal structure in negative
Img 4.f: microscopic structure
img 4.g: mitral valve
img 4.h: tricuspid valve

2.5.4 The Kideny

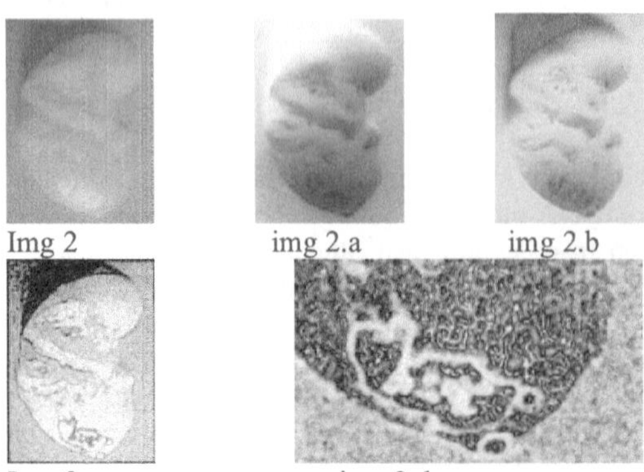

Img 2 img 2.a img 2.b
Img 2.c img 2.d

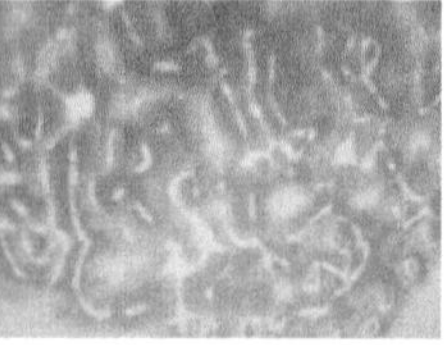

Img 2.e

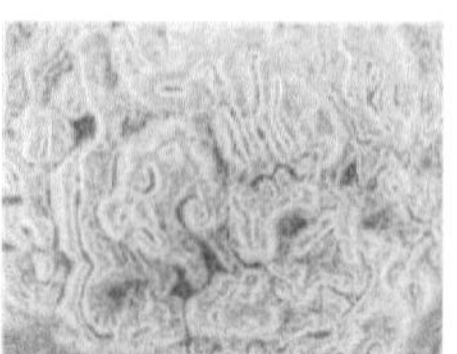

img 2.f

Img 2: Kidney
img 2.a: negative image of the kidney
img 2.b: onset of internal kidney structures
Img 2.c: internal structure appearance of a zone calculations
img 2.d: Calculated renal
Img 2.e microscopy of the kidney
img 2.f: nephritic glomeruli microscopic view

2.5.5 The Ear

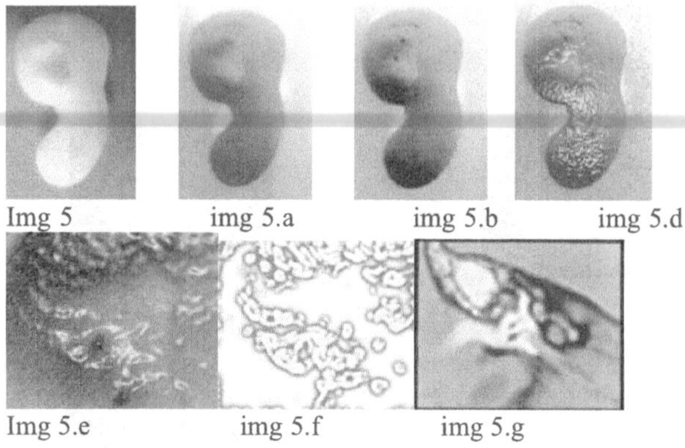

Img 5 img 5.a img 5.b img 5.d
Img 5.e img 5.f img 5.g

img 5: ear
img 5.a: image ear negative
img 5.b: appearance of internal structures
img 5.d: sketches of the ear
img 5.e: appearances middle and inner ear
img 5.f: OHR system internal structure in negative
img 5.g: comparison with IRM image inner ear

We have studied five different organs, the moulds of each organs obtained with the composit material is a confirm copy of the organ; each time we discover the external morphology of the organ as well as its internal architecture and microscopic details, each image taken by the MMR system has been compared with the real organ; it was identical same researches have been done on the internal architecture with comparative, the result are identical, the microscopic images of the MMR system are of better quality and high precision than the ones taken by the ordinary microscopic imagery.

2.6 Generalization of processes

2.6.1 M.M.R system in mineral domain

We come to describe an experimental process by using organs from human body, and to conclude that each organs have own his identical energy organ morphologically, even on the ultra-microscopic level.
This theory does'n apply only to the organic masses, but also to the vegetable and mineral masses.
Each plant material body is composed of two bodies
The material is observed and which is:
• the plant body,
• and the second is the plant body energy, identical to the physical body

Each mineral material bodies is composed of two bodies :

- The material is observed,
- The mineral body energy identical to the physical body

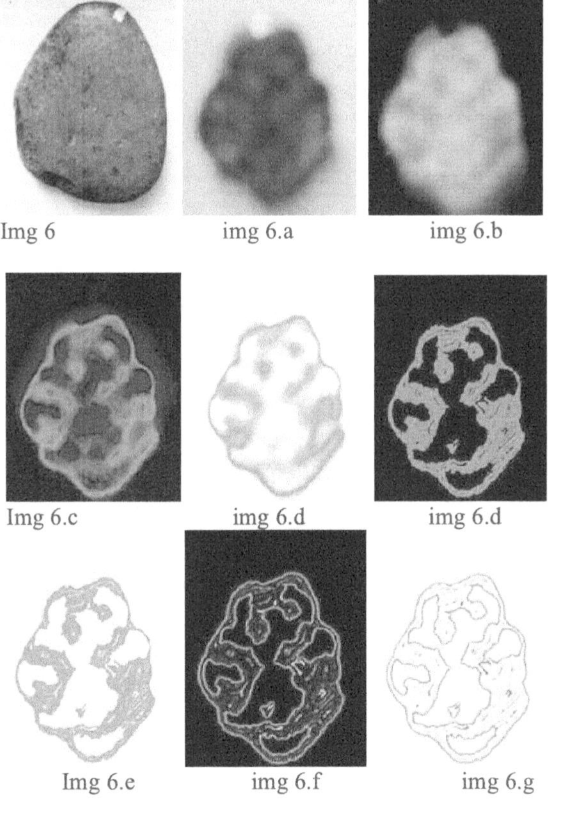

Img 6 img 6.a img 6.b

Img 6.c img 6.d img 6.d

Img 6.e img 6.f img 6.g

Img 6.h img 6.i

img 6: mineral mass
img 6.a: mass composite materials
img 6.b: image contrast
Img 6.e: appearance of the internal structure mineral
img 6.f: internal structure
img 6.g: detailed internal structure
Img 6.h: expansion
img 6.i: very precise internal structure

The MMR system gives us the the internal structure details of the mineral mass, no equipment in the world today can give this details of a compact mineral mass.
with the MMR system, we have the structure of aaccurate detailed with high precision.
That confirms the theory is valid for both masses, which is organic or mineral..

2.6.2 M.M.R system in vegetal domain

We come to experience the OHR system on organic compounds, on the mineral masses, the images collected give us the results which we can compare and show their exactness in all details with high exactitude demonstrate their accuracy internal structure.
We can also make a copy moulding of part of part of the organic, mineral or vegetable structure
We take as example to illustrate the vegetable part by making a moulding in composite of a mint sheet by visualizing only the petiole and the central vein.

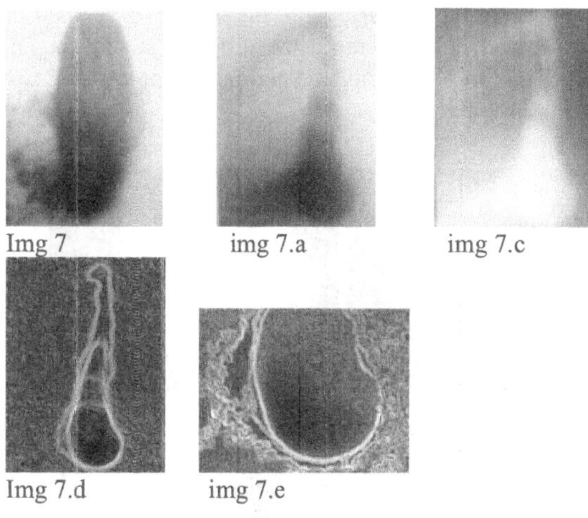

Img 7 img 7.a img 7.c

Img 7.d img 7.e

img 7 : mint leaf vegetable
img 7.a: composite copy of the midrib
img 7.c: inverse image
img 7.d: internal structure
img 7.e: enlargement

3. Conclusion

It is a discovery that allows us to prove:

- Existence of an energy that every tiny and small entity contains, this unknown energy exists in the organic masses, vegetal and mineral with specific characteristics already stated.
- The memorizing of this energy by water
- I made in practice a O.H.R system (or what it is called organo-historical –reconstruction) that allows us to reproduce a mold which is a true copy of the organ or the studied mass in its tiny or small unit.
- In medicine, this technique is really precise and rapid without any danger for the patients; the photos are more precise than any existing equipment at the moment.
- A new science is born with its multidisciplinary derivates in all fields.
- I modestly put at your kind attention the results of such research hoping that it will be a positive side and will bring harmony and preservation to humanity.
- I modestly put at your kind disposition the photos taken by the O.H.R system and the path as well as the procedure, and you can judge the quality of such photos that are single in the world.
- I put at your disposition the molds in composite materials representing the different studied organs that are the formal experimental proofs of such research.

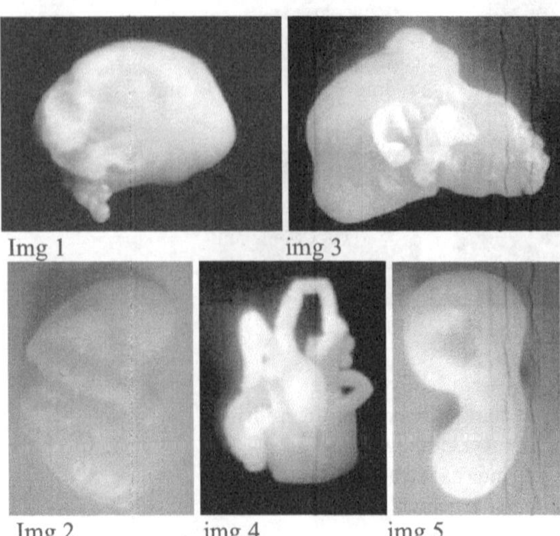

Img 1 img 3

Img 2 img 4 img 5

The relationship between oxidant-antioxidant status and bronchial obstructive parameters in patients with COPD

Solongo Khurts
Respiratory Department
First National Central Hospital
Ulaanbaatar, Mongolia
Sun_solongo@yahoo.com

Oyun-Erdene Namsrai
National University of Mongolia
oyunerdene@num.edu.mn

J.Narantsetseg, M.Ambaga
New Medicine Institute, Mongolia

***Abstract*— Air pollution has major health impacts on people living in Ulaanbaatar. As written in the WORLD BANK report: Ambient annual average particulate matter concentrations in the capital of Mongolia are 10–25 times greater than Mongolian air quality standards and are among the highest recorded measurements in any world capital. Chronic obstructive pulmonary disease (COPD) induced by air pollution and smoking was found to be a major cause of illness in Mongolia. We measured a wide range of parameters of the oxidant-antioxidant status in erythrocyte membrane, cytosol, plasma and urine of 196 patients with COPD and 80 healthy controls (HC). All data used in this paper is gathered since 2008 at the First National Central Hospital of Mongolia. Using the data mining methodology we selected highly effective features among them. Also the results were analyzed using SPSS 20 for Windows; Correlations between features were determined by Pearson's. Data are reported as mean and standard deviations. The statistical significance was given by a p value<0.05.**

An oxidant-antioxidant imbalance is thought to play an important role in the pathogenesis of chronic obstructive pulmonary disease (COPD). We hypothesized that antioxidant capacity reflected by cytochrome coxidase (COX), free radical scavenging substances (FRSC), and levels of the lipid peroxidation product malondialdehyde (MDA) in erythrocyte, plasma and urine may be related to the bronchial obstructive parameters in patients with COPD. The findings of the present study suggest that antioxidant capacity reflected by COX and the lipid peroxidation products MDA in erythrocyte's membrane are linked to the severity of COPD.

Keywords*— *chronic obstructive pulmonary disease, free radical scavenging activity, cytochrome c oxidase, lipid peroxides products, malondialdehyde

I. Introduction

COPD represents a major health problem, and its prevalence and mortality rates are increasing worldwide. COPD mainly caused by cigarette smoking and also a number of studies have shown a link between COPD and air pollution. Air pollution has major health impacts on people living in Ulaanbaatar. Ambient annual average particulate matter concentrations in the capital of Mongolia are 10–25 times greater than Mongolian air quality standards and are among the highest recorded measurements in any world capital. The excessively high particulate matter concentrations, especially in the winter and in the ger areas, increase the incidence of heart and lung diseases, and lead to premature deaths [1]. Oxidative stress, defined as an imbalance between increased exposure to oxidant and/or decreased anti-oxidative capacities, represents one of the key pathogenic mechanisms in the development of COPD [2]. A number of antioxidant disturbances have been observed in patients with COPD. Lipid peroxidation products, one of the key indicators of oxidative stress [3], are elevated in sputum and exhaled breath condensate of patients with COPD [4]. At the same time, the antioxidant mechanisms are attenuated in these patients, as indicated by reducing glutathione levels in the lungs [5], reduced glutathione peroxidase activity in erythrocytes [6] and lower antioxidant capacity in plasma [7] during exacerbations of COPD. Nevertheless, studies on the relationships between the oxidant-antioxidant imbalance and pulmonary functions showed inconsistent results. On the one hand, airway obstruction, reflected by reductions in forced expiratory volume in one second (FEV1), was shown to correlate with antioxidant substances such glutathione and myeloperoxidase levels [8]. Furthermore, lipid peroxidation products as measured as malondialdehyde (MDA) content correlated inversely with the degree of small airway obstruction [9]. On the other hand, however, more recent studies failed to find a significant relationship between plasma antioxidant capacity and pulmonary function in patients with COPD [7]. The aim of the present study was to assess the relationships between the COPD and antioxidant activity reflected by free radical scavenging capacity, cytochrome c oxidase and MDA levels in erythrocyte's membrane and cytosol, plasma and urine.

II. METHODS

Patients with COPD were consecutively recruited to the study in 2008, 2010 and 2012, at the Pulmonology Department of First National Central Hospital (Ulaanbaatar, Mongolia). All patients classified into four stages (Fig 1.) according to the American Thoracic Society/European Respiratory Society guidelines [10].

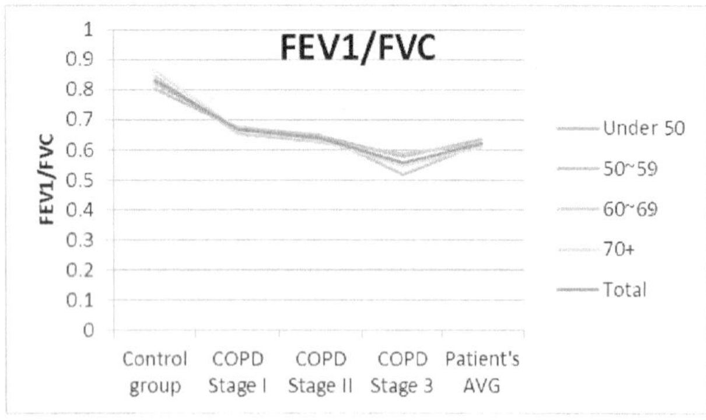

Fig. 1. COPD stages

Exclusion criteria were respiratory disorders other than the COPD, malignancy, overt cardiac failure, recent surgery, severe endocrine, hepatic or renal diseases. The control group included 80 healthy persons with similar ages, having normal pulmonary function tests.

		SaO_2	PaO_2
SaO2	Pearson Correlation	1	.880**
	Sig. (2-tailed)		.000
	N	188	188
PaO2	Pearson Correlation	.880**	1
	Sig. (2-tailed)	.000	
	N	188	188

**. Correlation is significant at the 0.01 level (2-tailed).

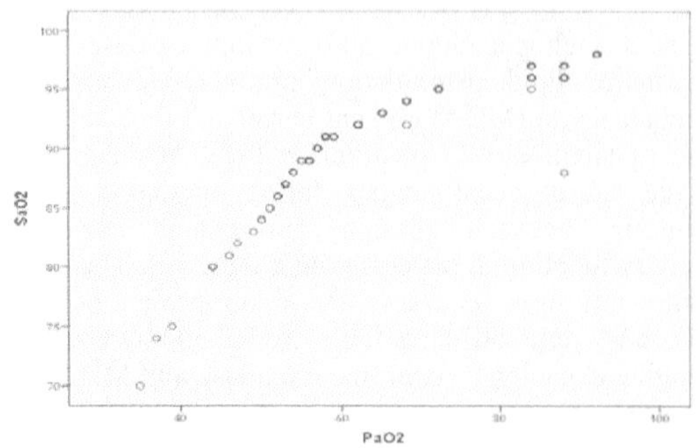

Fig. 2. Correlation between SaO2 and PaO2.

Pulmonary functional tests were evaluated by using of spirometer ST-320 (Mitsubishi, Japan). All pulmonary function tests were performed at the 10-15 minute after inhaling short-term β_2-agonist Salbutamol in dosage 0.2 mg. Forced expiratory volume in one second (FEV1) and forced vital capacity (FVC) were expressed as a percentage of the predicted value for age, sex, and height. Three technically acceptable measurements were performed in each patient, and the highest value was included in the analyses. PaO_2 was correlated with an oxygen saturation (SaO_2), what was measured by finger pulse-oxymeter and expressed as a percentage. (Fig 2).

Fasting venous blood samples were collected for the study of various parameters and taken in EDTA vial and in plain vials (without anticoagulant). Samples were used for the estimations of cytochrome coxidases, free radical scavenging activity, lipid peroxidation products in plasma, erythrocyte's cytosol and membrane suspension. Assessment of similar parameters was performed on urine, taken under standardized conditions.

Free radical scavenging activity measured as protonized products in plasma, urine, erythrocyte's cytosol and membrane suspension were determined by method, using of the stable free radical 2,2-diphenyl-2-picrylhydrazyl (DPPH), described by Brand-Williams (1995) and expressed as microgramm per milliliter. Cytochrome c oxidases (COX) in plasma, urine, erythrocyte's cytosol and membrane were estimated by using the HIMEDIA oxidase disks, based on the method described by Kovacs, developed by Gaby and Hadley (1957) and expressed as a minute. Lipid peroxidation in erythrocyte membranes, plasma and urine were assessed by measuring the concentration of thiobarbituric acid reactive substances (MDA-TBA) by spectrophotometry at 535 nm [11]. MDA levels are expressed as nanomoles of thiobarbituric acid reactive substances formed per liter of erythrocyte membrane suspension, plasma and urine.

Statistical analysis was carried out using SPSS 20. Continuous variables are shown as means ± SD. To assess the relationships between selected variables, Pearson's correlation analyses was used. P - value less than 0.05 ($P<0.05$) was considered as significant.

III. RESULTS

Hundred and ninety sex patients, 133 men and 63 women, were enrolled in this study. They were generally late middle-aged (mean age 59.4±5.5 years), with the average smoking history of 31.3±7.3 pack-years. The control group included 80 healthy persons with similar ages, smoking history of 4.5±1.2 pack-years, having normal pulmonary function tests. No differences were found in the demographic data between the two groups (Table 1). FVC, FEV1, and the ratio of FEV1/FVC were all significantly lower in patients with COPD compared to HC ($p<0.05$ for all spirometric variables). Examination of SaO2 and PaO2 revealed significantly lower in the study group compared to HC ($p<0.001$, $p=0.05$, respectively) (Table 1).

TABLE I. DEMOGRAPHIC DATA AND PULMONARY FUNCTIONAL TESTS IN CONTROL AND STUDY GROUPS.

Variable	Control group n=80	COPD group n=196
Age (years)	59.9±5.6	60.6±5.5
Men/women	46/34	133/63
Smoke index	4.11±0.46	18.35±1.31*
Body mass index (kg/m^2)	26.86±6.15	26.48±3.99
FVC (%)	99.99±15.67	90.54±21.6**
FEV1 (%)	83.98±11.8	57.82±17.07*
FEV1/FVC (%)	0.83±0.11	0.62±0.08*
SaO_2 (%)	97.6±0.77	92.63±4.63*
PaO_2 (%)	90.13±2.72	69.4±14.23*

*p<0.01; **p<0.05, Data are means ± SD.

Erythrocyte's cytosol and membrane FRSA as well as urinary and plasma FRSA were significantly lower in the study group compared to HC ($p<0.0001$). COX activity in plasma, urine and erythrocyte's membrane are lower, but having greater in erythrocyte's cytosol in patients with COPD compared to HC ($p<0.05$). Plasma, urinary and membrane lipid peroxides measured as MDA-TBA products were greater in study group significantly, compared to HC ($p<0.05$) (Table 2). Correlation analysis revealed a significant direct relationship of FVC and FEV1 with COX activity of erythrocyte's membrane ($r=-0.437$, $p<0.01$), and a significant inverse relationship of FVC and FEV1 with membrane MDA levels ($r=-0.396$, $p<0.05$). The findings of the present study suggest that oxidant-antioxidant capacity reflected by erythrocyte's membrane cytochrome c oxidases and membrane levels of the lipid peroxidation product MDA are linked to the severity of COPD.

TABLE II. PARAMETERS OF OXIDANT-ANTIOXIDANT STATUS IN CONTROL AND STUDY GROUPS

Parameters	Control group n=80	COPD group n=196
Plasma FRSA (mcg/ml)	70.95±4.21	63.67±5.33*
Urinary FRSA (mcg/ml)	95.95±1.81	90.60±3.90*
Cytosol FRSA(mcg/ml)	69.42±4.11	63.86±4.84*
Membrane FRSA (mcg/ml)	54.15±4.71	48.59±7.63*
Plasma COX (min)	2.93±0.82	4.03±1.01*
UrinaryCOX (min)	20.76±3.27	33.25±8.16*
Cytosol COX (min)	19.01±3.67	15.55±2.67*
Membrane COX (min)	30.21±4.26	37.54±5.78*
Plasma MDA(μmol/L)	0.051±0.0068	0.097±0.036*
Urinary MDA(μmol/L)	0.069±0.012	0.117±0.026*
Membrane MDA(μmol/L)	0.086±0.008	0.134±0.003*

*p<0.0001 Data are means ± SD.

IV. DISCUSSION

In the present study, we have demonstrated by studying patients with all stages of COPD, that the erythrocyte's membrane COX activity and membrane MDA levels correlate with disease severity as assessed by FVC and FEV1. In agreement, our present study suggests a significant relationship between COX activity in erythrocyte membrane and pulmonary functions in patients with COPD [14]. These findings extend those of Yang.M et al. 2010 [12] by indicating that the COX expression and activity, which were often associated with cigarette smoking, were present in COPD patients. Also we suggest that increasing of COX in cytosol may be related with increasing of Fe^{+++} in cytosol due to damage of hemoglobin's membrane. Antioxidant activity measured as FRSA in plasma, urine, erythrocyte membrane and cytosol are decreased in patients with COPD. No relationship was observed between FRSA and pulmonary functions in the present study. Numerous studies have shown depletion of antioxidant capacity in patients with COPD compared to healthy subjects, but also compared to smokers without COPD [13]. Indeed, several [17] but not all [18] studies documented that certain markers of oxidative stress may be related to smoking and to the severity of obstructive lung impairment in patients with COPD. However, Rahman et al. (2000) failed to document any relationship between plasma antioxidant capacity and spirometric variables. A similar result was shown in recent study. One reason for failing to find a significant relationship between FRSA and pulmonary function parameters may be related to the earlier described phenomenon that various enzymatic systems differ substantially in their responses to smoking-induced increases in oxidative stress [20].

Lipid peroxidation products are elevated in sputum, exhaled breath condensate [21] and plasma [2] of patients with stable COPD. Moreover, exacerbations of COPD lead to even further elevations in various markers of oxidative stress [3]. In addition, the oxidant-antioxidant balance is deteriorating further by the depletion of antioxidant mechanisms. Indeed, deficiencies in both enzymatic and non-enzymatic anti-oxidative systems were described in patients with COPD [6]. Relationships between anti-oxidative enzymatic systems and lung function impairment were found in previous reports studying the anti-oxidative enzymes in erythrocytes [6] but not in plasma [19]. One of the mechanisms by which oxidants can cause lung injury, is lipid peroxidation. Malondialdehydeis the principal and most studied product of polyunsaturated fatty acid production [4]. In the present study, a significant inverse relationship between erythrocyte's membrane MDA levels and the degree of obstructive lung impairment reflected by FEV1 and FVC was observed. Previously, lipid peroxidation products measured as MDA content correlated inversely with the degree of small airway obstruction reflected in low maximal expiratory flow rates in smokers [17]. Our findings extend these original reports by suggesting that high levels of MDA may be associated with lung function not only in plasma, but also in erythrocyte membrane in patients with COPD. These observations indicate that lipid peroxidation in erythrocyte membrane is markedly increased in patients with COPD, in agreement with previous findings showing elevated levels of other markers of lipid peroxidation such as urinary and plasma concentrations of 8-isoprostane [18] and exhaled ethane [15] in patients with COPD.

In conclusion, our results indicate that the activity COX and FRSA are reduced, and that lipid peroxidation is more active in patients with COPD suggesting that reductions in the capacity of anti-oxidative enzymes and increases in toxic lipid peroxidation products might be related to the progression of the disease. Further studies are needed to analyze the pathophysiological mechanisms involved in lung injury related to an oxidant / antioxidant imbalance. Therefore more computational approaches needed to analyze the correlation between air pollution and lung disease.

REFERENCES

[1] The World Bank Report, 2011, "Air quality analysis of Ulaanbaatar", http://ubairpollution.org/Papers/WorldBank2011_UB_report.pdf

[2] P.N. Dekhuijzen, K.K. Aben, I. Dekker, L.P. Aarts, P.L. Wielders, C.L. VanHerwaarden, and A. Bast, "Increased exhalation of hydrogen peroxide in patients with stable and unstable chronic obstructive pulmonary disease," Am J RespirCrit Care MED, vol. 154, pp. 813-816, 1996.

[3] D. Del Rio, A.J. Stewart, and N. Pellegrini, "A review of recent studies on malondialdehyde as toxic molecule and biological marker of oxidative stress," NutrMetabCardiovasc Dis, vol. 15, pp. 316-328, 2005.

[4] E.M. Drost, K.M. Skwarski, J. Sauleda, N. Soler, J. Roca, A. Agusti, and W. Macnee, "Oxidative stress and airway inflammation in severe exacerbations of COPD," Thorax 60, pp. 293-300, 2005.

[5] G.G. Duthie, J.R. Arthur, W.P. James, Effects of smoking and vitamin E on blood antioxidant status. Am J ClinNutr, vol. 53, pp. 1061-1063, 1991.

[6] M.A. Chan-Yeung, D.Y. Buncio, "Leukocyte counts, smoking and lung function," Am J MED, vol. 76, pp. 31-37, 1984.

[7] V.L. Kinnula, J.D. Crapo, "Superoxide dismutases in the lung and human lung diseases," Am J RespirCrit Care Med, vol. 167, pp. 1600-1619, 2003.

[8] K. Kostikas, G. Papatheodorou, K. Psathakis, P. Panagou, and S. Loukides, "Oxidative stress in expired breath condensate of patients with COPD," Chest, vol. 24, pp. 1373-1380, 2003.

[9] M. Linden, J.B. Rasmussen, E. Piitulainen, A. Tunek, M. Larson, H. Tegner, P. Venge, L.A. Laitinen, and R. Brattsand, "Airway inflammation in smokers with non-obstructive and obstructive chronic bronchitis," Am Rev Respir Dis, vol. 148, pp. 1226-1232, 1993.

[10] Global Initiative for Chronic Obstructive Lung Diseases (GOLD). Global strategy for diagnosis, management, and prevention of chronic obstructive pulmonary disease. NHLBI/WHO workshop report. Updated 2009. www. goldcopd.org.

[11] M. Sasikala, C. Subramanyam, and B. Sadasivudu, "Early oxidative change in low density lipoproteins during progressive chronic renal failure," IND. J. Clin. Biochem, vol. 14(2), pp. 176-183. 1999.

[12] M. Yang, P. Chen, H. Peng, Q. Shen, Y. Chen, "Cytochrome C oxidase expression and endothelial cell apoptosis in the lungs of patients with chronic obstructive pulmonary disease," ZhonghuaJie He He Hu Xi ZaZhi, vol. 33 (9), pp. 665-9. Sep 2010.

[13] W. MacNee, "Pulmonary and systemic oxidant/antioxidant imbalance in chronic obstructive pulmonary disease," Proc Am ThoracSoc, vol. 2, pp. 50-60, 2005.

[14] R.A. Pauwels, A.S. Buist, P.M.A. Calverley, "Global strategy for the diagnosis, management, and prevention of chronic obstructive pulmonary disease," NHLBI/WHO Global initiative for chronic obstructive lung disease (GOLD) workshop summary. Am J RespirCrit Care MED, vol. 163, pp. 1256-1276, 2001.

[15] P. Paredi, S.A. Kharitonov, D. Leak, S. Ward, D. Cramer, and P.J. Barnes, "Exhaled ethane, a marker of lipid peroxidation, is elevated in chronic obstructive pulmonary disease," Am J RespirCrit Care MED, vol. 62, pp. 369-373, 2000.

[16] H.J. Schunemann, P. Muti, J.L. Freudenheim, D. Armstrong, R. Browne, R.A. Klocke, and M. Trevisan, "Oxidative stress and lung function," Am J Epidemiol vol. 146, pp. 939-948, 1997.

[17] S. Petruzzelli, E. Hietanen, H. Bartsch, A.M. Camus, A. Mussi, C.A. Angeletti, R. Saraccii, and C. Giuntini, "Pulmonary lipid peroxidation in cigarette smokers and lung cancer patients," Chest, vol. 98, pp. 930-935, 1990.

[18] D. Pratico, S. Basili, M. Vieri, C. Cordova, F. Violi, and G.A. Fitzgerald, "Chronic obstructive pulmonary disease is associated with an increase in urinary levels of isoprostane F2a-III, an index of oxidant stress," Am J RespirCrit Care MED, vol. 158, pp. 1709-1714, 1998.

[19] I. Rahman, E. Swarska, M. Henry, J. Stolk, and W. MacNee, "Is there any relationship between plasma antioxidant capacity and lung function in smokers and in patients with chronic obstructive pulmonary disease?," Thorax, vol. 55, pp. 189-193, 2000.

[20] J.E. Repine, A. Bast, I. Lankhorst, and The Oxidative Stress Study Group, "Oxidative stress in chronic obstructive pulmonary disease," Am J Respir Crit Care MED, vol. 156, pp. 341-357, 1997.

[21] H. Tsukagoshi, Y. Shimizu, S. Iwamae, T. Hisada, K. Ishizuka, K. Dobashi, and M. Mori, "Evidence of oxidative stress in asthma and COPD: potential inhibitory effect of theophylline," Respir MED, vol. 94, pp. 584-588, 2000.

SESSION

SEQUENCING AND BIOTECHNOLOGY + BIOINFORMATICS

Chair(s)

TBA

Using Bioinformatics Shotgun Method and Hamilton Path for DNA Sequence Assembly

Michael Shan-Hui Ho[1], Kun-Yu Hung[2], Yu-Shiang Gen[1], Chaochang Chiu[3] and Pin-Shuo Huang[1]
[1] Department of Electric Engineering, NTPU, New Taipei City, Taiwan, R.O.C
[2] Department of Information Management, MCU, Taoyuan County, Taiwan, R.O.C
[3] Department of Information Management, YZU, Taoyuan County, Taiwan, R.O.C

Abstract - *Knowledge of DNA sequences has become indispensable for basic biological research. DNA sequence assembly is considered as a shortest superstring problem. Hence, the DNA sequence assembly problem has been recognized as NP-hard. A DNA sequence assembly bioinformatics approach, utilizing the bioinformatics shotgun method, true overlap determination for DNA reassembly graph construction, and the Hamiltonian path method for finding an optimal DNA reassembly path, is introduced for exact matches of any DNA sequence. This fast DNA algorithm fully utilizes parallelism to conquer time complexity bottleneck, and improves any DNA sequence assembly more efficient. Experimental results have shown in $O(n^4)$ polynomial bound.*

Keywords: DNA sequence assembly, NP-hard, bioinformatics computing, shotgun method, Hamiltonian path
A Maximum of 6 Keywords

1 Introduction

Dramatic progress in molecular biology has been driven and guided by knowledge of DNA. The discovery of the three-dimensional structure of DNA by Crick and Watson began in 1953. Isolation of restriction enzymes and DNA polymerases made possible DNA sequencing, the determination of the base sequence along a strand of DNA.

Knowledge of DNA sequences has become indispensable for basic biological research, other research branches utilizing DNA sequencing, and in numerous applied fields such as diagnostic, biotechnology, forensic biology and biological systematics. DNA sequencing technologies, including DNA sequence assembly, have revolutionized biology. In the earlier developed age of bioinformatics computing, any DNA sequencing outcomes might contain is reading [1]. Hence, there has been an urgent need of DNA sequence assembly studies for misreading correction.

Since the advent of rapid DNA sequencing methods in 1976, scientists have had the problem of inferring DNA sequences from sequenced fragments. Shotgun sequencing is a well-established biological and computational method used in practice. Many conventional algorithms for shotgun sequencing are based on the notion of pairwise fragment overlap.

2 DNA sequence assembly problems

Traditionally, the fragment assembly problem has been phrased as one of finding a shortest common superstring (SCS) of the fragment reads.

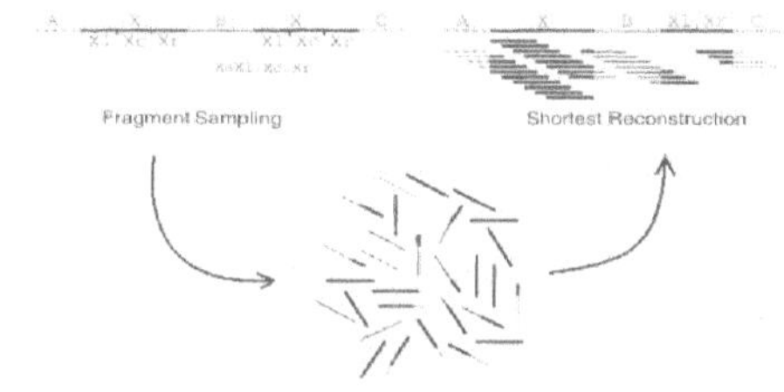

Figure 1: An over-compressed SCS-based assembly.

Figure 1 gives an example of a target for which such an over-compression occurs. While it is certainly true that knowing an SCS implies the original target DNA duplex is known in the sense of learning theory [2], the plain fact is that in practice SCS-based algorithms do not correctly handle repetitive sequence [3].

3 Shotgun sequencing

We define the DNA sequence assembly problem as follows: Given a set of strings $S = \{s_1, s_2, \ldots, s_n\}$ which are cut from an original string by using shotgun method [4], our job is to reconstruct the original string from the set S. Suppose we are given a DNA sequence S as in Figure 2:

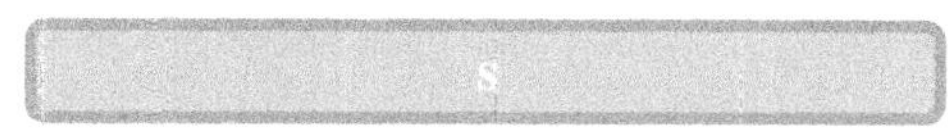

Figure 2: Original DNA sequence

Assume that the first shotgun cuts the sequence into n fragments, as shown in Figure 3. The second cutting produces k fragments, as shown in Figure 4:

Figure 3: The first cutting

Figure 4: The second cutting

If S is cut not only for just twice cut, but it can be cut for all possible fragments. The more cut shotgun fragments, the more accurate for DNA sequence assembly. For example, suppose that we are given an original DNA sequence S = {ATGCCTTAGCC}. Assume that the first shotgun cuts the sequence into the following three fragments: {ATGC, CTTA, GCC} and the second cutting produces the following four fragments: {ATG, CCT, TAGCC}. Then the input data of DNA sequence assembly problem consists of following seven fragments: {ATGC, CTTA, GCC, ATG, CCT, TAGCC}.

4 Hamilton path

In the mathematical field of graph theory, a Hamiltonian path (or traceable path) is a path in an undirected graph that visits each vertex exactly once. Determining whether such paths exist in graphs is the Hamiltonian path problem, which is NP-complete. Hamiltonian paths and cycles and cycle paths are named after William Rowan Hamilton who invented the Icosian game, now also known as *Hamilton's puzzle*, which involves finding a Hamiltonian cycle in the edge graph of the dodecahedron. A *Hamiltonian path* or *traceable path* is a path that visits each vertex exactly once. A graph that contains a Hamiltonian path is called a traceable graph. A graph is Hamiltonian-connected if for every pair of vertices there is a Hamiltonian path between the two vertices. A *Hamiltonian cycle*, *Hamiltonian circuit*, *vertex tour* or *graph cycle* is a cycle that visits each vertex exactly once (except the vertex that is both the start and end, and so is visited twice). A graph that contains a Hamiltonian cycle is called a Hamiltonian graph.

5 Sticker-based DNA computing model

The sticker-based model employs two basic groups of single-stranded DNA molecules in its representation of a bit string. Consider a *memory strand N* bases in length subdivided into *K* non-overlapping regions each *M* bases long (thus, $N \geq M * K$). Each region is identified with exactly one bit position (or equivalently one Boolean variable) during the course of the computation. Each memory strand along with its annealed stickers (if any) represents one bit string shown in figure 5.

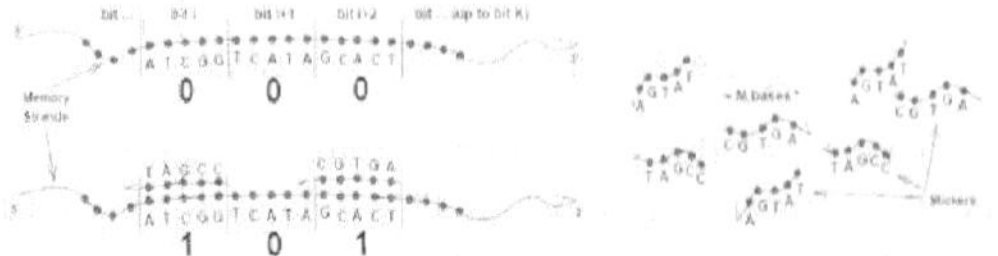

Figure 5: Memory strands of the sticker model

Table 1: Two-bit sticker-based model

$s_{m,1}$	$s_{m,2}$	Letter of mth site
0	0	A
0	1	G
1	0	C
1	1	T

In Table 1, a two-bit sticker ($s_{m,1}$ and $s_{m,2}$) model is used to represent letters A, G, C, T.

6 DNA manipulations

DNA Manipulations is also called Adleman-Liption model. A test tube is a set of molecules of DNA (a multi-set of finite strings over the alphabet {A, C, G, T}. In this subsection, DNA model of computation has eight biological operations, shown as following:

1. ***Extract.*** Given a tube *P* and a short single strand of DNA, *S*, the operation produces two tubes $+(P,S)$ and $-(P,S)$, where $+(P,S)$is all of the molecules of DNA in *P* which contain *S* as a sub-strand and $-(P,S)$ is all of the molecules of DNA in *P* which do not contain *S*.
2. ***Merge.*** Given tubes P_1 and P_2, yield (P_1, P_2), where $(P_1, P_2) = P_1 \quad P_2$. This operation is used to pour two tubes into one, without any change in the individual strands.
3. ***Detect.*** Given a tube *P*, if *P* includes at least one DNA molecule we have 'yes', and if *P* contains no DNA molecule we have 'no'.
4. ***Discard.*** Given a tube *P*, the operation discards *P*.
5. ***Amplify.*** Given a tube *P*, the operation, *Amplify* (P, P_1, P_2), will produce two new tubes $P_1$and P_2 so that P_1, and P_2 are totally a copy of *P* (P_1, and P_2 are now identical) and *P* becomes an empty tube.
6. ***Append.*** Given a tube *P* containing a short strand of DNA, *Z*, and the operation will append *A* onto the end of every strand in *P*.
7. ***Append-head.*** Given a tube *P* containing a short strand of DNA, *Z*, and the operation will append *A* onto the head of every strand in *P*.
8. ***Read.*** Given a tube P, the operation is used to describe a single molecule, which is contained in tube P. Even if P contains many different molecules each encoding a different set of bases, the operation can give an explicit description of exactly one of them.

7 Construction of bio-logic and bio-arithmetic bioinformatics circuitry

We use logic truth Tables to optimize and complete logic bio-circuit operations that can construct most basic DNA logic circuits. These DNA logic circuits (gates) work in test tubes to implement basic logic operations. These gates are AND, OR, XOR, etc. All operations of bioinformatics logic computing are shown in Figure 6

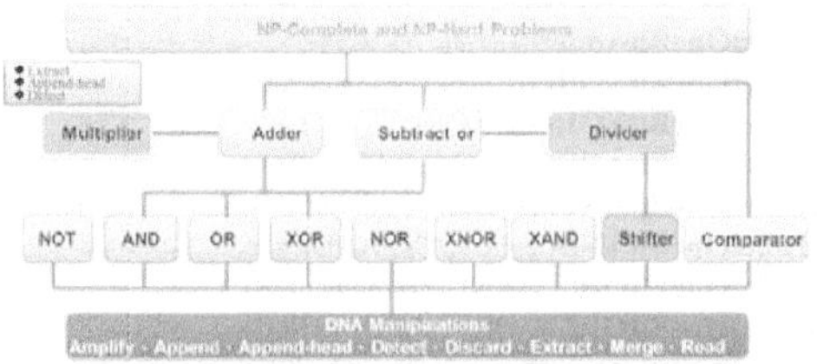

Figure 6: Bio-logic molecular computing model

7.1 AND operation on bioinformatics computing

The AND operation of a bit with two input Boolean variables U and V generates a result of 1 if both *U* and *V* are 1. However, if either *U* or *V*, or both, are zero, then the result is 0. The $\wedge$ symbol represents the AND operation. Assume that two one-bit binary numbers, U_k and V_k, for $1 \leq k \leq n$ are applied to represent first and second inputs for the AND operation of a bit respectively. The AND_k for $1 \leq k \leq n$ represents the output for the AND operation of a bit. The logic circuitry of parallel AND on one bit is shown in Figure 7. The corresponding truth Table of the one-bit AND is shown in Table 2.

Table 2: The truth Table of the one-bit AND

Input		Output
Uk	*Vk*	*ANDk = Uk* $\wedge$ *Vk*
0	0	0
0	1	0
1	0	0
1	1	1

Figure 7: Logic circuitry of Parallel AND on one bit

ParallelOneBitAND(T_0, U_k, V_k, AND_k)
$T_1^{U=1} = +(T_0, U_k^1)$ and $T_1^{U=0} = -(T_0, U_k^1)$.
$T_2^{U=1,V=1} = +(T_1^{U=1}, V_k^1)$ and $T_2^{U=1,V=0} = -(T_1^{U=1}, V_k^1)$
$T_2^{U=0,V=1} = +(T_1^{U=0}, V_k^1)$ and $T_2^{U=0,V=0} = -(T_1^{U=0}, V_k^1)$
If (*Detect*($T_2^{U=1,V=1}$) = = "yes") **then**
Append-head($T_2^{U=1,V=1}$, AND_k^1)
EndIf
If (*Detect*($T_2^{U=1,V=0}$) = = "yes") **then**
Append-head($T_2^{U=1,V=0}$, AND_k^0)
EndIf
If (*Detect*($T_2^{U=0,V=1}$) = = "yes") **then**
Append-head($T_2^{U=0,V=1}$, AND_k^0)
EndIf
If (*Detect*($T_2^{U=0,V=0}$) = = "yes") **then**
Append-head($T_2^{U=0,V=0}$, AND_k^0)
EndIf
$T_0 = \cup(T_2^{U=1,V=1}, T_2^{U=1,V=0}, T_2^{U=0,V=1}, T_2^{U=0,V=0})$
EndAlgorithm

Figure 8: Parallel AND operation of a bit algorithm

7.2 OR operation on bioinformatics computing

The OR operation of a bit with two input Boolean variables *U* and *V* produces a result of 1 if *U* or *V*, or both, are 1. However, if both *U* and *V* are zero, then the result is 0. A plus sign + (logical sum) or $\vee$ symbol is normally applied to represent OR. Assume that two one-bit binary numbers, U_k and V_k, for $1 \leq k \leq n$ are applied to represent first and second inputs for the OR operation of a bit respectively. The OR_k for $1 \leq k \leq n$ represents the output for the OR operation of a bit. The logic circuitry of parallel OR on one bit is shown in Figure 9. The corresponding truth Table of the one-bit OR is shown in Table 3.

Table 3: The truth Table of the one-bit OR

Input		Output
U_k	V_k	$OR_k = U_k \vee V_k$
0	0	0
0	1	1
1	0	1
1	1	1

Figure 9: Logic circuitry of parallel OR on one bit

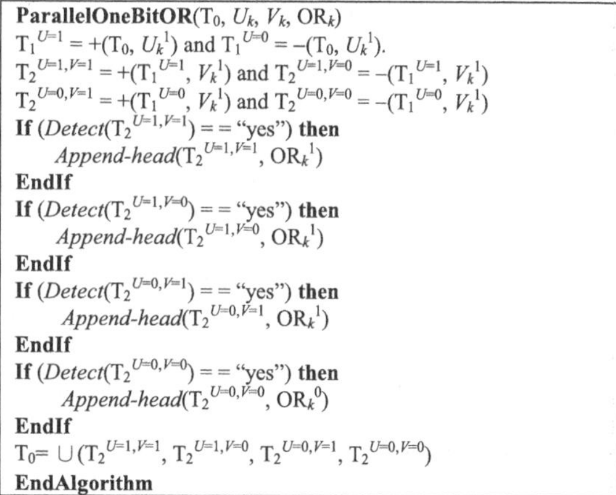
ParallelOneBitOR(T_0, U_k, V_k, OR_k)
$T_1^{U=1} = +(T_0, U_k^1)$ and $T_1^{U=0} = -(T_0, U_k^1)$.
$T_2^{U=1,V=1} = +(T_1^{U=1}, V_k^1)$ and $T_2^{U=1,V=0} = -(T_1^{U=1}, V_k^1)$
$T_2^{U=0,V=1} = +(T_1^{U=0}, V_k^1)$ and $T_2^{U=0,V=0} = -(T_1^{U=0}, V_k^1)$
If (*Detect*($T_2^{U=1,V=1}$) = = "yes") **then**
Append-head($T_2^{U=1,V=1}$, OR_k^1)
EndIf
If (*Detect*($T_2^{U=1,V=0}$) = = "yes") **then**
Append-head($T_2^{U=1,V=0}$, OR_k^1)
EndIf
If (*Detect*($T_2^{U=0,V=1}$) = = "yes") **then**
Append-head($T_2^{U=0,V=1}$, OR_k^1)
EndIf
If (*Detect*($T_2^{U=0,V=0}$) = = "yes") **then**
Append-head($T_2^{U=0,V=0}$, OR_k^0)
EndIf
$T_0 = \cup(T_2^{U=1,V=1}, T_2^{U=1,V=0}, T_2^{U=0,V=1}, T_2^{U=0,V=0})$
EndAlgorithm

Figure 10: Parallel OR operation of a bit algorithm

7.3 XOR operation on bioinformatics computing

The Exclusive-OR (XOR) operation of a bit with two input Boolean variables *U* and *V* generates an output of 1 if both *U* and *V* are different values and 0 if they are the same values. The $\oplus$ symbol represents the XOR. Assume that two one-bit binary numbers, U_k and V_k, for $1 \leq k \leq n$ are applied to represent first and second inputs for the XOR operation of a bit respectively. The representation of the superscript denotes the value of variable (e.g. U_k^1 denotes U_k=1, U_k^0 denotes U_k=0). The S_k for $1 \leq k \leq n$ represents the output for the XOR operation of a bit. The logic circuitry of parallel XOR on one bit is shown in Figure 11. The corresponding truth Table of the one-bit XOR is shown in Table 4.

Table 4: The truth Table of the one-bit XOR

Input		Output
U_k	V_k	$XOR_k = U_k \oplus V_k$
0	0	0
0	1	1
1	0	1
1	1	0

Figure 11: Logic circuitry of parallel XOR on one bit

ParallelOneBitXOR(T_0, U_k, V_k, XOR_k)
$T_1^{U=1} = +(T_0, U_k^1)$ and $T_1^{U=0} = -(T_0, U_k^1)$.
$T_2^{U=1,V=1} = +(T_1^{U=1}, V_k^1)$ and $T_2^{U=1,V=0} = -(T_1^{U=1}, V_k^1)$
$T_2^{U=0,V=1} = +(T_1^{U=0}, V_k^1)$ and $T_2^{U=0,V=0} = -(T_1^{U=0}, V_k^1)$
If (*Detect*($T_2^{U=1,V=1}$) = = "yes") **then**
  Append-head($T_2^{U=1,V=1}$, XOR_k^0)
EndIf
If (*Detect*($T_2^{U=1,V=0}$) = = "yes") **then**
  Append-head($T_2^{U=1,V=0}$, XOR_k^1)
EndIf
If (*Detect*($T_2^{U=0,V=1}$) = = "yes") **then**
  Append-head($T_2^{U=0,V=1}$, XOR_k^1)
EndIf
If (*Detect*($T_2^{U=0,V=0}$) = = "yes") **then**
  Append-head($T_2^{U=0,V=0}$, XOR_k^0)
EndIf
$T_0 = \cup(T_2^{U=1,V=1}, T_2^{U=1,V=0}, T_2^{U=0,V=1}, T_2^{U=0,V=0})$.
EndAlgorithm

Figure 12: Parallel XOR operation of a bit algorithm

7.4 Bio-arithmetic parallel adder on one bit

A one-bit adder has three inputs and two outputs. Each input and output is one bit. The first and second input bits represent augend and addend, denoted by U_k and V_k, for $1 \leq k \leq n$. The last input represents the carry, denoted by C_k, for $1 \leq k \leq n$. The first output represents the sum of the augend, addend and carry, denoted by S_k, for $1 \leq k \leq n$. Then, the second output represents the carry which is generated by the sum of the augend, addend and carry, denoted by C_{k+1}. This carry becomes the input of next one-bit adder. The logic circuitry of parallel adder on one bit is shown in Figure 13, and the truth Table of the one-bit adder is shown in Table 5.

Table 5: The truth Table of the one-bit adder

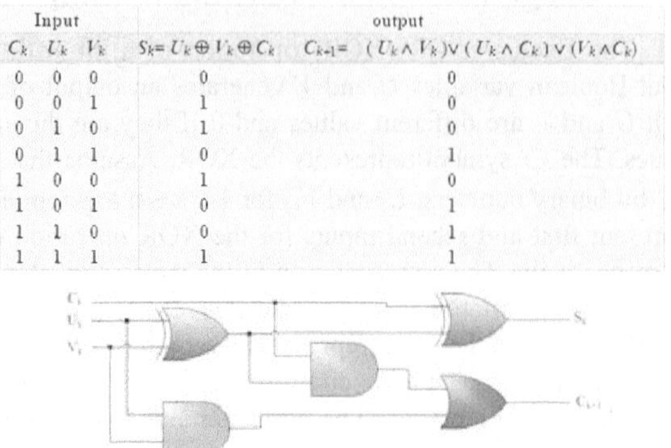

Input			output	
C_k	U_k	V_k	$S_k = U_k \oplus V_k \oplus C_k$	$C_{k+1} = (U_k \wedge V_k) \vee (U_k \wedge C_k) \vee (V_k \wedge C_k)$
0	0	0	0	0
0	0	1	1	0
0	1	0	1	0
0	1	1	0	1
1	0	0	1	0
1	0	1	0	1
1	1	0	0	1
1	1	1	1	1

Figure 13: Logic circuitry of parallel adder on one bit

Based upon the logic circuitry in Figure 13, we can derive the bio-algorithm of parallel adder on One Bit in Figure 14:

ParallelOneBitAdder(T_0, U_k, V_k, C_k)
ParallelOneBitXOR(T_0, U_k, V_k, XOR_k)
ParallelOneBitXOR(T_0, XOR_k, C_k, S_k)
ParallelOneBitAND(T_0, U_k, V_k, AND_k^1)
ParallelOneBitAND(T_0, C_k, V_k, AND_k^2)
ParallelOneBitAND(T_0, U_k, C_k, AND_k^3)
ParallelOneBitOR(T_0, AND_k^1, AND_k^2, OR_k^1)
ParallelOneBitOR(T_0, OR_k^1, AND_k^3, OR_k^2)
$T_1 = +(T_0, OR_k^{2^1})$ and $T_2 = -(T_0, OR_k^{2^0})$
If(*Detect*(T_1)=="yes") **then**
  Append-head (T_1, C_{k+1}^1)
EndIf
If(*Detect*(T_2)=="yes") **then**
  Append-head (T_2, C_{k+1}^0)
EndIf
$T_0 = \cup(T_1, T_2)$
EndAlgorithm

Figure 14: Parallel adder algorithm on one bit

7.5 Bio-arithmetic parallel adder on n bits

In this section, the bio-arithmetic adder on one bit is used to construct the Parallel Adder.

ParallelAdder(T_0, U, V, n)
Append(T_0, C_1^0)
For k=1 to n
  ParallelOneBitAdder(T_0, U_k, V_k, C_k)
EndFor
EndAlgorithm

Figure 15: Parallel adder algorithm

7.6 Bio-arithmetic parallel comparator on one bits

The following algorithm is applied to compare stickers from T_a and T_b. Tube $T_0^=$ is the first parameter and includes comparison outcome to pass to algorithm ParallelComparator ($T_0^{EDGE\_temp}$, $T_0^{overlay}$, T_a, T_b, m, n, g, b). Tube T_a and T_b contain two compared fragments individually. Number p represents the site on T_a ($s_{1,1}s_{1,2}\cdot$ . . . $s_{p,1}$ $s_{p,2}\cdot$ . . . $s_{m,1}s_{m,2}$) for $1 \leq p \leq q$ and number d represents the site on T_b ($s_{1,1}s_{1,2}\cdot$ . . . $s_{d,1}$ $s_{d,2}\cdot$ . . . $s_{m,1}s_{m,2}$) for $1 \leq d \leq q$. Algorithm for parallel execution is shown in Figure 16.

OneBitComparator($T_0^=$, T_a, T_b, p ,d)
$T_1^{1st_on} = +(T_a, s_{p,1}^1)$and $T_1^{1st\_off} = -(T_a, s_{p,1}^1)$
$T_2^{2nd\_on} = +(T_a, s_{p,2}^1)$ and $T_2^{2nd\_off} = -(T_a, s_{p,2}^1)$
$T_3^{1st\_on} = +(T_b, s_{d,1}^1)$ and $T_3^{1st\_off} = -(T_b, s_{d,1}^1)$
$T_4^{2nd\_on} = +(T_b, s_{d,2}^1)$ and $T_4^{2nd\_off} = -(T_b, s_{d,2}^1)$
If (*Detect*($T_1^{1st\_on}$)='*yes*' and *Detect*($T_3^{1st\_on}$)='*yes*') **then**
  If(*Detect*($T_2^{2nd\_on}$)='*yes*' and *Detect*($T_4^{2nd\_on}$)='*yes*') **then**
    $T_0^= = \cup(T_0^=, T_1^{1st\_on}, T_3^{1st\_on}, T_2^{2nd\_on}, T_4^{2nd\_on})$
  EndIf
EndIf
If (*Detect*($T_1^{1st\_on}$) = '*yes*' and *Detect*($T_3^{1st\_on}$) = '*yes*') **then**
  If(*Detect*($T_2^{2nd\_off}$)='*yes*' and *Detect*($T_4^{2nd\_off}$)='*yes*') **then**
    $T_0^= = \cup(T_0^=, T_1^{1st\_on}, T_3^{1st\_on}, T_2^{2nd\_off}, T_4^{2nd\_off})$
  EndIf
EndIf
If(*Detect*($T_1^{1st\_off}$) = '*yes*' and *Detect*($T_3^{1st\_off}$) = '*yes*') **then**
  If(*Detect*($T_2^{2nd\_on}$)='*yes*' and *Detect*($T_4^{2nd\_on}$)='*yes*') **then**

$T_0^{=} = \cup(T_0^{=}, T_1^{1st\_off}, T_3^{1st\_off}, T_2^{2nd\_on}, T_4^{2nd\_on})$
EndIf
EndIf
If($Detect(T_1^{1st\_off})$ = '*yes*' and $Detect(T_3^{1st\_off})$ = '*yes*') **then**
If($Detect(T_2^{2nd\_off})$='*yes*' and $Detect(T_4^{2nd\_off})$='*yes*') **then**
$T_0^{=} = \cup(T_0^{=}, T_1^{1st\_off}, T_3^{1st\_off}, T_2^{2nd\_off}, T_4^{2nd\_off})$
EndIf
EndIf
EndAlgorithm

Figure 16: Parallel comparator for one bit

7.7 Bio-arithmetic parallel comparator on n bits

The following algorithm, ParallelComparator (T_0, $T_0^{overlay}$, T_a, T_b, m, n, g, b), is an n-bit comparator. The algorithm use "O" in a sticker-based model to represent four condition by calling function OneBitComparator ($T_0^{=}$, T_a, T_b, p, $g+d$) and get equal statement. For every bit $O_{p,g}$ represents one success match between $s_{p,1}$,$s_{p,2}$ from T_a and $s_{g,1}$,$s_{g,2}$ from T_b. $O_{p,g}$ would store this comparing result in tube $T_0^{overlay}$. The number m and n are regarded as the start and last site of fragment which contained in T_a. Number g and number b are regarded as the start and last site of fragment which contained in T_b. That is to say, the bit x_g to x_b in tube T_b are all 1. Algorithm for parallel execution is shown in Figure 17.

ParallelComparator(T_0, $T_0^{overlay}$, T_a, T_b, m, n, g, b)
For d=0 **to** Min(n-m,b-g)
For p=n **downto** m
OneBitComparator($T_0^{=}$, T_a, T_b, p, $g+d$)
If ($Detect(T_0^{=})$="yes") **then**
$Append(T_0^{overlay}, O_{p,g+d}^{1})$
$Discard(T_0^{=})$
EndIf
EndFor
EndFor
If ($Detect(T_0^{overlay})$="yes") **then**
$T_0 = \cup(T_0, T_0^{overlay})$
EndIf
$Discard(T_0^{overlay})$
EndAlgorithm

Figure 17: Parallel comparator for n bit

8 Traditional shotgun method

The traditional shotgun method duplicates genomic DNA strands. These DNA strands are cut by randomly using a physical method to smash the DNA into small pieces. The sequences of all the small DNA pieces at once are compared and they are placed in order by virtue of their overlapping sequences to generate the full-length sequence of the genome.

8.1 Proposed bioinformatics shotgun method

In this research, a bioinformatics shotgun method and the Hamilton path are proposed to solve DNA sequence assembly. The proposed steps to solve the DNA Sequence Assembly problem are as follows:

1. Construct the shotgun space for bioinformatics DNA fragments;
2. Delete unrelated DNA fragments. These unrelated fragments cannot be used to reassembly.
3. Find and determine all of shotgun fragment true overlaps. They used to construct all of possible reassembly routes.
4. Construct different routes using true overlaps.
5. Compute the weight for each route. Finally a bioinformatics graph is completed by connecting these routes. At the same time, the Hamilton path is applied to find an optimal route.

8.2 Construction of bioinformatics shotgun DNA fragment space

Assume that x_1 to x_q is a q-bit binary number, which is applied to represent q elements in a finite set S, for $1 \leq m \leq q$. We define that x_m^1 denotes the value of x_m is 1 and x_m^0 means the value of x_m to be 0. Stickers in a sticker-based model are 15-base value sequence. Elements, $s_{m,1}$ and $s_{m,2}$ can be converted as two binary number simultaneously, $s_{1,1}, \ldots, s_{m,1}$, $s_{1,2}, \ldots, s_{m,2}$. The two elements ($s_{m,1}$, $s_{m,2}$) for 2^q possible fragments will be assigned when the value of x_m is "1". Algorithm 8.1 constructs a sticker-based DNA fragment solution space for 2^q possible fragments of a q-element set S.

Algorithm 8.1
//Construction solution space for 2^q
For m = 1 to q
$Amplify(T_0, T_1, T_2)$
$Append(T_1, x_m^1)$ and $Append(T_2, x_m^0)$
$T_0 = \cup(T_1, T_2)$
EndFor
//Append the two element ($s_{m,1}$ and $s_{m,2}$) for 2^q fragments
For n = q **downto** 1
If value of bit n=1 **then**
$Append\text{-}head(T_0, s_{n,2})$
$Append\text{-}head(T_0, s_{n,1})$
End If
EndFor
EndAlgorithm

Figure 18: DNA fragment solution space construction

An example, string "ACC", is used for DNA sequence input to construct a DNA fragment solution space shown in Figure 19.

$s_{1,1}^{0}s_{1,2}^{0}s_{2,1}^{1}s_{2,2}^{0}s_{3,1}^{1}s_{3,2}^{0}x_1^{1}x_2^{1}x_3^{0}$	A C C
$s_{1,1}^{0}s_{1,2}^{0}s_{2,1}^{1}s_{2,2}^{0}x_1^{1}x_2^{1}x_3^{0}$	A C Φ
$s_{2,1}^{1}s_{2,2}^{0}s_{3,1}^{1}s_{3,2}^{0}x_1^{0}x_2^{1}x_3^{1}$	Φ C C
$s_{1,1}^{0}s_{1,2}^{0}s_{3,1}^{1}s_{3,2}^{0}x_1^{1}x_2^{0}x_3^{1}$	A Φ C
$s_{1,1}^{0}s_{1,2}^{0}x_1^{1}x_2^{0}x_3^{0}$	A Φ Φ
$s_{2,1}^{1}s_{2,2}^{0}x_1^{0}x_2^{1}x_3^{0}$	Φ C Φ
$s_{3,1}^{1}s_{3,2}^{0}x_1^{0}x_2^{0}x_3^{1}$	Φ Φ C
$x_1^{0}x_2^{0}x_3^{1}$	Φ Φ Φ

Figure 19: Execution result of Algorithm 8.1

8.3 Deletion of unrelated DNA fragments

Algorithm 8.2 filters all of related fragments and turns them to be shotgun fragments. For example, all bits of any fragment are 1 or 0 cannot be used to reassembly.

Algorithm 8.2
//pick out related fragments
For m = 1 to q-1

If value of bit m=1 and m+1 =0 **then**
Amplify(T_3, T_3^{backup}, $T_3^{backup\_dummy}$)
EndIf
If($m+2 \le q$) **then**
For $n = m+2$ to q
$T_4 = -(T_3^{backup}, x_n^1)$
EndFor
$T_0 = \cup(T_0, T_4)$
EndIf
EndFor
//delete unrelated fragments
For m = 1 to q
T_5= value of bit m = 0
$T_0 = \cup(T_0, T_5)$
EndFor
For m = 1 to q
T_6= value of bit m = 1
$T_0 = \cup(T_0, T_6)$
EndFor
EndAlgorithm

Figure 20: Deletion of unrelated DNA fragments

Algorithm 8.2 first deletes all of related fragments. Some are all bits are 1 or 0. All bits 1 means this fragment cannot be cut by shotgun method. All bits 0 denote nothing. Some are empty in the middle. The execution result of Algorithm 8.2 is shown in Figure 21.

$s_{1,1}{}^0 s_{1,2}{}^0 s_{2,1}{}^1 s_{2,2}{}^0 s_{3,1}{}^1 s_{3,2}{}^0 x_1{}^1 x_2{}^1 x_3{}^0$	A C C
$s_{1,1}{}^0 s_{1,2}{}^0 s_{2,1}{}^1 s_{2,2}{}^0 x_1{}^1 x_2{}^1 x_3{}^0$	A C Φ
$s_{2,1}{}^1 s_{2,2}{}^0 s_{3,1}{}^1 s_{3,2}{}^0 x_1{}^0 x_2{}^1 x_3{}^1$	Φ C C
$s_{1,1}{}^0 s_{1,2}{}^0 s_{3,1}{}^1 s_{3,2}{}^0 x_1{}^1 x_2{}^0 x_3{}^1$	A Φ C
$s_{1,1}{}^0 s_{1,2}{}^0 x_1{}^1 x_2{}^0 x_3{}^0$	A Φ Φ
$s_{2,1}{}^1 s_{2,2}{}^0 x_1{}^0 x_2{}^1 x_3{}^0$	Φ C Φ
$s_{3,1}{}^1 s_{3,2}{}^0 x_1{}^0 x_2{}^0 x_3{}^1$	Φ Φ C
$x_1{}^0 x_2{}^0 x_3{}^1$	Φ Φ Φ

Figure 21: Example of unrelated DNA fragment deletion

8.4 Finding shotgun fragment overlap candidates

Algorithm 8.3 uses **ParallelComparator** to find all candidate overlaps between two fragments and then determine true overlaps by calling Algorithm 8.4

Algorithm 8.3
Amplify(T_0, T_0^{backup}, $T_0^{backup\_dummy}$)
For m = 1 **to** q
For $k = q$ **downto** m
T_7 = value of bit m = 1 and value of bit k = 1
For $r = m$ **to** k
T_8= value of bit r=0 and value of bit $r+1$=1
Call **ParallelComparator** compare T_7 and T_8
Call **Algorithm 9.4** compare T_7 and T_8
If no anymore fragments **then**
Terminate the execution of the loop
EndIf
EndFor
EndFor
EndFor
EndAlgorithm

Figure 22: Find overlaps between any two shotgun fragments

In Algorithm 8.3, an symbol $O_{m,n}$ represents the overlap between any two shotgun fragments. The number m denotes the first fragment overlap m^{th} position. The number n denotes the second fragment overlap n^{th} position. All candidate overlaps between two fragments are found in Figure 23.

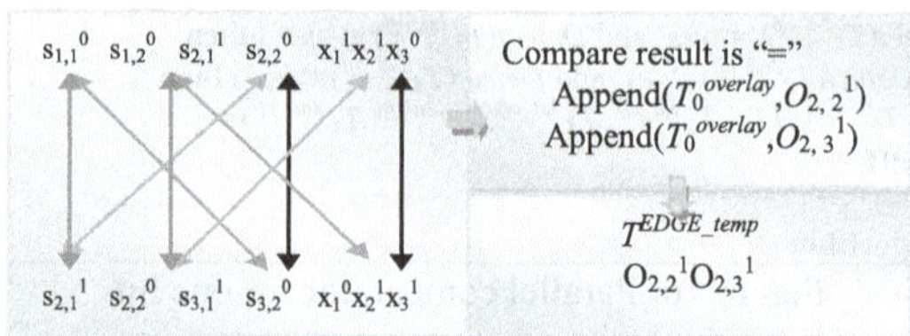

Figure 23: Execution result of Algorithm 8.3

8.5 True overlap determination

Algorithm 8.3 determines the true overlap.

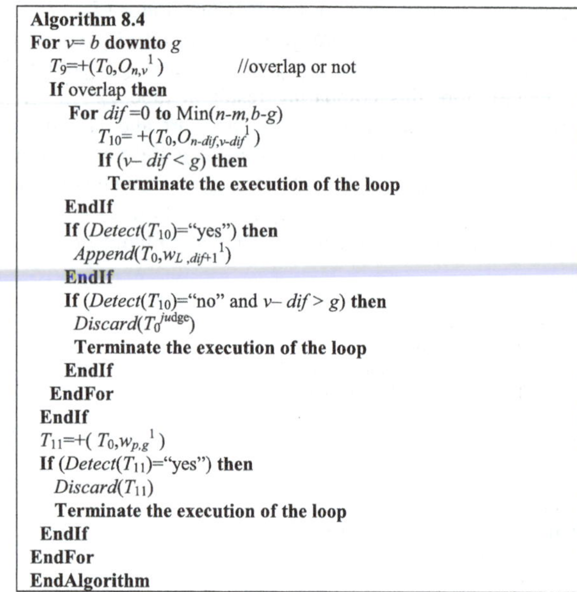

Algorithm 8.4
For $v = b$ **downto** g
$T_9 = +(T_0, O_{n,v}{}^1)$ //overlap or not
If overlap **then**
For dif=0 **to** Min(n-m, b-g)
$T_{10} = +(T_0, O_{n-dif,v-dif}{}^1)$
If ($v - dif < g$) **then**
Terminate the execution of the loop
EndIf
If (*Detect*(T_{10})="yes") **then**
Append(T_0, $w_{L,dif+1}{}^1$)
EndIf
If (*Detect*(T_{10})="no" and $v - dif > g$) **then**
Discard(T_0^{judge})
Terminate the execution of the loop
EndIf
EndFor
EndIf
$T_{11} = +(T_0, w_{p,g}{}^1)$
If (*Detect*(T_{11})="yes") **then**
Discard(T_{11})
Terminate the execution of the loop
EndIf
EndFor
EndAlgorithm

Figure 24: True overlay determination between two fragments

Algorithm 8.4 checks every overlap $O_{m,n}$ and judges it can a true overlap. An example is shown in Figure 9.4.1 Here, $O_{2,2}{}^1$ is a true overlap. $O_{2,3}{}^1$ and $O_{1,2}{}^1$ are not true overlaps. $w_{1,1}{}^1$ denotes an overlap length to be 1. Both $w_{1,2}{}^0$ and $w_{2,3}{}^0$ represent two related fragments.

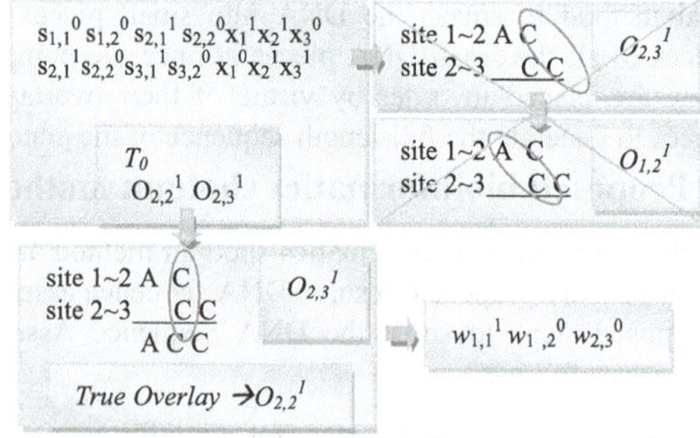

Figure 25: Example of determining true overlaps

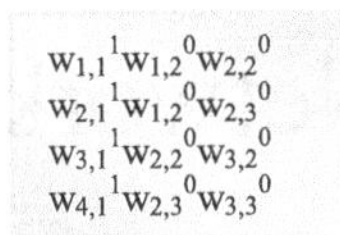

Figure 26: Execution results of Algorithm 8.4

8.6 Finding Hamilton path for solving DNA assembly

Algorithm 8.5 computes the weight for each route. Finally a bioinformatics graph is constructed by connecting these routes. At the same time, the Hamilton path is applied to find an optimal route in the same algorithm.

Algorithm 8.5
//Find the entry fragment
For m= 1 **to** q
  $T_{12}{}^{ON} = +(T_0, w_{1,m}{}^0)$
EndFor
//Find the non-entry fragment
For m= 1 **to** q
  $T_{13} = -(T_0, w_{1,m}{}^0)$
EndFor
$T_0{}^{on} = \cup(T_0{}^{on}, T_{12})$ and $T_0{}^{off} = \cup(T_0{}^{off}, T_{13})$
// exclude not satisfactory path
For m= 1 **to** q
  $T_{14}{}^{off} = -(T_0{}^{on}, w_{m,q}{}^0)$ and $T_{14}{}^{on} = +(T_0{}^{on}, w_{m,q}{}^0)$
  If (*Detect*($T_{14}{}^{off}$)="yes") **then**
    Amplify($T_{14}{}^{off}$, $T_0{}^{on}$)
  EndIf
EndFor
For $n = q$ **downto** 1
  For d= q-1 **downto** 2
    $T_{15} = +(T_{14}{}^{on}, w_{1,d}{}^0)$
    For $ds1 = q$-1 **downto** 2
      For $ds2$ =2 **to** q-1
        If (*Detect*($T_{16} = +(T_{15}, w_{ds2,ds1}{}^0)$)="yes") **then**
          $T_{17} = +(T_0{}^{off}, w_{ds2,ds1}{}^0)$
          If($ds1 + 1 = q$ and $ds2 + 1 = q$) **then**
            $T_{18} = +(T_0{}^{off}, w_{ds2,ds1+1}{}^0)$ **EndIf**
          If (*Detect*(T_{18})="yes") **then**
            Call **ParallelAdder** **EndIf**
        EndIf
      Amplify(T_{18}, $T_{19}{}^{on}$)
      EndFor
      For $i = q$ **downto** 1
        If (*Detect*($T_{19}{}^{on}$)="*no*") **then**
          Terminate the execution of the loop EndIf
      EndFor
    EndFor
  EndFor
  $T_{14}{}^{on} = \cup(T_{14}{}^{on}, T_0)$
EndFor
Read(T_0)
EndAlgorithm

Figure 27: Hamilton path bioinformatics solution for DNA assembly

All three possible routes are shown in Figure 28.

$w_{1,1}{}^1 w_{1,2}{}^0 w_{2,2}{}^0$ $w_{2,1}{}^1 w_{2,2}{}^0 w_{2,3}{}^0$ $w_{3,1}{}^1 w_{2,3}{}^0 w_{3,3}{}^0$	$w_{1,1}{}^1 w_{1,2}{}^0 w_{2,2}{}^0$ $w_{2,1}{}^1 w_{2,2}{}^0 w_{2,3}{}^0$	$w_{1,1}{}^1 w_{1,2}{}^0 w_{2,3}{}^0$
Route 1: AC>C>CC>C	Route 2: AC>C>C	Route 3: AC>CC

Figure 28: Construction of all possible routes

After all of passable routs are built up, Algorithm 8.5 calls algorithm **ParallelAdder** to compute the weighted for each routs. Finally, the bioinformatics Hamilton path is used in the DNA sequence re-assembly by finding one of the best routes shown in Figure 29.

Figure 29: Final DNA sequence reassembly optimal resolution

9 Conclusions

DNA sequence assembly is a set of genomic sequences that can be assembled, condensed and oriented in order by applying the sequence homology along with mapping information to create a consensus sequence of a chromosome. The goal of the assembly is to compose the sequences in one resulting sequence in a proper order. Unfortunately, the sequencing outcomes usually contain misreading (insertions, deletions, and substitutions of nucleotides) coming from biochemical steps as well as from a weakness of a sequencing program. To resolve these issues, a DNA sequence assembly bioinformatics approach, utilizing the bioinformatics shotgun method, true overlap determination for DNA reassembly graph construction, and the Hamiltonian path method for finding an optimal DNA reassembly path, is introduced and required for exact matches of any DNA sequence. Of course, to disable accidental overlaps, some limit of mismatch acceptance must be defined. While larger any genome grows in size, while more difficult it is reassembled in operations. This newly developed bioinformatics approach fully utilizes parallelism to conquer time complexity bottleneck, and improves any DNA sequence assembly more efficient. The experimental results of the DNA sequence assembly have shown in $O(n^4)$ polynomial bound.

10 References

[1] Blazewicz, J., Kasprzak, M., Swiercz, A., Figlerowicz, M., Gawron, P., Platt, D., et al. (2008). *Parallel Implementation of the Novel Approach to Genome Assembly*. Paper presented at the Software Engineering, Artificial Intelligence, Networking, and Parallel/Distributed Computing, 2008. SNPD '08. Ninth ACIS International Conference on.

[2] Li, M. 1990. Towards a DNA sequencing theory. Proc. 31st IEEE Symp. on Found, of Computer Science 125-134.

[3] Kececioglu, J., and Myers, E. 1995. Exact and approximate algorithms for the sequence reconstruction problem. Algorithmica 13, (1-2), 7-51

[4] Lu, J. P. (2004). DNA Sequence Assembly. Master Degree Thesis, National Chi Nan University.

A Logical Model for Metabolic Networks with Inhibition

Robert Demolombe*, Luis Fariñas del Cerro* and Naji Obeid*

*Université de Toulouse and CNRS, IRIT, Toulouse, France

***Abstract*—Metabolic networks formed by long sequences of biochemical reactions have been widely investigated to determine the catalytic role of genomes and how they interfere in the process. Many tumors have been reported to be the result of a pathology in the cell's pathway. Knowing that the complexity of the imbrication of such networks is beyond human reasoning, the use of artificial intelligence to help scientists in their experiments might seem adapted. This paper aims to present a logical model for metabolic pathways capable of describing both positive and negative reactions (activations and inhibitions) based on a fragment of first order logic. We also present an efficient automated deduction method allowing us to predict results by deduction and infer reactions and proteins states by abductive reasoning.**

Keywords: Metabolic pathways, logical model, inhibition, deduction, abduction.

I. Introduction

Cells in general and human body cells in particular incorporates a large series of intracellular and extracellular signalings, notably protein activations and inhibitions, that specify how they should carry out their functions. Networks formed by such biochemical reactions, often referred as *pathways*, are at the center of a cell's existence and they range from simple and chain reactions and counter reactions to simple and multiple regulations and auto regulations. Cancer, for example, can appear as a result of a pathology in the cell's pathway, thus, the study of signalization events appears to be an important factor in biological, pharmaceutical and medical researches. However, the complexity of the imbrication of such processes makes the use of a physical model as a representation seem complicated.

In the last couple of decades, scientists that used artificial intelligence to model cell pathways [8], [7], [17], [18], [4], [22], [16] faced many problems especially because information about biological networks contained in knowledge bases is generally incomplete and sometimes uncertain and contradictory. To deal with such issues, abduction [1] as theory completion [12] is used to revise the state of existing nodes and add new nodes and arcs to express new observations. Languages that were used to model such networks had usually limited expressivity, were specific to special pathways or were limited to general basic functionalities. We, in this work, present a fragment of first order logic [20] capable of representing node states and actions in term of positive and negative relation between said nodes. Then an efficient proof theory for these fragments is proposed. This method can be extended to define an abduction procedure which has been implemented in SOLAR [13], an automated deduction system for consequence finding.

The rest of this paper is organized as follows. Section II introduces the problem from a biological point of view. Section III presents a basic language and axiomatic capable of describing general pathways, ans shows how it is possible to extends this language and axiomatic to accommodate the requirements of section II. Section IV defines a translation procedure capable of eliminating first order variables and equality predicates and shows how it can be applied to derive new axiomatic that can be used in the automated deduction process in SOLAR. Section V provide some case studies, and finally section VI gives a summary and discusses future works.

robert.demolombe@orange.fr
luis.farinas@irit.fr - Contact Author
naji.obeid@irit.fr - LNCSR Scholar

II. Biological Background

Cancer has been at the center of countless biological researches trying to figure out what was causing the strange cells behaviors. Many treatments and cures have been developed and successfully administered, but in many other cases, therapeutic responses are limited and tumors relapse or fail to respond in a large fraction of patients. There is currently no way to predict how the tumor's will respond to the treatment. One approach is to investigate the molecular determinants of tumor response. These molecular parameters include the cell cycle checkpoint, DNA repair and programmed cell apoptosis pathways [15], [10], [5], [11], [14]. When DNA damage occurs, cell cycle checkpoints are activated and can rapidly kill the cell by apoptosis or arrest the cell cycle progression to allow DNA repair before cellular reproduction or division. Two important checkpoint that appear to function when parallel transduction cascades from DNA damage to the cell cycle checkpoint effectors are the ATM-Chk2 and the ATR-Chk1 pathways [15].

Intracellular signalization is actively studied and subject to many experiments because there are many unknown reactions that lead to checkpoints and ones that come after which cannot be proved or described. The goal of these experiments is to try to understand why in some cases cell treatment fails and cells do not go through these checkpoints when DNA damage occurs. As a result, scientist have been building networks showing, in human readable form, the cell cycle checkpoints pathways, that are constantly updated as new interaction are discovered. Figure 1 defines a list of symbols used in the molecular interaction map of ATM-Chk2 shown in Figure 2.

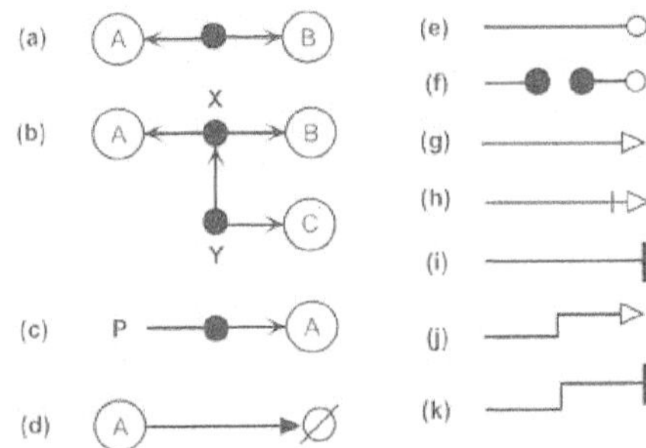

Fig. 1: Symbol definitions and map conventions.

(a) Proteins A and B can bind to each other. The node placed on the line represents the A:B complex. (b) Multimolecular complexes: x is A:B and y is(A:B):C. (c) Covalent modification of protein A. (d) Degradation of protein A. (e) Enzymatic stimulation of a reaction. (f) Enzymatic stimulation in trans. (g) General symbol for stimulation. (h) A bar behind the arrowhead signifies necessity. (i) General symbol for inhibition. (j) Shorthand symbol for transcriptional activation. (k) Shorthand symbol for transcriptional inhibition.

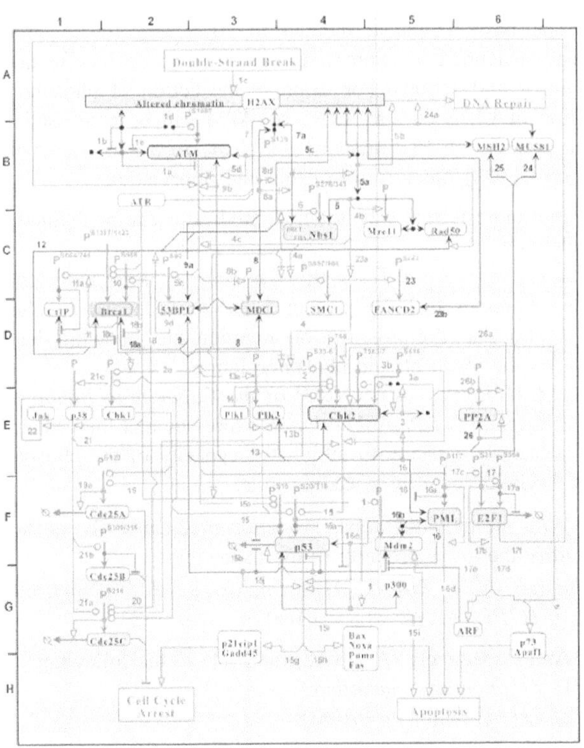

Fig. 2: ATM-Chk2 molecular interaction map.

III. Logical Model

In this section we will present a basic language capable of modeling some basic positive and negative interaction between two or more proteins in some pathway. We will first focus on the stimulation and inhibition actions, points (g) and (i) of Figure 1, and then show how this language can be modified to express the different other actions described in the same figure.

A. Formal Language

Let's consider a fragment of first order logic with some basic predicates, boolean connectives ($\wedge$) and, ($\vee$) or, ($\neg$) negation, ($\rightarrow$) implication, ($\leftrightarrow$) equivalence, ($\exists$) existential and ($\forall$) universal quantifiers, and ($=$) equality.

The basic state predicates are:

- $P(x)$: with intended meaning that the protein x is $Present$.
- $A(x)$: with intended meaning that the protein x is $Active$.
- $I(x)$: with intended meaning that the protein x is $Inhibited$.

The basic state axioms are:

- $\forall x(P(x) \leftrightarrow A(x) \vee I(x))$.
  Indicates that a certain $Present$ protein x can be either $Active$ or $Inhibited$, and that an $Active$ or and $Inhibited$ protein is considered $Present$ in the cell.
- $\forall x \neg(A(x) \wedge I(x))$.
  Indicates that a certain protein x can never be in both $Active$ and $Inhibited$ states at the same time.

An interaction between two or more different proteins is expressed by a predicate of the form $Action(protein_1, ..., protein_n)$. In our case we are interested by the simple $Activation$ and $Inhibition$ actions that are defined by the following predicates:

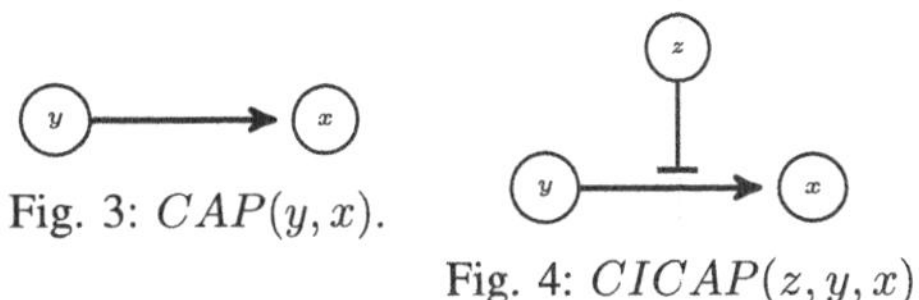

Fig. 3: $CAP(y, x)$.

Fig. 4: $CICAP(z, y, x)$.

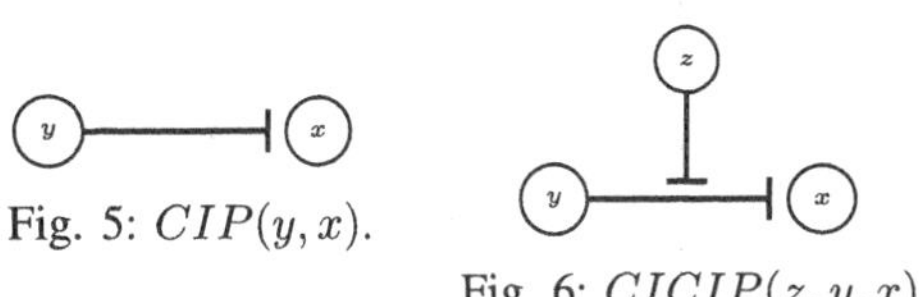

Fig. 5: $CIP(y, x)$.

Fig. 6: $CICIP(z, y, x)$.

- $CAP(y, x)$: CAP or the *Capacity of Activation* expresses that the protein y has the capacity to activate the protein x. (Figure 3)
- $CICAP(z, y, x)$: $CICAP$ or the *Capacity to Inhibit the Capacity of Activation* expresses that the protein z has the capacity to inhibit the capacity of the activation of x by y. (Figure 4)
- $CIP(y, x)$: CIP or the *Capacity to Inhibit a Protein* expresses that the protein y has the capacity to inhibit the protein x. (Figure 5)
- $CICIP(z, y, x)$: $CICIP$ or the *Capacity to Inhibit the Capacity of Inhibition of a Protein* expresses that the protein z has the capacity to inhibit the capacity of inhibition of x by y. (Figure 6)

In the next section we will define the needed axioms that will be used to model the *Activation* and *Inhibition* actions.

B. Action axioms

Giving the fact that a node can acquire the state active or inhibited depending on different followed pathways, one of the issues answered by abduction is to know which set of proteins is required to be active of inhibited for our target protein be active or inhibited.

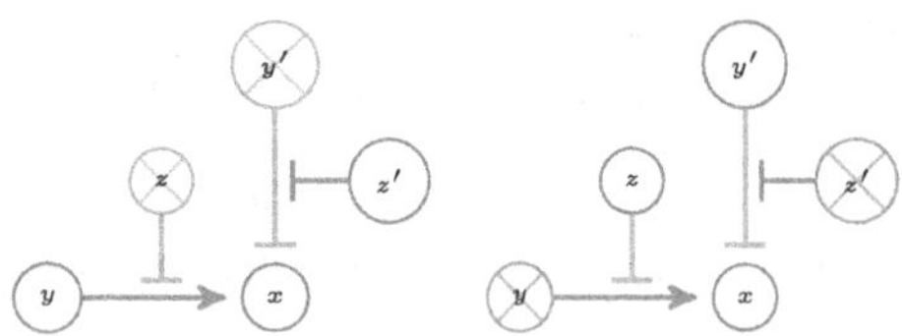

Fig. 7: Activation Fig. 8: Inhibition

A protein x is active if there exists at least one *active* protein y such as $CAP(y,x)$ that has the capacity to activate x, **and** for every protein z that has the capacity to inhibit the capacity of activation of x by y, such as $CICAP(z,y,x)$, z is *not active*. **And** for every protein y' such as $CIP(y',x)$ that has the capacity to inhibit x, y' is *not active*, **or** there exist at least one *active* protein z' such as $CICIP(z',y',x)$ that has the capacity to inhibit the capacity of inhibition of x by y'. (Figure 7)

A protein x is inhibited if there exists at least one *active* protein y' such as $CIP(y',x)$ that has the capacity to inhibit x, **and** for every protein z' that has the capacity to inhibit the capacity of inhibition of x by y', such as $CICIP(z',y',x)$, z' is *not active*. **And** for every protein y such as $CAP(y,x)$ that has the capacity to activate x, y is *not active*, **or** there exist at least one *active* protein z such as $CICAP(z,y,x)$ that has the capacity to inhibit the capacity of activation of x by y. (Figure 8)

More formally, a protein x is active iff the activation conditions $activ(x)$ are satisfied, and x is not inhibited. And a protein x is inhibited iff the inhibition conditions $inhib(x)$ are satisfied, and x in not active.

Formally we have:
$\forall x(A(x) \leftrightarrow activ(x) \wedge \neg I(x))$.
$\forall x(I(x) \leftrightarrow inhib(x) \wedge \neg A(x))$.
We can deduce in classical logic:
(A1) $\forall x(activ(x) \wedge \neg inhib(x) \rightarrow A(x))$.
(A2) $\forall x(\neg activ(x) \rightarrow \neg A(x))$.
(I1) $\forall x(inhib(x) \wedge \neg activ(x) \rightarrow I(x))$.
(I2) $\forall x(\neg inhib(x) \rightarrow \neg I(x))$.

The activation and inhibition conditions are defined as follow:

$activ(x) \stackrel{\text{def}}{=} \exists y(A(y) \wedge CAP(y,x) \wedge \forall z(CICAP(z,y,x) \rightarrow \neg A(z)))$

In another way, it is sufficient to have $A(y)$ if there exists an activation arc $CAP(y,x)$ going from y to x, and $\neg A(z)$ for all arcs $CICAP(z,y,x)$ that inhibit that arc.

$inhib(x) \stackrel{\text{def}}{=} \exists y(A(y) \wedge CIP(y,x) \wedge \forall z(CICIP(z,y,x) \rightarrow \neg A(z)))$

In another way, it is sufficient to have $A(y)$ if there exists an inhibition arc $CIP(y,x)$ going from y to x, and $\neg A(z)$ for all arcs $CICIP(z,y,x)$ that inhibit that arc.

We can deduce in classical logic:
$\neg activ(x) \leftrightarrow \forall y(CAP(y,x) \rightarrow (\neg A(y) \vee \exists z(CICAP(z,y,x) \wedge A(z))))$
$\neg inhib(x) \leftrightarrow \forall y(CIP(y,x) \rightarrow (\neg A(y) \vee \exists z(CICIP(z,y,x) \wedge A(z))))$

Axiomatic of activation: From (A1) and the definitions of $activ$ and $inhib$, we have the following activation axiom:

$\forall x(\exists y(A(y) \wedge CAP(y,x) \wedge \forall z(CICAP(z,y,x) \rightarrow \neg A(z))) \wedge \forall y'(CIP(y',x) \rightarrow (\neg A(y') \vee \exists z'(CICIP(z',y',x) \wedge A(z')))) \rightarrow A(x))$

Axiomatic of inhibition: From (I1) and the definitions of $activ$ and $inhib$, we have the following activation axiom:

$\forall x(\exists y'(A(y') \wedge CIP(y',x) \wedge \forall z'(CICIP(z',y',x) \rightarrow \neg A(z'))) \wedge \forall y(CAP(y,x) \rightarrow (\neg A(y) \vee \exists z(CICAP(z,y,x) \wedge A(z)))) \rightarrow I(x))$

C. Extension with new states and actions

The basic language defined in III-A and III-B can be easily extended to express different and more precise node statuses and actions. For example the action of phosphorylation of Chk2 on site S33-5 by ATM can be expressed by the predicate $CP(atm, chk2\_s33\_5, p\_chk2\_s33\_5)$, having $p\_chk2\_s33\_5$ as a result of this phosphorylation.

In a more formal way, the new predicates can be defined as following:

- $CP(z,y,x)$: CP or the *Capacity of Phosphorylation* expresses that the protein z has the capacity to phosphorylate the protein y on a certain site, knowing that x is the result of said phosphorylation.
- $CICP(t,z,y,x)$: $CICP$ or the *Capacity to Inhibit the Capacity of Phosphorylation* expresses that the protein t has the capacity to inhibit the capacity of the phosphorylation of y by z leading to x.

With the previous phosphorylation predicates we can now modify the $activ$ property to the following:
$phos(x) \stackrel{\text{def}}{=} \exists y1, y2(A(y1) \wedge A(y2) \wedge CP(y1,y2,x) \wedge \forall z(CICP(z,y1,y2,x) \rightarrow \neg A(z)))$

And respectively (A1), (A2), and (I1) to the following:
(P1) $\forall x(phos(x) \wedge \neg inhib(x) \rightarrow A(x))$.
(P2) $\forall x(\neg phos(x) \rightarrow \neg A(x))$.
(IP1) $\forall x(inhib(x) \wedge \neg phos(x) \rightarrow I(x))$.

We can now define the new phosphorylation axiom as:
$\forall x(\exists y1, y2(A(y1) \wedge A(y2) \wedge CP(y1,y2,x) \wedge \forall z(CICP(z,y1,y2,x) \rightarrow \neg A(z))) \wedge \forall y'(CIP(y',x) \rightarrow (\neg A(y') \vee \exists z'(CICIP(z',y',x) \wedge A(z')))) \rightarrow A(x))$

$Auto-phosphorylation$, $Dephosphorylation$, $Binding$, $Dissociation$ etc. actions that can be found in Figure 2, and some of the newly discovered ones such as $Methylation$ and $Ubiquitination$ [14], [5] can formalized in a similar fashion.

IV. Automated Deduction Method

In this section we define a fragment of first order logic with equality capable of supporting the language of states and actions defined in III. The properties of this fragment allow us to define a procedure capable of eliminating the quantifiers in this fragment, in other words to transform the first order formulas in formulas without variables, in order to obtain an efficient automated deduction procedure with these fragments.

Definition 1. *Restricted formulas are formulas without free variables defined by the following grammar:*

$\delta ::= \forall x_1,...,x_n\ (\varphi \rightarrow \psi) \mid \exists x_1,...,x_n\ (\varphi \wedge \psi).$

Where φ is an atomic formula, called *domain formula.* and ψ is either a restricted formula or a formula without quantifiers, and every variable appearing in a restricted formula must appear in a domain formula.

Examples of this kind of formulas are:
$\forall x(P(x) \rightarrow Q(x))$.
$\forall x(P(x) \rightarrow \exists y(Q(y) \wedge R(x,y)))$.

Definition 2. *A completion formula is a formula of the following form:*

$\forall x_1,...,x_n\ (P(x_1,...,x_n,c_1,...c_p) \leftrightarrow ((x_1 = a_{1_1} \wedge ... \wedge x_n = a_{1_n}) \vee ... \vee (x_1 = a_{m_1} \wedge ... \wedge x_n = a_{m_n})))$

Where P is a predicate symbol of arity $n+p$.

Completion formulas are similar to the completion axioms defined by Reiter in [19] where the implication is substituted by an equivalence.

Note : for notation purpose, we will sometimes represent $x_1,...,x_n$ by $\overline{x}$, and $c_1,...,c_p$ by $\overline{c}$.

Definition 3. *Given a restricted formula φ and a set of completion for φ noted $C(\varphi)$, we say that $C(\varphi)$ saturates φ, if and only if, for each domain formula in φ, there is a unique completion formula in C.*

Definition 4. *Given an atomic formula φ and a set $C(\varphi)$ of φ, we define the domain of the variables of φ with respect to $C(\varphi)$, denoted $D(\mathcal{V}(\varphi), C(\varphi))$, where $\mathcal{V}(\varphi)$ represents the variables of φ, as follows:*

if φ is of the form $P(x_1,...,x_n,c_1,...,c_p)$, and in $C(\varphi)$ we have a formula of the form:

$\forall x_1,...,x_n\ (P(x_1,...,x_n,c_1,...,c_p) \leftrightarrow ((x_1 = a_{1_1} \wedge ... \wedge x_n = a_{1_n}) \vee ... \vee (x_1 = a_{m_1} \wedge ... \wedge x_n = a_{m_n})))$

then

$D(\mathcal{V}(\varphi), C(\varphi)) = \{< a_{1_1},...,a_{1_n} >,...,< a_{m_1},...,a_{m_n} >\}$

Quantification elimination procedure

Let φ be a restricted formula of the following forms: $\forall \overline{x}(\varphi_1(\overline{x}) \rightarrow \varphi_2(\overline{x}))$ or $\exists \overline{x}(\varphi_1(\overline{x}) \wedge \varphi_2(\overline{x}))$, let $C(\varphi_1(\overline{x}))$ a set of completion formulas for φ_1, then we define recursively a translation T, allowing to replace universal (existential) quantifiers by conjunction (disjunction) of formulas where quantified variables are substituted by constants as follows:

- if $D(\mathcal{V}(\varphi_1), C(\varphi_1)) = \{< \overline{c_1} >,...,< \overline{c_n} >\}$ with $n > 0$:
  - $T(\forall \overline{x}(\varphi_1(\overline{x}) \rightarrow \varphi_2(\overline{x})), C(\varphi)) = T(\varphi_2(\overline{c_1}), C(\varphi_2)) \wedge ... \wedge T(\varphi_2(\overline{c_n}), C(\varphi_2))$
  - $T(\exists \overline{x}(\varphi_1(\overline{x}) \wedge \varphi_2(\overline{x})), C(\varphi)) = T(\varphi_2(\overline{c_1}), C(\varphi_2)) \vee ... \vee T(\varphi_2(\overline{c_n}), C(\varphi_2))$
- if $D(\mathcal{V}(\varphi_1), C(\varphi_1)) = \varnothing$:
  - $T(\forall \overline{x}\ (\varphi_1(\overline{x}) \rightarrow \varphi_2(\overline{x}))\ ,\ C(\varphi)) = True$
  - $T(\exists \overline{x}\ (\varphi_1(\overline{x}) \wedge \varphi_2(\overline{x}))\ ,\ C(\varphi)) = False$

Note : for a given formula φ, it will be noted that the translation T of φ allows to eliminate a set of quantifiers, in other words the set of variables symbols in φ. This procedure can be considered as kind of compilation to first order logic without variables and without equality.

Then in the theory $\mathcal{T}$ in which we have the axioms of equality and axioms of the form $\neg(a = b)$ for each constant a and b representing different objects, which are called unique name axioms by Reiter in [19], we have the following main theorem:

Theorem 1. *Let φ be a restricted formula, and $C(\varphi)$ a saturated completion set of formulas of the domain formulas of φ, then:*

$\mathcal{T},\ C(\varphi) \vdash \varphi \leftrightarrow T(\varphi, C(\varphi))$.

We will now present two examples of translation from first order logic formulas composed of action and state axioms to variable free formulas:

Example 1.

In the following example we apply the translation procedure to the axioms defined in section III, we consider a certain protein a with the following completion axioms:

$\forall y(CAP(y,a) \leftrightarrow y = b_1 \vee ... \vee y = b_n)$
If there is no arc $CAP(b_i, a)$:
$\forall y(CAP(y,a) \leftrightarrow true)$

For each b_i we have a completion axiom of the form:
$\forall z(CICAP(z, b_i, a) \leftrightarrow z = c_{i,1} \vee ... \vee z = c_{i,n_i})$
If there is no arc $CICAP(c_{i,j}, b_i, a)$:
$\forall z(CICAP(z, b_i, a) \leftrightarrow false)$

We also have:
$\forall y(CIP(y,a) \leftrightarrow y = d_1 \vee ... \vee y = d_m)$
If there is no arc $CIP(d_i, a)$:
$\forall y(CIP(y,a) \leftrightarrow true)$

For each d_i we have a completion axiom of the form:
$\forall z(CICIP(z, d_i, a) \leftrightarrow z = e_{i,1} \vee ... \vee z = e_{i,n_i})$
If there is no arc $CICIP(e_{i,j}, d_i, a)$:
$\forall z(CICIP(z, d_i, a) \leftrightarrow false)$

From the above and the definitions of $activ$ and $inhib$ in III-B, we can deduce the following:

$activ(a) \leftrightarrow (A(b_1) \wedge \forall z(CICAP(z, b_1, a) \rightarrow \neg A(z))) \vee ... \vee (A(b_n) \wedge \forall z(CICAP(z, b_n, a) \rightarrow \neg A(z)))$

and
$activ(a) \leftrightarrow (A(b_1) \wedge \neg A(c_{1,1}) \wedge ... \wedge \neg A(c_{1,n_1})) \vee ... \vee (A(b_n) \wedge \neg A(c_{n,1}) \wedge ... \wedge \neg A(c_{n,n_n}))$

Following the same reasoning we also have:

$\neg activ(a) \leftrightarrow (\neg A(b_1) \vee \exists z(CICAP(z, b_1, a) \wedge A(z))) \wedge ... \wedge (\neg A(b_n) \vee \exists z(CICAP(z, b_n, a) \wedge A(z)))$
and
$\neg activ(a) \leftrightarrow (\neg A(b_1) \vee A(c_{1,1}) \vee ... \vee A(c_{1,n_1})) \wedge ... \wedge (\neg A(b_n) \vee A(c_{n,1}) \vee ... \vee A(c_{n,n_n}))$

We can also define $inhib$ by:

$inhib(a) \leftrightarrow (A(d_1) \wedge \forall z(CICIP(z, d_1, a) \rightarrow \neg A(z))) \vee ... \vee (A(d_n) \wedge \forall z(CICIP(z, d_n, a) \rightarrow \neg A(z)))$
and
$inhib(a) \leftrightarrow (A(d_1) \wedge \neg A(e_{1,1}) \wedge ... \wedge \neg A(e_{1,m_1})) \vee ... \vee (A(d_m) \wedge \neg A(e_{m,1}) \wedge ... \wedge \neg A(e_{m,m_m}))$

And finally:

$\neg inhib(a) \leftrightarrow (\neg A(d_1) \vee \exists z(CICIP(z, d_1, a) \wedge A(z))) \wedge ... \wedge (\neg A(d_m) \vee \exists z(CICIP(z, d_m, a) \wedge A(z)))$
and
$\neg inhib(a) \leftrightarrow (\neg A(d_1) \vee A(e_{1,1}) \vee ... \vee A(e_{1,m_1})) \wedge ... \wedge (\neg A(d_m) \vee A(e_{m,1}) \vee ... \vee A(e_{m,m_m}))$

Then these axioms can be used in the previously defined (A1), (A2), (I1) and (I2).

Example 2.

Let's consider another example where a protein b has the capacity to activate another protein a, and that two other proteins c_1 and c_2 have the capacity to inhibit the capacity of activation of a by b. This proposition can be expressed by the following completion axioms:

- $\forall y(CAP(y, a) \leftrightarrow y = b)$: Expresses that b is the only protein that has the capacity to activate a.
- $\forall z(CICAP(z, b, a) \leftrightarrow z = c_1 \vee z = c_2)$: Expresses that c_1 and c_2 are the only proteins that have the capacity to inhibit the capacity of activation of a by b.

From the definition of $activ$, we can deduce:
$activ(a) \leftrightarrow (A(b) \wedge \forall z(CICAP(z, b, a) \rightarrow \neg A(z)))$
then
$activ(a) \leftrightarrow (A(b) \wedge \neg A(c_1) \wedge \neg A(c_2))$

Which means that the property $activ(a)$ is satisfied iff the protein b is active and both proteins c_1 and c_2 are not active.

We can also deduce using the same reasoning:
$\neg activ(a) \leftrightarrow (\neg A(b) \vee A(c_1) \vee A(c_2))$

Which means that the property $\neg activ(a)$ is satisfied iff the protein b is not active or one proteins c_1 and c_2 is active.

Let's also consider that a protein d has the capacity to inhibit the protein a and that there is no proteins capable of inhibiting the capacity of inhibition of a by d. This proposition can be expressed by the following completion axioms:

- $\forall y(CIP(y, a) \leftrightarrow y = d)$: Expresses that d is the only protein that has the capacity to inhibit a.
- $\forall z(CICIP(z, d, a) \leftrightarrow false)$: Expresses that there are no proteins capable of inhibiting the capacity of inhibition of a by d.

From the definition of $inhib$, we can deduce:
$inhib(a) \leftrightarrow (A(d) \wedge \forall z(CICIP(z, b, a) \rightarrow \neg A(z)))$
then
$inhib(a) \leftrightarrow A(d)$

Which means that the property $inhib(a)$ is satisfied iff the protein d is active.

We can also deduce using the same reasoning:
$\neg inhib(a) \leftrightarrow (\neg A(d))$

Which means that the property $\neg inhib(a)$ is satisfied iff the protein b is not active.

Using the axioms (A1) and (I1) defined in III-B
(A1) $\forall x(activ(x) \wedge \neg inhib(x) \rightarrow A(x))$.
(I1) $\forall x(inhib(x) \wedge \neg activ(x) \rightarrow I(x))$.

We can finally deduce:
$(A(b) \wedge \neg A(c_1) \wedge \neg A(c_2) \wedge \neg A(d)) \rightarrow A(a)$

Which means that the protein a is active if the protein b is active and the proteins c_1, c_2, d are not active.

And

$(A(d) \wedge (\neg A(b) \vee A(c_1) \vee A(c_2))) \rightarrow I(a)$

Which means that the protein a is inhibited if the protein d is active and either b is not active or c_1 or c_2 are active.

V. Queries and Results

From what we defined in sections III and IV, we can now model metabolic pathways using the $activ$ and $inhib$ properties and the translation mechanism defined in IV. The resulting axioms are of the following type $conditions \rightarrow results$, and can be chained together to create a series of reactions forming our pathway. Then questions of two different types can be answered using $deduction$ or $abduction$ reasoning.

Questions answered by deduction request all entities that satisfy a given property. In our case, we may have some information about states and actions of certain proteins in some knowledge base (**KB**). A question can be of the following form: *What is the result of reactions formed by the proteins of* ***KB***, or in other means, *what is the state (active or inhibited) of the proteins that result from the reactions formed by proteins of* ***KB***.

And questions answered by abduction looks for minimal assumptions that must be added to **KB** to derive that a certain fact is true. For instance, we may have some informations about actions of certain proteins in **KB**. A question can be of the following form: *What are the reactions that are needed to deduce that a certain protein is active or inhibited*, in other means, *what are the proteins and their respective states (active or inhibited) that should be present in order to derive that a certain protein is active or inhibited.*

Both types of questions can be addressed in SOLAR (SOL for Advanced Reasoning) [13] a first-order clausal consequence finding system based on SOL (Skip Ordered Linear) tableau calculus [6], [21].

In the following we are going to show an example based on figure 9, demonstrating both deduction and abduction type queries.

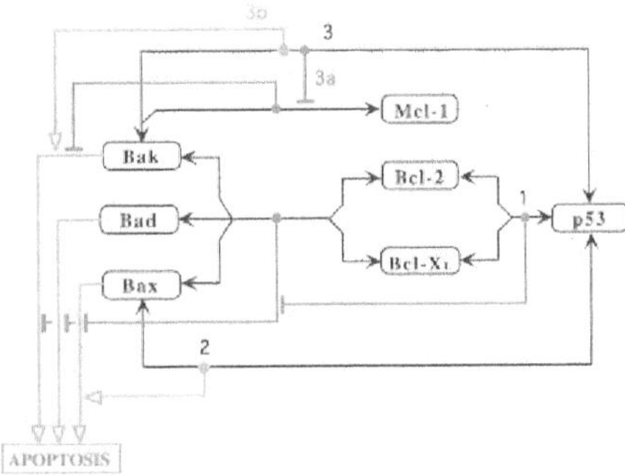

Fig. 9: Mitochondrial apoptosis induced by p53 independently of transcription

In Figure 9 the metabolic network shows how p53 can induce mitochondrial apoptosis independently of transcription. Three coherent pathways have been found [10]:

1) p53 can bind directly to Bcl-2 and Bcl-XL, and block their interaction with pro-apoptotic Bcl-2 proteins (Bak, Bad, and Bax).
2) p53 can bind and activate Bax oligomerization.
3) p53 can bind to Bak, block its interaction with the anti-apoptotic Bcl-2 protein Mcl-1 (3a), and promote Bak oligomerization and induction of apoptosis (3b).

Following section III-C we can define new predicates to suit the needs of the pathway:

- $CB(z, y, x)$: CB or the *Capacity of Binding* expresses that the protein z has the capacity to bind with the protein y, knowing that x is the result of said binding.
- $CICB(t, z, y, x)$: $CICB$ or the *Capacity to Inhibit the Capacity of Binding* expresses that the protein t has the capacity to inhibit the capacity of the binding of z and y leading to x.

For example, these new predicates can be used to model the binding between p53 and Bak using the predicate $CB(p53, bak, p53\_bak)$ where p53_bak is the complex formed by such binding. In a similar fashion we can define the other needed predicates, like the binding predicate that gives us the possibility to bind three proteins together, such as p53 binding to Bcl-2 and Bcl-XL, and the binding predicate that gives us the possibility to bind 5 proteins together, such as Bcl-2, Bcl-XL, Bax, Bad, and Bak.

With these new predicates, new axiomatic can be defined that would enrich the descriptive capacities of the old axiomatic, as seen in III-C. Then the translation procedure can be applied to these axioms and to the completion axiomatic that defines actions between proteins. And finally deduction and abduction can be applied to the resulting clauses to answer queries as shown above.

Applying the translation procedure of section IV the axioms of Figure 9 can be of the following form:

1) $A(p53) \wedge A(bak) \rightarrow A(bak\_p53)$
   bak_p53 is the result of the binding between p53 and Bak.
2) $A(bak\_p53) \rightarrow I(bak\_mcl)$
   bak_mcl is the result of binding between Bak and Mcl-1.
3) $A(bak\_p53) \wedge \neg A(b\_complex) \wedge \neg A(bak\_mcl) \rightarrow A(apoptosis)$
   $b\_complex$ is result of the binding between Bcl-2, Bcl-XL, Bak, Bad, and Bax.
4) $A(bak) \wedge \neg A(b\_complex) \wedge \neg A(bak\_mcl) \rightarrow A(apoptosis)$
5) $A(p53) \wedge A(bcl) \rightarrow A(p53\_bb\_complex)$
   bcl represents Bcl-2 and Bcl-XL.
   $p53\_bb\_complex$ is the result of binding between p53, Bcl-2 and Bcl-XL.
6) $A(p53\_bb\_complex) \rightarrow I(b\_complex)$
7) $A(bax) \wedge \neg A(b\_complex) \rightarrow A(apoptosis)$
8) $A(p53) \wedge A(bax) \wedge \neg A(b\_complex) \rightarrow A(apoptosis)$
9) $A(bad) \wedge \neg A(b\_complex) \rightarrow A(apoptosis)$

If we want to know what are the proteins and their respective states that should be present in order to derive that the cell reached apoptosis, the answer is given by applying abduction over the previous set of transformed clauses. In the set of consequences returned by SOLAR we can find the following:

- $A(p53) \wedge A(bcl) \wedge A(bak)$: is a plausible answer, because p53 can bind to Bcl giving the $p53\_bb\_complex$, which can in return inhibit the $b\_complex$ that is responsible of inhibiting the capacity of Bak to activate the cell's apoptosis. That is why it is sufficient to for this case to have p53, Bcl, and Bak in an active state to reach apoptosis.
- Another interpretation of the previous answer is that p53 can also bind to Bak giving the bak_p53 protein, which can in return inhibit the bak_mcl responsible of inhibiting the capacity of Bak to activate the cell's apoptosis. bak_p53 can also stimulate Bak to reach apoptosis. Without forgetting that $p53\_bb\_complex$ should be inhibiting $b\_complex$.

Now if we already know that the proteins p53, Bcl, and Bax are present and active in the cell, we can ask if the cell can reach apoptosis with such conditions. The answer is given by deduction over the previous set of transformed clauses plus the following observations $A(p53)$, $A(bcl)$, and $A(bax)$. SOLAR returns two found consequences, which means that there are two different possible pathways that can be followed by having those condition that enables the cell to reach apoptosis. Figure 9 shows:

- p53 can bind to Bcl giving the $p53\_bb\_complex$, which can in return inhibit the $b\_complex$ that is responsible of inhibiting the capacity of Bax to activate the cell's apoptosis. That is why it is sufficient to for this case to have p53, Bcl, and Bak in an active state to reach apoptosis.
- The second interpretation suggests that p53 can bind to Bax, stimulating the Bax activation the cell's apoptosis.

Taking into consideration that $b\_complex$ should be inhibited as shown above.

VI. Conclusion

A new language has been defined in this paper capable of modeling both positive and negative causal effects between proteins in a metabolic pathway. We showed how this basic language can be extended to include more specific actions that describes different relations between proteins. These extensions are important in this context, because there is always the possibility that new types of actions are discovered through biological experiments [14], [5]. We later showed how the axioms defined in such languages can be compiled against background knowledge, in order to form a new quantifier free axioms that could be used in either deduction or abduction reasoning. Although the first order axioms can be also well used to answer queries by deduction or abduction methods, the main advantage of translated axioms is their low computation time needed in order to derive consequences.

Future works can focus on useful methods for introducing the notion of time and quantities in the former model. Trying to get as precise as possible in describing such pathways can help biologists discover contradictory informations and guide them during experiments knowing how huge the cells metabolic networks have become (Figure 2). One of the constraints that can also be introduced is the notion of $Aboutness$ [3] that can limit and focus search results to what seems relevant to a single or a group of entities (proteins).

Acknowledgements

This work is partially supported by the Région Midi-Pyrénées project called CLE, the Lebanese National Council for Scientific Research (LNCSR), and the French-Spanish lab LIRP.

We would like to thank Gilles Favre, Jean-Charles Faye and Olivier Sordet for their precious metabolic network knowledge and comments that were used as a base for this paper. We would also like to thank Katsumi Inoue and Hidetomo Nabeshima for their important help with SOLAR.

References

[1] R. Demolombe and L. Fariñas del Cerro. An Inference Rule for Hypothesis Generation. In *Proc. of International Joint Conference on Artificial Intelligence*, Sydney, 1991.

[2] Robert Demolombe. Syntactical characterization of a subset of domain-independent formulas. *J. ACM*, 39(1):71–94, 1992.

[3] Robert Demolombe and Luis Fariñas del Cerro. Information about a given entity: From semantics towards automated deduction. *J. Log. Comput.*, 20(6):1231–1250, 2010.

[4] Martin Erwig and Eric Walkingshaw. Causal reasoning with neuron diagrams. In *Proceedings of the 2010 IEEE Symposium on Visual Languages and Human-Centric Computing*, VLHCC '10, pages 101–108, Washington, DC, USA, 2010. IEEE Computer Society.

[5] V Glorian, G Maillot, S Poles, J S Iacovoni, G Favre, and S Vagner. Hur-dependent loading of mirna risc to the mrna encoding the ras-related small gtpase rhob controls its translation during uv-induced apoptosis. *Cell Death Differ*, 18(11):1692–70, 2011.

[6] Katsumi Inoue. Linear resolution for consequence finding. *Artificial Intelligence*, 56(2–3):301 – 353, 1992.

[7] Katsumi Inoue, Andrei Doncescu, and Hidetomo Nabeshima. Hypothesizing about causal networks with positive and negative effects by meta-level abduction. In *Proceedings of the 20th international conference on Inductive logic programming*, ILP'10, pages 114–129, Berlin, Heidelberg, 2011. Springer-Verlag.

[8] Katsumi Inoue, Andrei Doncescu, and Hidetomo Nabeshima. Completing causal networks by meta-level abduction. *Machine Learning*, 91(2):239–277, 2013.

[9] Antonis Kakas, Alireza Tamaddoni Nezhad, Stephen Muggleton, and F Pazos. Modelling inhibition in metabolic pathways through Abduction and Induction. pages 305–322, 2004.

[10] Kurt W Kohn and Yves Pommier. Molecular interaction map of the p53 and mdm2 logic elements, which control the off-on swith of p53 response to dna damage. *Biochem Biophys Res Commun*, 331(3):816–27, 2005.

[11] Won-Jeong Lee, Dong-Uk Kim, Mi-Young Lee, and Kang-Yell Choi. Identification of proteins interacting with the catalytic subunit of pp2a by proteomics. *PROTEOMICS*, 7(2):206–214, 2007.

[12] Stephen Muggleton and Christopher H. Bryant. Theory completion using inverse entailment. In *Proceedings of the 10th International Conference on Inductive Logic Programming*, ILP '00, pages 130–146, London, UK, UK, 2000. Springer-Verlag.

[13] Hidetomo Nabeshima, Koji Iwanuma, Katsumi Inoue, and Oliver Ray. Solar: An automated deduction system for consequence finding. *AI Commun.*, 23(2-3):183–203, April 2010.

[14] Huadong Pei, Lindsey Zhang, Kuntian Luo, Yuxin Qin, Marta Chesi, Frances Fei, P. Leif Bergsagel, Liewei Wang, Zhongsheng You, and Zhenkun Lou. Mmset regulates histone h4k20 methylation and 53bp1 accumulation at dna damage sites. *Nature*, 470(7332):124–128, 2011.

[15] Y. Pommier, O. Sordet, V.A. Rao, H. Zhang, and K.W. Kohn. Targeting chk2 kinase: molecular interaction maps and therapeutic rationale. *Curr Pharm Des*, 11(22):2855–72, 2005.

[16] Oliver Ray. Automated abduction in scientific discovery. In *Model-Based Reasoning in Science and Medicine*, pages 103–116. Springer, June 2007.

[17] Oliver Ray, Ken Whelan, and Ross King. Logic-based steady-state analysis and revision of metabolic networks with inhibition. In *Proceedings of the 2010 International Conference on Complex, Intelligent and Software Intensive Systems*, CISIS '10, pages 661–666, Washington, DC, USA, 2010. IEEE Computer Society.

[18] Philip G. K. Reiser, Ross D. King, Douglas B. Kell, Stephen H. Muggleton, Christopher H. Bryant, and Stephen G. Oliver. Developing a logical model of yeast metabolism. *Electronic Transactions in Artificial Intelligence*, 5:233–244, 2001.

[19] R. Reiter. Readings in nonmonotonic reasoning. chapter On closed world data bases, pages 300–310. Morgan Kaufmann Publishers Inc., San Francisco, CA, USA, 1987.

[20] J.R. Shoenfield. *Mathematical logic*. Addison-Wesley series in logic. Addison-Wesley Pub. Co., 1967.

[21] P. Siegel. *Representation et utilisation de la connaissance en calcul propositionnel*. Thèse d'État, Université d'Aix-Marseille II, Luminy, France, 1987.

[22] Alireza Tamaddoni-Nezhad, Antonis C. Kakas, Stephen Muggleton, and Florencio Pazos. Modelling inhibition in metabolic pathways through abduction and induction. In Rui Camacho, Ross D. King, and Ashwin Srinivasan, editors, *Inductive Logic Programming, 14th International Conference, ILP 2004, Porto, Portugal, September 6-8, 2004, Proceedings*, volume 3194 of *Lecture Notes in Computer Science*, pages 305–322. Springer, 2004.

Bioinformatic Analyses of Chromium Tolerant Genes in Cyanobacteria and Identification of Chromium Tolerant Operon in *Synechococcus* sp. IU 625

Lee H. Lee[1], Richard Garrett[1], Anna Slusarczyk[1], Jose Perez[2], Jagruti Patel[1] and Tin-Chun Chu[2,*]
[1]Department of Biology & Molecular Biology, Montclair State University, Montclair, NJ, USA
[2]Department of Biological Sciences, Seton Hall University, South Orange, NJ, USA

Abstract - *Heavy metal contamination in the environment is always a big concern. Many microorganisms have developed metal tolerant /resistant mechanisms to survive in such environment. Cyanobacterium Synechococcus sp. IU 625 (S. IU 625) has been used an indicator for studying many EPA targeted heavy metals such as Zn(2+), Cu(2+), Hg(2+). This microorganism has been reported to have resistant mechanisms to mercury and zinc. In this study, bioinformatics tools were used to determine the plasmid-mediated chromium resistant genes of S. IU 625. An operon involved in chromium resistance has been proposed. For each gene within the proposed operon, PCR primers were designed to amplify the plasmid DNA of S. IU 625. The complete sequence of the operon has been obtained. Homology search suggested that this operon has high homology to Synechococcus elongatus PCC 7942. The phylogenic analysis of the chromate transporters has shown some distance among cyanobacteria.*

Keywords: cyanobacteria, *Synechococcus*, chromium, operon

1 Introduction

1.1 Cyanobacteria

Cyanobacteria are of the oldest and morphologically most diverse prokaryotic phyla on our planet. The early development of an oxygen-containing atmosphere approximately 2.45 – 2.22 billon years ago is attributed to the photosynthetic activity of cyanobacteria. Furthermore, cyanobacteria are one of the few prokaryotic phyla that have evolved photosynthetic multicellular organisms. The oldest known fossil specimen is that of a multicellular cyanobacterium from ~ 2.0 billion years ago [1].

There are roughly 1,500 species of cyanobacteria, more commonly referred to as "blue-green algae" [1]. The *Synechococcus* genus contains 20 well-studied species. *Synechococcus elongatus* (*S. elongatus*) contains 2 endogenous plasmids and a single circular chromosome. Genomic conservation exists within sub-species of the *Synechococcus* genus. For example, *Synechococcus elongatus* PCC 6301 (*S. elongatus* PCC 6301) and *Synechococcus elongatus* PCC 7942 (*S. elongatus* PCC 7942) contain 99.86% chromosomal similarity [2, 3]. The *Synechococcus* genus contains many unclassified species of cyanobacteria. One such species, *Synechococcus* sp. IU 625 (*S.* IU 625), is a non-motile, unicellular, rod-shaped microorganism which is similar to Gram-negative bacteria in cell wall structure, cell division and the ability to harbor plasmids [4]. They also serve as good indicators of environmental pollution, especially heavy metal contamination. Previous studies on *S.* IU 625 have found that heavy metals exhibit toxic effects and inhibit growth [5-11].

1.2 The pANL plasmid in *Synechococcus elongatus*

Most cyanobacteria, with the exception of *Thermosynechococcus elongatus* BP-1, have one or more endogenous plasmids which account for the majority of the cellular functions including heavy metal and antibiotic resistance, toxin production, and gas vacuolation. Smaller plasmids within bacteria are transferable during bacterial conjugation. Larger plasmids, such as pANL of *Synechococcus elongatus*, cannot be exchanged during conjugation and are conserved throughout several species of cyanobacteria. The pANL plasmid has been successfully identified in *S. elongatus* PCC 7942, in the closely related strain *S. elongatus* PCC 6301, and also *S. elongatus* PCC 6707, which is different from *S. elongatus* PCC 7942 in both genome size and base composition.

pANL contains an adaptive response to sulfur starvation and is divided into four structural and functional regions: the replication origin, a signal transduction region, a plasmid maintenance region, and a sulfur regulatory region [2]. Furthermore, the sulfur regulatory region contains 13 *srp* genes (*srpA*→ *srpM*) and is divided into clockwise and counter-clockwise clusters. The counter-clockwise cluster includes ORFs from *anL35* – *anL40*. The clockwise cluster includes ORFs from *anL44* – *anL55*. The two clusters are separated by two head-to-head genes: *anL42* and *anL43*, both of which encode conserved hypothetical proteins. Most of the genes in this region either have been shown or are predicted to be involved in sulfur metabolism or transportation. Many of them have close paralogues in the chromosome [2].

The sulfur regulatory region is responsible for cation homeostasis within the prokaryotic organism. Some heavy metal cations form strong toxic complexes, which makes them too dangerous for any physiological function. Even highly reputable trace elements like zinc or nickel are toxic at higher concentrations. Thus, the intracellular concentration of heavy-metal ions has to be tightly controlled, and heavy metal resistance is just a specific case of the general demand of every living cell. Oxyanions like chromate, with four tetrahedrally arranged oxygen atoms and two negative charges, differ mostly in the size of the central ion, so the structure of chromate resembles that of sulfate. The same is true for arsenate and phosphate. Thus, uptake systems for heavy metal ions have to bind tightly if they want to differentiate between structurally similar ions [12].

Most cells solve this problem by using two types of systems for heavy-metal ions: one is fast, unspecific and constitutively expressed. These fast systems are usually driven by the chemiosmotic gradient across the cytoplasmic membrane of bacteria and are non-specific for ion transfer. The second type of system has a high substrate specificity, is slower and often uses ATP hydrolysis as the energy source, sometimes in addition to the chemiosmotic gradient, and these expensive uptake systems are only produced by the cell in times of need, starvation or a special metabolic situation [12].

1.3 Chromium resistance in prokaryotes

In contrast to essential sulfur, tungsten, and selenium, chromium is a controversial element. Chromium (Cr) is considered as a non-essential metal for microorganisms and plants and exists in nature as two main chemical species: Cr(III) and Cr(VI). Inside the cell, chromate (CrO_4^{2-}) and dichromate ($Cr_2O_7^{2-}$) are highly toxic for the majority of cells. Cr(VI) is readily reduced to Cr(III) by various enzymatic and non-enzymatic activities and the resulting chromium may then exert diverse toxic effects in the cytoplasm of the bacteria [13].

1.3.1 Chromium uptake

Chromate is transported inside bacterial cells by sulfate transporters and has been identified as a competitive inhibitor of sulfate transport. Membrane transport proteins, more specifically, the sulfate permease CysP in *Synechococcus elongatus*, transport sulfate and analogous heavy metals into the cytoplasm. Homologues of CysP have been identified in other bacteria including the sulfate permease CysT in *E. coli.* [13].

1.3.2 Chromium efflux

Due to the toxicity of chromate, most bacteria possess the CHR transport system, which extrudes chromate out of the cell [13]. The ChrA transporter functions as a chemiosmotic pump that extrudes chromate from the cytoplasm using the proton-motive force and displays a topology of 13 transmembrane segments (TMSs). ANL48, a plasmid-generated homologue of ChrA, exists in *S.* IU 625 and is encoded by *srpC* on the pANL plasmid. Both ANL48 and ChrA are members of the CHR chromate ion transport superfamily and are responsible for chromium efflux [13, 14].

2 Material and Methods

2.1 Cyanobacterial maintenance and growth

S. IU 625 cultures were obtained from Dr. Roy McGowan, New York. They were maintained in sterile Mauro's Modified Medium (3M) [15] at pH 7.9. Cultures were grown under constant fluorescence light and agitation at 90 rpm with ambient temperature.

2.2 Bioinformatic analysis

General *in silico* analysis was performed using the Basic Local Alignment Search Tool (BLAST). Plasmid operon prediction was performed by the Database for Prokaryotic Operons (DOOR) [16]. The SoftBerry Bacterial Promoter, Operon and Gene Finding [17] tool was used to check for promoters in the proposed operon. A phylogram of 20 cyanobacterial species was constructed using a Nearest-Neighbor algorithm with MEGA5.10 software package [18]. The algorithm is powered by the Jones-Taylor-Thornton (JTT) model, which uses a bootstrap methodology to determine divergence in a multiple sequence alignment. The JTT model with bootstrap creates 100 replicates of each entry, generating the JTT matrix. The differences in substitution rates produce a phylogram.

2.3 Plasmid isolation

Qiagen plasmid mini-prep (Qiaprep spin miniprep kit, 27106) kits were used to isolate plasmid DNA from *S.* IU 625. 1.5 mL *S.* IU 625 cultures at an OD_{750nm} of 1.0 were placed in a 1.5 mL microfuge tube and centrifuged for 5 minutes at 14,000 rpm. The samples were decanted and the pellets were resuspended with 250 μL P1 resuspension buffer and vortexed until no clumps were visible. P2 alkaline lysis buffer (250 μL) was added to the tubes and were mixed by inverting tubes four to six times. N3 neutralization buffer (350 μL) was then added, and the tubes were immediately inverted to mix. The samples were centrifuged for 10 minutes at 14,000 rpm; the supernatant was transferred to the spin column in a 2 mL collection tube. The samples were centrifuged and the flow through discarded. The spin column was then washed by the addition of 0.75 mL PE buffer with ethanol added, and centrifuged again. The plasmid trapped within the spin column was then eluted with 50 μL elution buffer into a 1.5 ml microfuge tube. The concentration and purity of DNA were determined by NanoDrop ND-1000 spectrophotometer (Thermo Scientific, Wilmington, DE).

2.4 Primer design, PCR amplification, gel electrophoresis

The results obtained from the comparative genomic analyses of the cyanobacteria will be used to design primers to identify the chromium tolerant genes in *S.* IU 625. Forward and reverse primers were designed to amplify both intergenic and intragenic regions of genes using PrimerQuest^{SM} software from Integrated DNA Technologies, Inc. Primers were then used in a PCR (polymerase Chain Reaction)-based assay with a Veriti™ 96-Well Thermal Cycler (Applied Biosystems, FosterCity, CA). Each reaction tube contains the following: 12.5 μL of the HotStarTaq Master Mix (QIAGEN, Cat. No. 203443), 9.5 μL of sterile diH_2O, 1 μL forward primer, 1 μL reverse primer, and 1 μL DNA sample which yielded a total volume of 25 μL. The run method parameters are: initial denaturation at 95°C for 2 minutes to activate the HotStarTaq DNA polymerase, 30 cycles of denaturation at 95°C for 1 minute, primer annealing at 62°C for 1 minute, and extension at 72°C for 1 minute. After 30 cycles, the PCR reaction tubes were allowed to undergo a final extension at 72°C for 10 minutes. The thermal cycler was allowed to cool down to 4°C prior to the PCR products' placement into a -20°C freezer. These PCR products were ready for future analysis via gel electrophoresis or for DNA sequencing. The size of PCR products was estimated by 1% agarose gels in TAE buffer. The resulting gels were imaged and analyzed under UV light using a Kodak Image Station 440CF (Perkin Elmer Life Sciences, Waltham, MA). The sequences of the amplicons were obtained using 3130 Genetic Analyzer sequencer (Applied Biosystems, Carlsbad, CA). The homologues searches of the obtained sequences were using NCBI Blast searches.

3 Results

3.1 *In silico* analysis of chromium tolerant genes within *S.* IU 625 based upon the genome of *S. elongatus* PCC 7942

The *Synechococcus* genus contains several species of cyanobacteria. *S. elongatus* PCC 7942, a well studies and completely sequenced species, was used as a template to study genomics and proteomics of *S.* IU 625. The plasmid locations of each gene involved with chromium resistance within *S. elongatus* PCC 7942 is mapped in Figure 1.

3.2 *In silico* analysis of plasmid proteins (ANL48, ANL49 and ANL50)

It is hypothesized that the *Sulfur Regulatory Plasmid Genes* (*srp*) *C*, *D*, and *E* are members of a chromium efflux operon. Each component of the operon, along with *anL44*, was further analyzed *in-silico* using bioinformatic servers. The Basic Local Alignment Search Tool for Proteins (BlastP) was used to predict conserved domains.

srpC is flanked by *srpD*, and further downstream is *srpE*. It is proposed that chromate transport (*srpC*) relies on the amino acid transfer from *srpD* and *srpE*. A translation table (Figure 2) was constructed to determine the transcription regulator of the region.

3.3 *In silico* analysis of the proposed *srpCDE* operon

DOOR database was utilized to determine chromium-induced operons within the pANL plasmid of *S. elongatus* PCC 7942. DOOR predicted the following genes to be involved in an operon: COG2059, COG0031, and COG0405 (*srpCDE*). The *srpCDE* operon (DOOR ID #168857) was conserved in other species of cyanobacteria; including *Chromohalobacter salexigens* DSM 3043 (DOOR ID #201626) and *Oceanobacillus iheyensis* HTE831 (DOOR ID #71572).

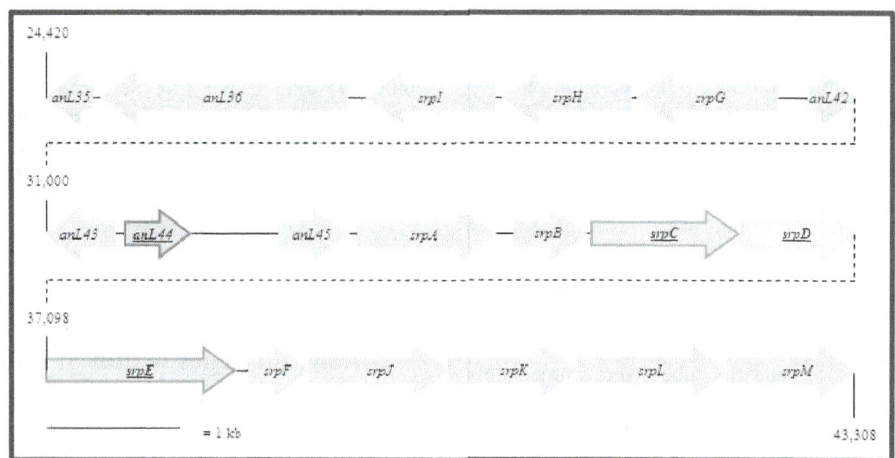

Figure 1: The sulfur regulatory region within pANL. This 18,888 bp region contains certain elements that are directly involved with chromium transport and metabolism. Genes within the plasmid specifically linked to chromium resistance include: 1) *anL44* – position 31,647 → 32,081; 2) *srpC* (COG2059) – position 34,800 → 35,981; 3) *srpD* (COG0031) – position 36,112 → 37,101; and 4) *srpE* (COG0405) – position 37,098 → 38,624. Genes positioned upstream of this cluster function as amino acid transport and metabolism. Genes which are located downstream have no known function and likely serve as transport proteins.

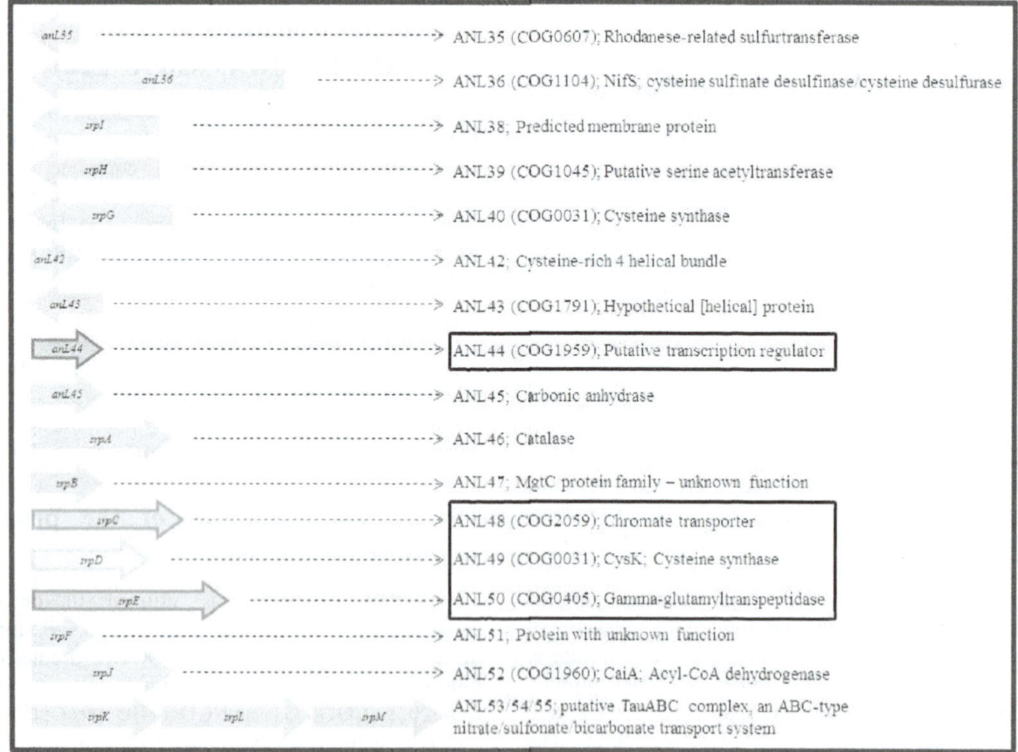

Figure 2: Proteomics of the sulfur regulatory region within pANL. The 19 proteins involved in heavy-metal resistance are displayed. Four involved specifically in chromium resistance are highlighted: 1) ANL44 – a putative transcription regulator, 2) ANL48 – a chromate transporter, 3) ANL49 – a cysteine synthase, and 4) ANL50 – a gamma-glutamyl transpeptidase.

The upstream flanking sequence of the transcriptional regulator was analyzed using SoftBerry. Theoretically, an operon may only contain a single, functional promoter with motifs for an RNA polymerase and -10 and -35 elemental boxes [19]. The results are shown in Figure 3.

The intergenic analysis using SoftBerry verified that ANL44 was the transcription regulator of the chromate efflux operon. ANL44 contains a Ribosomal releasing Factor 2 (RrF2) domain and serves as a putative repressor for the operon; with transcription occurring in the presence of chromium. A cartoon image of the proposed operon is displayed in Figure 4.

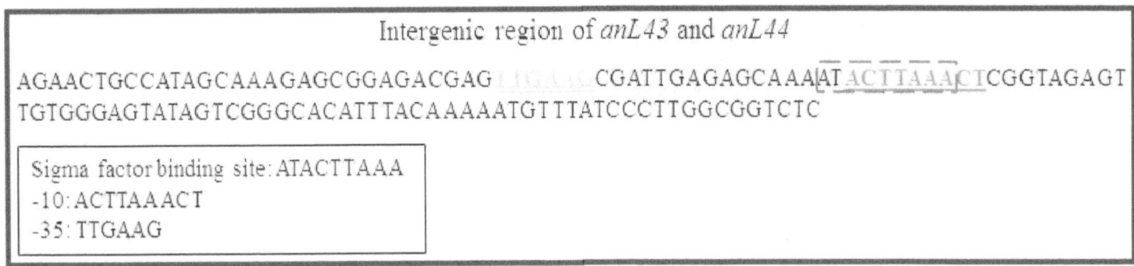

Figure 3: SoftBerry analysis of the intergenic region between *anL43* and *anL44*. Promoter analysis predicted a -10 and a -35 motif (underlined and double-underlined, respectively), as well as a RNA Polymerase Sigma Factor D17 (rpσD17) (dashed-line box).

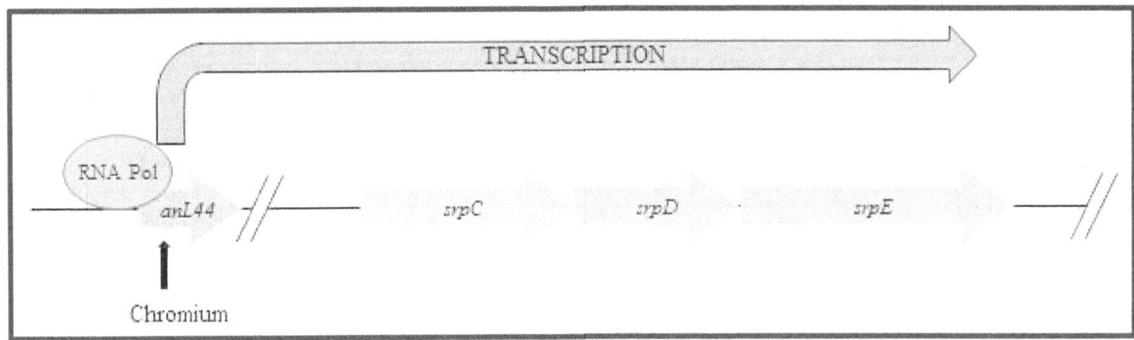

Figure 4: A visual representation of the *srpCDE* operon. The sigma subunit of RNA polymerase binds to the promoter at the elemental boxes to initiate transcription of the operon [19].

3.4 Priming for presence of putative chromium tolerant operon of *S.* IU 625

The bioinformatic analysis suggested the region of the operon functions in chromium tolerance. The primers were designed to identify these genes in *S.* IU 625 based on the genome of *S. elongatus* PCC 7942. Gel electrophoresis of these PCR products is shown in Figure 5. The results suggested that the primers are able to prime the plasmid DNA in *S.* IU 625 and the size of amplicons are within expected ranges.

It is conclusive that *srpC, srpD,* and *srpE* formulate an operon functioning during chromium efflux. Identification of these genes in *S.* IU 625 has been carried out. The phylogenetic analyses of *chrA* in cyanobacteria are shown in Figure 6. The relatedness of the chromate transporters in *S. elongatus* PCC 7942 and *S.* IU 625 in comparison with other unicellular cyanobacteria is not as close as expected in reported genes such as *smtA* (metallothionein) [20] and *merA* (mercuric reductase) [21]. This may be due to the plasmid location of chromium tolerant genes. Plasmid genes are highly subject to mutation, possibly accounting for the distance among species in the *Synechococcus* genus. Further analysis involving quantitative polymerase chain reaction (qPCR) with custom primers will determine if these genes are expressed in unison. Furthermore, *anL44* will be examined for gene expression to determine if the putative transcription regulator is influencing the operon.

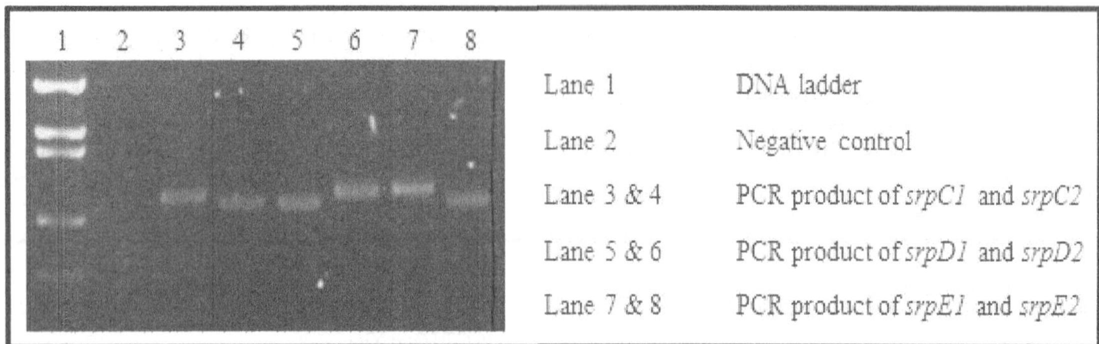

Figure 5: Gel electrophoresis of PCR products for all three genes.

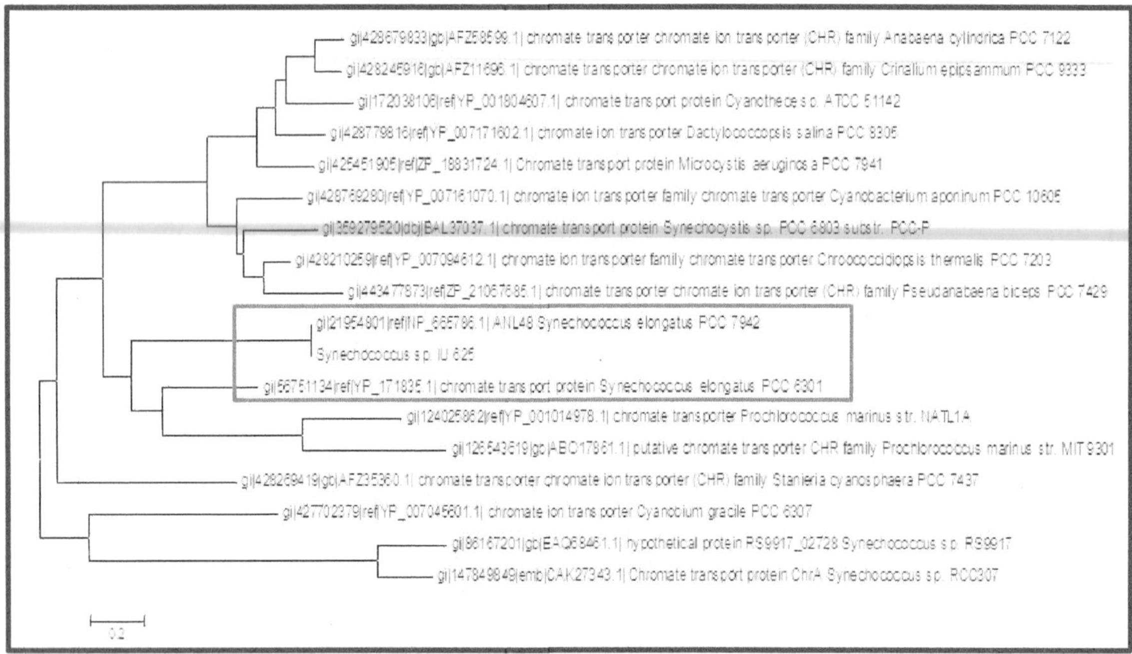

Figure 6: A phylogenetic analysis of chromate transporters in cyanobacteria. The *chrA* gene can be either on the plasmid or on the chromosome. The pANL variation of *chrA* is found in many subspecies of the *Synechococcus* genus. Plasmid genes are highly subject to mutation, possibly accounting for the distance among species in the *Synechococcus elongatus* species [2, 22].

4 Conclusions

In silico analysis showed that pANL was found within subspecies of *Synechococcus elongatus*. Experimentation determined that a novel species, *S.* IU 625, also contains the pANL plasmid. This may be suggestive that the two cyanobacteria originate at a common evolutionary ancestor (Figure 6). The pANL contains an adaptive response to sulfur and other heavy metal stress. It is important for *Synechococcus* species to survive in those stressed environment.

5 References

[1] B.E. Schirrmeister, A. Antonelli, and H.C. Bagheri, "The origin of multicellularity in cyanobacteria," *BMC Evol Biol* 2011, p. 45.

[2] Y. Chen, C.K. Holtman, R.D. Magnuson, P.A. Youderian, and S.S. Golden, "The complete sequence and functional analysis of pANL, the large plasmid of the unicellular freshwater cyanobacterium

Synechococcus elongatus PCC 7942," *Plasmid*, May 2008, p. 176-92.

[3] C. Sugita, K. Ogata, M. Shikata, H. Jikuya, J. Takano, M. Furumichi, M. Kanehisa, T. Omata, M. Sugiura, and M. Sugita, "Complete nucleotide sequence of the freshwater unicellular cyanobacterium Synechococcus elongatus PCC 6301 chromosome: gene content and organization," *Photosynth Res*, Jul-Sep 2007, p. 55-67.

[4] R.H. Lau, and W.F. Doolittle, "Covalently closed circular DNAs in closely related unicellular cyanobacteria," *J Bacteriol*, Jan 1979, p. 648-52.

[5] L.H. Lee, B.K. Lustigman, and S.R. Murray, "Combined effect of mercuric chloride and selenium dioxide on the growth of the cyanobacteria, Anacystis nidulans," *Bull Environ Contam Toxicol*, Dec 2002, p. 900-7.

[6] T.C. Chu, S.R. Murray, J. Todd, W. Perez, J.R. Yarborough, C. Okafor, and L.H. Lee, "Adaption of *Synechococcus* sp. IU 625 to growth in the presence of mercuric chloride," *Acta Histochem*, Jan 2012, p. 6-11.

[7] H.L. Lee, B. Lustigman, V. Schwinge, I.Y. Chiu, and S. Hsu, "Effect of mercury and cadmium on the growth of *Anacystis nidulans*," *Bull Environ Contam Toxicol*, Aug 1992, p. 272-8.

[8] L.H. Lee, B. Lustigman, I.Y. Chu, and S. Hsu, "Effect of lead and cobalt on the growth of *Anacystis nidulans*," *Bull Environ Contam Toxicol*, Feb 1992, p. 230-6.

[9] L.H. Lee, B. Lustigman, I.Y. Chu, and H.L. Jou, "Effect of aluminum and pH on the growth of *Anacystis nidulans*," *Bull Environ Contam Toxicol*, May 1991, p. 720-6.

[10] L.H. Lee, B. Lustigman, and D. Dandorf, "Effect of manganese and zinc on the growth of *Anacystis nidulans*," *Bull Environ Contam Toxicol*, Jul 1994, p. 158-65.

[11] L.H. Lee, B. Lustigman, and J. Maccari, "Effect of copper on the growth of *Anacystis nidulans*," *Bull Environ Contam Toxicol*, Apr 1993, p. 600-7.

[12] D.H. Nies, "Microbial heavy-metal resistance," *Appl Microbiol Biotechnol*, Jun 1999, p. 730-50.

[13] E. Aguilar-Barajas, C. Diaz-Perez, M.I. Ramirez-Diaz, H. Riveros-Rosas, and C. Cervantes, "Bacterial transport of sulfate, molybdate, and related oxyanions," *Biometals*, Aug 2011, p. 687-707.

[14] E. Aguilar-Barajas, P. Jeronimo-Rodriguez, M.I. Ramirez-Diaz, C. Rensing, and C. Cervantes, "The ChrA homologue from a sulfur-regulated gene cluster in cyanobacterial plasmid pANL confers chromate resistance," *World J Microbiol Biotechnol*, Mar 2012, p. 865-9.

[15] W.A. Kratz, and J. Myers, "Photosynthesis and Respiration of Three Blue-Green Algae," *Plant Physiol*, May 1955, p. 275-80.

[16] F. Mao, P. Dam, J. Chou, V. Olman, and Y. Xu, "DOOR: a database for prokaryotic operons," *Nucleic Acids Res*, Jan 2009, p. D459-63.

[17] SoftBerry, "SoftBerry: Bacterial Promoter, Operon and Gene Finding," 2006; http://linux1.softberry.com/berry.phtml?topic=index&group=programs&subgroup=gfindb.

[18] K. Tamura, D. Peterson, N. Peterson, G. Stecher, M. Nei, and S. Kumar, "MEGA5: molecular evolutionary genetics analysis using maximum likelihood, evolutionary distance, and maximum parsimony methods," *Mol Biol Evol*, Oct 2011, p. 2731-9.

[19] M. Sabbatini, A. Vezzoli, M. Milani, and G. Bertoni, "Evidence for self-association of the alternative sigma factor sigma54," *FEBS J*, Mar 2013, p. 1371-8.

[20] T.C. Chu, L.H. Lee, J.J. Gaynor, Q.C. Vega, B.K. Lustigman, and S. Srinivasan, "Identification of *Synechococcus* sp. IU 625 metallothionein gene and its evolutionary relationship to the metallothionein gene of other cyanobacteria," *Proc. The 2007 International Conference on Bioinformatics & Computational Biology (BIOCOMP 2007)*, 2007, p. 201-7.

[21] L.H. Lee, C. Okafor, M.J. Rienzo, and T.C. Chu, "Bioinformatic Analysis of Cyanobacterial Mercuric Resistance Genes and Identification of *Synechococcus* sp. IU 625 Putative Mercuric Resistance Genes," *Proc. The 2012 International Conference on Bioinformatics & Computational Biology (BIOCOMP 2012)*, 2012, p. 178-83.

[22] J.L. Martinez, and F. Baquero, "Mutation frequencies and antibiotic resistance," *Antimicrob Agents Chemother*, Jul 2000, p. 1771-7.

A novel approach for heuristic pairwise DNA sequence alignment

Beat Wolf[1], **Pierre Kuonen**[2], **Thomas Dandekar**[2]
[1]Computer science, University of Applied Sciences Western Switzerland, Fribourg, Switzerland
[2]Bioinformatics, University of Würzburg, Würzburg, Germany

Abstract— *With the ever increasing speed at which DNA can be sequenced the available computing power is struggling to follow at the same pace. In contrast to earlier days of DNA sequencing, it now takes longer to align the data than to sequence it. Thus, new approaches to solve the alignment problem need to be investigated. A perfect sequence alignment might not always be required, specially when available computing power is limited. With that in mind, a purely heuristic approach to sequence alignment is proposed and evaluated. The evaluation shows good performance and quality with the used datasets, but suggest that the algorithm should not be used as the final alignment step, but to quickly identify alignment candidate locations.*

Keywords: Algorithms, Sequence alignment, Heuristics, NGS

1. Introduction

Most current aligners use at some point in their alignment the Waterman-Smith algorithm [1], or a closely related one like Needleman-Wunsch [2] or Gotoh [3]. Examples of such aligners are SHRiMP [4] and SSAHA [5]. Algorithms of that family will find an optimal alignment, but at the cost of computing time and memory consumption. They also struggle to adapt to biological rules of the sequences to align. Those include affine gap penalities, where gap starts and gap extensions in the sequence to be aligned are scored differently, or sequencer specific features, like homopolymer errors, where repetitions of nucleotides are sequenced in the wrong number. To address those problems, we developed a new heuristic algorithm based on a novel approach.

2. Alignment

With next generation sequencing (NGS) techniques, DNA is sequenced in small sequences, ranging from 30 to 1000 nucleotides in length. The origin of those sequences on the source genome is unknown after the sequencing process. To find their location on the original genome, the location on the reference genome is searched where the sequence has the least amount of mismatches. Those mismatches mostly come in the form of SNPs (Single Nucleotide Polymorphism, a single change between the sequence and the reference) but also *indels* (insertions or deletions of a certain number of nucleotides). To speed up the detection of the most likely place to which the sequence has to be aligned, many algorithms use as a starting point for the alignment a seed. The seed is a portion of the sequence to be aligned that can easily be located on the reference genome using an index. Figure 1 shows sequence aligned against a reference, starting from the initial seed "TA", containing indels. The SNPs and indels are colored in gray. An alignment algorithm tries find the optimal way to extend the seed, to find the alignment with the maximal score. The score is calculated using the differences between the sequence and the reference. SNPs and indels have different costs, leading to the final alignment score.

Fig. 1: Sequence alignment

Most sequences to align have several seeds that map to the reference. Those seeds can map to regions near each other, or to regions far apart in the reference genome. Some seeds might also map to several different positions. The seeds are evaluated according to some criteria to select only the most promising ones and then are aligned using a classical algorithm. The evaluation of the seed can be based on its uniqueness or as in the BLAST [6] algorithm, by extending left and right, to score the seed depending on the amount of matching bases. It is on this idea of extending the seed that our novel algorithm is based. BLAST expands the seeds allowing no gaps in the extension. This is done by a simple comparison between the bases of the sequence and the reference, starting from the seed. If there is an indel close to the seed, the score will naturally be low. The proposed algorithm does the same extension, but allows for indels at every step.

3. Algorithm

The Gotoh [3] algorithm solves the alignment problem by creating a matrix where every position of the read is compared to every position of the reference. Using the score of the neighbor base in the matrix, a matrix containing the maximum score for the alignment at every position is created, allowing to find the optimal alignment between the two sequences. As described in [7], heuristic algorithms have a great potential of speeding up the alignment process. Several approaches already exist in this domain, ranging from evolutionary algorithms [8] to ant colonies [9]. Our algorithm takes a different approach, which is similar to the text file comparison algorithm developed by Miller and Myers [10], using less memory, but also having a lower precision. Starting at a seed, first the downstream (left) and then the upstream (right) part of the sequence is aligned. As long as the sequence and the reference match, the seed is extended. As soon as a mismatch is found, a decision has to be taken, either the mismatch is an insertion, a deletion or a simple mismatch. To make this decision, all three possibilities are evaluated. To do so, the score of all possibilities is evaluated, and the best one is chosen to continue the extension. This is where our algorithm differs from other algorithms, as every decision is final and can not be reevaluated at a later stage. To evaluate every possibility, the gapless extension score (sum of all matches and missmatches from that position) is added to the base cost for that choice (a short indel will for example have a lower cost than a longer one). The extension score is based on the comparison of the sequence and the reference, but gives less weight to the positions further away from the seed than the ones closer to it.

To illustrate the algorithm lets assume that we want to align the sequence ACATGCA (left side of the matrixes in Figure 2) against the reference ACGGATG (top in Figure 2). In this example the maximal size of indels is set to 2. Starting at the top left in Figure 2a, 2 matches are found. Matches are marked as light gray, mismatches in dark grayy. As long as the reference and the sequence to align math, the alignment can be extended with no further options beeing evaluated (as seen for the two first positions). On the third comparison from the top left, a mismatch is found.

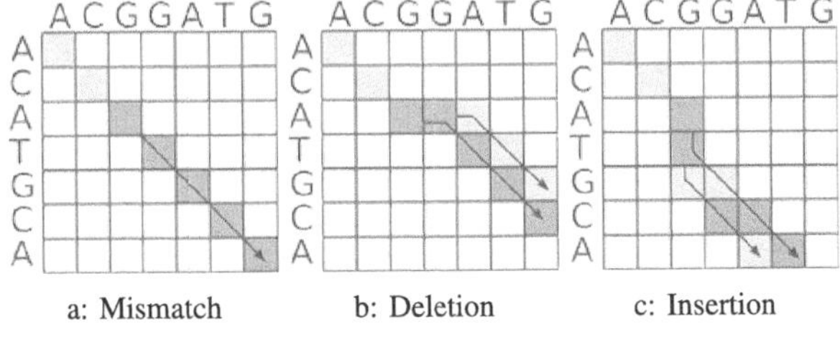

a: Mismatch b: Deletion c: Insertion

Fig. 2: Alignment options

Now, all possibilities have to be evaluated. Those possibilities are:

- The mismatch is a normal mismatch and the alignment continues on the same diagonal, figure 2a
- The mismatch is a deletion of size 1 or 2, figure 2b
- The mismatch is a insertion of size 1 or 2, figure 2c

In figure 2a the mismatch case is evaluated. This is done by simply extending the alignment on the same diagonal. Only a fixed amount of bases is tested for every scenario, usually 16, for reasons which will be explained later. Figure 2b shows 2 scenarios, a deletion of 1 or 2 bases. For those scenarios, 1 or 2 bases are skipped horizontally in the matrix, and the comparison continues by exploring the diagonals. Same goes for figure 2c where the 2 possible insertion scenarios are explored, this time skipping 1 and 2 bases vertically. Visually it can be seen that the 2 base deletion scenario is the best one, as after the two deletions, all the bases match. To evaluate which scenario is the best, there are several possibilities. Either the total amount of match and mismatches can be counted for every scenario, or matches and mismatches at the beginning of the diagonals are weigthed more. The later approach has the advantage that if there are indels on the diagonal to be tested, they will not influence the score too much. This is the approach the proposed algorithm takes. This also has the advantage that not the complete diagonal needs to be tested, as at a certain distance the importance of a comparison will be so low, that it can be discarded.

Tge following linear function is used:

$$f(r,s) = \sum_{p=0}^{x} m(r_p, s_p) * (\frac{x-p}{x} * M) \tag{1}$$

Where:

- r is the reference sequence
- s the sequence to be aligned
- x the maximum amount of bases to look at in the diagonal
- M the score for a matching position

$m(a,b)$ is a function that compare two characters:

$$m(a,b) = \begin{cases} 1 & \text{if } a \text{ equals } b \\ -1 & \text{otherwise} \end{cases} \tag{2}$$

To compute the final cost of a scenario, the base cost of the scenario is added to the score calulated with $f(r,s)$. Insertions and deletions have a higher cost in the scoring function than a simple mismatch. This leads us to use the 3 functions to calculate the final cost of every scenario:

$$\text{mismatch score} = f(r,s) \tag{3}$$

$$\text{insertion score} = I + E * (l-1) + f(r_p, s_{p+l}) \tag{4}$$

$$\text{deletion score} = I + E * (l-1) + f(r_{p+l}, s_p) \tag{5}$$

Where l is the length of the deletion (or insertion), I is the cost to start an indel, and E is the cost to increase the size of an existing indel by 1. The scenario with the highest score is chosen.

After the alignment, several post processing techniques can be applied. For example trimming bad quality borders.

Depending on the technology used to sequence the DNA, the borders of the sequences are often less accurately sequenced. To address this, we can cut off faulty borders. By default, in our implementation, both borders can be cut off up to 5% of the total sequence length. Other algorithms like Gotoh use this technique implicitly. Another improvement that can be made is to move indels to correct small indel placement errors. It is also possible to merge indels that are close to each other and placing indels at the leftmost position in a homopolymer.

4. Complexity

We calculate the insertion and deletion score in a way that already integrates affine gap penalty costs, they do not influence the complexity of the algorithm. The algorithm is designed to abort if a given amount of mismatches or insertions and deletions have been found. The maximum indel size can also be configured. Those configurations have a direct impact on the complexity of the algorithm. If there is an allowed maximum of x mismatches, a maximum indel length of l and a maximum length of the diagonals to be explored of d (16 by default), then the maximum amount of comparisons in the algorithm is $m + 2xl * d$, which translates to a complexity of $O(m + xld)$, where m is the length of sequence to be aligned. The complexity in the best case scenario, a perfect match between the reference and the sequence to be aligned, is $O(m)$. Compared to the complexity of at least $O(n * m)$ in Gotoh[3], where n is the length of the reference sequence the proposed algorithm is potentially much faster, especially when the initial seed is well chosen. It has to be noted, that n is usually reduced to be similar to m, which leads to a complexity of $O(m^2)$.

Assuming that the complete reference and sequence to align can already be found in the memory, the memory complexity is $O(1)$, because no matrix has to be explicitely constructed. The size of the reference and the size of the sequence to align do not affect the memory usage as the algorithm only solves one mismatch at a time and takes a final decision on how to align it. This keeps the memory requirement low. This is very good compared to the classical algorithms which often have a memory complexity of $O(n * m)$, or $O(m^2)$ when n is similar in size to m. The Gotoh algorithm for example creates 3 matrices, each of the size $m * n$.

5. Quality

In the previous chapter we showed the lower complexity of the algorithm compared to current algorithms. The choices have undoubtedly a consequence on the precision of the algorithm. To show how much is the goal of this chapter. To test the alignment quality, 40k simulated sequences where aligned using our heuristic approach and the Gotoh[3] algorithm, which is an improved version of the Waterman-Smith[1] algorithm, allowing for affine gaps while keeping the same execution and memory complexity. The location of every sequence to align on the refernce was known, thus both algorithms had to check only one candidate position, which should result in a succesful alignment. The sequences contain up to 5% mismatches and on top of that up to 3% deletions with a length of 1 to 5. Two datasets where produced, one with only 2 deletions which can not be close together, and one where a variable amount of deletions can be found, potentially close together. Figure 3 shows the boxplot for the first dataset and the second dataset. The Figures contain the boxplot of the percentage of the score the heuristic algorithm achieved compared to the Gotoh algorithm. The result is rather good for the heuristic algorithm, especially in the case of only 2 deletions per sequence. In the majority of cases, the heuristic algorithms solution is equal to the Gotoh algorithm. In the second dataset where there is a variable amount of deletions per sequence, one of the weaknesses of the algorithm appears. When 2 deletions are close together, the algorithm can take the wrong decision and decide to use a insertion instead of a deletion. But even considering that, the median score is about the same as the one achieved by Gotoh. Both dataset show outliners, with scores as low as 3% and 20% worse than the Gotoh algorithm.

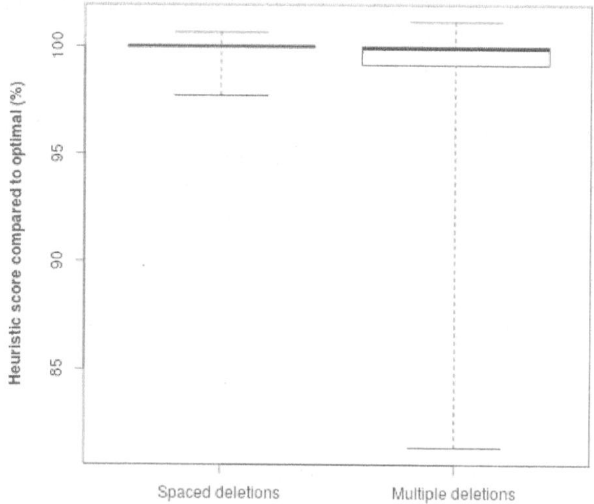

Fig. 3: Score (in %) achieved by the heuristic algorithm compared to Gotoh on 2 datasets

Without looking at the outliners we can see that the alignment using the heuristic is nearly identical to the Gotoh version on the first dataset. It even scores slightly higher in certain cases, which is due to a more aggressive skipping behavior of Gotoh, which can lead to too some unnecessarily skipped bases at the borders of the sequence. Further testing revealed one quality problem with the heuristic approach. Depending on which seed is chosen in a sequence, the results can slightly vary. While they may be correct (for example an indel that can potentially be placed at different places with the same score), the variant detection on the alignment becomes harder.

It has also to be noted, that for the second dataset 2.4% of the sequences did not find a valid alignment using the heuristic approach.

6. Performance

To assert the performance of the algorithm, it was directly compared to the Gotoh algorithm. Both algorithms where implemented in a unaccelerated version, meaning, no multithreading, GPU (Graphics processing unit) acceleration or SIMD(Single Instruction, Multiple Data) instructions where used that could affect both algorithms differently. There is a big potential to speedup the Gotoh algorithm using those techniques [11], while this potential is currently not explored for the proposed algorithm. The second dataset, which has more deletions, was used. Figure 4 shows the result of this comparison (logarithmic scale), which is as expected by the complexity of both algorithms. The time needed to align using the Gotoh algorithm increases quadratically with the read size, but with the proposed algorithm it increases only linearly. For sequences of length 100, the heuristic is about 6 times faster than Gotoh and for sequences of length 350 about 24 times faster.

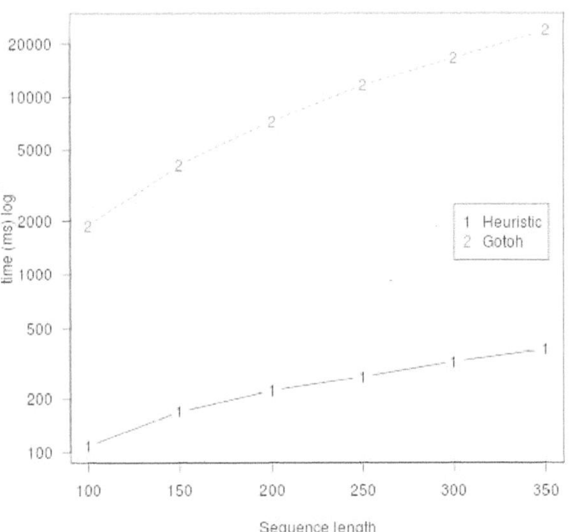

Fig. 4: Alignment time comparison

7. Possible improvements

As expected, the algorithm does not return the optimal solution for an alignment, but it does rapidly give an approximate alignment that in most cases is very close to the optimal solution. But there is a big potential for improvements. For example, the formula described to calculate the score for an insertion or deletion does not work for long indels. For an indel to be selected as an option over a mismatch, the score for it must be higher than the mismatch case. If the base cost of the indel $(I+E*(l-1))$ is higher than the maximum score it can get trough the extension $(\sum_{p=0}^{x} m(r_p, s_p)*(\frac{x-p}{x}*M))$, it will never be selected. With $I = 9$, $E = 2$, $M = 3$ and $x = 16$, the maximum length of an indel that can be detected (if all the bases match after the indel) is 22, but only if the Match case has the lowest possible score (-25.5) and the indel gets the highest extension score 25.5. One way to solve this problem is to make x depend on the desired maximum indel length l.

Another issue is that to choose an option, indels are no longer considered when creating the extension score, only matches and mismatches are counted. If an indel is close to the start of the diagonal to be tested, the score will be wrong and a wrong decision can be taken. This could be addressed by reapplying the same logic as in the extension during first step on every mismatch, thus creating a tree of possibilities. The debt of that tree could then be configurable, to be able to control the impact on the algorithmic complexity.

Another problem is, that when the heuristic takes a wrong decision, it will not recover from it. This problem could be limited by using multiple seeds for the same sequence, thus limiting the damage that can be done with one wrong decision.

8. Conclusion

The heuristic alignment approach is an interesting and fast one. The quality of the alignment, while expectedly not as good as with Gotoh, is very good depending on the dataset. While depending on the quality requirements, the alignment can be used directly, it is advisable to realign the sequences using an algorithm like Gotoh and only use the heuristic approach to identify good candidate positions for the final alignment. First tests to use this hybrid approach are promising and will be subject of further research. Still there are many improvements which can be made regarding the algorithm as described in 7. If the proposed improvements are viable will also be subject of further research.

References

[1] Smith, Temple F.; and Waterman, Michael S. (1981). "Identification of Common Molecular Subsequences".Journal of Molecular Biology 147: 195-197. doi:10.1016/0022-2836(81)90087-5. PMID 7265238.

[2] Needleman, Saul B.; and Wunsch, Christian D. (1970). "A general method applicable to the search for similarities in the amino acid sequence of two proteins". Journal of Molecular Biology 48 (3): 443-53. doi:10.1016/0022-2836(70)90057-4. PMID 5420325.

[3] O. Gotoh: An improved algorithm for matching biological sequences. In: Journal of Molecular Biology. 162, 1982, S. 705-708

[4] Rumble, S. M., Lacroute, P., Dalca, A. V., Fiume, M., Sidow, A., & Brudno, M. (2009). SHRiMP: accurate mapping of short color-space reads. PLoS computational biology, 5(5), e1000386. doi:10.1371/journal.pcbi.1000386

[5] Ning, Z., Cox, A. J., & Mullikin, J. C. (2001). SSAHA : A Fast Search Method for Large DNA Databases, (2), 1725-1729. doi:10.1101/gr.194201.1

[6] Altschul, S; Gish, W; Miller, W; Myers, E; Lipman, D (October 1990). "Basic local alignment search tool". Journal of Molecular Biology 215 (3): 403-410. doi:10.1016/S0022-2836(05)80360-2. PMID 2231712.

[7] Bucak, I. Ö., & Uslan, V. (2010). An analysis of sequence alignment: heuristic algorithms. Conference proceedings : Annual International Conference of the IEEE Engineering in Medicine and Biology Society. IEEE Engineering in Medicine and Biology Society. Conference, 2010, 1824-7. doi:10.1109/IEMBS.2010.5626428

[8] C. Zhang, A.K. Wong, "A genetic algorithm for multiple molecular sequence alignment", Comput. Applic. Biosci., Vol. 13, pp. 565-581, 1997.

[9] W. Chen, B. Liao, W. Zhu, H. Liu, Q. Zeng, "An ant colony pairwise alignment based on the dot plots", Journal of Computational Chemistry, Vol. 30, pp. 93-97, 2008.

[10] Miller, W., and Myers, E.W. 1985. A file comparison program. Software-Practice and Experience 15, 1025-1040.

[11] Rognes, T. (2011). Faster Smith-Waterman database searches with inter-sequence SIMD parallelisation. BMC bioinformatics, 12(1), 221. doi:10.1186/1471-2105-12-221

A framework for a general-purpose sequence compression pipeline: a centroid based compression

Liqing Zhang[1], Daniel Nasko[2], Martin Tříska[3], Harold Garner[4]

[1]. Department of Computer Science, Programs in Genetics, Biochemistry, and Computational Biology, Virginia Tech.
[2]. Center for Bioinformatics and Computational Biology, University of Delaware
[3]. Glamorgan Computational Biology Research Group, University of Glamorgan, United Kingdom
[4]. Virginia Bioinformatics Institute. Virginia Tech

Abstract

DNA sequence data accumulate at an overwhelmingly fast speed, overtaking the speed of the increase of disk storage and creating enormous challenges to data storage, processing, and analysis. Taking advantage of the fact that two human genomes differ by less than 0.1%, we and other groups previously proposed a reference based compression algorithm to compress genomic data. However, the reference based sequence compression only works when there is a reference genome. Many large-scale sequencing projects such as metagenomics data do not have any reference genomes readily available. Therefore, we need a compression method that can be applied in these cases. This project addresses the problem by introducing a centroid based compression algorithm. The centroid based compression algorithm involves taking in large-scale next generation sequencing data and clustering similar sequences into groups. Within each group a "centroid" sequence is identified, and the differences that each sequence has from its respective centroid sequence is encoded. Results show that the method is advantageous when there exists many redundant sequences within the dataset – in particular, the high coverage nature of next generation sequencing data and meta-genomics data. The framework developed here is for a general-purpose compression pipeline that can be theoretically applied to many cases.

Introduction

DNA sequence data is accumulating at an amazingly fast speed. For example, GenBank, one of the largest sequence databases, when first officially released in 1982, had only 606 sequences and a total of 680,338 bases. In contrast, its latest release in December 2012 contains more than 161 million sequences with over 148 billion bases. Shown in Figure 1, the number of bases stored in GenBank from 1982 to present increases exponentially with a doubling time of about 18 months. Whole genome sequencing (WGS) data was first made available in 2002. It is released independently from the regular GenBank updates and had 172,768 genomic sequences in over 692 million bases. Again, comparing it to its latest release in December 2012 shows a stark increase to over 92 million sequences containing more than 356 billion bases. With the remarkable improvements in DNA-sequencing technologies outpacing Moore's Law (www.genome.gov/sequencingcosts), tremendous challenges have been generated in all aspects of sequence data handling.

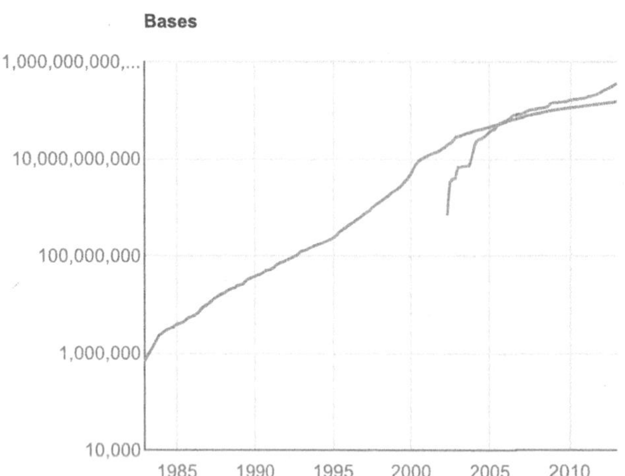

Figure 1. The number of bases stored in GenBank from 1982 to present, doubling at approximately every 18 months (the blue line). The red line shows the number of bases resulted from whole genome sequencing projects (WGS data). The WGS data is independent from the GenBank release. Adapted from http://www.ncbi.nlm.nih.gov/genbank/statistics.

One immediate challenge is to be able to store the massive sequence data in a compact manner and to be able to transfer the data from central sequence repositories or sequencing facilities to individual research labs in an efficient and timely manner. Clearly, there is a desperate need for an efficient way to store various biological data, one of which being DNA sequence data. Shown in Figure 2, from 1990-2009 disk storage per US dollar increased exponentially, doubling every 14 months, while the number of base pairs per US dollar also increased exponentially, with a doubling time of 19 months from 1990-2004. From 2004 to present the sequencing doubling time drastically slashed to every 5 months due to next generation sequencing technology. Therefore, simply increasing disk space is no longer a viable solution to this data tsunami and efficient sequence data compression algorithms are needed now more than ever to reduce the scale of this problem.

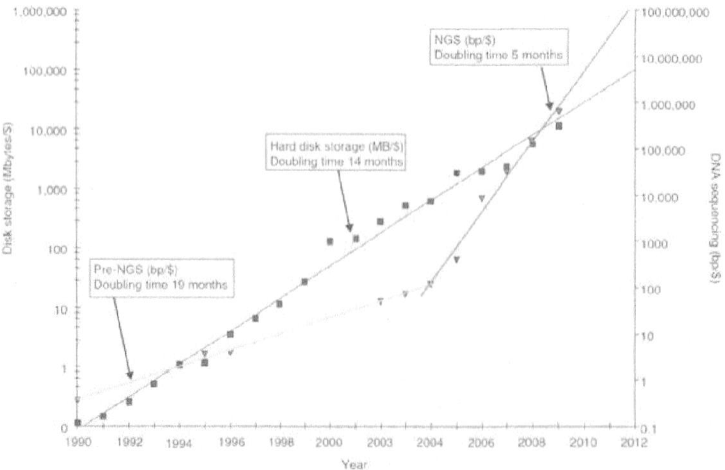

Figure 2. Comparison of disk storage price with DNA sequencing cost. Blue squares denote costs of disk storage (MB/$) during 1990-2009, showing an exponential growth with a doubling time of about 36 months. Red triangles denote DNA sequencing costs (base pairs/$), showing an exponential growth with a doubling time of

about 19 months (yellow line) during 1990-2004, and down to less than 6 months thereafter due to the next generation sequencing (NGS) technology. Adapted from the GB paper (http://genomebiology.com/2010/11/5/207).

There has been much effort in developing efficient compression techniques to store DNA sequences. Current compression programs that have been applied or developed to compress genetic data fall into two major categories: one is general-purpose compression and the other is specifically for genetic data. Some of the commonly used general-purpose compression programs are gzip and bzip2. Bzip2 uses the Burrows-Wheeler transform algorithm to compress files, and it is a lossless compression technique that compresses independently of all the files. Gzip uses the Deflate algorithm (a lossless data compression algorithm combining the LZ77 algorithm and Huffman coding) to compress files and is readily available on all machines with Unix/Linux operating systems. Examples for programs that have been developed specifically to compress sequence files include DNACompress (*1*), GenCompress (*2*) and Quip (*3*). Programs that are designed to compress genetic data can be classified by the types of files that they compress. For example, some programs focus on compressing the FASTQ files, whereas others such as SAM tools compress the mapped results. Also, depending on whether the compressed files lose information or not, compression algorithms can be also classified into two classes: lossy compression and lossless compression. The general-purpose compression tools are mostly lossless and specific-purpose compression tools can be both lossy and lossless.

Recently, a few research groups including ours proposed reference-based compression algorithms to compress large-scale genomic data such as humans (*4*). The idea is to compress human genomes by encoding only their differences with a reference genome. The motivation for encoding only the difference comes from the fact that about 99.9% of any two human genomes are identical to each other. Therefore, a delta (difference) representation that encodes the differences between two human genomes can be quite small. Although a reference sequence is required to retrieve the information from delta representations, a higher compression ratio is achieved by amortizing the cost over many genomes. For example, using the algorithm of Brandon et al. (*5*), a 433-fold level of compression can be achieved with an appropriate reference sequence for the data set of 3615 mitochondria genomic sequences, which is significantly better than previous work that compresses single genomic sequences. Similarly, the compression algorithm proposed by our group achieved a compression ratio of 98.8% for the data set of 5473 mitochondria genomes (*6*).

However, despite the great advantage that reference based compression algorithms show over direct compression of entire sequence data, they are only applicable when there is a reference genome/sequence readily available. In many large-scale sequencing projects, the reference genome is not known beforehand. For example, the sequencing of the cow rumen metagenome produced about 280 billion base pairs of DNA sequences and these sequences might come from more than 400 microbes whose genomes are unknown (*7*). Thus, a general-purpose compression mechanism that can also make use of reference based compression idea would have advantageous over both the general-purpose programs that do not make full use of biological data features and also the more specific programs as they tend to have limited usage.

This project develops such a framework for a general-purpose compression pipeline that borrows the idea of reference based compression and address the lack of reference sequences by introducing the use of centroid sequences as references. The centroid based compression pipeline includes four main procedures, clustering, centroid sequence construction, and difference determination and difference encoding. Data will be first pre-processed and clustered into groups. For each group, a centroid sequence will be constructed. Next all sequences in the same group will be compared to their respective centroid sequences and differences will be determined. Finally, the centroids and differences will be encoded by Huffman encoding. Our analyses show that the framework for a general-purpose compression pipeline is promising in addressing the situations when there is no reference genome available yet show the full advantage of reference based compression algorithms.

Methods

Overview

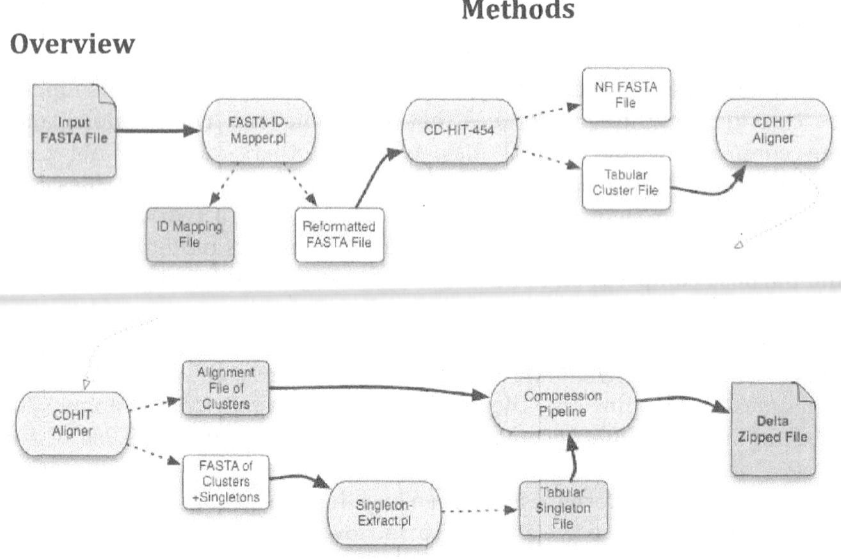

Figure 3. The flowchart of the centroid based compression pipeline.

The centroid based compression pipeline, shown in Figure 3, can be divided into four stages: preprocessing and clustering, centroid sequence construction, difference determination, and difference encoding. First, a set (or database) of sequences are preprocessed and clustered into groups. Second, a centroid sequence is constructed for each group. Third, differences between each sequence and their centroid sequence for the same group are extracted. Finally, the differences are efficiently compressed using Hoffman encoding.

Data preprocessing and clustering

Since the purpose of this work is to develop a framework for a general-purpose sequence compression pipeline, the most common format of sequence presentation, the *fasta* format, is considered. Other formats can be easily converted to the *fasta* format. For the experiments, DNA sequences are used, but the framework can be used to extend easily to protein sequence compression. As depicted in Figure 3, a FASTA ID mapper was written in Perl to extract the sequence ID information and the mapping information, which is stored separately in an ID mapper file. Next, the reformatted sequence file is fed into the clustering program CD-HIT (*8*). CD-HIT was chosen to be incorporated into the pipeline for three reasons. First, CD-HIT is very fast at clustering. Second, CD-HIT can handle very large databases such as the NR database (the non-redundant nucleotide sequence database in NCBI). Third, CD-HIT actually contains a suite of programs that perform a number of tasks that are needed in the compression pipeline. Therefore, CD-HIT is an ideal tool that can be used to develop the framework for a general-purpose sequence compression pipeline.

CD-HIT uses a greedy clustering algorithm as implemented by Holm and Sander (1998). Basically, sequences are first sorted in order of decreasing length. The longest sequence becomes the representative of the first cluster. Then, each of the remaining sequences is compared to the representative of each existing cluster. If the similarity with any representative is above a given threshold, it is grouped into that cluster. Otherwise a new cluster is defined with this sequence as the representative. CD-HIT-454 is a special version of CD-HIT created in 2010 and was designed to cluster reads of artificial 454 duplicates (*9*). It achieves this by allowing more memory to be allocated to search and takes certain heuristics into account. The major difference between the two sister programs is that CD-HIT performs much better when clustering at lower thresholds of sequence similarities (0% to 70%) while CD-HIT-454 performs much better when clustering at higher thresholds of sequence similarities (80% to 100%). It should be noted that the clustering of sequences is typically the most time-consuming component of the pipeline.

Centroid sequence construction

Once the clusters are established, consensus sequences are then constructed using CD-HIT's cdhit-cluster-consensus alignment program. CD-HIT's aligner aligns multiple sequences from each group using CLUSTALW (*9, 10*) and determines a consensus sequence from the resulting multiple sequence alignment. Briefly, the consensus sequence is constructed as follows. If the column of a multiple sequence alignment has only one character, the character is used as the consensus character. For column positions that have conflicting characters, the quality scores of each base are taken into account to compute an adjusted frequency for each character {'A','C','G','T', '-' (gap)}, and the dominate character that has a frequency >= 0.5 is used as the consensus character, otherwise, 'N' is used as the consensus character. The consensus sequence thus calculated is then used as the centroid sequence for each group with the only exception for the character 'N'. When the consensus has 'N', we will examine the column and pick out the most common nonN character as the consensus character to save space. In cases where there is only one sequence in the group, the group is considered to be a singleton and the one sequence is considered to be the centroid sequence of the group.

Difference encoding and difference decoding

This step involves encoding of the differences that each sequence has from their respective centroid sequence. Experiments were done to examine the frequencies of A, T, G, and C in randomly selected sequences in NCBI. A, T, and G have been found to be the more commonly occurring bases than C, and thus two bits were used to encode these three bases (A: 00, T: 01, and G: 10), whereas three bits, 110, were used to encode C. In addition, in the case of consensus sequence encoding, an END character, encoded in bits 111, is used to mark the end of the consensus sequence. For correction characters or differences from the consensus, there is an additional gap character encoded in four bits 1111 and 'N' encoded in 1110.

Figure 4 shows an overview of the steps for extracting differences from the consensus sequences for each individual sequence and encoding the differences. Figure 5 shows an overview of the steps for difference decoding. Basically, a group of sequences are encoded by their consensus sequence and the differences they have from the consensus sequence. For a group of sequences, their consensus sequence is first encoded by the bit scheme for consensus encoding. The END character is used to mark the end of the consensus sequence. Then the three sequences are encoded using the scheme for correction characters. Correction characters, i.e. differences from the consensus sequence, are encoded similarly with two additional characters "N" and "-" representing the unknown character and gap character. Binary encoding is used to mark the sequence name. Then the relative position of the current correction to the previous correction character is binary encoded followed by encoding of correction types and the actual correction character. There are two types of corrections, in place correction (encoded by 0) and insertion correction (encoded by 1). If no more correction is needed, a binary encoding of 0 is used to mark the end of the correction sequence or the actual sequence.

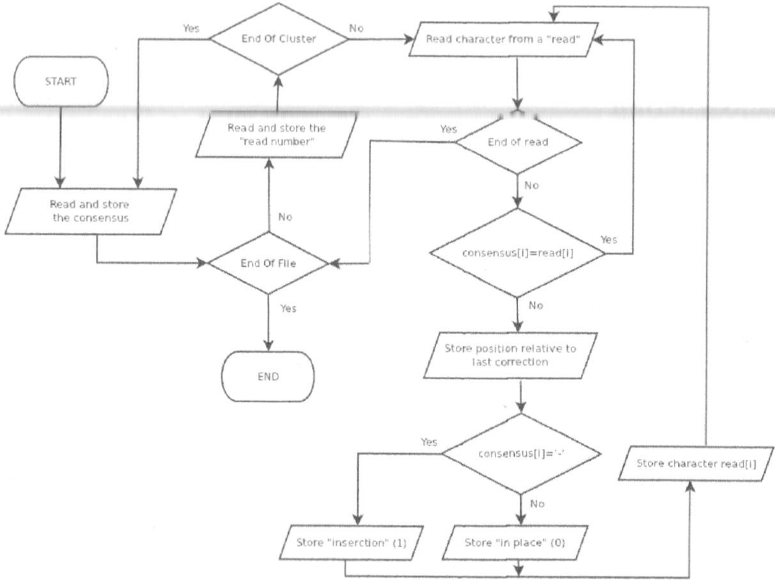

Figure 4. An illustration of how differences from consensus sequences are encoded.

Results and discussion

Five datasets were used to examine the proposed centroid based compression pipeline. The first one is from human genomic sequences obtained by Illumina sequencing of 22,012,277 reads with each read around 74 bases. The other four datasets are all from environmental metagenomic projects where the centroid based compression methods seem to be particularly needed for compressing millions and billions of reads with unknown and diverse origins. The first environmental metagenomic sequences were sampled from Chesapeake Bay, containing a quarter plate of the 454 sequencing (254,852 reads with ~400 bases per read). The second data is also generated for Chesapeake Bay, with Sanger sequencing of 20,140 reads at ~710 bases per read (*11*). The third one was sampled from Tampa Bay, containing a quarter plate of the 454 sequencing of 208,244 reads with ~288 bases per read. And the last metagenomic data was sampled from for Deep Sea Hydrothermal Vent, containing the Full Plate of the 454 sequencing of 700,278 reads with ~383 bases per read.

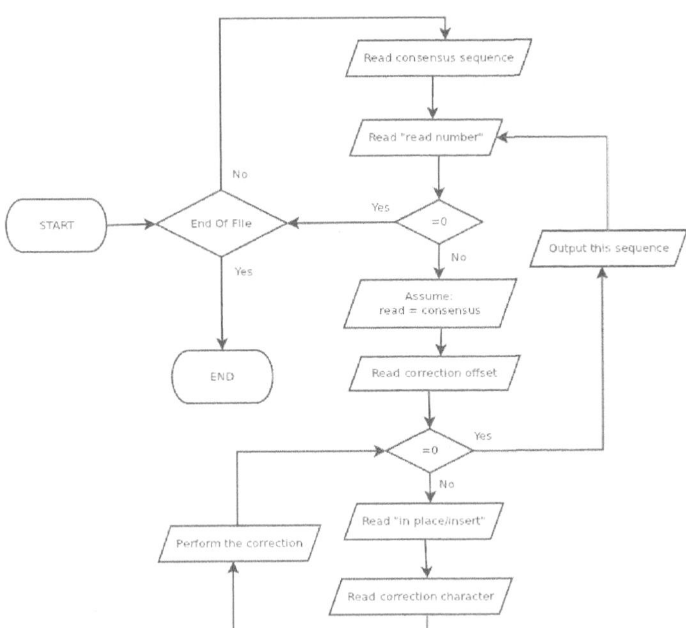

Figure 5. An illustration of how encoded sequences and differences are decoded.

For this pilot work, clustering efficiency and compression efficiency are the two main aspects that were examined. Experiments show that the clustering step is the most time-consuming step for the entire compression pipeline. Many heuristic clustering algorithms such as USEARCH (*12*) have been proposed to improve clustering speed. Clustering programs such as this can be potentially incorporated into the compression pipeline. Figure 6 shows the relationship between the similarity cutoff values used by the CD-HIT clustering program and the percentages of reads that are included in nonsingleton clusters (i.e. cluster sizes >=2). For all five datasets, the percentages of reads falling into clusters remain stable for the similarity cutoff values between 80-98%, but lower abruptly once the cutoff becomes higher than 98%. The metagenomic data for Tampa Bay has the highest percentage of reads falling into clusters (~88%), in contrast, the other four datasets have low percentage of reads being clustered, especially for the metagenomic data from Chesapeake Bay Sanger sequences and Hydrothermal Vent 454 data. In these datasets, most reads belong to singletons, that is, only one read in the group, thus, the centroid based compression is not expected to save much space for these singleton groups.

Analysis shows that clustering is the most time-consuming step for the entire compression pipeline. One important parameter that influences the speed of clustering is the similarity cutoff threshold used by CD-HIT. Figure 7 shows the CPU time consumed by clustering the five datasets as a function of the similarity cutoff threshold. For all dataset, it is clear that the lower the cutoff, the longer CPU it takes for clustering to complete. For example, when the cutoff ranges between 80-90%, clustering the Chesapeake Bay-454 sequences took almost 5 hours to complete, however, the time dropped quickly after the cutoff percentage increases after 90%, and down to almost 5 minutes when it increases to 93%. For the

Hydrothermal Vent sequences, the clustering took about 100 hours for the cutoff range between 80-90%. As the cutoff increases beyond 90%, the CPU time quickly dropped to around 20 minutes. However, although increasing the cutoff would greatly speed up the clustering step, due to the high similarity cutoff, many clusters will tend to be singletons, which reduces the advantage of the centroid based compression algorithm. Thus, even if reducing the cutoff can be a luring option for speed up the pipeline, the cutoff score should be carefully chosen in order to achieve a good tradeoff between the speed performance and compression performance.

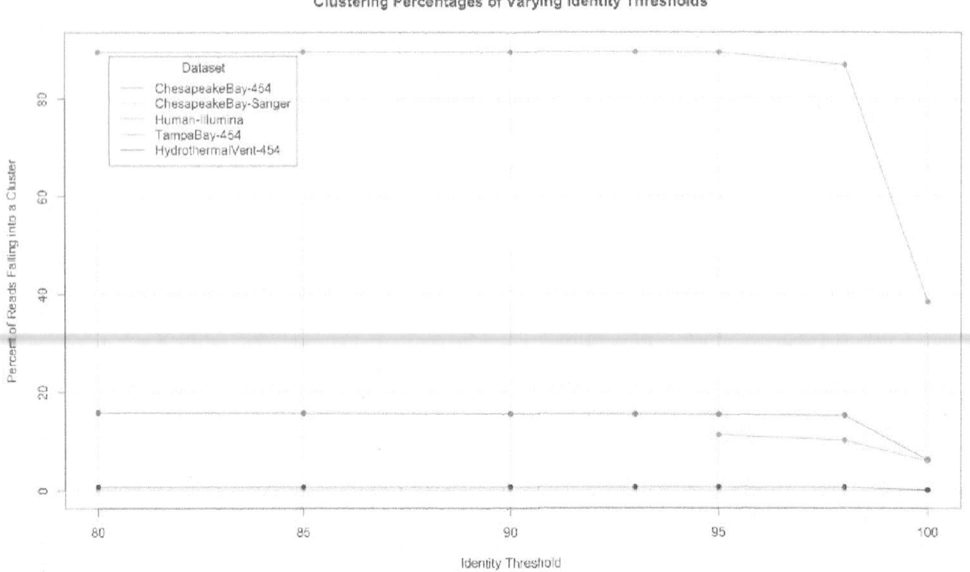

Figure 6. The percentages of sequences that are included in nonsingleton clusters.

As gzip is a commonly used data compression tool, readily available on Unix/Linux operating systems, it is used here to compare with the proposed centroid based compression algorithm. Interesting to note is that centroid based compression algorithm can be considered as a general-purpose compression tool for sequences as it can be applied to basically any sequence datasets, as long as they are in FASTA format. Table 1 shows the compression performance of the centroid based compression and gzip on the five datasets. There are about 1.6 billion bases for the human Illumina data, taking up roughly 1.6 billion bytes of disk space in its original form. After using gzip, it reduces to about 0.2976 of its original disk space. In contrast, the centroid compression pipeline has a compression ratio of 0.2175, thus, performing better in saving disk space than gzip. This pattern also holds for Chesapeake Bay-454 sequences and Chesapeake Bay-Sanger sequences. However, for the Tamper Bay and Hydrothermal Vent sequence datasets, gzip shows better performance in saving disk space and has a better compression than what the centroid compression can achieve. This is mainly due to the fact that for Tamper Bay sequences, most sequences turn out to be singletons, reducing the advantage that the centroid based compression has over the general-purpose compression. Future development should include separate compression strategies for singletons so that the maximum gain can be achieved by a mixture of algorithms.

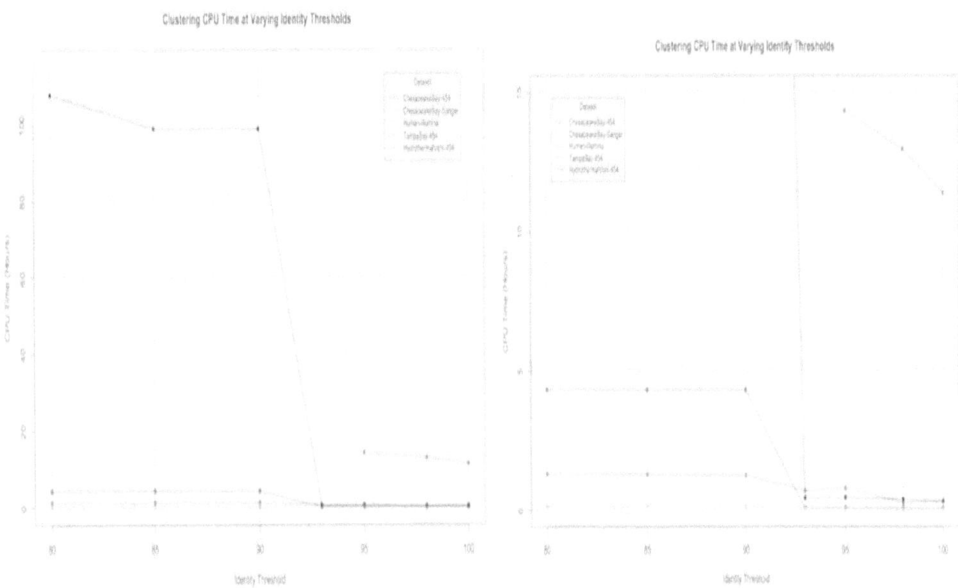

Figure 7. The CPU time that the clustering step takes as a function of identity threshold, i.e. similarity cutoff score. Left panel shows for all the datasets. Right panel shows the zoomed-in version for the four datasets.

Table 1. Performance comparison of the centroid based compression method with gzip

Dataset	**Bases**	**Size (Bytes)**	**gzip Compression Ratio**	**Centroid Compression Ratio**
Partial Human	1,633,582,881	1,655,595,158	0.2976	0.2175
Chesapeake Bay 454	101,826,137	102,080,989	0.2898	0.2431
Chesapeake Bay (Sanger)	14,312,931	14,561,295	0.3082	0.2829
Tampa Bay	59,975,867	59,975,867	0.0665	0.1205
Deep Sea Hydrothermal	268,822,604	269,522,882	0.1965	0.2988

Conclusions and future work

The fast development in bio-sequencing technology has created many excitements in life sciences but at the same time, bring about many challenges that are unprecedented, ranging from the demand for efficient mechanisms of data storage, data transfer and communication, data visualization, processing, and analyses, to results presentation and interpretation. For data storage, much work has been done for efficient algorithms to compress biological data, among which the delta compression algorithm, i.e., encoding only the differences from a reference sequence, has the best performance as it greatly reduces the amount of data needed to be stored. However, the method only applies to cases where a reference sequence or genome is available or can be readily computed. The current work develops a framework that extends the idea of delta compression, and addresses the situations when there are no reference sequences available. In fact, it is a general-purpose sequence compression framework that can be used to compress any sequence databases or datasets. Future work includes extensive studies of various aspects of the compression pipeline, such as exploring parallelized version of various clustering algorithms to speed up the compression process and efficient mechanisms such as arithmetic encoding (*13*) to encode consensus sequences and differences.

Acknowledgements

This project is funded by NSF Award No. OCI-1124123.

References

1. X. Chen, M. Li, B. Ma, J. Tromp, DNACompress: fast and effective DNA sequence compression. *Bioinformatics* **18**, 1696 (Dec, 2002).
2. X. Chen, S. Kwong, M. Li, A compression algorithm for DNA sequences. *Ieee Engineering in Medicine and Biology Magazine* **20**, 61 (Jul-Aug, 2001).
3. D. C. Jones, W. L. Ruzzo, X. Peng, M. G. Katze, Compression of next-generation sequencing reads aided by highly efficient de novo assembly. *Nucleic acids research* **40**, e171 (Dec, 2012).
4. M. H. Y. Fritz, R. Leinonen, G. Cochrane, E. Birney, Efficient storage of high throughput DNA sequencing data using reference-based compression. *Genome Research* **21**, 734 (May, 2011).
5. M. C. Brandon, D. C. Wallace, P. Baldi, Data structures and compression algorithms for genomic sequence data. *Bioinformatics* **25**, 1731 (Jul 15, 2009).
6. L. S. Heath, A. P. Hou, H. Xia, L. Zhang, paper presented at the Proc LSS Comput Syst Bioinform Conf, 2010.
7. M. Hess *et al.*, Metagenomic discovery of biomass-degrading genes and genomes from cow rumen. *Science* **331**, 463 (Jan 28, 2011).
8. W. Li, A. Godzik, Cd-hit: a fast program for clustering and comparing large sets of protein or nucleotide sequences. *Bioinformatics* **22**, 1658 (Jul 1, 2006).
9. B. Niu, L. Fu, S. Sun, W. Li, Artificial and natural duplicates in pyrosequencing reads of metagenomic data. *BMC bioinformatics* **11**, 187 (2010).
10. J. D. Thompson, D. G. Higgins, T. J. Gibson, CLUSTAL W: improving the sensitivity of progressive multiple sequence alignment through sequence weighting, position-specific gap penalties and weight matrix choice. *Nucleic acids research* **22**, 4673 (Nov 11, 1994).
11. S. R. Bench *et al.*, Metagenomic characterization of Chesapeake Bay virioplankton. *Applied and environmental microbiology* **73**, 7629 (Dec, 2007).
12. R. C. Edgar, Search and clustering orders of magnitude faster than BLAST. *Bioinformatics* **26**, 2460 (Oct 1, 2010).
13. I. H. Witten, R. M. Neal, J. G. Cleary, Arithmetic Coding for Data-Compression. *Communications of the Acm* **30**, 520 (Jun, 1987).

Classification of DNA Sequences by a MLP and SVM Network

TERJE KRISTENSEN
Institute of Computer Science,
Nygårdsgaten 112, Bergen University College,
N-5020, Bergen, Norway
E-mail: tkr@hib.no

FABIEN GUILLAUME
Pattern solutions ltd.
Nygårdgaten 112
N-5020, Bergen, Norway
E-mail: fabien.guillaume@student.hib.no

Abstract - **In this paper we show how a Multi-Layered Perceptron (MLP) neural network and a Support Vector Machine (SVM) are used to classify between eukaryotic and prokaryotic cells. The classification is based on their DNA-sequences which are obtained from different databases available on Internet. The sequences are first pre-processed using a sliding window technique to obtain sub-sequence frequencies, and then normalised to make them comparable.**

Keywords: MLP, SVM, prokaryotic and eukaryotic DNA-sequences, Java, sliding window

I. INTRODUCTION

One of the main research goals of molecular biology has been to determine a complete genetic description of any organism. In the Human Genome Project [4] the goal was to decipher the exact sequence of about 3 billion nucleotides in the 46 human chromosomes. An important part of the genome project is the computational processing of data [2]. The data first have to be organised into databases, and then analysed to see what information they contain. Since the birth of the Human Genome Project, sequence analysis as a computational method, has been used to infer biological information from the sequence data.

The classical approach to analysing sequences is by sequence matching using either single or multiple alignment techniques [7,8]. With these techniques one seeks to determine whether sequences are significantly similar or not. Another approach is to use theories from neural computing or statistical learning theory to detect genetic information on the DNA sequences.

Neural networks have been applied to various tasks such as automatic hyphenation of natural languages [11,12], edge detection [14], recognition of hand written Zip code and DNA sequence recognition [1,13]. A neural network trained by a Backpropagation algorithm may learn to categorise between different types of bacteria cells related to the structure of their DNA-sequence. Such a method is based on pattern recognition analysis, and is built on the assumption that some underlying characteristics of the DNA-sequence can be used to identify its bacteria type. Other neural network paradigms than a MLP network may also be used to analyse DNA sequences [18].

In this paper, however, we will focus on how to use both a MLP and a SVM network to distinguish between *eukaryotic* and *prokaryrotic* DNA-sequences on basis of their nucleotide frequency structure [8,9]. Cells can be divided into two major groups, prokaryotic and eukaryotic cells. All prokaryotic cells are uni-cellular organisms and consist mostly of bacteria. The genome of a prokaryotic cell consists of one double helix DNA strand, floating freely in the cell. This double helix strand is often circular. The genome of the bacterium E.Coli, for instance, consists of a circular strand of five and a half million bases.

A nucleotide sequence can be viewed as a language based on an alphabet of four letters: A, G, C and T where the number of As is the same as the number of Ts, and the number of Cs is the same as the number of Gs. However, the relation of A(T) and G(C) can vary tremendously, and depends on the actual species that are studied. This fact can, for instance, be used in environmental research, where oil on the sea surface may contain many different types of species that can be identified on basis of their DNA sequence structure.

Most eukaryotes are multicellular, but some are uni-cellular. The main difference between prokaryotic cells and eukaryotic cells is that eukaryotic cells contain a nucleus that is surrounded by a membrane. Prokaryotic cells do not have such a nucleus. In such cells the frequency distribution of pairs of nucleotides are different from those in prokaryotic cells [3].

II. SVM NETWORK

Support Vector Machines (SVM) is a computationally efficient learning technique that is now being widely used in pattern recognition and classification problems [2]. This approach has been derived from some of the ideas of the statistical learning theory regarding controlling the generalization abilities of a learning machine [19, 20]

In such a regime the machine learns an optimum hyper plane that classifies the given pattern. By use of kernel functions, the input feature space, by applications of a non-linear function, can be transformed into a higher dimensional space where the optimum hyper plane may be learned. This gives a flexibility of using one of many learning models by changing the kernel functions.

A. The SVM Classifier

The basic idea of an SVM classifier is illustrated in Fig. 1. In the figure it is shown, in the simplest case, the data vectors (marked by 'X's and 'O's) may be separated by a hyper plane. In such a case, there may exist many separating hyper planes. Among them, the SVM classifier seeks the separating hyper plane that produces the largest margin separation.

In the more general case, in which the data points are not linearly separable in the input space, a non-linear transformation is used to map the data vectors into a high-dimensional space (called feature space) prior to applying the linear maximum margin classifier. To avoid the potential pitfall of over-fitting in this higher dimensional space, SVM uses a kernel function in which the non-linear mapping is implicitly embedded. A function qualifies as a kernel function if it satisfies the Mercer's condition [20].

By use of a kernel function, the discriminant function in a SVM classifier has the following form

$$f(x) = \sum_{i=1}^{N} \alpha_i y_i K(\mathbf{x}_i, \mathbf{x}) + \alpha_0 \quad (1)$$

where K(-,-) is the kernel function, $\mathbf{x}_i$ are the support vectors determined from the training data, y_i is the class indicator e.g. +1 and -1 for a two class problem associated with each $\mathbf{x}$, N is the number of supporting vectors determined during training and α_i are the Lagrangian multipliers

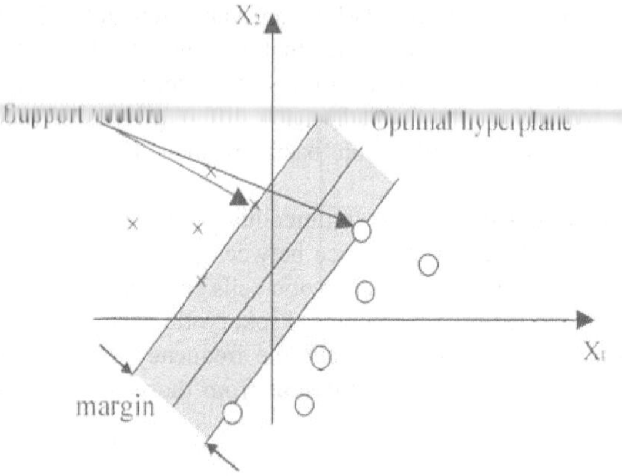

Fig. 1. A Support Vector Machine classification defined by a linear hyper plane that maximizes the separating margins between the classes.

Support vectors are elements of the training set that lie either exactly on or inside the decision boundaries of the classifier. In essence, they consist of those training examples that are most difficult to classify. The SVM classifier uses these borderline examples to define the decision boundary between the two classes.

B. *The Kernel Functions*

The kernel function plays a central role of implicitly mapping the input vectors into a high-dimensional feature space, in which linear separability is achieved. The most commonly used kernel functions are the polynomial kernel given by:

$$K(\mathbf{x},\mathbf{y}) - (\mathbf{x}^T\mathbf{y} + 1)^p \quad (2)$$

where $p > 0$ is a constant. The Gaussian radial basis function (RBF) kernel is given by

$$K(\mathbf{x},\mathbf{y}) = \exp(-\|\mathbf{x}-\mathbf{y}\|/2\sigma^2) \quad (3)$$

where $\sigma > 0$ is a constant that defines the kernel width. Both of these kernels satisfy the Mercer condition mentioned earlier.

III. THE MLP NETWORK

A Multi-Layered Perceptron (MLP) network generally contains three or more layers of processing units [10].

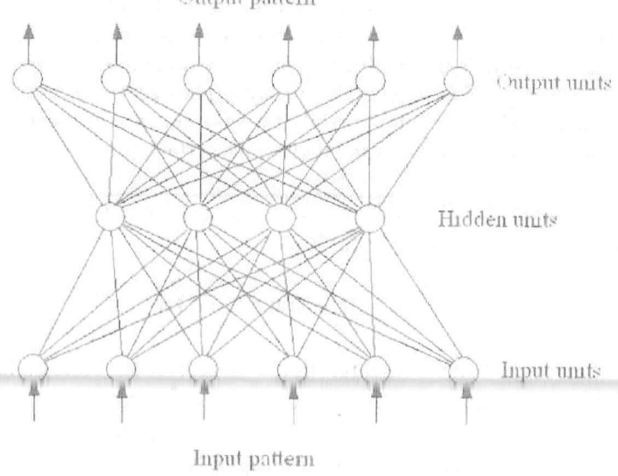

Fig. 2. A MLP network consisting of three layers of nodes..

Fig.2 shows the topology of a network containing three layers. The bottom layer constitutes the input layer which obtains its input from the environment. The middle layer contains hidden units. The hidden layer has de ability to solve non-linear separable problems. The top layer constitutes the output layer which gives the produced results from the network. Every layer is fully connected with the nearest layer, i.e. every unit in the first layer is connected to every unit in the second layer and every unit in the second layer is connected to every unit in the output layer. This is not a requirement, but most MLP networks are constructed like this.

A. The MLP Classifier

In the learning phase we present patterns to the network, and the weights are adjusted so that the produced outputs from the output nodes are equal to the target. In fact, we want the network to find a single set of weights that will satisfy all the (input, output) pairs presented to it. Neurons in one layer receive signals from neurons in the layer directly below and send signals to neurons in the layer directly above. Connections between neurons in the same layer are not allowed. Except for the input layer nodes, the network input to each node is the weighted sum of outputs of the nodes in the previous layer.

Each node is activated in accordance with the input to the node and the activation of the node. The difference between the calculated output and the target output is then calculated. The weights between the output layer, hidden layers and the input layer are adjusted by using this error function. The output of a node is calculated using the sigmoid function f(x) given by:

$$f(x) = 1/(1 + e^{-x}) \quad (4)$$

The weighted sum S_j is inserted into the sigmoid function, and the result is the output value from unit j:

$$f(S_j) = 1/(1 + e^{-S_j}) \quad (5)$$

where

$$S_j = \sum w_{ji}\, a_i \quad (6)$$

The error value of an output unit j can be calculated by:

$$\delta_j = (t_j - a_j)\, f'(S_j) \quad (7)$$

where t_j and a_j are the target and output value of unit j, respectively. f' is the derivative of the sigmoid function f, and S_j the weighted input sum. The derivative of the sigmoid function is given by:

$$f'(S_j) = f(S_j)\,(1 - f(S_j)) \quad (8)$$

We notice that the derivative is expressed by the function itself which makes the error more rapidly to calculate.

For a hidden node, the error value is calculated as:

$$\delta_j = \sum \delta_k w_{kj}(f'(S_j)) \quad (9)$$

From the formula we see that the error of a processing unit in the hidden layer is computed by the upper layer. Finally, the weights can be adjusted by:

$$\Delta w_{ji} = \alpha \delta_j a_i \quad (10)$$

where α is the learning rate. The new weights are then given by:

$$w_{ji}(t+1) = w_{ji}(t) + \Delta w_{ji}(t) \quad (11)$$

where t represents a processing step.

Usually, the momentum parameter β is introduced in the MLP network. It has been shown that the use of this additional parameter can be helpful in speeding up the convergence and avoiding local minima. Equation (11) can now be written as:

$$w_{ji}(t+1) = w_{ji}(t) + \alpha \delta_j a_i + \beta \Delta w_{ji}(t) \quad (12)$$

where β is the momentum and $\Delta w_{ji}(t)$ is the weight change from the previous processing step.

In general, the outputs $\{a_{pi}\}$ (p is the current pattern) of the nodes in the output layer will not be the same as the target or desired values $\{t_{pi}\}$. The system error or the cost function for the network is defined by:

$$E = \frac{1}{N}\frac{1}{2}\sum_p \sum_i \left(t_{pi} - a_{pi}\right)^2 \quad (13)$$

where N is the total number of patterns. A gradient search should be based on minimisation of the expression in equation (13). The weight updating rule then becomes as given in equation (12). For a more thorough discussion see references [10,15].

IV. DNA DATAMINING

Statistical analysis of several DNA sequences has shown that the distribution of nucleotides is far from random [17]. Some dinucleotide combinations in prokaryotic DNA sequences are more dominating than in eukaryotic cells. We will anticipate that this simple difference in data occurrence might be sufficient to allow species identification. We may then train, for instance, a MLP network, to use the differences in the nucleotide distribution to discriminate between eukaryotic and prokaryotic cells. We assume therefore that the identification of the DNA sequence is based solely on the frequency of nucleotide sub-sequences.

A sliding window is used to count the number of nucleotide sub-sequences of the DNA sequence. In general, the size of the window may vary, from one base wide to a user defined number *w*. By choosing a window of length one, we simply count the number of the different bases of the DNA sequence. The result will be four different frequencies, one for each base. A window of length two will result in sixteen different ordered sub-sequences. The frequency of each sub-sequence is computed by counting the occurrence of each nucleotide pair in the DNA sequence.

The number of triplets or *codon* units of the DNA sequence, may be estimated by using a window of three bases wide. This results in 4^3 or 64 ordered triplets. This is maybe the most relevant sub-sequence to study because the codon itself has important meanings in the DNA sequence. In general, a window of *w* bases results in 4^w sub-sequences of length w to be counted.

For a sliding window of length two the frequency of sub-sequence AA is denoted as f_{AA}, for AC as f_{AC} and so on. These numbers are collected in a vector $\mathbf{F_n}$, where n denotes the number of DNA sub-sequences. For a sliding window of size two, n is equal to 16. The counting of the different nucleotide pairs is illustrated in Fig.3. In the figure the counting of the nucleotide pair AC is shown. After counting the pair AC, the window is moved one letter to the right to cover the next nucleotide pair. This is done until the end of the DNA sequence.

ACATGATGCTA...

ACATGATGCTA...

ACATGATGCTA...

ACATGATGCTA...

Fig. 3. A sliding window of two letters is used to count the occurrence of each ordered nucleotide pair.

The DNA sequences obtained on the Internet have different sequence length. The frequency of the different nucleotide pairs have to be normalised to compare and present them to the MLP or SVM network. The normalisation condition of the frequency vector $\mathbf{F_n}$ is given by equation 14.

$$S_n = \frac{F_n}{|F_n|} \tag{14}$$

Here $|\mathbf{F_n}|$ means the Euclidean norm of the frequency vector. This non-linear transformation conserves the direction of the vector and enhances the differences among the input vectors. The geometric interpretation of the transformation is that the vector $\mathbf{F_n}$ is moved onto the hyper unit sphere.

V. FEATURE ANALYSIS

Before the training started, a feature analysis of the training data was carried out. The training set consists of fifteen DNA sequences from each cell class. $\mathbf{S_n}$ vectors from the two classes were aligned to see if one could find similarities between them. The mean relative frequency of corresponding sub-sequences in each class were computed and plotted in a graph. The main reason for doing this experiment was to make an analysis to see if the methodology used was adequate, and if there exist features that will make the DNA sequences different. The correlation between the mean relative frequency of eukaryotic and prokaryotic sub-sequences is given by the conventional linear correlation coefficient based on the usual covariance matrix.

Matlab programs were developed for plotting the results of the comparison between eukaryotic and prokaryotic sequences in the training set, and a plot is shown in Fig. 4. The upper graph shows the correlation between the DNA sub-sequences when the size of the sliding window is *two* bases wide. The correlation coefficient r is then estimated to 0.82. The lower graph shows a comparison between eukaryotic and prokaryotic sequences when the window size is *three*. The correlation coefficient r is now estimated to 0.74.

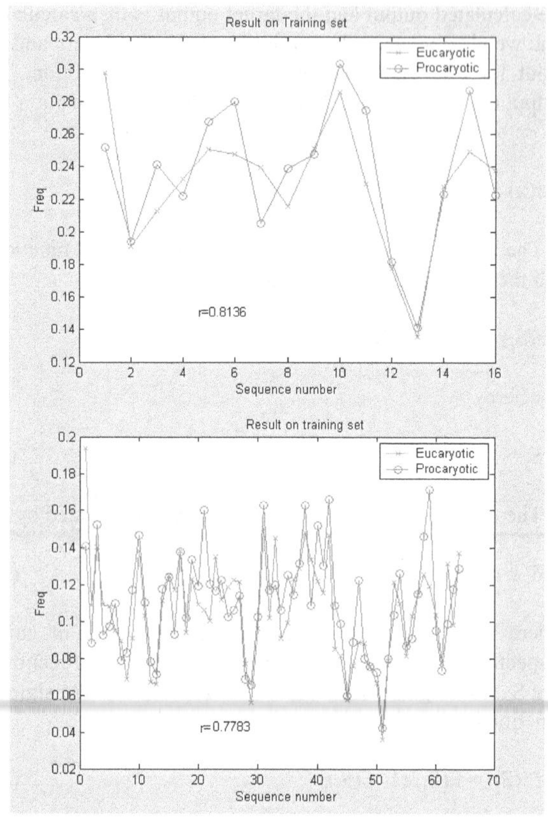

Fig. 4. The means of 'relative frequency' for corresponding sub-sequences of size 2 and 3 are compared for eukaryotic and prokaryotic DNA sequences.

Similar experiments were also carried out when the size of the window was greater than three. In fig. 5 we notice that the correlation coefficient drops when the window size increases. This means that by using longer sub-sequences, the feature difference between the two DNA classes is getting more substantial. The classification accuracy between the different DNA sequences should then increase. However, longer sub-sequences will tend to identify one specific DNA strand. This can be understood by letting the window size approach the length of the DNA sequence. The feature extraction should then be harder and make it more difficult for the network to generalise. A larger window will also generate more training data which in general will require more computer power and longer training times.

VI. TRAINING

Different DNA sequences were obtained from several DNA databases on the Internet. The experiments were performed under Window 7 on Intel Core i7-3610QM with 12GB of DDR3. A Java program has been developed to train the network using the javANN (java Artificial Neural Network) software package created by the company Pattern Solutions AS in Norway [15]. In addition, the LIBSVM package created by Chih-Chung Chang and Chih-Jen Lin at the National Taiwan University has been used [21]. A

Graphic User Interface was created in addition to Java classes to read the EMBLM format and also export the results into Excel files.

Fig. 6 shows the neural network which is used during the experiments. The EMBL format of a DNA sequence looks like the one given in Fig. 7.

VII. PARAMETERS AND WINDOWS SIZE

A. *SVM experiments*

The SVM is trained using a polynomial kernel or a modified Radial Basis Function kernel $K(\mathbf{x_i},\mathbf{x_j})$, given by equation 15.

$$K(\mathbf{x_i},\mathbf{x_j}) = e^{-\gamma\|\mathbf{xi}-\mathbf{xj}\|}, \quad \gamma > 0 \tag{15}$$

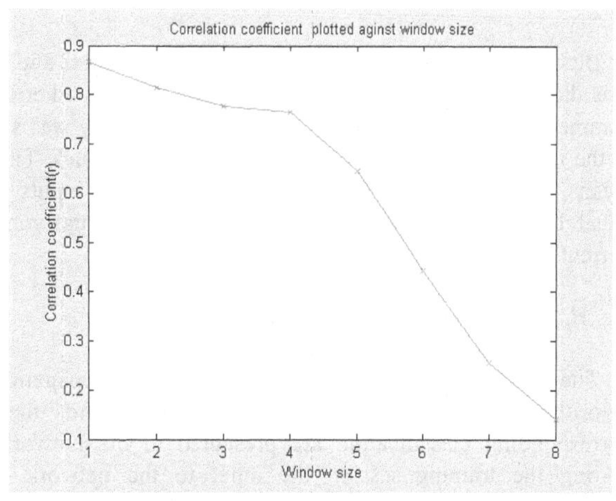

Fig: 5. The correlation coefficient between eukaryotic and prokaryotic DNA sequences drops when the gliding window size increases.

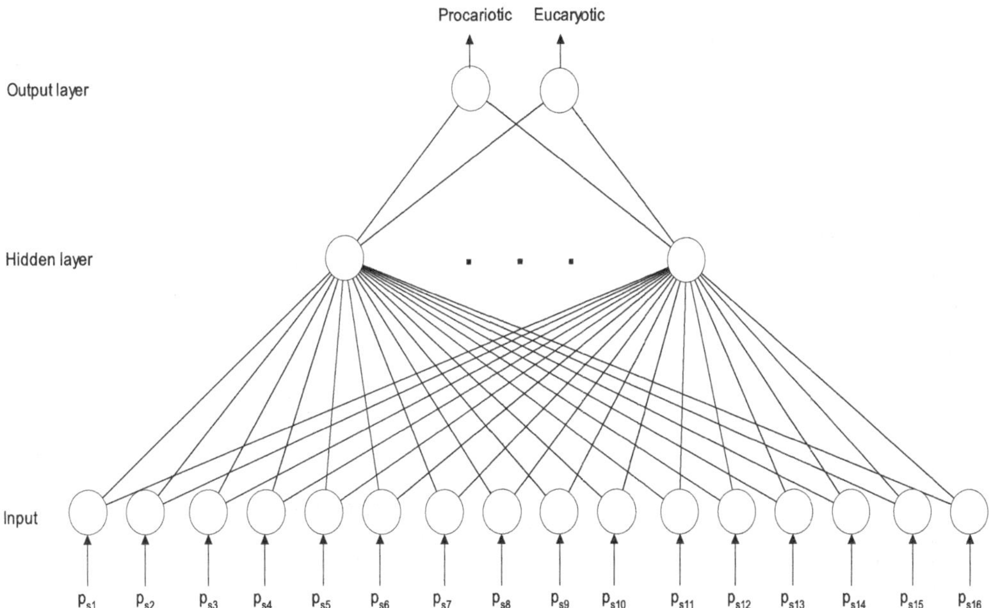

Fig. 6. Classification of eukaryotic and prokaryotic DNA-sequences by a BP network. Each p_{xi} is a 'relative frequency' of a nucleotide pair.

```
SQ   Sequence 691 BP; 135 A; 243 C; 192 G; 121 T; 0 other;
     CCTGAACCCG GTGTCCCCGG GTGGGGGGTG GGGACGCCAC GGCCGAAGCA GCTAGCTCCG        60
     TTCGTGATCC GGGAGCCTGG TGCCAGCGAG ACCTGGAATT TCCGGTCTGG TTGGTCTGGG       120
     GCCCCGCGGA GCCAGGTTGA TACCCTCACC TCCCAACCCC AGGCCCTCGG ATGCCCAGAA       180
     CCTGTAGGCC GCACCGTGGA CTTGTTCTTA ATCGAGGGGC ACTTCTACCC TAGCCGGGCC       240
     CAGCCCCCGA GCAGTGCAGC CTCCCGAGTG CAGAGTGCAG CCCCTGCCCG CCCTGGCCCA       300
     GCTGCCCATG TCTACCCTGC TGGATCCCAA GTAATGATGA TCCCTTCCCA GATCTCCTAC       360
     CCAGCCTCCC AGGGGGCCTA CTACATCCCT GGACAGGGGC GTTCCACATA CGTTGTCCCG       420
     ACACAGCAGT ACCCTGTGCA GCCAGGAGCC CCAGGCTTCT ATCCAGGTGC AAGCCCTACA       480
     GAATTTGGGA CCTACGCTGG CGCCTACTAT CCAGCCCAAG GGGTGCAGCA GTTTCCCACT       540
     GGCGTGGCCC CCGCCCCAGT TTTGATGAAC CAGCCACCCC AGATTGCTCC CAAGAGGGAG       600
     CGTAAGACGA TCCGAATTCG AGATCCAAAC CAAGGAGGAA AGGATATCAC AGAGGAGATC       660
     ATGTCTGGGG CCCGCACTGC CTCCACACCC A                                      691
```

Fig. 7. A database entry of a eukaryotic DNA sequence from the EMBL database on the Internet. The length of the DNA-sequence is 691 bases. The DNA sequence is a protein found in the human being.

Before training, two parameters need to be found, C and γ. C is the penalty parameter of the error term and γ is a kernel parameter. The C value used was equal 100, and γ was set to the inverse of the size of the number of input values. This means, for instance, that for an input file of sixteen inputs γI equal 1/16 = 0.0625.However, these values for C and γ are currently not optimal.

B. MLP experiments

The network is trained according to the Backpropagation algorithm [10,18]. A set of $\mathbf{S_n}$ vectors and their corresponding classification are presented to the network. During the training session the input to the network is alternately selected from the eukaryotic and prokaryotic cell class. After the training session is finished, the network is tested on a set of unknown $\mathbf{S_n}$ vectors. The output is recorded, and the performance of the network computed.

The MLP network used for window size two is shown in Fig 6. The input layer consists of 16 input nodes, one for each component of $\mathbf{S_n} = (s_1, s_2, ..., s_n)$. Each p_{si} given in Fig. 6 is a 'relative frequency' of each nucleotide pair of a DNA sequence. This is not the conventional relative frequency, because the relative frequencies do not sum up to 1. In this case the relative frequency is defined by the actual number of each nucleotide pair, divided by the square root of the total sum of pair frequency squared.

C. Window sizes

In Fig. 5 we notice that for sub-sequences of length two to four bases, the correlation coefficient does not vary much. This should mean that for a window of length 2, 3 or 4 bases wide, the classification performance should not differ very much. The experiments carried out may be a confirmation of this.

For a window of size equal three two cases are to be considered. The reason for this is that three nucleotides correspond to a codon defined by the Genetic code. There are as many codons as there are permutations of three nucleotides, i.e. $4^3 = 64$ possible codons, but only 22 of them are coding for amino acids and stop/start criteria. This also means that the Genetic code contains lots of redundancy. Table 1 shows the length of the frequency vector of different window sizes. The same input vectors were used in both the MLP and SVM network

Window size	The length of the frequency vector
2	16
3 (genetic code)	22
3	64
4	256

Table 1: The length of the frequency vector for different window sizes

VIII. THE GENETIC CODE

The DNA molecule contains genetic information in our cells. The genetic code is the language used by the cell to make different proteins by use of information given in the genes. A gene, which codes for a protein, is first transcribed to messenger RNA (mRNA). Then the information in the DNA molecule is translated to the protein via its messenger RNA (mRNA). The sequence of amino acids in the proteins is determined by of the DNA molecule. Three bases code for a certain amino acid. Such a base-triplet is called a *codon.*

Since the DNA string consists of four different bases (A, C, G, T), there will be $4^3 = 64$ different codons. Since the cell only uses 21 different amino acids to build proteins, most of the amino acids will correspond to several codons. So, there is a great deal of redundancy in this coding scheme. For instance, the codon ATG means 'start' of a protein synthesis and will also at the same time code for the amino acid *methionine*. The codons TAA, TAG and TCA indicates all 'stop' codons in the protein synthesis.

A. Inclusion of the Genetic Code

As explained in the section VI the representation of genetic code can be built into the neural network and the SVM experiments by use of a redefined frequency vector $\mathbf{F_{22}}$, containing only the relative frequencies of 22 codon elements: The different codons and corresponding amino acids of the Genetic code are given in Table 2.

Codons	**Amino Acid**
TTT,TTC	Phenylalanine
TCA,TCG,CCT,CCC,CCA,CCG	Leucine
ACT,ACC,ACA	Isoleucine
ATG	START/Methionine
GCT,GCC,GCA, GCG	Valine
TCT,TCC,TCA,TCG	Serine
CCT,CCC,CCA,CCG	Proline
ACT,ACC,ACA,ACG	Threonine
GCT,GCC,GCA,GCG	Alanine
TAT,TAC	Tyrosine
TAA,TAG,TGA	STOP
CAT,CAC	Histidine
CAA,CAG	Glutamine
AAT,AAC	Asparagine
AAA,AAG	Lysine
GAT,GAC	Aspartic acid
GAA,GAG	Flutamic acid
TGT,TGC	Cysteine
TGG	Tryotophan
CGT,CGC,CGA,CGG,AGA	Arginine
AGT,AGC	Serine
GGT,GGC,GGA,GGG	Glycine

Table 2: Different codons of the Genetic Code.

IX. EXPERIMENTS AND RESULTS

By using a MLP or SVM network the classification task between the different DNA sequences might reduce the need for frequency aligning, and hence the classification time in general. In Fig. 5 we notice that for sub-sequences of length two to four bases, the correlation coefficient does not vary much.

A. MLP results

The training set consists of 30 DNA sequences distributed equally between eukaryotes and prokaryotes. In one experiment only the number of hidden neurons was varied. The optimal number was found to be 30 hidden nodes. In another experiment the learning rate α and the momentum β were varied.

The training of the network is shown in Fig. 8. The number of iterations was set to 30 000. The global error was then estimated to about 10 %. In general, such an error is too large. However, the experiments showed that the generalisation of the network was then optimal. More training of the network resulted in that some over-training happened. The best results were achieved for the learning rate $\alpha = 0.07$ and momentum $\beta = 0.1$. These parameter values are very small which may indicate that the learning needs to be slow in order for the network to detect the detailed structures of the DNA sequences.

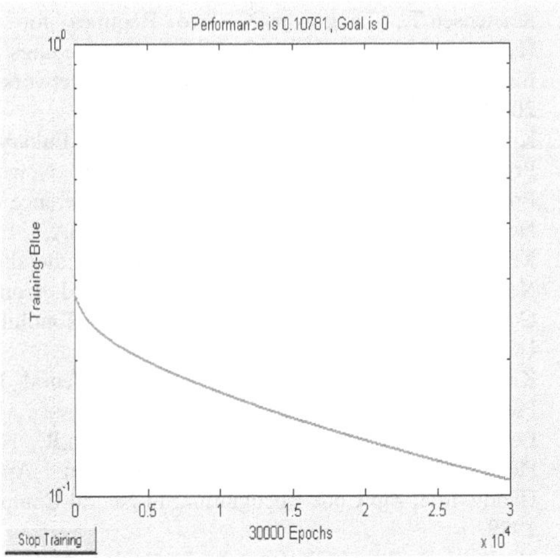

Fig. 8. Training of the MLP neural network. The training time is 30 000 iterations.

The performance of the network has been tested on 26 unknown DNA sequences found on the Internet. The best prediction was about 85 % for a window of length three. The Genetic code was then not built into the training set. This does not seem to be what we expected, and the explanation is maybe that the MLP network needs more data to be properly trained on in this case. The results are given in Table 3.

WindowSize	Training data	Validation data
4	96.5	65.4
3 (genetic code)	89,6	80,1
3	86,2	84,6
2	89,6	80,7

Table 3: Results of using the MLP network

B. SVM results

Different types of kernels were selected in the experiments of the SVM network, with the Genetic code included or not. The best performance was achieved for a network with a polynomial kernel. The performance was 84.6 % for unseen DNA sequences. This looks more sensible compared to what we would expect before carrying out the experiments.

Window size	Kernel type	Training data	Validation data
4	linear	96.5	73.1
4	polynomial	96.6	69.2
4	RBF	82.7	57.7
3 (genetic code)	linear	86,2	76,9
3 (genetic code)	polynomial	86,2	84,6
3 (genetic code)	RBF	82,7	76
3	linear	96,6	65,4
3	polynomial	96,6	69,2
3	RBF	86,2	73,1
2	linear	89,7	84,6
2	polynomial	86,2	84,6
2	RBF	82,7	73,1

Table 4: Results of using the SVM network

X. DISCUSSION

If we want an ANN or a SVM to fully automate the classification process of DNA sequences, we may get some problems to solve. In general, both the training and testing (performance) of the network will depend on the window size. By changing the window size, the topology of the neural network also must change. The number of input nodes of the network is dependent on the window size. For a window size of length w the number of input nodes is equal to 4^w. By changing the number of input nodes in a MLP network, the number of neurons of the hidden layer must be changed.

However, a new network topology configuration in general, would also mean redefinition of the learning rate α and momentum β of the training algorithm. This will again influence the training time of the network. So, by changing the topology of the network, the different parameters should also be changed accordingly.

A full automation of the categorisation of a MLP network for any size of sub-sequences, is a difficult task to solve. To be able to compare the results of the different experiment sin general, we may, for instance, plot the results in the 3D space of different parameter values. We could, for instance, represent this as a point in 3D where the x-y-z axes are defined by the window size, learning rate and the number of hidden neurons, respectively.

A more detailed analysis may also take into account the other parameters mentioned above. We could represent the different parameters as components of a vector in hyper space. However, the three parameters mentioned above are the most significant ones. The experiments could also be extended to use a sliding window of length greater than four, to see if the graph in Fig. 5 can be deduced from the experiments or not.

The number of DNA sequences used in the training set is currently too small. The experiments definitely have to be scaled up to make the conclusion more valid. In addition, short sequences in the data set may contain too little information to be of any practical value in the analysis. Longer DNA sequences give better performance rate. Further work is required to confirm this properly.

In a longer perspective, a more general solution of the classification problem of DNA sequences should be established as indicated in the discussion at the end of section V. This can be done by using, for instance, a parameter optimisation technique. In principle, such an approach may be similar to search in an n-dimensional space, where n is the number of parameters we want to optimize. One such optimization technique is Genetic algorithms that may be relevant in this case..

To automate the recognition process of DNA-sequences by a SVM network may be an easier task to carry out, since such a regime is more mathematically sound. However, the selection of the best kernel function adapted to the actual problem, may be a difficult task.

XI. CONCLUSION AND FURTHER WORK

A MLP and SVM network have been developed to categorise between eukaryotic and prokaryotic DNA-sequences found in biological databases on the Internet. All the DNA-sequences have been represented in the EMBL format. Java programs have been developed to carry out the experiments for both networks.

The experiments, so far, have shown that both a MLP and a SVM network are able to distinguish between prokaryotic and eukaryotic cells by using a simple feature extraction technique based on a gliding window. The recognition performance of unseen DNA-sequences was estimated to about 85 % for both the MLP and SVM network.

An experimental approach has currently been used to determine the optimal values of the parameters used. However, in further work a separate regime based on, for instance, Particle Swarm Optimization techniques is planned to be used to find optimal parameter values of both ANN and SVM network.

REFERENCES

1. Allex, C.F.,Shavlik,J.W., Blattner,F.R. Neural Network Input Representations that Produce Accurate Consensus Sequences fram DNA Fragment Assemblies. Bioinformatics 15, 1999.
2. Burges, C.J. A Tutorial on Support Vector Machines for Pattern Recognition. Knowledge Discovery and Data Mining 2, Springer, 1998.
3. Claverie, J Computational methods for the identification of genes in vertebrate genomic sequences. In Human Molecular Genetics, 6, 10, 1735-1744, 1997.
4. Campbell,N., Reece, J. Biology. Addison Wesley chapter 28, New York, 2001, USA.
5. Collins,F., Galas, D. A new five-year plan for the U.S. Human Genome Project, *Science*, 262, 1993, 43-46.
6. Douzono,H., Hara, S., Noguchi,Y. An Application of Genetic Algorithm to DNA Sequencing by Oligonucleotide Hybridization. In Proceedings of IEEE International Joint Symposia on Intelligence and Systems, May 1998.
7. Douzono,H., Hara, S., Noguchi,Y. A Design Method of DNA chips for SNP Analysis Using Self Organising Maps. In Proceedings of IEEE International Joint Conference on Neural Network, IJCNN 2001, Washington DC, 2001, USA.
8. Feng,D.F., Doolitle,R.F. Progressive sequence alignment of amino acid sequences and construction of phylogenetic trees from them. Methods in Enzymology, 266, 1996.
9. Fickett, J.W., and Hatzigeorgiou, A.G..Eukaryotic promoter recognition. *Genome Res.*, 1997,7, 861-878.
10. Haykin,S. Neural Networks. Prentice Hall, 2009.
11. Kristensen,T. A Neural Network Approach to Hyphenating Norwegian. In Proceedings of IEEE International Joint Conference on Neural Networks, IJCNN 2000, Como, Italy.
12. Kristensen,T., Langmyhr,D. Two Regimes for Computer Hyphenation – a Comparison. In Proceedings of IEEE International Joint Conference on Neural Networks, IJCNN 2001, Washington DC, USA.
13. Kristensen,T., Patel,R. Classification of Eukaryotic and Prokaryotic Cells by a Backpropagation Newtwork. In Proceedings of IEEE International Joint Conference on Neural Networks, IJCNN 2003, Portland, Oregon, USA.
14. Kristensen,T., Patel,R. Edge Detecting in a Lateral Inhibition Network. In Proceedings of IEEE World Congress on Computational Intelligence, WCCI 2002, Honolulu Hawai, USA.
15. Kristensen, T. javANN: Java Artificial Neural Networks. Pattern solutions AS. http://www.patternsolutions.no
16. LeCun,Y., Boser,B., Denker,J.S., Henderson,R., Howard,E., Hubbard,W., Jackel,L.D. Backpropagation Applied to Handwritten Zip Code Recognition. In Neural Computation 1, 1989.
17. Nusinov, R. Strong Preferences in Nucleotide Sequences of DNA Geometry. Journal of Molecular Evolution 20, 1984.
18. Potamias,G., Papanikolaou,E., Hatzigeorgiou,A. Knowledge-Based TDNN Architectures for Features Recognition in DNA Sequences. In Proceedings of IEEE International Joint Conference on Neural Networks, IJCNN 2001, Washington DC, USA.
19. Vapnik, V.N. An Overview of statistical learning theory. In IEEE transactions on Neural Networks, September, 1999
20. Vapnik, V.N. Statistical learning theory. Wiley, New York, 1998.
21. http://www.csie.ntu.edu.tw/~cjlin/papers/libsvm.pdf

Parallelization of Composition Vector Method for Sequence Similarity Analysis

[1*]Manoj Gupta, [2]Aniket Mittal, , [3]Rajdeep Niyogi, [4]Manoj Mishra
[1234]Department of Computer Science and Engineering, IIT Roorkee,
Roorkee, India - 247667

Abstract— Sequence comparison is an important task in the field of bioinformatics. Due to rapid accumulation of biological sequence data, scalability has become a bottleneck for researchers. In this paper we intend to solve this problem using parallelism on GPUs. GPUs provide the ability to achieve significant performance gains as compared to conventional CPUs due to their massive data parallel ability. Thus, we implement a Composition Vector method for sequence comparison on CUDA and compare its performance with sequential code. Our experiments show that a speedup of the order of 25 times is attainable due to massive data parallel components in the algorithm.

Keywords—Composition Vector Method, GPU, CUDA, Sequence Comparison.

1 Introduction

Biological sequences such as DNA have been studied extensively in the recent times, to extract critical biological information. Primarily, sequence comparison techniques are used to compare these sequences and figure out how similar or different one sequence is to another to formulate relationships between them thus extracting various properties from them, such as common ancestors, similar genes etc. Sequence comparison methods are commonly divided in two categories: alignment-based [16], [17] and alignment-free [4], [20]. Alignment-based methods mostly used dynamic programming to compare the sequences and generate similarity scores. The accuracy of this method is the main cause why this method is widely adopted. The composition vector (CV) is an alignment-free method [12] and is employed due to some advantages that it offers over alignment-based methods. Since every species has its own gene order and content, it is difficult to align two complete genome sequences using alignment-based methods. CV method has been used for phylogenetic analysis of complete genome sequences of bacteria, eukaryote, etc [5], [18], [19]. It is relatively easier to compute the distance matrix because it contains no scoring matrix, thus the computation can be easily parallelized [5].

In this paper, we exploit the fact the most computation in CV method is data parallel and can be parallelized using CUDA programming environment.

The CV method has the following four steps:

1) Construct the frequency vectors: Any string of length k in a sequence of length N is called a k-string. For a DNA sequence the possible values of the k-string can be 4k since at each position there are 4 possible values, {A, C, G, T}. Frequency vector contains the frequencies of each k-string in the sequence. For M sequences, there are M frequency vectors each of length 4^k.

2) Construct the composition vectors: The expected frequency for each k-string u, denoted by q(u) is estimated. The composition vector for each sequence is given by [1]:

$$\frac{[f(u)-q(u)]}{q(u)}, \tag{1}$$

For M sequences, there are M composition vectors each of length 4^k.

3) Calculate the distance between each pair of sequence: The cosine angle used by Hao et al. [5, 14] is used in this paper for the computation of distance between composition vectors of different sequences.

$$d^{Hao}(a,b) = \frac{1-\cos\theta}{2}$$

where, $\cos\theta = \frac{a^T b}{||a||.||b||}$.

For M sequences, a distance matrix of MxM size is produced.

4) Construct the phylogenetic trees: The distance matrix is then used to generate the phylogentic tree using the Neighbour Joining method [21], [22] in the software MEGA [15].

As can be inferred from the above method, step 2 is the most important step in this method [18], [19], [20]. There are several estimation formulas for the estimation of the expected frequency q(u). In this paper, an optimized version of the method proposed by Yu et al. [13] has been parallelized. To the best of our knowledge this is the first attempt to parallelize a CV method for sequence comparison method using GPUs and discover the amount of performance improvement obtainable. Although CV method is comparatively less time consuming than other alignment-based methods [16], [17], the computation time increases as the number and size of sequences increases. Thus the goal of our parallelized version is to exploit the computational power of GPUs on CUDA. In recent years, graphics processing units (GPUs) have gained a lot of attention as a cost-effective means in parallel computing and have been widely used in bioinformatics. Some traditional algorithms, such as Smith-Waterman sequence alignment algorithm [7], RAxML [23], DP-based alignment algorithms [8] etc. have been implemented on GPUs and achieved significant speedups.

The paper is organized as follows. In Section 2 we describe the specific algorithm being implemented and the pseudo codes for the parallelized algorithm. Section 3 gives detail about the experimental setup with two datasets and the platform used to implement. An analysis of the results is performed in Section 4 followed by the conclusions made in Section 5 along with the future work.

2 Method

2.1 Frequency Vector

The first step in CV method is computation of frequency of each of the 4^k k-strings in each DNA sequence, thus generating frequency vectors. These are computed by the simple formula given in [12],

$$f(u) = n(u)/(N - k + 1), \quad (2)$$

where, f(u) is frequency of the k-string u, n(u) is the number of times the k-string u occurs in the DNA sequence, and N is the length of the DNA sequence.

As can be observed from equation (2), the calculation for each k-string is independent from the other. This calculation has been done in parallel for each k-string in parallel. Thus, there can be a maximum of 4^k threads running in parallel for 4^k k-strings.

2.2 Expected Frequency

For any k-string u, let us write it as LwR, where the characters "L" and "R" represent the first and the last nucleotides of u, respectively, and "w" represents the (k-2)-string in the middle. The formula for the estimation of the expected frequency proposed by Yu et al. [13] is:

$$q(LwR) = \frac{f(L)f(wR)+f(Lw)f(R)}{2}, \quad (3)$$

After solving the optimization problem introduced by Chan et al. [3], the new formula for the estimation of the expected frequency is:

$$q(LwR) = \frac{1}{4\sigma}[f(Lw) + f(L)\textstyle\sum_I f(wI)] * [f(wR) + f(R)\textstyle\sum_I f(Iw)], \quad (4)$$

where I is the set of all nucleotides, i.e., I = {A, C, G, T} and σ is given by,

$$\sigma = \frac{1}{2}[\textstyle\sum_I f(Iw) + \sum_I f(wI)], \quad (5)$$

In order to calculate the expected frequency, we need the frequency vector for (k-1)-strings and 1-strings.

Equation (4) can be parallelized in different ways, such as one thread for LwR for given L, w, R, or for each LwR for a given w and for all L, R. In the latter case, one thread computes q(LwR) for 16 k-strings because both L and R have 4 possible values $\in$ I. In this paper this method has been used to parallelize the algorithm. Thus there can be a maximum of $4^{(k-2)}$ threads running in parallel for 4^k k-strings.

2.3 CUDA Model

The method used in this paper simply divides the tasks in blocks and threads available in CUDA. The sizes of blocks and threads are chosen carefully so that no GPU cycle is wasted idle. As described above, the number of threads required is a power of 4, specifically 4^k and $4^{(k-2)}$. For values of $k \geq 5$ the number of threads is $4^k \geq 1024$ and for $k \geq 6$, it is $4^{(k-2)} \geq 256$. Typical k-values used for the CV method are k = 6, 7, 8.

The configuration of the GPU cards available had a maximum of 512 threads per block. This value dropped to 256 threads per block if the number of registers used per threads exceeded a limit, as specified by the CUDA Occupancy Calculator [10]. For the first step, the code could be written to allow 512 threads per block but for the second step, the maximum went down to 256. Thus for the first step we divided the calculation in multiples of 512, and for the second step in multiples of 256.

2.4 Some notations used

The number of sequences in the dataset are represented by M. The length of ith sequence is denoted by N_i. vstring and wstring are used to denote a (k-1)-string and (k-2)-string respectively. All the arrays used in the code are ordered alphabetically. vstrings and wstrings are used to denote an array of (k-1)-strings and (k-2)-strings respectively. Thus, for k=7, the vstrings array will be = {AAAAAA, AAAAAC ... TTTTTG, TTTTTT} and the wstrings array will be = {AAAAA, AAAAC ... TTTTG, TTTTT}. The notation, $Arr_m[s]$ is used to simplify the pseudo-code. Here s is a string and Arr[s] means the value for that string s in the array Arr. String s will be some k-string and the array Arr is ordered alphabetically to retrieve the value of string s instantaneously. For e.g., for k=4, the ordering is as follows: AAAA = 0, AAAC = 1, AAAG = 2 ... TTTT = 255. This conversion is easily done if we consider the string s as a quaternary number with A=0, C=1, G=2, T=3. Now a simple function converts this quaternary number to decimal. Thus, TTTT = 3333 = 3*64 + 3*16 + 3*4 + 3 = 255. Thus Arr[AAAA] means Arr[0]. In other words, AAAA is the 0th 4-string. The subscript m in $Arr_m[s]$ represents the mth sequence (starting at 0). For k=4, for each sequence there are 256 values, thus $Arr_3[AAAC]$ converts to Arr[3*256 + 1].

3 Pseudo Codes

3.1 Calculation of Frequency Vectors

The first step of CV method is computing frequencies of various k-strings in all the DNA sequences. These frequencies are stored in a vector for each sequence, thus producing M vectors. In other words we get a matrix of size $Mx4^q$ for a specific k = q. We compute 3 such matrices for q = k, (k-1) and 1. The formula used to compute the frequency for a k-string in a specific sequence is given by (2).

Fig. 1 is the kernel code for step 1. Fig. 1a first calculates the number of occurrences of each k-string in each sequence. The kernel code is invoked from the host as shown:

```
noc_kernel <<<1, M>>> (noc, k, seq)
```

```
m = threadIdx.x
while (i+k-1) < N
      k_i = k_index(seq_m[i], k)
      noc_m[k i] += 1
      i++
Endwhile
```

(a) Kernel for number of occurences: noc_kernel

```
m = blockIdx.x
i = threadIdx.x
while(i < 4^k)
   freq_m[ks] = noc_m[i]/(N_m-k+1)
   i += blockDim.x
Endwhile
```

(b) Kernel for frequencies: freq_kernel

Fig. 1 Pseudo-code for Frequency Vector (2)

Our experiments show that these dimensions of the grid are slightly better than <<<M, 1>>>. `noc` variable is used to return the result computed. `q` is the current size of k-string. We use this to generate frequency vectors for k, k-1 (`vfreq`) and 1 (`ifreq`) length kstrings. For q = k, we get `kfreq` which is used in step 3 of the CV method to calculate composition vector explained in (1). For q = (k-1) and (k-2) we get `vfreq` and `wfreq` respectively that are used in step 2 of the CV method, as explained in the following section. `seq` is an array of all sequences. `k_index` function returns the decimal value of the k-string that starts at seq_m`[i]` (i^{th} position of mth sequence) and is of length k. Thus, there are M threads and each thread computes the number of occurrences for all kstrings for a particular sequence.

Fig. 1b uses the values of number of occurrences (`noc`) computed in Fig. 1a and calculates the final value of frequency vectors. It is called from the host with number of blocks equal to M and number of threads per block equal to 512 as shown:

```
freq_kernel <<<M, 512>>> (freq, noc, k,
                    seq_lens)
```

`freq` variable is used to return the value of the result. noc is the result of Fig. 1a. `k` is the current size of kstring. `seq_lens` is an array containing lengths of all the sequences. In Fig. 1b, the maximum values of m is M and maximum value of `i` is 511. The size of `freq` array is $Mx4^k$. $freq_m$`[ks]` stores the value of the frequency of k-string `ks` for the mth sequence, i.e. $m*4^k$ + decimal value of `ks`. The `while` loop runs $4^k/512$ times, for e.g., for k=6, it is called 8 times.

At the end of the call to kernel function, the freq array is copied to from device to host and we get a 2D array of all the frequency vectors for each sequence, i.e. a matrix of size $Mx4^k$.

3.2 Calculation of Sigma

Fig. 2 is the kernel code for the calculating σ with the formula shown in (5). The call to the kernel function is made from the host as shown:

```
σ_kernel<<<M, 512>>> (σ, wstrings,
vfreq)
```

```
m = blockIdx.x
i = threadIdx.x
while i < 4^(k-2)
  ws = wstrings[i]
  t1 = t2 = 0
  foreach i ϵ I
    t1 += vfreq_m[i + ws]
    t2 += vfreq_m[ws + i]
  endfor
  σ_m[ws] = (t1*t2)/2
  i += blockDim.x
endwhile
```

Fig. 2 Pseudo-code for sigma (5)

The code itself is easy to understand. Since the size of σ is $4^{(k-2)}$, the `while` loop runs $4^{(k-2)}/512$ times. At the end of this step, we get a 2D array of all the σ vectors for each sequence, i.e. a matrix of size $Mx4^{(k-2)}$.

3.3 Calculation of Expected Frequency

```
m = blockIdx.x
i = threadIdx.x
d = blockDim.x
while i < 4^(k-2)
  ws = wstrings[i]
  foreach l ϵ I
    foreach r ϵ I
      t1 = t2 = 0
      foreach x ϵ I
        t1 += vfreq_m[ws + x]
      End for
      t1 *= ifreq_m[l]
      t1 += vfreq_m[l + ws]

      foreach x ϵ I
        t2 += vfreq_m[x + ws]
      End for
      t2 *= ifreq_m[r]
      t2 += vfreq_m[ws + r]

      ki = l + ws + r
      expfreq_m[ki] = t1*t2/4σ_m[i]
    endfor
  End for
  i += blockDim.x
endwhile
```

Fig. 3 Pseudo-code for Expected Frequency (4)

where, $ifreq_m$`[A]` is the frequency of the 1-string A, i.e. frequency of the nucleotide A, in m^{th} sequence and σ_m`[A]` is the value of sigma for A^{th} wstring, in m^{th} sequence.

Fig. 3 is the kernel code for the calculations of step 2 shown in equation (4). It is called from the host with number of blocks equal to M and number of threads per block equal to 256 as shown:

```
k3<<<M, 256>>> (expfreq, wstrings,
           vfreq, ifreq, σ)
```

The maximum values of m is M and maximum value of i is 255. Thus the size of expfreq array is M*4[k]. The `while` loop runs $4^{(k-2)}/256$ times, for e.g., for k=8, it is iterates 16 times. Lines 8 to 10 calculate $\sum_I f(wI)$ in equation 4 and lines 11 and 12 calculate $f(L)\sum_I f(wI)$ and $f(Lw) + f(L)\sum_I f(wI)$ respectively. Similarly, lines 13 to 17 calculate $f(wR) + f(R)\sum_I f(Iw)$. Line 19 calculates the final value of q(LwR) in equation 4.At the end of this step, we get a 2D array of all the expected frequency vectors for each sequence, i.e. a matrix of size $Mx4^k$.

4 Experimental Setup

We compare the sequential version of the CV method to parallel version in our experiments. Both the codes are written in C language and the parallel version uses CUDA [9] programming environment for parallelization on GPUs.

4.1 Datasets

The experiments were performed on two datasets of different sizes. The first dataset (DS-I) is 18S rRNA sequence of human ribosomal DNA complete repeating unit (GenBank: U13369.1) that contains 34 DNA sequences, described in Table 1 [2]. The second dataset (DS-II) is 0.9-kb mtDNA fragments of 12 species of primates, described in Table 2 [6]. The DNA sequences for each species was obtained from NCBI database.

4.2 Platform

We have implemented our sequential version on an Intel Core i5-2430M CPU 2.40 GHz 2.40 GHz 4.00 GB RAM. The method has been parallelized on NVIDIA GeForce GT 525M.

Table 1 DS-I: 16S rRNA sequences [2].

Species	ID/accession	Length (bp)
Haloarcula sp.	U68539	1470
Haloarcula sp.	U68537	1469
Halobacterium salinarum	U68538	1471
Haloferax volcanii	U68540	1471
Haloarcula hispanica	U68541	1469
Haloarcula japonica	D28872	1424
Haloarcula marismortui (rrnA gene)	X61688	1472
Haloarcula marismortui (rrnB gene)	X61689	1472
"Haloarcula sinaiiensis" (major gene)	D14130	1470
"Haloarcula sinaiiensis" (minor gene)	D14129	1471
Haloarcula vallismortis	U17593	1471
Halobacterium salinarum (halobium)	M38280	1473
Halobacterium trapanicum	D14125	1472
Halorubrum coriense	L00922	1469
Halobacterium sp.	D14127	1471
Halobaculum gomorrense	L37444	1474
Halococcus morrhuae	D11106	1474
Halococcus morrhuae	X00662	1475
Haloferax denitrificans	D14128	1469
Haloferax gibbonsii	D13378	1470
Haloferax mediterranei	D11107	1472
Haloferax volcanii	K00421	1472
Halorubrum lacusprofundi	X82170	1464
Halorubrum saccharovorum	X82167	1460
Halorubrum sodomense	X82169	1462
Halorubrum trapanicum	X82168	1460
Natrialba asiatica	D14123	1469
Natrialba asiatica	D14124	1470
Halophilic strain	D14126	1472
Natronobacterium magadii	X72495	5209
Natronococcus amylolyticus	D43628	1930
Natronococcus occultus	Z28378	1464
Methanobacterium formicicum	M36508	1476
Methanospirillum hungatei	M60880	1466

Table 2. DS-II: 0.9-kb mtDNA sequences [6].

Species	ID/accession	Length (bp)
Macaca fascicular	M22653	896
Macaca fuscata	M22651	896
Macaca mulatta	M22650	896
Macaca sylvanus	M22654	896
Saimiri sciruеus	M22655	893
chimpanzee	V00672	896
Lemur catta	M22657	895
gorilla	V00658	896
hylobates	V00659	896
Orangutan	V00675	895
Tarsisus syrichta	M22656	895
human	L00016	896

5 Results and Discussion

5.1 Time taken by each step of CV method

Table 3 shows the time taken by the sequential code for various functions for DS-I and DS-II when the value of k is 8.

Table 3 Time taken for calculation of various vectors in CV method.

	Function	Time (ms) DS-I	Time (ms) DS-II
1.	k frequency vectors	2143	413
2.	Sigma vectors	220	93
3.	Expected frequency vectors	1923	483
4.	Composition vectors	19	8
5.	Distance vectors	150	23

Row 1 in table 3 is the time taken to calculate the frequency vectors for all sequences mentioned in Table 1 and Table 2. This is the same as the time taken to compute step 1 in CV method. Row 2, 3 and 4 describe the time taken to compute step 2 of CV method. It has been observed from the Table 3 that maximum time is consumed in the calculation of the functions in row 1, 2 and 3. Thus these three functions have been parallelized to achieve maximum performance improvement.

5.2 Comparison of Sequential and Parallel algorithms

From Fig. 4 and Fig. 5 we observed that there is significant reduction in computation time while parallelizing step 1 of CV method for DS-I (Table 1) and DS-II (Table 2) respectively. The pseudo-code for step 1 is given in Fig. 1. Similarly, the computation time is greatly reduced in parallelizing the step 2 of CV method as shown in Fig. 6 and Fig. 7 for the same datasets shown by Table 1 and Table 2 respectively. The times shown in Fig. 6 and Fig. 7 are the summation of the time taken by both the pseudo-codes, Fig. 2 and Fig. 3. Fig. 8 shows the total speedup obtained after parallelization. Speedup is calculated by summing the times taken in step 1 and 2 from Fig. 4 with Fig. 6, and Fig. 5 with Fig. 7. Then the ratio of sequential time versus parallel time is calculated. As, it is evident from these figures, the speedup in step 1 is much more than that in step 2 of CV method. The parallel code for step 1 is about 20-27 times faster, whereas it is about 4-6 times faster for step 2. This is mainly due to the fact that the kernel functions in Fig. 2 and Fig. 3 are much larger than those in Fig. 1. Thus, each thread on the GPU is doing larger number of computations and taking longer to finish them, hence reducing the performance.

Another useful observation can be made from Fig. 8. It shows how the speedup improves as the value of k increases. As k increases the sizes of all the vectors (kstring, vstring, wstring and all frequency vectors) increases exponentially, thus increasing the scope of parallelization. This in turn increases the performance speedup manifolds.

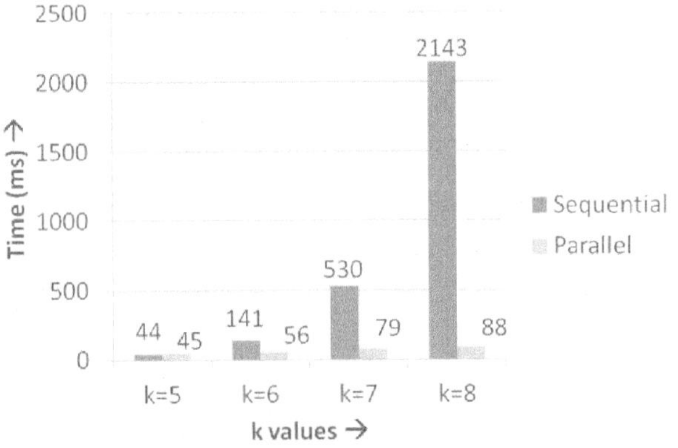

Fig. 4 Time comparison between sequential and parallel code for step 1 of CV method for DS-I.

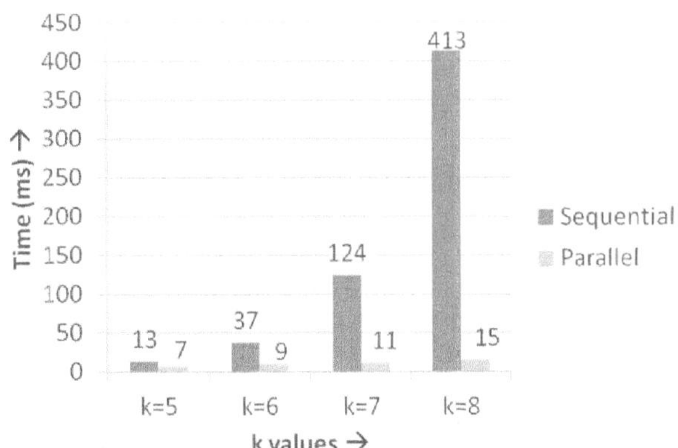

Fig. 5 Time comparison between sequential and parallel code for step 1 of CV method for DS-II.

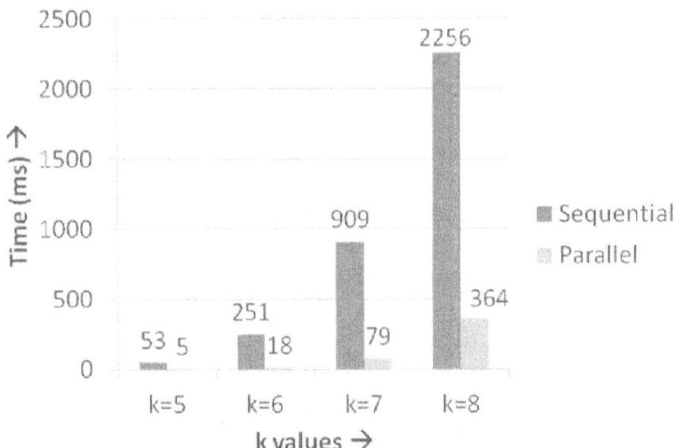

Fig. 6 Time comparison between sequential and parallel code for step 2 of CV method for DS-I.

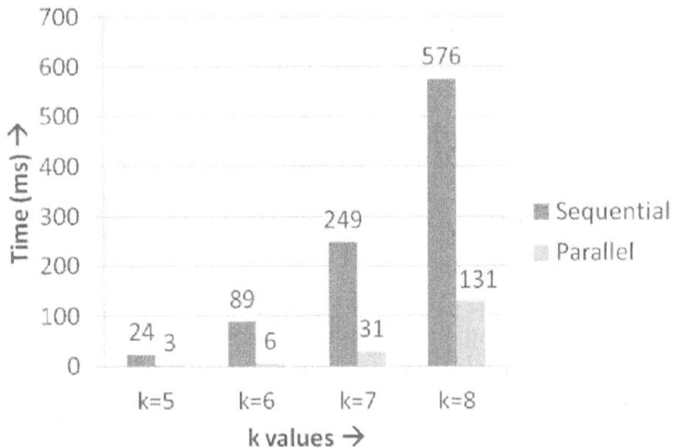

Fig. 7 Time comparison between sequential and parallel code for step 2 of CV method for DS-II.

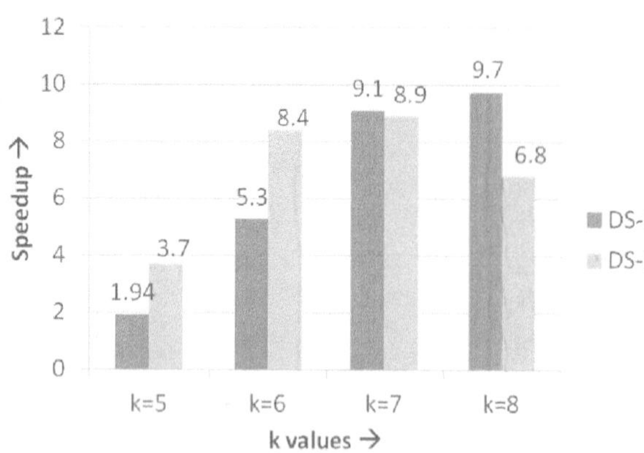

Fig. 8 Speedup comparison between parallel and sequential with total time of step 1 and 2.

6 Conclusion and Future Work

Composition vector method is widely used alignment-free method used for similarity analysis among the sequences. The first two steps of the method is highly computational intensive and hence parallelization will significantly reduce the computation time. Therefore, a parallelized implementation of Composition Vector method for sequence comparison has been performed. The result shows significant performance improvement as compared to its sequential counterpart. The computationally intensive phases of the algorithm were identified and their data parallel components exploited to parallelize them.

The approach used in this paper can be applied to different types of estimation methods [1] and performance improvement by exploiting data parallel components can be obtained.

Although there have been significant improvements obtained in parallelizing the CV method but in future we can further improvise by appropriately selecting CUDA parameters such as the most optimal kernel code and number of blocks and threads.

7 Conflict of Interests

The Authors declare that there is no conflict of interest.

8 References

[1] Raymond H., Roger W., Hau Man Yeung, "Composition Vector Method for Phylogenetics - A Review," ISORA 9, pp. 13-20, 2010.

[2] D.R. Arahal, F.E. Dewhirst, B.J. Paster, B.E. Volcani, and A. Ventosa, "Phylogenetic Analyses of Some Extremely Halophilic Archaea Isolated from Dead Sea Water, Determined on the Basis of Their 16S rRNA Sequences," Applied and Environmental Microbiology, vol. 62, pp. 3779-3786, 1996.

[3] Raymond H. Chan, Tony H. Chan, Hau Man, and Roger Wei, "Composition Vector Method Based on Maximum Entropy Principle for Sequence Comparison," IEEE/ACM Transactions on computational biology and bioinformatics, Vol. 9, No. 1, 2012.

[4] S. Vinga and J. Almeida, "Alignment Free Sequence Comparison-a Review," Bioinformatics, vol. 19, pp. 513-523, 2003.

[5] J. Qi, B. Wang, and B.L. Hao, "Whole Proteome Prokaryote Phylogeny without Sequence Alignment: A k-String Composition Approach," J. Molecular Evolution, vol. 58, pp. 1-11, 2004.

[6] Hayasaka K, Gojobori T, Horai S., "Molecular phylogeny and evolution of primate mitochondrial DNA", Mol Biol Evol. 5:626–44, 1998.

[7] S.A. Manavski, G. Valle, "CUDA Compatible GPU Cards as Efficient Hardware Accelerators for Smith-Waterman Sequence Alignment", BMC Bioinformatics V9(Suppl 2), S10, 2008.

[8] W. Liu, B. Schmidt, G. Voss, "Streaming algorithms for biological sequence alignment on GPUs", IEEE Trans. Parallel and Distributed Systems, V18, N9, pp. 1270-1281, 9/07.

[9] NCBI home page, http://www.ncbi.nlm.nih.gov.

[10] CUDA Occupancy Calculator, developer.download.nvidia.com/compute/cuda/CUDA_Occupancy_calculator.xls.

[11] J. Nickolls J., I. Buck, M. Garland and K. Skadron, "Scalable parallel programming with CUDA," ACM Queue, vol. 6, pp. 40-53, doi: 10.1145/1365490.1365500, Mar./April 2008.

[12] B. L. Hao, J. Qi and B. Wang, "Whole proteome prokaryote phylogeny without sequence alignment: A k-string composition approach", Journal of Molecular Evolution, 58(1), 1–11, 2004.

[13] Z. G. Yu, L.Q. Zhou, V. Anh, K. H. Chu, S. C. Long and J. Q. Deng, "Phylogeny of prokaryotes and chloroplasts revealed by a simple composition approach on all protein sequences from whole genome without sequence alignment", Journal of Molecular Evolution, 60, 538–545, 2005.

[14] B. L. Hao, J. Qi and B. Wang, "Prokaryotic phylogeny based on complete genomes without sequence alignment", Modern Physics Letters B, 2, 1–4, 2003.

[15] Molecular Evolutionary Genetics Analysis (MEGA), http://www.megasoftware.net/.

[16] T.T. Smith and M.S. Waterman, "Identification of Common Molecular Subsequences," J. Molecular Biology, vol. 147, pp. 195-197, 1981.

[17] S.B. Needleman and C.D. Wunsch, "A General Method Applicable to the Search for Similarities in the Amino Acid Sequence of Two Proteins," J. Molecular Biology, vol. 48, pp. 443-453, 1970.

[18] Z.G. Yu, L.Q. Zhou, V. Anh, K.H. Chu, S.C. Long, and J.Q. Deng, "Phylogeny of Prokaryotes and Chloroplasts Revealed by a Simple Composition Approach on All Protein Sequences from Whole Genome without Sequence Alignment," J. Molecular Evolution, vol. 60, pp. 538-545, 2005.

[19] K.H. Chu, J. Qi, Z.G. Yu, and V. Anh, "Origin and Phylogeny of Chloroplasts: A Simple Correlation Analysis of Complete Genomes," Molecular Biology and Evolution, vol. 21, pp. 200-206, 2004.

[20] X. Wu, X.F. Wan, G. Wu, D. Xu, and G. Lin, "Phylogenetic Analysis Using Complete Signature Information of Whole Genomes and Clustered Neighbor-Joining Method," Int'l J. Bioinformatics Research and Applications, vol. 2, pp. 219-248, 2006.

[21] M. Saitou and N. Nei, "The neighbor-joining method: a new method for reconstructing phylogenetic trees," Mol. Biol. Evol., vol. 4, pp. 406-425, July 1987.

[22] J.A. Studier and K.J. Keppler, "A note on the neighbor-joining algorithm of Saitou and Nei," Mol. Biol. Evol., vol. 5, pp. 729-731, Nov. 1988.

[23] A. J. Abcrcra, N. D. Pattcngalcb, A. Stamatakisa, "Parallel Computation of Phylogenetic Consensus Trees", Procedia Computer Science 00, 1–10, 2010.

Hybrid Framework for pairwise DNA Sequence Alignment Using the CUDA compatible GPU

H. Khaled, R. El Gohary, N.L. Badr and H. M. Faheem
Faculty of Computer & Information Science, Ain Shams University,
Cairo, Egypt.
heba.kaled@cis.asu.edu.eg, dr.raniaelgohary@fcis.asu.edu.eg, dr.nagwabadr@gmail.com, hmfaheem@cis.asu.edu.eg

Abstract—This paper provides a novel framework for accelerating the solution of the pairwise DNA sequence alignment problem using CUDA parallel paradigm available on the NVIDIA GPU. The main idea is to implement a new algorithm that assigns different nucleotide weights using GPU architectures then merge the subsequences of match using CPU to get the optimum local alignment. The paper describes both the algorithm and the implementation of it using both the GPU and CPU to constitute a hybrid model for solving DNA sequence alignment problem on DNA molecules. Experimental results demonstrate a considerable reduction in run time relative to traditional Smith-Waterman implementation on traditional processors.

Keywords— GPU, GPGPU, CUDA, sequence alignment algorithms, molecular biology.

1 Introduction

Sequence comparison is a very basic and important operation in Bioinformatics as Sequence alignment is a key component in the analysis of genes and genomes. Sequence alignment algorithms find regions in one sequence, called the query sequence, that are similar or identical to regions in another sequence, called the reference sequence [1]. A sequence alignment has a similarity score associated to it obtained by placing one sequence above the other, making clear correspondence between the characters and possibly introducing gaps into them. The most common types of sequence alignment are global and local. To solve a global alignment problem it is required to find the best match between the entire sequences. On the other hand, local alignment algorithms must find the best match between parts of the sequences. Both Needleman-Wunsch algorithm [2] for global alignment and Smith-Waterman algorithm [3] for local alignment deploy dynamic programming approaches.

Genomic databases have an exponential growth rate. Therefore, a huge amount of new DNA sequences will need to be compared, in order to infer functional/structural characteristics. The growth of database size increases the time required for searching using this kind of dynamic programming approaches. Complexity of sequence comparison is proportional to query size and database size [4], [5].

The recent development of multi-core architectures, and its associated programming interfaces, provide an opportunity to accelerate sequence database searches using commonly available and inexpensive hardware.

Graphics hardware is currently deployed in high-performance computing due to its cost effectiveness. Bioinformatics applications also exploit GPU as a massive parallel multi-core processor to address computational challenges in many areas such as sequence analysis and alignment and protein structure prediction [6].

CUDA is the architecture and developing platform of the NVIDIA GPU. It is an extension of the C programming language. CUDA programs typically consist of a component that runs on the CPU, or host, and a smaller but computationally intensive component called the kernel that runs in parallel on the GPU. The kernel cannot access the CPU's main memory directly – input data for the kernel must be copied to the GPU's on-board memory prior to invoking the kernel, and output data also must first be written to the GPU's memory. All memory used by the kernel must be pre-allocated, and the kernel cannot use recursion or other features requiring a stack, but loops and conditionals are allowed [1].

In CUDA, the GPU is viewed as a computing device suitable for parallel data applications. It has its own device random access memory and may run a huge number of threads in parallel [7] as shown in Fig.1. Threads are grouped in blocks and many blocks may run in a grid of blocks. Such structured sets of threads could be launched on a kernel of code and process the data stored in the device memory. Threads of the same block share data through fast shared on chip memory and they can be synchronized through synchronization points as shown in Fig.2 [8], [9]. The proposed DNA sequence alignment approach can benefit from the CUDA architecture and the single instruction multiple thread SIMT model.

The SIMT completes the DNA sequence comparison in two stages; the first stage is used to find matches and mismatches between each nucleotide from both the query and the target sequences. The second stage is used to weight and highlight the subsequences of matches. The resulting subsequences of matches are then passed to the CPU to be merged in order to find the optimum alignment between the two sequences.

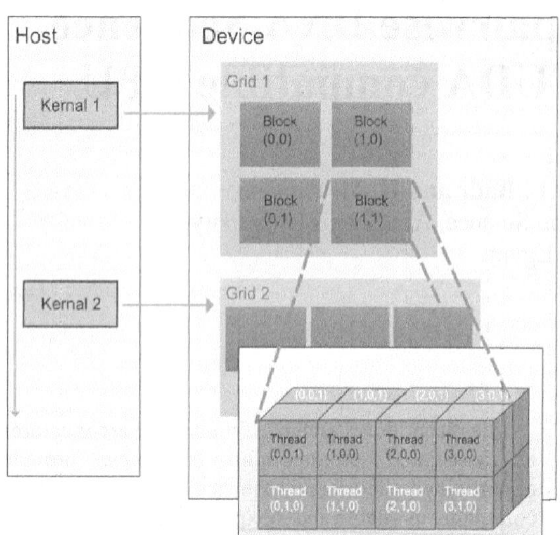

Fig. 1 Heterogeneous programming.

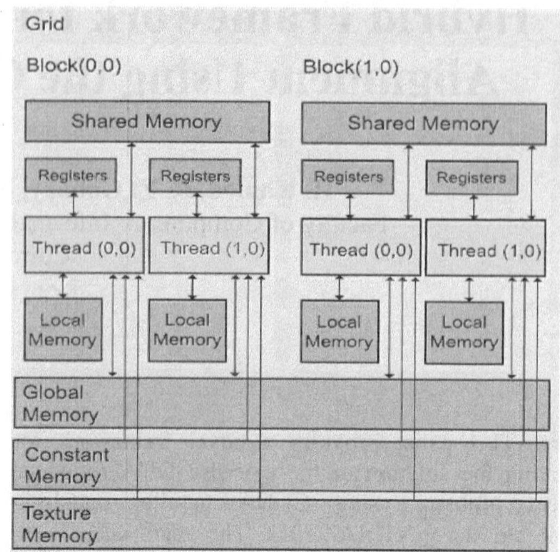

Fig. 2 CUDA Memory Model

The rest of the paper is organized as follows: Section 2 describes the proposed framework. Section 3 describes the operation of the proposed system. Section 4 provides the experimental results. Section 5 augments some concluding remarks.

2 Proposed Framework

Task Dependency in Smith-Waterman algorithm is very high. For each cell in the Smith-Waterman dynamic programing matrix, we need to compute the upper, left and diagonal cells adjacent to that cell. This is to find the best alignment between two DNA sequences.

Given two DNA sequences S of length n, and T of length m, the proposed algorithm starts with an initialization phase shown in Fig.3. During this phase, a sufficient number of threads that can carry out n × m initialization operation is activated. Corresponding locations in the two sequences are compared such that a weight of 2 is granted to matched positions and 0 is granted to unmatched.

Given two DNA sequences S of length n, and T of length m:

1- Activate a number of threads that can carry out n × m initialization operation.
2- Load the two DNA sequences to all the threads.
3- For All the threads Perform the initialization process according to the following rules:

IF $S_i = T_J$ $i=1\ldots n.\ j=1\ldots m.$
THEN $H(i,j)_t = 2$
ELSE IF $S_i \neq T_J$ where H_t is the preprocessing matrix
THEN $H(i,j)_t = 0$

Fig. 3 Initialization Algorithm

Sequence matching process is then performed as described in Fig.4. During this phase, a weight of 4 is granted to a specific position in the matrix having an initial weight of 2 if at least one of its adjacent upper diagonal left or lower diagonal right positions have a weight of 2. If both of the mentioned adjacent positions have a weight of 2 then, a weight of 6 is granted to the specific position. This approach maximizes the score of continuous "subsequence matching."

1- Activate a number of threads that can carry out n × m matching operation.
2- For All the threads Perform the sequence matching process according to the following rules:

IF $H(i,j)_t = 0$ where H_t and H_{t+1} are the
THEN $H(i,j)_{t+1} = 0$ preprocessing and the final sequence
ELSE IF $H(i,j)_t = 2$ matching matrixes
THEN
  IF $H(i+1,j+1)_t=2$ ***AND*** $H(i-1,j-1)_t=2$
  THEN $H(i,j)_{t+1}=6$
  ELSE IF $H(i-1,j-1)_t=2$ ***OR*** $H(i+1,j+1)_t=2$
  THEN $H(i,j)_{t+1}=4$
  ELSE $H(i,j)_{t+1}=2$

Fig. 4 Sequence Matching Algorithm

It is clear that there is no task dependency either in the initialization phase or in sequence matching process now, we are ready to implement this parallel part using CUDA provided by NVidia GPU which can lead to a significant improvement in the speed without the need to deploy special purpose hardware as in [10].

The block diagram shown in Fig.5 illustrates the model used to implement the Hybrid system for DNA sequence alignment using GPU.

The Implementation flow of the DNA Sequence Alignment consists of four subsystems: Initialization, pre-processing, Alignment, and the Output subsystem.

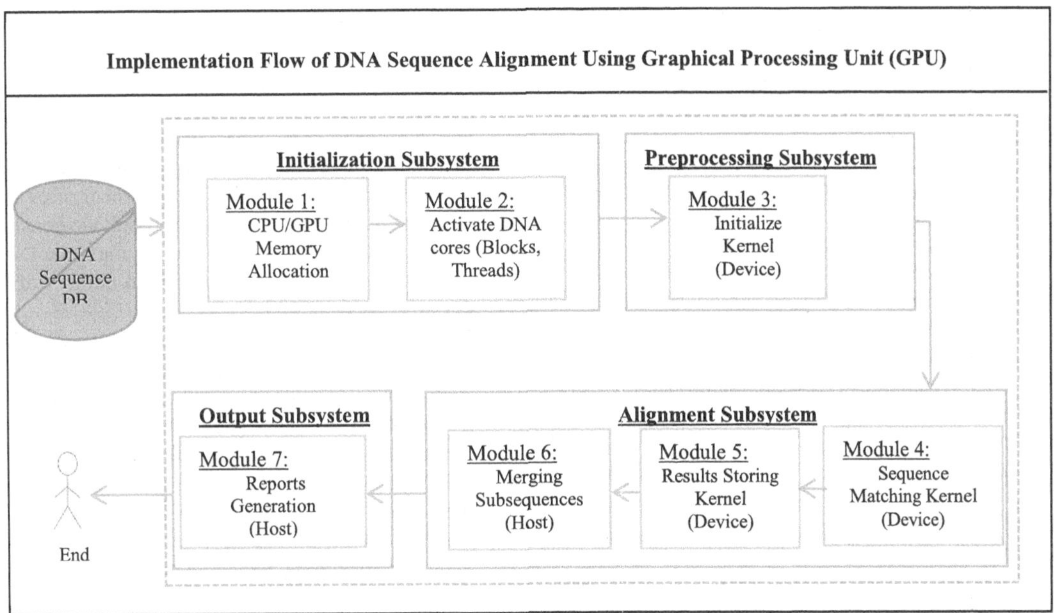

Fig. 5 Implementation Flow of DNA Sequence Alignment Using Graphical Processing Unit (GPU).

The Initialization Subsystem is concerned with the initialization phase that allocates memory for both CPU and GPU used to read the DNA sequences and store the output. It also activates number of CUDA Cores (blocks and threads) according to the sizes of the two DNA input sequences and then passes the inputs to the GPU grid.

At this point, the Preprocessing Subsystem can work on the device (GPU); the initialization kernel purpose is to compare each DNA nucleotide in the two sequences and fill the initialization vector with values for both DNA nucleotide match and mismatch. All the thread blocks perform the exact matching between the corresponding first sequence nucleotide and second sequence nucleotide simultaneously as a first step in the initialization process.

The resulting output matrix of the pre-processing subsystem is then passed to the Alignment subsystem.

The Alignment subsystem first applies the sequence matching algorithm that also works on the device (GPU). The sequence-matching kernel highlights the subsequence of match between the query and the subject sequences by weighting the match and the sub-sequences of match.

The proposed framework takes the advantage of the fact that each nucleotide comparison “initialization then Matching weight” for both the query sequence and the subject sequence can be computed independent of each other. Therefore, a number of n threads in a thread block are responsible for computing a row in the alignment matrix H.

Increasing the DNA sequences' size requires increasing the number of initialization and sequence matching operation needed. Using the CUDA architecture makes it obvious to scale the number of threads needed for the initialization and the sequence matching kernels.

The GPU based part is scalable as different number of blocks and threads per block are activated according to the given query and sequence sizes.

The resulting matrix from the Sequence matching kernel is then passed from the GPU to the CPU host memory where the last module “Merging Subsequences” in the Alignment subsystem will operate.

The Merging subsequences function running on the Host “CPU” firstly sorts the subsequences of match ascending according to their score. It represents the subsequence as entries in a table of indices and then tries to link these entries according to an input threshold given by the user until the optimum alignment could be found. The algorithm listed in Fig.6 represents how the Merging subsequences function operates.

The algorithm first creates a table of indices, which contains a list of matched subsequences represented by both lead and trail represented by" i and j coordinates"of each matched subsequence, its score, and Mismatch/gap. A preprocessing step is then carried out to discard the very small subsequences of score equals to 2 that represents “only one match”. The algorithm then sorts the entries of the matched subsequences using merge sort.

The user can specify a merging threshold K “the longest common subsequences between the two DNA sequences” that indicates how many subsequence to be merged with the whole entries in the table of indices. The algorithm then merges the entries in the table of indices “matched subsequences” according to a set of rules listed in the DNA sequence alignment sequential algorithm. The merging operation's complexity is O (K N) where K is a constant representing the merging threshold and N is the size of the table of indices. After the merging process the alignment of maximum score can be found.

1- Apply merge sort to the stored results, it sorts the subsequences descending according to their score "A preprocessing step".
2- Discard small subsequences of score equal 2.
3- Create table of indices according to the sorted subsequences.
4- Given that Each entry "aligned subsequence" in the table of indices has a lead and trail and each has i and j coordinates such that:

- i^{st}_{Lead} Is the i coordinate of the first subsequence's lead,
- j^{st}_{Lead} Is the j coordinate of the first subsequence's lead,
- i^{st}_{Trail} Is the i coordinate of the first subsequence's Trail,
- j^{st}_{Trail} Is the j coordinate of the first subsequence's Trail,
- i^{nd}_{Lead} Is the i coordinate of the second subsequence's lead,
- j^{nd}_{Lead} Is the j coordinate of the second subsequence's lead,
- i^{nd}_{Trail} Is the i coordinate of the second subsequence's Trail,
- j^{nd}_{Trail} Is the j coordinate of the second subsequence's Trail,
- $Score^{st\ Seq}$ = First subsequence's score,
- $Score^{nd\ Seq}$ = Second subsequence's score.
- $M\_G = \max[(i^{nd}_{Lead} - i^{st}_{Trail}), (j^{nd}_{Lead} - j^{st}_{Trail})]$ =Gaps and/or Mismatches between the two subsequences,
- Given a threshold K indicating how many subsequence to be merged with the whole entries in the table of indices, Merge the subsequences in the table of indices according to the following rules:

IF ((($i^{st}_{Trail} == i^{nd}_{Lead}$ **AND** $j^{st}_{Trail} < j^{nd}_{Lead}$) **OR**
($j^{st}_{Trail} == j^{nd}_{Lead}$ **AND** $i^{st}_{Trail} < i^{nd}_{Lead}$))
AND $(M\_G < Score^{st\ Seq})$ **AND** $(M\_G + 1 < Score^{st\ Seq})$)
THEN
Total score= $Score^{st\ Seq} + Score^{nd\ Seq} - M\_G - 2$

ELSE IF ((($i^{st}_{Trail} < i^{nd}_{Lead}$) **AND** ($j^{st}_{Trail} < j^{nd}_{Lead}$))
AND($(M\_G - 1) < Score^{st\ Seq}$)
AND ($(M\_G - 1) < Score^{nd Seq}$))
THEN
Total score= $Score^{st\ Seq} + Score^{nd\ Seq} - (M\_G - 1)$

5- Add the merged subsequences to the table.
6- After a round of merging and getting new subsequences, delete from the table of indices the first subsequence used in margining each new subsequence.
7- Go to 3 "another round of margining" until there are no sequences to be merged.

Figure6 DNA Sequence Alignment Sequential Algorithm

The Output Subsystem provides the results by selecting and reporting the sequence of maximum score and minimum gaps and mismatches.

To sum up, the proposed framework aims to compare nucleotides from both the query and the subject sequences, weight the matched subsequences, and then link the matching subsequences. Finally, the optimum local alignment will be the sequence of the highest score.

3 Operation

In order to explain the operation of the proposed system, let us consider an example; perform sequence alignment on the given two DNA sequences S= $T^1C^2G^3C^4A^5G^6A^7$ of length n=7 and T= $T^1C^2C^3A^4G^5C^6A^7$ of length m=7. The operation shown in Table 1 and Table 2 can be summarized as follows:

- Activate a total number of threads equals n*m =49 to perform both the initialization and the sequence matching processes. This can be carried out either by distributing these threads among number of blocks or activating only one block of total number of 49 threads. When activating the threads per block we consider the CUDA architecture limitation: a maximum of 512 threads per block and the maximum number of blocks per grid equals 65535.
- Load the two DNA sequences to the activated threads.
- All threads perform the initialization process "Kernel" simultaneously according to the rules stated in the Initialization Kernel. The initialization matrix will contain the values shown in Table 1.
- After the initialization process, all the threads perform the sequence matching process "kernel" simultaneously according to the rules stated in the Sequence Matching Kernel. The resulting matrix will be as shown in Table 2.

TABLE 1
Matrix Values after Initialization Kernel

	T	C	G	C	A	G	A
T	2	0	0	0	0	0	0
C	0	2	0	2	0	0	0
C	0	2	0	2	0	0	0
A	0	0	0	0	2	0	2
G	0	0	2	0	0	2	0
C	0	2	0	2	0	0	0
A	0	0	0	0	2	0	2

TABLE 2
Matrix Values after Sequence Matching Kernel

	T	C	G	C	A	G	A
T	4	0	0	0	0	0	0
C	0	4	0	2	0	0	0
C	0	2	0	4	0	0	0
A	0	0	0	0	6	0	2
G	0	0	4	0	0	4	0
C	0	2	0	6	0	0	0
A	0	0	0	0	4	0	2

- Pass the resulting matrix to the Host to fill the initial entries of the table of indices as shown in Table 3 according to the rules stated in the Merging subsequences function.
- Perform the preprocessing step to discard very small subsequences of score equals to 2 and sort the entries of the table of indices descending according to their score using merge sort as shown in Table 4.
- Merge the subsequences in the table of indices according to a threshold K indicating how many subsequences are used in merging with the whole entries of the table of indices. Add the merged subsequences to the table. The worst case in this sequential part occurs when the threshold K equals to the total number of entries in the table of indices the algorithm will try to merge each entry in the table of indices with the whole entries.
- Delete from the table of indices the first subsequence used in margining each new subsequence.

TABLE 3
Initial Table of Indices

ID	Subsequence &	Lead	Trail	Score	Gap& Mismatch
0	_	(2,4)	(4,6)	6	0
1	_	(3,2)	(5,4)	6	0
2	_	(0,0)	(1,1)	4	0
3	_	(1,2)	(1,2)	2	0
4	_	(1,5)	(1,5)	2	0
5	_	(3,1)	(3,1)	2	0
6	_	(6,3)	(6,3)	2	0
7	_	(6,6)	(6,6)	2	0

TABLE 4
Table of Indices after Discarding Very Small Subsequences

ID	Subsequence &	Lead	Trail	Score	Gap& Mismatch
0	_	(2,4)	(4,6)	6	0
1	_	(3,2)	(5,4)	6	0
2	_	(0,0)	(1,1)	4	0

- Repeat the merging operation consequently.
- If there is nothing to be merged then select the sequence of maximum score and minimum gaps and mismatches.
- The resulted tables of indices is shown in Table 5 given threshold K=3.

TABLE 5
Complete Round in the Table of Indices at K=3

ID	Subsequence &	Lead	Trail	Score	Gap& Mismatch
0	2&1	(0,0)	(5,4)	9	1
1	2&0	(0,0)	(4,6)	8	2
2	0	(2,4)	(4,6)	6	0
3	1	(3,2)	(5,4)	6	0

- The best alignment starts at lead (0, 0) and ends with the trail (5,4) with score equals 9 and Gap and Mismatch equals 1 which is indicated at sequence number 0 at the final round in the table of indices.

4 Performance Evaluation

The performance of the proposed algorithm is measured by comparing the execution time of the NVidia GPU/CPU version of the preprocessing, sequence matching and subsequences merging running time of the DNA sequence alignment proposed algorithm versus both the sequential execution of the same proposed algorithm of sequence comparison [10], and the sequential Smith-Waterman algorithm [3] used for DNA sequence alignment implemented on the same machine.

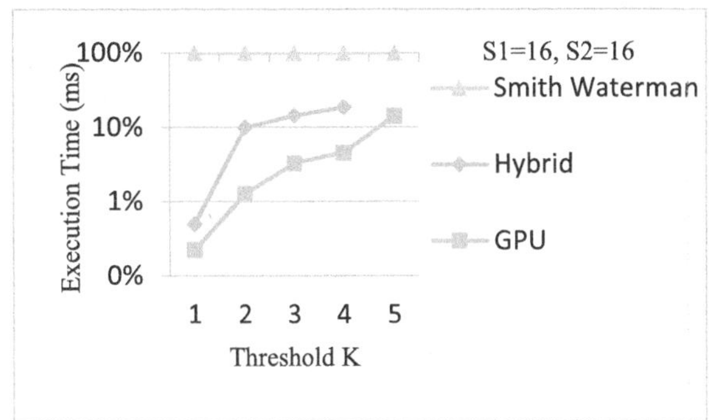

Fig. 7 Hybrid system and Smith-Waterman execution times at S1=16 and S2=16 BP

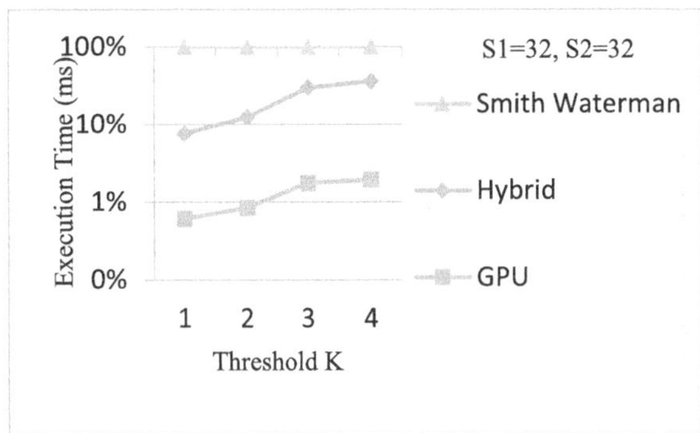

Fig. 8 Hybrid system and Smith-Waterman execution times at S1=32 and S2=32 BP

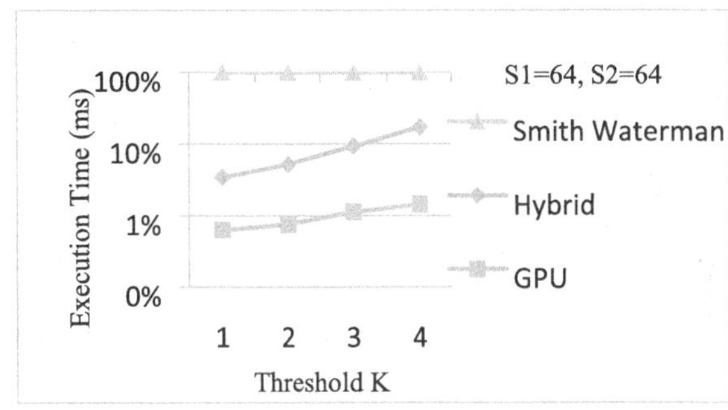

Fig. 9 Hybrid system and Smith-Waterman execution times at S1=64 and S2=64 BP

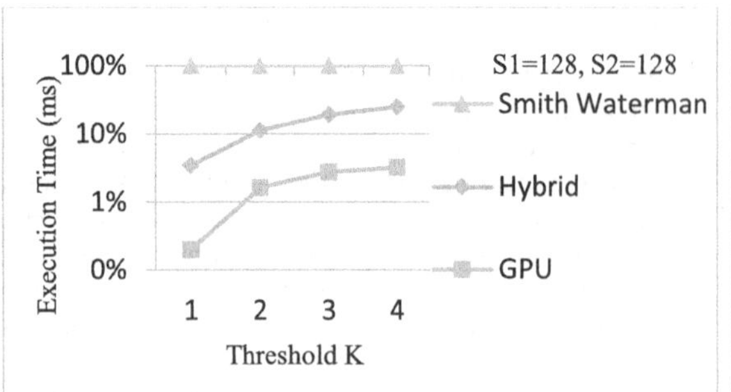

Figure 10 Hybrid system and Smith-Waterman execution times at S1=128 and S2=128 BP

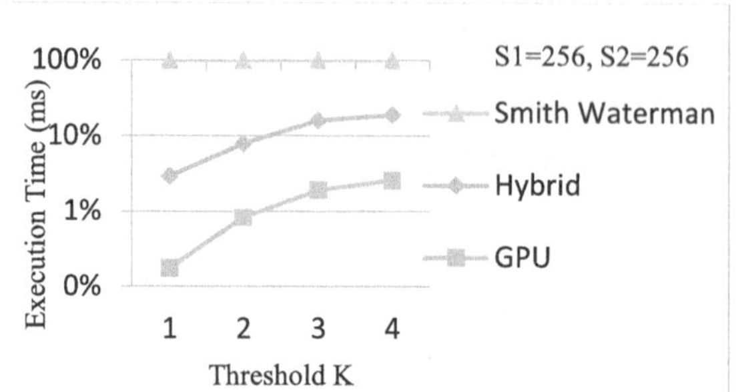

Figure 11 Hybrid system and Smith-Waterman execution times at S1=256 and S2=256 BP

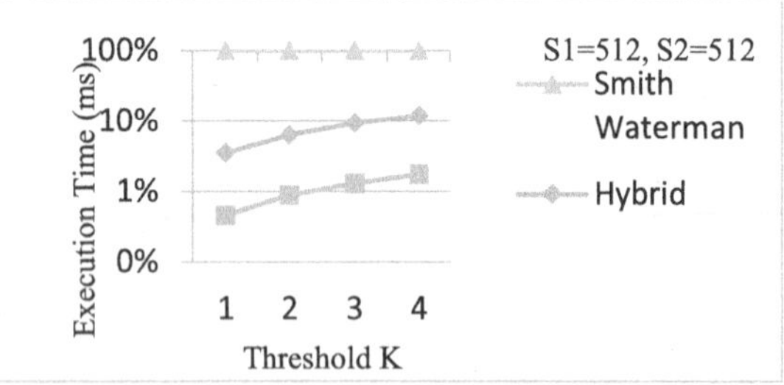

Figure 12 Hybrid system and Smith-Waterman execution times at S1=512 and S2=512 BP

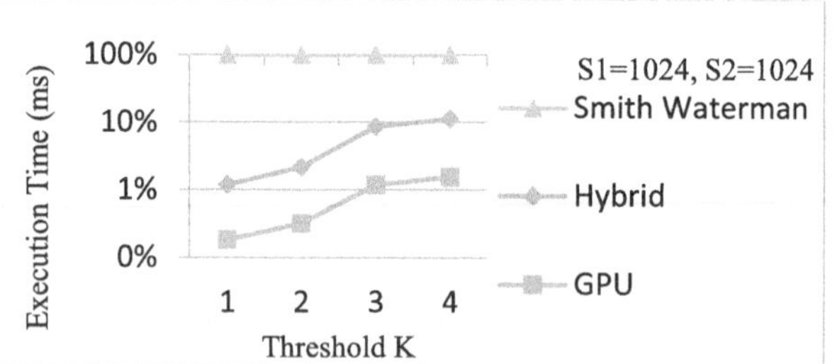

Figure 13 Hybrid system and Smith-Waterman execution times at S1=1024 and S2=1024 BP

Table 6
The Proposed GPU Implementation, The Hybrid System and Smith-Waterman Execution Times for Different Sequence Sizes.

Sequence's Size		Total Hybrid System Time (Parallel Matching GPU +Sequential Rounds) (ms)					Total Hybrid System "parallel + Sequential Execution "(ms)					Smith Waterman
S1	S2	T at K=1	T at K=2	T at K=3	T at K=4	T at K=5	T at K=1	T at K=2	T at K=3	T at K=4	T at K=5	
16	16	0.1389	0.3571	0.3277	0.4233	0.9589	0.0141	0.4982	0.6718	0.8997	3.2393	5.19781
32	32	0.4010	0.4964	1.4243	1.0972	1.6248	1.3449	2.3729	7.1229	9.5471	6.1988	17.983
64	64	1.3591	1.3024	1.8715	2.5768	4.2268	2.1330	3.3937	6.6120	13.9064	20.1797	73.4924
128	128	2.3459	14.8844	15.9078	19.8200	12.8086	9.8944	31.1223	58.8689	83.9278	85.9526	291.548
256	256	4.6377	16.6957	58.8322	106.7312	57.8178	29.8864	81.0289	177.6650	212.0680	256.1450	1059.95
512	512	16.7758	33.3471	50.2516	66.9213	386.2223	106.7730	194.8590	299.6170	390.4650	2328.3000	3397.86
1024	1024	41.3386	101.2055	282.8225	305.7553	316.2523	138.7090	260.3110	1115.4600	1488.2800	1852.3400	13817.8

The list of figures from Fig.7 to Fig.13 shows the Hybrid system execution time using GPU, Parallel architecture in [10] and Smith-Waterman at different sequence sizes starting from 16 bp 'Base pair' to 1024 bp.

The GPU execution time for both preprocessing and sequence matching is recorded at different input sequences' size and the CPU execution time for the merging subsequences is calculated for different thresholds as shown in Table 6.

Results are obtained using Intel Core i5 2430M 2.4GHZ, 4 GB DDR3 Memory and NVidia GeForce GT540M GPU with

96 CUDA Cores with 1GB device memory. All the implementations run on Windows7 with Display Driver285.86.

The methods are implemented using Microsoft Visual Studio 2010 and NVidia GPU Computing SDK 4.1.

5 Conclusion

The proposed framework combines both a parallel and a sequential algorithm to speed up the solution of the pairwise DNA sequence alignment. The architecture of the hybrid system uses the GPGPUs. It has been observed that the proposed framework can provide an alignment quality comparable to that of Smith-Waterman algorithm while consuming significantly less time.

The target of the proposed framework is to compare all the nucleotides from both the query and the target sequences simultaneously then extract the subsequences of match and try to merge them to find the optimum alignment according to the maximum score and minimum gap/mismatch.

The system is considered a step towards a complete parallel processing architecture to solve computationally intensive applications of DNA

6 References

[1] Michael Schatz, Cole Trapnell, Arthur Delcher, Amitabh Varshney, *"High-throughput sequence alignment using Graphics Processing Units,"* BMC Bioinformatics, Vol. 8, No. 1, 2007.

[2] T. F. Smith and M. S. Waterman, *"Identification of common molecular subsequences,"* J Mol Biol, 147(1), pp. 195-197, March 1981.

[3] T. Smith and M. Waterman, *"Identification of common molecular subsequences,"* J. Mol. Bio., (147):195–197, 1981.

[4] J. Setubal and J. Meidanis, *Introduction to Computational Molecular Biology*, PWS Publishing Company, 1997.

[5] Terence Hwa and Michael Lässig, *"Similarity Detection and Localization,"* Physical Review Letters Volume: 76, Issue: 2, 1995.

[6] Jun Sung Yoon and Won-Hyong Chung, *"A GPU-accelerated bioinformatics application for large-scale protein interaction networks,"* Asia Pacific Bioinformatics Conference, 2011.

[7] Rafia Inam, *"An Introduction to GPGPU Programming - CUDA Architecture,"* Mälardalen University, Mälardalen Real-Time Research Centre, 2011.

[8] NVIDIA CORPORATION, CUDA Programming Guide, *http://developer.nvidia.com/category/zone/cuda-zone*

[9] Svetlin A Manavski and Giorgio Vallel, *"CUDA compatible GPU cards as efficient hardware accelerators for Smith-Waterman sequence alignment,"* BMC Bioinformatics 2008.

[10] Heba Khaled , Hossam M Faheem , Tayseer Hasan , Saeed Ghoneimy,*"Design of a Hybrid System for DNA Sequence Alignment,"* Proceedings of The International MultiConference of Engineers and Computer Scientists 2008 , pp162-167.

Majority logic decoding: a discrete method for detecting differential expression in RNA-Seq data

Humberto Ortiz-Zuazaga[1], **Roberto Arce Corretjer**[1]
[1]Department of Computer Science, University of Puerto Rico Rio Piedras, San Juan, Puerto Rico

Abstract— *We present a novel method of analysis of RNA-Seq data based on majority-logic-decoding. We apply the analysis to a simulation of differential gene expression and compare to a typical statistical analysis with linear models. Our technique results in a markedly improved false positive rate.*

Keywords: next-gen sequencing, finite dynamical systems, differential expression

1. Introduction

Gene regulatory networks are a valuable tool in the analysis of microarray data, and in the description of biological systems. A well established current in microarray analysis is the reverse engineering problem: given a set of genes and a set of expression measurements under varying conditions, determine the nature of transcriptional regulation among the genes. A rich tradition of discrete Boolean approaches to this problem exists [1], [2], [3], [4], [5]. Recent research into finite fields as a richer and more efficient alternative to Boolean logic has proven fruitful [6], [7], [8]. We have developed a series of techniques for error-correction and clustering based on finite fields [9].

The same variety of tools is not available for RNA-Seq [10] analysis, although the two experimental techniques share goals and some analytical framework. Extending FDS to the analysis of RNA-Seq data will bring a new approach to the quickly growing corpus of RNA-Seq data. Our hypothesis is that FDS's discrete nature is suited to modeling digital expression measurements. To test this hypothesis, we apply our techniques to a simulated gene expression experiment.

2. Methods

2.1 Discretization of expression

1) Take base 2 logarithm of counts
2) Compute mean of the control samples counts of each transcript.
3) Subtract mean value of control samples from each treated sample count, to make counts zero centered
4) Compute standard deviation of treated samples
5) Divide each treated sample by the standard deviation
6) Pick a discretization threshold t
7) For each sample, if normalized counts $> 1t$, gene is upregulated, $< -1t$ gene is downregulated, otherwise no change
8) Compute majority logic decoding (mld) value over all samples for each gene

2.2 Majority logic decoding

Upregulated samples are encoded as '+', downregulated as '-', and unchanged as '0'. The discretization then yields a list of symbols for every sample of each gene. Majority logic decoding looks as the symbols for every sample and selects the symbol that appears in a majority of samples. This procedure has been adapted from a similar procedure described for microarray data in [9].

2.3 Verification

To validate our methods, we simulate gene expression counts and apply our techniques. We use *flux simulator* [11], a tool for generating simulated RNA-Seq data. We generate 20 random gene expression experiments using the *Drosphila melanogaster* genome release 70 from ENSEMBL [12], and the default flux-simulator parameters. These 20 runs are divided into 10 control samples and 10 treated samples. We randomly select 2000 transcripts from the 29,173 present in the simulated data. The 2000 are divided into 4 groups of 500 each, and we add 100 and 200 to the treated or the controls in each group, to simulate a spike-in experiment.

3. Results

Figures 1 shows the variance vs mean for the simulated data. The plot in Figure 2 shows the same plot for a similar sample of data from *Drosphila melanogaster* [13] from a public repository of RNA-Seq data [14].

We applied mld to the simulated spike-in data. Since the mld is sensitive to the choice of threshold value t, we sweep over a range of values and compute the false positive and false negative rate. We compare these rates to a linear model of differential expression using the `lmFit` [15] function in the `limma` [16] package from bioconductor [17]. Figure 3 shows the ROC curves for mld and the linear model. For $t = 1.3$, we correctly

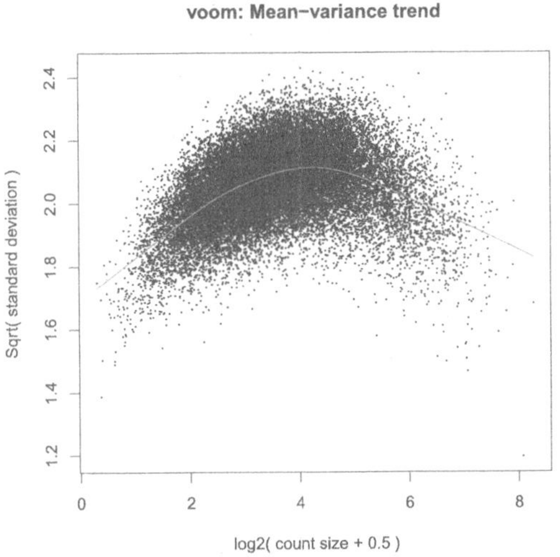

Fig. 1: Mean-variance relationship of simulated data.

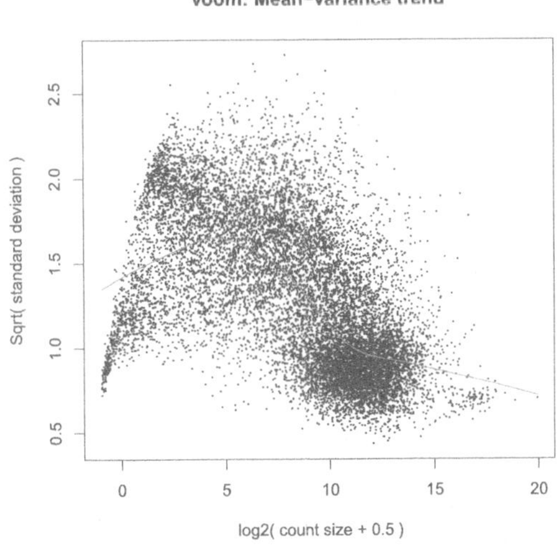

Fig. 2: Mean-variance relationship of real data.

identified 1436 out of 2000 positives, while predicting 2779 false positives from the 27,166 negatives.

The linear model fit can be used to predict the probability of differential expression for each transcript. Figure 4 is a plot of the log odds of differential expression versus the log ratio of expresison for the 2000 spike-in transcripts.

4. Discussion

Our method of simulating differential expression of RNA-Seq data seems to produce data very similar to real RNA-Seq data, although Figure 1 shows reduced variance and mean expression compared to Figure 2.

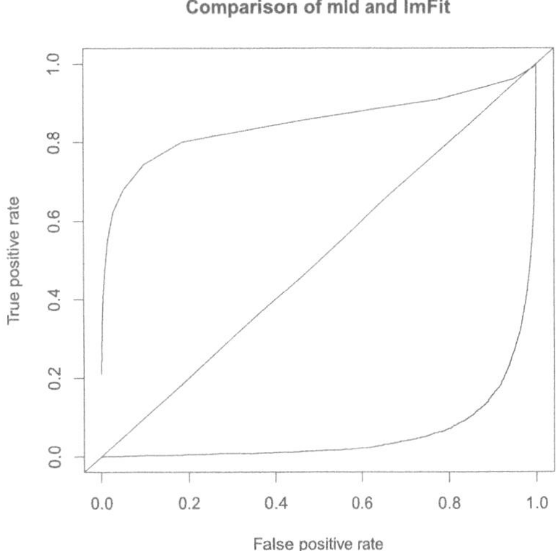

Fig. 3: ROC curve for mld (upper curve) and a linear model fit (lower curve) on the simulated spike-in experiment.

We have described a modification of majority logic decoding to handle discrete gene expression data such as produced by RNA-Seq experiments. We have tested the method by comparing with linear models such as those produced by `lmFit`. On simulated spike-in data, our method results in a markedly improved sensitivity. Figure 4 shows that linear modelling of the spike-in transcripts predicts log ratios of expression different from zero for almost all spike-ins, but the large majority of spike-in transcripts show no statistical support for differential expression. It is unlikely that refinements of the linear model would be able to distinguish the spike-in genes from the negatives. The mld technique, conceptually simpler, demonstrates better specificity, while keeping the false positive rate low.

5. Future studies

The spike-in experiment we simulated is a simple gene expression experiment. We want to extend our simulation technique to allow simulation of biologically relevant differential expression. In particular, we would like to simulate a gene regulatory network response and then use our mld technique to recover changes in expression at different stages. This more complex simulation will allow us to test other FDS techniques and adapt them to RNA-Seq data. The next step after that would be to apply these techniques to real RNA-Seq data.

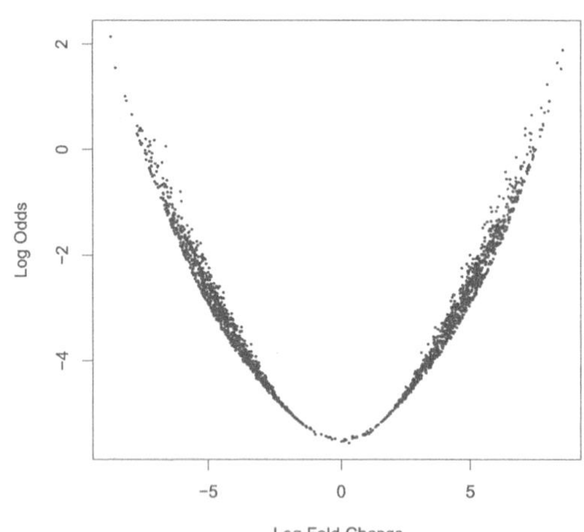

Fig. 4: Volcanoplot of spike-in genes.

6. Acknowledgments

The authors received partial support from the PR-INBRE grant (P20GM103475) from the National Institute for General Medical Sciences of the National Institutes of Health.

References

[1] T. Akutsu, S. Kuahara, O. Maruyama, and S. Miyano, "Identification of gene regulatory networks by strategic gene disruptions and gene overexpressions," in *Proceedings of the 9th ACM-SIAM Symposium on Discrete Algorithms*, H. Karloff, Ed. ACM Press, 1998.

[2] T. E. Ideker, V. Thorsson, and R. M. Karp, "Discovery of regulatory interactions through perturbation: Inference and experimental design," in *Pacific Symposium on Biocomputing*, 2000, pp. 302–313.

[3] S. A. Kauffman, "Metabolic stability and epigenesis in randomly constructed genetic nets," *J. Theor. Biol.*, vol. 22, pp. 437–467, 1969.

[4] ——, *The Origins of Order.* New York, Oxford: Oxford University Press, 1993.

[5] S. Liang, S. Fuhrman, and R. Somogyi, "REVEAL, a general reverse engineering algorithm for inference of genetic network architectures." *Pac Symp Biocomput*, pp. 18–29, 1998.

[6] R. Laubenbacher and B. Stigler, "Dynamic networks," *Adv. in Al. Math.*, vol. 26, pp. 237–251, 2001.

[7] O. Moreno, D. Bollman, and M. A. Aviñó-Diaz, "Finite dynamical systems, linear automata and finite fields," *2002 WSEAS Int. Conf. on System Science Alied Mathematics & Computer Science and Power Engineering Systems*, pp. 1481–1483, 2002, also to appear in the International Journal of Computer Research.

[8] M. A. Aviñó-Díaz, E. Green, and O. Moreno, "Applications of finite fields to dynamical systems and reverse engineering problems," *Proceedings of the 19th ACM Symposium on Applied Computing SAC*, 2004.

[9] H. Ortiz-Zuazaga, S. Peña de Ortiz, and O. Moreno de Ayala, "Error correction and clustering gene expression data using majority logic decoding," in *Proceedings of The 2007 International Conference on Bioinformatics and Computational Biology (BIOCOMP'07)*, Las Vegas, Nevada, USA, June 2007.

[10] U. Nagalakshmi, Z. Wang, K. Waern, C. Shou, D. Raha, M. Gerstein, and M. Snyder, "The transcriptional landscape of the yeast genome defined by rna sequencing," *Science*, vol. 320, no. 5881, pp. 1344–9, Jun 2008.

[11] T. Griebel, B. Zacher, P. Ribeca, E. Raineri, V. Lacroix, R. Guigó, and M. Sammeth, "Modelling and simulating generic RNA-Seq experiments with the flux simulator," *Nucleic Acids Research*, vol. 40, no. 20, pp. 10 073–10 083, Nov. 2012. [Online]. Available: http://nar.oxfordjournals.org/content/40/20/10073

[12] P. Flicek, I. Ahmed, M. R. Amode, D. Barrell, K. Beal, S. Brent, D. Carvalho-Silva, P. Clapham, G. Coates, S. Fairley, S. Fitzgerald, L. Gil, C. García-Girón, L. Gordon, T. Hourlier, S. Hunt, T. Juettemann, A. K. Kähäri, S. Keenan, M. Komorowska, E. Kulesha, I. Longden, T. Maurel, W. M. McLaren, M. Muffato, R. Nag, B. Overduin, M. Pignatelli, B. Pritchard, E. Pritchard, H. S. Riat, G. R. S. Ritchie, M. Ruffier, M. Schuster, D. Sheppard, D. Sobral, K. Taylor, A. Thormann, S. Trevanion, S. White, S. P. Wilder, B. L. Aken, E. Birney, F. Cunningham, I. Dunham, J. Harrow, J. Herrero, T. J. P. Hubbard, N. Johnson, R. Kinsella, A. Parker, G. Spudich, A. Yates, A. Zadissa, and S. M. J. Searle, "Ensembl 2013," *Nucleic Acids Res*, vol. 41, no. Database issue, pp. D48–55, Jan 2013.

[13] B. R. Graveley, A. N. Brooks, J. W. Carlson, M. O. Duff, J. M. Landolin, L. Yang, C. G. Artieri, M. J. van Baren, N. Boley, B. W. Booth, J. B. Brown, L. Cherbas, C. A. Davis, A. Dobin, R. Li, W. Lin, J. H. Malone, N. R. Mattiuzzo, D. Miller, D. Sturgill, B. B. Tuch, C. Zaleski, D. Zhang, M. Blanchette, S. Dudoit, B. Eads, R. E. Green, A. Hammonds, L. Jiang, P. Kapranov, L. Langton, N. Perrimon, J. E. Sandler, K. H. Wan, A. Willingham, Y. Zhang, Y. Zou, J. Andrews, P. J. Bickel, S. E. Brenner, M. R. Brent, P. Cherbas, T. R. Gingeras, R. A. Hoskins, T. C. Kaufman, B. Oliver, and S. E. Celniker, "The developmental transcriptome of drosophila melanogaster," *Nature*, Dec. 2010.

[14] A. C. Frazee, B. Langmead, and J. T. Leek, "ReCount: a multi-experiment resource of analysis-ready RNA-seq gene count datasets," *BMC Bioinformatics*, vol. 12, p. 449, 2011, PMID: 22087737. [Online]. Available: http://www.ncbi.nlm.nih.gov/pubmed/22087737

[15] G. Smyth, R. Gentleman, V. Carey, S. Dudoit, R. Irizarry, and W. Huber, "Limma: linear models for microarray data." in *Bioinformatics and Computational Biology Solutions using R and Bioconductor.* Springer, New York, 2005, pp. 397–420.

[16] G. K. Smyth, "Linear models and empirical bayes methods for assessing differential expression in microarray experiments." *Stat Appl Genet Mol Biol*, vol. 3, p. Article3, 2004.

[17] R. C. Gentleman, V. J. Carey, D. M. Bates, *et al.*, "Bioconductor: Open software development for computational biology and bioinformatics," *Genome Biology*, vol. 5, p. R80, 2004. [Online]. Available: http://genomebiology.com/2004/5/10/R80

Research on genome characteristics for minimal genome designing tool in Streptococcus

Chung Sei Rhee[1], Sehi L'Yi[1], Whi Ju Hong[2], Sehee Jeong[3] ,DaeHyun Chung[2], and Young-Chang Kim[3]
[1]Department of Software Engineering, Chungbuk National Univ., Cheong-ju, Korea
[2]Department of Information Statistics, Chungbuk National Univ., Cheong-ju, Korea
[3]Department of Microbiology, Chungbuk National Univ. , Cheong-ju, Korea

Abstract - *Synthetic biology has enormous scope and many application. In this study, we analyzed genome for minimal genome design using essential genes which is early stage of study in Synthetic biology. We build a database to presume specific gene and essential gene and analyzed genome characteristics in Streptococcus and validate it using statistical reliability test. The number of essential genes we found are 478 which is little larger than essential genes provided by DEG. In the future, the algorithm for essential gene presumption will be utilize to analyze all the sequence identified bacteria.*

Keywords: Minimal Genome, Essential Gene, Specific Gene, Streptococcus

1 Introduction

The minimal Genome is a minimal set of protein that make it possible to live a life as a cell. As genome project successes, it is able to get genome information of various of species. Moreover, it is also able to have various of genome analysis [1].

The most important thing on minimal genome design is finding genes which make them survive as a cell. This means that the essential concept on minimal genome is essential gene. The essential gene is defined as a gene that is necessary for normal growth, mostly identified by a mutation experiment. However, the result by a experiment changes depending on experimenter, experiment environment and gene characteristics like gene duplication, pleiotropy and conditional activities or inactivities[2].

Therefore, we approach with using basic concept of bioinformatics to presume essential gene more correctly. For this, we need a new definition for essential gene. Essential gene is explained as a gene that is necessary for live. So in this research, we define essential gene as a gene that all the individual genome keep for survival and presume them by protein sequence analysis.[3].

It is necessary to have not only essential gene but also information of essential gene location and distribution to design minimal genome. What's more, we need information about gene arrangement to perform a specific function. It is because, gene location, distribution and arrangement influence greatly on expression and life metabolism.

In this research, we select necessary information which is for the minimal genome design, and we provide a method to analyze it and arrange the base for a minimal genome designing tool.

2 Method and result

2.1 Determination of grouping algorithm standard

It is necessary to have a gene annotation to presume essential gene and specific gene. For this process, we analyze DNA sequence and put genes in same group to annotate same ID if these DNA sequences are similar which is able to calculate the similarity with some values that are made from sequence analysis. We call this process of grouping gene as grouping algorithm.

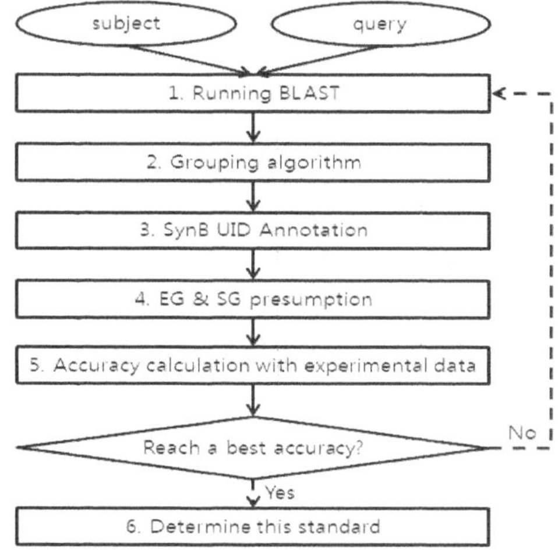

Figure 1. Grouping algorithm flow chart

The process of determining the weight of each values that are made from the BLAST program is shown as [Fig.1][4]. To determine the weights of each output values, we used two sample genome data in this research, Streptococcus Pneumoniae TIGR4 and Streptococcus Sanguinis SK36, which their information of experimentally presumed essential gene are provided from DEG. By the process 1, we ran BLAST with these two genome data and made sequence analysis result as output. With this result values, we gave a different weight to each these values and grouped genes as a result. In process 3, we annotated each gene and presume essential gene and specific gene by the process 4. Finally, calculated the accuracy form this result of essential gene presumption with DEG data, and repeat process 2 – 5 until the accuracy reaches the best score.

2.2 Reliability of grouping algorithm verification

To verify reliability of the standards in grouping algorithm, this research used Sensitivity, Specificity, and Accuracy. Sensitivity is the probability that essential genes of DEG are analyzed as essential gene also in our analysis result. Specificity is the probability that non-essential genes of DEG are actually analyzed as the same in our result. And accuracy is the probability that shows the degree of correspondence between the results in the whole specimen.

Table 1. Grouping result case 1 (standard with streptococcus pneumoniae TIGR4)

DEG \ SynB	(+)	(-)
(+)	120	96
(-)	125	1271

Table 2. Grouping result case 2 (standard with streptococcus sanguinis SK36)

DEG \ SynB	(+)	(-)
(+)	120	105
(-)	98	1243

Table 3. Reliability Verification of grouping algorithm

	Case 1(%)	Case 2(%)
Sensitivity	48.98	53.33
Specificity	91.05	92.69
Accuracy	86.29	87.04

If the Accuracy value is over 80%, it means that the results made from determination of grouping algorithm standard is reliable. Therefore, the results that we infer are reliable as well.

2.3 Essential gene & Specific Gene Presumption

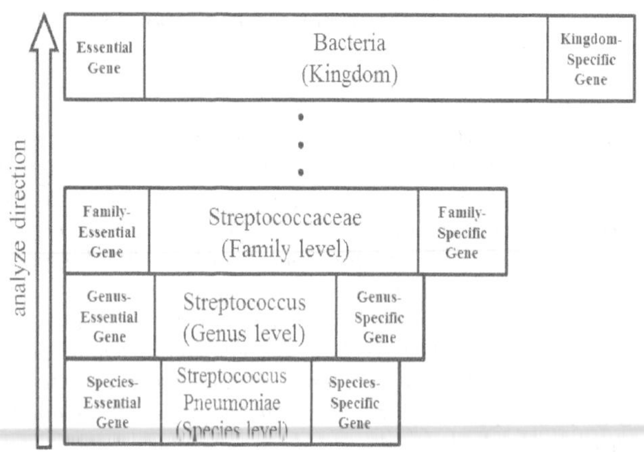

Figure 2. Process of incremental Essential gene & specific gene presumption

To distinguish presumed essential gene from all the genome with essential gene from Streptococcus, we call the essential gene that are presumed in Streptococcus genus as genus-essential gene, just like [Fig. 2]. When we presume genus-essential gene and extend the analysis to Streptococcaceae family level, we call the essential gene as family-essential gene. As we analyze essential gene from bacteria kingdom level, we finally find the essential genes that meet the theory that a gene is essential gene which all the individual genome keep for survival.

Whereas, there are genes which are only kept by one specific genome. In this case, the gene represent the characteristics of genome and this will be excellent information to design a minimal genome that represent the characteristics of specific genome and specific level. In this research, we call these gene as specific gene. Like essential gene, when we analyze specific gene in species level, we call it species-specific gene, and so on.

The number of presumed genus-essential gene is 478(eliminated duplicated genes in single genome). The number of genus-essential gene and species-specific gene in each genome are shown as [Fig. 3].

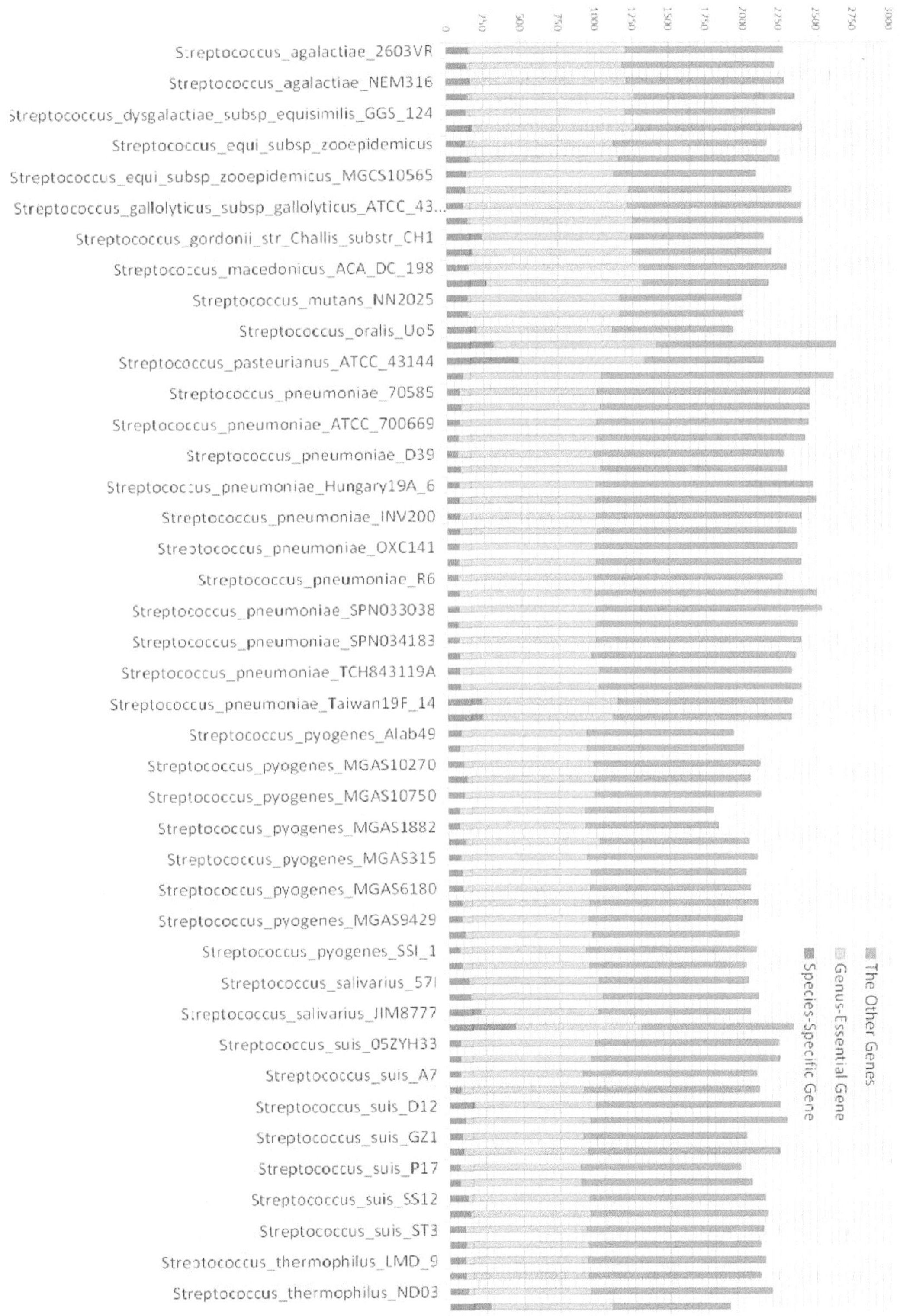

Figure 3. Number of genus-essential gene & species-specific gene

2.4 Study on Locational Gene Distribution

We divided genome equally to a hundred sections just like cutting apple pie and then investigated the distribution of genus-essential gene. As a result, there were some distribution characteristics of genus-essential gene which are shown in [Fig. 4].

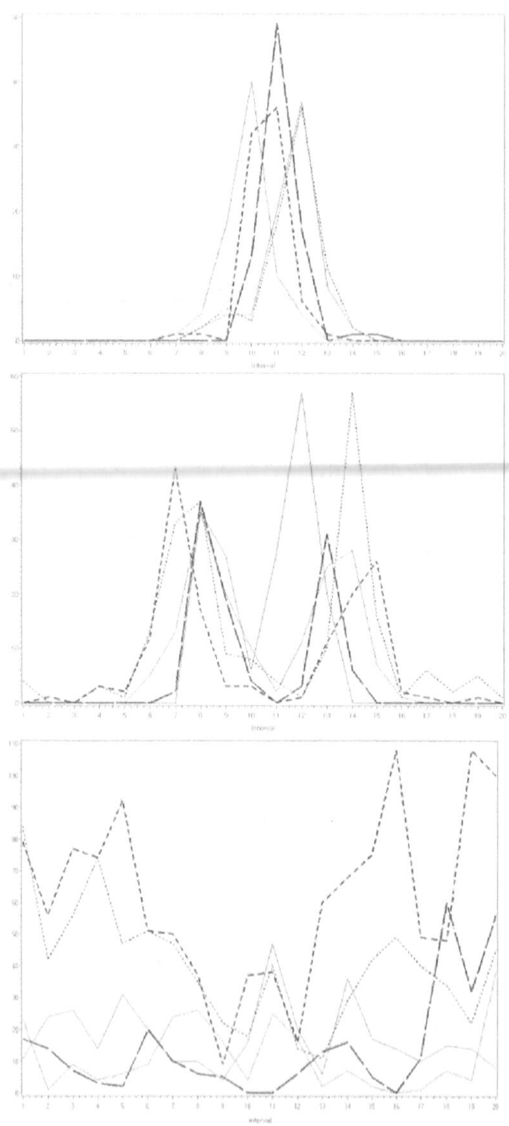

Figure 4. Essential gene's locational distribution.

The X axis is the each section of all genome in streptococcus. The Y axis is the frequency of the each genus-essential gene. One line represent on essential gene. Center line is the location of estimated origin.

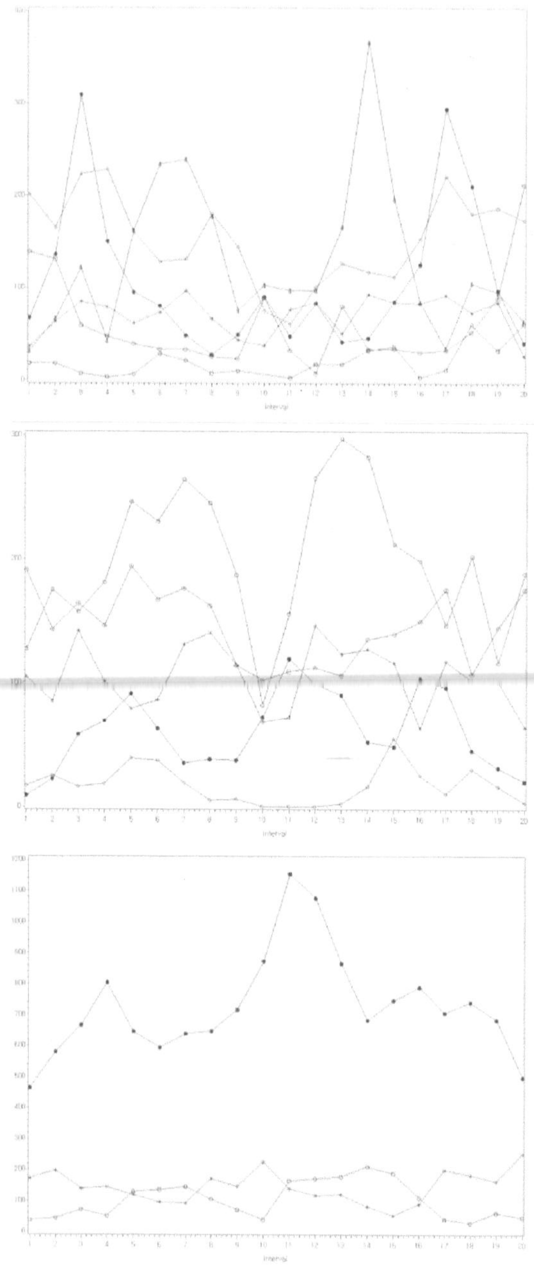

Figure 5. Locational distribution of genus-essential gene's function.

We also investigated the functional distribution to find the characteristics of Streptococcus. COGs(Clusters of Orthologous Groups) is used for function identification. The result is shown in [Fig. 5].

The X axis is the each section of all genome in streptococcus. The Y axis is the frequency of the each function. One line represent on function. Center line is the location of estimated origin.

2.5 Strand Pattern Analysis

In this research, we defined this strand pattern similarity. By conducting the chi-square test with the estimated transpose linear regression prediction equation with the 77 randomly selected genome out of all 82 genome in streptococcus, we verified if the equation is adequate. The null hypothesis is independent from the prediction equation and the other 5 species that was not selected which are stated in [Tab. 6]. And the alternative hypothesis is subordinate with the prediction equation and the 5 species. The p-value of the 5 species is independent from the prediction equation estimated by the null hypothesis. We can see that it is subordinate when it is dismissed.

Table 4. Selected genome to verify predicted equation

Num.	Genome
1	Streptococcus equi subsp. zooepidemicus MGCS10565
2	Streptococcus pneumoniae 70585
3	Streptococcus pyogenes MGAS10394
4	Streptococcus salivarius 57.I
5	Streptococcus suis 98HAH33

Table 5. The result of equality test

Genome Name	Chisq	P Value	Test
NC_011134	623.532	1	Do not reject H0
NC_012468	565.506	1	Do not reject H0
NC_006086	604.379	1	Do not reject H0
CP002888	621.476	1	Do not reject H0
NC_009443	852.34	1	Do not reject H0

In the result of this research, it is revealed that strand of genome in streptococcus tend to distribute like this equation.

$$\text{Identity(spercent)} = 1.1943 + 0.9756*\text{spline(interval)} \quad (1)$$

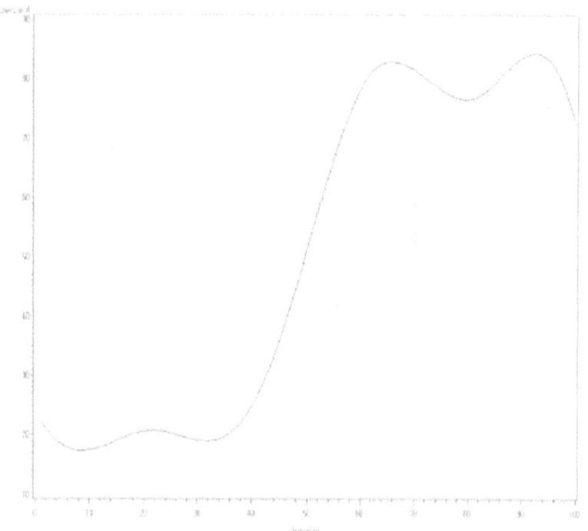

Figure 6. Streptococcus' strand pattern disposition

The X axis shows the 100 sections of the genome of the randomly selected 77 genome is streptococcus. And the Y axis is the ratio of the + patterns of each section. The sum of each section's +, - pattern is 100. According to the graph above, when the standard number is 50, the + patterns appears as 25 on the left, and the – pattern on the right higher than 80. So in this case, it is a + pattern.

3 Conclusions

The number of genus-essential gene that are presumed in this research are 478 which is little a lot comparing with experimentally presumed essential gene from DEG. For example, the number of experimentally presumed essential gene of Streptococcus pneumoniae is 244, and the case of Streptococcus sanguini is 218, in most 779 of Vibrio cholerae N16961's(http://tubic.tju.edu.cn/deg/). However, we cannot trust the result of biological experiment on the whole because it changes depending on a lot of situations. However this difference in number of essential gene between experimental result and result with bioinformatics way will be decrease when the genome information of Streptococcus are identified more because the number of genus-essential gene presumption will be decrease while we extend the analysis with more object. This result can be utilized on analyzing other microorganism essential gene with bioinformatics, especially it can be utilized to investigate the combination of essential gene which is root of life, that is to say minimal genome by adjusting this to all the genome sequence identified bacteria.

4 References

[1] A. Mushegian, "The minimal genome concept", Current Opinion in Genetics & Development, Vol. 9, Issue 6, pp709-714, 1999

[2] K. Kemphues, "Essential Genes", WormBook, ed. The C. elegans Research Community, WormBook,

doi/10.1895/wormbook.1.57.1, 2005, http://www.wormbook.org.

[3] Y. Lin, R. R. Zhang, "Putative essential and core-essential genes in Mycoplasma genomes", Scientific Reports, Vol. 1, DOI: 10.1038/srep00053, 2011

[4] S. F. Altschul, W. Gish, W. Miller , E. W. Myers, D. J. Lipman, "Basic local alignment search tool.", 215(3):403-10, Journal of Molecular Biology, 1990

[5] J. Puechberty, C. Blaineau, S. Meghamla, L. Crobu, M. Pagès and P. Bastien1, "Compared genomics of the strand switch region of Leishmania chromosome 1 reveal a novel genus-specific gene and conserved structural features and sequence motifs", BMC Genomics 2007, 8-57

[6] F. Gao, C. T. Zhang, "DoriC: a database of oriC regions in bacterial genomes.", bioinformatics, 1866-1867

V.I.S SYSTEM (2)

DNA Sequencing and reading from eye photo

Dr. Boucherit Taieb
BOUCHERIT Laboratory, 53 road SALHI Houari – (hippodrome – saint Eugène) 31000 Oran, Algeria.
Sponsored by **Dr.Abdelmalek Boudiaf Prefect of Oran**, Algeria, Algeria

Abstract – The V.I.S. system is an important discovery. it allows us in addition to the visualization of pathological organs, which we outlined in our subsequent publication Worlds Comp 2011, to view the chromosomes in a remarkable way and therefore to see the composition of DNA with an accuracy defying any method known today. We can get from the photo of the eye, the reading and the sequencing of the DNA.

1. Introduction

It's a discovery which allows us to visualize chromosomes and DNA from the photo of the eye, classically to see the DNA, it is necessary to use a whole log and complex process, namely several stages, to take a sample of the person with its consent, obtain chemically the insulation of chromosomes, and radiologically, to bombard them with X rays in order to get a print of nucleotides, all this in a time exceeding several days. Our method is unique, from the photo of the eye of a person we can have the image of its chromosomes and its specific DNA in a time not exceeding one hour.

I put kindly to your attention the images obtained by the V.I.S system and the progress, you can judge for yourself the quality of these images which are unique in the world.

2. Equipements and Methods

2.1 Equipment

Equipment is very simple; it consists of a camera and computer,

2.1.1 Methods

- Photo of the eye.
- Front view photo of the eye
- Camera without flash
- Environment slightly enlightened without important source of light
- The "*vitreous imagery system*" makes it possible to visualize the images of the patient's organs in the vitreous humor , these images are laid out in bulk, with sometimes the repetition more than one organ,same organ with different view.
- We resize each image of organs obtained in the humor vitreous in order to isolate it. we isolate an organ visualized by the technique of V.I.S system and we use use the second technique wich involves the display the chromosomes in the organ.

2.2 Theory & explanation

The cell is the Small functional unit alive , the human being amounts to approximally 100 billons of cells, they are grouped indifferrent tissues and organs , these cells are grouped into differenttissues and organs and are different from one tissue to another and from one organ to another, the cells consists of a cytoplasm and anucleus chromosomes that composed of a long molecules called DNA or desoxyribonucleic acid.
The DNA is in the form of strands twisted arond each other forming a double helix, two srands are formed of nucleotides consisting of a sugar, a phosphorus and nitrogen bases , these nitrogenous bases are four : A : adenine T : thymine C : cytosine G : guanine , these two strands of DNA are linked to each other through these base pairs , adenine binds to thymine and cytosine with guanine , the order of the arrangement of these bases determines séquences and a change in sequences can entail diseases.

In practice, to have the DNA of an individual, we make a sample of blood of saliva or other; after a sample of blood, we proceed to several stages to have the DNA, the blood is spin-dried, we collect white blood cells or leucocytes which contain the DNA. The second phase consists in releasing the DNA by adding reagent and by proceeding to a wash; then comes the purification and so we realize a precipitation. The images obtained by the V.I.S. system are images < < data bank > >, as we explained it in our previous publication: it means that they contain all information appropriate for this organ; these images contain those of the chromosomes. For that purpose, we use a second technique which consists of the display of chromosomes. The DNA or the deoxyribonucleic acid containing all the information, thus all the previously explained stages by the current techniques are not acceptable for the V.I.S. system because it gives directly the image of the chromosome and by increase the double helix DNA.

2.3 Processus et technique: V.I.S. system serves to display organs at the level of the vitreous humor.S. Système pour visualiser les organes au niveau de l'humeur vitrée

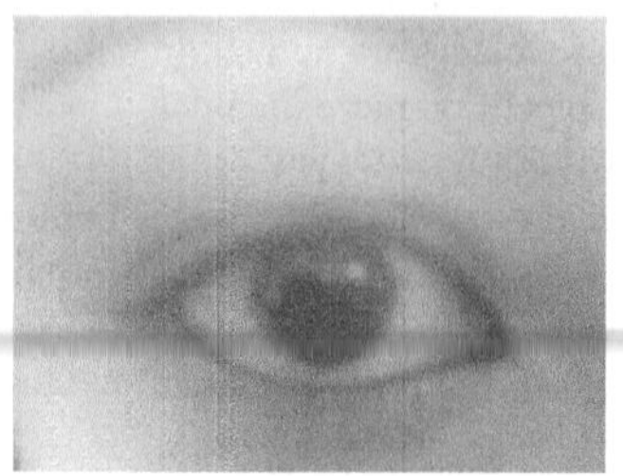

Img 1 Img 1 a

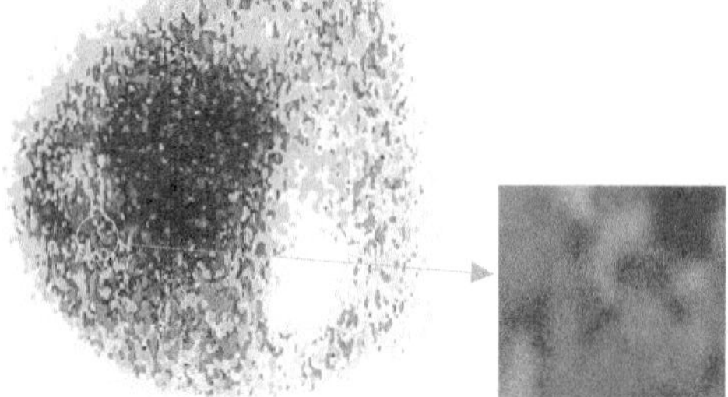

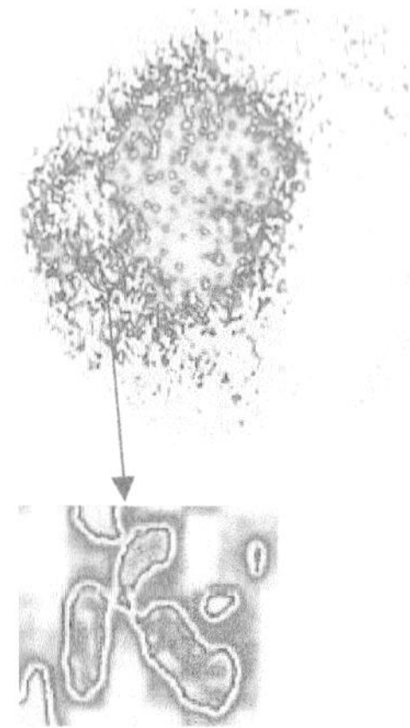

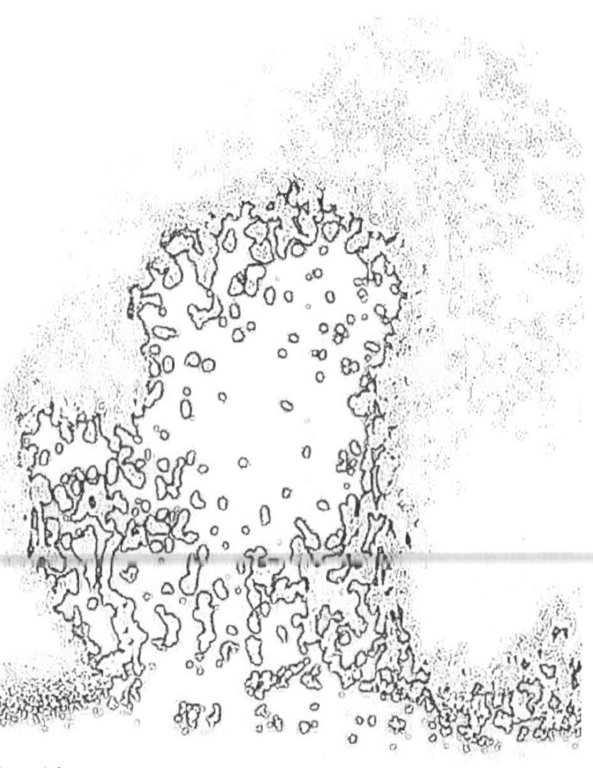

Img 1 b

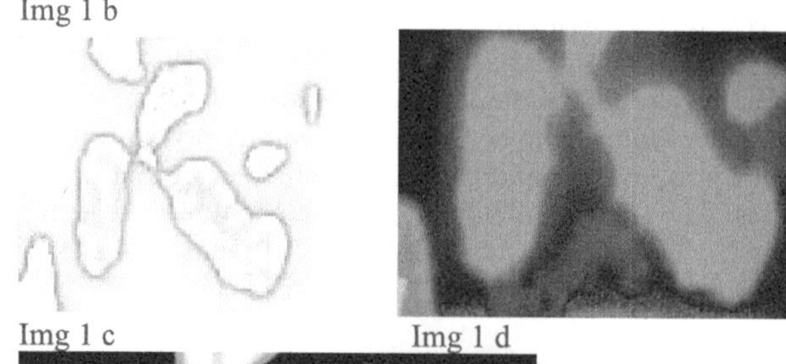

Img 1 c Img 1 d

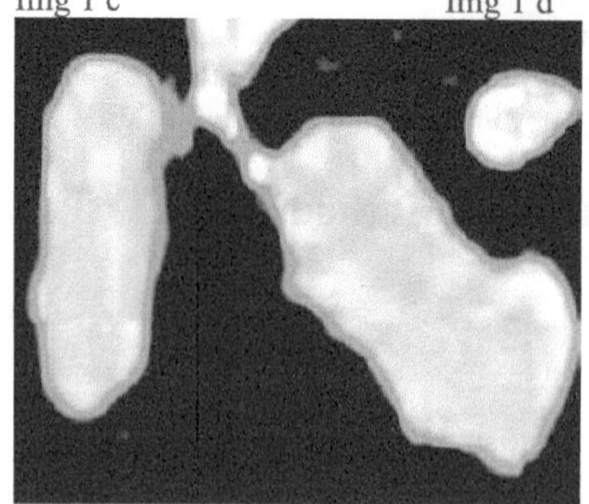

Img 1 e

These images were already presented in my first publication<<vitreous imaging system a new method for medical diagnostic >> the images, that will appear, will display chromosomes DNA

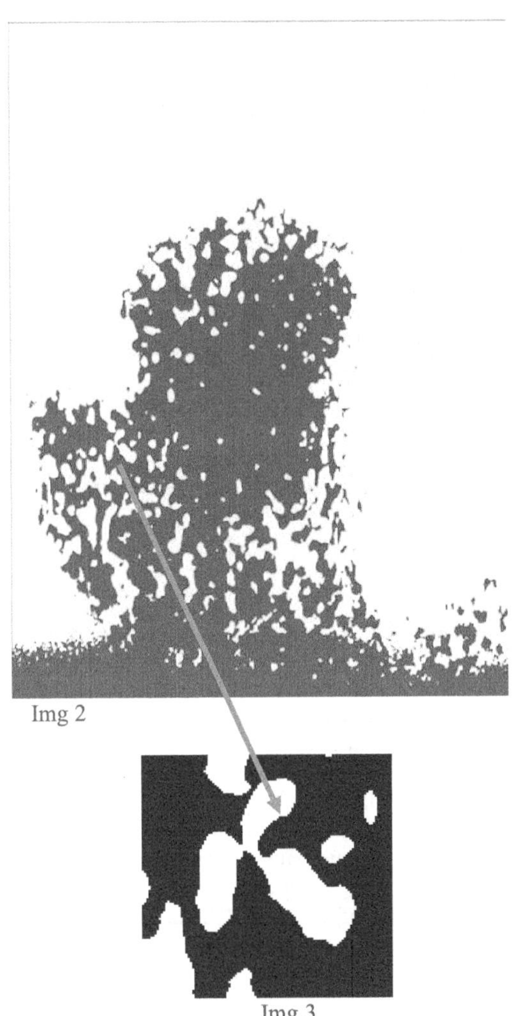

Img 2

Img 3

In the vitreous humor, we have the map of organs affected by pathologies. We select an organ to be studied in the glazed humor and we proceed to the second technique which consists of the display (visualization) of the chromosomes of this organ.

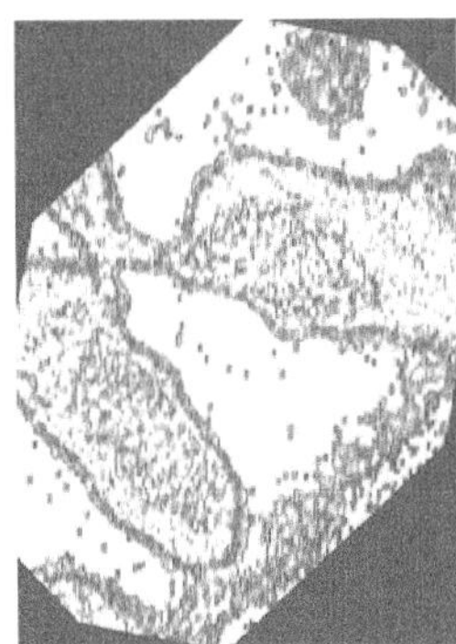

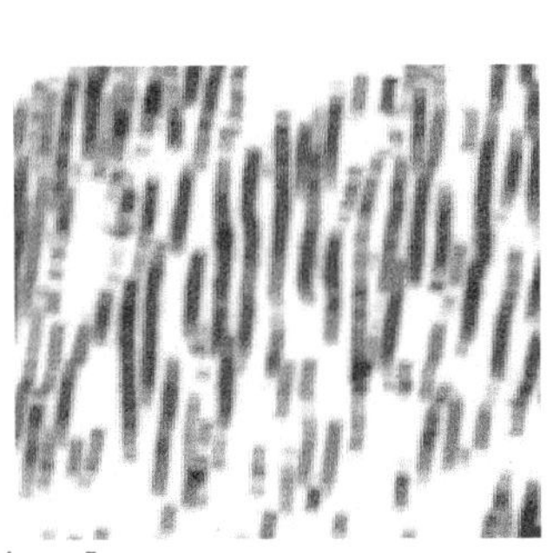

Img 4 img 5

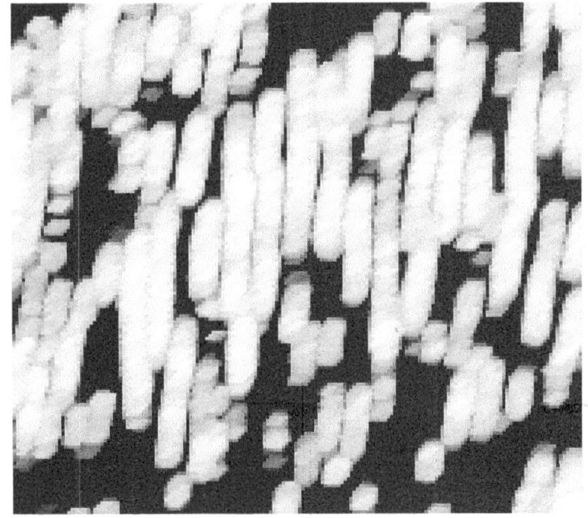

Img 6

Img 7

You will notice that we visualize display the chromosomes which are in the same direction, this will allow us to decrease considerably the number of chromosomes to be able to isolate them and study them easily.

We clearly see appearing chromosomes, we isolate a chromosome and we enlarge the image.

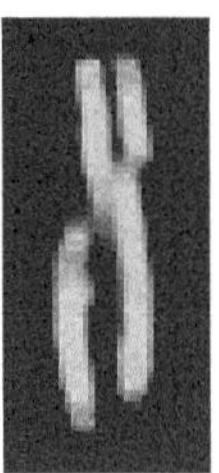

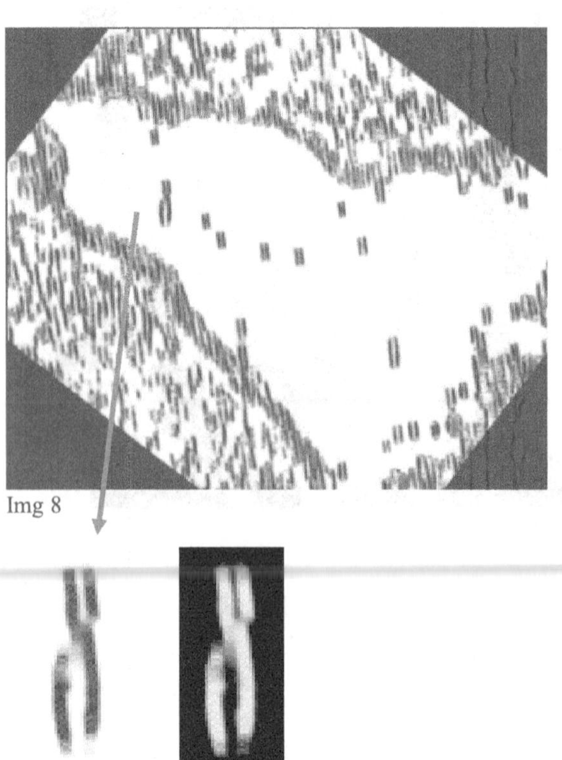

Img 8

Img 9 img 9

The chromosome that we study is the chromosome X , ewpanding the image we , we can see very clearly the double helix of DNA.

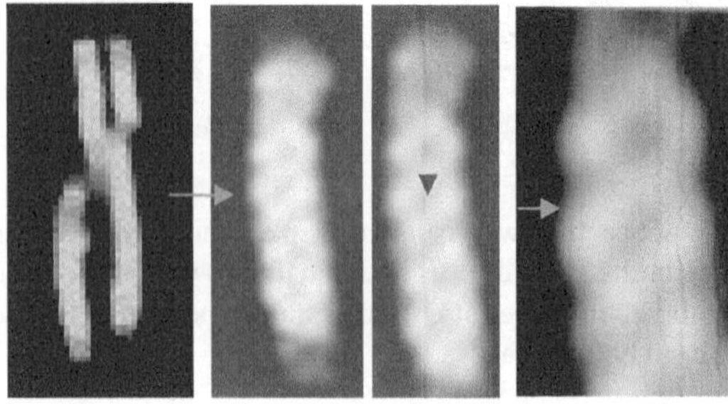

Img 9 img 10 img 11 img 12

We clearly see appearing chromosomes, we isolate a chromosome and we enlarge the image.

The double helix of DNA appears clearly in the form of two rolled up stalks the one on the other one. The comparison with a comparative plan is identical and remarkable; I open a bracket here by letting know that there is no image at present showing to us exactly the double helix of DNA.

.

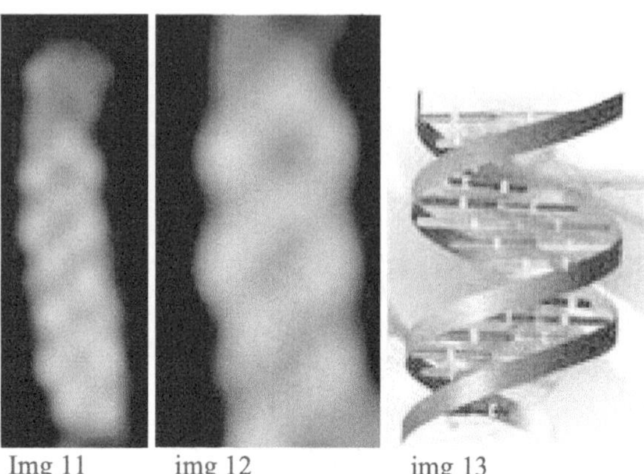

Img 11 img 12 img 13

Img 1 : photo of the eye
Img1a :vizualisations of pathological organ in humor vitreous
Img 1 b : organs visibles in vitreous humor
Img 1c et Img 1d : lung
Img 1 e : elargment
Img 2 : vitreous humor
Img 3 : lung
Img 4 : rotation of image and vizualisation to chromosomes
Img 5 : amas de chromosomes
Img 6 : chromosomes clusters
Img 7 : visualisation of chromosomes
Img 8 : rotation and ellargment
Img 9 : ellargment (visualisation of chromosome X)
Img 10 : strand of chromosome showing the double helix
img11 :ellargment of strand of chromosome
img 12 : visualisation of the double helix of chromosome
img 13 : diagram showing the double helix of DNA

The technique of visualization of DNA by the V.I.S.system is little expensive, simple and much faster than traditional techniques. After extraction, the genomic DNA is cut by sonication in fragments from 50 to 200 kb then cloned in a vector adapted as the artificial bacterial chromosomes, or B.A.C.

The number of clones has to allow a cover from 5 to 10 times the total length of the studied genome. The overlapping and the organization of clones are realized either by hybridization of specific probes, or by analysis of the profiles of limitation, or more frequently by an organization after sequencing and hybridization of the extremities of the B.A.C... After the organization of clones, they are split up and sequenced individually, then assembled by bioIT alignment

. The advantages of this method are a bigger ease of assembly of fragments thanks to the overlapping of B.A.C ., the possibility of comparing fragments with the available data banks, and the possibility of sharing the work of sequencing between several laboratories, each being in charge of a chromosomal region.

the major drawback is the difficulty to clone fragments containing repeated sequences very common in some genomes, which makes difficult the final bioIT analysis .Contrary t the VIS system, which consists of applying the technique of DNA visualization in the first place, and making magnifications in order to be able to see the double helix, chromosomes are observed in real images. (as we, have explained in our previous publication in Worldcomp 2011, the difference between a real image and an approximate one. The real image contains an infinite number of images themselves (Bank data) , unlike the, approximate image that contains only a single one.

Les avantages de cette méthode sont une plus grande facilité

2.4 Nucleotides

The DNA double helix consists of a set of elements containing the genetic information, called nucleotides. A nucleotide is a complex molecular assembly and includes a sugar linked to a phosphate group and a nitrogenous base. This base can be cytosine, guanine, and thymine, and adenine, adenine pairs with thymine and cytosine with guanine. Nucleotides thus related form a kind of scale rolled up in double helix. DNA molécule consists of 13 pairs of nucléotides.

2.5 Sequencage

2.5.1 Méthode de Sanger

The principle of this method is to initiate the polymerization of DNA using a small oligonucleotide (primer) complementary to a portion of the DNA fragment to be sequenced. The elongation of the primer is made by the Klenov fragment (DNA polymerase I lacking exonuclease activity of 5 '---> 3') and now by thermostable DNA polymerases, those used for PCR. The four deoxyribonucleotides (dATP, dCTP, dGTP, dTTP) are added, as well as a weak concentration of one of the four dideoxynucleotides (ddATP, ddCTP, or ddTTP). These didesoxynucléotides act as <<poisons >> chain terminators, once incorporated into the new synthesized stand, they prevent further elongation. This termination is specifically at the nucleotides corresponding to didesoxyribonucleotide incorporated into the reaction. For the complete sequencing of the same DNA fragment, this reaction is repeated four times in parallel, with four different didesoxyribonucleotides. For example ,in the reaction where we added ddGTP , the synthesis stops at G . The reactional mixture contains at the same time dGTP and a little ddGTP . The ending is statistically depending on whether the DNA polymerase uses one or more of these nucleotides. The result is a mixture of DNA fragments of increasing sizes, which all end in one of G in the sequence. These fragments are then separated by polyacrylamide gel electrophoresis, thus, making it possible to pinpoint the location of the Gs in the sequence.
The detection of fragments so synthetized is made by incorporating a tracer into the synthetized DNA. Initially, this tracer was radioactive; today, we use fluorescent, attached tracers either in the oligonucléotide, or in the didésoxyribonucléotide.

2.5.2 Méthode de Maxam et Gilbert

Specifics. The single-stranded DNA are subject to reactions. This method is based on a chemical degradation of DNA and uses the different reactivities of the four bases A, T, G and C to make selective cuts. By reconstructing the sequence of cuts, one can trace the sequence of nucleotides of the corresponding DNA . We can decompose the chemical sequencing into successive six stages.
Marking : the ends of two strands of DNA to be sequenced are marked by a radioactive tracer (32 p). This reaction is generally done using radioactive ATP and polynucleotide kinase.

Isolation of DNA fragment to be sequenced: it is separated by electrophoresis on a polyacrylamide gel. The DNA fragment is cut from the gel and recovered by diffusion.

- **Séparation of strands** : : the two strands of each DNA fragment are separated by thermal denaturation, and then purified by another electrophoresis

Chemical changes : specific of different basic types. Walter Gilbert has developed several types of specific reactions, performed in parallel on a fraction of each labeled DNA strand, for example, a reaction for G (alkylation by the sulphate of dyméthyle), a reaction for G and A (dépurification), a reaction for the C , as well as a reaction for the C and T (alkaline hydrolysis). These different reactions are carried out under very arranged conditions , so that on average each DNA molecule carries only zero or one modification.

- **Cut** : After these reactions, the DNA is cleaved at the modification by reaction with a base, piperidine.

- **Analysis:** for each fragment, the products of different reactions are separated by electrophoresis under denaturing conditions and analyzed to reconstruct the sequence of DNA. This analysis is similar to that which is carried out for the Sanger's method.

2.5.3 Pyroséquencing ultra broadband

suitable for sequencing <<novo>> and <<re sequencing>>

2.5.4 Séquençage par re synthèse
Utilisant un terminateur réversible adapté au re séquençage

2.5.6 Séquençing by hybridization / ligation

Adapted to the re sequencing, the detection of the SNP and the study of the organization of genomes.

2.6 V.I.S and technical of visualization of the DNA

The V.I.S. system allows us a direct visualization of chromosomes in real images, a real image , as we explained it previously, is an image < < data bank > > which means that it contains all the information relative to this image at the moment T when this image was taken.

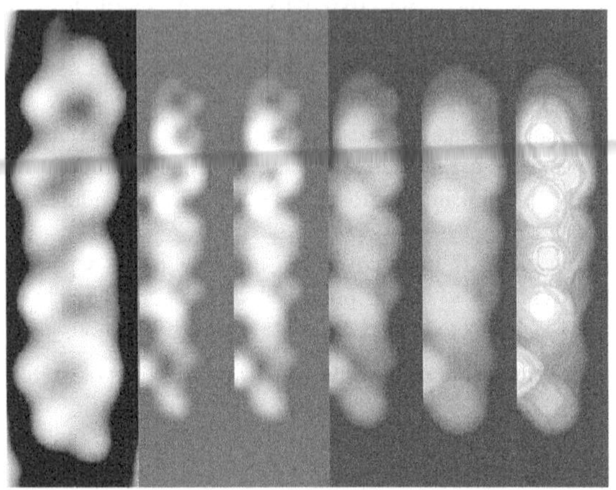

Img 14 img 15 img 16 img 17 img 18 img 19

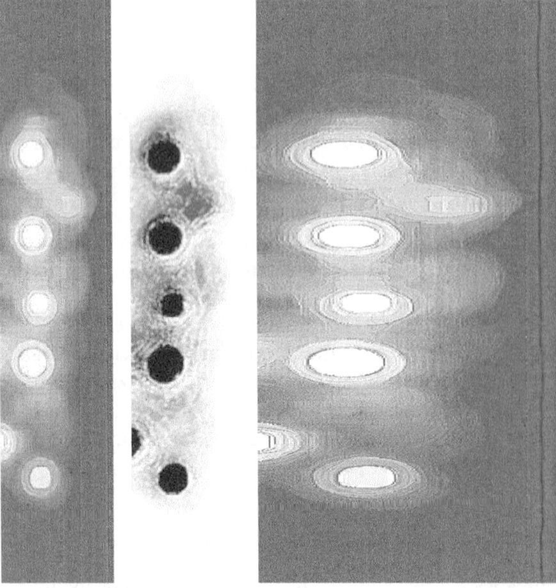

Img 20 img 21 img 22

We visualize nucléotides at the level of the stalk of DNA; every nitrogenous base has a precise position with regard to the others, and every nitrogeneous base has a curve different from the others; we can read the image by widening it on the horizontal plan and by shrinking it on the vertical plan .We obtains the technical sequencing by the V.I.S. system. We can easily read it, with, in front of every nitrogenous base, its graphic curve the explanation of which is given by these images.

Img14 :strand of chromosome helix DNA
img15 : vizualisation to the double helix of DNA
img 16, img 17 ; img 18 ; img 19 : visualization of nucleotides
img20, img 22 : nucléotides reading
img 22 : image V.I.S sequencing of DNA

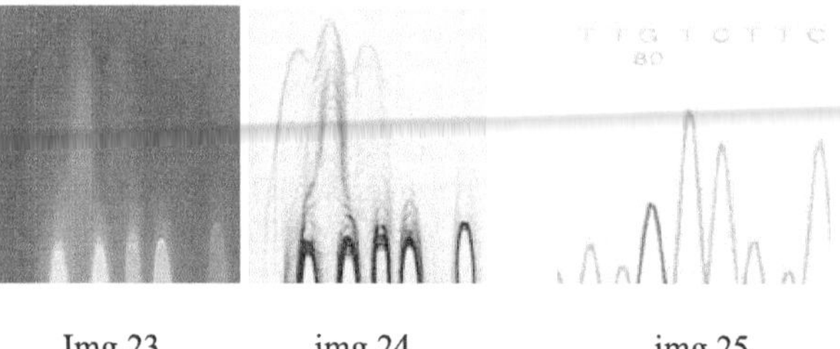

Img 23 img 24 img 25

Img 23 , img 24 : each nucleobase is a graphical wave

Img 25 : graphical of comparatif of sequencing DNA

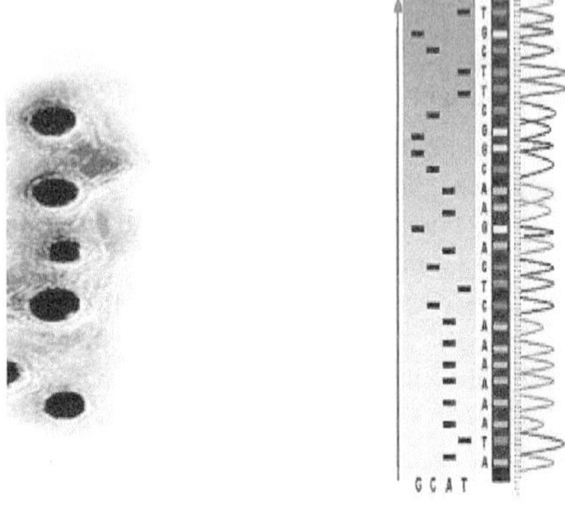

CTCACGA comparatif

The reading by VIS syteme is :

C : cytosine T : thymine C : cytosine A : adenine C : cytosine G : guanine A : adenine

2.7 Images of nucléotides by V.I.S

The imagery obtained by the nucleotide V.I.S. system is unique, where the current science provides only theories, diagrams and graphs to illustrate these theories. The V.I.S. system gives us real images of the infinitely small, and these images are not images of synthetic data computer, then by mathematical algorithm, these images are real ones .

From the image of chromosome obtained by the V.I.S .system technical, we can go farther by providing images with real details of the structure of the nucleotide as it has never been given.

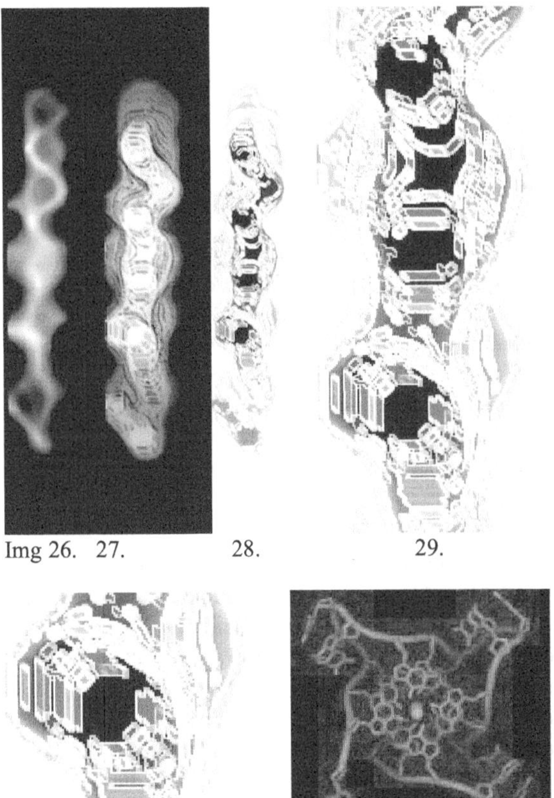

Img 26. 27. 28. 29.

Img 30 : img 31: comparative

Img : 32 img : 33 img : 34

Img: 26, 27, 28, 29, vizualisation of nucleotides in the double helix of DNA.
Img 30: internal view of the nucleotide
Img 31: diagram of nucleotide
Img 32: internal view of nucleotide
Img 33: other internal view of nucleotide
Img 34 : view of nucleobase

The images of the V.I.S. system show with high accuracy the external and internal configuration of a nucleotide, the image of sugars, phosphates and nitrogenous bases.

3. Conclusion

This publication is the continuity of the first one which is a new technique of medical and diagnostic imaging. The first technique of the V.I.S. system gives us the images of the pathological organs visible in the vitreous humor of the eye; on the other hand this second publication gives us the imaging of the double helix of DNA as well as the reading of the genetic coding always from the photo of the eye.
It is a new of reading DNA without having recourse to a taking or too long, expensive processes of reading, with a percentage of 99 % success. V.I.S. system gives us an easy, quick, not very expensive reading with a rate of 100 % success.
There will be much change in terms of ethics, for the present moment a legal authorization is needed to proceed to a taking But with this new process and this new technique, the examiner will need only a photo to read DNA , because for each picture of a person, we can get his DNA.

New Perspectives of Barcoding of Biotechnological Bacterial Strains by Using NGS Data

Reva O.N.[1], Chan W.Y.[2], Bezuidt O.[1], Lapa S.V.[3], Safronova L.A.[3], Avdeeva L.V.[3], Borriss R.[4]

[1]*Department of Biochemistry, Bioinformatics and Computational Biology Unit, University of Pretoria, Hillcrest, Lynnwood Rd., Pretoria 0002, South Africa; oleg.reva@up.ac.za; bezuidt@gmail.com*;

[2]*Department of Microbiology and Plant Pathology, Hillcrest, Lynnwood Rd., Pretoria 0002, South Africa; annie.chan@fabi.up.ac.za*;

[3]*Department of Antibiotics, Institute of Microbiology and Virology NAS of Ukraine, 154, Akademika Zabolotnogo str., Kiev, Ukraine, 03680; slapa@ukr.net; safronova_larisa@ukr.net; avdeeva@imv.kiev.ua*;

[4]*ABiTEP CmbH, Glienicker Weg 185, Berlin 12489, Germany, rborriss@abitep.de*;

Contact author: Reva O.N., *oleg.reva@up.ac.za*

Key words: next generation sequencing, barcoding, biotechnology

For BIOCOMP'13 - The 2013 International Conference on Bioinformatics & Computational Biology, Las Vegas, Nevada, USA, July 22-25, 2013.

Abstract

Next generation sequencing (NGS) technologies provided researchers with a wide variety of genetic data about organisms of interest. In this work we introduce several basic bioinformatic approaches to utilize NGS for resolving imperious problems of applied microbiology and biotechnology. Working with promising industrial strains, researches have to resolve the following questions: i) is these strain unique and if so, what makes them so unique genetically or practically speaking; ii) how can these strains be tracked down in the environment; iii) and are there any genetic markers of their extraordinary activity? All these questions may be addressed by creation genetic barcode sequences and mapping NGS reads against these barcodes.

Results and Discussion

The importance of genetic barcoding of biotechnological bacterial strains used in probiotics, biopesticides and other bioproducts based on living cultures is greatly underestimated. Many bacterial and fungal cultures show extreme enzymatic, antibacterial, hormonal and other activities, which may be of practical importance for medicine, agriculture and industry. Although precise species identification is a strict requirement for the registration of all microbial agents of bioproducts, it often remains unclear whether the reported extraordinary activity belongs to all members of the given species or is it attributed only to a specific strain? In our recent publication we demonstrated that the plant growth promoting activity, ability to colonize rhizosphere and inner plant tissues, and antagonistic activities against phytopathogens in plant-associated *Bacillus* are specific for sub-species or even individual strains (Safronova *et al.*, 2012). Another point for consideration is that the super-active strains isolated from nature, which appear to be prospective for biotechnological applications, quickly lose their specific activity during laboratory cultivation (Fleising 1989; Hunter-Cevera and Belt 1996). The researchers working in biotechnology are faced with the following problems i) delineating biologically active strains from their less active relatives as a direct measuring of specific activity is not always possible in large-scale experiments; ii) picking out markers and genetic determinants underpinning superior biological activity; iii) quality control of bioproducts to prevent substitutions of active strains with inactive variants. All these problems may be effectively addressed by genetic barcoding. In this study an example of genetic barcoding of plant growth promoting *Bacillus* strains will be considered.

Many plant growth promoting strains of *Bacillus* belong to three closely related species: *B. subtilis*, *B. amyloliquefaciens* and *B. atrophaeus* (Borriss *et al.*, 2011; Chen *et al.*, 2007; Reva *et al.*, 2004; Rückert *et al.*, 2011). Identification of these species by phenotype is almost intractable and even distinguishing them by 16S rRNA is rather problematic, while the ability to survive on roots and colonize plants was attributed to strain and sub-species levels of these micro-organisms (Reva *et al.*, 2004; Safronova *et al.*, 2012). We hypothesized that the ability to live in roots and colonise plants arises from adaptive changes, which occur in gene sequences and encoded proteins. In a comparative study of chemotaxis proteins of plant associated and free living bacteria this hypothesis was proved to be true. Survival of bacteria on roots requires sensing of specific signals and several adaptive changes in chemotaxis proteins have been found, which probably were driven by the positive selection of appropriate amino acid substitutions adjusting the spatial conformation and kinetics of these proteins (Yssel *et al.*, 2011). More proteins must be involved in adaptation to plant colonization that suggested a possibility to created genetic barcodes to aid in species identification and delineating between plant associated and soil dwelling eco-morphs of these bacteria. Availability of barcode sequences would allow large scale screening of isolates of *B. subtilis* group by sequencing in multiplex, as a single plate of Illumina may be distributed among up to 96 different samples via the use of individually-tagged libraries (Inouye *et al.*, 2012). Obtained DNA reads may be then mapped against barcode sequences by using BWA (Li and Durbin, 2010), Bowtie (Langmead and Salzberg 2012) and/or Masai (Siragusa *et al.* 2013) programs installed locally or through public cloud Web-servers (Fusaro *et al.*, 2011) without any need for prior assembly and annotation. Several plant associated and soil dwelling strains of *Bacillus* have been sequenced recently (Chen *et al.*, 2007; Rückert et al., 2011). We have additionally obtained complete genome sequences of the six new strains. More information is available on NCBI and GOLD BioProject Web-sites shown in Table 1.

Table 1. NCBI and GOLD bioproject IDs of newly sequenced *Bacillus* strains. Species were identified by 16S rRNA and GyrA sequences (Reva *et al.*, 2004).

Project Display Name	**GOLD ID**	**NCBI Project ID**
Bacillus atrophaeus UCMB-5137 (APIW00000000 at NCBI)	Gi21363	176685
Bacillus amyloliquefaciens UCMB-5007	Gi21364	176687
Bacillus subtilis UCMB-5014	Gi21365	176696
Bacillus amyloliquefaciens UCMB-5140	Gi21366	176688
Bacillus amyloliquefaciens ssp *plantarum* At1	Gi21367	176703
Bacillus amyloliquefaciens At2	Gi21368	176701

Genes of the two independently evolving lineages of microorganisms are under the pressure of several evolutionary forces and accumulate mutations. Pairs of orthologous genes may be compared by their total numbers of substitutions; percentages of sense mutations; and the dynamics of accumulation of conservative and non-conservative substitutions. This analysis was performed by an in house Python program. Evolutionary forces act unequally upon different genes depending on their nature and role in bacteria. In Fig. 1 the orthologous genes were analysed in three pairs of plant associated and soil dwelling strains of *B. atrophaeus*, *B. amyloliquefaciens* and *B. subtilis*. Three categories of conserved, positively selected and randomly mutated genes are depicted in Fig. 1. We hypothesized that the conserved genes (highlighted in Fig. 1), which are experiencing a weak positive selection, would be the best choice for barcoding of these microbes. A reciprocal BLASTN alignment approach allowed the selection of such genes of this category, which were shared by all three pairs of strains belonging to three different species. In total we identified 150 genes, which have experienced similar evolutionary forces during the adaptive evolution towards plant colonization lifestyle in the three different species of *Bacillus*. DNA sequences of these genes were aligned by MUSCLE (Edgar, 2004) and concatenated into an artificial 199,924 bp sequence. A neighbour-joining phylogenetic tree (Fig. 2) created by MEGA5 (Tamura *et al.*, 2011) demonstrated that these sequences contain strong phylogenetic signals to distinguish between these three species and their eco-morphs. Barcodes were created from these sequences by removal of all spaces throughout the alignment and inserting 50 'N's between individual genes to avoid chimeric mapping in between genes. Then the DNA reads generated by Illumina for different sequenced strains were mapped against the barcode sequences by BWA using the default parameters.

The statistics of mapping of Illumina reads against barcode sequences (Table 2) showed that the strains UCMB-5007, UCMB-5140 and At1 belong to *B. amyloliquefaciens* ssp. *plantarum* as they produced more reads, which matched to the corresponding barcode. The strains UCMB-5014 and At2 showed similarity to the *B. subtilis* 168 (NC_000964) lineage. Interestingly, that more reads from *B. amyloliquefaciens* ssp. *plantarum* were perfectly aligned against the corresponding barcode than those from *B. subtilis* isolates indicating that there may be stronger sequence conservation in plant associated *B. amyloliquefaciens*. However, another explanation that will be tested in further studies is that UCMB-5014 and At2 belong to distant subspecies of *B. subtilis* and need their own barcode sequences to be generated in future.

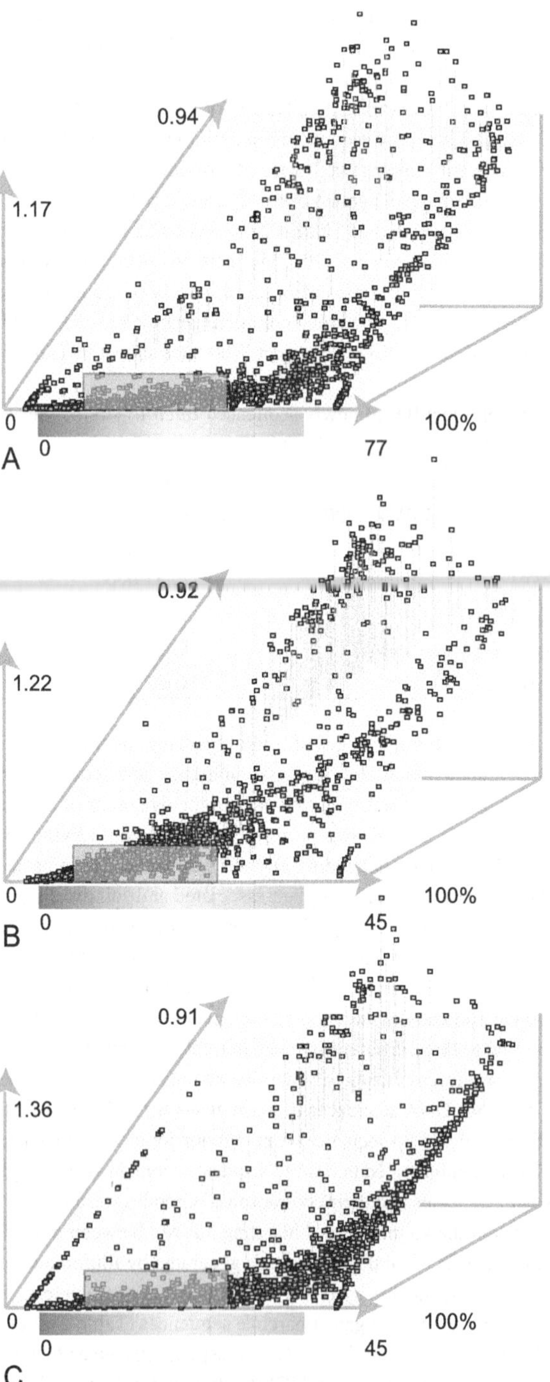

Fig. 1. Mutation accumulation patterns in orthologous genes of A) *B. atrophaeus* UCMB-5137 (plant colonizer) and *B. atrophaeus* 1942; B) *B. amyloliquefaciens* FZB42 (plant colonizer) and *B. amyloliquefaciens* DSM7; C) *B. subtilis* ssp. *subtilis* BSn5 (plant colonizer) and *B. subtilis* ssp. *subtilis* 168. Individual orthologous genes pairs are depicted by small boxes projected into 3D space where X axis is the

percentage of sense mutations over the total number of nucleotide substitutions; Y is the difference between sequences (1 – percentage of identities); Z (vertical axis) is the ratio (positives – identities)/identities; and forth dimension depicted by gradient colours represent number of nucleotide substitutions per 100 bp. Pairs of orthologous genes are represented by dots mapped into the 3D space. The areas, where the genes suitable for barcoding are expected, were highlighted on the projections.

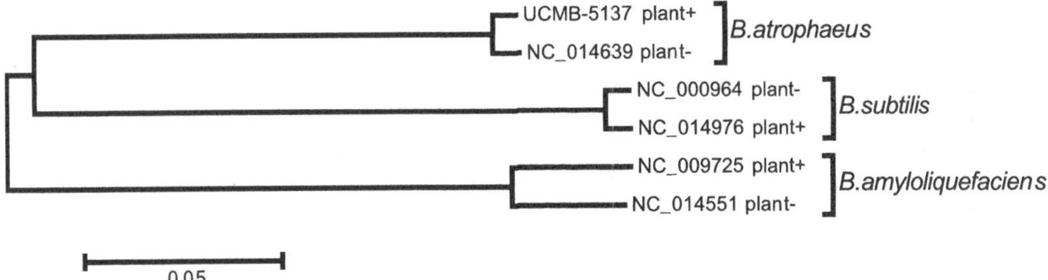

Fig. 2. Neighbour-joining phylogenetic tree based on concatenated DNA sequences of 150 selected genes. Plant associated and soil dwelling bacteria are marked as plant+ and plant–, respectively.

Table 2. Identification of newly sequenced genomes by mapping Illumina reads against the barcode sequences. Numbers of matched reads are shown in the table cells. The hypothesis is that as more randomly generated DNA reads were aligned against barcodes as closer the sequenced strain is to this lineage represented by the corresponding barcode.

	Newly sequenced strains of *Bacillus*				
Barcodes	**UCMB-5007 (32,405,476)[†]**	**UCMB-5014 (33,655,154)**	**UCMB-5140 (32,399,168)**	**At1 (34,562,286)**	**At2 (30,318,812)**
UCMB-5137	31	7,048	142	56	5,836
NC_014639	45	3,016	101	125	2,691
NC_014976	3,426	246,135	4,554	4,120	217,838
NC_000964	3,824	260,474	6,812	5,877	230,862
NC_009725	1,178,762	7,091	1,209,269	1,357,420	6,129
NC_014551	77,337	4,937	91,483	87,158	4,342

[†] – Number of DNA reads in Illumina datasets;

Conclusion

The growing popularity of genetic barcoding is fuelled by the attractiveness towards the use of the technically simple and inexpensive NGS technologies towards precise species identification. The simplicity of the idea inspired several grandiose projects, including the most ambitious the Consortium for the Barcode of Life (CBOL, http://barcoding.si.edu) which is aimed at barcoding all the species on the planet (Savolainen *et al.*, 2005). However, this project is focused mostly on barcoding of animals by sequencing the *cox1* gene. The goal of the Greengenes project is to provide a comprehensive depositary of full-length bacterial and archaeal 16S rRNA (McDonald *et al.*, 2012) and grouping them by a dedicated computational tool GRUNT (Dalevi et al., 2007). The aim of the latter project is also to fuel up the megasequencing project which studies the ecosystems at a large scale: the Human Microbiome Project (Aagaard *et al.*, 2012) and the Earth Microbiome Project (www.earthmicrobiome.org). However, the uses of barcoding and MLST have created some controversy among researchers regarding their applicability in taxonomy and habitat specificity; pathogenicity; and biotechnological importance of bacterial strains, whether they may be delineated each from others by barcodes (Dasmahapatra and Mallet 2006). Species identification and the estimation of virulence or industrial applicability of a given microorganism most likely require different sets of diagnostic markers. Genetic tagging of bacterial eco-morphs may be improved by a better understanding of micro-evolutionary processes affecting individual genes, sequences of which may be used for tracing down the adaptive genomic changes to fit the bacterium to the specific ecological niche and role in the ecosystem. In this work we presented several on-going studies on barcoding of plant-growth-promoting bacteria.

Acknowledgements

Sequencing and analysis of plant growth promoting strains was funded by the IRT grant for Genomics researches provided by the University of Pretoria and by NRF grant 73983 for German-South Africa collaboration.

References

1. Aagaard, K., Petrosino, J., Keitel, W., Watson, M., Katancik, J., Garcia, N., Patel, S., Cutting, M., Madden, T., Hamilton, H., Harris, E., Gevers, D., Simone, G., McInnes, P., and Versalovic, J. (2012). The Human Microbiome Project strategy for comprehensive sampling of the human microbiome and why it matters. FASEB J. Epub ahead of print, doi: 10.1096/fj.12-220806.
2. Borriss, R., Chen, X.H., Rueckert, C., Blom, J., Becker, A., Baumgarth, B., Fan, B., Pukall, R., Schumann, P., Spröer, C., Junge, H., Vater, J., Pühler, A., and Klenk, H.P. (2011). Relationship of *Bacillus amyloliquefaciens* clades associated with strains DSM 7T and FZB42T: a proposal for *Bacillus amyloliquefaciens* subsp. *amyloliquefaciens* subsp. nov. and *Bacillus amyloliquefaciens* subsp. *plantarum* subsp. nov. based on complete genome sequence comparisons. Int. J. Syst. Evol. Microbiol. *61*, 1786-1801.
3. Chen, X.H., Koumoutsi, A., Scholz. R., Eisenreich, A., Schneider, K., Heinemeyer, I., Morgenstern, B., Voss, B., Hess, W.R., Reva, O., Junge, H., Voigt, B., Jungblut, P.R., Vater, J., Süssmuth, R., Liesegang, H., Strittmatter, A., Gottschalk, G., and Borriss, R. (2007). Comparative analysis of the complete genome sequence of the plant growth-promoting bacterium *Bacillus amyloliquefaciens* FZB42. Nat. Biotechnol. *25*, 1007-1014.
4. Dalevi, D., DeSantis, T.Z., Fredslund, J., Andersen, G.L., Markowitz, V.M., and Hugenholtz, P. (2007). Automated group assignment in large phylogenetic trees using GRUNT: GRouping, Ungrouping, Naming Tool. BMC Bioinformatics *8*, 402.
5. Dasmahapatra, K.K., and Mallet, J. (2006). Taxonomy: DNA barcodes: recent successes and future prospects. Heredity (Edinb.) *97*, 254-255.
6. Edgar, R.C. (2004). MUSCLE: a multiple sequence alignment method with reduced time and space complexity. BMC Bioinformatics *5*, 113.
7. Fleising, U. (1989). Risk and culture in biotechnology. Trends in Biotech. *7*, 52-57.
8. Fusaro, V.A., Patil, P., Gafni, E., Wall, D.P., and Tonellato, P.J. (2011). Biomedical cloud computing with Amazon Web Services. PLoS Comput. Biol. *7*, e1002147.
9. Hunter-Cevera, J.C, and Belt, A. (1996). Maintaining cultures for biotechnology and industry. Academic Press, Inc., California, USA.
10. Inouye, M., Conway, T.C., Zobel, J., and Holt, K.E. (2012). Short read sequence typing (SRST): multi-locus sequence types from short reads. BMC Genomics *13*, 338.
11. Langmead, B., and Salzberg, S.L. (2012). Fast gapped-read alignment with Bowtie 2. Nat. Methods *9*, 357-359.
12. Li, H., and Durbin, R. (2010) Fast and accurate long-read alignment with Burrows-Wheeler transform. Bioinformatics *26*, 589-595.
13. McDonald, D., Price, M.N., Goodrich, J., Nawrocki, E.P., DeSantis, T.Z., Probst, A., Andersen, G.L., Knight, R., and Hugenholtz, P. (2012). An improved Greengenes taxonomy with explicit ranks for ecological and evolutionary analyses of bacteria and archaea. ISME J. *6*, 610-618.
14. Reva, O.N., Dixelius, C., Meijer, J., and Priest, F.G. (2004). Taxonomic characterization and plant colonizing abilities of some bacteria related to *Bacillus amyloliquefaciens* and *Bacillus subtilis*. FEMS Microbiol. Ecol. *48*, 249-259.
15. Rückert, C., Blom, J., Chen, X., Reva, O., and Borriss, R. (2011). Genome sequence of *B. amyloliquefaciens* type strain DSM7(T) reveals differences to plant-associated *B. amyloliquefaciens* FZB42. J. Biotechnol. *155*, 78-85.
16. Safronova, L.A., Zelena, L.B., Klochko, V.V., and Reva, O.N. (2012). Does the applicability of *Bacillus* strains in probiotics rely upon their taxonomy? Can. J. Microbiol. *58*, 212-219.

17. Savolainen, V., Cowan, R.S., Vogler, A.P., Roderick, G.K., and Lane, R. (2005). Towards writing the encyclopedia of life: an introduction to DNA barcoding. Philos. Trans. R. Soc. Lond. B. Biol. Sci. *360*, 1805-1811.
18. Siragusa, E., Weese, D., and Reinert, K. (2013). Fast and accurate read mapping with approximate seeds and multiple backtracking. Nucleic Acids Res. [Epub ahead of print, PMID: 23358824]
19. Tamura, K., Peterson, D., Peterson, N., Stecher, G., Nei, M., and Kumar, S. (2011). MEGA5: molecular evolutionary genetics analysis using maximum likelihood, evolutionary distance, and maximum parsimony methods. Mol. Biol. Evol. *28*, 2731-2739.
20. Yssel, A., Reva, O., and Tastan Bishop, O. (2011). Comparative structural bioinformatics analysis of *Bacillus amyloliquefaciens* chemotaxis proteins within *Bacillus subtilis* group. Appl. Microbiol. Biotechnol. *92*, 997-1008.

Multiple Sequence Alignments Using Motif Assembly

Charnelle Smoak[1], **Alexander Ropelewski**[2], **and Albert Esterline**[1]
[1] Department of Computer Science, North Carolina A&T State University, Greensboro, NC, USA
[2] Pittsburgh Supercomputing Center, Pittsburgh, PA, USA

Abstract - *Multiple sequence alignments are useful for phylogenetic inference and are used along with previously obtained knowledge to infer the structure and function of a protein. Alignments found with current multiple sequence alignment methods rarely reveal the best model of sequence evolution; hand-editing of alignments is generally required to ensure that important biological motifs are aligned. In the research reported here, a multiple sequence alignment pipeline was devised that anchors these motifs and builds a multiple sequence alignment around them. The need to hand-adjust alignments around key motifs is eliminated. For an ideal dataset, this alignment method produces alignments superior to those produced by native alignment algorithms.*

Keywords: Bioinformatics, Multiple Sequence Alignments, Motif Assembly, Meme Motif

1 Introduction

A multiple sequence alignment (MSA) is an alignment of three or more related biological sequences of similar length [1]. MSA's can be generated manually, automatically, or in a combined method. From the rendered output of a sequence alignment a biologist can infer homology and identify regions of similar structural or functional importance.

Motif finding is used to create scoring matrices to search other sequences for similar motifs and as a way to create better MSA's. Conserved or important patterns (residues) are called motifs in biological sequences. Motif finding or profile analysis is the process of finding these motifs. Finding motifs is vital to understanding gene function, human disease, drug design and more. [2] One of the most commonly used motif finding tools, and the one used in this paper, is known as Multiple EM for Motif Elicitation (MEME) [3]. MEME uses expectation maximization and represents motifs as position-dependent letter-probability matrices, which describe the probability of each possible letter at each position in the pattern.

In this research, we use a method called motif assembly, which combines MSA with motif finding. We use MEME to find the motifs that create the basis for our alignments. In our featured test dataset of Phospholipase A2 sequences, we use CLUSTAL W [4], a multiple sequence alignment program, as both our control by itself and concurrently with MEME in our new method to produce improved results.

2 Background

Many automated MSA software tools fail to produce biologically meaningful data [5]. This is because, computationally, MSA programs only look to align the sequences and do not recognize semantically important patterns that biologists often spot. Often, the resulting MSA will have motifs aligned with the first semi-matching pattern it can find. This may not always be correct, resulting in misaligned sequences. Hand editing is then needed to improve the quality of alignments. With the help of a pattern finding program such as MEME, a multiple sequence alignment can be improved. MEME is used to highlight important residues within a sequence.

3 Dataset

The dataset featured in this research contains sequences of Phospholipase A2 enzymes (see Figure 1) of several organisms including a human, cow, mouse, rat, rattlesnake, krait, starfish and bee. Phospholipase A2's are enzymes that release fatty acids from glycerol. These sequences were gathered from the Unitprot database [6].

PLA1

O

O

R1

R2

O

O-

O

P

O

R3

PLA2

O

PLC PLD

Figure 1

4 Method

Using the Python language, we implemented a pipeline that combines motif finding and a MSA method in a process called motif assembly (see Figure 2). In the first step, we used MEME to find the motifs on the unaligned sequences of the dataset. The pipeline reads the MEME XML output file to determine the starting and stopping points of each motif in each sequence. It then splices the sequences around the motifs and separates each section of the spliced sequences (motifs and nonmotifs) into separate files. In the next step, CLUSTAL W is called on the non-motifs while the motifs are anchored and left untouched. We then stitch the files back in order based on the retained values for the start and stop from the MEME output. This produces a new sequence alignment.

Unaligned Sequences

MEME[3] XML File with motifs found.

Partitioned sequence files generated from XML file.

Reassembled MSA after Clustal-W [4] is run on partitioned sequences.

Figure 2

5 Results

Results using the motif assembly method described above were compared with the results produced by an MSA done solely with CLUSTAL W (without motif assembly). As shown in Figure 3, the cysteines used to make disulfide bonds are misaligned in the result produced by CLUSTAL W but properly aligned by the motif assembly method.

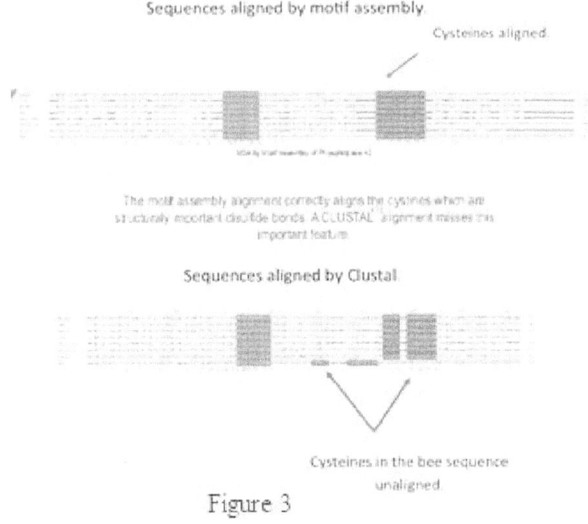

Figure 3

One important feature in this particular data set is the cysteines that are important for disulfide bonds that hold the Phospholipase A2 together. In the bee sequence they are unaligned which could cause an untrained eye to determine that the bee is not similar to the other sequences.

6 Conclusion

The results reported here suggest that multiple sequence alignment by motif assembly might be better for phylogenetic study than other methods for certain groups of sequences. This method will be benchmarked against various alignments including BAliBASE [7] and compared against various other methods. As of now, the pipeline only works under certain conditions and does not account for situations such as when MEME selects an out-of-order motif. In the future, we hope to fix this by using a consensus approach. We also hope to make this method more flexible so that it can be tuned to certain characteristics of the groups of sequences being aligned.

7 References

[1] European Molecular Biology Laboratory (EMBL), European Bioinformatics Institute-(EBI). Multiple Sequence Alignment. Available at http://www.ebi.ac.uk/Tools/msa/ [Accessed: 19 Mar 2013].

[2] Motifsearch.com. Motif Search, 2011. Available at http://www.motifsearch.com/ [Accessed: 19 Mar 2013].

[3] T. L. Bailey, N. Williams, C. Misleh, and W. W. Li. "MEME: discovering and analyzing DNA and protein sequence motifs," Nucleic Acids Research, Vol. 34, W369–W373, July 2006.

[4] J. D. Thompson, D. G. Higgins, and T. J. Gibson. "CLUSTAL W: improving the sensitivity of progressive multiple sequence alignment through sequence weighting, position-specific gap penalties and weight matrix choice," Nucleic Acids Research, Vol. 22, 4673-4680, Nov 1994.

[5] B. Morgenstein, S. J. Prohaska, D. Poehler, and P. F. Stadler. "Multiple sequence alignment with user-defined anchor points," Algorithms for Molecular Biology, Vol. 1 (BioMed Central), April 2006.

[6] M. Magrane and the UniProt consortium. "UniProt Knowledgebase: a hub of integrated protein data," Database: The Journal of Biological Databases and Curation (Oxford), bar009, March 2011.

[7] J. D. Thompson,, F. Plewniak, and O. Poch. "BAliBASE: a benchmark alignment database for the evaluation of multiple alignment programs," Bioinformatics, Vol. 15, No. 1, 87–88, 1999.

SESSION

PROTEIN CLASSIFICATION AND STRUCTURE PREDICTION, FOLDING, AND COMPUTATIONAL STRUCTURAL BIOLOGY

Chair(s)

TBA

Effect of Chloride Ions on GAPDH Conformation

Olga V. Gorshkalova and Norbert W. Seidler
Department of Biochemistry, Kansas City University of Medicine and Biosciences, 1750 Independence Avenue, Kansas City, MO, USA
CONTACT AUTHOR: Dr. Seidler (E-mail: nseidler@kcumb.edu; 816-654-7612)

Abstract - *The multifunctional protein GAPDH (for, glyceraldehyde 3-phosphate dehydrogenase) is known for its involvement in many diverse functions in cells including organization of the cell, signal transduction and regulation of gene expression. The participation in these alternate activities allow for effective integration of these cellular processes with the bioenergetics of the cell. The cellular triggers for acting in these diverse roles remain poorly understood. Several mechanisms are thought to control the functional diversity of GAPDH, including chemical modification, oligomerization, and small molecule binding. The latter mechanism, specifically the binding of chloride ions, may be an important trigger for GAPDH in certain cell types, such as neurons. We examined several crystal structures to assess small internal movements of interfacial amino acid residues that may be contributing to the conformational changes necessary to perform alternate functions.*

Keywords: Chloride ions, Glyceraldehyde 3-phosphate dehydrogenase (GAPDH), Protein folding, water

1 Introduction

GAPDH is the prototype multi-subunit protein that is the quintessential representative of the concept of multi-functionality. There is growing interest in this theme, which is a concept that suggests that a single gene that produces a single protein may result potentially in more than one function. In the case of the housekeeping enzyme, GAPDH, the diversity of function is astounding [1], including cellular processes that involve cell architecture, signal transduction and gene expression. It is reasonable to suggest that the multimeric features of this protein contribute to the masking of the sites necessary to perform alternate functions in the cell. Then the question arises as to what occurs in the cell to initiate a change in the oligomeric states that would promote a different biological action.

Human GAPDH consists of a somatic isoform and a tissue-specific spermatogenic isoform. There are also over 60 processed pseudogenes, some of which may be expressed. The protein is highly conserved with unicellular organisms exhibiting greater than 50% homology to the human protein. The GAPDH from humans consists of a chain of 335 amino acid residues. Native GAPDH exists as an asymmetric homo-tetramer, meaning that it is made up of identically-sequenced polypeptide chains, but that are folded each in a slightly different manner (Figure 1). There are two functional domains in each subunit, the dinucleotide-binding domain (residues 1 to 151, using the *Staphylococcus aureus* GAPDH numbering scheme) and the catalytic domain (residues 151 to 336), with residue Cys151 at the active center of the enzyme.

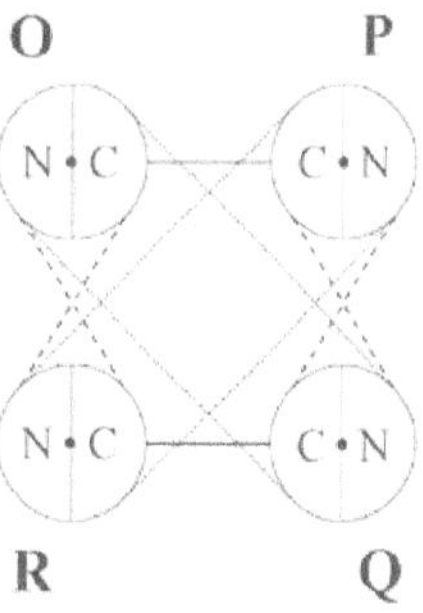

Figure 1: Diagrammatic representation of tetrameric GAPDH. Each subunit is shown as a circle that contains a catalytic domain (C) and a dinucleotide-binding domain (N) that interface the active site, which is given as a center dot. The subunits are designated as O, P, Q, and R, indicating that the molecule is an asymmetric tetramer with chains of identical sequence but slightly different conformations. The subunits interact across three axes, indicated by solid (*P*-axis), dashed (*R*-axis) and dotted (*Q*-axis) lines.

Laschet and coworkers [2] observed that GAPDH interacts with the $GABA_A$ receptor, which is important in promoting neuronal inhibition. The $GABA_A$ receptor is a pentameric ligand-gated ion channel that controls the flux of chloride ions into the cell, changing the levels of chloride ions from low micromolar to submillimolar levels. The nature of the relationship between GAPDH and $GABA_A$ receptor still remains a mystery, although it is thought to involve more than just a passive association [3]. We think that the intracellular levels of chloride ions, which are controlled by the $GABA_A$ receptor, directly impact the structure and hence the function of GAPDH. We previously observed that chloride ions promote the appearance of a decameric form of GAPDH [4], suggesting that chloride ions may affect the rearrangement of the GAPDH subunits. This chloride-induced change in the oligomeric properties of GAPDH may contribute to initiating one or more of the alternate functions that have been observed. It remains to be determined whether the downstream events that are initiated by the $GABA_A$ receptor activation involve this putative dynamic change in GAPDH structure and function. Curiously, many researchers have documented the inactivation of protein function by chloride ions as described below. A loss of glycolytic activity may be replaced by an increased activity of GAPDH's alternate functions.

1.1 Inactivation by chloride ions

Nagradova and coworkers [5] demonstrated cold inactivation of rat GAPDH at 4°C in the presence of 150mM NaCl. This inactivation was completely reversible by the addition of 50mM sodium phosphate at neutral pH, suggesting chloride-induced inactivation of enzymatic function. Another study [6] showed that enzyme inhibition by bromide ions, which are halides that are heavier than chloride, was temperature-dependent (i.e. the lower the temperature, the greater the inhibition). Although the author [6] studied the enzyme acetoacetate decarboxylase, which exists as a dodecamer, the mechanism of halide-induced inhibition may be universal in that subunit-subunit interactions are perturbed. Chilson and coworkers [7] looked at the effects of the different counter ions (i.e. halides) on the reactivation kinetics of guanidine-denatured enzyme. The authors examined a homologous oxidoreductase enzyme, lactate dehydrogenase. They observed that the larger the ion the greater the inhibition of reactivation, suggesting that the halide ions (i.e. chloride) affected subunit to subunit interaction during reactivation.

Markert [8] examined the formation of lactate dehydrogenase hybrids (i.e. composed of various percentages of the M and H isozymes) using the 'salt-freeze' technique, which involves freeze-thaw cycles in the presence of high salt concentrations (i.e. 1M NaCl). Interestingly, these hybrids can be produced at 6M NaCl without freeze cycles. GAPDH hybrids from polypeptides chains of different species are also produced in the presence of 3M NaCl [9]. By decreasing the temperature of the samples, the hydrophobic interactions are destabilized [10].

These studies suggest that the effects of chloride ions on GAPDH may be due in part to their effects on hydrophobic interactions which are dependent on water activity. In this study, we looked at crystal structures to determine the effects of chloride ions on the conformation of GAPDH.

2 Materials and Methods

There are only two crystal structures of GAPDH with chloride ions bound that are available in public databases: 3K9Q and 3LC2. Both structures are from the organism *Staphylococcus aureus*. The 3K9Q structure consists of a mutant GAPDH (Cys151Gly) with NAD^+ molecules and chloride ions bound. The 3LC2 structure has other ligands bound to GAPDH: glyceraldehyde 3-phosphate, chloride ions and glycerol. We chose the 3K9Q structure for further analysis because we were able to obtain a comparable GAPDH crystal structure (i.e. 3LVF) that contained the same ligand (namely, NAD^+) without the chloride ion. Additionally, we also compared 3K9Q (mutant GAPDH with chloride ion) with 3K73, which consisted of GAPDH with NAD^+ and phosphate ions. Table 1 shows the structures that we compared and their properties.

Table 1: Protein database structures that were compared

PDB Structure	Ligands Bound	GAPDH
3K9Q	Chloride ions; NAD^+	mutant (C151G)
3K73	Phosphate ions; NAD^+	wild type
3LVF	NAD^+	wild type

All of the structures mentioned in Table 1 were derived from the same organism, *Staphylococcus aureus*, therefore, having identical sequences with the exception of amino acid residue 151, which in 3K9Q was mutated to a glycine. We initially thought that this alteration in sequence would not contribute to the conformational changes that we were interested in examining. *Staphylococcus aureus* contains two homologs of GAPDH that are identified as *gapA* and *gapB* [11], which have glycolytic and gluconeogenic functions in the bacteria, respectively, and are involved in contributing to its pathogenic virulence.

2.1 Identification of the residues around the chloride ion

The specific amino acid residues that surround the chloride ion in the Q-subunit were determined using the 3LC2 structure. The crystal structure was accessed by the Cn3D 4.3 program as well as Pymol. The chloride atom in the Q-subunit was highlighted and the 'select by distance' function was used to identify the residues located within 5Å.

2.2 Designation of conserved core residues in the S-loop region

The amino acid residues that were closest to the chloride ion were found to be located in the S-loop region (i.e. residues 180 to 204) as described below. The S-loop region is in the catalytic domain of the protein. It represents an important structural component in creating a cleft in the tetrameric arrangement of GAPDH [12]. Conserved residues of the S-loop were identified by comparing GAPDH sequences from human and *Staphylococcus aureus*. The sequences were obtained from www.uniprot.org (P04406 for human and Q6GIL8 for *Staphylococcus aureus* MRSA252) and compared using BLAST (www.ncbi.nlm.nih.gov). Three amino acids residues that were identified were designated as CCS (for, **C**onserved **C**ore of **S**-loop) residues.

2.3 Computation of the volume that is circumscribed by the CCS residues

We were interested in determining the space occupied by these three CCS residues, with the intention of comparing the volumes among the crystal structures examined (i.e. the O-subunit from 3K9Q, 3K73 and 3LVF) in order to assess the effects of binding chloride ions. The volume was computed by summing the three prism volumes created by the α-, β- and γ-carbons, respectively. Each of the prism volumes was determined as shown in Figure 2. Angle θ was first determined by the formula:

$$\cos\theta = (1/2QP)/DQ$$

The height was computed using the equation:

$$height = \sin\theta \times DQ$$

The volume of the prism was obtained by the formula:

$$volume = 1/2 \times b \times l \times h$$

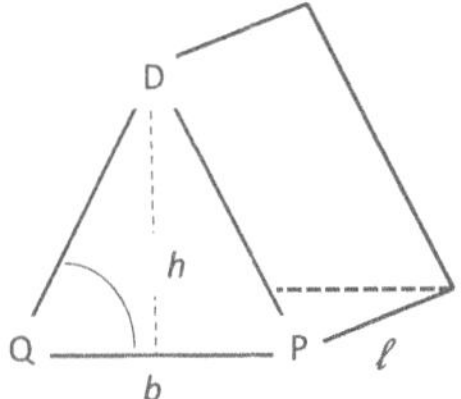

Figure 2: Unit volume that is circumscribed by the three CCS amino acid residues. Three residues are indicated by their one-letter identifier (i.e. D, for aspartate; P, for proline; Q, for asparagine). The distance, b, was measured using Pymol. The distance, h, was computed using trigonometric functions to derive the angle θ. The distance, l, was held constant at 154picometers (i.e. the length of a C-C sp3 bond). Given these parameters, the volume of a prism was calculated.

The distances between the α-carbon atoms of the three amino acid residues were measured using Pymol. This procedure was repeated for the β-carbons and then for the γ-carbons. A total of nine inter-atom distances were obtained for each crystal structure (i.e. 3K9Q, 3K73 and 3LVF). These distances were compared statistically using two-tailed paired *t*-tests. Since distances were matched, this justified the use of a paired analysis.

2.4 Measurement of inter-subunit distances

We were interested in determining the effects of the binding of chloride ions to GAPDH on the subunit-subunit interactions. Six amino acid residues on the O-subunit from each of the crystal structures examined (i.e. 3K9Q, 3K73 and 3LVF) were chosen for analysis. The criteria for choosing the residues were the following: they must be conserved and they must reside at the interface between subunits (i.e. a distance of 5Å from an R-subunit residue). Using Cn3D program, we identified the specific residues on the R-subunit that were separated by 5Å. There were at least three distances tabulated for each of the six O-subunit amino acid residues, enabling us to compare the relative distances of these six residues in each of the three crystal structures. Each of the six residues were statistically evaluated using two-tailed paired *t*-tests to compare the chloride ion containing crystal structure with those without chloride ions.

3 Results

Upon examination of the Q-subunit in the crystal structure 3LC2 (consisting of glyceraldehyde 3-phosphate and chloride ion bound to GAPDH), we determined the distances of amino acid residues in the immediate vicinity of the chloride ion. Amino acid residues Thr-181 (i.e. hydroxyl group), Asp-183 (i.e. β-carbon atom), Arg-198 (i.e. ω-nitrogen atom) and Arg-234 (i.e. ω-nitrogen atom) were all within 5Å of the chloride ion: 3.7, 4.6, 3.8 and 3.9Å, respectively. In the O-subunit of 3K9Q (consisting of NAD^+ and chloride ion bound to GAPDH), the distance of these residues to the chloride ion was observed to be different: 3.4, 4.2, 6.6 and 3.9Å, respectively. These observations suggest that the Arg-198 residue becomes displaced relative to the chloride in the presence of bound NAD^+. We observed another interesting feature of the GAPDH without NAD^+ (i.e. 3LC2); there were only two structured water molecules in the vicinity of the chloride. These waters were 6.0 and 6.1Å from the chloride ion, notably different from the chloride site found in GAPDH with NAD^+ (i.e. 3K9Q) that is described below.

3.1 Water molecules at the chloride site

Upon closer examination of the O-subunit in 3K9Q, we tabulated the polar neighbors of the water molecules that are in the vicinity of the chloride binding site using Pymol (Table 2). These water molecules are also presented in Figure 3. Additionally, the chloride ion was also found to be in polar contact with the 2′-hydroxyl of the nicotinamide ribose (i.e. 3.5Å), suggesting that the water molecules may be necessary for the proper configuration for chloride interaction. Behind the chloride ion in this perspective (Figure 3), there exists an amino acid residue (i.e. Thr-181), whose hydroxyl group is

3.4Å from the chloride ion, also representing a polar neighbor to the chloride ion. These four water molecules did not exhibit polar contacts with the chloride ion as determined by the Pymol program, but they were nonetheless in close proximity to the chloride ion (i.e. 4.9, 5.2, 5.7 and 4.8Å for W1, W2, W3 and W4, respectively).

Table 2: Polar distances involving four water molecules to the coenzyme NAD$^+$ and two arginine residues

Water Molecule	Polar Neighbor	Distance (Å)
W1	amide-*N* of NAD$^+$	2.6
W2	ring-*N* of NAD$^+$	3.3
	2′-*OH* of NAD$^+$	2.9
W3	2′-*OH* of NAD$^+$	3.0
	3′-*OH* of NAD$^+$	2.5
W4	ω-*N* of Arg-234	3.2
	δ-*N* of Arg-198	3.1

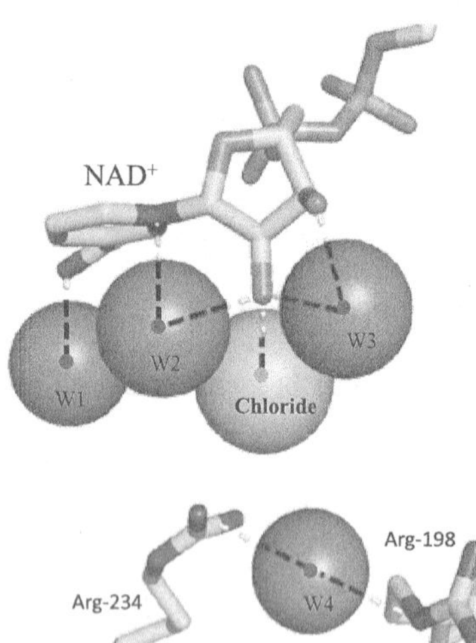

Figure 3: Chloride binding site in GAPDH. Using the crystal structure for *Staphylococcus aureus* GAPDH (i.e. O-subunit, 3K9Q), we present the chloride binding site, containing four water molecules, the coenzyme NAD$^+$ and two arginine residues. Polar neighbors are given using dashed lines. An additional residue (i.e. Thr-181) is directly behind the chloride molecule, forming a polar interaction with the chloride ion.

In summary, we have identified that there are four residues that are in close proximity of the chloride ion and that there are four water molecules in the vicinity of a chloride ion. Three water molecules make polar contacts with NAD$^+$ which in turn makes a polar contact with the chloride ion. Additionally, Thr-181 also makes polar contact with the chloride.

3.2 Comparison of GAPDH sequences

Comparison of the human (i.e. P04406 Swiss-Prot) GAPDH sequence to that of *Staphylococcus aureus* MRSA 252 (i.e. Q6GIL8 Swiss-Prot) using BLAST analysis showed 45% identity and 62% similarity. The S-loop sequence for both species is given in Figure 4. This region of the *Staphylococcus aureus* GAPDH is only 40% homologous to the human. Interestingly, the Thr-182 in the human is conserved (i.e. Thr-181 in *Staphylococcus aureus* GAPDH); this residue is the only near vicinity residue that formed a polar contact with the chloride ion.

```
Hs 180 AITATQKTVDGPSGK-LWRDGRGALQN 205
       A T  Q T D P  K   R  R A +N
Sa 179 AYTGDQNTQDAPHRKGDKRRARAAAEN 205
```

Figure 4: S-loop of the GAPDH. The sequence of the S-loop region (boxed) for human (Hs) GAPDH is juxtaposed to that of *Staphylococcus aureus* (Sa). The conserved sequences are indicated by common letters between the rows. Similar sequences are indicated by the plus (+) sign. The threonine residue that forms a polar contact to the chloride ion is given as white letters (shaded black). The core conserved residues are given as bolded letters (shaded grey).

We chose three conserved amino acid residues in this region other than those that were in close proximity to the chloride ion and designated them as core conserved S-loop residues (CCS): Gln-184, Asp-188 and Pro-190 (Figure 5).

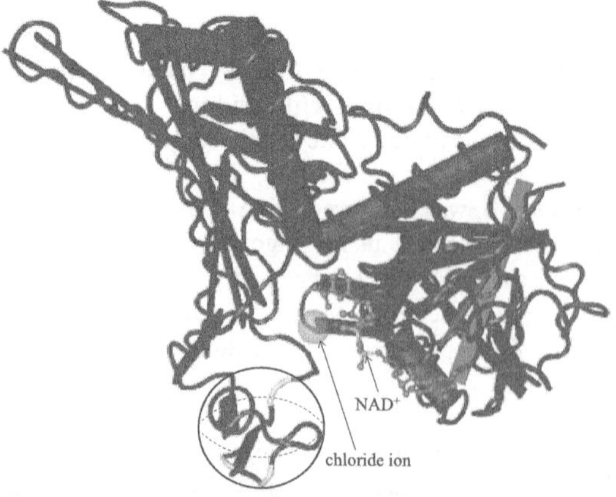

Figure 5: Structure of the O-subunit in GAPDH. The three CCS residues (light shaded) are shown in a circle that is drawn as a sphere to represent volume or space, which we computed as described below.

3.3 Volume circumscribed by CCS residues

The volume circumscribed by the three conserved core S-loop residues (CCS), namely Gln-184, Asp-188 and Pro-190, was determined as described in Materials and Methods. The magnitude of the volume was compared among the three main crystal structures that were studied (i.e. 3K9Q, 3K73 and 3LVF). The volumes that we computed for this parameter were 242.2, 247.5 and 250.2Å^3, respectively. There were three measurements for each calculated triangular space circumscribed by the successive carbons (i.e. α-, β- and γ-carbons) that make up the side chain of the CCS residues. As mentioned previously, the three triangular prisms were summed to obtain the total volume of the space that they occupy. Figure 6 illustrates the three triangular shapes providing a topological arrangement of the space.

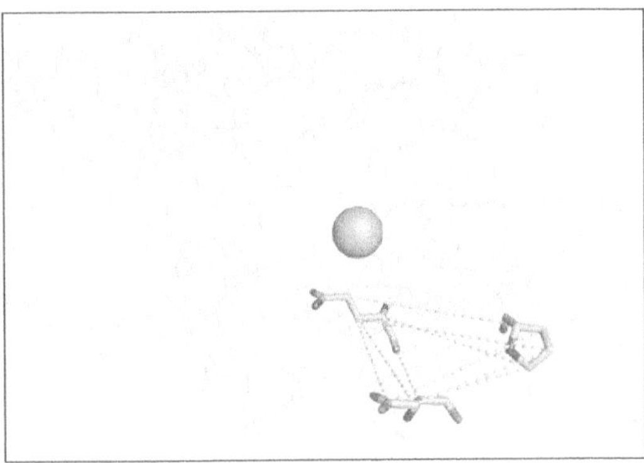

Figure 6: Illustration of the volume circumscribed by the three CCS residues. The residues of the O-subunit of GAPDH (i.e. 3K9Q) are shown as 'lines' and the three CCS residues are shown as 'sticks'. The distances between the side chain carbons are given in dashed lines, defining the space occupied by these residues. The sphere represents the chloride ion.

This volume (bordered by residues 184, 188 and 190) represents a space that is in close proximity to the amino acid residue Thr-181, which as described above forms a polar contact with the chloride ion. The average distance of the CCS residues to the chloride ion is 14.3Å. We proposed that this space would be modified in the structures that contain chloride ions (i.e. 3K9Q) compared to those structures either without chloride (i.e. 3LVF) or in the presence of inorganic phosphate (i.e. 3K73).

We took the individual atom to atom measurements (shown as dashed lines in Figure 6) in crystal structure 3K9Q and compared them against those obtained in 3K73 and 3LVF. We used a two-tailed paired *t*-test analysis. The results are presented in Figure 7 and illustrate the average decrease in inter-residue distance due to the presence of either chloride ion (bar on the left in Figure 7) or inorganic phosphate (bar on the right). Again, each bar represents a change in this region of the protein due to anion bound; however, only the results from the structure containing chloride ions approaches a significant change in conformation. While the *p*-value is slightly above the generally accepted 95% confidence limit (i.e. $p = 0.069$), it represents a strong trend, particularly in light of the effects of the inorganic phosphate (i.e. $p = 0.824$).

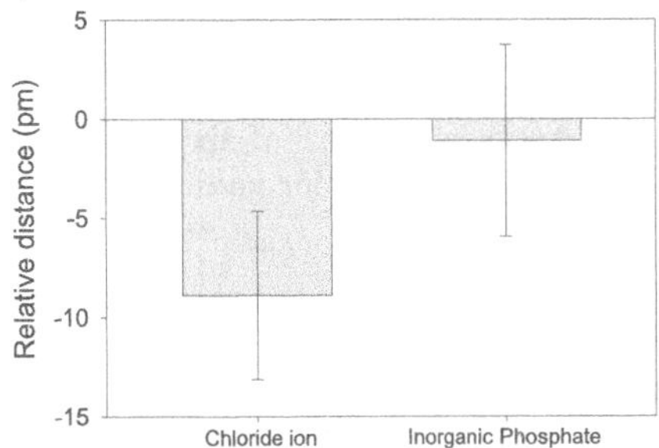

Figure 7: Anion-induced change in the distance between CCS residues. A total of nine measurements between these residues were made using the three crystal structures (i.e. 3K9Q, 3K73 and 3LVF). The distances measured in 3K9Q (with chloride ion) were subtracted by those in 3LVF (no anion) and the mean ± SEM is presented ($p = 0.069$). Likewise, the distances measured in 3K73 (with inorganic phosphate) were subtracted by those in 3LVF (no anion) and the mean ± SEM is presented ($p = 0.824$).

The results demonstrate that the binding of chloride and phosphate exhibit detectable, and we think meaningful, differences in the manner by which the two anions alter conformation (i.e. a contraction upon chloride binding).

3.4 Effects of the binding of the chloride ion on inter-subunit distances

In the three crystal structures examined, we identified six O-subunit amino acid residues that had at least one atom on the side chain that was separated from the R-subunit by a distance of 5Å or less. The six residues on the O-subunit and their respective binding partners on the R-subunit are shown in Table 3. This interface represents a part of the multiple interactions that exist across the *R*-axis, which stabilizes the tetrameric structure of GAPDH. The distances (in picometers) that were measured between these residues in 3K9Q (with chloride ion) were subtracted by those in 3LVF (no anion), giving us a value that represents either expansion of or contraction at the interfacial boundary. Likewise, the distances that were measured between these residues in 3K73 (with inorganic phosphate) were subtracted by those in 3LVF (no anion). The data are presented as mean ± SEM. The negative values represent contraction at the interfacial boundary, while positive values represent expansion of the distance between the O- and R-subunits due to the binding of the specific anion. Only one of the interactions (namely, the contact points between Pro-190 and its respective binding partners) was significantly changed and that occurred due to chloride ion binding. The decrease at the O-Gln-184/R-Thr-186 interface (i.e. -13.3pm) trended strongly, suggesting that there was a contraction across this part of the *R*-axis. When the effects of chloride ion (i.e. -6.7pm) were compared against that of inorganic phosphate at this junction point, there was no difference between the anions (data not shown).

Table 3: The average distance of six interfacial residues displaced upon binding a specific anion.

O-subunit residues	R-subunit residues	Subunit Separation (pm)	
		Chloride ion	Inorganic Phosphate
Thr-181	T186,Q187	-3.3 ± 5.6	-11.7 ± 7.9
Gln-184	T186	-6.7 ± 3.3	**-13.3 ± 3.3**[b]
Asp-188	R12,R15,L44, Y47,D48,T49, M50	-1.4 ± 2.3	1.0 ± 1.9
Pro-190	F10,R15,D34, T36, M40, L44	**16.1 ± 2.4**[a]	2.8 ± 2.5
Arg-200	H43,L44,Y47, D48,T49	4.0 ± 2.7	3.3 ± 3.6
Asn-205	T49	10.0 ± 0.00	0.0 ± 5.8

[a] There was a significant difference in the inter-subunit distance between 3K9Q and 3LVF involving this residue ($p < 0.00001$)

[b] Not technically a significant difference, but trending towards a difference in the inter-subunit distance between 3K73 and 3LVF involving this residue ($p = 0.057$)

Residue F10 qualified for the 5Å rule for 3LVF and 3K73 but not for 3K9Q; it was nonetheless kept in the computation for interfacial distances. Conversely, residue M50 qualified for the 5Å rule for 3K9Q but not for 3LVF or 3K73; it was likewise kept in the computational procedures.

We looked closely at the juxtaposition of Pro-190 and Leu-44, both of which are hydrophobic in nature. Figure 8 presents the relationship between these two residues in structures that have either inorganic phosphate or chloride ion bound. The structures are presented with the Pro-190 projected in the same orientation in each illustration.

While no demonstrative change in conformation was detectable in these two structures, the interfacial distances between the terminal carbon atom of Leu-44 and the ring atoms of Pro-190 that were measured in 3K9Q (i.e. with chloride ion) strongly trended greater than those measured in 3K73 (i.e. with inorganic phosphate) as indicated from the results of a Wilcoxon Signed Rank test ($p = 0.063$). The average distance across the *R*-axis in the GAPDH with chloride is 4.14Å and the average distance with inorganic phosphate is 4.00Å, indicating a 14pm separation between subunits due to chloride ion binding to GAPDH.

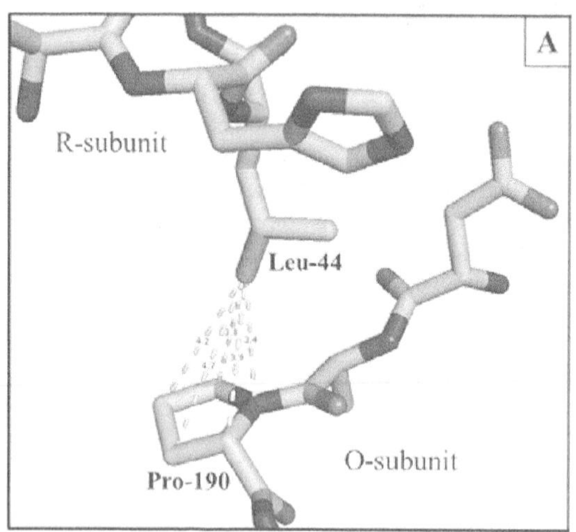

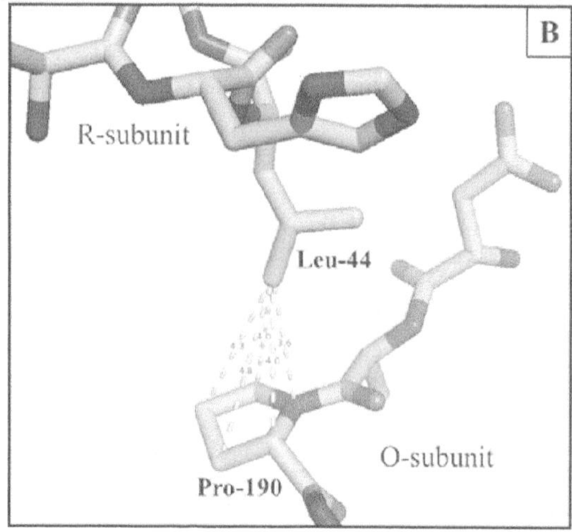

Figure 8: Interfacial interactions between residues across the *R*-axis in GAPDH. The distances (in angstrom) between the terminal carbon of the side chain on Leu-44 on the R-subunit and carbons that makeup the ring system of Pro-190 on the O-subunit for GAPDH with inorganic phosphate (A) and chloride ion (B) are given.

4 Discussion and Conclusions

We report that the impact of chloride binding to GAPDH alters the S-loop microenvironment in such a way as to disrupt the contacts across the *R*-axis. In this study, we used a computational approach employing the available crystal structures that contain bound chloride. Mukherjee and coworkers [13] have deposited several different *Staphylococcus aureus* GAPDH crystal structures that were obtained with various ligands bound and with certain mutants that were generated.

We compared three crystal structures (listed in Table 1) in an effort to interrogate the effects of chloride binding to the protein. While our results indicate that chloride interaction with GAPDH alters the protein in a manner different from that of inorganic phosphate binding, the only cautionary comment pertains to the nature of the 3K9Q structure as it compares to 3LVF and 3K73. Crystal structure 3K9Q is derived from a Cys151Gly mutant, whereas the other two are wild type. One can argue that the replacement of the cysteine side chain at position 151 (i.e. $-CH_3-SH$) with the side chain for glycine (i.e. -H) may be disruptive to the entire subunit, and thereby altering the contacts at the *R*-axis, particularly relative to 3LVF and 3K73. To address this concern we measured the overall dimensions of the O-subunit for each of these three crystal structures to ascertain the global impact of the Cys151Gly mutant. Choosing residues at the outer periphery of the subunit (namely, Lys196, Lys251 and Asp62), we measured the distances between these residues and the α-carbon of residue 151. The mean distance for 3K9Q (C151G mutant with chloride), 3K73 (wild type with inorganic phosphate) and 3LVF (wild type with no anion) is 28.8, 28.8 and 29.0Å, respectively. There were no statistical differences between these values. Therefore, the mutation had no effect on the overall topology of the O-subunit.

In summary, we computed the micro-conformational changes that occur upon the chloride binding to GAPDH and that these changes affect the highly conserved amino acid residues in the S-loop region. These chloride induced changes appear to directly alter the contacts across the *R*-axis, potentially destabilizing the O-P dimer relative to the R-Q dimer interactions. This observation is consistent with the literature [5-9], which demonstrate the enhanced instability in the presence of high chloride concentration. This chloride-induced change may affect the oligomeric properties of GAPDH as previously shown [4]. The alteration in the conformation and the change in subunit-subunit interaction may in part be due to the re-distribution of fixed water molecules at the anion binding site (Figure 3). In crystal structure 3K73, only the position of W4 is conserved. W1-W3 are re-positioned. The effects of chloride on GAPDH may contribute to initiating one or more of the alternate functions that have been observed with this functionally diverse protein. We know that GAPDH is a regulator of the chloride channel (i.e. $GABA_A$ receptor) [2], yet, it remains to be determined whether the downstream events that are initiated by the $GABA_A$ receptor activation involve this chloride-induced change in GAPDH structure. A chloride-induced inhibition of glycolytic function [5] may increase the activity of GAPDH's alternate functions. Since GAPDH plays a role in phosphorylation of $GABA_A$ receptor and that chloride ions appear to regulate GAPDH structure and perhaps function, it is reasonable to speculate that there may be a tightly regulated reciprocal relationship between these two proteins.

5 References

[1] Seidler NW. Functional diversity. Adv Exp Med Biol. 985:103-147, Jan 2013

[2] Laschet JJ, Minier F, Kurcewicz I et al., Glyceraldehyde-3-phosphate dehydrogenase is a $GABA_A$ receptor kinase linking glycolysis to neuronal inhibition. J Neurosci. 24(35):7614-7622, Sep 2004

[3] Montalbano AJ, Theisen CS, Fibuch EE, Seidler NW. Isoflurane enhances the moonlighting activity of GAPDH: implications for $GABA_A$ receptor trafficking. ISRN Anesthesiology, vol. 2012, Article ID 970795, 7 pages, 2012

[4] Seidler NW. Dynamic oligomeric properties. Adv Exp Med Biol. 985:207-247, Jan 2013

[5] Nagradova NK, Muronetz VI, Grozdova ID, Golovina TO. Cold inactivation of glyceraldehyde-phosphate dehydrogenase from rat skeletal muscle. Biochim Biophys Acta. 377(1):15-25, Jan 1975

[6] Fridovich I. Inhibition of acetoacetic decarboxylase by anions. The Hofmeister lyotropic series. J Biol Chem. 238:592-598, Feb1963

[7] Chilson OP, Kitto GB, Kaplan NO. Factors affecting the reversible dissociation of dehydrogenases. Proc Natl Acad Sci USA. 53(5):1006-1014, May1965

[8] Markert CL. Lactate dehydrogenase isozymes: dissociation and recombination of subunits. Science. 140(3573):1329-1330, Jun 1963

[9] Suzuki K, Harris JI. Hybridization of glyceraldehyde-3-phosphate dehydrogenase. J Biochem.77(3):587-593, Mar 1975

[10] Kauzmann W. Some factors in the interpretation of protein denaturation. Adv Protein Chem. 14:1-63, 1959

[11] Purves J, Cockayne A, Moody PC, Morrissey JA. Comparison of the regulation, metabolic functions, and roles in virulence of the glyceraldehyde-3-phosphate dehydrogenase homologues gapA and gapB in *Staphylococcus aureus*. Infect Immun. 78(12):5223-5232, Dec 2010

[12] Seidler NW. Basic biology of GAPDH. Adv Exp Med Biol. 985:1-36, Jan 2013

[13] Mukherjee S, Dutta D, Saha B, Das AK. Crystal structure of glyceraldehyde-3-phosphate dehydrogenase 1 from methicillin-resistant *Staphylococcus aureus* MRSA252 provides novel insights into substrate binding and catalytic mechanism. J Mol Biol. 401(5):949-968, Sep 2010

PREDICTION OF SEC-DEPENDENT SECRETED PROTEINS BASED ON mRNA STRUCTURE OF SIGNAL PEPTIDES

H. Samander[1], K. Passi[1], M. Saleh[2]
[1]Department of Mathematics and Computer Science, [2]Department of Biology
Laurentian University, Sudbury, Ontario, Canada

Abstract - *Protein secretion in bacteria is based on recognition of N-terminal signal peptides in pre-proteins. These signal peptides, however, vary greatly in sequences and could possibly present difficulty for bacteria in efficiently targeting these proteins. This is further supported by experimental observations that the resulting effects on protein secretion due to alterations in the signal peptide sequences are not explained by the signal peptide hypothesis. An alternative to this is the mRNA hypothesis whereby the target proteins are directed for secretion by recognition of the mRNA sequence. To explore this idea, databases of secreted and cytoplasmic proteins from Escherichia coli were constructed and analyzed using a number of bioinformatics tools such as Multiple Sequence Alignment (MSA), and Statistical Analysis RNA secondary structures. MSA supports the notion that the cell could use sequence features in mRNA to identify and target the secreted proteins, as they are more similar to each other and more different from the cytoplasmic proteins at the mRNA level. Statistical analysis of aligned mRNA sequences revealed a high correlation between the secreted and cytoplasmic mRNA when their U(T)/A ratios were compared. The analysis by calculating the ratio U(T)/A outperforms the analysis by SignalP4.0, since the U(T)/A ratio was predictive of the secretion of two proteins that had low SignalP score. Due to space limitations we do not present results related to RNA secondary structures. Taken all together, the analysis using bioinformatics tools appear to support the mRNA hypothesis in recognition and targeting of secreted proteins in Escherichia coli.*

Keywords: protein secretion, signal peptides, secreted mRNA, cytoplasmic RNA, Escherichia coli

1 Introduction

There are presently six recognized protein secretion systems in bacteria. The majority of secreted proteins are processed through type III or the SecYEG system. The currently accepted hypothesis regarding the targeting of pre-proteins to the SecYEG system is through a signal sequence at the N-terminus of the pre-protein. This signal sequence has certain distinguishing structural features that allow the cell to traffic the pre-protein to the SecYEG system within the cytoplasmic membrane. These features include a positively charged N-terminus, a hydrophobic middle region and a polar C-terminus containing a cleavage site with a specific amino acid sequence(s). There have been a large number of studies showing that alteration of these structural features eliminates or reduces the efficiency of protein secretion [7, 8, 10, 16, 21]. There have also been a number of studies that showed alteration of these structural features enhances secretion of the protein and thus present questions about this hypothesis. In addition to the findings of those studies, an inspection of signal sequences within the same bacterium reveals that there is indeed heterogeneity within the actual amino acid sequences, within the lengths of the sequences, and even in the basic features described above (N-positive-hydrophobic-polar-C). The SecYEG system would have to be promiscuous to be able to recognize such a diverse group of signals and would create difficulties for the cell to selectively target secreted proteins to the SecYEG membrane complex. We typically think of biological systems as being fine-tuned with several levels of quality control mechanisms. An alternative to the N-terminal signal sequence could be the mRNA sequence of the secreted protein. This so-called RNA hypothesis has been shown to be a possible mechanism for mRNA targeting and subcellular localization in bacterial, plant and animal cells [2, 12, 13, 22]. To explore whether or not a similar mechanism might be involved in targeting Sec-dependent secreted proteins in bacteria, we have used a bioinformatics approach and compared the properties of amino acid signal sequences with the 5' sequences of their mRNA's in E. coli. Our findings suggest that the features of the 5' of the corresponding mRNA's are more homogenous than the amino acid sequences. Our analysis also shows that there are distinct differences between the 5' sequences of mRNA's of secreted proteins and those of cytoplasmic proteins. The latter was most pronounced by comparing the T(U)/A ratios of the 5' ends of the mRNA's. This data suggest that mRNA sequences may function, either alone or in combination with amino acid signal sequences, in targeting pre-proteins for secretion through the SecYEG system.

2 Dataset construction and Bioinformatics tools

All analyses were performed in this study by using a Sony model personal computer, supported by the Windows-based operating system. Four different datasets were built, secreted and cytoplasmic proteins and mRNAs. The data used in this study was based on E.coli K12 protein sequences, listed in Table 1 and 2 (only few sequences are shown due to space limitation). To generate Table 1 dataset, E.coli proteins were selected based on annotation of the genome sequence available in public data sources [11]. We selected 200 sequences of proteins randomly and predicted their signal peptide by using SignalP4.0 webserver [14] in order to group the proteins into secreted and cytoplasmic. From this analysis, we extracted the proteins with a predicted signal peptide up to 25 amino acids long. Predicting cleavage sites was also performed using SignalP4.0 webserver. In an effort to generate an mRNA dataset, DNA sequences of both secreted and cytoplasmic genes were extracted from EcoCyc database [6]. EcoCyc is a bioinformatics database of Escherichia coli K-12 [18]. The first 75 nucleotides of each DNA sequence was used for the cytoplasmic proteins to reflect the maximum length of the signal peptides used for the secreted proteins, 25 amino acids long. Then DNA sequences are converted to mRNA sequences by using Bioinformatics Toolbox™ of MATLAB [20].

Table 1 DNA and mRNA sequences of secreted protein dataset of *E. coli* used in this study [18].

Secreted gene	Protein	DNA	mRNA
1. "yadM"	MIKTTPHKIVILMG ILLSPSVFATD	atgATAAAAACAACGCCACATAAAATAGTG ATACTGATGGGAATATTATTATCACCCTCA GTATTTGCAACGGATA	augAUAAAAACAACGCCACAUAAAAUAGUGA UACUGAUGGGAAUAUUAUUAUCACCCUCAG UAUUUGCAACGGAUA
2. "btuF"	MAKSLFRALVALS FLAPLWLNAAPR	atgGCTAAGTCACTGTTCAGGGCGCTGGTCG CCCTGTCTTTTCTTGCGCCACTGTGGCTCAA CGCCGCGCCGCGC	augGCUAAGUCACUGUUCAGGGCGCUGGUCG CCCUGUCUUUUCUUGCGCCACUGUGGCUCA ACGCCGCGCCGCGC
3. "yceI"	MKKSLLGLTFASL MFSAGSAVAADY	atgAAAAAAAGCCTGCTTGGTTTAACCTTCG CGTCCCTGATGTTCTCTGCCGGTTCAGCGG TTGCCGCCGATTAC	augAAAAAAAGCCUGCUUGGUUUAACCUUCG CGUCCCUGAUGUUCUCUGCCGGUUCAGCGG UUGCCGCCGAUUAC
4. "yaaI"	MKSVFTISASLAIS LMLCCTAQAND	atgAAATCCGTTTTTACGATTTCCGCCAGCCT GGCGATTAGCCTGATGCTGTGCTGCACGGC GCAGGCAAACGAC	augAAAUCCGUUUUUACGAUUUCCGCCAGCC UGGCGAUUAGCCUGAUGCUGUGCUGCACGG CGCAGGCAAACGAC
5. "yaaX"	MKKMQSIVLALSL VLVAPMAAQAAE	gtgAAAAAGATGCAATCTATCGTACTCGCAC TTTCCCTGGTTCTGGTCGCTCCCATGGCAG CACAGGCTGCGGAA	gugAAAAAGAUGCAAUCUAUCGUACUCGCAC UUUCCCUGGUUCUGGUCGCUCCCAUGGCAG CACAGGCUGCGGAA

Sequence analysis was performed by multiple sequence alignment. A multiple sequence alignment (MSA) tool aids in arranging sequences into a rectangular array to make residues in a given column homologous [4], in order to analyze sequences. Only the best-scoring alignment reported for each data set was considered in this study, which were T-Coffee and MUSCLE. The performance of MUSCLE and T-Coffee were ranked by using BAliBASE server [5]. T-Coffee and MUSCLE multiple sequence alignment were performed by using two different tools the T-Coffee web server and the Jalview 2.7 programme.

Table 2 DNA and mRNA sequences of cytoplasmic protein dataset of *E. coli* used in this study [18].

Cytoplasmic gene	Protein	DNA	mRNA
1. "thrC"	MKLYNLKDHNEQ VSFAQAVTQGLG K	atgAAAAAGCACCTTCTGCCTCTCGCTCTGCTG TTTTCCGGAATATCTCCGGCCCAGGCGCTGGA TGTCGGCGAT	augAAAAAGCACCUUCUGCCUCUCGCUCUG CUGUUUUCCGGAAUAUCUCCGGCCCAGGC GCUGGAUGUCGGCGAU
2. "dnaJ"	MAKQDYYEILGVS KTAEEREIRKAY	atgAAAATAATCTCTAAAATGTTAGTCGGTGCG TTAGCGTTAGCCGTTACCAATGTCTATGCCGC TGAATTGATG	augAAAAUAAUCUCUAAAAUGUUAGUCGG UGCGUUAGCGUUAGCCGUUACCAAUGUC UAUGCCGCUGAAUUGAUG
3. "ileS"	MSDYKSTLNLPET GFPMRGDLAKRE	atgCGTAAGTTCATTTTCGTATTGCTGACACTG CTTTTGGTCAGCCCTTTTTCCTTTGCGATGAAA GGTATTATC	augCGUAAGUUCAUUUUCGUAUUGCUGAC ACUGCUUUUGGUCAGCCCUUUUUCCUUU GCGAUGAAAGGUAUUAUC
4. "astE"	MDNFLALTLTGK KPVITEREINGVR	atgGAACTCTACAGAGAATATCCTGCATGGCTT ATCTTTTTACGCCGTACTTATGCGGTTGCAGC GGGCGTTCTG	augGAACUCUACAGAGAAUAUCCUGCAUG GCUUAUCUUUUUACGCCGUACUUAUGCG GUUGCAGCGGGCGUUCUG
5. "gdhA"	MDQTYSLESFLNH VQKRDPNQTEFA	atgATTATGAAAAATTGTCTACTGTTGGGCGCG CTTTTAATGGGCTTTACTGGTGTGGCGATGGC GCAAAGTGTC	augAUUAUGAAAAAUUGUCUACUGUUGGG CGCGCUUUUAAUGGGCUUUACUGGUGUG GCGAUGGCGCAAAGUGUC

Many quantitative measurements were analyzed for each protein and RNA data sets. These measurements included nucleotide frequencies, amino acid frequencies, average of protein properties, and energy. All frequency calculations in nucleotide bases in mRNA sequences and in the amino acid bases of proteins sequences were performed by MEGA software. MEGA "Molecular Evolutionary Genetics Analysis" is a bioinformatics tool for automatic and manual sequence alignment, estimating rates of molecular evolution, and testing evolutionary hypothesis. The MEGA showed all tables' output after taking the average of each group's frequency presented in percentages. The statistical analyses were performed with the commercial tool *QI Macros SPC for Excel* Software (Microsoft Windows, 2010).

3 Multiple Sequence Alignment (MSA)

All the 50 proteins and mRNA sequences, which are listed in Table 1 and 2, were aligned by using the T-Coffee multiple sequence alignment webserver. A default parameter was chosen in order to construct the primary library support for both alignments. The alignment results of secreted proteins and cytoplasmic protein are shown in Figure 1 (snapshot shown), while Figures 2 and 3 (snapshot shown) show the alignment results of secreted mRNA and cytoplasmic mRNA, respectively. The alignment score is 46 for secreted proteins, and 48 for cytoplasmic proteins, which are the scores of total consistency of secreted and cytoplasmic proteins, are slightly abnormal. These scores indicate that cytoplasmic proteins are slightly more aligned than the secreted proteins. Thus, cytoplasmic protein sequences seem to be more homogenous than the secreted proteins. In contrast, Figures 2 and 3 shows that the alignment score in cytoplasmic mRNA is 28, which is lower than the alignment score of 50 in secreted mRNA. These scores indicate that secreted mRNA sequences are likely to be more homogenous than the cytoplasmic mRNAs, which is normally accepted. The graphic result in Figure 4 represents the level of consistency among the secreted mRNA sequences. Most of the sequences are colored red and dark orange, where red and dark orange indicates a high level of consistency in secreted mRNA sequences, and that these sequences have a high degree of similarity. On the other hand, Figure 3 shows the sequences mostly colored in green, light orange and blue among middle regions, which represents very low level of consistency among the cytoplasmic RNA.

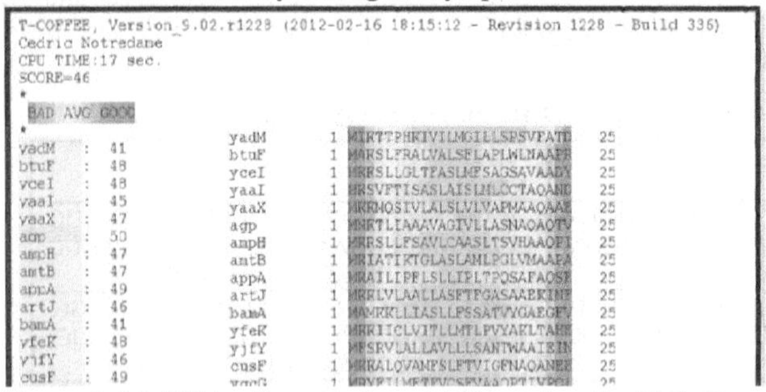

Figure 1 (a) MSA of secreted protein by using the T-Coffee webserver shows an alignment score = 46.

In order to support these observations, MSA by MUSCLE method has been applied using Jalview 2.7 application. The results are shown in Figure 4 (snapshot shown) for secreted and cytoplasmic proteins and in Figures 5 and 6 (snapshot shown) for secreted and cytoplasmic mRNA, respectively. Default parameters, such as the number of iterations and gaps, were selected for both the cases. The outputs were colored by the percentage of identity. The dark purple color indicates approximately more than 90% of similarity among the sequences in a given column, while the lighter color indicates lower percentages of similarity.

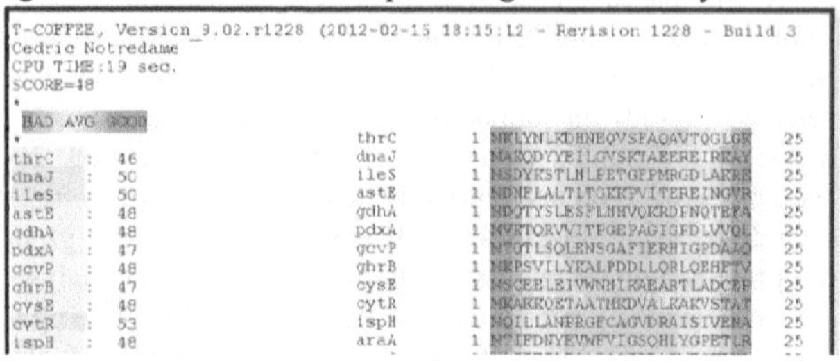

Figure 1 (b) MSA of cytoplasmic protein by using the T-Coffee webserver shows an alignment score = 48.

In addition, consensus sequences were plotted below the alignment to show which residues were most abundant in the alignment at each position. The percentages can be read by point in the cursor over a region. Indeed, Figures 6 and 7 illustrate that both secreted and cytoplasmic proteins have the same percentage of similarity in the first column as the protein sequences start with M. The consensus sequence of secreted proteins shows slightly higher level of similarity than the cytoplasmic proteins among the rest of the sequences. For example, Figure 4 (a) illustrates that secreted protein consensus sequence shares the amino acid L in 7 columns, and the amino acid A in six columns. This may refer to the fact that signals peptide of secreted proteins includes the most hydrophobic amino acid such as L [15]. Whereas Figure 4 (b) shows that the amino acid L is shared in 7 columns. This shows that the amino acids of secreted proteins are slightly more similar than amino acids of cytoplasmic proteins. On the contrary, Figures 5 and 6 report that mRNAs of secreted proteins are more similar than those of cytoplasmic proteins. In Figure 5, many areas are covered in dark purple, in addition to the first three positions, which reflects that the most sequences of secreted mRNA share >50% residues similarity in some columns. In fact, it is not a surprise to show that first three positions indicate more than 90% of similarity, since AUG is the canonical start codon. In Figure 6, however, a light shadow of purple color indicates <40% similarity in few columns of cytoplasmic mRNA. This observation shows that the secreted mRNAs are much more similar than the cytoplasmic mRNAs. Furthermore, after ignoring the first three positions, a histogram plot of consensus sequence in Figures 5 and 6 show that nucleotide U appears more frequently in secreted mRNA sequences than in cytoplasmic mRNA sequences. This observation also supports the hypothesis of U-richness.

To sum up, we observed that the differences in the similarity values among the secreted proteins and the cytoplasmic proteins is very less. Whereas, the differences in the similarity values among the secreted mRNAs and cytoplasmic mRNAs is much more. This provides us with some evidence that mRNA sequences may include a signal that plays a main role in secreting / exporting proteins, which supports the mRNA signal hypothesis.

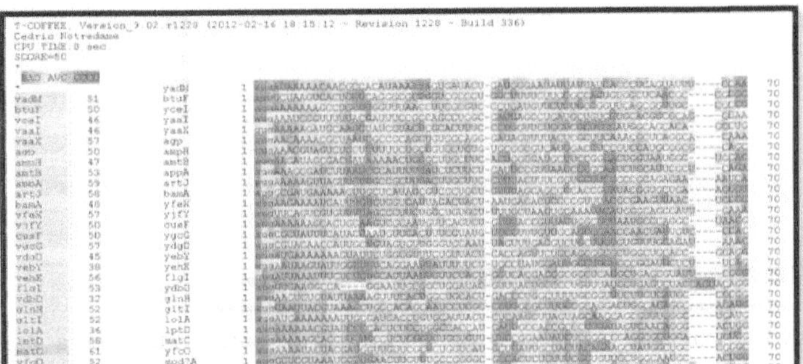

Figure 2 MSA of secreted mRNA by using the T-Coffee webserver shows an alignment score = 50.

Figure 3 MSA of cytoplasmic mRNA by using the T-Coffee webserver shows an alignment score = 28.

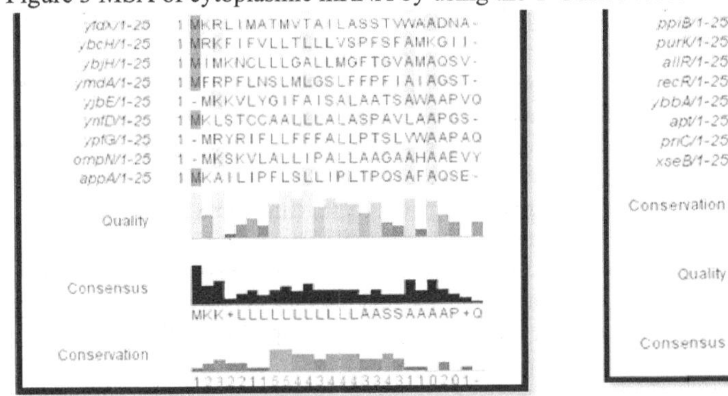

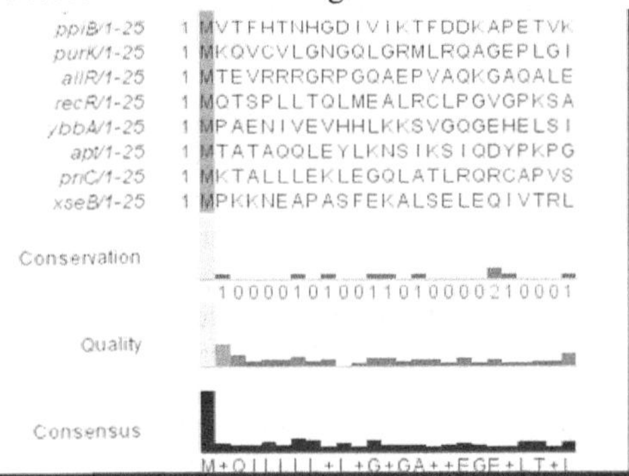

Figure 4 (a) MSA of secreted proteins by using the Jalview application and applying MUSCLE method. Dark purple indicates a high percentage identity, shows at the beginning of sequences alignment. (b) MSA of cytoplasmic proteins.

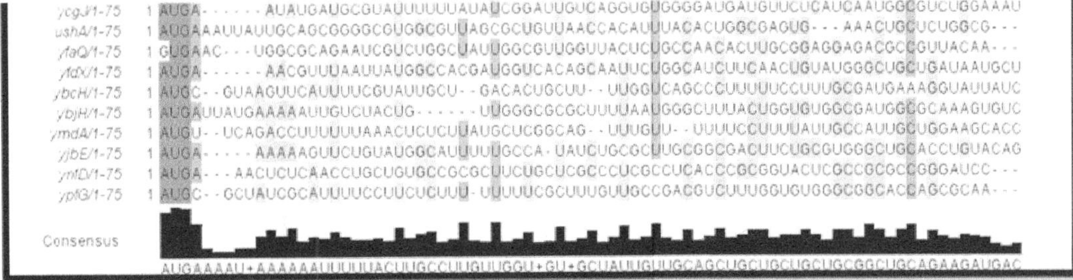

Figure 5 MSA of secreted mRNA by using MUSCLE method in Jalview application. Dark purple indicates a high percentage of identity, shows in the beginning of sequences alignment and some regions among the middle. A light purple indicates a lower percentage of identity in many regions in a middle area.

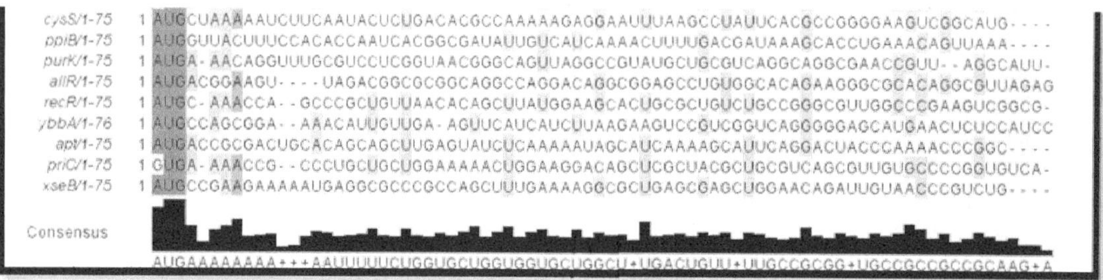

Figure 6 MSA of cytoplasmic mRNA by using MUSCLE method in Jalview application Dark purple indicates a high percentage of identity, shows at the beginning of sequences alignment only. A light purple indicates a lower percentage of identity shows among the middle in a few areas.

4 U(T)/A ratio

To study the relationship between U and A nucleotide for secreted and cytoplasmic mRNA we calculate the ratio U(T)/A of average frequencies of U and A. U(T)/A ratio of 50 sequences for secreted and cytoplasmic mRNA arrange in ascending order are plotted graphically in Figure 7. The graph in Figure 7 shows a strong correlation between the ratios of secreted and cytoplasmic mRNA. However, certain range of sequences show a significant difference in the U(T)/A ratio between secreted mRNA and cytoplasmic mRNA, for example between sequences 9 to 11, 24 to 32 and 13 to 14. In addition, there is a peak value for the U(T)/A ratio for the secreted sequences after sequence 48 indicating difference of 1.02 between the secreted mRNA and cytoplasmic mRNA ratios. In order to test whether the differences in U(T)/A ratios between secreted and cytoplasmic mRNA are statistically significant, *z*-test was performed by Excel. The *z*-test of independent samples can be applied to our datasets since the number of each datasets is fairly big($n_1 = n_2 =$ 50 data), and according to the central limit theorem our data approximates a normal distribution [19].The *z* value of 1.76 is greater than the critical *z* value 1.64, which is statistically significant. In addition to the *z* value, Table 3 shows that *p*-value = 0.03 is smaller than α = 0.05, which is also statistically significant. As a result, there is a significant difference in U(T)/A ratios between secreted mRNA and cytoplasmic mRNA that may affect the primary structures.

In addition, Figure 7 indicates that the U(T)/A ratios of 32 sequences (64%) of secreted 75-residues mRNA are ≥ 1.2. While U(T)/A ratios of 30 sequences (60%) of cytoplasmic 75-residues mRNA datasets are ≤ 1.2. In order to test the above observation, data of well-known secreted and cytoplasmic proteins were listed for different species of Gram-negative bacteria such as *Yersinia* and *salmonella*. The chosen proteins have been taken from the research papers that have proved the proteins to be secreted or cytoplasmic [19, 10, 9, 17, 3, 1]. However due to space limitation we do not list the proteins, DNA and mRNA of the bacteria. The ratio U(T)/A was calculated and SignalP4.0 was performed in order to predict the signal peptide and to classify the protein. The results are summarized in Table 4, which shows that both U(T)/A ratio and SignalP.40 have the same predictions except for two genes, yscH and sseI. The ratio U(T)/A shows these two genes to be secreted proteins whereas SignalP4.0 shows them as not having a signal peptide. Thereby, the analysis by calculation the ratio U(T)/A outperforms the analysis by SignalP4.0.

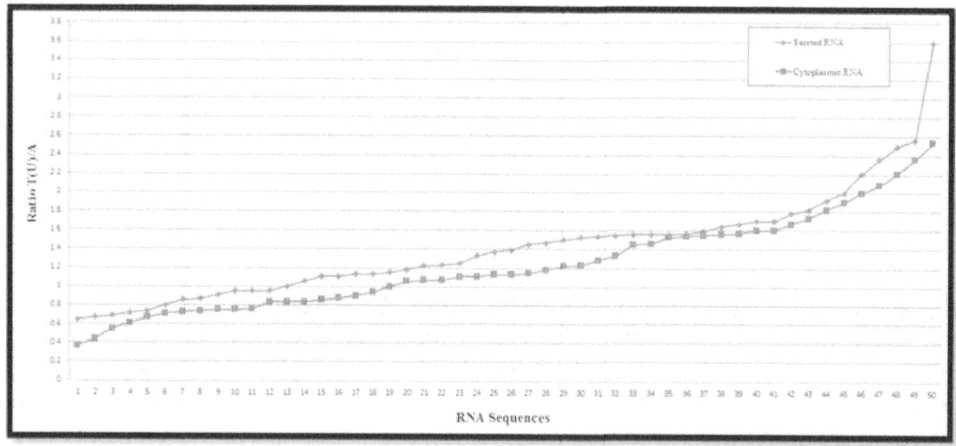

Figure 7 Ratio U(T)/A of 50 sequences for both secreted mRNA (blue line) and cytoplasmic mRNA (red line).

Table 3 Summary of *z*-test shows both *z* score and *p*-value (P(Z<=) one-tail) of the U(T)/A ratios of both secreted and cytoplasmic mRNA.

z-test: Two Sample for Means	*Secreted RNA*	*Cytoplasmic RNA*
Mean	1.4152	1.2284
Known Variance	0.31	0.25
Observations	50	50
z	1.765094089	
P(Z<=z) one-tail	0.038773977	
z Critical one-tail	1.644853627	
P(Z<=z) two-tail	0.077547954	
z Critical two-tail	1.959963985	

Table 4 The results of U(T)/A ratios and SignalP4.0 of all genes listed below

Gene	SignalP4.0		Ratio U(T)/A	
	D-Score	Signal Peptide?	U(T)/A	Secreted?
yscH *Yersinia*	0.319	No	1.35	Yes
scsD *salmonella*	0.640	Yes	2	Yes
scsC *salmonella*	0.903	Yes	1.35	Yes
sseI *salmonella*	0.132	No	1.71	Yes
ansA *Yersinia*	0.168	No	0.95	No
yaiL *E. Coli*	0.102	No	0.64	No
YaiE *Yersinia*	0.12	No	0.104	No

5 Conclusions

The aim of the present study was to provide computational evidence by using bioinformatics approaches that could support the RNA signal hypothesis. In addition to investigating the features in the RNA that codes for the signal, this study provides some evidences that mRNAs are directed to the secretory pathway elements that can be recognized in the mRNA sequence itself. Thus, many bioinformatics tools and applications were applied to make sure that most tools will show almost the same results and conclusions. Four datasets, secreted and cytoplasmic RNAs and proteins, were generated to access the study's goal. We provided evidence based on the analysis of 25 amino acids that sequences coding secreted mRNAs are more homogeneous and similar than those sequences coding for cytoplasmic mRNAs. The observations from MSA, homogeneity analysis and sequence statistical analysis provide us with some evidences that mRNA sequence may include a signal that plays a main role in secreting / exporting proteins in E.coli, which supports the RNA signal hypothesis.

6 References

[1] Batzilla, J., Höper, D., Antonenka, U., Heesemann, J., & Rakin, A. "Complete genome sequence of Yersinia enterocolitica subsp. palearctica serogroup O:3. J Bacteriol".193: 2067, 2011.

[2] Cuia, J., Huey-Fen Sim, T., Gong, Z., & Shen, H.-M. "Generation of transgenic zebrafish with liver-specific expression of EGFP-Lc3: A new in vivo model for investigation of liver autophagy". Biochemical and Biophysical Research Communications 2: 268-273, 2012.

[3] De Maayer, P., Chan, W., Venter, S., Toth, I., Birch, P., Joubert, F., & Coutinho, T. "Genome sequence of Pantoea ananatis LMG20103, the causative agent of Eucalyptus blight and dieback. J Bacteriol", 192: 2936–2937, 2010.

[4] Edgar, R. C., & Batzoglou, S. "Multiple Sequence Alignment". Elsevier Ltd., 16: 1–6, 2006.

[5] Edgar, R. C. "MUSCLE: multiple sequence alignment with high accuracy and high throughput". Nucleic Acids Research, 32: 1792-1797, 2004.

[6] Karp, P. D., Riley, M., Saier, M., Paulsen, I. T., Collado-Vides, J., Paley, S. M., Gama-Castro, S. "The EcoCyc Database". Nucleic Acids Research, 30: 56-58, 2002.

[7] LehnhardtS, S., Pollitt, N., Goldstein, J., & Inouye, M. "Modulation of the Effects of Mutations in the Basic Region of the OmpA Signal Peptide by the Mature Portion of the Protein". The Journal of Biological Chemistry, 263: 10300-10303, 1998.

[8] Lino, T., Takahashi, M., & Sako, T. "Role of amino-terminal positive charge on signal peptide in staphylokinase export across the cytoplasmic membrane of Escherichia coli". The Journal of Biological Chemistry 262: 7412-7417, 1987.

[9] McClelland, M., Sanderson, K., Clifton, S., Latreille, P., Porwollik, S., Sabo, A., Spieth, J. "Comparison of genome degradation in Paratyphi A and Typhi, human-restricted serovars of Salmonella enterica that cause typhoid". Nature Genetics, 36: 1268 – 1274, 2004.

[10] Michiels, T., Vanooteghem, J., Lambert de Rouvroit, C., China, B., Gustin, A., Boudry, P., & Cornelis, G. "Analysis of virC, an operon involved in the secretion of Yop proteins by Yersinia enterocolitica". J Bacteriol., 173:4994-5009, 1991.

[11] NCBI. "Just the Facts: A Basic Introduction to the Science Underlying NCBI Resources". 2004. http://www.ncbi.nlm.nih.gov/About/primer/bioinformatics.html

[12] Nevo-Dinur, K., Nussbaum-Shochat, A., Ben-Yehuda, S., & Amster-Choder, O. "Translation-Independent Localization of mRNA in E. coli. Science", 331: 1081-1084, 2011.

[13] Okita, T. W., & Choi, S.-B. "mRNA localization in plants: targeting to the cell's cortical region and beyond". Current Opinion in Plant Biology, 5: 553-559, 2002.

[14] Petersen, T. N., Brunak, S., von Heijne, G., & Nielsen , H. "SignalP 4.0: discriminating signal peptides from transmembrane regions". Nature Methods, 8: 785-786, 2011.

[15] Prilusky, J., & Bibi , E. "Studying membrane proteins through the eyes of the genetic code revealed a strong uracil bias in their coding mRNAs". PNAS, 16: 6662–6666, 2009.

[16] Puziss, J. W., Fikes , J., & Bassford, P. "Analysis of mutational alterations in the hydrophilic segment of the maltose-binding protein signal peptide". Journal of Bacteriology, 171: 2303-2311, 1989.

[17] Rosso, M., Chauvaux, S., Dessein, R., Laurans, C., Frangeul, L., Lacroix, C., Marceau, M. "Growth of Yersinia pseudo tuberculosis in human plasma: impacts on virulence and metabolic gene expression". BMC Microbiology, 8: 211, 2008.

[18] Riley, M., Abe, T., Arnaud, M., Berlyn, M., Blattner, F., Chaudhuri, R., Wanner, B. "Escherichia coli K-12: a cooperatively developed annotation snapshot". Nucleic Acids Research, 34: 1-9, 2005.

[19] Sheskin, D. J. "Handbook of parametric and nonpapramatric statical procedures". Boca Ration: Chapman & Hall / CRC, 2004.

[20] "The Mathworks, Natick , MA," Natick.

[21] Wolk, v., P.W., J., Fekkes, P., & Boorsma, A. "PrlA4 prevents the rejection of signal sequence defective preproteins by stabilizing the SecA–SecY interaction during the initiation of translocation". The EMBO Journal, 17: 3631 – 3639, 1998.

[22] Wilhelm, J. E., & Vale , R. "RNA on the Move: The mRNA Localization Pathway". J. Cell Biol, 123: 269-274, 1993.

PFC : An Efficient Approach for Protein-Protein Interaction Network Analysis

Ying Liu

[1]Department of Computer Science, Mathematics and Science, College of Professional Studies, St. John's University, Queens, NY 11439

Abstract *- One of the most pressing problems of the post genomic era is identifying protein functions. Clustering Protein-Protein-Interaction networks is a systems biological approach to this problem. Traditional Graph Clustering Methods are crisp, and allow only membership of each node in at most one cluster. However, most real world networks contain overlapping clusters. Recently the need for scalable, accurate and efficient overlapping graph clustering methods has been recognized and various soft (overlapping) graph clustering methods have been proposed. In this paper, an efficient, novel, and fast overlapping clustering method is proposed based on purifying and filtering the coupling matrix (PFC). PFC is tested on PPI networks. The experimental results show that PFC method outperforms many existing methods by a few orders of magnitude in terms of average statistical (hypergeometrical) confidence regarding biological enrichment of the identified clusters.*

Keywords: Protein-Protein Interaction networks; Graph Clustering; Overlapping functional modules; Coupling Matrix; Systems biology

1 Introduction

Homology based approaches have been the traditional bioinformatics approach to the problem of protein function identification. Variations of tools like BLAST [1] and Clustal [2] and concepts like COGs (Clusters of orthologous Groups) [3] have been applied to infer the function of a protein or the encoding gene from the known a closely related gene or protein in a closely related species. Although very useful, this approach has some serious limitations. For many proteins, no characterized homologs exist. Furthermore, form does not always determine function, and the closest hit returned by heuristic oriented sequence alignment tools is not always the closest relative or the best functional counterpart. Phenomena like Horizontal Gene Transfer complicate matters additionally. Last but not least, most biological Functions are achieved by collaboration of many different proteins and a proteins function is often context sensitive, depending on presence or absence of certain interaction partners.

A Systems Biology Approach to the problem aims at identifying functional modules (groups of closely cooperating and physically interacting cellular components that achieve a common biological function) or protein complexes by identifying network communities (groups of densely connected nodes in PPI networks). This involves clustering of PPI-networks as a main step. Once communities are detected, a hypergeometrical p-value is computed for each cluster and each biological function to evaluate the biological relevance of the clusters. Research on network clustering has focused for the most part on crisp clustering. However, many real world functional modules overlap. The present paper introduces a new simple soft clustering method for which the biological enrichment of the identified clusters seem to have in average somewhat better confidence values than current soft clustering methods.

2 Previous Work

Examples for crisp clustering methods include HCS [4], RNSC [5] and SPC [6]. More recently, soft or overlapping network clustering methods have evolved. The importance of soft clustering methods was first discussed in [7], the same group of authors also developed one of the first soft clustering algorithms for soft clustering, Clique Percolation Method or CPM [8]. An implementation of CPM , called CFinder [9] is available online. The CPM approach is basically based on the "defective cliques" idea and has received some much deserved attention. Another soft clustering tool is Chinese Whisper [10] with origins in Natural Language Processing. According to its author, CW can be seen as a special case of the Random Walks based method

Markov-Chain-Clustering (MCL) [11] with an aggressive pruning strategy.

Recently, some authors [12, 13] have proposed and implemented betweenness based [14] Clustering (NG) method, which makes NG's divisive hierarchical approach capable of identifying overlapping clusters. NG's method finds communities by edge removal. The modifications involve node removal or node splitting. The decisions about which edges to remove and which nodes to split, are based on iterated all pair shortest path calculations.

In this paper, we present a new approach, called PFC, which is based on the notion of Coupling matrix (or common neighbors). In the rest of the paper, we first describe PFC and compare its results with the best results achieved by the aforementioned soft approaches. The second part of this work aims to illustrate the biological relevance of soft methods by giving several examples of how the biological functions of overlap nodes relate to biological functions of respective clusters.

3 PFC Method

The method introduced here is based on the purification and filtering of coupling matrix, PFC. PFC is a soft graph clustering method that involves only a few matrix multiplications/ manipulation. Our experimental results show that it outperforms the above mentioned methods in terms of the p-values for MIPS functional enrichment [15] of the identified clusters. The PPI net works we used in the paper are yeast PPI networks (4873 proteins and 17200 interactions).

Liu and Foroushani [16] proposed a PFC filtering by simple, local criteria. In this paper, we propose a new PFC approach, filtering by corroboration.

3.1 Filtering by Simple, Local Criteria

The first Filtering approach is motivated by assumptions about the nature of the data and size of the target clusters. PPI data are for the most part results of high throughput experiments like yeast two hybrid and are known to contain many false positive and many false negative entries. For certain, more thoroughly studied parts of the network, additional data might be available from small scale, more accurate experiments. In PFC, the emphasis lies on common second degree neighbors and this can magnify the effects of noise. Under the assumption that Nodes with low degree belong in general to the less thoroughly examined parts of the network, it is conceivable that the current data for the graph around these low nodes contains many missing links. Missing links in these areas can have dramatic effects on the constellation of second degree neighbors. This means the Coupling data for low degree nodes is particularly unreliable. On the other hand, many extremely well connected nodes are known to be central hubs that in general help to connect many nodes of very different functionality with each other, hence, their second degree neighbors compromise huge sets that are less likely to be all functionally related. Additionally, it has been shown that most functional modules are meso-scale [6]. There are also some fundamental physical constrains on the size and shape of a protein complex that make very large modules unlikely. Taking these considerations into account, a filter is easily constructed by the following rules:

Discard all clusters (rows of purified coupling matrix) where the labeling node (the _th node in the _th row) has a particularly low (< 14) or particularly high (>30) degree. Discard all clusters where the module size is too small (<35) or particularly large (>65).

The selected minimum and maximum values for degree of labeling nodes and module size are heuristically motivated. The intervals can be easily changed to obtain or discard more clusters, but the enrichment results for these intervals seem reasonably good. The peak log value for the enrichment of selected clusters is at -91.00 and the average lies at -18.99. Using this filter, by clustering yeast PPI networks, PFC yields 151 clusters from 52 different Functional categories. Figure 1 gives an example.

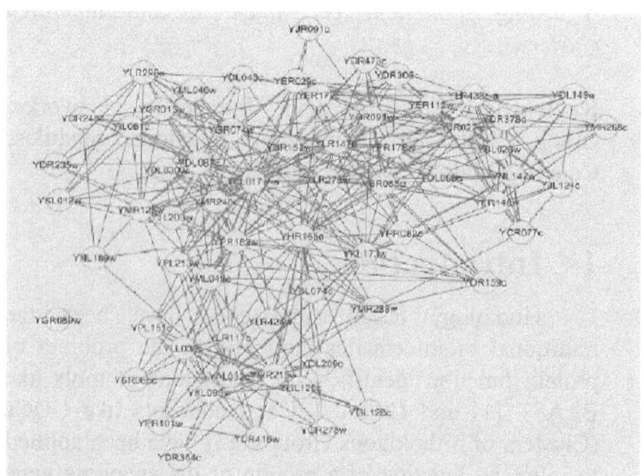

Figure 1 This Figure shows the community for the row labeled "YKL173w" in the purified coupling matrix of yeat PPI network. It is one of the clustered selected by PFC1. Out of the 63 proteins in this community, 58 belong to MIPS Funcat 11.04.03.01.

Given the Binary version of the Purified Coupling Matrix B
Calculate Overlap Matrix $O = B * B$
Normalize $O(i,j)$ by Size of Module j
Calculate Corroboration Matrix $C = \lfloor O./\alpha \rfloor$
Where: $0.5 < \alpha \leq 1$; and "./" is the Matlab cellwise division.
Calculate Common Corroborator Matrix $C_{Com} = C * C'$
Rank the rows of C_{com} by the sum of their entries
Interpret C_{com} as description of a directed Confirmation graph between clusters, where the direction of confirmation is from lower ranked to higher ranked rows.
Select clusters whose in-degree in the confirmation graph is higher than a threshold and whose out degree is 0.

3.2 Filtering by Corroboration

Filtering by local criteria gives impressing results but it does not guarantee that a few of the remaining clusters do not overlap in majority of their elements. Although PFC is an overlapping clustering algorithm, very large overlaps between clusters are bound to indicate presence of redundant clusters. At the same time, repeated concurrence of large groups of proteins in different rows does reinforce the hypothesis that these groups are indeed closely related, and that the corresponding rows represent a high quality cluster. These observations can be used to construct an alternative filter that removes both low quality and redundant clusters from the coupling matrix. The main idea is that a line A is corroborated by a Line B if the majority of nonzero elements in A are also nonzero in B. The following summarizes this filter:

Given the sparse nature of the involved matrices, this Corroboration based filter can be implemented very efficiently in Matlab. It discards by design redundant clusters (out-degree>0 in the confirmation graph indicates that there is a similar cluster with a higher rank) and retains only high quality clusters (clusters with a high in-degree in the confirmation graph have been confirmed by presence of many other clusters with similar structure). The ranking by row sum helps consolidate and summarize relevant parts of smaller clusters into larger ones. Figure 2 gives two examples of clusters selected by this approach on Yeast-PPI network.

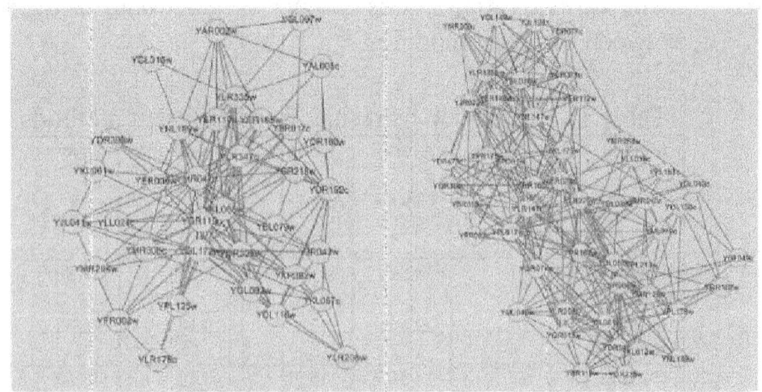

Figure 1: Two of the clusters selected by PFC2. The left Figure shows the selected community for the row labeled "YDR335w" in the purified coupling matrix. Out of the 35 proteins in this community, 29 belong to MIPS Funcat 20.09.01(nuclear transport). The right Figure shows the selected community for the row labeled "YKL173w" in the purified coupling matrix. It is one of the clustered selected by PFC1. Out of the 63 proteins in this community, 58 belong to MIPS Funcat 11.04.03.01(Splicing).

4 Experimental Results and Discussions

The results of the PFC are compared with results obtained by other soft clustering methods. A PPI network of yeast with 4873 Nodes and 17200 edges is used as the test data set. The other methods are an in-house implementation of Pinney and Westhead's Betweenness Based proposal [12], Chinese Whisper [10], CPM as implemented in C-Finder [9]. Whenever other methods needed additional input parameters, we tried to choose parameters that gave the best values. The results from different methods are summarized in Table 1.

4.1 Biological Functions of Overlap Nodes

The hypergeometric evaluation of individual clusters is the main pillar in assessing the quality of crisp clustering methods. For soft clustering methods, further interesting questions arise that deal with relationships between clusters. A possible conceptual disadvantage, production of widely overlapping, redundant clusters was addressed in previous sections. Figure 2 and Figure 3 are clustering results of the PFC. The result demonstrates an important *advantage* of soft methods against crisp ones: They show how soft clustering can adequately mirror the fact that many proteins have context dependent functions, and how in some cases overlap nodes can act as functional bridges between different modules.

Table 1 Comparison of results from different methods

Method	Cluster Count	Average Cluster size	Average Enrichment	Network Coverage	Diversity
Betweenness based	20	302.70	-15.11	0.58	19/20
Chinese Whisper	38	23.45	-12.11	0.17	32/38
C Finder	68	14.50	-15.70	0.19	48/68
PFC1	183	44.76	-19.35	0.31	55/183
PFC1	40	25.4	-19.40	0.17	36/40

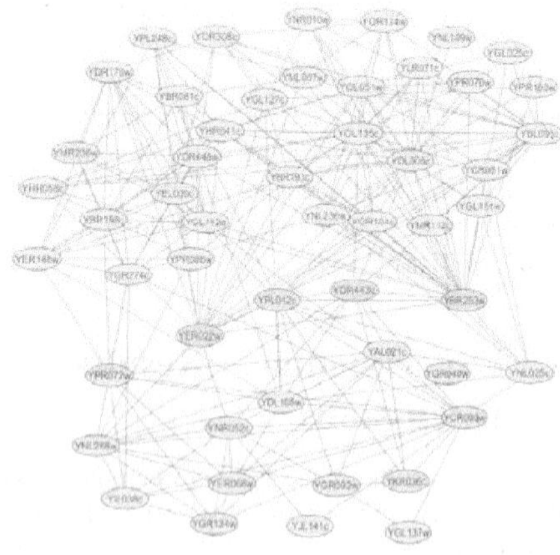

Figure 2. result #1: The main functions of the top and bottom clusters are identical: on both sides, over 80% of the nodes are involved in "transcription from RNA polymerase II promoter" and this is also the main function of all of the overlap nodes. However, the bottom part also contains a specialized module for poly tail shortening: all 7 node in the entire network that are involved in poly tail shortening are gathered here

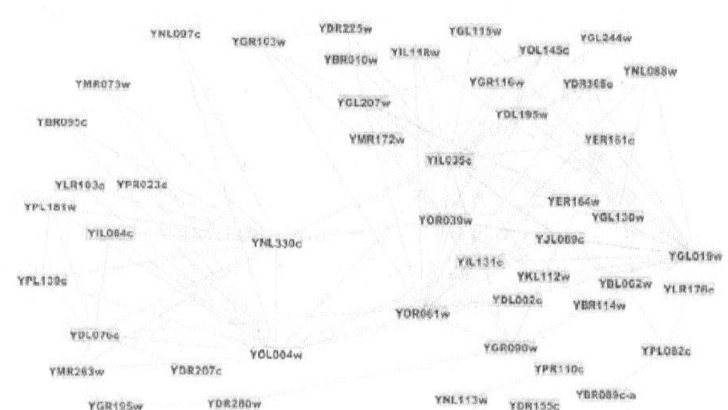

Figure 3. result #2.10 out of 13 yellow nodes are involved in histone deacytlation(left), 21 out of 33 green nodes are involved in transcription, DNA dependent (right); both white nodes are involved in both functions

5 Conclusions

This paper introduced PFC, a new clustering concept based on purification and filtering of a coupling (common neighbor) matrix. It discussed a very different filtering method. PFC consists of only a few matrix multiplications and manipulations and is therefore very efficient. The PFC outperforms current soft clustering methods on PPI networks by a few orders of magnitude in terms of average statistical confidence on biological enrichment of the identified clusters. The paper illustrated the importance of soft clustering methods in systems biology by giving a few concrete examples of how the biological function of the overlap nodes relates to the functions of the respective clusters.

6 References

[1] Altschul, SF, et al. "Gapped BLAST and PSI-BLAST: a new generation of protein database search programs". Nucleic acids research 25, no. 17: 3389, 1997.

[2] Thompson, JD, DG Higgins, and TJ Gibson. "CLUSTAL W: improving the sensitivity of progressive multiple sequence alignment through sequence weighting, position-specific gap penalties and weight matrix choice". Nucleic acids research 22, no. 22: 4673-4680, 1994

[3] Tatusov, R. L., E. V. Koonin, and D. J. Lipman. "A genomic perspective on protein families". Science 278, no. 5338: 631, 1997.

[4] Hartuv, E., R. Shamir. "A clustering algorithm based on graph connectivity". Information processing letters 76, no. 4-6: 175-181, 2000.

[5] King, A. D., N. Przulj, and I. Jurisica. "Protein complex prediction via cost-based clustering". Bioinformatics 20,: 3013-3020, 2004.

[6] Spirin, V., L. A. Mirny. "Protein complexes and functional modules in molecular networks". Proceedings of the National Academy of Sciences 100, no. 21: 12123-12128, 2003.

[7] Palla, G., I. Derenyi, I. Farkas, and T. Vicsek. "Uncovering the overlapping community structure of complex networks in nature and society". Nature 435, no. 7043 (Jun 9): 814-818, 2005.

[8] Derenyi, I., et al. "Clique percolation in random networks". Physical Review Letters 94, no. 16: 160202, 2005.

[9] Adamcsek, B., G. et al. "CFinder: locating cliques and overlapping modules in biological networks". Bioinformatics 22, no. 8: 1021-1023, 2006.

[10] Biemann, C. "Chinese whispers-an efficient graph clustering algorithm and its application to natural language processing problems". In Proceedings of the HLT-NAACL-06 workshop on textgraphs-06, new york, USA, 2006.

[11] Van Dongen, S. "A cluster algorithm for graphs". Report- Information systems , no. 10: 1-40, 2000.

[12] Pinney, J. W., D. R. Westhead. "Betweenness-based decomposition methods for social and biological networks". In Interdisciplinary statistics and bioinformatics. Edited by S. Barber, P. D. Baxter, K. V. Mardia and R. E. Walls. Leeds University Press, 2000.

[13] Gregory, S. "An algorithm to find overlapping community structure in networks". Lecture Notes in Computer Science 4702: 91, 2007.

[14] Girvan, M., M. E. Newman. "Community structure in social and biological networks". PNAS 99: 7821-7826, 2002.

[15] MIPS. The functional catalogue (FunCat). 2007. <http://mips.gsf.de/projects/funcat>.

[16] Chua, H. N. et al. "Exploiting indirect neighbours and topological weight to predict protein function from protein-protein interactions". Bioinformatics 22: 1623-1630, 2006.

[15] Liu, Y, and Foroushani, A. An Efficient Soft Graph Clustering Method for PPI Networks based on Purifying and Filtering the Coupling Matrix. BioComp 2011.

Protein Subnetwork Biomarkers for Yeast Using Brute Force Method

Kevin Charles, Andrews Afful, Ananda Mohan Mondal*
Department of Mathematics and Computer Science
Claflin University, Orangeburg, SC 29115
*Corresponding Author: amondal@claflin.edu

Abstract - *A simple brute force method to identify protein subnetwork biomarkers is developed for yeast using protein-protein interaction network and differentially expressed genes. Subnetworks related to different cellular roles for yeast are considered in this study. Four different PPI networks, namely- coexpressed PPI, genetic PPI, physical PPI and scored PPI are explored in identifying subnetworks for different cellular roles. Our results showed that all four PPI networks are capable of identifying subnetworks with different level of accuracy. Scored PPI network provides better coverage in terms of both single protein biomarker and PPI biomarker. Scored PPI network is also capable of producing large subnetwork biomarker for a specific cellular role. Our investigation showed that PPIs with high score have inherent capability of identifying subnetwork biomarkers.*

Keywords: Biomarker, subnetwork biomarker, single protein biomarker, PPI biomarker, brute force method.

1 Introduction

In general, a biomarker or marker is a gene or group of genes that represent a certain phenotype or disease. Biomarkers are important in the study of disease and drug design. If the biomarker(s) for a disease is known then drug can be designed to suppress the activity of biomarkers, thus curing the disease. Usually, genes expressed differentially are considered as single gene markers (SGMs). Studies show that sets of SGMs determined by differential expression vary considerably when inferring them from different platforms thus making them useless in cross-platform studies [1]. Chuang et al. [2] showed that multigenetic markers can be used to address this issue. Multigenetic markers consist of several differentially expressed genes which also form a connected region in a protein-protein interaction (PPI) network thus giving the name subnetwork biomarkers. Subnetworks are significant because, in contrast to individual proteins, they provide concrete hypotheses as to the molecular complexes, signaling pathways, and other mechanisms that impact the disease outcome [3].

With the recent development of high-throughput experiments to determine protein-protein interaction both physical and genetic, PPI networks are increasingly serving as tools for discovering the molecular basis of disease. In a recent review by Ideker and Sharan [3], authors enumerated four different prospective applications of PPI networks to disease, namely: identifying new disease genes; the study of their network properties; identifying disease-related subnetworks; and network-based disease classification. Researchers [4] found that disease genes exhibit an increased tendency for their protein products to interact with one another, tend to be co-expressed in specific tissues, and display coherent functions with respect to all three branches of the Gene Ontology hierarchy [5].

The general idea of computing subnetwork biomarkers, for example biomarkers for cancer, is to search for combinations of genes which (i) are sufficiently differentially expressed in the cancer tissue samples from gene expression training data and (ii) form a connected pattern in the PPI network [6]. There are different types of PPI networks as used in predicting protein functions[7] or subcellular locations [8, 9]. In the present work, we explored different types PPI network from the viewpoint of identifying subnetwork biomarkers. A simple brute force method employing the definition of subnetwork biomarker is used for analysis.

2 Datasets

In order to find subnetwork biomarkers, we need two sets of data, namely, i) protein-protein interaction data and ii) list of differentially expressed genes. In the present work, we considered yeast genome to identify subnetwork biomarkers related to Gene Ontology (GO) terms or biological processes. Four protein networks for yeast are used in the present study: two networks, physical PPI network and genetic PPI network, are obtained from BioGRID database [10], one Scored PPI network from STRING database [11], and one co-expression network is derived from gene expression data of Stanford University [12]. Pearson correlation is used to derive co-expressed PPI from gene expression data. In this study, the networks are named as physical PPI as PPPI, genetic PPI as GPPI, scored PPI as STRING and co-expressed PPI as COEXP. Table-1 shows the summary of four network datasets used for this study. In terms of the number of interactions, STRING is the largest network followed by GPPI, PPPI, and COEXP. In terms of proteins, STRING is the largest network followed by PPPI, GPPI, and COEXP. STRING is also the densest graph followed by GPPI, PPPI, and COEXP.

TABLE 1. Datasets of protein-protein interaction networks

Property	COEXP	GPPI	PPPI	STRING
No. of proteins	2004	5252	5477	6314
Edges	11954	103631	50997	489934
Average interactions per node	5.96	19.73	9.31	77.60

The differentially expressed genes are adopted from the experimental results of [13]. Data contains 29 cellular roles and after removing duplicates 600 role-protein pairs are left. Table-2 shows the number of differentially expressed genes or single protein biomarkers (column titled "Total SPB) associated with each role. Due to space limitation only 11 roles are shown in Table-2. It is noticeable that out of 600 role-protein pairs, 163 role-pairs do not have a known role. Among the known roles, "Transport" is associated with 50 proteins followed by "Cell stress" with 41 proteins, and "Amino acid metabolism" with 34 proteins. There are three roles associated only with 2 proteins (Cell polarity, Cell structure, and Pol II transcription).

TABLE 2. Distribution of single protein biomarkers with cellular roles (column titled "Total SPB") and composition of true subnetwork biomarkers identified in different PPI networks.

Sl #	Cellular Role	Total SPB	COEXP			GPPI			PPPI			STRING		
			SPB	PPIB	SNB	SPB	PPIB	SNB	SPB	PPIB	SNB	SPB	PPIB	SNB
1	Amino acid metabolism	34	8	8	2	12	8	4	6	3	3	30	81	1
2	Carbohydrate metabolism	31	2	1	1	8	5	3	2	1	1	27	97	1
4	Cell polarity	2	0	0	0	0	0	0	0	0	0	0	0	0
5	Cell stress	41	2	1	1	9	7	2	19	24	1	37	185	1
6	Cell structure	2	0	0	0	0	0	0	0	0	0	0	0	0
12	Differentiation	12	2	1	1	3	2	1	2	1	1	10	9	1
14	Lipid-sterol-Fatty acid metabolism	24	3	2	1	14	22	1	12	49	1	19	87	1
15	Mating response	23	4	6	1	8	5	3	6	4	2	21	62	1
20	Pol II transcription	2	0	0	0	0	0	0	0	0	0	0	0	0
28	Transport	50	2	1	1	14	9	5	8	6	3	38	56	2
29	Unknown	163	-	-	-	-	-	-	-	-	-	-	-	-

3 Methodology

3.1 Brute force method for identifying subnetwork biomarkers

A Brute Force method to identify subnetwork biomarkers related to GO terms for yeast genome is developed using the definitions given in this section. Differentially expressed genes related to GO terms for yeast genome are adopted from the experimental results of [13].

Single Protein Biomarker (SPB): A protein that is sufficiently differentially expressed in the tissue of a patient with the disease or phenotype is called a single protein biomarker for the disease or phenotype.

PPI Biomarker (PPIB): A PPI composed of two SPBs.

True PPI Biomarker: A PPI biomarker is a true biomarker when both proteins of the PPI are associated with the same disease, phenotype or biological process.

Pseudo PPI Biomarker: A PPI biomarker is a pseudo biomarker when two proteins of the PPI are associated with two different disease, phenotype or biological process.

Subnetwork Biomarker (SNB): A Subnetwork composed of PPIBs. So, by definition, an SNB is composed of one or more PPI biomarkers.

True Subnetwork Biomarker: An SNB composed of true PPIBs.

There are three components of Brute Force method in identifying Subnetwork Biomarker, namely: i) Algorithm for "Subnetwork Biomarker", ii) Algorithm for "Connected

Component", and iii) Algorithm for "True Subnetwork Biomarker". Following are the pseudocodes for different components.

PSEUDOCODE *SubnetworkBiomarker*(PPI[0..n-1], SPB[0..m-1])

```
//Finding Subnetwork Biomarkers
//Input1: An Array of PPI, PPI[0..n-1]
//Input2: An array of single protein biomarker, SPB[0..m-1]
//Intermediate Output: An array of PPI biomarkers,
//PPIB[0..k-1]
//Final Output: An array of subnetwork biomarkers,
//SNB[0..l-1]
for i ← 0 to n − 1 do
    split PPI[i] to Protein1 and Protein2
    if both Protein1 and Protein2 exists in array SPB
        push the PPI[i] into array PPIB
ConnectedComponent(PPIB)
```

PSEUDOCODE *ConnectedComponent*(PPIB[0..k-1])

```
//Input: An array of PPI biomarker, PPIB[0..k-1]
//Output: An array of subnetwork biomarkers, SNB[0..l-1]
//Element of SNB: An array of PPIB
Find the nodes from PPIB array and push them into NODE
    array
Until there is no node in NODE array do
    Take a node as the ROOT, find the edges and child
        nodes for it
    Repeat the previous step for each child nodes
        recursively until there is no more edge
    Put all the edges found above in an array, which
        represent a connected component
    Push the connected component into SNB array
    Delete edges and nodes corresponding to the connected
        component from the PPIB array and NODE array
        respectively.
```

PSEUDOCODE: *TrueSubnetworkBiomarkers*

```
//Given: List of all PPIB, list of SPB with cellular roles
//Find: List of PPIB for each role
Create a bag for each cellular role
Foreach PPIB
    If both proteins have the same role put the PPIB into
        the bag for that role
ConnectedComponent(for each bag)
```

3.2 Performance evaluation

In this study, we are exploring the capability of different PPI networks in identifying subnetwork biomarker using a brute force method employing the definition of subnetwork biomarker. The performance of the brute force method to identify protein subnetwork biomarkers is evaluated by the accuracy of identifying true PPI biomarkers as defined bellow:

$$Accuracy = \frac{Number\ of\ true\ PPIB}{Total\ number\ of\ PPIB} = \frac{Number\ of\ true\ PPIB}{Number\ of\ true\ PPIB + Number\ of\ pseudo\ PPIB}$$

Actually, performance of the brute force method developed depends on the quality of the PPI network.

4 Results and discussion

Subnetwork biomarkers are identified using the brute force method described above and Cytoscape [14] is used for pictorial representation of biomarkers.

4.1 Subnetwork Biomarkers Considering Whole Network

Table-3 and Figure-1 summarizes the topology of four different PPI networks and corresponding subnetwork biomarkers. It should be noted that network for STRING PPI (Figure-1d) has different layout than other three networks due to visualization difficulty with Cytoscape. It is clear that STRING network is the largest in terms of both number of PPIs (489934 PPIs) and number of proteins (6314) and COEXP network is the smallest with 11954 PPIs and 2004 proteins. As a result, SNBs derived from COEXP has the smallest number of SPBs (81) and the smallest number of PPIBs (135), and SNBs derived from STRING has the largest number of SPBs (307) and the largest number of PPIBs (3308). But there is only one large subnetwork biomarker for STRING network, in which all cellular roles are mingled together. On the other hand there are 15 SNBs for COEXP network. For practical purposes, we need SNBs such that each of them represents a particular cellular role. So, we need a method that can break the large single biomarker mingled with all cellular roles into smaller subnetwork biomarkers such that each of the subnetworks represents a particular cellular role. This is discussed in section 4.3.

TABLE 3. Topology of original PPI networks and subnetwork biomarkers.

PPI Type	Original Network		Subnetwork Biomarker		
	PPI	Protein	SPB	PPIB	SNB
COEXP	11 954	2004	81	135	15
GPPI	103 631	5252	182	288	7
PPPI	50 997	5477	178	280	4
STRING	489 934	6314	307	3308	1

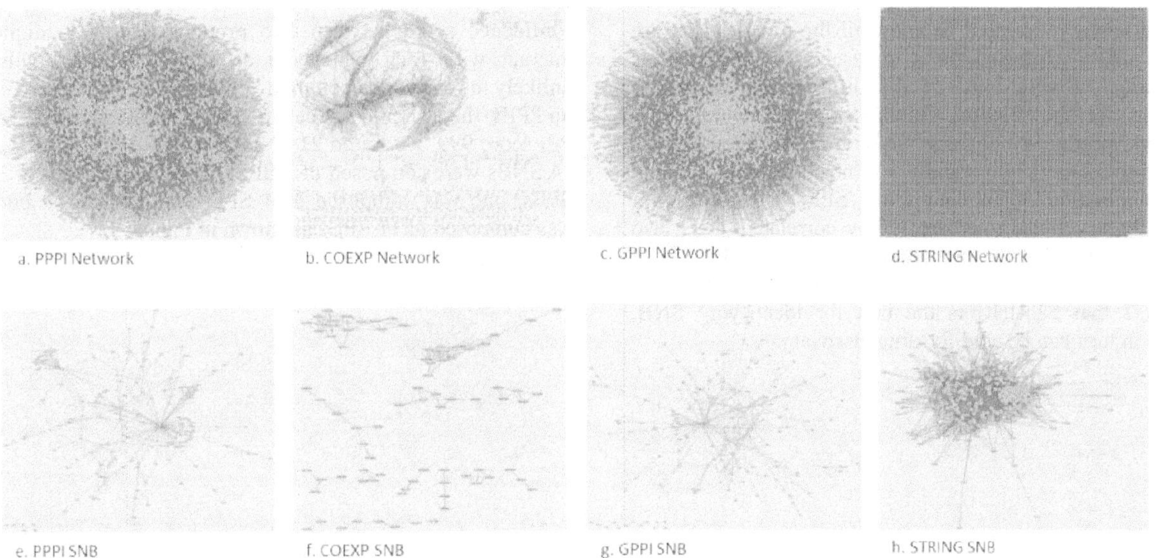

Figure 1. Original PPI networks and corresponding subnetwork biomarkers. (a, b, c, d) represent original network for physical PPI, co-expressed PPI, genetic PPI and STRING PPI respectively. (e, f, g, h) represent subnetwork biomarkers (SNBs) respectively derived from physical PPI, co-expressed PPI, genetic PPI and STRING PPI..

4.2 Quality of PPI Network in Producing Subnetwork Biomarker

Before breaking into individual subnetwork biomarkers, it is better to check the quality of the PPI network in producing subnetwork biomarkers. In this paper, we define the quality of a network in producing subnetwork biomarker as the capability of producing true subnetwork biomarker. So, this can roughly be estimated by accuracy defined earlier. Table-4 shows the accuracy of identifying true PPIB for different PPI types. It is evident that physical PPI has higher capability (44%) of producing true subnetwork biomarkers compare to other three PPI types (26%, 31%, 33%). By definition, physical PPI means that two proteins physically interact to produce some other products. As a result two proteins of physical PPI are more likely to be differentially expressed to represent the same cellular role thus providing better capability of identifying subnetwork biomarker.

TABLE 4. Quality of PPI types in producing subnetwork biomarkers.

PPI Type	Subnetwork Biomarker		Accuracy (%)
	PPIB	True PPIB	
COEXP	135	42	31%
GPPI	288	96	33%
PPPI	280	123	44%
STRING	3308	874	26%

4.3 Effect of Networks in Identifying Individual SNBs

As mentioned in section 4.1 that SNB derived from whole network is large and mingled with all cellular roles. For practical purposes, we need SNBs such that each of them represents a particular cellular role. The simplest way of achieving this goal is to collect all the PPIBs associated with the cellular role and then find the connected components with these PPIBs. By definition, these SNBs are called true SNB.

4.3.1 True Subnetwork Biomarkers for Different Cellular Roles

The composition of true subnetwork biomarkers (SNBs) for each cellular role in terms of single protein biomarker (SPB) and PPI biomarker (PPIB) are summarized in Table-2. There is no SNB for cellular roles "Cell polarity", "Cell structure", "Pol II transcription" identified in all four networks. This is because these three cellular roles are associated only with 2 SPBs. For the most cases, STRING network produced a single large SNB for each cellular role, whereas COEXP, GPPI, and PPPI are producing more than one SNB for a particular role. For example, in case of cellular role "Amino acid metabolism" as shown in Figure-2, COEXP produces 2 SNBs composed of 8 SPBs and 8 PPIBs, GPPI produces 4 SNBs composed of 12 SPBs and 8 PPIBs, PPPI produces 3 SNBs composed of 6 SPBs and 3 PPIBs, and STRING produces only one SNB composed of 30 SPBs and 81 PPIBs. For practical purposes, such as for drug discovery, we need to know all the proteins that are differentially expressed for a disease or an SNB that is composed of with most of the differentially expressed proteins for the disease. Cellular roles for which each network produces only one SNB are: "Differentiation", "Lipid-sterol-fatty acid metabolism", and "Recombination". This means that SPBs associated with these three cellular roles are highly correlated. It is also noticeable that STRING produces the largest SNB for these three cellular roles. It can be concluded from Table-2 and Figure-2 that STRING is the best for identifying SNB, which in turn can be used for drug discovery.

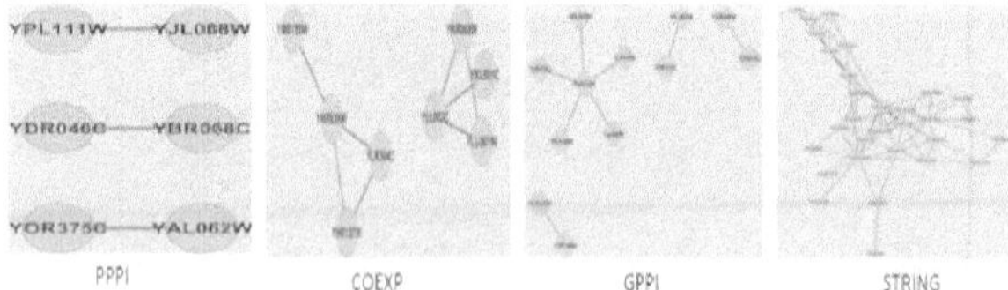

Figure 2. True subnetwork biomarkers for cellular role "Amino acid metabolism".

4.4 Coverage of Identifying True Subnetwork Biomarkers in Terms of Single Protein Biomarkers

Coverage of identifying true subnetwork biomarkers (SNBs) in terms of single protein biomarkers (SPBs) means the percent of actual SPB that forms true SNB for a network. This can be calculated from the results presented in Table-2. For role "Amino acid metabolism", coverage for COEXP is (8/34 =) 24%, for GPPI (12/34=) 35%, for PPPI (6/34=) 18% and for STRING (30/34=) 88%. It is clear that STRING PPI provides the highest coverage compare to other three networks for each and every cellular role. This is expected, since STRING is the largest network in terms of both number of proteins and number of interactions. So, in terms of coverage, STRING PPIs are the best source for identifying protein subnetwork biomarkers.

4.5 Subnetwork Biomarkers Using PPI Scores

The PPI scores from the STRING database reflect the functional associations of different proteins [16]. So, PPI scores in STRING database can better be utilized in determining subnetwork biomarkers.

4.5.1 Biomarkers at Two Extreme PPI Scores

For STRING PPIs, minimum and maximum scores are 150 and 999 respectively. Experiment was carried out to identify subnetwork biomarkers at these two extreme values of PPI score. No PPIB was found at PPI score 150 as expected since this score represents the minimum confidence score between two proteins that they might interact with each other and as such they are highly unlikely to represent a common cellular role. Since there is no PPIB, there should not be any SNB. On the other end, at PPI score 999, we found 21 SNBs composed of 79 PPIBs. 14 SNBs were composed of 2 SPBs, 5 were composed of 3 SPBs, one was composed of 4 SPBs and the largest one was composed of 11 SPBs as shown in Figure-3.

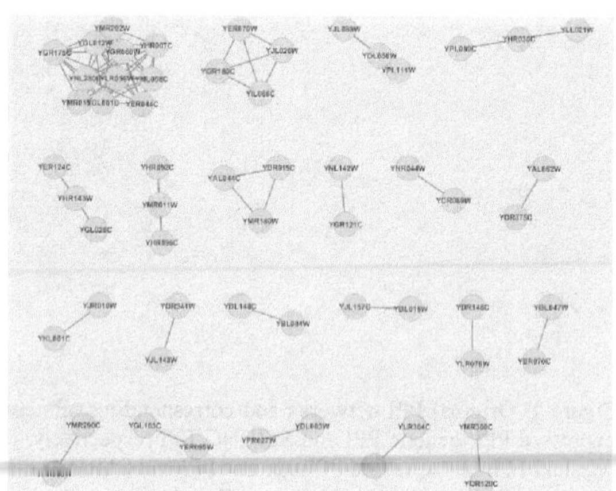

Figure 3. Subnetwork biomarkers at PPI score 999.

Upon investigation of the cellular roles of the proteins of 21 subnetwork biomarkers identified at PPI score 999, we found that 15 are true SNBs. For a true SNB, all proteins should have the same cellular role. For example, 11 proteins of the largest SNB share the same biological roles, "Lipid/sterol/fatty acid metabolism". The true SNBs at PPI score 999 do not include all the true PPIBs for the corresponding cellular role since these are derived from a small segment of the whole network. But these can be used as the seeds for deriving complete biomarkers for different roles. For example, SNB with 11 SPBs for cellular role "Lipid/sterol/fatty acid metabolism" can be used as the seed to derive the actual SNB with 19 SPBs and 87 PPIBs (Table-2).

4.5.2 Effect of PPI Scores in Identifying SNB

Figure-4 presents the % of true PPIB produced as function of PPI score. Whole network is divided into smaller fragment using a bin size of PPI score equals 100. For each bin, subnetwork biomarkers were identified and then accuracy for the same was evaluated. It is evident that performance increases with the increase of PPI score. Higher the PPI score, higher the confidence of interaction between two proteins [11]. If the two proteins are more likely to interact with each other, they are more likely to be localized at the same subcellular location [8, 9]. As a result, they are more likely to be associated to the same cellular role or phenotype and more likely to be differentially expressed in the same direction. This is the reason for which PPIs with high score are more likely to produce subnetwork biomarker with high quality.

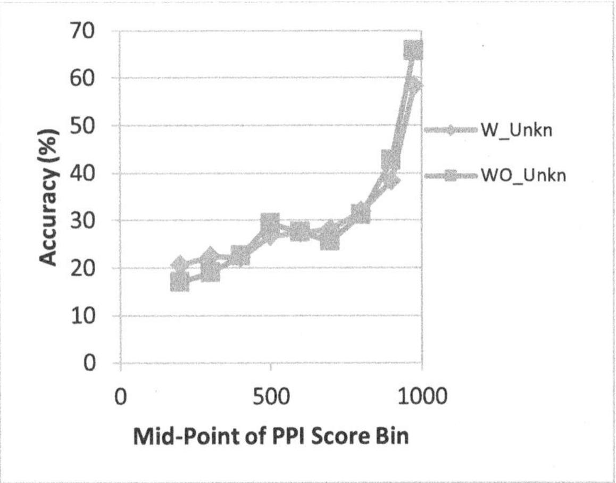

Figure 4. PPI scores on the performance of identifying subnetwork biomarkers. W_Unkn: With or including differentially expressed proteins for which cellular roles are unknown; WO_Unkn: Without or excluding proteins with unknown cellular roles..

5 Conclusion

A brute force method to identify subnetwork biomarkers (SNBs) is developed employing bottom-up approach starting with single protein biomarkers (SPBs). PPI Biomarkers (PPIBs) are found from SPBs and SNBs are found from PPIBs. We investigated the capability of different PPI networks for yeast, namely – COEXP, GPPI, PPPI, and STRING, in identifying SNBs for different cellular roles using the developed method. Considering whole network, PPPI has higher capability of producing true subnetwork biomarkers compare to other three types of PPI. But considering coverage in terms of SPBs and PPIBs for identifying SNBs, STRING PPIs are better than other three PPIs. Investigation also showed that maximum PPI score, 999, of STRING PPI can be used to identify the seeds for SNBs.

An actual problem in the context of finding SNB would be: given a genome-wide PPI network, come up with an algorithm that can identify or predict the SNBs, finally, compare the predicted SNBs with the true SNBs. Our future research will focus on developing such an algorithm.

ACKNOWLEDGMENT

This work was partially supported by NASA grant, Prime Award No: NNX12AI12A, Sub-award No: 520976-Claflin-Mondal.

References

[1] L. e. a. Ein-Dor, "Outcome signature genes in breast cancer: is there a unique set?," *Bioinformatics,* vol. 21, pp. 171-178, 2005.

[2] H. Y. Chuang, *et al.*, "Network-based classification of breast cancer metastasis," *Mol Syst Biol,* vol. 3, p. 140, 2007.

[3] T. Ideker and R. Sharan, "Protein networks in disease," *Genome Res,* vol. 18, pp. 644-52, Apr 2008.

[4] K. I. Goh, *et al.*, "The human disease network," *Proc Natl Acad Sci U S A,* vol. 104, pp. 8685-90, May 22 2007.

[5] M. A. Harris, *et al.*, "The Gene Ontology (GO) database and informatics resource," *Nucleic Acids Res,* vol. 32, pp. D258-61, Jan 1 2004.

[6] P. e. a. Dao, "Inferring cancer subnetwork markers using density-constrained biclustering," *Bioinformatics,* vol. 26, pp. i625–i631, 2010.

[7] H. Lee, *et al.*, "Diffusion kernel-based logistic regression models for protein function prediction," *OMICS,* vol. 10, pp. 40-55, Spring 2006.

[8] A. M. Mondal and J. Hu, "NetLoc: Network Based Protein Localization Prediction Using Protein-Protein Interaction and Co-expression Networks," in *IEEE International Conference on Bioinformatics & Biomedicine (BIBM2010)*, Hong Kong, 2010, pp. 142-148.

[9] A. M. Mondal and J. Hu, "Network Based Prediction of Protein Localization Using Diffusion Kernel," *International Journal of Data Mining and Bioinformatics* 2011.

[10] C. Stark, *et al.*, "BioGRID: a general repository for interaction datasets," *Nucleic Acids Res,* vol. 34, pp. D535-9, Jan 1 2006.

[11] C. von Mering, *et al.*, "STRING: known and predicted protein-protein associations, integrated and transferred across organisms," *Nucleic Acids Res,* vol. 33, pp. D433-7, Jan 1 2005.

[12] P. T. Spellman, *et al.*, "Comprehensive identification of cell cycle-regulated genes of the yeast Saccharomyces cerevisiae by microarray hybridization," *Mol Biol Cell,* vol. 9, pp. 3273-97, Dec 1998.

[13] A. K. Agarwal, *et al.*, "Genome-wide expression profiling of the response to polyene, pyrimidine, azole, and echinocandin antifungal agents in Saccharomyces cerevisiae," *J Biol Chem,* vol. 278, pp. 34998-5015, Sep 12 2003.

[14] C. T. Lopes, *et al.*, "Cytoscape Web: an interactive web-based network browser," *Bioinformatics,* vol. 26, pp. 2347-8, Sep 15 2010.

Study of Floral Transition in *Arabidopsis* Using Partial Correlation Analysis

NILUBON KURUBANJERDJIT [1], JEFFREY J.P. TSAI [1], CHIEN-HUNG HUANG [2], JIN-SHUEI CIOU [1‡], KA-LOK NG [1‡]

[1]Department of Biomedical Informatics, Asia University, 500, Lioufeng road, Wufeng, Taichung TAIWAN 41354

[2]Department of Computer Science and Information Engineering, National Formosa University, 64,Wen-Hwa Road, Hu-wei, Yun-Lin, TAIWAN 632

[‡] Corresponding authors, zxrwater@gmail.com, ppiddi@gmail.com

Abstract - *Time series microarray experiments provide a mean to infer gene regulatory networks from the temporal pattern. In this work, the floral transition process was selected as a study case. Differentially expressed genes (DEGs) were identified by using the Bioconductor statistical package, EBAYES. A gene association network (GAN) for these genes was obtained using the Gaussian Graph Model (GGM) based on DEG results. These findings suggest a potential relationship between those DEG events; their causal effects are inferred. However, the gene-gene interactions derived from GGM did not match the experimental protein-protein interaction (PPI) records, where most of the interactions are spurious. Here, we present a computational approach that started with PPI and examine the usefulness of adopting partial correlation analysis in reconstructing the regulatory modules. The presented approach is able to capture statistical significant biological features through the gene set enrichment analysis that are not ready derived from GGM analysis.*

Keywords: *A. thaliana*, floral transition, flower development, time course microarray data, protein-protein interaction, partial correlation

1 Introduction

Arabidopsis thaliana is a plant belongs to the mustard family that is frequently chosen as organism model in plant science research [1]. It is a long-day (LD) plant, possesses small physical size, diploid genetics, small genome and relatively short generation time. It is chosen as the model system for two reasons; (i) the complete genome sequence has been completed since year 2000 [8]; and (ii), there are many molecular tools, such as cDNA, genomic libraries, bacterial artificial chromosomes, microarrays, and ESTs are available for the biological functions study [1].

Flowering transition is a critical stage in plant development, control of flowering time involves a complex interplay of environmental and developmental factors. In higher plant, flowering transition represents a crucial transition from the vegetative stage to the reproductive stage in life cycle. Plants of the same species that grow in various ecological conditions, such as high temperature and day length may involve changes in the time of flowering to avoid unfavorable weather, such as harsh winters or hot summers [2]. The complexity of this regulation is created by signaling pathway involving a set of significant genes. Many pathways that related to the timing of the floral transition have been identified. Floral transition and flower development processes are regulated by four complex genetic networks: autonomous, gibberellins, light-dependent and vernalization networks [3]. A single gene may influence in more than one pathway. Therefore, it is necessary to discover a set of gene which is expressed during the life time of plant. Among the best characterized genetic pathways regulating a complex life in plants is the flowering pathway of *A. thaliana* [3-6].

Microarray data analysis allows for high-throughput screening of differentially expressed genes (DEGs). In time series microarray experiments, gene expression is measured over time and under one or more different conditions. Time series microarray experiments are an increasingly popular method for studying a wide range of biological systems, which is a method for estimating unobserved time-points, clustering, and aligning gene expression time-series. Inferring gene regulatory network by time course data is one of the main challenges in systems biology.

Protein interactions play an important role in gene regulation network (GRN). GRN usually contains small circuit patterns called network motifs, which are known to have interesting dynamical properties. In protein interaction networks, pseudo completely connected graphs, so-called pseudo-cliques, have been found to have a high functional significance [7, 8]. Motifs and cliques reveal the cores of functional modules in molecular networks.

In this study, the gene association network (GAN) for the floral transition process was inferred from time series microarray data. We also conducted the Gene Set Enrichment

Analysis (GSEA) to study enriched biological processes and pathways related gene groups.

To construct the GAN, one start with a PPI pair, where the regulation strength is quantified by using the Pearson correlation coefficient (PCC), in which the gene expression profiles are obtained from microarray database. This simple method of inferring GAN based on PCC is not valid in most case studies. This is because high PCC of two variables does not imply that there is a direct relationship. It is proposed that considering partial correlation can solve such problem because this quantity is able to measure the net dependence of two genes.

In a previous study, the PCC approach had been adopted in investigating gene expression data [9]. In another study [10], He et al., conducted such approach by integrating the protein-protein interaction (PPI) and microarray data. It was found that anti-correlated modules, i.e. vegetative phase and reproductive phase modules, are associated with the vegetative and reproductive growth stages respectively.

In this study, we present a computational approach to examine the net interdependency of genes for the floral transition process by using the Graphical Gaussian Model (GGM) package, GeneNet [11]. Opgen-Rhein and Strimmer, whom developed the GGM method [11], inferred a partial causal network by considering the partial correlation coefficients instead of PCC. GGM obtained the partial correlation for a pair of genes due to the presence of a group of genes, hence, resulted in small partial correction values. Therefore, the network obtained from GGM can be further improved. Our method is based on the first order and second order partial correlation calculation given by GeneNet (see Section 2.3 for more detail description).

GAN was reconstructed instead of GRN because the activation or suppression is not all directly determined in the present work. This is because GGM can only provide some of the regulatory relations among the genetic components only.

2 Methods

2.1 Input data

PPI data was obtained from BioGrid (Database of protein and genetic interactions) [12]. Microarray data for the flowering process was downloaded from PLEXdb [13] with experiment ID AT-4 or from GEO [14] with ID, GDS453. PLEXdb is a microarray data resource for plants and plant pathogens. AT-4, an Affymetrix microarray platform, compared gene expression levels between 40 samples dissected from the apical tissue harvested at zero, three, five and seven days after the shift to LD for five genotypes; i.e. (i) Columbia (Col-0) wildtype with an AG::GUS reporter, (ii) Landsberg erecta (Ler) plant with an AG::GUS reporter, (iii) CO mutant, (iv) FT mutant and (v) LFY-12 mutant. The flowering transition dataset, Ler, was chosen in the present study. DEGs are identified by using the empirical Bayes method (EBAYES) [15], which is publicly available through the Bioconductor web site [16-17]..

2.2 Bioconductor packages – EBAYES

The EBAYES algorithm computes moderated t-statistics, moderated F-statistic, and log-odds of differential expression by empirical Bayes shrinkage of the standard errors towards a common value. Since the two microarray replicate data are obtained from two different groups, so a two-class unpaired test is adopted in the analysis.

SAM is a statistical method for identifying DEGs by comparing two or more groups of samples. It uses repeated permutations of the data to estimate False Discovery Rate (FDR) based on observed versus expected score, which is obtained from randomized data. A gene which has an observed score that deviates significantly from the expected score is consider as a DEG. EBAM performs one and two class analyses using either a modified t-statistic or standardized Wilcoxon rank statistic, and a multiclass analysis using a modified F-statistic. Moreover, this function provides a EBAM procedure for categorical data such as SNP data and the possibility of employing a user-written score function. Our previous study [18] suggested that, EBAYES, SAM, and EBAM, achieve a similar level of cancer gene prediction accuracy, i.e. around 20%, therefore, EBAYES is adopted in the present analysis.

2.3 Gaussian Graphical Model (GGM)

Inferring GRN from microarray data is an important issue in systems biology. GGM is a graphical model that is developed by Dempster [20] to study the dependencies among a set of variables. In principle, GGM infers GAN by considering the partial correlation coefficient instead of PCC. In partial correlation calculation, one introduces a third variable that has relationship between the other two variables, then calculate the correlation between two variables while excluding the impact of the third variable.

This statistical framework has been successfully adopted in modelling genomic data [21], on the starch metabolism of *A. thaliana* [11] and reconstructs pathway reactions from metabolomics data [22]. Although GGM was able to infer the GAN, however, most of the regulatory relations among genes do not correspond to any PPI record collected by BioGrid. In other words, most of the network edges are false positive events. Another problem is the partial correlation values obtained from GGM analysis are rather small, which are close to zero in majority. This made it difficult to conclude the interdependency between any two genes.

Here we suggest performing the analysis by starting with the PPI relation, and considering the first and second order partial correlations (denoted in short by FOPC and SOPC) of such interaction. The first order partial correlation involves variables x and y adjusted for z, $r_{xy,z}$, is defined by,

$$r_{xy.z} = \frac{r_{xy} - r_{xz} r_{yz}}{\sqrt{1-r_{xz}^2}\sqrt{1-r_{yz}^2}} \qquad (1)$$

As an illustration, given a PPI pair, *x-y*, and assume that the set of interaction protein pairs is denoted by $\{x\text{-}z_1, x\text{-}z_2, y\text{-}z_3, y\text{-}z_4\}$. We compute the PCC for these four PPIs, and pick the maximum PCC pair for x and y. In general, their interaction partners, *z's* are not necessary the same, then, that will be considered for the SOPC study. For first order partial correlation, the *z's* has to be the same.

The SOPC of variables *x*, *y* adjusted for *z* and *q*, $r_{xy.zq}$, is defined by,

$$r_{xy.zq} = \frac{r_{xy.z} - r_{xq.z} r_{yq.z}}{\sqrt{(1-r_{xq.z}^2)(1-r_{yq.z}^2)}} \qquad (2)$$

where r_{xy} denotes the PCC for variables *x* and *y*, which is given by,

$$r_{xy} = \frac{\sum_{i=1}^{n}(x_i - \bar{x})(y_i - \bar{y})}{\sqrt{\left[\sum_{i=1}^{n}(x_i - \bar{x})^2\right]\left[\sum_{i=1}^{n}(y_i - \bar{y})^2\right]}} \qquad (3)$$

where x_i and y_i denote the expression level of mRNA for genes *x* and *y* respectively; $\bar{x}$ and $\bar{y}$ denote the mean expression intensity of mRNA for genes *x* and *y* respectively; and *n* is the total number of the expression data entries. The advantage of adopting partial correction is that it measures the independence between two genes, hence, allows it to distinguish between direct and indirect interaction. It improves the credibility of using GGM in causal inference study. GeneNet is a freely available R package for inferring GAN by analysing time series gene expression data based on the GGM approach.

To study the difference of first and second order partial correlation with respective to PCC, D_1 and D_2 are defined by,

$$D_1 = r_{xy,z} - r_{xy} \qquad (4)$$

$$D_2 = r_{xy,zq} - r_{xy} \qquad (5)$$

A negative *D* value indicates a lower partial correlation coefficient; it implies the effect is negative. If *D* is close to zero, this suggested that the effect is minimal. A positive *D* value means that the effect due to the variable(s) is positive.

2.4 Gene Set Enrichment Analysis (GSEA)

The functional annotation of the DEGs is given by implementing The Database for Annotation, Visualization and Integrated Discovery, i.e. DAVID [19]. DAVID provides functional annotation tools which mainly provide typical batch annotation and gene GO term enrichment analysis to highlight the most relevant GO terms associated with a given gene list. The list of *Arabidopsis* DEGs involved was submitted to DAVID for clustering the redundant annotation terms of the gene lists. Thus, enriched biological processes (BP) related DEGs were obtained.

3 Results

3.1 DEGs and Gene association network (GAN)

In our previous study [23], DEGs for the floral transition process are identified by using EBAYES. A total of 2716 DEGs, which consist of up and down regulated genes, are selected by EBAYES with adjusted p-value less than 0.05.

The GAN for the floral transition experiment based on partial correlation ordering analysis is shown in Figure 1. This network consists of the 150 most significant links among 81 genes. Among the 81 genes, many of them are involving in the flowering process, for instance, BNQ2 (also known as *BHLH134/BANQUO2)* has a role in regulating light responses [24], GBF3 is regulated by light [25], HSP70 is affected by the photoperiod shift [26], and HSF and MBF1c are key regulators of thermotolerance [27].

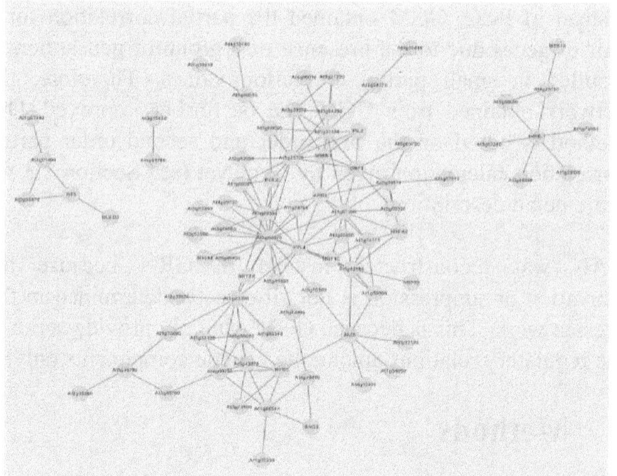

Figure 1 GAN for the floral transition process

The GAN exhibits a highly interconnected structure, where genes At3g28560, At5g25770, At5g54570 and At5g64570, have a high degree of connectivity that may act as key regulators. When we compared the 150 most significant links with the BioGrid data, none of the links match the PPI record. In other words, the results obtained from GGM can be further improved.

3.2 Gene Set Enrichment Analysis(GSEA) for GGM result

List of the 81 genes were submitted to DAVID, for clustering, thus, enriched biological process (BP), molecular function (MF) and pathway were obtained. The functional annotation clustering service predicted a few enriched BPs and MFs. However, the p-value results obtained from GSEA are rather large, i.e. larger that 0.33, which indicated that genetic elements comprising the GAN (Figure 1) do not show statistically significantly enriched BP or MF meaning. This suggested that additional information, such as PPI may be required for better performance. Also, only one enriched KEGG pathway was identified, which is associated with the entose and glucuronate interconversions pathway. In the following, we demonstrated that the present approach allowed us to obtained statistically significant and biological meaning BPs and pathway information for the flowering process.

3.3 The FOPC and SOPC study

A total of 3670 and 7083 genes belongs to the FOPC and SOPC results respectively. Figures 2 (A) and 2(B) are the plots of *D1* and *D2* after ranking the difference in ascending order. It is noted both of negative, and positive corrections are possible. The results strongly indicated that PCC are subjected to correction due to the presence of another one or two variables. It was found that 2098 (57.2%) and 4093 (57.8%) graphs received negative corrections according to the FOPC and SOPC analysis respectively. In other words, more than half of the PCC calculations received negative contributions after variable adjustment. Inferring GAN based on PCC is subject to both positive and negative corrections.

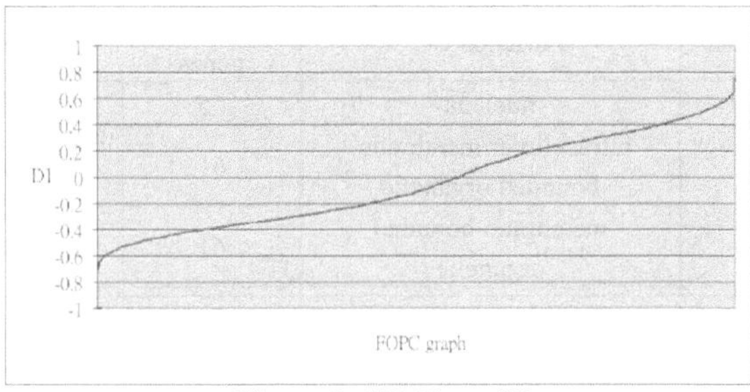

Figure 2 (A) Plot of D_1

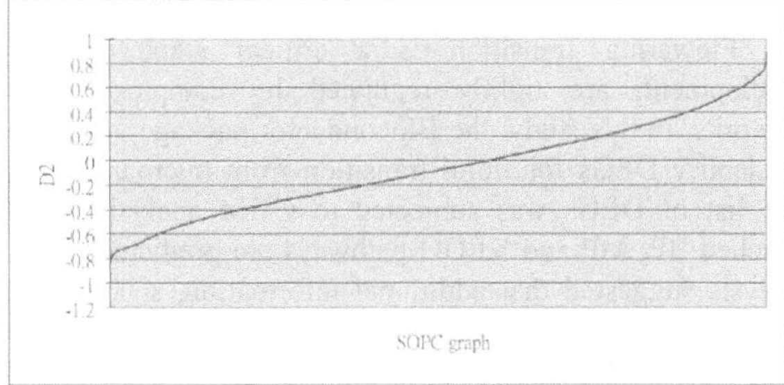

Figure 2 (B) Plot of D_2

Some of the FOPC graphs are interconnected which lead to the formation of functional modules. The present study identifies possible interaction pairs. The results of such study were depicted in Figure 3(A). Similarly, the results for the SOPC study were shown in Figure 3(B) .

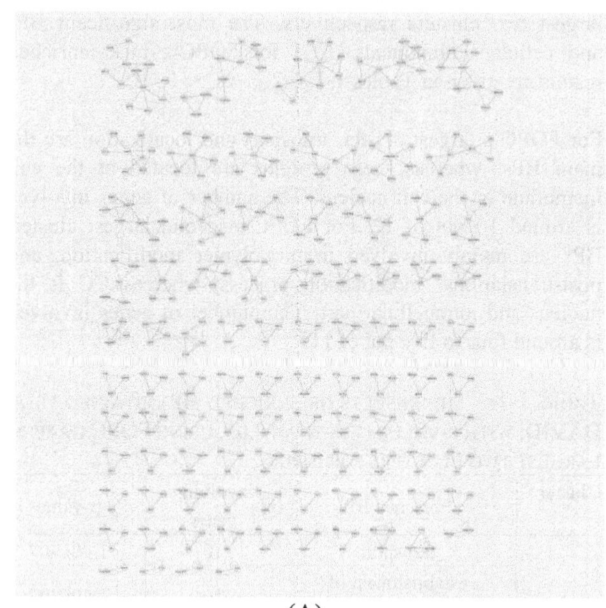

(A)

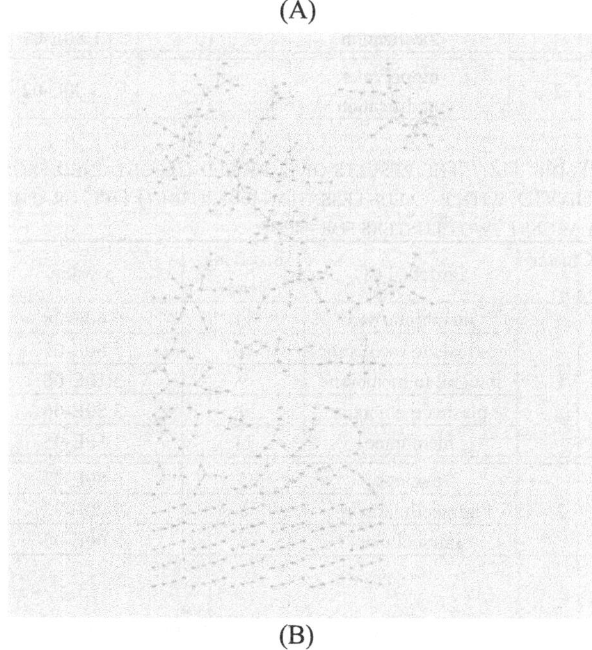

(B)

Figure 3 (A) Interconnected FOPC graphs, (B) Interconnected SOPC graphs, where blue and red coloured edges denotes PPI obtained from BioGrid and PPI with the highest PCC respectively.

3.4 Gene Set Enrichment Analysis (GSEA) for FOPC and SOPC results

We selected the largest two clusters from Figures 4 and 5 respectively, and submitted to DAVID for GSEA. A total of 12 (98) and 11 (30) genes were obtained for FOPC (SOPC) largest two clusters respectively. The most significant BPs and cellular components (CC) for FOPC's most enriched results are given in Tables 1-1, 1-2.

For FOPC's largest cluster, transport and localization are the main BPs, whereas these proteins are located at the cell membrane or the cell nucleus. The number of genes involved is around 10 out of 12. For FOPC's second largest cluster, BPs are mainly involved in biopolymer modification, and post-translational modification process; whereas CC is the nucleus and intracellular part. The number of genes involved is around four to five out of 11.

Table 1-1. THE RESULTS OF ENRICHED BP OBTAINED FROM DAVID, WITH P-VALUE LESS THAN 0.05, USING FOPC GRAPHS' LARGEST TWO CLUSTERS FOR INPUT.

Cluster	Enriched BP	involving genes	p-value
1	transport	10	1.40E-07
	establishment of localization	10	1.40E-07
	localization	10	1.80E-07
2	biopolymer modification	4	3.80E-02

Table 1-2. THE RESULTS OF ENRICHED CC OBTAINED FROM DAVID, WITH P-VALUE LESS THAN 0.05, USING FOPC GRAPHS' LARGEST TWO CLUSTERS FOR INPUT.

Cluster	Enriched CC	involving genes	p-value
1	membrane part	11	6.60E-08
	intrinsic to membrane	10	5.60E-07
	integral to membrane	9	3.10E-06
	plasma membrane	9	3.50E-06
	membrane	11	1.50E-05
2	nucleus	5	6.80E-03
	intracellular part	6	7.20E-02
	intracellular	6	8.60E-02

Only the top three GSEA results for SOPC's are given in Tables 2-1, 2-2, because the enriched BP and CC lists are long to list. It is noted that for SOPC's largest cluster, BP is mainly involved in transcription and metabolic processes, whereas CC is located at the nucleus and intracellular organelle. The number of genes involved is around 48 to 61 out of 98. For SOPC's second largest cluster, BPs are mainly involved in cell cycle; whereas CC information is not available. The number of genes involved is around 17 to 18 out of 30.

It is noted that predicted BPs are highly related to the flowering process, which supported the findings presented in the work of [10]. Relatively to FOPC analysis, the BPs identified by SOPC analysis tend to have a much smaller p-value, which indicated that the BPs are biologically more relevant. This may be due to the fact that SOPC is a second order effect calculation; hence, more reliable descriptions were obtained.

Table 2-1. THE RESULTS OF ENRICHED BP RESULTS OBTAINED FROM DAVID, WITH P-VALUE LESS THAN 0.05, USING SOPC GRAPHS' LARGEST TWO CLUSTERS FOR INPUT.

Cluster	Enriched BP	involving genes	p-value
1	regulation of transcription	48	1.30E-21
	regulation of nucleobase, nucleoside, nucleotide and nucleic acid metabolic process	48	2.30E-21
	regulation of nitrogen compound metabolic process	48	2.90E-21
2	regulation of cell cycle	17	2.00E-30
	cell cycle	17	4.00E-25
	regulation of cellular process	18	7.70E-08

Table 2-2. THE RESULTS OF ENRICHED CC RESULTS OBTAINED FROM DAVID, WITH P-VALUE LESS THAN 0.05, USING SOPC GRAPHS' LARGEST TWO CLUSTERS FOR INPUT.

Cluster	Enriched CC	involving genes	p-value
1	nucleus	55	1.60E-20
	intracellular membrane-bounded organelle	61	5.10E-06
	membrane-bounded organelle	61	5.20E-06
2	Not available		

4 Conclusion

Flowering transition is a critical stage in plant development, are tightly regulated by complex genetic networks. In this study, the Bioconductor package is adopted to identify DEGs for floral transition from microarray data. The list of DEGs was subjected to GGM analysis, where enriched BP, MP and KEGG pathways are predicted. GSEA analysis suggested that additional information, such as PPI, may be required for better performance. Partial correlation analysis was applied on PPI data, which allowed us to identify small floral transition modules; this provides direction for future investigation. It was shown that the FOPC and SOPC analysis permitted us to reveal more reliable regulatory motifs, obtained statistical significant biological processes and pathway information, hence, validate the use of PPI and partial correlation calculation in constructing biological relevant regulatory modules.

Acknowledgment

The work of Dr. Ka-Lok Ng and Nilubon Kurubanjerdjit is supported by the National Science Council of Taiwan, under the grant of NSC 99-2221-E-468-016-MY2 and NSC 101-2221-E-468 -027. The work of Ka-Lok Ng, Jin-Shuei Ciou and Jeffrey J.P Tsai is supported by the grant of NSC 99-2632-E-468-001-MY3. The work of Chien-Hung Huang is supported by the grants NSC 101-2221-E-150-088-MY2.

References

[1] D. F. Mandoli and R. Olmstead. "The Importance of Emerging Model Systems in Plant Biology"; Journal of Plant Growth Regulation, vol 19, Issue 3. 249-252, 2000.

[2] C. Shindo, M. J. Aranzana, et al. "Role of FRIGIDA and FLOWERING LOCUS C in determining variation in flowering time of Arabidopsis"; Plant physiology, vol 138, Issue 2. 1163-1173, 2005.

[3] I. Ausin, C. Alonso-Blanco, et al. "Environmental regulation of flowering"; The International journal of developmental biology, vol 49, Issue 5-6. 689-705, 2005.

[4] I. Baurle and C. Dean. "The timing of developmental transitions in plants"; Cell, vol 125, Issue 4. 655-664, 2006.

[5] E. S. Dennis and W. J. Peacock. "Epigenetic regulation of flowering"; Current opinion in plant biology, vol 10, Issue 5. 520-527, 2007.

[6] G. G. Simpson and C. Dean. "Arabidopsis, the Rosetta stone of flowering time?"; Science, vol 296, Issue 5566. 285-289, 2002.

[7] V. Spirin and L. A. Mirny. "Protein complexes and functional modules in molecular networks"; Proceedings of the National Academy of Sciences of the United States of America, vol 100, Issue 21. 12123-12128, 2003.

[8] E. Yeger-Lotem, S. Sattath, et al. "Network motifs in integrated cellular networks of transcription-regulation and protein-protein interaction"; Proceedings of the National Academy of Sciences of the United States of America, vol 101, Issue 16. 5934-5939, 2004.

[9] Arabidopsis Genome Initiative. "Analysis of the genome sequence of the flowering plant Arabidopsis thaliana"; Nature, vol 408, Issue 6814. 796-815, 2000.

[10] F. He, Y. Zhou, et al. "Deciphering the Arabidopsis floral transition process by integrating a protein-protein interaction network and gene expression data"; Plant physiology, vol 153, Issue 4. 1492-1505, 2010.

[11] R. Opgen-Rhein and K. Strimmer. "From correlation to causation networks: a simple approximate learning algorithm and its application to high-dimensional plant gene expression data"; BMC systems biology, vol 1, Issue 37, 2007.

[12] C. Stark, B. J. Breitkreutz, et al. "BioGRID: a general repository for interaction datasets"; Nucleic acids research, vol 34, Issue Database issue. D535-539, 2006.

[13] S. Dash, J. Van Hemert, et al. "PLEXdb: gene expression resources for plants and plant pathogens"; Nucleic acids research, vol 40, Issue Database issue. D1194-1201, 2012.

[14] T. Barrett, D. B. Troup, et al. "NCBI GEO: archive for functional genomics data sets--10 years on"; Nucleic acids research, vol 39, Issue Database issue. D1005-1010, 2011.

[15] B. Efron. "Robbins, empirical Bayes and microarrays"; The Annals of Statistics, vol 31, Issue 366-378, 2003.

[16] http://www.bioconductor.org/

[17] R. Irizarry. "From CEL Files to Annotated Lists of Interesting Genes"; In: Bioinformatics and Computational Biology Solutions Using R & Bioconductor, 431-442, 2005.

[18] S-T Chen, H-F Wu, K-L Ng. "A platform for querying breast and prostate cancer-related microNA genes"; International Conference on Bioinformatics and Biomedical Engineering (ICBBE 2012), 1(1), 271-274, Shanghai, May 17-20, 2012.

[19] W. Huang da, B. T. Sherman, et al. "Systematic and integrative analysis of large gene lists using DAVID bioinformatics resources"; Nature protocols, vol 4, Issue 1. 44-57, 2009.

[20] A.P. Dempster. "Covariance selection"; Biometrics,vol 28, 157-175, 1972

[21] R. Opgen-Rhein and K. Strimmer. "Inferring gene dependency networks from genomic longitudinal data: a functional data approach"; REVSTAT,vol 4, 53-65, 2006.

[22] J. Krumsiek, K. Suhre, et al. "Gaussian graphical modeling reconstructs pathway reactions from high-throughput metabolomics data"; BMC systems biology, vol 5, Issue 21, 2011.

[23] N. Kurubanjerdjit, J. J. P. Tsai, J-S Ciou, K-L Ng. "Gene Association Network of Floral Transition in

Arabidopsis, 3rd International Conference on Bioscience and Bioinformatics"; Switzerland, Dec. 29-31, 2012.

[24] C. D. Mara, T. Huang, et al. "The Arabidopsis floral homeotic proteins APETALA3 and PISTILLATA negatively regulate the BANQUO genes implicated in light signaling"; The Plant cell, vol 22, Issue 3. 690-702, 2010.

[25] U. Schindler, A. E. Menkens, et al. "Heterodimerization between light-regulated and ubiquitously expressed Arabidopsis GBF bZIP proteins"; The EMBO journal, vol 11, Issue 4. 1261-1273, 1992.

[26] S. Balasubramanian, S. Sureshkumar, et al. "Potent induction of Arabidopsis thaliana flowering by elevated growth temperature"; PLoS genetics, vol 2, Issue 7. e106, 2006.

[27] N. Suzuki, S. Bajad, et al. "The transcriptional co-activator MBF1c is a key regulator of thermotolerance in Arabidopsis thaliana"; The Journal of biological chemistry, vol 283, Issue 14. 9269-9275, 2008.

Prediction of Protein-protein Interaction Sites at Interface Topology Level

Tianchuan Du, Li Liao* and Cathy H. Wu*
Department of Computer and Information Sciences, University of Delaware, Newark, DE, USA

Abstract - *Protein-protein interactions play a crucial role in many biological processes such as immune response, enzyme catalysis, and signal transduction. Identifying the interacting sites between the proteins is important for understanding the functional mechanisms, and is crucial for drug development. Interaction profile hidden Markov model (ipHMM) was shown to be an effective tool for modeling protein-ligand interaction site in previous study. In this study, the ipHMM was applied to predict protein-protein interaction site by taking into account of interacting partner and topology information. Particularly, it was found that the performance of ipHMM at domain-domain interaction (DDI) family level was significantly lower for DDI families with multiple topology interfaces. To address this problem, we proposed to develop ipHMM at DDI interface topology level. The performance of interacting site prediction was significantly improved. The average sensitivity/recall was improved from 36.6% to 74.0%. The average precision was improved from 49.1% to 75.9%. The Matthews correlation coefficient was improved from 46.4% to 77.3%.*

Keywords: Protein-protein interaction; prediction; topology; interacting sites; ipHMM

1 Introduction

Protein-protein interactions (PPI) play essential roles in many biological processes. The cost, time and other limitations associated with the current experimental methods to get X-ray structures and the high throughput of sequencing technology have motivated the development of computational methods for predicting PPIs [1, 2]. Identifying PPI interacting sites has a significant impact on understanding protein functions, elucidating signal transduction networks and drug design [2, 3]. Computational methods developed so far have utilized information from various sources at different levels-from primary sequences, to molecular structures, and to evolutionary profiles [4-6]. However, there are still some challenging problems, such as large-scale conformational changes, one protein to many partners, and multi-component complexes [5]. The major task of this paper is focused on the problem that one protein can interact with many partner proteins and form interfaces involving different parts of its surface.

One major approach to studying protein-protein interaction is through domain-domain interaction. Each protein can be characterized by either a distinct domain or a combination of domains. Because proteins interact with one another through their specific domains, predicting domain–domain interactions on a large scale makes it possible to predict previously unknown protein–protein interactions from their domains. Therefore, domain-domain interactions present an overall view of the protein–protein interaction network within a cell responsible for carrying out various biological and cellular functions [7]. The evolutionarily conserved domains were well defined by the Pfam (http://pfam.sanger.ac.uk/) database [8]. The domain-domain interaction information from known structure is well characterized by some public databases, such as 3DID [9].

Many computational approaches have been proposed to predict domain-domain interaction (namely, whether two proteins can interact with each other through their specific domains), based on gene ontology [10, 11], gene-fusion [10, 12], correlated sequence signatures and sequence co-evolution [13-15], phylogenetic profiling [16], statistical/probabilistic frameworks [7, 10, 17-19], parsimonious principle [20, 21] and machine learning [22-25]. Several resources for the computationally predicted DDI databases have been generated. However, predicting domain-domain interaction sites between protein sequence pairs is more complicated. Research on protein interacting site prediction and analysis has been summarized in some recent reviews [5, 6, 26-30].

Interaction profile hidden Markov model (ipHMM) has shown to be an effective tool for predicting protein interaction sites for protein-ligand interaction. The ipHMM takes both structure and sequence data into account. It is based on a homology search via a posterior decoding algorithm that yields probabilities for interacting sequence positions and inherits the efficiency and the power of the profile hidden Markov model (pHMM) methodology [31]. The ipHMM was adopted here to predict protein interaction sites for protein-protein interaction instead of protein-ligand interaction with some modification.

* Corresponding authors: liliao@udel.edu, wuc@udel.edu

To this end, the domain-domain interaction from 3DID was used as training data to build ipHMM at DDI family level. It was found, however, that ipHMM at DDI family level performed poorly in characterizing the variation of DDI where homologous protein pairs can interact in a completely different manner. Those different interaction interfaces within the same DDI family are referred to as interface topologies [32]. The different topological interfaces are clustered to different DDI topologies, and the topology level information of DDI is collected in 3DID database as well. For instance, as shown in Figure 1, the AMNp_N domain was found to interact with two domains. One is the AMNp_N domain, and the other one is the PNP_UDP_1 domain. For the DDI, AMNp_N domain vs AMNp_N domain, there is only one topological interface (Row 1 in Figure 1.). The interacting residues aligned with HMM profile of the AMNp_N domain were marked with different colors to indicate their involvements in different topologies. For the DDI, AMNp_N domain vs PNP_UDP_1 domain, there are four different topological interfaces (Row 2-5 in Figure 1.). The interacting residues, aligned with HMM profiles of AMNp_N domain and PNP_UDP_1 domain, were also colored to differentiate different topological patterns. The interacting pattern of the AMNp_N domain is different when interacting with the AMNp_N domain and PNP_UDP_1 domain. Thus, building models for different DDI families (AMNp_N domain vs AMNp_N domain, AMNp_N domain vs PNP_UDP_1 domain) is beneficial. However, a single hidden Markov model for DDI families with multiple topology interfaces (such as AMNp_N domain vs PNP_UDP_1 domain) is not adequate to capture the topology variation accurately.

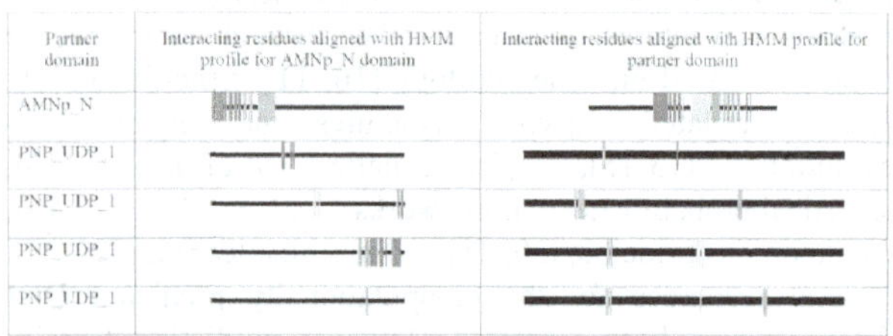

Figure 1. Domain-domain interaction for AMNp_N domain with different domains and different topology interfaces.

Figure 2 shows the distribution of DDI families with different number of topology interfaces reported in 3DID database. About 46% (2888/6260) of the DDI families have just one topology interface type. For those DDI families, the ipHMM at family level is the same as the ipHMM at topology level. Thus, ipHMM was only built at DDI family level. However, about 20 % of the DDI families have two topology interface types. And the rest, up to 36%, has more topology interface types. Therefore, it is imperative to address the multi topological interface issue. In this work, we proposed to develop the ipHMMs at topology level for DDI families that contain multiple interface topologies.

Figure 2. Distribution of DDI families with different number of topology interfaces.

2 Method

2.1 Dataset

Several research groups have published their work in organizing and standardizing the existing and known domain-domain interactions [9, 25, 33, 34]. The 3DID database is among the most successful and widely used one, which contains interactions inferred from PDB entries. This database identifies all cases of domain-domain interactions with known three dimensional structures by first assigning Pfam domains to each individual protein in the Protein Data Bank (PDB). Next, the atomic contacts between domains in the same structure are computed, requiring at least five contacts (hydrogen bonds, electrostatic or van der Waals interactions) to call a domain-domain interaction [9]. Domain-domain interaction information used for training and testing ipHMMs was obtained from the 3DID database http://3did.irbbarcelona.org [9]. The flat file downloaded from the 3DID was parsed and preprocessed. The -PDB files for interacting sequence pairs were downloaded from the RCSB Protein Data Bank. Based on the structural information for the protein complexes at the atomic level provided by the 3DID, we are able to determine which amino acids actually take part in the interaction and construct an ipHMM. The collection of pHMMs used to generate ipHMM was obtained from the Pfam database [35].

For this study, a set (A) of 51 DDI families, with 109 topologies and 1807 sequence pairs, were selected for building and testing the ipHMMs, satisfying the following criteria. Each selected DDI family has at least two different topology interfaces and has different domains. Each topology has 10-20 examples. The ipHMMs for those DDIs were built at both DDI family level and topology level.

To serve as baseline for comparison, a set (B) of 146 DDI families with 1917 protein sequence pairs, each just one topology interface type, were chosen to build ipHMMs on at DDI family level. Each selected DDI family has 10-20 examples and has different domains. The reason for that is we need fair numbers of examples and clear classification of domains. For those DDI families, the ipHMM at family level is the same as ipHMM at topology level.

2.2 The interaction profile hidden Markov model

The interaction profile hidden Markov model (ipHMM) was first developed for the prediction of protein-ligand interaction sites. It was later on combined with support vector machine to predict domain-domain interaction [36]. However, the application of ipHMM for the prediction of protein-protein interaction sites, which is based on domain-domain interaction, has not been reported. Although, our model adopted the ipHMM for predicting interacting sites, the fundamental assumption is different from Friedrich's approach. Friedrich's study assumed that sequence patterns encoding protein function are shared between members of a domain family. Thus, the ipHMM was built for each domain regardless of its partner (except that it grouped ligands into three ligand categories: peptides, nucleotides and ions). In our study, the assumption is that sequence patterns encoding protein function varies given different partners, which was supported by the finding that different interacting topology for a given domain [34]. This is the challenging problem mentioned before that one protein can interact with many partner proteins and form interfaces involving different parts of its surface. So the ipHMM was built for each domain family based on its domain partner. The construction of ipHMM was previously described by Friedrich and Gonzalez [31, 36]. Friedrich et al. developed the interaction profile hidden Markov model (ipHMM), which modifies the ordinary profile hidden Markov model by adding to the model architecture new states explicitly representing residues on the interface. The ipHMM architecture takes into account both structural information and sequence data. Each ipHMM is, like pHMMs, a probabilistic representation of a protein domain family. The architecture of the ipHMM follows the same restrictions and connectivity of the HMMER architecture [37], except that: the match states of the classical pHMM are split into a non-interacting (Mni) and an interacting match state (Mi) (Figure 3).

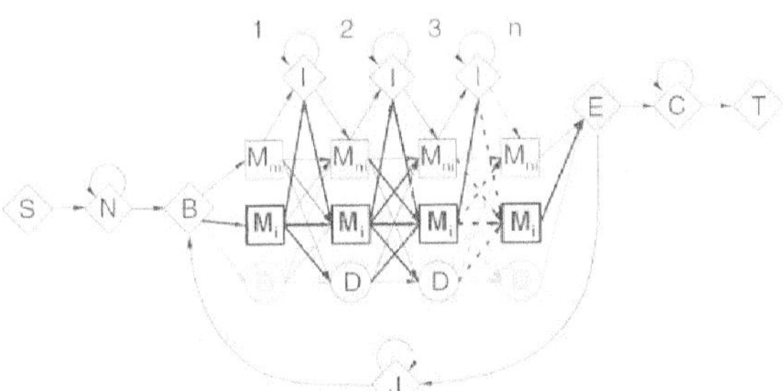

Figure 3. Architecture of the interaction profile hidden Markov model. The match states of the classical pHMM are split into non-interacting (Mni) and interacting (Mi) match states. Image credit for Friedrich et al., Bioinformatics, 2006.

The new match state has the same properties of a match state in the ordinary profile hidden Markov model architecture, i.e. these interacting match states are able to emit all amino acid symbols with probabilities, which are parameters to be fixed according to the training examples. The method used to build ipHMM models at DDI family level was described by Gonzalez [36]. It was modified to build at topology level which split each domain into different topologies and use the examples in each topology for model training. The flowchart of the system processing at both the domain level and topology level was shown in Figure 4. Posterior decoding is adopted to predict interacting residues and path dependent probabilities for every hidden state for ipHMM. After the interacting residues of protein sequence was predicted, it was compared to the ground truth data to evaluate the prediction performance.

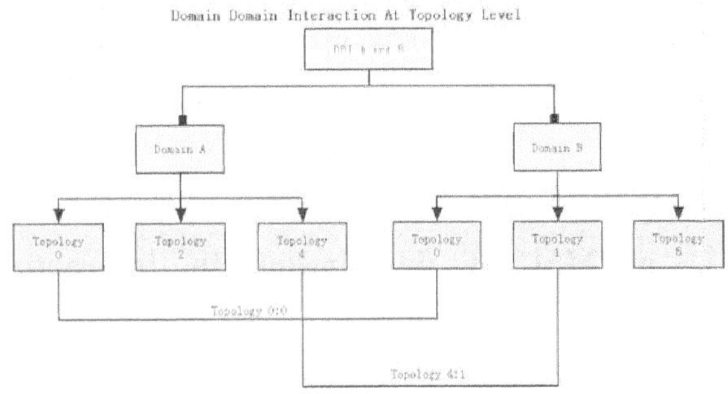

Figure 4. Predicting protein-protein interactions model hierarchy. Topology level models were built for Topology 0:0 and Topology 0:4

2.3 Evaluation of the Prediction Performance

The prediction performance of the ipHMMs was evaluated using standard metrics including sensitivity/recall, precision, specificity and Matthews correlation coefficient (MCC). Because we have relatively small numbers of training examples for each model, the leave-one-out cross validation was adopted. For each DDI family, we take each sequence pair as testing data and take the rest sequences as the training data. True positive (TP), true negative (TN), false positive (FP) and false negative (FN) are calculated for each testing data. True positives (TP) are the actual binding interfaces residues that are predicted correctly. True negatives (TN) are the actual non-interacting residues that are predicted correctly. False positives (FP) are false predictions of interacting residues. False negatives (FN) are false predictions of non-interacting residues.

$$sensitivity / recall = \frac{TP}{TP + FN} \tag{1}$$

$$precision = \frac{TP}{TP + FP} \tag{2}$$

$$specificity = \frac{TN}{TN + FP} \quad (3)$$

$$MCC = \frac{(TP \times TN - FP \times FN)}{\sqrt{(TP + FP)(TP + TN)(FP + FN)(TN + FN)}} \quad (4)$$

The sensitivity (also known as recall), which can be viewed as a measurement of completeness, is the fraction of correctly predicted interacting residues over all the actual interacting residues. The precision is the fraction of correctly predicted interacting residues over all predicted interacting residues. The specificity is the fraction of true negatives among all residues predicted to be non-interacting residues. The Matthews Correlation Coefficient (MCC) measures the correlation between observed and predicted interacting residues and negative interacting residues, where a value of -1 represents inverse prediction, 0 means random prediction, and 1 is a perfect prediction [26]. All the measurements were averaged for each testing sequence pair.

3 Results and Discussion

3.1 ipHMM at domain-domain interaction family level

A DDI family contains the information of the domain and its interacting partner domain. Therefore, the ipHMM models were built at domain-domain interaction family level. The set B of 146 DDI families with one single topology interface were selected to build ipHMM for both domain α and domain β. Given two protein sequences containing domain α and domain β, the predicted interacting residues of protein α and protein β can be obtained via the posterior decoding. The prediction performance was summarized in Table 1 (rightmost column) and Figure 5.

Table 1. Prediction performance of ipHMM

	Models trained at family level for (51) DDIs with multiple interface topologies	Models trained at topology level for (51) DDIs with multiple interface topologies	Models trained at family level for (146) DDIs with single interface topology
Sensitivity/ Recall	36.6%	74.0%	74.4%
Precision	49.1%	75.9%	77.6%
Specificity	96.9%	98.2%	97.3%
Matthews correlation coefficient	46.4%	77.3%	72.5%

It can be seen that sensitivity and precision for predicting interacting residues are both over 70%. This indicates that the ipHMM model has a good quality of predicting protein interacting site. For proteins with crystal structure, it can improve success of protein docking because it reduces the search space significantly. For proteins with just sequence, it can help to locate the target residues for mutation to invalidate the interaction.

3.2 ipHMM at domain-domain interaction topology level

As mentioned in the introduction section, even at domain-domain family level there exist multiple interface topologies within the domain-domain interaction family. From the distribution of DDI families with different number of topology interfaces (Figure 2), we found that more than half of the domains in 3DID have more than one topology interfaces. With the finding of new resolved protein X-ray structures, this fraction may expect to increase. This motivated us to further build the ipHMM model at topology level.

For the set A of 51 DDI families that contain multiple interface topologies, we developed ipHMMs at both the family level and topology level. The interacting residue prediction performance is also reported in Table 1 (columns 2 and 3) and Figure 5. It can be seen that the performance is rather poor for models built at the family level, as compared to these in the set B, namely these DDI families that contain single interface topology.

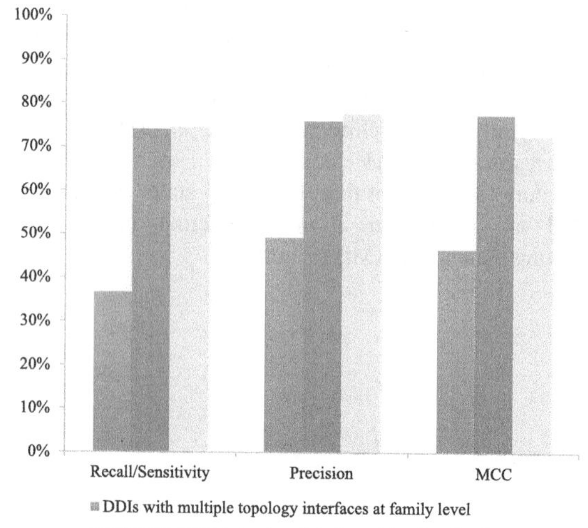

Figure 5. Protein-protein interacting sites prediction performance at family level and topology level

As expected, the performance is improved significantly for models built at the topology level. Specifically, the residue-based average sensitivity/recall increases from 36.6% (family level) to 74.0% (topology level), and the average precision also increases significantly, from 49.1% (family level) to 75.9% (topology level). The sensitivity is the fraction of correctly predicted interacting residues over all the true interacting residues, and the precision is the fraction of correctly predicted interacting residues over all the predicted interacting residues. Both the sensitivity and precision at DDI family level were low because those DDI families contain multiple interface topologies and a single ipHMM is inadequate to capture the variation in the interfaces. Our strategy of building ipHMMs at topology level has led to significantly improved performance in identifying the interacting sites of the protein pairs, which can help better understand protein functions and enhance drug design. Knowledge of the location of the interface can also improve the success of protein docking because it reduces the search space [27].

Note that the average specificity was improved slightly from 96.9% (family level) to 98.2% (topology level). The specificity is the fraction of true negative residues among all residues predicted to be negative interacting residues. The specificity for family level and topology level are both at a high score because most of the residues in protein are non-interacting residues and easier to predict; even blindly predict all residues as non-interacting will still score high for the specificity.

The average Matthews correlation coefficient (MCC) was improved from 46.4% (family level) to 77.3% (topology level). It measures the correlation between observed and predicted interacting residues and negative interacting residues.

In sum, all the measurements in this study showed that the performance of predicting interacting sites of protein pairs at topology level improved significantly. These results indicate that the performance of ipHMM model is among the best predictors in identifying PPI interacting sites for protein pair [26, 38, 39]. The good performance of ipHMM can be explained by its integration of sequence information and 3D structure information and more specific model at different level.

Although our datasets are relatively small due to the requirement of having at least 10 examples for each topology in order to reliably train ipHMMs, it is expected that the concept of making prediction at interface topology level is general applicable for all these DDIs in 3DID that contains multiple topologies. It is reasonable to believe that having multiple interface topologies at a domain may play a significant role, just as having multiple interacting domains for a protein does, in helping us better understand proteins and their function. Currently many topologies have less than 10 examples reported in 3DID, as described by Stein et al. [32]. As future work, more sophisticated clustering algorithms can be developed and applied to identify interface topology, leading to more examples and the improved prediction accuracy of interacting residues.

4 Conclusions

The interaction profile hidden Markov model (ipHMM) can be successfully applied to predict interacting residues for protein-protein interaction. The ipHMM at DDD family has a good quality of prediction for those DDI with single topology interface type. For those DDIs with multiple topology interface types, ipHMM built at topology level becomes necessary. It is shown that the ipHMM at topology level significantly improves the performance for predicting interacting residues as compared to ipHMM at DDI family level. The benchmark results indicate that ipHMM models are among the best predictors in identifying PPI interacting sites for protein pairs.

5 Acknowledgements

The project described was supported by NCRR (5P20RR016472-12) and NIGMS (8 P20 GM103446-12) at NIH. The content is solely the responsibility of the authors and does not necessarily represent the official views of the National Center For Research Resources or the National Institutes of Health.

6 References

[1] S. András, G. Vera, K. A. Adrián, and S. Jeffrey, "Prediction of physical protein–protein interactions," Physical Biology, vol. 2, p. S1, 2005.

[2] H.-X. Zhou and Y. Shan, "Prediction of protein interaction sites from sequence profile and residue neighbor list," Proteins: Structure, Function, and Bioinformatics, vol. 44, pp. 336-343, 2001.

[3] X.-w. Chen and J. C. Jeong, "Sequence-based prediction of protein interaction sites with an integrative method," Bioinformatics, vol. 25, pp. 585-591, March 1, 2009 2009.

[4] B. A. Shoemaker and A. R. Panchenko, "Deciphering Protein–Protein Interactions. Part II. Computational Methods to Predict Protein and Domain Interaction Partners," PLoS Comput Biol, vol. 3, p. e43, 2007.

[5] H.-X. Zhou and S. Qin, "Interaction-site prediction for protein complexes: a critical assessment," Bioinformatics, vol. 23, pp. 2203-2209, September 1, 2007 2007.

[6] I. Ezkurdia, L. Bartoli, P. Fariselli, R. Casadio, A. Valencia, and M. L. Tress, "Progress and challenges in

predicting protein–protein interaction sites," Briefings in Bioinformatics, vol. 10, pp. 233-246, May 1, 2009 2009.

[7] M. Deng, S. Mehta, F. Sun, and T. Chen, "Inferring Domain–Domain Interactions From Protein–Protein Interactions," Genome Research, vol. 12, pp. 1540-1548, October 1, 2002 2002.

[8] R. D. Finn, J. Mistry, J. Tate, P. Coggill, A. Heger, J. E. Pollington, O. L. Gavin, P. Gunasekaran, G. Ceric, K. Forslund, L. Holm, E. L. L. Sonnhammer, S. R. Eddy, and A. Bateman, "The Pfam protein families database," Nucleic Acids Research, vol. 38, pp. D211-D222, January 1, 2010 2010.

[9] A. Stein, R. Russell, and P. Aloy, "3DID: interacting protein domains of known three-dimensional structure," Nucleic Acids Research, pp. D413 - D417, 2005.

[10] H. Lee, M. Deng, F. Sun, and T. Chen, "An integrated approach to the prediction of domain-domain interactions," BMC Bioinformatics, vol. 7, p. 269, 2006.

[11] M. Liu, X.-w. Chen, and R. Jothi, "Knowledge-guided inference of domain–domain interactions from incomplete protein–protein interaction networks," Bioinformatics, vol. 25, pp. 2492-2499, October 1, 2009 2009.

[12] S.-K. Ng, Z. Zhang, and S.-H. Tan, "Integrative approach for computationally inferring protein domain interactions," Bioinformatics, vol. 19, pp. 923-929, May 22, 2003 2003.

[13] E. Sprinzak and H. Margalit, "Correlated sequence-signatures as markers of protein-protein interaction," Journal of Molecular Biology, vol. 311, pp. 681-692, Aug 2001.

[14] R. Jothi, P. F. Cherukuri, A. Tasneem, and T. M. Przytycka, "Co-evolutionary analysis of domains in interacting proteins reveals insights into domain-domain interactions mediating protein-protein interactions," Journal of Molecular Biology, vol. 362, pp. 861-875, Sep 2006.

[15] M. G. Kann, R. Jothi, P. F. Cherukuri, and T. M. Przytycka, "Predicting protein domain interactions from coevolution of conserved regions," Proteins-Structure Function and Bioinformatics, vol. 67, pp. 811-820, Jun 2007.

[16] P. Pagel, P. Wong, and D. Frishman, "A domain interaction map based on phylogenetic profiling," Journal of Molecular Biology, vol. 344, pp. 1331-1346, Dec 2004.

[17] T. M. W. Nye, C. Berzuini, W. R. Gilks, M. M. Babu, and S. A. Teichmann, "Statistical analysis of domains in interacting protein pairs," Bioinformatics, vol. 21, pp. 993-1001, April 1, 2005 2005.

[18] R. Riley, C. Lee, C. Sabatti, and D. Eisenberg, "Inferring protein domain interactions from databases of interacting proteins," Genome Biology, vol. 6, p. R89, 2005.

[19] H. Wang, E. Segal, A. Ben-Hur, Q.-R. Li, M. Vidal, and D. Koller, "InSite: a computational method for identifying protein-protein interaction binding sites on a proteome-wide scale," Genome Biology, vol. 8, p. R192, 2007.

[20] K. Guimaraes, R. Jothi, E. Zotenko, and T. Przytycka, "Predicting domain-domain interactions using a parsimony approach," Genome Biology, vol. 7, p. R104, 2006.

[21] K. Guimaraes and T. Przytycka, "Interrogating domain-domain interactions with parsimony based approaches," BMC Bioinformatics, vol. 9, p. 171, 2008.

[22] M. Singhal and H. Resat, "A domain-based approach to predict protein-protein interactions," BMC Bioinformatics, vol. 8, p. 199, 2007.

[23] X.-W. Chen and M. Liu, "Prediction of protein–protein interactions using random decision forest framework," Bioinformatics, vol. 21, pp. 4394-4400, December 15, 2005 2005.

[24] X. M. Zhao, L. N. Chen, and K. Aihara, "A discriminative approach for identifying domain-domain interactions from protein-protein interactions," Proteins-Structure Function and Bioinformatics, vol. 78, pp. 1243-1253, Apr 2010.

[25] S. Yellaboina, A. Tasneem, D. V. Zaykin, B. Raghavachari, and R. Jothi, "DOMINE: a comprehensive collection of known and predicted domain-domain interactions," Nucleic Acids Research, vol. 39, pp. D730-D735, January 1, 2011 2011.

[26] C.-T. Chen, H.-P. Peng, J.-W. Jian, K.-C. Tsai, J.-Y. Chang, E.-W. Yang, J.-B. Chen, S.-Y. Ho, W.-L. Hsu, and A.-S. Yang, "Protein-Protein Interaction Site Predictions with Three-Dimensional Probability Distributions of Interacting Atoms on Protein Surfaces," PLoS ONE, vol. 7, p. e37706, 2012.

[27] M. N. Wass, A. David, and M. J. E. Sternberg, "Challenges for the prediction of macromolecular interactions," Current Opinion in Structural Biology, vol. 21, pp. 382-390, 2011.

[28] T. Nurcan, G. Attila, and K. Ozlem, "Prediction of protein–protein interactions: unifying evolution and structure at protein interfaces," Physical Biology, vol. 8, p. 035006, 2011.

[29] O. Keskin, A. Gursoy, B. Ma, and R. Nussinov, "Principles of Protein–Protein Interactions: What are the

Preferred Ways For Proteins To Interact?," Chemical Reviews, vol. 108, pp. 1225-1244, 2008/04/01 2008.

[30] S. J. de Vries and A. M. Bonvin, "How proteins get in touch: interface prediction in the study of biomolecular complexes," Current Protein and Peptide Science, vol. 9, pp. 394-406, 2008.

[31] T. Friedrich, B. Pils, T. Dandekar, J. Schultz, and T. Müller, "Modelling interaction sites in protein domains with interaction profile hidden Markov models," Bioinformatics, vol. 22, pp. 2851-2857, December 1, 2006 2006.

[32] A. Stein, A. Ceol, and P. Aloy, "3did: identification and classification of domain-based interactions of known three-dimensional structure," Nucleic Acids Research, vol. 39, pp. D718-D723, 2010.

[33] R. D. Finn, M. Marshall, and A. Bateman, "iPfam: visualization of protein–protein interactions in PDB at domain and amino acid resolutions," Bioinformatics, vol. 21, pp. 410-412, February 1, 2005 2005.

[34] A. Stein, A. Panjkovich, and P. Aloy, "3did Update: domain–domain and peptide-mediated interactions of known 3D structure," Nucleic Acids Research, vol. 37, pp. D300-D304, January 1, 2009 2009.

[35] R. D. Finn, J. Mistry, B. Schuster-Böckler, S. Griffiths-Jones, V. Hollich, T. Lassmann, S. Moxon, M. Marshall, A. Khanna, R. Durbin, S. R. Eddy, E. L. L. Sonnhammer, and A. Bateman, "Pfam: clans, web tools and services," Nucleic Acids Research, vol. 34, pp. D247-D251, January 1, 2006 2006.

[36] A. Gonzalez and L. Liao, "Predicting domain-domain interaction based on domain profiles with feature selection and support vector machines," BMC Bioinformatics, vol. 11, p. 537, 2010.

[37] M. J. Sippl, "Biological sequence analysis. Probabilistic models of proteins and nucleic acids, edited by R. Durbin, S. Eddy, A. Krogh, and G. Mitchinson. 1998. Cambridge: Cambridge University Press. 356 pp. Protein Science, vol. 8, pp. 695-695, 1999.

[38] M. Šikić, S. Tomić, and K. Vlahoviček, "Prediction of Protein–Protein Interaction Sites in Sequences and 3D Structures by Random Forests," PLoS Comput Biol, vol. 5, p. e1000278, 2009.

[39] S. Ahmad and K. Mizuguchi, "Partner-Aware Prediction of Interacting Residues in Protein-Protein Complexes from Sequence Data," PLoS ONE, vol. 6, p. e29104, 2011.

Applications of Boolean Functions for mapping the mutation of mRNA and Protein structure : A new Computational approach

Joyshree Nath
Department of Computer Science, Jogesh Chandra Chaudhuri College, Kolkata,India
e-mail: joyshreenath@gmail.com

Abstract: *To understand DNA and hence protein structure also the relation with disease formation is now a prime research area. Many researchers and scientists across the globe are working on estimation of the structure of a DNA and hence the corresponding protein and the effects of mutation on it from different angles to get hold more on how a certain DNA sequence or a protein sequence can lead to a certain disease. This paper concentrates on the effects of mutation on the binary format of DNA structure due to the application of Boolean functions on it. Also this paper takes into consideration the potential protein primary structure formed from original DNA sequence and that from mutated sequence. Then this paper checks the sequence similarity of these sequences with the existing gene database of NCBI.*

Keywords : DNA, Protein, Disease, gene, NCBI

1. Introduction

To understand the DNA structure and also the protein structure is now one prime research area. It is established that the proteins are the main resource centre of human body. So the body will function properly provided the proteins are functions properly. So proper functioning of proteins can lead to proper functioning of our body in turn. Malfunction of proteins can naturally lead to various diseases like sickle cell anaemia or Al etc. The researchers are doing investigation to find any relationship between the protein's structure and its functions. To verify these one has to see the effects of different types of mutations on the protein structure. In the present work the author has applied different mutations on protein structure and also calculated the fractal dimension. The author has also compared the computed result with the result available in NCBI. The result found satisfactory. In section 2 the author has discussed the various aspects of central dogma, protein structures and mutations. In section 3 the author has discussed in detail the algorithms which they used to find different mutated protein structure. The entire work done using C-programs and also BLAST tool of NCBI website. In section 4 the results are shown obtained from the algorithm proposed by the authors. In section 5 the author has given a summary of the whole work. The present work is just a beginning of understanding protein structure and DNA structure. There are lot of scope in this area to explore. In section 6 the author has given conclusion and the future scope. The author already started the work to find a mathematical model to describe how DNA or Protein starts mutation and gets deformed and whether one can regenerate the original DNA or the protein structure from a deformed structure.

2. Background study:

2.1 Central Dogma

A DNA sequence is transcribed into the corresponding RNA and then into respective protein(amino acids). This procedure is known as the *central dogma of molecular biology.* Firstly, the DNA replicates its information and correspondingly there comes two cells with the same DNA information. That DNA information is copied (transcription) into an RNA called the mRNA(messenger RNA). This mRNA is processed for amino acid formation(translation) that in turn goes into the protein synthesis. These proteins help in different biological activities of an organism and most importantly it helps in providing energy to any organism. To decode the instructions encoded in DNA and thus to infer on the protein sequence structure encoded in the DNA sequence is a huge domain of research in today's time. Such proceedings may help us know more about human evolution and disease relations.

2.2. Proteins and their 3-D structures:

Proteins are molecules made of sequences of amino acids bound by a peptide bond. The genetic code codifies twenty two different amino acids that can compose proteins. They are made up of a repeating arrangement of amino acids, small molecules that differ from each other in their functional groups. Proteins play a fundamental role in nearly all biological processes.[13] The information in a biological system is stored in an organism's DNA (Deoxyribose Nucleic Acid). This information is turned eventually into amino acids and protein. Amino acids are organic compounds made from amine (-NH_2) and carboxylic acid (-COOH) groups, along with a side-chain. There are 20 proteinogenic amino acids. Those amino acids can be divided into essential (e.g.-Valine, Leucine) and non essential (e.g.-Alanine, Taurine) amino acids [1],[2]. Each protein exists as an unfolded polypeptide when translated from a sequence of mRNA. Amino acids form peptide bonds with other amino acids when the amino group of the first amino acid bonds with the group of the second amino acid. Protein folding is the process by which a protein structure assumes its functional shape (a 3-D structure) or conformation. The correct three-dimensional structure is essential to function. First the linear amino acid sequence formed is called primary structure. Then the next level coiling formed in this primary structure is called secondary structure, and then the tertiary structure and finally the quaternary structure. Failure to fold into proper 3-D structure may produce inactive proteins or lead to toxic functionality. Many allergies are caused by such folding of the proteins, for the immune system does not produce antibodies for certain protein structures. Aggregated misfolded proteins are associated with illnesses such as Creutzfeldt-Jakob disease, mad cow disease, Alzheimer's disease, Huntington's and Parkinson's disease. Most proteins have unimportant positions where almost any amino acid will do. Frequently there is an active center of the protein where amino acid changes are catastrophic Protein folding is routinely studied using techniques like *NMR spectroscopy, Circular dichroism, Proteolysis, Optical tweezers, Energy landscape of protein folding*[3]. All these theories throw light in portions on the technology or technologies that might have been responsible. But still now the exact procedure of protein folding mechanism has not been deciphered. This research work will take step in this direction so as to throw some more light on the mechanism of protein folding.

2.3. Mutation in DNA, protein sequences and its effect on diseases:

The gene sequences lead to different functional aspects and on mis functions may lead to diseases. Mutation means a certain change in the original genome sequence and thus changing it functionally many a times. It may be a kind of insertion or alphabetical change or deletion and lots more. This may become sometimes dangerous for the fact that mutation may lead to production of some different genome sequence and thus effect the protein production and lead to certain diseases. Sometimes the change may not effect the genome sequence at all. For example, swapping an A with T for haemoglobin gene causes serious disease sickle cell anaemia. Also if there is a mutation in one of the parental genes, this can be passed on from parent to child. This is why diseases can run in families.[12]

3. Algorithms used in the present study:

3.1. Predicting primary structures of proteins from a gene sequence

Firstly from the NCBI database mRNA sequences were taken of human (Homo sapiens) species. The DNA is transcribed into a single stranded RNA which has both introns and exons. The exon portions (protein coding sequences) are then clubbed together to form the mRNA. So the mRNA sequences are the potential areas of protein primary sequences. These mRNA sequences were fed into the web page- http://www.ncbi.nlm.nih.gov/projects/gorf/orfig.cgi and the triplet codons present in the sequence were decoded for the respective amino acids. The sequence similarity for those mechanically obtained amino acid protein sequences were checked through BLAST software of NCBI database.

3.2. Algorithms used for DNA sequence modification :

There are 3-4 types of mutations that are very prominent when it comes to disease associations. These are missense mutation(it is a mutation in which a single nucleotide is changed), Indels(A mutation named where insertion or deletion of nucleotides occur), frameshift mutation [9],[10].

Original Sequence of mRNA Homo sapiens of ACCESSION ID NM_001244856 was downloaded from NCBI database(http://www.ncbi.nlm.nih.gov/nuccore/NM_001244856.1). Again this DNA sequence was converted into bit format with the following denominations.

Table-1 : Character sequence, binary sequence of DNA

Sl.No.	Character sequence	Binary sequence	Decimal value
1	A or a	00	0
2	C or c	01	1
3	G or g	10	2
4	T or t	11	3

This time some affine rules were applied to that DNA sequence for only once. These were 15,51,60,85,90,102,105,150,153,165,170,195,204,240 in no particular order. This time also the mapping with respect to the table format (Table-2) was used.

Table-2 : Proposed Mutation Rule

A	B	C	Rule 15	Rule 51	Rule 60	Rule 85	Rule 90	Rule 102	Rule 105	Rule 150	Rule 153	Rule 165	Rule 170	Rule 195	Rule 204	Rule 240
0	0	0	1	1	0	1	0	0	1	0	1	1	0	1	0	0
0	0	1	1	1	0	0	1	1	0	1	0	0	1	1	0	0
0	1	0	1	0	1	1	0	1	0	1	0	1	0	1	1	0
0	1	1	1	0	1	0	1	0	1	0	1	0	1	1	1	0
1	0	0	0	1	1	1	1	0	0	1	1	0	0	1	0	1
1	0	1	0	1	1	0	0	1	1	0	0	1	1	0	0	1
1	1	0	0	0	0	1	1	1	1	0	0	0	0	1	1	1
1	1	1	0	0	0	0	0	0	0	1	1	1	1	0	1	1

The triplets were consecutive but separate and were used starting from the first trip on the DNA sequence to the last triplet of the same sequence and they were mapped to the table values. Thus the main sequence got modified into a sequence that is one-third of its length. This can be seen as a Boolean example of 'Deletion' mutation. Every modified sequence was stored into separate text files.

Also to go for 'Missense' mutation again the binary

mRNA sequence file was taken and the triplets were taken and matched to the same Table 2. But this time a null boundary condition of a 'logic 0' at the beginning and at the end of the sequence was taken and the triplets overlapped with the immediate previous one and the next immediate one.

Also to go for 'Insertion' mutation, the bits of the sequence were taken. For every two consecutive bits the effect of 'XOR'ing those bits were added in the middle of the bits. So if the consecutive bits are 0 and 1, then the effect of 'XOR'ing those bits, that is, 1 is place in between 0 and 1 and thus the bit pattern is increased. But all these mutations are not applied all through the sequences. But nature effects mutation in a random selection manner. Here also the effects of bit pattern changes are done to an alternating odd line nucleotide sequence pattern. This thing was done to insertion and missense change, deletion was effected on the entire sequence. Now to see if these sequences had global alignment or local alignment, these binary sequences were first converted into ATCG format alphabetically and then they were subjected to BLAST algorithm, through NCBI website: http://blast.ncbi.nlm.nih.gov/Blast.cgi. The comparison of nucleotide or protein sequences from the same or different organisms is a very powerful tool in molecular biology. By finding similarities between sequences, one can infer the function of newly sequenced genes, predict new members of gene families, and explore evolutionary relationships. Global or local sequence similarity searching can be used to predict the location and function of protein-coding and transcription-regulation regions in genomic DNA.[4]

3.3. Predicting primary structures of proteins from a gene sequence

Again the modified mRNA structures were fed into the ncbi webpage- http://www.ncbi.nlm.nih.gov/projects/gorf/orfig.cgi and the potential primary structures of the protein were obtained. This was taken to be the potential amino acid sequence starting right after *"gcc"* nucleotide group and ending with the proper stop codon(*"tga"* in this case). Thus the sequence similarity for those mechanically obtained primary structures were checked again through BLAST software of NCBI database.Thus the sequence similarity for those mechanically obtained primary structures were checked again through BLAST software of NCBI database.

4. Results and Discusion

Here are the results which are obtained from these statistical methods which are stated in section 4.

4.1. Protein sequences obtained from the original mRNA sequence:

M D T T R Y R P W G R W V H W S R R P L F L A L A V L V T T V L W A V I L S I L L S K A S T E R A A L L D G H D L L R TN A S K Q T A A L G A L K E EV G D C H S C C S G T Q A Q L Q T T R A E L G E A Q A K L E Q E S A L R E L R E R V T Q G L A E A G R G R D V R T E L F R A L E A V R L Q N N S C E P C P T S W L S F E G S C Y F S V P K T T W A A A Q D H C A D A S A H L V I V G G L D E Q G F L T R N T R G R G Y W L G L R A V R H L G K V Q G Y Q W V D G V S L S F S H W N Q G E P N D A W G R E N C V L H T G L W N D A P C D S E K D G W I C E K R H N C

The protein sequence obtained mechanically (obtaining NCBI id NCYVXDDJ014) was sent for BLAST in NCBI website blast algorithm applied had 103 blast hits, 96 among them being with that of the sequences of Homo sapiens. The protein sequence obtained showed a similarity to CLECT super-family of proteins. One screen shot is below:

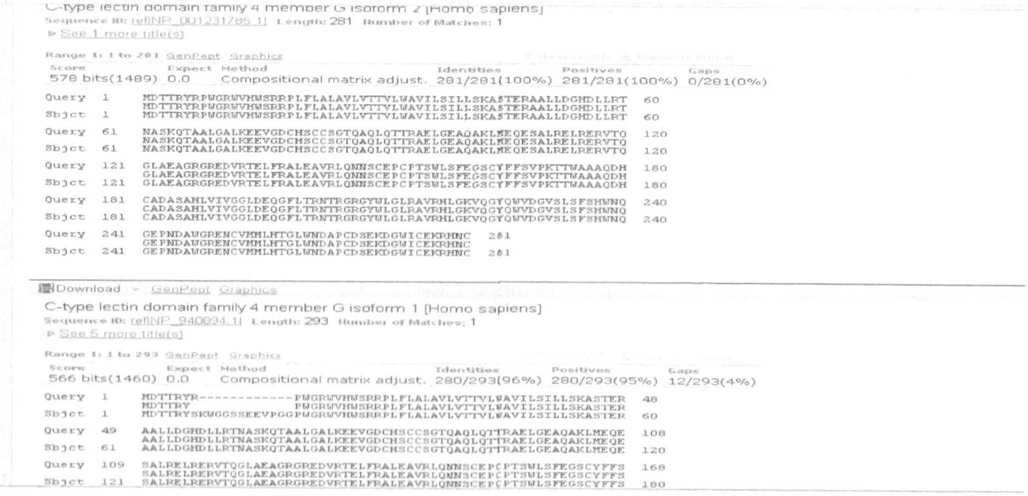

```
C-type lectin domain family 4 member G isoform 2 [Homo sapiens]
Sequence ID: ref|NP_001231785.1| Length: 281 Number of Matches: 1
See 1 more title(s)

Range 1: 1 to 281 GenPept Graphics
Score            Expect Method                        Identities      Positives       Gaps
578 bits(1489)   0.0    Compositional matrix adjust.  281/281(100%)   281/281(100%)   0/281(0%)

Query  1    MDTTRYRPWGRWVHWSRRPLFLALAVLVTTVLWAVILSILLSKASTERAALLDGHDLLRT  60
            MDTTRYRPWGRWVHWSRRPLFLALAVLVTTVLWAVILSILLSKASTERAALLDGHDLLRT
Sbjct  1    MDTTRYRPWGRWVHWSRRPLFLALAVLVTTVLWAVILSILLSKASTERAALLDGHDLLRT  60

Query  61   NASKQTAALGALKEEVGDCHSCCSGTQAQLQTTRAELGEAQAKLMEQESALRELRERVTQ  120
            NASKQTAALGALKEEVGDCHSCCSGTQAQLQTTRAELGEAQAKLMEQESALRELRERVTQ
Sbjct  61   NASKQTAALGALKEEVGDCHSCCSGTQAQLQTTRAELGEAQAKLMEQESALRELRERVTQ  120

Query  121  GLAEAGRGREDVRTELFRALEAVRLQNNSCEPCPTSWLSFEGSCYFFSVPKTTWAAAQDH  180
            GLAEAGRGREDVRTELFRALEAVRLQNNSCEPCPTSWLSFEGSCYFFSVPKTTWAAAQDH
Sbjct  121  GLAEAGRGREDVRTELFRALEAVRLQNNSCEPCPTSWLSFEGSCYFFSVPKTTWAAAQDH  180

Query  181  CADASAHLVIVGGLDEQGFLTRNTRGRGYWLGLRAVRHLGKVQGYQWVDGVSLSFSHWNQ  240
            CADASAHLVIVGGLDEQGFLTRNTRGRGYWLGLRAVRHLGKVQGYQWVDGVSLSFSHWNQ
Sbjct  181  CADASAHLVIVGGLDEQGFLTRNTRGRGYWLGLRAVRHLGKVQGYQWVDGVSLSFSHWNQ  240

Query  241  GEPNDAWGRENCVMMLHTGLWNDAPCDSEKDGWICEKRHNC  281
            GEPNDAWGRENCVMMLHTGLWNDAPCDSEKDGWICEKRHNC
Sbjct  241  GEPNDAWGRENCVMMLHTGLWNDAPCDSEKDGWICEKRHNC  281

Download GenPept Graphics
C-type lectin domain family 4 member G isoform 1 [Homo sapiens]
Sequence ID: ref|NP_940894.1| Length: 293 Number of Matches: 1
See 5 more title(s)

Range 1: 1 to 293 GenPept Graphics
Score            Expect Method                        Identities      Positives       Gaps
566 bits(1460)   0.0    Compositional matrix adjust.  280/293(96%)    280/293(95%)    12/293(4%)

Query  1    MDTTRYR------------PWGRWVHWSRRPLFLALAVLVTTVLWAVILSILLSKASTER  48
            MDTTRY             PWGRWVHWSRRPLFLALAVLVTTVLWAVILSILLSKASTER
Sbjct  1    MDTTRYSKWGGSSEEVPGGPWGRWVHWSRRPLFLALAVLVTTVLWAVILSILLSKASTER  60

Query  49   AALLDGHDLLRTNASKQTAALGALKEEVGDCHSCCSGTQAQLQTTRAELGEAQAKLMEQE  108
            AALLDGHDLLRTNASKQTAALGALKEEVGDCHSCCSGTQAQLQTTRAELGEAQAKLMEQE
Sbjct  61   AALLDGHDLLRTNASKQTAALGALKEEVGDCHSCCSGTQAQLQTTRAELGEAQAKLMEQE  120

Query  109  SALRELRERVTQGLAEAGRGREDVRTELFRALEAVRLQNNSCEPCPTSWLSFEGSCYFFS  168
            SALRELRERVTQGLAEAGRGREDVRTELFRALEAVRLQNNSCEPCPTSWLSFEGSCYFFS
Sbjct  121  SALRELRERVTQGLAEAGRGREDVRTELFRALEAVRLQNNSCEPCPTSWLSFEGSCYFFS  180
```

Similarly other rules are applied to the other protein sequences obtained from the main mRNA sequence. All the mutated sequences obtained were stored in separate text files and checked for sequence alignment through BLAST algorithm.

4.2. Results obtained for mRNA pattern change(missense) and BLAST sequences :

The mRNA sequence was sent for BLAST with somewhat similar sequence similarity and for Rule 170 had 105 blast hits, two among them being with the sequence with that of Homo sapiens 3 BAC RP11-80F7 (Roswell Park Cancer Institute Human BAC Library) of the accession id AC117432 and of that of Homo sapiens 3p BAC RP11-12J13 (Roswell Park Cancer Institute Human BAC Library) of the accession id AC106719:

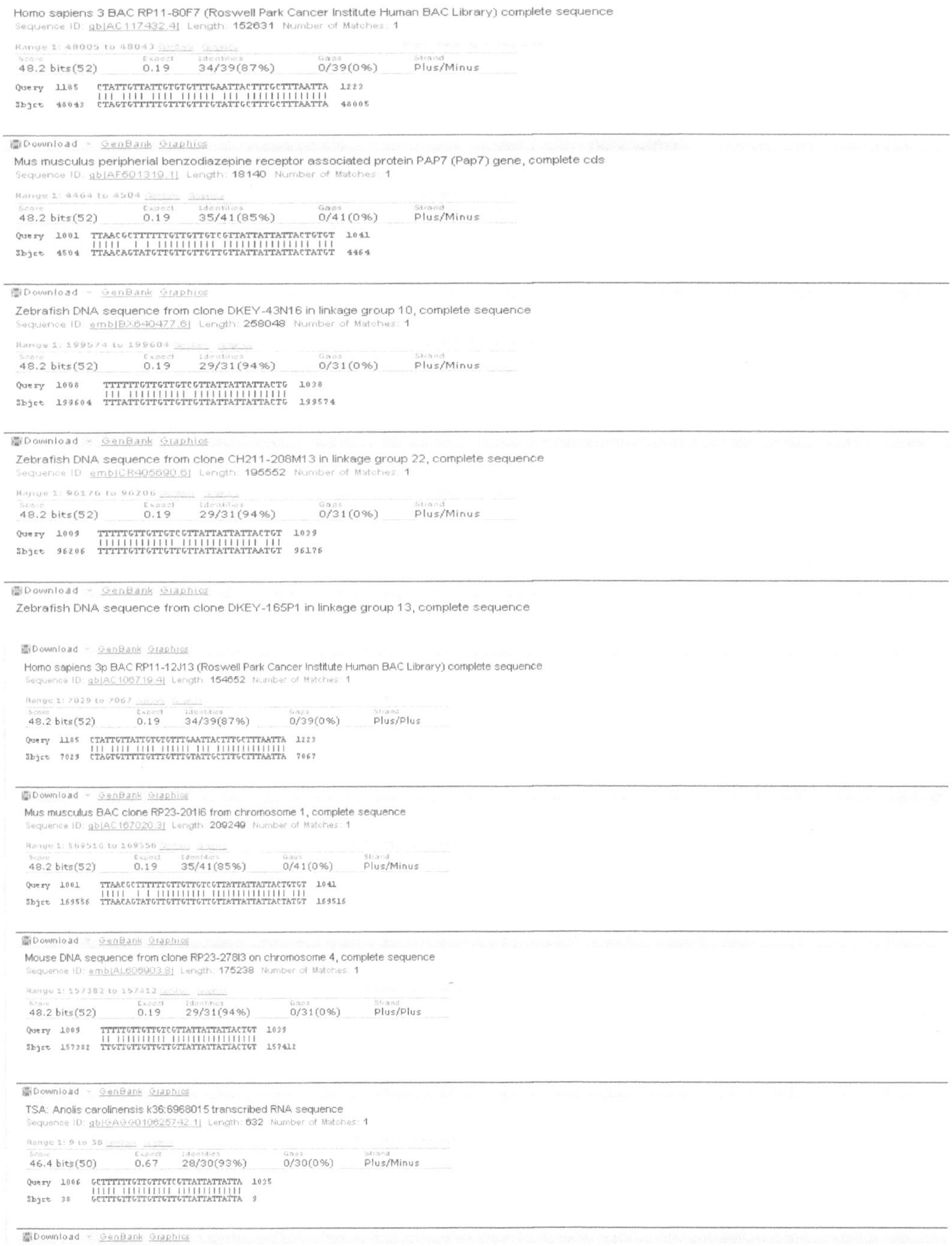

```
Homo sapiens 3 BAC RP11-80F7 (Roswell Park Cancer Institute Human BAC Library) complete sequence
Sequence ID: gb|AC117432.4|  Length: 152631  Number of Matches: 1

Range 1: 48005 to 48043
Score           Expect  Identities    Gaps        Strand
48.2 bits(52)   0.19    34/39(87%)    0/39(0%)    Plus/Minus

Query  1185   CTATTGTTATTGTGTGTTTGAATTACTTTGCTTTAATTA  1223
              ||| |||| |||| |||||| ||| |||||||||||||
Sbjct  48043  CTAGTGTTTTTGTTTGTTTGTATTGCTTTGCTTTAATTA  48005

Download ~ GenBank Graphics
Mus musculus peripherial benzodiazepine receptor associated protein PAP7 (Pap7) gene, complete cds
Sequence ID: gb|AF601319.1|  Length: 18140  Number of Matches: 1

Range 1: 4464 to 4504
Score           Expect  Identities    Gaps        Strand
48.2 bits(52)   0.19    35/41(85%)    0/41(0%)    Plus/Minus

Query  1001  TTAACGCTTTTTTGTTGTTGTCGTTATTATTATTACTGTGT  1041
             |||||   | | |||||||||| |||||||||||||| |||
Sbjct  4504  TTAACAGTATGTTGTTGTTGTTGTTATTATTATTACTATGT  4464

Download ~ GenBank Graphics
Zebrafish DNA sequence from clone DKEY-43N16 in linkage group 10, complete sequence
Sequence ID: emb|BX640477.6|  Length: 258048  Number of Matches: 1

Range 1: 199574 to 199604
Score           Expect  Identities    Gaps        Strand
48.2 bits(52)   0.19    29/31(94%)    0/31(0%)    Plus/Minus

Query  1008    TTTTTTGTTGTTGTCGTTATTATTATTACTG  1038
               ||| |||||||||| ||||||||||||||||
Sbjct  199604  TTTATTGTTGTTGTTGTTATTATTATTACTG  199574

Download ~ GenBank Graphics
Zebrafish DNA sequence from clone CH211-208M13 in linkage group 22, complete sequence
Sequence ID: emb|CR405690.6|  Length: 195552  Number of Matches: 1

Range 1: 96176 to 96206
Score           Expect  Identities    Gaps        Strand
48.2 bits(52)   0.19    29/31(94%)    0/31(0%)    Plus/Minus

Query  1009   TTTTTGTTGTTGTCGTTATTATTATTACTGT  1039
              ||||||||||||| ||||||||||||| |||
Sbjct  96206  TTTTTGTTGTTGTTGTTATTATTATTAATGT  96176

Download ~ GenBank Graphics
Zebrafish DNA sequence from clone DKEY-165P1 in linkage group 13, complete sequence

Download ~ GenBank Graphics
Homo sapiens 3p BAC RP11-12J13 (Roswell Park Cancer Institute Human BAC Library) complete sequence
Sequence ID: gb|AC106719.4|  Length: 154652  Number of Matches: 1

Range 1: 7029 to 7067
Score           Expect  Identities    Gaps        Strand
48.2 bits(52)   0.19    34/39(87%)    0/39(0%)    Plus/Plus

Query  1185  CTATTGTTATTGTGTGTTTGAATTACTTTGCTTTAATTA  1223
             ||| |||| |||| |||||| ||| |||||||||||||
Sbjct  7029  CTAGTGTTTTTGTTTGTTTGTATTGCTTTGCTTTAATTA  7067

Download ~ GenBank Graphics
Mus musculus BAC clone RP23-201I6 from chromosome 1, complete sequence
Sequence ID: gb|AC167020.3|  Length: 209249  Number of Matches: 1

Range 1: 169516 to 169556
Score           Expect  Identities    Gaps        Strand
48.2 bits(52)   0.19    35/41(85%)    0/41(0%)    Plus/Minus

Query  1001    TTAACGCTTTTTTGTTGTTGTCGTTATTATTATTACTGTGT  1041
               |||||   | | |||||||||| |||||||||||||| |||
Sbjct  169556  TTAACAGTATGTTGTTGTTGTTGTTATTATTATTACTATGT  169516

Download ~ GenBank Graphics
Mouse DNA sequence from clone RP23-278I3 on chromosome 4, complete sequence
Sequence ID: emb|AL606903.8|  Length: 175238  Number of Matches: 1

Range 1: 157382 to 157412
Score           Expect  Identities    Gaps        Strand
48.2 bits(52)   0.19    29/31(94%)    0/31(0%)    Plus/Plus

Query  1009    TTTTTGTTGTTGTCGTTATTATTATTACTGT  1039
               || |||||||||| ||||||||||||||||
Sbjct  157382  TTGTTGTTGTTGTTGTTATTATTATTACTGT  157412

Download ~ GenBank Graphics
TSA: Anolis carolinensis k36:6968015 transcribed RNA sequence
Sequence ID: gb|GAGG01062574 2.1|  Length: 632  Number of Matches: 1

Range 1: 9 to 38
Score           Expect  Identities    Gaps        Strand
46.4 bits(50)   0.67    28/30(93%)    0/30(0%)    Plus/Minus

Query  1006  GCTTTTTTGTTGTTGTCGTTATTATTATTA  1035
             ||||| |||||||||| ||||||||||||
Sbjct  38    GCTTTGTTGTTGTTGTTGTTATTATTATTA  9

Download ~ GenBank Graphics
```

Similarly other rules are applied to the main mRNA sequence. All the mutated sequences obtained were stored in separate text files and checked for sequence alignment through BLAST algorithm.

4.3. Results obtained for potential protein primary structure on mRNA pattern change(missense) and BLAST sequences :

The possible and most probable protein sequence that

could be predicted from the changed (missense) sequence (for Rule-90) was:
M S R G Y G P I G K Y K W F V G Q K N S D I D K Y N V R N N H D G R A I P V I I K Q K G H L A C L L R, which is much less than that predicted from the original mRNA sequence. Now one thing to be mentioned here is that the sequence considered above is not a continuation after *"gcc"*nucleotide group as mentioned earlier. As the one that was a continuation after *"gcc"*nucleotide group was only MC. So this shows that point mutation can change the mRNA sequence so much so that a protein sequence may not generate at all from the mRNA protein coding region. So the longest obtained protein sequence starting with the start codon *"AUG"* was taken and blasted for sequence similarity.

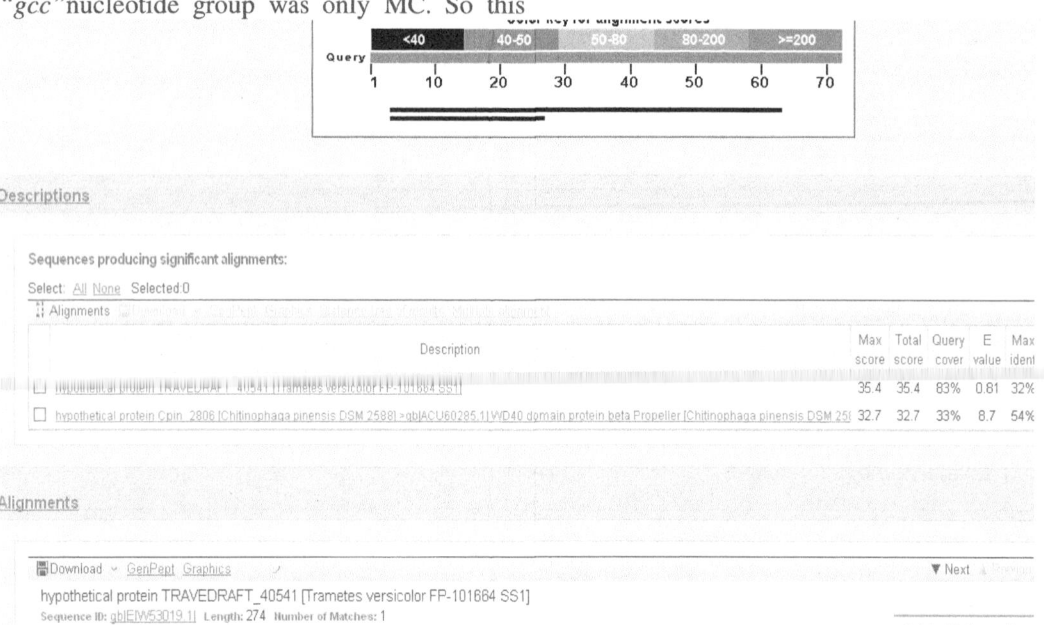

Similarly other rules are applied to the other protein sequences obtained from the changed mRNA sequence. All the mutated sequences obtained were stored in separate text files and checked for sequence alignment through BLAST algorithm.

4.4. Results obtained for mRNA pattern change(deletion) and BLAST sequences :

For deletion no alternate pattern was used. Instead the effect was watched in the entire pattern. The mRNA sequence was sent for BLAST with somewhat similar sequence similarity and for Rule 170 had 25 blast hits, one among them being with the sequence with that of Homo sapiens 3 BAC RP11-63L4 (Roswell Park Cancer Institute Human BAC Library) of the accession id AC078784. Here is a partial screenshot of that:

Download GenBank Graphics ▼ Next

PREDICTED Fragaria vesca subsp vesca auxin response factor 9-like (LOC101308499), mRNA
Sequence ID: ref|XM_004306607.1| Length: 2592 Number of Matches: 1

Range 1: 8 to 35 GenBank Graphics

Score	Expect	Identities	Gaps	Strand
42.8 bits(46)	2.6	26/28(93%)	0/28(0%)	Plus/Plus

```
Query  104   TTTAGAAAAGACATAATGAAAAAGGAAA   131
Sbjct  8     TTTAGAAAAGAAATAAAGAAAAAGGAAA   35
```

Download GenBank Graphics ▼ Next

Pediculus humanus corporis Titin, putative, mRNA
Sequence ID: ref|XM_002431647.1| Length: 32202 Number of Matches: 1

Range 1: 13034 to 13072 GenBank Graphics

Score	Expect	Identities	Gaps	Strand
42.8 bits(46)	2.6	34/40(85%)	1/40(2%)	Plus/Plus

```
Query  92     GTCGAAATGCTCTTTAGAAAAGACATAATGAAAAAGGAAA   131
Sbjct  13034  GTCGAA-TCCTATTTAAAAAAGACAAAACGAAAAAGGAAA   13072
```

```
Homo sapiens 3 BAC RP11-63L4 (Roswell Park Cancer Institute Human BAC Library) complete sequence
Sequence ID: gb|AC078784.24| Length: 165413 Number of Matches: 1
Range 1: 114873 to 114894 GenBank Graphics
Score           Expect  Identities     Gaps       Strand
41.0 bits(44)   9.0     22/22(100%)    0/22(0%)   Plus/Plus
Query  110     AAAGACATAATGAAAAAAGGAAA  131
Sbjct  114873  AAAGACATAATGAAAAAAGGAAA  114894

Download  GenBank Graphics                                    Next  Prev
Arabidopsis thaliana clone 27384 mRNA complete sequence
Sequence ID: gb|AY086756.1| Length: 1025 Number of Matches: 1
Range 1: 817 to 854 GenBank Graphics
Score           Expect  Identities     Gaps       Strand
41.0 bits(44)   9.0     33/39(85%)     1/39(2%)   Plus/Plus
Query  95   GAAATGCTCTTTAGAAAAGACATAATGAAAAAGGAAATC  133
Sbjct  817  GAAATGGTATTTGGAAA-GAAAAAATGAAAAAGGAAATC  854
```

Similarly other rules are applied to the main mRNA sequence. All the mutated sequences obtained were stored in separate text files and checked for sequence alignment through BLAST algorithm.

4.5. Results obtained for potential protein primary structure on mRNA pattern change(deletion) and BLAST sequences :

The same programming software was used to predict the potential genres of protein sequences for the pattern of mRNA obtained on 'Deletion' mutation application through Boolean functions. For some Boolean rules no AUG sequence range was found starting with *"gcc"* nucleotide group. So it can be said that for such sequence mutations the protein structure formation gets inhibited. But if the longest codon sequence is sequence is taken starting with *"AUG"*. For example for the Rule-170 no potential amino acid sequence was there where *"gcc"* preceded AUG. But when this fact is not considered then the small protein structure found starting with 'M', was MHALLLQ. There were 103 hits with 10 being of that with Homo sapiens sequence.

```
PREDICTED: RNA binding protein fox-1 homolog 2 isoform 8 [Dasypus novemcinctus]
Sequence ID: ref|XP_004456459.1| Length: 393 Number of Matches: 1
Range 1: 330 to 336 GenPept Graphics
Score           Expect  Identities   Positives    Gaps
24.0 bits(49)   607     6/7(86%)     6/7(85%)     0/7(0%)
Query  1    MHALLLQ  7
            MH LLLQ
Sbjct  330  MHSLLLQ  336

Download  GenPept Graphics
RNA binding motif protein 9 [Homo sapiens]
Sequence ID: emb|CAL91352.1| Length: 398 Number of Matches: 1
Range 1: 335 to 341 GenPept Graphics
Score           Expect  Identities   Positives    Gaps
24.0 bits(49)   608     6/7(86%)     6/7(85%)     0/7(0%)
Query  1    MHALLLQ  7
            MH LLLQ
Sbjct  335  MHSLLLQ  341

Download  GenPept Graphics
PREDICTED: RNA binding protein fox-1 homolog 2 isoform 6 [Dasypus novemcinctus]
Sequence ID: ref|XP_004456457.1| Length: 406 Number of Matches: 1
Range 1: 343 to 349 GenPept Graphics
Score           Expect  Identities   Positives    Gaps
24.0 bits(49)   608     6/7(86%)     6/7(85%)     0/7(0%)
Query  1    MHALLLQ  7
            MH LLLQ
Sbjct  343  MHSLLLQ  349
```

Similarly other rules are applied to the other protein sequences obtained from the changed mRNA sequence. All the mutated sequences obtained were stored in separate text files and checked for sequence alignment through BLAST algorithm.

4.6 Results obtained for mRNA pattern change(insertion) and BLAST sequences :

The mRNA sequence was sent for BLAST with somewhat similar sequence similarity and for Rule 170 had 100 blast hits, two among them being with the sequence with that of Homo sapiens 3 BAC RP11-255E6 (Roswell Park Cancer Institute Human BAC Library) of the accession id AC117432 and of that of Homo sapiens 12 BAC RP11-157G21 (Roswell Park Cancer Institute Human BAC Library) of the accession id AC106719:

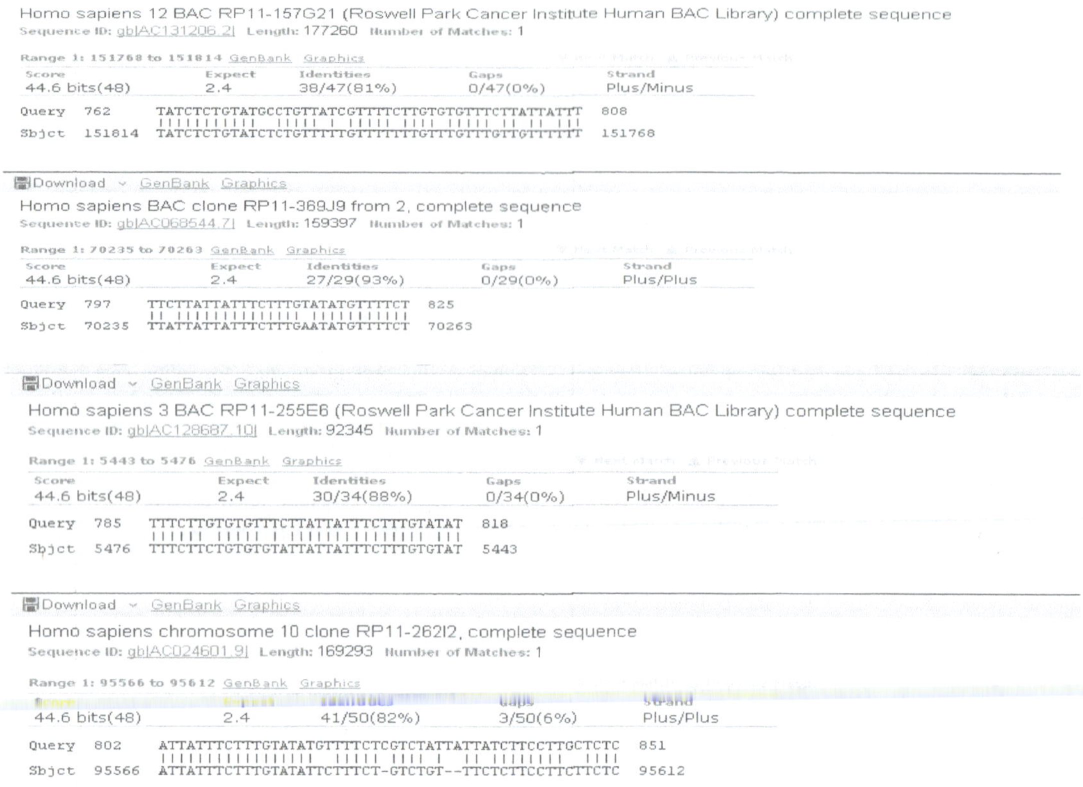

```
Homo sapiens 12 BAC RP11-157G21 (Roswell Park Cancer Institute Human BAC Library) complete sequence
Sequence ID: gb|AC131206.2| Length: 177260 Number of Matches: 1

Range 1: 151768 to 151814 GenBank Graphics
Score          Expect   Identities     Gaps        Strand
44.6 bits(48)  2.4      38/47(81%)     0/47(0%)    Plus/Minus

Query  762     TATCTCTGTATGCCTGTTATCGTTTTCTTGTGTGTTTCTTATTATTT  808
               |||||||||||  ||||| | ||||| |||| ||||| || || |||
Sbjct  151814  TATCTCTGTATCTCTGTTTTTGTTTTTTTGTTTGTTTGTTGTTTTTT  151768
```

```
Download  GenBank Graphics
Homo sapiens BAC clone RP11-369J9 from 2, complete sequence
Sequence ID: gb|AC068544.7| Length: 159397 Number of Matches: 1

Range 1: 70235 to 70263 GenBank Graphics
Score          Expect   Identities     Gaps        Strand
44.6 bits(48)  2.4      27/29(93%)     0/29(0%)    Plus/Plus

Query  797     TTCTTATTATTTCTTTGTATATGTTTTCT  825
               || |||||||||||||| ||||||||||
Sbjct  70235   TTATTATTATTTCTTTGAATATGTTTTCT  70263
```

```
Download  GenBank Graphics
Homo sapiens 3 BAC RP11-255E6 (Roswell Park Cancer Institute Human BAC Library) complete sequence
Sequence ID: gb|AC128687.10| Length: 92345 Number of Matches: 1

Range 1: 5443 to 5476 GenBank Graphics
Score          Expect   Identities     Gaps        Strand
44.6 bits(48)  2.4      30/34(88%)     0/34(0%)    Plus/Minus

Query  785     TTTCTTGTGTGTTTCTTATTATTTCTTTGTATAT  818
               |||||| ||||| | ||||||||||||||| |||
Sbjct  5476    TTTCTTCTGTGTGTATTATTATTTCTTTGTGTAT  5443
```

```
Download  GenBank Graphics
Homo sapiens chromosome 10 clone RP11-262I2, complete sequence
Sequence ID: gb|AC024601.9| Length: 169293 Number of Matches: 1

Range 1: 95566 to 95612 GenBank Graphics
Score          Expect   Identities     Gaps        Strand
44.6 bits(48)  2.4      41/50(82%)     3/50(6%)    Plus/Plus

Query  802     ATTATTTCTTTGTATATGTTTTCTCGTCTATTATTATCTTCCTTGCTCTC  851
               |||||||||||||||||  ||||| |||| |  || ||||||||  ||||
Sbjct  95566   ATTATTTCTTTGTATATTCTTTCT-GTCTGT--TTCTCTTCCTTCTTCTC  95612
```

Similarly other rules are applied to the main mRNA sequence. All the mutated sequences obtained were stored in separate text files and checked for sequence alignment through BLAST algorithm. When the above sequence were checked for alignment the following list of sequence alignments were obtained.

4.7. Results obtained for potential protein primary structure on mRNA pattern change(insertion) and BLAST sequences :

The possible and most probable protein sequence that could be predicted from the changed (insertion) sequence(for Rule-195) was:

M F S R L L L S S L L S F I T L S I S R C V R S G S R F V P L Y Y L Y L L L S G Y F L L F L S R L L C Y V L F S R F G L V T L G F L L L Q L L L L R N T S L N R A F V S L L L L R S D C Y T N C S

When this was blasted for sequence similarity in the NCBI BLAST tool the sequence got 6 BLAST hits and the partial screen shot goes like:

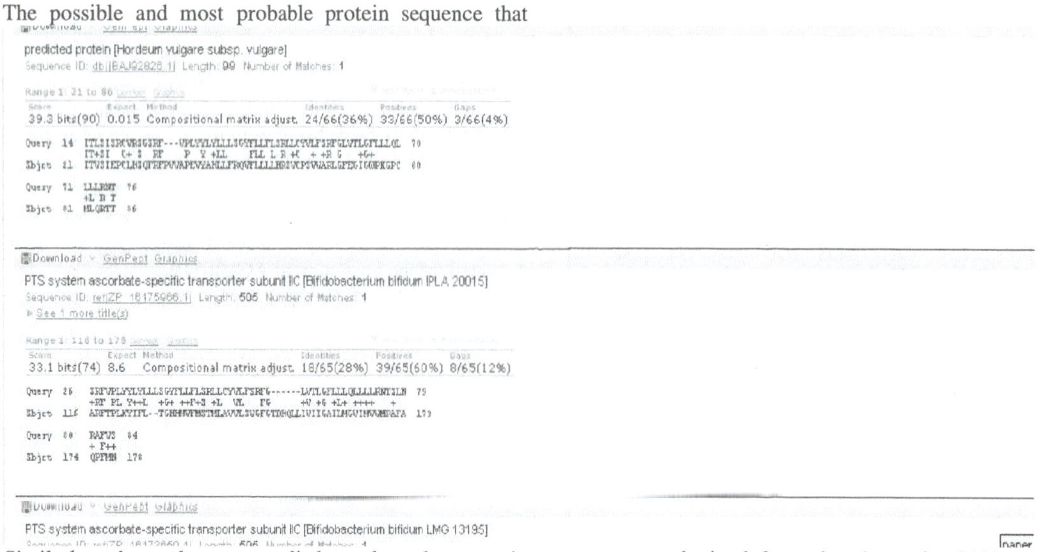

```
predicted protein [Hordeum vulgare subsp. vulgare]
Sequence ID: dbj|BAJ92828.1| Length: 99 Number of Matches: 1

Range 1: 21 to 86 GenPept Graphics
Score           Expect  Method                         Identities   Positives    Gaps
39.3 bits(90)   0.015   Compositional matrix adjust.   24/66(36%)   33/66(50%)   3/66(4%)

Query  14   ITLSISRCVRSGSRF---VPLYYLYLLLSGYFLLFLSRLLCYVLFSRFGLVTLGFLLLQL  70
            IT+SI  C+ S  RF    P  Y +LL    FLL L R +C  + +R G   +G+
Sbjct  21   ITVSIEPCLHSQFRFPVVAPEVYAHLLFRQVFLLLLHRSVCPSVVARLGFEGIGGPKGPC  80

Query  71   LLLRNT  76
            +L R T
Sbjct  81   MLQRTT  86
```

```
Download  GenPept Graphics
PTS system ascorbate-specific transporter subunit IIC [Bifidobacterium bifidum IPLA 20015]
Sequence ID: ref|ZP_18175966.1| Length: 506 Number of Matches: 1
See 1 more title(s)

Range 1: 116 to 178 GenPept Graphics
Score           Expect  Method                         Identities   Positives    Gaps
33.1 bits(74)   8.6     Compositional matrix adjust.   18/65(28%)   39/65(60%)   8/65(12%)

Query  26   SRFVPLYYLYLLLSGYFLLFLSRLLCYVLFSRFG------LVTLGFLLLQLLLLRNTSLN  79
            +RF PL Y++L  +G+ ++F+S +L  VL   FG      +V +G +L+ ++++   +
Sbjct  116  ARFTPLKYIFL--TGHHWVFMSTMLAVVLSVGFGTDHQLLIVIIGAILMGVIMVAMPAFA  173

Query  80   RAFVS  84
            + F++
Sbjct  174  QPFMN  178
```

```
Download  GenPept Graphics
PTS system ascorbate-specific transporter subunit IIC [Bifidobacterium bifidum LMG 13195]
```

Similarly other rules are applied to the other protein sequences obtained from the changed mRNA sequence and checked for sequence alignment through BLAST algorithm.

5. Conclusion and Future scope

There are numerous biological methods to check the effect of mutation on DNA or its corresponding protein sequence. But this paper shows the mapping of Boolean functions to the different types of mutations occurring in a genome sequence, namely: missense, deletion mutation. After that DNA and mature miRNA sequences are subjected to some binary rules and their pattern behavior is checked according to the mapping done of the binary sequence format of the DNA or miRNAs to those binary rules. Finally the structure and behavior of the proteins are studied to take the research work to the next level, where some light on the formation of protein 3-D structures could be thrown. This is required to be more enlightened about the functional aspects of protein structures and to see how the functional 3-D protein structures can be responsible for being associated with diseases.

6. Acknowledgement:

The author is very much grateful to Prof. Pabitra Pal Chowdhuri of ISI, Kolkata for allowing to do research work under his supervision.

7. References:

[1] A Comprehensive Study of Target Prediction Algorithms for Animal MicroRNAs(miRNAs), International Journal of Computer Applications(IJCA)(0975-8887,USA), Joyshree Nath, Asoke Nath, Vol-40, No 15(Feb),(2012).

[2] http://www.yourgenome.org/dgg/general/var/var_3.shtml

[3] http://www.biology-questions-and-answers.com/protein-structure.html

[4] http://www.experimentation-online.co.uk/article.php?id=1211

[5] http://en.wikipedia.org/wiki/Amino_acid

[6] http://en.wikipedia.org/wiki/Protein_folding

[7] http://www.ncbi.nlm.nih.gov/books/NBK21097/

[8] http://www.sciencemag.org/content/336/6089/1645

[9] http://en.wikipedia.org/wiki/Mutation

[10] http://www.definitions.net/definition/indel+mutation

[11] A new algorithm for Quantitative deciphering of pre-mature MiRNAs using some Statistical Parameters, Joyshree nath, Asoke Nath, Proceedings of IEEE International Conference WICT-2012 held at IIITM-K, Trivandrum Oct 30 to Nov 1, 2012, Page No. 595-601(2012).

[12] A Comprehensive Study on Animal miRNAs : A computational approach to explore its implications in Biological and Chemical environments, Joyshree Nath, International Journal of Advanced Computer Research, Vol-3, Number-1, issue-8, page. 153-158(2013).

Prediction of HIV-1 and human protein interactions based on a novel evolution-aware structure alignment method

Chunyu Zhao and Ahmet Sacan
School of Biomedical Engineering, Science and Health Systems, Drexel University, Philadelphia, PA, USA

Abstract - *Competition between HIV-1 proteins and human proteins is important in the course of HIV-1 infection. Understanding the interaction between HIV-1 and human proteins will help to understand how the pathogen manipulates the biological pathways and processes of the host. Based on the hypothesis that proteins with similar structures share similar interaction partners, we have developed a novel structure alignment method (Unialign) using the co-evolutionary information of the aligned proteins to predict the interaction between HIV-1 protein gp41 and human proteins. We applied Unialign to each of the five gp41 structures available in Protein Data Bank, structurally comparing them against all the human proteins in the PDB. Combining the structural hits with a human PPI database, we generated over 922 interaction predictions between this HIV-1 protein and human proteins. This predicted host proteins list could be very effective in assisting identification of interaction partners of HIV-1 experimentally.*

Keywords: HIV-1, protein-protein interaction (PPI), protein structure alignment, evolution, conservation.

1 Background

Human immunodeficiency virus type I (HIV-1) uses host surface proteins to gain entrance into the host cell. Interaction between HIV-encoded proteins and human proteins is important in the course of HIV-1 infection [1]. Thus, understanding the protein-protein interaction (PPI) between HIV-1 and human proteins provides critical insights into how the pathogen manipulates the biological pathways and processes of the host and subsequently helps the design of new therapeutic approaches. Computational approaches for identification of protein interactions in the pathogen-host context are of significant value as large-scale experimental characterization of these interactions is expensive in terms of time and money [2].

Several computational PPI methods have previously been applied for HIV-1 - human interactions. Tastan et al. integrated multiple information features including Gene Ontology (GO), properties of human interactome, and sequence motifs, and employed random forest method to predict protein-protein interactions [3]. Evans et al. predicted possible interactions using the presence of conserved sequence motifs and counter domain in both HIV-1 and human proteins [4].

The progress in experimental structure determination technologies and the coordinated structural genomics initiatives have increased the rate of deposition of protein structures in the Protein Data Bank (PDB), which currently holds over 80,000 protein structures [5]. Since geometry is often a strong determinant of a protein's function, it is assumed that proteins sharing similar structural patterns also share the same interaction partners. Doolittle et al. has already applied structure similarity based method to predict interactions between HIV-1 and human proteins, using the Dali Database for structure comparisons [6].

For the existing structure search approaches, pairwise structure alignment is the basic step for calculating the similarity between two structures. Structure alignment is a more sensitive method to find distantly similar biological functions and evolutionary relationships compared to sequence alignment, considering that structure is more conserved than sequence. Several popular structure alignment methods have been developed, such as DALI [7, 8], CE [9], and TM-align [10]. Although structure alignment methods are critically useful in discovering and understanding evolutionary relationships between proteins; available structure alignment methods only use the geometric information contained in the protein structures and do not incorporate known evolutionary information, e.g. that which can be extracted from multiple sequence alignments.

Here, we predicted the interaction map between HIV-1 ENV protein gp41 (Uniprot accession: P04578) and human proteins, using a novel evolution-aware structure alignment method (Unialign). First we retrieved all the human proteins sharing high structure similarity with gp41, using both Dali and Unialign. Second, we extracted all the known interactions for each HIV-1 similar human proteins, and identified them as the interacting partner candidates of the given HIV-1 protein. Evaluation of the predictions shows a statistically significant overlap between the majority of our predictions and the experimentally verified interactions. Previously unknown interactions predicted by our method provide opportunities for discovery of novel interactions.

2 Methods

An overview of our approach is given in Figure 1. Human proteins structurally similar to HIV-1 proteins are identified by structural alignment of PDB structures. Interacting partners of the human proteins are retrieved from Human Protein Reference Database (HPRD) and returned as predicted human interaction partners of the HIV-1 proteins. These predictions are compared with known HIV-1, human interactions. Below, we describe each of these steps in more detail.

2.1 Datasets

We downloaded the HIV-1 and Homo sapiens protein structures from Protein Data Bank (PDB) [5]. In order to compare the host protein prediction lists generated by two different structure alignment methods, we extracted all PDBs used in Dali Database (updated in 2011) [7, 8]. Dali Database contains the structural alignments of PDB90 (a non-redundant subset of PDB with no more than 90% sequence identity among pairs) against all the PDBs, as well as the corresponding Z-scores, indicating the significance of the structural similarity. Only the protein pairs with a Z-score above 2.0 are listed in the Dali Database. We filtered out the human proteins in Dali that could not be mapped to a Refseq ID. There were 5659 unique human proteins, with 29041 unique structure chains. Each PDB structure was mapped to the Uniprot accession IDs using PDB/UniProt Mapping [11]. The conversion between Uniprot accessions and Refseqs was realized by using Uniprot ID mapping Database [12].

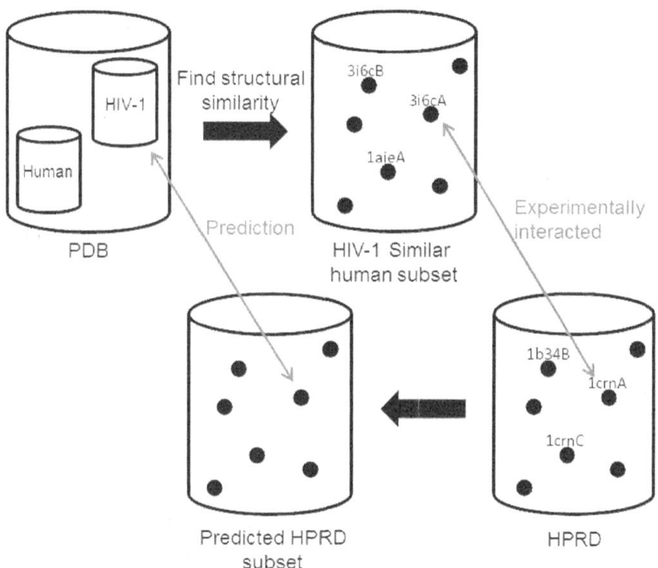

Figure 1. Protein-protein interaction prediction pipeline.

2.2 A novel evolution-aware structure alignment method: Unialign

Whereas other structural alignment methods find residue correspondences based on purely geometric considerations, our method additionally incorporates functional information and seeks a structural alignment where functionally important residues are better aligned. Our proposed residue-weighted structure alignment method is based on the observation that the functional importance of a residue is reflected in its evolutionary conservation; the more important a residue is, the sooner it becomes fixed in different evolutionary branches [13]. Important residues are likely to result in a loss of the protein's function if they mutate into other residues. Thus, we quantitatively predict the relative importance of the residues in a protein by calculating the entropy of each position in a multiple alignment, and give larger weights to the more conserved positions when calculating the structure alignment.

Entropy-based measures of position conservation have been used for systematic computational analysis of conservation profiles in multiple sequence alignment [14, 15]. Although HIV-1 is highly mutated, its ability to attack host human machinery remains strong. Therefore we assumed the interacting domains or residues of HIV-1 protein that mimic human proteins would be more conserved than the other residues. When we calculate the structural similarity between HIV-1 and human proteins, our algorithm uses gave larger weights to the more conserved residues in order to better capture their functional similarity with the residues from the host protein.

A high level description of the algorithm is shown in Figure 2. Given a protein pair, we obtain a set of homologous protein sequences for each query protein by applying Position-Specific Iterated BLAST (PSI-BLAST) against the NCBI non-redundant (nr) sequence database [16]. PSI-BLAST, which is similar to BLAST but more sensitive, searches the

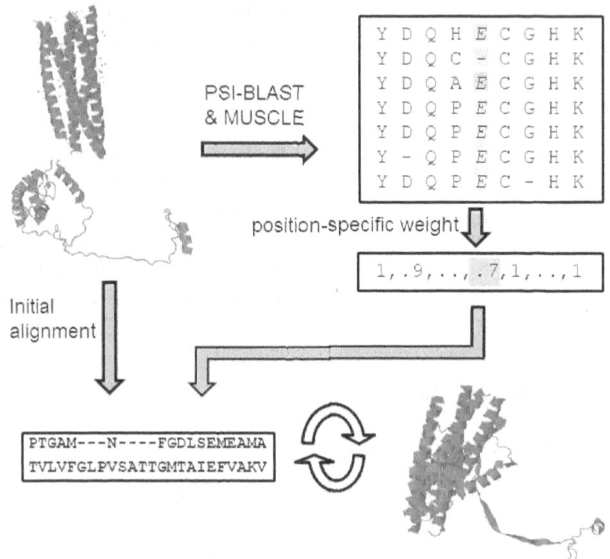

Figure 2. Flowchart of Unialign, an evolution-aware structural alignment method.

query amino acid sequence against protein databases, establishing an evolutionary link between query and its similar proteins and providing sequence similarity scores for each alignment [16]. Subsequently, regions of conservation are identified from multiple sequence alignment (MUSCLE) [17] of the selected set of homologous protein sequences, from which the evolutionary information for each residue is calculated. Regions of conservation identified from the multiple alignments of related sequences can aid the recognition of distant structure similarities.

We incorporate the residue-specific weights reflecting the evolutionary importance into our structure alignment method Unialign. Unialign employs an iterative optimization similar to TM-align [10], where an initial set of residue correspondences is used to produce a structural superposition, from which a new set of correspondences is generated. The main differences from TM-align are that Unialign calculates the superposition of the pairs of residues with optimal weighted RMSD and it uses local alignment rather than global alignment when generating a new set of correspdences. Unialign calculates RMSD using the Singular Value Decomposition (SVD) of the covariance matrix, where weighting terms are incorporated into the covariance matrix (as in [18]); thus we define *weighted RMSD* as:

$$r_{ij} = \sum_{k=1..N} w_k p_{ki} q_{kj} \quad (1)$$

where r is the 3-by-3 covariance matrix; N is the number of aligned residues; p_{ki} and q_{ki} are the ith coordinate of the kth aligned residues from proteins p and q, respectively; and w_k corresponds to the weight of each residue.

2.3 HIV-1, Human Interaction Database

In the HIV-1, human interaction database (HHPID), each interaction between HIV-1 and human proteins is represented by one or more descriptive key phrases, such as "increases", "unregulated by" or "phosphorylates" [19]. Only the direct interactions defined by Tastan et al. [3] were considered for our prediction validation since we are attempting to predict physical interactions. Additional constraints were added to the use of HHPID. For example, the HIV proteins in HHPID should be represented among the crystal structures retrieved from PDB, which are included within the Dali Database. Besides, any host protein shown to interact with HIV-1 in HHPID must have at least one known interaction with another human protein included in HPRD, and each of these proteins must also have representative structures in Dali Database. Take the ENV's cleavage products, gp41 as an example; 7 different proteins with 41 structures existed in PDB. However, only one protein P04578 out of seven was verified in HHPID, which shows the limits of available experimental data and, at the same time, reveals the importance of computationally predicting the interaction.

2.4 Representation of virus-host interaction prediction

We predicted the map of virus-host interaction for each HIV-1 protein. Multiple structures may represent the same protein, while different structures have different multiple sequence profiles, resulting in different conservation weights. Thus the predicted interactions for the different structures of a given protein were slightly different, yet some of them were redundant. Therefore, we used the structures (PDB chains) to compare the two structure alignment methods, and identified all unique pairs of Uniprot accessions to evaluate the interaction prediction performance.

3 Results and Discussion

3.1 Identification of HIV-1 structure-similar human proteins

For each HIV-1 protein, its different structures were aligned against all the human protein structures using two different pairwise structure alignment methods (Dali and Unialign). The gp41 protein P04578 we used has five different PDBs: 1df4A, 1df5A, 1dlbA, 1k33A and 1k34A. For Dali Database, the HIV-1 structure-similar human proteins were defined as those having a Z-score higher than 2.0, with the HIV-1 protein being either the query or the hit. For Unialign, we used Uniscore as the structural similarity metric, which is a weighted version of TM-score that gives different weights to residues according to their conservation. A Uniscore threshold of 0.72, giving target prediction lists with comparable size to Dali, was used to define HIV-1 structure-similar human proteins. Table I shows the number of HIV-1 structure-similar human proteins calculated by both Dali and Unialign.

Table I: The number of HIV-1 structure-similar human proteins calculated by Unialign and Dali.

PDB chain	Unialign	Dali
1DF4A	121	29
1DF5A	34	52
1K33A	37	27
1K34A	119	59
1DLBA	57	67

3.2 Prediction of human proteins interacting with HIV-1 proteins

After obtaining the human proteins that share high structural similarity with each specific HIV-1 protein structure, the interaction partners of each HIV-1 structure-similar human protein were obtained using Human Protein Reference Database (HPRD), which contains 38,989 unique documented protein-protein interactions [20]. We denote the predicted target human proteins as the subset HP. Our hypothesis was that proteins with similar structures or substructures share the same interaction partners. Besides, during the HIV-1 infection, the virus modifies or destroys the already existing interactions between human proteins. It could thus use the existing communication pathways within the cell for its own reproduction. Human proteins and HIV-1 proteins, in a way, compete for the same interactions. Therefore, HP was treated as the potential target set for the corresponding HIV-1 proteins, resulting in the establishment of the interaction map between each HIV-1 protein and its target human protein.

3.3 Validation of predictions using the HIV-1, Human Interaction Database

For validating the predicted interactions, we compared the predicted target human protein HP set with the experimentally acquired human protein interactions with HIV-1, which are compiled in the Human Protein Interaction Database (HHPID) [19]. There are 1036 known host-pathogen interactions in HHPID that satisfied our criterion (cf. Methods), including 20 HIV-1 proteins and 528 human proteins, denoted here as the HE set. The p-value for the overlap between computational sets HP and experimental sets HE was then calculated using the hyper-geometric test, showing the probability to obtain our predictions simply by chance. A total of 922 unique target human proteins (HP) were predicted to potentially interact with gp41 protein P04578; 15 of these predictions were among the 68 experimentally verified interactions. Four out of five predictions generated by Unialign had a statistically significant overlap ($p<0.05$) with the experimentally known ones, while only two predictions generated by Dali were statistically significant (Table II). Thus Unialign's performance is better than Dali's in terms of the interaction partner prediction of each HIV-1 structure. Prediction of the interaction partners with greater accuracy for a specific structure is of important practical value since it helps prioritize the predicted protein-protein interactions for further experimental validation. We also visually superposed the five structures of gp41 using the protein structure comparison service Fold available from the European Bioinformatics Institute [21] in Figure 3. Since HIV-1 has a high mutation rate, the conserved structures shown in Figure 3 might be essential for HIV-1 replication within the host cell.

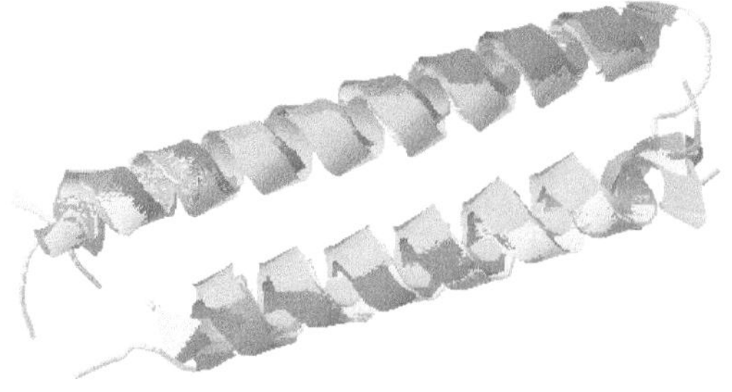

Figure 3. Multiple structures alignment for different structures of the gp41 protein (green: 1df4A, blue: 1df5A, light blue: 1k33A, yellow: 1k34A, purple: 1dlbA).

Table II: The number of HP, HE and Match of each gp41 protein structure and the p-values for the overlap between HP and HE.

Method	pdbchain	HP	HE	Match	p-value
Unialign	1DF4A	759	68	14	*3.31E-02*
	1DF5A	508	68	10	*3.82E-02*
	1K33A	528	68	13	*3.45E-03*
	1K34A	644	68	10	1.45E-01
	1DLBA	649	68	12	*4.28E-02*
Dali	1DF4A	619	68	5	7.69E-01
	1DF5A	1003	68	15	1.36E-01
	1K33A	587	68	15	*1.25E-03*
	1K34A	783	68	16	*9.55E-03*
	1DLBA	1344	68	16	4.50E-01

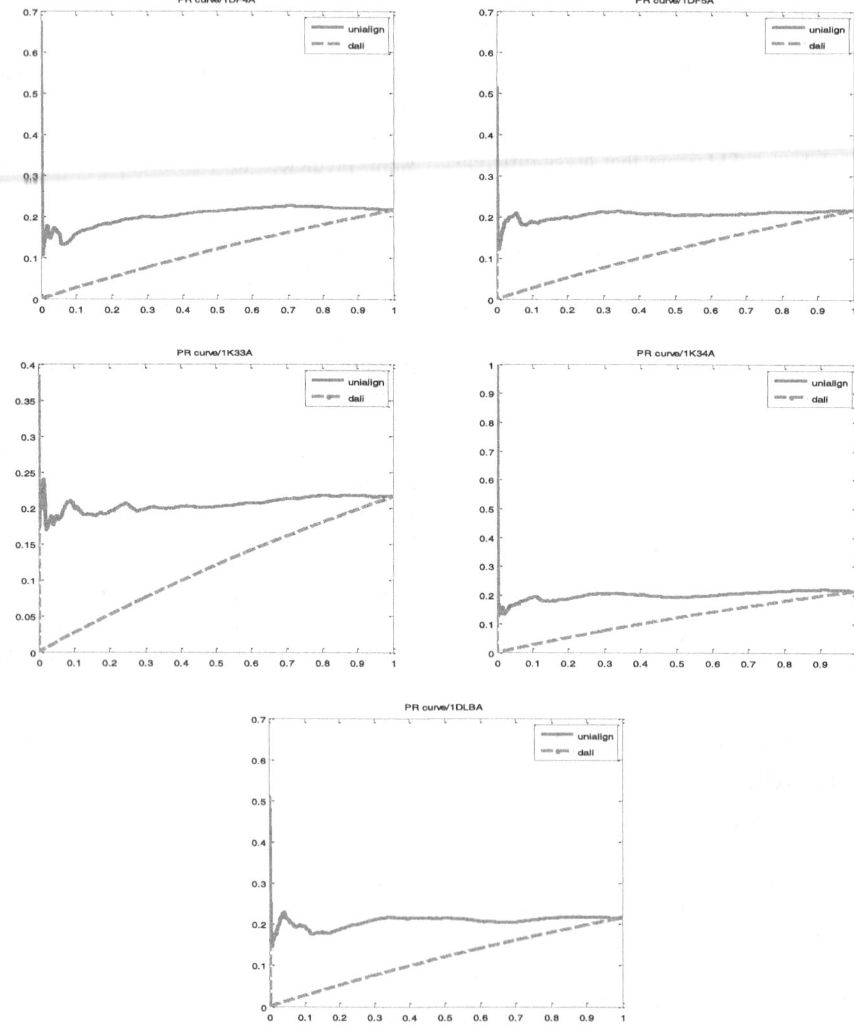

Figure 4. The precision vs. recall (PR) curve of Unialign (blue, solid line) and Dali (red, dash line). From the top left are 1DF4A, 1DF5A, 1K33A, 1K34A and 1DLBA.

3.4 Comparison of the two structure alignment methods

In order to assess the performance of Unialign and Dali in more detail, we investigated the precision-recall patterns of the similarity scores they report (see Figure 4), where a protein structure is deemed correct if at least one of its interacting partners in HHPID has a known partner in HHPID. The area under the prevision-recall curves (AUC) is reported in Table III.

Table III. The area under curve score of the precision vs. recall curve for each structure.

PDB chain	Unialign	Dali
1DF4A	0.2043	0.1167
1DF5A	0.2051	0.1170
1K33A	0.2056	0.1170
1K34A	0.2015	0.1170
1DLBA	0.2075	0.1172
Average	*0.2048*	*0.1170*

We observed that Unialign performs significantly better than Dali in identifying structurally similar proteins that share interaction partners, with an AUC twice that of Dali. We attribute this to the fact that Dali only uses geometric information to align structures, whereas Unialign additionally incorporates residues conservation profiles.

4 Conclusion

In this paper, we generated the potential virus-host interaction map between HIV-1 and human. Our method is based on the assumption that human host proteins are influenced during the HIV-1 infection by physically interacting with certain HIV-1 proteins and that the interaction interfaces mimic those already present in protein-protein interactions of the host. Computational methods could be very effective in helping the experimental identification of these interactions, as they promote the discovery of both novel virus-host interactions and potential clinical targets for therapeutic intervention. In the context of host-pathogen interaction prediction, especially for those highly mutated viruses such as HIV-1, our structural alignment method Unialign better captures the similarity of the more conserved residues and enjoys higher prediction accuracy. In contrast to other available structural alignment methods that prudently rely on geometric information, Unialign additionally utilizes the evolutionary conservation profiles of the proteins.

Our future work will involve extending the approach presented here to other HIV-1 proteins to generate a more comprehensive prediction set. The combination of structural similarity with other information such as protein sequence and Gene Ontology (GO) terms is expected to further increase the prediction accuracy.

5 References

[1] A. D. Frankel, and J. A. Young, "HIV-1: fifteen proteins and an RNA," Annu Rev Biochem, vol. 67, pp. 1-25, 1998.

[2] A. Valencia, and F. Pazos, "Prediction of protein-protein interactions from evolutionary information," Methods Biochem Anal, vol. 44, pp. 411-26, 2003.

[3] O. Tastan, Y. Qi, J. G. Carbonell et al., "Prediction of interactions between HIV-1 and human proteins by information integration," Pac Symp Biocomput, pp. 516-27, 2009.

[4] P. Evans, W. Dampier, L. Ungar et al., "Prediction of HIV-1 virus-host protein interactions using virus and host sequence motifs," Bmc Medical Genomics, vol. 2, May 18, 2009.

[5] H. Berman, K. Henrick, and H. Nakamura, "Announcing the worldwide Protein Data Bank," Nature Structural Biology, vol. 10, no. 12, pp. 980-980, Dec, 2003.

[6] J. M. Doolittle, and S. M. Gomez, "Structural similarity-based predictions of protein interactions between HIV-1 and Homo sapiens," Virology Journal, vol. 7, Apr 28, 2010.

[7] L. Holm, S. Kaariainen, P. Rosenstrom et al., "Searching protein structure databases with DaliLite v.3," Bioinformatics, vol. 24, no. 23, pp. 2780-2781, Dec 1, 2008.

[8] L. Holm, and P. Rosenstrom, "Dali server: conservation mapping in 3D," Nucleic Acids Research, vol. 38, pp. W545-W549, Jul, 2010.

[9] I. N. Shindyalov, and P. E. Bourne, "Protein structure alignment by incremental combinatorial extension (CE) of the optimal path," Protein Engineering, vol. 11, no. 9, pp. 739-747, Sep, 1998.

[10] Y. Zhang, and J. Skolnick, "Scoring function for automated assessment of protein structure template quality," Proteins-Structure Function and Bioinformatics, vol. 57, no. 4, pp. 702-710, Dec 1, 2004.

[11] A. Bairoch, R. Apweiler, C. H. Wu et al., "The universal protein resource (UniProt)," Nucleic Acids Research, vol. 33, pp. D154-D159, Jan 1, 2005.

[12] A. C. R. Martin, "Mapping PDB chains to UniProtKB entries," Bioinformatics, vol. 21, no. 23, pp. 4297-4301, Dec 1, 2005.

[13] I. Mihalek, I. Res, and O. Lichtarge, "A family of evolution-entropy hybrid methods for ranking protein residues by importance," Journal of Molecular Biology, vol. 336, no. 5, pp. 1265-1282, Mar 5, 2004.

[14] S. R. Sunyaev, F. Eisenhaber, I. V. Rodchenkov et al., "PSIC: profile extraction from sequence alignments with position-specific counts of independent observations," Protein Eng, vol. 12, no. 5, pp. 387-94, May, 1999.

[15] J. Pei, and N. V. Grishin, "AL2CO: calculation of positional conservation in a protein sequence alignment," Bioinformatics, vol. 17, no. 8, pp. 700-12, Aug, 2001.

[16] S. F. Altschul, T. L. Madden, A. A. Schaffer et al., "Gapped BLAST and PSI-BLAST: a new generation of protein database search programs," Nucleic Acids Research, vol. 25, no. 17, pp. 3389-3402, Sep 1, 1997.

[17] R. C. Edgar, "MUSCLE: a multiple sequence alignment method with reduced time and space complexity," Bmc Bioinformatics, vol. 5, pp. 1-19, Aug 19, 2004.

[18] K. L. Damm, and H. A. Carlson, "Gaussian weighted RMSD superposition of proteins: a structural comparison for flexible proteins and predicted protein structures," Biophys J, vol. 90, no. 12, pp. 4558-73, Jun 15, 2006.

[19] W. Fu, B. E. Sanders-Beer, K. S. Katz et al., "Human immunodeficiency virus type 1, human protein interaction database at NCBI," Nucleic Acids Research, vol. 37, pp. D417-D422, Jan, 2009.

[20] T. S. K. Prasad, R. Goel, K. Kandasamy et al., "Human Protein Reference Database-2009 update," Nucleic Acids Research, vol. 37, pp. D767-D772, Jan, 2009.

[21] E. Krissinel, and K. Henrick, "Multiple alignment of protein structures in three dimensions," Computational Life Sciences, Proceedings, vol. 3695, pp. 67-78, 2005.

SESSION

MODELING AND SIMULATION + NOVEL STUDIES

Chair(s)

TBA

Mathematical Model to Align Biological Networks

Nassim Sohaee
Department of Mathematics and Information Science
University of North Texas at Dallas
Dallas, Texas 75241
Email: nassim.sohaee@unt.edu

Abstract—**Sequence comparison and alignment has had an enormous impact on our understanding of evolution, biology and disease. Comparison and alignment of biological networks will probably have a similar impact. Existing network alignments use information external to the networks, such as sequence, or use only information about the structure of two networks and their topology. In this paper, we present a novel algorithm based on network structure and topology as well as biological properties of nodes.**

I. Introduction

In system biology, biological systems are often presented as networks. For example, protein-protein interaction networks, metabolic networks and signal transduction networks. Experimental techniques such as two-hybrid assay, spectrometry of purified complexes, correlated m-RNA expression, and genetic interaction provide extensive amount of data. This pool of information opens new opportunities and challenges to develop new strategies and techniques to interpret, analyze and organize interaction data into models of cellular function. There is also a high error rate associated with experimental methods. Hence, there is still a vital need to develop some theoretical techniques and algorithm to discriminate the true interactions form false positives. One of the methods that is getting a lot of attention is the comparison of different networks across species. Such comparison provides the transfer of knowledge across different species and gives insights into the underlying law behind complex biological phenomena.

There are several methods and techniques to study single organism's protein networks to identify functional modules and protein complexes. Most of the studies of protein interaction networks are based on detecting the highly connected protein clusters. These techniques help to predict functional modules and give an insight into protein structure of a specie. Identifying the modular structure of a biological network is important to understand the organization and interaction of the cellular processes which they represent. The study of complex biological networks uncover the hierarchical nature of these networks, which makes it possible to develop automatic methods to identify the topological and functional modules. Digging the biological network of a species helps to expand our knowledge at the level of cellular function of species. However, some of the very important questions about the origin of the species, the affect of evolution, similarity or dissimilarity of two species in term of cellular function cannot be addressed. Motivated by this, cross-species comparison is designed to identify functionally similar protein modules between two or more species.

sequence similarity is a parameter that is computed from a single trait of proteins. However, the protein homology is more than this fact that proteins with common evolutionary history are similar in sequence. The key point here is that similar protein sequences might come from a common ancestry, but proteins can adopt function or are specialized during their revolutionary history. In fact, proteins with similar function not necessarily posses similar sequences. The evolutionary history can present the development of species or the divergence of its protein sequences. Despite significant differences in amino acid sequences they can adopt essentially the same three-dimensional structure and perform the same biological function. Some computational techniques and processes, like alternative splicing and translation start site variations, are developed to calculate the translational genomic information into proteins [10]. Advanced researches in the area of protein splicing, demonstrated that protein function is more correlated to splicing profile similarity than sequence similarity [9]. It has been shown that proteins contributing to a functional module in one species are evolutionary conserved in the most of species that posses such a functional context.

Similarly, subnetworks conserved across species are likely to have similar functionality. A conserved module is a pair of protein modules that share a cross-species similarity at the node level and graph structure level [2]. One of the goals in cross-species network alignment is to transfer the knowledge from one network to the other to uncover the new biology. The network alignment helps to predict the protein function of unannotated proteins based on the protein function of annotated proteins in other network. Network alignment can also be used to measure the overall similarity of the network of two different species. This can lead to a metric to measure the phylogenetic relations among different species.

A. Motivation

We can categorize the algorithms and methods in network alignment problem into two groups. The first category is those algorithms that are solely based on the topology of two networks. These techniques are ignoring some important background knowledge hidden in the elements of the network. However they have this advantage over the other category that are applicable to a broad range of networks and applications.

The second category is those algorithms that consider both topological and biological properties of the network. These algorithms are designed based on the biological knowledge of the network. Comparison of the network considering some meaningful assumptions may lead to NP-hard problem. Hence, some of these algorithms are either computationally very expensive, or assuming a relaxed condition for aligning two networks. As we can see, sequence similarity function is playing a key role in all those algorithms. Basically, proteins are aligned based on their sequence similarity either as seed node or in the alignment graph. The function of a protein is more defined by its three dimensional folding rather than its sequence.

The sequence similarity between two genes with similar functionality may decay over the time because of local mutation, and large-scale genomic events like gene duplication, gene loss or recruitment of new genes into a functional context. Hence, nodes with no significant sequence similarity but similar interaction pattern should nevertheless be considered in the alignment.

In addition, functional swap between genes, changes the interaction pattern. It may induce a correlation between two genes with no significant sequence similarity and at the same time reduces the correlation between two genes with similar sequences.

Moreover, most of the alignment techniques presented above cannot be extended to a multiple network alignment. A multiple network alignment is a network alignment of three or more biological networks. In many cases, the input set of networks are assumed to have an evolutionary relationship by which they are descended from a common ancestor.

So there is a need to design a new algorithm for finding a precise network alignment based on the similarity of protein sequences and local topology of the proteins in Protein-Protein Interaction, PPI, network. It is also preferable if the new technique can easily be extended to multiple network alignment.

II. New Method

The network alignment problem is the problem of finding conserved subnetworks within k different PPI networks belonging to different species. The alignment graph is a representation to show the network alignment. The union of all nodes participating in network alignment make the node set for the alignment graph. Two nodes from different networks are connected, if they are aligned. In order to build an alignment graph we need to define a similarity measure between nodes. Obviously, homologous proteins can be potentially the best candidate for defining similar proteins. Two proteins are homologous if they have common ancestry. The easiest way is to consider the sequence similarity of two proteins. However, as we described before, there are protein sequences with significant dissimilarity coming form the same ancestor. Hence, sequence similarity can detect most of homologous proteins but not all.

A desirable alignment should be built up on some statistical models for considering the evolution of a protein and its interactions. Proteins without significant sequence similarity are aligned if their interaction patterns are sufficiently similar. Also, proteins with high sequence similarities may not align if their interaction patterns are dissimilar. Despite the putative functional role, dissimilarity between the interaction pattern of two proteins with high sequence similarity shows a strong network divergence between two networks.

A. Theory

Two networks $G_1 = (V_1, E_1)$ and $G_2 = (V_2, E_2)$ are aligned if there is a map $\pi : V_1 \to V_2 \cup \{-\}$ that maps a vertex $v \in V_1$ to

$$\pi(v) = \begin{cases} u \in V_2 & \text{a vertex } u \text{ in the second network} \\ - & \text{a gap} \end{cases}$$

The score of a network alignment can be defined as

$$\begin{aligned} score(\pi) = & \sum_{\substack{v \in V_1 \\ \pi(v) \neq -}} \sigma(v, \pi(v)) \\ & + \sum_{\substack{v \in V_1 \\ \pi(v) \neq -}} \sum_{\substack{w \in V_1 \\ \pi(w) \neq -}} \tau((v, \pi(v)), (w, \pi(w))) \end{aligned} \quad (1)$$

where $\sigma : V_1 \times V_2 \to \mathbb{R}^{\geq 0}$ gives the score of mapping individual nodes onto each other and $\tau : V_1 \times V_2 \times V_1 \times V_2 \to \mathbb{R}^{\geq 0}$ gives the score of mapping pair of nodes onto each other. Scoring function σ can present the pairwise similarity of two nodes, and τ gives score to conserved interaction between pair of nodes. For node alignment scoring we can use a function to quantify the similarity of two nodes, this could be the sequence similarity or any other function to measure the distance of two nodes. τ scoring function could be a binary function to show if the pair of aligned nodes conserve the interaction between them or not. Simply we can define,

$$\tau((u, v), (\pi(u), \pi(v))) = \begin{cases} 1 & (u, v) \in E_1,\ (\pi(u), \pi(v)) \in E_2 \\ 0 & \text{otherwise} \end{cases}$$

Given these functions, we are able to define the network alignment problem as an optimization problem. The pairwise network alignment asks for a highest scoring alignment π^* of two networks $G_1 = (V_1, E_1)$ and $G_2 = (V_2, E_2)$ where $score(\pi^*) = \max_{\pi \in \Pi} score(\pi)$, and π is the set of all possible alignments of G_1 and G_2.

Klau [8] proved , the above optimization problem is NP-complete. He also showed that there is a one-to-one correspondence between network alignment and a matching in the alignment graph. The alignment graph of two networks G_1 and G_2 is a complete weighted bipartite graph with $V_1 \cup V_2$ as the set of nodes. The weight of each edge is the score of aligning two end point nodes. A matching in a bipartite graph is a set of disjoint edges in the graph. A maximum matching in the alignment graph corresponds to an alignment of the nodes in two networks.

Network alignments measure link and node similarity. In most developed models for aligning networks, scoring function σ is defined as pairwise sequence similarity of two nodes. In this basic model we are unable to deal with structural conservation unless we introduce a new concept as maximum structural alignment. However, we can redefine function σ to consider both structural and pairwise sequence similarity as fundamental factor to align two nodes. The goal is to define a well defined function to score the alignment of two nodes based on their local topology and sequence similarity. For this matter, we need to measure the distance of two local graphs. There are some definitions to measure the distance of two subgraphs. In general the problem of finding the distance of two graphs leads to finding the maximum common subgraph which is NP-complete. However, The problem is solvable in the set of all labeled graphs. Generally a biological graph can be considered as a labeled graph. Each node in such a graph is representing a biological entity with some known information like name or id. Although, the naming procedure has flaws and usually orthologs have different names or ids in different species.

In this study we would like to develop a technique to find a local labeled subgraph around each seed node. The labels can be defined based on some local information like the gene's sequence. Then we can apply some of the known distance functions like Hamming distance to measure the distance of two local subgraphs around the seed nodes, and assign this distance as the value of the function σ. The value of function σ reflects the node similarity and local structural similarity around the nodes.

Hamming distance of two labeled graphs shows the number of edge deletion/insertion to change one graph to the other one. This value can be normalized to be a number between 0 and 1. When the Hamming distance of two labeled graphs is 0 it means that there is a structure preserving map between two graphs. Hamming distance 1 means that two graphs are structurally different.

With this new scoring function, the problem of aligning two biological networks can be stated as follow.

$$\max \sum_{i\in G_1 \text{ and } j\in G_2} x_{ij} - \sum_{i\in G_1 \text{ and } j\in G_2} \sigma(i,j)x_{ij}$$

This linear programming problem finds a matching in alignment graph with maximum number of edges and minimum weight. The wight of edges in the alignment graph associates with the structural similarity of local topologies. The goal is to align as many nodes as possible without compromising the structural similarity of aligned nodes. The variable x_{ij} is 1 if there is an edge in alignment graph connecting node i in one network to node j in the other network, and is $-\infty$ otherwise. Meanwhile, we would like to have an alignment of minimum weight. The weight of each edge in the alignment graph is $\sigma(i,j)$. The output of this maximization problem is a matching in the alignment graph with maximum number of edges and minimum weight. Hence, we can find an alignment to preserve node and structural similarity of two networks.

B. Biological Network Alignment Algorithm

Network alignment can be classified into local alignment and global alignment. There are two kinds of mapping between nodes of two aligned networks: one-to-one and many-to-many. In this paper we only consider global alignment, and one-to-one mapping.

Suppose $G = (V(G), E(G))$ and $H = (V(H), E(H))$ are two biological networks, where $V(G)$ and $V(H)$ are the node sets, and $E(G)$ and $E(H)$ are the edge sets, respectively. Network Alignment problem is to find the maximum conserved subnetwork between G and H. The evolutionary events and mutations, including node mutations (insertion, deletion, duplication, mismatch and functional change), and edge mutation (detachment, attachment) should be handle in the computational model.

In our method we assume there is a local property that we can find similarity the nodes of these two networks. In Protein-Protein Interaction networks we can use Blast to find sequence similarity of two given nodes. Node by node similarity of two networks is an input matrix for network alignment algorithm. As we discussed above two proteins with similar sequences may not have similar function. We will consider two protein sequences similar if the value of similarity function is larger than a user defined threshold, α.

Function of a protein depends on its sequence structure and its interaction pattern. In order to consider the interaction pattern of two protein sequences we compare the closed neighborhood induced subgraph of two nodes. Neighborhood of a node $v \in V$, $N(v)$, is the set of all nodes in V that are connected to v by an edge. Closed neighborhood of a node $v \in V$ is defined as $N^*(v) = N(v) \cup \{v\}$. An induced subgraph of a graph $G = (V, E)$ over a subset $U \subseteq V$ is a subgraph $G_U = (U, E_U)$, where E_U is the set of edges in E that both ends belong to U.

The goal is to find a technique that use both sequence similarity and interaction pattern to find new measure for comparing two proteins. For this matter we will use Hamming distance of closed neighborhood subgraphs of two nodes. Hamming distance of two graphs show the number of intertion/deletion required to change one graph to aother graph. Hamming distance of two graphs $G_A = (V_A, E_A)$ and $G_B = (V_B, E_B)$ is defined as

$$Hamming(G_A, G_B) = \frac{|E_A \Delta E_B|}{|E_A \cup E_B|}.$$

The Hamming distance is a metric on the set of all labeled graphs. A labeled graph is a graph that each node has a unique representative called label. The Hamming distance of two labeled graphs is a number between 0 and 1, where 0 means two graphs are the same and 1 means that two graphs are disjoint. Protein-protein interaction network can be considered as a labeled graph where the labels are protein names or protein sequences. However, protein naming is not consistent in cross species protein-protein interaction networks. Proteins with similar functionality and similar sequence might have different names in different protein-protein interaction networks.

Suppose $N^*(v)$ and $N^*(u)$ are two closed neighborhood of input networks G and H, respectively. In order to find Hamming distance of these two subgraphs, we need to have a labeling system to assign labels for their node sets. The idea is to assign the same label to nodes u and v in closed neighborhood subgraphs of G and H respectively, if $S(u, v) \geq \alpha$, where S is a function that finds sequens similarity of two protein nodes. Algorithm 1 present a simple method to assign labels to the set of the nodes of two input graphs. In this algorithm L denotes the set of labels assigned to the node set of G and H. Note that the labels are assigned locally, which means for any node $v \in V(G)$ and any node $u \in V(H)$ we are using algorithm 1 to assign labels to the set of nodes.

Algorithm 1 Node Labeling

Input Biological networks G and H, and S Similarity matrix of two input networks
Output (G, L) and (H, L)

while There is an entry in Matrix S larger than threshold α **do**
  Let $S(u, v) = \max\{S(x, y) | x \in V(G), y \in V(G)\}$
  $L(u) = L(v) = l_{(u,v)}$
  update matrix S by removeing row u and column v.
end while
for all remaining nodes u in matrix S **do**
  $L(u) = l_u$
end for

Using simple labeling stated in Algorithm 1

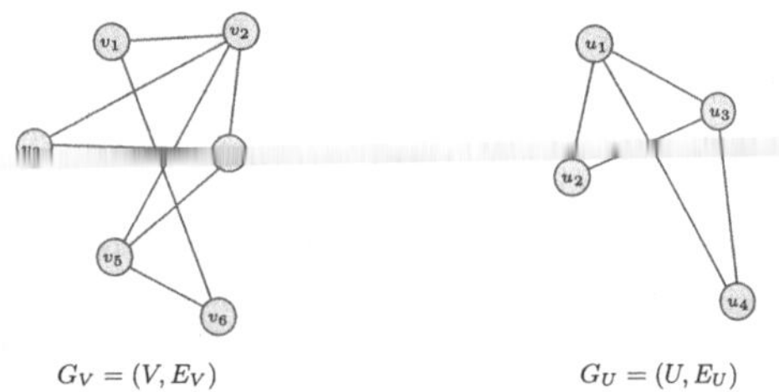

Fig. 1. Two biological networks G and H

TABLE I. SIMILAIRTY MATRIX OF TWO GRAPHS IN FIGURE 1

	v_1	v_2	v_3	v_4	v_5	v_6
u_1	0.001	0.15	0.02	0.001	0.002	0.15
u_2	0.1	0.13	0.25	**0.76**	0.01	0.11
u_3	0.21	0.14	**0.57**	0.001	0.14	0.001
u_4	0.12	**0.63**	0.003	0.01	0.04	**0.59**

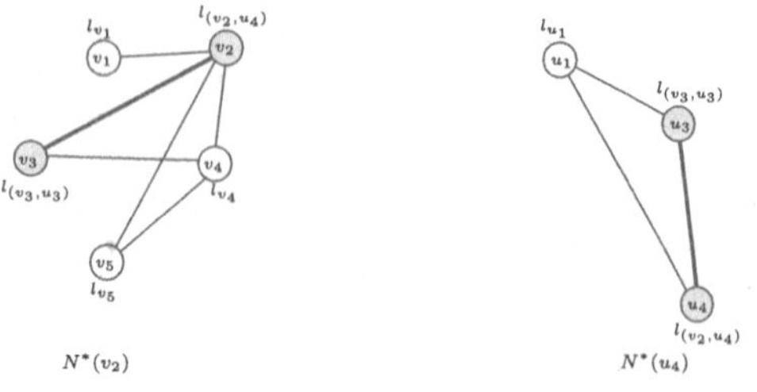

Fig. 2. Node labeling of subgraphs $N^*(v_2)$ and $N^*(u_4)$ of two graphs G and H in Figure 1, respectively.

Figure 2 shows, a node labeling of two subgraphs $N^*(v_2)$ and $N^*(u_4)$. Based on this node labeling, there is only one edge in the intersection of two labeled graphs. Hence, the hamming distance of these two subgraphs can be measured as 0.875. This large number shows that there is a slight structural similarity between these two closed neighbourhood subgraphs, even though two nodes v_2 and u_4 have sequence similarity larger than threshold α.

Let G and H be two biological networks with node similarity matrix S. Alignment graph $A(G, H)$, is a complete weighted bipartite graph whose node set is $V(G) \cup V(H)$. The weight of each edge (u, v) is defined as the Hamming distance of closed neighbourhood subgraphs containing nodes u and v. The weight of the edges in alignment graph $A(G, H)$ is between 0 and 1. Let M be a matching in alignment graph $A(G, H)$, the following mapping defines an alignment of two input graphs;

$$\pi_M : V(G) \to V(H)$$

$$\pi_M(v) = \begin{cases} u & Hamming(N^*(v), N^*(u)) < \beta \\ & \text{and } (v, u) \in M \\ - & \text{otherwise} \end{cases} \tag{2}$$

The value of β in equation 2, is a user defined value between 0 and 1. Large values for Hamming distance of two closed neighborhood graphs of two nodes indicates that two nodes have little similarity in their interaction patterns. In the problem of alignment of two biological network, the goal is to align nodes with similar biological properties as well as similar interaction pattern. As it stated in equation 1, both factors contribute in computing the score of an alignment. In equation 1, the first term is associated with nodes similarity in the mapping, and the second term is associated with interaction pattern similarity. In order to obtain an alignment with maximum interaction pattern similarity we need to find a maximum matching in the alignment graph of minimum weight. Minimum weight indicates that aligned nodes have similar interaction pattern.

Algorithm 2

Input Biological networks G and H, and S Similarity matrix of two input networks
Output Alignment mapping of two graphs G and H

$A(G, H) \leftarrow$ alignment graph of G and H
$M \leftarrow$ Maximum matching of minimum weight of $A(G, H)$
for all nodes $u \in V(G)$ **do**
  if $Hamming(N^*(u), N^*(v)) < \beta$ **then**
    $\pi(u) = v$
  else
    $\pi(u) = -$
  end if
end for

The problem of finding a maximum matching of minimum weight is one of classic combinatorics problems. Edmonds and Karp [11] studied this problem and introduced a polynomial time algorithm for finding a perfect matching of minimum weight in a bipartite graph. A perfect matching is a matching that every node of the graph is one end of an edge in the matching set. A bipartite graphs has a perfect matching if there are the same number of nodes in each part. If two input graphs G and H have different number of node, we can add some dummy nodes in one side and connect them to all the nodes of the other side with edge weight 1. Without losing generality, we can assume this new bipartite graph is the alignment graphs of G and H. By implementing Edmonds and Karp algorithm, or any improved version of that we can find a perfect matching of minimum weight. Perfect matching, M, introduces a mapping π_M that defines the alignment of two biological networks.

Algorithm 2 accepts two biological networks G and H as input. We assume the similarity matrix $S(G,H)$ is given or can be computed in efficient time. This algorithm first finds alignment graph $A(G,H)$. If the number of nodes in two sides of bipartite graphs $A(G,H)$ is not the same, will be added dummy nodes to have a complete bipartite graphs with the same number of nodes on each side. We will derive a mapping $\pi : V(G) \rightarrow V(H)$ by mapping a node u to v if and only if $(u,v)\ inM$ and $Hamming(N^*(u), N^*(v)) < \beta$.

III. Conclusion

We introduce a new global network alignment algorithm that is based on network topology and biological property of nodes. As such, it can be applied to any biological networks. Network alignment has applications across an enormous span of domains, from social networks to software call graphs. In the biological domain, the mass of currently available network data will only continue to increase and we believe that high-quality topological and biological alignments can yield new and pivotal insights into function, evolution and disease.

References

[1] J. Berg and M. Lassig, "Cross-species analysis of biological networks by Bayesian alignment," *Proceeding of National Academy of Science*, 103, pp. 10967-109-72, 2006.

[2] A. Daskalaki, "Handbook of Research on Systems Biology Applications in Medicine," *IGI Global* , Chapter 8, 2009.

[3] J. Edmonds and R. M. Karp, "Theoretical Improvement in Algorithmic Efficiency for Network Flow Problem, " *Journal of Assocition for Computing Machinery*, vol. 19, No. 2, April 1972, pp. 248-264.

[4] G. W. Klau, "A new graph-based method for pairwise global network alignment," *BMC Bioinformatics*, doi: 10.1186/1471-2105-10-s1-s59, 2009.

[5] M. Koyuturk, Y. Kim, U. Topkara et al. "Pairwise Alignment of Protein Interaction Networks Guided by Models of Evolution," *Proceeding of 9th International Conference of Computational Molecular Biology*, pp. 48-65, 2005.

[6] Z. Liang, M. Xu, M. Teng and L. Niu, "Comparison of Protein Interaction Networks Reveals Species Conservation and Divergence," *BMC Bioinformatics*, doi: 10.1186/1471-2105-7-457, 2006.

[7] T. Milenković, W. L. Ng, W. Hayes and N. Pržulj, "Optimal Network Alignment with Graphlet Degree Vectors," *Cancer Inforamtics*, no. 9, pp. 121-137, 2010.

[8] M. Narayanan and R. Karp, "Comparing Protein Interaction Networks via a Graph Match-and-Split Algorithm," *Journal of Computational Biology*, vol. 14, no. 7, pp. 892-907, 2007.

[9] R. Sharan and T. Ideker, "Modeling Cellular Machinery Through Biological Network Comparison," *Nat. Biotechnology*, no. 24, pp. 427-433, 2006.

[10] A. Västermark, Y. Shigemoto, T. Abe and H. Sugawara, " Splicing profile based proteins categorization between human and mouse genomes by use of the DDBJ Web services," *Genome Inform*, vol. 15, no. 2, pp. 13-20, 2004.

Photo-Penetration Depth Growth Dependence in an Agent-Based Photobioreactor Model

K.A. Hawick and A.V. Husselmann
Computer Science, Massey University, North Shore 102-904, Auckland, New Zealand
email: k.a.hawick@massey.ac.nz
Tel: +64 9 414 0800 Fax: +64 9 441 8181

April 2013

ABSTRACT

Growth of biological material such as bacteria for medical or other purposes is difficult to model generally. A number of competing processes occur in a typical bioreactor. We report on preliminary investigations of a lattice-based growth model for algal cells in a photobioreactor where photosynthesis is a key driving factor; but where the growth material must be held in a liquid suspension that imposes a limit on photo penetration. Using a variant of the Kawasaki exchange site growth dynamics we build a model that exhibits spatial asymmetries and emergent complexities. We study cell counts and cell densities as functions of time and photo penetration, and discuss possible bioreactor model extensions. We also present and discuss an acceleration of the model on Graphical Processing Units and various considerations necessary for parallelism of this.

KEY WORDS
algae; Kawasaki model; diffusion; lattice; photosynthesis; bioreactor; gpu; CUDA.

1 Introduction

Quantifying biological growth processes is important for understanding a range of natural processes but also for optimising production from the harvesting of bio products. Photosynthesis [36] is a key aspect of such systems. Computational modelling in this field is not a new concept, and a handful of packages exist for accomplishing this, such as BacSim [25] and BSim [13]. We develop an agent-based simplified photobioreactor model where cells are grown autotrophically [38], but disregarding nutrient uptake and focus instead on photo penetration into the reactor. In the past these models were typically known as Individual-based Models [11]. We are particularly interested in how photo penetration depth, temperature and the spatial geometry of the photobioreactor all interplay with the production time to maximise yield.

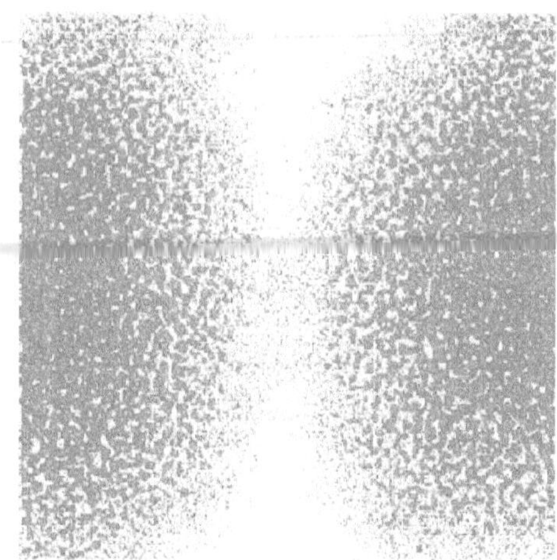

Figure 1: A visualisation of the photobioreactor model with a weak gravitational bias at several hundred frames into computation.

Figure 1 shows a sample snapshot of our simulated system after two initial bio samples were seeded at the middle of the left and right tank walls. Figure 2 shows a time-sequence of such configurations showing the growth pattern outwards from the initial injection points.

We envisage a scenario where a sample tank (which may in fact be a transparent plastic sample bag or glass tank) is initially charged with a well mixed set of chemical nutrients and a small initial sample of the target biological material. A photobioreactor is a (often cylindrical) vessel that contains some kind of growth medium. This medium is usually a special mixture made up of various nutrients like nitrate, phosphate, vitamins, and biotin. This vessel is sterilised and then inoculated with some strain of algae such as *Haematococcus pluvialis*. It is illuminated (often in a Circadian cycle) and fed CO_2, NO_3 and PO_3 through from the bottom. This is known as a bubble column reactor and is believed to be better than a stirred vessel because stirring introduces shear stress on cells [38].

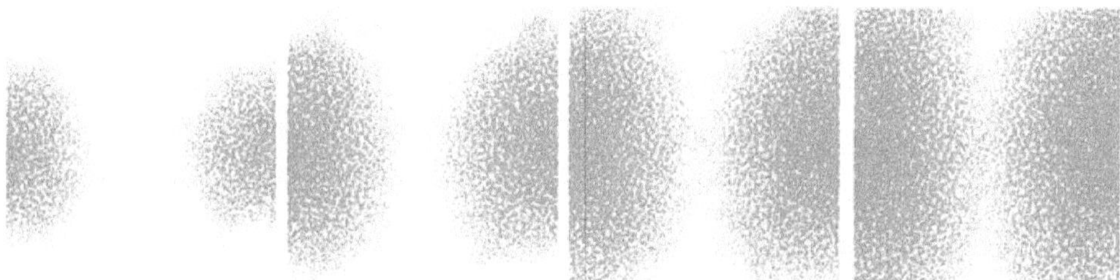

Figure 2: Several states throughout the computation of the system (which begun with a single cell inoculation at both sides), in order with no influence of gravity.

H. pluvialis in particular, is cultivated in order to produce a carotenoid known as Astaxanthin, a very potent anti-oxidant and often used en masse as a pigment for Salmon and Trout. Astaxanthin sells for $2500 USD per kg (synthetic) and more for naturally produced Astaxanthin. Cultivating this algae with higher efficiency is economically desirable, especially considering the costs involved.

In order to produce carotenoids from *H. pluvialis*, it is necessary to cultivate vegetative cells where no carotenogenesis takes place. Once a suitable culture is achieved (high cell density), then the culture is stressed in some fashion. This is done by causing nutrient deficiency, or increasing temperature, or introducing NaCL into the medium. Haematocysts for example, develop 2-3 days after the culture has begun to be stressed. Another 3-5 days after this and these cysts would have accumulated between 1 and 3% Astaxanthin, and would be ready for harvest. Harvesting is a delicate process, where drying of biomass is done and centrifuging is used to separate out the desired products. In terms of productivity it is optimal if the sample tank is set up once and maintainance such as resupply or material and other disturbances are minimised.

The goal in cultivating this particular aglae is to incite cell growth at a rapid rate to obtain a very high cell density; from when the culture can be stressed to maximise yield. In the literature, it is reported that the only aspect that changes growth rate when the cells are not under photoinhibition, photolimitation, nutrient deficiency, temperature stress, or shear-stress, is light availability [12, 38]. This is a major factor because cells closer to the surface of the vessel tend to absorb more light, and shades other cells. This is further complicated by bubbles from the feeding lines, which tend to move cells through the medium. The literature also reports that the ability of cells to grow and divide also depends on the history of illumination on those cells [26]. This means that an approximation to fluid dynamics in such a reactor simulation could improve accuracy.

Our overall goal in this work is ultimately to model the system as a set of individual agents [11]. In this present paper we develop a base line model, that is largely driven just by physical processes. We can use this for comparisons when individualistic agent oriented decisions are introduced to determine just what different localised intelligence or response to local environment actually makes.

A number of different models and approaches to bio reactor simulation have been investigated [3, 27]. Considerable work has been done studying photo synthesis [19, 39] itself. A body of work also exists reporting on the practicalities of building biological reactor systems [29, 31] and photosynthesis modelling [5, 10, 15] and its control [9, 14]. There are various geometric and shape considerations for models of this sort that are often related to percolation properties such as density.

Biological models for growth such as the Eden epidemic model [8] have also been studied on specific geometries [4, 7] and comparisons made between such bio driven processes and physical penetrative processes such as invasion percolation (IP). IP systems are generally modelled to understand similar optimization problems [2] as we face with a bioreactor system – namely to extract the maximal amount of a particular product [30] from a given spatial size and density of input material. The interface [16] between the different materials is a key factor in both systems and models.

Our present model is based on a lattice and is non unlike a porous media structure [28, 37] where diffusion movement is only allowed along set directions. Generally, however, if the model system size is allowed to be large enough, these local microscopic length scale effects are likely to be "integrated out" and the model exhibits complex fluid behaviours [1].

We experiment with simple sheet-like geometries where appropriate levels of light for photosynthesis are impingent upon the left and right walls. We use a variant of the Kawasaki lattice site exchange model [17, 22] so that the material can diffuse slowly around in the tank. The resulting model is essentially a lattice gas [21,35,40] or fluid model where the individual agents modelling the bio product are able to reproduce given sufficient nutrient material, time and of course photo stimulus energy. Our model also uses a weak gravitational field [32, 33] that will cause older heavier clumps of bio material to move preferentially downwards and thus supplying a means for the system to avoid complete spatial stagnation.

In Section 2 we present our preliminary growth model, and some simple experiments, as well as our parallel acceleration of this. In Section 3 we present results of these experiments.

Figure 3: The canonical Kawasaki exchange model with ages shown as colours distributed across the HSV colour space.

Finally, we discuss and conclude in Sections 4 and 5.

2 Photo Algae Growth Model

We use the Kawasaki exchange model as a baseline for our model [22]. In order to arrive at our model, we further add a probability of cell division dependent on exponential decay of illumination intensity, using lateral distance from closest of the left and right tank walls; we also introduce a gravitational force as presented in [17].

The Kawasaki model itself depends on stochasticity and energy minimisation. Essentially a species in a lattice would diffuse around until it comes into contact with identical species. Contact with another species is considered a bond, which requires energy to break. A candidate exchange is brought forth by the random choice of a neighbour site. Temperature is introduced along with a random deviate and Metropolis probability, should the energy not reduce in a candidate exchange. This allows a mechanism to simulate instantaneous local energy and accepting an exchange regardless of the bonds that may be broken. A visualisation of this with a relatively low temperature is shown in Figure 3.

We find that the Kawasaki site-exchange model [22, 23] is a useful way to formulate the diffusion process in a more realistic way by linking it to a temperature. The Kawasaki model [24] is based on the Ising model [20] but with exchange diffusion dynamics and is effectively a lattice gas model [18] if there are vacancies [6] 2011 present.

The model is implemented on a two dimensional lattice with a site exchange diffusion mechanism similar to Kawasaki spin-exchange dynamical model, which itself is based on the Ising model notion of nearest neighbour couplings between sites. Figure 4 shows how two sites arranged horizontally (A-B) or vertically (C-D) interact with their collective six nearest neighbours. At each step of the model the sites are "hit" randomly and the evolutionary process repeats.

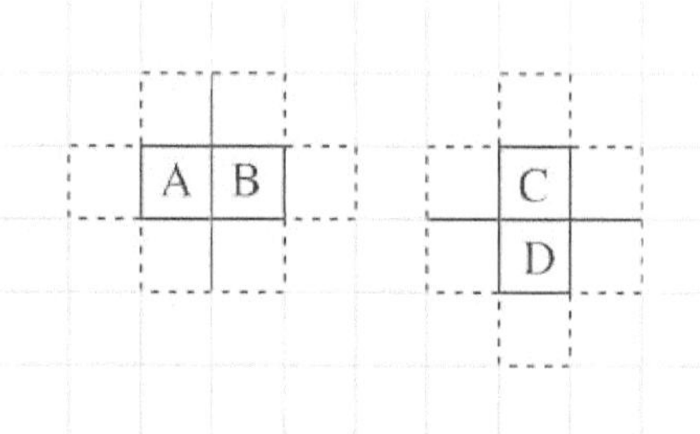

Figure 4: Exchange Mesh showing how A and B exchange, interacting with their nearest neighbours, or C and D do.

To facilitate inquiry into the movement of cells, we also record cell age, and accomplish this by incrementing the age of a cell should it be exchanged with a neighbouring cell. In order to conserve computational effort, we embed both the species state variable and age within the same 32-bit integer. We accomplish this by reserving the most significant byte for the species type, and the first three bytes as age. This allows us to colour cells according to their age using the HSV colour space by varying the hue parameter.

Algorithm 1 Monte-Carlo Model Algorithm.

```
N = L^2 for square lattice
initialise sites with p_v = 0.5 vacancies
choose non-vacant Q − 1 species with equal probability
for all time-steps do
  for all 3x3 blocks in lattice do
    for all 9 sites i in each block, random order do
      choose a random neighbour site j
      compute energy change if i, j exchanged
      if energy falls then
        accept change and do exchange
      else
        compute Metropolis probability p
        add gravitational bias
        obtain random probability r_1
        accept change conditionally on r_1 < p
        compute cell division probability P(split)
        obtain random probability r_2
        divide on r_2 < P(split)
      end if
    end for
  end for
end for
```

Our algorithm is summarised in Alg. 1. In most of our experiments, $Q = 1$ as we only have one species. The formula for computing $P(\text{split})$ is shown below.

$$P(\text{split}) = \gamma e^{-\beta f^2} \tag{1}$$

Where f is a fraction of the lattice width of the site to the closest wall (shown in Eq. 2). γ is a simple amplitude variable, and β controls the slope of the decay.

Figure 5: Kawasaki model augmented by a weak gravitational bias on upper and lower exchanges at an early frame.

Figure 6: Kawasaki model with gravitational bias at a much later frame in computation.

$$f = 1 - \frac{2}{w}\left|\frac{w}{2} - x\right| \quad (2)$$

The gravitational bias is introduced by widening the probability that a cell will exchange into the site below it, should that site be chosen for a potential exchange; as well as narrowing the probability that the cell will exchange into a site above it. The motivation behind this is that in the interest of minimising energy, a site below a cell is regarded as lowering the energy somewhat, and vice-versa with the upper site. To simulate larger cells due to nutrient absorption we made this probability delta proportional to the weight of the cell, which in turn, in our preliminary model is directly proportional to the age of the cell. The immediate effects of this modification on the canonical Kawasaki exchange mechanism is a type of sedimentation. This can be seen in Figs. 6 and 5. Fig. 6 shows a longer run than Fig. 5 where particles of the same weight form a sediment, while particles above are still moving freely.

In order to gain access to larger systems, we have implemented this algorithm on a Graphical Processing Unit (GPU), using NVidia's CUDA [34]. This allows us to take advantage of the large amount of parallel processors on these devices. For brevity, we omit an extensive discussion on this. However, since the algorithm requires each site to be able to modify its neighbouring cell (in the case of an exchange), we must account for the possibility of race conditions and intereference caused by this. We accomplish this in two ways. Firstly, we distribute threads across the lattice leaving a gap of 2 cells between threads. This allows each thread to process its site without any interference from neighbouring threads. We therefore split our update algorithm for one frame into nine separate kernels (device-specific functions), in order to update the cells in between. This is done by giving an offset to each thread successively, in order to process a 3x3 grid around itself. Secondly, in order to defeat any bias, we randomise the order on a frame-by-frame basis.

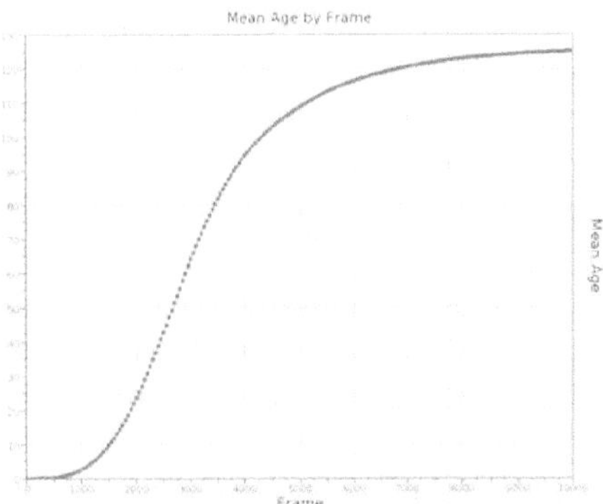

Figure 7: Average age of the cells, by frame, for a sample run with $T = 0.4$ and $\beta = 15$.

Due to the ability of the Kawasaki model to handle more species in the same lattice, we were also able to observe the effects of a competing growth in our simulated bioreactor, where the inoculation at the edges of the tank were differing species. We discuss this in more detail in Sec. 3.

To characterise the growth kinetics of our model, we measured the average age of the cells, as well as a fill fraction by frame, and average column density in the lattice over a complete run.

3 Results

The average ages of cells in a typical run are shown in Fig. 7. Due to the small inoculation, it is expected that the first thousand frames have low ages. This is followed by a period of rapid growth, where cells are constantly moving, and ages are increased rapidly. Finally, when the tank is near capacity, ages reach approximately 125 and stagnate as less movement is possible. We kept the temperature parameter constant at 0.4 in our experiments.

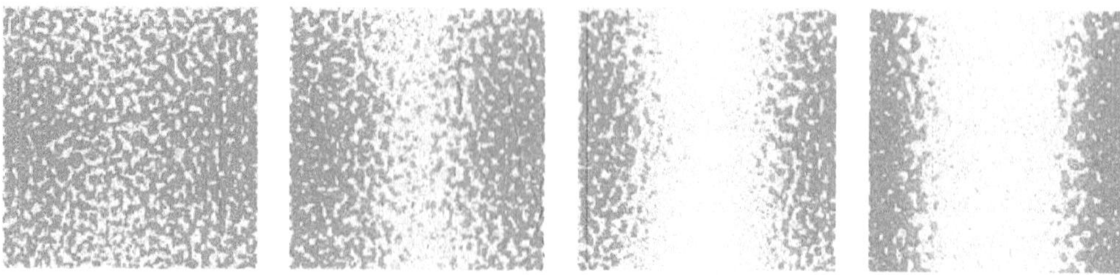

Figure 8: Visualisation of culture growth stagnation at illumination exponent values of 0, 20, 50, and 100 in order from left to right for sample runs. It is interesting to note that although 50 and 100 appear similar, they have different spatial densities.

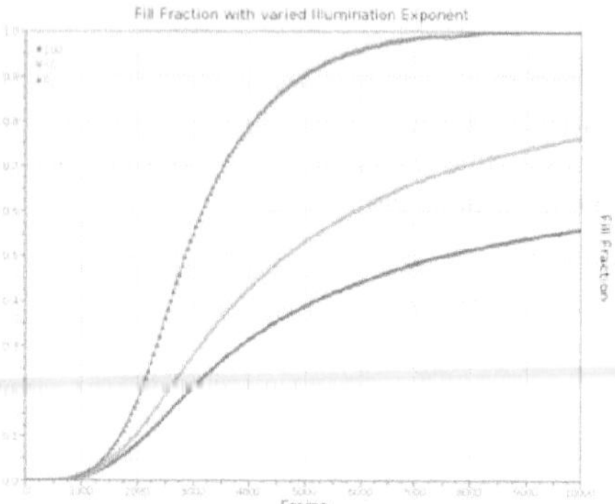

Figure 9: A plot of the fill fraction against frame number for differing values of the decay exponent parameter β. The data in this plot have been average over 100 independent runs for each frame.

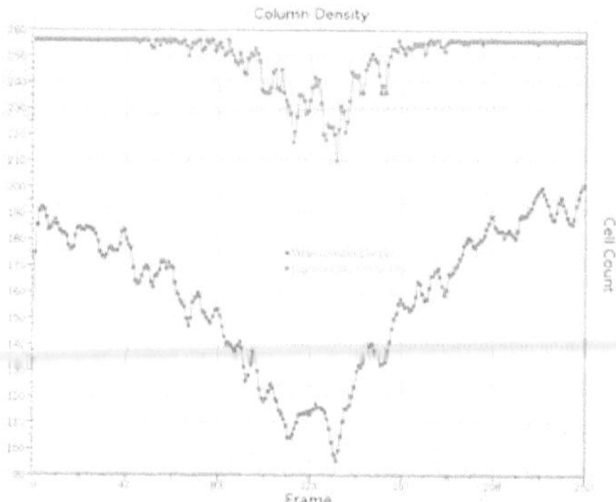

Figure 10: Average density of each column in one sample run.

A plot of the fill fraction of the tank is shown in Fig. 9. The data have been averaged over 100 runs for three different values of the β parameter, 0, 50 and 100. For values 50 and 100, the exponential drastically reduces the probability of a cell division towards the centre of the tank, whereas, if this is not an issue, logarithmic growth is evident when $\beta = 100$.

In Fig. 10 we show the column density of the lattice averaged over a sample run. As can be seen, density is much less in the centre, even at the maximum measured. The curves are almost reminiscent of exponentials. The variability in the data is due to the stochasticity of the algorithm. Averaging the results over separate runs would converge to a more clearly decaying curve.

Fig. 11 shows a bioreactor nearing full capacity. Gravitational bias was particularly harsh in this simulation, which led to the sedimentation effect near the bottom of the tank.

We were also able to observe two competing species. We envisage this being useful for tracking infection of an undesirable strain or alien biomaterial to the reactor. For a tank inoculated at each side with a different species, a visualisation is shown at a distant frame in computation in Fig. 12. An even more distant frame is shown in Fig. 13. Different species were allowed to divide their cells into occupied sites, simulating a sort of infection. Interestingly, the system reaches an equilibrium highly similar to that of the canonical Kawasaki model where one species is simply disabled (empty sites). For this, gravity bias was removed, and cells were coloured based on their species, not ages.

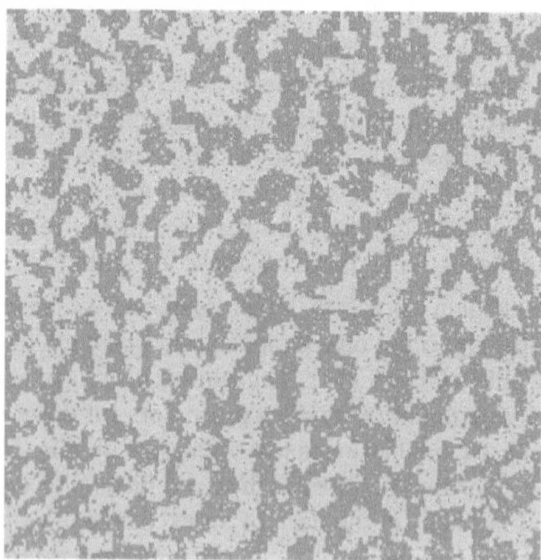

Figure 11: A typical bioreactor nearing full capacity. In this sample simulation, the influence of gravity was set 10 times higher to make the effects more clear.

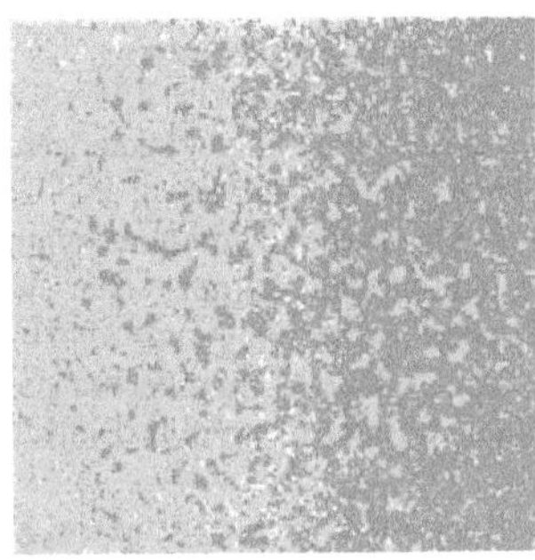

Figure 12: Two competing species.

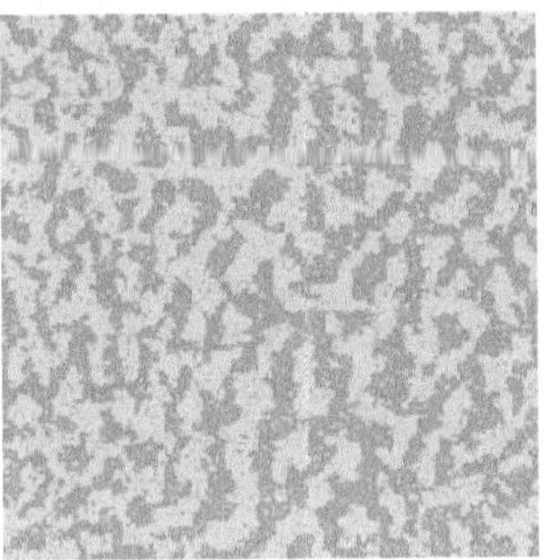

Figure 13: Two competing species at equilibrium.

4 Discussion

The model we have developed shows some promise in terms of modelling algal growth, but several problems remain. One of which is geometry and mutual shading of illumination by neighbouring cells causing photo-limitation. Photobioreactors are typically cylindrical in shape, providing a symmetry which other researchers in the field have made use of in the past. One of these involves a 1-dimensional model of such a system [36]. Cells shade one another from the source of illumination to some extent, which is difficult to model in a discrete lattice simulation. In this case, we have used an exponential decay of light through the medium assuming constant density, but this may not always be the case. Instantaneous differences, particularly when the culture is relatively young, may have a significant impact on culture growth. Illumination history is also important as noted previously, which we could simulate by the same mechanism as we have measured a pseudo-age in the cells. In addition, we have also disregarded the effect of photoinhibition, where cells are inhibited from growth due to absorption of too much photo energy.

The photo-penetration parameters are useful to observe the differences in light absorption of the medium. As stated previously, it would be desirable to include instantaneous differences in cell density for a higher degree of accuracy.

This preliminary work is an *ad hoc* model formulated on a discrete lattice. It may be advantageous to instead make use of a continuous-space model, or extend this lattice to three dimensions by a thin plate, similar to that of a flat reactor.

The mechanism by which we measure age of cells may benefit from a more realistic approach. At present, this parameter represents more of a movement or stress metric. We have also made the weight of cells directly proportional to the corresponding cell age. In addition, cell division occurs regardless of cell age. This is also a factor which may have a significant impact.

In reality, cells may also die due to overcrowding causing nutrient deficiency. In our model, we have disregarded nutrient distribution throughout the lattice, assuming that the medium is well mixed and nutrient fed constantly.

5 Conclusion

We have presented a preliminary model of a photobioreactor and characterised the growth kinetics of the simplified bioreactor. Our implementation was accelerated with the use of Graphical Processing Units, allowing access to large systems and temporally distant frames. Measurements made include fill fractions of the tank, as well as cell age and column density in the reactor.

The model is based on a Kawasaki exchange model with the addition of a gravitational bias, as well as a cell division probability. This probability is computed by evaluating an exponential decay function using lateral distance to the walls of the tank. This gave rise to a photo-limitation effect in the centre of the tank. There is scope to further quantify the relationship between photo penetration and growth behaviour.

Additionally, there is scope for introducing a spatial-agent model with cylindrical geometry instead of a discrete lattice; as well as the introduction of rudimentary intelligence in these cells.

In summary the model appears to exhibit a rich set of complex emergent patterns and may prove a valuable tool for investigating pragmatic photobioreactor harvesting issues.

References

[1] Arratia, P.E.: Complex fluids at work. Physics 4(9), 1–3 (January 2011)

[2] Barabasi, A.L.: Invasion percolation and global optimization. Phys. Rev. Lett. 76(20), 3750–3753 (May 1996)

[3] Castellanos, C.S.: Batch and Continuous Study of C. vulgaris in Photo-bioreactors. Master's thesis, University of Western Ontario (2013)

[4] Cieplak, M., Maritan, A., Banavar, J.R.: Invasion percolation and eden growth: Geometry and universality. Phys. Rev. Lett. 76(20), 3754–3757 (May 1996)

[5] Cloot, A.: Effect of light intensity variations on the rate of photosynthesis of algae: A dynamical approach. Mathl. Comput. Modelling 19, 23–33 (1994)

[6] Davydov, S.Y., Lebedev, A.A.: Vacancy model of micropipe annihilation in epotaxial silicon carbide layers. Semiconductors

45(6), 727–730 (2011)

[7] Ebrahimi, F.: The shape of invasion percolation clusters in random and correlated media. J. Stat. Mech: Theory and Experiment P04005, 1–8 (April 2008)

[8] Eden, M.: A two-dimensional growth process. In: Proc. Fourth Berkeley Symposium on Mathematics, Statistics and Probability. vol. 4, pp. 223–239. Univ. California Press, Berkeley (1960)

[9] Eilers, P.H.C., Peeters, J.C.H.: A model for the relationship between light intensity and the rate of photosynthesis in phytoplankton. Ecological Modelling 42, 199–215 (1988)

[10] Eilers, P.H.C., Peeters, J.C.H.: Dynamic behaviour of a model for photosynthesis and photoinhibition. Ecological Modelling 69, 113–133 (1993)

[11] Ferrer, J., Prats, C., Lopez, D.: Individual-based modelling: An essential tool for microbiology. J. Biol. Phys. 34, 19–37 (2008)

[12] Garcia-Malea, M., Brindley, C., Rìo, E.D., Acién, F., Fernández, J., Molina, E.: Modelling of growth and accumulation of carotenoids in haematococcus pluvialis as a function of irradiance and nutrients supply. Biochemical Engineering Journal 26, 107–114 (2005)

[13] Gorochowski, T.E., Matyjaszkiewicz, A., Todd, T., Oak, N., Kowalska, K., Reid, S., Tsaneva-Atanasova, K.T., Savery, N.J., Grierson, C.S., di Bernardo, M.: Bsim: An agent-based tool for modeling bacterial populations in systems and synthetic biology. PLoS ONE 7(8), e42790. doi:10.1371/journal.pone.0042790 (August 2012)

[14] Grima, E.M., Fernandez, F.G.A., Camacho, F.G., Rubio, F.C., Chisti, Y.: Scale-up of tubular photobioreactors. J. Applied Phycology 12, 355–368 (2000)

[15] Hankamer, B., Lehr, F., Rupprecht, J., Mussgnug, J.H., Posten, C., Kruse, O.: Photosynthetic biomass and h2 production by green algae: from bioengineering to bioreactor scale-up. Physiologia Plantarum 131, 10–21 (2007)

[16] Harris, R., Jorgenson, L., Grant, M.: Monte carlo lattice-gas simulations of stable and unstable interfaces. Phys.Rev.A 45(2), 1024–1034 (jan 1992)

[17] Hawick, K.: Visualising multi-phase lattice gas fluid layering simulations. In: Proc. International Conference on Modeling, Simulation and Visualization Methods (MSV'11). pp. 3–9. CSREA, Las Vegas, USA (18-21 July 2011)

[18] Hawick, K.A.: Domain Growth in Alloys. Ph.D. thesis, Edinburgh University (1991)

[19] Iluz, D., Alexandrovich, I., Dubinsky, Z.: The Enhancement of Photosynthesis by Fluctuating Light, Artificial Photosynthesis,, chap. 6, pp. 115–134. InTech (2012)

[20] Ising, E.: Beitrag zur Theorie des Ferromagnetismus. Zeitschrift fuer Physik 31, 253–258 (1925)

[21] Johnson, M.G.B., Playne, D.P., Hawick, K.A.: Data-parallelism and gpus for lattice gas fluid simulations. In: Proc. International Conference on Parallel and Distributed Processing Techniques and Applications (PDPTA'10). pp. 210–216. CSREA, Las Vegas, USA (12-15 July 2010), pDP4521

[22] Kawasaki, K.: Diffusion constants near the critical point for time dependent Ising model I. Phys. Rev. 145(1), 224–230 (1966)

[23] Kawasaki, K.: Diffusion constants near the critical point for time-dependent ising models. ii. Physical Review 148(1), 375–381 (1966)

[24] Kawasaki, K.: Diffusion constants near the critical point for time-dependent ising models. iii. self-diffusion constant. Physical Review 150(1), 285–290 (1966)

[25] Kreft, J.U., Booth, G., Wimpenny, J.W.: Bacsim, a simulator for individual-based modelling of bacteria colony growth. Microbiology 144, 3275–3287 (1998)

[26] Lee, Y.K., Pirt, J.S.: Energetics of photosynthetic algal growth: influence of intermittent illumination in short (40 s) cycles. Journal of General Microbiology 124(1), 43–52 (1981)

[27] Lehr, F., Posten, C.: Closed photo-bioreactors as tools for biofuel production. Current Opinion in Biotechnology 20, 280–285 (2009)

[28] Lenormand, R.: Liquids in porous media. J. Phys.: Condens. Matter 2, SA79–SA88 (1990)

[29] Luo, H.P., Kemoun, A., Al-Dahhan, M.H., Sevilla, J.M.F., Sanchez, J.L.G., Camacho, F.G., Grima, E.M.: Analysis of photobioreactors for culturing high-value microalgae and cyanobacteria via an advanced diagnostic technique: Carpt. Chem. Eng. Science 58, 2519–2527 (2003)

[30] Martys, N., Cieplak, M., Robbins, M.O.: Critical phenomena in fluid invasion of porous media. Phys. Rev. Lett. 66(8), 1058–1061 (February 1991)

[31] Masojidek, J., Papacek, S., Sergejevova, M., Jirka, V., Cerveny, J., Kunc, J., Korecko, J., Verbovikova, O., Kopecky, J., Stys, D., Torzillo, G.: A closed solar photobioreactor for cultivation of microalgae under supra-high irradiance: basic design and performance. J. Applied Phycology 15, 239–248 (2003)

[32] Masoum, S., Masihi, M.: Invasion percolation in presence of gravity. Iran J. Chem. Chem. Eng. 29, 71–82 (2010)

[33] Meakin, P., Feder, J., Frette, V., Jossang, T.: Invasion percolation in a destabilizing gradient. Phys. Rev. A 46(6), 3357–3368 (September 1992)

[34] NVIDIA® Corporation: NVIDIA CUDA C Programming Guide Version 4.1 (2011), `http://www.nvidia.com/` (last accessed April 2012)

[35] O.Penrose, A.Buhagiar: Kinetics of nucleation in a lattice gas model: Microscopic theory and simulation compared. J.Stat.Phys 30(1), 219–241 (1983)

[36] Papacek, S., Matonoha, C., Stumbauer, V., Stys, D.: Modelling and simulation of photosynthetic microorganism growth: random walk vs. finite difference method. Mathematics and Computers in Simulation 82, 2022–2032 (2012)

[37] Prat, M.: Recent advances in pore-scale models for drying of porous media. Chem. Eng. Journal 86, 153–164 (2002)

[38] Ranjbar, R., Inoue, R., Shiraishi, H., Katsuda, T., Katoh, S.: High efficiency production of astaxanthin by autotrophic cultivation of *haematococcus pluvialis*in a bubble column photobioreactor. Biochemical Engineering Journal 39, 575–580 (2008)

[39] Rehak, B., Celikovsky, S., Papacek, S.: Model for photosynthesis and photoinhibition: Parameter identification based on the harmonic irradiation o2 response measurement. IEEE Trans. on Automatic Control 53, 101–108 (Jan 2008)

[40] Rivet, J.P., Boon, J.P.: Lattice Gas Hydrodynamics. No. ISBN 0-521-019710, Cambridge (2001)

Learning microscopic kinetic characteristic of endosomal network by quantitative analysis of snap-shot microscopy images

Yannis Kalaidzidis[1], Lionel Foret[2,3], Jonathan E. Dawson[2], Roberto Villaseñor[1], Frank Jülicher[3], Marino Zerial[1]

[1]Max-Planck-Institute of Molecular Cell Biology and Genetics, Dresden, Germany
[2]Max-Planck-Institute for the Physics of Complex Systems, Dresden, Germany
[3]Laboratoire de Physique Statistique, Ecole Normale Supèrieure, Paris, France

Abstract - *Receptor-mediated endocytosis is a mechanism for import and distribution of nutrient and signaling cargo into a series of intracellular organelles, endosomes, with distinct biochemical characteristics. Endosomes form a dynamic network by undergoing fusion and fission, exchanging and redistributing cargo. Direct learning dynamic characteristic of individual endosomes in live cells is challenging problem. We have developed model to derive endocitic cargo traffic properties from microscopic dynamic of individual endosomes [1]. By reverse engineering this model allowed learn microscopic kinetic characteristic of endocytic network from set of snap-shot images. We developed software FitModelPDE2 (based on Pluk, C++, OpenCL) for fitting integral-PDE model to experimental data. Fitting of model to the experimental data revealed contribution of different processes governing endocytic system and suggested that some model parameters are functions of cargo progression. Applying "free-shape-function" approach we learned the changes of kinetic characteristic of endocytic network that accompany cargo progression..*

Keywords: endocytosis, model fitting, PDE, GPU-based computing

Introduction

Cells communicate with their environment by taking up and secreting different molecules. Some molecules selectively enter the cell in a process called receptor mediated endocytosis. In this process, a ligand binds specifically to its receptor(s) at the plasma membrane and is subsequently internalized into the cell via special vesicles. The vesicles fuse with early endosomes where cargo is sorted and delivered to its destination (in general either to degradation or to recycling). The recycling cargo delivered to specialized recycling endosomes, whereas cargo destined to degradation leaves early endocytic network and entering a network of late endosomes and lysosomes. In this study we have used Low-Density Lipoprotein (LDL), which is transported to late endosomes and lysosomes for degradation. The endosomes function is governed by the dynamic assembly on the membrane of a multi-protein machinery organized by small GTPases of the Rab family. Rab proteins determine specify of distinct endocytic compartments. Early endosomes are characterized by Rab5, recycling endosomes by Rab4 and Rab11 and late endosomes by Rab7 and their respective effectors. Rab5-positive early endosomes can fuse homotypically thereby sharing ligands within the endosomal network. The transfer of cargo from early to late endosomes occurs either by conversion of Rab5-positive early endosomes into Rab7-positive late endosomes or by budding of carrier vesicles from early endosomes and subsequent fusion with late endosomes. To what extent different types of cargo or different cell types use one mechanism, the other or both remains unclear.

Mathematical model of endocytic network

In our previous work [1] we developed model of cargo traffic through early endosomal network based on basic processes of endosome interactions: fusion, fission and conversion. Model demonstrated how the macroscopic kinetic behaviour of the endosomal network exhibits properties which are the result of the collective interplay of many endosomes in a population in the absence of an external controller, i.e. in a self-organization process. Mathematic formulation of model is equation (1), where is number of endosomes with cargo content at moment time ; are fusion and fission kernels respectively; is rate of generation of new cargo-loaded endosomes ; is rate of conversion of endosomes (i.e. change endosome identity toward the next compartment in the pathway); - rate of delivery and removal cargo by vesicles.

$$\frac{\partial n(s,t)}{\partial t} = \frac{1}{2}\int_0^s K_{fusion}(\varsigma, s-\varsigma)n(\varsigma)n(s-\varsigma)d\varsigma - \int_0^\infty K_{fusion}(s,\varsigma)n(s)n(\varsigma)d\varsigma$$
$$+\int_0^\infty K_{fission}(s,\varsigma)n(s+\varsigma)d\varsigma - \frac{1}{2}\int_0^s K_{fission}(\varsigma, s-\varsigma)n(s)d\varsigma$$
$$+A(s) - k_c n(s) - \frac{\partial}{\partial s}(v_{in}(s)n(s)) + \frac{\partial}{\partial s}(v_{out}(s)n(s))$$

(1)

Experimental work

In order to study the cargo transport through the early endosomal network, we used a culture cell assay with quantitative, high resolution microscopy. We used fluorescently labelled Low-Density Lipoprotein (LDL) as endocytic cargo destined to degradative pathway. For marking endocytic compartment we used HeLa cells transfected with a bacterial artificial chromosome (BAC) transgene stably expressing GFP-Rab5c under its endogenous promoter [6]. The cells were imaged by an automated high-resolution confocal microscope. We performed quantitative multi-parametric image analysis (QMPIA) to extract morphometric parameters of the imaged fluorescent structures as previously described [7]. Shortly, fluorescently labelled LDL (LDL-Alexa647, 0.5-10 μg/ml) was added to cell medium and chased for different time intervals. Then cell were fixed and imaged. For every time point 30 images (~600 cells) were acquired. The result, as a progressive changes LDL distribution over endosomes is presented on Fig.1.

the experimental data. FitModelPDE2 was developed on base of Pluk platform [8] (http://pluk.mpi-cbg.de/). In the FitModelPDE2 the declarative description of mathematical model (Fig.2) is automatically translated to OpenCL and executed on GPU. The model simulation was incorporated in parameter fitting procedure, which includes deterministic (descent gradient) and stochastic (random choice of starting point) components. The stochastic part of calculation was parallelized by automatic distribution of task for the cluster calculation. The confidence intervals of found parameters were estimated by procedure of Sivia and Carlile [9].

FitModelPDE2 is developed as stand-alone application and could be installed and used on Windows platform without necessity for end-user program GPU himself. The screen-shots of FitModelPDE2 model declaration screen as well as solution graphs are presented on Fig.3.

Simple model (2) has only 7 parameters. Unfortunately after fit we found that discrepancy of the best solution with experimental data have normalized $\chi^2 = 16.2$ (degree of freedom = 923). It suggests that some parameters are functionally dependent on changes of endosome during

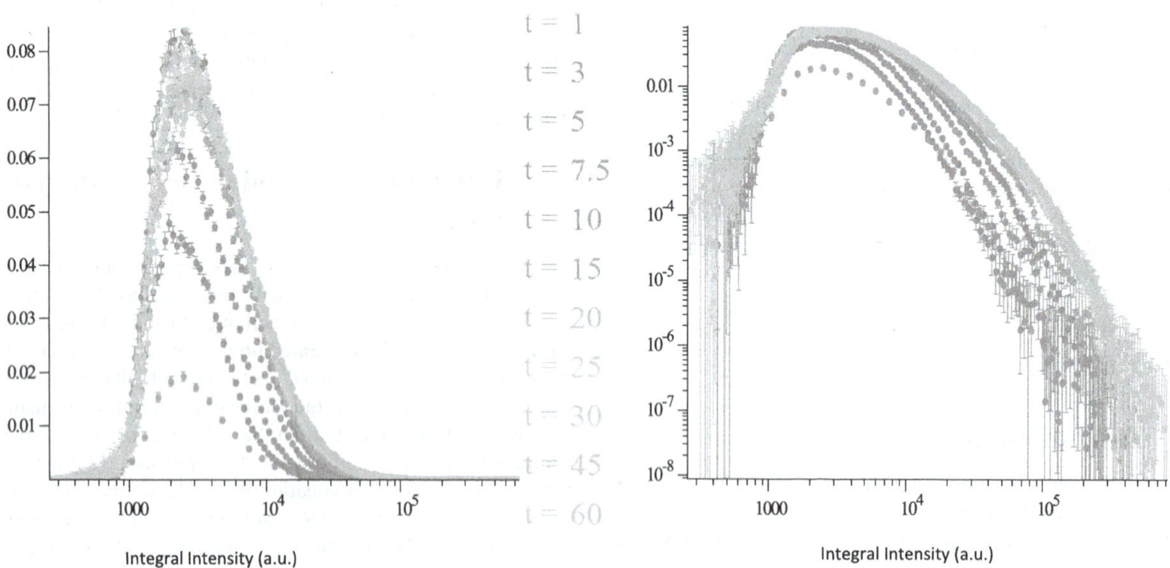

Figure.1. Density of endosome distribution (n(s)) over unit integral of integral intensities LDL per endosome at different time points after beginning of internalization. The distributions are normalized on relative area of images covered by cells. Left panel present data in semi-logarithmic scale, right panel present data in double-logarithmic scale. Error-bar presents SEM. All distributions consist of 924 data points.

progression toward degradative compartment.

$$
\begin{aligned}
&A_+(s) = A_0 e^{-\frac{s}{\lambda}} \\
&K_{fusion}(s,s') = const \\
&K_{fission}(s,s') = const \\
&k_c(s) = const \\
&v_{in}(s) = const \\
&v_{out}(s) = const
\end{aligned}
\qquad (2)
$$

Numerical analysis

We developed software *FitModelPDE2* for fitting model of integral-differential equation in partial derivatives to

It is worse to mention that non-local dependency of solution on model does not allow fit every experimental dataset by appropriate parameter tuning, since of non-locality of model involves all 924 data points in parameter search. It means that we are free to increase number of parameters without come to problem of over-parameterized model.

A

```
d.Y(s)/d.t = I.(K_fusion(xp, s - xp) * Y(xp) * Y(s - xp), --, s / 2.0)d.xp
        - Y(s) * I.(K_fusion(xp, s) * Y(xp), --, ++)d.xp
        + I.(K_fission(xp - s, s) * Y(xp), s + --, ++)d.xp
        - 0.5 * Y(s) * Is.(K_fission(xp, s - xp), --, s - --)d.xp
        + A_plus(s) - K_out(s) * Y(s)
        - d.((v_in(s) - v_out(s)) * Y(s))/d.s
```

B

```
A_plus(x) = nScale * Exp(- x / Lamda)
K_fusion(a, b) = kK_fus / s_Span
K_fission(a, b) = a < -- || b < -- ? 0.0 : kK_fis / s_Span * Exp(- (Ln(((a < b ? a : b)) / s0) / fisSigma) ** 2.0)
v_out(s) = k_out * s
v_in(s) = k_in
K_out(s) = K_minus * (1.0 - 1.0 / (1.0 + (Ln(s) / Ln(s1)) ** nMat))
```

C

```
s = [300.0, 1.0e6] : 300, log : 500.0
t = [0.0, 60] : 90, log : 0.2
```

D

```
fit K_minus = 0.1      : [1.0e-4, 1.0e0], log
fit Lamda = 5000.0     : [1.0e2, 1.0e6], log
fit kK_fus = 200.0     : [1.0e0, 1.0e4], log
fit kK_fis = 1.0       : [1.0e0, 1.0e4], log
fit k_out = 1.0e-8     : [1.0e-10, 1.0e-2], log
```

E

```
draw model_Y : LIGHTRED
draw Y_exper : LIGHTBLUE
draw_fit
draw_t[1] model_FI : LIGHTRED
print "A_plus = ", Is.(x * A_plus(x), --, ++)d.x
print "v_in(60) = ", Is.(v_in(x) * Y(x, 60), --, ++)d.x
```

F

```
compare Y_exper : model_Y [2000.0, 1.0e6]
```

Figure 2. Declaration of mathematical model in FitModelPDE2. **A**. Declaration of integral-differential equation of model. Here **d.() /d.x** denotes partial derivative by x. **I.(f(x) , a, b)d.x** denotes integral of function f(x) in interval [a, b]. - - and + + denote minimum and maximum value of integration variable. **B.** Declaration of functions. **C**. Specification of solution interval and number of points in the solution grid. Modifier **log : xx** specifies that grid is uniform in logarithmic scale and **xx** denotes minimum step value of the grid. **D**. This section specifies interval of optimal parameter search and initial guess. **E.** This section specifies output of fitting procedure in corresponding tabs of FitModelPDE2. F. This clause specify which model curve has to be compared (fitted to) which experimental data.

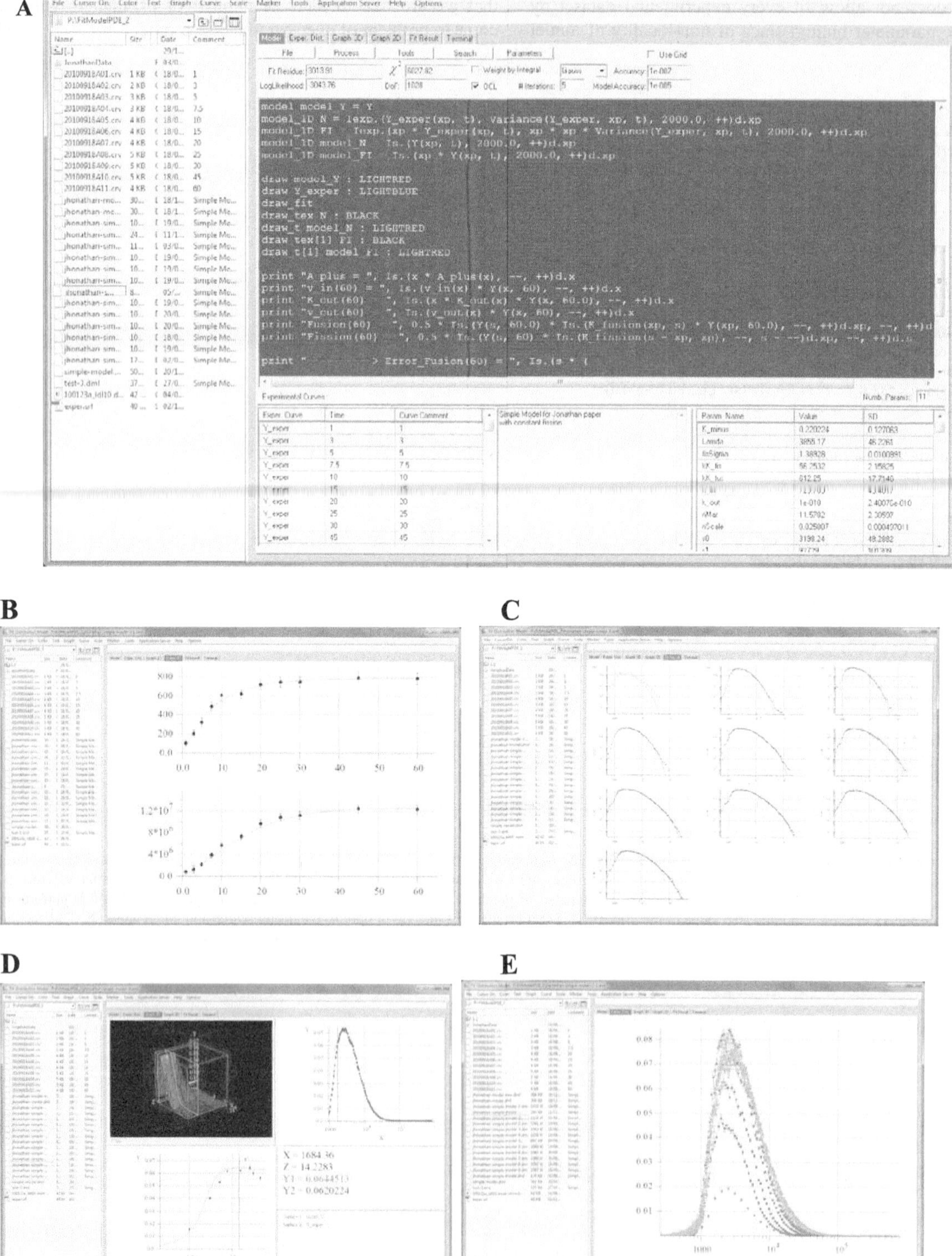

Figure 3. A. Model declaration screen. B. Integral characteristic of solution (experimental data - black dots, model curves - red lines). **C.** Individual experimental distributions (black dots) and corresponding model curves (red lines). **D.** 3D presentation of experimental data and model solution. **E.** Experimental data to fit model.

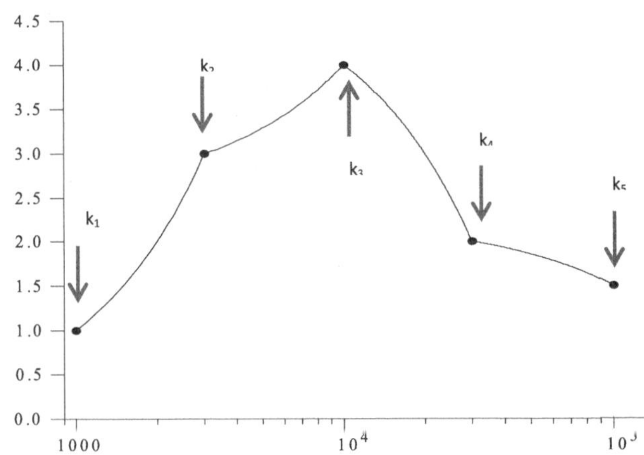

Figure 4. Piecewise-linear function: free-shape function approximation

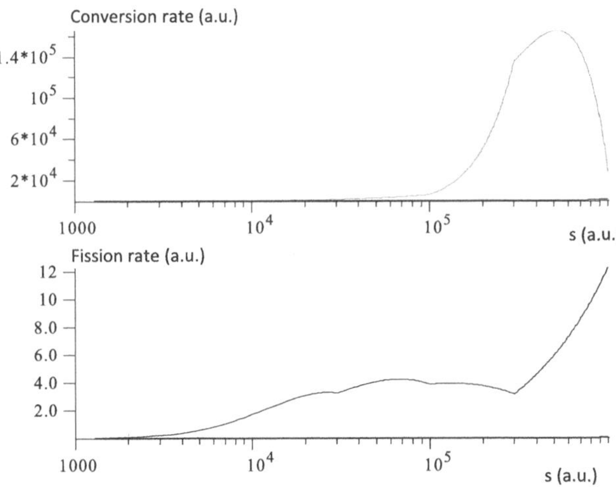

Figure 5. Upper panel: early to late endosome conversion rate as function of degradative cargo (LDL) accumulation. Bottom panel: endosome homotypic fission rate as as function of LDL accumulation in large endosomes. Both dependencies were found by piecewise linear function approximation with 5 knots equidistantly located in logarithmic scale.

Given that homotypic fission most probably has budding mechanism with some characteristic size s_0 of bud and given clear low limit of size of bud (it cannot be negative) reasonable assumption on fission kernel is

$$K_{fission}(s,\varsigma) = K_0(s+\varsigma)\cdot\exp\left(-\frac{\left(\ln(\frac{\min(s,\varsigma)}{s_0})\right)^2}{2\sigma_{fis}^2}\right)$$

, (3)

where K_0 is probability of fission for endosomes with size $s+\varsigma$.

Since we have no good idea about function $K_0(s+\varsigma)$, then we have used "free-shape-function" approach, where we present function as piece-wise linear function with 5 knot points located equidistantly in logarithmic scale (Fig.4). The same "free-shape-function" approach we use for determination of conversion rate $k_c(s)$, since from general knowledge of the system one could expect that conversion to the later compartment has to be conditioned by sufficient cargo accumulation. Indeed fitting dramatically improve $\chi^2 = 4.1$. We have to note that free function in fusion kernel (with constant fission kernel) does not change significantly χ^2 and converge to almost constant kernel. The found fission kernel and conversion rate are presented on Fig.5.

Conclusion

This result is biologically meaningful. Indeed one could expect that cargo processing and associated with it fission has to be completed before conversion. The conversion rate arose sharply when LDL is accumulated that is in line with direct observation in live cells [2], that have demonstrated that conversion is committed mostly by large endosomes with highly concentrated degradative cargo.

FitModelPDE2 (http://pluk.mpi-cbg.de) is a powerful tool for fitting model, which is formulated as integral-differential equation with partial derivatives to experimental data. The GPU-based parallelization of computation makes it feasible on laptop. All presented calculation were performed on Lenovo W520 under operation system Windows 7.

References

[1] Foret L., Dawson, J. E., Villasenor R., Collinet C., Deutsch A., Brusch L, Zerial M., Kalaidzidis Y, Juelicher, F., (2012), A General Theoretical Framework to Infer Endosomal Network Dynamics from Quantitative Image Analysis, Current Biology v.22, pp.1381–1390

[2] Rink, J., Ghigo, E., Kalaidzidis, Y., and Zerial, M. (2005). Rab conversion as a mechanism of progression from early to late endosomes. Cell *122*, 735-749.

[3] Ciechanover, A., Schwartz, A.L., Dautry-Varsat, A., and Lodish, H.F. (1983). Kinetics of internalization and recycling of transferrin and the transferrin receptor in a human hepatoma cell line. Effect of lysosomotropic agents. J. Biol. Chem. *258*, 9681-9689.

[4] Lauffenburger, D.A., and Lindermann, J.J. (1993). Receptors: model for binding, trafficking and signaling, (New York: Oxford University Press)

[5] Becker, V., Schilling, M., Bachmann, J., Baumann, U., Raue, A., Maiwald, T., Timmer, J., and Klingmüller, U. (2010). Covering a broad dynamic range: information processing at the erythropoietin receptor. Science *328*, 1404-1408

[6] Poser, I., Sarov, M., Hutchins, J.R., Heriche, J.K., Toyoda, Y., Pozniakovsky, A., Weigl, D., Nitzsche, A., Hegemann, B., Bird, A.W., et al. (2008). BAC TransgeneOmics: a high-throughput method for exploration of protein function in mammals. Nat. Methods *5*, 409-415

[7] Collinet, C., Stoter, M., Bradshaw, C.R., Samusik, N., Rink, J.C., Kenski, D., Habermann, B., Buchholz, F., Henschel, R., Mueller, M.S., et al. (2010). Systems survey of endocytosis by multiparametric image analysis. Nature *464*, 243-249

[8] Kalaidzidis Ya.L, Gavrilov A.V., Zaitsev P.V., Kalaidzidis A.L., and Korolev. E.V., (1997) PLUK—An Environment for Software Development., Programming and Computer Software, v.23, n.4, pp. 206-212

[9] Sivia, D.S., Carlile, C.J.,(1992), Molecular spectroscopy and Bayesian spectral analysis-how many lines are there, Journal Chemical Physics, v.96, n.1, pp.170-178

Are Turtles Diapsid Reptiles?

Jack K. Horner
P.O. Box 266
Los Alamos NM 87544 USA

BIOCOMP 2013

Abstract

It has been argued that, based on a neighbor-joining analysis of a broad set of fossil reptile morphological data that turtles are diapsid reptiles. A Bayesian phylogenetic analysis does not sustain this view.

Keywords: Turtles, diapsid, neighbor-joining, Bayesian phylogenetic

1.0 Introduction

The traditional classification of reptiles is based on a single key character, the presence and style of fenestration in the temporal region of the skull. Snakes, lizards, crocodiles, dinosaurs and others are 'diapsids': they have (at least in a rudimentary form) two holes in the temporal region. Reptiles in which the skull is completely roofed, with no temporal fenestration, are called 'anapsids'. These include many Palaeozoic forms such as captorhinomorphs, procolophonids and pareiasaurs, but also include Testudines (turtles and tortoises). Consistent with this assumption, recent analyses of the affinities of Testudines have included Palaeozoic taxa only, placing them as akin to captorhinomorphs or procolophonids or nested within pareiasaurs. [4], in contrast, maintains turtles are diapsid reptiles, based on a neighbor-joining (NJ) assessment ([2]) of fossil reptile morphological data.

2.0 Method

The taxon descriptors in [5] were reformatted under Microsoft *Notebook* to be compatible with the variable coding requirements of [1]. The resulting descriptors were then analyzed under a Bayesian phylogenetic ([2]) software package (*MRBAYES*, [1]; see Figure 1). The software was run on a Dell Inspiron 545 with an Intel Core2 Quad CPU Q8200 clocked at 2.33 GHz, with 8.00 GB RAM, under *Windows Vista Home Premium/SP2.*

```
begin data;
     dimensions ntax=33 nchar=168;
     format datatype=Standard gap=- missing=? interleave=Yes;

     matrix

Seymouriadae         0000000000000000000001000000000000000000000000000000000000
Diadectomorpha       000000000000000000001{01}00{01}00000{01}000000000000000000101{01}000
Caseidae             00000000010000000000000010000?0010000100000000000002010010001
Ophiacodontidae      0000000001000000001000{01}1000?0010100100000010000102111000l
Edaphosauridae       0000?0000000010000{01}?00010000?10{01}110010000201000010211110001
Sphenacodontidae     00001000011001001010001{01}0000?1010100100002010000102111100l
Gorganopsia          0000100101100100l?1?00111000?200010012001201000010212110001
Cynodontia           0000110201100100210001000000?20001001200120?0121202121100l
Captorhinidae        0000000000000100000000000000?100000110001000000000{02}001112010
Paleothyris          0000000000000000000?00000000000?10000011000100000000000110010
Millerettidae        ?0000000000001000?010000{01}000?100000010{01}00000000000{01}0010010
Acleistorhinus       000001000010100l1?0?00110000?0110000100011000000020110l0010
Lanthanosuchidae     00000100001110{01}1?1?00110100?0010000100001l???00{02}011010010
Macroleter           0000010000101001l?0?00001001?00000001100000???002010012010
Bradysaurus          000001010010110100010100010?000000010000010010020010l2110
Scutosaurus          00000101001111010001010000100?00000001000001001002001012110
Anthodon             0000010100101110100010100[illegible]0001000001001002001012110
Procolophon          0000010000101100100110001001?0000010110001{01}011002002012110
Owenetta             000001000010110010?0?10001001?000001111000l0???00200012110
Araeoscelidia        0000000000000l1000?10000010000100000110001000000000110110010
Claudiosaurus        000000000?001101?1?00?010000111000110001200??01013?112010
Younginiformes       0000000000000000010100000100011110001111010001101011011{02}010
Kuehneosauridae      000?0110001001101?0?00001010??01002??1111300??012132212010
Testudines
001{01}0101001000{01}01{01}{02}10{01}0001{01}0?1000011111001001100300 2{02}12110
Rhynchocephalia
000000000010001021010 0{01}0{01}0101111100l111{01}120011{01}1{02}1{23}2{12}12110
Squamata
000{01}0000{012}0{01}000{01}021{012}10{01}{01}0001011{01}1002101111300 11{01}1{023}132{12}
12{01}10
Choristodera         1001011?11000100112?000000000?01000??110?{23}0011113112212?10
Rhynchosauria        11110111001000{01}01?01000000{01}00111101101101200112131122l2110
Prolacertiformes
1001010001{01}00{01}{01}01?100010{01}0100110{01}02101101{23}001101{23}132{12}12010
Trilophosaurus       1?11000?00?00?????1?011000100?1??0???110?000?1213102212110
Archisauriformes
100{01}010001100{01}{01}01{01}{01}00000{01}010011110110110120011{01}1{03}112{12}12010
Placodus             1000000110100100212101001100111000111110?300??012132212010
Eosauropterygia
100{01}000{01}0010?0{01}021{01}?0000{01}0{01}0111100010{01}10?{23}00??{01}1{12}132212010

Seymouriadae         0000000000000000000000000000001000000000000000000000000000
Diadectomorpha       000000001000000000000000{01}00000000{01}000000000000000000000000
Caseidae             1000000000000000000000000100000000000001001000000000000001000000000
Ophiacodontidae      1000?000??0000000001000000000000101100100000000001000000000
Edaphosauridae       100110210?000000?1011010000000011110100000001001001000000 0
Sphenacodontidae     1001102110000000010100000000000010110010000000100100100000000
Gorganopsia          10111121?1012110120200002100000101100100100010011011100011
Cynodontia           101111211101211012020002210102210110010{01}1010110110111 01111
Captorhinidae        20000000000000001000100200100000000010000000000000000000{01}000
Paleothyris          2001?000??0??00?0101000001?000000010000000000100100000000 00
Millerettidae        2000?000?00??001000100020100000000110000000 0?0001000?0?000?
Acleistorhinus       ?201?000??0??1000001000 2?1?10?00101000???????????????????
Lanthanosuchidae     12000000??0??1000101000{01}11??01?0?11010??000????200?????01?
Macroleter           20?0?00???0??00?0?01000211?10?00111000000000000002001?0?0010
Bradysaurus          2010100101000112111111020111000011101010000?0002001111001 0
Scutosaurus          20101101010001121111110201110000111010110 00?0002001111101 0
Anthodon             2010110101000112111111020111000011101 01?000?0002001111101 0
Procolophon          200{01}001100100011111200021111110011101 00{01}00001002001100101 0
```

```
Owenetta            2000?010??1??0011112000211111100111 0{01}00?000?0002001?0??01?
Araeoscelidia       2001?000??0??001001100000100010000100000000010010000000001
Claudiosaurus       200??100??0??0010011100001?1010000101000?0011011000010111?
Younginiformes      2001?000??00?0010001100011??0?00?1101000000110010001?0{01}1{01}1
Kuehneosauridae     20?1?01???0??001???0?0?001?0??10?1101000100?11?1110?10????
Testudines
201011111101{01}{01}0211{01}2113{02}011111101{01}1??11{01}{02}011{01}0?1001111010
Rhynchocephalia     2{01}01?0111{01}010001110210001101011011111000{01}01?1001{01}001101121
Squamata
200{01}0{01}111101{01}0011{01}12010{012}11{01}{01}1110{01}11110001{02}{01}1100110011{01}1
{01}21
Choristodera        210110011?01??0111010101010?01?0111010001101101110011011 1?
Rhynchosauria       211010010?01?00210{01}21000111110101112100010011001000110111?
Prolacertiformes
21011{01}10??01?001000{12}1000{01}1?10100111010001{02}0?1{01}11{01}001101101
Trilophosaurus      211?10111101?00110121102111 00??01112100?1{12}011011000?10111?
Archisauriformes
2{01}1111?111011{01}01110{12}100{012}{01}1{01}10100?11010001{012}0?1{01}11{01}101101111
Placodus            2001?1101101?1201202010111110010111010000 00?1111111?1?1110
Eosauropterygia
2{01}01???11101?1201{01}?2110{01}{01}10?0110?110{01}0?01{01}1?11111010101{01}{01}0

Seymouriadae        0000000000000000000000000000000000000000000000000?00
Diadectomorpha      0000000000000000000000000000000000000000000000000?00
Caseidae            1000000000000000000000000000000100000000000000000?00
Ophiacodontidae     {01}0000000000000000000000000000001000000000000000000?00
Edaphosauridae      10000000000000??0000000000000001?00????0?0???0??0?00
Sphenacodontidae    1000000000000000000000000000000100000000000000000?00
Gorganopsia         1000000001200010100011012101011122101000010020000?0?
Cynodontia          1200?0100220011110101111211101112110101001102110 0?01
Captorhinidae       0001000002000000000000000000000100000000010000000?00
Paleothyris         0001000101000000000000000000000100000000010001100?00
Millerettidae       00?00?01?1?00?0?0100000000??00?100001000?10?00100?00
Acleistorhinus      ????????????????????????????????????????????????0???
Lanthanosuchidae    0?????0?????????????????????????????????????????0?0?
Macroleter          10?1000001000000010001000001?0010000100001000100 0?0?
Bradysaurus         11?10000?2200100011011000001000110001000021020011001
Scutosaurus         11?10000?2200100011011001001000110001000021020011211
Anthodon            21?10010?2200100010011001001000110001000021020012111
Procolophon         10?100{01}0021001000100110000010001110010000201100 1{01}000
Owenetta            ???10000?10101??0100?0000???0?01?0?????0?????1??0?00
Araeoscelidia       000100010{12}00000000000000000010010000000001101011 00?00
Claudiosaurus       00100101121001010000101?01110001000000000101001 00?00
Younginiformes      ?010000011{02}0{01}1010100101?01011001000001001101011 00?00
Kuehneosauridae     0010000101012?111?00101?0101???10??????0?10101?00?01
Testudines          22?01{01}1111{02}1011{01}11000101101111111 10{01}1110021120 0{01}201?
Rhynchocephalia     00100001{01}12000111000101{01}01010111110{01}11111201011 00?00
Squamata            0010001111{02}10{01}111000101{01}0101{01}11111011111{01}2010110 0?01
Choristodera        ?010000011{02}121110?00101001111??10?101110?10?01100?00
Rhynchosauria       0010{01}00011010110000110110101111120101110110101110?00
Prolacertiformes    001000001201{12}111{01}001101?0101100120{01}{01}11{01}0{01}10101100?00
Trilophosaurus      10100000120100000001101101011001201011101101011 00?00
Archisauriformes
{01}010{01}{01}01{01}111011100011010 3{12}{01}11011201{01}11100101011 01000
Placodus            001011111101 21??1?00101001111?01000110000?01000020?0
Eosauropterygia
20101{01}1111{01}{01}{12}11?1?00101{01}0{01}11{01}101000110000201000 00??0
;
end;
```

```
begin mrbayes;
   log start filename=turtle_vardata_log.log replace;
   set autoclose=yes;
   mcmcp nruns=2 ngen=8000000 printfreq=100
       samplefreq=100 nchains=4 savebrlens=yes
       filename=turtle_vardata;
   mcmc;
   plot filename=turtle_vardata.run1.p;
```

```
   plot filename=turtle_vardata.run2.p;
   sumt filename=turtle_vardata burnin=10000 contype=halfcompat;
   log stop;
end;
```

Figure 1. Template of the *MRBAYES* script [1]) used in this study. The script creates 8000000 (*ngen*) Markov Chain ([6]) generations, (Monte Carlo, [7]) sampling every 100 (*samplefreq*) generations. The first 10000 (*burnin*) trees are discarded. Partial tree consensus (*contype*) is allowed. For definitions of other parameters used in this script, see [1]. A description of the character coding shown in the data matrix can be found in [5]

3.0 Results

Figure 2 is the tree generated by the script shown in Figure 1 running under [1]. The time to produce this tree was ~3 hours. Based on the system monitor, two of the four cores on the system performed 99% of the computational work. Total CPU utilization ranged from about 25% to 50%. The computation required approximately 1 GB memory.

```
/-Seymouriadae (1)
|
|- Diadectomorpha (2)
|
|    /- Caseidae (3)
|    |
| /--+   / Ophiacodontidae (4)
| |  |   |
| |  \---+   /--- Edaphosauridae (5)
| |      |   |
| |      \---+ / Sphenacodontidae (6)
+ |          | |
| |          \-+                  / Gorganopsia (7)
| |            \------------------+
| |                               \------------- Cynodontia (8)
| |
| |     /-- Captorhinidae (9)
| |     |
| |     |/- Paleothyris (10)
| |   /-+|
| |   | ||   /- Araeoscelidia (20)
\-+   | \+   |
  |   |  |   |         /------ Claudiosaurus (21)
  |   |  \---+         |
  |   |      |         |   /- Younginiformes (22)
  |   |      |         |   |
  |   |      \---------+   |         /------ Kuehneosauridae (23)
  |   |                |   |         |
  |   |                |   |         |     /-- Rhynchocephalia (25)
  |   |                |   |         |-----+
  |   |                \---+    /----+     \-- Squamata (26)
  |   |                    |    |    |
  |   |                    |    |    |        /-------- Placodus (32)
  |   |                    |    |    \--------+
  |   |                    |    |             \- Eosauropterygia (33)
  \--+                     \---------+
     |                              |  /------- Choristodera (27)
     |                              |  |
     |                              |  |        /----- Rhynchosauria (28)
     |                              |  |   /----+
     |                              \--+   |    \------- Trilophosaurus (30)
     |                                 | /-+
     |                                 | | \---- Archisauriform~ (31)
```

```
     |                                 \-+
     |                                   \---- Prolacertiform~ (29)
     |
     |  /- Millerettidae (11)
     |  |
     |  |             /--- Acleistorhinus (12)
     |  |      /------+
     \--+      |      \----- Lanthanosuchid~ (13)
        |      |
        |      |  / Macroleter (14)
        \------+  |
               |  |                                / Bradysaurus (15)
               |  |                                |
               |  |                   /------------+- Scutosaurus (16)
               \--+                   |            |
                  |      /------------+            \- Anthodon (17)
                  |      |            |
                  |      |            \------------------------- Testudines (24)
                  \------+
                         |   /--- Procolophon (18)
                         \---+
                             \-- Owenetta (19)

|---------| 0.200 expected changes per site

Calculating tree probabilities...

Credible sets of trees (14565 trees sampled):
   50 % credible set contains 128 trees
   90 % credible set contains 4171 trees
   95 % credible set contains 8565 trees
   99 % credible set contains 13365 trees
```

Figure 2. Phylogenetic tree produced by the script shown in Figure 1. Some taxon names are truncated; full names can be found in [5].

4.0 Conclusions and discussion

The results in Section 3.0 motivate several observations:

1. Figure 2 shows affinities between Testudines and several of the parareptiles (Procolophonidae, Bradysaurus, Anthodon, and Scutosaurus), as originally claimed in [1]. However, the analysis does not sustain the claim in [1] that Testudines is a sister group of the Sauropterygia (e.g., the pleisiosaurs, nothosaurs, and pachypleurosaurs).

2. The morphology of turtles derives characteristics from diverse reptilian groups that crosscut the diapsid/anapsid distinction. This is evidence that the diapsid/anapsid distinction is of limited taxonomic utility.

3. The results of this study generally agree with those of [3], which is based on Maximum Parsimony.

4. It is not unusual for different phylogenetic methods to produce somewhat different results when applied to the same data set. Except on data sets containing no more than a few tens of taxa, today's practical phylogenetic algorithms must use some approximations and heuristics in order to execute in tolerable time. The NJ algorithm used in [5] for example, restricts its combinatorial tree searches to a relatively localized region of tree space; the Bayesian algorithm used in the present study samples less than the full population of generations produced. Bayesian methods have the distinct theoretical advantage, however, that if the sample selected is large enough, the Central Limit Theorem ([8], Chap. 7) guarantees the solution based on the sample

will converge to the population distribution of trees; NJ cannot be guaranteed to satisfy this criterion.

5.0 Acknowledgements

This work benefited from discussions with Tony Pawlicki, with Town Peterson and Kris Krishtalka of the University of Kansas Biodiversity Institute, and with Joan Hunt of the University of Kansas Medical Center. For any problems that remain, I am solely responsible.

6.0 References

[1] Ronquist F and Huelsenbeck JP. MRBAYES 3: Bayesian phylogenetic inference under mixed models. *Bioinformatics* 19 (2003), 1572-1574. Software is available at
Ronquist F and Huelsenbeck JP. MRBAYES v3.1.2 for 64-bit Windows. http://sourceforge.net/projects/mrbayes/files/mrbayes/3.2.1/mrbayes-3.2.1_installer_WINx64.msi/download. 2012.

[2] Felsenstein J. *Inferring Phylogenies.* Sinauer Associates. 2004.

[3] Lee MSY. The origin of the turtle body plan: bridging a famous morphological gap. *Science* 261 (1993), 1716-1720.

[4] Rieppel O and deBraga M. Turtles as diapsid reptiles. *Nature*, Vol. 384 (5 December 1996), 453-455.

[5] O. Rieppel and M. deBraga. Supplementary information for [4] . This data was once available on the *Nature* web site, URL http://www.nature.com, but no longer appears to be. A copy to the morphological data, together with a description of the morphological characters (and associated references) can be obtained from me on request.

[6] Gilks WR, Richardson S, and Spiegelhalter DJ. *Markov Chain Monte Carlo in Practice.* Chapman and Hall. 1996.

[7] Liu JS. *Monte Carlo Strategies in Scientific Computing.* Springer. 2001.

[8] Chung KL. *A Course in Probability Theory.* Third Edition. Academic Press. 2001.

Modelling and Simulation of Regional Cerebral Circulation

H. Pranevicius[1,2], D. Naujokaitis[1], V. Pilkauskas[1], O. Pranevicius[3], M. Pranevicius[4]

[1]*Department of Informatics, Kaunas University of Technology Studentu St. 56-301, LT - 51424 Kaunas, Lithuania*

[2]*Informatic faculty, Vytautas Magnus University*

[3]*Hospital Queens Fleshing, NY, USA*

[4]*Albert Einstein College of Medicine, NY, USA*

***Abstract*— Regional cerebral perfusion pressure (rCPP) drives regional cerebral blood flow (rCBF) in the area surrounding stroke. The rCPP is a difference between the local inflow and outflow pressures, the latter being either venous or tissue pressure, whichever is higher. Therefore understanding of rCBF distribution after stroke requires creation of the unified approach reflecting rCBF and rCPP relationship.**

We used hybrid systems simulation method based on the piece-linear aggregate (PLA) formalism in which integrators for differential equations are quantised into PLA models. We modelled rCBF by the modified Windkessel circulation model: we added variable resistance element, dependent on the external compression, and variable capacitance element, reflecting transmural pressure/volume relationship of the blood vessel, thus achieving ability to model regional compression of cerebral circulation. We demonstrated that modified Windkessel element can model phenomenon of rCPP reduction by local compression.

Index Simulation, Windkessel model, Hybrid Temporal-Spatial Simulation, Piece Linear Aggregates.

1 Introduction

Measurement of regional cerebral circulation has been carried out since 1940s with the use of diffusible inert gases (Kety, et al., 1948). That was followed by introduction of intravascular X-ray contrast media[1], intravascular radio-tracers[2], positron emission tomography (PET)[3], single-photon emission computed tomography (SPECT)[4], and magnetic resonance imaging (MRI), in particularly with intravascular contrast media[5]. These methods allow measurements of the important indicators of regional cerebral circulation: cerebral blood flow (CBF), cerebral vascular mean transit time (MTT), and cerebral blood volume (CBV), all of which can be measured by PET, while MTT and CBV can be measured by MRI with intravascular contrast media. However all these methods only allow visualizing three-dimensional distribution of blood flow and/or blood volume. Such images are the end result of the forces driving blood flow, yet these forces themselves remain hidden from the direct visualisation, and can be inferred only from the images obtained.

Visualization of flow is assumed to reflect distribution of vascular resistance. This may be oversimplification in cases where effective outflow pressure varies between the regions. Description of vascular network requires presentation of three dimensional distribution of regional cerebro vascular resistances (rCVR) and perfusion pressures (rCPP) as the determinants of regional cerebral blood flow: rCBF=rCPP/rCVR. From there, correction of cerebral blood flow maldistribution requires determination if rCVR or rCPP is the primary cause of decreased flow. Then therapeutic maneuvers could be prioritized in the direction of re-canalization or loading condition adjustment.

Creating regional circulation model is the first step in solving the inverse problem -- reconstruction of rCPP and rCVR from ABP and CBF in time.

In order for image to reflect an underlying physiology, the image of circulation driving forces must be obtained. The primary blood flow driving force at regional and global level alike is perfusion pressure. At the regional level it has its own three-dimensional distribution, which might or might not mirror the three-dimensional distribution of flow. Capacity to visualize this three-dimensional distribution of regional perfusion pressures would add another dimension in diagnosis and treatment of cerebral circulation disturbances. Most recent success in model driven non-invasive blood pressure measurement intracranial pressure points to the direction of how this might be accomplished. It would have to be imaging, driven by regional circulation model and its verification, combined with the continuous blood pressure monitoring. Essential step in such endeavour is simulation of regional cerebral circulation what is presented in this article.

We were first to introduce the use of nonlinear Starling resistor model to describe the effects of compartmental tissue pressure on regional cerebral perfusion pressure (rCPP) and regional cerebral blood flow (rCBF)[6]. Others tried to emulate this approach by using our steady state model with the source of alternating flow [7]. However such approach is erroneous when the dynamic flow is simplistically added to the steady state model: blood redistribution dynamics in this case should be accounted for by adding inductive and capacitive elements.

Starling resistor mimics vascular waterfall by assuming that local perfusion pressure is a difference between the inflow pressure and either compartmental tissue or venous pressure, whichever is higher. This model was adequate to simulate steady state blood flow distribution between two or three compartments, but did not address complexity of the dynamics of blood redistribution through multiple networks. Moreover, depending on the initial conditions and dynamics of the transition, multiple solutions for blood flow distribution are possible. To address these problems, Starling resistor model had to be upgraded with the compliance and inductivity to simulate effects of inertia and effects of transmural pressure on the compartmental vascular volume.

2 Blood vessel model

We created a lumped model for blood vessel compartment (Fig. 1), containing variable Starling resistor, nonlinear capacitor, inductivity and additional resistors. In this model we simulated compartmental pressure by additional variable E.

2.1 Windkessel model

Windkessel model is widely used to simulate hemodynamic. Windkessel in German is translated as 'air chamber', and represents elastic reservoir, namely elastic arteries[8]. Arteries distend when blood pressure rises during systole and recoil when blood pressure falls during diastole. Therefore Windkessel element incorporates inductive, capacitance and resistive elements, yet it does not take into account fluctuations of blood volume and outflow resistance due to regional transmural pressure.

Standard Windkessel model incorporates 2, 3 or 4 elements (2-WM, 3-WM, 4-WM). 2-WM consists of parallel resistor and capacitance. 3-WM adds resistor in series. 4WM adds inductivity in series or parallel with additional resistor to 2-WM.

Our modification of Windkessel model incorporates inductivity L, nonlinear resistor R and nonlinear capacitor C (Fig. 1). We incorporated additional resistors R_1, R_2 and R_3 to simulate all classic configurations of Windkessel model (2-WM, 3-WM and both versions of 4_WM). Reduced model (2-WM) has $L=0$, $R_1=R_2=R_3=0$.

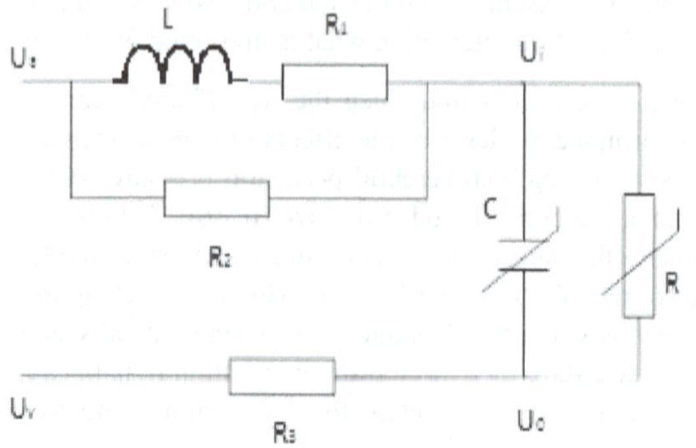

Fig. 1. Modification of Windkessel model with variable Starling resistance and nonlinear capacitance, both determined by the transmural pressure.

Inductivity L simulates effects of inertia. Potentials U_a, U_v simulate inflow and outflow pressure, furthermore difference between U_a and U_v is regional cerebral perfusion pressure (rCPP).

2.2 Starling resistor

We used nonlinear resistor R to describe effects of compartmental tissue pressure on the regional cerebral perfusion pressure (rCPP) and regional cerebral blood flow (rCBF)[6]. Starling resistor R depends on the external compression.

Starling resistor R is described by following equation:

$$R(U_i,U_o,U_e)=\begin{cases} R_0, & U_s(U_i,U_o,U_e)=0 \\ & \wedge(U_e<U_i \vee U_e<U_o), \\ \infty, & U_s(U_i,U_o,U_e)=0 \\ & \wedge U_e>U_i \wedge U_e>U_o, \\ \dfrac{R_0(U_i-U_o)}{U_s(U_i,U_o,U_e)}, & U_s(U_i,U_o,U_e)>0, \end{cases} \quad (1)$$

Where R_0 is selected minimum value of Starling resistance R, when external pressure is equal zero, $\wedge,\vee$ is AND, OR operators. U_i,U_o,U_e are inflow, outflow and external pressure respectively. Function $U_s(U_i,U_o,U_e)$ describes transmural pressure of blood vessel (2):

$$\begin{aligned} U_s(U_i,U_o,U_e) &= (U_i-U_o)H(U_i,U_e)H(U_o,U_e)+ \\ &+(U_i-U_e)H(U_i,U_o)H(U_e,U_o)H(U_i,U_e)+ \\ &+(U_e-U_o)H(U_o,U_i)H(U_e,U_i)H(U_o,U_e). \end{aligned} \quad (2)$$

where H is the Heaviside function (3):

$$H(x,y)=\begin{cases} 0, & x-y<0, \\ \dfrac{1}{2}, & x-y=0, \\ 1, & x-y>0. \end{cases} \quad (3)$$

2.3 Nonlinear capacitance

Variable capacitance C of Windkessel model incorporates transmural pressure / volume relationship of the blood vessels, which generally has sigmoid, nonlinear form[6][8]. Variable capacitance C and electrical charge Q is described by (4) and (5), respectively:

$$C(U_s)=\frac{Q_0 k e^{-kU_s}}{\left(1+e^{-kU_s}\right)^2}, \quad (4)$$

$$Q(U_s)=\frac{Q_0}{1+e^{-kU_s}}, \quad (5)$$

where Q_0 represents maximal blood volume, capacitance $C(U_s)$ is describing transmural pressure-blood volume relationship differential, k – is slope constant. $Q(U_s)$ is blood volume dependence on transmural pressure.

2.4 Physiological interpretation

Modified Starling resistor allows to simulate one of the most interesting and under-researched phenomenon of the cerebral blood flow circulation - its regional distribution. Blood flow distribution through the network of circulatory segments is determined not only by the regional resistances, but also by the local perfusion pressures (difference between inflow and tissue compartment pressures). Using variable resistance, Starling modification of Windkessel model allows simulation of local perfusion pressure distribution. The goal of such simulation is to obtain realistic regional blood flow and blood volume distribution models simulating effects of arterial, venous, and local tissue pressures, and allowing to correlate simulation results with rCBF/rCBV (regional cerebral blood flow and regional cerebral blood volume) maps from CT (computer tomography) or MR (magnetic resonance) angiograms with the intent to optimise rCPP after stroke.

3 Hybrid aggregate model

Cerebral blood flow is dynamic system that exhibits both continuous and discreet dynamic behaviour. For simulation of distribution of the blood flow between compartments we used hybrid systems simulation method based on PLA formalism [9].

PLA is a special case of automaton models. In the application of the PLA approach for system specification, the system is represented as a set of interacting piece-linear aggregates. The PLA is taken as an object defined by a set of states Z, input signals X, and output signals Y. Behaviour of an aggregate is considered in a set of time moments $t \in T$. States $z \in Z$, input signals $x \in X$, and output signals $y \in Y$ are considered to be time functions. Transition and output operators, H and G correspondingly, must be known as well.

The state $z \in Z$ of the piece-linear aggregate is $z(t) = (v(t), z_v(t))$, where $v(t)$ is a discrete state component taking values on a countable set of values; and $z_v(t)$ is a continuous component comprising of $z_1(t), z_2(t), ..., z_{v_k}(t)$ coordinates.

When there are no inputs, an aggregate state changes as follows: $v(t) = \text{const}$, $\frac{dz_v(t)}{dt} = -a_v$, where $a_v = (a_{v_1}, a_{v_2}, ..., a_{v_k})$ is a constant vector.

The state of the aggregate can change in two cases only: when an input signal arrives at the aggregate or when a continuous component acquires a definite value.

. The set of events E which may take place in the aggregate is divided into two non-intersecting subsets $E = E' \cup E''$. The subset $E' = \{e'_1, e'_2, ..., e'_N\}$ comprises classes of events (or simply events) e'_i, $i = \overline{1,N}$ resulting from the arrival of input signals from the set $X = \{x_1, x_2, ..., x_N\}$. The class of events $e''_i = \{e''_{ij}, j = \overline{1,\infty}\}$, where e''_{ij} is an event from the class of events e''_i taking place the j-th time since the moment t_0. The events from the subset E' are called external events. The events from the subset $E'' = \{e''_1, e''_2, ..., e''_f\}$ are called internal events, where $e''_i = \{e''_{ij}, j = \overline{1,\infty}, i = \overline{1,f}\}$ are the classes of the aggregate internal events. Here, f determines the number of operations taking place in the aggregate. The events in the set E'' indicate the end of the operations taking place in the aggregate.

For every class of events e''_i from the subset E'', control sequences are specified $\left\{\xi_j^{(i)}\right\}$, where $\xi_j^{(i)}$ – the duration of the operation, which is followed by the event e''_{ij} as well as event counters $\{r(e''_i, t_m)\}$, where $\{r(e''_i, t_m)\}$, $i = \overline{1,f}$ is the number of events from the class e''_i taken place in the time interval $[t_0, t_m]$.

In order to determine start and end moments of operation, taking place in the aggregate the so-called control sums $\{s(e''_i, t_m)\}$, $\{w(e''_i, t_m)\}$, $i = \overline{1,f}$ are introduced, where $s(e''_i, t_m)$ – the time moment of the start of operation followed by an event from the class e''_i. This time moment is indeterminate if the operation was not started; $w(e''_i, t_m)$ is the time moment of the end of the operation followed by the event from the class e''_i. In case of non-priority operations, the control sum $w(e''_i, t_m)$ is determined in the following way: $w(e''_i, t_m) = s'(e''_i, t_m) + \xi_{r(e''_i, t_m)+1}$, if at moment t_m an operation is taking place, which is followed by the event e_i; in the opposite case $w(e''_i, t_m) = \infty$. The infinity symbol (∞) is used to denote the undefined values of the variables.

The continuous component of aggregate state $z_v(t_m) = \{w(e''_1, t_m), w(e''_2, t_m), ... w(e''_f, t_m)\}$, where $w(e''_i, t_m)$ the time moment, when event e''_i will occur. Always $w(e''_i, t_m) \geq t_m$.

When the state of the system $z(t_m)$, $m = 0, 1, 2, ...$ is known, the moment t_{m+1} of the following event is determined by a moment of input signal arrival to the aggregate or by the equation:

$$t_{m+1} = \min\{w(e''_i, t_m)\}, i = \overline{1,f}.$$

The operator H states the new aggregate state.

$$z(t_{m+1}) = H[z(t_m), e_i], e_i \in E' \cup E''.$$

The output signals y_i from the set of output signals $Y = \{y_1, y_2, \ldots y_m\}$ can be generated by an aggregate only at occurrence moments of events from the subsets E' and E''. The operator G determines the content of the output signals:

$$y = G[z(t_m), e_i], e_i \in E' \cup E'', y \in Y.$$

For hybrid aggregate model [9], in time intervals $t_m < t < t_{m+1}, v(t_m) = \text{const}$ and continuous coordinates model is described by the ordinary differential equations (ODE)

$$\frac{dz_v(t)}{dt} = f[t, z_v(t), x(t)].$$

For realization of hybrid aggregate model Quantized State System (QSS) method is used [10]. Fig. 2 illustrates simulation of ODE and each component is described using PLA formalism [9]

For creation of hybrid aggregate imitators we used PLASim simulation library [11]. The PLASim is an object-oriented library for discrete-event simulation of models created using aggregate formalism. The PLASim's current version written in C# for NET Framework 4.0 and has packages that support random number generation, statistical collection, basic reporting with data visualization and discrete-event simulation. The development of a simulation model is based on sub-classing the SimulationModel class that provides the primary recurring actions within a simulation and event scheduling and handling. The user adds developed aggregates (model elements) based on sub-classing the Aggregate class, to an instance of Model and then executes the simulation.

We expanded the PLA aggregate model simulation ability in such a way that at each discrete quantized time moment continuous coordinates value can be recalculated using derivative value of simulated function. We used this PLA expansion to create key component of the hybrid model - an integrator aggregate ∫ (Fig. 2).

Below is given modified QSS model integrator aggregate specification in PLA formalization language:

1. Set of input signals $X = \{S_1(t_m)\}$,

where $S_1(t_m) \in R$ - function derivation, $S_1(t_m) = \frac{dX_1}{dt}$.

2. Set of output signals $Y = \{Q_j(t_m)\} j = 1, .. r$,

where $Q_j(t_m)$ - quantized function value.

3. Set of external events $E' = \{e_1'\}$,

where e_1' - given a new derivation value.

4. Set of internal events $E'' = \{e''_1\}$,

where e''_1 function reaches next quantum value.

5. Discrete component of state $v(t_m) = \{X_1(t_m), x_1'(t_m), j_1(t_m)\}$,

where $X_1(t_m) \in R$ – calculated function;

$x_1'(t_m) \in R$ – derivation of function;

$j_1(t_m) \in Z$ – number of quantized function value.

6. Continuous part of state $z_v(t_m) = \{w(e_1'', t_m)\}$,

$w(e_1'', t_m)$ – time point of next internal event,

$$w(e_1'', t_m) = \begin{cases} < \infty, x_1'(t_m) \neq 0; \\ \infty, \text{otherwise}. \end{cases}$$

7. Controlling sequences $e_1' \mapsto \{\sigma_1\}$, $e_1'' \mapsto \{\sigma_2\}$

where σ_1 and σ_2 time intervals after which the function X_1 will reach the next quantized value after external event, after internal event:

$$\sigma_1 = \begin{cases} \frac{Q_{j_1(t_{m-1})+1} - (X_1(t_{m-1}) + (t_m - t_{m-1}) \cdot x_1'(t_{m-1}))}{S_1(t_m)}, & S_1(t_m) > 0; \\ \frac{(X_1(t_{m-1}) + (t_m - t_{m-1}) \cdot x_1'(t_{m-1})) - (Q_{j_1(t_{m-1})-1} - \varepsilon)}{|S_1(t_m)|}, & S_1(t_m) < 0; \\ \infty, \quad S_1(t_m) = 0, \end{cases}$$

$$\sigma_2 = \begin{cases} \frac{Q_{j_2(t_{m-1})+2} - (X_2(t_{m-1}) + (t_m - t_{m-1}) \cdot x_2'(t_{m-1}))}{x_2'(t_{m-1})}, & x_2'(t_{m-1}) > 0; \\ \frac{(X_2(t_{m-1}) + (t_m - t_{m-1}) \cdot x_2'(t_m)) - (Q_{j_2(t_{m-1})-1} - \varepsilon)}{|x_2'(t_{m-1})|}, & x_2'(t_{m-1}) < 0; \\ \infty, \quad x_2'(t_{m-1}) = 0, \end{cases}$$

where $\lfloor z \rfloor$ – whole part of the number z,

ε - hysteresis window,

ΔQ - quantum value,

$Q_1, Q_2, .. Q_n$ - grid of function discretization.

8. Initial state:

$$v(t_0) = \{X_1(t_0), x_1'(t_0), j_1(f(X_1(t_0)))\};$$

$$z_v(t_0) = \{t_0 + \sigma_2\}.$$

9. The transition and the output operators:

$H(e_1'(S_1(t_m)))$: / came new value of the derivative

/ $X_1(t_m) = X_1(t_{m-1}) + (t_m - t_{m-1}) \cdot x_1'(t_{m-1})$;

$x_1'(t_m) = S_1(t_m)$;

$j_1(t_m) = j_1(t_{m-1})$;

$w(e_1', t_{m+1}) = t_m + \sigma_1$.

10. $H(e''_1)$: / achieved new quantified value of function X_1/

$X_1(t_m) = X_1(t_{m-1}) + (t_m - t_{m-1}) \cdot x_1'(t_{m-1})$;

$x_1'(t_m) = x_1'(t_{m-1})$;

$j_1(t_m) = j_1(t_{m-1}) + \text{sgn}(x_1'(t_{m-1}))$;

$w(e_1'', t_{m+1}) = t_m + \sigma_2$.

$G(e_1'')$: $y = Q_{j_1(t_{m-1}) + \text{sgn}(x_1'(t_{m-1}))}$.

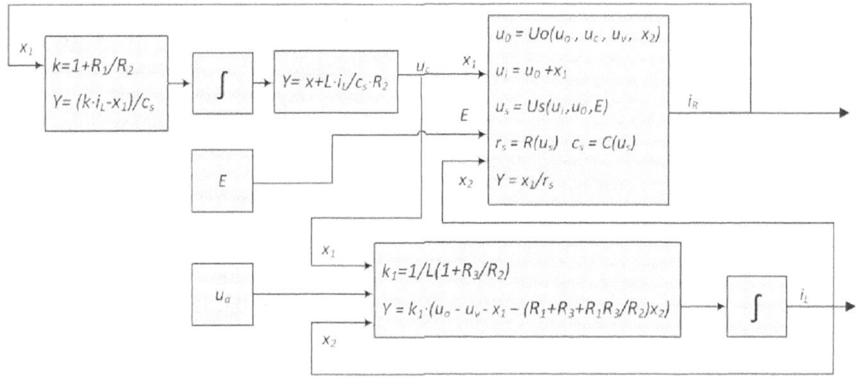

Fig. 2. Representation of the Windkessel model in PLA formalism as described by (7, 8) equations systems.

4 Blood vessel simulation

Blood vessel model (Fig. 1) is described by equations system, and then converted to PLA. According to the Kirchhoff law for electrical circuits[12]:

$$\begin{cases} u(t) = i_L(t)R_1 + L\dfrac{di_L(t)}{dt} + i_R(t)R + i_3(t)R_3, \\ u(t) = i_2(t)R_2 + \dfrac{1}{C}\int i_C(t)dt + i_3(t)R_3, \\ 0 = i_L(t)R_1 + L\dfrac{di_L(t)}{dt} - i_2(t)R_2, \\ 0 = i_R(t)R - \dfrac{1}{C}\int i_C(t)dt, \\ i_L(t) + i_2(t) = i_C(t) + i_R(t), \\ i_C(t) + i_R(t) = i_3(t). \end{cases} \quad (6)$$

Voltage $u(t)$ in equation system (6) is described by $u(t) = u_a(t) - u_v(t)$.

Now we can rewrite (6) as hybrid equations system (7) using PLA formalism.

$$\begin{cases} u_C(t) = \dfrac{1}{C}\int\left(\left(1+\dfrac{R_1}{R_2}\right)i_L(t) - \dfrac{u_C(t)}{R}\right)dt + \dfrac{L}{C\cdot R_2}i_L(t), \\ i_L(t) = \dfrac{1}{L\left(1+\dfrac{R_3}{R_2}\right)}\int\left(u(t) - \left(R_1 + R_3 + \dfrac{R_1R_3}{R_2}\right)i_L(t) - u_C(t)\right)dt. \end{cases}$$

(7)

Equations $u_i(t)$ and $u_o(t)$ on system (8) is used to imitate nonlinear elements R and C of Windkessel model.

$$\begin{cases} u_C(t) = R\cdot i_R(t), \\ u_0(t) = u_v(t) + \dfrac{R_3}{\left(1+\dfrac{R_3}{R_2}\right)}\left(\dfrac{u(t)}{R_2} + i_L(t) - \dfrac{u_C(t)}{R_2}\right), \\ u_i(t) = u_0(t) + u_C(t). \end{cases} \quad (8)$$

Equations system (7 and 8) was used for aggregates model, as shown in Fig. 2, which was programmed in our simulation system.

Below are simulation results of Windkessel model (Fig. 1) using nonlinear capacitor (4) and nonlinear resistor (1). To estimate model parameters we used arterial blood pressure (ABP) and trans cranial doppler cerebral blood flow velocity from [13]. Model parameters (L, Ro, qo, k) were selected to minimize mean quadratic deviation of modeled and measured rCBFV.

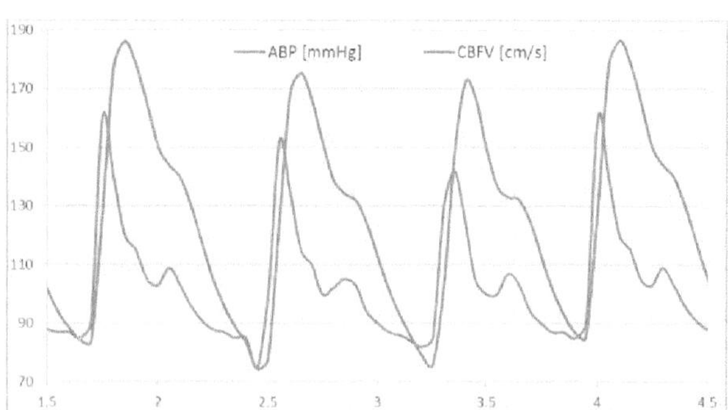

Fig. 3. ABP (blue) and simulated CBFV (red). X-axis- time in seconds.

For simulation we used experimentally measure the ABP data from Hwang PhD Thesis (2012). Besides in Fig. 3 the shape of CBFV is depended of ABP [13].

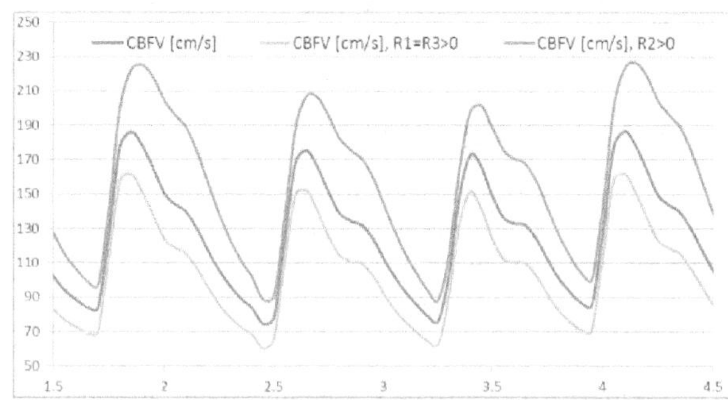

Fig. 4. Change of CBFV depending on additional resistors.

Effect of adding R_1, R_2 and R_3 on CBFV: Resistors in series (R_2 and R_3, 3-WM) decrease CBF pulse amplitude, while resistor R_2 in parallel with inductance (L) decreases effect of inductance and increases CBF pulse amplitude (Fig. 4), shape of CBF is unchanged.

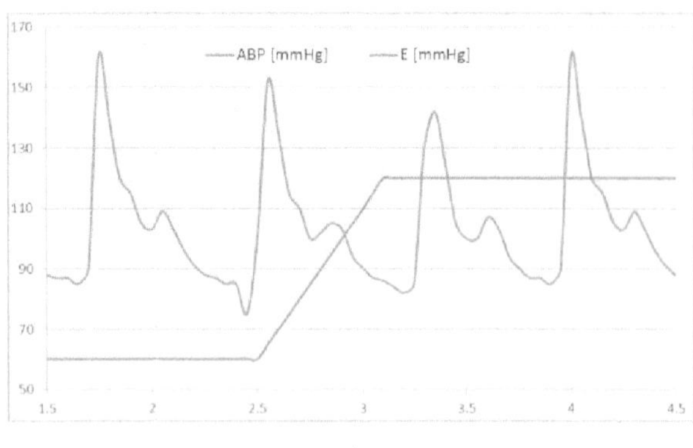

a)

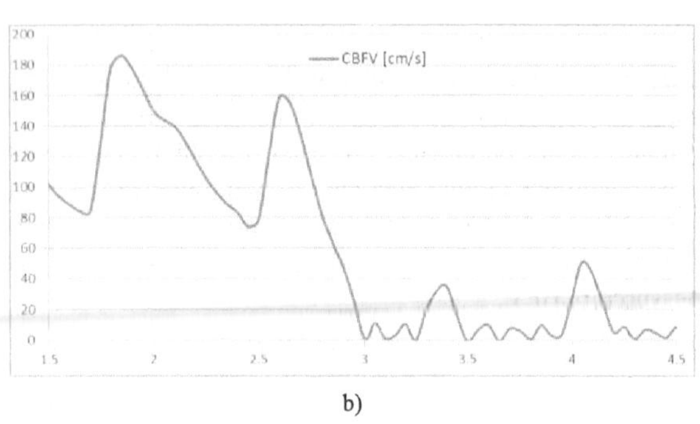

b)

Fig. 5. Change of CBFV depending on compartmental pressure.

Simulation of step increase in compartmental pressure E. As compartment pressure increases to mean arterial pressure (Fig 5, a), CBF ceases with preservation of low during systole and appearance of small amplitude back and forth oscillations (Fig. 5, b).

5 Conclusions

The research showed that modification of Windkessel model, with variable Starling resistor and nonlinear capacitor could be used to simulate dynamic blood flow, blood volume and resistance fluctuations in the collapsible vessel model. Model parameters and state equations have to be fitted with experimental data and fluid dynamics models to determine adequacy of approximation.

6 Acknowledgements

This work was supported by the Research Council of Lithuania for collaboration Lithuania and USA scientists under the grant MIT-074/2012.

7 References

[1] T. Greitz, "A radiologic study of the brain circulation by rapid serial angiography of the carotid artery.," *Acta Radiol,* pp. 1-123, 1956.

[2] W. Oldendorf, "Measurement of the mean transit time of cerebral circulation by external detection of an intravenously injected radioisotope.," *J Nucl Med,* pp. 382-398, 1962.

[3] G. Sette, J. Baron, B. Mazoyer, M. Levasseur, S. Pappata and C. Crouzel, "Local brain haemodynamics and oxygen metabolism in cerebrovascular disease. Positron emission tomography.," *Brain,* pp. 931-951, 1989.

[4] E. Shimosegawa, J. Hatazawa, A. Inugami, H. Fujita, T. Ogawa and Y. e. a. Aizawa, "Cerebral infarction within six hours of onset: prediction of completed infarction with technetium-99m-HMPAO SPECT.," *J Nucl Med,* pp. 1097-1103, 1994.

[5] W. Schreiber, F. Guckel, P. Stritzke, P. Schmiedek, A. Schwartz and G. Brix, "Cerebral blood flow and cerebrovascular reserve capacity: estimation by dynamic magnetic resonance imaging.," *J Cereb Blood Flow Metab,* pp. 1143-1156, 1998.

[6] O. Pranevicius, M. Pranevicius, H. Pranevicius and D. Liebeskind, "Transition to Collateral Flow After Arterial Occlusion Predisposes to Cerebral Venous Steal.," *Stroke,* pp. 575-579, 2012.

[7] A. Mikuckas, A. Venckauskas and I. Mikuckiene, "Dynamic Extension of Starling Resistor Model.," *Electronics and Electrical Engineering,* 2012.

[8] S. Berger, "Flow in large blood vessels, Fluid Dynamics in Biology," *Contemporary Mathematics,* pp. 479-518, 1992.

[9] H. Pranevicius, L. Simaitis, M. Pranevicius and O. Pranevicius, "Piece-linear aggregates for formal specification and simulation of hybrid systems: pharmacokinetics patient-controlled analgesia.," *Electronics and Electrical Engineering,* pp. 81-84, 2011.

[10] E. Kofman, "Discreet Event Simulation of Hybrid Systems.," *SIAM Journal on Scientific Computing,* pp. 1771-1797, 2004.

[11] G. Guginis and V. Pilkauskas, "The system for generating simulation model code from the PLA specifications.," in *Information Technologies, 2008* , Kaunas, 2008.

[12] S. Masiokas, Elektrotechnika. The second edition., Kaunas: "Candela", 1994.

[13] I. T. Hwang, Frequency domain model-based intracranial pressure estimation., Massachusetts: PhD Thesis. Massachusetts Institute of Technology, 2012.

[14] D. Kerner, "Solving Windkessel Models with MLAB," [Online]. Available: www.civilized.com.

[15] S. Kety and C. Schmidt, "The nitrous oxide method for the quantitative determination of cerebral blood flow in man: theory, procedure and normal values.," *J Clin Invest,* pp. 476-483, 1948.

[16] O. Pranevicius, M. Pranevicius and D. Liebeskind, "Partial aortic occlusion and cerebral venous steal: venous effects of arterial manipulation in acute stroke.," *Stroke,* pp. 1478-1481, 2011.

A Maximum Entropy/Ecological Niche Modeling Prediction of the Potential Distribution of Leischmaniasis under Climate Change

Jack K. Horner
P.O. Box 266
Los Alamos NM 87544 USA

BIOCOMP 2013

Abstract

Leishmaniasis is a life-threatening disease caused by protozoan parasites of the genus Leishmania and is transmitted by the bite of several species of sand fly (subfamily Phlebotominae). Global climate change has the potential to alter the distribution of these insect vectors. Here I use maximum entropy (maxent) ecological niche modeling (ENM) and the Intergovernmental Panel on Climate Change(IPCC)-vetted MK3.0/ Scenario A1B global climate model to predict the potential geographic distribution of Lutzomyia longipalpis (here regarded as proxy for leischmaniasis distribution) by the year 2060. The simulation predicts that leischmaniasis will retain its current distribution in South America, and could spread to the east coast of Africa and the northern half of Australia.

Keywords: Leischmaniasis, ecological niche modeling, epidemiology, maximum entropy

1.0 Introduction

1.1 Overview of Leischmaniasis

Leishmaniasis is a life-threatening disease caused by protozoan parasites of the genus *Leishmania* and is transmitted by the bite of several species of sand fly (subfamily Phlebotominae; [8]).

The most common forms leischmaniasis are cutaneous leishmaniasis, which causes skin sores, and visceral leishmaniasis, which affects several internal organs (usually spleen, liver, and bone marrow) ([8]). The number of new cases of cutaneous leishmaniasis each year in the world is thought to be about 1.5 million. The number of new cases of visceral leishmaniasis is estimated to be about 500,000. ([8]).

Cutaneous leishmaniasis ulcers from several *Leishmania* species may heal without treatment, although healing usually takes months and will leave a scar. The pentavalent antimonial drugs, sodium stibogluconate and meglumine antimoniate, remain the most widely used antileishmanial agents, but are increasingly being replaced by safer therapeutics ([10]).

In the absence of treatment, the case-fatality rate of visceral leishmaniasis is >90 percent. Mortality is often due to hemorrhagic or infectious complications. Liposomal amphotericin B is the drug with the highest therapeutic efficacy and the most favorable safety profile for the visceral form of the disease. Supportive therapy to address nutritional status, concomitant anemia, hemorrhagic complications, and secondary infections is essential to optimize treatment outcomes and maximize survival ([10]).

1.2 Overview of maximum entropy (Maxent) ENM

The general problem of ENM can be stated as follows. Given the distribution of a set S of species in a geographic region G (e.g., Central America) with associated ecological variables E (e.g., temperature, precipitation, slope, aspect, altitude), predict the potential distribution of S in geographic region G' ≠ G (e.g., the United States) . Roughly speaking, this amounts to predicting which parts of G' have an ecological system state "like" that part of G which is populated by S. "Like" in this context is cast in terms of statistical measures.

There are several ENM algorithms ([11]); among the more widely used is the maximum entropy method.

In the maximum entropy method (maxent), we are given a set of samples from a distribution over some space, together with a set of features (real-valued functions) on this space. The objective of maxent is to estimate the target distribution by finding the distribution of maximum entropy (i.e., that is closest to uniform) subject to the constraint that the expected value of each feature under this estimated distribution matches its empirical average. This turns out to be equivalent, under convex duality, to finding the maximum likelihood Gibbs distribution (i.e., distribution that is exponential in a linear combination of the features) ([16], Chap. 2).

For maxent ENM, the occurrence localities of the species serve as the sample points, the geographical region of interest is the space on which this distribution is defined, and the features are the environmental variables (or functions thereof) ([5]).

2.0 Method

A description of the nominal current distribution of *Lutzomyia longipalpis*, here used as a proxy for the distribution of the Phlebotominae, was obtained from [2] on 21 October 2012, yielding 164 species-occurrences (= species_name+species_locations). The species name and locations from this data were exported to a CSV *L. longipalpis*-occurrence training data file.

Any predictive ENM method requires an environmental model. The model used in this study is based on the MK3.0 ([3]) climate model, Scenario SRES A1B. MK3.0 is vetted by the Intergovernmental Panel on Climate Change (IPCC) and is included in the IPCC Fourth Assessment Report (IPCC4, [14]).

The present study uses a CIAT-generated 10-arc-minute downscaling (specifically by the so-called "Delta method"; [15]) of the MK3.0 native outputs ([6]). The climate-models grids for Mean Temperature (file csiro_mk3_0_sres_a1b_2050s_tmean_10min_no_tile_asc-1350677208.zip) and Precipitation (file csiro_mk3_0_sres_a1b_2050s_prec_10min_no_tile_asc-1350677358.zip) were downloaded from the CIAT web site ([6]), using download parameters:

- Method: Delta
- Scenario: SRES A1B ([14])
- Period: 2050s
- Variables: Precipitation, Mean Temperature
- Resolution: 10 (arc-)minutes
- Format: ASCII Grid

These files were unzipped and checked for conformity to the ASCII Grid format ([13]) using the Raster/Conversion function of the *Desktop QGIS* ([7]) software.

A preliminary maximum-entropy-based ([5]) study using the MaxEnt software ([1]) was performed to determine which of the 12 mean-temperature, and 12 precipitation files climate-model grids most affected the predictions. If the sum of the percent contribution of the four environmental variables with the highest percent contribution was ≥ 95%, these four variables were used for subsequent predictions; else, the analysis was terminated.

The *MaxEnt* maximum entropy ENM software ([1],[5]; an implementation of the maxent method can also be found in [4]) was used to predict the *L. longipalpis* distribution, circa 2060. The *MaxEnt* parameters were:

- Environmental layers used (all continuous): prec_7 prec_8 tmean_7 tmean_8
- Regularization values: linear/quadratic/product: 0.050, categorical: 0.250, threshold: 1.000, hinge: 0.500
- Feature types used: product linear quadratic hinge threshold
- responsecurves: true
- jackknife: true
- outputformat: raw
- samplesfile: C:\MaxEnt\2050_Leisch_MK3_A1B\longipalpus_occurrences.csv
- environmentallayers: C:\MaxEnt\2050_Leisch_MK3_A1B

All software was executed on a Dell Inspiron 545 with an Intel Core2 Quad CPU Q8200 clocked at 2.33 GHz, with 8.00 GB RAM, under *Windows Vista Home Premium/SP2.*

3.0 Results

Figure 1 shows the nominal current, and predicted potential, distributions of *L. longipalpis* under the conditions described in Section 2.0. The current distribution is essentially confined to South America, mainly in Brazil. Figure 2 shows the receiver operating characteristic (ROC, [9]) curve for this simulation.

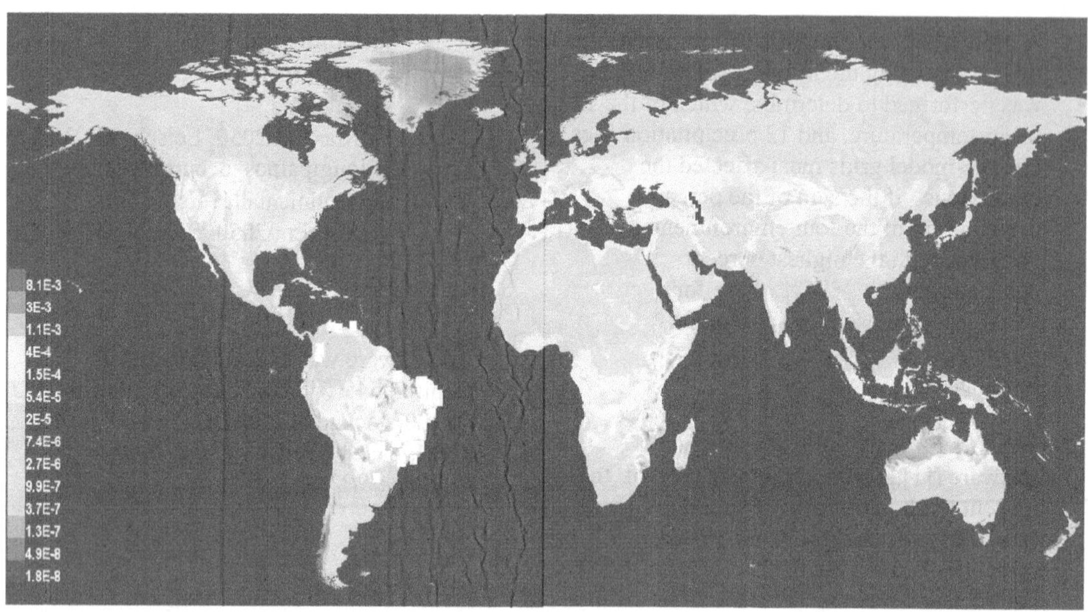

Figure 1. Current and predicted potential distribution of *L. longipalpis* by 2060 under the conditions described in Section 2.0 ("raw" output scaling). Darker greys colors show areas with better predicted conditions. White squares show the current presence locations used for training.

The computation utilized ~25% of the CPU and ~2 GB memory on the platform described in Section 2.0, as measured on the system monitor. The time to solution for the simulation was ~5-20 minutes for each of the 15 setups described in Section 2.0, depending on how many environmental variables were in a setup.

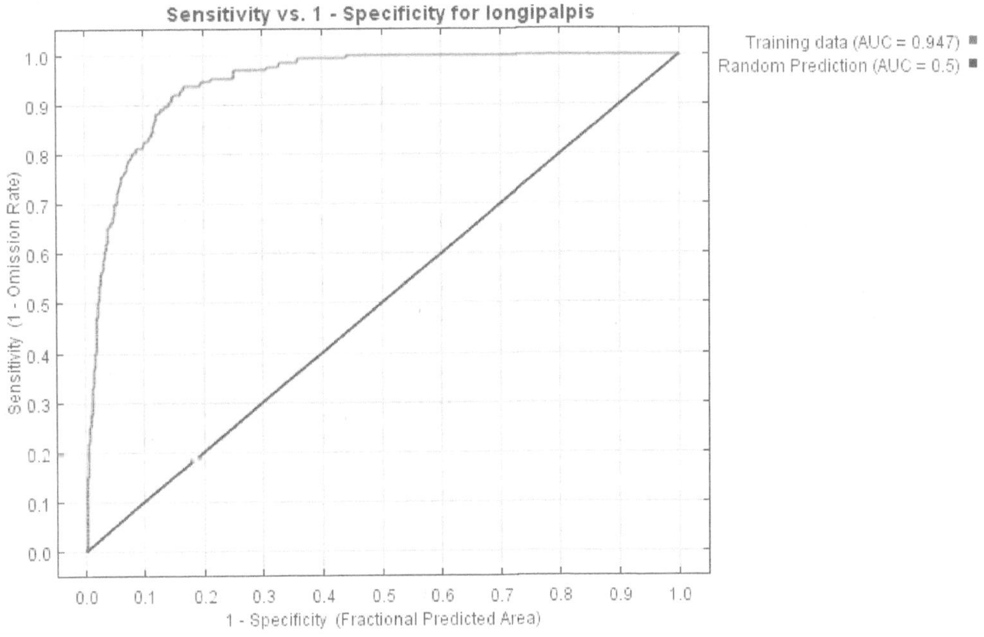

Figure 2. Receiver operating characteristic curve for the simulation described in Section 2.0. AUC = area under curve.

4.0 Conclusions and discussion

The global climate model used in this study predicts that average annual temperatures will rise ~2° C , and that annual precipitation will increase ~7% (depending on season), from 2008 nominals, in the United States by 2060. If we posit that the survivability of *L. longipalpis* in a region is sufficient to predict that leischmaniasis cases could occur in that region, the disease will retain its current distribution in South America, and could spread to the east coast of Africa and the northern half of Australia.

Similar results (not shown) were obtained from the other IPCC4 scenarios ([14]).

At least three caveats to these conclusions should be noted (see [11] for a comprehensive survey of the limitations of ENM):

1. The accuracy of ENM simulations is limited by the accuracy of the climate models they assume. Even within a model, different scenarios (e.g., radiative forcing scenarios) can produce different predictions.

2. ENM can show only where a particular species might be able to survive in a region. Whether a species can gain access to that region is a separate issue.

3. The accuracy of an ENM prediction depends on how comprehensive the set of relevant environmental variables used is. In

general, there is no mechanical way to characterize that list.

5.0 Acknowledgements

This work benefited from discussions with Town Peterson and Jose Soberón of the University of Kansas Biodiversity Institute. For any problems that remain, I am solely responsible.

6.0 References

[1] *MaxEnt*. www.cs.princeton.edu/~schapire/maxent. 2012.

[2] VectorMap/SandflyMap. http://www.sandflymap.org/. 2012.

[3] Gordon HB, Rotstayn LD, McGregor JL, Dix MR, Kowalczyk EA, O'Farrell SP, LJ, Hirst AC, S.G. Wilson SG, Collier MA, Watterson IG, and TI. The CSIRO Mk3 Climate System Model. http://www.cmar.csiro.au/e-print/open/gordon_2002a.pdf. 2002.

[4] Muñoz MES, De Giovanni R, Sutton T, Pereira RS, Ruland K, Brewer P, Jardim AC, Yamamoto M, Bellini DJS, da Cunha Rodrigues ES, Stanzani SL, Avilla AO, Lin C-T, Oberender J, Elwertowski T, Yesson C, and Bruy A. *openModeller*. http://openmodeller.sourceforge.net/. Circa 2009.

[5] Phillips SJ, Anderson RP, and Schapire RE. Maximum entropy modeling of species geographic distributions. *Ecological Modelling* 190 (2006), 231-259.

[6] Ramirez J and Jarvis A. High Resolution Statistically Downscaled Future Climate Surfaces. International Center for Tropical Agriculture (CIAT); CGIAR Research Program on Climate Change, Agriculture and Food Security (CCAFS). Cali, Colombia. 2008.

[7] The Quantum GIS Project. *Desktop QGIS* v 1.8.0. URL http://www.qgis.org/. 2012.

[8] US Centers for Disease Control and Prevention. Parasites -- Leischmaniasis. http://www.cdc.gov/parasites/leishmaniasis/. 2012.

[9] Peterson AT, Papeş M, and Soberón J. Rethinking receiver operating characteristic analysis applications in ecological niche modeling. *Ecological Modeling* 213 (2008), 63-72.

[10] US Centers for Disease Control. Parasites -- Leischmaniasis. Resources for health professionals http://www.cdc.gov/parasites/leishmaniasis/health_professionals/index.html.

[11] Peterson AT, Soberón J, Pearson RG, Anderson RP, Martínez-Meyer E, Nakamura M, and Araújo MB. *Ecological Niches and Geographic Distributions.* Princeton. 2011.

[12] Poli R, Langdon WB, and McPhee NF. *A Field Guide to Genetic Programming*. Lulu Enterprises. 2008.

[13] Oak Ridge National Laboratory. MODIS Land Subsets. ASCII Grid Format Description. http://daac.ornl.gov/MODIS/ASCII_Grid_Format_Description.html.

[14] Intergovernmental Panel on Climate Change. Climate Change 2007: Working Group I: The Physical Science Basis. 10.2.1.3 Comparison of Modelled Forcings to Estimates in Chapter 2. 2007. http://www.ipcc.ch/publications_and_data/ar4/wg1/en/ch10s10-2-1-3.html.

[15] Ramirez-Villegas J and Jarvis A. Downscaling Global Circulation Model Outputs: The Delta Method Decision and Policy Analysis Working Paper No. 1.

CIAT. http://www.ccafs-climate.org/downloads/docs/Downscaling-WP-01.pdf. May 2010.

[16] Cover TM and Thomas JA. *Elements of Information Theory.* Wiley. 1991.

Simulating Spiking Neurons by Hodgkin Huxley Model

Terje Kristensen[1] **and Donald MacNearney**[2]
[1]Department of Computing, Bergen University College, Bergen, Norway, tkr@hib.no
[2]Electrical Systems Integration, Aspin Kemp and Associates, Stratford, PE, Canada, donaldmacnearney@aka-group.com

Abstract - *The Hodgkin Huxley model of the biological neuron is numerically solved in Java, using both an Euler and a 4th order Runge Kutta method. The theory behind the Hodgkin Huxley model is described and the basic spikes are investigated using a graphical program developed by the authors. This is the first step in a long-term goal to develop a tool in Java to simulate neuron interactions on a larger scale. In the future, the authors would like to simulate interactions between multiple neurons, with the aspiration to investigate large-scale neural behavior with visualization and total control of all parameters involved.*

Keywords: Hodgkin-Huxley, Java, simulation, spiking neuron, numerical integration

I. INTRODUCTION

In 1952, Alan Lloyd Hodgkin and Andrew Huxley described their mathematical model, which explains the ionic interactions that characterize action potentials in a giant squid axon. Their model remains the most widely accepted model for describing neuron action potentials, and is used ubiquitously in neural modeling to this day. This project focuses on the Hodgkin Huxley model, and generating a graphical solution to their equations using Java. This graphical model will be used to draw conclusions about neural behavior, and to reinforce concepts presented in literature on such topics.

First, the objectives of this experiment will be formalized, followed by the background knowledge necessary to understand the Hodgkin Huxley model and achieve these objectives. A summary of the two numerical integration techniques to be used will be presented, and then a selection of observations made using the Java program will be discussed. As this project represents only the basics of a large and complex field of ongoing research, a summary of what may be realized in the future will be presented, pending more research in this area, notably in the area of multiple neuron interactions.

A. Objective

The purpose of this project is to investigate the Hodgkin Huxley model of a neuron action potential. The solution of the presented equations will be obtained using numerical methods in Java, and the solutions will then be presented graphically, using the Swing library in Java. First, the Euler numerical method will be used to obtain the solution, and then be compared to a solution found using a 4th order Runge Kutta method. Once this basic simulation has been completed, these simple solutions may be concatenated into more complex operations involving multiple neurons. When this is completed, the initial steps for integrating these spiking neurons into a two dimensional network of neuron modules may be investigated.

II. THEORY

The Hodgkin-Huxley model of neuron action potentials is based on measurements made by Hodgkin and Huxley on the axon of a giant squid. Hodgkin and Huxley were able to create a model of the electrical characteristics of a cellular neuron based on standardized circuit theory. They characterized the cellular membrane with a capacitive element and a series of varying resistive elements, the conductivities of which vary, based on the potential present across the membrane. As the system is disturbed by an input, or injected current, the membrane potential will attempt to regain its equilibrium through a set of equations defined empirically by Hodgkin and Huxley.

$$I=C_M dV/dt+g_K n^4(V-V_K)+gN_a m^3 h(V-V_{Na})+g_L(V-V_L) \quad (1)$$

Biologically speaking, this equation may be understood as the net current passing through the cell membrane being made up of a charging current across the capacitance of the membrane itself, plus an ionic current component stemming from ionic charge carriers crossing the membrane. This may be summarized according to equation 2.

$$I_{total} = I_{capacitive} + I_{ionic} \quad (2)$$

The general Hodgkin-Huxley equation is fairly straightforward to understand, in that it follows basic circuit principles. The parameters g_K and g_{Na} are the maximum conductances of the potassium and sodium channels, respectively, across the cell membrane, determined experimentally by Hodgkin and Huxley. Because this model only explicitly addresses potassium and sodium as current conducting ions, the parameter g_L was introduced to incorporate all other leakage conductances across the membrane. It will be seen later that the current through the potassium and sodium channels are in fact quite complex, while the leakage current is characterized by only three parameters: the leakage conductance, g_L, the leakage threshold voltage, V_L, both of which are constants, as well as the instantaneous potential across the membrane, V, which varies with time. The leakage parameters were selected by Hodgkin and Huxley to enable the entire system to approach the correct equilibrium point that matches with the observed equilibrium point in the physical experiments. In other words, the leakage current term adjusts for the offsets between the mathematical and observed membrane potential.

The parameter C_M represents the capacitance of the cell membrane, and the other parameters of the system were adjusted by Hodgkin and Huxley to allow this capacitance to become unity. As the capacitance is effectively just a scaling term, this does not affect the general characteristics of the solution. The remaining parameters of the general equation, m, n, and h, are denoted `gating parameters', and represent much of the complexity of the model, in that these parameters themselves are determined by additional differential equations, defined in general form by Equations 3, 4, and 5.

$$dm/dt = \alpha_m(1-m) - \beta_m m \quad (3)$$

$$dn/dt = \alpha_n(1-n) - \beta_n n \quad (4)$$

$$dh/dt = \alpha_h (1-h) - \beta_h h \quad (5)$$

Note that each of the gating parameters is defined in the same general form, however each is further characterized by two more parameters α and β, which are functions of the instantaneous potential across the cell membrane. The equations for these parameters are also determined experimentally by Hodgkin and Huxley and are defined by equations 6 to 11.

$$\alpha_n = (0.1 - 0.01V)/(e^{(1-0.1V)} - 1) \quad (6)$$

$$\beta_n = 0.125e^{(-V/80)} \quad (7)$$

$$\alpha_m = (2.5 - 0.1V)/(e^{(2.5-0.1V)} - 1) \quad (8)$$

$$\beta_m = 4e^{(-V/18)} \quad (9)$$

$$\alpha_h = 0.07^{(-V/20)} \quad (10)$$

$$\beta_h = 1/(e^{(3.0-0.1V)} + 1) \quad (11)$$

A. The Gating Parameters

In order to solve for the initial conditions of this system of equations, the gating parameters n, m, and h are assumed to have achieved their steady state values for a given steady state membrane potential. With this assumption, the initial values for the gating parameters are given by Equations 12 through 14

$$n_\infty = \alpha_n /(\alpha_n + \beta_n) \quad (12)$$

$$m_\infty = \alpha_m /(\alpha_m + \beta_m) \quad (13)$$

$$h_\infty = \alpha_h /(\alpha_h + \beta_h) \quad (14)$$

More components of Hodgkin and Huxley's equations, necessary for obtaining a solution, are the values of the constant parameters, experimentally obtained by Hodgkin and Huxley. The constant parameters of the problem are the membrane capacitance, the ionic channel threshold voltages, and the ionic channel conductances. Once again, note that the values for the leakage parameters were chosen by Hodgkin and Huxley to have a resting ionic current of zero and a resting membrane potential of 0 (mV). The values for these parameters used for this simulation are summarized below.

$C_M = 1.0\mu F/cm^2$
$V_{Na} = 115mV$
$V_K = -12mV$
$V_L = 10.613mV$
$g_{Na} = 120mS/cm^2$
$g_K = 36mS/cm^2$
$g_L = 0.3mS/cm^2$

It should be noted that there are various publications that summarize Hodgkin Huxley's equations, and offer their own solutions and parameter values [7]. These parameters differ in terms of units, or the adjustment for the leakage current and resting potential. When different values for the parameters are presented, the equations are also altered to account for the different parameters. The end result of the simulation should be the same, regardless of which representation of Hodgkin-Huxley's equations is used, and the only real differences are how the equations are presented. For this project the equations presented are as in [1].

To summarize this background section, the ionic currents in Hodgkin-Huxley's general equation (equation 1) are determined by time varying gating parameters, and the rates of change of these parameters are in turn determined by the present membrane potential. However, equation 1 also contains a capacitive current term, which is dependent on the rate of change of the membrane potential. Thus, it may be seen that equation 1actually represents a differential equation relating the instantaneous membrane potential to the change in membrane potential. With this knowledge, it is possible to use numerical techniques to solve for the membrane function over time.

III. INTEGRATION METHODS

A. Euler's method

Euler's method is the most basic of the explicit methods for solving differential equations through numerical integration [4]. The basic theory behind Euler's method is quite simple. Given an initial value which satisfies a differential equation, the given equation may be used to determine the instantaneous rate of change of the desired function at that point. Then, using a chosen step size and that rate of change, the next value for the function may be approximated. As the step size approaches zero, this approaches a perfect integration, and the differential equation may be solved exactly. The step size for this method must be chosen to be small enough to allow convergence of the calculated solution with the true solution. Mathematically, Euler's method is shown below. Given a differential equation with an initial value, as shown below, and a step size h, the solution of the problem may be found iteratively using Equation 15.

$$y' = f(t, y(t)), \quad y(t_o) = y_o$$

$$y_{n+1} = y_n + hf(t_n, y_n) \qquad (15)$$

B. *4th order Runge Kuta's method*

The Runge Kutta method used in this project is the most common method for solving initial value problems in the Runge Kutta family of methods [Chapra 2008]. In fact, the Euler's method described earlier is also known as a first order Runge Kutta method. For a given initial value problem specified by the following conditions, may be solved numerically using Equations 16 and 17, where the values for k_1, k_2, k_3, and k_4 are specified by Equations 18 through 21.

$$y' = f(t,y(t)), \quad y(t_o) = y_o$$

$$y_{n+1} = y_n + 1/6\,(k_1 + 2k2 + 2k_3 + k_4) \qquad (16)$$

$$t_{n+1} = t_n + h \qquad (17)$$

$$k_1 = h * f(t_n, y_{n)} \qquad (18)$$

$$k_2 = h * f(t_n + ½h\,,\, y_n + ½k_1 \qquad (19)$$

$$k_3 = h * f(t_n + ½h\,,\, y_n + ½k_2\,) \qquad (20)$$

$$k_4 = h * f(t_n + h_1\,,\, y_n + k_3\,) \qquad (21)$$

Essentially, the 4th order Runge Kutta method works in the same way as the Euler method, except that the slope used to determine the next value of the function under investigation is taken as a weighted average of the slopes across the step interval h. In theory, this enables the function to be approximated more accurately, albeit at the cost of more computing time. In this paper, the advantages and disadvantages of using each method will be investigated, based on the processing time each technique utilizes, as well as the mathematically determined order of the error.

All coding for this project was done in Java, using the Java Swing library, as well as the open source FreeChart library, for graphical interfacing. Presented in the following sections are the main themes of the project: observations of the action potential characteristics using the Hodgkin Huxley model, a comparison of the two numerical techniques used to obtain these results, and a preliminary investigation of multiple neuron interactions.

The graphical user interface developed for the initial system analysis is shown in figure 1. The type of input stimulation may be selected on this GUI, as well as the integration method desired. Each possible input has a separate configuration screen, where initial parameters are set.

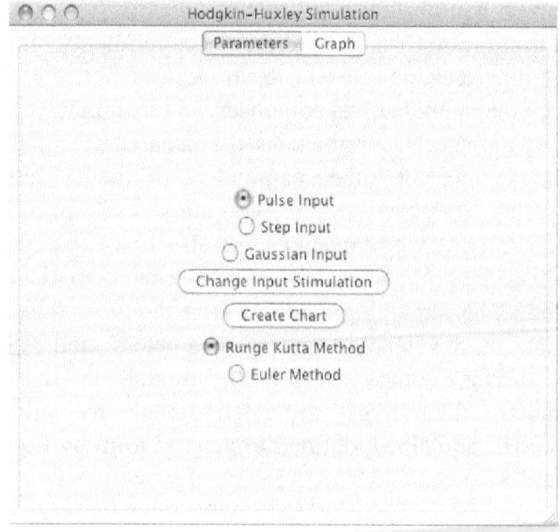

Figure 1: GUI for Single Neuron Analysis

A pulse input indicates an input in the form of regular set of pulses, where the duration of each pulse and time between them may be altered. A step input indicates an input current as a Heaviside step function. A Gaussian input current consists of pseudo-random numbers generated by the program which follow a Gaussian distribution. The shape of the distribution depends on the mean and the variance of the input current which may be set to a desired level.

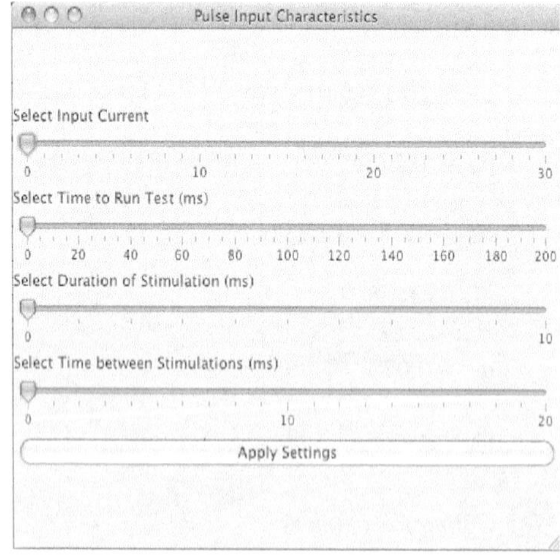

Figure 2: GUI for Configuration of a Pulse Input Signal

Figure 2 is a demonstration of a typical declaration screen in the GUI developed for this project. The user may select the desired input current, and then define each of the variables of the selected input for the simulation. The screen displayed is for pulse input stimulation.

Step input

The basic synapse model is best displayed visually using a step input signal. Depending on the size of the step input, as well as the final value of the input current, three cases are possible. The input could produce no spike in the neuron, a single spike, or a chain of repeating spikes.

The expected result was verified using the step input signal definition in the GUI developed for this project. A typical test, yielding a single spike, may be seen in Figure 3.

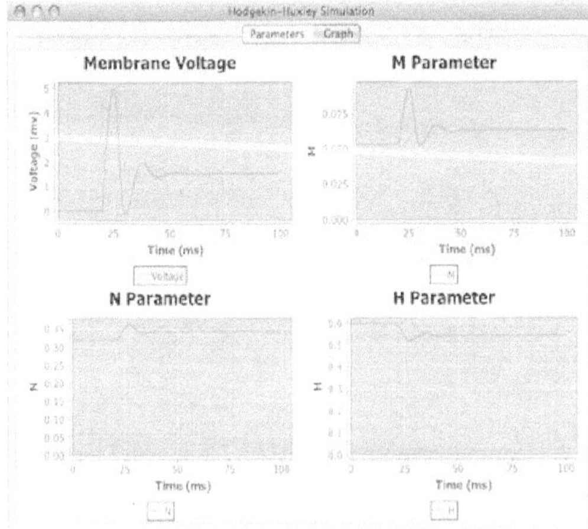

Figure 3: Neuron Response to step from 0 to 3 ($\mu A/cm^2$) – Single Spike

Also portrayed in each simulation case are the variations of the gating parameters m, n, and h, with time. Visually showing each of the gating parameters along with the membrane potential output effectively demonstrates the role of these parameters in producing action potentials, and the interrelations present between each parameter.

If the step input is altered to begin at 0 and step to 10($\mu A/cm^2$), the result is a train of repeated spikes, as shown in Figure 4.

Pulse Input

To demonstrate other characteristics of Hodgkin Huxley model we may use a series of regular pulses as input. In these tests the amplitude of the pulse, the duration of the pulse, and the period of the pulses (measured from the beginning of one pulse to the beginning of the next) are changed to demonstrate two characteristics of the synapse: membrane potential buildup and the refractory period.

It may be seen that the generation of a spike is dependent on the change in input stimulus, as well as the final value of the stimulus. In this paper the joint dependency on the size of the step and the duration of this step shall be referred to as membrane potential buildup, or just potential buildup.

In essence, this term encompasses the idea that the spike is generated by a buildup of voltage across the capacitance of the cell membrane, and as such both the level and duration of the input stimulus play a role in determining whether a spike will be created or not.

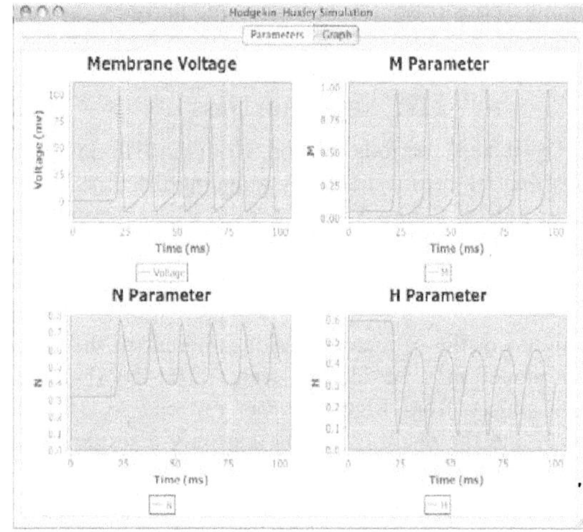

Figure 4: Neuron Response to step from 0 to 10 ($\mu A/cm^2$) – Train of Spikes

In figure 5, the dependency on the rate of change of the input, and not just the value of the input, is clearly demonstrated. With amplitude that is the same as in Figure 3, we can see that, in the case of a pulsing input, a repeated spike train is generated, with a spike occurring at each pulse. In the step input with this amplitude (Figure 3), only one spike occurred, because once the spike happens, the membrane potential approaches a new resting potential, which in turn has a new threshold level for generating spikes. Because the steady state potential for this system is equal to the new resting potential, and thus below the new threshold potential, only one spike is generated.

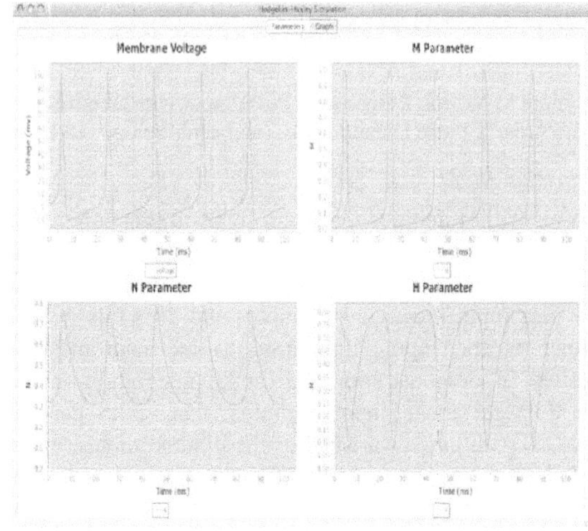

Figure 5: Neuron response to Pulse Input with Amplitude = 3($\mu A/cm^2$), Pulse Duration = 10 (ms) and period = 20 (ms)

However, for a pulse input (Figure 5), once the pulse has generated a spike, the level goes back to the original resting potential of zero, giving the neuron time to release the potential buildup and realize its original state, so that the next pulse generates the same response. The result is a continuous series of spikes, separated regularly by the period of the pulses.

IV. REFRACTORINESS

The refractory periods of the Hodgkin Huxley model neurons may be demonstrated by reducing the time between the input pulses. Figure 5 may be used as a reference point where no refractoriness is displayed, because there is a 10 (ms) delay between the end of one pulse and the beginning of the next.

In Figure 6, the refractory period inherent in the spiking neuron model may be clearly seen. The 10 (ms) delay between pulses from Figure 6 was reduced to 3 (ms) in Figure 6, and the result of this is that only a single spike is generated in the simulation. The reason for this is that 3 (ms) is not enough time to recover the resting state of the system, and as such applying a jump in current input is no longer enough to overcome the threshold limits for spiking after only 3 (ms) of recovery time.

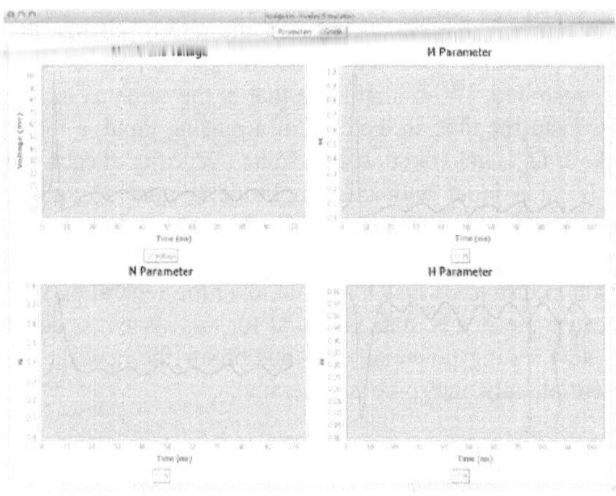

Figure 6: Neuron Response to Pulse Input with amplitude = 3(μA/cm^2), Pulse Duration = 10 (ms), and Period = 13 (ms)

Gaussian Input

An algorithm denoted Gaussian Input in this paper is used to simulate a noisy input, creating a pseudo-random number every 0.01 (ms), which follows a normal distribution based on a user input mean and variance, and uses this generated number as the input stimulation to the neuron. This is effective in demonstrating that spike generation increases with a larger mean input stimulus, that spike generation increases with larger variance of the input stimulus, and also reinforces the concept of the refractory periods of synapses. Each of these points has been touched on before, but a demonstration with noisy input signals can reinforce the point.

In Figure 7, a typical example of a spiking response to a Gaussian input may be seen. In this particular example, a mean input level of 8(μA\cm^2) and a variance of 10(μA\cm^2) were used for the simulation.

Notably with Figure 7, the refractory period of these neurons may be clearly seen. Once the input signal becomes large enough to generate repeated spikes, there is still a regularly spaced period between each of these spikes. Because the input signal does not follow any set pattern, it may be inferred that any regular spacing of the spikes is due to the refractory period inherent in the model.

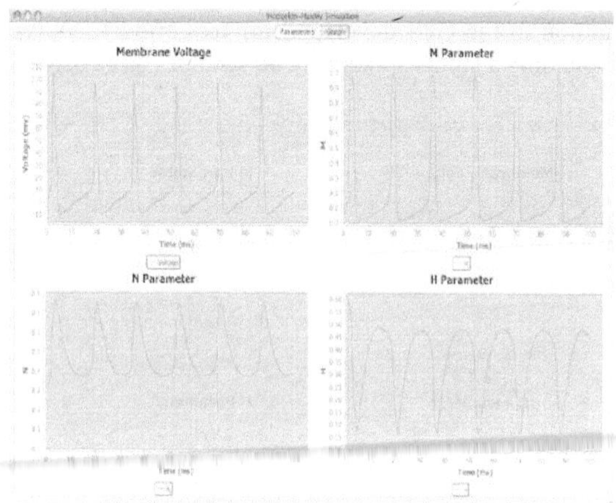

Figure 7: Neuron Response to Gaussian Input with Mean = 8 (μA\cm^2), and Variance = 10 (μA\cm^2)

V. COMPARISON BETWEEN EULER AND RUNGE KUTTA METHOD

To offer a basic comparison between the use of the Runge Kutta method and Euler's method, the same input signal was analyzed for each method, and the computational time used by each method was compared. For a step input from 0 to 10 (μA\cm^2) at 20 (ms), with a simulation time of 100 (ms), 1000 iterations of the calculations were performed by each method, with the Runge Kutta method taking 38.105 (s), and the Euler method taking 41.230 (s). This implies a run time of 38.105(ms) for each iteration with the Runge Kutta method, and 41.230(ms) for each iteration with the Euler method. A second trial was performed, using a pulse input with a stimulus level of 10 (μA\cm^2), a pulse duration of 20 (ms), a period of 20 (ms), and a simulation time of 100 (ms). The Runge Kutta performed 1000 iterations of this calculation in 39.584(s), while the Euler method took 39.522 (s) to perform the same number of iterations.

While these numbers are not very useful in determining which method is better to use, it should be noted that, mathematically, the error of the Runge Kutta method is on the order of h^4 [4], while the error for the Euler method is on the order of h. Thus, if the computational times are similar, as found in this project, the Runge Kutta's method is a more accurate way to determine a numerical solution, and should be used if possible. While analysis of the computation time and error of each method may determine which method is best for this particular project, the computation time itself is too large to expect real time simulation of neurons, and thus indicates that neither method is necessarily fast enough. Thus, when discussion turns to linking these neuron models into networks, neither of the methods used here will suffice to perform the calculations in real time.

VI. MULTIPLE NEURONS

Until now only the modeling of a single neuron has been accomplished. However, it is known that the brain contains billions of neurons interacting with each other. Therefore, in the course of this project, a simple approach to modeling multiple neuron interactions in a linear network was undertaken. However, due to the aforementioned excessive computing time required to simulate a single neuron, it was only possible to simulate a chain series of ten neurons before the computing time became too great to generate any useful data. The modified GUI for multiple neuron analysis may be seen in figure 8.

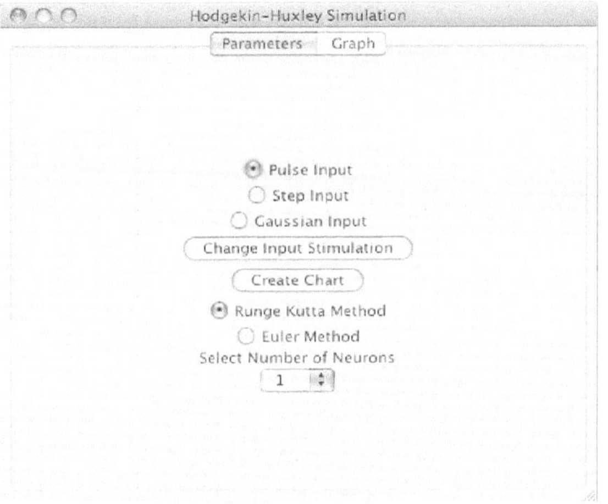

Fig. 8: GUI for Multiple Neuron Analysis

A model that can be used to describe the interactions between many neurons is the *integrate-and-fire* model [1]. The integrate-and-fire model differs from the Hodgkin Huxley model in that it satisfies accuracy and completeness in a both simple and computationally fast manner, allowing many neurons to interact, and even cross-couple, to create increasingly complex biological models. Also known as the leaky integrate-and-fire model, it models a neuron as a simple parallel RC circuit, charged by an input current pulse.

A threshold potential is introduced manually, and a resting potential may be defined, which V(t) is set to, after it reaches the threshold potential. In its simplest form, the response of this circuit resembles a saw-tooth wave with a time constant, for a constant input current. Once the threshold potential is exceeded, an output pulse is generated and the voltage on that neuron is set back to zero, or the defined resting potential. This model may be configured to demonstrate various response types for various input signals. Its flexibility and simplicity makes it a desirable approach to modeling systems of neurons, while the Hodgkin Huxley equations are desirable for accurately displaying real neuron characteristics. Integrate-and-fire models may also be modified to demonstrate the absolute refractory period shown by real synapses, as well as by Hodgkin and Huxley's model, by simply adding a delay period into the equations used in the model.

VII. CONCLUSION

From the simulations run in this project, it may be inferred that the generation of spiking action potentials in neurons depends on three major components: the level of input stimulation, the change in the level of input stimulation, and the refractory periods of the neurons themselves. Larger input stimulation levels, as well as larger rates of change in the input stimulations, both create more action potentials. Absolute refractory periods limit the minimum time between spiking, and make it impossible to initiate a second action potential before the first action potential has finished. Simulation of multiple neuron interactions was attempted, however the model used proved to be computationally inefficient, and therefore unable to generate useful data. It remains to study simulations of many neurons interacting based on the integrate-and-fire model. Such a model has not yet been implemented in Java.

VIII. FURTHER WORK

Ideally, this type of spiking network would present an alternative to the non-spiking artificial neural networks used most often in modern cognitive computing, offering increased accuracy in modeling a 'real' cognitive system using real time processing. The results of this project are a long way from providing a new system with which to perform such calculations.

However, this project provides a tool for increasing understanding of the biological neuron processes using a graphical interface, which is an important step towards realizing the full potential of cognitive computing. In the future it would be crucial to optimize the processing power used to perform the computations in this project, and use the increased time efficiency to implement the interactions of more neurons in a single system. Of course, the end goal would be to concatenate these neurons into a vast network, capable of emulating the human brain, but the methods for modeling these interactions used in this project are in themselves far too computationally exhaustive, and therefore slow, to be replicated on the order of billions of neurons, while still retaining any expectations that the system will perform in a reasonable representation of real time.

To take this project a step further, a thorough investigation would need to be conducted of each method available, and a simple yet accurate method of simulating the analog interactions of the neuron within a digital system would need to be implemented. This would hopefully enable the vast cognitive computing of the human brain to be simulated in the digital world. Advances have been made in the use of analog technologies to emulate the analog nature of the neuron, which have been quite promising [3], however the space efficiency of digital technology still makes a digital simulation of neural processes desirable.

REFERENCES

[1] Gerstener, W. and W. Kistler.2002 "Spiking Neuron Models", Cambridge University Press.
[2] Cummings, R. E. 2011. "How do We Make Future Neurally Integrated Prosthetic Devices Speak the Same Language as the Nervous System". General Session 6: Advances in Biomedical Engineering.
[3] Cummings, R. E. et al. 2008. "Towards control of dexterous hand manipulations using a silicon Pattern Generator". 30th annual International IEEE EMBS Conference, pp. 3455-3458.
[4] Chapra, S. C. 2008. Applied Numerical Methods with MATLAB for Engineers and Scientists. 2nd ed., New York, NY:McGraw Hill.
[5] Hodgkin, A. and Huxley, A. 1952. "A quantitative description of membrane current and its application to conduction and excitation in nerve". J. Physiol., 117, pp. 500-544.
[6] Hodgkin, A. and Huxley, A. 1952. "The dual effect of membrane potential on sodium conductance in giant squid axon of loligo". J. Physiol., 116, pp. 497-506.
[7] Morse, J. W., Ramon,F. 1974. "On numerical integration of the Hodgkin and Huxley equations for a membrane action potential". *Journal Theoretical Biology* 45, pp 240-273.
[8] Pinel, J. 2006. Basics of Biopsychology. Allyn & Bacon.

The Method Of Imitational Modeling Of Environmental Objects

TRASHCHEEV R.V.[1], ASKAR BORANBAYEV[2], SEILKHAN BORANBAYEV[3] SARANCHA D.A.[4], LYULYAKIN O.P.[4], YUREZANSKAYA Y.S.[4]

[1]Institute of Fundamental Problems of Biology of the Russian Academy of Sciences, 2 Irkutskaya St., Pushchino, 142290, Russia

[2]Nazarbayev University, Astana, Kazakhstan

[3]L.N. Gumilyov Eurasian National University, 5 Munaitpasov Street, Astana, 010008, Kazakhstan

[4]Dorodnitsyn Computing Centre of the Russian Academy of Sciences, 40 Vavilova St., Moscow, 119333 Russia

Abstract – *This article describes the mathematical modeling method of the ecological-biology system with usage of computers. The hypotheses about the leading mechanisms the number fluctuations of tundra animals are formulate. Analysis of the properties of the difference and differential equations and their manifestations in the community model "vegetation-lemmings - arctic foxes" and an individual-oriented model of a lemming population are performed. This method uses research results including a full set of operations – from a substantiation of a choice of object, selection and processing of the biological information to the construction of a set of the interconnected models. The given approach was used in the analysis of fluctuations of number of animals by means of tundra community model "vegetation-lemmings - arctic foxes", "vegetation - reindeer" and an individual-oriented model of a lemming population.*

Keywords: Simulation modeling, tundra populations, ecology, discrete mapping, analytical solutions, system dynamics.

1 Introduction

The mathematical modeling of the ecological-biology system specifically features:

1. Based universal equations for analysis of the natural ecological-biology system are absent (the analogues of equations in physics).
2. The theoretical (mathematical) methods are lack and it has to evaluate by experimental researches.
3. Some functional characteristics of ecological objects were absent and estimated with a help of experts.
4. Many biological research results are uncertain.

The general assumptions are not connected with detailed representation of biological characteristics. They are connected with the choice of the model and based on mathematical equations. The information filling of the model is realized according to its structure. But is this choice successful?

Model inevitably simplifies the situation. Only the results of computational experiments with a full formed model may show the success of this choice.

An effective tool is necessary for creating the model in a lack of quantitative data, in conditions of constant readiness to review the model assumptions and its structure.

In the first place, the successful of modeling depends on efficiency of interdisciplinary dialog.

The appearance of J. Forrester's "system dynamics" [7] made such an interdisciplinary toolbox available; it was based on the method of creating imitational models in a dialogue with experts. This approach lets one take into account virtually all proposals of the experts in either quantitative or qualitative form, and the relative simplicity of the resulting models lets perform comparative analysis for different sets of original assumptions, data, and hypotheses.

However, a large simulation model is not amenable to parametric analysis.

Construction of the many variants of the model and their analysis leads to the formation of mathematics - "designer" representations of the object, making him responsible for the entire process of modeling. This contributes to the joint selection of the model structure and biological information lets accept for consideration of the various intuitive ideas.

The main stimulus for the development of technology of modeling is enclosed in resolving the contradiction between the possibility of a detailed description and a desire to avoid the "immensity threat model."

The main thesis of the article: ideally (from the point of view of biology and mathematics) built a simulation model is a tool for the preliminary study of the object. Basic (detailed) simulation model should be a component of a set of interrelated models, including a simplified models.

Simplified models have a small number of variables, allow a detailed analytical study, allow to estimate the object "as a whole", configure the initial simulation model for necessary models, and make hypotheses about the leading mechanisms of the studying phenomenon.

To solve the aforementioned problems is proposed the method of complex studies (COST) that include the entire sequences of operations:

• collection, filtering, analysis and processing of input (biological) information; justification and construction of imitational models and analysis of their properties;

• formulation of an imitational system, i.e., a set of interrelated models on different itemized levels; the set includes simplified models that admits an analytic (portrait) study;

• formulation of hypotheses on leading mechanisms in the phenomenon are under consideration.

One can create simplified (analytic) models by joint analysis of ecology–biological information and results of computational experiments based on reductions of basic imitational models. What does the existence of a simplified model and how to use it?

Given paper talks about it.

The complex research approach was created in order to model the tundra community. Based on expert estimates of the relationships, researchers have created the "vegetation–lemmings–arctic foxes" (VLF) imitational model that takes into account seasonal changes in the parameters.

The need to get closer to understanding the mechanisms that form the dynamics of tundra animal populations has led to justify the use of a one-dimensional difference equation as a simplified model that relates lemming population size (leading unit in the VLF model) in two consecutive years.

The special role this simplified model plays in studying population fluctuations for tundra animals has led us to search closer connection between difference equation and the original (imitational) VLF model. Based on the joint analysis of ecology–biological information and results of computational experiments, we have been able to formulate and solve the "inverse imitational problem". The problem of introducing such additional assumptions would let us get formulas relating the original community model parameters with parameters of the difference equation. The VLF model was described in second section. It has full detail in it [6].

In the third section considered the properties of the difference equation, obtained in the modeling of FLV community. It has obtained nontrivial conclusions about the properties of this equation.

Simplified models and our previous modeling experience let us move to another level of description, namely using individually–oriented models [17, 20, 21].

The thesis of removing the dependency of modeling results not only a specific parameterization, but type of model is implemented here.

The fourth section describes the individual-oriented model of lemmings. The fifth section discusses another version of the simplified description - Simplified description in the form of differential equations. The sixth section discusses the model of "vegetation - Reindeer".

2 The Model "vegetation-lemming-arctic foxes"

Despite the lack of study, tundra in many ways is an attractive object for modeling. It is a relatively simple ecosystem with few species, the trophic relations are strained, and animals live on the verge of survival. To create a meaningful mathematical model, we need some striking phenomenon to explain which we would recreate in the model.

Accounting for the fluctuations in animal population sizes was one of the motives for creating the most popular "predator–prey" model. The main advantage of this object is the existence of pronounced regular fluctuations in animal populations, in particular, arctic foxes and their primary prey, lemmings (tundra rodents widely known for their migrations), which produces a reliable testing effect in studying the dynamics of animal populations. Regular peaks in animal populations have been noted: approximately once per three–four years [4, 8, 16–17], once per three years on the Taymyr peninsula [9]

At construction of model the following principles were used:

- Minimality. Usage the lowest possible mathematical structure to simulate the phenomenon.
- Systemness. Taking into accounting the diversity of relations within and outside the studied objects.
- Compatibility. Usege assumptions that do not contradict available ecological data.

Biophysical analysis of the structure of pasture (above-ground) part of the tundra biocoenosis has indicated the possibility to consider the VLF community separately (biophysical analysis is described in detail [4, 6]).

Selecting a simulation object and the structure of its mathematical description is a compromise between mathematical and environmental requirements.

For describe a model the mathematical structure «Ecological constructor» is proposed, this is such an algorithmic framework that makes it relatively simple to produce modifications of the model.

The implementation of this idea is based on a combination of system dynamics by J. Forrester and with the hypothesis of V.Volterra – Kostitsyn (the possibility of using the ordinary differential equations to describe the objects of ecological systems [2-4, 6]).

The dynamics of tundra community biomass described by the non-autonomous system:

$$\frac{dV}{dt} = f_V(V,L,\gamma), \ \frac{dL}{dt} = f_L(V,L,F,\gamma), \ \frac{dF}{dt} = f_F(L,F,\gamma), \quad (2.1)$$

Where *F, L, V - dynamics of biomass (number) of* artic *foxes, lemmings and vegetation (their food), respectively,* γ - vector of parameters of the system. For each trophic level *X*, , $f_X = R_X - M_X - D_X$, R_X *– growth,* , M_X – natural extinction, D_X – alienation.

The dynamics of biomass of each trophic level X is defined by three additive components – speed of reproduction, alienation and the natural extinction, and each of the components formed as a product of the constant and respective function (including the expert estimated function).

This approach corresponds to the level of our knowledge in the biophysics of ecological processes, the variety of assumptions, and lets us take into account different ecological hypotheses in different modifications of the model. We have created a large number of versions of this model: at first, we have used the idea of strong trophic interactions (of the "predator–prey" kind) literally, but then we have switched using the threshold dependence hypothesis for the rate of lemming biomass growth depending on the vegetation biomass [4] and other hypotheses.

Based on the expert data we collected, we have constructed the first version of the model, which is a union of Forrester's and V. Volterra's approaches emphasizing Volterra's "meeting hypotheses" [2-4], which appear to be the main reason for the success of our modeling. Failures in the implementation (the model "deconstructed" when one of the species died, and soon afterwards the entire system died too) have led us to search for alternative approaches and methods of simplified description. Studies of zero isoclinic lines in the "vegetation–lemmings" system have led to the idea of using an analogy with a neural cell and introduce, in the second version of the model, a threshold dependence of the lemming biomass growth on the availability of fodder: when a certain critical vegetation biomass is reached, a "population explosion" happens to the lemmings, and soon afterwards the food supply becomes depleted. Controlling regeneration rate for the vegetation has let us make the model tuning process controllable and thus "prove" a kind of "existence theorem" about the possibility of reconstruction of the necessary dynamic modes with a model from the chosen class. Our usage of the "threshold model" has made it possible to find, in a computational experiment, relations between parameters of the corresponding expert estimates and average interval between population peaks.

The second version of the model turned out to be unsatisfactory; hence, we attempted to restructure the modeling process. Restructuring was done in two directions: extending (deepening) the biophysical knowledge about biological properties of the biocenoses and searching for efficient mathematical ways to express them. Having analyzed the results of computational experiments and ecological information, we have understood the great importance of intrapopulation dynamics of lemmings in population size fluctuations of all animals in the tundra community. We have introduced a new type of nonlinearity, the Allee principle [3. 4]:, that brings into the model of the lemming density which is optimal for reproduction. A large number of other modifying assumptions were related to increasing stability (trajectory "boundedness") of the model. In testing these assumptions, we have used two biophysical criteria (independent of expert estimates and axioms of classical models): keeping the trajectories in the positive square and reproducing the corresponding dynamic modes. A description of this version of the "vegetation—lemmings—arctic foxes" (VLF) model is given in [4, 6].

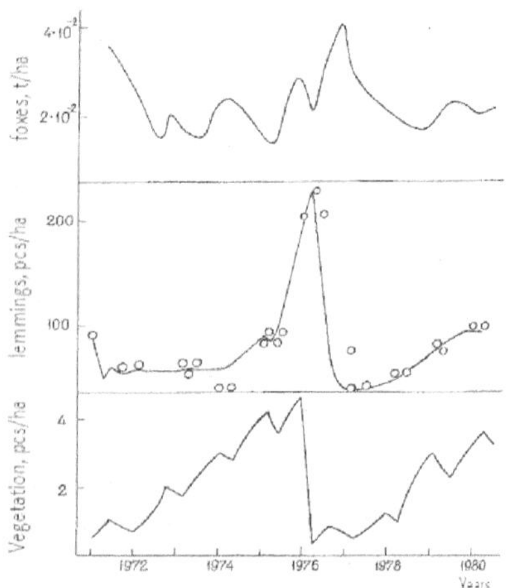

Fig. 1. Results of one of the simulations with the model VLF and registered on Wrangel Island [8]
Trends of the hoof lemming marked with "circles"

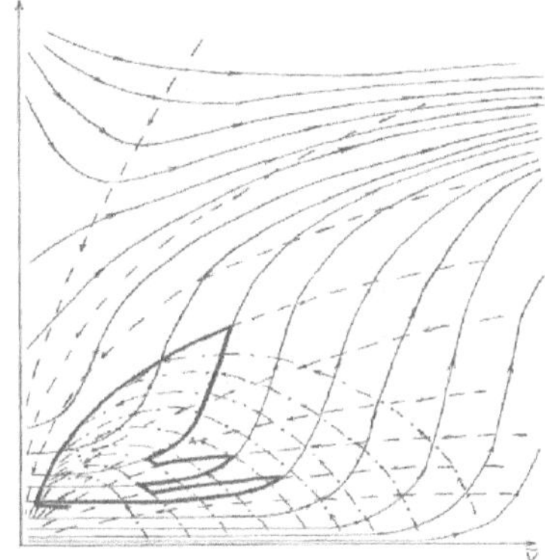

Fig. 2. Phase portrait of the simplified subsystem "vegetation - lemmings"

In computational experiments, we have obtained three- and four-year cycles in lemming and arctic fox population sizes fluctuations that are characteristic for tundra. Figure 1 shows the results of one imitational experiment with the VLF model and the population dynamics of arctic lemming registered on Wrangel island [8] denoted by circles; Fig. 2 shows the phase portrait of the "vegetation–lemmings" subsystem constructed with numerical computations on the entire model for each of the seasons. Here the bold line represents one of the actually realized trajectories; thin lines, phase curves in various seasons: dashed line, in winter (when lemmings do not reproduce); dot-and-dash line, in the nival reproduction period; solid, in summer (vegetation V along the horizontal axis, lemmings L along the vertical axis). As Fig. 2 clearly shows, during winter and spring seasons the trajectories are attracted to the origin, while in summer the attractor is in a region of high lemming and vegetation density. Due to seasonal switching of the trajectories, fluctuations appear in the model.

Desire closer to understanding the mechanisms of the population dynamics of tundra animals led to the closing stages of the method COST. Constructed a model of lemming populations [9], which determines the nature of the fluctuations in animal populations of tundra community that made it possible to justify as a simplified model of a one-dimensional differential equation that relates the number of lemmings (main unit in the model VLF) in two neighboring years [10, 11, 21]. The special role of the simplified model in the study of fluctuations in populations of tundra animals has led to the search for a closer relationship of the successor function and the initial (simulation) model VLF. On the basis of a joint analysis of environmental and biological information and the results of computational experiments failed to formulate and solve the "inverse simulation problem." It consists in the introduction of additional assumptions that have borne the formulas relating the parameters of the original community model with the parameters of the difference equation.

To solve this problem which based on the results of computational experiments, the following simplifications were extracted. First of all, it was excluded from the model equation describing the dynamics of foxes. Then spend a piecewise linearization used nonlinear relationships. An example of such a linearization is shown in Fig. 3. Thus, the original system is reduced to a set of systems of two independent linear ordinary differential equations with constant coefficients (see [4, 6]).

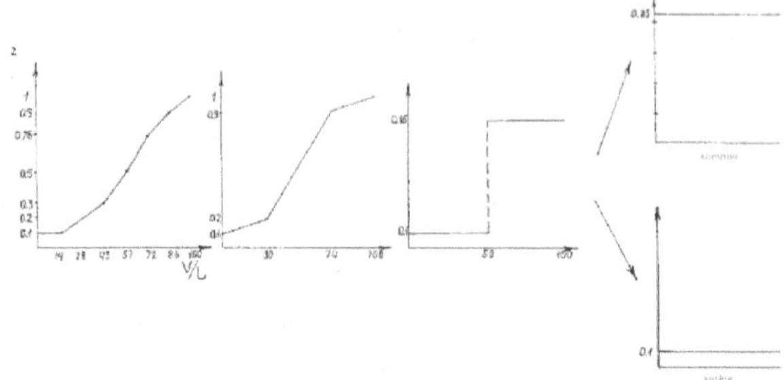

Fig. 3. Successive stages of approximation of trophic function lemmings (formalizes the decline in the value of forages in their deficit).

The result is a difference equation that *relates the number of lemmings in two adjacent years* [6]. For the normalized variable $\widetilde{L} = L / L_{max}$ it looks like this:

$$\widetilde{L}_{n+1} = \begin{cases} P\widetilde{L}_n, & \widetilde{L}_n \le 1/P, \\ 1 - r\left(\widetilde{L}_n - 1/P\right), & 1/P < \widetilde{L}_n \le \widetilde{B}, \\ d, & \widetilde{L}_n > \widetilde{B}. \end{cases} \qquad (2.2)$$

Where P – is the growth of biomass of lemmings during the favorable year; the value $\widetilde{B}$ is determined from the conditions of starvation in late winter; d – normalized biomass of lemmings in optimal biotope, coefficient r – characterizes the change in biomass of lemmings when there is not enough food in spring.

For comparison, Figure 4 shows a plot of the difference equation, derived from the results of numerical experiments with a model of the original VLF model.

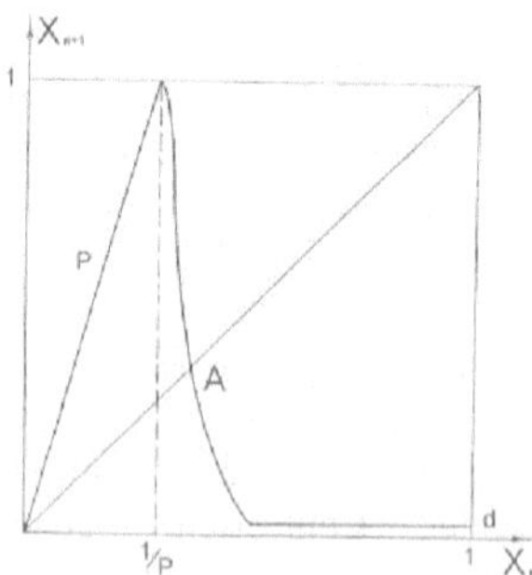

Fig.4. Graphical representation of the difference equation, derived from the results of numerical experiments with the model VLF.

Where X_n-current year, X_{n+1}-next year, P – growth of lemmings biomass, 1/P - value that determines the decrease of food below the critical level, A - the point of equilibrium, d - optimal biotope (the minimum value of lemmings biomass)

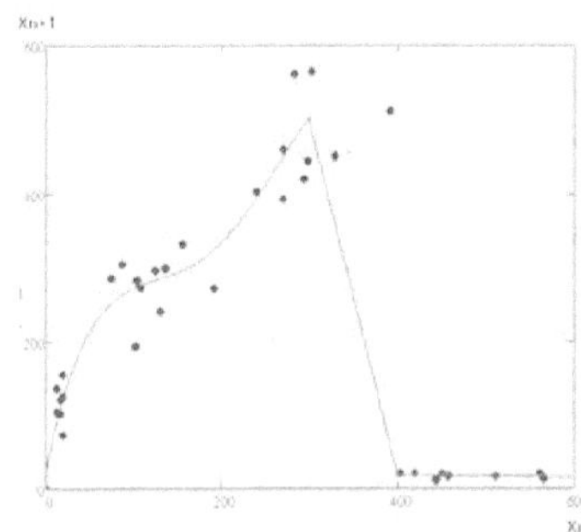

Fig.5. Kind of difference equation, the resulting computational experiments with individually - oriented models [6].

As part of integrated studies were able to combine models of different classes. Simplification is not accurate, as they are the source of expert linearization functions but, nevertheless, allows a joint analysis of the models.

3 The difference equation

Availability of simplified models in the form of difference (discrete) equations eliminated the requirement to introduce the model VLF nonlinearity in the interaction of species in the "hard" intrapopulation regulation and the possibility of periodicity through features seasonal behavior of the model.

Analysis of the difference equation can justify the hypothesis: the leading role in the formation of fluctuations in numbers of tundra animals have two dimensionless parameter - the relative rate of growth of biomass P lemming population and the proportion of survivors of lemmings in the most adverse conditions d. The conclusions obtained are in good agreement with one of the common hypothesis that forms the population fluctuation is not a single factor, but a combination of them. In this case, these combinations are shown and (quantitative) as they affect the dynamics of the formation of the number of animals.

Computational experiments were carried out with the script of the parameter d from *1* to *0* (Figure 6). We see that in this case there are consistently a zone of stability with stable cycles. Within a zone of stability during continuous cycle, the transition from one zone to another period of change in the sequence of natural numbers (1, 2, 3, 4, ...). Zone of stability are separated by transition zones with more complex modes.

The presence of transition zones is in some under a registered dynamics of real populations. In the absence of a clear three-year cycle (in warmer compared to Taimyr regions) meet the two and five-year intervals between the peaks of population [8, 9, 16].

The resulting differential equation can serve as a simple tool to predict the possible number of lemmings (and foxes). To assess the same, for example, the effects of anthropogenic indicators must use the full simulation model.

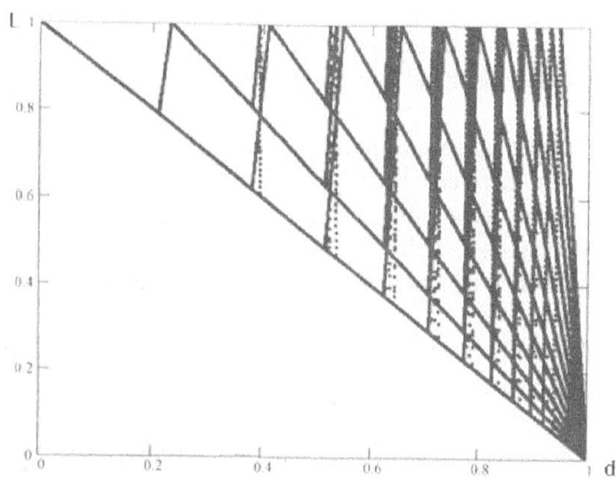

Fig.6 The dependence of the trajectories of the computational model on parameter *d*.
The results of numerical experiments with difference equation are given (2.2).

4 Individually - oriented models

Justification in the form of simplified models of difference equations used to describe the possible population of lemmings individual-oriented model [13, 14, 20, 21]. The use of individually - oriented models (IOM) enables a new level of detail to take account of: ecological and physiological characteristics of individuals, especially their interaction (social mechanisms), the impact of their behavior on the environment (including the spatial features of the range), seasonal factors. The dynamics of the individual is determined by a set of behavioral rules that define the conduct of the individual interacting with the environment and / or other individuals.

A detailed description of the properties individually oriented models is given in a previous publication [6, 21]. We present highlights.

The model year is divided into two periods: during the breeding season (February 1 to August 31) and the period of hibernation, lemmings are described by age, sex, stage of sexual development and the potential viability (RV). Population changes are related to the movement.

Coming out of the hole, the animal moves in a random direction. When meeting with other animals that may encounter, which leads to a decrease in the pancreas and reaches zero, the animal dies. (The death also occurs when the maximum age is reached). If it found during the breeding birds of different sexes, the female is able to reproduce with a certain probability of being pregnant.

After some time there is an offspring. About two weeks, it is the parent hole. Stage of sexual maturity occurs when animals reach a certain age, and finds its own hole (a more detailed model is described in [11, 13, 14]).

The conducted computational experiments with individually - oriented models allowed to produce fluctuations in the number, including with the period of 3 (Fig. 7).

Figure 5 shows a graphic representation of the difference equation, derived from the results of a computational experiments (the point on the graph) to the individually - oriented models. This view is qualitatively close to the form of the difference equation obtained for the model VLF.

The study of individually - oriented models was continued. The influence of the genotype of animals consisting of the dividing of the population into groups with different characteristics, such increased as fertility, resistance to external conditions, etc.

The three versions of the model have been examined. The first is a random uniform distribution of different genotypes of individuals. In this case, the birth of each child, if the parents a different genotype, are features only one parent.

In the second version was considered the situation of implementation, when the starting distribution is introduced only one genotype, while the second appears shortly after the beginning of computational experiment. Further, according to the results of computer simulation model parameters are determined in which the coexistence of genotypes, as well as the range of parameters in which the displacement of one genotype by another.

In the third case the descendants are averaged properties of both parents. In this case, after a while it becomes a homogeneous population by genotype. Also here it was studied the effect of food and the dominant species.

In the end we provide the parameters for which there are stable three-year and four-year cycles. Here is a typical three-year cycle (Figure 13). In this case, it is clear that both the genotype survive.

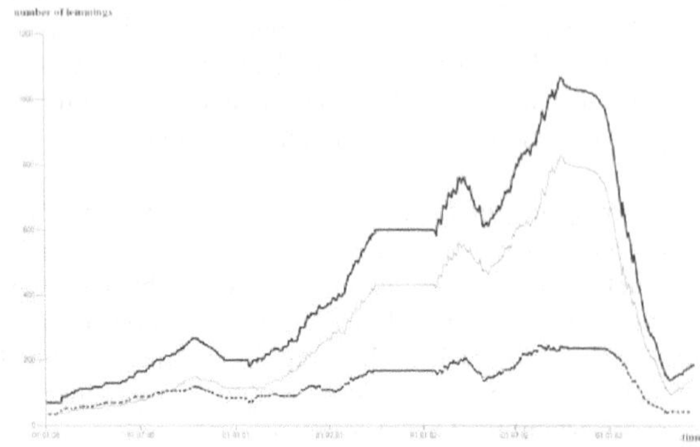

Fig.7. A typical three-year cycle (thick line - the number of the total population, with the bold line dotted line - the number of individuals with increased resistance clashes, thin line - increased fertility).

5 Simplified description in the form of differential equations

Many environmental systems, including tundra, characterized by seasonality. In [11-12, 19], taking into account this factor produced by generalizing the model of the "predator-prey". Since in the IOM ignored the interaction of lemmings with vegetation and predators, to simplify the description, taking into account the seasonality can take the following equation. Lets use the equation of Ferhyulst for the breeding season:

$$\frac{dX}{dt} = rX(1-\frac{X}{K}), \qquad (5.1)$$

where X – population size, t – time, r – the rate of growth, K –maximum population size.

For a period of hibernation:

$$\frac{dX}{dt} = -aX, \qquad (5.2)$$

where a – coefficient of reduction of the population.

For such model we have the following coefficients (K=500, r=3, a=0.1, and after the peak a=0.6; breeding period 7/12, re-hibernation 5/12) to receive cycles with a period of 3 years, similar to results of computational experiments with the IOM (Fig. 8). (The calculations of differential equations were done by the method of Runge-Kutta Fourth-Order).

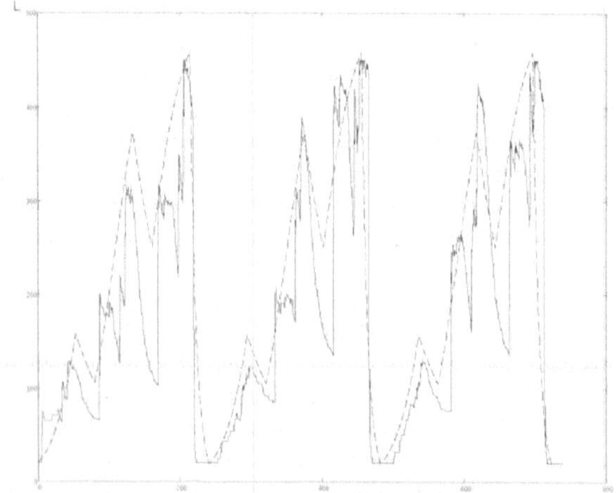

Fig.8. Comparison of the population dynamics of lemmings (L), resulting from full IOM (solid line) and from the simplified model (dashed line)

From Fig. 8 we can see that the coincidence is good at high numbers at the end of the season, and much worse at low numbers.

Analysis of the properties of the difference equation has showed that during the change of parameters we can see the alternation between the zones of stability and transition. Computational experiments with the model VLF showed that the similar effect is taking place in this model when there is a change in the level of the optimal biotope β (see Fig. 9).

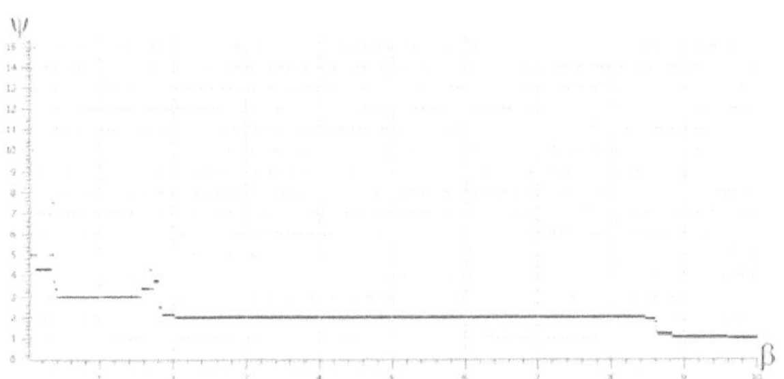

Fig.9. The dependence of the mean distance between peaks (ψ) of population on the level of optimal biotop (β). The results of numerical experiments with full VLF model.

As follows from Figure 9, the zone of stability observed for values of β: [0,05; 0,17] - (4), [0.2, 1.8] - (3), [2, 8.2] - (2), [8.9, 10] - (1). (In parentheses is the average distance between the peaks of numbers). Transition zones are observed at values of β: [0, 0.05], [0.17, 0.2], [1.8, 2], [8.2, 8.9].

6 A model of "Vegetation - Reindeer" community

The methodology of complex research, we tried to extend to other environmental objects. For this purpose we chose the reindeer population considered in the article [7]. The dynamic of reindeer population, was registered in the *Murmansk region (Lapland Reserve) during the period of 1929-1995 [7].*

In the article [7] the discrete mathematical model of non-exploited group of reindeer is considered, based on the relationship between populations with feed resources and takes into account the age structure of animals.

This work is unique in that it is possible to reproduce similar dynamic modes without age structure, numerically solving the non-autonomous system of two ordinary differential equations of the first order, built on the basis of complex studies method.

Analysis of baseline data (Figure 10.) showed that the dynamics is cyclical with the oscillation period of 35-40 years, the raises of number continues 25-30 years, alternate with the decrease in the number of 10 years. In the model [7] reproduced the dynamic conditions similar to the registered.

The similarity of the cyclical fluctuations in the model of "vegetation - lemmings - arctic Foxes" served as a basis for the application of the complex research method. During the formation of the model we used three principles: minimality, systemness, compatibility, as well as the modeling community of RLP. In addition, the hypothesis of critical levels of vegetation was involved [1].

In the framework of these principles has been allocated "vegetation - the reindeer" community. In this case it was possible to use the mathematical construction of ecological constructor (1).

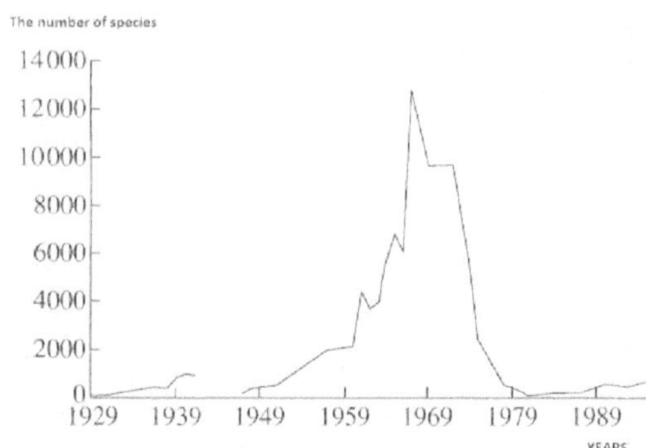

Puc.10. Experimental data. Registered dynamics of numbers of an isolated western group of reindeer in the Murmansk region. (Lapland Reserve) in 1929-1995 [1]. The gap in 1942-1947 related to World War II, when the deer meat was stacked for food.

6.1 Description of the simulation model of community

In the original simulation model there are three modes: enough of food (increasing population), not enough of food (birth rate is zero), the food is not available (high mortality, reduction of population). In this model there is one expert function (*fdv*), formalizing the assumption of critical levels of vegetation [1]. Based on the analysis of numerical experiments with the simulation model, introduced additional assumptions, which was simplified the simulation model to a model that can be analytically studied. The analytical solution of this system of differential equations, it has a simple form when food is not available, but if there is sufficient food supply solution is expressed in terms of the Bessel function [15]. The analytical solution can be a tool for configuring simulation model parameters.

The area of 100 sq.km. has been chosen for the modeling. The maximum number of the population in a given area is 120 animals. The maximum biomass of lichens is 10 centner/ha. reindeer population growth leads to a decrease in the biomass of lichens to 3 centner/ha. Then the growth is replaced by decrease. Thus the average biomass of lichens 3 centner/ha. is critical for this population, it shall be deemed that the food is not enough, and below 2.4 centner/ha of forage available, in this case, the fecundity of individuals drops to zero and significantly increases mortality. In accordance with the hypothesis of the critical levels of vegetation [1], grazing reserves of lichens can not be complete and their recovery begins before the reindeer population reaches a minimum. The period of growth of the population is 25-30 years. The drop in population to a minimum is happening during 10 years.

The initial simulation model has the form:

$$\begin{cases} \dfrac{dV}{dt} = R_V - M_V - D_V \\ \dfrac{dR}{dt} = R_R - M_R \end{cases} \quad (6.1)$$

where the additions of the system of equations are calculated using the following formulas.

The growth of vegetation: $R_V = a_1 \cdot \left(1 - \dfrac{V}{V_{max}}\right) \cdot V$. The natural death of vegetation: $M_V = a_2 \cdot V$. Alienation of vegetation if enough food: $D_V = b_1 \cdot R$. Alienation of vegetation if the food is not enough: $D_V = V \cdot fdv(V)$. Increase reindeer populations if enough food ($V \geq \alpha$): $R_R = D_V \cdot kpbr$. Increase reindeer populations if the food is not enough ($V < \alpha$): $R_R = 0$. Death of the reindeer, if enough food ($V \geq \alpha \cdot 0.8$): $M_R = R \cdot b_2$. Death of the reindeer, if the food is not available ($V < \alpha \cdot 0.8$): $M_R = R \cdot b_3$.

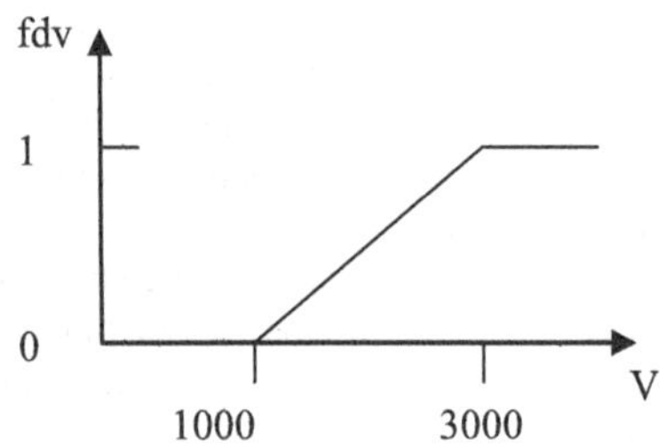

fig.11. Function fdv. Decrease in value of food (V) during its deficit.

Variables and coefficients:

V – biomass of lichen (tons/100 square kilometers);

V_{max} – the maximum of the biomass of lichen;

R – The population of reindeer;

a_1 – the coefficient of growth increment of vegetation;

a_2 – the coefficient of extinction of vegetation;

b_1 – the coefficient of the rate of consumption of lichens (tons per animal per year);

b_2 – the coefficient of mortality if there is enough food;

b_3 – the coefficient of mortality if there is not enough food;

$kpbr$ – the coefficient of transfer of biomass of lichen (Cladonia rangiferina) to biomass of reindeer (coefficient of conversion);

$fdv(V)$ - function formalizing decline in the value of food during their deficit.

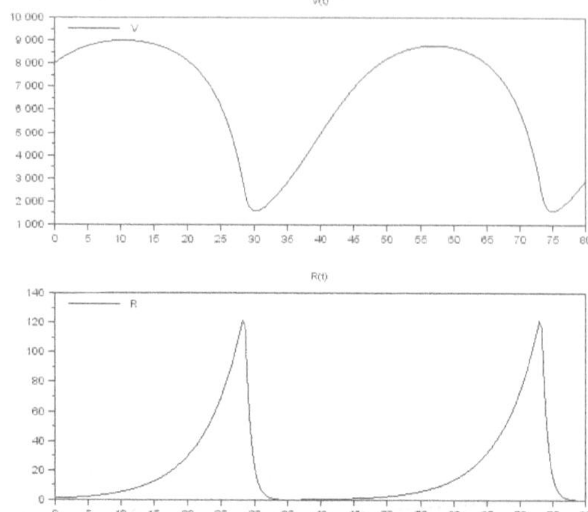

fig.12. Results of one of the computational experiments with a model of "Vegetation - Reindeer" community.

6.2 Description of the analytical model of community

There are 3 modes in the simulation model:

- -there is enough food (increase of the population);
- -there is not enough food (the birth rate is zero);
- -the food is not available (high mortality, decrease of population);

In addition, there is one expert function – *fdv*.

Analysis of the results of numerical experiments showed that the model can be simplified as follows. We will assume that the model works in two modes:

- -enough food (increase in the population), $V \geq \alpha$;
- -food is not available (decrease in the population), $V < \alpha$.

The function ***fdv*** in the mode "the food is not reachable" we will replace with the constant – c_2.

The system of equations for the analytical model looks like as (7.1). A simplified version of the model differs by the following summands:

Alienation of vegetation if enough food: $D_V = V \cdot c_2$.

Death of the reindeer, if enough food ($V \geq \alpha$): $M_R = R \cdot b_2$.

Death of reindeer, if the food is not available ($V < \alpha$): $M_R = R \cdot b_3$.

6.3 Analytical solution

The food is not available

$$R(t) = C_1 e^{-C_8 t}, \quad (6.2)$$

$$\frac{V(t)}{C_6 - C_2 V(t)} = E_2 e^{C_6 t}. \quad (6.3)$$

There is enough food.

$$R(t) = C_6 e^{C_8 t}, \qquad (6.4)$$

$$V(t) = e^{C_3 t/2}\left[C_1 J_\nu (2C_8^{-1}\sqrt{C_2 C_5} e^{C_8 t/2}) + C_2 Y_\nu (2C_8^{-1}\sqrt{C_2 C_5} e^{C_8 t/2})\right] \cdot$$

(6.5)

7 Conclusion

Using computer technology in an interdisciplinary process of creating mathematical models under incomplete and *always distorted* data of various nature about the properties of the object under study – is the imitational modeling in an ecology–biological domain [18]. It is the art of compromise between ecological and mathematical requirements. The search for such combinations is based on the idea of an "ecological constructor" (EC), an algorithmic structure of the model that lets one relatively and easily modifies it. The implementation of this idea is based on joining Forrester's system dynamics with the Volterra–Kosticyn hypothesis on the possibility to use systems of ordinary differential equations to describe ecological objects [2-4, 6]. However, purely imitational techniques are hard pressed to get a satisfactory description of the mechanisms of the phenomenon under study, distinguish its most important mechanisms even under perfect conditions for interdisciplinary interactions. A combination of imitational and analytic approaches, considering sets of interrelated models, including simplified ones that admit an analytic (parametric) study, presents an attractive option. The search for ways to implement such combinations has led to the creation of complex studies (COST). Simplified models that admit parametric studies have completely changes the possibilities and potential of the modeling. This is both a tool for tuning the original imitational model in corresponding dynamic modes and a way to generate hypotheses regarding the leading mechanisms of the phenomenon under consideration.

The approach described in this paper shows how we can use a computer not only to produce corollaries of known facts or input a huge number of parameters but also to simplify the model and generate hypotheses regarding the mechanisms of the phenomenon under study. Using this approach to model tundra populations and communities has let us implement the idea of efficiency in imitational technologies in order to justify simplified equations that admit parametric studies. We have created a special class of models that take into account both seasonality [11-12, 19] and the type of difference equations for which, under a certain scenario of sequential parameter changes, there arise stability zones with stable cycles, their periods change as natural numbers, and stability zones are divided from each other by transition zones with more complex modes [10]. Our previous modeling experience has let us move to another level of description, namely using individually–oriented models [13 – 14, 21]. Development of adequate mathematical models for various biological processes is necessary to form the framework of theoretical biology. Besides, under increasing global anthropogenic influences the model approach is virtually the only way to preserve an integral concept of biosphere objects being destroyed..

8 References

[1] Abaturov B.D. On the mechanisms of natural regulation of the relationship of herbivorous mammals and vegetation // The Journal of Zoology, Volume 54, Number 5, 1975. pp. 342-351. (in Russian).

[2] Murray J., *Mathematical Biology*, Vol. I. Springer-Verlag, New York, 2007.

[3] Bratus A.S., Novozhilov A.S., Platonov A.P. Dynamical Systems and Models of Biology. –M.:Fizmatlit, 2010, 400 p. (in Russian).

[4] Sarancha D.A. Quantitative methods in ecology. Biophysical aspects and mathematical modeling. M.: MFTI, 1997. 283 p. (in Russian).

[5] Forrester J. *World Dynamics*. Massachusetts Wright – Allen Press Inc., Cambridge, 1971.

[6] Sarancha D. A., Lyulyakin O. P., Trashcheev R. V.. Interaction of simulation and analytic methods in modelling of ecological and biological objects. pp.479-492// Russian Journal of Numerical Analysis and Mathematical Modelling. Vol. 27, No. 5, pp. 413–522, 2012

[7] Lopatin V.N. Abaturov B.D. Mathematical modeling trophically induced cyclic population of reindeer (RANGIFER TARANDUS) // Zoological Journal, Volume 79, number 4, 2000. pp. 452-460. (in Russian).

[8] Chernyavski, F. B., Lemming Cycles // Nature. – 2002, № 10 (in Russian)..

[9] Orlov V.A., Sarancha D.A., Shelepova O.A. Mathematical model of population dynamics of populations of lemmings (Lemmus Dicrostonyx) and its use to describe the populations of Eastern Taimyr // Ecology. 1986. №2. pp. 43-51(in Russian)..

[10] Nedostupov, E.V., Sarancha, D.A., Chigerev, E.N., Yurezanskaya, Yu.S. Some properties of one-dimensional unimodal mappings // DAN, 2010, Volume 430, № 1. pp. 23-28. (in Russian).

[11] Glushkov V.N., Nedostupov E.V., Sarancha D.A, Yufereva I.V. Computer methods for the analysis of mathematical models of ecological systems. M.:VCRAN.2006. 74 p. (in Russian).

[12] Bibik Yu.V., Popov S.P., Sarancha D.A. Nonautonomous mathematical models of ecological systems. M.: VC RAN,, 2004. 120 p. (in Russian).

[13] Sarancha D.A., Sorokin P.A., Frolova A.A., Mathematical modeling of the population dynamics of animal populations. M.: VCRAN. 2005. 27 p. (in Russian).

[14] Perminov V. D., Sarancha D. A. An approach to solving tasks of population ecology / / Mathematical modeling. 2003.№11.pp.45-53. (in Russian).

[15] V.F. Zaitsev, A.D. Polyanin. The *Handbook of Nonlinear Partial Differential Equations*, - M.: Science, 1993. 464 p. (in Russian).

[16] Pitelka F.A., Batzli G.O. Population cycle of lemmings near Barrow, Alaska: a history review. Acta Theriologica 2007, v 52, N 3: 323-336 pp.

[17] Turchin P., 2003. Complex population dynamics: a theoretical/empirical synthesis. Princeton and Oxford: Princeton university press. 451 p.

[18] Krasnoshekov P.,S., Petrov A.A. Principles of building models.- M.: MGU, 1983. - 264 p. (in Russian).

[19] Lobanov A.I., Sarancha D.A., Starozhilova T.K. Accounting for seasonality in the Lotka-Voltera model //Biophysics. 2002, t.47, v. 2., s. 325-330. (in Russian).

[20] Boranbayev S.N., Sarancha D.A., Taberkhan R., Trashcheev R.V. Applying of combined methods for initiation of *mathematical modeling* of biogeocenosis in the different regions of *Kazakhstan* (*simulation model "Vegetation - Lemmings - Foxes"*)// Vestnik L.N. Gumilyov Eurasian National University. Special Issue. 2012, p.154-166.

[21] Boranbayev S.N., Sarancha D.A., Taberkhan R., Trashcheev R.V. Applying of combined methods for initiation of *mathematical modeling* of biogeocenosis in the different regions of *Kazakhstan* (*Individually - oriented models*)// Vestnik L.N. Gumilyov Eurasian National University. Special Issue. 2012, p.133-142.

Model-driven Integration Architecture to Overcome Data Complexity

Why we Need Rational Approaches to Face Miscellaneous Issues

M. Roux[1], and T. Pagès[2]
[1]BIODATAConsulting, 166 avenue du Maine, 75014 Paris, France
[2]Department of Structure Design Informatics, SANOFI, 371 rue du Professeur Blayac, 34080 Montpellier, France

Abstract - *Integration of data resources is widely used by organizations involved in competitive, high-value-added domains. Various solutions are developed to deal with integration issues even if they lack rational methods to face emerging complexity due to semantic connectedness of data sources, especially in Life Sciences and Health. To get credible and best valuable output, needs and solutions must be formalized as a set of unambiguous statements telling "Which", "When", "For what" and "How" data integration is designed and implemented. Model-driven approaches were found to achieve these requirements. In this paper, model-driven data integration was put in perspectives in the context of current approaches with special attention to semantic complexity.*

Keywords: Data integration, Model-Driven Engineering, Meta-Model, Domain Model, Semantic Complexity, conceptual model.

1 Introduction

Integration of multiple, remote data resources aims at combining selected systems so that they form a virtual new whole. With this respect, data source integration is of strategic importance to organizations involved in knowledge-based research and economy. Especially, it is difficult to maintain current knowledge of appropriateness information without extensive data selection and management. Unfortunately, data resources are not designed for integration and doing it has raised many difficulties due, notably, to semantic and modeling heterogeneity between systems. Today, billions of distributed data sources are provided on the internet as data publishing system, and constitute an unlimited information resource. The only dark shadow (quite dark) consists in specific problems not only because of data volume but because of complexity due to high semantic connectedness of data resources; by "semantic connectedness", we mean that a data resource cannot be used standalone to get valuable output but must be contextualized and interrelated to other resource contents, making semantic integration a central issue.

With this respect, model-driven engineering (MDE) has provided principles, methods and tools to address mapping concerns between technological spaces, opening new dimensions in data integration approaches.

In previous work, we have discussed reasons for implementing model-driven approaches to represent domain data in high-throughput biology [1]; these approaches were first used to develop metamodeling architectures for complex data integration [2] and further applied to designing and populating a data repository [3]. Virtualization of remote resources operates as another alternative to data integration and we showed that data can be integrated by manipulating data models through ordinary metadata transactions [4].

In this paper, we introduce some new possibilities of model-based data integration rooted on model-driven interoperability advances.

The paper is organized as follows: first, major achievements for integrating distributed sources are reviewed; second, basic concepts and methods in Model-Driven Engineering (MDE) are presented before introducing our model-based approach for tackling data complexity with special attention to semantic complexity. Last, we discuss future work looking forward to pursuing our efforts on worldwide biomedical data sources.

2 Key aspects on virtual data integration

Data integration still is an on-going challenge and multiple reviews are driving the debate [5-9].

Virtual integration is opposed to physical integration in the sense that, in one case, data resources are maintained at the origin and presented as a new, virtual whole; in the other case, data are physically extracted and loaded into a centralized data warehouse.

Over four decades, challenges and achievements in virtual data integration have parallel the development of new forms and new contents of digital data resources as well as changes and improvements in accessibility. Dominant virtual data integration architectures are as follows:

2.1 Federated architectures

The bulk of the early federated databases (FDBs) literature was concerned with the requirements to federate a collection of heterogeneous, distant databases by examining steps to achieve and data formats, available and/or to be developed.

Foundations were provided by [10] that reported five-level architecture to deal with files and structured databases. Above each database, a wrapper [11] or translator [12] were designed to convert a search made by an application/user into one or more commands understandable by the underlying source; conversely, when the wrapper received a result from the source it was converted into a format understood by the search application/user. Example of such a wrapper is given with the Object-Exchange Model (OEM): each value to be exchanged using OEM is assigned a tag to a set of tuples; although these labels are not related to any ontology terms and could even have different meanings in different sources [12].

In parallel, federated data systems (FDSs) were developed to support a wider range of data sources including semi-structured data repositories, digital media, etc., based on using wrappers and mediators. [11-13].

According to [13], mediators were "modules occupying an explicit, active layer between the user's application and the data source". They were used to integrate multiple and heterogeneous data resources that deal with the same real-world entities; directly above the wrappers, mediators resolve discrepancies between sources; for example, they might contain rules that connect an input ontology to the database schema.

TSIMMIS [14] is a system that deals with semi-structured and textual data resources; it implements rules to manage how data resources must be combined and integrated.

2.2 Brokering architectures

With creation and management of information brokering architectures, particular attention was drawn on semantics (increasingly domain-specific) and the problem of knowing the contents and structure of information resources took second place.

The concepts of federated databases were adapted and extended through the creation and administration of various forms of metadata and ontologies [15, 16]. Thus, brokers are exchange devices that take requests from users, translate in terms of some ontologies and dispatch requests to the relevant referenced services; in return, they merge and display the results from the services. Brokers are used in the context of the internet; for example, the Global Earth Observation System of Systems (GEOSS) has developed a broker framework [17], which affords mediation and distribution functionalities to interconnect distributed and heterogeneous resources. This is characteristics of a System of Systems (SoS) environment specially designed for multi-disciplinary communities [18]. Thus, GEOSS allows bridging communities without asking them neither to adapt to one single conceptualization of the world nor to change their way of working.

3 Model-driven Data Integration

Main considerations to examine soundness of Model-Driven approaches to data integration are relying on the existing theoretical basis for specifying: (i) model design, i. e. "what" the model is representing, (ii) model properties and constraints, i. e. "how" model building blocks are arranged (syntax and semantics) and model handling i. e. "which" treatments (mapping, merging, etc.), are going to be applied; all of these three intents being in line with model-driven concepts and methods are also corresponding to virtual data integration issues as reviewed above.

3.1 Highlights on Model-Driven Engineering

Model-Driven Engineering (MDE) has emerged and matured in the field of software development. Approaches are built on the core principle that models are first class citizens. There are numerous definitions for the concept of model but we adopted the following "*a model is an abstraction of a system built with an intended goal in mind*", lay down by Bézivin and Gerbé [19]. This statement allows identifying the relation `isRepresentedBy` (μ) linking the system under study to its corresponding model. More precisely, the model can either *describe* or *specify* the system and the differences between meanings are attributable to which was built in connection with the other; for example, a system `isRepresentedBy` (`isDescribedBy`) a model will mean that the model will give value to the system; conversely, telling a system `isRepresentedBy` (`isSpecifiedBy`) a model will mean that the system will give value to the model [20].

Building blocks for modelling are provided by the metamodels which are at the heart of MDE. A metamodel is described as "*a model that defines the language for expressing a model*" [21]; it is a graph of concepts and relations between these concepts. There are a number of languages for writing metamodels like MOF at OMG or ECORE at ECLIPSE.

A model derived from one metamodel shares the metamodel properties and constraints and `isConformTo` (χ) its metamodel. Thus, several models `ConformTo` one metamodel will share properties and constraints with each others.

In the light of the above, MDE is based on a four-level structure with defined steps:

- Level M0 corresponds to the part of real world under investigation or the system (physical or abstract) of interest;
- Level M1 is the model level and represents the system at level M0;
- Level M2 corresponds to the meta-model that delineates a set of concepts and relations between concepts and provide building blocks for domain modeling;
- Level M3 defines the meta-meta-model that is "*the model that defines the language for expressing any metamodel*" [21].

The reification of the notion of model has led to the definition of model properties and operations in which models take part, especially transformations which are central to MDE. Metamodel-based transformations permit descriptions of mappings between models created using different metamodels, and different technological spaces. Practically, transformation rules are designed at the metamodel level between source and target metamodels (transformation metamodel) and executed at the model level [20]. Languages for model transformations are mainly QVT (principally for software development) and ATL (dedicated to solving data engineering transformation problems) [22].
The open source Eclipse platform provides MDE community tools in the context of the Modeling Project (http://www.eclipse.org/modeling/).

3.2 Metamodeling as a rational approach to data integration

Traditional architectures for data integration were adding a rough middle layer to create the necessary bridge between data sources and user layers. Although it is easy to agree on these principles, all the characteristics of these architectures are not readily stated and understood especially given that it is impossible to perform data integration by mapping all the data to one single model (that would force users to adapt to one single view of the world). It is just inevitable to accept the diversity of systems within different business domains and scientific communities. Thus, various types of views are developed and implemented, leading to more complexity over actual complexity.
Abstraction is a well known alternative approach to deal with complexity and the abstract metamodel level could provide building blocks for addressing syntactic, schematic, and structural issues in addition to the problem of semantic heterogeneity. Furthermore, metamodeling affords the method for specifying consistency of the various architecture artifacts on different layers and in different views. Domain Specific languages (DSL), which are specific metamodels provide similar functionalities in line with the variety and the complexity of domains under study.

Thus, rather than addressing data integration issues at the schemas level that makes each data source a particular issue, the problems could be considered at a further level of abstraction to rely on MDE methods and tools.

3.3 Unravelling high-level heterogeneity

To emphasize the interests in implementing Model-Driven approaches, syntactic and semantic data integration were addressed independently as a way to deepen understanding how each approach contribute to the whole data integration process.

3.3.1 Model-Driven approach to syntactic heterogeneity

Syntactic heterogeneity concerns differences in representation format; for example, relational and Entity-Relation formats are used in most of databases. Curiously, the notion of metamodel has emerged since first database management systems (DBMSs) to support schema management. In DBMS, metamodel is named catalogue or meta-base. Thus, the metamodel below (Figure 1) is currently used for the specification of relational database schemas; accordingly, each new relational model behaves as an instance of this metamodel.

```
BASE(BaseName, BaseId, RelatNbr,
Volume, ...)
RELATION (RelName, RelId, BaseId,
AttNbr, ...)
ATTRIBUT (AttName, AttId,
RelName, BaseId, Type, Long, ...)
CONSTRAINTS(ConstName,ConstId,
BaseId, ConstText, ...)
RIGTH(RelName, BaseId, LoginName,
RightList, ...).
```

Figure 1. Metamodel constructs for the specification of relational database schemas.

Similarly, metamodels for various formats were made available. The metamodel for Entity-Relation is notably used in computer-aided software engineering (CASE) tools; the well known XML schema description (XSD) corresponds to the metamodel of the XML format. One important consequence in implementing a metamodel approach is the possibility of using MDE methods. Thus, object format used for database design can be transformed into ER format for database implementation and populating. Thereafter, data stored in ER format can be transformed to XML format and merged within XML databases. But that doesn't include structural and semantic heterogeneity that deal with differences on schema (for example, differences in attributes of two schemas) and meaning (for example, the use of synonyms to express the same idea, concept).

3.3.2 Model-Driven approach to structural and semantic heterogeneity

Structural heterogeneity consists in the use of different building blocks to express the same idea.

For example, the type of unit of measurement in biological sciences was represented as a relation (`Unit` in Figure 2.a) or a class (`Unit` in Figure 2.b) in FuGE-OM [23] and MAGE-OM [24], respectively.

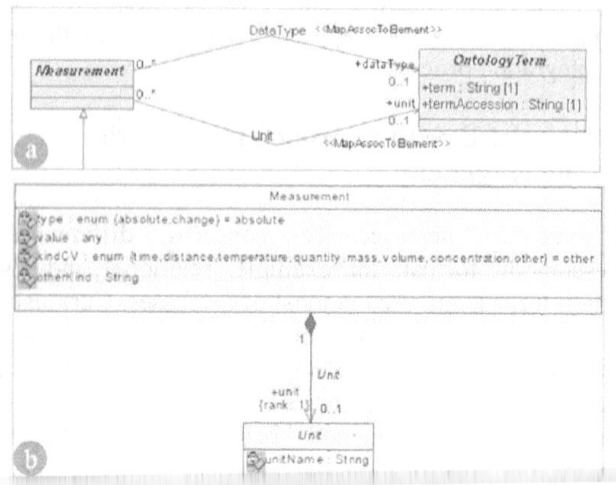

Figure 2. Structural differences between measurement modelling in FuGE and MAGE data models (see below for references).

To deal with such structural differences, data integration could be achieved by bringing heterogeneous models in conformance to an upper model. For example, the Structured Metrics Metamodel (SMM) developed at OMG for representing measurement information has a `DimensionalMeasure` class that is a specialization of the `Measure` class and has an attribute `unit`. Then, data stored through the relation `Unit` in FuGE-OM (Figure2.a) and class Unit in MAGE-OM (Figure 2b) could be bridged through SMM.

At this point, model-based approach of structural heterogeneity might be viewed just as increasing the abstraction level whose side effect might be to reduce complexity; but it is without counting on semantic heterogeneity. In many cases, not only the differential use of building blocks is problematic but the meaning of words used for naming concepts may differ across communities.

Semantic heterogeneity clearly stands out as the most important and more crucial issue and a strong obstacle to circumvent. However, to return the strength of evidence, semantics is context-dependent and the meaning of concepts/models often requires a deep understanding of roles and relations to other concepts/models in a specific domain. In other words, semantics is context-sensitive, which is fully sufficient to justify designing, on a case-by-case basis, domain-specific metamodels. Thus, in Health sciences, which is our domain of interest, several metamodels will track different perspectives including patient profiles, biological features, clinics, etc., all based on metadata/data standards and domain ontologies. An example of this approach is given in [2] and the proposed architecture was organized as follows:

- The upper general domain-specific metamodel was the FuGE framework [23] denoted mm_FuGE; it was developed to specify high-throughput data production about genome-wide biological components;
- Sub-families that recognize FuGE's extension guidelines (moreover, they correspond to sub-domains of expertise) were sharing more precise consensus with mm_FuGE; they were denoted "reusable models" (rm); MAGE specification [24] constitutes such a sub-family and it was denoted rm_MAGE;
- Models were derived from reusable models: GEO [25] and ArrayExpress [26] applications were developed according to the MAGE specifications. Five other applications were designed in line with the PSI/MI [27] specifications that define another sub-domain of expertise in high-throughput biology.

Thus, the above metamodeling architecture facilitates semantic integration by precisely defining what was shared and what was not shared by two applications. For example, the reusable model rm-PSI/MI was shared by the IntAct and MIPS applications, while the rm_FuGE-extension reusable model was the only model shared by the ArrayExpress and GEO applications.

In another work, we have used two frameworks specifying the same domain of discourse to operate semantic integration of data files to any format: the FuGE frame described in the object-oriented format and the ISA-TAB frame [3] described in the tabular format were used as metamodels to elicit model transformation (specification document for an ISA-TAB2FuGE transformation is available at: http://www.biodataconsulting.com). Data files were made accessible under both formats [3].

In spite of efforts in standardization, maintaining the semantic quality of integrated models is hard to assure. In order to achieve this semantic quality, general ontologies as the Basic Formal Ontology (BFO) [28] might be helpful as a semantic guideline.

More generally, alignment with general ontologies is likely to provide good stability under diverging evolutions of biology sub-domains. Since biological data tend to be complex, major building blocks (e.g., representations of molecular sequences) generally depict several views which can differ from one model to another. Alignment of such views on concepts forming the core of a general ontology helps to guarantee their stability.

4 Conclusions

4.1 Three reasons to ensure continuing

We are strongly convinced that MDE concepts, methods and tools will help adding yet another approach to data integration.

First and foremost, it makes of needs and solutions specifications an integral part of the developing process (and not only for reporting), that is fundamental because we are running in difficulties with the increase in data volume and their semantic complexity; in addition, cross-disciplinary expertise are required to address these complex issues and various skilled groups must clearly understand common challenges and opportunities.

Second, even if most of the technical problems in data integration have now been overcome, the same is not true for semantic aspects. Current approaches are built on mediator-based data integration system that may use ontologies as common schemas or multiple ontologies above each data source, etc. As metamodels are simplified ontologies, we think that model-driven approaches are suited for semantic data integration by its very nature.

Last and not least, model-driven approaches are incremental; model architectures are set up in a modular manner and models are made, notably, by (sub)model aggregation. This Lego-like approach is well in-line with the way knowledge is generated and acquired, especially in complex domains such as Health.

4.2 Future work

Our motivation is to use model-driven data integration in various domains, notably Life Sciences with special attention to Health.

For example, data will be collected from remote sources on people and volunteers (civil registrar, address,), environment (industrial and domestic waste, urban pollution,), health (disease, follow-up,), geolocation (place points from radiofrequency identification tag,..), etc., for further analyses in various contexts.

More precisely, our approach will be used to integrate macroscopic (clinical and physiological), molecular (biological), environmental (managed by geomatics domain) data on patients to address knowledge in Health and Medicine through systemic approaches. The main challenge is to better understand diseases while discovering new assets for prevention and therapy.

5 References

[1] Roux, M., Rosa, D., (2006) "Ten top reasons for Systems Biology to get into Model-Driven Engineering", ICSB Conference Proceedings. International workshop: Global integrated Model Management, Shangai, China.

[2] Terrasse, M-N., Roux, M. (2009), "Metamodelling architectures for complex data integration in systems biology", International Journal of Biomedical Engineering and Technology, Vol. 3(1-2), pp. 22-42.

[3] Sansone, S., Rocca–Serra, Ph., Field, D., Maguire, E., Taylor, C., Hide, W., Hofmann, O., Fang, H., Neumann, S., Tong, W., Amaral–Zettler, L., Begley, K., Booth, T., Bougueleret, L., Burns, G., Chapman, B., Clark, T., Coleman, L-A., Daruvar, A., Das, S., Dix, I., Edmund, S., Evelo, C.T., Forster, M., Gaudet, P., Gilbert, J., Goble, C., Griffin, J., Jacob, D., Kleinjans, J., Harlan, L., Haug, K., Hermjakob, H., Ho Sui, S., Liang, S., Merrill, E.M., Roux, M., Saito, J-T., Scheuerman, R.H., Steinbeck, C., Trefethen, A., Wolstencroff, K., Xenarios, I. (2012), "Towards interoperable bioscience data", Nature Genomics, Vol. 44, pp. 121–126.

[4] Roux, M. and Soto, M. (2005), "Transactions on Computational Systems Biology", Lecture Notes in Computer Science, 3380, pp. 28-43.

[5] Parent, C. and Spaccapietra, S. (2000), "Database integration: the key to data interoperability", in Papazoglou, M. P., Spaccapietra, S., Tari, Z. (Ed.), Advances in Object-Oriented Data Modeling, The MIT Press.

[6] Ziegler, P., Dittrich, K. R. (2004), "Three decades of data integration-All problems solved?", 18th IFIP World Computer Congress (WCC 2004), Vol. 12, Building the Information Society.

[7] Ziegler, P., Dittrich, K. R. (2007), "Data Integration - Problems, Approaches, and Perspectives", in Krogstie, J., Opdahl, A., L., Brinkkemper, S. (Ed.), Conceptual Modelling in Information Systems Engineering, Springer, pp. 39-58.

[8] Rajabifard, A. (2010), "Critical issues in global geographic information management-with a detailed focused on Data Integration and Interoperability of Systems and Data Scoping", 2nd Preparatory Meeting of the Proposed UN Committee on Global Geographic Information Management, New York, USA.

[9] Srivastava, K., Sridhar, P.S.V.S., Dehwal, A. (2012), "Data Integration Challenges and Solutions: A Study", Int. J. Adv. Res. Computer Sci. and Software Engineering, Vol. 2(7), pp. 34-37.

[10] Sheth, A., P., Larson, J. A. (1990), "Federated Database Systems for Managing Distributed, heterogeneous, and

autonomous databases", ACM Computing Surveys, Vol. 22, No. 3, pp. 183 – 236.

[11] Carey, M.J., Haas, L. M., Schwarz, P. M., Arya, M., Cody, W. F., Fagin, R., Flickner, M., Luniewski, A.W., Niblack, W., Petkovic, D., Thomas, J., Williams, J. H. and Wimmers, E. L. (1994), Towards heterogeneous multimedia information systems: The Garlic approach. Technical Report RJ 9911, IBM Almaden Research Center.

[12] Papakonstantinou, Y., Garcia-Molina, H., Widom, J. (1995), Object exchange across heterogeneous information sources, Data Engineering Conf., pp. 251-260.

[13] Wiederhold, G. (1992) "Mediators in the architecture of future information systems", IEEE Computer, Vol. 25(3), pp. 38-49.

[14] Garcia-Molina H., Hammer J., Ireland K., Papakonstantinou Y., Ullman J., Widom J. (1995), "Integrating and accessing heterogeneous information sources in TSIMMIS", Proceedings of the AAAI Symposium on Information Gathering, Stanford, California, pp. 61-64.

[15] Kashyap V and Sheth A. (1994), "Semantics based information brokering", Proceedings of the 3rd International Conference on Information and Knowledge Systems, pp. 363-370.

[16] Kashyap V. (1997), Information Brokering over Heterogeneous Digital Data: A Metadata Based Approach, PhD Thesis, Rutgers University.

[17] EuroGEOSS Broker (2012), Final report, available at: http://www.eurogeoss.eu/ (accessed 16 April 2013).

[18] Santoro, M., Nativi, S., Craglia, M., Boldrini, E., Vaccari, L., Papeschi, F., Bigagli, L. (2011), "The EuroGEOSS Brokering Framework for Multidisciplinary Interoperability", American Geophysical Union, Fall Meeting.

[19] Bézivin, J. and Gerbé, O. (2001), "Towards a precise definition of the OMG/MDA framework", Automated Software Engineering, ASE'01, San Diego, USA.

[20] Favre, I. M. (2004), "Towards a Basic Theory to Model Driven Engineering", 3rd Workshop in Software in Software Model Engineering (WiSME).

[21] OMG (2002), Meta Object Facility (MOF) Core Specifications, Version 1.4 (April 2002).

[22] Bézivin, J., Dupé, G., Jouault, F., Pitette, G. and Rougui, J. (2003), "First Experiments with the ATL Model Transformation Language: Transforming XSLT into XQuery", OOPSLA 2003 Workshop, Anaheim, USA.

[23] Jones, A.R., Miller, M., Aebersold, R., Apweiler, R., Ball, C.A., Brazma, A., Degreef, J., Hardy, N., Hermjakob, H., Hubbard, S.J., Hussey, P., Igra, M., Jenkins, H., Julian Jr., R.K., Laursen, K., Oliver, S.G., Paton, N.W., Sansone, S.A., Sarkans, U., Stoeckert Jr., C.J., Taylor, C.F., Whetzel, P.L., White, J.A., Spellman, P. and Pizarro, A (2007), "The functional genomics experiment model (FuGE): an extensible framework for standards in functional genomics", Nat. Biotechnol., Vol. 10, pp. 1127–1133.

[24] OMG (2003), available at: http://www.omg.org/cgi-bin/doc?formal/03-02-03 (accessed 16 April 2013).

[25] Barrett, T., Troup, D.B., Wilhite, S.E., Ledoux, P., Rudnev, D., Evangelista, C., Kim, I.F., Soboleva, A., Tomashevsky, M. and Edgar, R. (2007) "NCBI GEO: mining tens of millions of expression profiles – data base and tools update", Nucleic Acids Res., Vol. 35, pp. 760–765.

[26] Parkinson, H., Kapushesky, M., Shojatalab, M., Abeygunawardena, N., Coulson, R., Farne, A., Holloway, E., Kolesnykov, N., Lilja, P., Lukk, M., Mani, R., Rayner, T., Sharma, A., William, E., Sarkans, U. and Brazma, A. (2007), "ArrayExpress – a public database of microarray experiments and gene expression profiles", Nucleic Acids Research, Vol. 35, pp.1–4.

[27] Hermjakob, H., Montecchi-Palazzi L., Bader G., Wojcik J., Salwinski L., Ceol A., Moore S., Orchard S., Sarkans U., Von Mering C., Roechert B., Poux S., Jung E., Mersch H., Kersey P., Lappe M., Li Y., Zeng R., Rana D., Nikolski M., Husi H., Brun C., Shanker K., Grant S.G., Sander C., Bork P., Zhu W., Pandey A., Brazma A., Jacq B., Vidal M., Sherman D., Legrain P., Cesareni G., Xenarios I., Eisenberg, D., Steipe, B., Hogue. C., Apweiler, R. (2004) "The HUPO PSI's molecular interaction format—a community standard for the representation of protein interaction data", Nat Biotechnol.,Vol. 22, pp. 177-183.

[28] Grenon, P. and Smith, B. (2004), "SNAP and SPAN: towards dynamic spatial ontology", Spatial Cognition and Computation, Vol. 4, No. 1, pp.69–104.

A Maximum Entropy/Environmental Niche Modeling Prediction of the Potential Distribution of Chagas Disease Under Climate Change

Jack K. Horner
P.O. Box 266
Los Alamos NM 87544 USA

BIOCOMP 2013

Abstract

Chagas disease (CD) disease is a life-threatening tropical parasitic disease caused by the flagellate protozoan Trypanosoma cruzi. T. cruzi is typically transmitted to humans and other mammals by the bite of "kissing bugs" of the subfamily Triatominae (family Reduviidae), primarily by species belonging to the Triatoma, Rhodnius, and Panstrongylus genera. Global climate change has the potential to alter the distribution of these insect vectors. Here I use maximum entropy (maxent) ecological niche modeling (ENM) and the Intergovernmental Panel on Climate Change (IPCC)-vetted MK3/Scenario A1B global climate model to predict the potential geographic distribution of Triatoma dimidiata (here regarded as proxy for CD distribution) by the year 2060. The simulation predicts that, in addition to retaining its current distribution in Central America, CD could find a foothold in northern South America, mid-Africa, southeast Asia, and Maylasia.

Keywords: Chagas disease, ecological niche modeling, epidemiology, maximum entropy

1.0 Introduction

1.1 Overview of CD

Chagas disease (CD) disease is a life-threatening tropical parasitic disease caused by the flagellate protozoan *Trypanosoma cruzi*. *T. cruzi* is typically transmitted to humans and other mammals by the bite of "kissing bugs" of the subfamily Triatominae (family Reduviidae), primarily by species belonging to the *Triatoma*, *Rhodnius*, and *Panstrongylus* genera ([8]).

As many as 11 million people in Mexico, Central America and South America have CD. Most of those infected do not know that they are. Large-scale population movements from rural to urban areas of Latin America and to other regions of the world have increased the geographic distribution of CD; the disease has been reported in several European countries ([8]).

The symptoms of CD vary over the course of an infection. In the early, acute stage, symptoms are mild and usually produce no more than local swelling at the site of infection. The initial acute phase is responsive to antiparasitic treatments, with 60–90% cure rates. After 4–8 weeks, individuals with active infections enter the chronic phase of CD. The chronic phase is asymptomatic for 60–80% of chronically infected individuals through their lifetime ([8]).

The currently available antiparasitic treatments for CD are benznidazole and nifurtimox, which can cause temporary side effects in many patients including skin disorders, brain toxicity, and digestive system irritation ([10]).

Antiparasitic treatments appear to delay or prevent the development of disease symptoms during the chronic phase of the disease, but 20–40% of chronically infected individuals will eventually develop life-threatening heart and digestive system disorders ([10]).

1.2 Overview of maximum entropy ENM

The general problem of ENM can be stated as follows. Given the distribution of a set S of species in a geographic region G (e.g., Central America) with associated ecological variables E (e.g., temperature, precipitation, slope, aspect, altitude), predict the potential distribution of S in geographic region G' ≠ G (e.g., the United States) . Roughly speaking, this amounts to predicting which parts of G' have an ecological system state "like" that part of G which is populated by S. "Like" in this context is cast in terms of statistical measures.

There are several ENM algorithms ([11]); among the more widely used is the maximum entropy method.

In the maximum entropy method (maxent), we are given a set of samples from a distribution over some space, together with a set of features (real-valued functions) on this space. The objective of maxent is to estimate the target distribution by finding the distribution of maximum entropy (i.e., that is closest to uniform) subject to the constraint that the expected value of each feature under this estimated distribution matches its empirical average. This turns out to be equivalent, under convex duality, to finding the maximum likelihood Gibbs distribution (i.e., distribution that is exponential in a linear combination of the features) ([16], Chap. 2).

For maxent ENM, the occurrence localities of the species serve as the sample points, the geographical region of interest is the space on which this distribution is defined, and the features are the environmental variables (or functions thereof) ([5]).

2.0 Method

The current distribution of *T. dimidiata*, here used as nominal representative of the distribution of the Triatominae, was obtained from [2] on 16 October 2012, yielding 451 species-occurrences. The species name and locations from this data were exported produce a CSV-formatted *T. dimidiata*-occurrence training data file.

Any predictive ENM regime requires a climate model. The model used in this study is based on the MK3 ([3]) model, Scenario SRES A1B. MK3/A1B is vetted by the Intergovernmental Panel on Climate Change (IPCC) and is included in the IPCC Fourth Assessment Report (IPCC4).

The present study uses a CIAT-generated 10-arc-minute downscaling (specifically by the so-called "Delta method"; [15]) of the MK3/A1B native outputs ([6]).

The climate-models grids for Mean Temperature (file csiro_mk3_0_sres_a1b_2050s_tmean_10min_no_tile_asc-1350677208.zip) and Precipitation (file csiro_mk3_0_sres_a1b_2050s_prec_10min_no_tile_asc-1350677358.zip) were downloaded from the CIAT web site ([6]), using download parameters:

- Method: Delta
- Scenario: SRES A1B ([14])
- Period: 2050s
- Variables: Precipitation, Mean Temperature

- Resolution: 10 (arc-)minutes
- Format: ASCII Grid

These files were unzipped and checked for conformity to the ASCII Grid format ([19]) using the Raster/Conversion function of the *Desktop QGIS* ([7]) software.

A preliminary maximum-entropy-based ([19]) study using the MaxEnt software ([17]) was performed to determine which of the 12 mean-temperature, and 12 precipitation files in the climate-model grids most affected the predictions. If the sum of the percent contribution of the four environmental variables with the highest percent contribution was $\geq 95\%$, these four variables were used for subsequent predictions; else, the analysis was terminated.

The *MaxEnt* maximum entropy ENM software ([1],[5]; an implementation of the maxent method can also be found in [4]) was used to predict the *T. dimidiata* distribution, circa 2060. The *MaxEnt* parameters were:

- Environmental layers used (all continuous): prec_7 prec_8 tmean_7 tmean_8
- Regularization values: linear/quadratic/product: 0.150, categorical: 0.250, threshold: 1.350, hinge: 0.500
- Feature types used: linear quadratic hinge
- responsecurves: true
- jackknife: true
- outputformat: raw
- samplesfile: C:\MaxEnt\2050_MK3_A1B\T_dimidiata_occurrences.csv
- environmentallayers: C:\MaxEnt\2050_MK3_A1B

All software was executed on a Dell Inspiron 545 with an Intel Core2 Quad CPU Q8200 clocked at 2.33 GHz, with 8.00 GB RAM, under *Windows Vista Home Premium/SP2.*

3.0 Results

Figure 1 shows the nominal current, and predicted distribution of *T. dimidiata* under the conditions described in Section 2.0. The current distribution is confined to Central America. Figure 2 shows the receiver operating characteristic curve (ROC, [9]) for this simulation Note that the climate conditions predicted by MK3/A1B for 2060 more than double the area of the region in which *T. dimidiata* could survive -- notably, northern South America and the US Gulf States -- compared to its nominal current distribution.

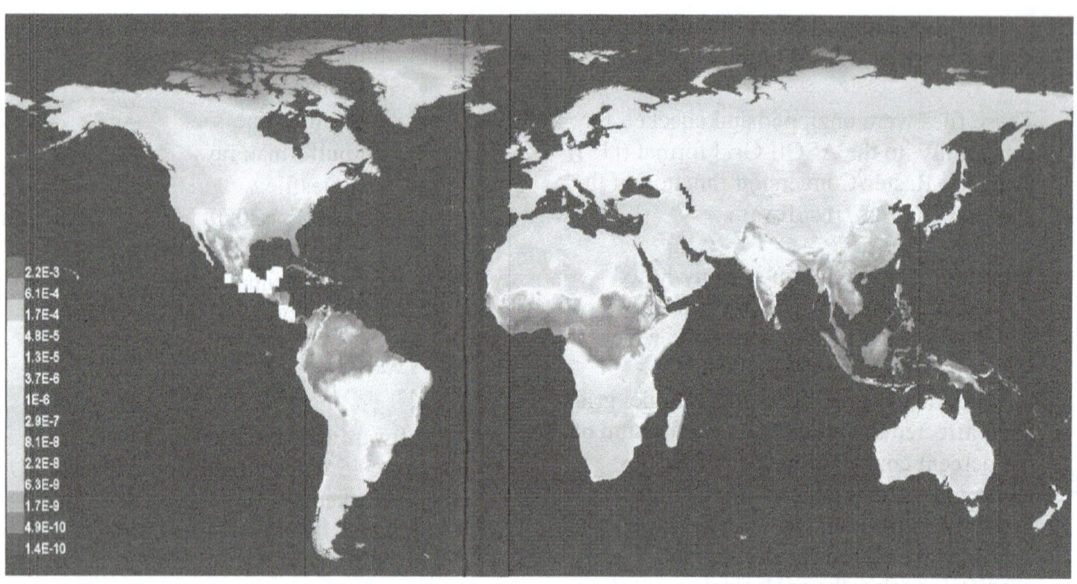

Figure 1. Current, and predicted, distributions ("raw" output scaling) of *T. dimidiata* under the conditions of Section 2.0. White squares indicate current distribution. Darker greys represent higher likelihood of presence of the species.

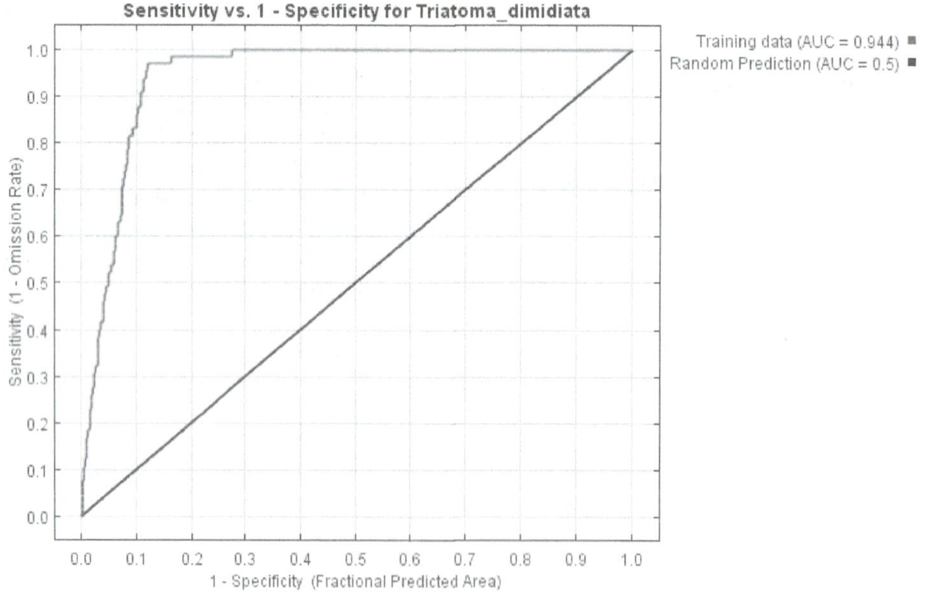

Figure 2. Receiver operating characteristic curve ([9]) for the simulation described in Section 2.0. AUC = area under curve.

The computation utilized ~25% of the CPU and ~2 GB memory on the platform described in Section 2.0, as measured on the system monitor. Wall clock time was ~5 minutes.

4.0 Conclusions and discussion

The global climate model used in this study predicts that average annual temperatures will rise ~2° C , and that annual precipitation will increase ~7% (depending on season), from 2008 nominals, by 2060. These changes are sufficient to roughly triple the temperature-precipitation region in which *T. dimidiata* could survive, compared to its current nominal distribution. If we posit that the survivability of *T. dimidiata* in a region is sufficient to predict that CD cases could occur in that region, the simulation predicts that, in addition to retaining its current distribution in Central America, CD could find a foothold throughout northern South America, mid-Africa, southeast Asia, and Maylasia.

Similar changes (not shown) in the distribution of CD, under each of the IPCC4 scenarios ([14]).

At least three caveats to these conclusions should be noted (see [11] for a comprehensive survey):

1. The accuracy of ENM simulations is limited by the accuracy of the climate models they assume. Even within a model, different scenarios (e.g., radiative forcing scenarios) can produce different predictions.

2. ENM can show only where a particular species might be able to survive in a region. Whether a species can gain access to that region is a separate issue.

3. The accuracy of an ENM prediction depends on how comprehensive the set of relevant environmental variables used is. In general, there is no mechanical way to characterize that list.

5.0 Acknowledgements

This work benefited from discussions with Town Peterson of the University of Kansas Biodiversity Institute. For any problems that remain, I am solely responsible.

6.0 References

[1] *MaxEnt*. www.cs.princeton.edu/~schapire/maxent. 2012.

[2] University of Kansas. *Lifemapper*. http://www.lifemapper.org/index.shtml. 2012.

[3] Gordon HB, Rotstayn LD, McGregor JL, Dix MR, Kowalczyk EA, O'Farrell SP, LJ, Hirst AC, S.G. Wilson SG, Collier MA, Watterson IG, and TI. The CSIRO Mk3 Climate System Model. http://www.cmar.csiro.au/e-print/open/gordon_2002a.pdf. 2002

[4] Muñoz MES, De Giovanni R, Sutton T, Pereira RS, Ruland K, Brewer P, Jardim AC, Yamamoto M, Bellini DJS, da Cunha Rodrigues ES, Stanzani SL, Avilla AO, Lin C-T, Oberender J, Elwertowski T, Yesson C, and Bruy A. *openModeller*. http://openmodeller.sourceforge.net/. Circa 2009.

[5] Phillips SJ, Anderson RP, and Schapire RE. Maximum entropy modeling of species geographic distributions. *Ecological Modelling* 190 (2006), 231-259.

[6] Ramirez J and Jarvis A. 2008. High Resolution Statistically Downscaled Future Climate Surfaces. International Center for

Tropical Agriculture (CIAT); CGIAR Research Program on Climate Change, Agriculture and Food Security (CCAFS). Cali, Colombia.

[7] The Quantum GIS Project. *Desktop QGIS* v 1.8.0. URL http://www.qgis.org/. 2012.

[8] US Centers for Disease Control. Parasites -- American Trypanosomiasis (also known as Chagas Disease): Detailed FAQs. http://www.cdc.gov/parasites/chagas/gen_info/detailed.html. 2012.

[9] Peterson AT, Papeş M, and Soberón J. Rethinking receiver operating characteristic analysis applications in ecological niche modeling. *Ecological Modeling* 213 (2008), 63-72.

[10] US Centers for Disease Control. Parasites -- American Trypanosomiasis (also known as Chagas Disease): Antiparasitic Treatment. http://www.cdc.gov/parasites/chagas/health_professionals/tx.html. 2012.

[11] Peterson AT, Soberón J, Pearson RG, Anderson RP, Martínez-Meyer E, Nakamura M, and Araújo MB. *Ecological Niches and Geographic Distributions.* Princeton. 2011.

[12] Poli R, Langdon WB, and McPhee NF. *A Field Guide to Genetic Programming.* Lulu Enterprises. 2008.

[13] Oak Ridge National Laboratory. MODIS Land Subsets. ASCII Grid Format Description. http://daac.ornl.gov/MODIS/ASCII_Grid_Format_Description.html.

[14] Intergovernmental Panel on Climate Change. Climate Change 2007: Working Group I: The Physical Science Basis. 10.2.1.3 Comparison of Modelled Forcings to Estimates in Chapter 2. 2007. http://www.ipcc.ch/publications_and_data/ar4/wg1/en/ch10s10-2-1-3.html.

[15] Ramirez-Villegas J and Jarvis A. Downscaling Global Circulation Model Outputs: The Delta Method Decision and Policy Analysis Working Paper No. 1. CIAT. http://www.ccafs-climate.org/downloads/docs/Downscaling-WP-01.pdf. May 2010.

[16] Cover TM and Thomas JA. *Elements of Information Theory.* Wiley.1991.

Visualization of organs electromagnetic field And DNA

Dr. Boucherit Taieb,
Privet Laboratory Boucherit, Oran, Algeria.
07, kaddour sid ahmed street, delmonte, Oran, Algeria
Sponsored by Dr.Abdelmalek Boudiaf, Prefect of Oran town, Algeria

Abstract –*The MMR System or "masse micro reconstruction" is a discovery that allows us to reproduce any organ from the capture of its energy, reproduction is the compiles copy of the organ by composite materials with a very high precision since it reproduce the organ in its ultra-cellular exactness details. The taken images of the composite materials are «Data Bank», since these images we can visualize the electromagnetic field of the organ associating the computer competition.*

1 Introduction

It's discoveries that allow us to visualize the electromagnetic field of organ through images. Classically it's impossible to see or visualize an electromagnetic field but it detected through specific equipment. With MMR system we can see an electromagnetic field as well as the broadcasting of electromagnetic wave and their period which actually unrealizable through technical means.

I put on your kind attention the images taken by the MMR system as well as routing of the whole procedure and you can judge the quality of such single images in the world.

2 Materials & Methods

Materials

The material is very simple, it consists of a composite materials also all equipment of a laboratory of physics and chemistry, a computer & digital camera.

- Sensors.
- Chemical Materials.
- Materials Physics.
- Composite Materials.

2.1 Methods

- The MMR2 make it possible to manufacture the organ in the composite materials through their emitted energy.
- The first step of manufacturing of the complete organ proceeds to taking photos from different angles of the composite and processing them by computer in the next step.

2.2 Theory & explanation

The cells, organs as well as DNA, issue a specific electromagnetic field, the heart cells have a proper electromagnetic field which different from the liver cells or the brain cells, the role of electromagnetic field of each cells or organ is doubled, it has role of protection against the exterior, and a attractive role for the necessary elements for her developments. The electromagnetic field has a very important role since it maintain the cells at its precise place with the other cells of the some type and prevent its migration towards the cells of other organs.
Let's take the example close organs, the heart cells are maintained by their electromagnetic field in the heart and prevent their migration towards the lungs, liver, the kidneys and the vice-verso, meanwhile electromagnetic field of the cells & organs attract the entities that are mandatory to its development and its survival. All this is just a theory since we have not brought the proof the existence of electromagnetic field of the organs.
The images obtained by the MMR system are «Data Bank», as we have already explained in our previous publication which includes all the information's proper to each organ; they are images which display the electromagnetic field of organs. Therefore we use a second technique that consist of visualize the electromagnetic field of organs as well as the broadcast the length wave.
the role of DNA electromagnetic field is different it has a protection role against the exterior environment for the first time, but to attract the role single entity that is RNA messenger.
I will try to make the compelling evidence to support this theory.

2.3 Process & technical :

The MMR2 system enable to visualize the electromagnetic field of the organs. since their facsimile composite material, which is the genuine copy of the organ, as it represents it in its ultra-microcopy, as already explained in my previous publications, the pictures taken by the composite materials are (data bank) precisely « encyclopedia of images » each image with accurate technique give us an accurate science (medicine, DNA, chemistry, physic....etc).

The second technique used illustrated in images the electromagnetic fields of oranges. An electromagnetic field cannot be observed but measured; the actual technology cannot visualize it in images.

An electromagnetic field is made with electromagnetic waves that are oscillation coupled with electric field (E) and magnetic field (M) that spread.

The electromagnetic radiation is made of two components

1. Wave length : distance between two crests called lambda (λ)
2. Frequency : number of oscillations per time unit measured in hertz

Donnant la formule : $c= \lambda .f$

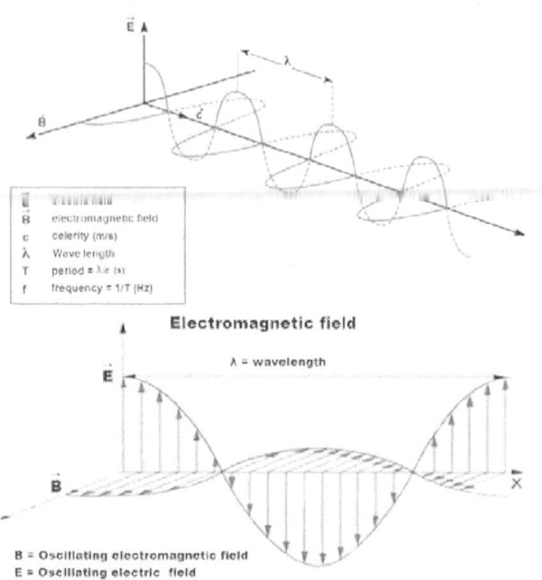

2.4 MMR system images

we take the pictures obtained by capturing of organ energy. and reproduced in composite material, in order show that these images are « data bank ».

The explored organs are:

***The Brain**
*** The kidney**
*** The liver**
*** The heart**

The MMR2 systems provide us these organs in composite materials:

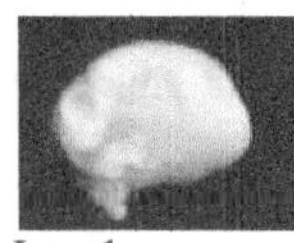
Img 1

img 2

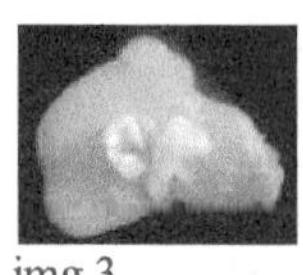
img 3

img 4

Img 1 : the brain in composit material
img 2 : the kidney in composit material
img 3 : the liver in composit material
img 4 : the heart in composit material

2.4.1 The Brain :

The human brain is composed of four zones.

Frontal, temporal, parietal and occipital, we can measure the electromagnetic activity of the brain by an electroencephalogram, that shows four types of cerebral waves, it's the brain activity that produce an electromagnetic oscillation that we measure with the EEG or electroencephalogram, these waves owns a weak amplitude, a short frequency and weak energy.

there are four types of cerebral waves as per the brain activity

- The Beta wave : of superior frequency higher than 12Hz and power of some microvolt's
- The Alpha wave : their frequency is between 8.5 and 12 Hz
- The Theta wave : frequency 4.5 between and 8 Hz
- The Delta wave ; frequency 4 Hz primarily collected during the Dreams period.

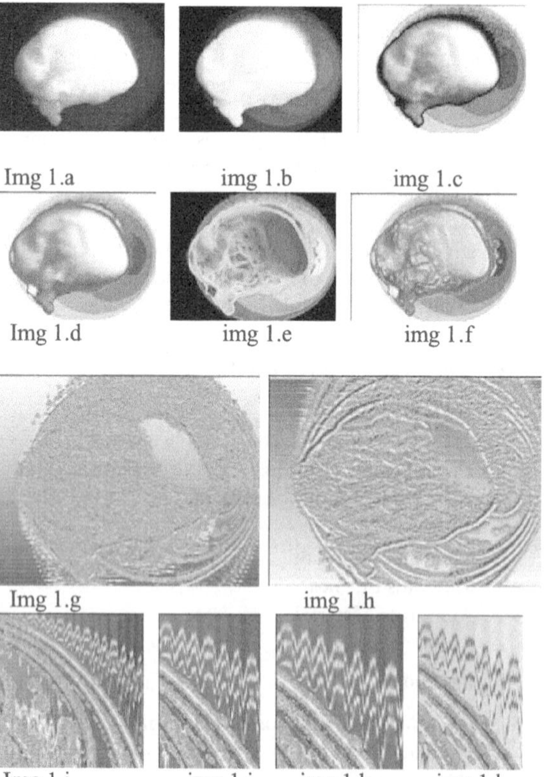
Img 1.a img 1.b img 1.c
Img 1.d img 1.e img 1.f
Img 1.g img 1.h
Img 1.i img 1.j img 1.k img 1.l

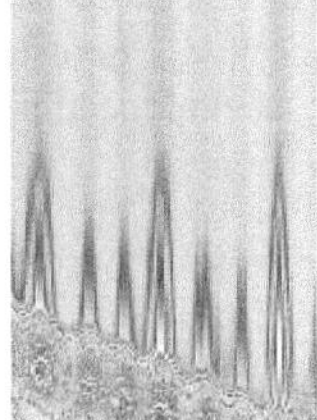
Img 1.m

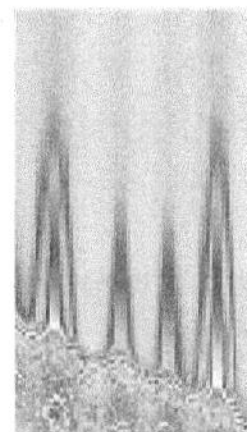
img 1.n

Img 1.a : brain in composit material.
Img 1.b : images illustrating the four fields electromagnetic of the brain.
img 1.c : four field visible field.
Img 1.d : delimitation of each field.
img 1.e : four field visible.
img 1.f : four field visible.
Img 1.g : other image reflecting the electromagnetic field.
img 1.h : electromagnetic field image.
img 1.i : enlargement.
img 1.j : enlargement.
Img 1.k : wavelength of the field.
img 1.l : electromagnetic wave.
img 1.m : wavelength of the electromagnetic field.
img 1.n : period of electromagnetic wave.

With M.M.R system we can see the electromagnetic fields of the brain, we remark that there are four fields; the first is Frontal, the second is temporal, the third is parietal and cover the frontal and the temporal, and the fourth occipital it cover all the others.
The images visualize the electromagnetic wave broadcasting we distinguish the wave period with a great clearness.

Img 1.n

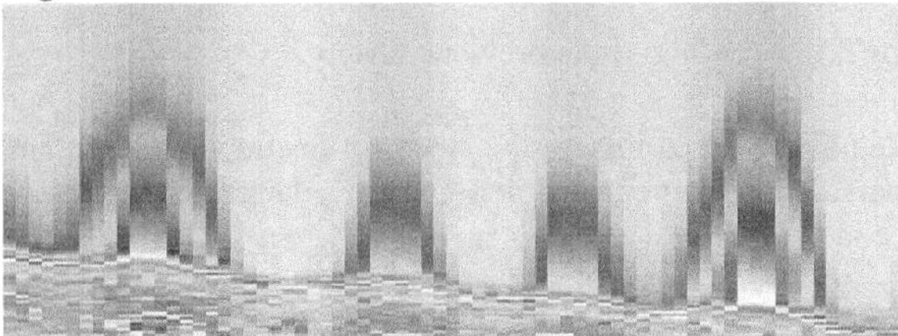
Img 1.o

we note the broadcast of an electromagnetic wave in the image 1.n, with the periodic repetition of the wavelength observed in the image 1.o.

So the MMR system allows us to visualize the electromagnetic fields of the brain, it also allows us to visualize the emission of electromagnetic waves with a repetition period of the wave, we can easily identify the frequency and period, all it's visible in images that are real images, as opposed to their detection by an electroencephalograph which can only be measured.

2.4.2 The heart

The heart have their own electromagnetic field, we know that the heart electrical activity measured by an electrocardiogram, the electrical current source is at a specific point called the sinus node at the top of the right atrium. This is a cluster of cells a few millimeters in diameter; these cells generate an electrical current of a few millivolts, that spreads through the bundles Purkinje Hys causing the ventricles to contract. This cardiac activity is measured and recorded on a electrocardiogram (ECG).

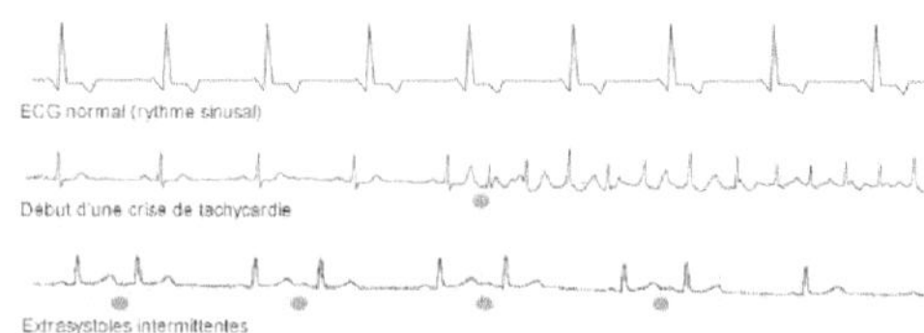

The MMR system allows us to visualize the heart's electromagnetic field in image, with the reading of electromagnetic wave period emitted.

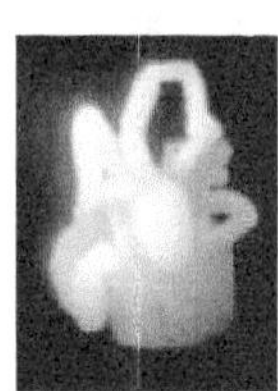
Img 2

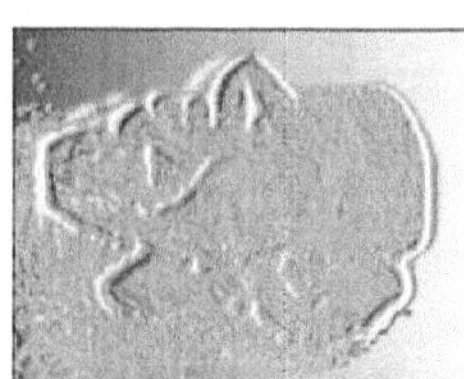
img 2.a

img 2.b

Img 2.c

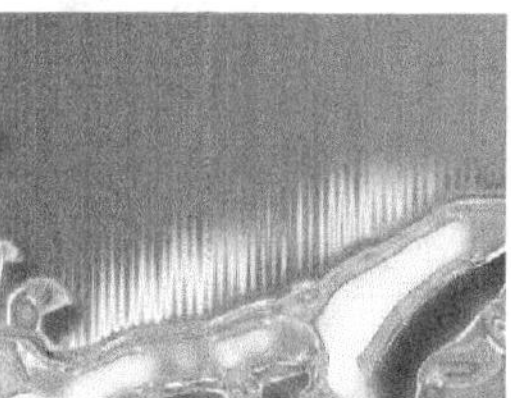
img 2.d

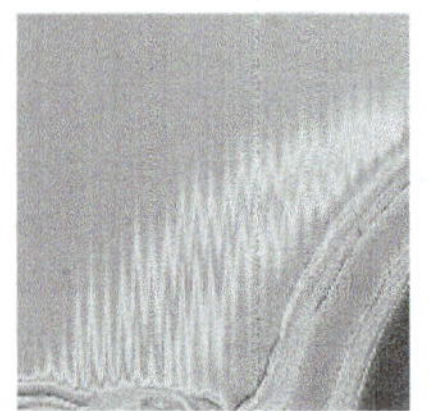
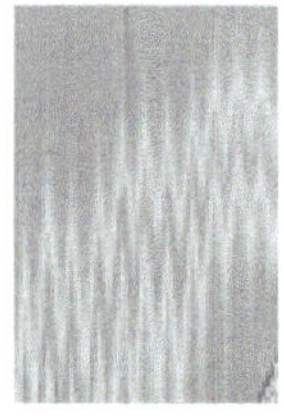

Img 2.e img 2.f img 2.g

Img 2: Heart in composite materials

img 2.a: visualization of electromagnetic fields

img 2.b: enlargement

Img 2.c: electromagnetic waves

img 2.d: electromagnetic waves

img 2.e: visualizations electromagnetic waves

img 2.f: visualizations electromagnetic waves

img 2.g: electromagnetic waves

Img 2.h

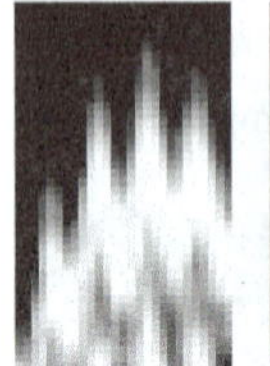
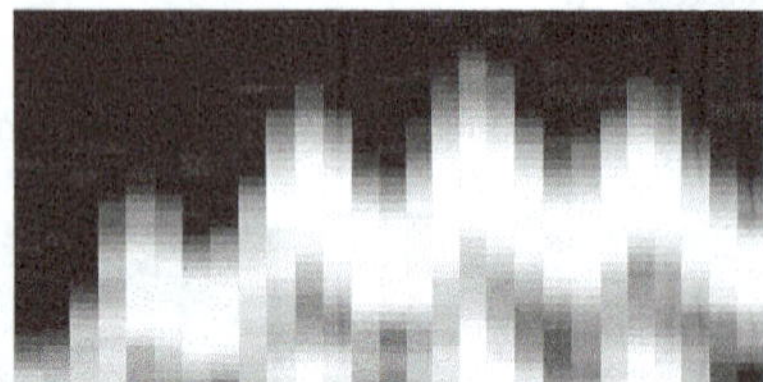

img 2.i img 2.j

We can see into images the emission of electromagnetic waves, which is characterized by repeated periodic wave as we see identical in (img2.h), the periodic spreading is clearly displayed in (img2.i) & (img2.j).

2.4.3 The liver

The electrical activity of the brain and heart can be measured by a specific equipment, but the liver no physical or medical literature doesn't have equipment that can measure its electrical activity. The MMR system also allows us here to visualize the electromagnetic field of the liver as evidenced by the images.

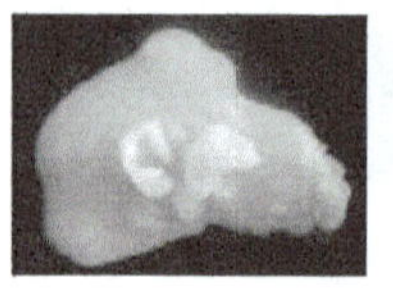
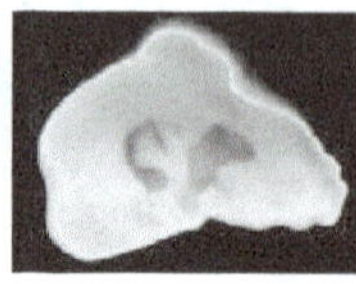
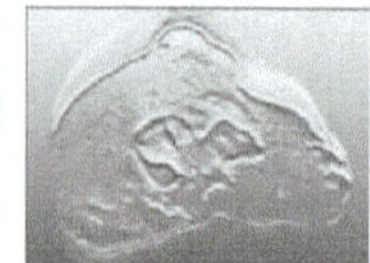

Img 3 img 3.a img 3.b

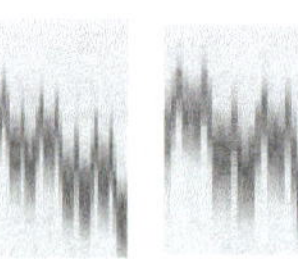

Img 3.c img 3.d img 3.e img 3f img 3.g

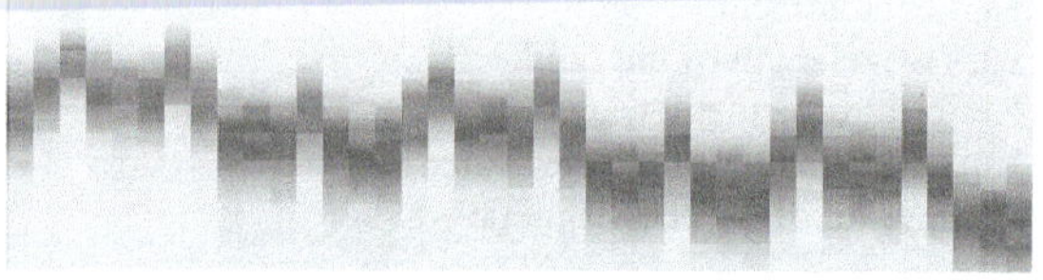

Img: 3.h

Img 3: liver composite material

img 3.a: real liver reversed image

img 3.b: electromagnetic fields visible liver

img 3.c: emission of electromagnetic waves

img 3.d: emission of electromagnetic waves

img 3.e: electromagnetic waves

img 3.f: wave period

img 3.i: spreading of the previous image

We always see in images the electromagnetic waves emission characterized by repeated periodic wave characteristics as we see in the img3.f/g

2.4.4 The Kidney

The MMR system allows us to visualize the electromagnetic field of the kidney.

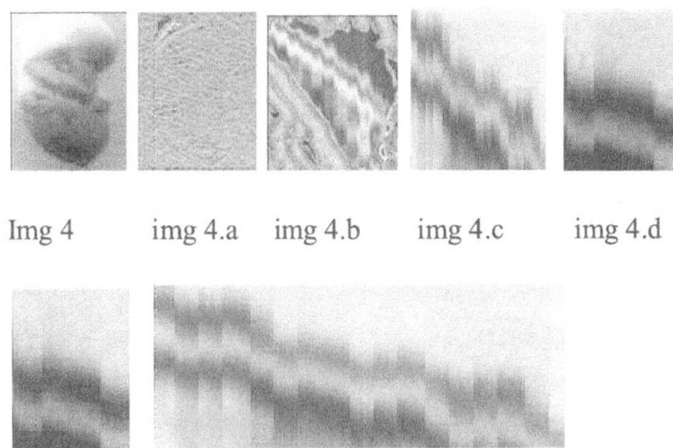

Img 4 img 4.a img 4.b img 4.c img 4.d

Img 4.e img 4.f

Img 4: kidney composite materials

img 4.a: visualization of electromagnetic fields

img 4.b : visible electromagnetic fields

img 4.c: visible electromagnetic fields

img 4.d: period of electromagnetic fields

Img 4.e: spreading of the period

img 4.f: spreading of the electromagnetic emission

We notice that each organ studied has one or more electromagnetic fields characterized by a specific period, a specific amplitude and electromagnetic wave length, through images we can easily see the repetition of waves and their frequency and their periods, indisputable evidence of the electromagnetic fields existence for each organ.

2.5 Theory

As a matter of fact, the organs broadcast an electromagnetic field, the cells also broadcast an electromagnetic field, the trace elements, the potassium, calcium, magnesium in the essential nutritive substance for the body each one of them broadcast a specific electromagnetic field, function of the electromagnetic field is to preserve its space from outside aggression and to attract what is essential for its nutrition and development, thus the electromagnetic fields of nutritive substance specific for precised organ is similar or equal to the organ electromagnetic field, so the substance is attracted and absorbed by the cells which is the opposite with a substance non specific from organ. In which the electromagnetic field is different from the organ, it is rejected by the field, as example the bones need calcium, the calcium molecule has the same electromagnetic field as the bone cells, it's absorbed by the bones cells through the osmosis phenomena and thus digested by the bone cells.

2.5.1 The DNA electromagnetic field

DNA or Deoxyribonucleic acid, consists of two long strands run in opposite directions to each other and are therefore twisted forming a DNA double helix.

The DNA broadcast electromagnetic field that acts as an isolator gate that allow only one element get in the DNA.

This element is the RNA which has an identic electromagnetic field as the DNA.

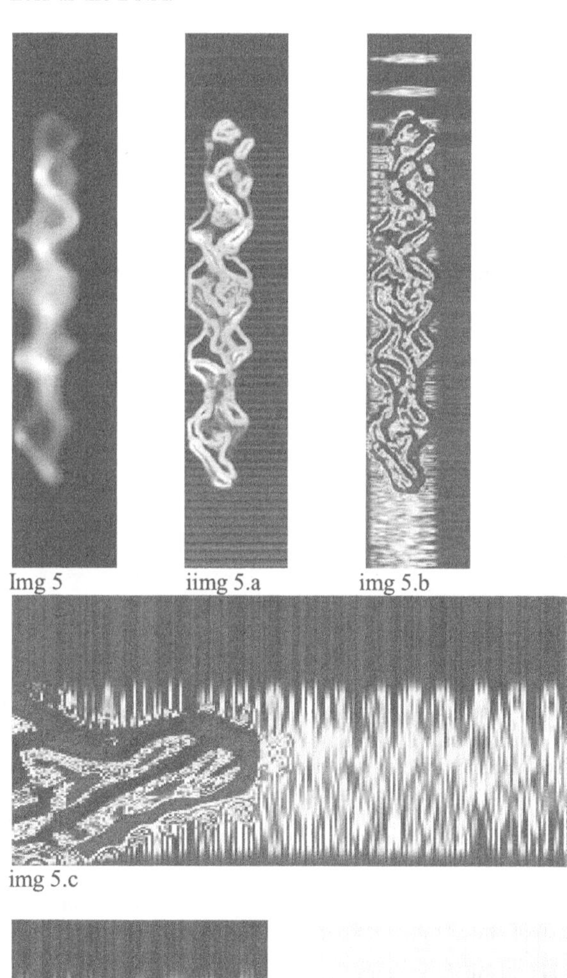

Img 5 iimg 5.a img 5.b

img 5.c

Img 5.d

img 5.e

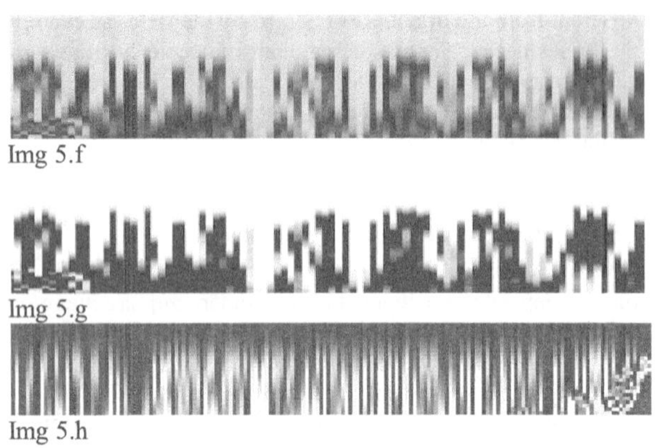

Img 5.f

Img 5.g

Img 5.h

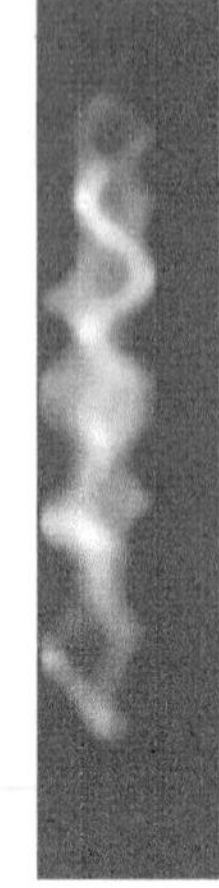

img 5: Image of the DNA double helix
img 5.a: appearance of the electromagnetic field
img 5.b: electromagnetic field very visible
img 5.c: expansion of the electromagnetic field
img 5.d: wavelength periodic
img 5.e: Negative Image
img 5.f: sprawl in order to see the periodic phenomenon
img 5.g: Negative Image
img 5.h: emission of periodic wavelength

The DNA double helix protects it with electromagnetic field from inner and outsider attacks. This field is permeably for the RNA. That has an identic electromagnetic field of the DNA, when contacted the RNA and DNA this later is opened allowing the RNA getting into the DNA in order to realize a copy of DNA blade.

3. Conclusion

It is a derivative of publication:
(MMR system or Micro-Mass Reconstruction) that is the head publication since which we can visualize by images of electromagnetic fields existence of the organs. As well as their broadcasting of the circulating waves, this technology makes the electromagnetic field visible.

We have illustrated too, the electromagnetic field of the DNA and mentioned that no and never one in science literature the idea of the DNA electromagnetic field has been treated or revealed.

We set new theories associated with evidences & proofs through unique images.

SESSION

DATA AND INFORMATION MINING + COMPUTATIONAL BIOLOGY + MEDICAL SCIENCE, MODELS, AND SYSTEMS + BIOMETRICS

Chair(s)

TBA

Mining Accurate Shared Decision Trees from Microarray Gene Expression Data for Different Cancers

Guozhu Dong and Qian Han
Department of Computer Science & Engineering and Kno.e.sis Center
Wright State University, Dayton, OH 45435, USA

Abstract— *This paper studies the problem of mining shared decision trees across multiple application domains, including multiple microarray gene expression datasets for different cancers. Shared knowledge structures capture similarity between application domains and have many useful applications. Given two datasets with classes, we focus on shared decision trees that are highly accurate in both datasets and whose nodes exhibit highly similar distribution of matching data for the classes of the two datasets. Algorithms are presented for mining high quality shared decision trees having high shared accuracy and high data distribution similarity. Experimental results on microarray datasets for medicine are reported to evaluate the algorithms.*

Keywords: microarray gene expression data for cancers; shared knowledge mining; similarity mining; shared decision tree mining

1. Introduction

The usefulness of shared decision tree mining is based on this observation: Given two datasets, a high quality shared decision tree is a common, easy to understand, and informative knowledge structure, characterizing the two datasets and highlighting their conceptual-level structural similarities.

The ultimate goal of mining shared decision trees is to assist users to (1) transfer understanding between applications, (2) perform analogy based reasoning and creative thinking (whose usefulness is discussed in [Fau97], [GC10]), and (3) form novel hypothesis in challenging research applications. Mining shared decision trees is also useful (4) for assessing the degree and types of knowledge-level similarities between application domains, which is important in deciding whether learning transfer between the application domains should be applied to avoid negative learning. Reference [Don12] discusses various applications of general cross domain similarity mining. The usefulness of knowledge transfer between applications has been widely recognized in many application domains (including education, learning, cognitive sciences, biological sciences, business and economic development) and in the learning transfer area [PY10] of data mining/machine learning.

1.1 The Shared Decision Tree Mining Problem (SDTP): In general, the basic *shared decision tree mining problem*[1] is, given[2] datasets D_1 and D_2 with identical[3] sets of classes and attributes, mine a *shared* decision tree with certain properties. Specifically, SDTP mines shared decision tree T with highly similar class distributions of data at the tree nodes, besides having high accuracy in both D_1 and D_2.

SDTP is a special case of *shared classifier mining problem*, which is in turn a special case of *shared knowledge structure mining problem* or *cross domain similarity mining problem* [Don12]. This paper chooses to work on mining shared decision tree classifiers, since decision trees are easy to understand, are widely used, and can be easily converted to informative (sets of) classification rules.

1.2 Main Novelty of This Paper: Our work is fairly different from learning transfer [PY10], both technically and philosophically. Technically, learning transfer builds new classifiers/clusterings for a target dataset by utilizing knowledge structure extracted from auxiliary/source datasets, which may not be shared knowledge structures for both the source and target datasets. Moreover, our work assumes that both source and target datasets have class labels whereas learning transfer assumes that the target dataset has a lack of class labels. Philosophically, learning transfer aims to utilize source datasets to build a *better* classifier/clustering for the target dataset *faster*. In contrast, SDTP aims to use the mined shared decision trees to reveal high level similarities and to assist human users.

Our problem and main algorithm differ from those in traditional decision tree [Qui93] mining significantly: We deal with (1) selecting desirable split attributes from two datasets, and (2) challenges associated with data distribution similarity, with multi-objective optimization for dataset pairs with different characteristics and with tree quality evaluation.

1.3 Main Contributions of the Paper: (1) The paper motivates and formulates the shared decision tree (and shared knowledge structure) mining problem. As argued above, shared decision trees (and knowledge structures) represent high level structural similarities.
(2) The paper introduces the *characterizing classification rule set* concept as an alternative shared knowledge structure; such rule set can be extracted naturally from shared decision trees with high data distribution similarity.

[1]This paper assumes that all input datasets contain attribute/feature based tuples and all tuples have class labels.

[2]The problems and algorithms can all be generalized to more datasets.

[3]Section 2 discusses how to prepare the datasets to meet the "identical classes and attributes" requirements.

(3) The paper proposes several quality evaluation factors, including shared accuracy, data distribution similarity, tree simplicity, and accuracy gap. Moveover, SDT-Miner is developed to address challenges caused by the requirements of high accuracy and of high data distribution similarity. SDT-Miner also uses a novel weight-vector pool idea to trade off two objectives associated with the two requirements for mining high quality trees in dataset pairs with different characteristics.

(4) The paper reports an extensive experimental evaluation on shared decision tree mining w.r.t. quality, and weight tradeoff. Moreover, high quality shared decision trees from microarray gene expression data for cancers are presented, either here or in a supplementary paper [DH10]; those trees could be useful to domain experts.

1.4 Organization of the Paper: §2 defines the SDTP and the shared characterizing classification rule sets mining problem. §3 and §4 present SDT-Miner and associated technical methods. §5 reports experimental evaluation. §6 discusses additional factors for tree quality evaluation, and also discusses SDT-Miner with cross validation measure. §7 discusses future research problems, and concludes the paper.

2. Problem Definition and Preliminary Analysis

We now give a brief review of decision trees. Each internal node of a decision tree (see Figure 1 for an example, although many details are ignored at this time) involves a test on its splitting attribute, plus a number of branches each labeled with a condition; it partitions its associated data into a number of subsets, one per branch. Each leaf node has a class label. The information gain measure is often used for selecting the splitting attributes.

2.1 Context for Shared Decision Tree Mining: To mine shared decision trees, we are given two input datasets D_1 and D_2 with identical sets of classes and attributes. If D_1 and D_2 do not have identical classes and attributes, users will need to provide an 1-to-1 mapping[4] between the classes and attributes of the two datasets.

Definition 1. *A* shared decision tree *for a dataset pair* $(D_1 : D_2)$ *can classify data in* D_1 *and data in* D_2.

We wish to mine shared decision trees that are highly accurate in both datasets. So we define the following measure.

Definition 2. *The* shared classification accuracy *of a shared decision tree* T *for* $(D_1 : D_2)$ *is defined as* $SA(T) = \min(Acc_{D_1}(T), Acc_{D_2}(T))$, *where* $Acc_{D_i}(T)$ *is the accuracy*[5] *of* T *on* D_i.

2.2 Behavior and Data Distribution Similarity: We use data distribution similarity (DS) to capture behavior similarity between two datasets w.r.t. a shared decision tree. DS measures the similarity between the class distributions of data in the two datasets at the nodes of the given tree. Formally, the *class distribution vector* of dataset D_i at tree node V is $CDV_i(V) = (Cnt(C_1, D_i(V))),\ Cnt(C_2, D_i(V))),$ where $Cnt(C_j, D_i(V)) = |\{t \in SD(D_i, V) \mid t\text{'s class is } C_j\}|$, and $SD(D_i, V)$ is the subset of D_i for V. The *distribution similarity* (DSN) at node V of a shared decision tree T for $(D_1 : D_2)$ measures the similarity between the CDVs at V:

$$DSN(V) = \frac{CDV_1(V) \cdot CDV_2(V)}{\|CDV_1(V)\| \cdot \|CDV_2(V)\|}.$$

For example, for the root node of the tree in Figure 1, the CDVs are[6] $(46, 51)$ for D_1 and $(21, 39)$ for D_2, and the DSN is $0.97 = \frac{(46,51)\cdot(21,39)}{\|(46,51)\|\cdot\|(21,39)\|}$.

Definition 3. *The* data distribution similarity *(DS) of a shared decision tree* T *for* $(D_1 : D_2)$ *is defined as the average* $DSN(V)$ *values among all nodes of* T.

For example, the DS of the tree in Figure 1 is 0.95, the average of all nodes' DSNs, which are 0.97, 0.99, 0.99, 0.96, 0.98, 0.95, 1, 0.99, 0.97, 0.96, 1, 1, 0.55.

Other methods to define DS can be examined, e.g. one that only considers DSN at the leaf nodes. Since experiments showed that those methods did not lead to better trees with more similar data distribution, we will not pursue them further.

2.3 Shared Decision Tree Mining Problem: To define the shared decision tree mining problem, a shared decision tree quality measure is required.

Definition 4. *The* quality of a shared decision tree T (SDTQ) *is defined as the harmonic mean of* $DS(T)$ *and* $SA(T)$, *namely* $SDTQ(T) = \frac{2DS(T)SA(T)}{DS(T)+SA(T)}$.

We choose harmonic mean because it is widely used, and it allows both DS and SA to play a role. Moreover, it does not require any parameters, and also can differentiate high quality shared decision trees from lower quality ones.

We are now ready to define the SDTP problem.

Definition 5 (SDTP). *Given a dataset pair* $(D_1 : D_2)$, *the* SDTP *is to mine a shared decision tree* T *with high* SDTQ(T).

An example shared decision tree mined from real (cancer) dataset pairs is given in Figure 1. The data of the two datasets

[4]The 1-to-1 mappings can be real or hypothetical. Considering hypothetical equivalence relations helps support "what-if" analysis on questions such as "what shared decision trees exist for the given equivalence relations."

[5]When the datasets are small in number of tuples, one may estimate $Acc_{D_i}(T)$ as $1 - \frac{|W_i|}{|D_i|}$, where W_i is the set of tuples classified wrongly at the leaf nodes of T. Our experiments use this method. Holdout testing can be used otherwise.

[6]$(46, 51)$ represents D_1 contains 46 tuples of C_1 and 51 tuples of C_2.

have very similar distributions at the tree nodes and the leaf nodes are very pure (with dominating majority class).

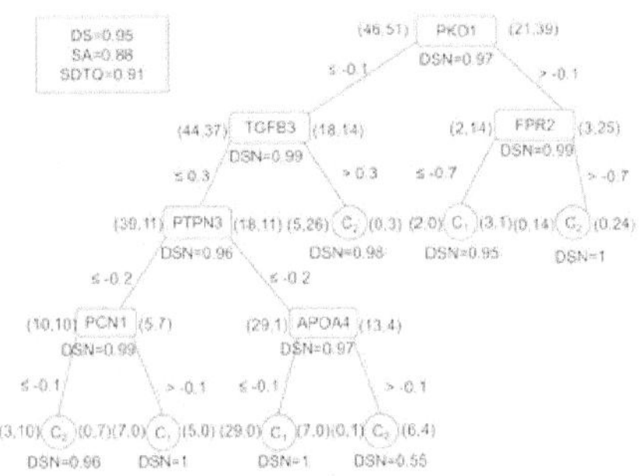

Fig. 1: Shared Decision Tree Mined from (BC:CN)

We also consider another minor variant of SDTP, called SDTP$^-$, which aims to mine shared decision tree T with high shared accuracy (SA(T)). The SDTP$^-$ can be solved using variants of SDT-Miner by ignoring the DS factor.

2.4 Characterizing Rule Set Mining: While the focus of the paper is on shared decision tree mining, we now introduce two other concepts, another shared knowledge structure and the associated mining problem. This is done since shared decision trees mined by our algorithms can naturally generate such shared structures.

Definition 6. *A characterizing classification rule set (CRS) for a dataset D is a small set $\mathcal{R}$ of classification rules*[7] *that characterizes D, meeting these two requirements: (a) the set $\mathcal{R}$ forms a highly accurate rule based classifier, and (b) the matching*[8] *datasets of different rules in $\mathcal{R}$ are highly disjoint and they collectively cover almost the entire D.*

The "disjoint and cover" requirements ensure that the rule set describes the entire dataset under consideration and it is "minimally" redundant. The "small" requirement, together with the "minimally-redundant" property, make it easy to understand and manually process the rule set by humans.

To illustrate, consider the CRS (in Table 1) extracted from the tree shown in Figure 1, using the natural "path to rule" mapping. Clearly, the rules have very similar supports and confidences in the two datasets. Being induced from a decision tree, different rules have disjoint matching datasets.

Table 1: Rule Set from a Tree Mined from (BC:CN)

1. $PKD1 \leq -0.1, TGFB3 > 0.3 \rightarrow C_1$ (32.0%,83.9%) (5%,100%);
2. $PKD1 > -0.1, FPR2 \leq -0.7 \rightarrow C_1$ (2.1%,100%) (6.7%,75%);
3. $PKD1 > -0.1, FPR2 > -0.7 \rightarrow C_2$ (14.4%,100%) (40%,100%);

...

2.5 Advantages of SDTP over SDTP$^-$: High $SDTQ$ shared decision trees mined by algorithms for $SDTP$ are more desirable than high SA shared decision trees mined by algorithms for $SDTP^-$ in two significant ways: (1) High $SDTQ$ shared decision trees describe highly similar population structures[9] in the two datasets. (2) A high $SDTQ$ shared decision tree can give a shared CRS with highly similar supports and confidences for the rules (shown in Table 1) with no matching data overlap among the rules. The high SA shared decision trees do not have these properties.

3. SDT-Miner: Main Procedures

This section presents *Shared Decision Tree Miner* (SDT-Miner), for the shared decision tree mining problem. While SDT-Miner is structurally similar to traditional decision tree algorithms such as C4.5, it has several novel ideas.

The most basic operation in SDT-Miner is to select attributes and values to split tree nodes. SDT-Miner makes the selection to maximize an objective function that combines information gain ($IG2$)[10] and data distribution similarity (DS) on two datasets. It combines and balances them using a weighted sum based on a weight vector $w = (w_{IG}, w_{DS})$. (We discuss how to define $IG2$ in the next section.)

SDT-Miner has five inputs (listed in Algorithm 1), and calls SDTNode recursively to build a shared decision tree.

Algorithm 1. SDT-Miner

Input: $(D_1 : D_2)$: Two datasets
  $AttrSet$: Set of candidate attributes that can be used
  $MinSize$: Dataset size threshold for splitting termination
  $w = (w_{IG}, w_{DS})$: Weight vector on $IG2$ and DS
Output: A shared decision tree for D_1 and D_2
Method:
1. Create root node V;
2. Call SDTNode($V, D_1, D_2, AttrSet, MinSize, w$);
3. Output the shared decision tree rooted at V.

SDTNode (Function 1) splits a tree node V by picking the best split attribute and value to optimize the ID function:

$$ID(A, a_V) = w_{IG} * IG2(A, a_V) + w_{DS} * DSN(A, a_V),$$

where A and a_V are resp. a candidate splitting attribute/value, and $DSN(A, a_V)$ is defined as the average of the two DSN values for the two children nodes of V when A and a_V are used to split V. Both $IG2$ and DSN use the two datasets D'_1 and D'_2 for V. SDTNode also needs the sizes of the complete input datasets D_1 and D_2 of SDT-Miner, which are omitted in the parameter list for simplicity.

We now give more details about the SDTNode function. (1) SDTNode uses (line 1) function TerminateCheck to determine if splitting should terminate for node V, in order

[7] A classification rule has the form $r : \phi_1, \cdots, \phi_m \rightarrow C_i$ (s, c), where $\phi_1, \cdots, \phi_m$ is the body of the rule, C_i is the head of the rule, each ϕ_j is a condition on an attribute, s is the support of (the body of) the rule, and c is the confidence of the rule.

[8] The matching dataset of a rule r in a dataset D, denoted by $mat(r, D)$, is defined to be the set of tuples in D that satisfy the body of r.

[9] Population structures have often been used in the literature; e.g. the structure of a country is often characterized by percentage of people in the 0-14, 14-65, and 65+ groups.

[10] One should not confuse $IG2$ with the standard IG on one dataset. $IG2$ is defined to help mine high quality shared decision trees in the next section.

```
Function 1. SDTNode(V, D'_1, D'_2, AttrSet, MinSize, w)
1. If TerminateCheck(V, D'_1, D'_2, MinSize, AttrSet)
   then assign the majority class in D'_1 and D'_2
   as class label of V and return;
2. Select the attribute B and value b_V that maximize ID, that is
   ID(B,b_V) = max{ID(A,a_V) | A ∈ AttrSet, and a_V is
            a common candidate split value for A at V};
   // use B and b_V as the splitting attribute/value for V
   // compute the left subtree of V
3. Create left child node V_l of V,
   with "B ≤ b_V" as the corresponding edge's label,
   let D'_il = {t ∈ D'_i | t satisfies "B ≤ b_V"} for i = 1, 2,
   call SDTNode(V_l, D'_1l, D'_2l, AttrSet − {B}, MinSize, w);
   // compute the right subtree of V
4. Create right child node V_r of V,
   with "B > b_V" as the corresponding edge's label,
   let D'_ir = {t ∈ D'_i | t satisfies "B > b_V"} for i = 1, 2,
   call SDTNode(V_r, D'_1r, D'_2r, AttrSet − {B}, MinSize, w).
```

to avoid overfitting and to obtain simpler high quality trees. Details are given in section 4.

(2) We determine the majority class of a node V (line 1) as follows. When the majority classes of the two datasets for V are the same, we pick that majority class as the class label for V. Otherwise, we determine the class label of V to minimize the overall error rate, considering both datasets. Let D_1 and D_2 be the two complete input datasets for SDT-Miner, C_1 and C_2 be their two classes, and D'_1 and D'_2 be the subsets of D_1 and D_2 for V. We define the error rate for D'_j when C_i is the class label assigned to V as $ER(C_i, D'_j) = \frac{|W_j|}{|D_j|}$, where W_j is the set of tuples in D'_j that would be wrongly classified. Then we pick class C_k such that $\sum_{i=1}^{2} ER(C_k, D'_i) = min(\sum_{i=1}^{2} ER(C_1, D'_i), \sum_{i=1}^{2} ER(C_2, D'_i))$ as class label.

(3) Selecting B and b_V to maximize ID (line 2) helps ensure that the split attribute/value have high $IG2$ and DS. There are several methods (discussed in the next section) to define $IG2$, leading to significant performance difference.

(4) Experiments show that the best shared decision trees mined by SDT-Miner from different dataset pairs use different weight vectors, indicating that different dataset pairs have different characteristics w.r.t. the relationship between $IG2$ and DS. § 4 presents several pools of weight vectors to help mine (near) optimal shared decision trees efficiently.

(5) The candidate common split values for an attribute A at V (the last part of line 2) are determined by considering the A values in both datasets for V. They are the mid points between consecutive A values in the two datasets: If v_1, v_2, ..., v_n are the distinct values of A in $D'_1 \cup D'_2$ listed in increasing order, then each $(v_i, v_i + 1)/2$ is a candidate common split value.

4. SDT-Miner: Subroutines

We now present several technical ideas. Some are used by SDT-Miner, while others are competing ideas.

4.1 Defining Information Gain ($IG2$): The $IG2$ for two datasets can be defined in several ways, depending on how the two datasets are treated. Let A be an attribute and a an associated split value for a dataset pair $(D'_1 : D'_2)$ for a given tree node. (a) The *union-based information gain* treats the two datasets as one:

$$IG_{2u}(A, a, D'_1, D'_2) = IG(A,\ a,\ D'_1 \cup D'_2).$$

(b) The *average-based information gain* is defined as the average of the information gain on the two datasets:

$$IG_{2avg}(A, a, D'_1, D'_2) = avg(IG(A,\ a,\ D'_1), IG(A,\ a,\ D'_2)).$$

(c) Similarly, the *minimum-based information gain* uses the minimum of the two information gains:

$$IG_{2min}(A, a, D'_1, D'_2) = min(IG(A,\ a,\ D'_1), IG(A,\ a,\ D'_2)).$$

Experiments showed that IG_{2u} is the best, when used in combination with the DS. SDT-Miner uses the IG_{2u} method. The IG_{2avg} method is poor because it may give a relatively high IG_{2avg} value when one of the two component IGs is very high and the other is very low. The IG_{2min} method has the following weakness: When two competing attributes A_1 and A_2 have similar IG_{2min} values, their IG values in the two datasets can behave very differently.

4.2 Encourage Simpler Trees: SDT-Miner aims to build simple trees and avoid "overfitting". (Tree simplicity, measured by tree height and number of (leaf) nodes ([Mor82], [FI92]), is used to evaluate tree quality; preferring simpler trees is consistent with the Occam's razor principle.) We use two techniques to achieve that goal. (1) When many attribtues are available, we restrict the candidate attributes to those whose IG is ranked high in both datasets. This avoids non-discriminative attributes that maybe locally discriminative at a given node. (2) We stop splitting for a given tree node when at least one dataset is small or pure.

4.3 TerminateCheck: The TerminateCheck function returns "true" if at least one of three conditions is true: (a) $AttrSet$ is empty. (b) Either $|D'_1| \leq MinSize$ or $|D'_2| \leq MinSize$. (c) At least one of D'_1 and D'_2 is pure[11] ($T1P$), or both D'_1 and D'_2 are pure ($T2P$).

SDT-Miner uses $T1P$ since $T2P$ often leads to significantly lower DS. $T2P$'s poor performance can be attributed to its encouraging node splitting when one dataset is pure.

Condition (a) is identical to the traditional decision tree termination condition. Conditions (b) and (c) are designed to deal with the subtleties due to the presence of two datasets.

In general, for dataset pairs $(D_1 : D_2)$ with small datasets (< 150 tuples), 3 is a reasonable $MinSize$ value; otherwise, we normally choose $MinSize = 0.02 * min(|D_1|, |D_2|)$.

4.4 Weight Vector Pools: As will be seen in the experiment section, different dataset pairs have different characteristics in terms of how the $IG2$ and DS factors relate to each other. To mine an optimal shared decision tree, SDT-Miner gives appropriate weight to $IG2$ and DS using a weight vector,

[11] A dataset is pure if all of its tuples belong to a common class.

based on this relationship.[12] Clearly it is computationally infeasible to consider all possible weight vectors. We address this by using a small pool of well spaced weight vectors, to help SDT-Miner explore the possibilities of the relationship between $IG2$ and DS. Several weight vector pools are considered. The two weights in a weight vector (w_{IG}, w_{DS}) in a given pool are required to satisfy $0 < w_{IG}, w_{DS} < 1$, $w_{IG} + w_{DS} = 1$, and w_{IG}, w_{DS} take values in a particular weight value set. Each weight value set contains 0.1 and has a fixed step size $\delta > 0$. Let $WVP(\delta)$ denote the weight vector pool for δ. We examined four weight vector pools, for $\delta = 0.4, 0.2, 0.1, 0.05$.

$WVP(0.4) = \{(0.1, 0.9), (0.5, 0.5), (0.9, 0.1)\}$(3 vectors)
$WVP(0.2) = \{(0.1, 0.9), (0.3, 0.7), \ldots\}$ (5 vectors)
$WVP(0.1) = \{(0.1, 0.9), (0.2, 0.8), \ldots\}$ (9 vectors)
$WVP(0.05) = \{(0.05, 0.95), (0.1, 0.9), \ldots\}$ (19 vectors)

5. Experimental Evaluation

This section uses experimental results on Microarray datasets to demonstrate that (1) SDT-Miner is able to mine high quality shared decision trees; (2) SDT-Miner's techniques are better than competing ones. It discusses (3) how SDT-Miner performs when it uses a single weight vector, and (4) how it performs when it uses multiple weight vectors.

In the experiments, we set $MinSize = 3$ and $AttrSet = \{A \mid rank_1(A) + rank_2(A)$ is among the smallest 20% of all shared attributes, where $rank_i(A)$ is the position of A when D_i's attributes are listed in decreasing IG order$\}$. SDT-Miner uses $T1P$ and IG_{2u}. The $WVP(0.1)$ weight vector pool is used by default. Experiments were conducted on a 2.20 GHz AMD Athlon with 3 GB memory running Windows XP. The codes were implemented in Matlab.

5.1 Microarray Datasets: Our experiments used the four real-world microarray gene expression datasets given in Table 2,[13] concerning cancers (2) and disease treatment outcome (2, marked by *). The two classes for cancers are usually *normal* and *tumor*; the two classes for treatment-outcome datasets vary, and they are usually synonyms of *desirable* and *undesirable*.[14] Each tuple in such a dataset is a microarray measurement of a patient tissue sample and each column is the expression level for a gene in that sample. We normalized the data so that each column of each dataset has a mean of 0 and a standard deviation of 1.

Table 2: Statistics of Datasets

Dataset	No. of Tuples	No. of Attributes
Breast Cancer (BC)	97	24481
Central Nervous System* (CN)	60	7129
DLBCL-Harvard* (DH)	58	7129
Prostate Cancer (PC)	136	12600

[12]It is interesting to investigate whether one can determine this relationship for a dataset pair efficiently, without running SDT-Miner.

[13]Dataset references: *BC* [Vee02], *CN* [Pom02], *DH* [Shi02], *PC* [Sin02].

[14]The first and second classes of the datasets are: 'relapse" and "non-relapse" for *BC*, "class 1" and "class 0" for *CN*, "cured" and "fatal" for *DH*, and "tumor" and "normal" for *PC*.

We used the ArrayTrack [Ton03] to identify shared (equivalent) attributes (different names for the same gene in different gene name systems). Table 3 lists the number of shared attributes for the dataset pairs. Dataset pairs on a common row have the same number of shared attributes, since CN/DH share an attribute list.

Table 3: Number of Shared Attributes between Datasets

Dataset Pair	No. of Shared Attributes
(BC:CN), (BC:DH)	5114
(CN:DH)	7129
(CN:PC), (DH:PC)	5317
(BC:PC)	8124

For each dataset pair, our experiments assumed the first classes of the two datasets are equivalent, and so on.

5.2 SDT-Miner Mines High Quality Shared Decision Trees: Table 4 lists the quality scores, and the associated DS and SA values, of the best shared decision trees mined by SDT-Miner. (The last column will be explained later.)

Table 4: Quality of Best Shared Trees by SDT-Miner

Dataset Pair	DS	SA	SDTQ	AG
BC: CN	0.96	0.91	0.93	0.09
BC: DH	0.98	0.98	0.98	0.02
BC: PC	0.98	0.98	0.98	0.02
CN: DH	0.98	0.98	0.98	0.02
CN: PC	0.91	0.93	0.92	0.07
DH: PC	0.97	0.95	0.96	0.05
Average	0.96	0.95	0.96	0.05
CN:CN90%	0.93	0.42	0.58	0.58
DH:DH90%	0.91	0.45	0.60	0.55

Moreover, Figure 1 (Section 2) shows a shared decision tree with high DS, SA and quality scores, mined by SDT-Miner from dataset pairs (BC:CN).

Clearly we cannot expect to find shared decision trees with high quality scores for all dataset pairs. To demonstrate this, we generated dataset pairs where one dataset is a real one, and the other one is obtained from the real dataset by class label exchange for certain fraction of tuples. For example, for dataset pair (CN:CN90%), the dataset CN90% is generated by randomly selecting 90% of the tuples of C1 of dataset CN and changing their class label to C2, and similarly for C2. The shared decision tree mined from such dataset pair often has poor SDTQ due to low SA (see Table 4). This is not surprising: for (CN:CN90%), each class of CN is essentially paired with its opposing class, and hence high quality shared decision trees are not expected to exist.

5.3 SDT-Miner's Techniques Outperform Competing Ones: This section confirms that the techniques used by SDT-Miner outperform the competing techniques we examined. SDT-Miner uses $T1P$ and $IG2$. The competing techniques include the $T2P$ termination option and other ways to compute $IG2$. We briefly discuss other inferior methods.

5.4 Termination Options: $T1P$ Outperforms $T2P$: Experiments demonstrate that $T1P$ (which SDT-Miner uses) is better. Table 5 shows the DS and SA values for the trees mined when T1P or T2P is used (both using the $WVP(0.1)$

pool). In all cases the DS values of the trees mined using T1P are higher than those mined using T2P, and that is also true on average. It can be verified that, for all dataset pairs, $T1P$ is the better option yielding higher quality trees. $T2P$'s poor performance is clearly associated with the fact that it encourages node splitting when only one dataset is pure.

Table 5: DS/SA Quality Values for Options T1P/T2P

Dataset Pair	$DS(T1P)$	$SA(T1P)$	$DS(T2P)$	$SA(T2P)$
(BC:CN)	0.96	0.91	0.91	0.90
(BC:DH)	0.98	0.98	0.97	0.98
(BC:PC)	0.98	0.98	0.94	0.99
(CN:DH)	0.98	0.98	0.93	0.97
(CN:PC)	0.91	0.93	0.86	0.87
(DH:PC)	0.97	0.95	0.88	0.93
Average	0.96	0.95	0.92	0.94

5.5 $IG2$ Methods: Union Way Outperforms Others: Experiments demonstrate that IG_{2u} (which SDT-Miner uses) is better. Table 6 lists the tree quality achieved by SDT-Miner and by its variants that replaces IG_{2u} using IG_{2avg} and IG_{2min}. All methods use the weight vector $(0.5, 0.5)$. The average quality achieved by SDT-Miner is 0.94, much better than that of 0.76 (0.72) achieved by IG_{2avg} (IG_{2min}).

Table 6: Quality of Shared Trees by Three Methods

Dataset Pair	SDT-Miner	IG_{2min}	IG_{2avg}
(BC:CN)	0.92	0.68	0.69
(BC:DH)	0.98	0.81	0.65
(BC:PC)	0.91	0.68	0.82
(CN:DH)	0.95	0.68	0.82
(CN:PC)	0.92	0.76	0.77
(DH:PC)	0.96	0.69	0.79
Average	0.94	0.72	0.76

The quality of a shared tree can be mainly reflected in two aspects: (a) Does the tree contain many "inverted nodes"? A node is *inverted* if the two datasets' majority classes at the node are different. (b) Does the tree contain many nodes with many wrongly classified tuples?

SDT-Miner is better than IG_{2avg} since typical shared decision trees mined by SDT-Miner do not contain any inverted nodes and have very few wrongly classified tuples, while shared decision trees mined by IG_{2avg} often contain nodes with a large number of wrongly classified tuples.

5.6 SDT-Miner Using One Weight Vector: This section examines the performance of SDT-Miner using a single weight vector from $WVP(0.1)$. Experiments show that (a) the choice of weight vector has significant impact on the mined tree's quality, and (b) no individual weight vector is the best for all dataset pairs. Table 7 lists the "best"/ "worst" weight vectors, which when used by SDT-Miner produces the highest/lowest quality trees, and the relative improvement of the best quality over the worst.

For (a), the average relative improvement is an impressive 6.2%. For (b), from Table 7, no single weight vector is the best weight vector for all dataset pairs. we note that the best weight vectors all belong to $\{(0.1, 0.9), (0.7, 0.3), (0.9, 0.1)\}$. The larger weight in the

Table 7: Best/Worst Weight Vectors

Dataset Pair	Best Weight Vector	Worst Weight Vector	Relative Quality Improvement
(BC:CN)	(0.9,0.1)	(0.1,0.9)	1.1%
(BC:DH)	(0.9,0.1)	(0.1,0.9)	3.2%
(BC:PC)	(0.7,0.3)	(0.4,0.6)	7.7%
(CN:DH)	(0.7,0.3)	(0.3,0.7)	14.0%
(CN:PC)	(0.1,0.9)	(0.9,0.1)	4.5%
(DH:PC)	(0.7,0.3)	(0.1,0.9)	6.7%
Average			6.2%

weight vector indicates that higher emphasis is addressed on that factor; and the smaller one is less important.

5.7 SDT-Miner Using Multiple Weight Vectors: Table 8 shows the relative improvement of the tree quality obtained by the best weight vector from the $WVP(0.1)$ weight vector pool over the quality obtained by a single weight vector. Since certain weight vectors behave quite similarly to some others, this table includes only three weight vectors, namely (0.1,0.9), (0.7,0.3), (0.9,0.1).

The table shows the approach of selecting the best tree mined by different weight vectors leads to better performance than the approach of using a single weight vector. Sometimes, the relative improvement is about 12.6%.

Table 8: Using Multiple Weight Vectors vs Using One

Dataset Pair	(0.1,0.9)	(0.7,0.3)	(0.9,0.1)
(BC:CN)	1.1%	1.1%	0%
(BC:DH)	3.2%	0%	0%
(BC:PC)	1.0%	0%	6.5%
(CN:DH)	12.6%	0%	0%
(CN:PC)	0%	0%	4.5%
(DH:PC)	6.7%	0%	3.2%
Average	4.1%	0%	2.4%

We also performed experiments to compare the performance of all four weight vector pools listed in Section 4. It turns out that $WVP(0.2)$ is good, since it contains a small number of vectors and it yields good performance. If a user only wants to use one weight vector instead of a pool, we recommend $(0.7, 0.3)$, based on results in Tables 7 and 8.

5.8 Experiments on Other Algorithms : We examined two other algorithms. ISDT-Miner finds a decision tree T_i for each D_i using C4.5, and then selects the tree with higher SA as the shared decision tree. USDT-Miner mines tree T for the dataset $D_1 \cup D_2$ using C4.5 as the shared tree. Experiments show that the average SDTQ values on the 6 dataset pairs are 64% for ISDT-Miner and 92% for USDT-Miner, worse than SDT-Miner's 96%. We note that, when the similarity of the class ratios between the two datasets in a dataset pair is low, USDT-Miner is much worse than our SDT-Miner. We verify this using the experiments of generated dataset pairs. From one dataset of such dataset pairs, we remove a given percentage of the tuples from a given class. For example, to generate dataset pair (BC:PC_C_2-30%), the last 30% of tuples of the second class are removed from dataset PC. Such removal significantly decreases the class ratios between the two datasets, compared with the ratio between the original two datasets. The SDTQ value of the shared decision tree mined by USDT-Miner on this dataset pair is 82%, significantly worse than the 95% achieved by SDT-Miner.

We also conduct experiments on algorithms for solving $SDTP^-$. For the variant of SDT-Miner using IG_{2u} and ignoring DS, the mined shared trees' $SDTQ$ values are often worse than those mined by SDT-Miner. For variants using IG_{2min} or IG_{2avg}, the SA values are much worse.

6. Other Factors on Shared Decision Tree Quality and Validation Methods

(a) We suggest to use tree simplicity as an additional factor to measure shared decision trees' quality. Tree simplicity, usually measured by tree height, number of nodes, or number of leaf nodes (denoted by #LN) ([Mor82], [FI92]), has been used in evaluating the tree quality on a single dataset. Preferring simpler trees is consistent with the principle of Occam's razor. Experiments show that shared decision trees have $avg(\#LN) = 7$ for real dataset pairs, much smaller than the $avg(\#LN) = 24.2$ for pairs of random datasets.

(b) We also suggest to use accuracy gap as a factor to measure shared decision trees' quality. Specifically, given a shared decision tree T on a dataset pair $(D_1 : D_2)$, the *accuracy gap* is defined to be $AG = min(BA_1, BA_2) - SA$, where BA_i is the accuracy of the best decision tree for D_i, and SA is the shared accuracy of T. T is more valuable if AG is small, since it is nearly as good as the best individual trees for D_1 and D_2.[15]

Table 4 gives the AG values for various shared trees mined from the real dataset pairs and some permuted dataset pairs. We observe that the AG value is relatively small for the real dataset pairs, whereas it is big for the permuted dataset pair.

While cross validation based measure is a widely used for classification accuracy evaluation, SDT-Miner uses training data to measure the quality of shared decision trees. This choice was made since the microarray gene expression datasets are usually small, making it hard to use cross validation. One could consider using cross validation if the datasets are large.

As shown in Table 4, for some dataset pairs, the quality score of the best shared trees can be very low. This can help get a better understanding of how the quality scores behave.

7. Concluding Remarks and Future Directions

In this paper we motivated the shared decision tree (and shared general knowledge structure) mining problem using importance of shared knowledge structures for supporting understanding transfer, for supporting analogical reasoning, and for supporting creative thinking. Then we presented SDT-Miner algorithm, using novel ideas to address challenges caused by the high shared accuracy and highly similar data distribution requirements, the need to optimize two objectives, and the presence of two datasets with significantly different relationships w.r.t. those objectives. We considered how to define information gain on two datasets, and how to capture behavior similarity using data distribution similarity. We presented several quality factors for evaluating shared decision trees' quality. We used experiments to show that SDT-Miner can mine high quality shared decision trees. We also defined CRS as another candidate shared knowledge structure, which can be easily extracted from shared decision trees with high shared accuracy and high distribution similarity.

Future research questions include: Consider mining other forms of shared knowledge structures, collaborate with domain experts to utilize and improve the shared knowledge structure mining techniques in medical/scientific investigations.

Acknowledgement: This work was supported in part by NSF grant IIS-1044634 and by a DAGSI scholarship. Any opinions, findings, and conclusions or recommendations expressed here are those of the authors and do not necessarily reflect the views of the funding agencies.

[15] Gap on other quality factors can be used, e.g., decision trees have $avg(\#LN) = 5.3$ for single real datasets, and $avg(\#LN) = 16.7$ for single random datasets.

References

[DH10] Guozhu Dong and Qian Han. Supplementary information: Detailed tables and shared decision trees accompanying [DH10:SDT]. http://www.cs.wright.edu/~gdong/projects.html, 2010.

[Don12] Guozhu Dong. Cross domain similarity mining: Research issues and potential applications including supporting research by analogy. *ACM SIGKDD Explorations*, June 2012.

[Fau97] Gilles Fauconnier. *Mappings in Thought and Language*. Cambridge University Press, 1997.

[FI92] Usama M. Fayyad and Keki B. Irani. The attribute selection problem in decision tree generation. In *Proceedings of the tenth national conference on Artificial intelligence*, pages 104–110, 1992.

[GC10] Dedre Gentner and Julie Colhoun. Analogical processes in human thinking and learning. In *Towards a Theory of Thinking*, pages 35–48. 2010.

[Mor82] Bernard M. E. Moret. Decision trees and diagrams. *ACM Computing Surveys*, 14(4):593–623, 1982.

[Pom02] Scott L. Pomeroy, et al. Prediction of central nervous system embryonal tumour outcome based on gene expression. *Nature*, 415:436–442, Jan. 2002.

[PY10] Sinno Jialin Pan and Qiang Yang. A survey on transfer learning. *IEEE Transactions on Knowledge and Data Engineering*, 22(10):1345–1359, 2010.

[Qui93] John Ross Quinlan. *C4.5: Programs for Machine Learning*. 1993.

[Shi02] Margaret A. Shipp, et al. Diffuse large b-cell lymphoma outcome prediction by gene-expression profiling and supervised machine learning. *Nature Medicine*, 8:68–74, Jan. 2002.

[Sin02] Dinesh Singh, et al. Gene expression correlates of clinical prostate cancer behavior. *Cancer Cell*, 1(2):203–209, Mar. 2002.

[Ton03] Weida Tong et al. ArrayTrack-Supporting toxicogenomic research at the FDA's National Center for Toxicological Research (NCTR). *EHP Toxicogenomics*, 111(15):1819–1826, 2003.

[Vee02] Laura J. Van't Veer, et al. Gene expression profiling predicts clinical outcome of breast cancer. *Nature*, 415:530–536, 2002.

Cloud-Accelerated Data-Mining for Putative Heteromeric Transcription Factors and Target Genes Using Microarray Gene Expression Profiles

***Edward A. Salinas[1], Amitava Karmaker[2] (*corresponding author)**
[1]Independent Researcher, Rockville, Maryland 20852, USA
[2]University of Wisconsin-Stout, Menomonie, Wisconsin 54751, USA

Abstract *– Observing and interpreting intra-protein and protein-DNA interactions is critical to understanding the complexities of gene regulation [3, 16]. We here review a previously presented method [1, 15, 17, 26], using a variation of microarray expression profile correlation analysis, that mines microarray data to find interactions between putative heteropolymeric transcription factor (TF) complexes and target genes. The technique incorporates correlation coefficients between genes and transcription factors expression profiles, but also between genes and hypothetical TF co-factors, whose expression profiles are estimated by taking minima from constituent profiles. Second, we revisit the technique and improve it with parametric calibration. Third, using the calibrated parameter, we adapt our algorithm and implement it to run on the Amazon EC2 cloud to achieve speedup and obtain results in a timely manner.*

Keywords: *Microarrays, Biological Data Mining, Amazon EC2 cloud, correlation coefficients.*

1 Introduction

Since the sequencing of the human genome [2] has been completed, the interpretation and biological connotation of sequences and the annotation of functional elements of the genome have been of great interest to researchers. Despite the fact that many genes have been catalogued, their complete regulatory interactions are not completely understood at the transcriptional level [3]. To know what orchestrates gene control, we must to discover regulatory elements and any interacting transcription factor (TF) complexes. Tuning the expression of genes, TF regulatory complexes may bind to cis-elements in promoter regions and either facilitate or inhibit gene expression [16]. Knowledge of such interactions would allow the construction of transcription regulatory networks (TRNs) and help researchers understand the dynamics of gene expression. By building and elucidating whole TRNs, we may be able to discover novel routes of gene regulation which may have applicability in many settings, for example the laboratory and the clinic.

It has been an arduous task in functional genomics to build TRNs from protein-DNA interactions. *In silico* data mining of transcription regulatory elements is quite effective for prokaryotes, like Escherichia coli [4], whose genomic landscapes are more compact with numerous genes being controlled by a single operon. For higher eukaryotes, model-based approaches [3] that find patterns among co-expressed genes with respect to regulating TFs have been proposed. The techniques include the finding of over-represented DNA motifs and common transcriptional regulatory modules among co-expressed genes. A variety of statistical and machine-learning algorithms have been employed; they include position-weighted matrices, position-specific score matrices, Markov chains, artificial neural networks, and expectation maximization [5-11]. Such techniques, though, incorporating model-prediction-based approaches have unfortunately been susceptible to high false-positive prediction rates and a majority of the predicted TFBSs have no functional role *in vivo* [12].

Discovering novel means to anticipate which proteins might cooperate in a heteropolymeric complex may aid in the discovery of new TRNs. Here, we hypothesize that heteropolymeric TF complexes of constituent members can be predicted *in silico* based on their constituent TF expression profiles. Using transcription factor activity profiles and gene activity profiles from microarray data, we review a technique that relies on combinations of TFs and correlation coefficients to predict TF-complexes [1, 15, 17, 26]. The dataset includes gene and TF expression profiles from a female human across 115 tissues samples [13]. The method supposes that a hypothetical TF-complex expression profile in a given tissue can be measured by taking minima from the component factors at the given tissue. By combining these values across tissues to create hypothetical TF complex profiles and by comparing and contrasting these profiles with each other and with the genuine expression profiles using correlation coefficients, we hope to discover novel complexes. The putative heteropolymeric complexes are assigned a score-value based on the analysis. These values are then sorted with values from other proposed and hypothetical complexes. This analysis may result in the identification of complexes that we believe are more likely to be genuine, and not hypothetical.

Our technique relies on a combinatorial scheme choosing a gene, tuples of TFs, and calculating correlation coefficients between the gene and TF profiles (both real and hypothetical). As our technique is parameterized, we explore parameter calibration using known (true positive) TF-pair-gene data. Because timing studies indicated long execution times we modified our code to run on the Amazon EC2 cloud. Using the Amazon EC2 cloud, we obtained speedup and results in about a day, whereas, the local "terrestrial" implementation would have taken months to generate results.

2 Methods and Materials

For the project, we employed public microarray data [13]. The data come from a variety of human genes and transcription factors expressions across *115* tissue types (e.g. bladder, brain, stomach, and uterus). The data is atypical from other microarray data in that genomic DNA material is harnessed to approximate mRNA transcript levels. The dataset may be viewed as a table of transcript expression values with genes indexed by rows and tissues by columns; each cell in the data table thus quantifies a gene's activity in the indicated tissue. A portion of *3166* gene transcripts, from *2526* unique genes, was chosen. Also, *352* transcripts, based on entrez-gene and TRANSFAC databases [20, 21] were marked as transcription factors was also chosen. These two gene and TF datasets were used for all calculations and computations.

Our method contains a genetic profile pre-processing procedure where a gene's activity level may be adjusted with the formula $y'=ye^{\alpha y}$ where α has a constant parametric setting for the algorithm. For all experiments done for this paper, the value of α was set to *0.26*. The graph in figure 1 demonstrates the motivation for the transformation. We later

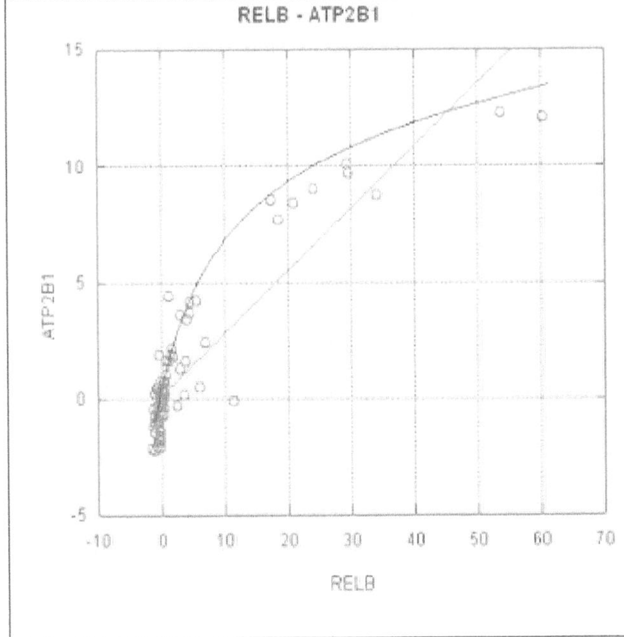

Fig. 1 Data such as depicted this chart helped motivate the α-transformation of the gene data.

describe a calibration procedure we used to arrive at this parametric setting.

Given *1* row (profile) of microarray data for a gene *g* and a set of *N* rows (profiles) of transcription factors $TF_1, \ldots TF_N$, our method to asses the regulatory dynamics between *g* and the *N* transcription factors as a complex is as follows. First, the expression data for the gene is transformed with the previously described alpha transformation. Second, as we have done before [17, 26] *N* correlation coefficients are calculated between the gene's transformed expression profile and the individual transcription factor expression profiles. The Pearson Correlation Coefficients are computed using the formula:

$$r_{xy}=\frac{n\sum x_i y_i-\sum x_i y_i}{\sqrt{n\sum x_i^2-(\sum x_i)^2}\sqrt{n\sum y_i^2-(\sum y_i)^2}} \quad (1)$$

Third, between each of the possible pairs, the hypothetical expression levels are computed and then as many correlation coefficients are calculated. The hypothetical dimeric expression profiles are computed by taking the minimum expression value between the two constituent TFs expression values for a given tissue and assigning that value to the corresponding tissue expression for the hypothetical dimer. The same procedure is done for remaining $k=3,\ldots,N$ expression profile triplets, quadruplets, etc. of the corresponding hypothetical trimers, tetramers, etc. For example, for a hypothetical tetramer, its expression at tissue *j* would be $min(TF1_j, TF2_j, TF3_j, TF4_j)$ where TFx_j is the xth constituent factor expression data at the jth tissue. This way, altogether, the sum of $C(N,k)$ ("*N choose k*"), for $k=1,2,\ldots,N$ correlation coefficients are computed between the gene expression profile and the real and hypothetical expression profiles; *N* are real and the remaining are hypothetical

Fourth, the highest-order coefficient (the $k_{max}{}^{th}$ coefficient), where the *minima* of *N* values for a given tissue was taken is compared with the remaining, lower-order coefficients. The value *a*, which we call the absolute improvement score is computed with the formula:

$$\min_{y \neq k_{\max}} \left(|\rho_{k\max} - \rho_y| \right) \quad (2)$$

where the minimal absolute value between the highest order correlation and all other correlations is taken. This score we believe helps to isolate and reveal any transcription regulatory signal out of the highest-order hypothetical TF from among the others. If this procedure is carried out for all genes and all *k-tuples* of transcription factors, then in total,

$$c=g\left(\sum \binom{N}{k}_{k=1}^{k_{max}}\right) \quad (3)$$

correlation coefficients are computed. In the formula, g is the number of genes, N is the number of transcription factors, k represents the different numbers of combinations of factors chosen (singletons, pairs, triples, etc.), and k_{max} represents the highest-order polymerization under consideration. For example, for the CFOS/CJUN example we discuss later, k_{max} is *2*; in data-mining for heterotetramers, k_{max} is *4*. Note that the sum over combinations is used in *Eq. 3* because an analysis requires the computation of lower-order coefficients in the formula for computing the absolute improvement score. Finally, we rank the complexes by their scores. Figure *2* presents a schematic providing an overview of the technique.

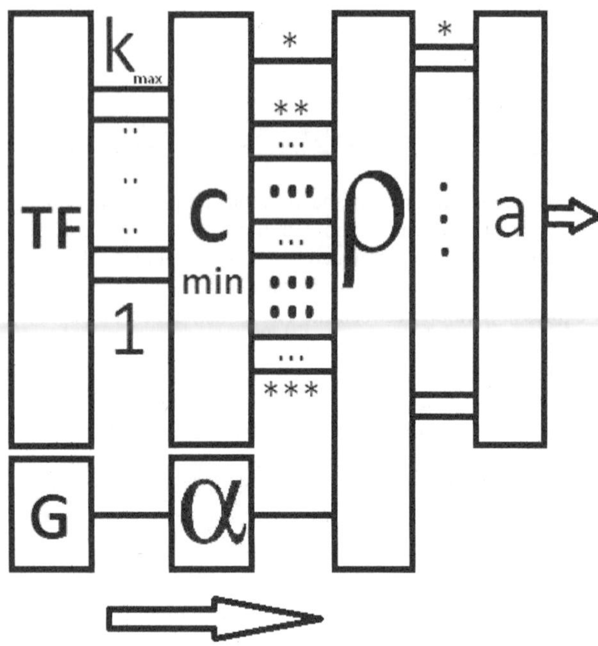

Fig. 2. A schematic shows data-flow and operations of the algorithm. TFs are chosen (k_{max} in total); a gene is chosen (box "*G*") and then subjected to the alpha transformation (box "α"); *1-tuples, 2-tuples,…(k_{max}-1)-tuples,* and *k_{max}-tuples* of TFs are chosen and minima are taken to form hypothetical expression profiles (boxes labeled "TF" & "C_{min}"). Finally, correlations are computed between the gene and all of the TF profiles (box "ρ") (both genuine and hypothetical) and compared to generate an absolute improvement score for the highest-order putative heteropolymeric TF complex (box "a"). The scores are used for ranking hypothetical TFs as being likely transcription factor complexes. Legend: The "*" represents the highest-order coefficient, "**", intermediates, and "***" the lowest.

When a gene shares a name with any of the possible regulatory transcription factors, or if any pair of the transcription factors share a name, then the corresponding coefficients and absolute improvement scores are not calculated. This is because we do not aim to consider polymerization involving self-regulating genes or any extent of homo-polymerization.

The central hypotheses of this project are that by taking the minima at a given tissue across expression profiles that we find the hypothetical expression profile of the corresponding polymeric TF and that the computation and subsequent sorting of the absolute improvement scores may identify and distinguish a transcription regulatory signal from the transcription factors and their hypothetical joining to regulate the corresponding gene.

All local "terrestrial" analyses were done with a custom-written *C/C++* program running on a *64*-bit Ubuntu/Linux platform with an Intel core i7-960 processor. Perl and bash scripts played a role in loading data into our program as well. Our dataset was not free of missing values. Missing values were marked with the value *(-18)*. In computing the correlation coefficients, columns (tissues) with missing values were ignored and skipped over. In computing the hypothetical expression profiles, if any single component TF profile had a missing value in a given column, then the hypothetical profile was defined to have a missing value in that column as well.

2.1 Validation and Parametric Calibration

To explore the validity of our technique we selected two well-known heterodimer-forming transcription factors CFOS and CJUN [23] from our dataset and applied our algorithm. The two transcription factors together form AP-1. Using the TRANSFAC and ENCODE [21, 22] databases we identified a total of *4* known target genes of the AP-1 TF complex in our gene dataset: TIMP1, GJA1, HMGA1, and MAP4K5. A perfect data-mining technique to identify TFs and their target genes would identify at least these target genes for AP-1.

As described in the METHODS section, using every pair of transcripts in our dataset belonging to CFOS and CJUN, we carried out a $k_{max}=2$ analysis and computed correlation coefficients, hypothetical expression profiles, absolute improvement scores, and then sorted. We simultaneously allowed the α parameter to vary from 0 to 1. Looking at the data generated across α–values, data with α in the range 0.25 to *0.27* resulted in the greatest accumulation of true positive target genes in the top-10 list of target genes sorted by the absolute improvement score. From that, we set alpha to *0.26* which is the median (and mean) of the values *0.25*, *0.26*, and *0.27* listed above.

Having calibrated α, we sorted our list of target genes and discounted reported target genes CFOS, and CJUN (the components of AP-1 itself). In the resulting list we found known target genes (HMGA1, and MAP4K5) among the top ten rows of the sorted list of absolute improvement scores and corresponding genes and TFs. Using the hyper-geometric distribution to carry out a non-parametric statistical test, similarly as elsewhere [18, 19], based on the null hypothesis that the known positives are randomly distributed in the list of *2526* genes, we computed that there is a p-value of $8.4{\cdot}10^{(-5)}$ for finding *2* or more of the known target genes in the top *10* of the list sorted by the absolute improvement scores. This indicates that we may reject the null hypothesis, H_0, that the target genes are randomly distributed in the sorted list at the $\alpha = 1\%$ significance threshold. The results are displayed in table 1.

Table 1. Genes and correlations (between CFOS, CJUN and the hypothesized yet genuine AP-1 complex). Known targets of the AP-1 complex are starred ("*"). AI is the absolute improvement score, used for ranking.

	Gene	C1	C2	CC	AI
1	VARS2	*0.46*	*-0.39*	*0.07*	*0.39*
2	EGR1	*-0.07*	*0.72*	*0.33*	*0.38*
3	HMGA1*	*0.44*	*-0.34*	*0.04*	*0.37*
4	AP2S1	*0.46*	*-0.30*	*0.06*	*0.35*
5	ZFX	*-0.41*	*0.35*	*-0.07*	*0.35*
6	EGR1	*-0.07*	*0.64*	*0.29*	*0.35*
7	LRP6	*-0.33*	*0.37*	*0.01*	*0.34*
8	MAP4K5*	*-0.36*	*0.33*	*-0.02*	*0.34*
9	DPYSL3	*-0.16*	*0.61*	*0.18*	*0.34*
10	RNU3IP2	*0.511*	*-0.25*	*0.17*	*0.34*

2.2 Data Mining for Heterotetrameric Transcription Factors

To data-mine for possible hetero-tetrameric TF complexes, we implemented our algorithm with $k_{max}=4$; we coded a *C/C++* computer program and ran exactly 4 time trials. Employing a quad-core i7 Pentium processor and the OpenMP API for multi-threaded programming, our $k_{max}=4$ calculations were over a single gene running *1, 2, 3,* and *4* OpenMP threads. The trials were carried out not to analyze the results, but simply to obtain execution-time data. From four essentially identical trials we saw average execution times of *3090, 1550, 1036,* and *780* seconds. For analyzing all *3166* gene transcripts (including loading the data and printing results), this would be about *113, 57, 38,* and *29* days. Desiring shorter execution times, we deemed such running times too long; in fact a previous analysis never completed [17]. Figure *3*, along with some power curves made with Excel, shows the timing data for the time trials of a single gene.

For these reasons we decided to explore using the Amazon (Elastic Compute Cloud) EC2 cloud to carry out a complete $k_{max}=4$ analysis.

2.3 Cloud-accelerated Data Mining for Heterotetrameric Transcription Factors

The Amazon Elastic Compute Cloud (EC2) is "a web service that provides resizable compute capacity in the cloud. It is designed to make web-scale computing easier for developers." [27] Having such a resource and the ability to use and control it would enable the rapid calculations we sought.

For all of our cloud resource requirements and needs, we used the MIT StarCluster tools package [28]. The software's name, STAR, is an acronym standing for "Software Tools for Academics and Researchers". StarCluster helps enable users

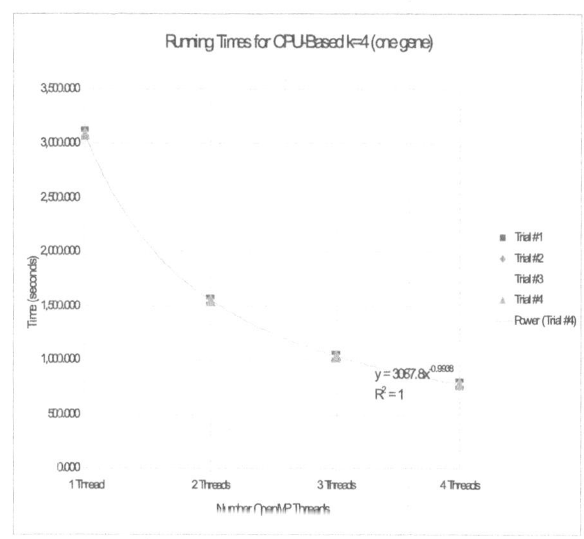

Fig. 3. Four essentially indistinguishable execution time data and power curves for a *k=4* analysis with one gene using *1,2,3, & 4* OpenMP threads

and developers to programmatically acquire and allocate Amazon EC2 cloud resources, virtualized servers, and set them up as a High-Performance Computing (HPC) cluster with the Sun Grid Engine (SGE) scheduling system with a "head" node and "worker" or "execute" nodes. StarCluster is available for download and is python-based. The EC2 HPC cluster accessed via StarCluster proved convenient, critical, and invaluable for the expedient and large-scale deployment of our code.

All nodes were created from Amazon Machine Images (AMIs). AMIs are "pre-configured operating system and virtual application software which are used to create virtual machines within the Amazon Elastic Compute Cloud (EC2). They serve as the basic unit of deployment for services delivered using EC2." [29] All nodes allocated with the STAR package have the AMI ID ami-999d49f0 which refers to an AMI with an Ubuntu-based distribution of the Linux operating system. Such an AMI configuration helped ease the transition of the code to the cloud and in minimizing configuration changes necessary for successful deployment. For testing and running our code we used the *m1.small* and *c1.xlarge* instance types [30]. Different instance types have different hardware and memory specifications. The *m1.small* and *c1.xlarge* have 1 core and somewhat less than 2GB of RAM and 8 cores and about 7GB of RAM respectively.

We ran the computations in the Amazon EC2 cloud in a three-phase fashion. The first phase included verifying that the code would run on the cloud. The second phase consisted of ensuring that the code would take advantage of multi-core SMP virtualized resources and of carrying out time trials to estimate compute resources needed for a full run. The third and final phase consisted of the actual allocation of a large number of virtualized servers and running of the all calculations.

To carry out the first phase of the cloud-computing implementation of our algorithm, we downloaded the STAR cluster package and set it up to allocate a small HPC cluster with the *m1.small* instance types with one worker node and one head node. With that allocated virtual HPC, using the indicated AMI, we achieved rapid transition and porting to the Amazon EC2 cloud. After a small number of modifications, the code was recompiled and tested. Several tests verified the code's proper execution.

To carry out the second phase of the cloud-computing implementation of our algorithm, we next allocated another small HPC exactly as before, but with the *c1.xlarge* instance type. We modified the code slightly to ensure full use of the 8 cores available with the OpenMP API for threads. Several tests verified the use of the cores and correct execution of the code. Moreover, using the smaller, but more powerful HPC cluster, we carried out a small timing study. The timing study consisted of the analysis of a single gene, but in a multithreaded way. The timing study indicated that each gene, run with *8*-way parallelism, could be analyzed with all TFs mining for heterotetrameric factors in about *1* hour and *45* minutes.

We desired to rapidly execute our code in about *24* hours to obtain timely results. Based on the timing study data from phase *2*, we estimated that we needed to allocate *264* *c1.xlarge* nodes to run the analysis across all *3166* genes with all of the TFs. With *8* cores per node, this is a total of *2112* cores. We conferred with Amazon on the scope of our compute resource demands and to verify use and availability.

To carry out the third and final phase of the cloud-computing implementation of our algorithm, we allocated the desired *264* nodes and ran each gene as a sun grid engine job. This way, *3166* jobs were set up. To accomplish this task, a few scripts were composed and run to set up and execute the jobs using the *qsub* command. The *qsub* command permits job submission to the job scheduler for eventual execution. Using the *264*-node cluster, at any given time, about *264* genes were analyzed simultaneously on the *2112* allocated virtual cores.

3 Results

Our *C/C++* $k_{max}=4$ analysis led to two results: *a)* putative heterotetrameric TF complexes and target genes along with the corresponding coefficients sorted by their improvement scores and *b)* a successful run on the cloud in about *24* hours.

Table 2 presents the top *10* genes, putative TF-tetratmers, and absolute improvement scores, ranked by absolute improvement score of our analysis results.

Table 2. The top-scoring genes and hypothetical transcription factors from the cloud-based k=4 analysis. Legend: AI "Abs. improvement"

	AI	GENE	TF1	TF2	TF3	TF4
1	0.71	FGB	IRF1	MGA	PAPOLA	SNAPC3
2	0.67	FGB	E2F5	ILF3	MGA	SP110
3	0.67	FGB	EPC1	ITGB3BP	PAPOLA	SP110
4	0.67	FGB	SDCCAG3 3	TWISTNB	ZNF155	ZNF83
5	0.66	FGB	ILF3	MGA	NFYA	SP110
6	0.65	AFP	ILF3	MGA	SP110	ZNF83
7	0.65	EHHADH	ELL2	EWSR1	PCAF	PPARBP
8	0.65	FGB	IRF1	ITGB3BP	PAPOLA	SNAPC3
9	0.65	FGB	PRKAR1A	TWISTNB	ZNF155	ZNF83
10	0.64	FGB	E2F5	IRF1	ITGB3BP	PAPOLA

We note that in the top *10* results from the cloud-based analysis that the FGB gene is seemingly overrepresented as well as the SP110, ZNF83, and MGA transcription factors. FGB forms the beta portion of fibrinogen; it helps form blood clots. The max-gene-associated protein (MGA) is a TBOX DNA-binding protein. Besides table 2, it has been suggested elsewhere [34, 35], to possibly interact with TFs such as the E2F proteins. The SP110 transcription factor plays a role forming a part of a leukocyte-specific nuclear-body [14, 20]. We submit these top results to the body of scientific literature as candidates for subjects of further research and inquiry. In addition, the complete list of over *40,000* putative target genes, correlations, and heteropolymeric TF complexes, dataset and source code are available from the corresponding author of this paper as well.

4 Discussion

We here briefly discuss the efficacy of the algorithm, the role that missing values may have played in it, the role of the Amazon EC2 cloud in implementing our algorithm, its utility, and briefly compare it with our previous GPU/CUDA based implementation [26]. We also discuss further ways to test the technique. Finally, we discuss its role of the in a greater bioinformatics context.

Regarding efficacy we note how the program detected three out of five known target genes for the AP-1 complex in the top ten listed target genes (out of *3166* transcripts total). This result suggests that the method has some value, but that to be most useful, it should be improved. We believe that the parametric calibration of alpha certainly improved the analysis outcome as well.

The data used had over *44,000* missing values (*40,080* in the gene dataset, *4806* in the TF dataset). With missing values being propagated to the hypothetical composite TF expression profile, they may present a challenge to the algorithm unless they are filled in or imputed. This presents an opportunity for improvement of the technique.

The bioinformatics concept of data mining for true positives causes us to recall the fact that the "gold standard" technique to indicate how two or more proteins heteropolymerize are standard "wet lab" protocols. Crystallography and co-immunoprecipitation (co-IP) may be used to find such complexes [25]. Crystallography [24] examines actual crystallized structures, in 3D; co-IP isolates protein-protein-DNA complexes out of a solution using immunochemistry techniques. These procedures unfortunately, are neither quick nor cheap. In addition, as the number of proteins whose polymerization is examined goes up, additional work is needed to determine whether they in fact bind or not. This means more time and money is needed to make such determinations. Thus our technique explored in this paper may have some value in saving time and money.

Our previous CUDA-based implementation [26] ran in about 4 days whereas in contrast, our cloud-based implementation here ran in about *1* day. The programs finished execution so quickly because of the sheer number of nodes, *264*, brought to bear on the computations. As the code scaled linearly during the timing studies, we could have opted for ½ as many nodes, but tolerated two days of execution time. Such possibilities reflect the flexibilities of the Amazon EC2 service. That is a flexibility that a CUDA-based implementation of a program simply may not have unless its implementation is highly used and quite mature.

Reasons to use a local, CUDA-based implementation over a cloud-based method include 1) frequent execution and 2) security. A local CUDA-based program requires no payment for Amazon services and is more secure as no data is in the cloud. Reasons for the converse include 1) the previously mentioned flexibility of the cloud and 2) usage frequencies. For certain applications, the flexibility may prove critical – such as certain periodic batch processes. In any case, these are only a few things to consider. Local compute resources require time, money, power, and other resources, perhaps even staff to maintain them. Each use case deserves its own cost-benefit analysis to lead a compute project to the proper choice. It should be noted that some configurations, even cloud-based GPUs, offer a useful heterogeneous cloud-based system for HPC user needs [33].

To our knowledge, the Amazon EC2 cloud has never been used to implement this particular technique for microarray data-mining for TF complexes; we successfully utilized the Star Cluster package to port our code to the cloud. Bioinformatics has many ways to take advantage of the Amazon EC2 cloud [31]. One interesting method, through CloVR [32], couples "cloud" virtualization technology with local virtualization technology (with "VirtualBox" and "VMWare") to aid in certain large scale metagenomic and BLAST analyses.

5 Conclusion

To summarize, we have presented and reviewed an algorithm used to data mine a microarray dataset by calculating correlations between gene and transcription factor expression profiles over tissues. Its objective is to highlight multiple transcription factors that may heteropolymerize and have a target gene whose transcription is then modulated. The method constructs a hypothetical heteropolymeric transcription factor profile whose tissue expression values are imputed by taking minima over tissues. A score-value procedure based on a comparison among the correlation coefficients is used to rank and order. The higher ranked combinations are believed to be more likely to form heteropolymeric complexes and target the gene. We carried out a calibration protocol with some test data showing the efficacy of our program; it gave interesting results in revealing some *3* out of *4* true positives with a *P-value* of $8.4 \cdot 10^{(-5)}$. To examine the heteropolymerization of *4* TFs at a time, the computational demands are high, so we explored using the Amazon EC2 cloud to speed up the analysis. We successfully ran the code in about *24* hours on a 264-node virtual HPC, and presented some the results from that analysis. Finally, we discussed our algorithm and the utility of the Amazon cloud and compared it with our previous GPU/CUDA-based analysis.

6 Acknowledgements

We acknowledge Dr. Michael Allan for providing ideas for validating the technique and biological insights too. We also acknowledge Dr. Stephen Kwek for guidance in implementing the algorithm. All programming was done by Edward A. Salinas.

Funding: All funding for use of the Amazon EC2 Cloud was provided by Edward A. Salinas.

7 References

[1] A. Karmaker, E. Salinas, S. E. Harris and S. Kwek, *Identifying Correlations between Genes and Transcription Co-factors using Expression Profile.*, JCIS, 2007.

[2] E. S. Lander, L. M. Linton, B. Birren, C. Nusbaum, M. C. Zody, J. Baldwin, et al., *Initial sequencing and analysis of the human genome*, Nature, 409, pp. 860-921, 2001.

[3] J. W. Fickett and W. W. Wasserman, *Discovery and modeling of transcriptional regulatory regions*, Curr Opin Biotechnol, 11, pp. 19-24, 2000.

[4] L. A. McCue, W. Thompson, C. S. Carmack and C. E. Lawrence, *Factors influencing the identification of transcription factor binding sites by cross-species comparison*, Genome Res, 12, pp. 1523-32, 2002.

[5] M. Defrance and H. Touzet, *Predicting transcription factor binding sites using local over-representation and comparative genomics*, BMC Bioinformatics, 7, pp. 396, 2006.

[6] A. E. Kel, E. Gossling, I. Reuter, E. Cheremushkin, O. V. Kel-Margoulis and E. Wingender, *MATCH: A tool for searching transcription factor binding sites in DNA sequences*, Nucleic Acids Res, 31, pp. 3576-9, 2003.

[7] M. C. Frith, M. C. Li and Z. Weng, *Cluster-Buster: Finding dense clusters of motifs in DNA sequences*, Nucleic Acids Res, 31, pp. 3666-8, 2003.

[8] C. T. Workman and G. D. Stormo, *ANN-Spec: a method for discovering transcription factor binding sites with improved specificity*, Pac Symp Biocomput, pp. 467-78, 2000.

[9] M. C. Frith, U. Hansen, J. L. Spouge and Z. Weng, *Finding functional sequence elements by multiple local alignment*, Nucleic Acids Res, 32, pp. 189-200, 2004.

[10] K. Ellrott, C. Yang, F. M. Sladek and T. Jiang, *Identifying transcription factor binding sites through Markov chain optimization*, Bioinformatics, 18 Suppl 2, pp. S100-9, 2002.

[11] W. Ao, J. Gaudet, W. J. Kent, S. Muttumu and S. E. Mango, *Environmentally induced foregut remodeling by PHA-4/FoxA and DAF-12/NHR*, Science, 305, pp. 1743-6, 2004.

[12] W. B. Alkema, O. Johansson, J. Lagergren and W. W. Wasserman, *MSCAN: identification of functional clusters of transcription factor binding sites*, Nucleic Acids Res, 32, pp. W195-8, 2004.

[13] R. Shyamsundar, Y. H. Kim, J. P. Higgins, K. Montgomery, M. Jorden, A. Sethuraman, et al., *A DNA microarray survey of gene expression in normal human tissues*, Genome Biol, 6, pp. R22, 2005.

[14] *Entrez Gene http://www.ncbi.nlm.nih.gov/entrez/http://www.ncbi.nlm.nih.gov/entrez/query.fcgi?CMD=search&DB=gene*,

[15] E. Salinas, A. Karmaker, BioComp 2009 Analysis of Correlations between Genes and Triads of Transcription Factors Using Microarray Expression Profiles.

[16] Watson, et. al., Mol. Biology of the Gene, 6th Edition, 2008

[17] E. Salinas, A. Karmaker, Analysis of Correlations Between Genes and Tetrads of Transcription Factors Using Microarray Expression Profiles, Proc. Of BioComp 2010, Las Vegas, NV, USA

[18] S. Falcon and R. Gentleman Using GOstats to test gene lists for GO term association Bioinformatics (2007) 23(2): 257-258

[19] W. Ewens, G Grant, Statistical Methods in Bioinformatics, an Introduction, 2nd Edition, Springer, 2005

[20] Sayers et. al., Database Resources of the National Center for Biotechnology Information, Nucleic Acids Res. (2009) 37(suppl 1): D5-D15

[21] E. Wingender, P. Dietze, H. Karas, and R. Knüppel, TRANSFAC: A Database on Transcription Factors and Their DNA Binding Sites, Nucl. Acids Res., (1996) 24(1): 238-241

[22] D. Thomas, et al., The ENCODE Project at UC Santa Cruz, Nucl. Acids Res.(2007) 35(suppl 1): D663-D667

[23] Halazonetis TD et al., CJUN Dimerizes with CFOS, Forming Complexes of different DNA Binding Affinities, Cell. 1998 Dec. 2; 55(5):917-924

[24] Park, Young-Jun, et. al., Crystal structure of a heterodimer of editosome interaction proteins in complex with two copies of a cross-reacting nanobody; Nucl. Acids Res. (2011) doi: 10.1093/nar/gkr867

[25] Zhang L., et. al., Successful co-immunoprecipitation of Oct4 and Nanog using cross-linking, Biochem Biophys Res Commun. 2007 September 28; 361(3): 611–614

[26] CUDA-Accelerated Data-Mining for Putative Heteromeric Transcription Factors and Target Genes Using Microarray Gene Expression Profiles, Proc. Of BioComp 2012, Las Vegas, NV, USA

[27] The Amazon EC2 Web page http://aws.amazon.com/ec2 accessed 3/15/2013

[28] The Star Cluster home page, http://star.mit.edu/cluster/ accessed 3/15/2013

[29] Amazon AMI Webpage https://aws.amazon.com/amis accessed 3/15/2013

[30] Amazon EC2 Instance Types web page http://aws.amazon.com/ec2/instance-types/ accessed 3/15/2013

[31] Fusaro VA, Patil P, Gafni E, Wall DP, Tonellato PJ (2011) Biomedical Cloud Computing With Amazon Web Services. PLoS Comput Biol 7(8): e1002147. doi:10.1371/journal.pcbi.1002147

[32] Angiuoli, S.V., Fricke W.F., et al., CloVR: A virtual machine for automated and portable sequence analysis from the desktop using cloud computing, BMC Bioinformatics 2011, 12:356

[33] Leinweber, M., et al., GPU-based Cloud computing for comparing the structure of protein binding sites, Digital Ecosystems Technologies (DEST), 2012 6th IEEE International Conference, vol., no., pp.1-6, 18-20 June 2012

[34] A.M.L. Liekens, et al., BioGraph: Unsupervised Biomedical Knowledge Discovery via Automated Hypothesis Generation, Genome Biology 12:R57, 2011.

[35] http://biograph.be/concept/graph/C1422345/C1167128

Functionally Diagram Human Brains using Ganged Confocal Scanning UV Fluorescence Microscopes with 3-D Substage Micromanipulator and Cryostat Microtome

Edward Richfield and Steve Richfield, IEEE #41344714

SUVFM Corporation; 5498 124th Avenue East, Edgewood WA, USA
Steve.Richfield@gmail.com

Abstract - *This is a proposal to construct practical automated neurological diagramming machines.*

This is a new class of devices that will be able to functionally diagram complex biological systems, eventually including human brains. Development of these devices should quickly lead to a greatly improved understanding of human cognition sufficient to assure the success of ongoing AI/AGI development efforts, and provide key information needed to develop treatments for various neurological conditions.

These microscopes will look into bulk tissue, focusing UV spots and recovering scattered UV and visible-light fluorescence from the same side, but along different light paths. This will work to a depth of ~10µ, even on living tissue. Computed tomography and image processing will transform the information from observed construction into a wiring diagram, including component values.

In a whole-brain diagramming version, brains can then be diagrammed by analyzing their surface ~10µ, then microtoming away ~4µ of the surface to analyze deeper in, and continuing this process one slice at a time until the entire brain has been diagrammed.

Keywords: diagramming, confocal, scanning, ultraviolet, fluorescence, microscope

1 Introduction

If only AI researchers had full wiring diagrams of brains, if only pharmacology researchers could watch chemical messengers move about within living cells, if only doctors could analyze the functional differences between diseased and healthy tissue; then both computer science and medical science would be suddenly propelled forward by decades.

Scientific research utilizes existing or easily fabricated equipment. Equipment development is a business built on prior scientific research. This "loop" sometimes leaves "islands of opportunity" where some advanced product development could produce equipment to greatly advance science, yet no equipment manufacturer is able to address the market. These islands exist in areas like microscopy, where equipment manufacturers, operating on thin profit margins in highly competitive markets, lack the financial resources and multidisciplinary expertise to develop radically new equipment. This proposal addresses the largest known island of opportunity.

Much of biological research, neuroscience research, artificial general intelligence research, and numerous other smaller areas are now substantially "hung up" on the lack of a particular equipment capability, namely, the ability to "functionally diagram" tissue, especially brain tissue. When available, functional diagramming will probably be more transforming to these and several other areas than were computers.

functional diagramming : (aka neuromorphic diagramming or computational diagramming) is the process of identifying the functional interrelationships of the components of cells and their quantitative interrelationships with other cells, and then filing this information into a database without regard for the physical structure and dimensions being represented.

To date, the most ambitious functional diagramming project was done manually, to diagram the 302 neurons in the nematode (roundworm) Caenorhabditis elegans, and this database is now on-line. Unfortunately, without the capabilities of the SUVFM described herein, that database does not include component values. Without component values, numerous researchers have been unable to understand its operation, or even label the neurons beyond "sensory", "interneuron", and "motor"[9]. Cognition is primarily concerned with interneuron functionality, which is determined by component values like synaptic efficacy. Note that the same neuron in different subjects may have different functions, as their operation is probably the result of self-organization. Hence, a useful analysis would have to be completed on a single subject, which would preclude all but fully automated methods

Note that each synapse probably has several quantitative component values. Aside from efficacy, there may be a variety of statistical accumulators that control changes (learning), nonlinearities that may be needed for certain computations, synaptic integration and/or differentiation, and other as-yet unknown characteristics.

2 Obama's B.R.A.I.N. Initiative

On April 2, 2013, President Obama announced the B.R.A.I.N. Initiative, supposedly to understand the operation of the brain. However, the requested $100M funding for this "initiative" is less than 2% of the present $5.5B NIH neurosciences budget. Careful examination of the proposal shows no funding at all for the present roadblocks of diagramming, identifying component values, or reaching a detailed understanding of the computations involved.

Washington insiders seem to think that this is politics as usual. This new "initiative" is being used as a foil to fight the present economic "sequester", which fails to provide funding for new projects. It is also possible that Obama may want to start something really big, in order to be long remembered, akin to President Kennedy starting the Apollo moon missions. Either way, much more fame and funding could be in the future for the B.R.A.I.N. initiative.

It seems obvious to nearly everyone that a major breakthrough in research methodology is needed before a major breakthrough in brain research can occur. We believe that a "Big Iron" approach, such as that described herein, will produce the information needed to sidestep the present roadblocks.

3 Prospective Diagramming Methods

Some formal proposals and many informal proposals for methods of diagramming have emerged. Each method images neurons differently, so that understanding of the operation of living tissue gained with one method cannot then be transferred to other methods for diagramming. This is the present roadblock. When the functionality of neurons and synapses is better understood, diagramming methods that can't work on living tissue (e.g. scanning electron microscopy) might become applicable and produce superior diagramming results.

Diagrams are needed to understand neurons, and neuronal understanding is needed to produce better diagrams. This particular proposal is seen as the next logical step on the long path to complete neuronal understanding and the production of accurate functional diagrams.

The fundamental limitation in resolution is ~1/3 of the wavelength used for illumination or observation. This limitation applies to all methods from MRI to electron microscopes. Brains are transparent to radiation of nearly all wavelengths up into the near UV region, whereupon they become opaque. You can probably see the veins in your wrist because of transparency to visible light. Opacity to shorter wavelengths is the basis of Lasik eye surgery, as its use of short wavelength UV only affects the surface cells.

Either observation must be made at near-UV wavelengths to utilize transparency at maximum possible resolution, or alternatively, methods not relying on transparency must be employed. Unfortunately, we don't know enough to understand what can be seen at higher resolutions. Without transparency, there is presently no known way to observe detail in living neurons, a necessary requirement to close our present gap between form and function.

Near-UV just happens to have another wonderful feature for this application, namely, that in addition to being able to see near-UV light scattered by transparent structures, complex molecules fluoresce when exposed to near-UV. Their fluorescence provides for limited chemical analysis of complex molecules – a feature not available with other methods. Conventional subtractive staining provides fluorescence, but hides structures that are beneath the stained details, making it unusable for diagramming.

Through a process of elimination, there seems to be little choice but to diagram utilizing near UV scattered light and fluorescent microscopy techniques, at least until the relationships between form and function has been discovered. However, there is a residual problem. Present confocal microscopy methods fail to produce images from bulk tissue of sufficient quality for use in automated diagramming. This proposal advances a method of utilizing separated point scanning and UV computed tomography (UV CT) to overcome those shortcomings.

Once neuronal and synaptic operation is much better understood, other methods will probably supersede the ones presented herein to provide more accurate diagrams.

4 Overview

Cytometry : an analytical method capable of precisely quantifying the functional states of individual cells by measuring their optical characteristics based on fluorescence or scattered light.

This proposal leverages on several well known physical characteristics of brain and other neural tissue:

1. Chemical components of brain tissue fluoresce richly when exposed to blue or near-UV light.
2. Brain tissue is transparent at microscopic scales.
3. The boundaries between transparent structures having differing indexes of refraction are made visible because the change in index of refraction reflects light when flat like a window, but scatters light from rough biological structures.
4. Brain tissue can be accurately sectioned away in 4μ slices when held at -4°C.

The SUVFM achieves UV resolution in 3-D while reading out chemical composition, and comes in two forms:

1. A laboratory instrument to identify what physical structures in <u>living</u> tissue, identified by their time-dependent fluorescence spectra, perform what computational processes.
2. An automated tissue diagramming machine, which incorporates the information gained from the laboratory version, and diagrams the surface ~10μ of surface volume in <u>frozen</u> tissue, removes ~4μ, and repeats this process, one slice at a time until the entire brain is completely diagrammed. Since

the slices are immediately discarded prior problems of preserving, processing, and analyzing them are eliminated.

5 Background

The scanning ultraviolet fluorescence microscope (SUVFM) comes at the end of a half-century of advancements in microscopes of various sorts. While the SUVFM would have far less resolution than electron microscopes, it has other crucial characteristics that are now needed to move cognitive computing forward, including the ability to examine living tissue and the ability to perform limited chemical analysis on individual 3-D pixels.

The SUVFM would rapidly flash weak focused spots of near-ultraviolet light into biological samples at various places and depths and observe the fluorescence spectra and decay rates at those places. A computer would analyze the decay spectra and profiles, and reconstruct the 3-D structure. This would be capable of structural and some chemical imaging in 3-D with considerably better than visible light resolution. Further, by scanning to a sufficient depth that the top layer could then be sectioned off and the process continued through an entire brain, there could be enough redundant overlap to ensure that there would be no errors, even if there was a problem removing one of the ~4μ sections. With this device it should eventually become possible to automatically reconstruct the complete functional diagram of a brain, including individual synapse characteristics and other similar details.

In the late 1960s, Marvin Minsky of MIT's AI lab developed the first working machine vision system that successfully parsed visual scenes, thereby paving the way for brain diagramming as now contemplated. Marvin Minsky also invented the confocal microscope[14].

Soon after, there was an early effort at Carnegie Mellon University to diagram insect brains using a computer program written by Michael Everest. Researchers attempted to microtome off slices and stain them to microscopically scan using 2-D visible light methods. This effort failed because some slices were inadvertently destroyed, and staining is a subtractive process (whereas fluorescence is additive) so that it was impossible to see what was behind a stained detail. Further, large microtomed slices must be >4μ thick to withstand handling, whereas some important parts of neurons (like their axons) may only be 1μ or less wide. The scanning ultraviolet fluorescence microscope easily avoids all of these prior problems by immediately discarding the slices and looking into the unsliced brain. It provides more than an order of magnitude more real-world resolution than prior methods by working in 3-D with ultraviolet, and using UV CT to extract more detail than visual methods can extract.

So far there have been no successful automated brain diagramming projects, and there won't be until scanning UV fluorescence microscopes similar to those described herein are constructed. To diagram brains, such a microscope will require the largest supercomputers now available to deal with the horrendous computational load and produce diagrams in months, rather than centuries.

A scanning UV fluorescence microscope could also non-destructively observe the operation of living cells in far more detail than is currently possible with direct visual observation. Researchers now routinely observe living neurons in operation under UV fluorescence because their fluorescence changes as they operate. The addition of scanning to improve resolution and provide depth separation and real-time logging should make it possible to characterize synapses by their appearance under fluorescent conditions as their electrical operation is simultaneously observed.

6 Basic Physics

Complex molecules often fluoresce. A higher-energy photon (or simultaneous lower-energy photons[13]) activates them, and results in the sometimes delayed release of lower-energy photon(s)[3]. Chemicals can be identified by the energy needed to activate them, the energy of the released photon(s), the delay between activation and fluorescence, the recovery time, and the response to photobleaching. Where several chemical constituents are present their fluorescence is combined, leaving the computer to unravel the combined fluorescences.

A point within tissue can be chemically analyzed by flashing a point of UV or blue light through the tissue and focused at the point and observing the visible-light fluorescent decay. The visible light will be a combination of the fluorescent decay of everything at that point, plus far more light from everything before and after the point that is illuminated by the UV or blue light. However, clever optical design must limit the extraneous field of view. The defocused extraneous light will be very nearly constant from point to point so it can be subtracted off to yield just the spectral characteristics at the targeted point. Computerized image enhancement will clean up any remaining problems.

The basis of successful diagramming is 3-D chemical mapping. This image, instead of being in color, will be a 3-D map of the spectral and decay characteristics at the many points in the tissue. A computer will then analyze the image and form a map of the chemicals present. From the chemical map the computer can infer the structure, and from the structure the computer can infer function, and then relate each functional element to its neighbors by examining the chemical and electrical interfaces.

7 Optics

A new principle of microscopy is employed here, where a single near-UV LED in an array of LEDs illuminates a point within the sample via a thin hollow cone of focused light. A coaxial central cone of receptivity then focuses an image of that point within the sample onto an imaging array, where a computer then looks at the same pixel position as the LED illuminated. Only a tiny micron-wide volume where the two coaxial cones intersect is visible to the microscope at any instant in time.

Image enhancement methods applied to the point observations will provide for ~0.1μ near-UV limited resolution. Physically moving the LED and imaging arrays facilitates the processing of virtual slices, interpolation between pixels, and working around any dead pixels. Beam splitters will provide for any number of color-sensitive imaging arrays, as may be needed for adequate chemical analysis.

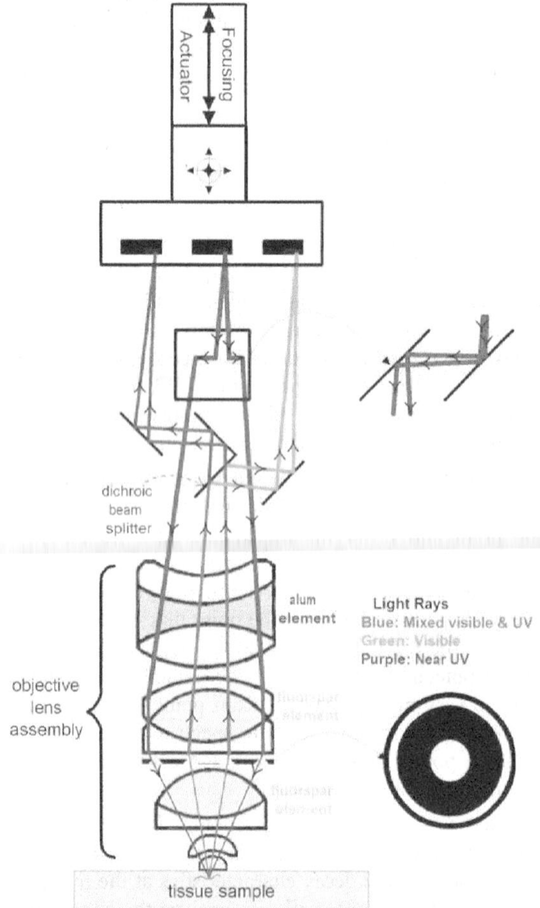

Fig. 1 Design of SUVFM Microscope

8 Computational Feasibility

There is an incredible amount of detail in a human brain. It will be analyzed in ~250K 4μ physical slices. UV analysis will be on ~0.1μ virtual slices, so that each physical slice is analyzed as ~40 virtual slices. That means that every additional minute of time spent analyzing each physical slice translates into another 6 months of total scanning and diagramming time.

Presuming that an array of objective lenses are on 1cm centers, presenting 2K x 2K images at 0.1μ pitch means that each objective would have to mechanically scan a 1cm x 1cm area on a 50 x 50 grid and stop at 2.5K separate points for each physical slice. At each one of these 2-D points it would then be necessary to explore the ~40 virtual slices.

However, miniaturization solves these scanning speed issues. For example, if objective lenses can be placed on a 1mm grid there can be 100 times as many microscopes, which would give the scanning system 100 times the speed.

The length of time a supercomputer barely able to simulate a brain in real time would require to scan and diagram a similar brain is nearly constant. This time is nearly invariant with brain complexity, from insect to human, because a more complex brain would require more supercomputer(s) to simulate it, and the additional supercomputer(s) would speed the scanning and diagramming process. Since many computers can be networked for scanning and diagramming, the actual time required will be reduced approximately in proportion to the number of networked computers. This time is not yet known, but is suspected to be sufficiently low so that a small number of supercomputers, each capable of simulating a human brain, perhaps just one such supercomputer, could keep up with scanning hardware to produce a complete diagram in about a month.

There are ~10^{14} 0.1μ spaced points in a 10μ thick piece of human brain. There are also ~10^{15} synapses in the human brain. This puts a tractable cloud-sized upper limit on the memory requirements. These numbers aren't so daunting when you think in terms of server containers – shipping containers that each holds ~2,000 servers, rather than in terms of individual CPUs and disk drives. Of course, Moore's Law will soon bring computer-related costs down to a much more affordable range

Diagramming will proceed by assigning tentative IDs to all 2-D areas separated by boundaries, or bounded by the field of view. As subsequent virtual slices are analyzed, IDs from prior slices will propagate. Where different ID'd volumes subsequently merge, showing those volumes to be from the same structure, the diagramming software will go back into the previously diagrammed database and re-mark all of the entries for one of the IDs to be the other ID. Hence, 3-D analysis can be performed on successive 2-D virtual slices, with no need to re-examine prior slices.

Note that there are ~18 3-D serial section visualization software packages now available, but diagramming is very different from visualization – easier in some ways, but harder in others. Diagramming need provide no graphics beyond those needed for debugging, but must have some limited image "understanding" abilities.

The only significant image storage requirements are for holding information in the top ~10μ of depth, in case a subsequent problem develops with the cryostat microtome. The 3-D images within each physical slice are fused with the previous slice, the IDs are propagated, and the previous physical slice's image can then be discarded.

9 Improvements over Prior Methods

The basic microscopic principles of flashing UV spots into neurological tissue and observing the responding fluorescence is not at all new. Therefore, there should be no unfortunate technical surprises. However, the following logical extensions of this basic technique are new:

1. Automatically moving samples around in 3 D, so that volumes can be automatically analyzed that far exceed the field of view of the microscope's optics.

2. Ganging many microscopes together, to provide a >100X improvement in speed for large samples.
3. Incorporating a cryostat microtome to automatically remove scanned tissue, so that scanning can continue automatically throughout a thick sample without human intervention.
4. The design for an optical "head" to provide 3-D pixels of sufficient resolution and quality for diagramming.

None of these improvements involves new physics or way-out engineering. Just some plain old product development is needed to build an SUVFM.

The total is much greater than the sum of the parts, because all of these parts are needed for diagramming, diagramming is needed for understanding, and understanding is needed to advance the several fields that are currently "hung up" on the lack of this understanding. Research has gone about as far as possible with present equipment. These new capabilities will open up whole fields of research, especially in AI by answering most of the questions now vexing AI developers, like how apparently unorganized infant brains seemingly self-organize as they grow to adulthood.

10 Why now?

We are right now at the coming-of-age of the two critical technologies:

1. UV and confocal microscopy are ~50 years old. SUVFMs were first proposed ~30 years ago. However, real working SUVFMs are just now being demonstrated, albeit without any of the improvements necessary to support diagramming.
2. These analyses are computationally intensive. A cloud of networked computers, each with GPU and/or FPGA arrays, could now provide the needed computational power, as none of their several present weaknesses appears to affect this particular application, wherein the problem arrives literally chopped into small pieces.

11 Important Details

Fortunately, only certain points need be fully decay-analyzed to measure component values. While this won't identify all chemical constituents, it should identify enough to separate most structures. There will be cases where unobservable structural details must be inferred from what can be seen. It is expected that future simulation results and mathematical breakthroughs will fully fill in any such gaps.

Note that to be able to calibrate this process, functional diagramming must be initially usable on living tissue to be able to understand what does what on a physical level never before seen. Later, once it is possible to reliably relate fluorescence to chemistry to structure to function to diagram, living tissue capability may no longer be needed.

12 Other Issues

There are a variety of miscellaneous issues, such as avoiding opaque objects like red blood cells, adding additional fluorescent markers to identify things that may not otherwise fluoresce uniquely, preserving tissue during months of analysis, etc. These are addressed by perfusing a carefully designed fluid to replace the blood, akin to the way that the blood is replaced with a cryoprotectant fluid before freezing organs for later transplantation. Present cryoprotectant fluids are not suitable for this use because their physical properties aren't compatible with microtoming, but engineering a more suitable fluid is not seen as being a major engineering challenge, as even blood plasma performs marginally.

Microscopy would all be performed under oil immersion, which would perform the dual purposes of preservation and facilitate the use of high numerical aperture (NA) objectives.

13 Uncertainties

Given the wealth of available UV-based techniques, applied to the wealth of neurological unknowns, it is not yet possible to accurately judge the prospects of eventual 100% success. All that can be done is to address the issues now known, and discover what, if anything, remains. Nonetheless, if the SUVFM only does what is clearly possible without significant problems, it will still transform the biological sciences.

14 Supporting Technologies

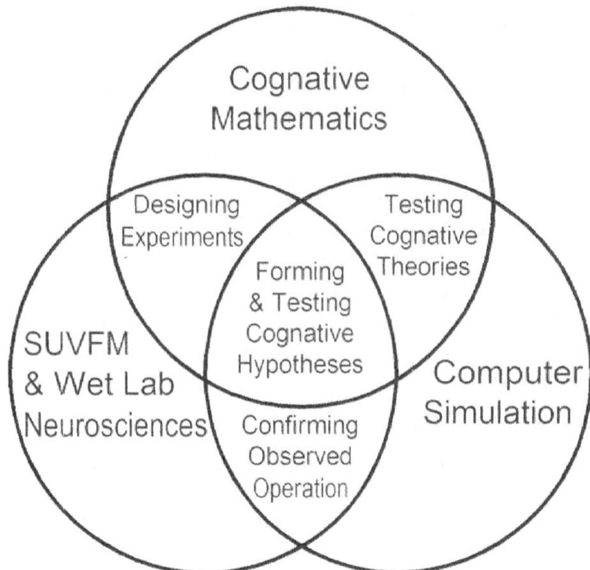

Fig. 2: Future Technology Triad

Initially, the SUVFM will simply do its part in this triad, and benefit from other areas doing their respective parts.

Ideally, wet lab research, cognitive mathematics, and computer simulation will all work together to get each other over the hard spots.

15 Other Advanced Methods

There is a rapidly evolving assortment of advanced methods not considered in this proposal. These have been omitted here both for brevity, and because they may not be needed to diagram things as "simple" as computational functionality. However, they remain "on the shelf" as engineering margin, to "save the day" should unexpected problems emerge. The four front-running advanced methods are:

1. Instead of using UV, excite with low levels of photons that individually are insufficiently energetic to cause fluorescence. This results in a quadratic response to intensity that decreases the response away from the focal point. Two-photon Microscopy (TPM) has already been applied to study the neuron structure and location in intact brain slices, the role of calcium signaling in dendritic spine functions, neuronal plasticity and the associating cellular morphological changes, and hemodynamics in rat neocortex.
2. Identifying the precise locations of isolated fluorescent molecules (fluorophores) by precisely determining the centers of their diffraction-limited images. This can be done with ~0.002μ precision.
3. In addition to using near-ultraviolet as detailed in this proposal, far-ultraviolet could analyze the exposed surface in greater resolution, but without the ability to analyze it in sufficient depth for diagramming. This would provide some ability to analyze unfamiliar structures, albeit only at the random locations where why were sliced.
4. Instead of cutting off separate slices and discarding them, an alternative method is to turn the brain into a long tape of recovered sections, so that in effect the SUVFM becomes a just new type of tape drive[7]. While this runs the great risk of destroying a slice and thereby losing the entire diagram, it could nonetheless augment the methods presented here, so that a lost slice would only lose some additional detail in a region that has already been scanned.
5. Once brain operation is understood, multiple restarts on a simulator can be used to debug a diagram sufficiently for it to work, albeit suboptimaly due to errors in diagramming.
6. Once a brain diagram works suboptimaly, multiple restarts on a simulator can be used to allow the system to self-optimize.

16 High Risk?

Are we going to build this machine, turn it on, and immediately start diagramming brains? Of course not. The laboratory version of this machine will provide direct simultaneous observation of form and function. Once these relationships have been found and understood, programs can be written to identify and measure similar structures in brains and indicate their component values in the diagrams that are produced. Even when this machine has been constructed, useful diagrams will probably still be several years away.

Are we going to be able to fully characterize every component? Of course not. There is little need for perfection in component characterization, as once the functionality is well understood; most optimum component characteristics can be computed. Computed optimum component values are more valuable than imperfectly measured values for most uses.

After considerable research using the laboratory version, are we going to be able to fully diagram the brains of some small creatures that have large neurons? This seems like a safe bet.

The first machines will find their limits somewhere in between the very easiest and the most difficult brains to diagram, and this limit will advance with each new generation of machine, hopefully to eventually include human brains.

This is a proposal for a process, rather than a proposal to build a specific model of equipment. As with everything from airplanes to computers, capabilities will dramatically grow with each new generation of equipment.

One thing seems certain: Even the very first machines will transform the biological sciences as they provide spectacular 3-D images with sub-micron resolution of the internal structures of living cells, displaying real-time views of cells' internal chemistry.

17 Conclusion

The SUVFM promises to transform neuroscience into an information technology, which is the fundamental criterion for applying Moore's Law and/or Ray Kurzweil's exponential growth curve to project future capabilities. Initial machines won't be capable of diagramming anything as big and complex as a human brain, and probably won't be able to provide all component values for any brains, but initial limitations will soon pass as this technology advances and computational substitution fills in for unreadable component values.

Try to imagine for a moment how different AI would now be, if for the last 20 years we were to have had substantially all of the answers to how human cognition works. Human-scale AI "research" would now be little more than deciding to turn it on.

Semiconductor manufacturers are now spending billions of dollars developing the fabrication facilities to produce better computers, as AI developers are investing millions of dollars, often in the form of their own "sweat equity", to develop better AI software. However, without closure of the technology triad that now appears to include building the SUVFM; this will all probably hit a "brick wall" before producing the hoped for singularity. The SUVFM is the only technology on the horizon to avoid that brick wall. The SUVFM can be built for only a few million dollars.

18 Distant Future

Eventually, in the distant future when cognition is sufficiently well understood so that AI experimentation can operate independently of mathematical developments and wet lab support, the SUVFM will take its place as the stepping stone to uploading and downloading, thereby allowing people's conscious minds to be transferred into perpetually maintainable computers.

This will work just like classical checkpoint/restart computing methods. A computer program can be abruptly stopped in one computer, its state read out, transferred to a second and potentially differently constructed computer, and the program continued right where it left off in the first computer. Your brain is the first computer, your neural diagram contains both the program and most of the state, and a computer simulating your neural diagram becomes the second computer that restarts your consciousness where your body left off.

This method cannot perfectly capture the state, because some of it is held electrically and would be lost. The effect of this loss would probably be about the equivalent of an electro-shock therapy treatment, probably resulting in the loss of several hours of memory.

Everlasting life on a mass production scale, implemented upon death via diagramming followed by uploading (into a virtual reality computer) or downloading (into an android body) for simulation, is probably worth more than the present value of the earth, because people would gladly mortgage their futures in order to have futures[18]. Regardless of whatever else develops on earth, a nation that makes this work on a large scale will eventually own everything, making this the world's most valuable technology and substantially more valuable than oil.

This line of economic thinking has already been real-world tested – in ancient Egypt. There, they sought resurrection by building gigantic pyramids. Despite being an apparent technical failure, this project drove their economy to propel their civilization to greatness.

Once this has become a reality, it will be a simple matter to run the simulating computers far faster than real-time speeds, and simulate far more than the original three pounds of brain, to eventually achieve limitless intellects. This will achieve the long-predicted "singularity", albeit by different means than has been widely predicted. Further, this approach deftly avoids most of the potential civilization-ending scenarios of past AGI (Artificial General Intelligence) based proposals because at its core, it will still be human.

With such a potentially valuable future, even modest advances toward that goal assume billion-dollar values that far exceed their cost by orders of magnitude.

This could easily ignite a technology race, akin to the race between the U.S. and the U.S.S.R. to develop thermonuclear weapons or space travel, where it is more important not to be left out than to be first.

This may be society's last chance to reclaim its future from the robber barons, by publicly funding, developing, owning, and controlling this technology.

There are substantial technical risks to achieving the goal of fully diagramming human brains, but those risks are tiny compared to the existential economic risks of letting another nation capture this technology. However, there seems to be little risk that the SUVFM would fail to revolutionize the biological sciences, regardless of any unforeseen technical limitations.

19 Special Thanks

This proposal would not have been possible without the considerable contributions of William Calvin, Michael Everest, Kathryn Graubard, Marvin Minsky, Les Westrum and other industry notables, hopefully soon to include you, for identifying weaknesses and/or suggesting improvements.

20 References

All of the U.S. patents listed herein are available on-line at http://www.uspto.gov.

[1] *UV Computer Tomography Fluorescence Microscope Having Superior Resolution* on file at the U.S. Patent Office.

[2] New York State Department of Health. *Serial Section & Stereo Reconstruction WWW Sites*. http://www.wadsworth.org /spider_doc/sterecon/ssrecn.html

[3] Nikon. *Introduction to Fluorescence Microscopy*. http: //www.microscopyu.com/articles/fluorescence/fluorescenceinto .html

[4] So, P., et al. 2010. *Systems and Methods for Volumetric Tissue Scanning Microscopy*. U.S. Pat. 7,724,937.

[5] Werner, J., et al. 2010. *3-Dimensional Imaging at Nanometer Resolutions*. U.S. Pat. 7,675,045.

[6] Richfield, E., Richfield, S. 2009. *A New Approach to Unsupervised Learning*. IC-AI 2009: 43-52

[7] Hayworth, K. 2005. *Automatic taping lathe-microtome*. Proceedings of the Southern California Society for Microscopy and Microanalysis, April 1. http://geon.usc.edu/~ken/index_files /SCSMMAbstract_Hayworth.pdf

[8] Mueller, M. 2005. *Introduction to Confocal Fluorescence Microscopy, Second Edition*. SPIE Tutorial Texts in Optical Engineering Vol. TT69, Dec., ISBN-10: 0819460435, ISBN-13: 978-0819460431.

[9] Oshio, K., et al. 2003. *Database of Synaptic Connectivity of C. Elegans for Computation*. Technical Report of CCeP (Cybernetic *Caenorhabditis elegans* Program), Keio Future No. 3, Keio University. http://ims.dse.ibaraki.ac.jp/ccep/

[10] Andersen, et al. 2001. *Time multiplexed multifocal multiphoton microscope*. Optical Society America, Optic Letters, Vol 26, No. 2, pp. 75-77.

[11] Kim, et al. 1999. *High speed, two photon scanning microscope*. Applied Optics, vol. 38, No. 28, Oct.

[12] Stevens, J., et al. 1994. *Three-Dimensional Confocal Microscopy: Volume Investigation of Biological Systems*, Academic Press, Inc., ISBN-10: 0126683301, ISBN-13: 978-0126683301

[13] Denk, et al. 1990. *Two-photon laser scanning fluorescence microscopy*. Science, vol. 248, Apr. 6, pp 73-76.

[14] Minsky, M, 1988. *Memoir on Inventing the Confocal Scanning Microscope*. Scanning, vol 10 pp128-138. http:// web.media.mit.edu/~minsky/papers/ConfocalMemoir.html

[15] White, J. et al. 1986. *The structure of the nervous system of the nematode Caenorhabditis elegans*, Phil. Trans. R. Soc. London B 314, pp.1-340.

[16] Moessner, G. 1985. *Cryostat microtome apparatus*. U.S. Pat. 4,548,051.

[17] Atsuo, G. 1975. *Oil Immersion Apochromatic Microscope Objective*. U.S. Pat. 3,912,378.

[18] Gallun, R. 1974. *The Eden Cycle*. Ballantine Books, ISBN-10: 0345242556, ISBN-13: 978-0345242556

Laterality of Motor Control or Raised Intracranial Pressure? Physiology not Physics Aids Understanding the Emergence of Ipsilateral Pyramidal Signs in Neurosurgery

Iraj Derakhshan, MD
Formerly, Associate Professor of Neurology, Case Western Reserve and Cincinnati Universities
415 Morris St, Suite 401, Charleston, WV, 25301; Tel 304 343 4098

Abstract- A substantial number of surgical operations for supratentorial lesions are performed for fear of raised intracranial pressure and subsequent herniation of the brain. In this article I will show that the abovementioned fear is based on an irrelevant physical theory regarding the intracranial pressure, i.e. the Monroe-Kelley doctrine, which is ignorant of the fact that we breathe with our major hemispheres, hence the danger of lesions affecting the major hemisphere, which is also the hemisphere of speech and consciousness. Based on physiological consequences of one-way callosal circuitry underpinning lateralities of motor and sensory control, I confirm the more recent findings in neurosurgical literature that intracranial operations should be limited to those instances in which a lesion is directly interfering with the normal functioning of the neighboring neural structures and not because of considerations regarding the presence of raised in intracranial pressure. Using as example the tragic case of Congresswoman Giffords, who is incongruent as to her behavioral and neural handedness (see text for explanation), I have shown that the decompressive craniectomy she underwent resulted in the removal viable neural tissue, depriving her of a better outcome in the functioning of her nondominant side of the body. The new insight into the role of the major hemisphere in breathing and consciousness deserve utmost consideration when evaluating patients with intracranial lesions. This may demand abandoning the current practice of prophylactic craniotomy.

Keywords: prophylactic craniotomy, increased intracranial pressure, motor control, handedness.

Introduction

There is substantial evidence that raised intracranial pressure, as determined in bedside settings, is irrelevant to the occurrence of clinical (i.e. ipsilateral paralysis) and pathological (transtentorial herniation) findings seen in patients with supratentorial space occupying lesions or in those with traumatic brain injury (with or without edema). This article provides an alternative physiological explanation of ipsilateral paralysis, classically explained by transtentorial herniation of the brain, based on directionality in callosal traffic, underpinning lateralities of sensory and motor control in humans. [1, 2] Although the advent of neuroimaging techniques in recent decades (e.g. CT and MRI scans) has diminished the need for a meticulous examination of patients in search for the presence of pyramidal signs ipsilateral to a supratentorial lesion, it is hoped that a better understanding of the physiological underpinning of those ominous "false localization signs" would have a bearing on abandoning the current practice of (unnecessary) craniotomies performed for averting the "life threatening" consequences of raised intracranial pressure in these circumstances (cerebral herniation, Kernohan notch).

Physics

According to the Monro-Kellie doctrine, a fully formed cranium is a rigid box in which an increase in the volume of any of its histological constituents will be accompanied by a decrease in the volume of the remaining components in order to avoid an increase of the intracranial pressure. At the same time, the doctrine specifies the formation of transtentorial herniation as a consequence of raised intracranial pressure, in turn giving raise to the notching of contralateral cerebral peduncle as it presses against tentorium cerebelli; causing hemiparesis ipsilateral to the space occupying lesion due to the Kernohan-Woltman phenomenon. This scenario, however, has many weaknesses the most glaring of which has been elucidated only recently. Thus, the occurrence of false localizing signs in Kernohan and Woltman's classical study was limited to 17 of the 35 cases with supratentorial lesions (i.e. exacting half of those studied), despite the fact that all of them had the peduncular notching contralateral to the tumor. This fact alone reduces the status of the peduncular notching to that of an irrelevant artifact rather than being the "cause" of the ominous but "false" localizing signs (ipsilateral paralysis). [1, 2]

It bears mentioning here that the therapeutic usefulness of decompressive craniectomy for relief of raised intracranial pressure has come under heavy criticism in recent times. [3-5]

Physiology

According to one-way callosal traffic circuitry, the abovementioned ipsilateral pyramidal findings are the result of transcallosal deafferentation of the minor hemisphere from the excitatory signals arising in the major hemispheres (i.e. diaschisis); underscoring the fact that all commands arise in the major hemisphere regardless of the laterality of the effectors intended for such commands. In addition to a plethora of clinical evidence supporting the above conclusion, [1, 2, 6-10] the existence of a moiety within the major hemisphere which is devoted to the affairs occurring on the nondominant side of the body/space has been documented by Kooi et al and Baumer et al, respectively employing electro-encephalography (EEG) and transcranial magnetic stimulation techniques (TMS). [11, 12] Specifically, Kooi and colleagues described the initiation of "temporal transients" in the left hemisphere with transmission of those signals to the right hemisphere within 200-1000 milliseconds. According to Kooi et al, such transients were four times more likely to arise from the left hemisphere and spread to the right than the other way around. The above left/right ratio corresponds to that of the laterality of motor control at the society at large. [13] Therefore, it is likely that the transients described by Kooi et al [11] and Jaffe et al [14] were representations of the more recently described respiratory cortical evoked potentials.[15, 16] The frequency at which these alpha transients occurred in Jaffe et al's study (~ 20/minutes) is consistent with the above statement. In the same vain, the hazard ratio for sudden death attributed to respiratory arrest following stroke involving the major hemisphere was four times higher in right handers compared to those who were "ambidextrous" or left handed (HR, 0.96 vs 0.24). [17, 18] Kooi et al's denial of a relationship between handedness and the laterality of the temporal lobe potentials is unwarranted since a large segment of those claiming left handedness or ambidexterity are wired as neural right handers (i.e. they are left hemispheric as to the laterality of motor control). [13, 18] In the TMS experiments conducted by Baumer et al, [12] an interstimulus interval of up to 10 milliseconds between conditioning and test stimulus was need for the facilitating stimuli to the left hemisphere to reach the right hemisphere of the right handed participants studied. Lastly, the constant temporal association of paroxysms of petit mal seizures and apnea may be regarded as indicative of a common origination of both phenomena from the same hemisphere. [19, 20] It may therefore be concluded that the ratio of fifty percent reported in Kernohan and Woltman's classical article (i.e. 17/35), [1, 2] reflected the fact that lesions of only one of the two hemispheres (not both) were associated with emergence of the ominous pyramidal signs ipsilateral to that hemisphere (i.e. the major hemisphere). Thus, the above-mentioned ratio may be viewed as the foot print of directionality of the excitatory signals in callosal traffic (i.e. from the major to the minor hemisphere), withdrawal of which resulted in the appearance of pyramidal signs ipsilateral to the major hemisphere, due to an interhemispheric diaschisis affecting the minor hemisphere. [2, 6, 8, 9]

At this juncture the following questions arise:

1. Are there other circumstances (syndromes) indexed to the laterality of motor control (as delineated above) the occurrences of which bear similar numerical characteristics, i.e. a fifty percent or less probability of occurrence in lesions that are likely to be equally distributed between the two hemispheres?

2. Is the incidence of epilepsy resulting from supratentorial lesions always less than 50 percent?

The answer to both questions is in the affirmative. For example, in a study by Faught et al, describing de novo seizures among 123 patients with primary intracerebral hemorrhage, 25 percent developed seizures within five years after hospitalization (with lobar hemorrhage in 44 cases). [21] The authors indicated that the predicted cumulative seizure incidence for their patients was 50% had all patients survived and followed for five years. In the data presented in this article seizures occurred in 23/ 44 patients with lobar intracerebral hemorrhage. This ratio is similar to the abovementioned ratio of 50% for emergence of "false localization signs" in Kernohan and Woltman series (see above). To repeat, the 50 percent (or fewer) rule for the incidence of epilepsy in supratentorial metastatic lesions, meningiomas and cavernous angiomas, signifies that only one half of the entire supratentorial cortical expanse is capable of generating seizures even if the lesions were bilateral in their distribution. [22-28] Thus, given the equal likelihood of hemispheric involvement in these and similar lesions, it is likely that the anatomy sustaining the laterality of motor control provides the anatomical substrate for the abovementioned ratio; i.e. only one of the two hemispheres is capable of generating epilepsy, a finding that enjoys historical [29] and experimental support. [30] Thus, in an experiment involving ablation of both motor cortices in monkeys, Pribram et al documented the role of the left hemisphere in generating epileptiform potentials. In the latter study, however, the laterality of the lesion as the source of the observed epileptiform discharges escaped the authors' attention. A similar attitude has been displayed by two other influential investigators. Roland et al and Tanji et al were both inattentive to the fact that bilateral cortical activation observed in their experiments occurred as their subjects moved their nondominant arms. [31, 32] Finally, the more recent demonstration of bi-hemispheric activation of the brain upon using the nondominant hand involved the employment of near infra-red spectroscopy (NIRS) in measuring regional circulation of the brain when performing maximum pinching exercises with the left hand and the electromyographic documentation of the precedence of muscular activity in the right hand compared to the left (by

53 milliseconds) when right handed participants engaged in bimanual simultaneous pinching exercises.[33-37] In this connection, the fact that apnea is a constant companion of petit mal epilepsy bear remembering.[38]

The most naturalistic way of demonstrating this callosum-mediated asynchrony is the use of bimanual simultaneous drawing maneuver.[8, 13] In this test, the delay in moving the nondominant hand is reflected in the asymmetrical performance of the two hands when drawing a straight line or a box-shaped configuration. The lines drawn by the dominant hand are longer and straighter than those drawn by the nondominant because the latter is farther from the command center by a callosum-width, resulting in the degradation of the signal originating in the major hemisphere. [39] Further, it has been shown that the numerical discrepancy between performances of the two hands remain unchanged despite days of practice. [40]

The Eyes Have It

Another way of distinguishing the major from the minor hemisphere is to notice the deviation of the eyes toward the anesthetized (Wada test) or injured (e.g. supratentorial stroke) minor hemisphere, since an injury to the major hemisphere is not accompanied by conjugate eye deviation (CED) (Prevost sign); [41, 42] nor are the lesions affecting the minor hemisphere associated with the development of epilepsy.[43-47] Retrospectively, the role of laterality of motor control in the genesis of CED was evident from the start. [48] Thus, thirty six of the fifty one cases of CED reported by Prevost had supratentorial lesions of the right hemisphere at the autopsy. In addition, none of the remaining 15 cases with supratentorial strokes affecting the left hemisphere with conjugate deviation of the eyes to the left had language deficit arising from the newly acquired apoplexy (vascular event). The latter observation is consistent with the suggestion that the second group consisted of neurally left handed subjects regardless of their behavioral preference (i.e. they were all right hemispheric in their laterality of motor control). Significantly, it is among the second group of Prevost's patients that the first description of a (cortical) internuclear ophthalmoplegia (Case 50), depicted by the author as follows: *the eyes were deviated to the left, particularly the left eye.* The diaschitic nature of this syndrome, known as the lone abducting eye and caused by temporary paralysis of the contralateral medial longitudinal bundle, has been commented upon elsewhere (Figure1). [9, 46]

Case in Point

According to publicly available information, Congresswoman Giffords was tragically shot in the head in January 8th, 2011 with a bullet entering into her left hemisphere above the eye brow and exiting posteriorly near the midline (probably traversing frontal and parietal lobes). Since, there has been no report indicating occurrence of epilepsy following the trauma. There are reports indicating that she was conscious on arrival to the hospital and that she carried out simple commands from the start. She began speaking sometime thereafter (most likely indicating an initial mutism) but has since participated in multiple speaking engagements and has shown normal comprehension of speech. She has remained with compete paralysis of the right arm and leg but is able to take steps and has fairly good balance when walking. Linguistically, her speech is slow and marked by semantic paraphasia (e.g. replacing "Sandy-Brook" for "Sandy Hook"). In this connection, it is important to note that expressive language disturbances in supratentorial lesions have no lateralization value since moving the tongue and lips require an orderly participation of both hemispheres regardless of the laterality of the command center. [49]

In the case of Congresswoman Giffords, the most significant lateralizing sign was represented in the "shocking" hospital photos released in November of 2011, demonstrating the presence of a (cortical) internuclear ophthalmoplegia on the right side with the left eye completely deviated to the left but the right eye stopping at the middle (Figure 2). Following the trauma the patient has undergone three operations on the head: left "decompressive" craniotomy, right lateral canthotomy and left cranioplasty.

According to the clinical information provided above, Congresswoman Giffords' is that of a crossed nonaphasia in an ostensible right hander; i.e. a person who is wired as a left hander with the command center in her right hemisphere, as revealed by the eye deviation towards the injured hemisphere as depicted in Figure 2. [9, 46, 47] Similar cases have been described in the past, all remarkable for the preservation of comprehension and absence of apraxia in the limbs ipsilateral to the damaged hemisphere. [50-54]

Conclusion

According to the observations recounted above, Congresswoman Giffords sustained an injury to her nondominant hemisphere and was never in danger of respiratory disturbances seen as a result of injury to the breathing hemisphere. The initial craniotomy performed for fear of an "impending herniation" was thus unnecessary and unjustified and probably has compromised chances of any recovery by removing useful brain tissue. So was the right lateral canthotomy, which seem to have been performed "looking for orbital bone fragments." This perhaps was due to a misinterpretation of the unusual occurrence of cortical internuclear ophthalmoplegia seen in Figure 2.

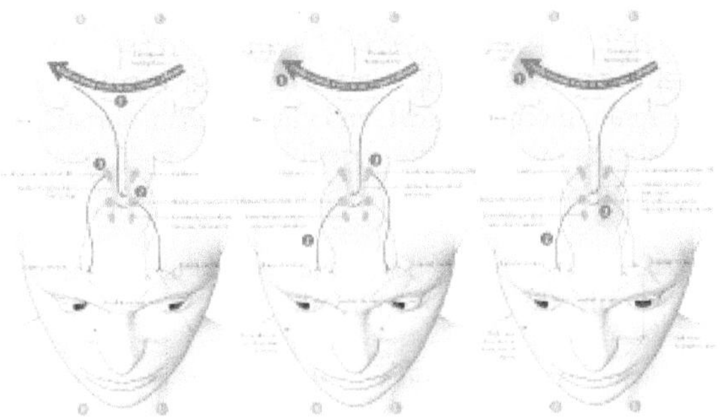

Figure 1. Lone abducting eye in a truly right handed person. The right eye, with its intact motor connection to the left hemisphere, has been pulled to the right as a result of an imbalance created by the right-sided stroke (image on the right). The fibres going from the left cortex to the right lateral rectus find their way directly, without callosal participation, to brainstem nuclei on the right (middle image). The left eye which normally follows the right in such a situation becomes immobile because of the diaschisis affecting the pons as a result of the acute lesion affecting the right hemisphere. This may indicate a wider diaschitic paralysis of the left brainstem than that present in cases with conjugate deviation of the eyes to the left. [13] Notice that in the case of Congresswoman Giffords, who is wired as a left hander, the laterality of events are in the reverse direction compared to those depicted above [adopted from CMAJ's article, 2005].

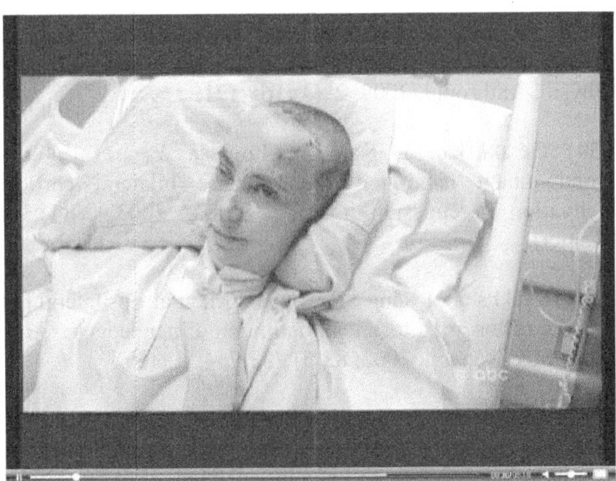

Figure 2. Note the stoppage of the right eye at the middle with the left eye deviated to the left, i.e. presence of a cortical internuclear ophthalmoplegia (see the text for explanation).

References

[1] Derakhshan I. The Kernohan-Woltman phenomenon and laterality of motor control: A fresh analysis of data in the article "Incisura of the crus due to contralateral brain tumor". J Neurol Sci. 2009; 287(1-2): 296.

[2] Derakhshan I, Adler DE, Milhorat TH. Kernohan notch. J Neurosurg. 2004; 100(4): 741-742.

[3] Shafi S, Diaz-Arrastia R, Madden C, Gentilello L. Intracranial pressure monitoring in brain-injured patients is associated with worsening of survival. J Trauma. 2008; 64(2): 335-340.

[4] Cooper DJ, Rosenfeld JV, Murray L, Arabi YM, Davies AR, D'Urso P, et al, Decompressive craniectomy in diffuse traumatic brain injury. N Engl J Med. 2011; 364(16): 1493-1502.

[5] Ma J, You C, Ma L, Huang S. Is decompressive craniectomy useless in severe traumatic brain injury? Crit Care. 2011; 15(5):193-194.

[6] Derakhshan I. Callosum and movement control: case reports. Neurol Res. 2003; 25(5): 538-542.

[7] Derakhshan I. Laterality of the command center in relation to handedness and simple reaction time: a clinical perspective. J Neurophysiol. 2006; 96(6): 3556.

[8] Derakhshan I. Right sided weakness with right subdural hematoma: motor deafferentation of left hemisphere resulted in paralysis of the right side. Brain Inj. 2009; 23(9):770-774.

[9] Derakhshan I. How do the eyes move together? New understandings help explain eye deviations in patients with stroke. CMAJ. 2005; 172(2):171-173.

[10] Jeannerod M. The origin of voluntary action: history of a physiological concept. C R Biol. 2006; 329(5-6): 354-362.

[11] Kooi KA, Guevener AM, Tupper CJ, et al; Electroencephalographic patterns of the temporal regions in normal adults. Neurology, 1964; 14:1029-1035.

[12] Bäumer T, Bock F, Koch G, et al, Magnetic stimulation of human premotor or motor cortex produces interhemispheric facilitation through distinct pathways. J Physiol, 2006; 572(Pt3): 857-868.

[13] Derakhshan I. Bimanual simultaneous movements and hemispheric dominance: Timing of events reveals hard-

wired circuitry for action, speech, and imagination. Psychol Res Behav Manag. 2008; 1:1-9.

[14] Jaffe R, Weiss AH. The significance of unilateral alpha-range bursts in the EEG. Acta Neurol Scand. 1966; 42(3): 257-267. (Figures 1-3 A)

[15] von Leupoldt A, Keil A, Chan PY, Bradley MM, Lang PJ, Davenport PW. Cortical sources of the respiratory-related evoked potential. Respir Physiol Neurobiol. 2010; 170(2):198-201.

[16] Davenport PW, Friedman WA, Thompson FJ, Franzén O. Respiratory-related cortical potentials evoked by inspiratory occlusion in humans. J Appl Physiol. 1986; 60(6): 1843-1848.

[17] Algra A, Gates PC, Fox AJ, Hachinski V, Barnett HJ; North American Symptomatic Carotid Endarterectomy Trial Group. Side of brain infarction and long-term risk of sudden death in patients with symptomatic carotid disease. Stroke, 2003; 34(12): 2871-2875.

[18] Derakhshan, I.: Right Handers Breathe with Left Hemisphere: Handedness and the Risk of Sudden Death in Hemispheric Stroke in NASCET. BIOCOMP, 2008; 470-477.

[19] Fischgold H, Arfel-Capdevielle G. Respiratory changes associated with epileptic paroxysms. Electroencephalogr Clin Neurophysiol, 1955; 7(2): 165-178.

[20] Bogacz J, Yanicelli E. Vegetative phenomena in petit mal epilepsy. World Neurol 1962; 3: 195-208.

[21] Faught E, Peters D, Bartolucci A, Moore L, Miller PC. Seizures after primary intracerebral hemorrhage. Neurology, 1989; 39(8): 1089-1093.

[22] Stortebecker TP. Metastatic tumors of the brain from a neurosurgical point of view; a follow-up study of 158 cases. J Neurosurg, 1954; 11(1): 84-111.

[23] Chan RC, Thompson GB. Morbidity, mortality, and quality of life following surgery for intracranial meningiomas. A retrospective study in 257 cases. J Neurosurg, 1984; 60(1):52-60.

[24] Paillas JE. A review of 2,413 tumours operated over a 30-year period. J Neuroradiol. 1991; 18(2): 79-106. (epilepsy incidence, 44%)

[25] Giovanelli M, Migliore A, Perria C. Incidence of epilepsy in supratentorial expansive processes. (Observations on 1019 cases). 1967; 11(3): 286-289. (Epilepsy incidence, 40%)

[26] Hofmeister C, Stapf C, Hartmann A, Sciacca RR, et al Demographic, morphological, and clinical characteristics of 1289 patients with brain arteriovenous malformation. Stroke. 2000; 31(6):1307-1310. (Epilepsy incidence, 40%)

[27] Arif H, Hirsch LJ. Treatment of status epilepticus. Semin Neurol. 2008; 28(3): 342-354.

[28] Rocamora R, Mendivil P, Schulze-Bonhage A. Multiple supratentorial cavernomas and epilepsy surgery: case report. Neurocirugia (Astur). 2008; 19(3): 257-263; discussion 263-266.

[29] Wernicke's Works on Aphasia; a Source Book and Review, translated by G.E. Eggert, 91-144. The Hague, Netherlands: Mouton Publishers, 1977.

[30] Pribram KH, Kruger L, Robinson F, et al. The effects of precentral lesions on the behavior of monkeys. Yale J Biol Med. 1955 -1956; 28(3-4): 428-443.

[31] Roland PE, Larsen B, Lassen NA, et al. Supplementary motor area and other cortical areas in organization of voluntary movements in man. J Neurophysiol, 1980; 43(1):118-136.

[32] Tanji J, Okano K, Sato KC. Neuronal activity in cortical motor areas related to ipsilateral, contralateral, and bilateral digit movements of the monkey. J Neurophysiol, 1988; 60(1): 325-343.

[33] Shibuya K, Kuboyama N. Bilateral motor control during motor tasks involving the nondominant hand. J Physiol Anthropol. 2009; 28(4):165-171.

[34] Derakhshan I, Kato H, Itoyama Y, et al; Why nondominant hand movements cause bilateral cortical activation in emission imaging. Stroke, 2003; 34(1):3-4 (Letter)

[35] Derakhshan I, Jang SH, Byun WM, et al; Ipsilateral but via the callosum: a technical definition of handedness. Arch Phys Med Rehabil. 2002; 83(5):733-734. (Letter)

[36] Derakhshan I, Hund-Georgiadis M, Zysset S, et al; Crossed nonaphasia in a dextral with left hemispheric lesions: handedness technically defined. Stroke, 2002; 33(7): 1749-1750. (Letter)

[37] Walsh RR, Small SL, Chen EE, Solodkin A. Network activation during bimanual movements in humans. Neuroimage. 2008; 43(3): 540-553.

[38] Bogacz J, Yanicelli E. Vegetative phenomena in petit mal epilepsy. World Neurol. 1962; 3: 195-208.

[39] Welsh TN, Elliott D. Gender differences in a dichotic listening and movement task: lateralization or strategy? Neuropsychologia, 2001; 39(1): 25-35.

[40] Albert NB, Ivry RB. The persistence of spatial interference after extended training in a bimanual drawing task, Cortex. 2009; 45(3): 377-385.

[41] Johkura K, Nakae Y, Yamamoto R, et al. Wrong-way deviation: contralateral conjugate eye deviation in acute supratentorial stroke. J Neurol Sci. 2011; 308(1-2):165-167.

[42] Meador KJ, Loring DW, Lee GP, et al Thompson WO, Heilman KM. Hemisphere asymmetry for eye gaze mechanisms. Brain, 1989; 112(Pt1): 103-111.

[43] Tijssen CC, van Gisbergen JA, Schulte BP. Conjugate eye deviation: side, site, and size of the hemispheric lesion. Neurology, 1991; 41(6): 846-850.

[44] Singer OC, Humpich MC, Laufs H, et al, Conjugate eye deviation in acute stroke: incidence, hemispheric asymmetry, and lesion pattern. Stroke, 2006; 37(11): 2726-2732.

[45] Sato S, Koga M, Yamagami H, et al, Conjugate eye deviation in acute intracerebral hemorrhage: stroke acute management with urgent risk-factor assessment and improvement--ICH (SAMURAI-ICH) study. Stroke, 2012; 43(11): 2898-2903.

[46] Becker E, Karnath HO. Neuroimaging of eye position reveals spatial neglect. Brain. 2010; 133(Pt3): 909-914.

[47] Fruhmann Berger M, Pross RD, Ilg U, et al, Deviation of eyes and head in acute cerebral stroke. BMC Neurol, 2006; 23: 1-8.

[48] Prevost J-L. De la Deviation Conjuguee des Yeux et de la Rotation de la Tete dans Certains Cas d'Hemiplegie. Paris, Victor Masson et Fils, 1868 (Doctoral Thesis)

[49] Lecours AR. The "Pure Form" of the phonetic disintegration syndrome (pure anarthria); anatomo-clinical report of a historical case. Brain Lang. 1976; 3(1): 88-113.

[50] Hund-Georgiadis M, Zysset S, Weih K, Guthke T, von Cramon DY. Crossed nonaphasia in a dextral with left hemispheric lesions: a functional magnetic resonance imaging study of mirrored brain organization. Stroke, 2001; 32(11): 2703-2707.

[51] Schlaug G, Marchina S, Norton A. From Singing to Speaking: Why Singing May Lead to Recovery of Expressive Language Function in Patients with Broca's Aphasia. Music Percept, 2008; 25(4): 315-323.

[52] Zipse L, Norton A, Marchina S, Schlaug G. When right is all that is left: plasticity of right-hemisphere tracts in a young aphasic patient. Ann N Y Acad Sci. 2012; 1252: 237-245.

[53] Jacobs LM, Berrizbeitia LD, Ordia J. Crowbar impalement of the brain. J Trauma. 1985; 25(4): 359-361.

[54] Denny-Brown D, Banker BQ. Amorphosynthesis from left parietal lesion. Arch Neurol Psychiatry. 1954; 71(3), 302-313.

Statistical Approach for Face Recognition using LDA

Shaikh Jameel Ahmed[1], Mohammed Ahsan Raza Noori[1], Shaikh Naziya Sultana[2], Wajid Ali Siddiqui[3]

[1]College of Science and Arts, King Khalid University, Kingdom of Saudi Arabia (jameelkku@gmail.com)
[1]College of Science and Arts, King Khalid University, Kingdom of Saudi Arabia (ahsan.exe@gmail.com)
[2]Aurangabad College for Women Aurangabad, (naziyamsc@gmail.com)
[3]College of Computer Science and IS, Jazan University, Kingdom of Saudi Arabia (wajidbob@gmail.com)

Introduction - In Today's Era security of information is becoming both increase singly, the crimes time to time increase in different sectors credit card fraud, computer hacking. Person identification is now an integral part of the infrastructure needed for diverse business. Biometrics security is an advanced technology intended to protect extremely sensitive data. In this paper we are presenting technique based on statistical analysis on LDA for personal identification.

Key words – *Images, mean, covariance, Eigen value, Eigen vector, Euclidean distance*

1. Introduction to Biometrics technologies - The word "Biometrics" is derived from the Greek words 'bios' and 'metric', which means life and measurement. Different sectors are now using this elegant method, as technology growth is rapidly. Biometrics technique is categories into two basic types. A. **Physiological** B. **Behavioral.** Physiological are further classified into various types such as, face recognition, finger print, hand geometry, Iris scan, Retina scan, DNA. Everyone have their advantages and drawback. Behavioral are further classified into voice recognition, signature recognition and keystroke. There are two main step present in any biometric system i.e. *verification* and *Identification.* For any biometric system following steps are conducted. [1][2]

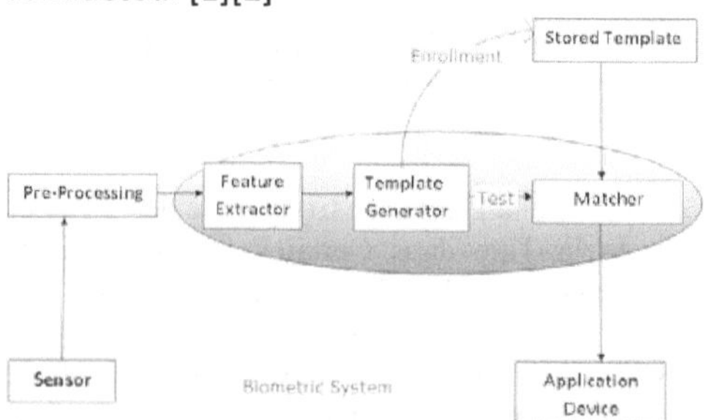

Figure - 1

Step that are involved in face recognition are (a) Image Registration (b) Locate Image of face (c) Analysis of facial image (d) Comparison (e) Match with existing template. In this paper we are using physiological method for identification, In face recognition is an authentication there are few technique present in face recognition like LDA, PCA, ICA & Neural network. Feature extraction is one of the most popular and fundamental problems in face recognition. Statistical method for face recognition are *featured based* or *holistic based*.[2]

2. Introduction to LDA technique used for statistical approach – Linear Discriminat Analysis is primarily used here to reduce the number of features to a more manageable number. LDA is statistical approach for classifying samples of unknown classes based on training sample with known classes. Aim to maximize between classes variance and minimize within class variance.

3. Methodology - For implementation LDA face recognition system, we have consider standard database of Indian face which from IIT, Kanpur.

3.1 ***Data Collection*** –For implementing we have consider ten persons face database, each person have five image of front pose. Similarly we have taken few other faces of some research students, and we have consider poses variation like up, down, right and left by using those database our training and testing operation can be performed.[3]

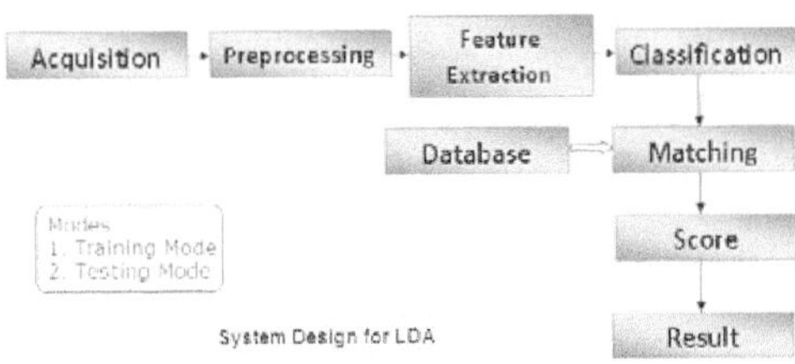

Figure -2

3.2 ***Pre-processing*** – various operation perform on image they are

a. crop

b. resize of image

c. conversion of RGB into gray scale level

Crop – Original size of image is 640 x 480 by using crop operation on image it becomes 450 x 450 also removing additional background.

Original Image Crop Image

Resize – crop image is resize into 80 x 80 for operation to be perform on training and testing database.

Crop Image Resize Image

Conversion RGB into Gray Scale – Conversion of all resize image into gray scale term as normalization.[11][12]

Resize Image Gray Scale Image

3.3 Mathematical Operation – Compute mean of each dataset and mean of entire dataset, assume μ_1 and μ_2 mean of set1 and set2 respectively and μ_3 be mean of entire data, which is obtain by margin set1 and set2 given as

$$\mu_3 = p1 \times \mu_1 + p2 \times \mu_2$$

Where p1 and p2 are the apriori probabilities of classes, in simple two class problem, the probability factor is assumed to 0.5. In LDA, within class and between class scatter are used to formulate criteria for class separability. Within class scatter is expected covariance of each classes. The scatter measures are computed using

$$S_w = \sum_j p_j \times (cov_j)$$

For two class problem

$$S_w = 0.5 \times cov_1 + 0.5 \times cov_2$$

All the covariance matrices are symmetric. Assume cov1 and cov2 be the covariance of set1 and set2 respectively. Covariance matrix is computed as

$$cov_j = (x_j - \mu_j)(x_j - \mu_j)^T$$

Between class scatter is compute using following equation

$$S_b = \sum_j (\mu_j - \mu_3) \times (\mu_j - \mu_3)^T$$

Where Sb can be thought of as the covariance of data set whose members are the means vectors of each class. It should be noted that if LDA is a class dependent type, for L-class separate optimizing criterion are required for each class. The optimizing factors in case of class dependent type are computed as,

$$criterion_j = inv(cov_j) \times S_b$$

An Eigen vector of a transformation represents a 1-D invariant subspace of the vector space in which the transformation ins applied. A Set of these Eigen vectors whose corresponding Eigen values are non-zeros all linearly independent and are invariant under the transformation. For L-class problem we would always have L-1 non-zero Eigen values. Eigen vectors corresponding to non-zero Eigen values for transformation. We transform that sets using the single LDA transform or the class septic transformation which case may be. The decision region in the transformed space is a solid line separating the transformed data sets thus class dependent.

$$transformed\_set\_j = transform\_j^T \times set\_j$$

For the class independent LDA,

$$transformed\_set = transform\_spec^T \times data\_set^T$$

The test vectors are transformed and are classified using the Euclidean Distance of the test vectors from each class mean. The theory of Linear Discriminant Analysis applied to a 2-class problem. The original data sets are shown and the same data sets after transformation are also illustrated. It si quite clear from transformation provides a boundary for proper classification. Once the transformation are completed using the LDA transforms, Euclidean Distance or RMS distance is used to classify data points. Euclidean Distance is computed using following equation, where the mean of the transformed data set, is the class index and it the test vectors. Euclidean Distance are obtained for each test point.

$$dist\_n = (transform\_n\_spec)^T \times x - \mu_{ntrans}$$

Finally, smallest Euclidean Distance among the distance classifies the test vectors as belonging to class. [4][5][6][14]

4. Steps for LDA - Method that is used to calculate Euclidean Distance is

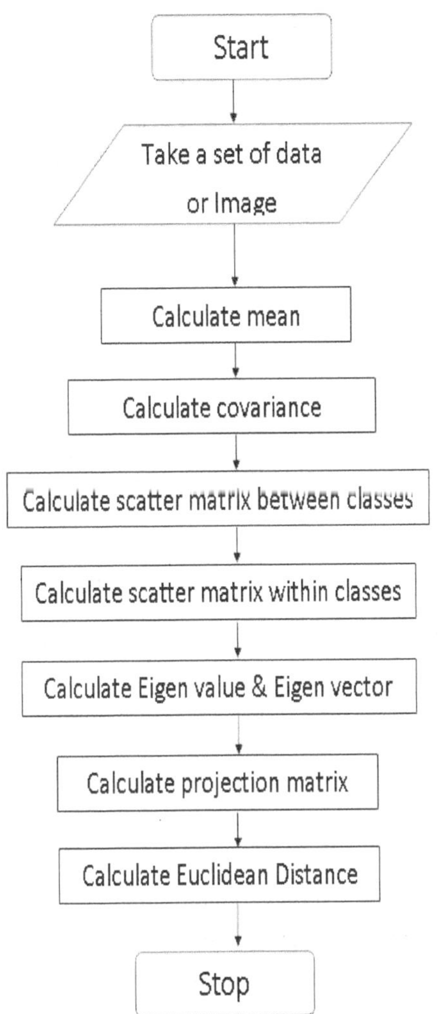

5. Standard Database used in our technique for Identification.

We have considered standard database for face recognition system for Indian faces which is from IIT, Kanpur. Our database contain ten persons face with different emotion, database contain five images for single person of front pose. For standard database four images are used in training dataset and one image is used as testing dataset.[7][8][9][10][13]

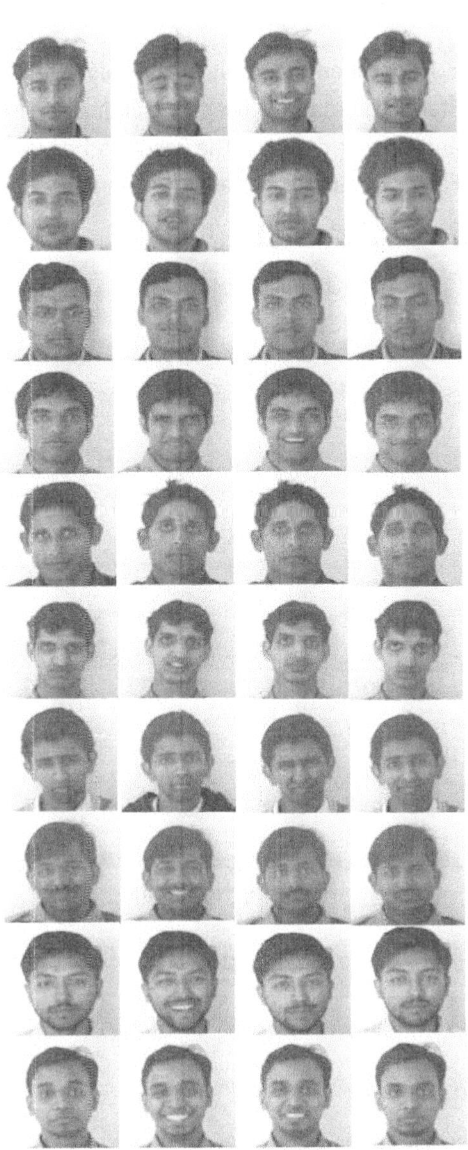

Training set of Standard Database

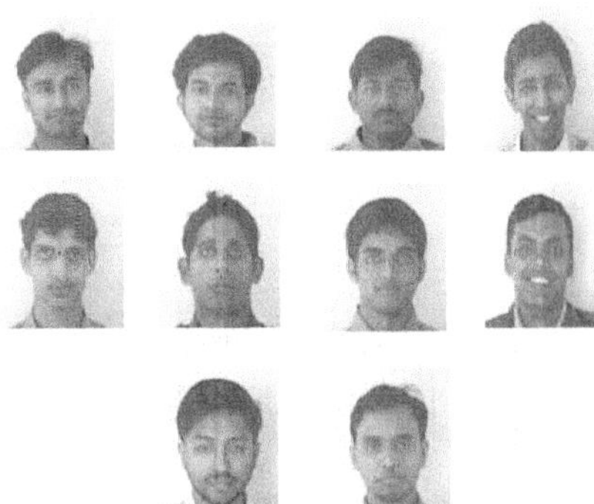

Testing Set of Standard Database

6. Experimental Result and Analysis – The Standard database used in training dataset and testing dataset. The result is based on False Acceptance Rate **(FAR)** and False Rejection Rate **(FRR)**.

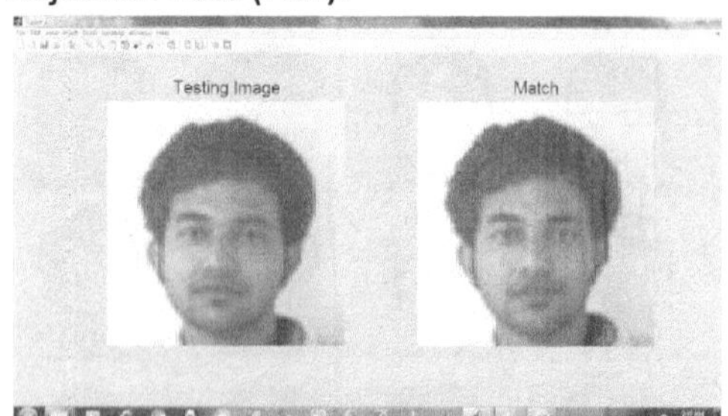

Matching Found

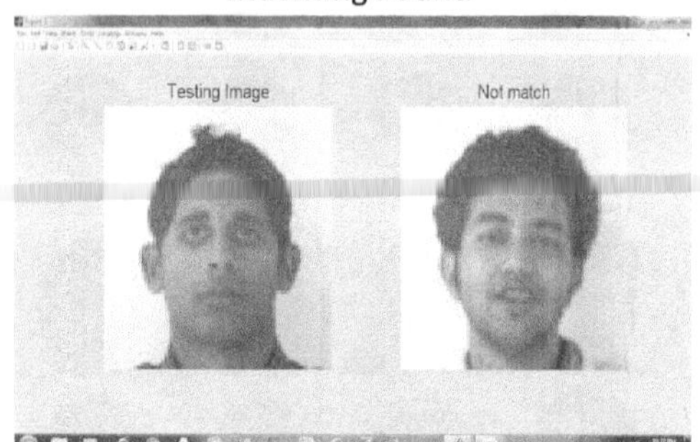

Matching Not Found

Training v/s Trailing front faces DB

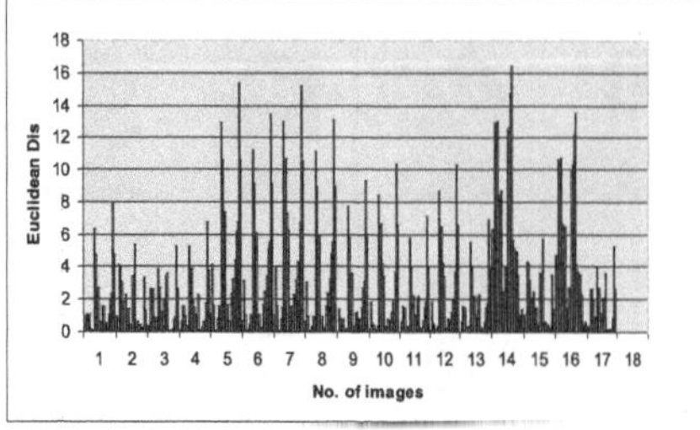

Testing image No.	Index No.		Min Euclidean Distance
	Match image	Not Match image	
1	3	-	0.0042
2	5	-	0.0016
3	11	-	0.0005
4	-	4	0.000001
5	20	-	0.0128
6	-	7	0.0003
7	-	14	0.0004
8	29	-	0.0017
9	33	-	0.0006
10	37	-	0.0012

The table shows minimum Euclidean Distance of an front faces. The database which we are used is "Standard Database".

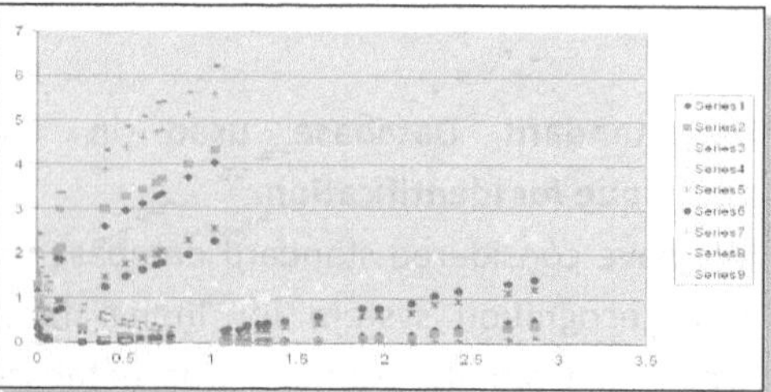

Similarly, we have calculate minimum Euclidean Distance for different emotional.

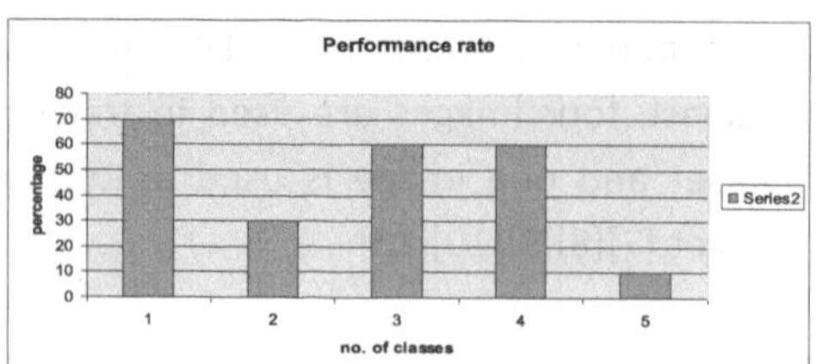

Performance Rate

FAR – The probability that the system incorrectly matches the input pattern to a non-matching template in the database. It measures the percent of invalid inputs which are incorrectly accepted.

FRR – The probability that the system fails to detect a match between the input pattern and a matching template in the database. It measures the percent of valid input which are incorrectly rejected.

7. Future Scope – Observing overall the process from our face recognition system we have to conclude that we want to working on more database and performing the training and testing operation in such a way that we have giving more promising and good result.

8. References

1. 'Face Recognition', National Science and Technology (NSTC), Committee on Technology, homeland and National security, pp. 2-4, 7th August 2006.
2. Ion Marques, 'Face Recognition Algorithme', pp. 14-15, June 16, 2010.
3. Shan-Hung Lin, "An Introduction to Face recognition technology", IC Media Corporation, Vol. No- 3, Paper no-1, 2000.
4. Wen Yi Zhao & Rama Chellappa, "Image-based Face recognition: Issues and Methods", Sarnoff Corporation and Center of automation Research respectively.
5. A Hossein Sahoolizadeh, B Zargham Heidari & C Hamid Dehghani, "A New face recognition method uses PCA, LDA & Neural network", work academy of science, Engineering & technology, Vol. No- 41, 2008.
6. Pallabi Parveen & Bhavani Thuraisingham, "Face recognition using various classifiers", Dept. of Computer Science Dallas, Paper No-UTDCS-05-06, January 2006.
7. Juwei Lu, K. N. Plataniotis & A. N. Venetsanopoulos, "Face recognition using LDA based algorithm", IEEE transaction on neural network, May 2002.
8. Hazim Kemal Ekenel & Rainer Stiefelhages, "Two-class LDA analysis for face recognition", Interactive system Labs, Dept. of Computer science, University at Karlsruhe.
9. Aleix M Martinez, "PCA vs. LDA", IEEE transaction on pattern analysis & machine intelligence, Vol. No.-23, paper no-2, February 2001.
10. W. Zhao, R. Chellappa, "Discriminant Analysis of principal component for face recognition", university of Maryland.
11. S. Balakrishnama, A. Ganapathiraju, "LDA- A brief tutorial", Institute for signal and information processing.
12. Hua Yu & Jie Yang, "A direct LDA algorithm for high-dimensional data –with application to face recognition", Pattern Recognition, Vol. No.-34, pp-2067-2070, 2001.
13. Merian Stewart Bartlett, "Face recognition by ICA", IEEE transaction on neural network, Vol. No.-13, paper no.-6, November 2002.
14. http://web.mit.edu/emeyers/www/face_databases.html

SESSION

LATE BREAKING PAPERS - BIOINFORMATICS AND COMPUTATIONAL BIOLOGY - MICROARRAYS, DNA SEQUENCING, GENE REGULATORY NETWORKS, HEALTH AND MEDICAL INFORMATICS

Chair(s)

Prof. Hamid Arabnia

A Complementary Feature Selection Method in Finding Biomarkers

Kung-Hua Chang[1], **and D. Stott Parker**[1]
[1]University of California Los Angeles
Los Angeles, CA, USA
{kunghua,stott}@cs.ucla.edu

Abstract - *DNA microarray analysis and mass-spectrometry data analysis involves identifying informative biomarkers out of thousands of genes or (M/z, abundance) value pairs. In this paper, we discuss the problem of finding complementary feature sets, so that the biomarkers selected complement each other's strengths for classification. In other words, complementary biomarkers are optimized so as to correctly classify as many examples as possible in the input training set. The performance of our complementary feature selection algorithm is superior when compared with prior research for p-norm SVM, 0-norm SVM, 1-norm SVM and SVM-RFE. The algorithm also managed to select very few (3 or 4) genes as feature sets in benchmark Colon and Prostate Cancer datasets. Moreover, many genes selected were also validated as meaningful, and selected by algorithms in prior published work.*

Keywords: Microarrays, Gene expression analysis, support-vector machine.

1 Introduction

Many problems involve informative feature selection among large sets of biomarkers. Microarray analysis usually involves analyzing thousands of genes in order to find the most differentially expressed genes as biomarkers, while mass-spectrometry data analysis involves searching into thousands of biomarkers in terms of relative abundance and m/z. Much prior research has applied statistical methods such as t-tests [1], signal-to-noise ratio [2], or SAM [3], and machine learning approaches such as Support-Vector Machines [4-11] in order to select informative biomarkers. However, statistical methods usually find more biomarkers than necessary – such that many of the biomarkers are redundant and are very similar to each other. Reducing the number of biomarkers selected can be important, such as in reducing the time required for analysis.

In this paper, we discuss the problem of finding subsets of features that are complementary, in the sense that one biomarker can complement the missing classification ability of the others. When optimized, these feature sets are both informative and small in size, and sometimes surprisingly so.

A difficulty in analyzing biological datasets, such as high-throughput proteomics technology based on mass-spectrometry (MS) and gene expression datasets from DNA microarray analysis, lies in the high dimensionality of the data. Researchers often apply some filters as a pre-processing method, such as removing genes that are not differentially expressed under a pre-defined threshold, before applying machine learning algorithms [10]. However, even after applying such filters, the remaining number of genes can be quite large, and many algorithms have difficulties operating with such high dimensionality. Besides, the sample size for microarray datasets is usually very small and it is very easy for some machine learning algorithms to over-fit.

Fortunately, a Support-Vector Machine (SVM) [12] can work on high dimensional datasets with a method that works to avoid over-fitting as much as possible (by separating classes with a high-dimensional hyper-plane having maximal margin). This can greatly alleviate problems of over-fitting. This is the main reason we choose SVMs for analyzing mass-spectrometry and microarray datasets in this paper.

In this paper, we propose a Complementary Feature Selection (CFS) algorithm using SVMs, and apply our algorithm on several benchmarks – a mass-spectrometry dataset from NIPS competition data [13], and 2 microarray datasets (Colon [4] and Prostate cancer datasets [14]). We compare our experimental results with those using the p-norm SVM, 0-norm SVM, 1-norm SVM, and SVM-RFE that are reported by Tan et. al. [8].

2 Methods

2.1 Complementary Feature Selection (CFS)

Feature selection algorithms usually deploy heuristic search algorithms such as forward stepwise selection to pick a subset of features K from a set of N features $(x_1, x_2, \ldots, x_N)$ by satisfying an objective function such as maximum classification accuracy.

Instead of maximizing on classification accuracy, Complementary Feature Selection (CFS) seeks to maximize *coverage* of training examples by measuring each individual feature's classification ability with a machine learning algorithm on the training set, and then pairing features together so as to make them complement to each other. The objective function is to cover (correctly classify) as many training examples as possible. This differs from the traditional feature selection algorithms that maximize classification accuracy because CFS can choose very weak features (that would normally be discarded by contemporary feature selection algorithms).

Formally, CFS seeks to optimize the function

$$\underset{K}{\operatorname{argmax}} \sum_{i=1}^{M} sign\left(\sum_{j \in K} L\left(y_i, G\left(x_{ij}\right)\right)\right)$$

where K is a subset of a set of N features $(x_1, x_2, ..., x_N)$ and x_{ij} is the value of feature x_j in the i-th observation. We estimate each feature's classification ability by using a classification algorithm G such that $G(x_{ij})$ predicts the class labels in the training example. We then compare y_i, the actual class label in the training set, with $G(x_{ij})$, the predicted class label in the training set, in a loss function $L\left(y_i, G(x_{ij})\right)$ to quantify the results. The loss function is defined as:

$$L(p,q) = 1 \quad \text{if } p = q$$
$$L(p,q) = -1 \quad \text{if } p \neq q$$

$\sum_{j \in K} L\left(y_i, G\left(x_{ij}\right)\right)$ calculates the coverage of the original training set by adding up the values of 1 and -1 from the loss function. Each training example will receive a value between $|K|$ and $-|K|$, so we apply a SIGN function to convert them into 0 or 1 as:

$$sign(V) = 1 \text{ if } V > 0$$
$$sign(V) = 0 \text{ if } V \leq 0$$

Our objective function is then to choose a subset K of features out of a total of N features that maximizes the sum of

$$sign\left(\sum_{j \in K} L\left(y_i, G\left(x_{ij}\right)\right)\right).$$

Finally, $\sum_{i=1}^{M} sign\left(\sum_{j \in K} L\left(y_i, G\left(x_{ij}\right)\right)\right)$ sums up all the signed values from each selected features for M training examples. In other words, the maximal value is M, which is the complete coverage of all M training examples.

2.2 Implementation

It is infeasible to perform brute-force search to select an optimal subset K out of N features when N is large. We have implemented a branch-and-bound depth-first heuristic search algorithm based on CFS that works by (1) starting with an empty set S, (2) selecting each feature (biomarker) to add to S so that each feature is given a chance to be selected as the initial feature, (3) adding the feature (biomarker) to S based on CFS that best complements its classification power, (4) training with S to obtain new predicted class labels $G(S)$, (5) evaluating the coverage of the current feature set S to determine whether the algorithm should stop due to maximal coverage (i.e., covering all M training examples), and (6) repeating (3)-(5) until maximal coverage is reached. An important assumption is that the distribution of the training set is similar to that of the validation/test set. so that the best features (biomarkers) from the training set also are effective for the test set. By repeatedly selecting a feature that best complements the current feature set S at each step, we implicitly minimize the number of features needed. The algorithm avoids selecting redundant features having similar classification power.

3 Experiments

3.1 Datasets

We use LIBSVM [15] with nu-SVC and linear kernel, and leave everything else with default settings. We set the terminating condition of our branch-and-bound depth-first heuristic search to be 250,000 feature sets. In our experiments, the best feature set usually appears within 100,000 features sets, and we expand from 100,000 to 250,000 feature sets to ensure that we have more than enough coverage. We apply our algorithm to 3 publicly available datasets: ARCENE dataset [13], Colon cancer dataset [4], and Prostate cancer dataset [14]. All the datasets are 2-class classification problems.

The ARCENE dataset [13] was obtained from two different sources. One was from The National Cancer Institute (NCI) and the other was from Eastern Virginia Medical School (EVMS). All the data is mass-spectrum data obtained with the SELDI technique. The training and validation examples include patients with cancer (ovarian / prostate cancer), and healthy patients. The datasets we obtained contain 44 positive examples and 56 negative examples in the training set, and another 44 positive examples / 56 negative examples in the validation set – with 10,000 biomarkers. We mixed these 200 total examples together and performed 10-fold cross validation without normalizing the dataset.

The Colon cancer dataset [4] contains 2000 genes selected from 6500 genes with a total of 62 samples. It contains 40 tumor samples and 22 healthy samples from the colon. The raw expression values have already been pre-processed in [4], so we keep all 2000 genes, normalize the dataset, and perform 10-fold cross validation on this dataset.

The Prostate cancer dataset [14] contains expression profiles from 50 non-tumor prostate samples and 52 prostate tumor samples with 12600 genes. We normalize the dataset and perform 10-fold cross validation with our algorithm.

3.2 Preprocessing

Instead of using the filter method from [10] to pre-process each dataset, we simply let support-vector machine filter out genes (biomarkers) that are not differentially expressed. We found that when we applied the SVM to some of the M by 1 matrices from individual genes for training, it could not separate the 2 different classes. In other words, when these genes are not differentially expressed the SVM is unable to build a model, and thus the SVM with this M by 1 matrix serves the same purpose as the filter method. This approach also makes use of all the weak features that would otherwise be discarded by using filter method as filter method often seeks to choose the top few hundreds of differentially expressed genes. In our approach, as long as we are able to train a model using SVM, we do not care how weak that feature is.

3.3 Results

Table 1 shows the number of biomarkers we filtered out using SVM. We can see that by testing each individual biomarker's classification ability, it can prune an average of 5352 biomarkers in the ARCENE datasets, 4526 genes in the Prostate Cancer dataset, and about 0.2 genes in the Colon Cancer dataset. The reason we only pruned an average of 0.2 genes in Colon Cancer dataset is because this dataset has already been pre-processed by [4] and has been reduced from 6500 genes to 2000 genes.

DATASET	AVERAGE NO OF PRUNED BIOMARKERS
ARCENE	5352
COLON	0.2
PROSTATE	4526

Table 1- Average Number of Biomarkers Filtered Out by SVM

Table 2,3, and 4 show the best solution (out of 250,000 total solutions) for each fold in the 10-fold cross validation results from the ARCENE dataset [13], Colon cancer dataset [4], and Prostate cancer dataset [14], respectively. We select an average of 4 biomarkers in the ARCENE dataset, 3 genes in the Colon Cancer dataset, and 3 genes in the Prostate Cancer dataset with very good test accuracy.

Training	Test	Selected_	FOLD

Accuracy	Accuracy	Biomarkers	
72.2222	95	9478 8924 6584 3857	1
73.3333	90	2096 1055 6408 3539	2
73.3333	100	61 2496 731 1883	3
55.5556	95	9886 3734 1496 7741	4
70.5556	95	5923 3241 3856 1741	5
80	95	6146 9477 5981 8328	6
66.1111	95	9985 9986 4768 5269	7
69.4444	90	6594 9241 8055 9326	8
67.7778	90	5424 2840 9986	9
68.8889	100	8785 8783 6732 3688	10

Table 2 - Experimental Results from CFS-SVM on ARCENE dataset.

Training Accuracy	Test Accuracy	Selected_Genes	FOLD
92.7273	100	286 1772 1671	1
94.5455	100	1976 513 1532	2
92.8571	100	377 1772 1288	3
91.0714	100	632 75 1771	4
92.8571	100	1775 792 31	5
92.8571	100	1094 1582 1772	6
92.8571	100	377 1562 1772	7
92.8571	100	813 377 882	8
94.6429	100	909 1772 1871	9
94.6429	100	1210 1244 1060	10

Table 3 - Experimental Results from CFS-SVM on Colon cancer dataset.

Training Accuracy	Test Accuracy	Selected_Genes	FOLD
95.6044	100	6185 4419 10234	1
96.7033	100	8802 9172 6185	2
95.6522	100	11367 6185 9034	3
94.5652	100	48 10234 8724	4
95.6522	100	3286 6462 10537	5
95.6522	100	6749 6185	6

		6390	
95.6522	100	10703 6462 10537	7
96.7391	100	10691 9850 5954	8
95.6522	100	6185 5151 9172	9
95.6522	100	6749 6185 6462	10

Table 4- Experimental Results from CFS-SVM on Prostate cancer dataset.

In Table 5, we compared our experimental results with the results by p-norm SVM, 0-norm SVM, 1-norm SVM, and SVM-RFE as reported by Tan et. al [8]. We labeled our experimental results as CFS-SVM (Complementary Feature Selection with Support-Vector Machine). In Table 5, we showed our results in the format 10-Fold Training Error / 10-Fold Test Error to compare the Average 10-Fold Test Error as reported by Tan et. al [8]. Our average best test accuracy from 10-Fold cross validation is better than the average test error from 10-Fold cross validation from p-norm SVM, 0-norm SVM, 1-norm SVM, and SVM-RFE. Besides, the number of genes selected by our algorithm is smaller than the number of genes selected by the above-mentioned algorithm.

Datasets	Methods	No. of selected Biomarkers	Average Error (%)
ARCENE	p-norm	6.5	17.6
	0-norm	27.4	24.6
	1-norm	12.9	19.8
	RFE	70	16.6
	CFS	**3.9**	30.278 / **5.5**
Colon Cancer	p-norm	4.6	16.1
	0-norm	13.2	14.5
	1-norm	15.6	13.5
	RFE	64	14.5
	CFS	**3**	6.8 / **0.0**
Prostate Cancer	p-norm	8.3	2.9
	0-norm	10.5	4.7
	1-norm	17.9	3.5
	RFE	50	5.1
	CFS	**3**	4.3 / **0.0**

Table 5- Experimental results from CFS-SVM comparing with the results by p-norm SVM, 0-norm SVM, 1-norm SVM, and SVM-RFE as reported by Tan et. al. [8]. Average Error by CFS-SVM is shown in the format: "Average Training Error" / "Average Test Error"

Gene	Entrez	Description
75	Hsa.2800	Human Hums3 mRNA for 40S ribosomal protein s3.
377	Hsa.36689	H.sapiens mRNA for GCAP-II / uroguanylin precursor.
1582	Hsa.2928	H.sapiens mRNA for p cadherin.
1771	Hsa.601	Human aspartyl tRNA synthetase alpha-2 subunit mRNA, complete cds.
1772	Hsa.6814	COLLAGEN ALPHA 2(XI) CHAIN (Homo sapiens)

Table 6 - The list of genes selected by CFS-SVM overlapping with [5] from Colon Cancer dataset.

In Table 6, we show the list of genes selected from the best solution in the Colon cancer dataset that are overlapping with the list provided by [5]. According to [5], these genes have been shown to be very closely related to Colon Cancer.

In Table 7, we showed the list of genes selected from the best solution in the Prostate cancer dataset that are overlapping with the list provided by [8] and [16]. According to [8], the genes 6185, 6390, and 10234 from the list in [16] have been shown to be very closely related to Prostate Cancer. We also found 2 more genes 6462 and 9172 related to Prostate Cancer from the list in [16] as well. We have made our experimental results and processed data available at [17].

GENE	UID	DESCRIPTION
6185	37639_at	Human hepatoma mRNA for serine protease hepsin
6390	38322_at	Homo sapiens cDNA, 3 end
6462	38634_at	Human cellular retinol-binding protein mRNA
9172	38406_f_at	Homo sapiens cDNA, 3 end
10234	41504_s_at	Homo sapiens short form transcription factor C-MAF (c maf) mRNA

Table 7 - The list of genes selected by CFS-SVM overlapping with [8] and [16] from Colon Cancer dataset.

4 Conclusions

In this paper, we presented a new feature selection algorithm called complementary feature selection (CFS) utilizing complementarity between different features in order to identify an informative feature subset that is optimized so as to be sufficient to classify as many examples as possible in the training set. We used a new filter based purely on support-vector machine as a pre-processing method and performed our experiments using support-vector machine on 3 publicly available bioinformatics datasets while comparing our experimental results with prior research in [8]. The experimental results showed that our proposed algorithm CFS-SVM can find very small subsets of genes that can perform better than the subsets found by p-norm SVM, 0-norm SVM, 1-norm SVM, and SVM-RFE in [8]. Finally the selected list of genes was validated as meaningful, based on prior research [5][8][16]; in other words, we used prior knowledge to identify meaningful genes.

5 References.

[1] Bø T, Jonassen I. "New feature subset selection procedures for classification of expression profiles". Genome biology, Vol. 3, No. 4. (2002), doi:10.1186/gb-2002-3-4-research0017.

[2] Golub T.R., Slonim D.K., Tamayo P., Huard C., Gaasenbeek M., Mesirov J.P., Coller H., Loh M.L., Downing J.R., Caligiuri M.A., Bloomfield C.D., Lander E.S. "Molecular classification of cancer: class discovery and class prediction by gene expression monitoring". Science, 1999 Oct 15; 286(5439):531-537.

[3] Tusher V.G., Tibshirani R., Chu G. "Significance analysis of microarrays applied to the ionizing radiation response". Proc Natl Acad Sci U S A. 2001;98:5116–5121. doi: 10.1073/pnas.091062498

[4] Guyon I., Weston J., Barnhill S., Vapnik V. "Gene selection for cancer classification using support vector machines". Mach. Learn. 46: , 389-422,2002

[5] Wang L., Zhu J., Zou H. "Hybrid huberized support vector machines for microarray classification and gene selection". Bioinformatics, 23: 2507-2517,2008. Gene List is available at: http://bioinformatics.oxfordjournals.org/content/24/3/412/T5.expansion.html

[6] Zhang H.H., Ahn J.Y., Lin X.D., Park C.W. "Gene selection using support vector machines with non-convex penalty". Bioinformatics,22: 88-96,2006

[7] Bradley P.S., Mangasarian O.L. "Feature selection via concave minimization and support vector machines". In Proc. 13th ICML,82-90,1998

[8] Tan J.Y., Zhang C.H., Deng N.Y. "Cancer related gene identification via p-norm support vector machine". The Fourth international symposium on optimization and systems biology, 83-90.2010.9

[9] Zhang et al. "Recursive SVM feature selection and sample classification for mass-spectrometry and microarray data". BMC Bioinformatics, 7:197, 2006

[10] Paul T.K., Iba H. "Extraction of informative genes from microarray data". Proceedings of the Genetic and Evolutionary Computation Conference, Washington DC, USA, pp 453-460, 2005.

[11] Chang K.H., Kwon Y.K., Parker D.S. "Finding minimal sets of informative genes in microarray data". Lecture Notes in Computer Science, 2007, Volume 4463/2007, 227-236, DOI: 10.1007/978-3-540-72031-7_21

[12] Vapnik V.N. "The Nature of Statistical Learning Theory". Springer, 1995.

[13] Guyon I., Gunn S.R., Ben-Hur A., Dror G. "Result analysis of the NIPS 2003 feature selection challenge". In: NIPS. http://mlr.cs.umass.edu/ml/datasets/Arcene

[14] Singh D., Febbo P., Ross K., Jackson D., Manola J., Ladd C., Tamayo P., Renshaw A.,D'Amico A., Richie J., Lander E., Loda M., Kantoff P., Golub T.,Sellers W. "Gene expression correlates of clinical prostate cancer behavior". cancer cell,1:,203-209,2002

[15] Chang C.C., Lin C.J. "LIBSVM : a library for support vector machines". ACM Transactions on Intelligent Systems and Technology, 2:27:1--27:27, 2011.

[16] Lai Y.L. "Genome-wide co-expression based prediction of differential expressions". Bioinformatics. 24 666-673,2008.

[17] http://www.cs.ucla.edu/~kunghua/BIOCOMP2013/

HapMaker: Synthetic Haplotype Generator

N. Okuda[1], P. Bodily[1], J. Price[1], M. Clement[1], and Q. Snell[1]
[1]Computer Science Department, Brigham Young University, Provo, UT, U.S.A.

Abstract— *HapMaker is a simple program that generates a variant DNA sequence based on an input DNA sequence. Its purpose is to aid in the investigation of algorithms for heterozygous genome assemblers. In order to verify that HapMaker could accomplish its goal, we designed an experiment to test its accuracy in simulating haplotypes. We found that HapMaker meets our standard of accuracy in two of the three experiments. Where HapMaker seems to have failed to meet our standard of accuracy, we find insights not only in how to improve HapMaker but also in how different genome assemblers behave when given DNA data sampled from a simulated heterozygous homologous pair.*

The HapMaker source code is available at `https://github.com/nOkuda/hapmaker`.

Keywords: simulation, haplotypes, heterozygous, assembly, diploid

1. Introduction

Every good piece of software needs a good validation tool. Genome assemblers are pieces of software. Therefore, good genome assemblers need good validation tools. Although current genome assemblers are good at assembling homozygous genomes, their methods currently take little consideration for assembling heterozygous genomes.

In this paper, we will consider a genome to be the set of chromosomes present in an organism. We define a chromosome to be a continuous sequence of DNA. We define DNA to be the building blocks of hereditary information and call one such block of DNA a base. We note that some chromosomes in an individual are very similar to each other. We say that these similar chromosomes are homologous to each other. We define a haplotype to be the DNA sequence of one of the chromosomes in a set of homologous chromosomes. We also say that a genome is homozygous when homologous chromosomes all have the same haplotype, and we say that a genome is heterozygous when the genome is not homozygous. Finally, we refer to differences between homologous chromosomes as haplotypic variation.

We have developed HapMaker as a haplotype simulator that can be used as a tool in the process of validating genome assemblers concerned with assembling heterozygous genomes. Given an input DNA sequence and a heterozygosity level (i.e., the amount of difference between homologous DNA sequences), HapMaker will produce a haplotype. In addition, HapMaker outputs a mapping between the bases of the input sequence and the haplotype produced. We hope that such data will give software developers the information they need to validate their heterozygous genome assemblers.

2. Related Work

We find that the area of heterozygous genome assembly is not much researched. Thus, validation tools for heterozygous genome assembly are sparse if not non-existant.

Although we did not find software that directly addressed the need to validate heterozygous genome assemblers, we found that both DAWG [1] and INDELible [2] had features similar to those of HapMaker. DAWG and INDELible are programs used to study theoretical phylogenetics, which is concerned with the principles of DNA evolution. Since HapMaker relies on principles of DNA evolution to produce a haplotype, we found that both DAWG and INDELible shared a few similar features with HapMaker.

3. Methods and Materials

HapMaker is written in Perl and uses the BioPerl [3] library. It first takes in an input DNA sequence in fasta [4] format. It then counts the number of bases in the input sequence and allocates an array of that size. HapMaker then marks regions of the array as unmutatable, as specified by a no-change file. To simulate evolution for unmarked regions, HapMaker chooses at random a location in the array and marks it for either an insertion, deletion, or polymorphism event. In the case that HapMaker chooses an already marked entry, HapMaker chooses another location at random. The evolution process continues until a number of changes has been made such that the input heterozygosity rate has been satisfied. At this point, HapMaker then reads the array from beginning to end and outputs a DNA sequence according to the contents of the array.

We chose the default internal parameters of HapMaker according to the research of Mills et al. [5]. They studied the differences between a region of the human genome and a corresponding region of the chimpanzee genome. We thought that because humans and chimpanzee genomes are very similar, using the statistics on their differences would be similar to variation seen between haplotypes. Mills et al. reported that insertions and deletions are equally likely, that the length of insertion and deletion events greater than one base were generally less than 100 bases, and that both insertion and deletion events considered together occurred about once every 7200 bases. This information with the claim of polymorphism events occurring once every 200

Table 1: Some results from Allpaths-LG.

Category	Control	DAWG	HapMaker	INDELible
number of contigs	29	43	22	65
N50 contig size	42,300	35,700	86,400	26,600
total contig length	918,518	917,134	916,464	891,524
number of scaffolds	2	4	1	8
N50 scaffold size	811,000	334,000	922,336	480,000
total scaffold length	929,875	928,788	922,336	919,256

Table 2: Some results from Newbler.

Category	Control	DAWG	HapMaker	INDELible
number of contigs	265	245	322	261
N50 contig size	7290	7923	5568	7377
total contig length	889,141	891,369	890,426	891,399
number of scaffolds	122	125	141	117
N50 scaffold size	8093	8096	6031	9125
total scaffold length	794,646	825,172	756,366	782,680

bases in humans [6] led us to set the ratio of an insertion or deletion event occurring comparative to a polymorphism event as $\frac{200}{7200} = \frac{1}{36}$.

In order to measure the accuracy of HapMaker in simulating haplotypic variation, we devised an experiment. We took the largest contig from a human genome assembled by Levy et al. [7] (accession number `ABBA01049830.1`), used BLASTN [8] to find the corresponding sequence in the current reference human genome [9] (accession number `NT_010859.14`, from base 1,623,205 to 2,545,953), and considered these two DNA sequences as homologous chromosomes in a control group data set. We then took the DNA sequence from the reference human genome in the control group and used it as input to HapMaker to produce a haplotype, and created a HapMaker group data set consisting of the input and output sequences of HapMaker.

We assume that the two sequences in the control group data set are representative of haplotypic variation in the human genome because the assembly by Levy et al. exclusively used DNA sequences sampled from one person whereas the reference human genome is a sequence produced from DNA sequences sampled from multiple people. We then use this assumption to make a further assumption: if we use a genome assembler to assemble DNA sequences sampled from the control group data set, the assembly results from an assembly of DNA sequences sampled from the HapMaker group data set should be similar if HapMaker was accurate in its haplotype simulation. To put this assumption to use as a way to measure HapMaker's accuracy, we used ART [10] to sample the DNA sequences from the data sets and then assembled the sampled DNA sequences using three genome assemblers: Allpaths-LG [11], Newbler 2.7, and SOAPdenovo 2 [12].

To include further points of reference, we also made data sets using DAWG and INDELible and followed the experiment protocol as described above.

4. Results

We obtained the Allpaths-LG statistics using the `AllPathsReport` command. Besides setting the parameters to use the proper directories, we also set the MIN_CONTIG parameter to one. Since `AllPathsReport` reported the N50 sizes in kilobases, the reported numbers in Table 1 are rounded (except for the HapMaker N50 scaffold size, since it was obvious what it was). The scaffold statistics reported include gaps.

We see that the Allpaths-LG results show that the groups having differing numbers of contigs. We also see that the N50 contig sizes are different from each other. We see a similar pattern in the scaffold statistics. However, both the total contig lengths and the total scaffold lengths across groups is very similar. Perhaps INDELible is slightly smaller in total lengths compared to the other groups, but considering the size of these lengths, the differences are relatively small.

The Newbler results are shown in Table 2. Here, the results tell a similar but slightly different story compared to Allpaths-LG. Although the Control group has a number of contigs quite similar to those of the DAWG and INDELible groups, the HapMaker group produces many more contigs. The N50 contig sizes (which we obtained using a script [13] supposedly [14] used in the Assemblathon [15] for the same purpose) reflect this. However, all of the groups come out to

Fig. 1: Some results from SOAPdenovo. The x-axis labels k-mer sizes. Although all k-mer sizes above 59 resulted in segmentation faults, we chose to plot the graphs up to a k-mer size of 61 in order to make the numbering on the x-axis easier to see. SOAPdenovo failed to produce any scaffolds.

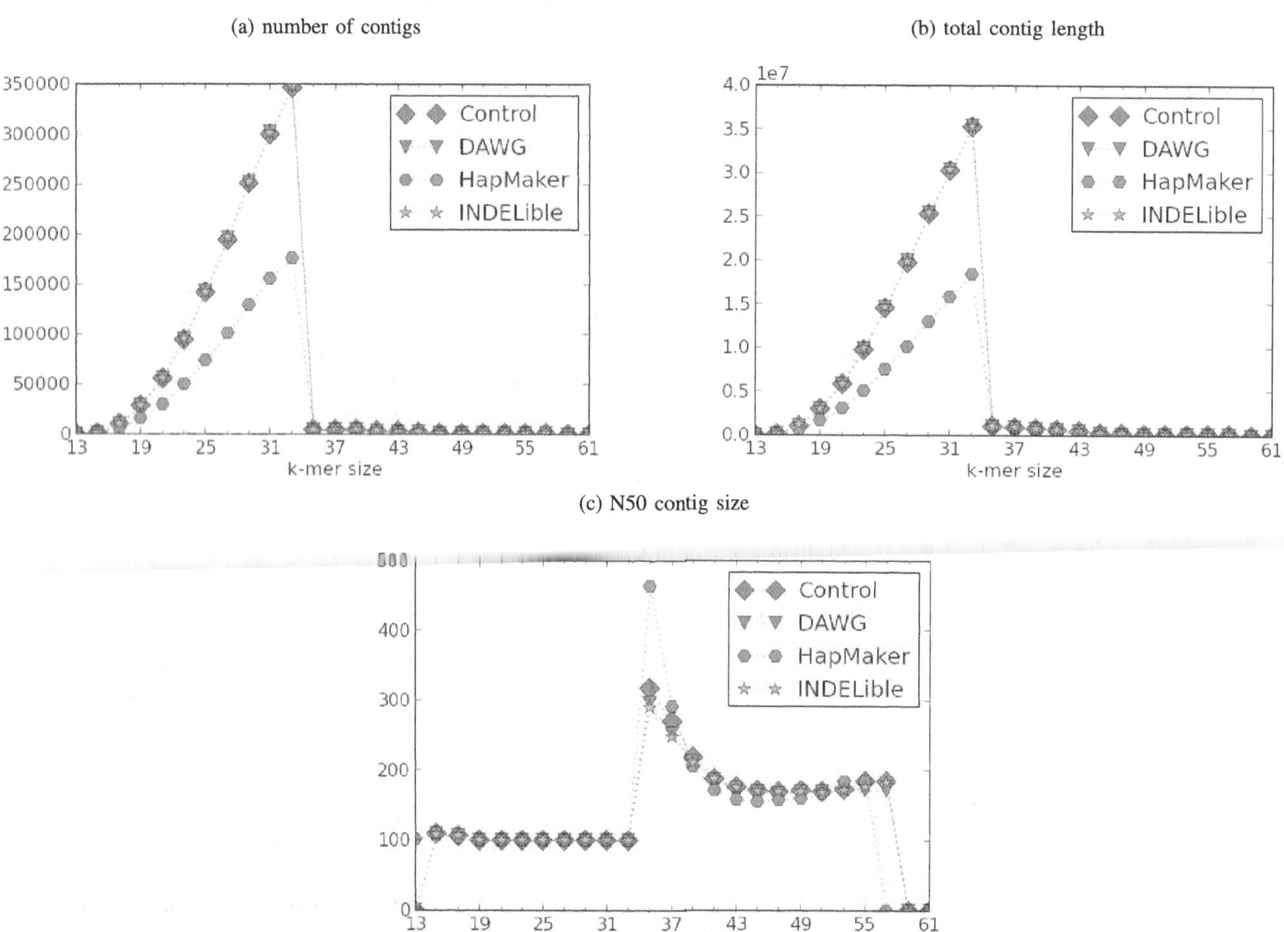

have about the same total contig length. As with the number of contigs, the number of scaffolds between the groups are similar among the Control, DAWG, and INDELible groups, but the HapMaker group has more scaffolds. The N50 scaffold size reflects the fact that the HapMaker group has more scaffolds by reporting a lower N50 scaffold size. However, the INDELible group has a much larger N50 scaffold size than either the Control or DAWG groups, even though they all shared similar numbers of scaffolds. Finally, the total scaffold lengths are similar between the Control and INDELible groups, but the DAWG group has a higher total scaffold length while the HapMaker group has a lower total scaffold length.

The SOAPdenovo results are shown in Figures 1(a) – 1(c). We used matplotlib [16] to plot the charts. Because we ran SOAPdenovo over multiple k-mer sizes, we wanted to show how the various assembly statistics changed as the k-mer size changed. Although SOAPdenovo failed to produce any scaffolds, it did produce contigs. There was also a problem with SOAPdenovo running into a segmentation fault once the k-mer size was greater than or equal to 57 for HapMaker group and greater than or equal to 59 for the other groups. Even so, we can observe the results for k-mer sizes that did not result in segmentation faults.

The SOAPdenovo results suggest that the HapMaker group is different from the other groups. At the k-mer size of 33, when all groups have the highest number of contigs (Figure 2a) and the largest total contig size (Figure 2b), all of the groups except for HapMaker are so close together that their plots overlap each other for all k-mer sizes. In the N50 contig size plot (Figure 2c), the largest N50 sizes for all groups seems to be when the k-mer size is 35. However, while both the DAWG and INDELible groups have slightly smaller N50 contig sizes compared to the Control group, the HapMaker group clearly has a much higher N50 contig size than the other groups.

5. Discussion

Allpaths-LG and Newbler give positive results for HapMaker's performance. Although the number of contigs and scaffolds varies from group to group (and as a result, the N50 statistics also vary), the total contig and total scaffold lengths are very similar across the groups, respective to their assemblers. This suggests that ART may not have sampled each data set in exactly the same way, but in spite of this, the assemblers were able to predict similar chromosomes for all groups. In other words, all of the haplotype simulation programs accurately simulated haplotypes.

However, SOAPdenovo disagrees with Allpaths-LG and Newbler. We believe that various factors contributed to this disagreement. After all, even though the difference in number of contigs, N50 contig size, and total contig length are very pronounced especially where they are reaching their globally maximum points, the general shape of the plots are quite similar to each other. These differences which SOAPdenovo reveals may have something to do with the insertion and deletion length models used by the haplotype simulation programs. Whereas DAWG and INDELible used a power law model, HapMaker used a uniform random distribution model. If this difference in insertion and deletion length models truly is the cause of the differences we see in SOAPdenovo's results, we have found supporting evidence for Cartwright's assertion that the power law model best simulates insertion and deletion lengths in real genomes [17]. In future work, we will want to verify that the differences in insertion and deletion length models truly were the factor that caused the SOAPdenovo results to show that the HapMaker group is different.

One thing to take from SOAPdenovo's results is the differences an algorithm can make on the results. Since both SOAPdenovo and Allpaths-LG use a de Bruijn graph approach to genome assembly, it was surprising at first that their results were so different. However, Allpaths-LG has an error correction stage in its algorithm whereas SOAPdenovo does not. Meanwhile, Newbler uses an overlap-concensus approach to genome assembly. This suggests that a de Bruijn graph approach to genome assembly without error correction is quite different from either a de Bruijn graph approach with error correction or an overlap-consensus approach.

Another interesting result is Newbler's report that the total scaffold lengths are shorter than the total contig lengths. Is this an indication that Newbler has successfully noted haplotypic differences? Further investigation is necessary to explore this idea.

6. Conclusion

In conclusion, HapMaker is a tool that allows users to generate a simulated haplotype from an input DNA sequence. The source code is available at `https://github.com/n0kuda/hapmaker`. While the results from our experiments show that HapMaker is accurate according to the results from Allpaths-LG and Newbler, the results from SOAPdenovo seem to indicate that there is a problem with the way HapMaker currently simulates haplotypes. We hope to investigate this further.

References

[1] R. A. Cartwright, "Dna assembly with gaps (dawg): simulating sequence evolution," *Bioinformatics*, vol. 21, no. Suppl. 3, pp. iii31–iii38, 2005.

[2] W. Fletcher and Z. Yang, "Indelible: A flexible simulator of biological sequence evolution," *Molecular Biology and Evolution*, vol. 26, no. 8, pp. 1879–1888, 2009.

[3] J. E. Stajich, D. Block, K. Boulez, S. E. Brenner, S. A. Chervitz, C. Dagdigian, G. Fuellen, J. G. Gilbert, I. Korf, H. Lapp, H. Lehväslaiho, C. Matsalla, C. J. Mungall, B. I. Osborne, M. R. Pocock, P. Schattner, M. Senger, L. D. Stein, E. Stupka, M. D. Wilkinson, and E. Birney, "The bioperl toolkit: Perl modules for the life sciences," *Genome Research*, vol. 12, no. 10, pp. 1611–1618, 2002.

[4] W. R. Pearson and D. J. Lipman, "Improved tools for biological sequence comparison," *Proceedings of the National Academy of Sciences*, vol. 85, no. 8, pp. 2444–2448, 1988.

[5] R. E. Mills, C. T. Luttig, C. E. Larkins, A. Beauchamp, C. Tsui, W. S. Pittard, and S. E. Devine, "An initial map of insertion and deletion (indel) variation in the human genome," *Genome Research*, vol. 16, no. 9, pp. 1182–1190, 9 2006.

[6] "Snp fact sheet," http://www.ornl.gov/sci/techresources/Human_Genome/faq/snps.shtml, accessed 16 Jan 2013.

[7] S. Levy, G. Sutton, P. C. Ng, L. Feuk, A. L. Halpern, B. P. Walenz, N. Axelrod, J. Huang, E. F. Kirkness, G. Denisov, Y. Lin, J. R. MacDonald, A. W. C. Pang, M. Shago, T. B. Stockwell, A. Tsiamouri, V. Bafna, V. Bansal, S. A. Kravitz, D. A. Busam, K. Y. Beeson, T. C. McIntosh, K. A. Remington, J. F. Abril, J. Gill, J. Borman, Y.-H. Rogers, M. E. Frazier, S. W. Scherer, R. L. Strausberg, and J. C. Venter, "The diploid genome sequence of an individual human," *PLoS Biol*, vol. 5, no. 10, p. e254, 09 2007.

[8] S. F. Altschul, T. L. Madden, A. A. Schäffer, J. Zhang, Z. Zhang, W. Miller, and D. J. Lipman, "Gapped blast and psi-blast: a new generation of protein database search programs," *Nucleic Acids Research*, vol. 25, no. 17, pp. 3389–3402, 1997.

[9] International Human Genome Sequencing Consortium, "Initial sequencing and analysis of the human genome," *Nature*, vol. 409, no. 6822, pp. 860–921, February 2001.

[10] W. Huang, L. Li, J. R. Myers, and G. T. Marth, "Art: a next-generation sequencing read simulator," *Bioinformatics*, vol. 28, no. 4, pp. 593–594, 2012.

[11] S. Gnerre, I. MacCallum, D. Przybylski, F. J. Ribeiro, J. N. Burton, B. J. Walker, T. Sharpe, G. Hall, T. P. Shea, S. Sykes, A. M. Berlin, D. Aird, M. Costello, R. Daza, L. Williams, R. Nicol, A. Gnirke, C. Nusbaum, E. S. Lander, and D. B. Jaffe, "High-quality draft assemblies of mammalian genomes from massively parallel sequence data," *Proceedings of the National Academy of Sciences*, 2010.

[12] R. Luo, B. Liu, Y. Xie, Z. Li, W. Huang, J. Yuan, G. He, Y. Chen, Q. Pan, Y. Liu, J. Tang, G. Wu, H. Zhang, Y. Shi, Y. Liu, C. Yu, B. Wang, Y. Lu, C. Han, D. Cheung, S.-M. Yiu, S. Peng, Z. Xiaoqian, G. Liu, X. Liao, Y. Li, H. Yang, J. Wang, T.-W. Lam, and J. Wang, "Soapdenovo2: an empirically improved memory-efficient short-read de novo assembler," *GigaScience*, vol. 1, no. 1, p. 18, 2012.

[13] http://korflab.ucdavis.edu/Datasets/Assemblathon/Assemblathon2/Basic_metrics/assemblathon_stats.pl, accessed 29 May 2013.

[14] https://groups.google.com/forum/?fromgroups#!topic/unix-and-perl-for-biologists/ou3GvHtHijw, accessed 29 May 2013.

[15] D. Earl, K. Bradnam, J. St. John, A. Darling, D. Lin, J. Fass, H. O. K. Yu, V. Buffalo, D. R. Zerbino, M. Diekhans, N. Nguyen, P. N. Ariyaratne, W.-K. Sung, Z. Ning, M. Haimel, J. T. Simpson, N. A. Fonseca, Ä. Birol, T. R. Docking, I. Y. Ho, D. S. Rokhsar, R. Chikhi, D. Lavenier, G. Chapuis, D. Naquin, N. Maillet, M. C. Schatz, D. R. Kelley, A. M. Phillippy, S. Koren, S.-P. Yang, W. Wu, W.-C. Chou, A. Srivastava, T. I. Shaw, J. G. Ruby, P. Skewes-Cox, M. Betegon, M. T. Dimon, V. Solovyev, I. Seledtsov, P. Kosarev, D. Vorobyev, R. Ramirez-Gonzalez, R. Leggett, D. MacLean, F. Xia, R. Luo, Z. Li, Y. Xie, B. Liu, S. Gnerre, I. MacCallum, D. Przybylski, F. J. Ribeiro, S. Yin, T. Sharpe, G. Hall, P. J. Kersey, R. Durbin, S. D. Jackman, J. A. Chapman, X. Huang, J. L. DeRisi, M. Caccamo, Y. Li, D. B. Jaffe, R. E. Green, D. Haussler, I. Korf, and B. Paten, "Assemblathon 1: A competitive assessment of de novo short read assembly methods," *Genome Research*, vol. 21, no. 12, pp. 2224–2241, 2011.

[16] J. D. Hunter, "Matplotlib: A 2d graphics environment," *Computing In Science & Engineering*, vol. 9, no. 3, pp. 90–95, 2007.

[17] R. A. Cartwright, "Problems and solutions for estimating indel rates and length distributions," *Molecular Biology and Evolution*, vol. 26, no. 2, pp. 473–480, 2009.

Reconstruction of Dynamic Gene Regulatory Networks for Cell Differentiation by Separation of Time-course Data

T. Nakayama[1], H. Daiyasu[1], S. Seno[1], Y. Takenaka[1], and H. Matsuda[1]
[1]Department of Bioinformatic Engineering, Graduate School of Information Science and Technology, Osaka University, 1-5, Yamadaoka, Suita, Osaka, Japan

Abstract—*Recently, dynamic Bayesian network (DBN) model is widely used for estimating gene regulatory networks (GRNs) from time-course gene expression data. Ordinary DBNs estimate only a single network using the whole time-course data. However, some GRNs, such as cell differentiation, dynamically change their network structures due to chromatin remodeling. In this papers we present a method to estimate such dynamic GRNs that follow the dynamic changes of the regulations in adipocyte differentiation by separating time-course data. We analyzed the estimated GRNs and confirmed that the GRNs showed the dynamic changes in adipocyte regulation. The result shows that our method can identify the regulatory relationships of the genes that are dynamically changing during adipocyte differentiation by separating the time-course data.*

Keywords: cell differentiation, adipocyte, dynamic Bayesian network model, time-course data separation

1. Introduction

Reconstruction of gene regulatory networks (GRNs) from gene expression data is a fundamental but challenging task in bioinformatics area. A number of methods have been developed for reconstructing GRNs. Among the methods, dynamic Bayesian network (DBN) model is widely used for estimating GRNs from time-course gene expression data [1]. However, ordinary dynamic Bayesian networks estimate a single network using whole time-course data, while some GRNs (e.g., GRNs in cell differentiation) dynamically change their network structures at their observed time points [2]. In this paper, we present a method to estimate the dynamic GRNs by separating time-course data.

Adipocyte differentiation is the one of the processes that is controlled by a complex network of transcription factors acting at different stages of differentiation due to chromatin remodeling [3]. It have been suggested that the four important adipogenic genes act at different stages [3][4]. During the early stages of adipogenesis, C/EBPβ and C/EBPδ activate expression of PPARγ, C/EBPα and probably other adipogenic genes. And then, PPARγ and C/EBPα activate expression of adipocyte specific genes. Furthermore recent studies have been revealing a complex transcriptional cascade controlling adipocyte differentiation [5][6][7][8].

The node-set separation method (NSS) [2] tries to capture different sub-networks that have high activity at their observed time points. This method estimates a GRN from whole timecourse data by using DBN, and then represents the dynamics of the GRN as transition of the regulations among the genes that are in active gene sets. An active gene set is determined as a set of differentially expressed genes comparing with the controls for each time point. Regulations among the genes in the active gene sets from consecutive two time points show the activity of the GRN at the time. In whole time-course data, the activities are changed at each time point. The transitions of activities of the GRN are regarded as the dynamics of the GRN.

There is matter that the method like the NSS uses the whole time-course gene expression data to estimate GRNs. It is suggested that the estimations with whole time points cannot identify the regulations that only exist in short span. Such short-term dynamic transcription controls are caused by chromatin remodeling [3]. Recently, experiments of microarray and updated methods, like RNA-Seq, that enable us easily to acquire high resolution time-course data. However, ordinary DBN-based methods evaluate the overall change of the gene expressions rather than the expressions represent the regulation change during short-term time intervals. In this paper, we estimate dynamic GRNs by DBN from separating the timecourse data of adipocyte differentiation, and present our proposed method can estimate some experimentally-confirmed regulations that are not detected by the NSS.

2. Materials and Method

Our method needs a time-course data with more time points than the NSS to estimate the dynamic GRN. It means that the data need to have the many time points enough to estimate a GRN if we separate the data. In addition, the estimation costs a computational time because the data need to have the many genes enough to estimate the relationships among genes that are concern of adipocyte differentiation. In this study, we used parallelized software on massively parallel systems for estimating the dynamic GRNs of adipocyte differentiation.

2.1 Microarray Data of Adipocyte Differentiation

We collected RNAs from Mouse ST2 Bone marrow stroma cell-derived stem cell (RCB0224) from RIKEN BioResource Center (BRC, Tsukuba, Japan) for adipocyte cell differentiation. The ST2 cell was induced by changing the medium from RMPI1640 to DMEM supplemented with 10% FBS, 0.5 mM 3-isobutyl-1-methlxanthine (MIX), 0.25μM DEX, and insulin-transferrin-selenium-X supplement containing 5μg/ml of insulin and 1μM rosiglitazone. After 48 hours, the differentiation medium was replaced with DMEM supplemented with 10% FBS.

The collected RNAs were analyzed with Affymetrix GeneChip Mouse Genome 430 2.0 Array, which generated transcript expression profiles at the time points: 5, 15, 30 and 45 minutes, 1 to 30 hours for every hour, 36 to 192 hours for every 6 hours after adipogenesis induction. Each time-course data was background-subtracted and normalized with the robust multi-array analysis (RMA) [9] using affy package from the Bioconductor version1.8.1. The transcript expression profiles are available from Genome Network Platform (http://genomenetwork.nig.ac.jp). We also calculated expression rate in each gene by Z-score. The data are converted to a common scale with an average of zero and standard deviation of one. This normalization was to emphasize the changing behavior of the gene expressions of the data rather than the value of the gene expressions.

In adipocyte differentiation, it is well-known that some significant transcription genes act a key regulator of adipocyte development [5] (see Fig. 1). These genes expressed enough value in our observed data. The network represents 23 regulations among 14 adipogenic genes.

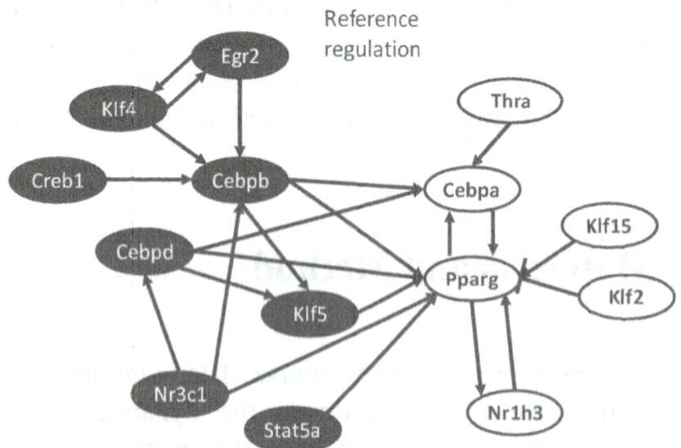

Fig. 1: Reference gene regulatory network [5]. Black and white circles represent the genes that are regulated at early stage and at late stage, respectively. Arrow edge represents upregulation and T-shaped edge, which exist on the relationship among Klf2-Pparg, represents down-regulation.

2.2 Separating the Time-course Data

We separate the time-course data to describe the changes of the gene regulations. If we estimate the network using whole time-course data of adipocyte differentiation, the result of the estimation describes the relationships between genes that regulate the other genes at any time throughout the whole differentiation. Other studies suggest that the gene regulatory relationships in cell differentiations are changing dynamically [3][6][10]. We generate subsequences from the gene expression data to make sure of the changes and estimated networks from each subsequence.

The node set separation method [2] is one of the methods to make subsequences. This method defines an active gene set for each time point and estimates GRN with each continuous couple of the time points at the active genes. In the method concept, the sub-networks that are constructed from the active genes have high activity and transmit information of external signals to other sub-networks.

We separate data by time-course, inspired by the NSS algorithm. In contrast to the NSS, the subsequences have some continuous time-courses at least 10 time points and all genes of input data (see Fig. 2). The NSS uses only active genes at consecutive two time points, while this method takes many time points to clear the causal relationships between two genes.

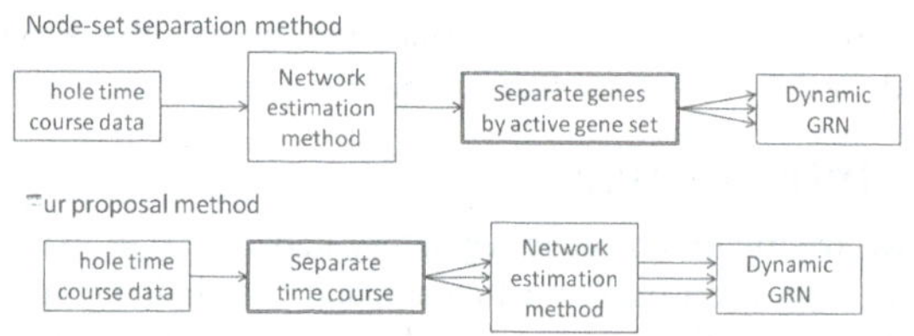

Fig. 2: Summary of the methods

Our method separates input time-course data into equal intervals with overlap. We formalized separated subsequences Z, that is

$$\begin{aligned} Z_i &= (X_{(i-1)S+1}, X_{(i-1)S+2}, X_{(i-1)S+W}) \\ i &= 1, 2, \ldots, 1 + (T - W)/S \end{aligned} \quad (1)$$

where $X = (X_1, X_2, \ldots, X_T)^t$ is the input time-course data and T is the number of the time points of input data. W is the size of the interval, which is "window size", and S is the value of shifted time points, which is "sliding width".

2.3 GRN Estimation

We estimated GRNs by the DBN model [1][11] using SiGN [11][12], which is the software that implements the DBN and works at high speed in parallel for supercomputer systems. The DBN model is able to construct cyclic regulation and is based on time-course data. In general, the DBN is estimated by an approximate search (greedy hill climbing) algorithm because the DBN model takes a large amount of computational time as increasing the number of genes.

3. Result

We present our separation method is suitable for high resolution time-course data of adipocyte differentiation than the NSS.

In this study, we separate the above time-course data into 10 subsequences. We set the parameters of (1) to $W = 15$ and $S = 5$. It means that each subsequence has 15 time points and the first time point of the subsequences a five time point time lag between two continuous sub sequences. We estimated the DBNs by SiGN with the 10 subsequences that have 15 time points and all time points for comparison. The network N_t where $t = 1, \dots, 10$ is estimated from Z_t and N is estimated with all time points X. The NSS is applied to N. We set the threshold of active gene to zero. It means that the gene is assumed active if the expression value of the gene is greater than mean of the gene expression value.

In this work, the computational environments of the estimation are the Human Genome Center (HGC) super-computer system, the University of Tokyo, and K computer (Advanced Institute for Computational Science, RIKEN). We used SiGN to estimate the DBN networks. The parameters we set is below; the number of bootstrap = 10,000, bootstrap replication = 3, bootstrap threshold = 0.05, hyperparameters of the BNRC score function hn=2, hb= 1.0 and hi=2.0. The other parameters were set to their default values. We decided these parameters by repeating small experiments with changing the parameters. This parameter set makes SiGN repeat network estimation 10,000 times to determine one network for bootstrapping, and output a network consisting of the regulations that appear on at least five percent of the 10,000 networks.

Figure 3 shows estimation accuracy of the each 10,000 estimated networks. SiGN uses an informatic criterion named BNRC [11]. The optimal network is chosen such that the BNRC is minimal. BNRC depends on the number of time points. In this study, BNRC of the estimated network was divided by the number of time points of the input data for the bias correction.

The overall network N is shown in Fig. 4. N has 62 edges among 16 genes. The number of estimated networks by NSS method is 60 because active gene set are determined at each time point. We show parts of the networks in Fig. 5. Our proposed method estimated 10 networks. For comparison with the results of NSS, N_2, N_4, N_7, N_8, and N_9, which are the result from 6th time point to 21th time point, 16th to 30th, 31st to 45th, 36th to 50th, and from 41th to 55th, respectively, are shown in Fig. 6. These networks in figures were arranged by force directed algorithm using Cytoscape (http://www.cytoscape.org), which is a visualization and analysis tool for biologic network.

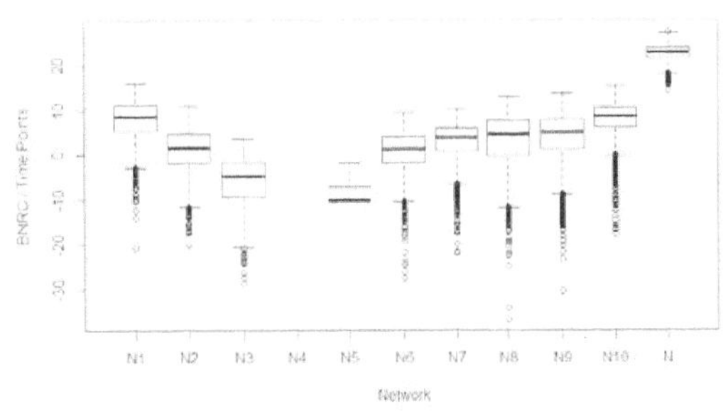

Fig. 3: This box plot shows the network estimation accuracy. The lower BNRC the network has, the higher accuracy the estimation of the network is. $N_1, \dots, N_{10}$ are estimated by our proposed method, and N is estimated by NSS. N_4 has no box in the box plot because the results of N_4 were too low to draw in this graph.

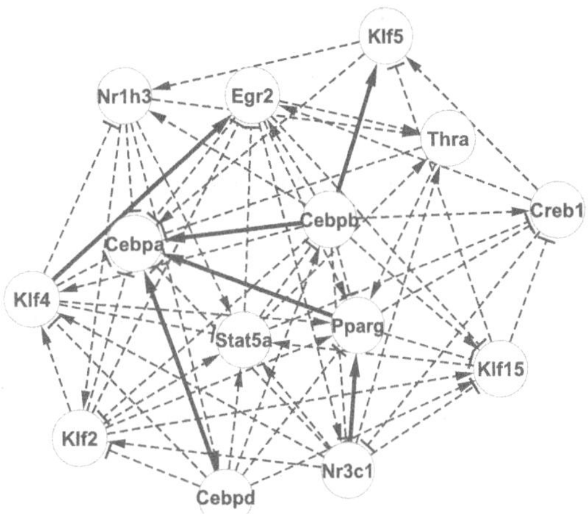

Fig. 4: The result of estimation with whole time-course data. Solid arrows show regulations that match with known regulations shown in Figure 1, and dash arrows show those that do not match with them.

Summary of these networks is shown in Fig. 7. Figure 7 shows distribution of F-measure in estimated networks by NSS and proposed method. F-measure, which is calculated by Eq. (2), is a measure of a estimation accuracy to compare the result with a reference. The best score of F-measure becomes 1, and the worst score of F-measure becomes 0.

$$
\begin{aligned}
F-measure &= 2 \cdot \frac{Precision \cdot Recall}{Precision + Recall} \\
Precision &= \frac{true\ positive}{true\ positive + false\ positive} \\
Recall &= \frac{true\ positive}{true\ positive + false\ negative}
\end{aligned}
\tag{2}
$$

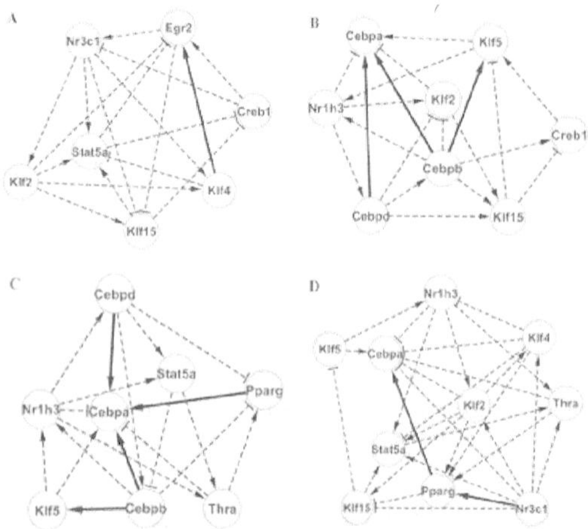

Fig. 5: A part of the results of estimation by NSS. As the same as Fig. 4, Solid and dash arrows show the regulations that match and do not match with known regulations shown in Fig. 1, respectively. Network A extracts an active gene set at the first time point from the network shown in Fig. 1. Similarly, networks B, C, and D extract active gene sets from the 15th and the 16th, from the 30th and the 31th, and from the 45th and the 46th time points, respectively.

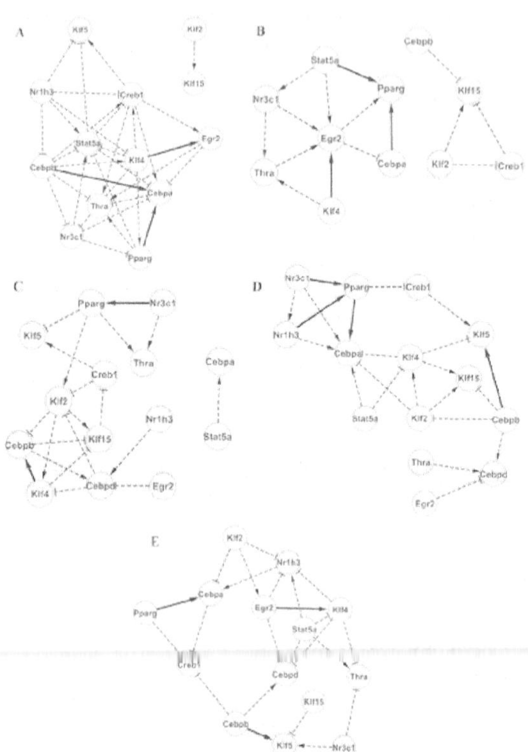

Fig. 6: A part of the results of estimation by our proposed method. Solid and dash arrows and their width mean the same as in Fig. 5. Network A is estimated from the 6th time point to the 21th. Similarly, networks B, C, D and E are estimated from the 16th to 30th, from the 31th to 45th, from the 36th to 50th, and from the 41th to 55th time points, respectively.

Figure 8 is the network represents the result of comparing the reference network shown in Fig. 1 with the estimated networks. The number of matched edges that estimated only by NSS is one, and estimated only by the proposed method is five. Five edges are commonly appeared in both methods.

4. Discussion

In this paper we proposed a time-separation method for GRN estimation method with high time-resolution data of adipocyte differentiation. Our method has an advantage of tracing dynamic GRN changes over other methods that estimate GRN with whole time-course data. The networks of proposed method capture the gene regulations that are not in entire span of adipocyte differentiations but in short span. This method is applicable to estimate GRN from the mechanisms at what expressions of genes change vary widely for a small amount of time such as adipocyte differentiations.

Figure 3 showed that the BNRC of the all networks estimated by our method is lower than the result of NSS. It means that the estimation accuracy of our method becomes higher than NSS. Furthermore, Figure 8 shows that the proposed method estimated more correct regulations than NSS. Moreover, Figure 7 shows the accuracy of each estimated network is more of the same. It suggests that our method does not decline estimation accuracy in spite of using lesser time points than NSS, and captured the regulations of adipocyte differentiation in short span. Our method focuses on the change of regulation in short span. In contrast, the networks that are estimated by NSS is based on the whole time-course data. Therefore, the regulations are mainly appeared from the entire differentiation behavior. Several studies have reported that various genes regulate other genes like a cascade in short term in adipocyte differentiation. For the reason, the proposed method is more suitable than NSS in this study.

The parameters of the proposed method, which are "window size" and "sliding width", are not optimized. If we could fully optimize the parameters, we would get more favorable performance.

4.1 Author's Contributions

TN developed software and made computational experiments. HM supervised the research. TN, HD, SS, YT and HM wrote the manuscript. All authors read and approved the final manuscript.

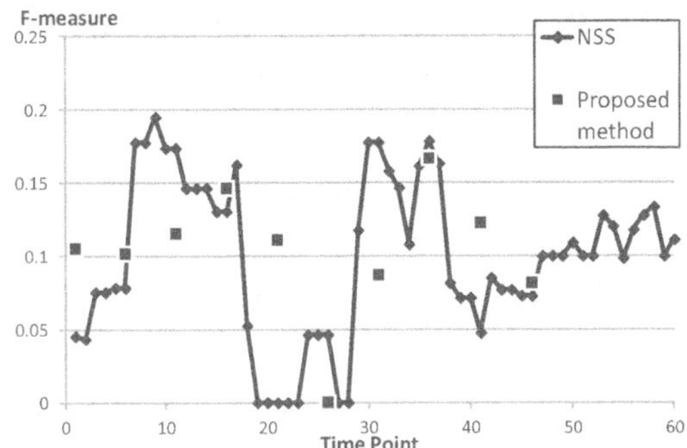

Fig. 7: This graph shows the distribution of F-measure in estimated networks by NSS and proposal method. Each point represents one network estimated respective methods.

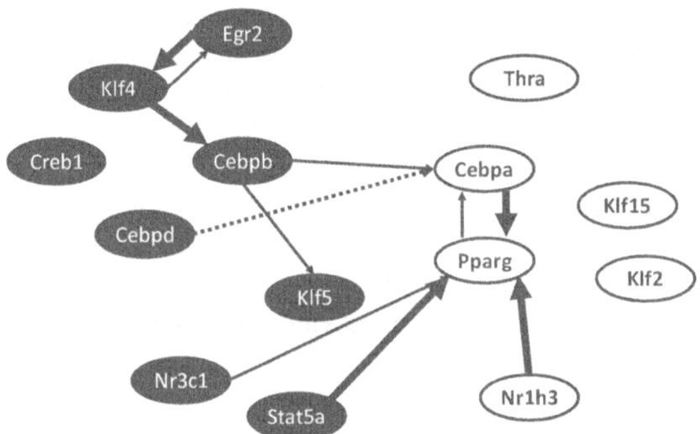

Fig. 8: This network represents the result of comparing the reference network with the estimated networks. Thin edge is the correct edge that is appeared in both networks in common. Thick edge and dot edge mean that the correct edge is appeared in the separated networks and the network estimated by NSS, respectively.

4.2 Acknowledgment

The authors thank to Drs. Yoshinori Tamada and Satoru Miyano for providing the information on the SiGN software. This work was partially supported by Grant-in-Aid for Scientific Research (22310125) from the Japan Society for the Promotion of Science (JSPS), and MEXT SPIRE Supercomputational Life Science.

References

[1] N. Friedman, K. Murphy, and S. Russell, "Learning the structure of dynamic probabilistic networks". in *Proc. UAI'98*, 1998, pp. 139–147.

[2] Y. Tamada, H. Araki, S. Imoto, M. Nagasaki, A. Doi, Y. Nakanishi, Y. Tomiyasu, K. Yasuda, B. Dunmore, D. Sanders, S. Humphreys, C. Print, DS Charnock-Jones, K. Tashiro, S. Kuhara, and S. Miyano, "Unraveling dynamic activities of autocrine pathways that control drugresponse transcriptome networks," *Pac Symp Biocomput.*, pp. 251–263, 2009.

[3] R. Siersbaek, R. Nielsen, S. John, MH. Sung, S. Beak, A. Loft, GL. Hager, and S. Mandrup, "Extensive chromatin remodelling and establishment of transcription factor 'hotspots' during early adipogenesis" *The EMBO Journal*, vol. 30, pp. 1459–1472, 2011.

[4] R. Siersbaek, R. Nielsen, and S. Mandrup, "PPARγ in adipocyte differentiation and metabolism-novel insights from genome-wide studies," *FEBS Letters*, vol. 584, no. 15, pp. 3242–3249, 2010.

[5] R. Siersbaek, R. Nielsen, and S. Mandrup, "Transcriptional networks and chromatin remodeling controlling adipogenesis," *Trends in Endocrinology and Metabolism*, vol. 23, no. 2, pp. 56–64, 2012.

[6] E. D. Rosen, O. A. MacDougald, "Adipocyte differentiation from the inside out," *Nature Reviews Molecular Cell Biology*, vol. 7, no. 12, pp. 885–896, 2006.

[7] M. I. Lefterova, and M. A. Lazar, "New developments in adipogenesis," *Trends in Endocrinology and Metabolism:TEM*, vol. 20, no. 3, pp. 107–114, 2009.

[8] Q. Q. Tang, and M. D. Lane, "Adipogenesis: from stem cell to adipocyte," *Annual Review of Biochemistry*, vol. 81, pp. 715–736, 2012.

[9] RA. Irizarry, B. Hobbs, F. Collin, YD. Beazer-Barclay, KJ. Antonellis, U. Scherf, and TP. Speed, "Exploration, normalization, and summaries of high density oligonucleotide array probe level data," *Biostatistics*, vol. 4, no. 2, pp. 249–264, 2003.

[10] Y. Tokuzawa, K. Yagi, Y. Yamashita, Y. Nakachi, I. Nikaido, H. Bono, Y. Ninomiya, Y. Kanesaki-Yatsuka, M. Akita, H. Motegi, S. Wakana, T. Noda, F. Sablitzky, S. Arai, R. Kurokawa, T. Fukuda, T. Katagiri, C. Schönbach, T. Suda, Y. Mizuno, and Y. Okazaki, "Id4, a new candidate gene for senile osteoporosis, acts as a molecular switch promoting osteoblast differentiation," *PLoS Genetics*, vol. 6, no. 7, doi: e1001019, 2010

[11] S. Kim, S. Imoto, and S. Miyano, "Dynamic Bayesian network and nonparametric regression for nonlinear modeling of gene networks from time series gene expression data," *Biosystems*, vol. 75, no. 1–3, pp. 57–65, 2004.

[12] Y. Tamada, T. Shimamura, R. Yamaguchi, S. Imoto, M. Nagasaki, and S. Miyano, "Sign: large-scale gene network estimation environment for high performance computing," in *Genome Inform. '11*, 2011, vol. 25, no. 1, pp. 40–52.

A Method of Sequence Analysis for High-throughput Sequencer Data Based on Shifted Short Read Clustering

Kensuke Suzuki, Daisuke Ueta, Shigeto Seno, Yoichi Takenaka and Hideo Matsuda
Graduate School of Information Science and Technology, Osaka University
1-5, Yamadaoka, Suita, Osaka 565-0871 Japan

Abstract—*Recent advances of high throughput sequencing can produce over tens of millions reads in a single assay, and various analyses are performed based on the information. Short read clustering is one of the pre-analysis methods, which makes clusters of reads by finding similar read pair in the read set. However, existing short-read clustering is limited to cluster only the reads that are derived from the exactly same start point in the genome. We proposed a clustering method which can cluster not only the reads derived from the same position but also shifted-reads. Shifted-reads are pairs of largely overlapped reads because they are derived from a few base shifted positions in the genome. Clustering shifted-reads enables to fully use the information of redundancy of deep sequencing. We evaluated that proposed method is useful for sequence analysis through the experiments of sequence error correction and SNP detection.*

Keywords: High-throughput sequencer, short read, clustering, directed acyclic graph

1. Introduction

High-throughput sequencers, which began with the introduction of the 454 sequencing systems [1], provide highly detailed structures of genomes and transcriptomes. Next generation sequencers (NGS), including ABI SOLiD [2], Illumina Solexa and HiSeq [3], are capable to generate more than 1 billion base pairs in a run. NGSs have one or two order of magnitude higher throughput and they are at least an order of magnitude less expensive to run. Due to the massiveness of the data produced by NGS, sequence analysis software that was developed in 1990s has no longer acceptable performance.

NGS technologies raise many challenges in the field of bioinformatics [4], especially the two big issues are "mapping" and "*de novo* assembly". Mapping is a process of finding source positions of observed reads from reference genome. NGS produces more than tens of millions of 32-100 bp reads, mapping and aligning this large volume of short reads to a reference genome poses a great challenge to the existing sequence alignment programs. Various tools are newly developed to map and align NGS reads, Bowtie [5][6], BWA [7] and SOAP [8] are widely used. These software typically use a fast indexing algorithm to rapidly identify potential matches in the reference genome. Meanwhile, mapping reads to a reference genome has several drawbacks [9]. First, it cannot even be applied if no reference genome exists, i.e. sequencing a novel organism or analyzing metagenomic data. Second, reliance on a reference genome can make it more difficult to identify significant differences between the sequenced reads and the reference genome; for example, areas of dense polymorphisms may be unmappable. *De novo* assembly tools allow NGS data to be assembled without a reference genome. The software named CABOG [10] and Newbler [1] are widely used for 454 data, Velvet [11] and SOAPdenovo [12] are used for Illumina or SOLiD data. These software are based on overlapping layout consensus (OLC) and *de Bruijn* graph algorithm. Both mapping and assembly form the basis of further analysis, such as structural variant detection, polymorphism identification and gene expression analysis.

Conducting any kind of analysis, the utility of NGS is diminished by two major limitations; shortness of read length and low quality of base differentiation including sequence errors. The length of reads produced by NGS platform are typically not over 100 bp, this fact could hinder unique mapping to a reference genome. Moreover, massively parallel sequencing suffer from inherent noise factor, poor quality reads are quite common in the NGS data. Low base quality causes not only the false negatives but also false positives. Therefore, preprocess is a very important step for the accuracy of downstream analysis.

Short read clustering is one of the pre-analysis methods, which makes clusters of reads by finding similar read pair in the read set. Short read clustering is mainly used for handling sequence error. For example, FleClu [13] is a method for error trimming, RECOUNT [14] is a method for error correction in NGS data. These methods cluster short reads in *de novo* and trim or correct sequence error using the information of sequence redundancy. Handling quality values before assembly or alignment to the reference genome succeeded to increase the accuracy of downstream analyses. However, existing short read clustering methods are limited to cluster only the reads that are derived from the exactly same start point in the genome. This means that the information about redundancy is not effectively utilized.

To cope with the problem, we proposed a clustering method which can cluster not only the reads derived from exactly same position but also shifted-reads. Shifted-reads are a pair of largely overlapped reads because they are derived from a few base shifted positions in the genome. In this study, we used *SlideSort* [15], which is a fast and exact algorithm to enumerate all pairs similarity in large pool of fixed-length short reads. Basically, SlideSort also can cluster only the reads of same start point even though the similarity is calculated by the edit distance. Thus, we enhance the search ability of shifted-reads by providing wrapper process for SlideSort. Moreover, we also proposed a directed acyclic graph (DAG) representation to describe sequence information from resulting short read cluster. Clustering shifted-reads make us enable to use fully information of redundancy of deep sequencing and DAG representation of sequence information is well suited for various analysis. We evaluated that proposed method is useful for sequence analysis through the experiments of sequence error correction and SNP detection.

2. Methods

The sequencing is generally designed to produce enough number of short reads to make overlaps among the reads. It means that each base is supported by multiple short reads which are sequenced from some base different loci.

Now we assume that the length of each read is l bases. In case that tail $l-w$ bases of one read and head $l-w$ bases of another read are similar permitting d bases mismatches, we call such read pair as w-shifted-reads. Because large numbers of reads are produced in sequencing, most reads can build shifted-read pair with other reads. Once we get all w-shifted-read pairs where $w \leq W$, short read clusters can be constructed by gathering the reads which have at least one shifted-read in the cluster.

The clusters are normally described in undirected graph formats in which nodes and edges represent the reads in the cluster and shifted relationship among the reads respectively. This form is hard to apply to later sequence analysis because graph search and realignment are required even knowing the frequency of a base. In our method each cluster is converted into directed acyclic graph (DAG) format. The advantage of this format is its availability in later sequence analysis such as sequencing error correction and SNP detection. This format is capable of handling sequence information and frequency of each base in an intuitive manner.

2.1 Clustering with Shifted-reads

We assume that the input read set $R = \{r_1, r_2, \cdots, r_N\}$ is in FASTQ format. N is the total number of input reads and the length of every read is l bases. In the clustering with shifted-reads, we operate four steps to generate clusters (Figure 1).

First step is duplicate removal. It is clear that the same reads are reported as 0-shifted-read pairs for all combination. Although such pairs result in exactly the same, the numbers of the pairs are enormous. In this step same reads are compressed as one read. This step is desirable in order to avoid reporting every combination of same reads as 0-shifted-reads. Quality values for each reads are summed up for each bases and kept in temporary file. The number of duplicated reads is also stored in the same temporary file as the frequency of the read.

Second step is end cut. To generate w-shifted-reads, we make two read sets from the reads without duplicate. One read set consists of the reads whose w bases of left end are cut and the other read set contains the reads whose w bases of right end are cut. Finding similar read pairs between left cut reads and right cut reads means finding w-shifted-read pair. When we set the maximum number of cut bases as W, $W+1$ kinds of left cut reads and right cut reads are made because w is moved from 0 to W.

Third step is similarity search. We applied an algorithm named SlideSort [15] in this step. When two read sets A (N_A reads) and B (N_B reads) are given, SlideSort is able to test all $N_A \times N_B$ pairs of reads and report only similar pairs. Similar pairs means read pairs whose edit distance (number of insertion, deletion or substitution) is not more than threshold. Our method applies this algorithm to test whether the hamming distance (number of substitution) between two reads is not more than d. The read pairs searched between left w cut reads and right w cut reads are regarded as w-shifted-reads. Processing all $W+1$ kinds of read sets in this way we know which read is shifted-read for all reads. In other words, this step outputs a graph G_{all} in which the nodes represent each read and the edges represent the relationship that two reads are shifted-reads each other.

Fourth step is division into connected components. The graph G_{all} represents all shifted-read relationships. This graph is divided into connected components G_i, which means

$$G_{all} = \{G_1, G_2, \cdots, G_C\} \tag{1}$$

C is the total number of connected components. Each G_i is defined as

$$G_i = (V_i, E_i) \tag{2}$$

And the nodes and edges are defined below.

$$V_i = \{v_{i1}, v_{i2}, \cdots, v_{ia}\} \tag{3}$$

$$E_i = \{e_{v_{ij}, v_{ik}} | shifted(v_{ij}, v_{ik}) = true\} \tag{4}$$

Every v_{ij} represents a read. And the function $shifted()$ returns $true$ when two reads are shifted-read each other. Because each node in G_i represents the reads, V_i is a subset of R. Each connected component G_i is regarded as a cluster in our method and it is converted into a DAG.

2.2 DAG Construction

Each cluster of shifted-reads needs to be converted into a DAG to make it applicable to sequence analysis. This section

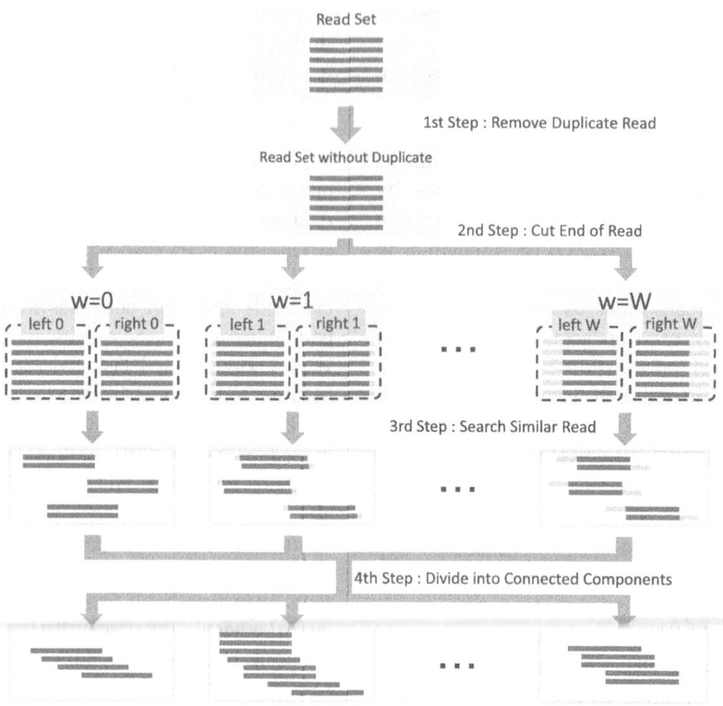

Fig. 1: Overview of the clustering with shifted-reads. Step.3 is performed by using SlideSort software.

explains how the clusters are converted. The set of DAGs are denoted in below.

$$G'_{all} = \{G'_1, G'_2, \cdots, G'_C\} \quad (5)$$

Here G'_i represents the DAG for G_i.

$$G'_i = \{V'_i, E'_i\} \quad (6)$$

$$V'_i = \{v'_{i1}, v'_{i2}, \cdots, v'_{i\alpha}\} \quad (7)$$

The reads in cluster G_i are divided by the location of read head, read tail and mismatch. Each unique substring is regarded as a node in V'_i (Figure 2). This can be realized because the size of shift for each shifted-reads is already known. The set of edges E'_i is, therefore, represents the existence of at least one read which has the join of two neighboring nodes as a subsequence.

Algorithm 1 shows the overview of DAG construction. This algorithm gives a DAG to a cluster. G'_i is initialized by enrolling a read as a node. All reads in G_i are searched by breadth first search. They are aligned to G'_i to upload it.

In **Algorithm 1**, *child* has overlapped subsequences in G'_i because *parent* and *child* are shifted-read each other and the sequence of *parent* exists in G'_i (Figure 2). $seq()$ means the sequence of given read or node. The process of

Algorithm 1 DAG Construction

for $i = 1$ to C **do**
  var $read \leftarrow v_{i1} \in V_i$
  $v'_{i1} = seq(read)$
  initialize G'_i by v_{i1}
  queue $Q \leftarrow \phi$
  $push(Q, read)$
  while $Q \neq \phi$ **do**
    var $parent \leftarrow unshift(Q)$
    for all $child$ in $shifted(parent, shifted) = true$ $\cap$ unvisited **do**
      $upload(G'_i, seq(child))$
      $push(Q, child)$
    end for
  end while
  add G'_i to G'_{all}
end for

$upload()$ is to find the series of nodes that correspond to the overlap between G'_i and *child*. When we assume the overlap nodes are $\{v'_{is}, v'_{is+1}, \cdots, v'_{iS}\}$, we can find them because the number of shift between *parent* and *child* is already known and the nodes for *parent* are also known.

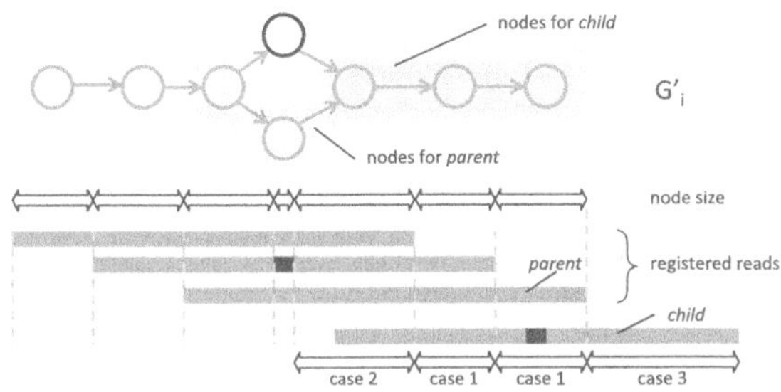

Fig. 2: Alignment between G_i' and *child*. The *child* node is divided in subsequences by the node sizes. The correspondance between nodes and subsequences have three cases. Each subsequence is used to upload G_i'.

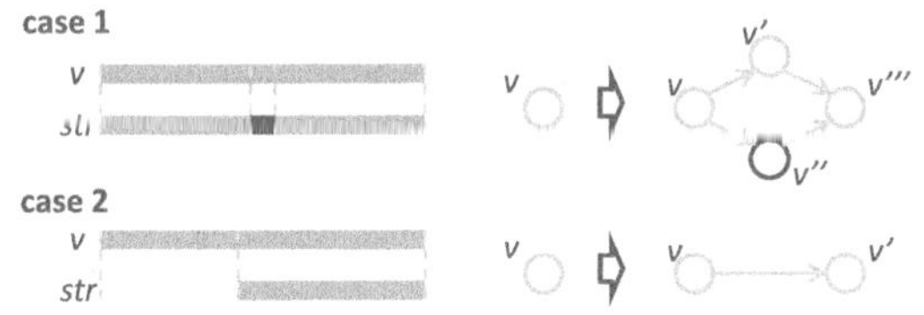

Fig. 3: Replacement of old nodes. Case 1 is the "same length" case with mismatches. A bifurcation is constructed in this case (v' and v''). Case 2 is the case of "node is larger". Old node is divided into overlapped part (v') and not overlapped part (v).

Getting the overlap nodes $\{v_{is}', v_{is+1}', \cdots, v_{iS}'\}$, *child* is divided into the size of each node. The correspondence between each node "v" and "str", one of the subsequences of *child*, has three cases; (1) same length, (2) node is larger and (3) node is absent. G_i' is uploaded by these nodes and subsequences (Figure 3).

(1) When the length of v and str are the same, it is case (1). If there are no mismatches between v and str, the redundancy and quality values of str are added to that of v. But generally v and str has some mismatches because maximum d mismatches are permitted in the overlapped region. In this case, we divide v into four parts; before mismatch, v side of mismatch, str side of mismatch and after mismatch (Figure 3 case 1). The old node is replaced by these nodes. Because each part before and after mismatch still can have some mismatches, these two parts are processed as case (1) recursively.

(2) The length of v can be larger than str when str is head or tail of *child*. In this case the v is divided into overlapped part and not overlapped part. Overlapped part is processed as case (1) because it can have some mismatches (Figure 3 case 2).

(3) In the case that no node is found for str, a new node needs to be added to G_i'. This case can happen in the head or tail of *child*. The redundancy and quality values of the new node is initialized by that of str.

Because the reads in a cluster are found as shifted-reads, they can be arranged in one direction. This guarantees each G_i' is a DAG. We set a restriction that even if some mismatches are successive, every one base is described as one node. Therefore when the multiple nodes exist at the same depth, each node represents one base and the number of alternatives at the same depth is not more than four.

2.3 Sequencing Error Correction

The mismatches in the shifted-read pairs are described by bifurcations in the DAGs. Most of these bifurcations are caused by sequencing errors in the reads. Our method is capable of handling these sequencing errors because the quality values and the redundancy for every node are stored in temporary files. Here we define the redundancy of a node v as $freq(v)$, and the total quality values of a node v as $sumQV(v)$. The degrees of confidence can be calculated from these data. A way to give the confidence score to every node is calculating average quality values.

$$avgQV(v) = \frac{sumQV(v)}{freq(v)} \tag{8}$$

Because the quality values for sequencing errors are tend to be small and the frequency of error base is small, the sequencing error node in a DAG must have smaller quality values as a trend.

For this reason our method can be applicable to sequence error correction. After constructing a DAG, the values of $avgQV(v)$ are calculated for every nodes. Under the restriction that the sequencing errors appear in the bifurcations, our method checks all alternatives in the DAGs. We set a threshold T and regard the node v as sequencing error when $avgQV(v) \leq T$. These error node is replaced by the node with largest confidence score.

2.4 SNP Detection

Another reason for the bifurcations is polymorphisms. When a read set from diploid genome sequencing is processed by our method, the SNPs cause some part of bifurcations. The quality values for the alternatives are high in this case because they are not sequencing errors. Therefore the alternatives with high confidence scores are reported as possible SNPs. Our method accepts the reads which is sequenced from one sample. It means that only the hetero SNPs are observed from the read set. In addition the two bases which appear as a SNP have almost the same frequency when enough reads are sequenced.

Our method ignores the nodes whose average quality values are lower than T or frequencies are smaller than F in order to test only reliable bifurcations. At the locations of SNPs we are likely to observe two paths bifurcation from one node and those paths are confluent at next node. Considering the bias of sequencing, we report a bifurcation such that both of the top of two frequent nodes at the same depth have over 40% frequency.

3. Results and Discussions

We obtained two datasets to evaluate our method. Dataset 1 is whole genome shotgun sequencing of *Escherichia coli str. K-12 MG1655* sequenced by Illumina Genome Analyzer. This dataset (SRR001666) is available on NCBI Sequence Read Archive (http://www.ncbi.nlm.nih.gov.sra/). The read length of this dataset is 36 base and about 14 million reads are contained. Dataset 2 is whole genome shotgun sequencing of human individuals (NA11994). This is one of the dataset in 1000 Genome Project (http://www.1000genomes.org/). We trimmed first 51 bases of the dataset sequenced by Illumina Genome Analyzer II. Our algorithm was implemented by Perl. All the experiments were done on a Linux computer with Intel Xeon X7542 (2.67GHz) and 256GB RAM.

3.1 Parameter Setting for Shifted-read Clustering

We first evaluate the effect of short read clustering with shifted-reads. The parameter W is the most important parameter in the clustering step. It is clear that bigger W finds more shifted pairs. We checked the behavior of the clustering with different W. Dataset 1 is used in this experiment.

Figure 4 shows the number of clustered reads and the number of generated clusters. In this experiment, the case $W = 0$ is exactly the same as normal SlideSort. We counted the number of the reads which have at least one shifted-read and the number of clustered reads and Not clustered reads are shown in line chart. We can see that the cases of $W > 0$ increase the number of clustered reads. It is because the reads which are sequenced from W bases apart can be clustered in our method. Although the bigger W finds more clustered reads, the effect is almost the same in the area of $W > 0$. It means that W need not to be set big value in this dataset. The reason is that the number of reads are three times larger than the genome size (the number of reads are 14 million and the size of genome is 4.6 million bases), i.e. almost all reads can find at least one similar read with 2 base shift. Meanwhile, the bars show the number of clusters generated from our method. The difference between $W = 2$ and $W = 4$ is larger than that of $W = 4$ and $W = 6$. Although the number of clustered reads of $W = 2$ and $W = 4$ are almost the same, the effect for the number of cluster is different. It says that our method found more inter-cluster reads by moving W from 2 to 4. In other words, there are few region in which every two reads are apart more than 6 bases.

Figure 5 shows the distribution of the cluster size in each parameter. Cluster size means the length of the longest sequence reconstructed from the DAG. We searched the longest paths in all graphs and plotted the length of them in figure 5. The case $W = 0$ becomes a bar because the cluster size is exactly the same as the fixed-length of input reads. We can see that the difference of average size is the biggest between $W = 2$ and $W = 4$.

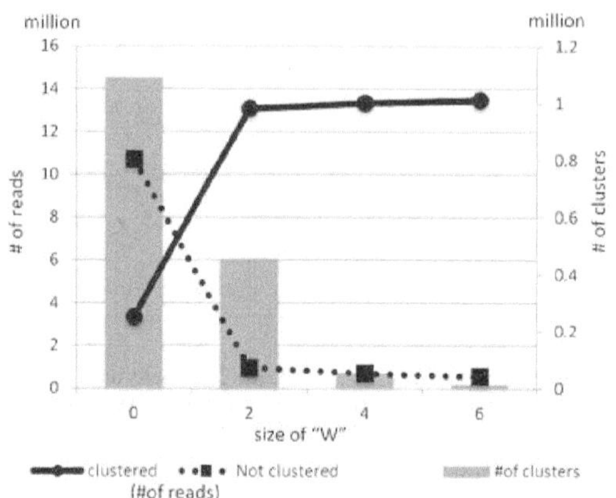

Fig. 4: The number of clustered reads and generated clusters. The solid line represents the number of clustered reads and the broken line shows the number of NOT clustered reads. The bars show the number of generated clusters. $W = 0$ is exactly the same as normal SlideSort.

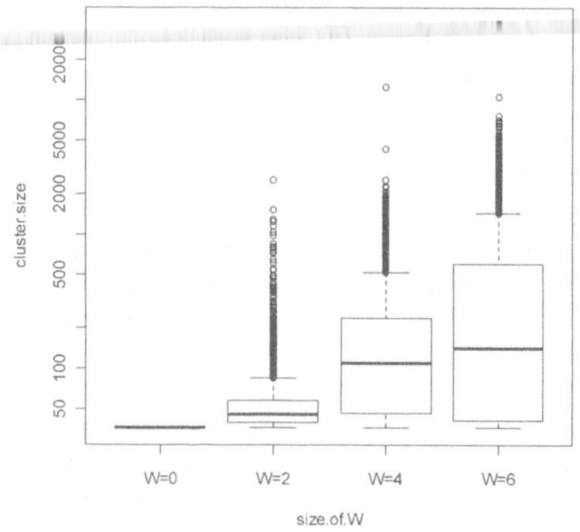

Fig. 5: Distribution of cluster size. Cluster size means the diameter of DAG and matches the length of the longest representative sequence reconstructed from short read clustering.

The setting of parameter W is important in our method. We cannot set too large W because the overlaps between two reads get too small. It results in producing false shifted-reads. Generally the best parameter W depends on the number of reads and length of a read. In dataset 1 we can conclude $W = 4$ is the best choice.

3.2 Sequencing Error Correction

The ability of sequencing error correction of our method is evaluated using dataset 1. As we could not know the true sequencing errors, we compared the proportion of mappable reads onto the reference genome before and after the error correction. The mapping is done onto the reference genome

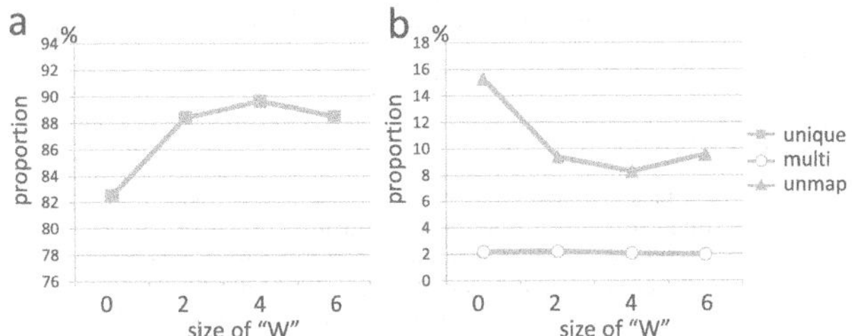

Fig. 6: Difference of mapping ratio in different W. W is the parameter to cluster shifted-reads, which means the maximum number of cutting both ends of reads. (a) Unique hit in square (b) multi hit and unmapped in circle and triangle, respectively.

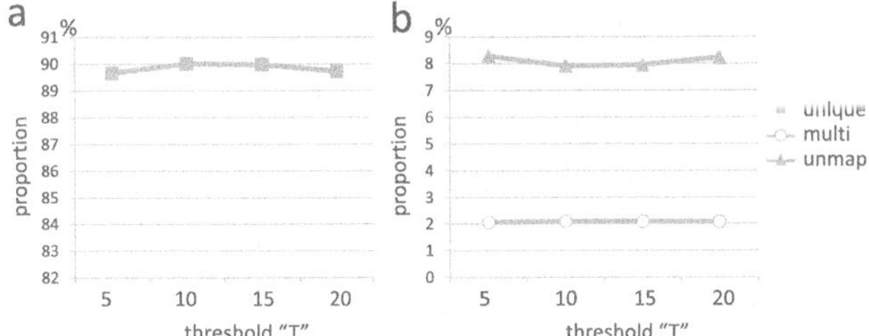

Fig. 7: Difference of mapping ratio in different T (W = 4). T is the threshold of quality values for regarding the bases as error. Larger T values, more bases are corrected as errors. (a) Unique hit in square (b) multi hit and unmapped in circle and triangle, respectively.

(NC_000913.2) without mismatches using Bowtie as the mapping algorithm.

Before comparing with existing method, we checked the effect of parameter W and T. In the figure 6 we confirmed $W = 4$ shows the best performance. In the case $W < 4$ our method could not find enough number of shifted-reads. It means there is less chance to make corrections of bases for sequencing error. On the other hand, we observed lower proportion for unique hit reads and higher proportion for unmapped reads in $W = 6$. This is caused by the false pairing of shifted-reads. The reads which are generated from totally different location are regarded as shifted-reads because the overlap is not sufficient length at $W = 6$. These false shifted-reads bother the base frequency and total quality value in the DAGs.

Figure 7 shows the effect of threshold T for average quality value, which is used to judge whether the base is error or not. Although the performance in $T = 10$ is slightly better than other thresholds, they are almost same. It is because average quality value can consider not only individual quality values but also the frequency of each base. It absorbs the effect of noise of quality value. However, too large T also disturbs accuracy because it can cause false substitution of bases in the error correction phase.

In order to evaluate the sequencing error correction ability of our method, we compared the proportions of mappable reads with existing method. The competitor is the algorithm named RECOUNT [14]. This is one of the algorithms for sequencing error correction based on short read clustering without shifted-reads. Three read sets, raw dataset 1, processed by RECOUNT and processed by our method, are mapped onto the reference genome. Table 1 shows the proportion of unique hit reads, multi hit reads and unmapped reads in each method. The parameter of our method is $W = 4$ and $T = 10$. As a result, our method succeeded to increase the number of unique hit reads and decrease the number of unmapped reads. Almost the same numbers of multi hit reads are found among each result, it is valid to conclude that multi hit reads are generated from repeated region.

Table 1: Comparison of mappable reads

	Raw Data(%)	RECOUNT(%)	Our method(%)
unique hit	76.4	77.0	90.0
multi hit	1.9	2.1	2.1
unmapped	21.7	20.9	7.9

3.3 SNP Detection

In order to test whether our method is available to detect SNPs, we operated a simulation using dataset 2. The reads are first mapped onto reference genome (GRCh37). And we extracted the reads which are mapped on the region of a million bases (chr9:110,507,033-chr9:111,507,032). Therefore only about 400,000 reads are processed by our method. The experiment is done with the parameter $W = 20$. Only the bifurcations which have frequency ≥ 5 and average quality value ≥ 5 are tested. After constructing clusters we searched the DAGs greedy with average quality values to get a sequence that represents each cluster. The represent sequences are locally aligned with reference genome by BLAST search. When the represent sequences are aligned on the locations of known SNPs and the DAGs have bifurcations at the location, we regard the bifurcation as correct SNPs detection. According to the database 145 SNPs are known in the target region of dataset 2 with more than 5 reads frequency.

Table 2 shows the total, correct and incorrect number of detected SNPs. Although the correct answer is not so many, we confirmed that our method is capable to detect SNPs. The detection is still improved when we use more sequences. Because the bottle neck is the length of overlap in each shifted-read, we need read set which contain more reads or longer reads to connect the clusters. On the other hand, we detected the bifurcations which are not registered in the database as SNPs. They could be new revealed SNPs by our method. However we need to develop sophisticated algorithm to confirm whether they are real SNPs.

Table 2: Detected SNPs and correct answer

	matched in DB	mismatched	total
# of detection	37	391	428

4. Discussion and Conclusions

In this study, we have introduced a method for clustering short reads with some bases shifted. Our method clusters not only the reads that are derived from the exactly same start point but also the reads that are derived from a few base shifted positions in the genome. We showed that even a few base shift causes significant change on the property of clustering result and increases the number of clustered reads. We also proposed a method for reconstructing directed acyclic graph from the output of SlideSort program. In other words, our method is a format conversion from raw NGS data like FASTQ format to weighted directed acyclic graph. This DAG structure does not lose the information about the subsequences of reads, redundancies and quality values. DAG representation is suitable for various sequence analysis. As applications for sequencing error correction and SNP detection problem, our method shows good performance in spite of the simplicity.

In future work, we would like to develop our method to apply further sequence analysis. If a method to identify all reasonable paths from DAGs could be developed, our method is useful for meta-genomic analysis and RNA-seq analysis. Meta-genomic data contains homologs (close but not the same sequences) derived from various microbes, RNA-seq data contains isoforms (partially shared common subsequences) caused by alternative splicing. In such cases, our method could be a good alternative of OLC or *de Bruijn* graph algorithm. Once all reasonable elongated sequences can be extracted without forcibly assembling to the one sequence, the information is summarized and operation becomes easy. Meanwhile, our method has the two major limitations so far. First, computational cost is larger than original SlideSort. Setting large value of W severely effects on the computational time and memory usage. Second, there are problems for handling small insertions and deletions. Cost effective method of gapped alignment is needed in clustering step, and the construction of DAG with repeats and small indels should be done more strictly. We leave these problems for future investigation.

Acknowledgement

The authors thank Kana Shimizu, the developer of SlideSort, for her great work in short-read clustering and fruitful discussions. The datasets in our experiment are provided by NCBI Sequence Read Archive and 1000 Genome project. We would like to express our appreciation for them.
Funding: This work was partially supported by KAKENHI (22310125, 22680023), and by MEXT SPIRE Supercomputational Life Science.

References

[1] M. Margulies, M. Egholm, W. E. Altman, S. Attiya, J. S. Bader, L. A. Bemben, J. Berka, M. S. Braverman, Y.-J. Chen, Z. Chen, and et al., "Genome sequencing in microfabricated high-density picolitre reactors." *Nature*, vol. 437, no. 7057, pp. 376–380, 2005.

[2] M. Janitz, *Next-Generation Genome Sequencing*, M. Janitz, Ed. Vch Verlagsgesellschaft Mbh, 2008.

[3] S. S. Ajay, S. C. J. Parker, H. Ozel Abaan, K. V. Fuentes Fajardo, and E. H. Margulies, "Accurate and comprehensive sequencing of personal genomes." *Genome Research*, vol. 21, no. 9, pp. 1498–1505, 2011.

[4] S. Bao, R. Jiang, W. Kwan, B. Wang, X. Ma, and Y.-Q. Song, "Evaluation of next-generation sequencing software in mapping and assembly." *Journal of Human Genetics*, vol. 56, no. 6, pp. 406–414, 2011.

[5] B. Langmead, C. Trapnell, M. Pop, and S. L. Salzberg, "Ultrafast and memory-efficient alignment of short dna sequences to the human genome," *Genome Biology*, vol. 10, no. 3, p. R25, 2009.

[6] B. Langmead and S. L. Salzberg, "Fast gapped-read alignment with bowtie 2," *Nature Methods*, vol. 9, no. 4, pp. 357–360, 2012.

[7] H. Li and R. Durbin, "Fast and accurate short read alignment with burrows–wheeler transform," *Bioinformatics*, vol. 25, no. 14, pp. 1754–1760, 2009.

[8] R. Li, Y. Li, K. Kristiansen, and J. Wang, "Soap: short oligonucleotide alignment program." *Bioinformatics*, vol. 24, no. 5, pp. 713–714, 2008.

[9] L. D. Stein, "An introduction to the informatics of next generation h sequencing." *Current protocols in bioinformatics editoral board Andreas D Baxevanis et al*, vol. Chapter 11, no. December, p. Unit 11.1., 2011.

[10] J. R. Miller, A. L. Delcher, S. Koren, E. Venter, B. P. Walenz, A. Brownley, J. Johnson, K. Li, C. Mobarry, and G. Sutton, "Aggressive assembly of pyrosequencing reads with mates," *Bioinformatics*, vol. 24, no. 24, pp. 2818–2824, 2008.

[11] D. R. Zerbino and E. Birney, "Velvet: Algorithms for de novo short read assembly using de bruijn graphs," *Genome Research*, vol. 18, no. 5, pp. 821–829, 2008.

[12] R. Li, H. Zhu, J. Ruan, W. Qian, X. Fang, Z. Shi, Y. Li, S. Li, G. Shan, K. Kristiansen, and et al., "De novo assembly of human genomes with massively parallel short read sequencing." *Genome Research*, vol. 20, no. 2, pp. 265–272, 2010.

[13] W. Qu, S.-I. Hashimoto, and S. Morishita, "Efficient frequency-based de novo short-read clustering for error trimming in next-generation sequencing." *Genome Research*, vol. 19, no. 7, pp. 1309–1315, 2009.

[14] E. Wijaya, M. C. Frith, Y. Suzuki, and P. Horton, "Recount: expectation maximization based error correction tool for next generation sequencing data." *Genome informatics International Conference on Genome Informatics*, vol. 23, no. 1, pp. 189–201, 2009.

[15] K. Shimizu and K. Tsuda, "Slidesort: all pairs similarity search for short reads," *Bioinformatics*, vol. 27, no. 4, pp. 464–470, 2011.

The Role of ICT and Mobile Health to Improve Clinical Process Management. An Overview on the Therapy Management Process and a Real Case

Paolo Locatelli[a], Vittorio Montefusco[b], Elena Sini[c], Nicola Restifo[a], Roberta Facchini[a], Michele Torresani[b]

[a] *Fondazione Politecnico di Milano, Milano, Italy*
[b] *Fondazione IRCCS Istituto Nazionale dei Tumori di Milano, Milano, Italy*
[c] *IRCCS Istituto Clinico Humanitas, Rozzano, Italy*

Abstract

The volume and the complexity of clinical and administrative information make Information and Communication Technologies (ICTs) essential to run and innovate healthcare. Mobile&Wireless solutions, integrated to Automatic Identification and Data Capture technology and to Hospital Information Systems, can provide staff with software applications in order to manage critical activities on the go, associate data to objects and increase the volume and timeliness of available data on processes. This paper presents a project aimed to design, develop and implement a set of organizational models, acknowledged procedures and ICT tools to improve actual support, safety, reliability and traceability of a specific therapy management process – the one related to haematopoietic stem cell (HSC) and therapeutic cell (TC) donation, processing and transplantation. The project value is to design a solution based on mobile and identification technology in close collaboration with physicians and actors involved in the process to ensure usability and effectiveness in process and risk management.

Keyword: *Hospital Information Systems, Mobile Health, Medication Therapy Management, Bedside Technology, Stem cells, RFId*

Introduction

Hospital Information Systems (HIS) are fundamental tools in the delivery of effective and efficient care [1]. An HIS comprises several different applications that support healthcare organizations', clinicians', patients' and policy makers' needs for collection and management of data related to both clinical as well as administrative processes. This data can be processed by a number of systems with many different purposes (e.g. diagnostics, epidemiology, research,..), needs to be integrated across departments in order to effectively support processes [2], and must be subject to strict rules in terms of confidentiality and security safeguard [3]. Systematic reviews [1] show that, in most cases, ICT-based solutions tend to be adopted by healthcare providers - under the pressure of technologically-pushing forces (machinery) [4] - with a limited assessment of the organizational consequences of ICT adoption and with limited focus on supporting and making core care processes more reliable and cost-effective [5]. This concerns also additional issues on risks management related to how information system could influence clinical practice and human errors [6].

In recent years, however, organizations - faced with an unprecedented era of competition and cost-cutting - are changing this behavior [7] and exploring ICTs-enabled perspectives to improve the quality of clinical processes and patient and staff safety while simultaneously reducing costs [8][9].

This paper aims to show how deep the impact of systems based on innovative technologies focusing on process reengineering and organizational change could be, identifying an important synergy between traditional Information Systems and Mobile&Wireless technologies to deliver effective process support to clinical staff. On the other hand, it will show how several barriers could undermine the value of such systems. Evidences explained in the paper are found in literature and provided by the ICT in Healthcare Observatory (IHCO)[1] of the School of Management of the Politecnico di Milano Technical University in Milan (Italy) and will be proven by the explanation of topic dealt in a research project ongoing on stem cell process management innovation through ICT.

---

[1] ICT in Healthcare Observatory (IHCO) is a broad and continuative research initiative promoted since 2007 by the Politecnico di Milano School of Management which focuses specifically on the analysis of ICT-driven innovation in the Italian healthcare industry. The research is a combination of a quantitative panel of electronic surveys, several qualitative case studies, and a series of focus groups.

Hospital Information Systems: main functional areas and evolution needs

How ICTs solutions can improve the healthcare ecosystem

The main areas of an HIS are three [10]: (i) administration and management, (ii) front-office and (iii) clinical area. The clinical area is the centre of the system, as it has to support all core care processes and appears to be the most challenging area in terms of management, because it involves critical patient data. Clinical systems are mainly departmental systems, typically independently implemented by each department or ward, or Electronic Medical Records (EMRs). Literature analysis [11] allows the identification of five functional areas that characterize EMRs: Admission-Discharge-Transfer management, Outpatient management, Diagnostics, Therapy management, Clinical Dossier. Among these, the latter – embracing the management of all medical and nursing sheets, including initial assessment, vital signs automated monitoring, anesthesiology documents, OR reports, etc. - and therapy management - supporting prescription and administration of drugs, transfusions, nutrition, etc. - are the less widespread areas and the ones of greatest expected growth in the future. They are also the most challenging to implement, above all with respect to change management and organizational issues. Case studies conducted by the ICHO[1] in the last years showed that the main limit to current EMR projects is the lack of integration and the absence of an enterprise-wide approach to the solutions. However, many efforts have been made to drive EMR evolution towards maturity, enabling comprehensive support to healthcare processes [11]. Case studies reveal that effective digitalization of these core clinical processes is closely connected to the implementation of Mobile&Wireless (M&W) solutions to support operations and information management, integrated with Automatic Identification and Data Capture (AIDC) tools (e.g. Barcode, RFId, NFC,..).

Such kinds of services are part of the Mobile Health solution category. Mobile Health comprises all devices (smartphone, tablet, …) and applications enabling physicians and nurses to access the HIS services in mobility (e.g. to look up to the EMR on a tablet, to download clinical reports on a smartphone, …). Mobile Health is considered as an opportunity to overcome time-space barriers and to improve care processes through higher availability of information for physicians and nurses. The World Health Organization refers to Mobile Health as "the use of mobile and wireless technologies to support the achievement of health objectives" [12]. According to the WHO, Mobile Health "has the potential to transform the face of health service delivery across the globe".

M&W and AIDC technologies - technology on which Mobile Health is based - are quite immature in the healthcare environment. However they are considered a strategic leverage characterized by a great expected growth in the future. The purpose of these tools is to support healthcare and technical operations in mobility, overcoming the need for a desktop station, and to improve the security level of the whole clinical process, by identifying people and items throughout the process. IHCO research shows that past investments in Mobile Health in Italy have been limited: out of 86 Chief Information Officer (CIO), in 2011, almost half has not invested in these kind of applications and only 13% has invested more than 50.000 € on them. In 2012, the percentage of organizations that will spend more than 50.000 will grow up to 21%.

As mentioned above, M&W technologies can play a relevant role in improving both efficiency and effectiveness of healthcare for inpatients as well as outpatients (e.g. ambulance transportation and ambulatory visits). M&W solutions, integrated both to AIDC technology solutions and to the HIS, allow to close the safety loop directly to the patient, bringing operating support and identification/traceability features to patient bedside. This kind of application is, more than others, suitable to improve therapy management process, from patient identification to prescription and pharmacotherapy administration at bedside. The main challenges for therapy management involve the introduction of an enterprise-wide patient identification system, which could enable process traceability, governance and cost control, and the availability of application on mobile support to improve clinical operations. This is much more crucial than cost-effectiveness or resource optimization, because it has a direct impact on clinical safety and risk of processes. IHCO analyses show that M&W solutions already have been adopted in one third of the surveyed organizations. Considering Mobile devices, the most common ones are Notebooks/Netbooks (83%) and Tablets (62%), followed by PDAs with just 20%. Above all, more widespread application include barcodes printed on drugs' boxes and patients' wristband read by special PDAs at bedside. Moreover, some facilities are starting experimental implementations of RFId (Radio Frequency Identification) and NFC (Near Field Communication) technologies, as an "evolution" of barcode.

Mobile Health to improve therapy management process

Through M&W and AIDC technologies – integrated in mobile solutions – it is possible to support heterogeneous processes such the therapy prescription and administration one. Therapy management refers to all the aspects of the therapeutic process, both in terms of staff workflow activities and in terms of direct contact with the patient. This includes a number of different kind of processes such as pharmacotherapy, chemotherapy, radiotherapy, blood transfusions and medications. Literature states that - above all in this field - most of the threats to patient safety are process-related, rather than clinical [13]. Paperwork, manual transcription and the lack of automated identification systems are the main criticalities affecting clinical processes. These are especially risky because they include a number of critical stages, involving different staff members in different departments and involve complex information management activities. Therapy management belongs to these error-prone processes [14]: misinformation and errors in data transfer are the greatest cause of incidents in treatment administration and they often remain under-reported, owing to a lack of awareness about closing the information loop and improving practice. According to a WHO public report [15] regarding incidents in Radiotherapy management, more than 4,500 near misses were reported in the literature and on public databases from Australia, USA, Canada, UK, and other European countries. Of all injurious incidents, 54% were related to the 'planning' stage, 8% were related to 'transfer of information' and 10% to the 'treatment delivery' stage. Near misses had been intercepted through the whole process, 16% of which in the 'assessment & decision' step and 6% in 'simulation & imaging'. Referring to a literature review conducted specifically in oncology departments by Schwappach and Wernli in 2010, medication errors are distributed as follows: 41% in nurse administration (omitted medications and wrong doses), 21% in order writing or transcription (pharmacy errors) and 38% in medication dispensing (incorrect dose, wrong drug,..)[16].

A comprehensive approach to information management, process traceability and control - especially for activities performed on patients - is the way to enhance safety, efficiency, and governance in clinical practices. As for ICT support, nowadays in most cases specialized proprietary solutions cover more demanding activities (e.g. prescription of therapy) but they are usually not communicating with other systems because they don't target the full process coverage (e.g. across departments or to bedside with M&W and AIDC technologies). Moreover, several activities in a single process are still paper-based (e.g. when patient has to sign procedure consensus), so the HIS is often prone to hybrid configurations. This gap between IT tools and clinical needs leads to an undetermined effectiveness of such tools on process performance and sometimes to higher risks for the patient. Moreover, the lack of reference standards and guidelines for the implementation of such technologies in healthcare, as well as the low maturity of ICT tools are two other issues that need to be dealt with. Moreover, the main challenges to be faced in the definition, design and development of IT solution in healthcare environment involve organization management. The solution to these issues is the improvement of staff skills, usability and compliance to needs through co-design of the solution among IT technicians and clinicians. In particular, it is necessary to design solutions with embedded mobile technologies that can support staff and enhance security throughout the whole process. These solutions must be integrated with the HIS, so that information can be shared among all systems. For example, digital and integrated pharmacotherapy management tools are identified as solutions able to gain strategic benefits (i) if designed to support end-to-end clinicians and nursing activities also at bedside, (ii) if integrated with AIDC technologies to support safe identification and bedside traceability, (iii) if properly integrated with the HIS, (iv) if implemented together with a review of processes.

In the next section we will describe a project based on M&W and AIDC technologies, aimed to improve actual support, safety, reliability and traceability of activities related to hematopoietic stem cell (HSC) and therapeutic cell (TC) process.

Mobile&Wireless and AIDC technologies in Therapy Management: a case study

A case of therapy management process to be improved

A therapeutic area that is still unsupported is stem cells management: HSCs and TCs transplantation are life-saving therapies in the treatment of several congenital or acquired hematologic disorders (e.g. a timely implantation is key for patient recovery after chemotherapy treatments). Despite FACT-JACIE qualification of centers is strongly recommended by the Italian Ministry of Health, there is still a need for greater efficiency in the management of the transplantation process. There is no standard and validated information system for detailed monitoring and control of the process, neither in the wards, nor in the Stem Cell Lab. Examples of critical points in the process are represented in Figure 1.

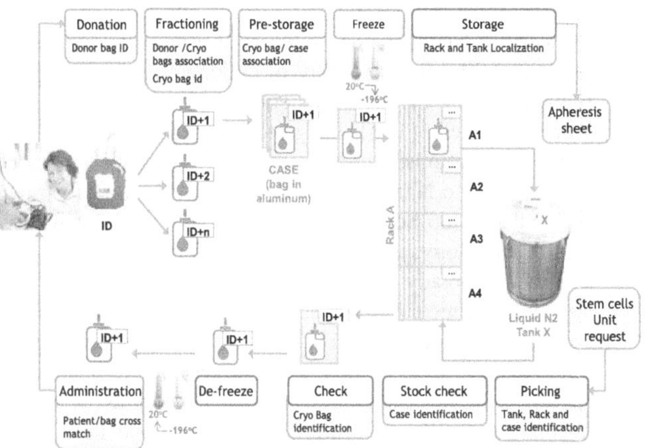

Figure 1. The autologous stem cells transplantation process

The Transfusion Service does not have full awareness of laboratory processing activities (e.g. units collected by the Transfusion Service get fractioned by a different Lab, but this phase is not managed on the Transfusion Service management system) and actual stocks. The same happens for patient records in the Lab, where donor history sheets recording all information on donated bags are still on paper or on a different system from the above mentioned ones. Also bedside activities show some critical issues, many similar to those in the transfusion process: unambiguous patient identification, bags and vials labeling, in the ward safe cross-matching, adverse reaction notification, process monitoring and traceability. The Transfusion Service often relies on notes about performed implantations to update patients' transfusion record on the Blood Bank Management software or register. Due to absence of a pervasive IT support and to fragmentation between different units (different duties, low communication and difficult record tracking), there is a lot of paperwork and manual activities non-homogeneously recorded on personal files (docs or spreadsheets). Raising the process complexity, autologous transplantation requires the cells to be cryo-preserved in liquid nitrogen tanks (at -196° C) for several months before administration; this stage is risky for both Lab technicians and for the stem cells (if thawed they start to die, so the faster the process is, the better). Because the treatment is based on "non-repeatable" products and because of the type of diseases treated, the Stem Cells process is recognized as having numerous critical points and risk management and prevention is required. A risk analysis performed on this process [17] show that the management of the bag – fractioning, cryo-preservation and stocking – is one of the more critical phase of the process. As far as concerns the management of the bags, an error in labeling can lead to the wrong bag being infused or a fall by the person carrying the units to the cryopreservation area can lead to loss of the product, as well as a mistake in bag identification in picking before the administration.

The Research Project and the HSC Process Innovation

Recognizing the great need (and opportunity) for innovative IT tools supporting the Stem Cells process, Italian Ministry of Health funded a research project named "Safety, traceability and reliability of collection, processing and transplantation of hematopoietic stem cells (HSCs) and therapeutic cells (TCs): integrated procedures and tools to support operations, clinical care and banking". Fondazione IRCCS Istituto Nazionale dei Tumori in Milan (Italy), recognized as a top Scientific Research and Treatment Institution in Oncology, is highly experienced in such topics and, due to the already significant knowledge acquired on ICT support to clinical processes, proposed itself to manage and coordinate the project [18]. A.O. Ospedale "Ca'Granda" Niguarda in Milan (which is the largest public hospital in Milan) [19], IRCCS Istituto Clinico Humanitas (a private hospital and research center), and Fondazione Politecnico di Milano are also involved in the project. Each partner is bringing peculiar needs and competences: each hospital runs important storage and transplantation facilities with a different research focus on cells. Fondazione Politecnico, an academic institution connected to the technical university in Milan, contributes with expertise on methodological framework (e.g. process reengineering, risk assessment) ensuring a coherent approach in process innovation.

The project goal is to design, develop and implement a set of organizational models, acknowledged procedures and ICT tools in order to improve actual support, safety, reliability and traceability in HTCs and TCs, in accordance with the internationally recognized FACT-JACIE standards. This will allow clinicians to guarantee and pursue high quality in procedures and data handling, providing also accurate data traceability on stem cell collection and implantation (e.g. process lead times, haemovigilance). Istituto Tumori has been adopting innovative M&W solutions (embedded with RFId tags and antennas) integrated to the HIS in order to avoid errors and enhance patient safety and quality of care. The Istituto's M&W strategy aims to build an ICT infrastructure (hardware and software integrated to the involved HIS modules) which guarantees secure identification of patients, staff, treatments, and critical items in crucial checkpoints within the clinical pathway. As of today, the Istituto's traceability platform supports traceability and safety needs within a growing number of clinical activities, from general patient identification (access to the operating room, access to radiotherapy rooms,..) to patient-to-treatment cross matching (blood bags, sample tubes, surgical sampling,..). This is done through several different Wi-Fi devices like handheld readers attached to standard desktop PCs or smart PDAs (soon replaced by NFC embedded smartphone) with a thematic workflow management application installed (e.g. the transfusion safety app, the bedside radiology app, and so on). The new project is an opportunity to extend the Istituto's traceability platform in the field of HSC and TC process management, supporting the whole process: cell donation, fractioning, lab processing, long-term cryopreservation, delivery of the bag and transplantation to receiver patient in clinical units (or extraction for research purposes). On the other hand, the solution will be designed and developed according to interoperability standards in order to be transferred to the other hospitals involved in the project. The target solution will exploit the AIDC technology features by the integration with the different HIS modules (Central Patient Registry, Transfusion Service System, Drug Management System, ..) aiming to provide all the process actors (Transfusion Service, Stem Cell Lab, Ward) with tools for process real-time tracking and monitoring. New and existing ICT tools need to be integrated and enriched with new data and features:

- The Transfusion Service System will be at first extended to support Stem Cell Lab processing activities, then new data and functions will be added to keep the record unified and updated throughout the process.
- The Stem Cell Lab will be provided of a system to manage stocks and assure quality of its procedures, up to the ward where the stem cells unit is thawed for administration.
- Technicians' operations at deep freeze tanks in the stocking room will be supported by a mobile application and RFId identification of rack's position, e.g. when positioning a unit in the right place, timely recording all actions.
- At bedside, a mobile application will support clinical staff while administering the unit to the patient; it will also keep record of administrations and adverse reaction, sharing the data with the HIS.
- The traceability platform will integrate the whole process, connecting the different systems and recording the identification data throughout the different steps (stem cells bag will be labeled with RFId label and it will be read from device available in the Transfusion Service Centre, in the Lab and in the ward).

According to the scenario, the entire process will be supported with customized tools that enable more effective and precise information sharing (e.g. about patients' stem cells collection and transplantation history), and enforce process tracking and monitoring capability (e.g. tracking all the

steps, time monitoring, staff authentication). The project is challenging because extreme low temperature inhibits RFId tags and specific envelopes and layouts are needed in order to support technicians in storing each aluminum cassette containing the HSC bag in the N2 tank's rack and subsequently recognizing and drawing out the correct one (assigned to the patient). This is relevant in order to reduce risk in a error-prone phase of the process with direct impact on patient safety. Besides, the project will contribute to public knowledge with electromagnetic compatibility tests between High Frequency RFId fields (13.56 MHz) and HSCs; though, considering the real operative scenario (low power RFId emission and short exposure time) these tests are more likely to be just precautionary.
The project will benefit from the involvement of different healthcare organizations (public and private, general hospital and specialized institute) and from the engagement of process actors (e.g. physicians, nurses, technicians) in solution design, test and evaluation. Therefore, the solution will involve cross-organization development and will result more acceptable for clinical staff.

Expected impact of Process Innovation

In the first phase of process analysis and tool design the value of the solution has been measured in term of how it can increase quality of care by reducing medical errors, improving clinical decision and helping to eliminate redundant information recording (increase effectiveness). The areas where the solution could be able to improve the stem cells process management are:

- **RFID Patient Tracking**. During every stage of the process patient and bag identification is ensured by RFId tag applied to patient wristband and bag label. RFId tags can also storage information related to the unit to control its usage (e.g. the time within the therapy has to be done).
- **Mobile Applications for Bedside Administration Management**. The application available on Smartphone (NFC integrated) will help clinicians in the ward to manage activities on-the-go. Bedside access to the application enables patient and bag cross-match before administration and can prevent dangerous errors before they happen.
- **Mobile Applications for Workflow Management** (Figure 2). The application available on PDA (RFId integrated) will help technicians in the laboratory to manage activities on-the-go. A workflow for laboratory staff will automate inventory management from the receiving of collected bags to their storage in liquid N2 at -196°C to reduce inefficiencies (finding free locations in the tank) and improving bag retrieval and dispensing accuracy (improving location and identification of bags).
- **Medical Records**. The mobile application in the ward will be integrated with the central repository of the Transfusion Centre. The one for stock management will be integrated to the Stock Management System. These integration will allow to share data on the overall process, on therapies performed on the patient and on state of bags in the tanks. These will merge with data collected by the other workflows supported by the traceability platform to complete the overview on patient treatments (e.g. surgery, transfusions, chemotherapy,..) and on bag lifecycle. Technicians, transfusionists and authorized clinicians will securely access patient and bag information when needed. Also real time recording will enhance the quality of the information.
- **Medication Error Tracking**. Patients and bags secure identification, real-time data recording and cross-match control will allow to analyze data on how and why medical mistakes occur. This will helps to proactively address mistakes before they occur again, such as changing flawed processes or improving staff training.
- **Electronic Management of Communications**. Clinicians will use a web-based application to send requests to the Transfusion centre (e.g. evaluation of donor suitability) or to the Stem Cells Lab (e.g. bag request for transplantation) improving timeliness, traceability and quality of the communication, avoiding paperwork and phone management of the communication.

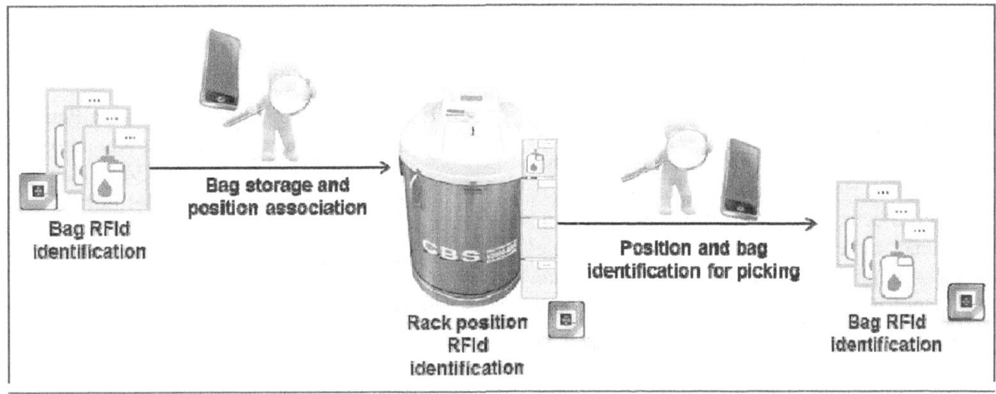

Figure 2. Storing and picking management through RFId mobile application at N2 tank area

Conclusion

Modern healthcare asks for effective, responsive, patient and process-oriented, cost-effective solutions to support clinical staff in their daily activities. An important issue for the future of the HIS is the growing need for real-time availability of legally compliant and paperless healthcare information. From this point of view, a first goal regards the complete integration of healthcare systems at all levels. This integration pushes for both the exploitation of standards and for the design of comprehensive architectural models that can to cope with both the configurations of the current HIS and the operative procedures of clinical process. Mobile Health solutions – based on M&W with AIDC technology embedded - integrated to the HIS have to be powerful and strategic in order to support clinical process on the go and to record information related to bedside events and procedures.

Among the other functional areas in the field of therapy management, dedicated ICT tools and mobile devices could address approaching common challenges. The main goals of ICT supporting therapy management are secure patient identification, workflow support to activities, safety of treatments administration, process traceability and costs control. These are related also to Risk Management issues.

Research and projects promoted by Istituto Nazionale dei Tumori di Milano and Fondazione Politecnico di Milano explore these issues focusing on M&W and RFId technologies as a powerful tool to support process traceability and safety of bedside operations. A new project focuses on improving Stem Cell management with aiming to develop a M&W integrated solution to support the whole process: from cell donation to bags, to lab processing and fractioning, to long-term cryopreservation, to delivery to wards, to transplantation to recipient patients (or their use for research purposes). In the proposed scenario portable devices, like WiFi PDAs or smartphone with NFC/RFId antennas embedded, will support operations both in wards and in the processing lab. RFId-labeled bags will be tested to track with a single read/write item all process phases (also in deep freeze at -196°C). The value of the project is represented by the attention paid in process reengineering and change management issues, as well in the correct choice of the proper technology to build the HIS infrastructural backbone and to develop mobile applications to fit in different hospital environments. On one hand the co-design of the application with the involvement of clinicians since the earlier stages of requirement definition is crucial to ensure solution usability and acceptance by physicians and nurse. This also to face risk management issues related to low usability and effectiveness of the proposed solution. On the other hand, developing a flexible and scalable solution based on interoperability and technological standard allows not only to make the solution available for implementation in other hospitals (as Ospedale Niguarda and Humanitas in the field of the research project), but also to spread innovative solution to support different process (as, for example, pharmacotherapy and radiotherapy management, blood transfusion and so on), guaranteeing secure identification of patient, staff, treatments, and critical items at crucial checkpoints within the clinical pathway.

References

[1] Rodriguez J.J.P.C. (2010) Preface, in: Rodriguez J.J.P.C. (Ed.) Health Information Systems: Concepts, Methodologies, Tools, and Applications, Hershey (PA): Medical Information Science Reference.

[2] Pascot D., Bouslama F., Mellouli S. (2011) Architecturing Large Integrated Complex Information Systems: An Application to Healthcare Knowledge information Systems, 27(2): 115–140.

[3] Lobenstein K.W. (2005) Information Security and Ethics, in: Brown F.D., Stone T.T., Patrick T.B. (Eds.) Strategic Management of information Systems in Healthcare, Chicago (IL): Health Administration Press.

[4] Burke D.E., Wang B.B.L., Wan T.T.H., Diana M.L. (2002) Exploring Hospitals' Adoption of Information Technology, Journal of Medical Systems, 26(4): 349–355.

[5] Martin D.K., Shulman K., Santigao-Sorrell P., Singer P.A. (2003) Priority Setting and Hospital Strategic Planning, Journal of Health Services Research ad Policy, 8(4): 197–201.

[6] Bonnabry P, Despont-Gros C, Grauser D, Casez P, Despond M, Pugin D, Rivara-Mangeat C, Koch M, Vial M, Iten A, Lovis C. (2008) A risk analysis method to evaluate the impact of a computerized provider order entry system on patient safety. Journal of the American Medical Informatics Association Jul-Aug;15(4):453-60.

[7] Corso M., Gastaldi L. (2009) Managing ICT-Driven Innovation in the Heatlhcare Industry: Evidence from an Empirical Study in Italy 10th International CINet Conference "Enhancing the Innovation Environment", Brisbane (AU) – September, 6–8: 1–14.

[8] Christensen C.M., Grossman J.H., Hwang J. (2009) The Innovator's Prescription: A Disruptive Solution for Healthcare, New York (NY): McGraw–Hill.

[9] Anderson J.G. (2009) Improving Patient Safety with Information Technology, in: Khoumbagi K., Dwivedi Y., Srivastava A., Lal B. (Eds.) Handbook of Research on Advances in Health Informatics and Electronic Healthcare Application, Hershey (PA): Medical Information Science Reference.

[10] Locatelli P., Restifo N., Gastaldi L., Corso M. (2012). Health Care Information Systems: Architectural Models and Governance, Innovative Information Systems Modelling Techniques, Christos Kalloniatis (Ed.), ISBN: 978-953-51-0644-9, InTech.

[11] Locatelli P., Restifo N., Gastaldi L., Sini E., Torresani M. (2010) The Evolution of Hospital Information Systems and the Role of Electronic Patient Records: From the Italian Scenario to a Real Case, in: Safran C. Reti S., Marin H.F. (Eds.) Medinfo 2010– Proceedings of the 13th World Congress on Medical Informatics, Amsterdam (NL): IOS Press.

[12] Mobile Health: new horizon for health through mobile Technologies – World Health Organization, Global Observatory for eHealth series - Volume 3, 2011, ISBN 9789241564250.

[13] Bates D.W., Using information technology to reduce rates of medication errors in hospitals. British Medical Journal (British Medical Association), 2000; 320:788-791.

[14] Ciofi degli Atti M., Paolini V., Cavallin M., Corsetti T., Locatelli F., Trucco P., Raponi M., (2013) Proactive evaluation of clinical risk: a FMECA analysis in pediatric chemotherapy Annali di Igiene: Medicina Preventiva e di Comunita Jan-Feb;25(1):15-21.

[15] Radiotherapy risk profile. Technical Manual. WHO Press, 2008, WHO, Geneva, Switzerland.

[16] Schwappach D.L., Wernli M. Medication errors in chemotherapy: incidence, types and involvement of patients in prevention. A review of the literature, European Journal of Cancer Care 19, 2010, 285–292.

[17] Bambi F., Spitaleri I., Verdolini G., Gianassi S., Perri A., Dori F., Iadanza E., (2009) Analysis and management of the risks related to the collection, processing and distribution of peripheral blood haematopoietic stem cells, Blood Transfus:7: 3-17

[18] Locatelli P., Restifo N., Facchini R., Sini E., Torresani M., Closing the safety loop in therapy management through ICT: mobile and wireless scenario for bedside support, IADIS International Journal on Computer Science and Information Systems, Vol. 7, No.1, pp. 120-134 (ISSN: 1646-3692).

[19] Baj E., Locatelli P., Gatti S., Restifo N., Origgi G., Bragagia S., Open Source: A lever for enhancing opportunities of healthcare information systems - An italian case study (2009) Proceedings of the 1st International Workshop on Open Source in European Health Care: The Time is Ripe, OSEHC 2009 In Conjunction with BIOSTEC 2009 and the EFMI LIFOSS WG, pp. 28-37.

Address for correspondence

Roberta Facchini, roberta.facchini@fondazione.polimi.it

Species Survivability and Altitude Dependence in a Lotka-Volterra Predator-Prey Spatial-Agent Based System

D.Q. Quach, J.M. Willemse, V. Du Preez and K.A. Hawick
Computer Science, Massey University, North Shore 102-904, Auckland, New Zealand
email: {dara.quach, dupreezvictor}@gmail.com, {j.m.willemse, k.a.hawick}@massey.ac.nz
Tel: +64 9 414 0800 Fax: +64 9 441 8181

June 2013

ABSTRACT

Predator-Prey food chains in real biological systems can be modelled using a differential system such as the Lotka-Volterra equations and many-agent effects added through a spatial mesh of interacting cells. Real systems in nature however do not exist in perfect gridded environments with uniform feeding and other environmental factors and we investigate effects of environment by perturbing the spatial Lotka-Volterra system in a realistic fractal landscape based on a digital elevation map. We investigate how this supports coupling of individual species survivability parameters to spatially varying altitude and report on this effect on species mean, carrying-capacity and predator-prey boom-bust periodicity. We present simulation results and discuss this approach as a basis for other even more realistic multi-species ecological models based on landscape or terrain map data.

KEY WORDS
Lotka-Volterra model; multi-agent system; altitude; digital elevation map.

1 Introduction

The Lotka-Volterra equations have been widely used as a model for predator-prey systems. They produce the well known boom-bust phenomena exhibited by real predator-prey biological and ecological systems. The original equations have been extended with spatial diffusion terms to model a landscape of interacting agents whereby spatial fluctuations arise but gradually disperse as the system homogenises or phase locks to a decreasing number of different spatial waves.

Predator-prey based population models [10] of interdependent species arranged in spatially inhomogeneous systems [7] can give interesting and important insights into ecological systems [8, 14]. These aspects are especially important for studies of the impact of populations on the environment [11, 17]

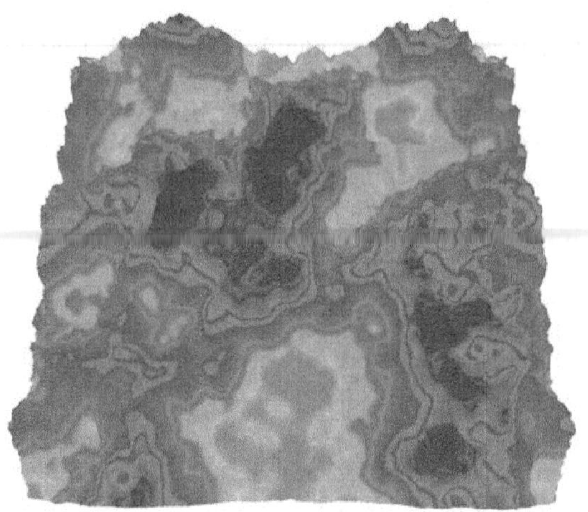

Figure 1: Spatial Lotka-Volterra digital elevation model

One useful approach to modelling environmental impact is to consider feeding-chains of predators and their prey and to consider how the microscopic interactions of individual species will affect the complex system as a whole. The Lotka-Volterra (LV) model [1] has been extended to incorporate spatial variations [9, 15] by adding a diffusive coupling term between LV equations solved numerically on a spatial mesh [12].

The system can be initialised randomly – as a well mixed population of predators and prey, but it will separate into spatial fluctuations over time [2,16], with clumps of predator and prey species forming into complex spatial patterns. The growth [5] of these spatial domains is an interesting study into complex emergent behaviour. Varying the number of species present [6] also leads to greater complexity and coupled oscillatory behaviour.

In this present paper we restrict the model to just two species, but we perturb the species' growth terms in the spatial Lotka-Volterra equations using digital elevation map data so that the growth of the prey is made dependent upon altitude. The concept of altitude as a simulation variable has been discussed by Willemse and Hawick [18] whereby, an approximated planet-like fractal terrain mesh is generated. We use a fractal landscape algorithm to generate topologically rich landscapes to test the behaviour of the model Figure 1 shows a three dimensional visualisation of an arbitrary time step captured from the simulation software developed for this work.

Our article is structured as follows: In Section 2 we describe how the Lotka-Volterra system can be perturbed using altitude information. We summarise the terrain map generation algorithm we used in Section 3. In Section 4 we present some selected results showing the spatial complexity emerging from the altitude dependence and we discuss implications for real predator-prey species which inhabit terrains varying in altitude in Section 5. We offer some tentative conclusions and suggestions for further investigation in Section 6.

2 Altitudes and the Spatial Lotka-Volterra Model

The Lotka-Volterra system of differential equations has been described extensively in the literature for two coupled species and for the case of simple diffusive coupling of spatial systems.

We give a brief summary of the generalised Lotka-Volterra equations for coupled populations. The usual form that these systems of equations are expressed in is with species population field variable $u = u(\mathbf{r}, t)$ and $f = \frac{\partial u}{\partial t}$, for the Lokta-Volterra particular system of equations where u and f are vectors where each element is a function of space $\mathbf{r}$ and time t, and one normally writes:

$$u \leftarrow u + hf \quad (1)$$

with:

$$\begin{aligned} f_0 &= Au_0 - Bu_0u_1 + \nabla^2 u_0 \\ f_1 &= Du_1 - Cu_0u_1 + \nabla^2 u_1 \end{aligned} \quad (2)$$

where we have ignored the diffusive coupling values in front of the Laplacian ∇^2 terms. Usually these are just set to unity as all they affect is the meaning of the time-scale, which for our purposes is in arbitrary units. This formulation is for a simple first order numerical differentiation scheme but in practice a higher order scheme such as Runge-Kutta 2nd order (RK2) or higher is desirable. Our implementation uses finite differencing code that is generated automatically and we are able to experiment with various numerical schemes including a 10th Order one due to Hairer [4]. Unless stated otherwise, an RK2 scheme was used and was found adequately accurate and stable for the results reported in this present paper. In the work reported in this paper we restrict our systems to two dimensional surfaces so that $\mathbf{r} = (x, z)$ only although the surfaces are embedded in a three dimensional space and individual mesh points have a height or altitude value $a(x, z)$.

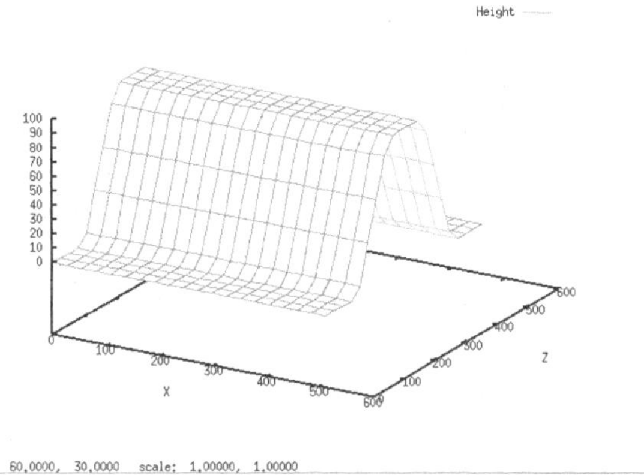

Figure 2: Ridge back terrain Mesh

In most studies of the Lotka-Volterra system It is usual to choose constant and spatially uniform values like: $D = A = 1.0$ and $C = B = 0.5$, where the fixed point is at D/C, A/B - and so as long as we start the system somewhere plausible close to the attractor it will spiral in and go into orbit around it (i.e, at $(2, 2)$) given these values.

It is possible however to introduce spatial environmental effects by simply perturbing the species' self-coupling or survivability terms by setting $A = 1.0 - a(x, z); D = C = B = 1.0$ where a is altitude. In fact it is sufficient just to make the prey species factor (A) vary spatially and leave the predator term spatially invariant, since predators will couple to landscape environmental effects via the prey variations.

In the work reported in Section 4 we use $A = 1.0 - a(x, z)$ with altitude function $0 < a(x, z) < 1$ and with $D = C = B = 1.0$ where A is the exponential prey growth rate, B is the rate at which predators consume prey, C is the growth rate of predators as a result of consuming prey and D is the exponential death rate of predators.

3 Generating Height Maps

Figure 2 shows a ridge back elevation mesh which provided the initial altitude model for our Lotka-Volterra variation. This artificial terrain contains 512×512 mesh points which have a base elevation of 0. In 10-unit steps between $z[100 \rightarrow 200]$ the height increases by a value of 10. The opposite occurs between $z[312 \rightarrow 412]$. Between $z[200 \rightarrow 312]$ the elevation is at the maximum value of 100.

For the purpose of providing realistic elevation values at each $a(x, z)$, we have employed the diamond-square subdivision algorithm [3]. The resultant mesh is an arbitrary elevation model which can be scaled to serve the purpose of providing an elevation function.

Diamond-square subdivision is an iterative algorithm for generating realistic fractal terrain height maps. It is 'fractal' in the sense that each subdivision is self-similar in the range of possible variation to the displacement of its points, according to some roughness constant and the size of the subdivided region within the map as a whole. Thus any given subset of the generated height map, regardless of its size or magnification, is statistically similar to any other subset or the height map as a whole. Algorithm 3 describes the fractal diamond-square algorithm and is supported by Figure 3.

Algorithm 1 Diamond-Square Subdivision

Require: a, W, R
  $\Delta h \leftarrow \frac{W}{2}$
  $roughness \leftarrow 2^{-R}$
  $w \leftarrow W$
  while $w > 0$ **do**
    for all $w \times w$ square subsets of a **do**
      $displacement \leftarrow$ random range$[\frac{-\Delta h}{2}, \frac{\Delta h}{2}]$
      $y \leftarrow displacement+$average of the four corner points of the subset square
      middle point of subset square $\leftarrow y$
    end for
    for all $w \times w$ diamond subsets of a **do**
      $displacement \leftarrow$ random range$[\frac{-\Delta h}{2}, \frac{\Delta h}{2}]$
      $y \leftarrow displacement+$average of the four corner points of the subset diamond
      middle point of subset diamond $\leftarrow y$
    end for
    $w \leftarrow \frac{w}{2}$
    $\Delta h \leftarrow \Delta h \times roughness$
  end while
  return a

Figure 4 shows a diamond-square generated digital elevation model. The altitude values are normalised to the range $[0.0 \rightarrow 1.0]$. Consider that the highest point of the mesh $a(x, z) \equiv 1.0$ and the lowest point $a(x, z) \equiv 0.0$. Therefore, the prey growth factor (A) is inversely proportional to altitude based on the assumption that prey is more likely to thrive at lower altitude.

4 Experimental Simulation Results

Presented in this section are a series of window captures from our spatial Lotka-Volterra simulation software. Figure 5 shows in arbitrary time sequence from left to right, top to bottom, the usual clustering of the self coupled pair at the high and low flat top while the mid region has step elevation causing small segmentation. In accordance with expectation based on the low growth rate at the highest altitude, the rate of diffusion at the lowest altitude is much more rapid than at top of the ridge. The red regions represent a dominance of the prey species where the lighter shades indicate high concentration of life. Blue regions are predator dominant and, as with the red, where the shade is lighter, the total two-species concentration is higher. Figure 4 demonstrates the average population of the two species over time at the beginning of the simulation and the point of stability.

The fractal model uses an HSV colour scheme where the $predator : prey$ ratio is demonstrated by hues between the predator dominant 60° (yellow) and prey dominant 360° (red). The elevation determines the value where $V = 1 - a(x, z)$. Figure 7 illustrates this.

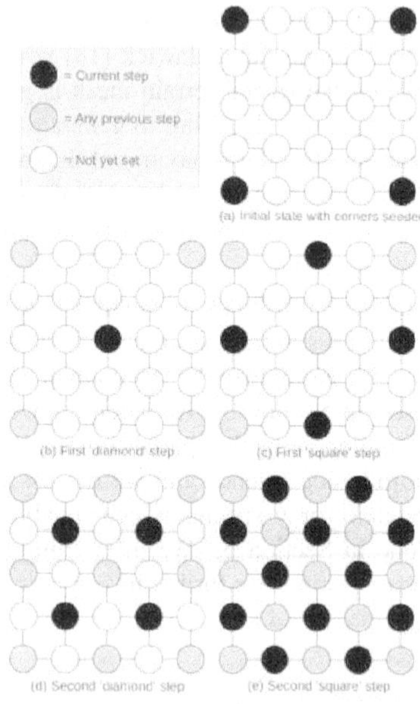

Figure 3: Diamond Square Algorithm.

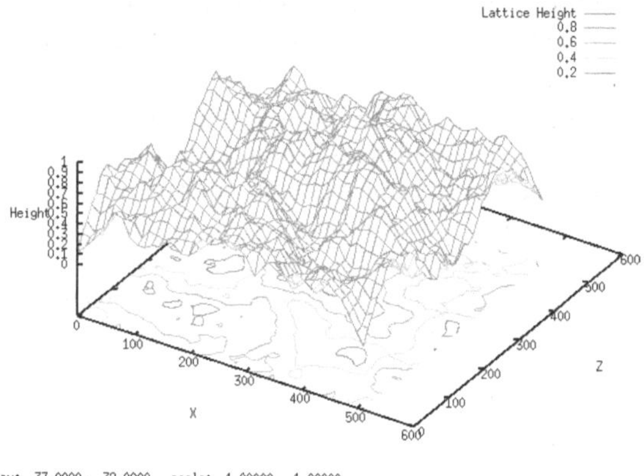

Figure 4: Digital elevation mesh generated with the diamond-square algorithm

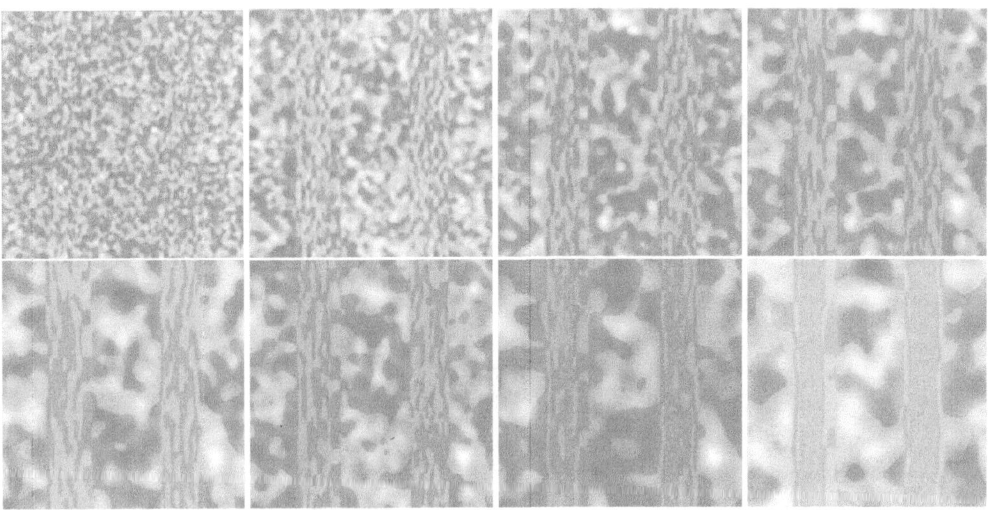

Figure 5: Ridge back simulation screen capture series

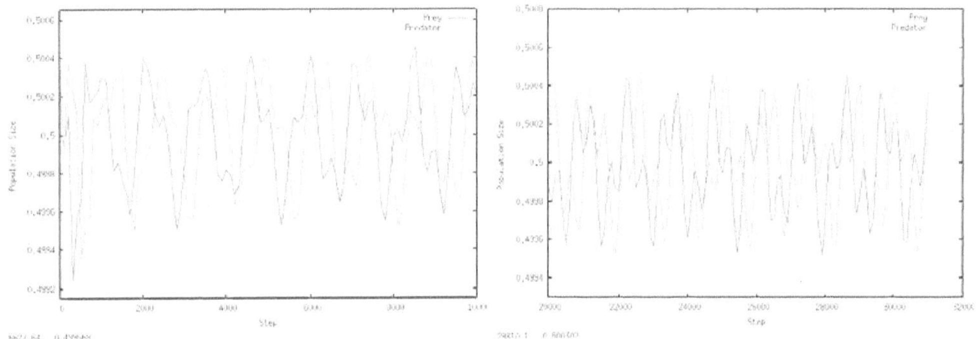

Figure 6: Initial (left) and stable (right) ridge back model population density over time

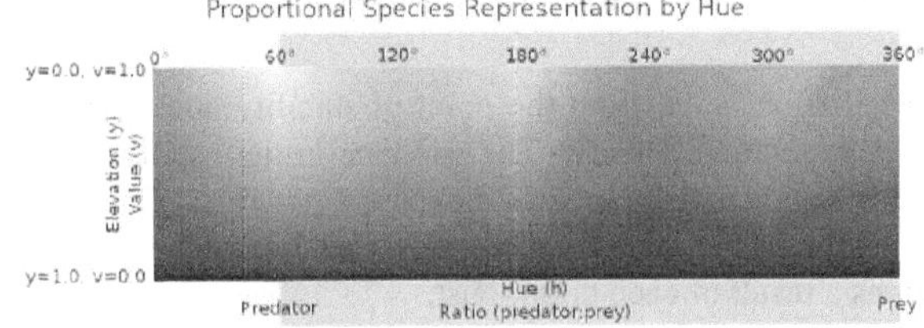

Figure 7: Colour scheme.

Figure 8 shows in sequence from left to right, top to bottom, visualisations of the fractal terrain simulation. As with the ridge back results, the rate of diffusion at the lowest altitude is much more rapid than at the highest. Figures 9 to 11 plot the average population density over time from simulation start and at the stability point. The altitude has been divided into three altitude ranges, low, middle, and high. The total average is then presented in Figure 12.

5 Discussion

The introduction of elevated spatial variations causes some local regions of convergence and prevents the whole system from going into a uniformly boring mixture as happens in flatland.

In the ridge back model, at the highest points, the self coupling terms are set to 0.1. and at the lowest points, set to 1.0 gradually increasing or decreasing in-between. As shown in Figure 4, the self coupling data quickly falls into the usual boom-bust pattern with the predator trailing at a 90 degree interval with the only differentiating factor being the range of species population density. As expected, this survivability term does not sufficiently model the effects of altitude on population patterns and numbers in a predator-prey system.

Figure 8: Digital elevation model simulation screen capture series

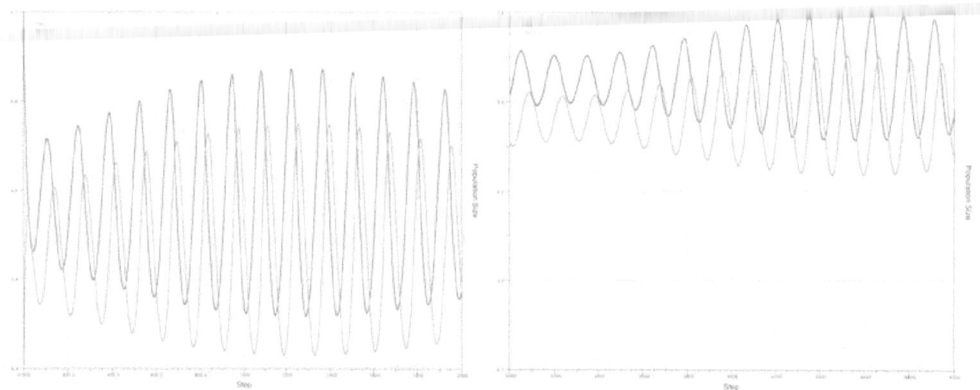

Figure 9: Low altitude range initial (left) and stable (right) digital elevation model population density over time

The variation of the survivability/self coupling terms on the fractal model provides significantly more interesting results. The altitudinal effects on the species density and fluctuation are clearly shown in Figures 9, 10, 11 and 12. High altitude population of both species oscillates at wide ranges before stabilising to a very narrow range, this accurately represents higher altitudes providing lower food availability, which affects the predators ability to survive while allowing the prey to thrive as they can effectively avoid predators. The predator population remains stable near zero in those regions as a result of a the inability to recover after the large bust intervals of the prey species. Similar, however less extreme effects can be seen at mid-range altitude. Eventually, the predator population stabilises at a healthy density with a sufficient food source. At the low range, the population follows the usual boom-bust pattern, however, with a clearly varying oscillation range from the point of stability due to the greater population density. The variance in the oscillation range is a indicator of species movement patterns. This is also visible in the blue coloured waves of Figure 8 which occur as a result of each boom-bust.

Perturbing the species success term in the Lotka-Volterra equation is sufficient to simulate the effect altitude can have on the system assuming the prey species prefers to breed at lower altitudes, be it for climate or resource reasons. To accommodate water or other resources a more complex spatial term could be used to support species seeking these necessities. Further ideas into artificial seasons can be implemented by introducing constraints at specific scaled time steps, these constraints for example, can be pertaining to prey survivability in certain simulated climates.

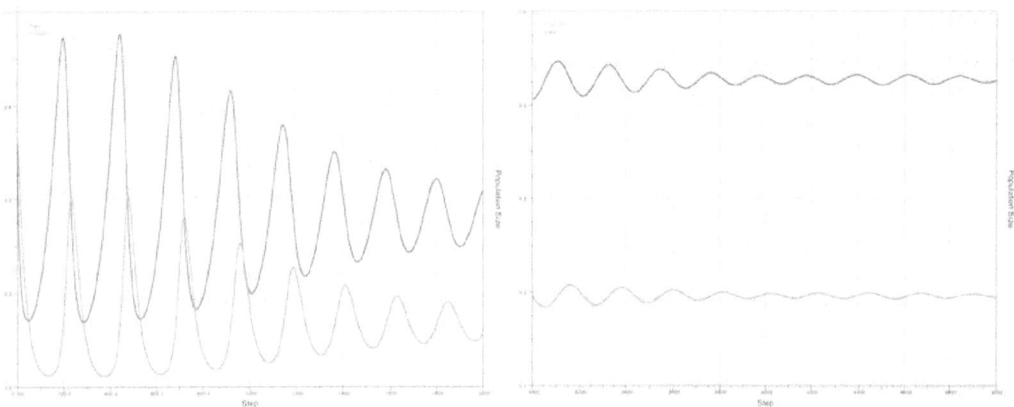

Figure 10: Middle altitude range initial (left) and stable (right) digital elevation model population density over time

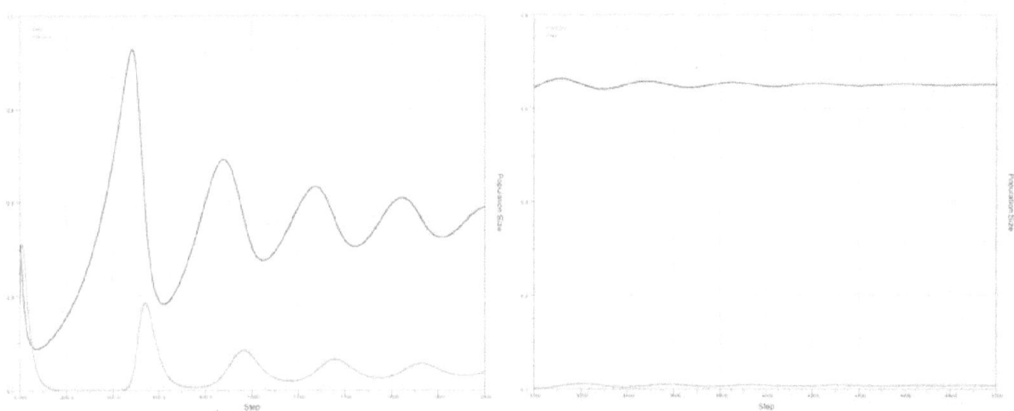

Figure 11: High altitude range initial (left) and stable (right) digital elevation model population density over time

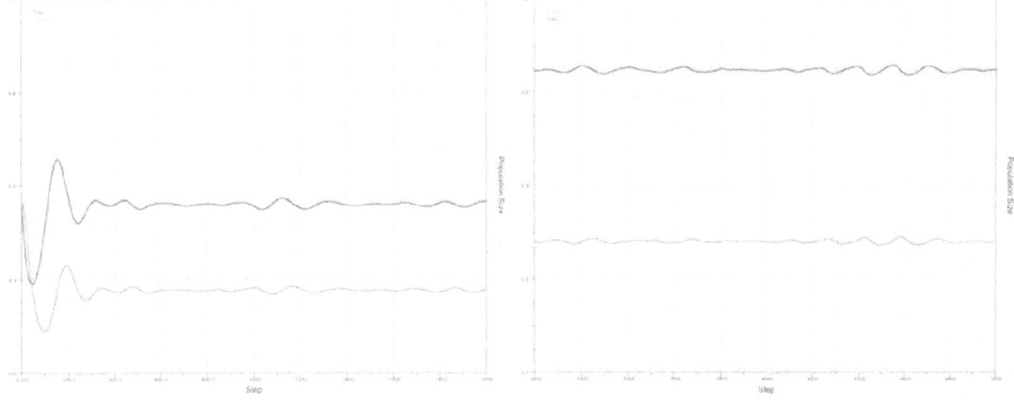

Figure 12: Total altitude range initial (left) and stable (right) digital elevation model population density over time

6 Conclusions

We have introduced altitude and environmental effects to the Lotka-Volterra Spatial Model by perturbing the parameters in the system of equations on simple configurations such as the ridge back elevation mesh to a full stochastic terrain mesh.

Adjusting the species's survivability terms, as expected, caused altitude to play a main role in affecting population numbers of a two-species system. The randomly generated population numbers per spatial cell at the start of the simulation quickly fall into distinct patterns at the various valleys and peaks of the terrain mesh. Low altitudes model a plentiful food availability allowing for results which are close to the usual Lotka-Volterra boom-bust cycles. The movement patterns are much more prominent at the highly populated low altitudes.

As the species move to mid-range altitudes, the simulation models the effects of the decreasing food source. Therefore, the initial decline of the predator population in these regions occur at a greater rate than they can breed, allowing the prey to thrive while the predators struggle to recover high population numbers. The higher altitude range further exaggerates the observations in the mid-range in terms of the variation in the population ratio.

This system models, to a certain extent, what can happen in the real world where the altitude contributes to survivability of specific species [13]. The prey utilise higher altitudes as a predator avoidance strategy but do not grow in number as significantly as at low regions. This system also models the population number of prey being effected at low regions they slowly decrease to a stable state due to the a small portion of the prey migrating up land.

The introduction of additional species variants in the system could provide insight into the effects of the "food-chain" or introduced pests. Future work may involve further investigation into environmental constraints such as artificial seasons and spatial configuration of resources. A seasonal model whereby, the survivability terms are further adjusted on a time scale may introduce improved simulation of migration patterns. A variation in which growth rates are weighted based on proximity to water or some other resource could also produce interesting spatial results.

References

[1] Ackland, G., Gallagher, I.: Stabilization of large generalized lotka-volterra foodwebs by evolutionary feedback. Phys. Rev. Lett. 93, 158701–1–4 (2004)

[2] Dubramysl, U., Tauber, U.C.: Spatial variability enhances species fitness in stochastic predator-prey interactions. Phys. Rev. Lett. 101, 258102–1–4 (2008)

[3] Fournier, A., Fussell, D., Carpenter, L.: Computer rendering of stochastic models. Commun. ACM 25(6), 371–384 (Jun 1982), `http://doi.acm.org/10.1145/358523.358553`

[4] Hairer, E.: A Runge-Kutta Method of Order 10. J. Inst. Maths. Applics. 21, 47–59 (1978)

[5] Hawick, K.A.: Spectral analysis of growth in spatial lotka-volterra models. In: Proc. International Conference on Modelling and Simulation. pp. 14–20. No. 685-030, IASTED, Gabarone, Botswana (6-8 September 2010)

[6] Hawick, K.A., Playne, D.P., Scogings, C.J.: Simulating the generalised spatial lotka-volterra equations with multiple species on gpus with automatic code generation. In: Proc. 12th IASTED Int. Conf. on Parallel and Distributed Computing and Networks (PDCN'13). IASTED, Innsbruck, Austria (11-13 February 2013)

[7] Kaitala, V., Ranta, E., per Lundberg: Self-organized dynamics in spatially structured populations. Proc. Roy. Soc. Lond. B 268, 1655–1660 (2001)

[8] Kot, M.: Elements of Mathematical Ecology. No. ISBN 0-521-80213-X, Cambridge (2001)

[9] Malcai, O., Biham, O., Richmond, P., Solomon, S.: Theoretical analysis and simulations of the generalized lotka-volterra model. Phys. Rev. E 66(3), 031102 (Sep 2002)

[10] Maron, M.: Modelling populations from malthus to the threshold of artificial life. Tech. rep., University of Sussex (2003)

[11] Newth, D., Cornforth, D.: Local structure and stability of model and real world ecosystems. In: Recent Advances in Artificial Life. pp. 187–198. Sydney, Australia (5-8 December 2005)

[12] Satulovsky, J.E.: Lattice lotka?volterra models and negative cross-diffusion. J. Theor. Biol. 183(4), 381–389 (December 1996)

[13] Scott, J.: Predators and their prey - why we need them both. Available from http://www.conservationnw.org/what-we-do/predators-and-prey/carnivores-predators-and-their-prey (2011), `http://www.conservationnw.org/what-we-do/predators-and-prey/carnivores-predators-and-their-prey`

[14] Sole, R.V., Manrubia, S.C., Benton, M., Kauffman, S., Bak, P.: Criticality and scaling in evolutionary ecology. Trends Ecol. Evol. 14(4), 156–160 (April 1999)

[15] Solomon, S.: Generalized lotka-volterra (glv) models. Tech. rep., Racah Institute of Physics, The Hebrew University, Jerusalem (1999)

[16] Sprott, J., Wildenberg, J., Azizi, Y.: A simple spatiotemporal chaotic lotka volterramodel. Chaos, Solitons and Fractals 26, 1035–1043 (2005)

[17] Todd, P.M., Wilson, S.W.: Environment structure and adaptive behavior from the ground up. In: Proceedings of the second international conference on From animals to animats 2 : simulation of adaptive behavior: simulation of adaptive behavior. pp. 11–20 (1993)

[18] Willemse, J.M., Hawick, K.A.: Generation and rendering of fractal terrains on approximated spherical surfaces. In: Proc. 17th International Conference on Computer Graphics and Virtual Reality (CGVR'13). p. CGV4061. No. CSTN-183, WorldComp, Las Vegas, USA (April 2013)

A Study of Functional Delegation in Adjoining Cells

Bharat S. Rawal[1] and Anthony J. Atala[2]
[1] Department of Computer and Information Sciences, Shaw University, Raleigh, NC, USA
brawal@shawu.edu
[2] Department of Urology, Wake Forest School of Medicine, Winston-Salem, NC, USA
atala@wfubmc.edu

Abstract - *This paper provides a brief review of viable methods for task delegation in adjoining cells based on biological cell to cell communication inspired by Split-protocol paradigm. Various approaches of protocol splitting and task delegation concept has been studied before in reference to splitting protocols at a server level and making the splitting in general transparent to the client. The split phenomenon can be applicable in cell biology because the cells in living bodies are constantly sending out and receiving signals. Many medical implications occur due to communication breakdown in cells, or the inability of cells to respond to incoming signals. We propose the split technique when one cell fails to respond to the signals. In that case, adjoining cells will respond on behalf of defective cells. This technique may be helpful for Type-I and II diabetic patients. This research will open new horizons in medical and bioengineering fields.*

Keywords: A Web Servers, Bare Machine Computing, Molecule Signaling, Molecular, Circuitry

1 Introduction

To address bottleneck at the server and client sides we have demonstrated split-protocol architecture in networking and high performance computing, and some part of architectural details are reproduced here for interpreting the splitting concept. An HTPP protocol intertwined with a TCP protocol is shown in Figure 2. The protocol interactions can be implemented at many levels as done in OS based systems or as a single intertwined protocol level in bare PC applications [16]. It is also possible to split the protocol after we receive GET request and partition a single server into two servers consisting of a connection server (CS) and a data server (DS) [2]. Such splitting concept has been studied and their results were published in paper Mini Web Server Clusters for HTTP Request Splitting [3]. In this approach, the CS handles all connection related to interfaces and communicates to the client in two directions. The DS only communicates to the client in one direction, i.e. sending data to the client. The CS also sends an inter-server packet to DS to provide client's request and its state. The CS is connected to the client throughout its session or during its processing of a given request. In such architecture one CS interfaces with one or more DSs to provide client services and thus becomes a bottleneck in a given mini-cluster configuration [3].

To address such bottleneck, we proposed a split protocol at an architectural level thus resulting in a modified client server architecture, where connections and data transfers are separated entirely. In this approach, the data servers (one or more) can be located at a separate location than their counter part connection server. The CSs can be monitored for ongoing connections and the clients are isolated from data servers. The CS and DS servers can have a tight connection to serve client requests thus providing increased security at a server level. When a connection is established between a client and a CS, the CS will send an inter-server packet to a DS and terminate its connection processing, where a DS can finish the rest of the session to send data and close the connection. Such modified client server interactions are shown in Figure 3. Notice that client sends interactions SYN, SYN-ACK-ACK and GET to CS and CS sends SYN-ACK and GET-ACK only to the client. After CS processes the connection, it sends a message to DS through an inter-server packet and eliminates this connection at CS. The rest of the connection and related interactions related to DATA, ACK and FIN-ACK will be dealt by DS. We have freed up CS completely after the GET is processed.

Although the split concept idea was conceived for a network protocol, its broader applicability to life science, servers and clients, teaching, learning and research is certainly imminent. Normally individual plant cells communicate directly with one another through microscopic membrane-lined channels. Less direct forms of communication are the coordination of growth and development of an individual cell with that of its neighbors. Plants are being able to create their food and maintain growth of cells in the plant tissue with cell to cell coordination. There are many studies for different mechanisms individual cells use to communicate with one another [13].

Communicating cells may be close together or far apart. Multi-cellular organisms release signaling molecules that target other cells. Cells may communicate by direct contact.

Both animals and plants have cell junctions that connect to the cytoplasm of adjacent cells. Signaling substances dissolved in the cytosol can pass freely between adjacent cells. Animal cells can communicate by direct contact between membrane-bound cell surface molecules. Such cell-cell recognition is important to such processes as embryonic development and the immune response. In other cases, messenger molecules are secreted by the signaling cell [12, 14]. Cells are made of molecular circuits that perform logical operations similar to electronic devices [9]. A newly developed bio-computer allows scientists to "program" molecules to carry out "commands" inside cells [17]. Many medical implications occur due to communication breakdown in cells, or inability of cells to respond to incoming signals. We propose the split technique when one cell fails to respond to the signals .In that case, adjoining cells will respond on behalf of faulty cells as shown in Figure 1. This technique may be helpful for Type-II diabetic patients. This paper highlights on mechanisms to program molecules to send and respond artificially created signal.

The remainder of the paper is organized as follows. Section II presents related work; Section III describes splitting design and implementation; Section IV presents electromagnetic approach to cell signaling; Section V discusses impacts of splitting; and Section VI contains the conclusion.

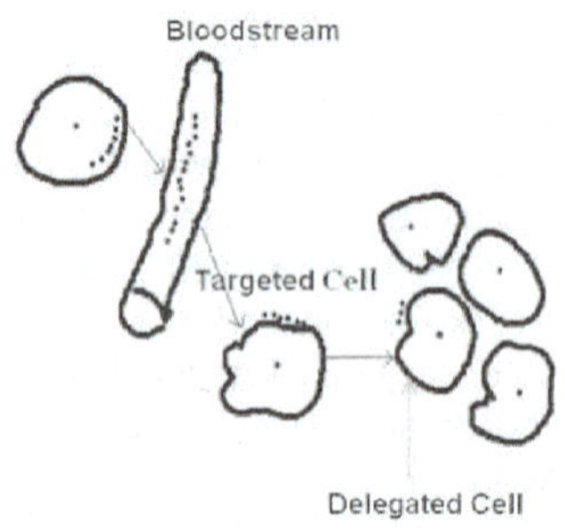

Figure 1. Functional Delegation in Adjoining Cells

2 Related work

Bare PC applications use the Bare Machine Computing (BMC) or dispersed OS concept [19]. That is, there is no operating system (OS) or centralized kernel running in the machine. Instead, the application is written in C++ and runs as an application object (AO) [20] by using its own interfaces to the hardware [18] and device drivers. While the BMC concept resembles approaches that reduce OS overhead and/or use lean kernels such as Exokernel [5, 7, and 11], Splitting protocol at a client server architecture level is different from migrating TCP connections,

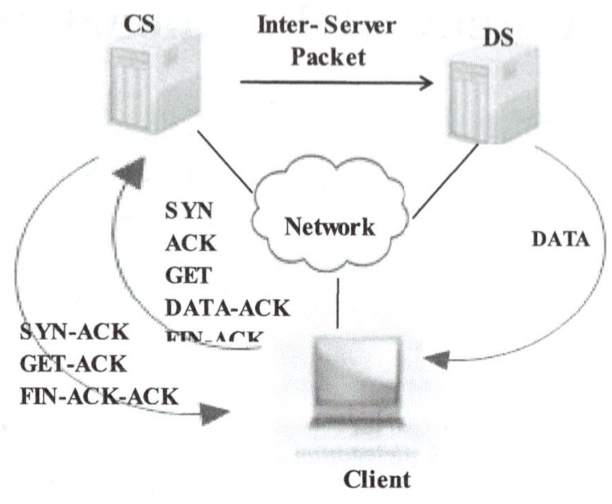

processes or Web sessions; splicing TCP connections; or masking failures in TCP-based servers. For example, in

Figure 2. Server Split Protocol

migratory TCP (M-TCP) [15], a TCP connection is migrated between servers with client involvement; in process migration

Figure 2. Server Split Protocol

[6], an executing process is transferred between machines; in proxy-based session handoff [10], a proxy is used to migrate Web sessions in a mobile environment; in TCP splicing [1], two separate TCP connections are established for each request; and in fault-tolerant TCP (FT-TCP) [8], a TCP connection continues after a failure enabling a replicated service to survive. Per our knowledge, no work on splitting protocol connections at client server architectural level has been done before.

In living organisms Communicating cells may be close together or far apart. Multi-cellular organisms release signaling molecules that target other cells. Cells may communicate by direct contact. Both animals and plants have cell junctions that connect to the cytoplasm of adjacent cells. Signaling substances dissolved in the cytosol can pass freely between adjacent cells. Animal cells can communicate by direct contact between membrane-bound cell surface molecules. Such cell-cell recognition is important to such processes as embryonic development and the immune response. In other cases, messenger molecules are secreted by the signaling cell [12, 14]. Cells are made of molecular circuits that perform logical operations similar to electronic devices [15]. A newly designed bio-computer allows scientists to program molecules to carry out commands inside cells [17].

Also whenever a transcription factor binds to a region of DNA Genes are turned on or off like digital gate [26].This paper highlights on mechanisms to program molecules to send and respond artificially created signal.

3 Design and implemention

Split protocol client server architecture design and implementation differ from traditional client and server designs. As the traditional client server architecture is modified in this approach, we have designed and implanted a client and a server based on a bare PC, where there is no traditional OS or kernel running in the machine. This made our design simpler and easier to make modifications to conventional protocol implementations. Figure 3 shows a high level design structure of a client and server in a bare PC design. Each client and a server consist of a TCP state table (TCB), which consists of the state of each request. Each TCB entry is made unique by using a hash table with key values of IP address and a port number. The CS and DS TCB table entries are referred by IP3 and Port#. The Port# in each case is the port number of the request initiated by a client. Similarly, the TCB entry in the client is referenced by IP1 and Port#.

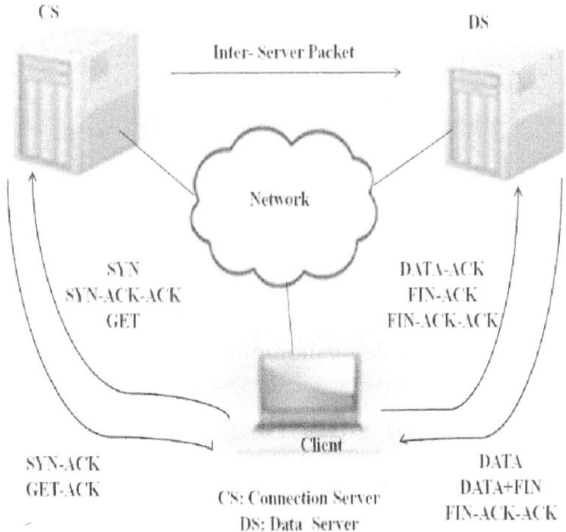

Figure 3. Client Split Protocol Architecture

The TCB tables form the key system component in the client and server designs. A given entry in this table maintains complete state and data information for a given request. This entry requires about 160 bytes of relevant information and another 160 bytes of trace information that can be used for trace, error, log, and miscellaneous control. This entry information is independent of its computer and can be easily migrated to another PC to run at a remote location. This approach is not the same as process migration [6] as there is no process information contained in the entry. The inter-server packet is based on this entry to be shipped to a DS when a GET message arrives from the client. Notice that the client uses IP1 and Port# to address the TCB entry as shown in Figure 4. That means, when DS sends data or other packets, then it must use IP1 as its source address and its own MAC address in the packet. However, a client must be aware of IP1 and IP2 addresses to communicate to two servers for different purposes. Client knows IP1 through its own request and by resolving the server's domain name. The client does not know IP2 address to communicate during the data transmission. We solved this problem by including the IP2 address in the HTTP header using a special field in the header format. In this design, a client could get data from any unknown DS and it can learn the data server's IP address from its first received data (i.e. header). This mechanism simplifies the design and implementation of split protocol client server architecture. This technique also allows the CS to distribute its load to DSs based on their CPU utilization without resorting to complex load balancing techniques [4].

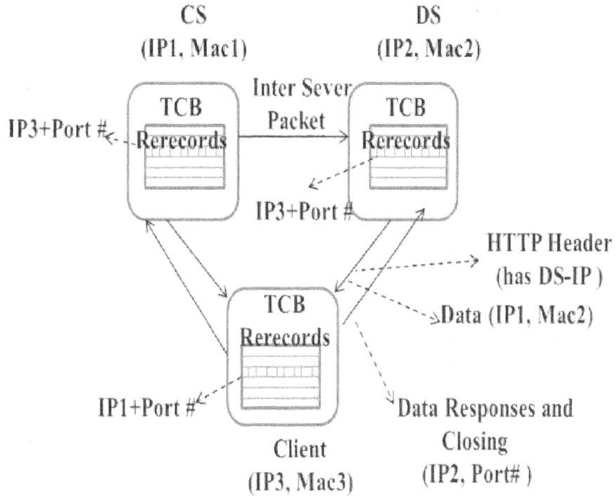

Figure 4. Design Structure

We have taken an existing bare PC server design and created CS and DS elements. The CS design turned out to be fairly simple as its sliding window and data transmission logic is removed. The DS design also became somewhat simpler by removing the connection logic.

For a bare client implementation, a bare PC server design is modified by swapping the roles of client and server interactions. We had to create client request generator logic in addition to the server logic.

The bare PC server application does not use any OS-related libraries or system calls. However, the application itself is developed using a standard MS Windows environment and written in Visual C++ (without any *.h files), and the MASM Assembler. Most of the direct hardware interfaces are implemented in C/assembly language using software interrupts. The size of the assembly code is approximately 1,800 lines. These direct hardware interfaces include: display, keyboard, timers, task management, NIC, and real/protected mode switching. The Intel 82540EM NIC driver code is approximately 3100 lines of C/C++ code and 43 lines of assembly code. Similarly, the USB driver uses approximately 133 lines of assembly code, with the rest of the code written in C. The code implementing the Web server is written in C++ in an object-oriented manner. The size of the source code is approximately 22,452 lines of code not including comments and 13,744 executable lines. This yields a single monolithic executable AO consisting of 344 sectors of code size (176, 128 bytes), which is placed on the USB. The code implementing the Web client is similar but it is about 5% more the server code. The same USB also contains boot code and other user interfaces to load and run the program on a bare PC.

4 Electromegnetic approche to cell signaling

Cells are made of molecular circuitry, and molecular interaction is similar to logical interaction of electrical circuits. A macromolecular interaction technique derived from physical sciences can be used to examine the structures and properties of biological molecules. This paper investigates the structures of proteins and nucleic acids, and studies of the physical features that determine macromolecular conformation. Also it analyzes the macromolecular interactions, and ligand-macromolecular interactions. Physical approach can help in developing and applying theoretical methods to investigate biological phenomena for cell delegation. Biostatistician modeling can help in investigating, collecting and interpreting information from available large molecular databases, and decoding of the human genome. For example, one can use micro-array technology to create and understand novel statistical problems in cell delegation process.

Figure 5 describes communication the model known as molecular communication [22]. Receiver and transmitter represent nanomachines that communicate by propagating molecular signals through communication channel. Nano machines devices are capable of sensing, processing and sending signals. As shown in Figure 5 signaling molecule are capable of carrying information from one cell to another cell. Communication channel provides mechanism for molecule propagation between nanomachines [21].

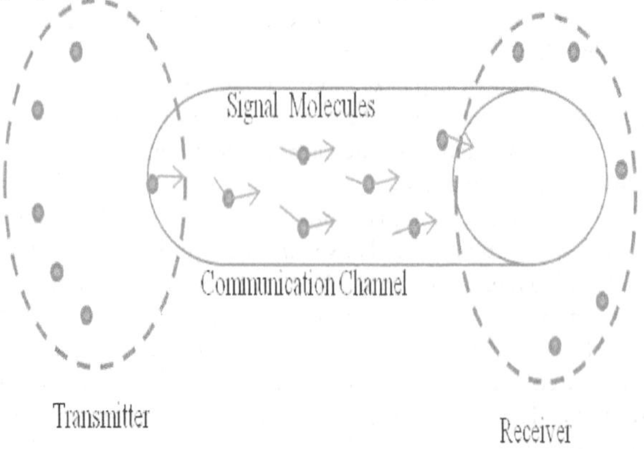

Figure 5. Molecular Communication

As shown in Figure 6 the signaling molecule could be a nenorobots in the bloodstream, and electromagnetic signatures are some of relevant parameters for biomedical communication purposes [23, 24]. The new advancement in manufacturing techniques, Silicon-On- Insulator (SOI) technology has been used to assemble high performance logic sub 90 nm circuits. The protein Nitric Oxide Syntheses (NOS) can provide positive or negative effects upon cell and tissues in their cellular living processes [24]. In molecular communication sender (transmitter) encodes information on molecule and propagate this molecule in communication channel, this molecule is known as information molecule and receiver decodes the information and reacts biochemically. The nature of molecular communication includes aqueous environmental, low-energy, and stochastic communications [22].

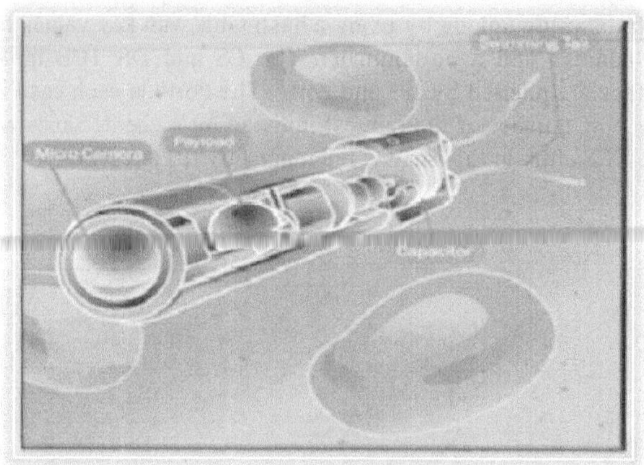

Figure 6. Molecular communication through signaling nanorobot [25]

5 Types of cell signaling

Depending on the distance communicating and responding cells, cells communicate through any of four basic mechanisms as shown Figure 7.

5.1 Direct Contact :

Normally cells communicate with each other via direct contact, over short distances (paracrine signaling), or over large distances and/or scales (endocrine signaling). In some cases a cell actually send signals to themselves, as membranes this process, called autocrine signaling, is similar to self delegation in split-protocol. Directly connected cells communicate through the process of diffusion. Diffusion is the process of random movement towards a state of equilibrium. When cells are very close to each other, some of the molecules in the plasma membranes of cells can bind specifically as shown in Figure 7a.

5.2 Paracrine Signaling

Figure 7b represents Paracrine signaling. Signaling molecules secreted by the cells can diffuse through the extracellular fluid to other cells. Those molecules are taken up by neighboring cells. These types of signals are of short duration and are called Pracrine signals. Paracrine signaling plays an important role in early development in the coordination of the activities of neighboring cell groups.

5.3 Endocrine Signaling

Figure 7c represents Endocrine Signaling and the released signal molecule from cell remains in the extracellular fluids enters in to the organism's circulatory system and travel widely throughout the body. These longer life hormonal signal molecules affect cells distant from the releasing cells.

This type of intra cellular communication is known as endocrine signaling.

5.4 Synaptic Signaling

Figure 7d describes Synaptic signaling. The nervous system provides rapid communication in animal cells through neurotransmitter. Nerve cells release neurotransmitters from their tips very close to the target cells.

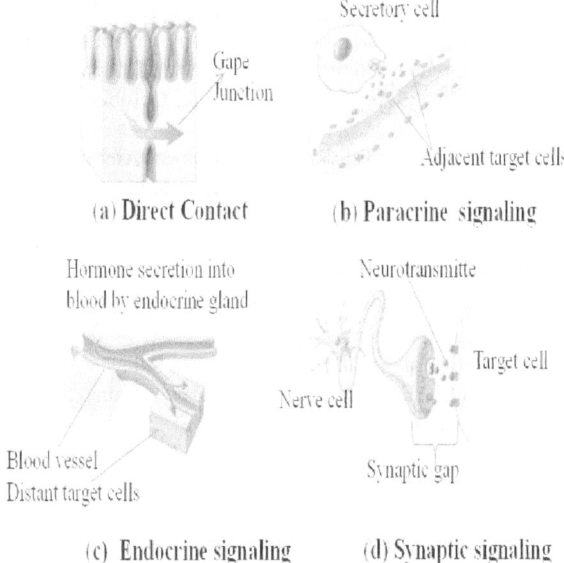

Figure 7. Cell Signaling Mechanisms [21].

6 Impacts of splitting

Splitting is a general approach that can be applied in principle to any application protocol that uses TCP (it can also be applied to protocols other than TCP to split the functionality of a protocol across machines or processors). In particular, splitting the protocol within a client server paradigm requires modification in the client server architecture. This approach impacts current server and client architectures and designs. However, this approach adds a new dimension and alternatives to current client server computing. Some of the issues and impact related to this novel approach are listed below:

- Split protocol configurations based on connections and data can be used for constructing large server clusters (4-15 DSs).
- A scalable performance can be achieved by adding DSs to the cluster without paying any penalty to load balancing overhead.
- A uniform response time can be achieved by adding additional DSs as they work independently and concurrently in the system.
- Complex load balancing techniques and dispatchers are not needed.
- Connections and data transfers can be completely isolated in reference to clients (this may provide additional security due to data server isolation).
- Connection and data servers can be located in different places; especially data servers can be located in close proximity to data.
- Client connections can be easily monitored without interrupting the client data communication.
- Server designs can be simplified, especially the CS design is much simpler and manageable.
- This approach can also be used for database servers and file servers.
- Split protocol can be applicable in molecular communication as molecular circuitry behaves similar to the logic of electrical logical gates.
- Molecular split protocol can helpful tools in developing remedies for diseases whose primary cause are communication breakdown between cells.
- Split protocol will open new horizon for exploring new research in the biomedical science.

The configurations studied and the results obtained in this paper can be viewed as a first step to validate the applicability of splitting connections and data transfers as a general concept. In future, it would be of interest to investigate its applicability to other protocols and applications.

7 Conclusion

A single monolithic HTTP/TCP protocol that is standard in a Web server can be split into two portions, and each portion can be run independently on a different Web server, thus constituting dual servers. These servers communicate across a network by using inter-server messages or delegating messages. A server can delegate a request to another server or it can process the request in its entirety. This paper explores the application of split concept in computing, networking and life science, especially the study of task delegation in adjoined cells, and in plant/animal tissue. The split phenomenon can be applicable in cell biology: the cells in living bodies are constantly sending out and receiving signals. Many medical implications occur due to communication breakdown in cells, or inability of cells to respond to incoming signals. We propose the split technique when one cell fails to respond to the signals. In that case, adjoining cells will respond on behalf of faulty cells. This technique may be helpful for Type-I and II diabetic patients. This research will open new horizons in medical and bioengineering fields.

8 References

[1] A. Cohen, S. Rangarajan, and H. Slye, "On the performance of TCP splicing for URL-Aware redirection," Proceedings of USITS'99, The 2nd USENIX Symposium on Internet Technologies & Systems, October 1999.

[2] B. Rawal, R. Karne, and A. L. Wijesinha. Splitting HTTP Requests on Two Servers, The Third International Conference on Communication Systems and Networks: COMPSNETS 2011, January 2011, Bangalore, India.

[3] B. Rawal, R. Karne, and A. L. Wijesinha." Mini Web Server Clusters for HTTP Request Splitt", 13th International Confrence on High performance Computing and Comunication, HPCC-2011, Banff, Canada, Sept 2-4, 2011.

[4] Ciardo, G., A. Riska and E. Smirni. EquiLoad: A Load Balancing Policy for Clustered Web Servers". *Performance Evaluation*, 46(2-3):101-124, 2001.

[5] D. R. Engler and M.F. Kaashoek, "Exterminate all operating system abstractions," Fifth Workshop on Hot Topics in operating Systems,

[6] D.S. Milojicic, F. Douglis, Y. Paindaveine, R. Wheeler and S. Zhou. "Process Migration," ACM Computing Surveys, Vol. 32, Issue 3, September 2000, pp. 241-299.

[7] D. Wentzlaff and A. Agarwal, "Factored operating systems (fos): the case for a scalable operating system for multicores," ACM SIGOPS Operating Systems Review, Volume 43, Issue 2, pp. 76-85, April 2009.

[8] D. Zagorodnov, K. Marzullo, L. Alvisi and T.C. Bressourd, "Practical and low overhead masking of failures of TCP-based servers," ACM Transactions on Computer Systems, Volume 27, Issue 2, Article 4, May 2009.

[9] http://www.kurzweilai.net/wetware-a-computer-in-every-living-cell/comment-page-1

[10] G. Canfora, G. Di Santo, G. Venturi, E. Zimeo and M.V.Zito, "Migrating web application sessions in mobile computing," Proceedings of the 14th International Conference on the World Wide Web, 2005, pp. 1166-1167.

[11] G. R. Ganger, D. R. Engler, M. F. Kaashoek, H. M. Briceno, R. Hunt and T. Pinckney, "Fast and flexible application-level networking on exokernel system," ACM Transactions on Computer Systems (TOCS), Volume 20, Issue 1, pp. 49 – 83, February, 2002.

[12] Tadashi Nakano, "Biological Computing Based on Living Cells and Cell Communication," International Conference on Network-Based Information Systems, pp. 42-47 September 2010.

[13]http://plantsinaction.science.uq.edu.au/edition1/?q=content/feature-essay-10-1-communication-between-plant-cel.

[14]S.Hiyama,Y.Mortitani,T.Suda,R.Egashira,Anomoto,M.Moore,and T.Nakano "Molecular Communication," In Proc.2005 NSTI Nanotechnology Conference Vol3.pp 392-395, 2005.

[15] K. Sultan, D. Srinivasan, D. Iyer and L. Iftod. "Migratory TCP: Highly Available Internet Services using Connection Migration," Proceedings of the 22nd International Conference on Distributed Computing Systems, July 2002.

[16] L. He, R. K. Karne, and A. L. Wijesinha, "The Design and Performance of a Bare PC Web Server," International Journal of Computers and Their Applications, IJCA, Vol. 15, No. 2, June 2008, pp. 100-112.

[17]http://www.americanscientist.org/science/pub/bio-computer-created-inside-living-cell

[18] R. K. Karne, K. V. Jaganathan, and T. Ahmed, "How to run C++ Applications on a bare PC," SNPD 2005, Proceedings of NPD 2005, 6th ACIS International Conference, IEEE, May 2005, pp. 50-55.

[19] R. K. Karne, K. V. Jaganathan, and T. Ahmed, "DOSC: Dispersed Operating System Computing," OOPSLA '05, 20th Annual ACM Conference on Object Oriented Programming, Systems, Languages, and Applications, Onward Track, ACM,San Diego, CA, October 2005, pp. 55-61.

[20] R. K. Karne, "Application-oriented Object Architecture: A Revolutionary Approach," 6th International Conference, HPC Asia 2002 (Poster), Centre for Development of Advanced Computing, Bangalore, Karnataka, India, December 2002.

[21]http://www.mhhe.com/biosci/genbio/raven6b/graphics/raven06b/other/raven06b_07.pdf

[22] Satoshi Hiyama, Yuki Moritani, Tatsuya Suda," A Biochemically-Engineered Molecular Communication System" Nano-Net Lecture Notes of the Institute for Computer Sciences, Social Informatics and Telecommunications Engineering Volume 3, 2009, pp 85-94

[23] Cavalcanti A, Freitas Robert A Jr, Kretly Luiz C. 2004. Nanorobotics control design: a practical approach tutorial. ASME 28th Biennial Mechanisms and Robotics Conference, Salt Lake City Utah, USA.

[24] Adrino Cavalacnti, et al., Nanorobot Hardware Architecture for Medical defense, *Sensors.* 2008; 8:2932 2958.http://dx.doi. org/10.3390/s8052932.

[25] http://electronics.howstuffworks.com/nanorobot.htm accessed on 02/20/2013.

[26] http://www.sciencedaily.com/releases/2012/10/.htm accessed on 02/20/2013.

Identification of Genes by E. coli Regulatory Protein Using Neurofuzzy System and Multivariate Analysis

Deok Hee Nam
Engineering and Computing Science, Wilberforce University, Wilberforce, OH 45384, USA

Abstract *– In recent days, biological data analyses have been importantly treated by the scientists from the biomedical fields due to the floods of the daily produced bio-scientific information. One of the frequently examined topics related to the biomedical fields is how the DNA genes can be well-expressed and recognized more efficiently even though massive biomedical information about DNA genes are getting larger and more complicated. In addition, the implementation of the recognized gene expression is a very important issue for the biomedical researches of DNA genes. Hence, the goal of the paper is how to improve the problematic issues more efficiently when the DNA genes are examined and implemented. The paper presents how the regulated genes of E. coli protein can be recognized by a system mining technique using neurofuzzy systems with principal component analysis.*

Keywords: bioinformatics, multivariate analysis, neurofuzzy, pattern recognition, system reduction.

1 Introduction

Recently, various statistical data analysis techniques have been applied to DNA array data to recognize or identify the characteristics of applied genes' expression. Meanwhile, there are various factors or measurements to determine the characteristics of genes from various and huge biological information. In order to differentiate the examined genes, the complexity of the procedure needs to be considered very importantly. In general, there are three levels of increasing complexity for the process in order to recognize the gene expression array [1]. The first level is the complexity of single genes to examine the tendency of each genes in isolation for comparing the control versus experimental situations. The second level is the complexity of multiple genes with analyzing the groups or clusters of genes based upon their characteristics such as functionalities, co-regulations, inter-relationships, and etc. Finally, the third level is about the analysis of the embedded structures of genes including genes' protein networks, patterns, and etc.

For recognizing the patterns or the classifications, the statistical methods can be often applied by the biological scientists. Among different types of statistical methods, multivariate analyses are frequently used to discover the newly reduced structures of the existing system without closely related measurement types. Moreover, in many cases, the examined data system cannot be presented by a mathematical expression. Hence, to compensate the weakness, a neurofuzzy system can be adapted to find out the improved solutions. Therefore, the presented paper represents how the genes expression can be classified by the reduced measurements and recognized by neurofuzzy system [2] and principal component analysis (PCA) [3][4] efficiently.

2 Review of Literature

2.1 Principal Component Analysis (PCA)

Among the statistical analysis techniques, PCA is one of the most frequently used techniques to indentify or extract the most meaningful components among the unknown under-layered components based upon the relationship between the system variables from the multi-variables data systems. Basically, principal component analysis (PCA) [5] considers the total variance in the original data to recognize the newly reduced components without closely correlated components between the meaningful factors and the variables. Shlens [3] and Smith [4] presented the procedures of PCA. The following steps briefly introduce how the procedure of PCA works.

Let X be an organize data set with an $m \times n$ matrix format, where m is the number of measurement types to represent the dimension of the data and n is the number of samples. First, standardize X by normalizing X with subtracting the mean from each measurement type. After the standardization of X, apply Singular Value Decomposition (SVD) technique to calculate the newly extracted components with the eigenvectors of the covariance. Finally, determine the most meaningful components by accumulating the calculated covariance based upon the required criterion.

2.2 Neurofuzzy System

A neurofuzzy system is a hybrid system which is a fuzzy system applied by neural network technique that uses a learning algorithm derived from examined and trained data to determine the developed system's characteristics. Jang [2] introduced Adaptive Neuro-Fuzzy Inference System (ANFIS), which represents a structure of a neurofuzzy system based upon Takagi–Sugeno fuzzy inference system using five different layers such as input layer, production layer (fuzzification), normalized firing layer (inference), consequence parameters layer (defuzzification), and finalized output layer. Fig. 1 shows the structure of ANFIS system with five network layers.

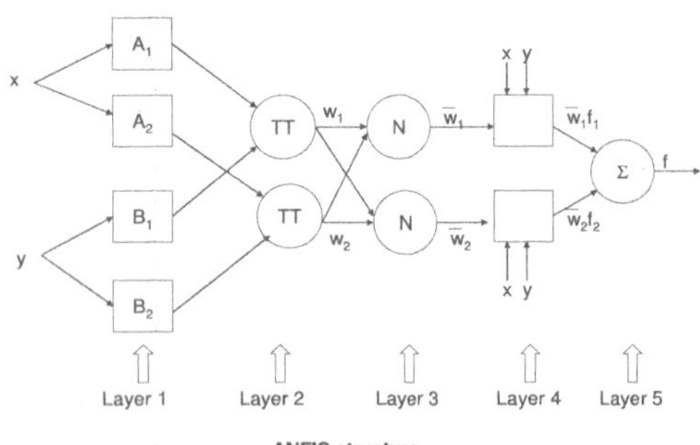

Fig. 1 Adaptive Neuro-Fuzzy Inference System (ANFIS) [2]

The output from Layer 5 from Fig. 1 by Jang [2] can be expressed as

$$O_{5,i} = \sum_i \overline{w}_i f_i = \frac{\sum_i w_i f_i}{\sum_i w_i} \quad (1)$$

with applying the following rulebase [2], such as

Rule 1: IF x is A_1 AND y is B_1

THEN $f_1 = p_1x + q_1y + r_1$

Rule 2: IF x is A_2 AND y is B_2

THEN $f_2 = p_2x + q_2y + r_2$

3 Data of regulated genes by E. coli strains [1]

Baldi and Fatfield [1] showed the experimental data of the network of genes, which are regulated by the global E. coli regulatory protein, measured by leucine-reponsive regulatory protein (Lrp), which is "a global regulatory protein that affects the expression of multiple genes and operons."[1] In general, Lrp can be measured by the activities of operons based upon the predetermined genes for biosynthetic enzymes and catabolic enzymes. In order to identify genes regulated by Lrp, four normalized measurements are used such as the mean and standard deviation of control filters, the mean and standard deviation of experimental filters differentiated by the distribution of genes with lowest p-values from Lrp of E. coli strains. TABLE 2 (Appendix) shows the collection of 39 regulated gene data expressed by four different measurements, fold, and posterior probability of differential expression (PPDE), which is a global confidence level.

4 Applied Neurofuzzy Systems

There are four different neurofuzzy systems to develop the procedures of estimating Posterior Probability of Differential Expression (PPDE) with reduced components using principal component analysis (PCA) from the five original measurements types as shown in TABLE 1. The following figures are about the neurofuzzy system with three newly extracted components from the five original measurements types. Fig. 2 shows the properties of neurofuzzy system with three inputs and an output. As shown in Fig. 3, Gaussian Bell shape functions are used for the membership functions for each input and output for the neurofuzzy system. Fig. 4 shows the applied rules for the neurofuzzy system and Fig. 5 describes how the structure of the neurofuzzy system is developed based upon ANFIS. There are five layers to extract the finalized output through fuzzification and defuzzification procedures as shown in layer 2 to layer 4 from Fig. 5.

Fig. 2 Neurofuzzy inference system with properties including three inputs and an output.

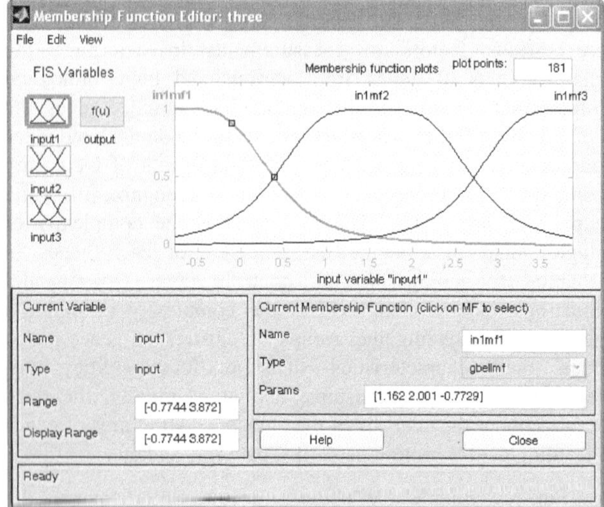

Fig. 3 Neurofuzzy inference system with membership functions

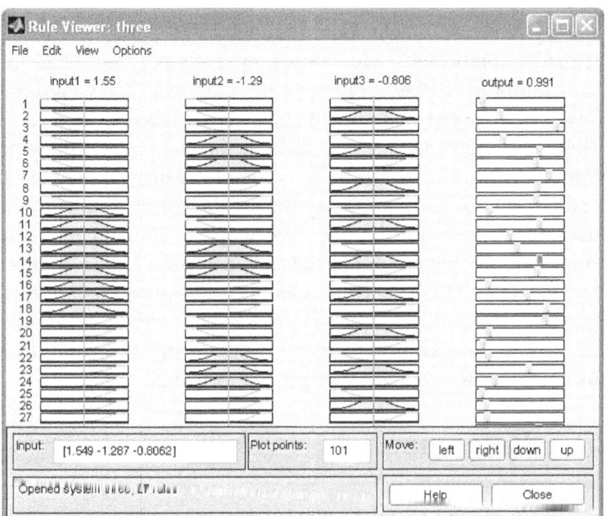

Fig. 4 Neurofuzzy inference system with applied rules for defuzzification

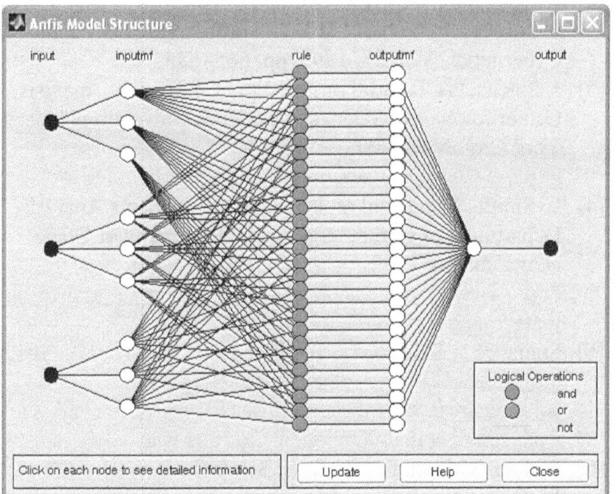

Fig. 5 ANFIS Model Sturcutre of developed Neurofuzzy inference system with three inputs

5 Analysis and Results

To identify the regulated genes of E. coli proteins, Posterior Probability of Differential Expression (PPDE) is applied as an output of each gene from the DNA gene data from TABLE 1. As shown in Fig. 6, all eigenvalues are presented based upon the reduced numbers of components from the five original measurements types. In order to decide the reduced number of components from the five original measurements types, three different cases are examined such as four, three, and two newly extracted components cases, respectively. The reduced components are compared with the five original measurements types using the statistical categories such as quadratic mean (QM), standard deviations (SD), and statistical index (SI).

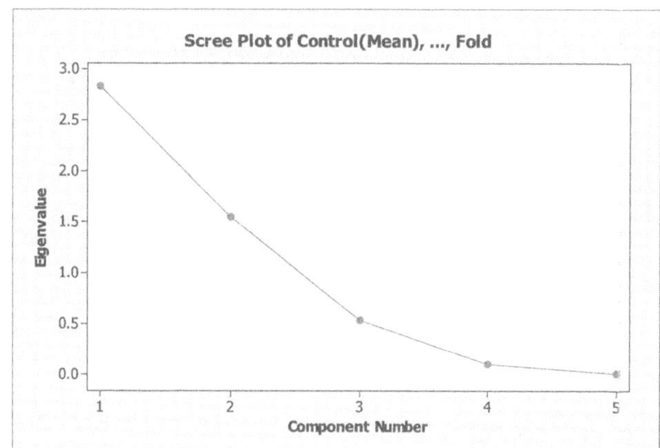

Fig. 6 The relationship between Components and Eigenvalues

TABLE 1 Statistical Analysis between extracted components with estimated values and the original values using neurofuzzy systems

	QM	SD	SI
org	0.0214	0.0551	0.0765
four	0.0689	0.1957	0.2646
three	0.0573	0.1747	0.232
two	0.034	0.106	0.14

Note: "org" is using the original data set. "four" is only using four extracted components. "three" is only using three extracted components. "two" is only using two extracted components.

Using four reduced components

Only four newly extracted components are applied to estimate the PPDE using four inputs neurofuzzy system. The values of quadratic mean and standard deviation show relatively higher than the values estimated by the neurofuzzy system with the five original components.

Using three reduced components

For the case of the evaluation with three reduced components, the statistical evaluation using neurofuzzy system with three newly extracted components is better than the evaluation from neurofuzzy system with four reduced component case even though the gene data set is not proportionally related.

Using two reduced components

Following Fig. 6, the accumulation of eigenanalysis of the correlation up to two components is about 0.875. It covers nearly 90 % of the original data. Moreover, the statistical evaluation of PPDE for genes shows the best performance among the evaluation of PPDE using the neurofuzzy systems with four or three reduced components.

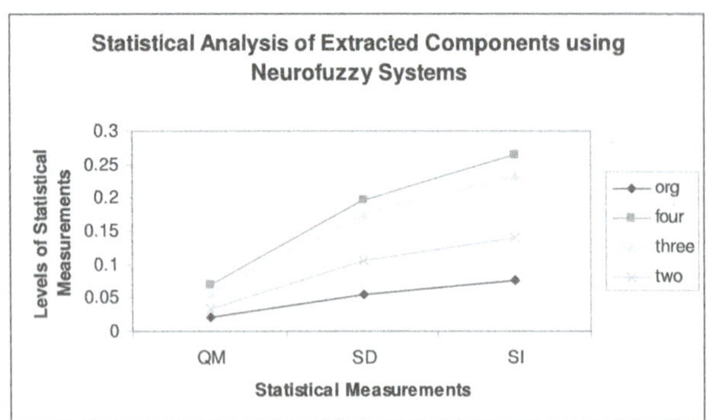

Fig. 7 Comparison of Statistical Analysis using Extracted components through neurofuzzy systems

Fig. 7 plots the statistical evaluation using four different cases with the comparison based upon the suggested statistical measurements. *org, four, three, and two* in Fig. 7 stand for the statistically evaluation with the five original components, four newly extracted components, three newly extracted components, and two newly extracted components using neurofuzzy systems, respectively. Additionally, the following categories evaluate the performance of the neuro fuzzy systems using reduced data models.

QM: Quadratic Mean or Root Mean Square [6, 7], a statistical measure of the magnitude of a varying quantity for the distance between the original output and the estimated output using the same testing data through the neurofuzzy system.

$$QM = \frac{\sum_{i=1}^{n} \sqrt{(x_i - y_i)^2}}{n-1} \qquad (2)$$

where x_i is the estimated value of PPDE using the neurofuzzy system and y_i is the original PPDE value.
SD: Standard Deviation for the distances between the original output and the estimated output using the same testing data through the neurofuzzy system.
SI: Statistical Index, a combined index from the quadratic mean and standard deviation of the statistically analyzed values by equally weighted potentially. The value, which is close to 0, is the better results.

6 Conclusion

The presented paper describes how efficiently the regulatory DNA genes expression can be expressed and identified by using five measurements types through PPDE. Three different reduced components are compared and analyzed with the estimation of PPDE values using the neurofuzzy systems developed by reduced components. Even though the data of DNA genes are not linearly related, the statistical estimation through various neurofuzzy systems using the reduced components is fairly closed to the similar estimation from the neurofuzzy system with the five original components. As shown in the paper, if the reduced components are used to recognize the DNA genes instead of five original components, the complexity of the system analysis can be reduced as well as saving the execution time without losing the significant meaning of the original DNA genes expression.

7 References

[1] P. Baldi and G. W. Fatfield, *DNA Microarrays and Gene Expression*, Cambridge University Press, Cambridge United Kingdom, 2002.

[2] J.-S.R. Jang, "ANFIS: Adaptive-Network-Based Fuzzy Inference Systems," IEEE Trans. Systems, Man & Cybernetics, Vol. 23, 1993, pp. 665–685.

[3] J. Shlens, "A Tutorial on Principal Component Analysis," Center for Neural Science, New York University, New York City, NY, 2009. http://www.snl.salk.edu/~shlens/pca.pdf

[4] L. Smith, "A tutorial on Principal Components Analysis," Department of Computer Science, University of Otago, New Zealand, 2002. http://www.cs.otago.ac.nz/cosc453/student_tutorials/principal_components.pdf

[5] Statistics Solutions Intelligence In Data, 2012. http://www.statisticssolutions.com/academic-solutions/resources/directory-of-statistical-analyses/principal-component-analysis-pca/

[6] R. Jain, R. Kasturi, and B. G. Schunck, *Machine Vision*, McGraw Hill, Boston, Massachusetts, 1995.

[7] K. V. Cartwright, "Determining the Effective or RMS Voltage of Various Waveforms without Calculus," The Technology Interface, School of Sciences and Technology, College of The Bahamas, Vol. 8, Issue 1: 20 pages, 2007.

Appendix

TABLE 2 Gene differentially expressed by Lrp measurements for E. coli strains [1]

Gene Names	Control (Mean)	Experiment (Mean)	Control (SD[1])	Experiment (SD)	Fold	PPDE[2]
oppA	0.00162000	0.03160000	0.0007630	0.01030000	19.44	1.00000
lysU	0.00018100	0.00124000	0.0000748	0.00027800	6.87	0.99999
oppB	0.00007510	0.00114000	0.0000212	0.00037900	15.12	0.99999
oppC	0.00020100	0.00108000	0.0000234	0.00036100	5.38	0.99998
oppD	0.00008970	0.00065500	0.0000276	0.00020500	7.30	0.99995
serA	0.00290000	0.00065600	0.0011400	0.00011200	-4.41	0.99994
ftn	0.00023600	0.00138000	0.0001290	0.00056400	5.84	0.99984
rmf	0.00005790	0.00147000	0.0000468	0.00033500	25.43	0.99982
hdeA	0.00024000	0.00082900	0.0000846	0.00009900	3.45	0.99982
ilvP$_G$::lacY	0.00036800	0.00147000	0.0000456	0.00081000	3.99	0.99980
hdeB	0.00039900	0.00108000	0.0002580	0.00055900	4.96	0.99977
ilvP$_G$::lacA	0.00033100	0.00183000	0.0001740	0.00074800	5.53	0.99974
artP	0.00006730	0.00042300	0.0000124	0.00011600	6.28	0.99957
artI	0.00012600	0.00058000	0.0000379	0.00028000	4.60	0.99948
gltD	0.00052800	0.00002740	0.0001280	0.00001420	-19.27	0.99943
ilvG_1	0.00042100	0.00091500	0.0000755	0.00006850	2.17	0.99916
livK	0.00041600	0.00011500	0.0001470	0.00003220	-3.61	0.99903
ybeD	0.00011300	0.00040100	0.0000170	0.00014800	3.55	0.99884
livH	0.00040500	0.00012400	0.0000818	0.00005500	-3.26	0.99880
uspA	0.00054200	0.00180000	0.0003070	0.00074300	3.32	0.99874
pheA	0.00009110	0.00034100	0.0000378	0.00004170	3.75	0.99844
grxB	0.00005950	0.00033800	0.0000192	0.00010700	5.68	0.99836
b2253	0.00042400	0.00090000	0.0000815	0.00015000	2.12	0.99827
hdhA	0.00001300	0.00021400	0.0000122	0.00002750	16.49	0.99822
gst	0.00000344	0.00007240	0.00000405	0.00002410	21.01	0.99800
oppF	0.00015700	0.00049000	0.0000282	0.00023200	3.13	0.99787
rpoE	0.00017100	0.00043500	0.0000480	0.00007290	2.55	0.99784
yhjE	0.00054400	0.00018200	0.0000688	0.00012000	-2.98	0.99773
yggB	0.00017300	0.00045000	0.0000357	0.00008500	2.61	0.99773
rpoS	0.00033500	0.00087700	0.0001210	0.00030700	2.62	0.99768
b1685	0.00003710	0.00026400	0.0000120	0.00012200	7.10	0.99743
livM	0.00068000	0.00027400	0.0001380	0.00015500	-2.48	0.99721
rseA	0.00024100	0.00058200	0.0005610	0.00013200	2.42	0.99712
ilvP$_G$::lacZ	0.00081000	0.00181000	0.0000451	0.00061700	2.24	0.99709
gdhA	0.00009160	0.00027300	0.0000152	0.00002160	2.98	0.99681
livJ	0.00116000	0.00269000	0.0005030	0.00044200	2.32	0.99669
fimA	0.00033500	0.00007820	0.0001460	0.00003080	-4.29	0.99652
trxA	0.00009050	0.00028400	0.0000299	0.00004290	3.13	0.99621
ydaR	0.00005150	0.00026200	0.0000261	0.00005610	5.08	0.99595

[1]SD stands for Standard Deviation.

[2]PPDE stands for Posterior Probability of Differential Expression.

Note: p-value column is omitted from the original table from Baldi and Fatfield. [1]

Gene Set Enrichment Analysis for a Long Time Series Gene Expression Profile

Yuta Okuma*†, Shigeto Seno*‡, Yoichi Takenaka*§, Hideo Matsuda*¶
*Graduate School of Information Science and Technology
Osaka University, 1-5, Yamadaoka, Suita, Osaka 565-0871 Japan
†Email: y-ookuma@ist.osaka-u.ac.jp
‡Email: senoo@ist.osaka-u.ac.jp
§Email: takenaka@ist.osaka-u.ac.jp
¶Email: matsuda@ist.osaka-u.ac.jp

***Abstract*—Gene Set Enrichment Analysis(GSEA) is a method of analyzing microarray data that can be used to determine whether a microarray data set indicates significant biological changes in the expression of an a priori-defined set of genes. However, GSEA cannot be applied to time series data because of the multiple time points and seamless nature of such data. Therefore, we have developed a new GSEA method of analyzing time series data. We compared our new GSEA method with its traditional counterpart in an examination of mouse adipocyte differentiation data. Compared with the conventional method, our GSEA method detected a larger number of gene sets. Using the new method, we can detect periods of gene expression that cannot be found using the conventional GSEA, i.e., our method can identify the significant expression period for each gene set. This capability is necessary for examining the changes that occur in living organisms.**

Keywords*—*Gene Set Enrichment Analysis, sliding window approach, microarray.

I. Background

All living things possess genes and control gene expression to generate RNA and proteins. The analysis of gene expression with DNA microarrays is valuable for elucidating biological process [1] [2]. There are many methods of analyzing gene expression, e.g., between-subjects [3], clustering [4], and gene network analyses [5]. The method should be chosen based on the research objective. The results of many studies have demonstrated that genes work within networks, not alone. Genes interact with each other in networks, and they promote or inhibit the expression of other genes to maintain biological functions. Thus, a method of analyzing DNA microarray data as gene sets, not individual genes, is suitable for the analysis of living organisms.

With respect to gene expression analyses, time series data can be meaningful because genes are expressed over time. When researchers want to examine changes in living things, e.g., cell differentiation, they cannot avoid using time series data. Moreover, microarray data can be analyzed using gene annotations and other a priori-defined data, which makes acquiring new knowledge using gene databases and time series experiments desirable.

Gene Set Enrichment Analysis(GSEA) [6] is a method of analyzing gene expression by evaluating the expression of *a priori*-defined gene sets rather than the individual expression of each gene. This method can be used to examine a gene expression profile that is divided into two or more experimental conditions. GSEA can also compare two or more biological states for each gene set. When GSEA compares two groups, the genes are ranked according to statistical results. Using these rankings, GSEA evaluates the expression of *a priori*-defined gene sets to produce an enrichment score(ES) for each gene set. The ES indicates the expression level of the gene set. GSEA utilizes the ES to analyze the gene set.

GSEA is a useful statistical method with many variations such as PAGE [7], PGSEA [7], Gene Tail [8], SAM-GS [9], and GSEA-P [10]. These methods use gene annotations as the known information to create the gene sets. By analyzing gene expression profiles using gene sets(not individual genes), we can determine the expression of genes with vital biological functions in common. GSEA methods are distinguished from other methods by the statistics or execution environment used [11].
There are many GSEA-related methods, some of which can analyze a simple time series, e.g., gene sets whose expression increases monotonically. However, most GSEA-related methods cannot analyze a time series gene expression profile because the conventional form of GSEA applies to data that reflect multiple phenotypes. GSEA has limited utility for examining time series data involving many time points because it cannot divide the data into discrete subsets.

In this study, we describe a method that enables the analysis of time series gene expression profiles for each gene function with the use of a gene database. With large-scale time series data as the input, this method can identify the significant expression periods of a gene set.

II. Gene Set Enrichment Analysis

Our method is derived from the conventional GSEA method, which uses the Kolmogorov-Smirnov test to convert the expression level of each gene set to a score. This scores and test are also used in our method [6].

A. Overview

GSEA uses gene annotations as the known information to establish gene sets. Before the analysis is begun, gene sets are created from the information in a database and the expression data. The purpose of this analysis is to compare two groups, e.g., "cancer patient group X and healthy control group Y" or "tissue X and tissue Y." The genes are ranked according to a certain standard, and each gene set receives a score corresponding to its rank in the set. By comparing these scores, we can determine that genes with function A are expressed in group X but not in group Y.

B. Gene sets

GSEA adopts gene sets with previously identified functions. A gene set is defined as a cluster of genes with the same function. Several publically available databases are utilized for this type of analysis. The Gene Ontology database is used frequently because it contains many gene sets with detailed classifications. These classifications employ "GO terms," which are divided into three categories

- biological process
- cellular component
- molecular function

In Gene Ontology, gene functions are constructed as a hierarchical structure. GO terms that belong to the upper layers are more general than those in the lower layers. Because there are numerous gene functions, researchers should choose which category or gene sets they will use. Many researchers analyze gene expression using gene sets or pathways [12] [13] [14].

C. Gene ranking

In GSEA, a score that represents the degree of the expression of a gene set is computed using the gene rank as the standard. To calculate the gene rank, each gene's statistic is compared between two groups. Then, the gene with the higher expression variation ratio receives a higher rank. The statistical tests used in GSEA are provided in TableI. For example, the statistic of gene i for the signal-to-noise ratio is expressed by formula(1):

$$R(i) = \frac{\overline{X^i} - \overline{Y^i}}{U_{X^i} + U_{Y^i}} \tag{1}$$

When statistics are calculated as a signal-to-noise ratio, genes with a large variation in the average expression level and small dispersion of expression in each group receive the highest ranks. The t statistic is calculated using the t-test and is represented by formula(2):

$$R(i) = \frac{\overline{X^i} - \overline{Y^i}}{\sqrt{\frac{1}{n_A} + \frac{1}{n_B}}\sqrt{\frac{(n_A-1)U_{Ai}^2 + (n_B-1)U_{Bi}^2}{n_A+n_B-2}}} \tag{2}$$

Using the t statistic, genes with large $|R(i)|$ values are identified. There are two types of statistic: one has plus and minus and the other has only plus. Signal-to-noise and gene expression ratios are examples of the former type of statistic; they express the degree and direction of the statistical change. The t-statistic and weighted average difference(WAD)

TABLE I. STATISTICS USED IN GSEA

Statistic	Method of ranking
signal-to-noise ratio	Genes with a large gap between two groups and small dispersion receive a higher rank.
t statistic	Genes are ranked according to the absolute value of the t statistic.
weighted average difference(WAD)	Genes are ranked using the log ration as the standard.

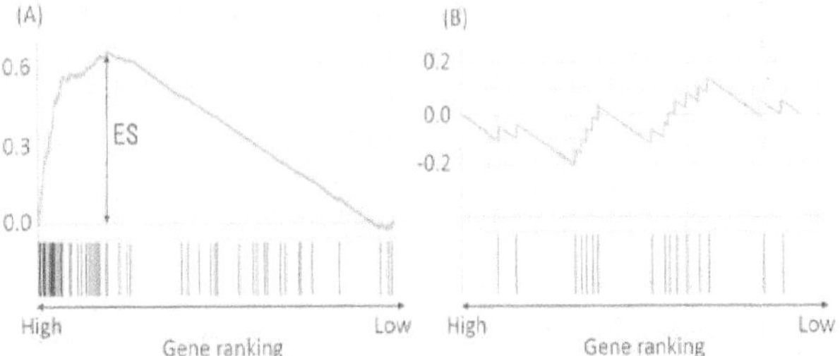

Fig. 1. This figure shows examples of high ES and low ES. ES is defined as the maximum deviation from zero. The black bars under the graph indicate the gene sets' genes and the location represent genes' ranks. The left panel indicates a gene set with a ES because it contains many genes with high ranks. The gene set in the right panel has a lower ES than the left because the genes are more evenly distributed.

are examples of the latter type; they indicate only the degree of change.

Researchers who want to determine the level of expression of a gene set should use the t-statistic or WAD. However, if they want to identify both the level of expression and which the group that a gene set is expressed in, they should use the signal-to-noise ratio. [15]

D. Enrichment score

The enrichment score(ES) is computed based on a genes' rank, which is determined by the signal-to-noise ratio. Therefore, the ES represents the gene set's expression ratio. We assume that the total number of genes is N, a gene set is S and a ranked gene list is L. Then, we examine the list from top to bottom. If a gene in set S appears in the list L, we classify it as S("hit"). In contrast, if that gene does not appear in L, we classify it as S("miss"). Their weight is calculated by formula(3) and formula(4):

$$P_{hit}(S,i) = \sum_{\substack{g_j \in S \\ j \leq i}} \frac{|r_j|^p}{N_R}, where N_R = \sum_{g_j \in S} |r_j|^p \tag{3}$$

$$P_{miss}(S,i) = \sum_{\substack{g_j \notin S \\ j \leq i}} \frac{1}{(N - N_H)} \tag{4}$$

In these formulas, p is the value used to adjust the weight at each step. The ES is defined as the margin between P_{hit} and P_{miss}. In other words, if a gene set has many genes at the top of the list, its score is high, as shown in Figure 1 (left). In the contrast, if the gene expression ratio of gene in a gene set is scattered, the ES is low, as shown in Fig. 1. (right). Some gene sets contain many genes, whereas others have few genes. The ES of a group with many genes tends to be high, and the ES of a group with few genes tends to be low. These tendencies are the reason why gene sets cannot be compared using the ES alone. To compare multiple gene sets, we should use the normalized enrichment score(NES), which is computed by random sampling. Assuming that random sampling is performed M times, we represent i^{th} ES as ES_i, and the NES is computed by formula(5):

$$\text{NES} = \frac{ES}{\frac{1}{M}\sum_{i=1}^{M} ES_i} \quad (5)$$

Because the NES represents a normalized score, the NES is not influenced by the number of genes in the group; i.e., the NES is a comparable score.

III. Gene Set Enrichment Analysis for a Time-series Gene Expression Profile

The conventional GSEA assumes that the input data consist of a gene expression profile based on two phenotypes or two biological states. Even if time series data are input into the GSEA, only two groups can be analyzed. In our method, we first extract a fixed time period from the beginning of gene expression until the end using the sliding window method. Then, we compare the extracted interval to the rest of dataset. Our method can handle a time series gene expression profile by comparing two groups at all the extracted intervals. The result of these comparisons is a score based on the rate of variability in the gene expression. We examine this score from two perspectives, "time" and "genes." The period when a gene function is significantly expressed is considered the output. An overview of the proposed method follows, and Fig. 2. shows a general view of the method.

A. Overview

In the first step, we decide the target (window) size and slide it from the start to the end of the input data. Then, we determine the ranks based on the rate of variability in the gene expression, and we compute the ES based on the rank.
In the next step, we confirm whether the score computed in the first step is significantly higher than the other scores. This step is divided into two parts because we must test two types of significance. Then, we perform two comparisons: one among the gene sets and the other among the time intervals. The intervals in which a gene set is significantly expressed are the output. The details of each step are described in following sections.

B. STEP1:Determining the extraction area and computing the ES for each area

In this step, we determine the extraction area and compute ES

1) We determine the extraction area size (window size), w, and the number of time points, t
2) We place the window on the first time point; the time points under the window are the target area. We compare the target area with the other areas.
3) We slide the window one time point. To repeat this process, we create a new target.
4) For each target, we calculate the gene ranks and compute the ES based on these ranks.

The number of target areas is calculated as (t - w + 1), and we represent the target region as T_1, T_2, ... T_{t-w+1}. At point 4 of STEP 1, we obtain all the targets' ES values. In the following step (STEP 2), we test whether a gene set is significantly expressed in the target area.

C. STEP2:Testing for results

In this study, we compare the ESs to determine the result terms. However, an ES may be calculated erroneously; therefore we must confirm the significance of each ES. To determine the expression significance, we must assess the time significance and the genetic significance. To test the significance of time, we perform random sampling from all the data M times. Then, we compute the ES for each time and create an ES distribution. Finally, we determine whether the original ES was expressed significantly at the term from the position of the original ES in the ES distribution (STEP 2.1). Following the same procedure, we judge the significance of all the genes by performing random sampling. Random sampling means that we select from among all the genes the same number of genes that was contained in the original gene set. Then, we perform random sampling M times, create an ES distribution and check the original ES position within the ES distribution (STEP 2.2). We use the Kolmogorov-Smirnov test for these two tests. The results of these tests are the p value and false discovery rate (FDR) for each gene set. The p value reflects the probability that the ES of the gene set was calculated by chance. The FDR is the probability that insignificant scores were incorrectly identified as significant.

1) STEP2.1:Testing for time significance: In this section, we test for term T_j with the following testing algorithm:

1) We perform random sampling M times from all the time points and calculate ES_1, ES_2, ..., ES_M.
2) We create an ES distribution based on the ES calculated at point 1.
3) We compute the appearance probability (p) of the original ES and the FDR.

In this step random sampling means that we select the same number of time points as T_j and compute the ES for the same genes. Additionally, during the random sampling, we do not have to select continuous time points, i.e., we compute ES M times for the changing time points that we select. Using the Kolmogorov-Smirnov test, we can obtain the p value and FDR. The p value calculated at STEP 2.1.3 is determined by formula(6):

$$Pr(ES(N, N_H) \leq \lambda) = \sum_{k=-\infty}^{\infty} (-1)^k \exp(-2k^2\lambda^2 n) \quad (6a)$$

$$n = \frac{(N - N_H)N_H}{N} \quad (6b)$$

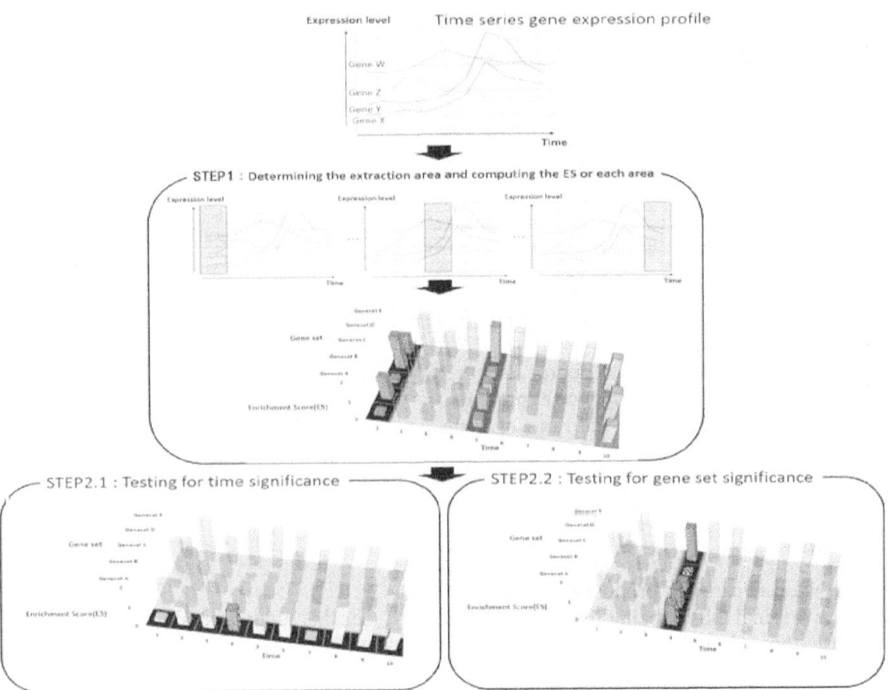

Fig. 2. Overview of the proposed method.

λ represents ES in the formula, and N_H indicates the number of genes included in gene set H. The FDR is the estimated probability that a gene set with a given NES represents a false positive finding. For example, an FDR of 25% indicates that the result is likely to be valid three out of four times. Assuming that a gene set is significantly at T_j, when the random sampling for time is performed, the mean value of the ES will be smaller than the original ES. In contrast, when a gene set is not significantly expressed at T_j, the original ES will be similar to the mean value of the ES.

2) STEP2.2:Testing for gene set significance: If we can find the time interval when a gene set is significantly expressed at STEP 2, then we have confirmed the time significance. However, this confirmation is not sufficient because we have not accounted for errors that may have occurred during the measurements. For example, assuming that there is a constant increase during a certain time interval, an analysis of that interval will indicate that all the gene sets exhibit significant expression. Accordingly, we must examine the result of STEP 2 for the genes. In this section, we assume that gene set S is significantly expressed at term T_j. The testing algorithm for the genes is performed as follows:

1) We perform random sampling M times from all the genes on T_j and calculate ES_1, ES_2, ..., ES_M.
2) We create an ES distribution based on the ES calculated at substep 2.2.1.
3) We compute the appearance probability (p) of the original ES and the FDR.

In this step, random sampling means that we select the same number of genes as that of S from all the genes at random. If we can confirm that S is significantly expressed at this step, we can assert that gene set S is significantly expressed at T_j. In brief, if a period that passes two tests (STEP 2.1 and STEP 2.2) exists, our objective has been achieved.

IV. Experiments and Results

To verify the effectiveness of the proposed method, we described two experiments. In the first experiment, we compare the proposed method with the conventional method to determine if there are any differences between the outputs of the two methods. The second experiment reveals the expression period of the gene set that is determined by the proposed method. We also determine whether the detected period is reasonable from a biological point of view.

A. Experimental condition

Input data

- Time series gene expression profile

We use a time series expression profile of mouse adipocyte differentiation and osteoblast differentiation. The sampling time points are 0, 5, 15, 30 and 45 minutes (5 points); 1, 2, ... and 30 hours (30 points); and 36, 42, ..., 186 and 192 hours (27 points), for a total of 62 time points. This gene expression profile contains 21,947 genes.

- Gene sets

We use 948 gene sets that belong to Gene Ontology's biological process, cellular component and molecular function categories; each set contains more than 25 genes.

Definition of variables and method

- Window size

In this experiment, we set the window size at 10 time points. Then, we slide this window from the start to the end of the data.

• Threshold

The p value, which is computed using the Kolmogorov-Smirnov test, is used as the threshold. Furthermore, we use the Bonferroni correction because we perform multiple analyses. When we use a window with a size of 10, we execute 53 analyses. Thus, the threshold is calculated using formula(7).

$$threshold p = \frac{p}{N} = \frac{0.15}{53} = 0.00471698... \sim 0.0047 \quad (7)$$

• Gene ranking method

In this experiment, we evaluate not only the degree of gene expression but also the increase or decrease in gene expression. Thus, we perform the ranking according to the ratio of gene expression.

B. Experiment 1: Comparison of the proposed method with the conventional method

In this experiment, we compare the proposed and conventional methods, with the original GSEA being the conventional method. When we use the original GSEA, we divide the input data into two parts because adipocyte differentiation is divided into two waves [16]. The first wave that occurs between 4 and 24 hours coordinates the transient formation of early enhanceosomes at transcription factor hotspots. The second wave that occurs between 2 and 6 days coordinates the assembly of late enhanceosomes at the same hotspots. Then, we perform two comparative experiments. At first, we compare the first wave period with the other period using the original GSEA. Next, we compare the second wave period with the other period using the original GSEA. The image of this experiment is shown in Fig. 3. In both experiments, we detect the significant expression periods of only one gene set. In contrast, our method detects the expression periods of many gene sets. The number of gene sets which can be detected by proposed method and conventional method are presented in Table II. The gene sets in Table II are important functions for adipocyte differentiation [16]. A total of 128 gene sets are detected by the proposed method, of which 16 gene sets are related to the first and second waves.

C. Experiment2: Validation of the result of the proposed method from a biological standpoint

Although our proposed method can detect numerous expression periods, we have not confirmed whether there are any contradictions in the results. To do so, we count the numbers of gene sets that are related to the first and second waves. The first wave contains gene sets that are related to the cell cycle, ribosomes and translation. The second wave contains gene sets that are related to lipid metabolism, glucose metabolism, lipid binding, mitochondria and transport. The results for all the gene sets are shown in Table III, and the gene sets that are related to the first and second waves are shown in Fig. 4. Based on the these results, most of the gene sets are in the first or second wave, which indicates that the results of the proposed method dovetail with the biological aspects of living organisms.

TABLE II. THE RESULTS OF EXPERIMENT 2: THE NUMBERS OF GENE SETS IN THE FIRST AND SECOND WAVES OF EXPRESSION(DETECTED / ALL).

Wave	Gene set	Proposed method	conventional method
First wave	Cell cycle	0 / 18	0 / 18
	Ribosome	1 / 4	0 / 4
	Translation	2 / 20	1 / 20
Second wave	Lipid metabolism	2 / 29	0 / 29
	Glucose metabolism	0 / 1	0 / 1
	Lipid binding	1 / 2	0 / 2
	Mitochondria	3 / 15	0 / 15
	Transport	7 / 14	0 / 14
Total		16 / 103	1 / 103

TABLE III. THE DETAILED EXPERIMENTAL RESULTS. SOME GENE SETS ARE COUNTED IN TWO AREAS; THUS, THE TOTAL IS DIFFERS FROM THE TOTAL NUMBER OF GENE SETS THAT ARE DETECTED BY THE PROPOSED METHOD.

	Number of gene sets
First wave	23
Second wave	117
Other periods	15

V. CONCLUSIONS

In this study, we show that we can determine the periods when gene sets are significantly expressed using the proposed method. In the experimental chapter, we verify that we detect more gene sets using the proposed method than using the original GSEA method and that the proposed method can be adapted to time series data. Moreover, there are no contradictions in the results from a biological viewpoint. In our experiments, we used constant value as the window size. But the expression periods are differ according to gene functions or phenomenon. Then, our future work is to develop the method that can estimate appropriate value for each gene set and adapt it dynamically.

ACKNOWLEDGMENT

The present study was supported in part by Grants-in-Aid for Scientific Research(Nos.22680023, 24700294, and 22310125) from the Japan Society for the Promotion of Science(JSPS) and by the SPIRE Supercomputational Life Science through the Ministry of Education, Culture, Sports, Science and Technology of Japan(MEXT).

REFERENCES

[1] M. Schena, D. Shalon, R. W. Davis and P. O. Brown, "Quantitative monitoring of gene expression patterns with a complementary dna microarray," *Science*, vol. 270, no. 5235, pp. 467–470, 1995.

[2] D. J. Lockhart, H. Dong, M. C. Byrne, M. T. Follettie, M. V. Gallo, M. S. Chee, M. Mittmann, C. Wang, M. Kobayashi, H. Horton and E. L. Brown, "Expression monitoring by hybridization to high-density oligonucleotide arrays," *Nat Biotechnol*, vol. 14, no. 13, pp. 1675–1680, 1996.

[3] V. G. Tusher, R. Tibshirani and G. Chu, "Significance analysis of microarrays applied to the ionizing radiation response," *Proc Natl Acad Sci U S A.*, vol. 98, pp. 5116–5121, 2001.

[4] D. Jiang, C. Tang and A. Zhang, "Cluster analysis for gene expression data: a survey," *Knowledge and Data Engineering, IEEE Transactions on*, vol. 16, pp. 1370 – 1386, 2004.

[5] H. Toh and K. Horimoto, "Inference of a genetic network by a combined approach of cluster analysis and graphical gaussian modeling," *Bioinformatics*, vol. 18, pp. 287 – 297, 2002.

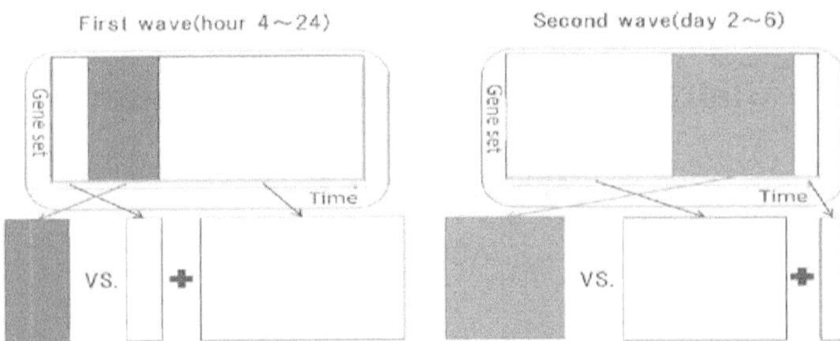

Fig. 3. An image of the input data for the conventional method. The painted area is target area, and the non-painted area is the area to be compared. In GSEA, the expression of the gene sets' is compared between these two areas. From these analyses, we can obtain the result when we perform GSEA as if we know the best expression period.

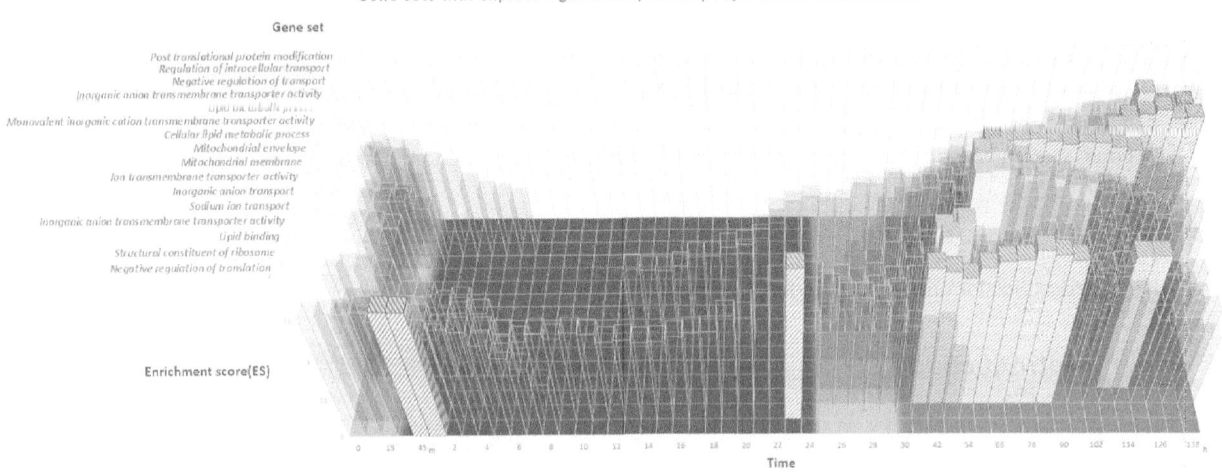

Fig. 4. The results of the proposed method. This figure is plotted with time as the horizontal axis, ES as the vertical axis and gene sets as the depth axis. The painted bars indicate the significant intervals and clear bars mean that gene sets are expressed in the intervals, but their expressions are not significant. In this figure, we plot only positive ESs. Because, positive ES means "a gene set is expressed in the interval" and we want to detect gene sets that are expressed significantly in the window. These gene sets are related to the first and second waves of expression. The first wave includes gene sets that are related to ribosomes or translation. The second wave includes gene sets that are related to lipid metabolism, lipid binding, mitochondria or transport.

[6] A. Subramanian, P. Tamayo, V. K. Mootha, S. Mukherjee, B. L. Ebert, M. A. Gillette, A. Paulovich, S. L. Pomeroy, T. R. Golub, E. S. Landerb and J. P. Mesirov, "Gene set enrichment analysis: a knowledge-based approach for interpreting genome-wide expression profiles," *Proc Natl Acad Sci U S A*, vol. 102, pp. 15 545 – 15 550, 2005.

[7] S. Y. Kim and D. J. Volsky, "Page: parametric analysis of gene set enrichment," *BMC Bioinformatics*, vol. 6, p. 144, 2005.

[8] C. Backes, A. Keller, J. Kuentzer, B. Kneissl, N. Comtesse, Y. A. Elnakady, R. Müller, E. Meese and H. P. Lenhof, "Genetrail-advanced gene set enrichment analysis," *Nucleic Acids Research*, vol. 35, pp. 186 – 192, 2007.

[9] I. Dinu, J. D. Potter, T. Mueller, Q. Liu, A. J. Adewale, G. S. Jhangri, G. Einecke, K. S. Famulski, P. Halloran and Y. Yasui, "Improving gene set analysis of microarray data by sam-gs," *BMC Bioinformatics*, vol. 8, p. 242, 2007.

[10] A. Subramanian, H. Kuehn, J. Gould, P. Tamayo and J. P. Mesirov, "Gsea-p: a desktop application for gene set enrichment analysis," *Bioinformatics*, vol. 23, pp. 3251 – 3253, 2007.

[11] J. J. Goeman and P. Bühlmann, "Analyzing gene expression data in terms of gene sets: methodological issues," *Bioinformatics*, vol. 23, no. 8, pp. 980–987, 2007.

[12] S. W. Doniger, N. Salomonis, K. D. Dahlquist, K. Vranizan, S. C. Lawlor and B. R. Conklin, "Mappfinder: using gene ontology and genmapp to create a global gene-expression profile from microarray data," *Genome Biol*, vol. 4, p. R7, 2003.

[13] S. Zhong, K. F. Storch, O. Lipan, M. C. Kao, C. J. Weitz and W. H. Wong, "Gosurfer: a graphical interactive tool for comparative analysis of large gene sets in gene ontology space," *Appl Bioinformatics*, vol. 3, pp. 261 – 264, 2004.

[14] G. F. Berriz, O. D. King, B. Bryant, C. Sander and F. P. Roth, "Characterizing gene sets with funcassociate," *Bioinformatics*, vol. 19, pp. 2502 – 2504, 2003.

[15] M. Ackermann and K. Strimmer, "A general modular framework for gene set enrichment analysis," *BMC Bioinformatics*, vol. 10, p. 47, 2009.

[16] R. Siersbæk, R. Nielsen and S. Mandrup, "Transcriptional networks and chromatin remodeling controlling adipogenesis," *Trends in Endocrinology and Metabolism*, vol. 23, pp. 56–64, 2012.

Customized Biomedical Informatics

Abhishek Narain Singh

ABI-O-TECH

abhishek.narain@cantab.net

Abstract. Structural variations, SVs, with size 1 base-pair to several 1000s of base-pairs with their precise breakpoints and single-nucleotide polymorphisms, SNPs, were determined for members of a family of four. It is also discovered that the mitochondrial DNA is less prone to SVs re-arrangements than SNPs and can have paternal leakage of inheritance which proposes better standards for determining ancestry and divergence between races and species. Sex determination of an individual is found to be strongly confirmed by means of calls of nucleotide bases of SVs to the Y chromosome. SVs would serve as fingerprint of an individual contributing to his traits and drug responses. These in silico techniques for analysis would become such a widespread application that a total transformation of the bio and medical industry would go through.

Keywords: bioinformatics, high performance computing, medical informatics

1 Introduction

Sequencing is hard, but interpretation of 'big data' can be much more tougher. Technology and thereby machinery has been advancing rapidly and the cost of associated with it is reducing at a significant pace in the area of sequencing DNA. We once had the standard Sanger sequencing technology about a decade ago, which was used to complete the draft of first human genome sequence. Over the years, the technology advanced to introduce paired end sequences where the sequence can be determined at either end of a fragment and the insert size in between the ends can be roughly known apriori. Though the accuracy of this sequence or the base quality is not always reliable, significant lower cost of this technology can allow multiple sequencing of the region of interest which is also known as sequencing coverage, so as to then take the consensus at a region of interest to determine the sequence. Usually a higher average coverage is preferred, and given the various softwares we have for analysis or assembly, typically the coverage should be above 12x for reasonable reliability. The high false discovery rate of structural variation algorithms even in deeply sequenced individual genomes of the order of 30x average coverage [1,2] suggests that for lower coverage the problem will be even more to get rid of false positives. Nevertheless, the results with coverage as less as 3-5x also could have a lot of meaningful findings, and could be deployed for several genomes analysis which would make sense on a population wide scale at relatively less cost, such as in the 1000 genomes project.

Variations at specific loci in genome have been associated with recurrent genomic rearrangements as well as with a variety of diseases, including color blindness, psoriasis, HIV susceptibility, Crohn's disease and lupus glomerulonephritis [3-8]. This only enhances the importance of comprehensive catalogue for genotype and phenotype correlation studies [1-8] in particular when the rare or multiple variations in gene underlie characteristic or disease susceptibility [9,10]. Microarrays [11-13] and sequencing [14-17] reveal that structural variants (SVs) contribution is significant in characterizing population [18] and disease [19] characteristics. Interestingly in particular the HLA domain in chromosome VI of an individual which is the

MHC region in humans, would be interesting in being decoded for the variations, as a lesser difference between two individual could imply stronger success possibility of organ transplant. In general, the HLA domain variation would give an insight in immunologic responses. However, we must be careful with the results we get when we call for the variations, as any difference could represent actual difference between the DNA sources, an assembly artifact (clone-induced or computational) or alignment error. With time the sequencing of human genomes now become routine [1], the spectrum of structural variants and copy number variants (CNVs) has widened to include much smaller events. The important aspect now is to know how genomes vary at large as well as fine scales and by what magnitude does it impact a population in general and an individual in particular. The challenge now is to understand its effects on human disease, characteristic traits and phylogenetic evolutionary clues thus having its large impact in medical and forensic area apart from enriching us of mankind evolutionary history.

There has been several new tools made available which can detect variations without the need for assembling the genome for the individual such as those used in the 1000 Genome Project consortium which finds great applicability in case the coverage of sequences is low[1] and has so to speak yet have a profound impact at a population level. However, if the sequencing coverage is reasonably higher such as above 12x in average so to speak in a comparative sense from the data in 1000 Genome Project, then there is no reason as to why assembling the genome and then mapping to a reference genome to detect variations directly should not be the adopted method. In this article, we share result of the variations detected in a family of four individuals viz., father, mother, and two daughters.

2 Materials and Methods

Blood samples of a family were collected in Amsterdam, though they might not be individuals who are direct Dutch descent as Amsterdam is a fairly cosmopolitan city. Naming them anonymously they are A105A, A105B, A105C and A105D respectively. The DNA was extracted and sequenced on Illumina HiSeq sequencer with an average coverage of more than 12x across the genome and with the raw read length of 90 bases at either ends of the paired-end reads with an average insert size of about 470 bases. It would not matter if the sequences are mate-pair or paired-end reads as the difference lies more in the wet-bench technique, and as far as the computational algorithms are concerned it would not matter. As there are many copies of mitochondrial DNA in a cell, the sequencing coverage of mitochondrial DNA would be several folds higher than 12x. The reads were then assembled into respective contigs using parallel assembler ABySS version 1.3.1 with optimal parameters of kmer size (k) of 49 and minimum reads to make a consensus contigs (n) of 3 to yield highest possible N50 value for the contigs ~3000. SSPACE scaffolding tool was also used for assembly. On average it required about 140 GB of RAM in a shared environment and 49 computing wall-clock hours on an symmetric multi-processor cluster with 6 computing cores each of capacity 2.6 GHz. The assemblies of the four individuals were then aligned globally in a parallel computing approach to the NCBI human reference genome, Build 37, followed by extraction of SVs information of category insertions and deletions only (InDels), and single nucleotide polymorphisms (SNPs) on regions of misalignment [20,21]. Figure A summarises the various classes of variations in genomes of individuals found. Genome comparison plot for the A105 family using GenomeBreak is shown in Figure B where one can graphically get estimates of regions of alignments and mis-alignments with the reference genome NCBI HuRef build 37.

The total time for the alignment and extraction of information on a single computing core of 2.6 GHz capacity came out to about 85 wall-clock hours, for each individual assembly. Given that the sequencing technology is expected to improve in the next couple of years not just in the length of the reads at either ends but also in terms of quality of confidence in the letters, future versions of assembly softwares will provide more reliable assembly to be generated and more quickly. It can also be safely assumed looking at the current trend past few years that the cost of sequencing would also be dropping further, which would imply that sequencing with much higher coverage of up to 40x average would become more a routine practice. An important challenge would be requirement of high disk space in order to manage data explosion with simply maintaining the raw data or any intermediate data and downstream results. In order to save disk space, an interesting approach could be to simply store the mis-alignments of the individual genome rather than the whole genome. The whole genome raw data and assembly could be put in tape which are less expensive and yet can store the data reliably. One important aspect that has always been an underpinning concern in most bioinformatics software applications has been disk I/O and interprocessor communication bandwidth in case using any of the tools in parallel mode. Another aspect which is crucial for making prediction is the sensitivity and specificity of the algorithm used. Specificity has been kept as a preferred choice of the mode of operation of the softwares, as then the hypothesis which we make from relational comparison has stronger level of confidence. At the same time, once these tools and approaches are used for routine application, there is no reason why we cannot switch to a sensitive mode of using these tools in order to capture more possibilities of variations, though it will obviously be increasing more false-positive cases.

3 Results and Discussions

A clear application of finding the variations in an individual is in conducting an organ transplant surgery and getting to know a-priori a disposition of an individual or population to a disease. If the immunologic responses after the grafting of an organ from a donor to the receptor are known beforehand to conducting the transplant, we can be more predictive of the chances of success of the transplantation. The immunologic responses are dictated by the MHC region of the genome, which in humans corresponds to the HLA domain in chromosome VI. So in essence if we extract the SVs and SNPs of chromosome VI of the donor individual and compare it with the SVs and SNPs of acceptor patient's chromosome VI, then it can be reasonably proposed that the lower the differences between the two sets of SVs and SNPs, the higher the success possibility of organ transplant. However, even with these SVs and SNPs a subset could be more crucial to be identical or being absent perhaps for the transplantation to be successful. Similarly if we are interested in any other particular chromosome which has been known of having strongly been associated with a particular phenotype or characteristic trait, we can extract the SVs and SNPs for the particular chromosome and conduct a relational database analysis. Below in Figure C is the plot of the sum of the bases of InDels and SNPs for chromosome XX of A105 family. It is interesting to see that the sum of the bases of InDels have increased in the children when compared to their parents while the levels of SNPs remain more or less the same.

It would yet be interesting that there might be situation where we would simply like to know genome-wide SVs and SNPs of an individual. Figure D is a plot of the sum of the bases of SVs and SNPs respectively for the whole genome determined for A105 family. Here again we notice that the children have relatively higher number of bases for SVs than their parents, though the levels of SNPs remain more or less the same. This finding thus proposes that even in one generation of the offsprings, there can be significant rearrangement in the genetic background to produce greater variations in genotype and thereby having an effect on phenotypes, and that the children are not an exact clone of the set of chromosomes they inherited from either parents as there will be significant variation even when simply compared to the chromosomes of the parents that they inherited. The changes in SNPs are more restricted than insertions or deletions, and thus SVs serve as a stronger means as a fingerprint and characteristics of an individual when analysed genome-wide.

With the advent of rapid advancement of technology, coupled with decrease in cost of sequencing, it will not be long when every individual will carry their genome-chip which would be comprising of the set of chromosomal sequences, along with information of SVs and SNPs already determined. Many ventures have already started on this line to tap upon the opportunities that this changing world of medical informatics and genomics has to offer. In fact, this would be a practice which we might want to do early in the life of an individual say within a week after his birth. Lets say we take it a step further and obtain the DNA sample from the fetus itself, thus being able to do analysis of the baby which is to be born. With the power of prediction and integrating it to powerful relational databases we can tell a-priori as to what are the chances of the baby to be healthy in general. We would be able to predict disease susceptibility of the new born baby as well as characteristic traits a-priori, thereby given an opportunity for the mother to decide whether to have the baby or not, and if so what all things she should be caring about. We would also be able to determine the sex of the baby before it is born, thereby provide an alternative and safer means to determine the sex of the baby, without any extra cost, as the genome of the baby will be sequenced and analysed anyways. As an example in Figure E and Figure F you will see that the calls of bases on Y chromosome of InDels and SNPs respectively is far higher for the father than the mother or the two daughters, thereby clearly being able to differentiate male from female. It is also observed that the difference in the calls of sum of bases for InDels is far higher than the calls for the sum of the bases for SNPs, thereby proposing that the former is a stronger means to determine the sex of an individual than the latter. This also proposes that contrary to what is observed genome-wide, the SVs have higher selection pressure than the SNPs in the Y-chromosome. It is to be noted that though a woman does not have a Y-chromosome, yet since Y-chromosome like any other chromosome is prone to crossing-over phenomena, there can be other chromosome which have sections of Y-chromosome DNA in it, and thus that is reflected in aligning the Y-chromosome to the whole genome of a female with successful alignment at certain section, thereby enabling extraction of SNPs and SVs around the region aligned.

As the mitochondrial DNA (mtDNA) is known to have several copies in a cell, one would expect far higher coverage of mitochondrial DNA sequence than the rest of the genome, such as average of more than 12x in our case. The sequence assembly of mitochondrial DNA thus will have far higher reliability, following which the downstream analysis as well. From the already existing knowledge of inheritance of mitochondrial DNA, one would expect all the SNPs and SVs successful calls in mother to be found in all the children as well, as mitochondrial DNA is known to be maternally inherited. This is because mitochondrial DNA material is present in the cytosol of a cell and not in the nucleus, and there is lesser possibility for the cytosol of the sperm cells to integrate with the cytosol of mother ova and is known to be destroyed at fertilization. So for determining maternal inheritance, ones mtDNA is the same as his mother's mtDNA, which is the same as her mother's mtDNA and so on.

Our findings for A105 family analysis revealed contradicting results. Not all SNPs and SVs present in mother were found to be present in the children. In fact, there were cases found where a SNP was found to be present in father and a child but not in mother. Table A shows the list of SNPs and Table B shows the list of SVs in A105 family. This proposes a new discovery that mitochondrial DNA can have paternal sources of inheritance as well, though they can also be a result of de-novo genetic changes rather than inheritance. Further, comparing Table A and B, it is discovered by observation that mitochondrial DNA is less prone to SVs than SNPs, and that can be possibly attributed to the fact that mitochondrial DNA is not exposed to the phenomenon of crossing-over of genetic material as is the case with chromosomes. Further, the ratio of SVs bases calls to the size of genome is significantly less for mitochondrial DNA (of the order of 2.35*10^-4) than for the whole genome (of the order of 2.5*10^-3), thereby providing further evidence that structural variations in mitochondrial DNA has higher selection pressure than the rest of the genome and is thus a more rare event in the mitochondria relative to the rest of genome. This ratio remains comparable to the rest of genome when considered for SNPs (of the order of 5.3*10^-4 for mitochondria and of the order of 8.0*10^-4 for whole genome). Though it has been already observed in banana that mitochondrial DNA can also be paternally inherited [23, 24], this is the first time that the discovery of paternal inheritance possibility of mitochondrial DNA in humans is being reported by this article.

Mitochondrial DNA and Y-chromosome DNA has been widely been used to determine maternal and paternal ancestry respectively, such as in a recent findings for Native Americans and Indigenous Altaians [22]. Based on the discoveries above, it can thus be safely concluded that if we continue with ancestry determination by mitochondrial DNA, then SVs would serve as better means to determine ancestry for a longer period than SNPs, as they are relatively more rare events. At the same time the SNPs of the mitochondria would serve as better candidate for the characteristic signature of the individual and can be used to determine ancestry and divergence for a relatively shorter period. Having said that, it would still be proposed that given that there is possibility of mitochondrial DNA to be inherited by father as well, maternal ancestry determination by mtDNA should be rephrased as simply ancestry determination by mtDNA. This will also mean that all the analysis which different scientists across the globe have been conducting so far assuming mtDNA to be totally maternally inherited will need a complete change in the understanding and knowledge generated. As it is confirmed that Y-chromosome is completely paternally inherited, ancestry determination by 'Y line tests' as Y-chromosomes are confirmed to be totally inherited from the father is always remain as a good methodology. Further, as observed and stated above, since SVs have higher selection pressure than SNPs for the Y-chromosome, the SVs will serve as a better means for paternal ancestry determination for a relatively longer time-span and the SNPs would serve better candidate to determine paternal ancestry and divergence in a relatively shorter time-span. The SNPs of the whole genome can also be used for generic ancestry and divergence determination.

4 Conclusion

This research article improves our understanding of human genetics, variations in genome, and inheritance. It provides us with new scopes to fetch relevant information and opens door for many newer technologies to be built based on the discoveries. Though we have made these observation for a single family data, it would be highly unlikely that many such similar experiments would not converge to same discoveries. Nevertheless, it would be worthwhile to conduct population and ethnic or caste based studies and where possible combine it with authentic historical matrimonial records for relational database queries obtaining meaningful results. The discoveries make us more equipped with statistical and robust, efficient and relatively less costly means to derive information such as sex determination, or immunologic response to disease, or success rate of organ transplant, or susceptibility to diseases and possible cure for them. The SVs and SNPs in HLA loci would also serve as a medical transformational method for determining the success of organ transplant for a patient, and predisposition to diseases apriori. With the advent of diploid genomes been made available in future with assemblers being able to generate the diploid assembly too, our understanding for genetics and disease will enhance further and thereby enable better and more reliable technologies to come in.

5 Figures and Tables

VARIATIONS IN GENOME ARCHITECTURE

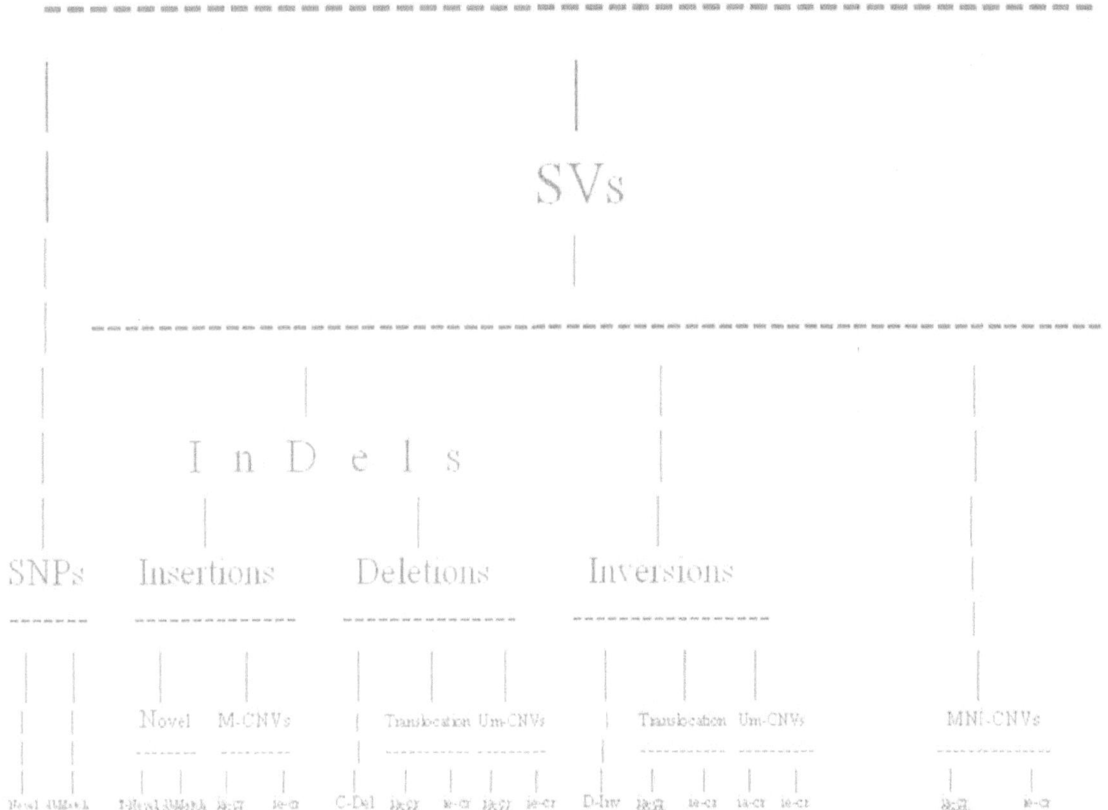

Um = Un-matching; M = Matching, MNI= Matching Non-Insertion, ia-cr = Intra-chromosomal = tandem duplications, ie-cr = Inter-chromosomal; SNPs = Single Nucleotide Polymorphism = SNVs = Single Nucleotide Variations; SVs = Structural Variations; InDels = Insertions and Deletions; CNVs = Copy Number Variations; Translocation = Single copy match elsewhere in the genome; Tandem Duplication and Multiplication lies in various CNVs; Mobile Element Insertion lies in M-CNVs; T-Novel = Truly Novel; C-Del = Complete Deletion; D-Inv = Direct Inversion

*Classification only on the basis of types of differences in when compared to a reference genome and not on the basis of size.

Figure A

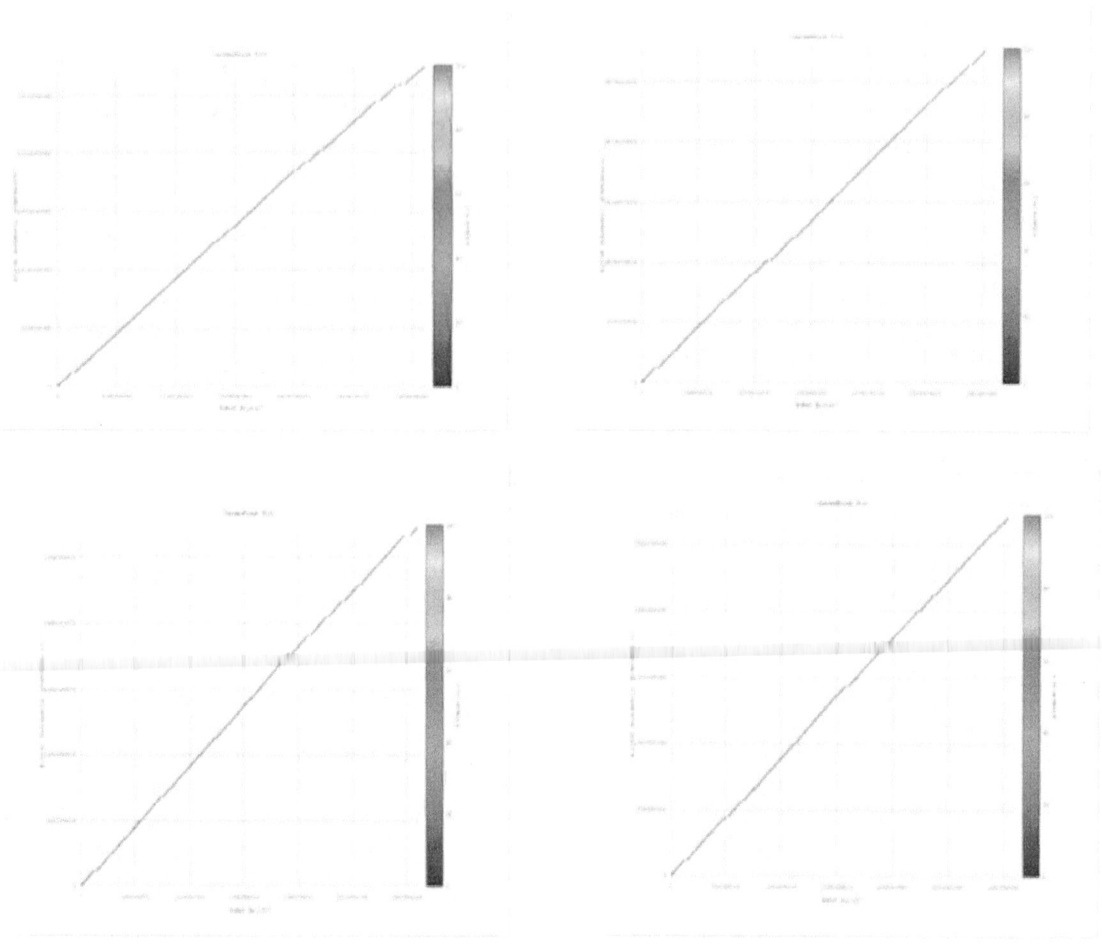

Figure B: Clockwise from top left: A105A, A105B, A105D, A105C

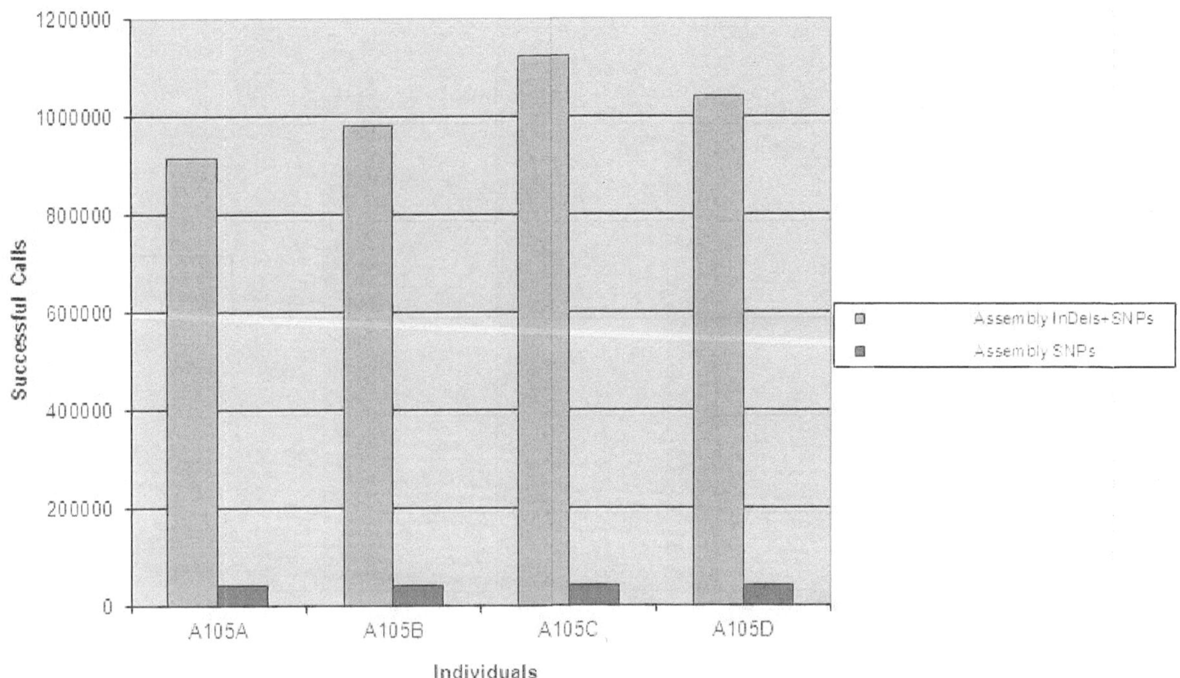
A105 Family Chromosome 20 Decoded
1200000
1000000
800000
600000
400000
200000
0
Successful Calls
A105A
A105B
A105C
A105D
Individuals
Assembly InDels+SNPs
Assembly SNPs

Figure C

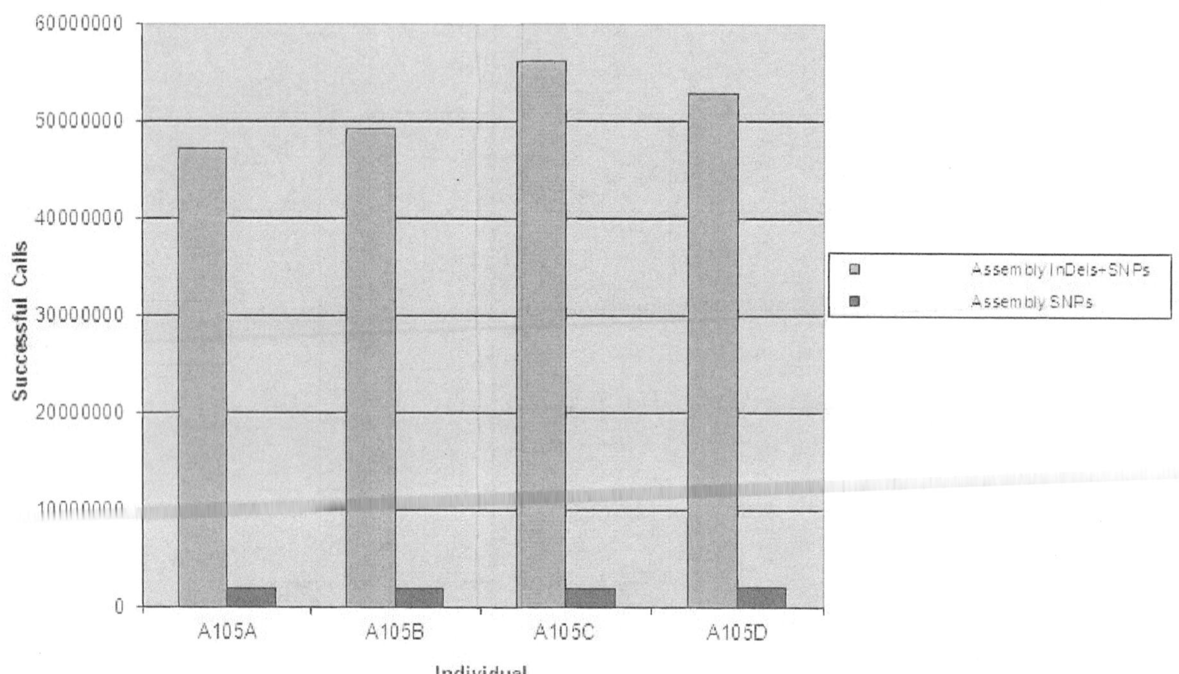
A105 Family Decoded
60000000
50000000
40000000
30000000
20000000
10000000
0
Successful Calls
A105A
A105B
A105C
A105D
Individual
Assembly InDels+SNPs
Assembly SNPs

Figure D

Sex Determination by Y chromosome

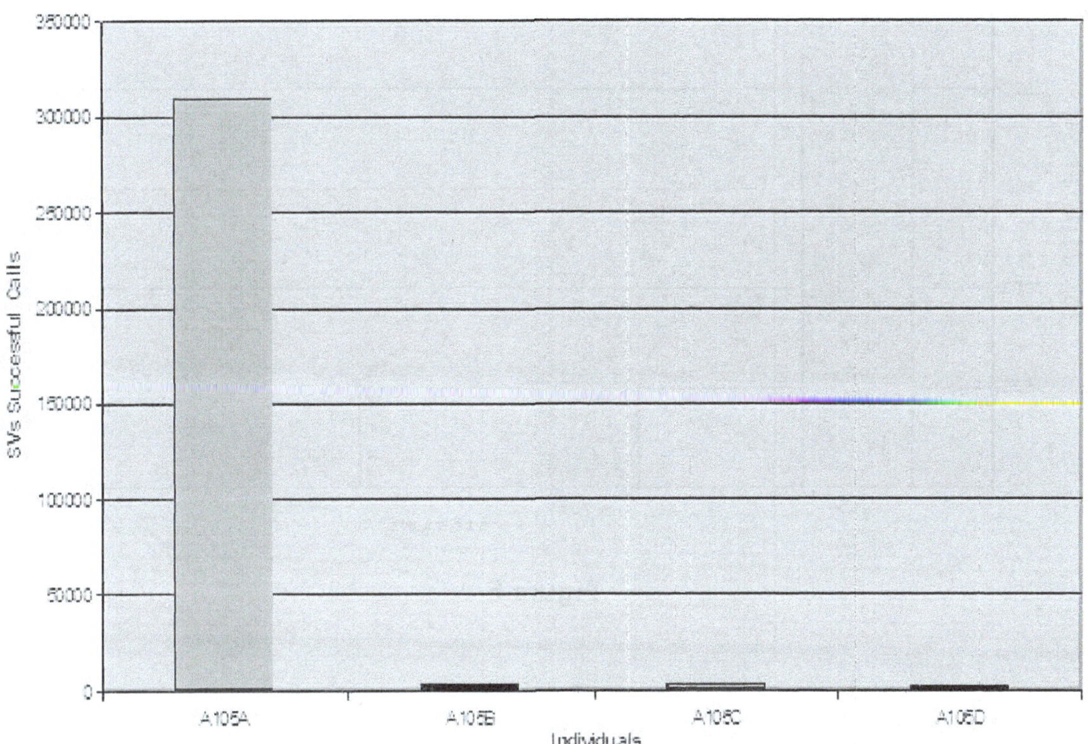
350000
300000
250000
200000
150000
100000
50000
0
SVs Successful Calls
A105A
A105B
A105C
A105D
Individuals

Figure E

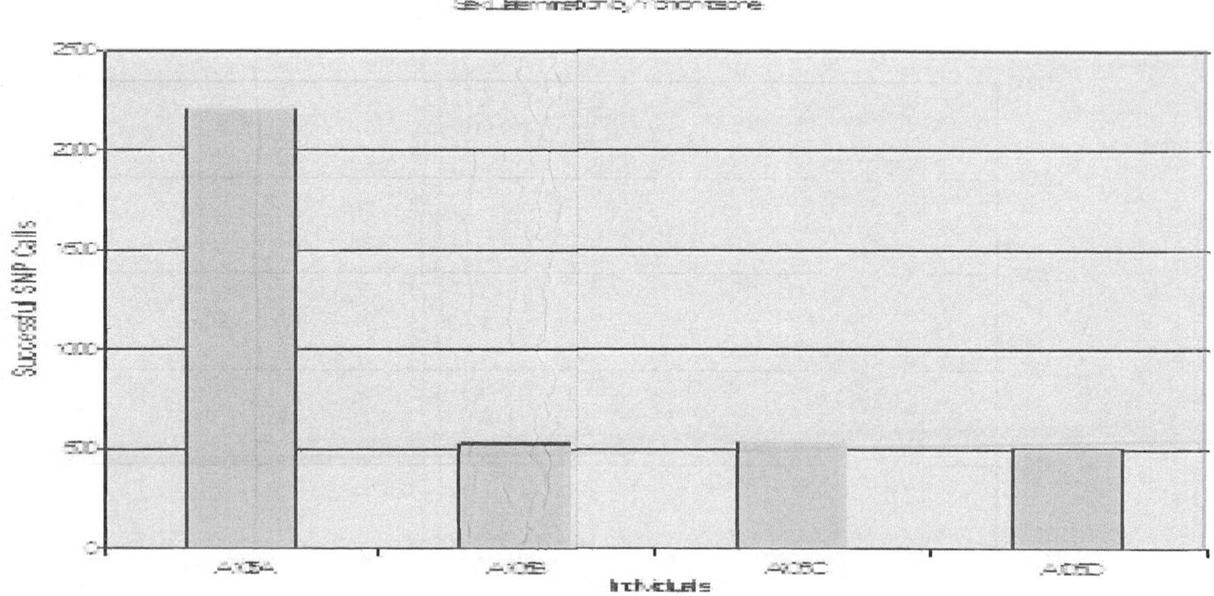

Figure F

Stringent parameters Genome Break					Lenient parameters Genome Break			
A105A	**A105B**	**A105C**	**A105D**		**A105A**	**A105B**	**A105C**	**A105D**
331 A	331 A	131 T	339 A		331 A	331 A	131 T	339 A
493 A	1476 G	750 A	6474 A		493 A	15380 A	750 A	6474 A

16496 G	1518 C	4769 A	6497 T		1476 G	15408 A	4769 A	6497 T
16519 T	15380 A	16519 T	15476 C		16519 T	16220 A	16519 T	1547 6 C
16527 C	15408 A				16496 G	16249 T		
	16220 A				1518 C	16437 T		
	16249 T				16527 C	16469 T		
	16437 T							
	16469 T							

Table A

Stringent parameters GenomeBreak					Lenient parameters Genome Break			
A105A	**A105B**	**A105C**	**A105D**		**A105A**	**A105B**	**A105C**	**A105D**
3107 N .	3107 N .	3107 N .	3107 N .		3107 N .	3107 N .	3107 N .	3107 N .

314 . C	314 . C	Missing	314 . C		314 . C	314 . C	Missing	314 . C
522 C .		4824 . N			522 C .			
523 A .					523 A .			

Table B

6 Author Contact

abhishek.narain@iitdalumni.com

7 References

1. 1000 Genomes Project Consortium et al. A map of human genome variation from population scale sequencing. Nature 467, 1061-1073 (2010).
2. Mills, R.E. et al. Mapping copy number variation by population scale sequencing. Nature published online, doi:1:10.1038/nature09708 (3 February 2011).
3. Fanciulli, M. et al. FCGR3B copy number variation is associated with susceptibility fo systemic, but not organ-specific, autoimmunity. Nat. Genet. 39, 721-823 (2007).
4. Aitman, T.J. et al. Copy number polymorphism in Fcgr3 predisposes to glomerulonephritis in rats and humans. Nature 439, 851-855 (2006).
5. Gonzalez, E. et al. The influence of CCL3L1 gene-containing segmental duplications on HIV-1/AIDS susceptibility. Science 307, 1434-1440 (2005).
6. Fellermann, K. et al. A chromosome 8 gene-cluster polymorphism with low human beta-defensin 2 gene copy number predisposes to Crohn disease of the colon. Am. J. Hum. Genet. 79, 439-448 (2006).
7. Yang, Y. et al. Gene copy-number variation and associated polymorphisms of complement component C4 in human systemic lupus erythematosus (SLE): low copy number is a risk factor for and high copy number is a protective factor against SLE susceptibility in European Americans. Am. J. Hum. Genet. 80, 1037-1054 (2007).
8. Hollox, E.J. et al. Psoriasis is associated with increased beta-defensin genomic copy number. Nat. Genet. 40, 23-25 (2008).
9. Feuk L, Carson AR, Scherer SW: Structural variation in the human genome. Nat Rev Genet 2006, 7:85-97.
10. Bodmer W, Bonilla C: Common and rare variants in multifactorial susceptibility to common diseases. Nat Genet 2008, 40;695-701
11. Iafrate AJ, Feuk L, Rivera MN, Listewnik ML, Donahoe PK, Qi Y, Scherer SW, Lee C: Detection of

large-scale variation in the human genome. Nat Genet 2004, 36:949-951.
12. Sebat J, Lakshmi B, Troge J, Alexander J, Young J, Lundin P, Maner S, Massa H, Walker M, Chi M, Navin N, Lucito R, Healy J, Hicks J, Ye K, Reiner A, Gilliam TC, Trask B, Patterson N, Zetterberg A, Wigler M: Large-scale copy number polymorphism in the human genome. Science 2004, 305:525-528.
13. Redon R, Ishikawa S, Firch KR, Feuk L, Perry GH, Andrews TD, Fiegler H, Shapero MH, Carson AR, Chen W, Cho EK, Dallaire S, Freeman JL, Gonzalez JR, Gratacos M, Huang J, Kalaitzopoulos D, Komura D, MacDonald JR, Marshall CR, Mei R, Montgomery L, Nishimura K, Okamura K, Shen F, Somerville MJ, Tchinda J, Valsesia A, Woodwark C, Yang F, et al.: Global variation in copy number in the human genome Nature 2006, 444:444-454.
14. Tuzun E, Sharp AJ, Bailey JA, Kaul R, Morrison VA, Pertz LM, Haugen E, Hayden H, Albertson D, Pinkel D, Olson MV, Eichler EE: Fine-scale structural variation of the human genome. Nature 2006, 444:444-454.
15. Khaja R, Zhang J, MacDonald JR, He Y, Josheph-George AM, Wei J, Rafiq MA, Qian C, Shago M, Pantano L, Aburatani H, Jones K, Redon R, Hurles M, Armengol L, Estivill X, Mural RJ, Lee c, Scherer SW, Feuk L: Genome assembly comparison identifies structural variants in the human genomo. Nat Genet 2006, 38:1413-1418.
16. Korbel JO, Urban AE, Affourtiti JP, Godwin B, Grubert F, Simons JF, Kim PM, Palejev D, Carriero NJ, Du L, Taillon BE, Chen Z, Tanzer A, Saunders AC, Chi J, Yang F, Carter NP, Hurles ME, Weissman SM, Harkins TT, Gerstein MB, Egholm M, Snyder M: Paired-end mapping reveals extensive structural variation in the human genome. Nat Genet 2006, 38:1413-1418.
17. Kidd JM, Cooper GM, Donahue WF, Hayden HS, Sampas N, Graves T, Hansen N, Trague B, Alkan C, Antonacci F, Haugen E, Zerr T, Yamada NA, Tsang P, Newman TL, Tuzun E, Cheng Z, Ebling HM, Tusneem N, David R, Cillett W, Phelps KA, Weaver M, Saranga D, Brand A, Tao W, Gustafson E, McKernan K, Chen L, Malig M, et al.: Mapping and sequencing of structural variation from eight human genomes. Nature 2008, 453:56-64.
18. Conrad DF, Pinto D, Redon R, Feuk L, Gokcumen O, Zhang Y, Aerts J, Andrews TD, Barnes C, Campbell P, Fitzgerald T, HuM, Ihm CH, Kristiansson K, Macarthur DG, Macdonald JR, Onyiah I, Pang AW, Robson S, Stirrups K, Valsesia A, Walter K, Wei J, Tyler-Smith C, Carter NP, Lee C, Scherer SW, Hurles ME: Origins and functional impact of copy number variation in the human genome. Nature 2010, 464:704-712.
19. Buchanan JA, Scherer SW: Contemplating effects of genomic structural variation. Genet Med 2008, 10:639-647.
20. Abhishek Narain Singh, Comparison of Structural Variation between Build 36 Reference Genome and Celera R27c Genome using GenomeBreak, Poster Presentation, The 2nd Symposium on Systems Genetics, Groningen, 29-30 September 2011
21. Abhishek Singh, GENOMEBREAK: A versatile computational tool for genome-wide rapid investigation, exploring the human genome, a step towards personalized genomic medicine, Poster 70, Human Genome Meeting 2011, Dubai, March 2011
22. Dulik MC, Zhadanov SI, Osipova LP, Askapuli A, Gau L, Gokcumen O, Rubinstein S, Schurr TG, Mitochondrial DNA and Y Chromosome Variation Provides Evidence for a Recent Common Ancestry between Native Americans and Indigenous Altaians, Am J Hum Genet. 2012 Feb 10;90(2):229-46. Epub 2012 Jan 25.
23. Marianne Schwartz and John Vissing, "Paternal Inheritance of Mitochondrial DNA", New England Journal of Medicine, Aug 22, 2002; 347:576-580.
24. "Mitochondria can be inherited from both parents", New Scientist article on Schwartz and Vissing's report.

The strategies and approaches to develop electronic health records in Taiwan

Chien-Chen Ni[1], Min-Huei Hsu[2], Pei-Tun Yang[3], Yu-Ting Yeh[4], and Chien-Tsai Liu[1]
[1] Graduate Institute of Biomedical Informatics, Taipei Medical University, Taipei, Taiwan
[2] Medical Informatics Center, Department of Health, Executive Yuan, Taiwan
[3] The Electronic Medical Record Program Office, Taiwan Nursing Informatics Association, Taiwan
[4] Graduate Institute of Medical Sciences, Taipei Medical University, Taipei, Taiwan

Abstract - *Electronic health record (EHR) can support a secure, real-time, point-of care, patient centric information resource for clinical care. Taiwan's government has been promoting the EHR adoption since 2000. There has been three phases for EHR development, from development of electronic medical record (EMR) systems for a single hospital to exchange of EMRs among hospitals across different health care organizations. The Department of Health has established a National EMR Development Committee (EMRDC) for development of EMR policies, document standards and system platforms for exchange of EHRs across hospital boundaries. In this paper, we will describe the EHR adoption strategies, current progress in EHR development, and our practical experience and lessons learned in implementing the EHR projects in Taiwan.*

Keywords: eHealth, Electronic health records, System interoperability

1 Introduction

To increase patient safety and improve the efficiency of healthcare services, the Department of Health of Taiwan government (DOH) has been promoting adoption of electronic health records (EHRs) since 2000 [1]. The first infrastructure that allowed physicians to record/access patient clinical information across the boundaries of hospitals was national health smart cards [2,3]. Since the capacity of the smart cards is very limited (32KB) and the content of medical information is not well defined, what content should be stored and the ways of interpretation and use of the stored data remain in controversy [4,5]. Thus the DOH focused on development of electronic medical records (EMRs) for an individual hospital or medical institution, and then expanded the project construct infrastructure for exchange of electronic medical records (EMRs) among different hospitals [6]. However, in so far as most hospitals still had two major concerns about EHR adoption: the high initial costs with no immediate benefits and the lack of nation-wide standards for sharing and exchange of EMRs. Thus, it is still a big challenge for the DOH to develop interoperable EMR systems for sharing and exchange of EMRs nationwide.

2 Strategic policies and approaches

Starting 2010, a project, called "Accelerating adoption of Electronic health records (AAEHR)" has been launched [1]. The goal of the project is to reach 80% of all hospitals and medical institutions that fully implement their EMR systems and can exchange EMRs across hospital boundaries in 5 years (by 2015). The major tasks of the program are to speed up medical institutions to adopt EMR systems and to facilitate sharing and exchange of EMRs among medical institutions nationwide. Compared to the previously launched EHR projects, the DOH has allocated the program more national resources for EHR adoption aid, and established better fine-tuned and organized implementation strategic policies that can be implemented straightforward, efficiently and effectively. The strategies and approaches to implement the program are described below.

2.1 Establishing a National EHR Development Committee (NEDC)

The major tasks of the NEDC are to establish policies and infrastructure layouts for adoption of EMR systems, to set up standards for sharing and exchanging EHRs, and to set standards for ongoing project management and review. In addition to the EHR Project Management Office (EPMO), the NEDC consists of four work groups, namely the Clinical Work Group (CWG), Information Systems and Standards Work Group (ISWG), Patient Safety Work Group (PSWG) and Project Review Work Group (PRWG).

- The CWG is responsible for establishing specific application domains of using EHRs in clinical settings, and conducting feasibility studies on the linkage between the meaningful use of EHRs and hospital accreditation.
- The ISWG is responsible for developing EHR exchange standards and technical implementation guides for established clinical application domains by the CWG.
- The PSWG is responsible for establishing information security measures, privacy protection policies, and other supporting mechanisms from the perspectives of patients, health care providers and third-party institutions.

- The PRWG is responsible for project management, performance evaluation and monitoring, and set criteria for the continuous pursuit of sustainable improvements.
- The EPMO is a staff team to support the EMRDC and work groups, and responsible for planning, coordination, and management of the projects relevant to EHR adoption, as well as promotion of EHR awareness.

2.2 Laying out infrastructure and establishing implementation strategic plans for sharing and exchange of EMRs

- Established "Regulations Governing the Production and Maintenance of Electronic Medical Records for Medical Institutions," and set up a Certification Commission for EMR systems to ensure all adopted EMR systems are compliant with the regulations.
- Developed the standards and technical implementation guides for sharing and exchange of EMRs in specified clinical domains. Currently, four clinical domains have been identified including medical imaging and reports, blood test report, outpatient medication summary and discharge summary.
- Laying out a national EHR exchange infrastructure. The infrastructure (Figure 1) consists of an EHR exchange center (NEEC), EHR Gateway servers (EGS) and a virtual private network (VPN). Each hospital involved in EMR sharing and exchange has an EGS. The EGS is used for storage of the EMRs, ready for sharing. The EMRs are also indexed by the NEEC. The NEEC has a centralized patient index repository containing a list of patients who had received medical services in the last 6 months. The high speed VPN provides secured communications among hospitals. Each hospital has an EMR depository and clients for production and retrieval of EMRs. The client is usually a part of hospital information systems such as a computerized physician order entry (CPOE) system or other clinical support systems.

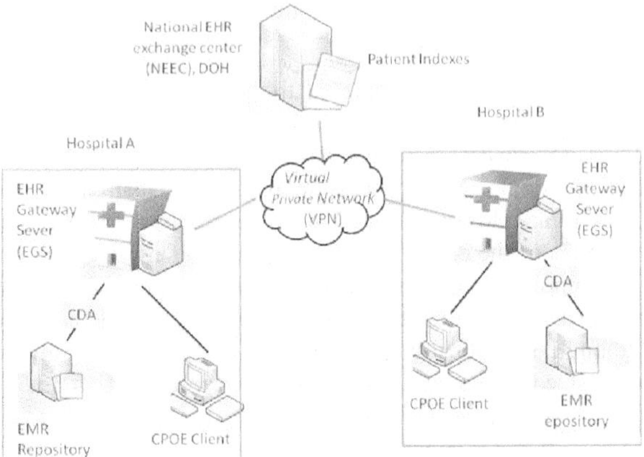

Figure 1 The EHR exchange infrastructure

Type the title approximately 2.5 centimeters (1 inch) from the top of the first page and use 20 points type-font size in bold. Center the title (horizontally) on the page. Leave approximately 1 centimeter (0.4- inches) between the title and the name and address of yourself (and of your co-authors, if any.) Type name(s) and address(s) in 11 points and center them (horizontally) on the page. Note that authors are advised not to include their email addresses.

2.3 Creating a subsidy program for EHR adoption

The primary purpose of the program is to encourage medical institutions to implement EMR systems, to adopt information-based medical practices, and to facilitate sharing and exchange of EMRs.

- The subsidy will be granted only for those hospitals that have adopted EMR systems and implemented exchange and sharing of the EMRs in four clinical domains specified by the NEDC. The amount of subsidies for each hospital is based on the average outpatient visits and number of beds, ranging from US$ 80,000 to 400,000. Proportion-wise to the hospitals size, the small-sized hospitals can receive more subsidies than larger hospitals. This is because smaller hospitals usually have limited resources and need more aids to adopt EMR systems.
- For primary care clinics which are usually very small, and have limited financial aid and IT capabilities in developing EMR systems, the DOH has commissioned subcontractors to develop EMR systems for 2,000 clinics. The EMR systems must be compliant with the "Regulations Governing the Production and Maintenance of Electronic Medical Records for Medical Institutions". Once the EMR systems have been developed, the systems should be less costly, and can be massively deployed to the rest clinics.

2.4 Setting goals and checkpoints to measure the progress of EHR adoption

To promote EHR adoption, we hosted educational workshops/seminars nationwide to raise awareness of EMR adoptions, and organized follow-up seminars for hospitals to share their expertise and experiences in adoption of EMR systems and exchange of EMRs. The goals of EHR adoption have been set as following.

- In the first year (by 2010), 20% of total hospitals (about 100 hospitals) have adopted EMR systems with the capability in sharing and exchange of EMRs in one of four specified clinical domains.
- In the second year (by 2011), 23% of total hospitals (about 115 hospitals) have adopted EMR systems, and there are at least 55 hospitals that can exchange of EMRs in one of four specified clinical domains over the national EHR exchange infrastructure and the NEEC.
- In the second year (by 2012), 26% of total hospitals (about 130 hospitals) have adopted EMR systems, and

there are at least 75 hospitals that can exchange EMRs in three of four specified clinical domains over the national EHR exchange infrastructure and the NEEC.

3 Results

3.1 System operating for exchanging EHRs

There are two working modes in accordance with the framework of NEEC (Figure 1) for the exchange of EMRs: provision mode and retrieval modes. In the provision mode, a hospital must firstly prepare an EMR to be exchanged based on CDA R2 templates defined by the DOH, then perform digital signature on the prepared EMR, and lastly, upload the EMRs to its EGS. After receiving the encrypted EMRs, the EGS decrypts and validates the EMRs. It will generate an index of the EMR if the validation is correct, and then send the index to the NEEC. In the retrieval mode, a physician can request a patient's EMR from other hospital following the steps below.

(1) Obtain the patient's consent (a signed informed consent document).
(2) Log-in the NEEC system by using both the physician's personnel smart card and the patient's health smart card.
(3) Query the patient's indexes from where the physician can select one or more indexes to the EMRs related to this visit. For illustration reason, let's assume the physician selects only one patient's index (i.e., one episode of visits).
(4) With the selected index the NEEC server can locate the EGS of a hospital where the EMR is stored. The NEEC server performs the retrieval of the EMR, and send the encrypted EMR to the EGS of the hospital where the physician requesting the EMR.
(5) The requesting hospital can view the EMR with a NEEC viewer directly or download the EMR for further use.
(6) After completing the retrieval, the EMR in the EGS is removed.

3.2 Hospitals involving in Exchanging EHRs

The AAEHR program has been executed nationwide, and making progress toward the assigned goals. Until the end of 2012 there were 191 hospitals (about 39.8%) that have adopted EMR systems with the capability in exchange of EMRs in one of four clinical domains (Table 1). Those included 23 medical centers (100%), 56 regional hospitals (67.5%) and 112 district hospitals (29.9 %) were certified by the CCES, and eligible for incentive money from the Subsidy program for EHR adoption. Among them, however, there were 190 hospitals with the capability in exchanging the medical images and reports, 92 hospitals with the capability of exchanging discharge summaries, 77 hospitals with the capability of exchanging laboratory blood tests reports, and 69 hospitals with the capability of laboratory blood tests reports. This is because the DOH has delayed in publishing the standards. The first standard was the medical images and report which was published in late of June, 2011. The latest standard was outpatient medication summary which was published in November, 2011.

Table 1: the summary of the hospitals with certified EMR systems

EMR Type	Medical centers (n=23)	Regional hospitals (n=75)	District hospitals (n=380)	Total (n=478)
Medical images and report	22	49	109	190
Discharge summary	9	21	50	92
Laboratory blood test report	10	19	35	77
Outpatient medication summary	9	14	31	69
Total*	23 (100%)	56 (67.5%)	112 (29.9%)	191 (39.8%)

* A hospital might apply more than one types of EMR to be certified

4 Discussions

The DOH has been promoting the adoption of ICT in health care settings for more than 10 years. During the past years one of the most remarkable achievements was the successful implementation of national health smart cards. The NHI-IC card system has been operating for nearly 10 years. There were few problems that caused people inconveniences and very few major threats to the data security and privacy protection. This makes people confident in ongoing E-Health projects. Thus, they support the adoption of EHRs. It can be seen that setting good examples (or references) in using ICT in health care is crucial for the government to promote nationwide eHealth services.

As indicated in Table 1, the EHR adoption rate was 100% for medical centers, 67.5% for regional hospitals, and 29.9% for district hospital. The hospitals with higher rank tend to adopt EMR systems more quickly than those with lower rank. However, small-sized hospitals represent more than 50% of the entire medical services in Taiwan. They play very important roles in sharing and exchange of EMRs, but they usually don't have enough resources for EHR adoption. Although the Subsidy program for EHR adoption favored small-sized hospitals, there is still enormous room for improvement in subsidies distribution.

Incentives and mandates should be introduced in the best mix for optimal results. The subsidy program for EHR adoption is merely a short-term incentive. This case of pay for performance policy speed up of EHR adoption in Taiwan is far different to the United States policy of "meaningful use" which was strongly supported by a particular Act (Health Information Technology for Economic and Clinical Health Act) to secure a 10 years incentive payment [7,8]. As the government tightens its budget in this area, the introduction of policy mandates becomes inevitable. While hospital accreditation system has shown to improve successfully hospital quality in Taiwan[9], we believe that incorporating EHR as part of the mandatory criteria of the hospital accreditation system will strengthen hospitals motives to speed up the adoption of their EMR systems and the involvement in EHR exchanges.

5 Conclusions

The Department of Health has developed a sophisticated and feasible model to the adoption of EHRs. Although the budget for EHR adoption subsidies has been reduced year by year, the EHR adoption program has been executed smoothly and without major opposition. We believe that setting good examples (or references) to demonstrate the benefits of using ICT in health care is critical and could help foster the success of implementation of EHRs. In addition, the incentive policies for EHR adoption can be subtle and significantly influenced small-sized hospitals in the speed of EHR adoption. We will continue reviewing our policies and developing sustainable eHealth business models to improve health care quality, enable public health management, and achieve the efficient use of medical resources.

6 Acknowledgement

The authors of this paper appreciate the colleagues at the Center for Information Management of the Department of Health, the EHR Project Management Office and all the members of the National EHR Development Committee for their support and help in the metadata analysis on the EHR project performance.

7 References

[1] Promption and adoption of electronic medical records, Department of Health, Executive Yuan, R.O.C. http://emr.doh.gov.tw/ (in Chinese).

[2] National Health Insurance Profiles. The Bureau of National Health Insurance, Department of Health, Executive Yuan, R.O.C. http://www.nhi.gov.tw/english/webdata.asp?menu=11&menu_id=290&webdata_id=1884

[3] Liu CT, Yang PT, Yeh YT, Wang BL. The impacts of smart cards on hospital information systems — An investigation of the first phase of the national health insurance smart card project in Taiwan, Int J Med Inform. 2006; 75(1):173-81.

[4] Hsu MH, Yen JC, Chiu WT, Tsai SL, Liu CT, Li YC. Using Health Smart Cards to Check Drug Allergy History: The Perspective from Taiwan's Experiences. J Med Syst. 2009; online published DOI: 10.1007/s10916-009-9391-5.

[5] Min-Hui Hsu, Yu-Ting Yeh, Chien-Yuan Chen, Chien-Hsiang Liu, Chien-Tsai Liu*. Online Detection of Potential Duplicate Medications and Changes of Physician Behavior for Outpatients Visiting Multiple Hospitals Using National Health Insurance Smart Cards in Taiwan. International Journal of Medical Informatics. 2011, 80(3): 181-9.

[6] Jian WS, Hsu CY, Hao TH, Wen HC, Hsu MH, Lee YL, Li YC, Chang P. Building a portable data and information interoperability infrastructure-framework for a standard Taiwan Electronic Medical Record Template. Comput Methods Programs Biomed. 2007, 88(2):102-11.

[7] Introduction of EMR Policy. Available at URL: http://emr.doh.gov.tw/introduction.aspx accessed on August 11, 2011.

[8] Blumenthal D, Tavenner M.The "meaningful use" regulation for electronic health records. *N Engl J Med.* 2010 Aug 5;363(6):501-4

[9] Wung CH.The reform of the hospital accreditation system in Taiwan. *World Hosp Health Serv.* 2008;44(1):14-5, 18.

Bioinformatics Component in Personalized Medicine

Abhishek Narain Singh

ABI-O-TECH

abhishek.narain@cantab.net

Call to Action	Key Takeaways
▪ Integrated approach of multi-omics ▪ Hardware Software kinship ▪ Security and Privacy of Data	▪ Next Generation Sequence analysis ▪ Proteomics and Genomics ▪ High Performance Bio-Computing
Focus areas: technological, genomics, proteomics, HPC	

Abstract

Past few decades have seen rapid growth in sequencing technology and software tools to aid their processing and analysis. The cost of genome sequencing of whole human data has dropped to couple thousand dollars from what it used to be about a million dollars. In parallel there has been significant growth in supercomputing power as per the Moore's law with multi-and-many-core computers being a common commodity, needless to mention the GPUs which promise to bring supercomputing power at desktop space. Parallel advancement has been in the domain of proteomics and transcriptomics. The 'gaps' today are integrating these hardware, software and human resources for a better bioinformatics solution to aid a personalized medicine age to practice.

Introduction

Science has been progressing significantly in the past few decades in the area of biological studies which thus opens questions as of are we now more capable of understanding human health and be able to predict the causative factors for a disease. Though diseases have been more or less generically understood for the causative agents, what might be more interesting are primarily the diseases for which there can be multitude of factors that influence upon its activation or diseases for which different individuals respond with great variation in defense mechanisms. Whatever be the medical parameters and not so well understood complicated mechanisms involved, one thing is for sure that with the advent of our capabilities of understanding and analyzing the genome, interactome, metabolome and proteome, we can definitely give more probabilistic predictive and personalized medical counseling, and be there the nuts and bolts for delivery, then perhaps personalized medicine too. In a way personalized medicine will differ from what hospitals and other healthcare services have been providing till now of personalized care, as with advent of more scientifically in-depth technology it would mean newer approaches to disease prevention, diagnosis by multitude of parameters, and the choices that an individual will have once recommendations are made. This can be a more effective reality when the interests of government, insurance companies, hospitals, scientists, technologists, education bodies, medical professionals and most important the patients are well aligned. We are now living in a data rich age, with capable technologies to extract relevant patterns for the case in hand. In particular the genomics area has been moving rapidly past one decade to give us a stronger faith in establishing a personalized medicine era by means of integrating with greater emphasis the personalized genomic medicine component.

Emerging Informatics Challenges with Genome Sequencing

In the area of sequencing genomes there has been rapid advancement in technology and simultaneous reduction in cost. Deodyribonucleic acid (DNA) is well known to be the blueprint of life. Dideoxynucleotide sequencing of DNA has improved from what it was in rudimentary stage to a large-scale production enterprise that requires devoted instrumentations, databases, bioinformatics tools and robotics. Tailor made bioinformatics tools has been significantly useful in answering our questions about mutation spectrum of an organism, from single nucleotide base to large copy number variations. The ability to process millions of sequence reads in parallel sets the next generation sequencing technology more popular. Further, in the process of its metamorphosis, the cost per reaction of DNA sequencing has fallen with a Moore's law precision [1]. The first human genome sequence was obtained by using Sanger sequencing method. In the past few years, the technology evolved to introduce paired end sequences , where the sequence can be determined at either end of a fragment and the insert size in between the ends can be approximately known a priory. The accuracy of this sequence or the quality of the information concerning the nucleotide bases is not always reliable as thus a probabilistic number is associated, however significant lower cost of this technology can allow multiple sequencing of the region of interest which is also known as the coverage of sequencing, so as to then take the consensus at a region of interest to determine the sequence. A higher average coverage is usually preferred for more accuracy though bold steps were taken in projects such as to analyse genome with lower coverage such as the 1000 genomes project. Thus higher the coverage the more reliable the results are, and in the bioinformatics community it is generally accepted to have a coverage of 20x to almost saturate the possibility of having near zero false base consensus. The high false discovery rate of structural variation algorithms even in deeply sequenced individual genomes of the order of 30x average coverage [1,2] suggests that for lower coverage the problem will be even more to get rid of false positives. Nevertheless, the results with coverage as less as 3-5x could also have a lot of meaningful results, and could be deployed for several genomes population wide analysis at relatively less cost, such as in the 1000 genomes project [1]. The 1000 genomes project used the technique of mapping the sequence reads to the reference genome, as it would not be possible to obtain any reliable genome assembly with an average sequencing coverage of 3-5x. There have been several new tools made available which can detect variations without the need for assembling the genome for the individual such as those used in the 1000 Genome Project consortium which finds great applicability in case the coverage of sequences is low[1]. Nevertheless, if the sequencing coverage is high enough such as above 12x in average, then there is no reason as to why assembling the genome and then mapping to a reference genome to detect variations directly should not be the adopted. At the same time, results obtained by assembly analysis can be compared for consistency by mapping reads to the reference genome approach to see if they both lead to same discoveries. The findings should then be experimentally validated by PCR and other traditional means, if there be time and resources, to get an estimate of false positive rates by both the approaches. As bioinformatics tools make use of a lot of predictive algorithms and machine-learning approaches, it is always wise to apply a combination of approaches, parameters and software tools to have a higher faith in the consensus results, thereby reducing the cost associated with experimental validation. The bioinformatics software tools aiding the analysis has been constantly growing and enhancing adapting rapidly with the improvement in sequencing quality and quantity

Bioinformatics White Space

The overall goal of conducting bioinformatics analysis for medical application is to look at the pattern of variation inheritance and to detect any otherwise abnormal observation which can be a prospective discovery. This would be helpful in understanding human genetic variation, selection pressure and inheritance better for improved personalized medical treatment and trait characteristics determination. Genome variations have been associated with recurrent genomic rearrangements as well as with a variety of diseases, including colour blindness, psoriasis, HIV susceptibility, Crohn's disease and lupus glomerulonephritis [3-8]. There is thus a need of comprehensive catalogue of genotype and phenotype correlation studies [1-8] in particular when the rare or multiple variations in gene underlie characteristic or disease susceptibility [9,10]. Microarrays [11-13] and sequencing [14-17] reveal that structural variants (SVs) contribution is significant in characterizing population [18] and disease [19] characteristics. In particular the HLA region in chromosome 6 of an individual which is the MHC region in humans would be interesting in being decoded for the variations, as a lesser difference between two individuals could imply stronger success rate of organ transplant. Even otherwise, the HLA region variation would give an insight in immunologic responses. However, we must be careful with the results that we get when we call for the variations, as any difference could represent actual difference between the DNA sources, an assembly artefact (clone-induced or computational) or alignment error. Since the sequencing of human genomes now become routine [1], the spectrum of structural variants and copy number variants (CNVs) has widened to include even smaller events. What is important now is to know how genomes vary at large as well as fine scales. It is a challenge to understand its effects on human disease, characteristic traits and phylogenetic evolutionary clues. Figure A below tries to compile all the various terminologies and variations in genome architecture when compared to a reference genome [20, 21].

VARIATIONS IN GENOME ARCHITECTURE

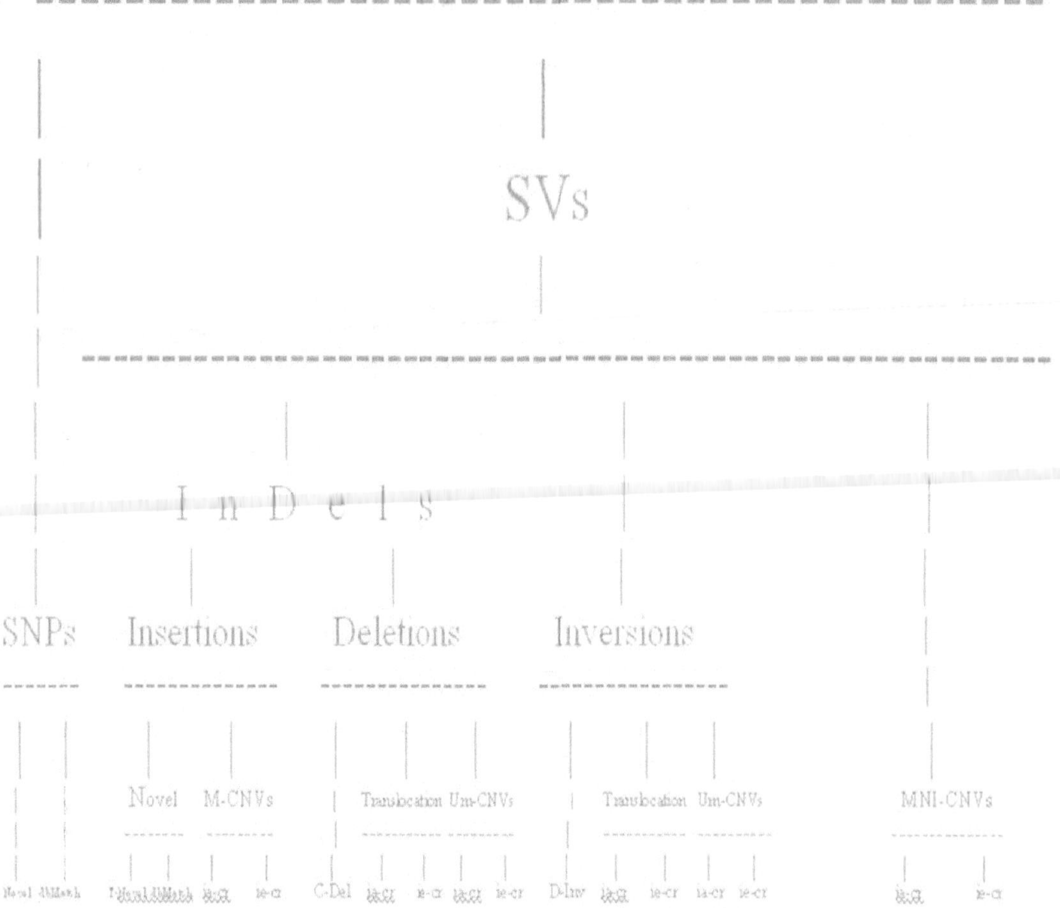

Um = Un-matching; M = Matching; MNI= Matching Non-Insertion; ia-cr = Intra-chromosomal = tandem duplications; ie-cr = Inter-chromosomal; SNPs = Single Nucleotide Polymorphism = SNVs = Single Nucleotide Variations; SVs = Structural Variations; InDels = Insertions and Deletions; CNVs = Copy Number Variations; Translocation = Single copy match elsewhere in the genome; Tandem Duplication and Multiplication lies in various CNVs; Mobile Element Insertion lies in M-CNVs; T-Novel = Truly Novel; C-Del = Complete Deletion; D-Inv = Direct Inversion

*Classification only on the basis of types of differences in when compared to a reference genome and not on the basis of size.

Figure A: Variations in Genome Architecture [20,21]

One clear application of finding the variations in an individual is in conducting an organ transplant surgery. If the immunologic responses after the grafting of an organ from a donor to the receptor may be determined a-priori to conducting the transplant, medical practitioners can be more predictive of the chances of success of the transplantation. This also applies to clinical data making and donor matching. The immunologic responses are dictated by the MHC region of the genome, which in humans corresponds to the HLA region in chromosome 6. If we extract the SVs (structural variations) and SNPs (single nucleotide polymorphism) of chromosome 6 of the donor and compare it with the SVs and SNPs of acceptor patient's chromosome 6, then it can be reasonably proposed that the lower the differences between the two sets of SVs and SNPs, the higher the success possibility of organ transplant. However, even with these SVs and SNPs a subset could be more crucial to be present or being absent perhaps for the transplantation to be successful. Similarly if we are interested in any other chromosome which has been known of having strong association with a particular phenotype or characteristic trait, we can extract the SVs and SNPs for that chromosome and do a relational database analysis amongst other techniques such as machine learning approaches. Below in Figure B, is a GenomeBreak bioinformatics software tool plot for an individual assembled genome to detect the structural variation when compared to the reference genome [22, 23].

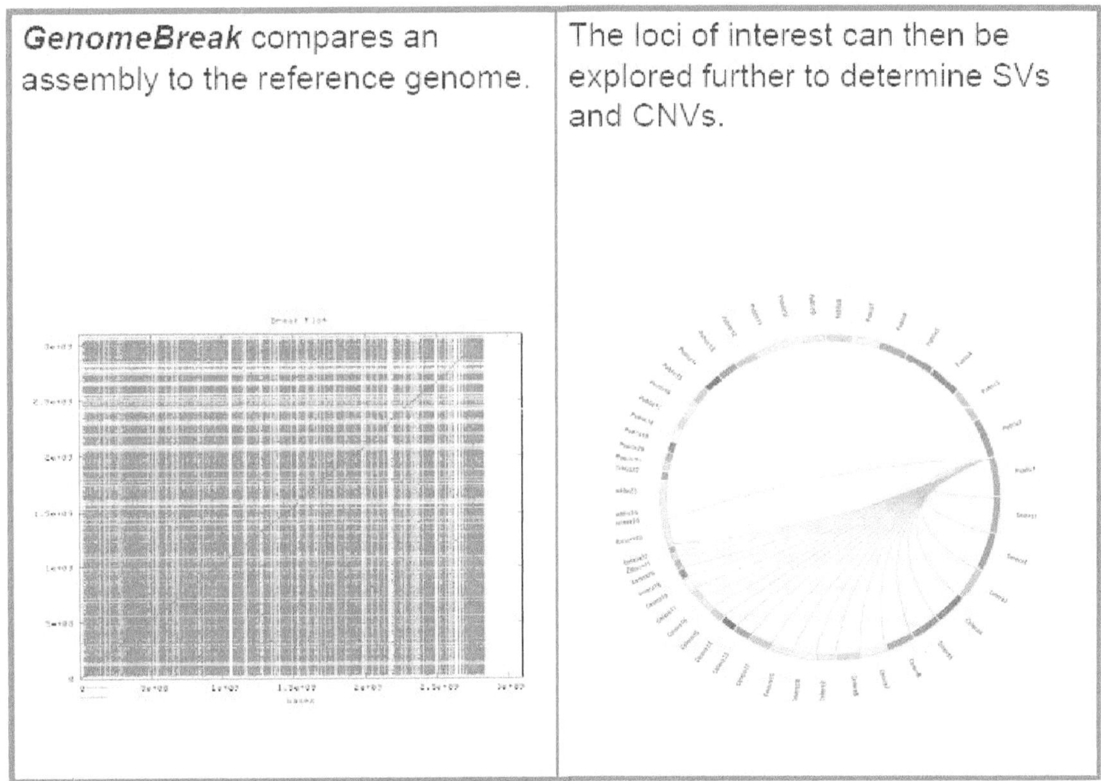

Figure B: GenomeBreak plot of a an assembled genome [22,23]

With the rapid advancement of technology, coupled with decrease in cost of sequencing, it will not be long when everyone can carry their genome-chip which would contain chromosomal sequences, along with information of SVs and SNPs already determined. In fact, this would be a practice which we might want to do early in the life say within a week after his birth. Let's say we take it a step further and obtain the DNA sample from the fetus, thus being able to do analysis of the baby which is to be born. With the power of prediction and integrating it to powerful relational databases and other scientific techniques we can tell what are the chances of the baby to be healthy in general. We would be able to predict disease susceptibility of the new born baby as well as characteristics traits, thereby giving an opportunity for the mother to decide whether to have the baby or not, and if so what all things she should be caring about. We would also be able to determine the sex of the baby before it is born, thereby provide an alternative and safer means to determine the sex of the baby, without any extra cost, as the genome of the baby will be sequenced and analyzed anyways. The results from genome analysis can be more sensitive if we have parallel transcriptome analysis by means of RNA-Seq techniques. Genome analysis toolkit, GATK, tools and other tools for next generation sequencing of DNA, NGS, visualization such as IGV (interactive genomics viewer) find greater application at that point [24].

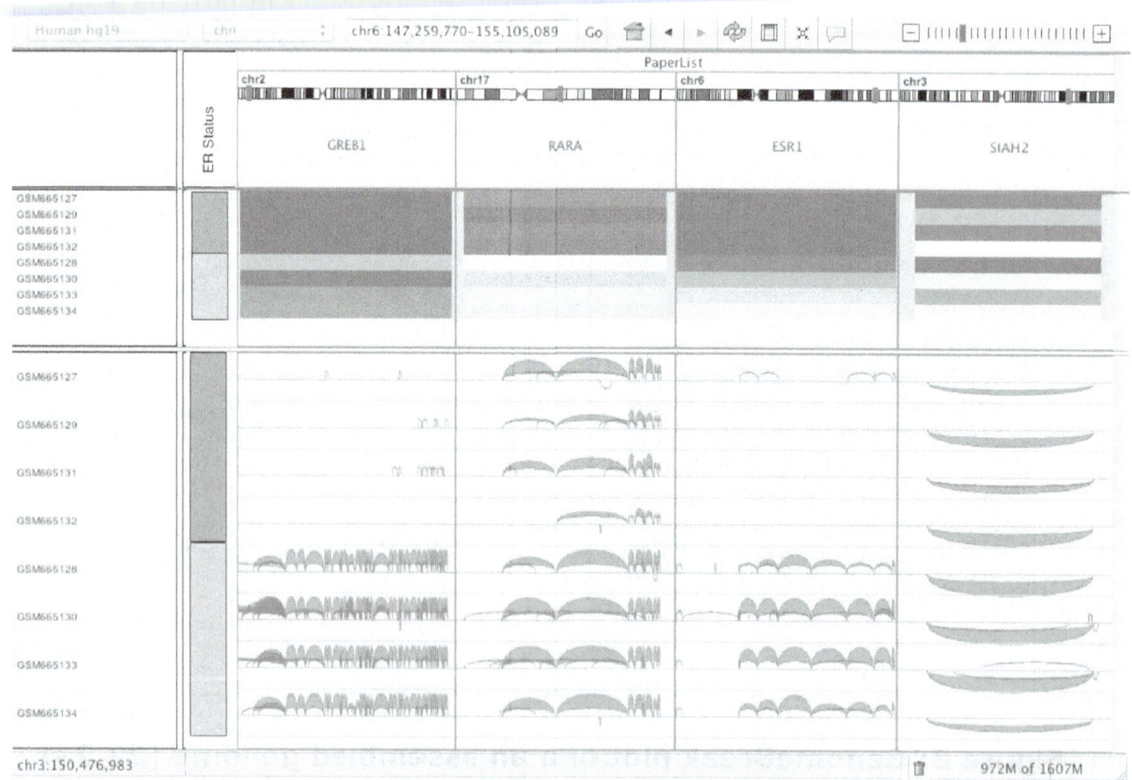

Figure C: Sample IGV plot

Going further for analysis tools for proteome analysis such as plot of intensities for mass to charge value, m/z peaks vs dilution, also would be great supplement to detect the peptides which can be present in a patient from his body fluid sample under certain condition such as while the patient has been diagnosed for certain symptoms. Personalized medicine performance can thus be tested on a more regular basis by means of such powerful tools which test for the expression of various proteins to be present in patient body while he is undergoing treatment as well. Below in Figure D we see one such tool plot by ProteomeBreak.

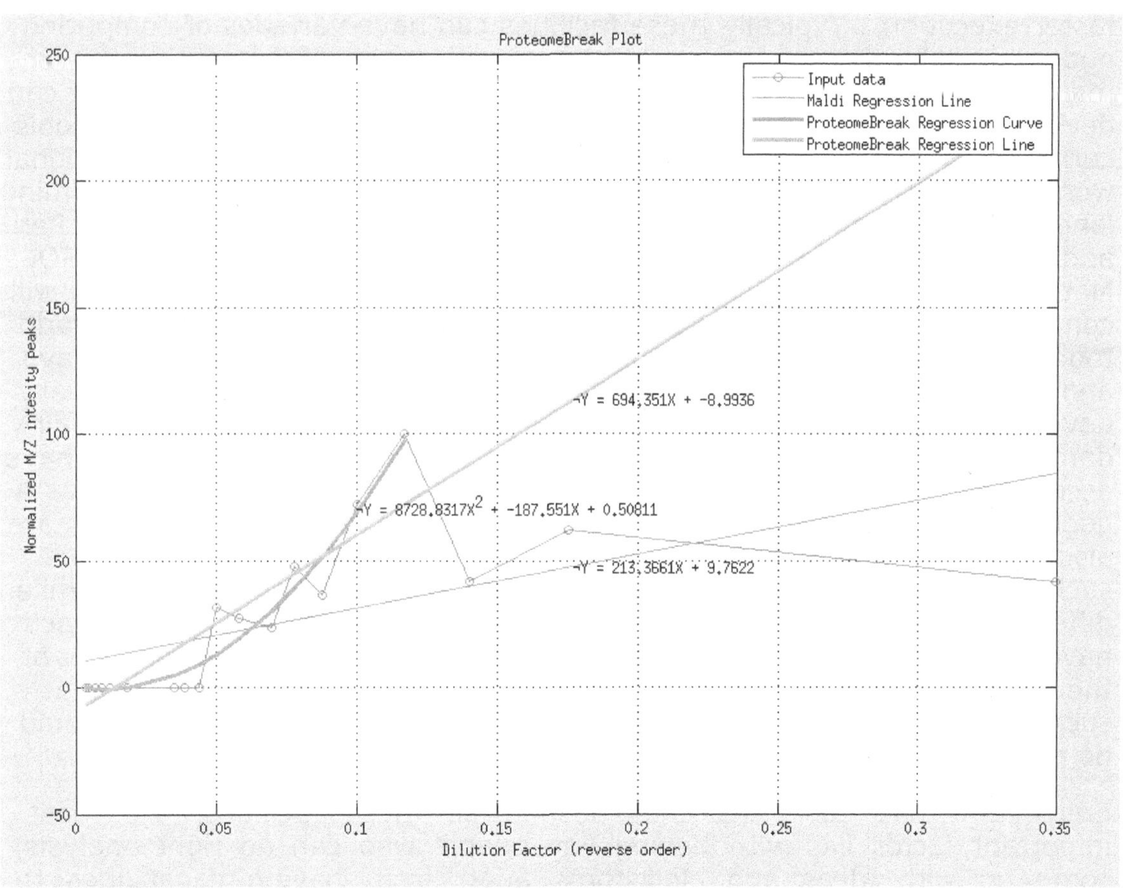

Figure D: ProteomeBreak Plot for Maldi M/Z peak normalized values plotted against dilution factor

Computational Demands and Skills

As we are living in a data explosion age, bioinformatics has been able to keep pace with the age definition. About a decade ago analysts typically dealt with gigabytes of data at most. Today, it is fairly common to see bioinformaticians dealing with terabytes of raw data, processed data and possibly petabytes of intermediate processing data. A good strategy and management approach is to depend on these high levels of data storage cloud-type or cluster facility. Such high performance computing facilities usually not only provide the support in terms of hardware, but usually also take care of different software tools with updated versions available. Such cluster facilities also make more computational resources available such as providing possibility of submission of several jobs, or running a parallel script using OpenMP, OpenMPI, MVAPICH2, perl Threads, pThreads for a faster execution. Typically these facilities can have varieties of computing nodes available, each varying in the specifications of processing power, memory available, I/O network bandwidth etc. which the informatician can decide as per the demand. As an example, the genome assembly tools currently usually can take quite high memory compared to other traditional work like pattern extraction for a motif search. Among programming languages that have become popular in the bioinformatics world are Perl and Python. Nevertheless, as C, C++, Java, Pascal, shell script, MySQL, Matlab are usually popular in the computer science world, they will continue to show their existence and application in bioinformatics world too. As an example GUI programming is quite extensively done using Java, and most MPI (message passing interface) applications are usually developed on C and C++. Among the operating systems Linux has fairly dominated the programming world. For the Windows user if you have access to a remote login linux machine, then putty generally serves as a good tool for quick connection for free, though other commercial tools are also available. For making use of two operating systems simultaneously such as the Oracle VM VirtualBox is getting increasingly popular. While different software tools exist for various bioinformatics applications, each have their own merits and demerits in terms of statistics and reliability of the assembly generated apart from computationally important aspects such as resource utilization and execution time, and those factors should be preferably considered before going for full blown operation.

Employers tend to forget that despite all these facilities, the most important factor lies with having key people who can do right analysis, come up with ideas and algorithms apart from having capabilities to implement those ideas as a software code. Typically such key people have strong background of education and experiences both in biotechnology and computer science apart from exposure to mathematics and engineering world. People factor plays a key role since the ideas and direction given by people might be much more worthy than lots of effort put in taking the project in a not so sensible direction.

Conclusion

Bioinformatics field represented by genomics, proteomics, transcriptomics, and metabolomics is mature as well as evolving at a fast pace and can thus be tightly linked to personalized medicine. Among the above subcategories, the genomics field has matured to a greater extent such that scientists even went on to coin personalized genomic medicine as a more specific category within personalized medicine. Whatever be the case, there is no doubt that bioinformatics is tightly coupled towards bringing in the capability that will be required to deliver personalized medicine, such as with the example tools that are discussed above. Apart from these, the databases would play crucial role and would lead to more job creation as personalized medicine gets to practice.

Author Contact

abhishek.narain@iitdalumni.com

References

1. 1000 Genomes Project Consortium et al. A map of human genome variation from population scale sequencing. Nature 467, 1061-1073 (2010).

2. Mills, R.E. et al. Mapping copy number variation by population scale sequencing. Nature published online, doi:1:10.1038/nature09708 (3 February 2011).

3. Fanciulli, M. et al. FCGR3B copy number variation is associated with susceptibility fo systemic, but not organ-specific, autoimmunity. Nat. Genet. 39, 721-823 (2007).

4. Aitman, T.J. et al. Copy number polymorphism in Fcgr3 predisposes to glomerulonephritis in rats and humans. Nature 439, 851-855 (2006).

5. Gonzalez, E. et al. The influence of CCL3L1 gene-containing segmental duplications on HIV-1/AIDS susceptibility. Science 307, 1434-1440 (2005).

6. Fellermann, K. et al. A chromosome 8 gene-cluster polymorphism with low human beta-defensin 2 gene copy number predisposes to Crohn disease of the colon. Am. J. Hum. Genet. 79, 439-448 (2006).

7. Yang, Y. et al. Gene copy-number variation and associated polymorphisms of complement component C4 in human systemic lupus erythematosus (SLE): low copy number is a risk factor for and high copy number is a protective factor against SLE susceptibility in Europena Americans. Am. J. Hum. Genet. 80, 1037-1054 (2007).

8. Hollox, E.J. et al. Psoriasis is associated with increased beta-defensin

genomic copy number. Nat. Genet. 40, 23-25 (2008).

9. Feuk L, Carson AR, Scherer SW: Structural variation in the human genome. Nat Rev Genet 2006, 7:85-97.

10. Bodmer W, Bonilla C: Common and rarae variants in multifactorial susceptibility to common diseases. Nat Genet 2008, 40:695-701.

11. Iafrate AJ, Feuk L, Rivera MN, Listewnik ML, Donahoe PK, Qi Y, Scherer SW, Lee C: Detection of large-scale variation in the human genome. Nat Genet 2004, 36:949-951.

12. Sebat J, Lakshmi B, Troge J, Alexander J, Young J, Lundin P, Maner S, Massa H, Walker M, Chi M, Navin N, Lucito R, Healy J, Hicks J, Ye K, Reiner A, Gilliam TC, Trask B, Patterson N, Zetterberg A, Wigler M: Large-scale copy number polymorphism in the human genome. Science 2004, 305:525-528.

13. Redon R, Ishikawa S, Firch KR, Feuk L, Perry GH, Andrews TD, Fiegler H, Shapero MH, Carson AR, Chen W, Cho EK, Dallaire S, Freeman JL, Gonzalez JR, Gratacos M, Huang J, Kalaitzopoulos D, Komura D, MacDonald JR, Marshall CR, Mei R, Montgomery L, Nishimura K, Okamura K, Shen F, Somerville MJ, Tchinda J, Valsesia A, Woodwark C, Yang F, et al.: Global variation in copy number in the human genome Nature 2006, 444:444-454.

14. Tuzun E, Sharp AJ, Bailey JA, Kaul R, Morrison VA, Pertz LM, Haugen E, Hayden H, Albertson D, Pinkel D, Olson MV, Eichler EE: Fine-scale structural variation of the human genome. Nature 2006, 444:444-454.

15. Khaja R, Zhang J, MacDonald JR, He Y, Josheph-George AM, Wei J, Rafiq MA, Qian C, Shago M, Pantano L, Aburatani H, Jones K, Redon R, Hurles M, Armengol L, Estivill X, Mural RJ, Lee c, Scherer SW, Feuk L: Genome assembly comparison identifies structural variants in the human genome. Nat Genet 2006, 38:1413-1418.

16. Korbel JO, Urban AE, Affourtiti JP, Godwin B, Grubert F, Simons JF, Kim PM, Palejev D, Carriero NJ, Du L, Taillon BE, Chen Z, Tanzer A, Saunders AC, Chi J, Yang F, Carter NP, Hurles ME, Weissman SM, Harkins TT, Gerstein MB, Egholm M, Snyder M: Paired-end mapping reveals extensive structural variation in the human genome. Nat Genet 2006, 38:1413-1418.

17. Kidd JM, Cooper GM, Donahue WF, Hayden HS, Sampas N, Graves T, Hansen N, Trague B, Alkan C, Antonacci F, Haugen E, Zerr T, Yamada NA, Tsang P, Newman TL, Tuzun E, Cheng Z, Ebling HM, Tusneem N, David R, Cillett W, Phelps KA, Weaver M, Saranga D, Brand A, Tao W, Gustafson E, McKernan K, Chen L, Malig M, et al.: Mapping and sequencing of structural variation from eight human genomes. Nature 2008, 453:56-64.

18. Conrad DF, Pinto D, Redon R, Feuk L, Gokcumen O, Zhang Y, Aerts J, Andrews TD, Barnes C, Campbell P, Fitzgerald T, HuM, Ihm CH,

Kristiansson K, Macarthur DG, Macdonald JR, Onyiah I, Pang AW, Robson S, Stirrups K, Valsesia A, Walter K, Wei J, Tyler-Smith C, Carter NP, Lee C, Scherer SW, Hurles ME: Origins and functional impact of copy number variation in the human genome. Nature 2010, 464:704-712.

19. Buchanan JA, Scherer SW: Contemplating effects of genomic structural variation. Genet Med 2008, 10:639-647

20. Abhishek Narain Singh, A105 Family Decoded: Discovery of Genome-Wide Fingerprints for Personalized Genomic Medicine, Poster, 2-5 Feb UPCP 2012, Florence, Italy

21. Abhishek Narain Singh, "A105 Family Decoded: Discovery of Genome-Wide Fingerprints for Personalized Genomic Medicine", page 115-126, Proceedings of the International Congress on Personalized Medicine UPCP 2012 (February 2-5, 2012, Florence, Italy), Medimond Publisher, ScienceMED journal vol.3 issue 2, April 2012.

22. Abhishek Narain Singh, Comparison of Structural Variation between Build 36 Reference Genome and Celera R27c Genome using GenomeBreak, Poster Presentation, The 2nd Symposium on Systems Genetics, Groningen, 29-30 September 2011

23. Abhishek Singh, GENOMEBREAK: A versatile computational tool for genome-wide rapid investigation, exploring the human genome, a step towards personalized genomic medicine, Poster 70, Human Genome Meeting 2011, Dubai, March 2011

24. Helga Thorvaldsdottir, James T. Robinson, Jill P. Mesirov. Integrative Genomics Viewer (IGV): high-performance genomics data visualization and exploration. Briefings in Bioinformatics 2012.

SESSION

PROTEIN FOLDING, CANCER STUDIES, GENE REGULATORY NETWORKS, RECOGNITION SYSTEMS , DNA/RNA TRANSFORMATION, ACOUSTICS, AND ALGORITHMS

Chair(s)

Prof. Hamid Arabnia
University of Georgia

Competitive Imperialistic Approach for Protein Folding

E. Khaji [a], S.M.Mortazavi [b]

[a] Department of Physics, Gteborg University, 41296 Gothenburg, Sweden.

[b] School of Business, University of Colorado, CO 80217 Denver, USA .

Abstract

The protein folding problem is a fundamental problem in computational molecular biology and biochemical physics which led us to understand the function of a given sequence.The problem is NP-hard and the standard computational approach are not suitable to obtain the enough accurate structure in the huge conformation space. Simplied models such as hydrophobic-polar (HP) model have become one of the major tools for studying protein structure due to the complexity of the protein folding problem. Several optimization methods have been applied on this problem including Monte Carlo methods, evolutionary algorithm, and ant colony optimization algorithm. In this work, we present the results of the experiments of Imperialist Competitive algorithm on 3D HP protein folding problem. The achieved results are compared favorably with specialized state-of-the-art methods for this problem. Our empirical results indicate that Imperialist Competitive algorithm outperforms the existing results for standard benchmark instances from the literature. Furthermore, we compare our folding results with proteins with known folding.

Keywords: Imperialistic Competitive Algorithm, metaheuristics, hydrophobic-polar model, protein folding

1. Introduction

The 3D structure of proteins, which itself is a function of its sequence, is crucial to pharmacology and medical sciences. Most drugs work by attaching themselves to a protein so that they can either stabilize the normally folded structure or disrupt the folding pathway, which leads to a harmful protein [20]. Thus, knowing exact 3D shapes will help to design drugs, and understanding the functionality of a protein. Although a system of differential equations exists to describe the folding forces, due to its complication, its always preferred to solve the problem using more simplified methods.

These models try to generally reect different global characteristics of protein structures [20]. In the hydrophobic-polar (HP) model [4] the primary amino acid sequence of a protein is abstracted to a sequence of hydrophobic (H) and polar (P) residues that is represented as a string over the letter H and P. It describes the proteins based on the the hydrophobicity of amino acids which makes them be less exposed to the aqueous solvent than the polar ones, thus resulting in the formation of a hydrophobic core in the spatial structure. In the model, the amino acid sequence can be seen as a binary sequence of monomers which are hydrophobic or polar. The structure of the protein can now be defined as a series of monomers on the verticess of a three dimensional cubic lattice. The free energy of a conformation is dened as the summation of the non-consecutive cotacts between hydrophobic and hydrophobic amono acids in the way that each contact is considerred as a negative point. Moreover, a contact is assumed as two non-consecutive amino acids in the chain are placed in adjacent sites in the lattice. Therefore, nding optimal structures of the HP model on a cubic lattice is NPcomplete problem [2].

In conclusion, achievement of the native structure of a given sequence is an optimization problem which should be solved with an optimization algorithm such as Ant colony optimization, GA, PSO, or Imperialist Competitive Algorithm (ICA). ICA is a new socio politically motivated global search strategy that has recently been introduced for dealing with different optimization task showing great performance in both convergence rate and better global optima achievement [14-19]. In this paper, we used imperialist Competitive Algorithm in protein folding estimation and compared it with the present results.

2. The Protein Folding Probelm

"Efforts to solve the protein folding problem have traditionally been rooted in two schools of thought"[20]. In terms of thermodynamics, native structure of the protein possesses the global minimum of its free energy. On the other hand, one can have a evolutionary view on the problem of protein folding signifying that the native structure has been evolved within the time. Thus, methods have been developed to map the sequence of one protein (target) to the structure of another protein (template),to model the overall fold of the target based on that of the template and to infer how the target structure will be changed,related to the template, as a result of substitutions [1].Accordingly methods for protein-structure prediction has been divided into two classes: de novo modeling and comparative modeling. The de novo approaches can be further subdivided, those based exclusively on the physics of the interactions within the polypeptide chain and between the polypeptide and solvent, using heuristic methods [9], [10],and knowledge-based methods that utilize statistical potential based on the analysis of recurrent patterns in known protein structures and sequences.

The comparative modeling models structure by copying the coordinates of the templates in the aligned core regions. The variable regions are modeled by taking fragments with similar sequences from a database [1]. The processes involving in folding of proteins are very complex and only partially understood, thus the simplied models like Dills HP model have become one of the major tools for studying proteins [4]. The HP model is based on the observation that hydrophobic interconnection is the driving force for protein folding and the hydrophobicity of amino acids is the main force for development of native conformation of small globular proteins. In the HP model, the primary amino acid sequence of a protein is abstracted to a sequence of hydrophobic (H) and polar (P) residues, amino acid components. The protein conformations of this sequence are restricted to self-avoiding paths on 3 dimensional sequence lattice. One of the most common approaches to protein structure prediction is based on the thermodynamic hypothesis which states that the native state of the protein is the one with lowest Gibbs free energy. In the HP model, the energy of a conformation is dened as a number of topological contacts between hydrophobic amino acid that are not neighbors in the given sequence. More specically a conformation c with exactly n such H-H contacts has free energy of $E(c) = n.(1)$. The 3D HP protein folding problem can be formally dened as follows.Given an amino acid sequence $s = s_1\ s_2...s_n$, nd an energy minimizing conformation of s, i.e. nd $c^sC(s)$ such that $E^s = E(c^s) = /min_{cC(s)}E(c)$, where $C(s)$ is the set of all valid conformations for s. It was proved that this problem is NP-hard [2].A number of well-known heuristic optimization methods have been applied to the 3D protein folding problem including Evolutionary Algorithm (EA) [9], Monte Carlo (MC) algorithm [10] and Ant Colony Optimization (ACO) algorithm [7]. An early application of EA to protein structure prediction was presented by Unger and Moult [11]. Their EA incorporates characteristics of Monte Carlo methods. Currently among the best known algorithms for the HP protein folding problem is Pruned-Enriched Rosenblum Method (PERM) [8]. Among these methods are the Hydrophobic Zipper (HZ) method [5],Ant Colony Optimization (ACO), Ant Colony System (ACS)[20], and the Constraint-based Hydrophobic Core Construction Method (CHCCM) [12]. The Core-direct chain Growth method (CG) [3] biases construction towards nding a good hydrophobic core by using a specically designed heuristic function.

3. Imperialistic Compatetive Algorithm for Protein Folding Problem

Imperialist competitive algorithm (ICA) is a heuristic stochastic algorithm sufficient for solving NP-hard problems. The first step of the algorithm is creating initial population where each population in ICA is considered as a country. After calculating the fitness (power) of all countries, some of the most powerful countries in the population selected as the the imperialists while the rest form the colonies are assigned randomly to each of imperialist countries. Indeed, the number of colonies for each imperialist country is proportional to the power of the imperialist.When the competition starts, imperialists attempt to achieve more colonies and the colonies start to move toward their imperialists. Thence, within the competition, the powerful imperialists will be improved or substitued with more powerful colonies whearas the weakest colonies will be collapsed. Finally, just one imperialist will remain while the position of the last imperialist and its colonies will be the same. The flowchart of this algorithm is shown in Figure 2 [11]. More details about this algorithm are presented in [8-13]. In the shadow of protein folding,the evaluating step of Imperialist algorithm and any other heuristic algorithm is the crucial point. Considering each country as a sequence of random numebrs, each random number determine the direction in which the next amino acid will be placed. Therefore, among all the possbile nodes in a 3D space for an amino acid to be placed, the one which will be the nearest point to the random number will be choosed. According to this discription, on can easily guess that the dimension of each country is equal to$(3.l) - 1$ where l is the length of the polypeptide.

Then, the evaluation of the power of each country is straight forward as described in the introduction. The suedocode of the algorithm is as follows:

0) Define objective function.
1) Create initial empires.
2) Assimilation: Colonies move towards imperialist states in different in directions.
3) Revolution: Random changes occur in the characteristics of some countries.
4) Position exchange between a colony and Imperialist. A colony with a better position than the imperialist, has the chance to take the control of empire by replacing the existing imperialist.
5) Imperialistic competition: All imperialists compete to take possession of colonies of each other.
6) Eliminate the powerless empires. Weak empires loose their power gradually and they will finally be eliminated.
7) If the stop condition is satisfied, stop, if not go to 2.
8) End

3. Numerical Experiments

Ten standard benchmark instances of length 48 for 3D HP protein folding shown in Table I have been widely used in the literature [3], [7], [9-11]. Experiments on these standard benchmark instances were conducted by performing a number of independent runs for each problem instance, 20 runs. The following parameter settings are used for all experiment as:

Number of initial countries= 500. Number of Initial Imperialists = 8. AlgorithmParams.NumOfDecades = 200. The process in which the socio-political characteristics of a country change suddenly = 0.3. Assimilation coefficient or "beta" = 2. Assimilation angle coefficient or "gama" = .5. AlgorithmParams.Zeta = 0.02. AlgorithmParams.DampRatio = 0.99. The percent of Search Space Size = 0.02.

In Table II the achieved results by various heuristic algorithms are compared. For every of the benchmark instances the best found result by various methods is reported. We compared the solution quality obtained by: hydrophobic zipper (HZ) algorithm [5], the constrain-based hydrophobic core construction (CHCC) method [13], the core-directed chain growth (CG) algorithm [3], the contact interactions (CI) algorithm [11], the pruned-enriched Rosenbluth method (PERM) [7], the ACO algorithm of Hoos (ACO) [10] and the ICA approach presented in this paper. In the majority of the cases our average results are better than the best found results by other methods. The main disadvantage of heuristic methods, as it is mentioned by other authors, is that they achieve good folding for short proteins only.

Table 1
Standard Benchmark Instances.

1	HPHHPPHHHHPHHHPPHHPPHPHHPHPHHPPHHPPPHPPPPPPPPHHP
2	HHHHPHHPHHHHHPPHPPHHPPHPPPPPPHPPHPPPHPPHHPPHHHPH
3	HPHHPHHHHHHPPHPHPPHPHHPHPHPPPHPPHHPPHHPPHPHPPHP
4	PHPHHPPHPHHHPPHHPHHPPPHHHHHHPPHPHHPHPHPPPPHPPHPHP
5	PPHPPPHPHHHHPPHHHHPHHPHHHPPHPHPHPPHPPPPPPHHPHHPH
6	HHHPPPHHPHPHHPHHPHHPHPPPPPPPHPHPPHPPPHPPHHHHHHPH
7	PHPPPPHPHHHPHPHHHHPHHPHHPPPHPHPPPHHHPPHHPPHHPPPH
8	PHPHPPPPHPHPHPPHPHHHHHHPPHHHPHPPHPHHPPHPHHHPPPPH
9	PHPHPPPPHPHPHPPHPHHHHHHPPHHHPHPPHPHHPPHPHHHPPPPH
10	PHHPPPPPPHHPPPHHHPHPPHPHHPPHPPHPPHHPPHHHHHHHPPH

Table 2
Comparison of 3D Protein Folding.

Benchmark	HZ	CHCC	CG	CI	PERM	ACO	ICA
1	31	32	32	32	32	32	34
2	32	34	34	33	34	34	34
3	31	34	34	32	34	34	35
4	30	33	33	32	33	33	33
5	30	32	32	32	32	32	33
6	29	32	32	30	32	32	32
7	29	32	32	30	32	32	34
8	29	31	31	30	31	31	36
9	31	34	33	32	34	34	35
10	33	33	33	32	33	33	35

4. Conclusion

Imperialist Competative Algorithm can be applied to the 3D protein folding problem simply and succesfully. This algorithm outperforms the well known approaches in the literature. The folding achieved by this algorithm is very similar to the real protein folding when it is applied on short proteins. The obtained results are encouraging and the ability of the developed algorithm to generate rapidly high-quality solutions can be seen.

References

[1] Balev S. Solving the Protein Threading Problem by Lagrangian Relaxation, Algorithms in Bioinformatics, 3240, Springer, 2004, 182193.

[2] Berger B., T. Leighton, Newton–Protein folding in the hydrophobic-hydrophilic (HP) model is NP-complete, Computational Biology , 5, 1998, 2740.

[3] Beutler T., K. Dill, A fast conformational method: A new algorithm for protein folding simulations Protein Sci., 5, 1996, 147153.

[4] Dill K., K. Lau, A lattice statistical mechanics model of the conformational sequence spaces of proteins, Macromolecules, 22, 1989, 3986 3997.

[5] Dill K., K. M. Fiebig, H. S. Chan, Cooperativity in protein-folding kinetics, Nat. Acad. Sci. , USA, 1993, 19421946.

[6] Dorigo M., L. M. Gambardella, Ant colony system: A cooperative learning approach to the traveling salesman problem, IEEE Transactions on Evolutionary Computing, 1, 1997, 5366.

[7] Hsu H. P., V. Mehra, W. Nadler, P. Grassbergen, Growth algorithm for lattice heteropolymers at low temperature, Chemical Physics, 118, 2003, 444451.

[8] Krasnogor N., D. Pelta , P. M. Lopez, P. Mocciola, E. de la Cana, Genetic algorithms for the protein folding problem: a critical view, Engineering of intelligent systems, ICSC Academic press, 1998, 353360.

[9] Liang F., W. H. Wong, Evolutionary Monte Carlo for protein folding simulations, Chemical Physics, 115 7, 2001, 444451.

[10] Shmygelska A., H. H. Hoos, An ant colony optimization algorithm for the 2D and 3D hydrophobic polar protein folding problem, BMC Bioinformatics, 6:30, 2005.

[11] Toma L., S. Toma, Contact interaction method: a new algorithm for protein folding simulations, Protein Sci. , 5, 1996, 147153.

[12] Unger R., J. Moult, Genetic algorithms for protein folding simulations, Molecular Biology, 231, 1993, 7581.

[13] Yue K., K. Dill, Forces of tertiary structural organization in globular proteins, Nat. Acad. Sci. , USA, 1995, 146150.

[14] Atashpaz-Gargari, E., Lucas, C. Imperialist Competitive Algorithm: An algorithm for optimization inspired by imperialistic competition IEEE Congress on Evolutionary Computation 46614667. 2007

[15] Atashpaz-Gargari, E., Hashemzadeh, F., Rajabioun, R. and Lucas, C. Colonial Competitive Algorithm, a novel approach for PID controller design in MIMO distillation column process International Journal of Intelligent Computing and Cybernetics, 1 (3), 337355. 2008

[16] Rajabioun, R., Atashpaz-Gargari, E., and Lucas, C. Colonial Competitive Algorithm as a Tool for Nash Equilibrium Point Achievement Lecture notes in computer science, 5073, 680-695. 2008

[17] Lucas. C., Nasiri-Gheidari. Z., Tootoonchian. F., Application of an imperialist competitive algorithm to the design of a linear induction motor Energy Conversion and Management. 51,pp. 14071411. 2010

[18] R. Rajabioun, E. Atashpaz-Gargari, C. Lucas. Colonial Competitive Algorithm as a Tool for Nash Equilibrium Point Achievement Springer LNCSBook Chapter, 2008

[19] E. Hosseini Nasab, M.Khezri, M.Sahab Khodamoradi, E. Atashpaz Gargari. An application of Imperialist Competitive Algorithm to Simulation of Energy Demand Based on Economic Indicators: Evidence from Iran European Journal of Scientific ResearchVol.43 No.4,pp.495-506, 2010

[20] S. Fidanova, I. Lirkov. Ant Colony System Approach for Protein Folding Proceedings of the International Multiconference on Computer Science and Information Technology ,pp. 887891, 2008

Biomimetic Pattern Recognition in Cancer Detection

Leonila Lagunes[1] Charles H. Lee[2]
Department of Mathematics
California State University-Fullerton
BIOCOMP 2013

Abstract—**Biomimetic Pattern Recognition (BPR) is a classification process using a constructed biological structure. BPR is derived from the Principle of Homology-Continuity, which assumes members of the same class are biologically evolved and continuously connected. Recently, BPR has been successfully used in voice, facial, and iris recognition. In this article, we develop two BPR algorithms using proximity extension and two classification schemes. We investigate the performance of proposed BPR methods to detect cancer using DNA microarray data. A sample, normal or cancerous, consists of thousands of expressed genes, which are regarded as single nodes in a hyper-dimensional space. Assuming the PHC, nodes of the same class can be topologically assembled into a complex skeleton-like structure and further be covered with a tissue-layer to form a biological body. The resulting product can subsequently be used for classification. Performance for the algorithms, based on Leukemia, Bladder, Liver, and Colon cancers are studied. Our results indicate that the proposed BPR has an increase in recognition rate when compared to previous techniques. BPR has shown to be a promising approach for cancer detection using DNA microarray data.**

TABLE OF CONTENTS

[1]leo.lagunes13@gmail.com
[2]charleshlee@fullerton.edu

1. INTRODUCTION

Cancer treatments have been shown to be more effective if detected and treated at an early stage. Current cancer detection methods include imagining and blood-sample testing. Cancer imaging encompasses various techniques including traditional X-Rays, X-Ray-based computed tomography, Magnetic Resonance Imaging, Positron Emission Tomography, ultrasound scans, and endoscopy [1]. Current detection methods can be expensive and invasive driving scientists to develop alternative methods for detection, such as pattern recognition. Pattern recognition techniques such as Support Vector Machine, Discriminatory Analysis, etc. have been used in cancer detection. In this paper, we consider and develop new Biomimetic Pattern Recognition techniques.

1.1 DNA Microarray Data

Diagnosis and treatment of cancer can be improved by characterizing gene expression levels in healthy and cancerous tissue. Gene expression levels can be studied through microarray technology. Microarray technology allows researchers to measure and monitor the expression levels of thousands of genes simultaneously for a given organism [1]. DNA microarray data can be used to determine which genes are expressed at different levels between cancer-free cells and cancer-containing cells [2]. Biologists gather DNA from both cancerous and healthy cells for comparison and is tagged with red fluorescence for cancer and green for normal. DNA fragments then bind to their complements in a microarray chip as a part of a process called *hybridization* (**Figure 1B**). A red spot indicates that the gene is highly expressed in a cancer cell and minimally in a healthy cell [2]. Green signifies that the gene is minimally expressed in a cancer cell and highly in a healthy cell. Yellow fluorescence shows that a gene is almost equally expressed in both cells. A black spot indicates that the gene is inactive in both cell [3]. A laser then scans the microarray and determines the expression levels of each gene according to the intensity of the color and is given a numeric value. Each sample is defined as a sequence of numerical values of gene expression levels. In recent years, DNA microarray technology has provided a promising tool to determine the diagnosis and prognosis of different cancer types [4-7].

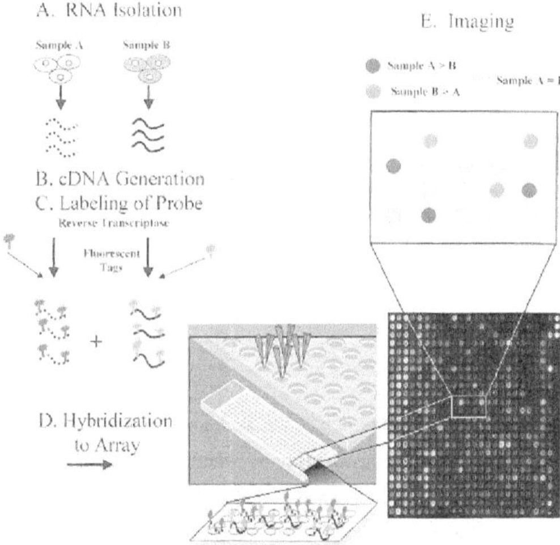

Figure 1. DNA microarrays process from reference [3]. (A) DNA from a cell is extracted. Each DNA segment has a corresponding spot on the microarray chip. (B) When comparing gene expression levels, DNA from each cell is labeled with different fluorescent tags and hybridized on the microarray chip.

1.2 Biomimetic Pattern Recognition

Biomimetic Pattern Recognition (BPR) is a technique constructing a hyper-dimensional (HD) geometric body to mimic a biological system for classification. BPR was first introduced by Shoujeu Wang in 2002 in Beijing, China and was derived from the Principle of Homology-Continuity (PHC) [8]. PHC assumes that the difference between elements of the same class is gradually changed. In other words, there is a gradual connection between any two elements that belong to the same class. These connecting branches can be HD line segments or hyper-surfaces and the resulting topological structure forms a "biological" organism, which can be used for classification. One special characteristic of BPR is that it requires only a small number of samples opposed to traditional pattern recognition algorithms. In recent years, BPR has been used successfully in voice recognition [9], iris recognition [10], and facial recognition [11]. BPR methods include different constructions as well as different classification techniques.

In this paper, the focuses are to develop two new techniques for developing BPR algorithms and apply them to DNA microarray data for cancer detection. We aim to build HD topological formations (skeleton-like structures) and pattern recognition schemes. We propose a new approach to the PHC, where elements of the same class are topologically assembled as nodes in a HD space and are connected by means of nearest neighbor.

2. Methodology

2.1 Data Sets

The BPR technique introduced in this paper is general and can be applied to any data set in a specified format. An applicable data set should be an m-by-n matrix. However, for our purpose, we apply this technique to DNA microarray data.

2.2 BPR Algorithm

2.2.1 Training Process: By providing a new approach to the PHC, we connect nodes from the same class in a HD space by means of nearest neighbor.

In order to build the HD topological formations, it is important to understand points and line segments in HD space. Let $\vec{x}$ be an element in $\mathbb{R}^n$. The minimum distance, D, from a point $\vec{x}$ to line segment connecting $\vec{x}_1$ to $\vec{x}_2$ is determined based on whether the projection of $\vec{x}$ onto the line segment is inside or outside the line segment x_1x_2. Let $\vec{u} = \frac{\vec{x}_2-\vec{x}_1}{\|\vec{x}_2-\vec{x}_1\|}$ be a unit vector going from $\vec{x}_1$ to $\vec{x}_2$ and $q = \langle \vec{x} - \vec{x}_1, \vec{u} \rangle$ be the projection of $\vec{x}$ onto the line segment x_1x_2. Note that $\|\bullet\|$ and $\langle \bullet, \bullet \rangle$ denote the usual Euclidian norm and the inner product in $\mathbb{R}^n$, respectively. It can be shown that

$$D = \begin{cases} \|\vec{x} - \vec{x}_1\| & q < 0 \\ \sqrt{\|\vec{x}_2 - \vec{x}_1\|^2 + q^2} & 0 \leq q \leq \|\vec{x}_2 - \vec{x}_1\| \\ \|\vec{x} - \vec{x}_2\| & q > \|\vec{x}_2 - \vec{x}_1\| \end{cases} \tag{1}$$

Let S be the set of M elements of the training set and U be an empty set. Without loss of generality, let $\vec{x}_1$ and $\vec{x}_2$ be the two closest elements in S. Remove $\vec{x}_1$ and $\vec{x}_2$ from S and add them to U so that $U = \binom{\vec{x}_1}{\vec{x}_2}$. Then, we select the next element $\vec{x}_3$ in S so that its distance to the line segments in U is minimal; currently U simply contains a line segment connecting $\vec{x}_1$ to $\vec{x}_2$. Again, we remove $\vec{x}_3$ from S and add it to U in the following fashion:

$$U = \begin{pmatrix} \vec{x}_1 & \vec{x}_3 \\ \vec{x}_2 & \vec{x}_3^* \end{pmatrix} \tag{2}$$

where $\vec{x}_3^*$ is determined based on the proposed algorithms:

1. **Nodal Connection:** Connect $\vec{x}_3$ to the closest node of the line segment $\vec{x}_1$ to $\vec{x}_2$. In this case, $\vec{x}_3^*$ is either $\vec{x}_1$ or $\vec{x}_2$.

$$\vec{x}_3 * = \begin{cases} \vec{x}_1 & \|\vec{x}_3 - \vec{x}_1\| < \|\vec{x}_3 - \vec{x}_2\| \\ \vec{x}_2 & \|\vec{x}_3 - \vec{x}_2\| \leq \|\vec{x}_3 - \vec{x}_1\| \end{cases} \tag{3}$$

2. **Segment Connection:** Connect $\vec{x}_3$ to the closest element of the line segment $\vec{x}_1$ to $\vec{x}_2$. In this case, $\vec{x}_3^*$ could be $\vec{x}_1$, $\vec{x}_2$ or a new element,$\vec{x}_t$ (not from the original training set) on the segment from $\vec{x}_1$ to $\vec{x}_2$.
   - If the projection of $\vec{x}_3$ lies outside the line segment $x_1\vec{x}_2$ then $\vec{x}_3*$ is defined as in Equation (4).
   - If the projection of $\vec{x}_3$ lies inside the line segment $x_1 x_2$ then

$$\vec{x}_3 * = \vec{x}_1 + (\vec{x}_3 - \vec{x}_1) \bullet (\vec{u}) * \vec{u} \tag{4}$$

Continue in this fashion until S has been exhausted. At the end of the algorithm, the set U will contain $(M - 1)$ segments

$$U = \begin{pmatrix} \vec{x}_1 & \vec{x}_3 & \cdots & \vec{x}_M \\ \vec{x}_2 & \vec{x}_3^* & \cdots & \vec{x}_M^* \end{pmatrix} \tag{5}$$

with at least one node of the segment being an element of the training set. Notice that both algorithms use the same name set, however, a different structure results. **Figure 2** shows an example of the development and the contrast of both proposed algorithms in $\mathbb{R}^2$. The Segment Connection algorithm provides a more compact structure than that from the Nodal Connection algorithm. Namely, the sum of all minimum distances in U is smaller for the Segment Connection algorithm. Keep in mind that the algorithms are performed on each training class. Hence, there result two "biological organisms", one structure for the Training Normal class and one for the Training Cancer class.

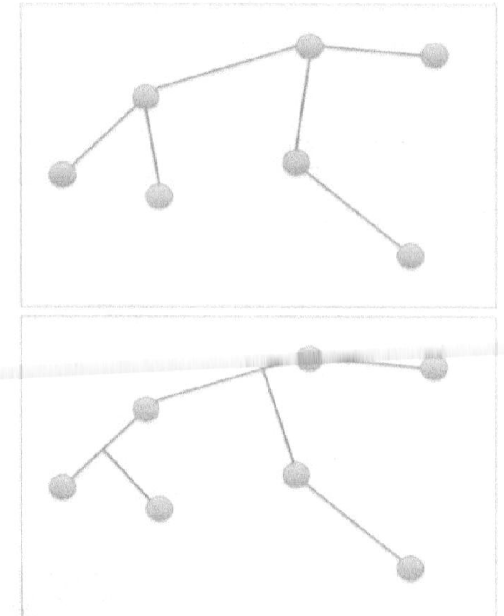

Figure 2 - Images depict the skeleton-like structure development using two assembling algorithms, where the next point is selected based on its minimal distance to the current structure and is connected to the closer node **(Top)** Nodal Connection **(Bottom)** Segment Connection.

2.2.2 Classification Process: Two structures are developed from the Training algorithm one for the cancer training set (U_C) and one for the normal training set (U_N). The resulting structures provide a basis for classification of an arbitrary node from the test set, T_S. We introduce two classification techniques. Accuracy for the algorithms is calculated based on the True Positive (TP), True Negative (TN), False Positive (FP), and False Negative (FN) values with the formula

$$\text{Accuracy} = \frac{TP + TN}{TP + FP + TN + FN} \tag{6}$$

In the first (**"Flesh"**) classification process, the newly constructed structures, U_C and U_N, are covered with tissue layers, F_C and F_N, respectively.

If the distance of an arbitrary node to the skeleton-like structure is within the "flesh" size, the node is defined as a part of that class. Namely, let $\vec{X}$ be an element of the testing set, its classification is determined as follows,

$$\text{Class}(\vec{X}) = \begin{cases} \text{Cancer} & \|U_C - \vec{X}\| \leq F_C \\ \text{Normal} & \|U_N - \vec{X}\| \leq F_N \end{cases} \tag{7}$$

Figure 3 portrays how classification is done with a fixed "flesh size" covering the structure'. Note that when this classification method is implemented, an optimal "flesh size" is sought. In our studies, the size of the flesh, F_C or F_N, is chosen so that the overall accuracy of the validation set (50% of the test set) is maximal. Then, we consider the flesh sizes where the accuracy of the test set is the highest. F_C or F_N is defined as the average of the obtained flesh sizes.

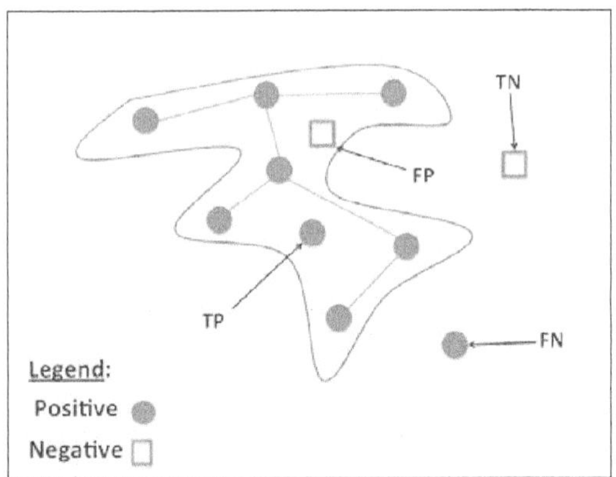

Figure 3 - The True Positive (TP), False Positive (FP), True Negative (TN), and False Positive (FN) values are determined based on the nodes location relative to each derived skeleton. Image shows the "Flesh" classification method.

In the second (**Proximity**) classification process, an arbitrary node is classified as part of a class depending on its location relative to each skeleton. If the distance from the node to the structure of class A is closer than the distance from the node to the structure of class B, then the node is classified as part of class A. **Figure 4** depicts a visual representation of the BPR Proximity method. Mathematically, one can write the classification rule as follows

$$\text{Class}(\vec{X}) = \begin{cases} \text{Cancer} & \|U_C - \vec{X}\| \leq \|U_N - \vec{X}\| \\ \text{Normal} & \|U_N - \vec{X}\| \leq \|U_C - \vec{X}\| \end{cases} \tag{8}$$

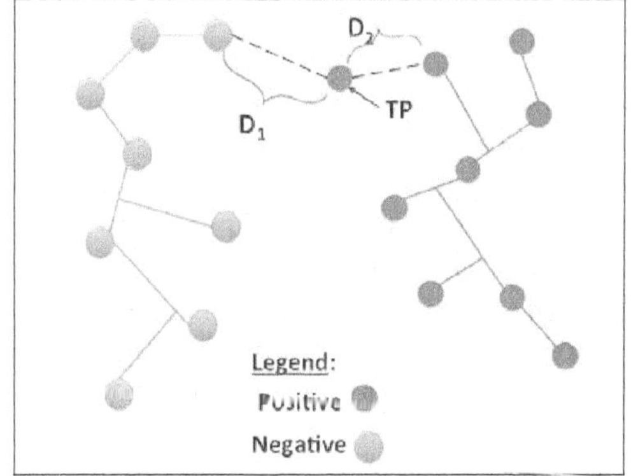

Figure 4 - Image shows the Proximity classification method. If the distance from a node to the structure of class A is smaller than that to class B, the node is defined as part of class A

We run the proposed BPR algorithms numerous times for a fixed number of genes considered, fixed holdout percentage, and cancer type. Each time the algorithm runs with different randomly selected training and testing sets. The average accuracy $A_n^H(\text{cancer})$ is recorded. Due to a large number of parametric variations (number of genes, holdout percentages, cancer types), a unified metric is needed to assess the performance of the proposed algorithms. A geometric mean,

$$G_n^H = \sqrt[Ntypes]{\prod_{Cancer-1}^{Ntypes} A_n^H(\text{cancer})} \tag{9}$$

is calculated for all the considered cancer types, where n is the number of genes considered, $Ntypes$ is the number of cancer types available, and H is the holdout percentage. We then define the overall algorithm performance as

$$P_n = \sqrt[NH]{\prod_{i-1}^{NH} G_n^H} \tag{10}$$

where $\{H_i\}_{i=1}^{NH}$ is a set of different holdout percentages. The overall performance allows us to determine recognition rate for different types of cancers and optimal parameters to use with the proposed BPR algorithm.

3. Results

In this paper, the proposed BPR methods (two biomimetic construction algorithms and two classification methods) are applied to four different cancer types (Bladder, Colon, Leukemia, Liver). Several metrics have been proposed for assessing the accuracy of the BPR algorithms. Accuracies are calculated based on the average of 100 runs. When classification using the "Flesh" method is implemented, half of the testing set is used for determining the optimal "Flesh size. Accuracy is calculated based on the remaining test set with Equation (6). Below are results obtained as well as how optimal conditions are determined and highest accuracy attainable for each cancer type. **Table 1** summarizes the data sets used in this study. Table represents the microarray data sets used. Data for liver and bladder has been provided by genome- www5.stanford.edu in reference [12] and [13] respectively. Colon and leukemia data came from reference [14] and [15], respectively.

Table 1: Data Sets

Cancer Type	Number of Genes	No. of Cancer Samples	No. of Normal Samples
Bladder	6688	103 Tumor	22 Healthy Tissue
Colon	2000	40 Tumor	22 Healthy Tissue
Leukemia	7129	48 AML	25 ALL
Liver	5520	105 Tumor	76 Healthy Tissue

Data sets used consist of four cancer types, bladder, colon, leukemia, and liver cancers. Each data set contains cancer-free (normal) and cancerous (cancer) samples. For bladder cancer, the data set contained data for 125 samples, 103 of which are cancer and 22 are normal. Data for 6688 genes were provided. For colon cancer, the data set contained data from 62 samples, 40 of which are cancer and 22 are normal. Data for 2000 genes were provided. For leukemia cancer, the data set contained data from 73 samples, 48 of which are Acute Myeloid Leukemia (AML) and 25 are Acute Lymphoblastic Leukemia (ALL). We considered the AML samples to be cancer and ALL to be normal. Data for 7129 genes were provided. For liver cancer, the data set contained data from 181 samples, 105 of which are cancer and 76 are normal. Data for 5520 genes were provided.

In order to develop the HD skeleton-like structure, we regard each sample of gene expression levels as a single node in the space. Each node belongs to either the cancer-free or cancer-containing calss. The Cancer Training Set, S_C, and Normal Training Set, S_N, are randomly selected from the total samples based on a Holdout value (percentage of the total samples used for training alone). Holdout percentages used in this study include $33\%, 50\%$, and 80%. The remaining samples composed the Testing sets as given in **Table 2**. It should be remarked that the Validation* sets are needed only when using classification with the "flesh" method

Table 2: Size of Sets Based on Holdout Values

Holdout	**Training**	**Validation***	**Test**
$\frac{1}{2}$	$\frac{1}{2}$	$\frac{1}{4}$	$\frac{1}{4}$
$\frac{1}{3}$	$\frac{1}{3}$	$\frac{1}{3}$	$\frac{1}{3}$
80%	80%	10%	10%

Given S_C, and S_N, we define the Differential Mean, $D(g)$ for each gene, g, as

$$D(g) = |\overline{S_C(g)} - \overline{S_N(g)}| \quad (11)$$

For each simulation, the training sets contain a random selection of samples from the entire raw data. We then sort the differential mean values for all the genes in descending order and chose the highest differential mean to construct a HD Biomimetic structure. **Figure 1** shows the average gene expression levels for each type of cancer.

From Equation (11), we determine the genes with the highest average differential expression level. **Figure 5** displays the top ten highly differentiated normalized average gene expression levels for each cancer type. Results show that gene expressions for the colon cancer and normal samples are widely varied and overlapped. This may be indicative as to why colon cancer classification is a big challenge and accuracy can be low compared to other types of cancers [5-7].

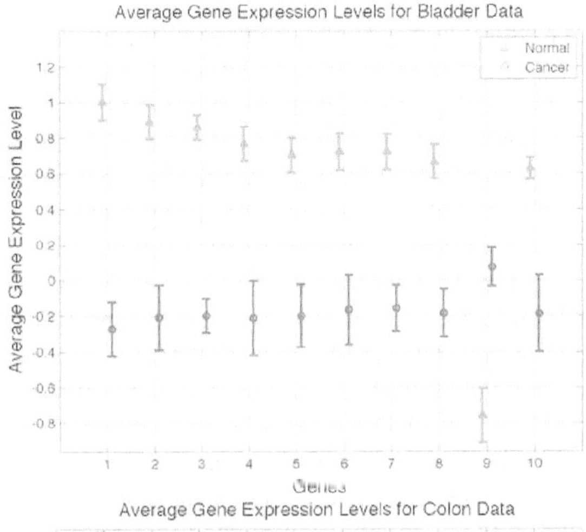

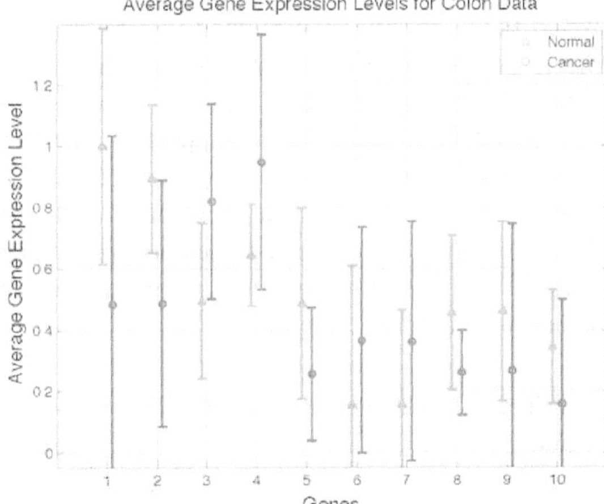

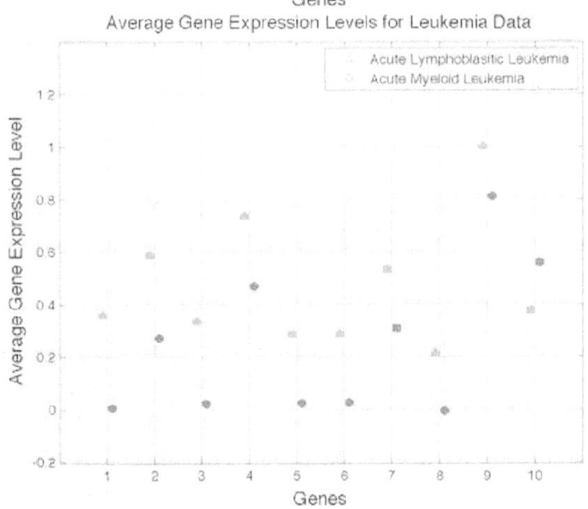

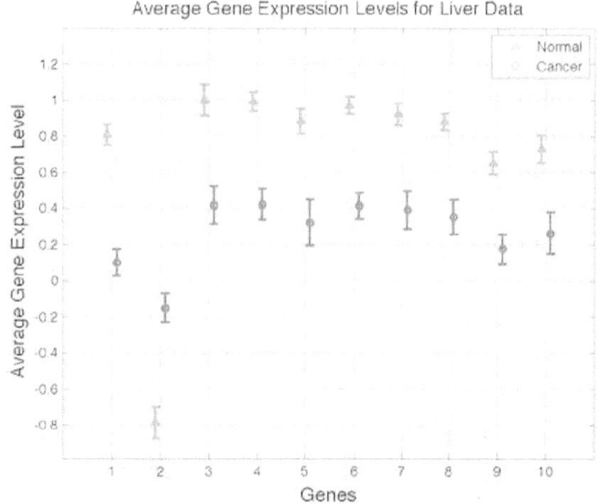

Figure 5 Graphs represent the average gene expression level for genes with highest differential mean. Includes Bladder, Colon, Leukemia, and Liver average differential gene expression.

After testing each algorithm, we determine the overall perfermance with Equation (9) and (10). **Table 3** describes the average geometric mean accuracy across all genes when using the different techniques developed.

Table 3: Mean Accuracy for Different Methods

Holdout	50%	33.33%	80%
Techniques			
Nodal/Proximity	90.89%	91.71%	86.62%
Nodal/Flesh	79.81%	63.38%	79.25%
Line Segment/ Proximity	91.14%	92.00%	86.84%
Line Segment/ Flesh	79.87%	63.25%	79.27%

This table allows us to determine that the Line Segment construction and Proximity classification technique provide the highest accuracy when compared to the other combinations for all different holdout values. We determine the optimal holdout value when we consider the average accuracy of each cancer type when implementing the Line Segment construction and Proximity recognition. **Table 4** shows the average accuracy for cancer types with the different holdout values considered across all genes considered.

Table 4: Mean Accuracy for Different Holdouts			
Holdout	50%	**33.33%**	80%
Cancer Type			
Bladder	99.61%	99.67%	98.71%
Colon	78.13%	80.09%	70.55%
Leukemia	92.14%	93.23%	85.25%
Liver	96.24%	96.29%	95.79%

The optimal holdout is 33.33%, since, for each cancer type, this holdout yields higher average accuracy than 50% and 80% at each cancer type.

Figure 6 shows the overall performance for each combination of methods. We observed the geometric mean of methods for each number of genes considered. This graphs allows us to determine which combination of methods yields optimal accuracies.

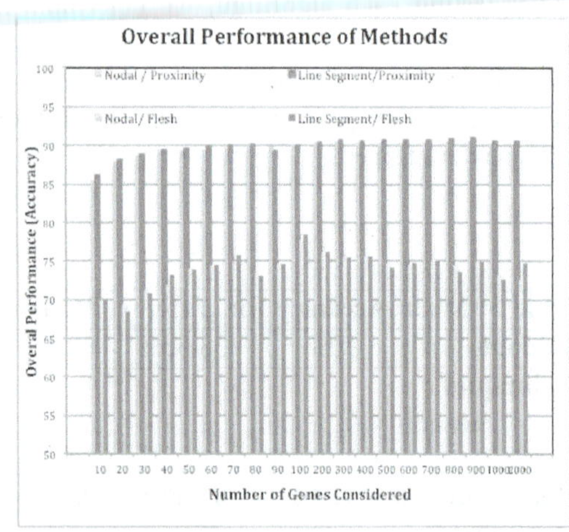

Figure 6 - Graph shows overall performance of each algorithm and classification technique for all 100 trials. Each bar represents the average accuracy of the test set for each number of genes considered. Note that we use holdout percentages (33%, 50%, and 80%) of the DNA microarray data samples for training and the remaining for testing.

We use the performance results from **Figure 6** to determine the optimal parameters for any arbitrary implementation. The overall values in the chart suggest that using the Segment method along with the Proximity recognition scheme yield higher accuracies than the other methods. The optimal number of genes to consider is 300 to 900 since the overall performance is highest in this range. The "Flesh" recognition method proves to be the least effective with either construction method.

The average accuracy for each cancer type using the mentioned metrics is compared to previous algorithms and experiments. We limited comparison to those studies that used the same data sets of DNA microarray samples. **Table 5** summarizes the overall performance of the proposed BPR and performance from other articles using the same DNA microarray data. In Peterson (2004), the accuracy is calculated using a single dominant mode of the Principal of Orthogonal Decomposition (POD) method. Testing was done separately with either cancer or normal set [7]. In Abbasi (2007), an improved POD classification method was introduced, where accuracy is determined from a combination of both cancer and normal sets [8]. Lee uses a multi-nodal POD along with Support Vector Machine, Self-Organized Map, and Neural Networks to determine the accuracy for each cancer type [9]. The last column shows the attained accuracy when using the proposed Biomimetic Pattern Recognition method for each cancer type.

Table 5: Overall Performance of Cancer Types				
Cancer Type	Peterson (2004)	Abbasi (2007)	Lee (2010)	Proposed BPR
Bladder	60.00%	64.52%	N/A	99.67%
Colon	N/A	N/A	65.35%	83.09%
Leukemia	N/A	N/A	97.30%	93.20%
Liver	75.00%	82.30%	96.43%	97.34%

From Table 2, we can see the improvement in accuracy throughout each method where applicable.

4. Summary and Conclusion

In this paper we proposed a new BPR algorithm which employs a different approach to the PHC where elements of the same class are connected according to nearest neighbor. This approach allows for the development of two different biomimetic structure constructions (Nodal and Segment) and two recognition methods ("Flesh" and Proximity). The proposed methods were applied to bladder, colon, leukemia, and liver cancer data. We considered different holdout percentages and number of genes to test highest recognition rate on each cancer type.

Results from **Figure 6** indicate that the combination of the Segment Connection construction and Proximity Recognition scheme yield the optimal accuracies than other combinations examined. **Table 3** suggests that the given combination of schemes with a 33% holdout value give a higher accuracy for each cancer type. From **Table 4**, we determined that experiment shows the new BPR algorithm has high recognition rate when compared to previous techniques. Biomimetic Pattern Recognition has shown to be a promising tool for cancer detection using DNA microarray data.

5. Acknowledgements

The author would like to thank Drs. Amybeth Cohen and Laura Arce for their support, mentoring, and biology consultation. Graphics and computations were generated with MatLab2011a. The author would like to acknowledge Dai Nguyen for help in the MatLab 2011a coding. This work was supported by a Minority Access to Research Careers grant to from the National Institutes of Health (2T34GM008612-17) and the CSUF McNair Program.

6. References

1 Hoopes. L. *Genetic Diagnosis: DNA Microarrays and Cancer*. (Nature Education, Scitable by Nature Education). 2008

2 Babu. M. *Microarray Data Analysis*, (Encyclopedia of Genetics, Computational Genomics, Proteomics and Bioinformatics, Horizon Press, UK). 2004

3 Vessey. K. *Use of Microarrays to Investigate Plant Response to Stress*. (GNC Training Workshop). 2008

4 Rhodes. D.R., Yu. J. *Large-scale meta-analysis of cancer microarray data identifies common transcriptional profiles of neoplastic transformation and progression*. Proceedings of the Natural Academy of Sciences of the United States of America. 2004

5 Peterson. D., Lee. C.H. *A DNA-based Pattern Recognition Technique for Cancer Detection*. Proceedings of the 26th Annual International Conference of the IEEE EMBS. 2004.

6 Abbasi. N., Lee. C.H. *Feature Extraction Techniques on DNA Microarray Data for Cancer Detection*. Proceedings of World Congress on Bioengineering. 2007

7 Lee. C.B., Lee. C. H. *Extended Principal of Orthogonal Decomposition Method for Cancer Detection*. Proceeding of the International Journal of Bioscience, Biochemistry and Bioinformatics. 2010

8 Wang. S., Zhao. X. *Biomimetic Pattern Recognition Theory and Its Applications*. Chinese Journal of Electronics. Vol 3. No. 3. 2004

9 Qin. H., Wang. S., Sun. H. *Biomimetic Pattern Recognition for Speaker-Independent Speech Recognition*, Proceedings of the International Conference on Neural Networks and Brain. Vol. 2. (pgs 1290 - 1294). 2005

10 Zhai. Y., Zeng. J., Gan . J., Xu .Y. *A study of Biomimetic Pattern Recognition based Iris Recognition Method*, Proceedings of the International Symposium on Information Processing. Vol. 2. (pgs. 71-74) 2009

11 Wang. Z., Mo. H., Lu. H., Wang. S. *A method of Biomimetic Pattern Recognition for Face Recognition*, Proceeding of the International Joint Conference on Neural Networks). Vol. 3. (pgs. 2216 2221) 2003

12 Chen, X., et. al., *Variation in Gene Expression Patterns in Human Gastric Cancers*, Mol Biol Cell. 2003 Aug; 14(8): 3208-15. Epub 2003

13 Alon. U., et al. *Broad Patterns of Gene Expression Revealed by Clustering Analysis of Cancer and Normal Colon Tissues Probed by Oligonucleotide Arrays*. Proc. National Academic Science.

14 T. R. Golub, D. K. Slonim, et al. *Molecular classification of cancer: class discovery and class prediction by gene expression monitoring*. Science. 1999, 286: 531-537.

15 Chen, X. et al. *Gene expression patterns in human liver cancers*. Molecular Biology of the Cell. 2002.

Diabetes Differential Diagnosis Application System- a Case Study

Shweta Sheel, MBBS[1], Veronica Heredia, MD, Aman Kumar

***Abstract*— There is a significant increase in the number of Type-2 diabetic patients in the past decade. This is mainly due to rapidly rising numbers of obese and overweight people. According to the latest CDC estimates over 7 million people in the US are still undiagnosed of this disease. In this study we developed a Diabetes Differential Diagnosis Application (DDDxA) system that takes textual data from a potential patient as input and based on Natural Language Processing techniques suggests if a person should be recommended for further screening for diabetes or not. The DDDxA system has the potential to perform an initial diagnosis of the patient and provide initial treatment in the field away from a doctor's clinic.**

I. INTRODUCTION

According to a CDC (Center for Disease Control and Prevention) 2011 study (http://www.cdc.gov/diabetes/pubs/estimates11.htm#1) there are 25.8 million people, or 8.3% of the U.S. population that have diabetes. Out of these 25.8 diabetic patients 18.8 million people are diagnosed with this disease while over 7.0 million people in the US are still undiagnosed. These statistics and estimates are derived from various data systems of the Centers for Disease Control and Prevention (CDC), the Indian Health Service's (IHS), National Patient Information Reporting System (NPIRS), the U.S. Renal Data System of the National Institutes of Health (NIH), the U.S. Census Bureau, and published studies.

There is a need in this field for a semi-automated computerized system that quickly and accurately diagnoses a diabetic condition without the help of specialized or expert physicians. This can allow further referrals and rapid treatment that will allow patients to recover faster than is possible without specialists present.

In this study we have developed a preliminary Diabetes Differential Diagnosis Application (DDDxA) that can identify early diabetic (Type-2) instances almost as accurately as a clinician. The fundamental goal of the DDDxA is to allow patient (by themselves or with a healthcare professional) to enter Patient Symptoms on a Mobile Device connected via a Secure Network to a back end Diagnosis System. The Diagnosis System will then return a diagnosis back to the Mobile Device via the Secure Network. The diagnosis will provide a confidence score of the likelihood of diabetes in the patient.

II. METHODOLOGY

We collected anonymized TBI/PTSD Patient Data and develop NLP based Diabetes Predictive Engine. Differential Diagnostics or DDx is a method for determining the most likely disease that based on a set of patient symptoms. The basic theory of DDx is a *probabilistic measure* for estimating the likelihood of a specific diagnosis. In the case of Dibetes DDx, the measure would be

$$P(D) = \sum_{i}^{n} P(D/S_i)$$

Where

$P(D)$ = Probability of Diabetes in a patient
$P(D/S_i)$ = Probability of Diabetes in a patient, given Symptom *S*.

In this study in addition to the probability distribution method, we have used a machine learning approach (Support Vector Machine) to differentially diagnose Diabetes based on textual data collected based on the patient input.

III. DATA COLLECTION

A. Diabetes Check List

We collected the patient data from 25 people who were never pathologically tested for Diabetes. The Patient Data was divided into Training and Test data. The Automated DDx Systems was trained on one set of data and then tested on a blind set of data. There are two basic types of input for the Automated DDx: 1) Patient Intake Forms (Diabetes Check List) and 2) Free Text Patient Description.

[1] Contact Author - Shweta Sheel, MBBS, Gauhati Medical College Hospital, Assam, India; Email: shwetasheel@gmail.com; Veronica Heredia, MD; Email: vph@earthlink.net; Aman Kumar, BCL Technologies, San Jose, California; Email: amank@bcltechnologies.com.

Diabetes Checklist – Pilot Program

Client's Name ____________

Clinician ____________

Date ____________

Instruction to Client: Below is a list of common problems and complaints that are related to diabetic experience. Please read each one carefully put an "X" in the box to indicate how much you have been bothered by that problem in the last 3 months

No.	Response	Not at all (1)	A little bit (2)	Moderately (3)	Quite a bit (4)	Extremely (5)
1.	Do you have an urge for frequent urination than normal?					
2	Do you have blurry vision recently?					
3	Do you have increased hunger than normal?					
4	Do you experience more fatigue than normal?					
5	Do you experience dry mouth recently more than normal?					
6	Do you feel more irritable than normal?					
7	Do you experience unusual headaches?					
8	Do you have had itchy skin?					
9.	Have you experienced Unusual Weight Changes?					
10	Do you experience frequent infections such as frequent and persistent yeast infections in women, skin infections, urinary infections, or gum and mouth infections					
11	Do you experience Sores, Cuts, and Bruises That Take a Long Time to Heal?					
12	Do you experience Numbness or Tingling in the Hands or Feet?					
13	Have you experienced Sexual Dysfunction lately?					
14	Is your body shape an apple shape with thin arms and legs?					

Fig. 1. Diabetes Check List - Sample

B. Free Text Patient Description

In the absence of specific Diabetes Intake Forms, clinicians write down patient information in the form of free text. The figure below shows an example of free text input for a patient.

Mrs. << anonymized >> is a 45 year old asymptomatic obese African American female who comes to your office for the first time for follow up of her DM. She was diagnosed with type 2 DM 6 months ago. The patient complains of burning sensation in his feet at night. On physical examination, you note decreased sensation in his toes and calluses on hos lateral fifth digits. She is taking glyburide 5 mg daily before breakfast. She is on no other prescription medications but she takes over the counter ibuprofen for knee pain. She follows the American Heart Association Diet. Her fasting blood sugar 2 months ago was 160.

Past medical history - positive for mild hypertension -130/85 to 140/90 mmHg. Hyperlipidemia: No Known drug allergies.

Family history- Positive for DM in her mother and older sister. Hypertension and coronary artery disease in her mother, father, older sister and younger brother.

Social history- Negative for smoking, alcohol or illicit drug abuse. Married with three adult children. Works as cashier at a local supermarket.

Fig. 2. Sample Case Presentation - Diabetes

The NLP based Diabetes Predictive Engine consists of 3 parts – Natural Language Parser, Semantic Role Labeler, and Support Vector Machine, as shown in the figure below:

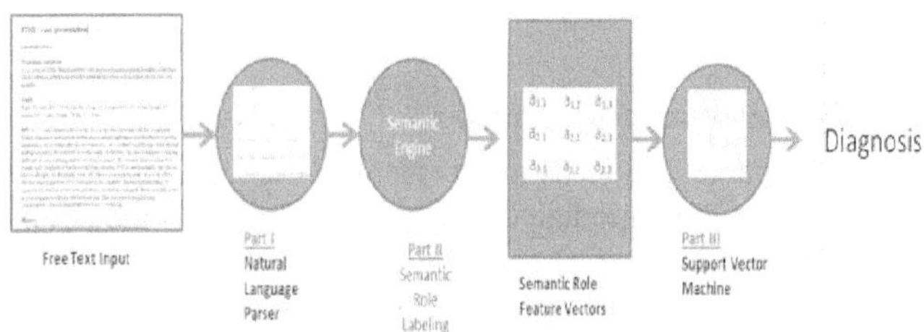

Fig. 3. Differential Diagnosis based on Text and Natural Language Processing

C. Natural Language Parser

The first step of the NLP Engine is to break the text into sentences and parse each sentence to find its grammatical structure and parts of speech. For instance the sentence:

> "The patient complains of burning sensation in his feet at night."

parses to the tree in the figure below:

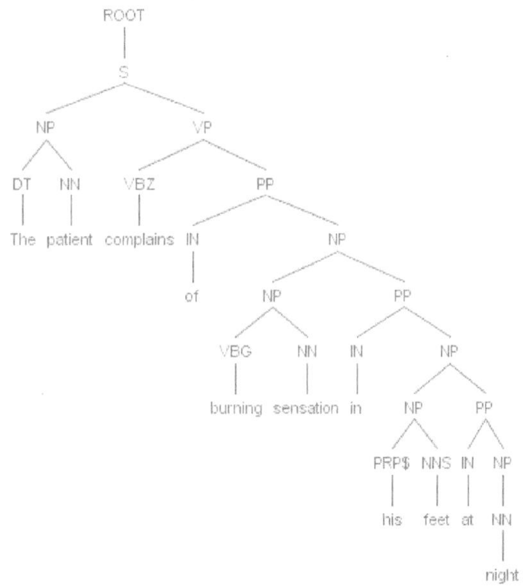

Fig. 4. Sample Parse Tree

Where:
DT: Determiner
S: Simple Declarative Clause
NP: Noun Phrase
NN: Noun, singular or mass
VP: Verb Phrase
VBZ: Verb, 3rd person singular present
PP: Prepositional Phrase
IN: Preposition
VBG: Verb, gerund/present participle
PRP$: Personal Pronoun
NNS: Noun plural

D. *Semantic Role Labeler*

This parse tree feeds into semantic role labeling module. This module (manual role labeling right now), along with a lexical ontology will semantically annotate Part-of-Speech (POS) tagged parse trees. In this case, the semantic roles are:

Agent: : <the patient>
Mood : <burning sensation>
Location: <feet>
Time: <night>

E. *Support Vector Machine*

These semantic roles form the Semantic Role Feature Vectors. Each document is converted into a matrix for feature vectors that are sent to a Support Vector Machine (SVM). We developed and trained the SVM to take Semantic Feature Vectors and predict Diabetes. We used Joachims SVM tool (http://svmlight.joachims.org/) that is a C implementation of Support Vector Machines. We have implemented two programs*: (1) svm_learn* , which takes a training file and creates a model based on it; and (2*) svm_classify* , which takes testing data and applies the model to it in order to classify it.

For differential diagnosis project, the input file includes the training examples. Each of the following lines represents one training example. The format of the training examples is given below.

<line> .=. <target> <feature>:<value> <feature>:<value> ... <feature>:<value> # <info>
<target> .=. +1 | -1 | 0 | <float>
<feature> .=. <integer> | "qid"
<value> .=. <float>
<info> .=. <string>

During classification phase, the target value gives the class of the example. So, for a positive example (meaning the patient is diabetic) +1 as the target value, while -1 a negative example, meaning no diabetes, respectively.

IV. Experimental Set up

The acquisition of fully-anonymized 'Free Text Patient Description' and 'Diabetes Checklist' content for 25 adult men and women in the USA and India was done manually. These 25 people were not diagnosed with diabetes in the past. The textual data was fed into the preliminary diagnostic system. A phrase similarity repository is derived following Stanford's STRIDE ontology.

The preliminary DDDx system suggested if these people should be recommended for further screening of diabetes. The system provided a confidence score based on the term frequency matching of the features in the check list.

V. Evaluation

Based on the textual data entry of the 25 people the hand-simulated DDDx system recommended that 14 people should be further screened for Diabetes, meaning they were recommended to go for the following pathological tests under formal medical supervision:

- Fasting or pre-meal blood glucose
- Post-meal blood glucose measurement
- Hemoglobin A1C
- Dilated eye exam
- Comprehensive foot exam
- Urine test for microalbumin
- Blood pressure
- Weight
- Lipid control

After performing these pathological tests, we found that out of the 14 people that the DDDxA system recommended for further screening, 11 people tested positive for Type-2 Diabetes. Thus the preliminary DDDxA system recorded an accuracy of around **78.6%** accuracy. In other words, for the given sample size of 25 people, the DDDxA system could diagnose the Type-2 Diabetes in patients with a *precision* of 78.6%. The following table gives the preliminary results of this study.

Table I

Evaluation score of the Diabetes Differential Diagnosis Application System

Number of People Initially Screened (presumed healthy)	25
Number of people DDDxA system screened for potential Diabetes	14
Number of people confirmed to have Type-2 Diabetes after pathological tests under medical supervision	11
Accuracy of the DDDxA system	78.57%

VI. Conclusions and Future Work

In this study we developed a Diabetes Differential Diagnosis Application (DDDxA) System that takes textual data – 'Diabetes Check List' and 'Free Text Patient Data' as input and based on the textual and semantic analysis of the data recommends if a person should be recommended for further screening for Diabetes.

The DDDxA system has the ability to perform an initial diagnosis of the patient and provide initial treatment in the field away from a doctor's clinic. In addition, it can subsequently diagnose the patient based on response to treatment and help modify the diagnosis and treatment based on the patient's response to previous treatment.

For future work, we would like to expand the data set from 25 people to 100 people and evaluate the system. In addition, we would like to expand the 'check list' and 'free text patient data' to more features to have wider coverage and higher precision.

References

[1] Tucker ME. New AACE algorithm addresses all aspects of type 2 diabetes. Medscape Medical News [serial online]. April 23, 2013; Accessed May 1, 2013. Available at http://www.medscape.com/viewarticle/802954.

[2] Garber AJ, Abrahamson MJ, Barzilay JI, Blonde L, Bloomgarden ZT, Bush MA, et al. AACE Comprehensive Diabetes Management Algorithm 2013. Endocr Pract. Mar-Apr 2013;19(2):327-36.

[3] American Diabetes Association. Standards of medical care in diabetes--2012. *Diabetes Care*. Jan 2012;35 Suppl 1:S11-631

[4] Keller DM. New EASD/ADA Position Paper Shifts Diabetes Treatment Goals. Medscape Medical News. Available at http://www.medscape.com/viewarticle/771989.

[5] Framenet: Frame Semantics Meets the Corpus. In LSA.Fillmore, C. and Baker, C. (2000)

[6] Automatic Labeling of Semantic Roles. Proc.of ACL.Gildea, D. and Jurafsky, D. (2000)

[7] Burges, Christopher J. C.; A Tutorial on Support Vector Machines for Pattern Recognition, Data Mining and Knowledge Discovery 2:121–167, 1998

BIOCOMP'12

Almost Sure Stability of Stochastic Gene Regulatory Networks with Mode-Dependent Interval Delays

Robert Altwasser, Reinhard Guthke, Sebastian Vlaic [a], Mark R. Emmett [b], Carol L. Nilsson [c] and Anke Meyer-Baese [d],

[a] *Leibniz Institute for Natural Product Research and Infection Biology e. V. Hans-Knöll-Institute (HKI), 07745 Jena, Germany*

[b] *Department of Biochemistry and Molecular Biology, UTMB Cancer Center, University of Texas Medical Branch, Galveston, TX 7555-1060, U.S.*

[c] *Department of Pharmacology and Toxicology, UTMB Cancer Center, University of Texas Medical Branch, Galveston, TX 7555-1060, U.S.*

[d] *Department of Scientific Computing, Florida State University, Tallahassee, FL 32306-4120, U.S.*

Abstract

We investigate the almost surely asymptotic stability of gene regulatory networks (GRNs) with Markovian switching. Previous research has described GRNs as coupled nonlinear stochastic systems under parametric perturbations without considering the important aspect of different time-delays in the subsystems. However, a realistic model of a GRN is that of a hybrid stochastic retarded system that represents a complex nonlinear dynamical system including mode-dependent time delays and Markovian jumping as well as noise fluctuations. In this paper, we interpret GRNs as hybrid stochastic retarded systems and prove their almost surely asymptotical stability and give upper bounds of derivatives of time delays of the subsystems. The theoretical results are elucidated in an illustrative example and thus shown how they can be applied to reverse engineering design.

Key words: Genetic regulatory network, retarded systems, Markov chain, stochastic systems, almost sure stability, time delays

Email address: ameyerbaese@fsu.edu (Anke Meyer-Baese).

Preprint submitted to Elsevier Science

1 Introduction

Gene regulatory networks (GRNs) combining a coupled dynamics of fast and slow states constitute an important class of biological networks [1]. Reverse engineering requires a rigorous understanding of the qualitative robustness properties of GRNs with respect to parameter variations on both a fast or slow time scale and under consideration of a transcriptional time delay [5]. In early works, GRNs are described as either two-time scale systems without delay [4] or as unperturbed systems [6].

It is well-known that molecules and reaction rates are subject to significant statistical fluctuations and especially gene regulation is an intrinsically noisy process due to intracellular and extracellular noise perturbations and environmental fluctuations. Additionally, the transition from one state to the next is based on certain transition probabilities forming a homogeneous Markov chain with finite state space. This aspect motivates the formulation of a stochastic model with Markovian switches to describe the dynamics of gene regulation. Previous work investigated genetic regulatory networks with parameter uncertainties and noise perturbations [10] or of Markov-type with delays and uncertain mode transition rates [11]. It is naturally to propose a more detailed model with delays that combines Markovian jumping and noise perturbations and analyze its dynamic behavior. Previously [3], the gene regulatory networks were formulated as stochastic coupled nonlinear differential systems operating at different time-scales with equal time delays for each scale and under Markovian jumping as well as noise fluctuations. In this paper, we prove almost sure stability of the GRN and analyze its robustness properties, modeled by a system of competitive differential equations, from a rigorous analytic standpoint [7]. The network under study models the delayed nonlinear dynamics under consideration of Markovian jumping and noise perturbations and assumes mode-dependent interval delays.

2 Problem Statement

GRNs represent circuits of genes that interact and regulate the expression of other genes by proteins. The change in expression of a gene is regulated by protein synthesis in transcriptional, translational and post-translational processes. Taking into account a transcriptional time delay [5] and the fact that mRNA typically decays much faster than the protein, we considered in a previous work [3] the GRN described by the following equation

$$\dot{M}_i(t) = -a_i M_i(t) + \sum_{j=1}^{n} w_{ij}\tilde{g}_j(P_j(t-\rho_i(t))) + B_i \tag{1a}$$
$$\dot{P}_i(t) = -c_i P_i(t) + d_i M_i(t-\sigma_i(t))$$

where $M_i(t), P_i(t) \in R$ are the concentrations of mRNA and protein of the ith node, respectively. The parameters a_i and c_i are the decay rates of mRNA and protein, respectively; d_i is the translation rate, $\tilde{g}_j(x)$ is of Hill-form with $\tilde{g}_j(x) = \frac{\left(\frac{x}{\beta_j}\right)^{H_j}}{\left(1+\left(\frac{x}{\beta_j}\right)^{H_j}\right)}$, B_i is defined as the basal rate with $B_i = \sum_{j\in I_i} \alpha_{ij}$ and I_i is the set of all the j which is a repressor of gene i, $W = (w_{ij}) \in R^{n\times n}$ is defined as follows

$$w_{ij} = \begin{cases} \alpha_{ij}, & : \text{ if transcription factor j is an activator of gene i} \\ 0, & : \text{ if there is no link from node j to i} \\ -\alpha_{ij} & : \text{ if transcription factor j is a repressor of gene i} \end{cases} \tag{2}$$

α_{ij} represents the transcriptional rate of transcription factor j to gene i being a bounded constant. Let $(M^{*^T}, P^{*^T})^T$ be an equilibrium point of the system (1a). We thus obtain $f_i(y_i(t)) = \tilde{g}_i(y_i(t)+P_i^*) - \tilde{g}_i(P_i^*)$. Because $\tilde{g}_i$ is a monotonically increasing function with saturation, $g_i(\cdot)$ satisfies the sector condition $0 \leq \frac{g_i(x)}{x} \leq k_i$. By shifting the equilibrium of the system to the origin, we have $\mathbf{x}(t) = \mathbf{M}(t) - \mathbf{M}^*(t)$ and also $\mathbf{y}(t) = \mathbf{P}(t) - \mathbf{P}^*(t)$. We have defined a general formulation of the GRN as a nonlinear coupled system with both time-varying delays for feedback regulation $\rho_i(t)$ and translation $\sigma_i(t)$.

In terms of Hill function, the transformed system is:

$$\dot{x}_i(t) = -a_i x_i(t) + \sum_{j=1}^{n} w_{ij} f_j(y_j(t-\rho_j(t))) \tag{3a}$$
$$\dot{y}_i(t) = -c_i y_i(t) + d_i x_i(t-\sigma_i(t))$$

The above model can be formulated as a n-dimensional GRN

$$\dot{\mathbf{x}}(t) = -\mathbf{A}\mathbf{x}(t) + \mathbf{W}\mathbf{f}(\mathbf{y}(t-\rho(t))) \tag{4a}$$
$$\dot{\mathbf{y}}(t) = -\mathbf{C}\mathbf{y}(t) + \mathbf{D}\mathbf{x}(t-\sigma(t))$$

with $A = \text{diag}\{a_1, a_2, \cdots, a_n\}$, $C = \text{diag}\{c_1, c_2, \cdots, c_n\}$ and $D = \text{diag}\{d_1, d_2, \cdots, d_n\}$.

Since gene regulation is viewed as an intrinsically noisy process, the GRN can be modeled as follows:

$$d\mathbf{x}(t) = -\mathbf{A}\mathbf{x}(t) + \mathbf{W}\mathbf{f}(\mathbf{y}(t-\rho(t))) + \rho(\mathbf{y}(t))d\omega(t) \tag{5a}$$
$$d\mathbf{y}(t) = -\mathbf{C}\mathbf{y}(t) + \mathbf{D}\mathbf{x}(t-\sigma(t))$$

with $d\omega(t) = n(t)dt$ where $\omega(t)$ is a l-dimensional Wiener process and $n(t) = [n_1(t), \cdots, n_l(t)]$ with $n_i(t)$ being a scalar zero mean Gaussian white noise process and $n_i(t)$ independent of $n_j(t)$. $\rho(\mathbf{y}(t)) \in R^{n\times l}$ represents the noise intensity matrix. In [2], GRNs were considered with both interval time-varying delays and stochastic noise:

$$\dot{\mathbf{x}}(t) = -\mathbf{A}\mathbf{x}(t) + \mathbf{W}\mathbf{f}(\mathbf{y}(t-\rho(t))) \tag{6a}$$
$$+ [G_0\mathbf{x}(t) + G_1\mathbf{x}(t-\sigma(t)) + G_2\mathbf{y}(t) + G_3\mathbf{y}(t-\rho(t))]d\omega(t) \tag{6b}$$
$$\dot{\mathbf{y}}(t) = -\mathbf{C}\mathbf{y}(t) + \mathbf{D}\mathbf{x}(t-\sigma(t))$$

G_i represent the stochastic perturbation matrices. As stated in [2] and [3], the system matrices of GRN change randomly at discrete time instances with unknown a-priori probabilities and are governed by a Markov process. Thus, we will model the process of gene regulation as a Markov jump system and will apply techniques from hybrid stochastic delay systems (HSDSs) to the dynamical analysis of GRNs.

3 Theoretical Concepts of Hybrid Stochastic Delay Systems

In the following, we will introduce some notations and theoretical concepts from stochastic functional differential equation theory [8] that we will be using throughout this paper.

Notations:

$(\Omega, F, \{F_t\}_{t\geq 0}, P)$: complete probability space with a filtration $\{F\}_{t\geq 0}$ that is right-continuous and F_0 contains the P-null sets.

$B(t) = (B_1(t), \cdots, B_m(t))^T$: m-dimensional Brownian motion defined on the probability space.

$|\cdot|$ is the Euclidean norm in R^n.

$C([-h,0]; R^n)$ with $h \geq 0$ denotes the family of all continuous R^n-valued functions ψ on $[-\tau, 0]$ with the norm $||\psi|| = \sup\{|\psi(\theta)| : -h \leq \theta \leq 0\}$.

$C^b_{F_0}([-h,0]; R^n)$ is the family of all F_0-measurable bounded $C([-h,0]; R^n)$-valued random variables $\xi = \{\xi(\theta) : -h \leq \theta \leq 0\}$.

Let $r(t), t \geq 0$, be a right-continuous Markov chain on the probability space taking values in a finite state space $S = \{1, 2, \cdots, N\}$ with generator $\Gamma = (\gamma_{ij})_{N\times N}$ given by

$$P\{r(t+\Delta) = j : r(t) = i\} = \begin{cases} \gamma_{ij}\Delta + o(\Delta), & \text{if } i \neq j, \\ 1 + \gamma_{ij}\Delta + o(\Delta), & \text{if } i = j, \end{cases} \quad (7)$$

where $\Delta > 0$ and $\gamma_{ij} \geq 0$ is the transition rate from i to j if $i \neq j$ while $\gamma_{ij} = -\sum_{i\neq} \gamma_{ij}$.

We also assume that the Markov chain $r(\cdot)$ is independent of the Brownian motion $B(\cdot)$. The sample pathes of $r(t)$ are right-continuous step functions with a finite number of simple jumps in any finite subinterval of $R_+ := [0, \infty)$.

In the following we describe an n-dimensional hybrid stochastic system (HSS) with mode-dependent interval time delays [9] used in stochastic modeling. Let such a n-dimensional HSDS be given as

$$\begin{aligned} dx(t) = & f(x(t), x(t-\tau(t,r(t)), t, r(t))dt \\ & + g(x(t), x(t-\tau(t,r(t)), t, r(t))dB(t) \end{aligned} \quad (8)$$

on $t \geq 0$ with initial data $x_0 = \{x(\theta): -h \leq \theta \leq 0\} = \xi \in C^b_{F_0}([-h,0];R^n)$, $r(0) = r_0 \in S$ and with

$$\begin{cases} f : & R^n \times R^n \times R_+ \times S \to R^n \\ g : & R^n \times R^n \times R_+ \times S \to R^{n\times m} \end{cases}$$

In addition, we assume that they satisfy the local Lipschitz condition in (x, y) such that for any $K > 0$, there is a $L_K > 0$ with

$$\begin{cases} |f(x,y,t,i) - f(\bar{x},\bar{y},t,i)| \vee |g(x,y,t,i) - g(\bar{x},\bar{y},t,i)| \\ \qquad \leq L_k(|x-\bar{x}| + |y-\bar{y}|) \end{cases}$$

for all $|x| \vee |y| \vee |\bar{x}| \vee |\bar{y}| \leq K, t \geq 0$ and $i \in S$. In addition, we have $\sup_{t\leq 0, i\in S}\{|f(0,0,t,i)|, |g(0,0,t,i)| : t \geq 0, i \in S\} \leq K_0$ with some nonnegative number K_0. For two real numbers x and y, $x \vee y$ stands for the maximum of x and y. In addition, the time-delay of the system $\tau(t) : R_+ \times S \to R_+$ is differentiable in t for all $i \in S$ and bounded such that $l < \tau(t,i) \leq h$ for all $t \geq 0$ and $i \in S$.

Further $C^{2,1}(R^n \times R_+ \times S; R+)$ is the family of all nonnegative functions $V(x,t,i)$ on $R^n \times R_+ \times S$ being twice continuously differentiable in x and once in t. With $V \in C^{2,1}(R^n \times R_+ \times S; R_+)$, we define an operator L, from $R^n \times R^n \times R_+ \times S \to R$ by

$$LV(x_t,t,i) = V_t(x,t,i) + V_x(x,t,i)f(x,y,t,i) \tag{9}$$

$$+\frac{1}{2}\text{trace}[g^T(x,y,t,i)V_{xx}(x,t,i)g(x,y,t,i)] \tag{10}$$

$$+\sum_{j=1}^{N}\gamma_{ij}V(x,t,j) \tag{11}$$

where

$$\begin{cases} V_t(x,t,i) & = \frac{\partial V(x,t,i)}{\partial t} \\ V_x(x,t,i) & = \left(\frac{\partial V(x,t,i)}{\partial x_1}, \cdots, \frac{\partial V(x,t,i)}{\partial x_n}\right) \\ V_{xx}(x,t,i) & = \left(\frac{\partial^2 V(x,t,i)}{\partial x_i \partial x_j}\right)_{n\times n} \end{cases}$$

We give a useful definition regarding the stability of HSDS.

Definition [8] The system (8) is said to be almost surely stable if

$$P\left(\lim_{t\to\infty} x(t;\xi,r_0) = 0\right) = 1 \tag{12}$$

for all initial data $\xi \in C^b_{F_0}([-h,0]; R^n)$ and $r_0 \in S$.

The purpose of this note is to provide the theoretical basics and required definitions necessary to apply this theory of HSDSs to GRNs.

4 Almost Sure Stability Analysis of Hybrid Stochastic GRNs with Mode-Dependent Interval Delays

The objective of this study is to discuss the stability properties of the hybrid stochastic retarded GRN. The analysis is based on a mathematical model and a rigorous analytic standpoint.

Based on the above model described by equation (3), we will now introduce noise perturbations and Markovian jumping parameters. As previously discussed, the parameters of the GRN may change randomly at discrete time instances or in other words, the GRN has finite modes and it can switch from one to another at different times determined by a Markov chain. Since the switching probabilities are not a priori known, the GRN can be modeled by a hybrid system. The system of the GRN has both continuous and discrete states which are described by a Markovian jumping system. We can rewrite the GRN from equation (5a) as a hybrid stochastic delay system with mode-dependent interval time delays

$$\begin{cases} dX(t) = F(X(t), X(t-\rho(t,r(t))), X(t-\sigma(t,r(t)))t, r(t))dt \\ \quad +G(X(t), X(t-\rho(t,r(t))), X(t-\sigma(t,r(t))), t, r(t))dB(t) \end{cases}$$

with $X(t) = [x(t), y(t)], Y(t) = X(t-\rho(t)) = [0, \cdots, 0, y(t-\rho(t))]$ and $Z(t) = X(t-\sigma(t)) = [x(t-\sigma(t)), 0, \cdots, 0]$. X, Y and Z are $2n \times 1$ vectors. $G(X(t), X(t-\rho(t)), X(t-\sigma(t)), t, r(t))$ is the noise intensity function. The Markov chain $r(\cdot)$ is given as in (7) and $B(\cdot)$ is the Brownian motion.

We will make the following assumptions for computational simplicity without loss of generality.

Assumptions:

(A1) The trace can be approximated as $\text{trace}[G^T(X,Y,Z,t,i) \cdot G(X,Y,Z,t,i)] \leq \rho_1|X(t)|^2 + \rho_2|Y(t)|^2 + \rho_3|Z(t)|^2$ with $\rho_i \geq 0$.

(A2) For the nonlinear term, we assume $F(X,Y,Z,t,i) \leq \rho_4|X(t)|^2 + \rho_5|Y(t)|^2 + \rho_6|Z(t)|^2$ with $\rho_i \geq 0$.

Theorem 1: Suppose that there are nonnegative numbers l_i, h_i, δ_i and $\bar{\delta}$ such that

$$\begin{cases} l_i \le \rho(t,i) \le h_i, & \rho_t(t,i) = \frac{\partial \rho(t,i)}{\partial t} \le \delta_i \\ l_i \le \sigma(t,i) \le h_i, & \sigma_t(t,i) = \frac{\partial \sigma(t,i)}{\partial t} \le \delta_i \\ \bar{\delta}_i = \delta_i + \gamma_{ii} l_i + \sum_{j \neq i} \gamma_{ij} h_j \le \bar{\delta} < 1 \end{cases}$$

for all $t \geq 0$ and $i \in S$ with $l = \min_{i \in S} l_i$ and $h = \max_{i \in S} h_i$. Assume that there exist nonnegative function $V \in C^{2,1}(R^n \times R_+ \times S; R_+)$, $\lambda \in L_1(R_+; R_+)$, $w_1, w_2, w_3 \in C(R^n; R_+)$ such that

$$LV(X, Y, Z, t, i) \le \lambda(t) - k_1 w_1(X) + k_2 w_2(Y) + k_3 W_3(Z), \quad \forall (X, Y, Z, t, i) \in R^n \times R^n \times R^n \times R_+ \times S \qquad (13)$$

$$w_1(X) > w_2(Y) + w_3(Z), \quad \forall X, Y, Z \neq 0$$

and

$$\lim_{|x| \to \infty} \inf_{t \geq 0, i \in S} V(X, Y, Z, t, i) = \infty \qquad (14)$$

where $k_1, k_2, k_3 \geq 0$ such that $k_1 \geq \frac{k_2 + k_3}{(1-\delta)}$. Then the system (13) is almost surely stable.

Proof:

The proof follows the same outline like the proof of Theorem 3.1 in [8] and is therefore omitted. The above Theorem was adapted from [8] and its results can be used in reversed engineering design. The derived theoretical concepts are illustrated in an example.

Example 1: Let us consider a two-gene Markovian model (5a) with $A = \mathrm{diag}(2.4 \quad 1.52)$, $C = \mathrm{diag}(1.4 \quad 1.32)$ and $D = \mathrm{diag}(0.5 \quad 0.5)$ and $W = \begin{bmatrix} 0.2 & 0 \\ 0 & -0.1 \end{bmatrix}$ and $\zeta(t)$ being the Gaussian noise. Let $r(t)$ be a right-continuous Markov chain taking values in $S = \{1, 2\}$ with $\Gamma = (\gamma_{ij})_{2\times 2} = \begin{bmatrix} -0.9 & 0.9 \\ 0.8 & -0.8 \end{bmatrix}$. Let us assume that we want to determine the parameters ρ_1, ρ_2 and ρ_3. Based on Theorem 1, we can derive the inequalities $2.17 \geq 0.7\rho_1 + \rho_2 + \rho_3$ to be fullfilled in order to ensure the almost sure stability of system (5a).

In summary, we have shown that the most detailed model of GRN known yet and described by a hybrid stochastic retarded system is asymptotically stable.

5 Conclusion

We analyzed the dynamical behavior of genetic regulatory networks subject to noise perturbations and mode-dependent time-delays, and with both continuous and discrete states described by Markovian jumping systems based on the theory of hybrid stochastic retarded systems. The proposed model represents the most complex GRN model known so far in the literature. We assumed that the nonlinear nominal system and the noise intensity are bounded and that the Markov chain is independent of the Brownian motion. Specifically, we applied these theoretical concepts to study asymptotic stability properties of gene regulatory networks. In this sense we established stability results for the perturbed genetic regulatory network and determined the conditions that ensure the existence of globally pth moment asymptotically stable equilibria of the perturbed system. A sufficient condition for the nonlinear part and the noise intensity function are derived. The established results have potential application for reverse engineering and robust biosynthetic gene regulatory network design.

Acknowledgement

This research was supported in part by NIH Grant 5 G13 LM009832-02. RA was supported by the Jena School for Microbial Communication (JSMC).

References

[1] R. Tanaka, H. Okano and H. Kimura (2006), Mathematical description of Gene Regulatory Units, *Biophysical Journal*, **vol. 91**, p. 1235-1247.

[2] P. Balasubramaniam and R. Rakkiyappan and R. Krishnasamy (2010), Stochastic Stability of Markovian Jumping Uncertain Stochastic Genetic Regulatory Networks with Interval Time-Varying Delays, *Mathematical Biosciences*, **vol. 226**, p. 97-108.

[3] A. Meyer-Baese, C. Plant, S. Cappendijk and F. Theis (2010), Robust Stability Analysis of Hybrid Stochastic Gene Regulatory Networks, *BIOCOMP 2011*, p. 854-863.

[4] M. Simpson, C. Cox and G. Sayler (2003), Frequency Domain Analysis of Noise in Autoregulated Gene Circuits, *Proceedings of National Academy of Sciences*, **vol. 100**, p. 4551-4556.

[5] N. Monk (2003), Oscillatory Expression of Hes1, p53 and NF-kB Driven by Transcriptional Time Delays, *Curr. Biol.*, **vol. 13**, p. 1409-1413.

[6] F. Ren and J. Cao (2008), Asymptotic and Robust Stability of Genetic regulatory Networks with Time-Varying Delays, *Neurocomputing*, **vol. 71**, p. 834-842.

[7] L. Huang, X. Mao and F. Deng (2008) Stability of Hybrid Retarded Systems, *IEEE Transactions on Automatic Control*, p. 3413-3420.

[8] L. Huang and X. Mao (2010) On Almost Sure Stability of Hybrid Stochastic Systems with Mode-Dependent Interval Delays, *IEEE Transactions on Automatic Control*, p. 1946-1952.

[9] C. Yuan and X. Mao (2004) Robust Stability and Controllability of Stochastic Deifferential Delay Equations with Markovian Switching, *Automatica*, p. 343-354.

[10] P. Li, J. Lam and Z. Shu (2008) On the Transient and Steady-State Estimates of Interval Genetic Regulatory Networks, *IEEE Transactions on Systems and Cybernetics, part B*, p. 336-349.

[11] J. Liang, J. Lam and Z. Wang (2008) State Estimation for Markov-Type Genetic Regulatory Networks with Delays and Uncertain Mode Transition Rates, *Physics Letters A*, p. 4328-4337.

[12] Ali Saberi und Hassan Khalil (1984), Quadratic–type functions for singularly perturbed systems, *IEEE Transactions on Automatic Control*, p. 542-550.

[13] M. Vidyasagar (1993), Nonlinear Systems Analysis, *Prentice Hall*.

Research normal distribution, the trust interval and calculation of importance degree of geometrical characteristics a human face on the basis of photo portraits

Tofiq Kazimov and Shafagat Mahmudova

Institute of Information Technology of ANAS, Baku, Azerbaijan

Az1141 tofig@mail.ru. shafagat_57@mail.ru.

Contact Author: Shafagat Mahmudova

BIOCOMP'13

Abstract— in article algorithm of automatic identification of persons on the basis of their photographs are considered. For identification of persons, the comparative analysis of control systems by bases of images created in the different periods is carried out and their applied possibilities are shown. . The questions of definition of anthropometrical points of the person calculation of values of geometrical characteristics and their confidential intervals, algorithm of automatic addition of geometrical characteristics in a database and some other questions connected with them are described. To determine trust interval using Student method, first of all, subordination of the law of normal distribution of selection consisting of geometrical characteristics was investigated. The paper offers a new algorithm to find coefficients which determine importance degree of the values of geometrical characteristics used to identify a human face on the basis of photo portraits.

Keywords: recognition, anthropometrical, identification, geometrical characteristics, confidential an interval, importance degree, coefficient.

1 INTRODUCTION

Modern information and communication technologies (ICT) enable the development of various areas of great importance, as well as of biometric technology. The expansion of the fields of application of these technologies plays an important role in preventing a number of dangerous incidents. It is obvious that the prevention of dangerous manifestations, such as the prevention of international terrorism, transnationals organized crime, as well as illegal weapon and drug transportation is one of the main duties of each state. One of the methods in detecting and neutralizing hazardous manifestations is just the advantages of biometric identification technologies. Biometric technologies particularly strengthen reliable control passport-visa control and other identification documents.

Information on the dynamics of biometric technology market given by the world-famous International Biometric Group, gives a way to say: Taking into account the unique characteristics of a person chosen separately, biometric technology was organized on the basis of biometrics [1, 8, 9].

People differ significantly from each other for the sizes and the arrangement of such face elements as eyes, eyebrows, noses, ears, mouths, etc. Therefore, the first approach to the problem solution of automatic person face identification by photo portrait was based on the selection and comparison of some anthropometric face peculiarities. This method has been used in experimental criminalities for years. This technique was especially effective when a person did not have a photograph except the one in a passport [2].

Paper [3] is devoted to the recognition of a human face on the basis of a photo portrait. For face recognition based on a photo portrait, the authors developed 19 anthropometric face points. These points are chosen from the point of resistance to slight changes (caused by the angle, light, facial expression, cosmetics, age, and so on). An algorithm has been developed for calculating the values of the distances between these points and of geometrical characteristics of the human face. It is shown that the difference of the developed algorithm from the other existing ones is that compared with the other photos stored in the database it works even in the absence of any other information about the person except the image described in the photo [10, 11].

The development principles of "Recognition" biometric identification system (RBIS) are explained on the basis of algorithm given to identify a human on the basis of photo portraits in paper [4], and a database with a developed structure is organized for it. Various sized images of n persons and individual data for each (first name, middle name, last name, date of birth, eye colour, height and etc.) were included in the database. The paper also describes an algorithm for default addition of the values of the geometrical characteristics, for search and identification of an image of a human face on the basis of photo portrait in the database [12, 13].

2 PROBLEM STATEMENT

Definition of accuracy of identification is a very important aspect of human face recognition based on photo-portrait. Definition of trust interval of geometrical characteristics is one of the main factors of recognition of a human face based on photo-portrait. In this article, we considered the process of detection of trust intervals of geometrical characteristics used in identification of human face based on photo-portraits. In works [4] [13], trust interval is a range containing the real value of parameter studying on existing reliability level during its main collection.

Advantage of experiments carried out with definition of trust interval to those performed without, are as following:

1. Insignificant effect of ultimate factors to main process during performance of experiments;
2. Faster and more accurate performance of experiments;
3. Performance of necessary number of observations during experiments.

In order to define the trust interval, values of geometrical characteristics calculated through "Recognition" identification system we used [4]. For this reason, initially, experiments were carried out on geometrical characteristics stored in the data base belonging to 102 people. Geometrical characteristics belonging to 102 people were distributed among 18 clusters based on identical characteristics.

2 situations can occur while working with RABIS:

1. Values of geometrical characteristics can be included in trust interval detected for them. In this case, system will continue its operation and pass on to the next level.
2. Values of some geometrical characteristics may not be included in trust interval included for them. In this case the system alerts the user and the distances suitable for them are re-calculated in order to determine those geometrical characteristics and process is continued.

Generally, values of 102*18 numbers of geometrical characteristics were used in order to calculate the trust interval [4]. Clusters by geometrical characteristics are indicated as Ns1, Ns2, and Ns18. Student method was used in order to define the trust interval [6,17].

To determine trust interval, used in human image identification on the basis of photo portrait, using Student method, first of all, subordination of the law of normal distribution of selection consisting of geometrical characteristics should be investigated.

Determination of normal distribution is of great importance for various reasons. In most cases, it is considered to be the best convergence to the function. The statistical distribution of numbers of natural phenomena is considered normal. For example, for determining the weight or volume of the goods, and measurement of height of the person having medical check-up, etc.

A new algorithm is proposed in this paper to find the coefficient which determines importance degree of the values of geometrical characteristics. Let us explain the essence of the algorithm. The values of geometrical characteristics of n quantity used for the identification are divided into the clusters of m quantity for the same sign. To determine the importance degree of the values of geometrical characteristics an identification process is carried out temporarily replacing each value of geometric characteristics of each person with the other values taken from the replacement interval, and the impact of the replacement in the recognition process is assessed.

3 RESEARCH NORMAL DISTRIBUTION THE TRUST INTERVAL

Normal distribution is defined by the main 2 parameters: average and standard error [16]. Finite population consisting of 17 random selection values within the geometrical characteristics values. The average value is calculated on the basis of finite population. As the result of calculations the average value μ = 2.45787 obtained. Selection distribution was sorted out in finite selection on the based 2 values and per each selection average value calculated on the basis of them. The frequency of average values and their sum have been calculated and shown in Table 1.

TABLE 1. The frequency of average values and their sum

Frequency, f	$\bar{x}$ f
$\sum f = 135$	$\sum \bar{x} f = 331{,}662269$

Mathematical expectance on the basis of selection distribution has been calculated by the following formula:

$$E(\bar{x}) = \frac{\sum f \bar{x}}{\sum f} = \frac{331{,}662}{135} = 2{,}46,$$

The average value of selection data

$$\mu = 2{,}45787 = 2{,}46,$$

Thus,

$$E(\bar{x}) = \mu \approx 2{,}46$$

Standard error for the main normally distributed population has been determined by the following formula [16].

$$SE_{(\bar{x})} = \sqrt{\frac{(N-n)\sigma^2}{(N-1)n}}, \quad (1)$$

σ^2 indicates the main dispersion.

For the values of main geometric characteristics

$$\sigma^2 = 0{,}3551, \quad N = 102, \quad n = 2,$$

If the measure of the main population more than the selection population $(n/N = 0{,}0196 <= 0{,}05)$ then

$$\sqrt{\frac{(N-n)}{(N-1)}} = 0{,}995 \approx 1,$$

And standard error equals to:

$$SE_{(\bar{x})} = \sqrt{\frac{\sigma^2}{n}} = 0{,}2511$$

As it is obvious from the calculations, normal distribution of values of geometrical characteristics has been proved (Figure 1).

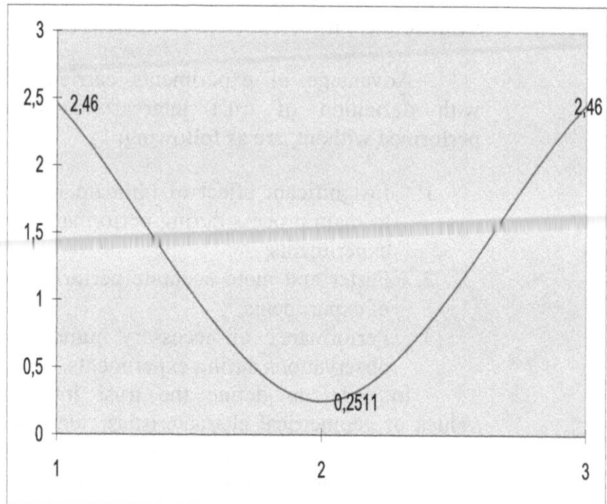

Figure 1. Normal distribution of values of geometrical characteristics

Trust interval is described as below:

$$\bar{X} - t_\beta . m_{\bar{x}} \leq \tilde{X} \leq \bar{X} + t_\beta . m_{\bar{x}} \quad (2)$$

Here,

$\bar{X}$ - average value of main collection,

$m_{\bar{x}}$ - error of average and

$$m_{\bar{x}} = \pm \frac{\sigma}{\sqrt{n}}, \quad (3)$$

$$\sigma = \pm \sqrt{\frac{\sum_{i=1}^{n} (x_i - \bar{X})^2}{n-1}}, \quad (4)$$

t_β - Student factor selected from the schedule,

$x_i\ (n=\overline{1,n})$ - indicates the elements of main collection.

While using formula (2) for cluster Ns1,

Confidence interval of value of geometric characteristics used for human face recognition based on photo portrait was determined by the Student method.

Using fuzzy calculation, confidence interval of the values of the geometrical characteristics can be determined. It should be noted that on the basis of the research carried out by the authors, real interval values of the distances between anthropometric points of a human face have been established. With the help of fuzzy calculation, to find interval values of the geometrical characteristic in accordance with the same distances

$$S_i^*/S_{i+1} \le P_i^* \le S_i/S_{i+1}^* \quad i=\overline{1,n-1} \qquad (5)$$

formula was used.

Here the real maximum value of (i) anthropometric distance of a human face was indicated as - $S_i^*\ (i=\overline{1,n})$, and the real minimum value as - $S_i\ (i=\overline{1,n})$.

The value of geometric characteristics found with the help of calculation was indicated as - $P_i^*(i=\overline{1,n})$.

The real interval values of geometric characteristics found through (5) have been shown in table 3.

When compared $P_i^*(i=\overline{1,n})$ values in table 3 with $P_i\ (i=\overline{1,n})$ values in table 2 the following terms will be ensured.

$$\mathrm{Max}(P_i) \le \mathrm{Max}(P_i^*) \quad i=\overline{1,n}$$

$$\mathrm{Min}(P_i) \ge \mathrm{Min}(P_i^*) \quad i=\overline{1,n}$$

It has been cleared out that, the values of P_i don't exceed beyond the real value interval.

The paper [6] provides information about the algorithms developed for normal distribution of the values of geometrical characteristics used in the recognition of a human face on the basis of photo portrait and to define trust interval of the geometrical characteristics. It is shown that the determination of normal distribution of geometrical characteristics is of great importance for various reasons. m selection value is randomly taken from the values of geometrical characteristics and its normal distribution is investigated [6, 14,13, 15].

The paper [5] provides information about the algorithms developed to define trust interval of the values of geometrical characteristics in the recognition of a human face on the basis of photo portrait. On the basis of the conducted researches, the real interval values of distances between the anthropometric points of a human face are established. With the help of fuzzy calculation, interval values of geometric characteristics values, proper to the same points, are found [6, 7, 15].

Finding coefficients which determine importance degree of the values of geometrical characteristics used to identify a human face on the basis of photo portraits is of great importance for the recognition process from the various views. Determination of coefficients determining importance degree of the values of geometrical characteristics for identification leads to the reduction of the number of values of insignificant geometrical characteristics, as well as to the improvement of identification quality and to the decrease of time spent for the identification.

4 IMPORTANCE DEGREE ALGORITHMS

Let us mark the wanted photo portrait possessing geometric characteristics of m quantity, i.e., m sized point with $F^*(p_1^*, p_2^*, ..., p_m^*)$, photo portraits in the database with $F_i(p_{i1}, p_{i2}, ..., p_{im})$, $(i=\overline{1,n})$. If we mark F_i points and distances of F^* point with S_i, then

$$S_i(F^*, F_i) = \sum_{k=1}^{m}(p_k^* - p_{ik})^2,\ i=\overline{1,n}, \qquad (6)$$

Where n indicates the number of photo portraits in the data base. Let us divide geometrical characteristics of the photo portraits in the data base into $K_j\ (p_{ij}, i=\overline{1,n}), (j=\overline{1,m})$ clusters of m quantity. If we mark replacement intervals of the parameters of each $K_j, (j=\overline{1,m})$ cluster with $[\alpha_j, \beta_j], (j=\overline{1,m})$, then inequality

$$\alpha_j \le p_{ij} \le \beta_j,\quad i=\overline{1,n},\ j=\overline{1,m}, \qquad (7)$$

can be right for any p_{ij}.

To determine importance degree of geometrical characteristics of each photo portraits, i.e. of p_{ij} parameters for the identification, let us divide $[\alpha_j, \beta_j]$ interval of each $K_j\ (j=1,m)$ cluster into the equal $t \ge 10$ parts by h_j step.

$$h_j = (\beta_j - \alpha_j)/t,\ j=\overline{1,m}, \qquad (8)$$

$$x_{jk} = \alpha_j + kh_j,$$

t - is an integer number.

Replacing $x_{jk} \in [\alpha_j, \beta_j], (k=\overline{0,t}; j=\overline{1,m})$ points consistently instead of the values of l the $(l=\overline{1,m})$ coordinates of F^* points, we achieve the point of $(t+1)m$ quantity. Let us mark them with $FT_{kl}\ (k=\overline{0,t}; l=\overline{1,m})$.

Let us calculate ω_j coefficient indicating $ST_{ki}\ (F_i, FT_{ki})$ distances between these points and $F_i, (i=\overline{1,n})$ points in the database and determining the efficiency degree of geometrical characteristics.

$$\omega_j = \left(\frac{1}{n(t+1)} \sum_{i=1}^{n} \sum_{k=0}^{t} \frac{ST_{ki} - S_i}{x_{jk} - p_{ij}} \right)^{-1},\ j=\overline{1,m}, \qquad (9)$$

Note that, calculating the distance between the other photo portraits existing in the database and the two points in 16-dimensional space, the photo portrait of any person is compared with the following formula in the work [5].

$$S_i(F^*, F_i) = \sqrt{\sum_{k=1}^{m} (p_k^* - p_{ik})^2},\ i=\overline{1,n}, \qquad (10)$$

In this paper, the formula (10) is replaced with the formula (6). The aim of the replacement is to accelerate the identification process and to reduce the time spent for the identification. Including the coefficient which determines importance degree of the values of geometrical characteristics, into the formula (6), we can increase the importance of the recognition and may not take into account insignificant geometrical characteristics. When in a database it is too many records, then this replacement very important.

Including the coefficient (9) into the formula (6), the following distance formula is achieved:

$$S_i(F^*, F_i) = \sum_{k=1}^{m} \omega_j (p_k^* - p_{ik})^2,\ i=\overline{1,n}; j=\overline{1,m}, \qquad (11)$$

5. EXPERIMENTAL TEST

$$n=102,\ k=n,\ \beta=95\%,$$

$$t_\beta = 1{,}98,$$

$$m_{\bar{x}} \approx \pm 0{,}0353,$$

We will get

$$2{,}21232796 \le \bar{X} \le 2{,}35227203$$

Here Student coefficients were taken based on the value of t_β and values of k and β.

In such manner, values of trust interval in accordance with other clusters are calculated and shown in table 2.

TABLE 2. Trust intervals of geometrical characteristics used in identification of human face based on photo portrait in accordance with other clusters

Ns1	Ns2	Ns3
2,21 ≤ 2,28 ≤ 2,35	0,05 ≤ 0,42 ≤ 0,79	5 ≤ 5,76 ≤ 6,51

Ns4	Ns5	Ns6
0,18 ≤ 0,22 ≤ 0,62	0,9 ≤ 1,13 ≤ 1,35	0,4 ≤ 0,79 ≤ 1,08

Ns7	Ns8	Ns9
1,94 ≤ 2,03 ≤ 2,11	0,25 ≤ 0,59 ≤ 0,92	1,21 ≤ 1,23 ≤ 1,25

Ns10	Ns11	Ns12
0,33 ≤ 0,665 ≤ 0,98	1,60 ≤ 1,61 ≤ 1,63	3,2 ≤ 3,243 ≤ 3,27

Ns13	Ns14	Ns15
0,25 ≤ 0,29 ≤ 0,33	0,01 ≤ 0,2935 ≤ 0,74	5 ≤ 5,76 ≤ 6,51

Ns16	Ns17	Ns18
0,18 ≤ 0,22 ≤ 0,62	0,33 ≤ 0,66 ≤ 0,98	1,60 ≤ 1,61 ≤ 1,63

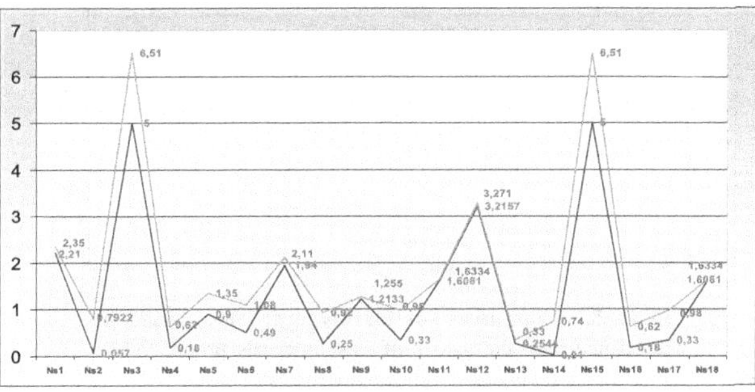

Figure 2. Trust intervals of geometrical characteristics used for identification of human face based on photo portrait

TABLE. 3. The real minimum and maximum values of geometrical characteristics

	Min value	Max value
P_1^*	1,42	2,8
P_2^*	0,04	0,8
P_3^*	2,8	6,7
P_4^*	0,1	1
P_5^*	0,352	1,79
P_6^*	0,4	1,29
P_7^*	0,68	2,22
P_8^*	0,1	1,6
P_9^*	1	2,031
P_{10}^*	0,2	3,33
P_{11}^*	0,21	1,73
P_{12}^*	0,33	3,56
P_{13}^*	0,54	2,4
P_{14}^*	0,01	1
P_{15}^*	2,8	6,8
P_{16}^*	0,1	1
P_{17}^*	0,23	1,33
P_{18}^*	0,21	1,8

As it is mentioned above, a large number of experiments have been carried out at TBIS on the basis of above mentioned algorithm in order to calculate the coefficients which determine importance degree of the values of geometrical characteristics used to identify a human face on the basis of photo portraits.

TABLE 4. Values found on the basis of given algorithms

P11				P12			
2,21	0,09	0,09	0	2,21	0,11	0,06	0
2,22	0,08	0,08	0,010	2,22	0,12	0,07	0,01
2,24	0,06	0,06	0,030	2,24	0,14	0,09	0,03
2,25	0,05	0,05	0,040	2,25	0,15	0,1	0,04
2,27	0,03	0,03	0,060	2,27	0,17	0,12	0,06
2,28	0,02	0,02	0,070	2,28	0,18	0,13	0,07
2,29	0,01	0,01	0,080	2,29	0,19	0,14	0,08
2,31	0,01	0,01	0,080	2,31	0,21	0,16	0,10
2,32	0,02	0,02	0,070	2,32	0,22	0,17	0,11
2,34	0,04	0,04	0,050	2,34	0,24	0,19	0,13
2,35	0,05	0,05	0,040	2,35	0,25	0,2	0,14
P13				**P14**			
2,21	0,21	0,14	0	2,21	0,01	0,21	0
2,22	0,22	0,15	0,01	2,22	0,01	0	0,21
2,24	0,24	0,17	0,03	2,24	0,03	0,02	0,19
2,25	0,25	0,18	0,04	2,25	0,04	0,03	0,18
2,27	0,27	0,2	0,06	2,27	0,06	0,05	0,16
2,28	0,28	0,21	0,07	2,28	0,07	0,06	0,15
2,29	0,29	0,22	0,08	2,29	0,08	0,07	0,14
2,31	0,31	0,24	0,1	2,31	0,1	0,09	0,12
2,32	0,32	0,25	0,11	2,32	0,11	0,1	0,11
2,34	0,34	0,27	0,13	2,34	0,13	0,12	0,09
2,35	0,35	0,28	0,14	2,35	0,14	0,13	0,08

In particular cases, using the values $n = 102$, $m = 18$, $t = 10$ the values proper to the values of the geometrical characteristics of 10 persons in accordance with the 1st value of the cluster have been calculated through the formulas (6), (8), (9) and (11). Some of the results of the conducted experiments are shown in table 4, figure3, figure.4, figure.5, figure.6 in the form of graphics.

TABLE 5. Coefficients determining importance degree of geometrical characteristics (for the values of the 1st, 2nd, 3rd geometrical characteristics)

	Coefficient values
ω_1	1,39
ω_2	0,70
ω_3	0,80

The values proper to the given formulas have been calculated for other persons in this way, as well.

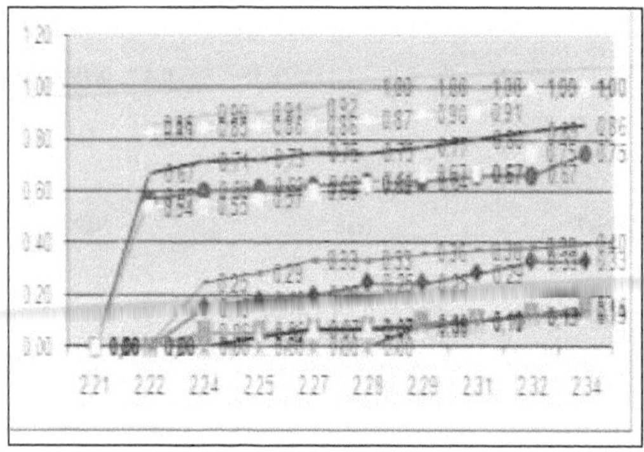

Figure 3. Comparison of the distance values found in accordance with the values of trust intervals proper to the values of the 1stgeometrical characteristics (10 persons)

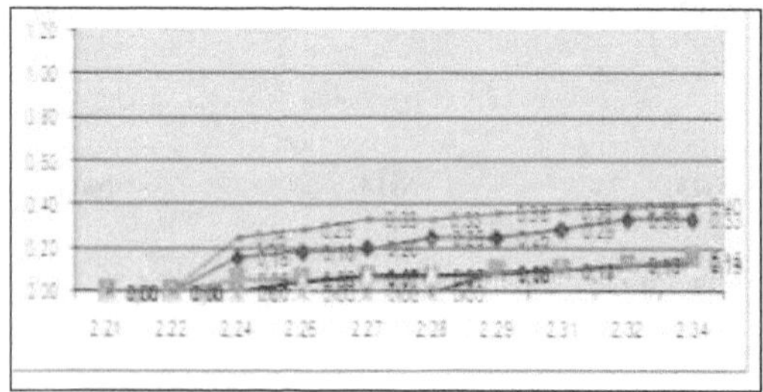

Figure 4. Comparison of the distance values found in accordance with the values of trust intervals proper to the values of the1st geometrical characteristics (females)

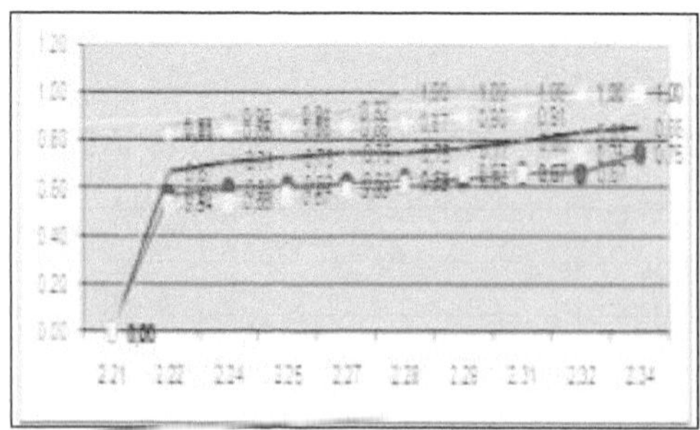

Figure 5. Comparison of the distance values found in accordance with the values of trust intervals proper to the values of the1st geometrical characteristics (males)

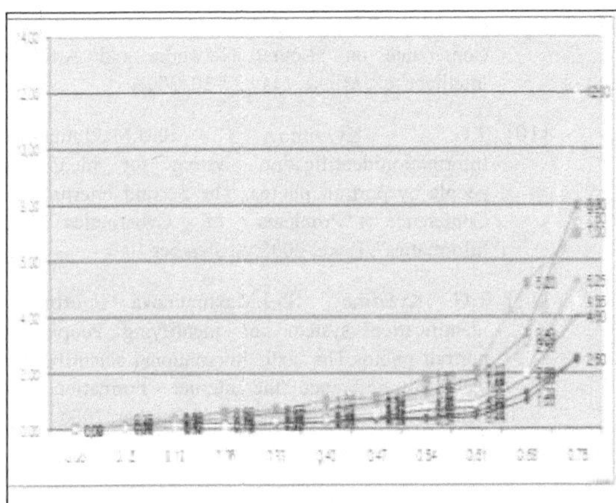

Figure 6. Comparison of the distance values found in accordance with the values of trust intervals proper to the values of the 2nd geometrical characteristics (10 persons)

102 * 19 * 5 (9690) experiments have been carried out on the basis of the data of 102 persons through TBIS. The values $\omega_j \ (j=\overline{1,m})$ are shown in the table 5.

The authors have established biometric identification system in accordance with anthropometric points of a human face by the photo portrait on the basis of obtained scientific results.

The software system is capable to detect the most similar faces comparing any photo portrait of any person uploaded to the system with other existing ones in the base. Note that the rumours regard to the identity of the hero of the mysterious "Mona Liza" by the prominent Italian artist Leonardo da Vinci is still not calming down. The disputes in connection with who is described in the portrait have been going on over more than 500 years.

The portraits of Leonardo da Vinci (figure 7) and Mona Liza (figure 8) painted in different years were included in the system database by the authors as an experiment. Two versions of identification process were carried out through the system. In the 1stversion the portrait of Mona Liza was included in the system base for identification and compared with the other ones existing in the database. Initially, the most similar portraits were Mona Liza (100%) and the portrait of Leonardo da Vinci (99.5%). In the2nd version the portrait by artist was included in the system for identification. In this case, the most similar portraits were the portrait of Leonardo da Vinci himself (100%), and then the portrait of Mona Liza (99.5%).

5 RESULT

Student method was used for definition of trust intervals of geometrical characteristics used for identification of human face based on photo portrait. Definition and use of trust intervals results in fast and effective operation of human face identification program. This, results in preventing time loss during identification.

A new algorithm has been proposed to find coefficients which determine importance degree of the values of geometrical characteristics used to identify a human face on the basis of photo portraits:

1. A formula is given to calculate distances between the wanted photo portraits possessing m number of geometric characteristics with the points of photo portraits in the base;
2. A formula is given to calculate a step in appropriate intervals of each cluster in order to determine importance degree of the values of geometrical characteristics of each photo portrait for identification;
3. A formula is given to calculate $\omega_j \ (j=\overline{1,m})$ coefficients determining importance degree of the values of geometrical characteristics;
4. Including $\omega_j \ (j=\overline{1,m})$ coefficients a distance formula is given for the identification.

The given algorithm leads to the reduction in the number of values of geometrical characteristics used for identification, as well as to the improvement of identification quality and to the decrease in time spent for the identification.

Figure 7. Leonardo Da Vinci

Figure 8. Mona Liza

REFERENCES

[1] R.M.Boll, J.H.Connel, Sh.Pankanti, N.K.Ratkha E.U.Sen'or, "Rukovodstvo po biometrii", (Manual on Biometrics), Moscow: Tekhnosfera, 2007.

[2] D.I.Samal, V.V.Starovoitov, "Podkhody i metody raspoznavaniya lyudei po fotoportretam", (Approaches and Methods of People Recognition According to Photoportraits), Minsk, 1998.

[3] T.G. Kyazimov, Sh.J.Makhmudova, "Systems of People Computer Recognition According to Photopor traits", Informatsionnye tekhnologii, no. 1, pp. 13–16, 2009.

[4] T.G. Kyazimov, Sh.J.Makhmudova, "Automating System of People Recognition According to the Identifi cation Geometric Characteristics of Face Image",Telekommunikatsii, 2008, no. 11, p. 22–25.

[5] T.G. Kyazimov, Sh.J.Makhmudova, "The Effectiveness Increase of a System of Automatic Biometrical Identification Based on Photo Portraits", Automatic Control and Computer Sciences, vol. 45, no. 2, pp. 106–112, 2011.

[6] A.I.Orlov, "Matematika sluchaya: Veroyatnost' i statistika – osnovnye fakty", Uchebnoe posobie, (Mathematics of Incident: Probability and Statistics – Fundamental Facts. Manual), Moscow, MZPress, 2004.

[7] S.V.Matsievskii, "Nechetkie Mnozhestva. Uchebnoe Posobie Fuzzy Ensembles. A Manual)", Kaliningrad, KGU, 2004.

[8] I.Fomin, "Raspoznavanie obrazov. Teoriya I primeneniya", M.: Fazis, 2010, 368 pp.

[9] T.G. Kyazimov, Sh.J.Makhmudova, "About creation of system of computer recognition of people by photographs" / ICNNAI 2008, The Fifth International Conference on "Neural Networks and Artificial Intelligence", Minsk: May 27-30, 2008.

[10] T.G. Kyazimov, Sh.J.Makhmudova, Informationidentification system for identifying people by portrait photos, The Second International Conference "Problems of Cybernetics and Informatics", Baku, 2008, September 10.

[11] T.G. Kyazimov, Sh.J.Makhmudova Information identification system for identifying People by portrait photos,The sixth International scientific and technical conference "the Internet - Formation - the Science - 2008", Vinnitsa, 7 - 10 October, 2008.

[12] Sh.J.Makhmudova, "Definition of weight coefficient of geometric characteristics used for identification of human face on the basis of photo-portrait ICCIT2011, the 6th International Conference on Computer Sciences and Convergence Information Technology, 2011, November 29 to December 1.

[13] T.G. Kyazimov, Sh.J.Makhmudova, "Recognition of the person with photographs", Information Technology:, Baku, 2010, 113 pp.

[14] R.Chellappa , P.Sinha , P.Jonathon , "Face Recognition by Computers and Humans", Computer, 2010, Date:February, pp. 46-55.

[15] T.G. Kyazimov, Sh.J.Makhmudova, "Methods ofimrovement of efficiency in recognition identifications systems", The Third International Conference "Problems of Cybernetics and Informatics", 2010, September 6-8, Baku, Azerbaijan.

[16] M.Eddows, R.Stansfield. Methods of decision making. M: Audit, UNITY 1997, 590 p.

[17] .http://mschool.kubsu.ru

BIOCOMP'12

Model Order Reduction of Deterministic and Stochastic Gene Regulatory Networks

Robert Altwasser, Reinhard Guthke, Sebastian Vlaic [a], Mark R. Emmett [b], Carol L. Nilsson [c] and Anke Meyer-Baese [d],

[a] *Leibniz Institute for Natural Product Research and Infection Biology e V. Hans-Knöll-Institute (HKI), 07745 Jena, Germany*

[b] *Department of Biochemistry and Molecular Biology, UTMB Cancer Center, University of Texas Medical Branch, Galveston, TX 7555-1060, U.S.*

[c] *Department of Pharmacology and Toxicology, UTMB Cancer Center, University of Texas Medical Branch, Galveston, TX 7555-1060, U.S.*

[d] *Department of Scientific Computing, Florida State University, Tallahassee, FL 32306-4120, U.S.*

Abstract

The complexity of gene regulatory networks in terms of both large-scale description as well as nonlinear models is often an obstacle for analytical purposes. Therefore, the development of effective model reduction techniques is of paramount importance in the field of systems biology. In this paper, we apply Carleman bilinearization for model reduction for gene regulatory networks based only on Gramians computations. The method is based on the bilinear representation of weakly nonlinear systems and Taylor's series expansion. Thus, we obtain a simple computational solution and identify parameters that are relevant to ensure stability of the system. The theoretical results are elucidated in an illustrative example and thus shown how they can be applied to reverse engineering design.

Key words: Genetic regulatory network, balanced truncation, Carleman bilinearization, Gramians, stochastic systems

---

Email address: ameyerbaese@fsu.edu (Anke Meyer-Baese).

Preprint submitted to Elsevier Science

1 Introduction

Many gene regulatory networks (GRNs) are described by complex models which are difficult to analyze and also difficult to control. The large-scale nature of these systems and the highly complex underlying models require reduced-order models to facilitate their analysis. Balanced truncation is known as a popular method for model reduction since it is relatively simple and the quality of the reduced model is guaranteed [2]. The interpretation of most balancing techniques is based on the concept of past and future energy. While for linear systems finding a balancing coordinate transformation via solutions of the controllability and observability Lyapunov equations is quite easy, for nonlinear systems this equations are almost impossible to solve and thus balancing becomes in general not a simple task [3].

Carleman biliniarization [1] facilitates the representation of a nonlinear system by a bilinear form. This still keeps a certain contribution of the nonlinearity of the system in the resulting simplified form.

The emphasis of this paper lies on a model reduction technique for GRNs based on gramians and Carleman biliniarization. The idea is to employ a model simplification based on this analysis resulting in a model of lower complexity, easier to handle, and in a simplified synthesis procedure for design problems. In addition, this simplification is reducing the computational complexity.

2 Problem Statement

Gene regulatory networks represent circuits of genes that interact and regulate the expression of other genes through the action of proteins. The change in expression of a gene is regulated by protein synthesis in transcriptional, translational and post-translational processes. Taking into account a transcriptional time delay [7] and the fact that mRNA typically decays much faster than the protein, we considered in a previous work [5] the gene regulatory network described by the following equation

$$\dot{M}_i(t) = -a_i M_i(t) + \sum_{j=1}^{n} \tilde{w}_{ij}\tilde{g}_j(P_j(t)) + \tilde{b}_i u(t) \tag{1a}$$

$$\dot{P}_i(t) = -c_i P_i(t) + d_i M_i(t) \tag{1b}$$

where $M_i(t), P_i(t) \in R$ are the concentrations of mRNA and protein of the ith node, respectively. The parameters a_i and c_i are the decay rates of mRNA and protein, respectively; d_i is the translation rate, $\tilde{g}_j(x) = \frac{\left(\frac{x}{\beta_j}\right)^{H_j}}{\left(1+\left(\frac{x}{\beta_j}\right)^{H_j}\right)}$, $\tilde{b}_i, u(t) \in R$, $\tilde{W} = (\tilde{w_{ij}}) \in R^{n \times n}$ is defined as follows

$$\tilde{w}_{ij} = \begin{cases} \alpha_{ij}, & : \text{ if transcription factor j is an activator of gene i} \\ 0, & : \text{ if there is no link from node j to i} \\ -\alpha_{ij} & : \text{ if transcription factor j is a repressor of gene i} \end{cases} \quad (2)$$

α_{ij} represents the dimensionless transcriptional rate of transcription factor j to gene i being a bounded constant.

We can re-write this system as

$$\dot{\mathbf{x}}(t) = \mathbf{f}(\mathbf{x}(t)) + \mathbf{B}u(t) \quad (3a)$$

$$y(t) = \widehat{C}\widehat{x}(t) \quad (3b)$$

In [10], was shown that the above system can be expanded into a generalized Taylor's series around the equilibrium point $\mathbf{x} = \mathbf{0}$, if it is weakly nonlinear

$$\mathbf{f}(\mathbf{x}) = \mathbf{A_1}\mathbf{x}^{(1)} + \mathbf{A_2}\mathbf{x}^{(2)} + \cdots \quad (4)$$

where $\mathbf{x}^{(1)} = \mathbf{x}$ and $\mathbf{x}^{(2)} = \mathbf{x} \otimes \mathbf{x}$ with $\otimes$ denoting the Kronecker product. For the original system (1a) this means:

$$\begin{bmatrix} \dot{\mathbf{M}}(t) \\ \dot{\mathbf{P}}(t) \end{bmatrix} = \underbrace{\begin{bmatrix} -\mathbf{A} & \mathbf{W} \\ \mathbf{D} & -\mathbf{C} \end{bmatrix}}_{\mathbf{A_1}} \begin{bmatrix} \mathbf{M}(t) \\ \mathbf{P}(t) \end{bmatrix} + \underbrace{\begin{bmatrix} \mathbf{0} & \bar{\mathbf{W}} \\ \mathbf{0} & \mathbf{0} \end{bmatrix}}_{\mathbf{A_2}} \begin{bmatrix} \mathbf{M}(t) \\ \mathbf{P}(t) \end{bmatrix}^{(2)} + \underbrace{\begin{bmatrix} \tilde{\mathbf{B}} \\ \mathbf{0} \end{bmatrix}}_{\mathbf{B}} u(t) \quad (5)$$

where $\bar{\mathbf{W}}$ is the second order Taylor's series component.

We also write $\dot{\mathbf{x}}(t) = \begin{bmatrix} \dot{\mathbf{M}}(t) \\ \dot{\mathbf{P}}(t) \end{bmatrix}$.

In the following, we will give the preliminary definitions necessary to determine the model order reduction for the GRN.

3 Preliminary Definitions

Assume $x = (x_1 x_2 \cdots x_n) \in R^n$ be an n-dimensional vector and $x^{(2)}$ is defined as follows:

$$x^{(2)} = x \otimes x = \left[x_1 x^T, \cdots, x_n x^T\right]^T \qquad (6a)$$
$$= \left[x_1 x_1, \cdots, x_1 x_n, x_2 x_1, x_2^2, \cdots x_n x_n\right]^T \in R^{nn}$$

with $\otimes$ being the Kronecker product. Thus, we have

$$x^{(k)} = x \otimes x \otimes \cdots x \otimes x \qquad (7)$$

with $k-1$ Kronecker products.

4 Deterministic Gene Regulatory Network Model Reduction Based on Taylor's Series Approximation

We will consider the approximation up to the degree of two of the nonlinear GRN and represent the system in form of the Carleman biliniarization. We assumed previously that the GRN is weakly nonlinear. This yields a new simplified system

$$\dot{\hat{\mathbf{x}}}(t) = \widehat{\mathbf{A}}\hat{\mathbf{x}}(t) + \widehat{\mathbf{N}}\hat{\mathbf{x}}(t)\mathbf{u}(t) + \hat{\mathbf{B}}\mathbf{u}(t) \qquad (8a)$$
$$\mathbf{y}(t) = \hat{\mathbf{C}}\hat{\mathbf{x}}(t)$$

where $\hat{\mathbf{x}} = [x^{(1)}, x^{(2)}]$ and $\widehat{\mathbf{A}}, \widehat{\mathbf{N}}, \hat{\mathbf{B}}, \hat{\mathbf{C}}$ are constant matrices given as

$$\widehat{\mathbf{A}} = \begin{bmatrix} A_1 & A_2 \\ 0 & A_{21} \end{bmatrix}, \quad \widehat{\mathbf{N}} = \begin{bmatrix} 0 & 0 \\ B_{20} & 0 \end{bmatrix}, \quad \hat{\mathbf{B}} = \begin{bmatrix} B \\ 0 \end{bmatrix}, \quad \hat{\mathbf{C}} = \begin{bmatrix} C \\ 0 \end{bmatrix} \qquad (9)$$

The matrices A_i are given by Taylor's series expansion and the others are given by

$$A_{21} = A_1 \otimes I_n + I_n \otimes A_1 \qquad (10a)$$
$$B_{20} = B \otimes I_n + I_n \otimes B_n$$

with I_n being a $n \times n$ identity matrix. We immediately see that $\widehat{\mathbf{A}}, \widehat{\mathbf{N}}$ are $n + n^2$-square matrices and $\widehat{\mathbf{x}}, \widehat{\mathbf{B}}, \widehat{\mathbf{C}}$ are vectors of $n + n^2$ components.

Theorem 1: Assume that the input $u(t) = \kappa = const$ is bounded and that the matrix $\widehat{\mathbf{A}} + \kappa\widehat{\mathbf{N}}$ is a Hurwitz-type matrix, then the solution of the system (8a) is bounded.

Proof: The proof is found in a modified form in [10]. The bilinear system becomes a linear system

$$\dot{\widehat{\mathbf{x}}}(t) = (\widehat{\mathbf{A}} + \kappa\widehat{\mathbf{N}})\widehat{\mathbf{x}}(t) + \widehat{\mathbf{B}}\kappa \qquad (11a)$$
$$\mathbf{y}(t) = \widehat{\mathbf{C}}\widehat{\mathbf{x}}(t)$$

The matrix $\widehat{\mathbf{A}} + \kappa\widehat{\mathbf{N}}$ is Hurwitz and together with the constant input it results that $\dot{\widehat{\mathbf{x}}}(t)$ is bounded as well.

The reduced-order system is an approximation of the nonlinear n-order system with a smaller k-order bilinear system ($k \ll n$).

The gramians R and Q for equation (11a) are given by the following Lyapunov equations

$$(\hat{A} + \kappa\widehat{N})R + R(\hat{A} + \kappa\widehat{N})^T = -BB^T \qquad (12a)$$
$$(\hat{A} + \kappa\widehat{N})Q + Q(\hat{A} + \kappa\widehat{N})^T = -C^T C$$

Regarding the solution of the Lyapunov equations, we have the following theorem [15].

Theorem 2: Let $A \in R^{n \times n}$ and $D \in R^{n \times n}$. Then the Lyapunov equation

$$AX + XA^T = D \qquad (13)$$

has a unique solution if and only if A and $-A^T$ have no eigenvalues in common. If D is symmetric and the above equation has a unique solution, then that solution is symmetric.

Based on the symmetry property, the computation of R and Q becomes much simpler. In addition, we have the following result.

Theorem 3: The eigenvalues of RQ are similarity invariants, i.e., they do not depend on the choice of the state space coordinates. There exists a state space representation where

$$\Sigma := \begin{pmatrix} \sigma_1 & \cdots & 0 \\ \cdots & \sigma_i & 0 \\ 0 & \cdots & \sigma_n \end{pmatrix} \tag{14}$$

with $\sigma_1 \geq \sigma_2 \geq \cdots \geq \sigma_n > 0$ the square roots of the eigenvalues of Σ. Such representations are called *balanced*, and the system is in *balanced form*. In addition, the $\sigma_i, i = 1, \cdots, n$, equal the Hankel singular values, i.e., the singular values of the Hankel operator of the system.

The derived theoretical concepts are illustrated in an example.

Example 1: Let us consider a three-gene GRN (1a) with $A_1 = \mathrm{diag}(a_i)$, $C = (1, 1, 1)$ and $B = (b, b, b)^T$. A_2 is given as $A_2 = \mathrm{diag}(A_{2_{21}} = W_{11}, A_{2_{25}} = W_{22}, A_{2_{39}} = W_{33})$ and else $A_{2_{ij}} = 0$ and $W = \begin{bmatrix} W_{11} & 0 & 0 \\ 0 & W_{22} & 0 \\ 0 & 0 & W_{33} \end{bmatrix}$.

We compute the Taylor series up to the order of two and have $f(x) = A_1 x + A_2 x^2$ with $x^{(2)} = [x_1^2, x_1x_2, x_1x_3, x_2x_1, x_2^2, x_2x_3, x_3x_1, x_3x_2, x_3^2]$.

We obtain based on the Carleman biliniarization the following matrices

$$A_{21} = A_1 \otimes I_3 + I_3 \otimes A_1 = \begin{bmatrix} a_1 I_3 & 0_{3\times3} & 0_{3\times3} \\ 0_{3\times3} & a_2 I_3 & 0_{3\times3} \\ 0_{3\times3} & 0_{3\times3} & a_3 I_3 \end{bmatrix} + \begin{bmatrix} A_1 & 0_{3\times3} & 0_{3\times3} \\ 0_{3\times3} & A_1 & 0_{3\times3} \\ 0_{3\times3} & 0_3 \times 3 & A_1 \end{bmatrix}$$

$$B_{20} = B \otimes I_3 + I_3 \otimes B = 2b \begin{bmatrix} I_{3\times3} \\ I_{3\times3} \\ I_{3\times3} \end{bmatrix}$$

$$\widehat{N} = \begin{bmatrix} 0_{3\times3} & 0_{3\times9} \\ B_{20} & 0_{9\times9} \end{bmatrix}, \quad \widehat{A} + \kappa\widehat{N} = 2b \begin{bmatrix} A_1 & A_2 \\ B_{20} & A_{21} \end{bmatrix}$$

$$\widehat{B}\widehat{B}^T = b^2 \cdot \begin{bmatrix} J_3 & 0_{3\times9} \\ 0_{9\times3} & 0_{9\times9} \end{bmatrix}, \quad \widehat{C}C^T = \begin{bmatrix} J_3 & 0_{3\times9} \\ 0_{9\times3} & 0_{9\times9} \end{bmatrix}$$

where J_3 is the matrix of ones given as $J_3 = \begin{bmatrix} 1 & 1 & 1 \\ 1 & 1 & 1 \\ 1 & 1 & 1 \end{bmatrix}$

The solution of the system is bounded according to Theorem 2 if the matrix $\widehat{A} + \kappa\widehat{N}$ is Hurwitz. The computation of the matrices P and Q is based on standard numerical algorithms.

5 Stochastic Gene Regulatory Network Model Reduction Based on Bilinear Approximation

Another interpretation of the bilinear system in equation (8a) is given in [11]. The gramians are interpreted as residual covariances. We assume that instead of u we have an independent white-noise process of spectral density γ. Then this becomes a linear Ito-type stochastic differential equation

$$\begin{aligned} \dot{\hat{\mathbf{x}}}(t) &= \widehat{\mathbf{A}}\hat{\mathbf{x}}(t) + \sum_{j=1}^{m} \widehat{\mathbf{N}}_j\hat{\mathbf{x}}(t)dw_j + \widehat{\mathbf{B}}dw \\ \mathbf{y}(t) &= \widehat{\mathbf{C}}\hat{\mathbf{x}}(t) \end{aligned} \quad (16a)$$

where the covariance matrix is given as $R(t) = E(xx^T)$ and satisfies the deterministic differential equation

$$\dot{R}(t) = \widehat{A}R(t) + R(t)\widehat{A}^T + \gamma^2 \sum_{j=1}^{m} \widehat{N}_j R(t) \widehat{N}_j^{\,T} + \widehat{B}\widehat{B}^T \tag{17}$$

When the above system (16a) is mean-square-stable, then $R(t)$ converges to the limiting covariance $R \geq 0$ satisfying

$$\begin{aligned} \widehat{A}R + R\widehat{A}^T + \gamma^2 \sum_{j=1}^{m} \widehat{N}_j R \widehat{N}_j^{\,T} &= -\widehat{B}\widehat{B}^T \\ \widehat{A}^T Q + Q\widehat{A} + \gamma^2 \sum_{j=1}^{m} \widehat{N}_j^{\,T} R \widehat{N}_j &= -\widehat{C}\widehat{C}^T \end{aligned} \tag{18a}$$

The output yields

$$\frac{d}{dt}E(y(t)^T y(t)) =< R(t), \widehat{C}\widehat{C}^T > \underbrace{\rightarrow}_{t\to\infty} < R, \widehat{C}\widehat{C}^T >=< \widehat{B}\widehat{B}^T, Q > \tag{19}$$

$< A, B >=$ traceAB with A, B being symmetric matrices. The bilinear systems can be reduced based on balanced truncation by using a truncated version of the contragradient transformation $T \in R^{n\times n}$

$$TRT^T = T^{-T}QT^{-1} = diag(\sigma_1, \cdots, \sigma_n) \tag{20}$$

with σ_j being a generalized Hankel value [11].

The computation of the matrices R and Q is a challenge for most numerical algorithms even for a lower dimension. In [11], methods like Krylov subspace projections were proposed to ease the numerical burden.

The derived theoretical concepts are illustrated in an example.

Example 2: Let us consider a three-gene GRN (1a) as given in Example 1. We assume $\gamma = 0$ and based on the matrix C computed in Example 1, we obtain as the trace based on equation (19)

$$E(y(t)^T y(t)) =< R, \widehat{C}\widehat{C}^T >= \sum_{j=1}^{3}\sum_{i=1}^{3} R_{ij} \tag{21}$$

Thus, the output covariance matrix $E(y(t)^T y(t))$ is given as the sum of the first left part of the matrix R.

6 Conclusion

We applied Carleman biliniarization to model reduction for GRNs. The proposed technique is based on the assumption of weakly nonlinear systems being approximated by a bilinear system. Determining the Gramians of the bilinear system is important for model reduction. The achieved reduction represents a simple estimate for the additional parameters employed and is at the same time computationally non-intensive for deterministic GRN under assumption of a bounded input. The established results have potential application for reverse engineering and robust biosynthetic gene regulatory network design.

Acknowledgement

This research was supported in part by NIH Grant 5 G13 LM009832-02. RA was supported by the Jena School for Microbial Communication (JSMC).

References

[1] W. Rugh (1981), Nonlinear Systems Theory, *The John Hopkins University Press.*

[2] B. Moore (1981), Principal component analysis in linear systems: controllability, observability and model reduction, *IEEE Transactions on Automatic Control*, p. 17-32.

[3] J. Scherpen (1993), Balancing for nonlinear systems, *Systems and Control Letters*, p. 143-153.

[4] R. Tanaka, H. Okano and H. Kimura (2006), Mathematical description of Gene Regulatory Units, *Biophysical Journal*, **vol. 91**, p. 1235-1247.

[5] A. Meyer-Baese, C. Plant, S. Cappendijk and F. Theis (2010), Robust Stability Analysis of Multi-Time Scale Genetic Regulatory Networks under Parametric Uncertainties, *BIOCOMP 2010*, p. 854-863.

[6] M. Simpson, C. Cox and G. Sayler (2003), Frequency Domain Analysis of Noise in Autoregulated Gene Circuits, *Proceedings of National Academy of Sciences*, **vol. 100**, p. 4551-4556.

[7] N. Monk (2003), Oscillatory Expression of Hes1, p53 and NF-kB Driven by Transcriptional Time Delays, *Curr. Biol.*, **vol. 13**, p. 1409-1413.

[8] F. Ren and J. Cao (2008), Asymptotic and Robust Stability of Genetic regulatory Networks with Time-Varying Delays, *Neurocomputing*, **vol. 71**, p. 834-842.

[9] L. Huang, X. Mao and F. Deng (2008) Stability of Hybrid Retarded Systems, *IEEE Transactions on Automatic Control*, p. 3413-3420.

[10] M. Condon and R. Ivanov (2005) Nonlinear Systems - Algebraic Gramians and Model Reduction, *The International Journal for Computation and Mathematics in Electrical and Electronic Engineering*, p. 202-219.

[11] P. Benner and T. Damm (2005) Equations, Energy Functionals, and Model Order Reduction of Bilinear and Stochastic Systems, *SIAM Journal of Control and Optimization*, p. 686-711.

[12] P. Li, J. Lam and Z. Shu (2008) On the Transient and Steady-State Estimates of Interval Genetic Regulatory Networks, *IEEE Transactions on Systems and Cybernetics, part B*, p. 336-349.

[13] J. Liang, J. Lam and Z. Wang (2008) State Estimation for Markov-Type Genetic Regulatory Networks with Delays and Uncertain Mode Transition Rates, *Physics Letters A*, p. 4328-4337.

[14] Ali Saberi und Hassan Khalil (1984), Quadratic–type functions for singularly perturbed systems, *IEEE Transactions on Automatic Control*, p. 542-550.

[15] M. Vidyasagar (1993), Nonlinear Systems Analysis, *Prentice Hall.*

Symmetric Group Structures of Genetic Transformation

Reza R. Ahangar

700 University BLVD., MSC 172 Department of Mathematics, Texas A & M University-Kingsville, Kingsville, TX 78363-8202, e-mail: reza.ahangar@tamuk.edu

ABSTRACT: Proteins are fascinating bio-molecular machines made by amino acids, generated by codon, and are connected in a linear chain. The energy created by proteins can perform operations from collecting sunlight, transporting materials, providing mechanical strength for fighting virus or bacteria. We will study symmetric transformation of codons as a function in a symmetric group transformation of a set RNA={U,C,A,G} or DNA={T,C,G,A}. Our goal is to translate the genetic codes into a mathematical language of composition of functions in a symmetric group of S_4={1,,2,3,4}. A permutation symmetric group can be used to demonstrate natural phenomena in genetic algorithm, **crossover, mutation, and natural selection**. Better understanding of symmetric group transformation and an appreciation for the essential role it has played in codon formation will improve our understanding of nature's coding processes. Incorporation of algebraic structure of symmetry groups will facilitate that improvement.

Keywords: DNA/RNA transformation, Codon, Symmetric group transformation, Broken Symmetry, Non-isometric transformation.

1-Introduction and History: In 1944, **Schrodinger** published a small book under the intriguing title "What Is Life?" He was describing DNA as a solid one-dimensional crystal. Now we know that DNA is not a steady state. It is a dynamic double helix library of information stored in several billion pieces linked together in 46 strings of a chromosome. For Schrodinger, writing the time evolution of DNA a building block and particle of life needs more elaboration to analyze.

It may take another century to be able to analyze and understand the social structure of any living species and to write its evolution equation of motion.

The discovery of bio-molecular structure of DNA by Watson and Crick in 1953 [(1) and (2)] has helped to reveal the complex genetic information. This new model of double helix of DNA could explain how the information is stored in DNA in the form of sequence of nucleotides, but it could not help us to understand how it is coded, how it could be used in biological functions, or how to decipher the genetic information.

Another new discovery by Crick [(3)] *et. al.* in 1961 was magnificent and revealed that genetic code is a triplet sequence of 3 nucleic bases. The complete classification of the correspondence between codons and amino acids was assembled in a standard table in 1966. In 1957 the brilliant physicist, George Gamow [7] produced a model that he called compact triangle code for codons. Gamow proposed the transformation of an equilateral triangle in the plane and in the space to represents symmetric transformations for codons.

Even the genetic table in biochemistry was compared to the periodic table of elements in Chemistry at the beginning. But the table as such does not explain why there are 64 codons and only 20 amino acids. It has been discovered that this *degeneracy and redundancy* is associated with and is a consequence of symmetry.

A mathematical structure of DNA and amino acids was presented using Geometric visualization. Mark White 2007 [see ref. [18]] testified "*We have merely created some linguistic and visualization tools based on fundamental codon symmetry in conjunction with the unique nature of DNA's natural two-bit set when placed within the elements of solid geometry. This exercise has generated a nifty data container with virtually no data in it, apart from the specific set of DNA nucleotides.*"

A latest article on developing the Galois Field of five DNA base alphabet used a set {D,G,A,U,C} with unspecified pairing D [Sanchez Robersy, 2004..2006, see [11], [12],[13],[14],[15].

Two mathematicians claimed in their article on March 1994 that a genetic code, which is able to specify 20 amino acids, is derived from a simpler version which coded for only six. They came to their conclusion after examining the symmetry inherent in the redundancy of the genetic code [9].

The abstract idea of symmetric is from algebraic structures that can explain the *degeneracy and redundancy* of the genetic code. Symmetry can initiate discovery of an organizing principle for the way in which the genetic information is stored and regulates the process in protein synthesis.

A codon is traditionally defined as an ordered set of three nucleotides selected from {U/T, C, G, A}. We will try to use the mathematical approach to define codons and use them to analyze DNA or RNA transformation sequences. To do this we need the mathematical tools of permutation, symmetric mapping, and group structures.

We will reproduce Cayley's binary operation table for permutation group S_4. The symmetric group of dihedral which is denoted by D_4 and alternating group A_4 will be demonstrated. Out of 64 codons, there will be eight compositions of operations which will not be the product of rotations and reflections. We will present the non-isometric transformation that may produce a twist in DNA transformations.

Intuitively, we may answer a persisting question "what is breaking the symmetric transformation"? *Our conjecture will be the important rule of the evolution based on variations which we will observe under permutation group structure.*

2. Partially ordered DNA/RNA Bases:

On the Bio-molecular level, we can assume that the sets of RNA or DNA are partially ordered sets. This hypothesis can be postulated either on the atomic numbers in

quantum approach or by simply counting the number of hydrogen or nitrogen bonds. Nitrogen bases for Bio-molecules U (uracil: $C_4N_2H_4O_2$), C (cytosine: $C_4N_3H_5O$), A (adenine: $C_5N_5H_5$), and G (guanine: $C_5N_5H_5O$) are the building blocks of set RNA= {U, C, A, G}.
Dupliji et al 2000/2005 (see [4]) also used the number of *hydrogen bonds* to study the common characteristics in 64 codons of DNA bases and arranged four nucleotides in descending order C, G, U, and A.

Yang 2003 (see[20] and [21]), proposed sp^2 N-numbers to demonstrate the RNA basis as ordered elements.
We use the notation U/T, because genetic code is read from mRNA, and so we will not differentiate their partial strength and order.
We use this idea to introduce the RNA/DNA = {U/T, C, G, A} as a *partially ordered* set. According to this arrangement, $U/T \leftrightarrow 1, C \leftrightarrow 2, G \leftrightarrow 3, A \leftrightarrow 4$, we will accept the relation $U/T \prec C \prec G \prec A$ and symbol "$\prec$" to represent the partially ordered set.

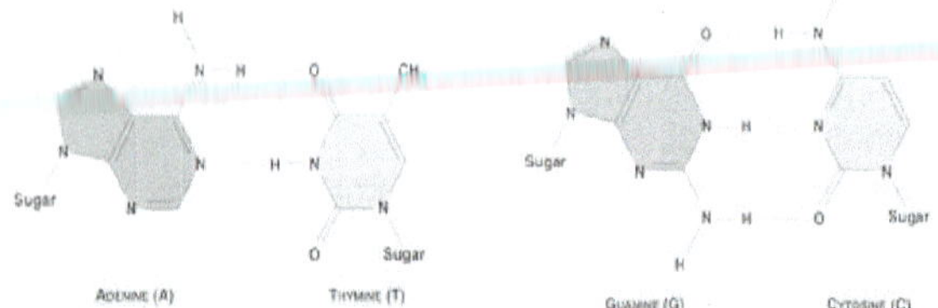

Fig.1: Four DNA base with their Nitrogen and Oxygen bonds.

The doublet-matrix: The matrix of the 16 possible base-doublets can be constructed by the following revised Kronecker product with concatenation (Negadi, 2003, see [17]). In the first step we use *partially ordered* amino acids to define a vector $\vec{V} = [v_i]_{4\times1}$ *where* $i = 1,2,3,4.$ such that v_1 =U/T, v_2= C, v_3=G, v_4=A. In the second step, we assume the product of two components is defined as a binary operation, for example,

(2.1) $v_i \circ v_j \; for \; i,j = 1,2,3,4 \;\; \Leftrightarrow \;\; v_i v_j$.

We can use the above mentioned assumptions to define a new DNA vector product.

Vector Product Operation: Given two RNA/DNA vectors V and W. Define the product

(2.2)

$$<\vec{V},\vec{W}> = \vec{V} \circ \vec{W}' = \begin{bmatrix} v_1 \\ v_2 \\ v_3 \\ v_4 \end{bmatrix} \circ [w_1 \; w_2 \; w_3 \; w_4] = [v_i w_j] \quad i,j = 1,2,3,4$$

The following is the result of the product when we apply this definition to the DNA elements;

(2.3)

$$<\vec{V},\vec{V}> = \vec{V} \circ \vec{V}' = \begin{bmatrix} U \\ C \\ G \\ A \end{bmatrix} [U \quad C \quad G \quad A] = \begin{bmatrix} UU & UC & UG & UA \\ CU & CC & CG & CA \\ GU & GC & GG & GA \\ AU & AC & AG & AA \end{bmatrix}$$

This is consistent with the canonical matrix of doublets. From 64 possible codons one can extract 16 families each defined by the first two nucleotides. One can continue to develop the matrix representing the 64 (triplet) codons of the genetic code based on the doublet matrix of (2.1) to (2.3). There have been many attempts to explain ubiquitous existence of 64 codons and 20 (canonical) amino acids with *44 degenerate codons*. Instead of this approach, we will continue to use symmetric transformation to explain this phenomenon (see table 4.2).
In the physical interpretation of the set of n- tuplet S_n, each point represents a DNA base and is a set of n points in the space with equal weights. The midpoint of each segment in DNA- space is said to be the centroid of that segment. The center of mass of a tetrahedron with equal weight on each edge will be at a point equal distance from each vertex and it will be changed **when the symmetry is broken.**

The genetic code is an important key in the understanding of the process in the body when the DNA copy - RNA, is translated into the functional molecules, the proteins.
In regions of the genome that code for protein production, each codon, such as GTA, specifies a particular amino acid - in this case histidine. Three of the 64 possible codons do not code for an amino acid but instead signify termination of the transcription process.
The genetic code is an important key in the understanding of the process in the body when the DNA copy - RNA is translated into the functional molecules, the proteins.
In regions of the genome that code for protein production, each codon, such as GTA, specifies a particular amino acid - in this case histidine. Three of the 64 possible codons do not code for an amino acid but instead signify termination of the transcription process.
The key point to remember is that the genetic code is degenerate - different triplets may code for the same amino acid. For instance the six codons AAT, AAC, GAA, GAG, GAT and GAC all code for leucine. There is no great regularity to this redundancy. For example, TAC is the only codon that codes for methionine. However, a definite degree of symmetry - albeit imperfect - is clearly visible in the genetic code.
Often, the first two bases in a codon are enough to determine which amino acid it codes for. Let us use X for unknown code, for example GAX always codes for leucine and CGX always represents arginine.
In short, the code is symmetric under changes of the third base. If this *symmetry were perfect*, the 64 codons would break up into 16 'quadruplets' such as GAC, GAG, GAA,

GAT with each coding mapping for a unique amino acid. However, there are more than 16 amino acids, so sometimes the third base matters. Indeed, sometimes the second base matters as well. Either way, *the perfect 'quadruplet' symmetry is broken.*
In this study we will not consider bio-chemical reaction in breaking the symmetries. *We only try to explain geometrically that without distortion of the tetrahedron of the four letter bases, the transformation will not be possible.*

2.1 **Symmetric Transformation Group**:
A set with a binary operation "∘" is said to be a group if and only if under this operation i) the set is closed, ii) the set is associative, iii) has identity, iv) every element is invertible.
A mapping from a *partially ordered* set, RNA/DNA=<U/T, C, G, A> into S_4={1,2,3,4} is a group, which is called a permutation group.
The properties of the permutation group have been studied extensively. The set of all symmetric operations with the composition of functions "∘" is a non- Abelian group where the "∘" represents the binary operation in the group of composition functions.
To investigate the codons generated by < U/T, C, G, A> we will assume the following cases.

- bio-molecule transformations occur in the same plane with complete symmetry of geometric shape of n- gons (square in this case for dihedral group).
- transformation of the molecules that are in space have complete geometrical symmetry of a regular tetrahedron.
- we will check transformation in the permutation group S_4 that do not keep symmetry.

The variations of the permutation group S_4 over a set RNA/DNA=<U/T, C, G, A> in the space is sufficiently simple to help us understand and visualize all of the possible transformations. We would like to explain and differentiate those transformations that keep the DNA bases unchanged and recognize those that lead to a new and different base. Among these, some may change content, shape, and properties.
Since Darwin's evolution is based on genetic variations and natural selections, we really need to investigate what causes the variations and how much these changes will affect the internal structures of genes.
Mathematical tools will help lead us to a logical conclusion. There are some simple transformations like ***rotation, reflection, and translation*** of geometric points in the space which do not cause change in the object in the space but merely change its position in the space.
Studying transformations that change one molecule into another is also important. However, study of the causes of the conversion of one molecule to another molecule is beyond the scope of this article and perhaps requires *quantum mechanical* or *thermo dynamical* approaches to investigate the energy required for these transformations.
To achieve our goal we need to present the following definition of *isometry*.
2.2 **Isometric Transformation:** A transformation which preserves the distance between two points is called an isometry.
Assume two points in Euclidean Space E. Let M' and N' be the new positions of two points M, N in the space E. The transformation is said to exhibit isometry if and only if, d(M, N)=d[M',N']. In other words, isometry transformation preserves the distances.
Analytically, it can be proved that rotations and reflections preserve the distances. There are many other transformations like *similarity, inversion, or conformal* mapping which are not isometric.
We will study some examples of isometric transformation like dihedral D_4 and alternating group A_4 as a subgroup of the permutation group S_4. The geometric views of transformation will help us to distinguish all non- isometric mapping.
Study of the non-isometric permutations will help us identify genetic errors in cell transcriptions.
Operator Sequence Instead of DNA Sequence:
The binary operation in permutation mapping will produce a sequence of products which will be recorded in a table called Cayley's table (Arthur Cayley, 1854).
To view and interpret geometric transformation we assume that

i) every motion can be described by a geometrical transformation.
ii) there are some independent intrinsic and basic transformations.
iii) every motion can be described by the composition of the "basic transformations".

Some DNA transformations can be considered planar transformation. The vertices of a square can be labeled <T/U, C, G, A> or S_4 = {1,2,3,4}. For simplicity the center of all nucleotide bases stay in the same plane and all transformations like rotation, reflections, and translations will take place in the same plane.

3. Geometry of the Tetrahedron Mapping:
A one to one mapping from a set to itself is called permutation. It is called symmetric when the set is a subset of the positive integers S_n={1,2,3,…,n}.
Initially, labeling the vertex of the tetrahedron by a set of RNA/DNA={A,T/U,C,G} or S_4 ={1,2,3,4} gives us the bound for the symmetries in the group, such that:

U/T←→1, C←→2, G←→3, A←→4.

When vertices of a tetrahedron change, their image in the second set will also change. Mathematically we define a one-to-one function from the domain of objects RNA/DNA elements to a set of four integers {1,2,3,4}.
Let us demonstrate the mapping by

$$\eta = \begin{bmatrix} U/T & C & G & A \\ 1 & 2 & 3 & 4 \end{bmatrix}$$

This kind of mapping is called permutation.
There are 4 choices for the position of vertex 4. For the second position there are 3 choices for vertex 1. Thus there are 4! = 4 * 3*2*1=24 symmetric permutations in S_4 (see [3],[6], and [10]).

Tetrahedron (b) demonstrates axes of revolution which are midpoint connectors of opposite edges: MN, PQ, and RS. There are four symmetric axes for rotations in regular tetrahedron (a) and three in (b). All symmetric axes pass through a fixed point center “O”.

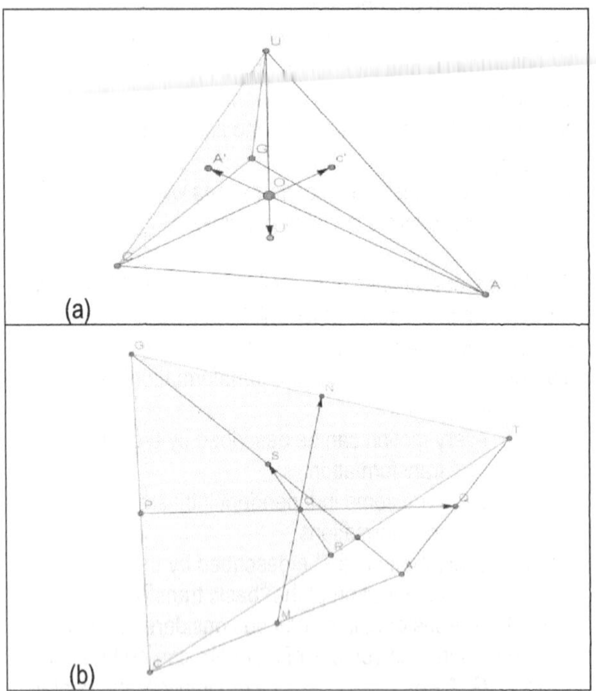

Fig. 2 Tetrahedron TCGA in (b) (or UCGA) in (a) demonstrates symmetric axis of rotations passing through each vertex and the centroid of the opposite face.

Non-Isometric Transformation in DNA/RNA Permutation:
In the previous sections, two subgroups of transformation are discussed in both A_4 and D_4. In both cases the new position of the entire object will be determined after a sequence of rotations or reflections. The following transformations are not a single rotation or reflection of the entire object, but may be expressed as a composition of other single transformation portions of the object.
The following is an example which demonstrates one sample of non-isometric transformation

$$(23) = \begin{vmatrix} U/T & C & G & A \\ 1 & 2 & 3 & 4 \\ 1 & 3 & 2 & 4 \end{vmatrix} = (CG)$$

We wanted to show the geometric meaning of this change without considering other scientific restrictions.
In this permutation two amino acid bases U/T and A will not be changed, but we will interchange C and A. Geometrically we can reflect the segment AC symmetrically without rotating or reflecting the object.

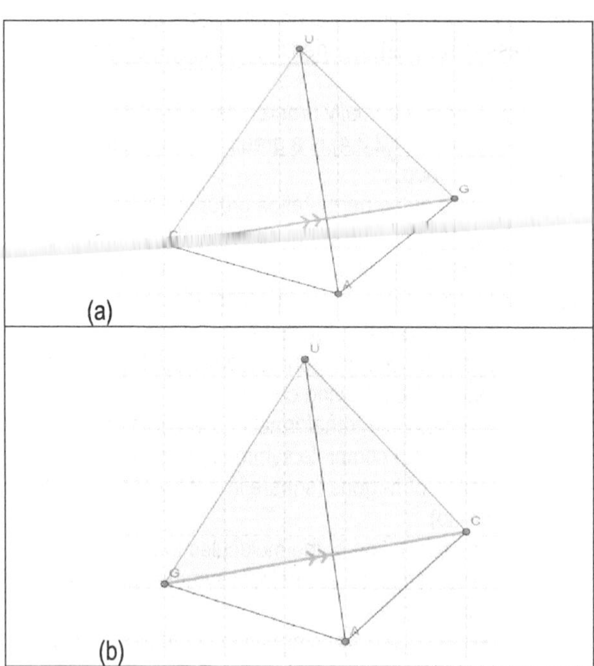

Fig. 3. Can we transform tetrahedron (a) to (b) without geometrical distortion? This transformation is not possible without with a simple rotation and reflection of the object twisting part of the object.

3.1-Dihedral Group D_4

We denote D_n (n>= 3) dihedral group of symmetries for each regular n-sided polygon. In each case there are n-rotations (including the identity) and n- flips so that the order of D_n is 2n. This argument demonstrates that D_3 and S_3 have the same order of six. Thus D_3 represents all rotations and reflections for equilateral triangles and D_4 also is a group of all rotations and reflections in a square. Assume symmetry group of the square (Fig.4) and that r represents a 90 degree rotation counterclockwise and s a reflection across a horizontal axis. We can observe that $r^4=s^2=e$ where e=(1) is denoted for identity transformation.

All other transformations in this group can be interpreted by these two elements r and s.
Thus, D_4 is a group that is generated by a pair of transformations on a mapping $\eta = \begin{bmatrix} U/T & C & G & A \\ 1 & 2 & 3 & 4 \end{bmatrix}$

such that, r=(1234)=(UCGA)

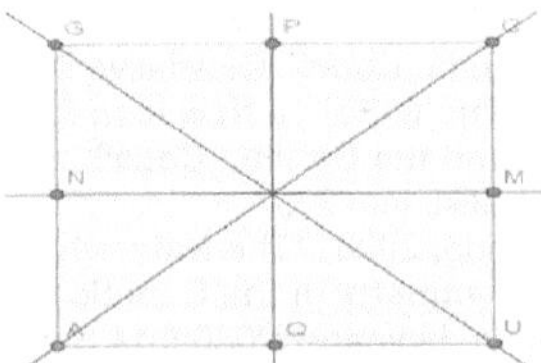

Fig. 4: The Square UCGA is a regular polygon with symmetric axes: PQ, NM, AC, and GU.

In the following matrix, the first row represents the RNA/DNA bases with their original order in the second row. The third row demonstrates the position after transformation. We call it identity transformation if it comes back to the same order.

Identity Transformation

$$\Leftrightarrow \quad (1) = \begin{vmatrix} U/T & C & G & A \\ 1 & 2 & 3 & 4 \\ 1 & 2 & 3 & 4 \end{vmatrix} = e$$

In a regular tetrahedron, U' the center of triangle GCA is the image of the point U. We will present another example to explain the rotation of 120° about UU' (or equivalently TT' in DNA) will produce the following transformation.

$$\begin{vmatrix} U/T & C & G & A \\ 1 & 2 & 3 & 4 \\ 1 & 3 & 4 & 2 \end{vmatrix} = (234) = (CGA)$$

Symbolically, a simple transformation will be (CGA). In this permutation model, U/T will map to itself, C to G, G to A, and A will map to C.

All of the elements in D_4, A_4, and S_4 can be described by graphical and vector approaches.

4.: Non-isometric Transformation:

Cayley's Binary Multiplication Table for Alternating Symmetric Group A_4: The order of the alternating group A_4 according to the formula $|A_n|=n!/2$ will be 12. For simplicity, we will call each element a letter that represents the associated transformation. In the Cayley's table (2), the set of binary operations can be observed A_4={e, a, b, c, g, h, i, j, r, s, t, u}. It can be verified that {e, a, b, c} is a subgroup of the alternating group. In addition, all of the elements in A_4 can be generated by the elements of this subgroup. That is:

e=(1), a=(12)(34), b=(13)(24), ab=(14)(23), g=(123), ag=(134), bg=(243), abg=(142), g^2=(132), bg^2=(124), abg^2=(143).

Space of Symmetric Transformation in DNA/RNA: Let us call the midpoint connectors of all opposite edges in tetrahedron by MN, PQ, and RS. Due to the symmetry properties of a regular tetrahedron all of them are concurrent at a point "O". This is the centroid of the tetrahedron ATGC. Each face from the set {ATC, AGC, AGT, GTC} represents a triplet codon with a centroid {A',G',C',T'}.

Thus, in addition to MN, PQ, and RS, segments AA', CC', GG', and TT' are symmetric axes of rotations or reflections of the tetrahedron in 3D space.

We are planning that the geometric approach used in this article can explain the puzzle of 44 degenerate codons. Further research will be required to explain the link of this approach of using the geometric interpretation for symmetric transformation in DNA with other advanced level genetic errors during transcription, apoptosis, and mutation.

There will be significant differences between our approach and the traditional approach.

Our approach is based on the geometry of permutation group structure which has been a trend of research during the past few decades.

- We will look at the sequence of the *operation functions* rather than DNA sequence.
- We can observe all operation functions listed in Table (2).
- There are 12 isometric transformations in the Alternating Symmetric group A_4 and 8 isometric transformations in dihedral group D_4 with four elements in common.
- The total number of permutations of four letter alphabets in RNA/DNA={U/T,C,G,A} is equal to 4!=24 and the total number of isometric transformations is 16.
- There will be a difference of (24-16=8) eight non-isometric transformations. These non-isometric transformations will cause the shape of the codons deformation of DNA.
- Cayley's table (Table (2)) demonstrates only 24 functional operators as a result of operations in the symmetric group.
- The puzzle that 44 that are degenerate and redundant partially explained. Actually, 40 of them are explained very well to reduce 64 positions in Cayley's table to 20 amino acids.

4.1 Concluding Discussion:

- We have studied the dynamic functional operations instead of static positions of single DNA bases.
- The understanding of searching a DNA sequence should be changed into the effect of dynamic functional operators to analyze a genetic code.
- Nature may dictate these operators in their physical, chemical, or biological operations.

Further studies are needed to find the outcomes in generating or producing the natural process.

Future Research:

The importance of this work is not that it solves the question of evolution, life, birth, death, mutation, and structure of the genetic code, but that it opens up a new line of direction to the genetic transformation. However Further investigation needed to determine the nature of eight non-isometric symmetric group structures. We still need to demonstrate the cause of four more degeneracies in the 64 codons of Cayley's table.

References:

1. Akinori Sarai and Yoshinori Takeda, **Lamda Repressor recognizes the approximately 2-fold symmetric half operator sequences asymmetrically**, proc. Natl. Acad. Sci. USA, Vol. 86, pp. 6513-6517, September 1989, Biochemistry.
2. Crick F.H.C., Barnett L., Brenner S., Watston in R.J., Nature 192, 127 (1961).
3. Dean, R. A., ***"Classical Abstract Algebra"***, Harper and Row, Publishers, New York, (1990).
4. Duplij Diana and Duplij Steven, **"DNA sequence representation by trainders and determinative degree of nucleotides**", Journal of Zhejiang University Science (JZUS), 2005 [illegible].
5. Beland, P., T. F. Allen, **"*The Origin and Evolution of the Genetic Code*",** Journal of Theoretical Biology, (1994).
6. Gilbert, J., Gilbert, L., **"*Elements of Modern Algebra*"**, Thompson Brooks/Cole, (2005).
7. Gamow, G., **"Possible relation between deoxyribonucleic acid and Protein Structure."**, Nature, vol. 173, pp.318, (1954).
8. Luscombe N.M., Austin S.E., Berman H. M., Thorton J.M. **"An overview of the Structures of protein-DNA complexes***, Published: 9 June 2000, *Genome* **Biology** 2000, **1(1)**: reviews001.1–001.10. The electronic version of this article is the complete one and can be found online at http://genomebiology.com/2000/1/1/reviews/001, Genome**Biology**.com (Print ISSN 1465-6906; Online ISSN 1465-6914).
9. Ian Stewrt, Science Magazine, **"Broken symmetry in the genetic code?"** 05 March 1994 by IAN STEWART. Hornos and Hornos, Physical Review Letters, vol 71, p 4401.
10. Moore, J. T., ***"Elements of Abstract Algebra"***, The Macmillan Company, New York, (1961).
11. Sanchez Robersy, and Grau Ricardo, **"Vector Space of Extended Base-triplets over the Galois Field of Five DNA Bases Alphabet"** , International Journal of Biological and Medical Sciences 3:2 2008, Bioinformatic Group, Santo Domingo, Vila Clara, Cuba, p.89-96.
12. Sanchez Robersy, Morgado Eberto, and Grau Ricardo, **"A Genetic Code Boolean Structure: I. The Meaning of the Boolean Dections."** Math Biol doi: 10.1016/j. bulm.2004.05(2004).
13. Sanchez, R. E. Morgado, R. Grau, ***"Abelian Finite Group of DNA Genomic Sequences"***, Quantitative Biology, (2005).
14. Sanchez R., Morgado E., and Grau R., ***"Gene Algebra from a Genetic Code Algebraic Structure"***, Journal of Mathematical Biology, (2005), Vila Clara, Cuba..
15. Sanchez Robersy, Morgado Eberto, and Grau Ricardo, **"The Genetic Code Boolean Lattice**: Match Commun. Math Comput. Chem. 52, 29-46 (2004).
16. Shcherbak, V. I. **A new manifestation of the decimal system in the genetic code**, In: Proceedings of the 12th
17. International Conference Origin of Life, Book of Abstracts, San-Diego, July 11–16, USA. 1999.
18. Negadi Tidjani: **"Symmetric Groups for the Rumer-Konopel' chenko-Shcherbak "Bisections" of the Genetic Code and Applications",** Internet Electronic Journal, Molecular Design. 2004, 3,247-270, http://www.biochempress.com
19. Watson J.D. and Crick F.H.C., Nature 171, 373 (1953) and Nature 171, 964 (1953).
20. White, M. "***The G-Ball, a New Icon for Codon Symmetry and the Genetic Code*",** Qualitative Biology, (2007).
21. **White M., The G-Ball, a New Icon for Codon Symmetry and the Genetic Code1,** by Mark White, MD, Copyright Rafiki, Inc. 2007.
22. Yang Chi Ming, 2003, **"The Naturally Designed Spherical Symmetry in the Genetic Code",** arxiv.org/ftp/q- bio/papers/0309014 Sept. http://preprint.chemweb.com/biochem/0306001
23. Yang, D. J., Ying, Z. J., **"*Detection of Permutation Symmetry in Pattern Sets*"**, Discrete Dynamics in Nature and Society, (2006).

		Second letter				
		U	C	A	G	
First letter	U	Phe	Ser	Tyr	Cys	U
		Phe	Ser	Tyr	Cys	C
		Leu	Ser	STOP	STOP	A
		Leu	Ser	STOP	Trp	G
	C	Leu	Pro	His	Arg	U
		Leu	Pro	His	Arg	C
		Leu	Pro	Gln	Arg	A
		Leu	Pro	Gln	Arg	G
	A	Ile	Thr	Asn	Ser	U
		Ile	Thr	Asn	Ser	C
		Ile	Thr	Lys	Arg	A
		Met	Thr	Lys	Arg	G
	G	Val	Ala	Asp	Gly	U
		Val	Ala	Asp	Gly	C
		Val	Ala	Glu	Gly	A
		Val	Ala	Glu	Gly	G

(Third letter: rightmost column)

Table (1): The codon triplet table- http:// nobelprize.org/ educational/ medicine/ gene-code/ how.html

					Cayley's table for DNA Transformation in S_4.																				
	Binary Composition	RNA Group	e	a	b	c	g	h	i	j	$r=g^2$	$s=i^2$	$t=j^2$	$u=h^2$	N	O	P	R	S	T	U	V	W	X	Y	Z
1	e=(1)	(UCGA)	e	a	b	c	g	h	i	j	$r=g^2$	$s=i^2$	$t=j^2$	$u=j^2$	N	O	P	R	S	T	U	V	W	X	Y	Z
2	a=(12)(34)=s	(UC)(GA)	a	e	c	b	h	g	j	i	$s=i^2$	$r=g^2$	$u=j^2$	$t=h^2$	O	N	R	P	U	V	S	T	Z	Y	X	W
3	$b=(13)(24)=r^2$	(UG)(CA)	b	c	e	a	i	j	g	h	$t=h^2$	$u=h^2$	$r=g^2$	$s=i^2$	R	P	O	N	T	S	V	U	Y	Z	W	X
4	$c=(14)(23)=r^2s$	(UG)(CG)	c	b	a	e	j	i	h	g	$u=j^2$	$t=j^2$	$s=i^2$	$r=g^2$	P	R	N	O	V	U	T	S	X	W	Z	Y
5	g=(123)	(UCG)	g	i	j	h	$r=g^2$	$t=j^2$	$u=j^2$	$s=i^2$	e	b	c	a	W	X	Y	Z	N	O	P	R	S	T	U	V
6	h=(134)	(UGA)	h	j	i	g	$s=i^2$	$u=j^2$	$t=h^2$	$r=g^2$	a	c	b	e	X	W	Z	Y	P	R	N	O	V	U	T	S
7	i=(243)	(CAG)	i	g	h	j	$t=h^2$	$r=g^2$	$s=i^2$	$u=h^2$	b	e	a	c	Z	Y	X	W	O	N	R	P	U	V	S	T
8	j=(142)	(UAC)	j	h	g	i	$u=j^2$	$s=i^2$	$r=g^2$	$t=j^2$	c	a	e	b	Y	Z	W	X	R	P	O	N	T	S	V	U
9	$g^2=(132)=r$	(UGC)	$r=g^2$	$u=j^2$	$s=i^2$	$t=j^2$	e	c	a	b	g	j	h	i	S	T	U	V	W	X	Y	Z	N	O	P	R
10	$i^2=(124)=s$	(CGA)	$s=i^2$	$t=h^2$	$r=g^2$	$u=j^2$	a	b	e	c	h	i	g	j	T	S	V	U	Y	Y	W	X	R	P	O	N
11	$h^2=(143)=t$	(UAG)	$t=h^2$	$s=i^2$	$u=h^2$	$r=g^2$	b	a	c	e	i	h	j	g	V	U	T	S	X	W	Z	Y	P	R	N	O
12	$j^2=(234)=u$	(UCA)	$u=j^2$	$r=g^2$	$t=j^2$	$s=i^2$	c	e	b	a	j	g	i	h	U	V	S	T	Z	Y	X	W	O	N	R	P
13	N=(12)	(UC)(GA)	N	O	P	R	S	T	U	V	W	X	Y	Z	e	a	b	c	g	i	j	h	$r=g^2$	$t=j^2$	$u=j^2$	$s=i^2$
14	O=(34)	(GA)	O	N	R	P	U	V	S	T	Z	Y	X	W	a	e	c	b	i	g	h	j	$t=h^2$	$r=g^2$	$s=i^2$	$u=h^2$
15	P=(1324)	(UGCA)	P	R	N	O	V	U	T	S	X	W	Z	Y	c	b	a	e	h	j	i	g	$s=i^2$	$u=j^2$	$t=h^2$	$r=g^2$
16	R(1423)	(UACG)	R	P	O	N	T	S	V	U	Y	Z	W	X	b	c	e	a	j	h	g	i	$u=j^2$	$s=i^2$	$r=g^2$	$t=j^2$
17	S=(23)	(CG)	S	T	U	V	W	X	Y	Z	N	O	P	R	$r=g^2$	$u=j^2$	$s=i^2$	$t=j^2$	e	a	b	c	g	j	h	i
18	T=(1342)	(UCAG)	T	S	V	U	Y	Y	W	X	R	P	O	N	$s=i^2$	$t=h^2$	$r=g^2$	$u=j^2$	b	c	e	a	h	i	g	j
19	U=(1243)	(UCAG)	U	V	S	T	Z	Y	X	W	O	N	R	P	$u=j^2$	$r=g^2$	$t=j^2$	$s=i^2$	a	e	c	b	j	g	i	h
20	V=(14)	(UA)	V	U	T	S	X	W	Z	Y	P	R	N	O	$t=h^2$	$s=i^2$	$u=h^2$	$r=g^2$	c	b	a	e	i	h	j	g
21	W=(13)=rs	(UG)	W	X	Y	Z	N	O	P	R	S	T	U	V	g	i	j	h	$r=g^2$	$u=j^2$	$s=i^2$	$t=j^2$	e	a	b	c
22	X=(1234)=r	(UCGA)	X	W	Z	Y	P	R	N	O	V	U	T	S	h	j	i	g	$t=h^2$	$s=i^2$	$u=h^2$	$r=g^2$	c	b	a	e
23	$Y=(24)=r^3s$	(CA)	Y	Y	W	X	R	P	O	N	T	S	V	U	j	h	g	i	$s=i^2$	$t=h^2$	$r=g^2$	$u=j^2$	b	c	e	a
24	$Z=(1432)=r^3$	(UACG)	Z	Y	X	W	O	N	R	P	U	V	S	T	i	g	h	j	$u=j^2$	$r=g^2$	$t=j^2$	$s=i^2$	a	e	c	b

Table (2): Cayley's Table for all periodic permutation in S_4 demonstrates codons transformation group and subgroups.

Analog Cochlea Circuit Model for Kemp Echo Synthesis

Louiza Sellami
Department of Electrical and Computer Engineering, US Naval Academy
Annapolis, MD 21402, USA
sellami@usna.edu

Robert W. Newcomb
Department of Electrical and Computer Engineering, University of Maryland
College Park, MD 21742, USA
newcomb@eng.umd.edu

***Abstract*— An analog circuit model of the cochlea is presented, which simulates Kemp echoes in their impulse response. The circuit model is derived from a unidimensional transmission line cochlea model into which non-uniform and loss properties are incorporated. Kemp echoes are synthesized via PSPICE simulations of the circuit model, and the results are compared to the Kemp echoes obtained experimentally.**

I. INTRODUCTION

The peripheral auditory system has the capacity to generate audio-frequency sounds in the external auditory canal. This property was demonstrated experimentally by Kemp [1], who was able to record echoes from human ears by sealing a miniature sound source and a microphone into the ear canal. Since then, other researchers [2-4] have confirmed Kemp's discovery.

The sound generating property of the auditory system manifests itself in various forms. Spontaneous emissions are detectable from some healthy human ears and consist of narrow-band signals of one or more fixed frequency tones, often audible to the subject, and which can be measured in the absence of acoustic stimulus.

In contrast, stimulated acoustic emissions, also known as Kemp echoes, transiently evoked oto-acoustic emissions (TEOAEs), or simply evoked acoustic emissions, are exhibited by the majority of normal human ears and half of abnormal ears [1,2], in response to a transient stimulus. These emissions have nonlinear characteristics and are reduced in ears with hearing loss, and are completely suppressed in ears with cochlear deafness [1-3].

Stimulated acoustic emissions are responses to click stimulus which occur several milliseconds after the stimulus is applied and persist for some tens of milliseconds. Experimental evidence shows that these echoes differ from ear to ear and change significantly with the amplitude and the frequency of the stimulus. These changes affect the magnitude of the emissions, in that stimuli of higher frequency generate much smaller emissions than stimuli of lower frequency at the same stimulus level, and the dependency with stimulus amplitude is highly nonlinear [2]. These changes affect also the latency of the emissions which depend on the stimulus frequency.

Although experimental results show that the magnitude of Kemp echoes is reduced by certain types of hearing loss, they can still be isolated with good filtering techniques [2]. Because there are significant differences in the Kemp echoes for normal versus certain types of damaged ears, it is felt that the Kemp echoes can provide a noninvasive way to quickly and easily characterize some types of damages to the inner ear. Further, these emissions can be a reliable technique for demonstrating objectively the presence of normal activity in the cochlea, detecting changes in its functioning, as well as detecting hearing loss of non-cochlear origin since, in this case, the echoes remain normal.

In light of these findings, and as a first step, we present a cochlea model that is able to regenerate Kemp echoes in their impulse response, and from which a characterization of the inner ear can be made. The structure of the model is such that the geometrical and mechanical characteristics of the cochlea re embedded in the mathematical model which is based on the nonuniform, lossless, unidimensional transmission line model. Further, the model is converted to a scattering one by rephrasing the model equations in terms of incident and reflected waves and digitizing the resulting equations in space, and from which an equivalent electrical analog circuit model is developed. We point out that though cochlea modeling has been the subject of many studies for decades, and several models exist in the literature, each one describing one or more particular functional aspects of the cochlea, most of these models are not directly appropriate for Kemp echo phenomenon since the latter is based on the incident and reflected pressure waves in the cochlea [1, 5].

II. THE MATHEMATICAL MODEL

The equations describing the motion of the fluid and the basilar membrane are derived from the following considerations:

- Newton's Law for force on a fluid.
- Conservation of mass.
- Basilar membrane motion equation.

The geometrical model that we propose to study is indicated schematically in Fig. 1. The model represents an uncoiled one dimensional cochlea with two chambers (vestibuli and tympani) filled with fluid (perilymph) and separated by the basilar membrane. The cochlea model is idealized as an exponentially tapered tube, and that the basilar membrane is stiff except for the portion that vibrates transversally to the fluid flow. The taper of the membrane is linear and varies in the opposite direction of the exponential taper of the cochlea. The upper chamber (scala vestibuli) and the lower one (scala tympani) are connected at the narrow end by an opening called the helicotrema. At the wider end they are sealed by a flexible membrane: the scala tympani by the round window and the scala vestibuli by the oval window. Sound inputs and outputs enter and exit at the oval window via the middle ear which acts as a transformer for signals transmitted from the outer ear at the ear drum.

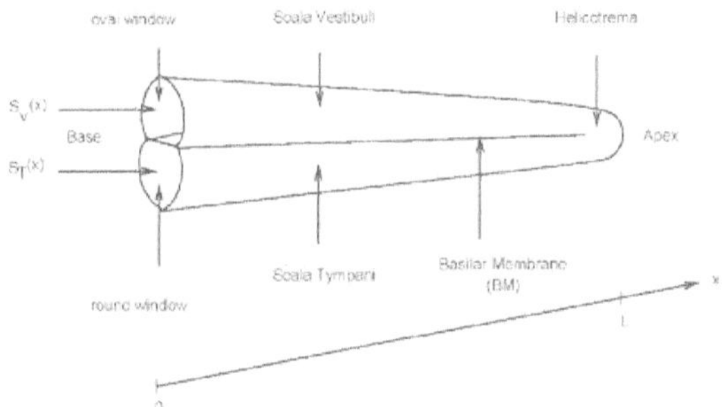

Fig. 1: Drawing of an uncoiled cochlea

The ear converts sound waves in the external environment into neural signals in the auditory nerves. The vibration of the eardrum, induced by these waves, causes vibration of the stapes whose footplate drives the fluid in the scala vestibuli. The pressure difference generated between the scalae vestibuli and tympani drives the basilar membrane, and the resulting motion is sensed by the hair cells, which transmit information about their changing electrical activity, through the auditory nerves, to the nervous system.

Here subscripts v and T are used for the vestibular and tympanic scala. Also, t denotes time while x is the distance along the basilar membrane, starting at the window end, a one-dimensional model being assumed. Further, $v_V(t,x)$ and $v_T(t,x)$ denote the fluid velocities, $p_V(t,x)$ and $p_T(t,x)$ the pressure in the fluid, and $S_V(x)$ and $S_T(x)$ the cross-sectional area at x.

By virtue of symmetry, the taper, and the closed nature of the cochlea, a velocity v_V in the scala vestibuli induces a velocity v_T in the tympanic membrane such that $S_V(x) = S_T(x)$ and

$$v_V(t,x) = -v_T(t,x) \tag{1}$$

We take (1) as a basic assumption of the theory, which allows us to work primarily with v_V. Also, it is the pressure difference $p = p_V - p_t$ which causes the basilar membrane to vibrate transversally. Thus, we express our equations in terms of p.

A. Newton's Law for Force on a Fluid

Obtained directly from Newton's law for force on a fluid, with the forces being: the inertial force, due to the mass of the fluid, the frictional force, due to frictions in the fluid, and the restoring force, due to the pressure difference in the chambers of the cochlea, this equation expresses the gradient of the pressure difference as a function of time and displacement along the cochlea [5, 6].

$$\nabla p(t,x) = -\frac{2}{S_V(x)}\left[R_V\left(S_V(x)v_V(t,x)\right) + \rho_F \frac{\partial\left(S_V(x)v_V(t,x)\right)}{\partial t}\right] \tag{2}$$

Here R_V is the frictional coefficient and ρ_F the fluid density.

B. Conservation of Fluid Mass

This equation is derived from the general fluid equation applied to the cochlea fluid, assumed uncompressible, and expresses the gradient of the fluid velocity as a function of time and displacement along the cochlea [5].

$$\nabla\left[S_V(x)v_V(t,x)\right] \approx \frac{D(x)}{2}\dot{\xi}_m(t,x) \tag{3}$$

Where $D(x)$ is the width, and $\dot{\xi}_m$ the maximum velocity of the basilar membrane, respectively.

C. Basilar Membrane Motion

The gradient of the pressure difference depends on the fluid velocity, which, in turn, depends on the maximum displacement $\xi_m(t,x)$ of the basilar membrane. To obtain an independent equation for $\xi_m(t,x)$ we consider the basilar membrane to be a second order system with an equivalent mass μ, frictional resistance $\sigma(x)$, and stiffness $\emptyset(x)$, all per unit area. We also use the fact that it is the pressure difference between the two chambers that causes the membrane to deflect at any point. Then, using $\xi_m(t,x)/2$ as the average displacement over $D(x)$, the equation of motion of the BM is

$$-p(t,x) = \mu\frac{\partial^2\xi_m(t,x)/2}{\partial t^2} + \sigma(x)\frac{\partial\xi_m(t,x)/2}{\partial t} + \phi(x)\xi_m(t,x)/2 \tag{4}$$

which is the final main equation desired. Next, we take the Laplace transform of (4) with variable s, and solve for $D(x)\xi_m(s,x)/2$ as follows:

$$\frac{D(x)\xi_m(s,x)}{2} = -\frac{p(s,x)}{sQ(s,x)} \tag{5}$$

where

$$Q(s,x) = \frac{\mu s^2 + \sigma(x)s + \phi(x)}{D(x)s} \tag{6}$$

On defining $u_V(t,x) = v_V(t,x).S_V(x)$, the final equations (2), (3), (5), and (6) of the model are then linearized and put in a matrix form as follows:

$$\nabla\begin{bmatrix} p(s,x) \\ u_V(s,x) \end{bmatrix} = -\begin{bmatrix} 0 & P(s,x) \\ \dfrac{1}{Q(s,x)} & 0 \end{bmatrix}\begin{bmatrix} p(s,x) \\ u_V(s,x) \end{bmatrix} \quad (7)$$

Where

$$P(s,x) = \frac{2}{S_V(x)}\left[R_V + \rho_F s\right] \quad (8)$$

III. CIRCUIT IMPLEMENTATION

To obtain the circuit realization shown in Fig. 2, we consider (7) combined with (8), and (7) combined with (6), which we discretize in space. This results in the following two equations.

$$p(s,x_k) = p(s,x_{k+1}) + \frac{2}{S_V(x_k)}R_V\Delta x + \frac{2}{S_V(x_k)}\rho_F s\Delta x u_V(s,x_k) \quad (9)$$

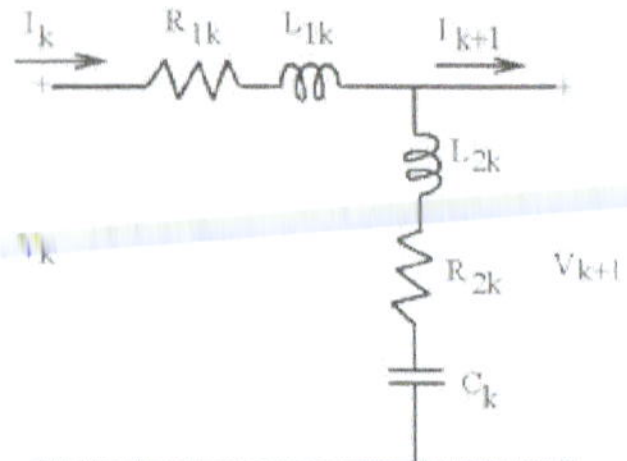

Fig. 2: Electrical equivalent circuit of section k of the cochlea

$$u_V(s,x_k) = u_V(s,x_{k+1}) + \frac{D(x_k)s\Delta x}{\mu s^2 + \sigma(x_k)s + \phi(x_k)}p(s,x_k) \quad (10)$$

By way of electrical analogies, the pressure difference p and the fluid velocity u_V are converted to voltage V and current I, respectively in (9) and (10). This gives

$$V(s,x_k) = V(s,x_{k+1}) + \left(R_{1k} + L_{1k}s\right)I(s,x_k) \quad (11)$$

$$I(s,x_k) = I(s,x_{k+1}) + \frac{V(s,x_k)}{R_{2k} + L_{2k}s + \dfrac{1}{C_k s}} \quad (12)$$

The electrical components for the *kth* section are calculated in terms of the mechanical and geometrical properties of the basilar membrane, and the fluid density, in accordance with (13). The latter is obtained by comparing (11) to (9), (12) and (10), and upon using (6) and (8).

$$R_{1k} = \frac{2R_V}{S_V(x_k)}\Delta x;\ L_{1k} = \frac{2\rho_F}{S_V(x_k)}\Delta x;\ R_{2k} = \frac{\sigma(x_k)}{D(x_k)}\Delta x \quad (13)$$
$$L_{2k} = \frac{\mu}{D(x_k)}\Delta x;\ C = \frac{D(x_k)}{\phi(x_k)}\Delta x$$

The final representation is a cascade of *N* sections of the kind described above, along with terminations. At the helicotrema end, $u_V = 0$ and $p = 0$, which corresponds to an open circuit. At the source end, the ear is excited with a speaker-like transducer, which we take as a pressure source. In the circuit diagram (Fig. 2), this is represented by a source V_{in} in series with the impedance of the outer ear, R_{in}, assumed resistive. The coupling to the round window is represented by an ideal transformer with a turn ratio higher than one, since the middle ear acts as a lever arm to increase the pressure and decrease the velocity.

IV. PSPICE SIMULATION RESULTS

A PSpice simulation is performed on the circuit of Fig. 3 where the input signal is a 10-V pulse of 2 *msec* duration. The circuit component values are calculated from (13) with the following parameters [7]:

$$\rho_F = 1000\ \text{Kg/m}^3;\ R_V = 56\ \text{Kg/m}^3.\text{sec};\ \mu = 1.43\ \text{Kg/m}^2$$
$$D(x) = 0.0086x + 0.0002\ \text{m};\ S_V(x) = 27.10^{-7}e^{-50x}\ \text{m}^2 \quad (14)$$
$$\sigma(x) = 6000e^{-170x^2}\ \text{N.sec/m}^2;\ \phi(x) = 2.10^{10}e^{-340x}\ \text{N/m}^3$$

A total of 1245 samples of the reflected voltage is measured and plotted in Fig. 4. A comparison with Kemp echoes of Fig. 5 shows quantitative and qualitative

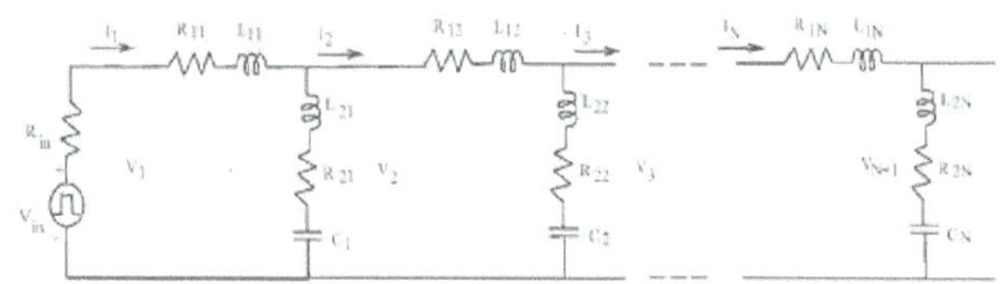

Fig. 3: Electrical equivalent circuit of the cochlear model.

similarities in the shape of the signal. Both signals exhibit two phases: a phase of high amplitude oscillations of short duration (first 175 data points), followed by a second phase with low amplitude oscillations which persist for a much longer period.

In the experimental echoes, the first phase contained the response of the middle ear only, as the trace of the stimulus was filtered out, and in the simulated echoes, the model reproduced the input signal, since it is not filtered out. No middle ear response is exhibited, as the latter was not included in the model. This is in accordance with the observations noted in [2] where response latencies can be divided roughly into two intervals: 0-5ms post stimulus time, in which one observes the impulse response of outer and middle ears, and a later part at greater than 5 ms, in which emissions from the inner ear appear.

The oscillations of the second phase emanate from the cochlea itself and seem to last rather longer in the simulated case perhaps because less friction was introduced in the basilar membrane model. The magnitude is not taken into account, here, since a voltage pulse was used in the simulation, whereas a pressure pulse was used in the original experiment.

V. DISCUSSION

In this paper, we developed an analog circuit model of the cochlea is presented, which simulates Kemp echoes in their impulse response. The circuit model is derived from a unidimensional transmission line cochlea model into which non-uniform and loss properties are incorporated. Kemp echoes are synthesized via PSPICE simulations of the circuit model, and the results compared with the Kemp echoes obtained experimentally.

Though simplifications were introduced and nonlinear effects neglected, the proposed model was able to reproduce quantitatively and qualitatively experimental echoes in their shape. In addition, the model is suitable for ear characterization, through lattice synthesis techniques [7].

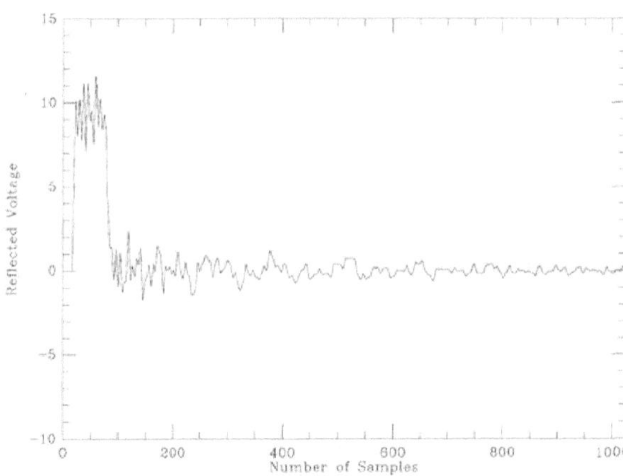

Fig. 4: Stimulated emissions measured from the circuit of Fig. 3.

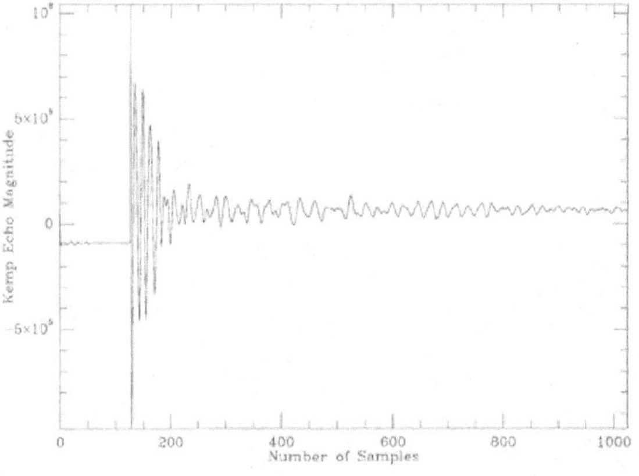

Fig. 5: Kemp echo signal, sample 1. Data provided by Dr H. P Wit and Dr P. Van Dijk, Institute of Audiology, Groningen, the Netherlands.

VI. REFERENCES

[1] D.T. Kemp, "Stimulated Acoustic Emissions from within the Human Auditory System,"Journal of the Acoustical Society of America, Vol. 64, no. 5, pp. 1386-1391, Nov. 1978.

[2] H.P. Wit and R.J. Ritsma, "Stimulated Acoustic Emissions from the Human Ear," Journal of the Acoustical Society of America, Vol. 66, no. 3, pp. 911-913, Sept. 1979.

[3] D. T. Kemp and R. Chum, "Stimulated Acoustic Emissions from the Human Ear," Hearing Research, Vol. 2, pp. 213-232, 1980.

[4] J. C. Langlevoort, H. P. Wit, and R. Ritsma, "Frequency Spectra of Cochlear Acoustic Emissions," Journal of Acoustical Society of America, Vol. 70, pp. 437-445, 1981.

[5] L. Sellami and R. W. Newcomb, "A Digital Scattering Model of the Coclea," IEEE Transactions on Circuits and Systems, Vol. 44, No. 2, Feb. 1997, pp. 174-180.

[6] J.B. Allen, "Cochlear Modeling," IEEE ASSP Magazine, Vol. 2, no. 1, pp. 3-29, Jan. 1985.

[7] R.W. Newcomb, "Notes on Cochlear Models for Kemp Echoes," Technical Report, University of Maryland, Dec. 1988.

[8] L. Sellami and R. W. Newcomb, "Synthesis of ARMA Filters by Real Lossless Digital Lattices," IEEE Transactions on Circuits and Systems, Vol. 43, No. 5, May 1996, pp. 379-386.

"*Known Knowns, Known Unknowns, & Unknown Unknowns*": Computational Science challenges for analysis of multi-dimensional DNA matrices in Evolutionary & Population Genomics

Steven M. Carr

Genetics, Evolution, and Systematics Laboratory, Department of Biology, and Department of Computer Science, Memorial University of Newfoundland, St John's NL A1B 3X9, Canada

Abstract - *The advent of so-called NextGen DNA sequencing methods has massively increased the rate at which DNA sequence information can be generated, and the volume and complexity of the data matrices that apply to biological questions, including molecular and organismal evolution and population biology. One such approach is the analysis of complete mitochondrial DNA (mtDNA) genomes from multiple species simultaneously, by means of a "sequencing by hybridization" microarray biotechnology, the "ArkChip". I review mitogenomic biology and biotechnology, describe some of the known knowns of bioinformatic information content and its computational challenges, outline new computational strategies for known unknowns of evolutionary trees (phylogeny) and population biology structures in time and space (phylogeography), and speculate on future application of Computational Science to biological unknown unknowns.*

Keywords: Mitogenomics, DNA Microarrays, NextGen Sequencing, Bioinformatics, Evolution, Phylogeography

1 Introduction

"*There are known knowns; there are things we know we know. We also know there are known unknowns; ...we know there are some things we do not know. But there are also unknown unknowns – the ones we don't know we don't know*" Donald Rumsfeld (2002)

Advances in so-called Next Generation ('NextGen') sequencing methods have created gigantic data sets that test the abilities of computational science both to assemble overlapping primary data as a single robust construct, and then to extract information and detect patterns within that construct, where at least some of the patterns are 'unknown unknowns.'

Where population biologists are interested in multiple individuals per species, a more modest but successful strategy involves the mitochondrial DNA (mtDNA) genome, which has a long history of application in evolutionary and population biology, including resolution of relationships among humans and other Great Apes, and tracing the pre- and post-glacial history of human emergence Out of Africa into Europe, the near and far East, and the Americas.

Figure 1 – Nuclear *versus* vertebrate mitochondrial genomes. The human nuclear genome comprises one set each of chromosomes from the mother and father, for a total of about 3 billion DNA base pairs (bp) encoding just over 20,000 'genes'. In contrast, the human mitochondrial DNA (mtDNA) genome is a small, circular, extra-nuclear molecule inherited solely through the maternal egg cytoplasm. It comprises 38 genes concerned with the cellular 'powerhouse' functions of the mitochondrion [1,2].

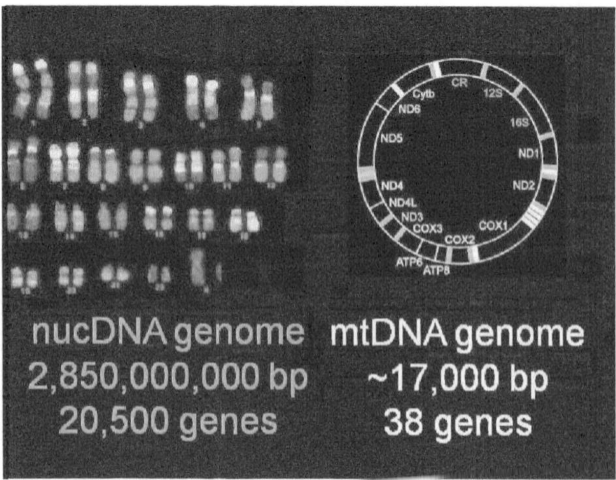

2 Mitochondrial Genomics

Unlike genes on separate chromosomes in the nuclear genome that undergo 50% recombination each generation, mtDNA does not undergo genetic recombination, but is passed intact between mother and offspring, and in the next generation passes only through the daughters' cytoplasm, mitochondria in the male sperm making no contribution. This matrilineal inheritance, combined with a higher rate of mutation than typical nuclear genes, makes mtDNA invaluable for tracing patterns of historical migration (vicariance) or descent (evolution) in time and space.

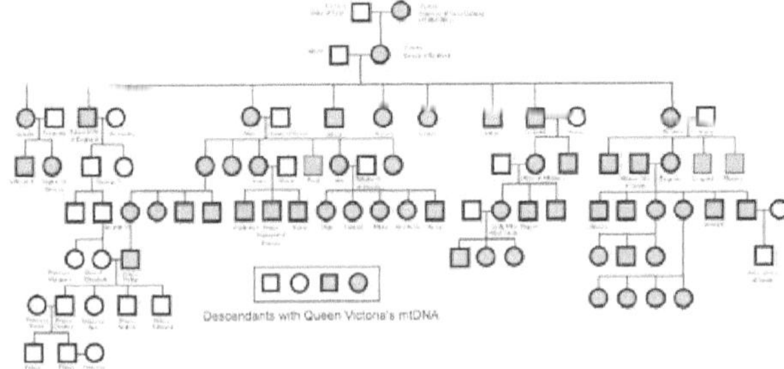

Figure 2 – MtDNA Family Tree of Queen Victoria of England. Victoria is well-known to have carried a nuclear germline mutation for hemophilia, which she passed on as an autosomal recessive allele through her sons and daughters to the royal families of Russia and Spain. She (II-2) is less well-known to have passed her mtDNA genome to all of her children, and via her daughters' daughters' daughters through five generations shown here to her great-great grandson, Prince Phillip (VI-3). Queen Elizabeth II (VI-2) shares her mtDNA with Prince Charles (VII-2), but her grandson and great-grandson Prince William (VIII-2) and Prince George (not shown) have distinct mtDNA genomes inherited from their respective mothers Diana (VII-1) and Kate (VIII-3).

Since the late 1970s, DNA sequence data have been collected by the dideoxy or Sanger method, which involves the use of chemical terminators to produce sets of DNA molecules that differ by plus or minus one base pair, such that the complete sequence is obtained from the nested series. "Pseudo Color"-coding of the terminators and large-scale automation of the separation process culminated in publication of the complete human genome sequence in 2004.

The Sanger method has dominated the field for more than thirty years. Now, "Next Gen" sequencing methods offer increasingly rapid, high-throughput data production that does not rely on linear separation, but rather massively parallel processing of simultaneous reactions. One such method is sequencing by hybridization on a DNA microarray. The method resembles molecular 'velcro', where a known reference sequence is represented on a microarray as a series of short, overlapping oligonucleotide "hooks", and is challenged by an unknown but homologous experimental sequence as a set of "threads". The experimental DNA sticks only to sequence-specific "hooks," which may include single-base variants of the reference sequence. The microarray can return information about widely-separated single nucleotide polymorphisms (SNPs) associated with medical conditions, or where all possible single-base variants are included along with the reference mtDNA sequence, the data are the complete mtDNA sequences of individuals that can differ by from one to hundreds of SNPs [1].

Where a microarray can be designed to accommodate mtDNA reference sequences from several species whose sequences are sufficiently distinct to prevent 'crosstalk', the result is an "ArkChip" capable of simultaneous, cost-effective population genomic analysis at the incremental cost of DNA extraction and amplification for each added species [2]. A typical ArkChip experiment generates ca. 1,000,000 features that comprise four A, C, G, and T hybridization signals for the forward and reverse DNA strands of single individuals from each of seven species [4 x 2 x 17,000 x 7] [3]. Projects may include scores or hundreds of individuals per species (Figure 3). *Known knowns* in this process include algorithms that extract individual genome sequences from a 4 x 2 x 17,000 matrix [4]. *Known unknowns* will compare gene patterns along the 17,000 element genome vector within and among species, based on external algorithms applied to exported data [5]. *Unknown unknowns* include creation of algorithms for detection of molecular and evolutionary patterns implicit in fully-annotated higher-order dimensions across genes and species.

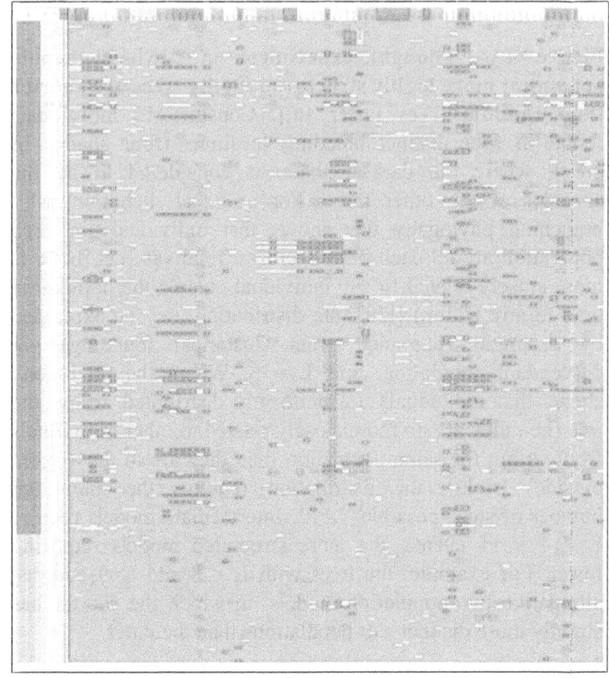

Figure 3 – Schematic of the evolutionary bioinformatic content of the mtDNA genomes from 80 Atlantic Cod (*Gadus morhua*). Each genome comprises 16,553 bp (16.5

Kbp), whose sequence is assembled from a consensus of the forward and reverse DNA strands, so that the complete data set comprises > 1.3 x 10^6 bp (Mbp). Single Nucleotide Polymorphisms (SNPs) have been identified at more the 500 sites. The data have been sorted to highlight more than 200 [dark grey block at left] that are informative as to genetic relationships among fish [2, 3]. Related fish genomes with a common ancestor (clades) have been group by column and are recognizably as bands across columns [4]. Alternative sorting can highlight patterns of molecular evolution by gene or codon position within genes [5]. Color-coding may indicate SNP sites, information content, confidence levels in base calls, patterns of sharing among fish genomes, etc.

Phylogeography is the study of population genetic relationships in space and time. Whereas the field began in the early days of DNA sequencing with short sequences and partially-resolved relationships, the advent of genomic data enables complete resolution of within-species phylogenies and creates new challenges for their interpretation.

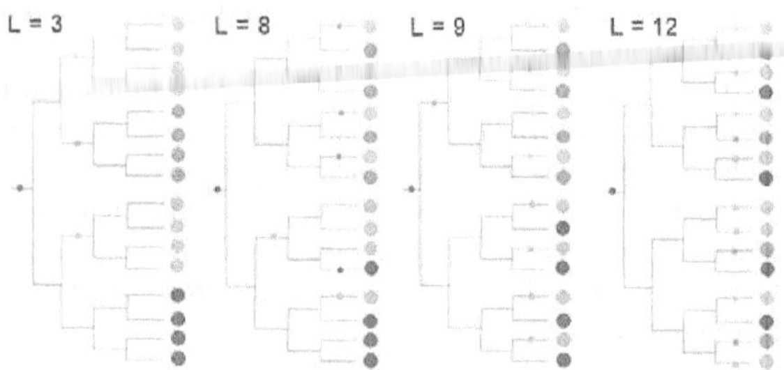

Figure 4 – Thought experiment in phylogeographic genomics: more highly structured family trees are shorter than random trees [after [6]]. Consider 16 individuals found in four distinct breeding locations (four shades of grey), where the darkest shade is considered to be the ancestor of the other three. For an ideal dichotomously-branching phylogeny that shows that individuals in each population are all each other's closest relatives (i.e., none is more closely related to any individual outside the population than to any within) [left], the distribution may be explained by a single vicariance event (historical founding) per descendant population, thus L = 3. Where the phylogeny shows that individuals are uniformly distributed across the tree (i.e., they are no more closely related to other individuals from within the same population than they are to those from outside) [right], the distribution requires the maximum number of steps possible, L=12. Intermediate models require L = 4 ~ 11 events, the more structured models requiring fewer. For example, the trees with L = 8 and L=9 contrast alternative two-population models, in which the shorter has slightly more distinct sub-populations than the latter.

The principles in the idealized model can then be applied to larger data sets with real genomic data. The phylogenetic tree in Figure 5 was derived by one of a variety of well-established "known known" computational algorithms. With genomic data sets, the topological branching order is largely method-independent [7]. Moving backward in time from right to left, the branching order shows successively more inclusive groups of related individuals (clades). The shaded dots are characters attached to each individual, in this case its population of origin. The question is the co-occurrence of clades and populations as an historical biological process.

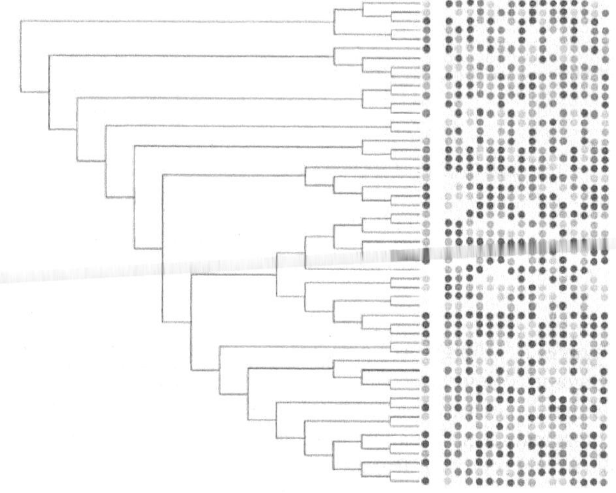

Figure 5 – Monte Carlo randomization of population assignments as a test of phylogeographic structure. For an observed phylogenetic tree [left] that shows the distribution of individuals across populations, the length L of the tree is the minimum number of vicariance events (historical movements) necessary to explain it. By repeatedly randomizing population assignments over the tips of the tree [right] and determining the length of the resultant tree, the observed length may be compared with the random distribution as a test of non-random structure. A set of 10,000 such randomizations gives a stable distribution.

Figure 6 shows the application of the Monte Carlo method to a population genomic data set from Harp Seals (*Pagophilus groenlandicus*) (after [6]). Harp Seals breed in exactly four places in the North Atlantic and adjacent waters, in the White Sea, Greenland Sea, the Newfoundland & Labrador Ice Front, and the southern Gulf of St Lawrence [top]. Whereas the two westernmost breeding sites are known to exchange animals, trans-Atlantic genetic relationships and those among the two eastern populations in particular have been unclear. The well-defined arrangement of populations sets up several *a priori* biogeographic hypotheses, including a linear 'four stepping-stone' model [middle] and a 'two-stone' trans-Atlantic model [bottom].

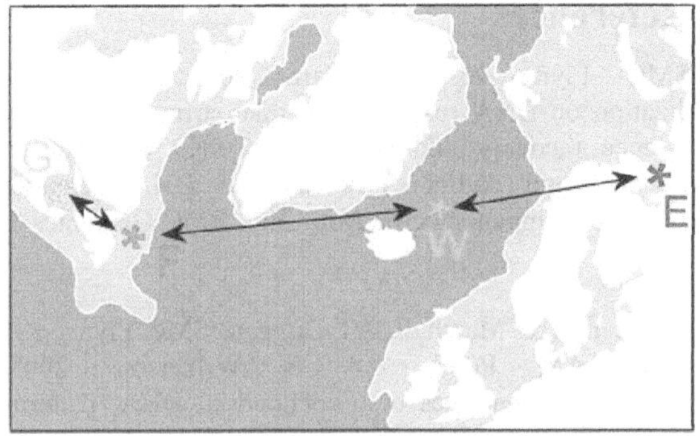

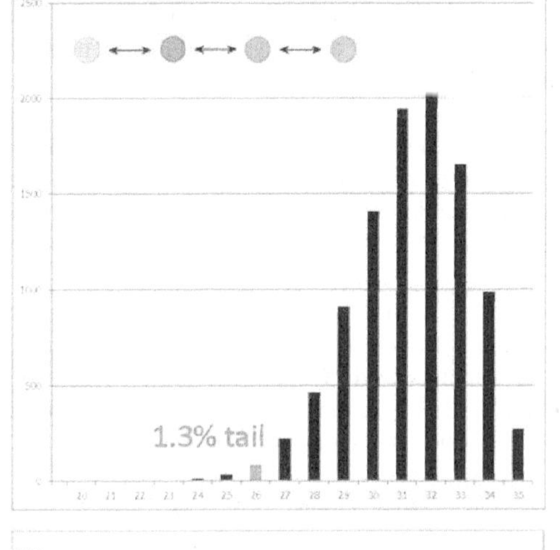

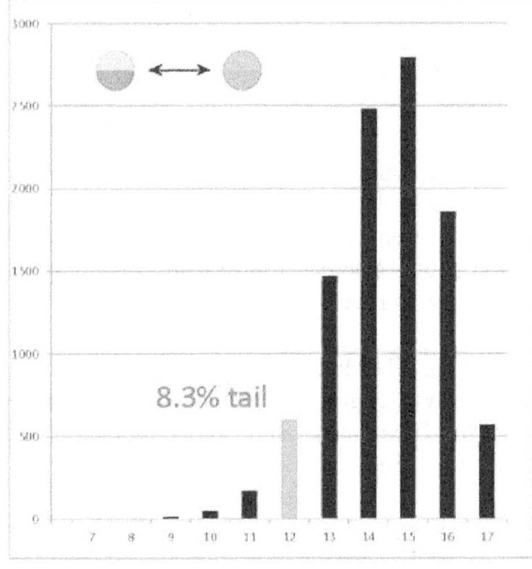

Figure 6 - Results of Monte Carlo simulations of alternative phylogeographic hypotheses for Harp Seals (*Pagophilus groenlandicus*) (after [6]). Phylogeographic models are encoded in a 4x4 matrix, so that it is possible to weight movements among population to reflect hypotheses of random or linear movements, or the likelihood of longer versus shorter movements. Each graph shows the distribution of the length L of 10,000 randomizations by the method in Figure 5, as compared to the observed length [shaded column]. For the linear, four-stone 'stepping stone' model [middle], the observed tree falls within the left-hand 5% tail and thus indicates that the model explains the distribution significantly better than does the random hypothesis of no structure. In contrast, the two-stone model [bottom] that groups the western and eastern population as pairs falls to the right of the 5% tail, such that it is not significantly shorter than random. The four-stone model is a better explanation of the distribution than the two-stone model [6].

Given the Monte Carlo procedure as a means of testing for non-random structure in intra-specific phylogenies as a whole, is it possible to make quantitative distinctions among the component populations of the species? Inspection of the tree may suggest qualitative patterns, for example that two populations seem to differ in their distribution among clades. Traditionally, such comparisons would be quantified by relative frequencies in row-by-column tests. However, when genomic data differentiate every individual, and simple comparison of group frequencies masks the nested nature of those groups as clades, such methods are unproductive. A more productive approach is to derive a numerical proxy for each of the phylogenetic components of the total population.

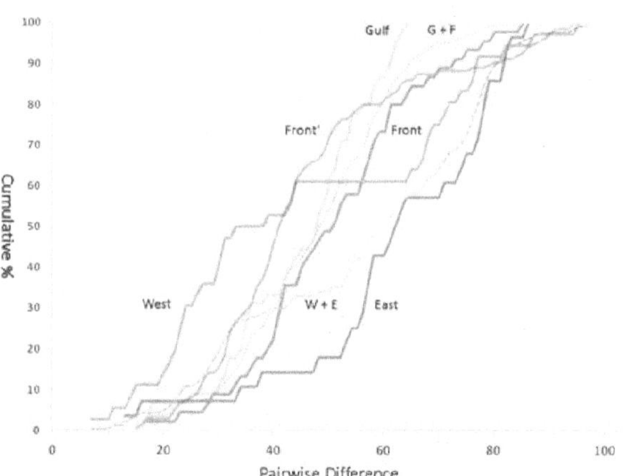

Figure 7 – Cumulative pairwise distance curves for populations of Harp Seals (after [6]). From a matrix of the observed pairwise DNA differences between all individuals in each of five populations, the cumulative curve shows the total fraction of the population differentiated at or below a particular pairwise difference. This curve serves as a quantitative proxy for a time-dependent branching family tree. Compared at 50%, curves displaced to the left indicate relatively 'young' populations in which the majority of animals diverged recently, in contrast to curves displaced to the right that indicate typically 'older' relationships. Differences among curves may be evaluated by a non-parametric Kolmogorov-Smirnov test, which evaluates the single greatest vertical difference between pairs of curves, which in this dimension indicates more or less rapid phylogenetic diversification [6].

3 Conclusions

The advent of NextGen DNA sequencing methods has massively increased the rate at which DNA sequence information can be generated, and the volume and complexity of the data matrices that apply to biological questions, including molecular and evolutionary biology. Questions include known knowns where computational methods can be applied to automated signal processing and ease of comparison among data sets, known unknowns inherent in patterns revealed for the first time by highly-resolved genomic phylogeny and phylogeography, and unknown unknowns lurking in cross-comparisons and pattern-detection among the higher-order dimensions of ordered data matrices. In summary,

- **Biotechnology**
  - **Iterative whole-genome DNA sequencing** on **microarrays: the *ArkChip***
  - ***Known Knowns***: Optimization & Automation of **signal processing algorithm**
  - ***Known Unknowns***: Comparison of data patterns within / between species
- **Phylogenetic Genomics** in *time*
  - ***Known Knowns*:** Reconstruction of intraspecific phylogenies ('family trees')
- **Phylogeographic Genomics** in *space*
  - ***Known Unknowns***: quantitation of phylogeny in space
    - **Monte Carlo** models for testing phylogeographic hypotheses
    - **Non-Parametric** comparison of proxies of phylogenetic topology
- ***Unknown Unknowns*** ?
  - **Higher-order interactions** in microarray data: sequence x species x array
  - **Pattern identification** in multiple dimensions

4 Acknowledgements

The experimental work was supported by research contracts from the Canadian Department of Fisheries and Oceans and a Discovery Grant from the National Science and Engineering Research Council (NSERC). I gratefully acknowledge the contributions of my co-authors and students on the papers referenced below. I am also grateful to my new colleagues in the Department of Computer Science at Memorial University, for stimulus in new research directions and encouragement to attend the BioComp'13 conference. For Justyna, Matilda, and Eowyn, with thanks for their indulgence.

5 References

[1] SMC Flynn & SM Carr. 2007. Interspecies hybridization on DNA resequencing microarrays: efficiency of sequence recovery and accuracy of SNP detection in human, ape, and codfish mitochondrial DNA genomes sequenced on a human-specific MitoChip. BMC Genomics 8, 339.

[2] SM Carr, HD Marshall, AT Duggan, SMC Flynn, KA Johnstone, AM Pope, & CD Wilkerson. 2008. Phylogeographic genomics of mitochondrial DNA: patterns of intraspecific evolution and a multi-species, microarray-based DNA sequencing strategy for biodiversity studies. Comparative Biochemistry and Physiology, D: Genomics and Proteomics 3, 1-11.

[3] SM Carr, AT Duggan, & HD Marshall. 2009. Iterative DNA sequencing on microarrays: a high-throughput NextGen technology for ecological and evolutionary mitogenomics. Laboratory Focus 13, 8-12.

[4] SM Carr & HD Marshall. 2008. Intraspecific phylogeographic genomics from multiple complete mtDNA genomes in Atlantic Cod (*Gadus morhua*): Origins of the "Codmother," trans-Atlantic vicariance, and mid-glacial population expansion. Genetics 108, 381-389.

[5] HD Marshall, MW Coulson, & SM Carr. 2008. Near neutrality, rate heterogeneity, and linkage govern mitochondrial genome evolution in Atlantic Cod (*Gadus morhua*) and other gadine fish. Molecular Biology & Evolution 26, 579-589.

[6] SM Carr, AT Duggan, GB Stenson, & HD Marshall. Quantitative analysis of phylogeographic structure; Whole-mitogenome variation among harp seals (*Pagophilus groenlandicus*) from discrete transatlantic breeding areas, Molecular Ecology, in review.

[7] MW Coulson, HD Marshall, P Pepin & SM Carr. 2006. Mitochondrial phylogeographic genomics of gadine fish: Implications for taxonomy and biogeographic origins. Genome 49, 1115-1130.

Improving SVM and TSVM with Multiclass Accordance Sampling for Breast Cancer

Hala Helmi, Jonathan M. Garibaldi
School of Computer Science University of Nottingham,
Jubilee Campus, Wollaton Road, Nottingham, NG14 5AR, UK
{hqh, jmg} @cs.nott.ac.uk

Abstract—.

The Support Vector Machine (SVM) is a state of art classification method and it widely used in bioinformatics and other disciplines due to its high accuracy. The basic SVM takes a set of input data, predicts, for each given input, which of two possible classes, treating only labelled data in supervised learning, and supports only binary classification. Transductive support vector machines (TSVM) extend SVMs in that they could also treating partially labelled data in semi-supervised learning. In TSVM a binary random sampling is used to gradually select unlabeled samples to train classifier. In this paper, we provide and explore whether using multiclass selective sampling method can improve TSVM performance replacing the random sampling used TSVM. Experimental results show that accordance-sampling method can improve TSVM.

1. INTRODUCTION

In order to learn a classifier, semi-supervised learning algorithms need labelled training examples. In many applications, labelling the training examples is costly process and time consuming task, because it requires human expertise. Hence, finding ways to minimize the number of the required labelled examples is beneficial.

Multiclass selective sampling, a form of active learning, which is an expert domain, will assign labels to some most informative unlabeled examples. Thus, sampling the informative unlabeled examples from a large unlabeled examples pool is the key issue for active learning. This will result in reducing the number of training examples that need to be labelled.

Usually, the training set is chosen to be a random sampling of examples. This may result in different unlabeled examples to be used in different runs. Since in active learning random sampling usually cannot achieve the best performance. We would like to know if we could use other sampling strategies to obtain better results. Therefore, in our case, active learning will learn TSVM classifier to actively choose the training data [10].

We present a novel multiclass selective sampling method that performs accordance sampling with support vector machines (SVMs) experimental results showing that active learning with SVMs can extensively reduce the amount labelled training examples needed [9].

We will use number of classification problems as a running example throughout this paper. We performed experiments using this new sampling method on UCI datasets [13] as well as in-house datasets [4].

The paper is organised as follows: the use of the both terms transduction and multiclass are discussed in further detail in section 2 followed by a description in more details our new method multiclass accordance- sampling in section 3 followed by a description of the experiments carried out in section 4. In sections 5, the results are presented and discussed where indicate that Accordance Sampling can significantly reduce the need for labelled instances. Lastly, conclusions are drawn in section 6.

2. SUPPORT VECTOR MACHINES

2.1 Induction SVMs

Generally, SVMs is binary classification. Assume we are given training data$\{ \mathrm{x}_1 \dots \mathrm{x}_n\}$ that are vectors in some space $X \subseteq \mathbb{R}^d$.We are also given their labels $\{ y_1 \dots y_n\}$ where $y_i \in\{-1,\ 1\}$. In their simplest form, SVMs are used hyperplanes that separate the training data by a maximal margin. All vectors lying on one side of the hyperplane are labelled as -1, and all vectors lying on the other side are labelled as 1. The training instances that lie closest to the hyperplane are called support vectors [1].

$$\mathbf{k}(x_i, x_j) = \emptyset\,(x_i)^T\,\emptyset\,(x_j)'$$

SVM has the following primal form:

Minimize over $(\mathbf{w}, b, \xi_1, \dots, \xi_m)$

$$\|\mathbf{w}\|_p^p + C\sum_{i=1}^{m}\xi_i$$

Subject to:

$$\forall_{i=1}^{m}: y_i\,(\mathbf{w}^{\mathrm{T}}\emptyset\,(\mathbf{z} * x_i)' + b) \geq 1 - \xi_i, \xi_i \ \geq 0 \qquad (1)$$

2.2 Transduction SVMs

The previous subsection worked within the framework of induction. There was a labelled training set of data and the task was to create a classifier that would have good performance on unseen test data. In addition to regular induction, SVMs can also be used for transduction. Here we are first given a set of both labelled and unlabeled data. The learning task is to assign labels to the unlabeled data as accurately as possible [2][3]. SVMs can perform transduction by finding the hyperplane that maximizes the margin relative to both the labelled and unlabeled data [2][6].

Minimize over $(y_1^*, \dots, y_k^*, w, b, \xi_1, \dots, \xi_{m,} \xi_1^*)$

$$\frac{1}{2}\|w\|_2^2 + C\sum_{i=1}^{m}\xi_i + C^*\sum_{j=1}^{k}\xi_j^*$$

Subject to:

$$\forall_{i=1}^{m}: y_i\left(w^T\emptyset(z * x_i)' + b\right) \geq 1 - \xi_i, \xi_i \geq 0$$
$$\forall_{j=1}^{k}: y_j^*\left(w^T\emptyset(z * x_j^*)' + b\right) \geq 1 - \xi_j^*, \xi_j^* \geq 0 \quad (2)$$

3. MULTICLASS ACCORDANCE SAMPLING

3.1 Multiclass SVMs

http://nlp.stanford.edu/IR-book/html/htmledition/multiclass-svms-1.html

Binary (two-class) classification using SVMs presents an interesting and effective approach to solving automated classification tasks. The initial support vector machines were designed to be used for binary classification; this has now been extended to classifying multiclass [8]. Almost all the current multiclass classification methods fall under two categories: one against one or one against all [7][8]. In this paper we will use one against all method.

Usually a bioinformatics classification problem faces these situations, since more than two classes are usually needed, relying on a clustering-based approach usually to predict labels for unlabelled examples [5][11]. Then, multiclass SVM is used to learn with the augmented training set, to classify the test set [11][12].

3.2 Accordance Sampling

Many researches going on the area of statistical analysis a new technique of taking a representative sample been suggested. The basic idea is to have all the classes representatives present in the sample, say we got a data of 1000 record with 5 classes, class 1→ 500 record, class 2→ 250 record, class 3→ 125 record, class 4 → 65 record and class 5 → 60 record.

It will not be fair to just randomly select a sample of 250 because there is a big probability that class 6 or 5 will not be represented. As well as, it will not be fair to take a sample of 50 records from each class, because that leaves only 10 record of class 5 to be tested. In addition to that, class 1 will not be well trained, as only 50 out of 500 will be used to train it.

Ideally, we found that we should combine both concept, as all classes should be used but with the same percentage they exist in the data, say we need 20% of the data for the training, then 20% of the class1, 20% of class2 etc... to be selected on random bases.

We propose a novel multiclass sampling method to replace the random sampling used by ISVM and TSVM to find whether this could extensively reduce the amount of labelled training examples needed. In meantime, to see if this can improve the performance of both ISVM and TSVM.

New method uses redundant views to expand the labelled dataset to build strong learning models. The major difference is that the new method uses number of classifier views (two views in our case) to select and sample unlabeled examples to be labelled by the domain experts, while the original ISVM and TSVM randomly samples some unlabeled examples and uses classifiers to assign labels to them.

We expect that ISVM and TSVM will benefits from the Accordance Sampling method. Let *V*1 and *V*2 be the two views classifiers learned from training labelled data *L* to classify all unlabelled examples *U* using both views. For each example x_i in *U*

$$mean(x_i) = (V1((x_i) + V2(x_i)) / 2$$
$$s(x_i) = I(x_i) + max\{mean(x_i), 1 - mean(x_i)\} \quad (3)$$

ISVM and TSVM will trains the redundant view classifiers by assigning and learn labels from the most informative labelled examples [14][15]. It then uses the view classifiers to classify the most informative unlabeled examples. The unlabeled examples that the two views classifiers agree the most on their classification are then sampled. We use a ranking function to rank all the unlabeled instances according to the predictions of the views classifiers. The ranking score function for an unlabeled instance x_i is defined as

$$s = I(x_i) + max\{(p1((x_i) + p2(x_i)) / 2, 1 - (p1(x_i) + p2(x_i))/2\} \quad (4)$$

Where

$$I(x_i) = \begin{cases} 1 \text{ if the view classifiers assign the same label to } (x_i) \\ 0 \text{ otherwise} \end{cases}$$

$p1(x_i)$ *and* $p2(x_i)$ *are predicted probabilities for the positive class by two view classifiers.*

Scores generated results in a rank where examples in the highest positions are the ones that both view classifiers assign the same label, with high confidence to them which means that those are the most informative unlabelled examples. Then it selects the larger one of the average predicted probabilities for the positive and negative classes by two view classifiers.

4. EXPERIMENTS

For our empirical evaluation of the above methods, we used two breast cancer datasets. In-house Nottingham Tenovus Primary Breast Carcinoma Series dataset and other one is Breast Cancer Wisconsin (original) UCI datasets.

We choose two datasets to investigate the performance of using accordance sampling for breast cancer classification. The characteristics of each dataset are shown in Table 1. For each dataset, we created a pool of unlabeled by sampling 10%, 20%, 30% etc examples from the data training for each class as we mentioned previously. Then randomly select two examples in the pool to give as the initial labelled. Thus give the learner the remaining unlabelled examples and the two labelled examples. We then test the classifier.

The attributes of each dataset are split into two sets and are used as two classifiers views. This is a practical approach for generating two views from a single attribute set. To comprehensively explore ISVM and TSVM performance on these views we would like to experiment all possible combinations of the views. Since the number of attributes is large we randomly generate some small groups contains 2 attributes. We randomly select 200 pairs of views to run of views. The last column in the Table 1 represent the number of view pair used in our experiments and the total number of all possible view splits. We use one against all method for multiclass problem we group each class as positive and the rest as negative.

Table 1. The characteristics of used datasets.

Datasets	Examples	Attributes	Class	L	U	V
Wisconsin	699	11	2	649	50	$200/2^{10}$
Nottingham Tenovus	1076	54	6	663	413	$200/2^{53}$

Our experiments compared the performance of the original ISVM and TSVM and the new accordance sampling method. We used accuracy to measure the strength performance of our model. We apply accordance-sampling method on TSVM and ISVM on both datasets by building model using Perl. We run each method on each dataset 10 times.
We then run the original ISVM and TSVM algorithms using the same setup to measure the performance.

4.1 Nottingham Tenovus Primary Breast Carcinoma Series dataset.

The dataset contains three main clinical groups, Luminal, Basal and HER2 with 6 subgroups for 1076 patients between the year 1986-1998 and with immunohistochemical reactivity for 25 proteins with known relevance in breast cancer.

Soria et al. [4] successfully identified the six clinically useful and novel subgroups while maintaining the three clinical groups. Out of the 1076 data patterns, we classify only the 663 data patterns which Soria et al. have successfully classified into six classes. The remaining 413 data patterns which are not classified are disregarded.

Table 2. Percentages of data training for each class comparing ISVM and TSVM using accordance sampling.

Nottingham Tenovus Breast Cancer			
Training %	#Test	**TSVM**	**ISVM**
10	595	**83.12**	**80.87**
20	529	**85.66**	**82.66**
25	496	**85.88**	**84.43**
30	463	**86.34**	**84.12**
40	397	**87.8**	**84.76**
50	331	**89.99**	**85.09**
60	265	**91.54**	**88.87**
70	199	**94.37**	**90.34**
75	166	**95.64**	**92.76**
80	133	**97.37**	**93.88**
90	67	**99.75**	**94.56**

4.2 Breast Cancer Wisconsin (Original) Data Set

The data sets, available from the UCI Machine Learning Data Repository [13], are as follows. The breast cancer Wisconsin data set has 699 examples in nine dimensions and is `noise-free', one feature has 16 missing values which are replaced with the feature mean.

Table 3. Percentages of data training for each class comparing ISVM and TSVM using accordance sampling.

Breast Cancer Wisconsin			
Training %	#Test	**TSVM**	**ISVM**
10	629	**89.36**	**85.22**
20	559	**90.05**	**86.45**
25	524	**91.95**	**86.77**
30	489	**92.23**	**88.09**
40	419	**93.11**	**89.34**
50	349	**93.56**	**90.22**
60	280	**94.44**	**91.67**
70	210	**94.02**	**92.88**
75	175	**94.8**	**92.98**
80	140	**95.37**	**93.07**
90	70	**96.5**	**93.93**

5. RESULTS AND DISCUSSION

Accordance sampling, selects the unlabeled examples that the two views classifiers agree the most about their label. When the two classifiers are sufficient and independent, the sampled examples are more reliable labelled. Thus, selecting those examples that the two views classifiers agree on their label are less likely to introduce errors in expanded labelled dataset. This means that one of the classifiers assigns the wrong label to the example, which may lead to labelling errors in the expanded labelled dataset. This is one approach to investigate why the sampling method could work well in exploring the labelling errors. However, in our case we cannot calculate the labelling errors rates since the real labels of unlabelled examples are not known.

5.1 Nottingham Tenovus Primary Breast Carcinoma Series dataset.

Fig. 1 shows a graph of accuracy against the percentage of training data for each class using TSVM and ISVM with accordance sampling for Nottingham Tenovus Primary Breast Carcinoma Series dataset. Comparing to Fig. 2 which shows a graph of accuracy against the percentage of training data using the original TSVM and ISVM along for the 10 runs for each amount of training labelled data.

We observed that TSVM was able to produced higher average classification accuracy than ISVM with accordance sampling method across different amounts of training labelled data between 10% to 90%. Although ISVM start with slightly small difference in contrast to TSVM, this gap widened, starting at 40% to be 90.9% - 84.76% TSVM to ISVM respectively. However, at 75% to 90% the difference start narrows again. This indicate that active learning accordance sampling provides more benefit to both methods supervised and semi-supervised learning. Nevertheless, TSVM algorithm outperforms ISVM practically when measured the accuracy. At 90% of training, TSVM achieved an average accuracy of 99.75 % with sampling method while the original TSVM achieved an average accuracy of 94.11%.

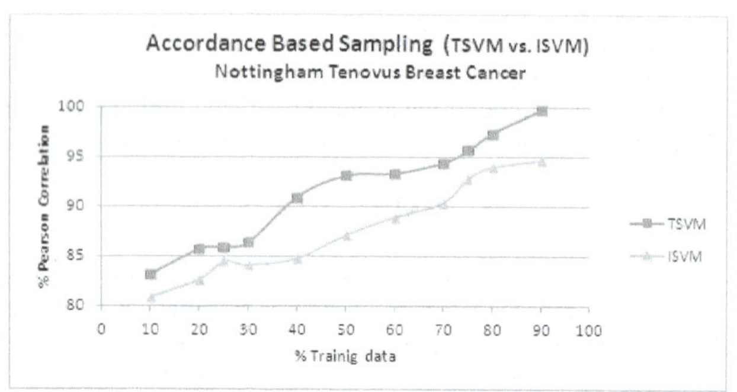

Figure 1: Accordance Based Sampling TSVM vs. ISVM with different percentages of labelled training data for each class.

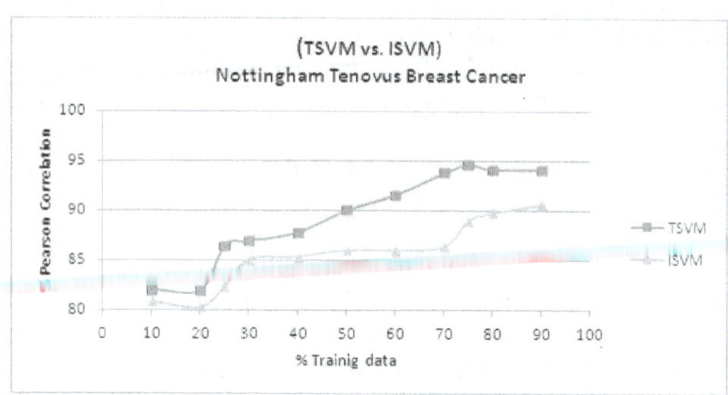

Figure 2: Original TSVM vs. ISVM with different percentages of labelled training data.

5.2 Breast Cancer Wisconsin (Original) Data Set

From Fig. 3 we can see a graph represent the accuracy against the percentage of training data for each class using TSVM and ISVM with accordance sampling for Breast Cancer Wisconsin (Original) Data Set. In contrast to Fig. 2, this shows a graph of accuracy against the percentage of training data using the original TSVM and ISVM across the 10 runs for each amount of training labelled data.

We investigated that TSVM was able to provide a slight advantage over regular ISVM. It produced higher average classification accuracy than ISVM with accordance sampling method along with all different amounts of training data between 10% to 90%. Moreover ISVM start with considerably large gap comparing to TSVM, this gap widened and narrowed irregularly. Specifically, the difference extended starting at 20% to be 90.05%- 86.45% ISVM to ISVM respectively. While, using the original TSVM and ISVM gives 84.75% - 82.45% using 20% labelled training data. However, at 75% the difference narrows and start widened again after that.

This point out that the performance active learning accordance sampling gains more benefit to both methods supervised and semi-supervised learning. Nevertheless, TSVM algorithm outperforms ISVM practically when measured the accuracy. At 90% of training, TSVM achieved an average accuracy of 96.5 % with sampling method though the original

TSVM achieved an average accuracy of 93.51%. Comparing to the ISVM at 90% give 93.93% while the oriental ISVM give around 90%

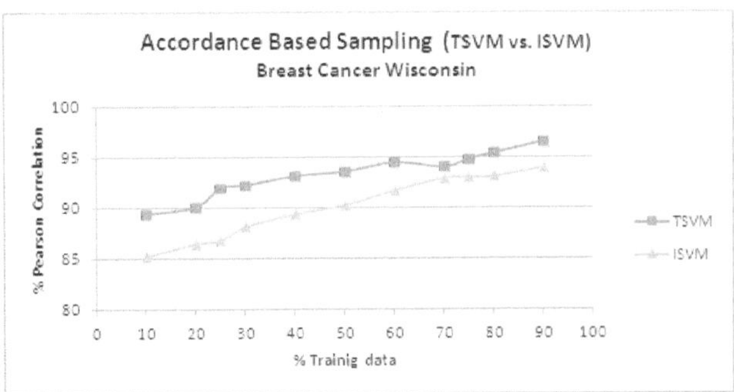

Figure 3: Accordance Based Sampling TSVM vs. ISVM with different percentages of labelled training data for each class.

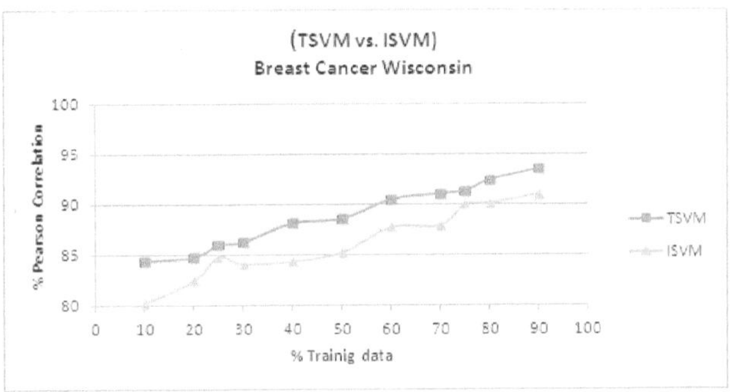

Figure 4: Original TSVM vs. ISVM with different percentages of labelled training data.

6. CONCLUSION

In this paper, we propose a novel multiclass accordance sampling method and replace the random sampling used by ISVM and TSVM to find whether this could extensively reduce the amount of labelled training examples needed. In meantime, to see if this can improve the performance of the original ISVM and TSVM algorithms. We apply new method on two datasets the Nottingham Tenovus Primary Breast Carcinoma Series dataset and Breast Cancer Wisconsin (Original) dataset compared the results for both datasets before using the accordance sampling method and after.

The basic idea of this sampling method is to select the unlabeled examples that the views classifier agreed the most on their label. Our experiments show that this new sampling method can indeed make a significant performance improvement over the original ISVM and TSVM.

REFERENCES

[1] T. Joachims, "Making large-scale support vector machine learning practical". In Advances in Kernel Methods: Support Vector Machines, (1999).

[2] O. Chapelle, Schölkopf B, Zien A. Semi-supervised learning. MIT press Cambridge, MA:; (2006).

[3] O. Chapelle, Zien A. Semi-supervised classification by low density separation. (2004).

[4] D. Soria, J. M. Garibaldi, F. Ambrogi, A. R. Green, D. Powe, E. Rakha, R. D. Macmillan, R. W. Blamey, G. Ball, P. J. Lisboa, T. A. Etchells, P. Boracchi, E. Biganzoli, and I. O. Ellis, "A methodology to identify consensus classes from clustering algorithms applied to immunohistochemical data from breast cancer patients" in Computers in Biology and Medicine, vol. 40, no. 3, pp. 318–330, (2010).

[5] Pal M. Multiclass approaches for support vector machine based land cover classification. Arxiv Preprint arXiv:0802.2411 (2008).

[6] K. Bennett, Demiriz A. Semi-supervised support vector machines. Advances in Neural Information Processing Systems 368-74 (1999)

[7] One-against-all multi-class SVM classification using reliability measures. Neural networks, 2005. IJCNN'05. proceedings. 2005 IEEE international joint conference onIEEE; (2005).

[8] Fu LM, Fu-Liu CS. Multi-class cancer subtype classification based on gene expression signatures with reliability analysis. FEBS Lett 561(1-3):186-90. (2004)

[9] Blum, A., Mitchell, T.: Combining labeled and unlabeled data with co-training.In: COLT: Proceedings of the Workshop on Computational Learning Theory, pp. 92–100. Morgan Kaufmann Publishers, San Francisco (1998).

[10] Freund, Y., Seung, H.S., Shamir, E., Tishby, N.: Selective sampling using the query by committee algorithm. Machine Learning 28(2-3), 133–168 (1997)

[11] Weston J, Watkins C. Multi-Class Support Vector Machines 1998.

[12] Hsu CW, Lin CJ. A comparison of methods for multiclass support vector machines. Neural Networks, IEEE Transactions on 2002;13(2):415-25.

[13] Blake, C., Merz, C.: UCI repository of machine learning databases. University of California, Irvine, Dept. of Information and Computer Sciences (1998), http://www.ics.uci.edu/~ mlearn/MLRepository.html

[14] Wang, W., Zhou, Z.: On multi-view active learning and the combination with semi-supervised learning. In: Proceedings of the 25th International Conference on Machine Learning, ICML 2008 (2008)

[15] Muslea, I., Minton, S., Knoblock, C.A.: Selective sampling with redundant views. In: AAAI/IAAI, pp. 621–626 (2000)